YALE JUDAICA SERIES

VOLUME XXXI

THE LIGHT OF THE EYES

THE LIGHT OF THE EYES

AZARIAH DE' ROSSI

Translated from the Hebrew with an introduction and annotations by

Joanna Weinberg

Yale University Press New Haven & London

Published with assistance from the foundation established in memory of Philip Hamilton McMillan of the Class of 1894, Yale College.

Set in Granjon Roman type by Keystone Typesetting, Inc. Printed in the United States of America by Edward Brothers, Inc., Ann Arbor, Michigan.

The paper in this book meets the guidelines for permanence and durability of the Committee on Production Guidelines for Book Longevity of the Council on Library Resources.

Library of Congress Cataloging-in-Publication Data

Rossi, Azariah ben Moses dei, ca. 1511-ca. 1578.
[Me'or 'enayim. English]
The light of the eyes / Azariah de' Rossi ; translated from the Hebrew with an introduction and annotations by Joanna Weinberg.
p. cm. — (Yale Judaica series ; v. 31)
Includes bibliographical references and index.
ISBN 0-300-07906-0 (alk. paper)

1. Jews—History. 2. Judaism—History. 3. Chronology, Jewish. 4. Jews—Historiography. I. Weinberg, Joanna. II. Title. III. Series.
DS116 .R68313 2000
909'.04924—dc21 99-055976

A catalogue record for this book is available from the British Library.

10 9 8 7 6 5 4 3 2 1

To the memory of my parents, my teachers
ELI AND ADELAIDE WEINBERG

אליקים בן מאיר ז״ל
אדל בת חיים ז״ל

CONTENTS

PREFACE		ix
ACKNOWLEDGMENTS		xi
TRANSLATOR'S INTRODUCTION		xiii
ABBREVIATIONS		xlvii
INTRODUCTION		1
VOICE OF GOD		7
SPLENDOR OF THE ELDERS		33
PART THREE ENTITLED WORDS OF UNDERSTANDING	Section 1	79
	Section 2	265
	Section 3	403
	Section 4	569
CHRONOLOGICAL TABLES		723
GLOSSARY		725
BIBLIOGRAPHY		727
BIBLIOGRAPHY OF WORKS CITED IN THE NOTES		743
INDEXES		757

PREFACE

"THIS is not a work for one man alone and there is much material in the author's work that remains to be annotated." Such was Zvi Hirsch Jaffe's justification for the publication of his new edition of Azariah de' Rossi's *Me'or Enayim* (*Light of the Eyes*) (Warsaw, 1899), only thirty-three years after David Cassel had published his indispensable edition of the text with its notes, references, and lists of sources.

Jaffe's pronouncement may still be invoked. For the polymathic erudition displayed by de' Rossi throughout the *Light of the Eyes* renders it an unwieldy work "for one man" (and indeed for one woman) to annotate. Furthermore, the interpretation of the work, which was an innovation in Hebrew literature, remains a complex and challenging task for scholars.

Apart from providing the first complete translation of the work, I have taken Jaffe's words to heart and traced all of de' Rossi's many, diverse references, explicating the text where necessary. My introduction is intended to help the reader confront a work of such length and complexity. A biography of the author and a short survey of the reception of the book are followed by a discussion of its genre, structure, and content. Some of the key issues of the book are evaluated in relation to its cultural context, together with a presentation of the use of sources. A short history of the controversy over the printing of the book concludes the introduction. It has not been possible to discuss all aspects of the book, but I hope the introduction will provide the reader with the means to make full use of the annotated translation.

Joanna Weinberg
London
November 1998

ACKNOWLEDGMENTS

The translation of the *Me'or Enayim* has been an awesome task. As the years have gone by, my debts to friends, colleagues, and institutions have accrued. From the very beginning, the late Arnaldo Momigliano supported my project and guided me with his inimitable scholarship. My work on de' Rossi was first completed as a Ph.D. dissertation for London University (1982) under the kind and helpful supervision of Chimen Abramsky. During my postgraduate years I received various grants and scholarships for my research on de' Rossi: I was Junior Fellow in the History of Classical Civilization at the Warburg Institute (1973–75); Research Scholar at the Scuola Normale Superiore, Pisa (1973–75); Fellow of the Villa I Tatti (1975–76); Recipient of a Research Scholarship from the Leverhulme Trust (1976–77). David Newman introduced me to the subject. My deepest thanks go to Eli Gutwirth, Louis Jacobs, Alastair Hamilton, Dilwyn Knox, Jill Kraye, Tali Loewenthal, and Anne Marie Meyer, who assisted me on many occasions. I gained great benefit from the incisive and critical observations of Giulio Lepschy, who encouraged my work throughout these long years. A special debt of thanks goes to Ada Rapoport-Albert, who gave unstintingly of her time to help me with many intractable problems. Although we often begged to differ, my discussions with Robert Bonfil were helpful, and I learned much from his studies on de' Rossi. Anthony Grafton was always prepared to allow me to profit from his profound expertise in sixteenth-century thought and chronology, in particular. I am especially grateful to David Ruderman, who suggested the publication of my work in the Yale Judaica Series. I am profoundly indebted to Sid Leiman, who read the entire manuscript with a careful eye, offering many useful suggestions and correcting all manner of errors. I am grateful to Jonathan Wittenberg, who assisted me in the difficult task of rendering de' Rossi's poems into readable verse. My colleagues Hyam Maccoby and Mark Solomon at Leo Baeck College assisted me on all manner of difficult points. I am grateful to the principal of Leo Baeck College, Jonathan Magonet, who ensured that my duties at the college did not curtail my freedom to pursue my research. I have used the facilities of many libraries and institutes, including the Bodleian Library, Cambridge University Library, the Vatican library, and the Angelica library. The staff of the Warburg Institute always offered me welcome support. Indispensable for my task were the Western and Oriental collections of the British Library, which gave me access to virtually the entire corpus of works consulted by de' Rossi. The heads of the Hebrew section of the British Library, David Goldstein of blessed memory and Brad Sabin-Hill, as well as the librarian Menahem Silver, were always generous with their help. My thanks go to Daniel van Boxel and Joop van Klink for technical assistance in preparing the manuscript.

I have been assisted by many, but "last is best." Piet van Boxel was by my side throughout these last years, helping and guiding me and reading the greater part of the manuscript. Without his help, this work would never have been completed.

TRANSLATOR'S INTRODUCTION

AZARIAH DE' ROSSI

Azariah de' Rossi (1511?–77?) is a well-known figure in the history of Jewish scholarship. His pioneering contributions to Jewish history enshrined in his magnum opus *Me'or Enayim* (the *Light of the Eyes*) are often invoked in modern studies. And yet we have only scant and fragmentary data about the life of this renowned scholar. With the exception of the documents bearing on the last years of his life, our information is drawn for the most part from the vague and impressionistic autobiographical asides that de' Rossi lets slip in the course of his writings.[1]

Azariah (or Buonaiuto) min ha-Adomin[2] (de' Rossi) was born in Mantua. He retained strong ties to his native city all his life,[3] but how long he lived there cannot be ascertained. He has little to say about his family, although he does claim descent from one of the four noble families brought to Rome by Titus after the destruction of the second Temple.[4] He even neglects to mention the name of his father, Moses, in his major works, an unusual omission for a Jewish writer.[5] A document published by Shlomo Simonsohn refers to a certain Moses de' Rossi, who is given permission to be a money changer in Mantua.[6] There is no conclusive evidence, however, that this Moses[7] is Azariah's father.

"I am about sixty years old," writes de' Rossi in 1571–72.[8] According to this state-

1. For other descriptions of his life, see L. Zunz, "Toledot"; D. Cassel, introduction to *Me'or Enayim,* i–xii. More recently, S. Baron, "Azariah de' Rossi: A biographical sketch," 167–73; R. Bonfil, *Kitve Azariah,* 16–37.

2. De' Rossi himself vocalizes his name as ha-Adomim (not Adumim, the more usual spelling of the plural adjective for "red") in the poem at the beginning of "Words of Understanding."

3. In ch. 60, p. 714, e.g., he refers to "Mantua, my land."

4. See ch. 60, p. 718. Other families which, according to this medieval tradition, claimed this lineage were the de Pomis, de' Vecchii, and de' Mansi.

5. The name of his father is given in the title of a poem by de' Rossi that is printed at the end of Isaac Abravanel's *Mirkevet ha-Mishneh* (Sabbioneta, 1551) and in the title of another poem published by J. Bergmann, "Gedichte," 55.

6. S. Simonsohn, *History,* 259.

7. Bonfil (*Kitve Azariah,* 19) inclines to the view that Moses the money changer was his father on the grounds that de' Rossi appears to have been brought up in fairly prosperous circumstances.

8. Ch. 1, p. 85.

ment, a conscious adaptation of the Mishnaic expression attributed to Rabbi Eleazar ben Azariah (Ber. 1:4), he must have been born about 1511. Nothing is known of his childhood and early youth. Judging from his writings, one may assume that he received an education typical of Italian Jews in the Renaissance: a thorough training in the texts of the Jewish tradition combined with secular subjects, including grammar, rhetoric, Italian, and Latin.[9] A copybook of de' Rossi, compiled when he was about twenty years old, yields some indication of the interests he was partly to develop in later life.[10] In the first fifty-one folios, he transcribes some of Abraham Zacuto's astrological treatises and horoscope[11] and Abraham Halevi's letter about the ten tribes and interpretation of the prophecies of the child Naḥman.[12] His interest in popular medieval texts is attested by his transcription of the *Alphabet of Ben Sira,*[13] the *Sefer ha-Sha'ashuim* (*Book of Delights*) by the twelfth-century Spanish writer Joseph ben Meir ibn Zabarra,[14] and the *Mishle Sindebar* (*Tales of Sindbad*).[15] He also transcribed a set of poems about women written at the end of the fifteenth century: Abraham da Sarteano's poem entitled *Sone Nashim* (*The Misogynist*); Avigdor da Fano's reply in defense of women, *Ezrat Nashim,* and a poem by Elijah da Genazzano which is a reaction against da Fano, in support of Abraham da Sarteano.[16] In addition, de' Rossi transcribed the prayer from the second part of Moses da Rieti's didactic poem *Miqdash Me'aṭ,* which was modeled on Dante's *Divine Comedy,*[17] and a short verse compilation of the laws on ritual slaughter, *Hilkhot Sheḥiṭot u-Ṭerefot.*[18] The final pages of the copybook include a short medical extract in

9. For a discussion of these texts, see D. Ruderman, "An exemplary sermon." Secular subjects were sometimes taught by Christian teachers, although this was not always the case. At the end of his *Shilṭe ha-Gibborim* (185b) Abraham Portaleone relates how he was taught Latin and logic by Abraham Provenzali. David Provenzali, one of the three brothers, whom de' Rossi designates as the "luminaries of Mantua," had proposed to found a Jewish university in Mantua in which grammar, Latin, and Italian, among other subjects, were to be taught. The objective of Provenzali's venture, which was not realized, was to prevent the immersion of Jewish students in their Christian surroundings. (The proposal is printed by S. Assaf, *Meqorot,* 115–19.)

10. The copybook is in the National Library, Jerusalem, Heb. 8° Ms. 3935.

11. These texts were printed and discussed by M. Beit-Arié and M. Idel, "Ma'amar." They contain Zacuto's eschatological calculations for the years 1504–31 based on the book of Daniel; a description of eclipses and their astrological significance; the horoscope which Zacuto composed in Tunis for the years 1504–17.

12. The letter on the ten tribes written in 1528 and the astrological interpretations were printed by M. Beit-Arié, "Iggeret," 371–78. In ch. 13 of the *Light of the Eyes,* de' Rossi discusses the subject of the ten tribes but does not refer to Halevi's work.

13. Ff. 52r–68r. There are many versions of this work. De' Rossi's transcription differs from all printed editions. On the work, which was first printed in Constantinople in 1519, see E. Yassif, *The tales.*

14. Ff. 68r–98r. The work was first printed in Constantinople in 1567.

15. Ff. 99r–110v. The work was translated into many languages. De' Rossi's transcription is different from the first Hebrew printing (Constantinople, 1516).

16. Ff. 111r–15r. Abraham da Sarteano's poem, composed of fifty tercets, was the first of that genre to be written in Italy. See S. de Benedetti Stow, "Due poesie," 9. The set of poems was printed by D. Kaufmann, "Eliezer," 309–11, and da Sarteano's poem was published in a critical edition by J. Schirmann, *Mivḥar,* 210–15.

17. Moses b. Isaac da Rieti (1388–ca.1460) wrote the work in circa 1429. The complete work was published by D. Goldenthal (Vienna, 1851). The prayer (ff. 118r–25v) is the second canto from the second section, entitled *ha-Hekhal* (*The sanctuary*). It was inserted into the *Maḥzor Romi* and also published separately with an Italian translation (Venice, 1550).

18. Ff. 119r–20v. The anonymous verses are followed by a short poem (f. 120 col. v).

verse by Judah Alḥarizi[19] and the whole of Kalonymus ben Kalonymus's satirical didactic work *Even Boḥan* (*The Tested Stone*).[20]

Whether the youthful de' Rossi espoused the eschatological tendencies displayed in the works of Zacuto and Halevi cannot be ascertained. What is clear, however, is that by the time he came to write on the subject in his *Light of the Eyes,* his sole purpose was to denigrate and emphasize the futility of all astrological and eschatological calculations.[21] De' Rossi did not refer to the other works transcribed in his copybook in his later scholarly work. These texts, as Robert Bonfil has noted,[22] may be characterized as the kind of literature used for pedagogical purposes in the education of young boys, the majority being in verse and therefore easily memorized. In part, they may also reflect de' Rossi's own literary proclivities—he was to set his hand to verse composition throughout his scholarly life.

De' Rossi married the sister of the Mantuan banker Hayyim Massaran.[23] He had several daughters (but does not specify how many), and he refers to one married daughter whose son died in childhood.[24] At the age of thirty-five, de' Rossi met the distinguished physician Amatus Lusitanus (Rodrigues João de Castelo Branco) (1511–68) in a bookshop, probably in Ferrara.[25] Amatus describes this meeting in his *Centuriae medicinales.*[26] He refers to their discussion of the anti-Jewish tract *Opus de arcanis catholicae veritatis* (Orthone, 1518) by Petrus Galatinus (Columna), which was written partly to defend Reuchlin, one of the interlocutors in the book.[27] According to Amatus, de' Rossi was particularly interested in the Hebrew verses written by two Jews which adorn the first page of the work.[28] The account of the meeting is simply a preface to Amatus's case history of de' Rossi, who, wracked by all manner of illness, had sought Amatus's professional help. Amatus gives a detailed description of his patient's symptoms, his

19. Ff. 121r–21v. These verse texts, *On the healing of the body* and *Discourse on all the limbs of the body,* were based on Maimonides' treatment of the subject. See I. Sonne, "Excursions," 225–26.

20. Ff. 123r–69r. Kalonymus ben Kalonymus (b. 1287) wrote the work as a satirical portrayal of the Jews of Provence. De' Rossi's transcription is identical with the first edition (Naples, 1489) (with omission of the poem on the last page).

21. See, e.g., his statement in ch. 43, p. 551: "Zacuto and Rabbi Abraham Halevi . . . set the end for 1490. All their visions were pleasant dreams, but their expectations for salvation were deluded."

22. Bonfil, *Kitve Azariah,* 50.

23. De' Rossi mentions his brother-in-law in ch. 15, p. 292. On Hayyim Massarano, see Simonsohn, *History,* 217 and n. 69.

24. At the end of the book, de' Rossi publishes the epitaph he composed on the death of his grandchild Benjamin.

25. Friedenwald gives an English translation of Amatus's case history of de' Rossi in "Two Jewish Physicians." According to Friedenwald (393), Amatus met de' Rossi in Ancona in 1548 or 1549, but his dating is based on the supposition that de' Rossi was born in 1514. If, however, de' Rossi was born in 1511 or 1512 it is possible that they met in Ferrara, where Amatus was professor of anatomy lecturing on Galen and Hippocrates. Amatus went to Ancona in 1547.

26. *Curationum medicinalium centuriae quatuor* . . . (Basel, 1556), Cent. IV, curatio 42, 355–62.

27. De' Rossi does not refer to Galatinus in his *Me'or Enayim;* but it is possible that in particular his discussion of the scribal emendations of scripture (*Tiqqun Soferim*) (see ch. 19) may be read partly as a response to Galatinus's treatment of the same subject.

28. The poems are written by a certain Moses Aharon hebraeus and Isaac Hyspanus hebraeus. There is a typographical error in Amatus's text: 'Iesuos' instead of 'Hebraeos.' See F. Secret, *Les Kabbalistes,* 106, n. 24.

own diagnosis and cure.[29] (According to Amatus, his treatment was successful and de' Rossi became as strong "as a boxer.") Amatus advises de' Rossi to avoid the foggy, damp climate of Mantua and Ferrara—where apparently he was living at the time. In the course of the case study, we are given a glimpse into de' Rossi's daily routine. He states that de' Rossi, like other Jews, was black-biled (*atrabiliarius*), a condition exacerbated by his devotion to study and medical work.[30] He also mentions that de' Rossi had pupils[31] but does not disclose any details about de' Rossi's medical work or teaching. The only other indication of the way de' Rossi may have earned his living derives from a casual statement he makes when treating the subject of the antiquity of the vowel points. He states, "Now in the past, when I was a censor, I came across two Mishnah texts which were five hundred years old." It is likely that he was working on behalf of the Jewish community, who had to ensure that all books in their possession contained nothing that might be regarded as derogatory to the Christian faith.[32] Whether de' Rossi was paid for his work as censor is not known.

De' Rossi lived for a time in Bologna. He relates how he attended a geometry class in Bologna's "mater studiorum," that is, the University of Bologna, famous in the sixteenth century for its faculty of mathematics. In 1567, two years before Jews were definitively expelled from Bologna,[33] de' Rossi, like many of his coreligionists, fled to the city of Ferrara, where the ruling Estense family pursued a favorable policy toward Jews and conversos.[34] There he participated in Jewish scholarly activities, attending study sessions in the *yeshivot* or *accademie.*[35] De' Rossi refers by name to some of his distinguished Jewish contemporaries, including Judah Moscato, Eliezer Ashkenazi, and the Provenzali brothers. He never divulges the names of the Christians whom he engaged in scholarly conversation, although on one occasion he does refer to his conversation with a Benedictine monk from the Abbazia di Polirone, which was situated near Mantua.[36]

The devastating earthquake which shook Ferrara in November 1570 and continued intermittently with minor tremors until the end of 1571 had a profound effect on

29. According to J. O. Leibowitz ("A Probable Case"), Amatus gives a correct description and effective treatment of peptic ulcer.

30 ". . . cum praeter caetera, studiosus sit et rei medicae quoque operam navet" (op. cit., 356).

31. Amatus prescribed a daily routine for de' Rossi. At a certain time in the day "discipulis suis lectionem suavi voce perlegebat" (op. cit., 360).

32. It appears that Jews undertook to censure their own books to ensure that they met the stipulations of the Index of 1554. In the same year, the rabbinical synod of Ferrara passed a resolution decreeing that no book was to be printed without the permission of three rabbis and the heads of the local community. (See L. Finkelstein, *Jewish Self-Government,* 301.) The purpose of this resolution may have been to ensure that Hebrew books would not be confiscated or burned. According to M. Benayahu, *Copyright,* 197, Jews were not involved in the censorship of printed books, and to corroborate his claim he cites de' Rossi's statement. On Jewish involvement in censorship, see Sonne, *Expurgation.*

33. On the edict of expulsion, see D. Capri, "The Expulsion," 145–65. De' Rossi describes his escape from Bologna in his account of his second life-threatening experience during the earthquake of 1570: "In the year 5327 [1567] He performed miracles for me when He delivered me from the grasp of the angel of destruction when I was staying among the holy congregation of Bologna."

34. See A. Balletti, *Gli ebrei,* and A. Pesaro, *Memorie.*

35. In ch. 19 he describes a session in the Sephardi yeshiva and in ch. 57, p. 677–78, refers to a recently established "accademia." Bonfil, *Rabbis,* 18–19, has shown that the term *yeshiva* was used as "studium" or "accademia" in sixteenth-century Italy.

36. See ch. 9, p. 189.

de' Rossi. Like many of his contemporaries, he took up the pen to describe his experiences and to explore the scientific and theological causes of the earthquake.[37] In a gripping account—it is in fact the most readable part of the *Light of the Eyes*—he describes how the Ferrarese had to leave their houses and encamp in the open or live in boats on the riverside. He refers to the generosity of the wealthy members of the community, who allowed people to take up temporary residence on their estates and supplied them with provisions.[38] Having lost most of his possessions when his home was hit by the earthquake, he encamped with his family south of the river Po. It was while he was living under canvas that he met the Christian who encouraged him to translate the *Letter of Aristeas* into Hebrew. Once this task had been accomplished, de' Rossi appears to have been stimulated into writing what must have been the fruit of a lifetime's labor, the *Light of the Eyes.*

The completion of his magnum opus brought de' Rossi into the public eye. The publication of the work was beset with difficulties. In Mantua he encountered opposition but was reassured by his friend the playwright Judah de' Sommi, who told him, "As a result of your immense effort you shall produce not silver but rather gold and precious stones."[39] But the fears that the book provoked were not easily allayed, and in 1574, he had to go to Venice to argue his case with certain rabbis who had objected to some of his views.[40]

Under attack, de' Rossi nevertheless sought to act in the interests of the Jewish community as a whole. His name appears on the list of Jews who volunteered to contribute to the funds being collected by members of the Ferrarese Jewish community in aid of the Jews expelled from Ancona in 1574.[41] On the death of the renowned patroness of arts Margaret, wife of Emmanuel Philibert, duke of Savoy, de' Rossi composed a set of elegies in Hebrew, Aramaic, and Italian with Latin translations.[42] Margaret had acted on behalf of Jews and conversos in Piedmont and had attempted to protect the conversos against the edict of expulsion which had been imposed under papal pressure.[43] De' Rossi's elegies for Margaret's widower may be seen as an expression of gratitude and a tacit plea that he should continue to support his Jewish subjects.[44]

Sickness and poverty assailed de' Rossi in the last years of his life. In a letter dated March 1576, de' Rossi wrote to the abbot of Montecassino, Stefano Cattaneo, thanking

37. Entitled "The Voice of God," it forms the first section of the *Me'or Enayim.* For details and bibliographical information, see n. 1 of the translation.

38. He mentions Isaac Abravanel, grandson of Don Isaac, Isaac Berechyah da Fano, Joseph Halevi, Aaron Degale, and Solomon Modena as well as "individual nobles of the Sephardi community."

39. Ch. 18, p. 322.

40. See below, on the controversy over the book.

41. De' Rossi's name appears in the list published by Sonne, *From Paul V,* 227. He also helped to raise money for the publication of Joseph Caro's *Kesef Mishneh* (see ch. 23, p. 363).

42. All the Hebrew and Aramaic poems were printed by A. Benjacob in *Halevanon* 7 (1870), 47–48; 63–64, and some published by D. Cassel at the end of his edition of the *Maṣref la-Kesef.* The Italian poems appear to have been torn out of the autograph Bodleian Ms. (Mich. 308), and the copies in the Turin Royal library were burned in the fire which destroyed the major part of the library's collection. Judah Moscato, de' Rossi's friend and mentor, also wrote elegies for Margaret. See A. Apfelbaum, *Toledot,* 57–59.

43. For the relevant documents, see R. Segre, *The Jews.*

44. The Jewish identity of the poet is never made explicit in the poems. He uses vocabulary and imagery that render them appropriate for Christian ears.

him for three scudi sent to him on receipt of a book (presumably the *Light of the Eyes*). He explains that he had been reduced to his impoverished state—having incurred expenses in producing his book, he was unable to get any financial return as a result of the "persecusione d'hippocriti malevoli"—and that he was so worn out by illness and other troubles that he was unable to tend to the daily needs of his family.[45] The persecutors to whom he alludes are presumably certain rabbis who had attempted to restrict the circulation of the *Light of the Eyes*.[46] While responding to their criticisms, he was trying to find favor in other quarters. The work received the imprimatur of Marco Marini, a renowned Christian Hebraist. He began to approach his scholarly pursuits in a somewhat different manner, writing in Italian rather than Hebrew, and for Christians rather than for Jews. He produced an Italian translation of chapter 35 of the *Light of the Eyes* from the controversial section on chronology at the request of the governor general of the church, Giacomo Boncompagni. In 1577, he wrote his pioneering study on the Syriac version of the Gospels entitled *Osservazioni di Buonaiuto de' Rossi ebreo sopra diversi luoghi degli Evangelisti nuovamente esposti secondo la vera lezione siriaca* (*Observations of Buonaiuto de' Rossi regarding various passages in the Gospels expounded anew according to the correct Syriac reading*).[47] The overall purpose of the work was to demonstrate that passages which had apparently become corrupt or obscure in the Vulgate, particularly where Aramaic expressions are used, could be emended or clarified by means of the ancient Syriac version (the Peshitta).[48] It opens with a letter addressed to the cardinal of Santa Severina, Giulio Antonio Santoro,[49] and is dedicated to Giacomo Boncompagni.[50]

All of these Christians were associated with oriental studies, but their interest in de' Rossi was not purely scholarly. The cardinal of Santa Severina was involved in the Casa dei Neofiti from its establishment in 1577.[51] It was at his request that the inquisitor general of Ferrara, Eliseo Capys, had spent two years between 1575–77 trying to persuade de' Rossi to convert to Christianity. In a letter addressed to the cardinal, the inquisitor writes that de' Rossi was adamant in his refusal to convert but nevertheless did not wish to present himself as a fanatical Jew ("pazzo ebreo") who was unable to speak favorably of other religions. He wished to present the cardinal with a discourse on certain problematic passages in the Gospels and hoped that he would receive some alms to enable him to publish the work, which would be to the glorification and confirmation of the Christian faith. The inquisitor indicates that he would continue his effort

45. The letter published by L. Modona, "Une lettre," 315–16, was written in Italian but contains some Hebrew expressions. According to M. Armellini, *Bibliotheca Benedictino-Cassinensis* (Assisi, 1731), 1:180–82, Cattaneo wrote a work on Italian, Syriac, Hebrew, and Arabic emblems.

46. De' Rossi's bitterness about his treatment may be reflected in an undated set of poems published by J. Bergmann, "Gedichte," 55–58. In the fifth poem, he writes, "May God destroy those who slander me; may those who hate me be eradicated; may God disperse them/then might workers of iniquity say in their hearts: Surely there is a God who works justice in the world."

47. The work is still in manuscript. I intend to publish the text with introduction and notes.

48. De' Rossi was one of the first Western scholars to learn Syriac—he used Theseo Ambrogio's introduction to the language.

49. Santoro's active involvement with the Eastern Church is documented by G. Levi della Vida, *Documenti.*

50. On this work and other related documents, see my article "Towards a Reappraisal," 493–511.

51. See K. Hoffmann, *Ursprung,* 182–83.

to save de' Rossi, whom he describes as an extremely ugly but brilliant Jew. He suspected that de' Rossi was a rabbi engaged in apostasizing activities or at least in circumcising Marranos and therefore feared that the gravity of such a crime rendered him liable to the punishment *Make the heart of this people fat [and make their ears heavy and shut their eyes; lest they see with their eyes and hear with their ears and understand with their heart and convert, and be healed* (Is. 6:10)].[52] In other words, de' Rossi was a lost cause.

The inquisitor's reference to the circumcision of Marranos reflects historical reality. Ferrara served as an asylum for many converso refugees, some of whom reverted to Judaism. Jews such as Menahem da Fano risked their lives in order to undertake the clandestine activity of circumcising conversos who wished to return to their former religion.[53] There is no evidence to corroborate the inquisitor's suspicions; what is certain is that de' Rossi never held an official rabbinic position in Ferrara.

The inquisitor's letter of 17 July 1577 is the last documentary piece of evidence we have relating to de' Rossi's life. According to Leon Modena, de' Rossi composed a poem in response to a dream in which he was informed of the correct date of his death.[54] Samuel David Luzzatto (Shadal) claimed to have seen the poem in an old memorial book in which it was said that the lines of the poem were inscribed on de' Rossi's tombstone.[55] According to the poem he died in Kislev 5338 (November–December 1577). These lines were said to have been inscribed on de' Rossi's grave:

> Resting on my bed Kislev 335
> An apparition to me appeared and said:
> You have yet three more years
> Then Kislev 338 shall my soul advance on high.
> Oh You who abounds in goodness forgive, let
> the darkness of years become white as snow.

APPRAISALS OF THE *LIGHT OF THE EYES*

It is often asserted that de' Rossi's contribution to Jewish scholarship was not properly recognized until the scholars of the Jewish Enlightenment resumed de' Rossi's "constructive quest" and adopted and developed his philological and historical methods.[56]

52. The inquisitor writes, "Ma perché ho grande coniettura ch'egli sia qui in ferrara quale Rabbino che fa apostatar o almeno circoncidere quelli Marani ch si fan Hebrei dubito che la gravità di questa impietà lo faci degno di questo castigo excaeca cor populi huius."

53. On this, see R. Bonfil, "New information." See also, P. C. Ioly Zorattini, *Processi,* 13–15.

54. Modena, *The Autobiography,* 110.

55. See S. D. Luzzatto, *Iggrot,* 291 n. 96. The poem and this information about his dream is given by S. Rapoport, in Zunz, "Toledot," 161. Cassel also publishes the quatrain and states that he came across the lines transcribed by an unknown writer in a gloss on the copy of the *Me'or Enayim* which belonged to Modena (now in Biblioteca Palatina, Parma, 983). The writer of the gloss supposed that the lines he was transcribing were written in Modena's hand. However, Modena's copy of de' Rossi's book held in the Biblioteca Palatina does not appear to contain the gloss indicated by Cassel. De' Rossi may have been buried in Mantua. If Luzzatto was correct, these lines rather than the epitaph de' Rossi publishes at the end of the book (on this epitaph, see below and ch. 60) were chosen for his tombstone. According to a note which D. Kaufmann found among the papers of Samuel Vita della Volta ("Contributions," 87), an inscription was found on the wall of one of the synagogues of Mantua in 1841 recording the virtues of de' Rossi and Abraham Provenzali.

56. See, e.g., S. Baron, "Azariah de' Rossi's Historical Method," 238; Y. H. Yerushalmi, "Clio," 635.

Although the *Light of the Eyes* failed to make an impact in Jewish circles in the two centuries after its publication, Christian scholars of all descriptions were recognizing the important scholarly contributions of the Jew they called Rabbi Azarias.[57] They discussed and translated de' Rossi's chapters on such topics as the Samaritan script, the *Letter of Aristeas,* and Jewish chronology and with few reservations regarded de' Rossi as a scholar worthy of being quoted alongside Maimonides, Abraham ibn Ezra, and Isaac Abravanel. He was even accorded an entry in Richard Simon's catalogue of authors cited in the *Histoire critique du vieux testament.*[58] Notwithstanding the vague criticism that de' Rossi occasionally put forward paradoxes, Simon appraised him favorably, judging him to be more erudite than the majority of Jews because "having knowledge of the Latin language, he consulted Christian authors."

The story of the fortune of de' Rossi's work before it was reclaimed as a model of Jewish scholarship may partly be told through the documentation relating to one legal ruling. In a well-known passage in his *Shulḥan Arukh,*[59] the sixteenth-century code of Jewish law that was to leave a lasting impact on traditional Judaism, Joseph Caro forbade the reading of all secular literature in any language at any time. The love poetry of Immanuel of Rome and histories of wars (probably a reference to the tenth-century *Josippon*) were classified by Caro as secular literature. Seventeen years later, Moses Isserles came to write his *Mappah* on Caro's code. Glossing this passage, he gave a less stringent ruling and permitted the reading of secular literature and histories of wars provided they were written in Hebrew.[60] As the centuries progressed, Caro's original ruling was modified. In his *Mor u-Qeṣiʿah,* glosses on the *Oraḥ Ḥayyim,*[61] the eighteenth-century scholar Jacob Emden[62] provided a detailed list of approved and banned reading for the Sabbath and the rest of the week. The first part of David Gans's *Ṣemaḥ David* and likewise the first part of Abraham Zacuto's *Sefer Yuḥasin,* both sixteenth-century chronicles, were regarded as permitted reading for the Sabbath because their subject matter dealt with scriptural and talmudic history, and likewise the first sections of the *Josippon* because it concerned the miracles which were performed for Israel.[63] Records of sad events contained in the sixth book of the *Josippon* and in the chronicle of Joseph

57. The first non-Jewish authors to refer to de' Rossi that I have been able to trace are Jacob Christmann in *Calendarium Palaestinorum,* Frankfurt on Main, 1594 (pp. 32–33) who refers to ch. 25 about the introduction of the anno mundi reckoning and Villalpandus, in chaps. 21 and 26 of his *Apparatus* of 1602, where he refers to de' Rossi's chapter (56) on ancient Jewish coins and inserts are extract from it in Latin which Benedictus Blancuccius had translated for him. According to S. Burnett, *From Christian Hebraism,* 208, Pierre Chevalier's reference to the *Sefer ha-Bahir* in his attack on Elijah Levita's argument about the invention of the Hebrew vowel points (in his Annotationes to the *Rudimenta Hebraicae linguae* of Antoine Chevalier [Geneva, 1590]) is taken from de' Rossi.

58. *Histoire critique du vieux testament,* 602.

59. The passage is in *Oraḥ Ḥayyim,* 307:16.

60. Moses ben Israel Isserles (1525/30–72), known by his acronym Rema, was born in Cracow. His glosses on the *Shulḥan Arukh* contain additions, explanations, and customs of Ashkenazi scholars ignored by Caro.

61. *Mor u-Qeṣiʿah* (Altona, 1761–68).

62. Jacob Emden (1697–1776) was a rabbinic authority, a kabbalist, and an anti-Shabbatean polemicist.

63. Emden stresses that the reading of these texts should not become a habitual occupation for the Sabbath because it might lead to the neglect of the study of Torah. He also adds that the interpolated material in the *Josippon,* "those useless stories about Alexander of Macedon and their like," are forbidden reading matter even for the weekday because they are a waste of time.

Hacohen were not allowed to be read on the Sabbath. For much the same reason Solomon ibn Verga's *Shevet Yehudah* was also consigned to weekday reading even though it too contained testimony of Gods protection of Israel throughout the centuries. As for the second part of the *Yuḥasin* and the final part of the *Ṣemaḥ David,* which pertained to the gentiles, they were to be read only in moments of leisure and relaxation from the study of the Torah. But they should be read, he stressed, as examples of good style and also because "a scholar should not be ignorant about the course of history. . . . Occasionally, history may even have a direct bearing on our people and we can learn from it to our benefit."[64]

This entire passage is taken over and abbreviated somewhat by the noted eighteenth-century kabbalist Hayyim David Azulai[65] in his *Maḥaziq Berakhah.*[66] But he adds to the section and, without explanation or comment, proceeds to give a transcript of a letter he found among the papers of a "great rabbi." The letter in question was the famous (or notorious) document sent from Safed to the Italian communities probably in 1574 by Joseph Caro's disciples, Moses Alshekh and Elishah Gallico. In it, they conveyed the opinion of their recently deceased master that Azariah de' Rossi's *Light of the Eyes* should be consigned to the flames.[67]

The exclusion of the *Light of the Eyes* from the list of approved historical literature and the appendage of the letter in this section of the glosses tell more than one story. On the one hand, Azulai seems to be approving the alleged ban of Caro, which in fact did not win the day.[68] Despite the controversy which raged over the publication of the book in the author's lifetime, the antagonism on the part of some leaders of the communities to the author and his book was not unanimous by any means. At the same time, it would appear that Azulai was conscious that if it were not for the suspect nature of the work, it should have merited a place among those other Jewish historical works and been put on the approved list, at least for weekday occasional reading. (In fact Azulai himself read the book—he uses it in his *Va'ad le-Ḥakhamim* without quoting his source.)[69]

But de' Rossi's work did not fall into total oblivion in the two hundred years which elapsed from the time of his death in 1577. A glance at David Cassel's and Leopold Zunz's lists of Jewish writers who quoted the work indicates that all manner of authors of the seventeenth and eighteenth centuries—talmudic commentators, kabbalists, scientists, and biblical exegetes—were acquainted with the work. Both the former converso Manasseh ben Israel[70] of Amsterdam and the learned rabbi and scientist Joseph del Medigo[71] put the work on their lists of required reading. Not all readers of the book

64. Ibid., f. 18r, col. a.

65. Hayyim David Azulai, known by his acronym, Ḥida (1724–1806), was also a rabbinic authority, emissary, and bibliographer.

66. *Maḥaziq Berakhah,* Kuntres Aḥaron, f. 173r, col. b.

67. On Caro's ban, see M. Benayahu, "The polemic," 238–42. The authenticity of the ban is open to doubt.

68. See, e.g., vol. 9 of Medini's *Sede Ḥemed,* 366 col. a, in which he quotes Solomon Ḥazan's eulogy of de' Rossi.

69. *Va'ad le-Ḥakhamim* (Livorno, 1795), 33v–34r. In "Toledot" (11), Leopold Zunz castigates Azulai for having failed to mention de' Rossi as the main source of his information.

70. In his *Dissertatio,* 2:134, he stresses the need to read only "good books." De' Rossi's name appears on the list, which includes Saadya, Maimonides, Kimḥi, ibn Ezra, and Rashi.

71. *Mikhtav,* 22.

were sympathetic. Indeed, many of the criticisms leveled against de' Rossi at the time of the publication of the book and the trenchant objections of Judah Loew ben Bezalel, the Maharal of Prague[72] were raised again during the seventeenth and eighteenth centuries.

The book, then, was read, but it would appear there was no direct follower of de' Rossi's method. In some ways this was inevitable. De' Rossi was not a Nachman Krochmal and did not impose a philosophy of history on his study of antiquity. His approach was that of an antiquarian with all its limitations, and his work was recognized and used as such.

There is no doubt that the *Light of the Eyes* acquired its prominence among the Jewish scholars of the Enlightenment. It was they who called its author "father of scholars." The highest praise which Zvi Hirsch Goldenberg could bestow on Solomon Rapoport (Shir), one of the pioneers of the circle for the Science of Judaism, was to compare him to de' Rossi: "Since the days of the great critic Azariah de' Rossi of blessed memory, no scholarship comparable to his was to be seen in all Israel." Zunz, in collaboration with Rapoport, wrote the basic biography and study of de' Rossi, which was published in volumes of the *Kerem Ḥemed* and reprinted in I. Benjacob's and Z. H. Jaffe's editions of the work.

The nineteenth-century Jewish scholars referred to de' Rossi as to a contemporary colleague and judged his work by their own standards. (In fact, Zunz compiled a list of de' Rossi's "mistakes.") Until quite recently, their perspective influenced most appraisals of de' Rossi's contribution to Jewish historiography. It was the pioneering work of Salo Baron[73] that has led scholars to recognize the need to give close scrutiny to de' Rossi's exceptionally manifold and diverse source material and to determine the historical and cultural context which informs all his work.

THE *LIGHT OF THE EYES:* GENRE

The historical works singled out above are among the standard texts submitted to analysis and discussion whenever the question of the historical productions of the Jews during the Middle Ages and Renaissance is raised. With the exception of the *Josippon,* they were all written in the fifteenth and sixteenth centuries. They may be loosely characterized as chronicles. Ibn Verga's *Shevet Yehudah* recounts the persecutions of the Jewish people from the second Temple period until his own time.[74] While containing a sociological analysis of exile, it also uses themes and motifs of Hispanic and converso

72. Maharal's invective in his *Be'er* (126 col. b–141a), in which he attacked de' Rossi, particularly for his interpretation of the Aggadot, without mentioning his name, and a briefer attack in his *Neṣaḥ* (35 col. a) has attracted much attention. See, A. Neher, *Le puits,* 98–116; L. Segal, *Historical Consciousness,* ch. 8; B. Carucci Viterbi, "La polemica." It should be pointed out that the Maharal and de' Rossi were proceeding from different premises and positions. What the Maharal defined as essence was called metaphor by de' Rossi. Thus investigation of Maharal's approach does not really assist understanding of de' Rossi's arguments.

73. Baron's three essays, "A Biographical Sketch" (published in Hebrew in 1929); "Azariah de' Rossi's Attitude to Life" (published in 1927), and "Azariah de' Rossi's Historical Method" (published in French in 1928), were printed in his *History and Jewish Historians.*

74. It was written at the beginning of the fifteenth century and published in Adrianople, 1553. For a general characterization of this and the other chronicles mentioned here, see Yerushalmi, *Zachor,* ch. 3, 57–75, and R. Bonfil, "How Golden," 78–102.

literary sources, as Eleazar Gutwirth has demonstrated.[75] Joseph Hacohen, the author of *Divre ha-Yamin le Malkhe Ṣarefat u-Malkhe bet Ottoman ha-Togar* (*The History of the Kings of France and of the Ottoman Turkish Sultans*), explicitly draws the reader's attention to the novelty of his work when he begins with a proclamation that he is a direct heir of Josephus and is renewing the line of chroniclers in Israel.[76] Zacuto's *Sefer Yuḥasin* is a history of rabbinic scholars in the "chain of tradition" genre, and the last section of the work comprises a chronicle of world history.[77] The disciple of Moses Isserles, David Gans, published his chronicle, the *Ṣemaḥ David,* in Prague in 1593—twenty years after de' Rossi had published his *Light of the Eyes.* Drawing on much of de' Rossi's data, Gans wrote a world chronicle divided into two parts, separating Jewish from gentile history or, in his own words, "separating the holy from the profane since uninspired history should not be confused with the words of the living God."[78]

Each of the works making up this motley collection of chronicles deserves individual treatment; all contain some novel material or investigation of either Jewish or gentile history, and all authors make some use of non-Jewish sources. Nevertheless, the annalistic form of literature is by its very nature restricted in scope and does not allow for extensive critical analysis or evaluation of source material. De' Rossi departed from previous Jewish modes of writing to produce a work which in structure and content was innovative. On his own admission, he modeled his work on the miscellanea used by encyclopaedists, philologists, and antiquarians. He defended his adoption of this genre of writing and argued that variegated studies were entertaining and broadened the reader's scholarly perspective. In his Italian work on the Gospels, de' Rossi referred to his *Light of the Eyes* as "libro di varie lettioni," surely a title intended to recall Pedro Mexía's popular *Silva de varia leçion.* In the opening chapter of the main body of the book, de' Rossi, who had read Mexía's *Forest* in an Italian translation, describes his chapters as a garden full of different plants and fruits from which visitors may pick whatever takes their fancy. The forest had simply been transformed into a garden. But Mexía's work served as a model for de' Rossi in respect not so much of content as of format. Mexía's *Forest* was, in the words of Marcel Bataillon, a hotchpotch of topics of insignificant erudition.[79] There can be no doubt that his discourses on "That it is praiseworthy to speak little" or "Who was the first person to tame the lion?" are a far cry from de' Rossi's erudite chapters.[80]

AN OVERVIEW OF THE CONTENT OF THE *LIGHT OF THE EYES*

The *Light of the Eyes* is divided into three unequal parts: "The Voice of God" (Qol Elohim), on the earthquake of Ferrara (1570); "The Splendor of the Elders" (Hadrat Zeqenim), de' Rossi's Hebrew translation of the *Letter of Aristeas;* and "Words of

75. E. Gutwirth, "The Expulsion," 141–61.
76. The work was published in Sabbioneta, 1554.
77. The work was published in Constantinople, 1566.
78. *Ṣemaḥ David,* 7.
79. M. Bataillon, *Érasme,* 673.
80. Baron described de' Rossi's chapters as essays, and this term has been adopted by most scholars. The term is anachronistic, however—Montaigne first coined it in 1580—and it is not an adequate description of de' Rossi's mode of composition.

Understanding" (Imre Binah), studies on Jewish history, chronology, and other antiquarian topics. The third part, "Words of Understanding," which forms the main body of the book, is in four sections and sixty chapters, of which the third section on chronology is given the title "Days of the World" (Yeme Olam).[81]

The first section of "Words of Understanding" contains a critique of Philo and a study of the Jewish and Christian traditions about the origins of the Septuagint in which de' Rossi puts forward his novel explanation of the discrepancies between the Hebrew and Greek texts. It also includes a lengthy chapter on the geographical and scientific notions of the rabbis considered in the light of the New World discoveries.

Section 2 is mainly devoted to the interpretation of the Aggadot, transmission of texts, and historical investigations related to the Seleucid era and the Jewish *anno mundi* era. The section ends with an apologia of the rabbis' lack of expertise in the area of history and, as a corollary, an argument in defense of the right to challenge rabbinic pronouncements on non-normative issues.

The third section, "Days of the World," consists of a major study of Jewish chronology, including historical chronology, the calendar, Daniel's prophecy of the seventy weeks, messianic speculation, and the three ages of the Tanna d've Eliyahu.

The final section includes four chapters on the priestly vestments with a comparative study of the treatment of the subject by medieval Jewish commentators, Aristeas, Philo, and Josephus, and Christian references, including the thirteenth-century liturgist Guglielmus Durandus. In the following chapters, a variety of topics is discussed, including the interpretation of Haggai's prophecy (2:9) and the significance of omens, which reflect de' Rossi's own notions about Jewish history of the second Commonwealth and divine providence, producing as it were an antidote to his diatribe against messianic speculation. A chapter on ancient Jewish coins is followed by a triad of chapters on the antiquity of the Hebrew language, script, and vowels. The book ends with the celebrated chapter on the nature of biblical poetry.

Clearly de' Rossi had designed a scheme for all the chapters.[82] The transitions between sections and chapters follow a tenuous but natural sequence, a detail of one chapter becoming the starting point of the next one.[83] The work begins and ends with a reference to the earthquake of Ferrara, to which event de' Rossi dates the genesis of his literary activity. Each section contains a preparatory general discussion in which de' Rossi defends his method of scholarship and alerts his reader as to the purpose of his inquiry. The apologetic strain which runs throughout the book unifies the disparate chapters, becoming most evident and reaching its climax just before and at the beginning of "Days of the World" (chaps. 27, 28, and 29). This is the most controversial section of the book. In it, de' Rossi challenges the traditional computation of the age of the universe, thereby invalidating all messianic speculation and in particular the fashionable

81. De' Rossi takes rhetorical license with the biblical expression usually translated as "Days of Old" to refer to his section on chronology.

82. He often states that he will treat a certain topic in a forthcoming chapter and invariably fulfills his promise.

83. For example, he follows his discussion of the topos of the monarch's cross-questioning of sages in ch. 10 by selecting one of the questions—Which distance is greater: from heaven to earth or from east to west?—to introduce the subject of the following chapter, an appraisal of some of the scientific and geographical notions of the rabbis.

eschatological reckoning for the year 1575. With the conclusion of the chronological section, the apologetic strain diminishes; the refutation of rabbinic chronology had been proved to de' Rossi's satisfaction. The remaining topics such as the identity of Aquila and Onqelos, the priestly vestments, the antiquity of the Hebrew language, and biblical poetry were less controversial and did not require the same careful defensive treatment.

THE *LIGHT OF THE EYES:* CULTURAL CONTEXT AND PURPOSE

The most eloquent testimony to de' Rossi's scholarly *Sitz im Leben* is exemplified in a gloss he wrote in relation to the epitaph he had composed for his grave and which he published at the end of the last chapter of the book. In the gloss, he writes that he had modeled his inscription on the text that Cardinal Contarini had prepared for his own sepulchral monument: "Venimus ad portum, Spes et fortuna valete, / nil mihi vobiscum, illudite nunc alios" (We have reached port; farewell hope and fortune, / I have nothing more to do with you; now make play with others). These couplets, like many epitaphs of the time, are devoid of Christian or religious sentiment[84] and could therefore be adopted by de' Rossi without impinging on his religious identity.[85] And yet it is a testament to de' Rossi's openness to the cultural world around him that he penned his farewell to the world under the inspiration of the renowned cardinal.[86]

Given the case of the epitaph, it comes as less of a surprise that Christian scholarship should pervade de' Rossi's writing. The majority of the subjects treated by de' Rossi were already under discussion by Christian scholars of all descriptions. For each topic, whether it be the *Letter of Aristeas,* chronology, or the Hebrew language, de' Rossi consulted the current textbooks. At the same time, he provided a Jewish dimension to the subjects in question. He adopts this method of writing even in the opening part of the book, the account of the earthquake which shook Ferrara in 1570. It contains recognizable features of contemporary tracts written in response to this momentous event but adds the Jewish material related to the interpretation of such natural disasters and a description of the behavior of the Jewish population of Ferrara at the time of the calamity.[87]

He "doth protest too much, methinks" are the words that come to mind on reading the *Light of the Eyes.* For one of the most conspicuous features of de' Rossi's discourse is his consistently apologetic stance. Having brought cogent arguments and authoritative sources to prove the rabbis' inadequacies in the historical domain, de' Rossi would then conclude, "Nor will anything be proposed that would mar the honor of our rabbis, may they rest in peace" (chap. 29). His own laborious and carefully woven arguments he dismisses time and time again with the talmudic dictum "Whatever happened happened." An entire chapter is devoted to a defense of his use of non-Jewish sources, and at appropriate moments the following leitmotiv appears: "Of course I would not accept their statements which hint at heresy or make light of our Torah, God forbid."

84. On the epitaph, which derives from the *Anthologia Palatina* (9, 49), see I. Kajanto, *Classical and Christian,* 48.

85. De' Rossi actually adds two more lines of a more religious sentiment to his epitaph. See ch. 60.

86. Gasparo Contarini (1483–1542) was one of the key figures at the colloquy between Catholics and Protestants at Regensburg in 1541.

87. See my article "The Voice of God."

De' Rossi, in other words, was fully aware that he was treading a new path, one which might not gain approval in all quarters. One of his most hostile critics, the Maharal of Prague, was perhaps not wrong when he accused de' Rossi of paying lip service to rabbinic authority and of employing such feeble arguments in their defense that he undermined their case to an even greater extent. For with all his apologetic pleas, he forges ahead in his quest for truth, which, in his view, "may emerge from all places." Truth, in de' Rossi's words, "is like a seal of the true God, the characteristic of the beautiful soul and the good to which all aspire." In this affirmation, redolent of Neoplatonic and talmudic notions,[88] de' Rossi discloses his true attitude toward his painstaking researches, which would appear to undermine all his token gestures toward rabbinic authority.

The truth that de' Rossi was seeking pertained to the proper way of reading rabbinic statements on matters that lay beyond Sinaitic tradition, nonlegal issues that could have no repercussion on a Jew's observance of the Torah. In particular, his aim was to differentiate the Aggadot, the nonlegal utterances and discourses in rabbinic tradition, from the main body of Oral Torah and to interpret the stories as didactic tales the purpose of which was summed up in the rabbinic dictum, "If you wish to know about Him who spoke and the world existed, go and study Aggadot." But ever since the controversy in Provence at the beginning of the fourteenth century the nonliteral interpretation of the Aggadot became a dangerous undertaking unless the exegete was a kabbalist. With the printing of the Zohar and midrashic texts in the sixteenth century there was a resurgence of interest in the Aggadot among Italian Jews. The Venetian rabbi Samuel Katzenellenbogen, however, denounced the study of Aggadot, which, in his view, had superseded that of the Talmud.[89] Moses Basola and Joseph Ashkenazi attacked the printers of works in which the Aggadot were submitted to philosophical or allegorical interpretation.[90]

De' Rossi's approach to the Aggadot was somewhat novel; for it was primarily as a historian that he analyzed the Aggadot. His purpose in the second section of "Words of Understanding" was not to fathom the depths of rabbinic wisdom, which he fully acknowledged, but to demonstrate that the historical and scientific data in the Aggadot did not concur with historical or scientific truths. By eradicating the intellectually untenable elements in the Aggadot and divesting the stories and pronouncements of their literal meaning, de' Rossi saw himself as removing the main barrier to a constructive reading of the texts. The facts were in themselves irrelevant, and in de' Rossi's view used as metaphors, symbols, and allegories in accordance with the principles of rhetoric. On the basis of a rather selective and partial reading of medieval appraisals of the status of the Aggadot, he concluded, "The Aggadot are definitely not traditionally transmitted *halakhah,* but merely invented suppositions."

88. De' Rossi applies the term "beautiful soul" to Christians as well as to Jews. In his work on the Syriac Gospels he constantly refers to those Christians who would appreciate knowledge of the true text of Scripture as "bei spiriti" or "elevati spiriti."

89. See R. Bonfil (*Rabbis,* 309), where he cites Katzenellenbogen's sermons: "In practically all congregations they avoid listening to the laws and look for Aggadot and Midrashim."

90. See M. Benayahu, *Copyright,* 87–89.

A significant proportion of the book is devoted to chronology. Even in the introduction to the entire work, which serves as a preamble to the *Letter of Aristeas,* de' Rossi already touches on some of the problems relating to the chronology issue: the succession of high priests at the beginning of the second Temple period, the dates of Alexander of Macedon and their connection with the Seleucid era. Chronology also penetrates the second section of "Words of Understanding," which is principally devoted to the interpretation of rabbinic Aggadot. Thus in chapter 18, de' Rossi draws attention to the homiletic device of identifying different people as one and the same person by reason of their affinity in character or behavior. The main example, the identification of Cyrus, Darius, and Artaxerxes as a single individual, is not chosen at random but has important implications for de' Rossi's refutation of the famous statement at the end of the Seder Olam, which compressed the duration of Persian rule at the beginning of the second Temple period into thirty-four years. In his controversial discussion of hyperbole[91] (chap. 20), de' Rossi discusses the recurring use of the number three hundred. Comparing this figure—which the Babylonian Talmud sets for the number of high priests who officiated in the second Temple—with the more modest figure of eighty to eighty-five in the Palestinian Talmud and fifty-two in Josephus, de' Rossi was able to discount the Babylonian evidence by dismissing the figure as a hyperbole. Then again in chapter 25, his argument that the traditional anno mundi computation was a convention which was not adopted before the close of the talmudic era had a bearing on his overall thesis that the conventional figure was at least one hundred years short. In other words, the ground was being prepared for his onslaught on traditional chronology in section 3. Central to his investigations were the popular forgeries of Annius of Viterbo. De' Rossi translates two of Annius's fakes (Metasthenes and Philo) into Hebrew and sets them together with a short extract from Xenophon's *Cyropaedia* and *Anabasis,* a section from Josephus's *Antiquities* and Eusebius's *Chronicle* as the primary source materials for his complicated discussions in the following chapters.

The starting point of de' Rossi's inquiries was the information found in scripture and rabbinic tradition. He scanned the relevant discussion of the subject in the works of such medieval authorities as Abraham bar Ḥiyya, Maimonides, and Isaac Israeli. But he also applied a comparative approach, referring to the classic questions regarding the Julian and Christian calendars and the date of the foundation of Rome. Ptolemy's *Almagest* also featured in the discussion, and the recently published *Chronologia* of Gerhard Mercator was brought to bear on Ptolemy's evidence about the eras and epochs.

Anthony Grafton has demonstrated unequivocally the importance of chronology in the sixteenth century. Together with philology it became a discipline in its own right: "By the 1570's, when [Joseph] Scaliger turned to chronology, intellectuals of very different kinds had long regarded it as a fascinating and important subject—indeed as part of the core of civilization."[92] Moreover, "the technical components of chronology formed part of the fabric of common life. The study of calendars, their relation to one another and their always inexact co-ordination with the movements of the sun and

91. See below, the section on the controversy over the publication of the book.
92. A. Grafton, *Joseph Scaliger,* 5.

moon belonged to the art of computus which the vast majority of intellectuals and many others knew intimately until the eighteenth century."[93] De' Rossi's endeavor fits the picture depicted by Grafton. Of course, his contribution to the subject was modest compared with Scaliger's—he was concentrating on the chronological and calendrical problem associated with one tradition, namely, his own rabbinic one. But his fearless critical approach to the subject bears comparison with that of Scaliger. De' Rossi's critique of rabbinic chronology was based on a detailed and comprehensive examination of all the figures pertaining to the duration of the bondage in Egypt, the middle years of the first Temple period, and the first years of the second Temple period. In addition, he had to take into account the Jewish calendrical system, which was reckoned from creation, because any alteration to the anno mundi reckoning would also affect the computation of the calendar. But he argued that the rabbinic reckonings were never meant to give the exact date. Rather it was "a mere convention which was established by the formulator of our calendar. . . . Addition or subtraction of years can in no way disrupt or defer any of the fixed times in our calendar."

Having debunked the conventional *aera mundi* computation, de' Rossi could proceed to a branch of chronology which permeated both Jewish and Christian writings—messianic speculation and schematized descriptions of the ages of the universe—and demonstrate the flimsy foundation on which they were based. De' Rossi's treatment of the famous statement of the Tanna d've Eliyahu that divided the duration of the world into three ages of two thousand years each was novel. Considering the variety of approaches to this theme, rabbinic, kabbalistic, and Christian, de' Rossi could underline its literary quality, thus divesting it of any real significance as far as figures and dates were concerned. In the final analysis, he invokes the famous statement attributed by Xenophon to Socrates that humans should not overstep the bounds of their human capabilities and investigate that which does not pertain to them. The pronouncement of the Tanna d've Eliyahu appears in the discourses of scholars as different from one another as Pico della Mirandola and Gilbert Génébrard, and the latter even begins his *Chronographia* with the talmudic quotation.[94] The widespread use of schemes like the Tanna d've Eliyahu highlights the iconoclasm in de' Rossi's approach and sets him apart from his contemporaries with only Scaliger for company. As Grafton has demonstrated, Scaliger "saw the dates he established—even those of events we would consider mythical—as mere dates, not symbols,"[95] and by concentrating on the technical and soluble he was able to preserve a certain scholarly objectivity. This was also de' Rossi's mode of pursuing his chronological quest. What could be established had to be established on the basis of reliable authorities and precise evidence. Those who are intent on truth "should abstain from absorbing everything that is put into their mouths and are not satisfied by taking implausible matters on trust."[96]

93. Ibid., 7.

94. On this subject, see R. Barnes, *Prophecy,* 51 and passim. De' Rossi certainly came across the reference to the Tanna d've Eliyahu in the non-Jewish sources he consulted. In Agostino Ferentilli's *Discorso,* which he quotes in ch. 16, for example, the Tanna d've Eliyahu is even mentioned in the title of the work.

95. *Joseph Scaliger,* 355.

96. Ch. 40.

The dazzling erudition that de' Rossi displays on every page of the book and in regard to a wide range of subjects militates against any facile interpretation. An important and challenging reevaluation of the book was proposed by Robert Bonfil.[97] He regarded the apologetic strain prevalent in the work as the key to its interpretation. According to Bonfil, it was written as a response to the anti-Jewish atmosphere of Counter-Reformation Italy. Thus the purpose of de' Rossi's prolix historical investigations, a New History of the Jews, as Bonfil recently termed the work,[98] was to defend rabbinic literature from the attacks of Christians and Jewish apostates by showing that non-normative matters discussed in the Talmud were open to criticism, that there was no precise chronology for the age of the universe, and that all messianic speculation was founded on false premises. At the same time, de' Rossi intended to buttress Jewish self-esteem by discussing the Jewish contribution to such subjects as poetry and language. The use of non-Jewish sources was de' Rossi's method of fighting his opponents with their own weapons and was thus a powerful tool of defense.

For Bonfil, then, de' Rossi's erudite research was "a means of fostering, as objectively as possible, his nationalistic perceptions of Jewish identity."[99] In an attempt to give an overarching rationale for de' Rossi's work, Bonfil has produced an attractive but also reductive interpretation. I would certainly admit that on occasion a polemical dimension can be discerned in some of de' Rossi's investigations. It may be detected in his attack on the sixteenth-century Massorete Elijah Levita, who had argued with good reason that the Hebrew vowel system had been invented by the Tiberian Massoretes after the redaction of the Talmud. De' Rossi's attempt to uphold the traditional view of the antiquity of the vowel points comes as something of a surprise. In fact, he goes so far as to say that Adam must have been familiar with the vowel points, for otherwise he would have been unable to determine the correct pronunciation of the words. It is appropriate to consider why in tackling such matters as Jewish chronology de' Rossi adopted a rather iconoclastic attitude while maintaining a conservative position when confronted with the untraditional but more correct views of the grammarian Levita. As I have shown, de' Rossi was conversant with Christian biblical scholarship; in his perusal of these texts he could hardly have failed to notice the allegation—which apparently always bore repeating—that Jews had invented the vowel points in order to conceal the true meaning of Scripture. Or, to quote from Perez de Valencia, whose work de' Rossi had read, Jews had deliberately falsified the vowel points in order to suppress Christian truths. De' Rossi's defense of Jewish tradition regarding the antiquity of the vowel points should perhaps be viewed not only as an attack on Levita, but also as a response to Christian detractors of the Hebrew Scriptures. Levita had attracted a large following of Christian scholars. It is not unlikely that de' Rossi's critique of Levita was dictated by a desire to put an end to the propagation of the Christian medieval view regarding the invention of the vowel points.

But one should not allow the polemical dimension of de' Rossi's arguments to obscure one's assessment of his real contribution to critical scholarship, which is illustrated

97. "Expression," 40; "Some Reflections"; "How Golden."
98. "How Golden," 100.
99. Ibid., 101.

on so many pages of the *Light of the Eyes.* One could point, for example, to his study of the ps. Philonic work the *Liber biblicarum antiquitatum.* This work, which was extant in a Latin version, recounted biblical history from Adam to Saul. De' Rossi was the first scholar to discern, and to discern correctly, that the text contained striking parallels to some of the nonlegal rabbinic Midrashim and Aggadot and to detect that the text probably represented the most ancient stratum of the stories. Joannes Sichardus, the editor of the first printed edition of the work, had indicated biblical references and variant readings in marginal glosses. Sixtus Senensis had noted that the Latin text was permeated with Hebraisms. De' Rossi went further and supplied the rabbinic parallels, a respectable undertaking for any textual critic.

De' Rossi's discovery can hardly be called nationalistic. Certainly, his mastery of the texts of Jewish tradition was greater than that of any Christian scholar of his time. He was therefore in a good position to provide the Jewish data where relevant. In this particular case, he was able to widen the horizons of his Jewish readers and make them consider the implications of the ancestry of some of the rabbinic material.[100]

Even Bonfil acknowledges that the polemical strain in de' Rossi's writings is veiled. Whether he was constrained by the power of the censor's pen cannot be determined. The question is whether de' Rossi's alleged refutation of Christian attacks on Judaism should be regarded as the master key to the interpretation of the work as a whole, particularly because occasionally he manifests a balanced openness toward Christianity. At the beginning of chapter 14, he prepares his readers for his critical evaluation of rabbinic literature by pronouncing on the inviolability of the Oral Torah in a clearly uncontroversial vein. Not content with giving the apposite Jewish sources, he then refers to Thessalonians (2 Thess. 2:15) and to Augustine's work against the Manichaean, in which the authority of oral tradition is stressed. It seems remarkable that de' Rossi should seek Christian corroboration of a concept which is the very essence of traditional Judaism.

In chapter 16, de' Rossi describes the rabbinic stories about the gnat that entered Titus's nostril after the destruction of the second Temple as a fiction invented in order to communicate the religious message by the most effective means. He compares the rabbinic treatment of Titus with Christian reflections on the attempt to rebuild the third Temple in the time of Julian the Apostate. Socrates and Nicephor Callistus[101] had claimed that the endeavor was foiled by an earthquake which had occurred at the time, thus fulfilling Jesus' prediction that *stone would not remain on stone.* De' Rossi asserts that there was no historical record of the earthquake and then states, "Nevertheless, one should not reproach them for this, because their intention was to inspire people to their belief." The Christians, no less than the rabbis, surrendered historical truth for the sake of propagating the faith. It may be that this expression of tolerant thinking on the part of de' Rossi can be seen in another light. Versed in Christian writings, he was certainly familiar with anti-Jewish attitudes toward the rabbinic Aggadot. Following Bonfil's reasoning, it might be suggested that the most effective defense de' Rossi could put for-

100. In a similar way (see ch. 16, n. 43), he pointed out the use of one of Aesop's fables in a Midrash—he was probably the first to mention this parallel.

101. De' Rossi found these sources in Antonio Buoni's *Del terremoto* (Modena, 1571), II, 26r, par. 239.

ward was by uniting rabbis and Christians and demonstrating that pious doctrine rather than history is the key to any religious argument. In fact, his statement was not received favorably by Christian authorities, for in some of the copies of the first edition it is censored. But the apologetic argument should be used with caution. De' Rossi expresses a similarly enlightened view when speaking about Christians who interpreted the word *son* in Philo and the Hermetic texts as a prefiguration of Jesus. De' Rossi writes in language reminiscent of the Passover Haggadah: "And truly, the upright will deem them worthy of praise for this, inasmuch as the more a person can transform something to the merit of his religion, the more deserving is he of praise."[102] The adaptation of the time-honored phrase, "The more a person relates the story of the exodus from Egypt, the more he is to be praised" is surely provocative. There may be a touch of irony in de' Rossi's words, but they are certainly not apologetic or, still less, polemical.

In the sixteenth century, both Catholics and Protestants scanned the ancient sources in the hope of recovering the requisite information to support their case. A high level of scholarship was attained by means of this ecclesiastical historiography of the Eusebian type. But as Grafton has shown with regard to Scaliger, the impetus to participate in scholarly debate was not necessarily motivated by ideology.[103] The task of compiling and evaluating accurately and precisely was sufficient in itself and, as the subject dictated, required taking issue with Catholics and Protestants alike. According to Bonfil, de' Rossi's pedantic assembling of figures and dates for his chronological investigations would not have interested his readers and was undertaken only to prove that there was no reliable chronology. It is clear, however, that de' Rossi was tackling the subject according to the book—the recording of all the figures and dates was indispensable. The conclusion of his research was significant, but equally, the method by which he arrived at his conclusion was a sine qua non for any self-respecting chronologer.

Baron has termed de' Rossi an antiquarian, comparing his method of studying ancient Jewish traditions to the manner in which Carlo Sigonio or Onofrio Panvinio studied Roman institutions. Indeed, de' Rossi's mode of assembling a wide variety of sources to establish one point and his occasional use of epigraphic and numismatic evidence sometimes gives the impression of the antiquarian at work.[104] And yet he does not attempt to reconstruct one particular period of ancient Jewish history. If a large part of his investigations relates to the history of the second Temple period, that is because the rabbinic sources throw up historical problems which he felt bound to address. For this purpose he assembled a wide variety of sources, often presenting them as *ḥiddushim* (original findings). For his Jewish readers, these texts were most certainly new, and, as he states in his work on the Syriac Gospels, he wrote his *lumen oculorum* (*Light of the Eyes*) for his "fratelli hebrei" (Jewish brethren). De' Rossi's quest for the truth thus brought him to mediate between the two worlds of Jewish and Christian scholarship. Rabbinic texts were elucidated by means of non-Jewish sources divested of all ideological or religious bias, while Jewish sources could be brought to bear on some of the fashionable debates of the day.

102. Ch. 4, p. 117.
103. *Joseph Scaliger,* 356.
104. The most important study of antiquarianism remains A. Momigliano, "Ancient History."

THE USE OF SOURCES

In the epigraph to the *Light of the Eyes,* the pious sentiment that God's name should be invoked prior to all undertakings is blazoned out by means of citations from the Palestinian Talmud, the Zohar, Philo, and Plato. The epigraph is illustrative of a phenomenon attested on virtually every page of the book, namely, the citation of a number of sources of diverse provenance, expressing unanimous views or proffering identical information, in order to establish the truth of a particular fact or idea. And although a hierarchy may be detected in the order in which these texts are cited, the presence of Philo and Plato in the august company of the Palestinian Talmud and Zohar signals de' Rossi's method of quoting the truth "from whatever place." Salo Baron rightly asserted that de' Rossi's contribution to historiography should not be seen in terms of originality of thought or even of method.[105] Rather, it lies in a remarkable synthesizing faculty whereby he applies the ideas and methods of his sources to the subject under discussion. De' Rossi uses more than 150 Jewish sources, excluding the Talmuds and midrashic literature, and more than 100 non-Jewish sources. Of these, some have a central role to play, while others are used simply to buttress his arguments. He often extrapolates the requisite information with complete disregard for context or simply truncates the passage he quotes to meet his requirements. There are also those texts to which he makes only passing reference but which provide him with more ideas or facts than he acknowledges. An apparent vagueness or mistranslation in his citation of primary sources can sometimes be attributed to his use of secondary sources, which on occasion provide the key to the scholarly background of de' Rossi's own investigations.[106]

Although there are countless examples of recourse to non-Jewish sources by Jewish writers, de' Rossi's relentless application of non-Jewish material for the purpose of correcting rabbinic statements was unprecedented. Conscious of his novel use of these sources, he devoted chapter 2 to a defense of his method, entirely drawn from Jewish sources.[107] Evolving his own criteria for accepting or rejecting non-Jewish evidence, he articulated two main principles: The authors should not present heretical views or ridicule the Torah, and they should not have vested interests in the issues at stake. This chapter is followed by his critique of Philo. In one respect, it may be regarded as a continuation of his argument in defense of the use of alien wisdom. Philo is a central figure in the book. Because Philo's status as a Hellenistic Jew presented something of an anomaly—"he fell between two stools"—de' Rossi felt bound to determine Philo's status in relation to Jewish tradition before incorporating the Philonic material into his work.

De' Rossi's interpretation of his self-imposed condition for using non-Jewish evidence was somewhat liberal. After all, a large number of his Christian sources tendered anything but a friendly attitude toward Judaism. On closer investigation, it becomes

105. Baron, "Azariah de' Rossi's Historical Method," 225–26.

106. See, e.g., my discussion of de' Rossi's reference to a passage in Jerome in ch. 5 which was taken from the forgeries of Annius of Viterbo ("An Apocryphal Source").

107. The discussion first revolves around the prohibition against *sefarim ḥiṣoniim* (profane literature), which de' Rossi argues was simply a precautionary measure aimed at limiting Jews' immersion in non-Jewish culture. He also proposes the argument used by Maimonides, Bibago, and other Jewish writers that the study of alien literature was part of the process of recovering the legacy which Jews had lost when they became subject to foreign domination.

clear that his condition applied only to the particular passage he was quoting rather than to the actual content of the book or intention of the author. Thus, for example, he cites the christological commentary to the Psalms[108] by "the Valencian," the Augustinian priest Perez (Pharez) de Valencia (1408–90).[109] De' Rossi, however, is not interested in the main thesis of the work. Rather, he focuses on a specific passage in which Perez reaffirms a notion popular with both Jews and Christians that the land of Israel was located "in the navel of the earth." Perez's evidence was particularly useful because he explicitly stated that Jerusalem is located in the middle of the inhabited world, thus apparently corroborating de' Rossi's own view of the relativity of the notion of centrality in this context. Perez discusses the question in order to establish the exact location of Jesus' crucifixion;[110] de' Rossi's argument takes a different direction; Perez's statement serves as one of the many connecting links in the construction of his argument.

De' Rossi's sources fall into four main categories: 1. Jewish writings, subdivided into rabbinic (talmudic and midrashic) and post-talmudic texts; 2. the works of ps. Aristeas, Philo, and Josephus; 3. Christian writings; 4. ancient Greek and Latin authors.[111]

1. Jewish Writings

THE RABBINIC TEXTS

The overwhelming majority of sources quoted by de' Rossi belong to Jewish tradition, and the bulk of these are from the Babylonian Talmud. Judging from the number of times he cites the Babylonian Talmud inaccurately, it would appear that he is quoting from memory. He may have been forced to do so because of the lack of texts in circulation following a papal decree in 1553 that ordered the destruction of all copies of the Talmud.[112] He demonstrates a remarkable familiarity and expertise with the entire corpus of rabbinic literature. For the most part he does not dispute the traditional attribution of authorship of early rabbinic writings. One exception may perhaps be detected in his somewhat hesitating description of the *Sefer Yeṣirah* as a work "attributed to Abraham our father."

The textual criticism which de' Rossi applies to the rabbinic writings is comparable to that used by humanists in the editing of classical texts. Philological precision is inextricably linked with the quest for historical truth. Thus, in discussing the story of the gnat that entered Titus's nostril in chapter 16, he indicates its unhistorical nature by demonstrating the many discrepancies between the different versions of the story. He also devotes an entire chapter (19) of the section on the Aggadot to the subject of textual

108. The *Expositiones in centum et quinquaginta Psalmos . . . ad illustrationem fidei nostrae* was first printed in 1484 and reprinted several times with Perez's other works, including an anti-Jewish tract, *Quaestiones . . . et resolutiones contra Iudaeos,* which was extensively used by a noted anti-Talmudist, the Ferrarese Finus Hadrianus Finus, in his *In Iudaeos.*

109. I am grateful to E. Gutwirth, who helped me to identify this source.

110. In reference to Ps. 74:12, "O God my King from of old, who brings salvation in the midst of the world," Perez interprets "God" as "Christ" and "in the midst of" as "the middle of the inhabited world," i.e., "secundum latitudinem quia distat ab aequinoctiali quasi triginta gradibus ubi Christus crucifixus est."

111. A significant part of the work on de' Rossi's sources was first written in my Ph.D. thesis and was used with acknowledgment by Bonfil in his *Kitve.*

112. See K. Stow, "The Burning," 435–59.

corruption. The standard explanations for corruption of texts enumerated by humanists like Coluccio Salutati and Angelo Poliziano are put forward by de' Rossi.[113] They include copyists' errors owing to negligence or misunderstanding of the text, the insertion of marginal glosses into the body of the text, and intentional alteration of the text. He accounts for the internal discrepancies within midrashic texts, collating different manuscripts and editions of the texts, giving preference to the readings in the oldest versions. In addition, he consulted the larger midrashic compilations in which the earlier Midrashim were quoted. Thus, in regard to the Seder Olam Rabbah, which, as has been shown, was a key text for his study of rabbinic chronology, he consulted not only various manuscripts and the printed edition of 1513, but also the printed and manuscript versions of the Yalqut Shimoni in which the Seder Olam was cited. Having accepted the traditional attribution of the work to Jose ben Ḥalafta, he accounts for the anachronisms in the texts as later accretions.

THE POST-TALMUDIC SOURCES

In the revised edition of the text published in 1575, de' Rossi appended a list of animadversions (*hassagot*) consisting of forty-one examples from the book (cited with page numbers) in which he criticized certain post-talmudic authorities. The list comprises references to such writers as Rashi, the Tosafists, and Maimonides.[114] The inclusion of the list in the final edition of the *Light of the Eyes* indicates that de' Rossi was not prepared to yield his ground but, on the contrary, wished to draw attention to his critical views.

From the time of Saadiah Gaon, animadversions had been used as a forum for debate. Of particular note are Nahmanides' hassagot on Maimonides' *Sefer ha-Miṣvot,* Rabad of Posquières' *hassagot* on Maimonides' *Mishneh Torah,* and Zerachiah Halevi's *Sefer ha-Maʾor,* which was primarily a critique of Isaac Alfasi and other rabbinic authorities in defense of the customs of the Jewish communities of Provence. This genre of writing was also used in non-Jewish literature of the fifteenth and sixteenth centuries.[115] De' Rossi's use of it was slightly different from that of previous Jewish and contemporary non-Jewish writers inasmuch as it is not a sustained invective against any single work or author. Since the book contains more than forty-one passages in which de' Rossi contests the views of other post-talmudic writers, one must assume that he regarded these examples as the most significant.

In the preface to the list, de' Rossi informs the reader why it is included in the book:

> Now although I wanted to compile an index of all particulars relating to the book, I must be content for the moment, kind reader, with presenting you with a list of animadversions against certain authorities of blessed memory which are contained in the book. I was confident that on seeing that each criticism was accompanied by some praise, the intelligent person could only regard my procedure in a favorable light. In fact, among the wise

113. On the terms for editing texts used by humanists, see S. Rizzo, *Il lessico.*

114. The writers mentioned are Rashi, Judah Halevi, Isaac Abravanel, Elijah Mizraḥi, Maimonides, Albo, Nathan ben Yeḥiel, Abraham ibn Ezra, the Tosafists, Rabbenu Nissim, Moses Isserlis, Isaac Alfasi, Meir Abulafia of Toledo, Abraham ibn David, Nahmanides, Rabbenu Ḥananel, Moses al-Ashqar, and Elijah Levita.

115. See the compilation of these works by J. Gruterus in *Lampas.*

> and instructive teachings of our sages, one should point out the useful statement cited in Bava Batra (142b) in connection with the controversy between six Amoraim, three on each side, about one of the laws regarding transfer of property. It reads:
> Rabbi Abbahu said to Rabbi Jeremiah: "Is the law according to your verdict or according to ours?" He said to him: "It is obvious that the law is decided according to our view since we are older than you. It cannot be according to your view since you are our juniors." He said to him: "Surely age cannot be the decisive factor in the matter; rather it should be decided by those whose opinion is supported by reason."
> Rabbi Jeremiah was silenced by him and did not resume the dispute. Nevertheless, the reader should know that should he set about to extricate those esteemed authorities from my hands, he has my approval; it is divine recompense itself that will come to his salvation.[116]
> Let us begin by praising the Tosafist of blessed memory for his discrimination in identifying a quotation from the book of Ben Sira called Ecclesiasticus by Greeks and Christians.[117] Likewise in chapter 57 I showed you that the Ḥokhmata Rabbata cited by Ramban (Nahmanides) is a quotation from the Wisdom of Solomon. As regards the possibility that some of the passages were tampered with, I have nothing to say—I simply do not know.

In this short preface, the reader is presented with typical de' Rossian apologetics. In order to preempt criticism of his refutations of the views of revered Jewish authorities, de' Rossi tries to mitigate the harshness of his verdicts by allocating some credit to his victims. Thus he praises the Tosafist for identifying the passage from Ben Sira in the knowledge that the list contains various examples in which he took the Tosafists to task fairly severely. Characteristic, too, is his citation from the Talmud. The passage quoted out of context is usefully applied to his case. Reason is on his side and must be the decisive factor in every argument. The allusion to interpolation used as an excuse for the errors of the "esteemed authorities" is couched in such vague terms that the reader is obviously not supposed to take the suggestion seriously. No one common feature characterizes the wide range of post-talmudic sources used by de' Rossi. According to the subject, he quoted from biblical commentaries and talmudic glosses, codes, astronomical and philosophical treatises, kabbalistic and historical writings.

The author whose approach to history bears greatest affinity to de' Rossi's is Isaac Abravanel (1437–1508), to whom de' Rossi invariably refers as Don Isaac. According to Fritz Baer, Abravanel acquired his interest in history at the Spanish court, where he became acquainted with the historiographical literature of the time.[118] Like de' Rossi, Abravanel asserted the importance of history for the understanding of the Bible and used non-Jewish evidence. The most striking similarity between the two authors may be found in their use of Josephus. Baer claims that Abravanel was the first Jewish writer to have read a Latin translation of Josephus's works. Abravanel frequently referred to Josephus, particularly in his commentary on Daniel. Many of the historical problems discussed by de' Rossi had already been broached by Abravanel in the course of his prolix commentaries on Scripture. It is not unlikely that Abravanel's work gave de' Rossi the impetus to investigate these questions in greater depth. De' Rossi's greater

116. "It is . . . salvation," cf. Is. 35:4.

117. De' Rossi gives here the reference to ch. 2. The Tosafist comments on B. B.Q. 92b: "Birds of a feather flock together and man does likewise." De' Rossi points out the parallel passage in Ben Sira, 13:15.

118. F. Baer, "Don Isaac Abravanel," 247.

familiarity with his primary source material and more systematic historical analysis enabled him to give a more thorough and precise presentation of the subject. Abravanel was not writing principally as a historian. Nevertheless, the differences between the two scholars are also indicative of the general features which distinguish sixteenth-century from fifteenth-century scholarship.

2. Aristeas, Philo, and Josephus

The works of Aristeas, Philo, and Josephus provided de' Rossi with some of the crucial evidence for his discussions of the historical problems related to the second Temple period and the description of the priestly vestments. In a play on a biblical expression about Noah's three sons,[119] he implicitly represents Aristeas as Ham, that is, the gentile, Philo as Japhet, the Hellenistic Jew, and Josephus as Shem, the Judean Jew. The differentiation between the three is, however, eclipsed by the nature of the evidence they could supply:[120] "They all lived in Temple times; their statements were not guess-work or hearsay but presented what they and not others had witnessed." In this statement one may perhaps detect an echo of Jerome's appraisal of Josephus. In an epistle with which de' Rossi was familiar Jerome had stated,[121] "In his time, the Temple was still standing; Vespasian and Titus had not yet destroyed Jerusalem. He was of priestly stock—and what is seen with the eye is much more comprehensible than that which is known through hearsay."

All three authors fared well in print in the sixteenth century. Editions galore, authentic and suppositious, in Greek, Latin, and the vernaculars poured from the presses. De' Rossi read the Latin and Italian texts and even a Castilian version of the *Antiquities*—but he was unable to read them in the original Greek. This, however, did not deter him from translating some of the texts, including the *Letter of Aristeas* in its entirety, into Hebrew. The translation of the *Letter,* which can hardly be described as easy reading material, was an enormous undertaking. As noted above, he claims that a Christian scholar who, like him, was living under canvas at the time of the earthquake which hit Ferrara in 1570 urged him to undertake the translation. De' Rossi went about his task with scholarly rigor. He based his translation on Matthias Garbitius's Latin rendering, which, he notes, had met unanimous approval according to most recent appraisals and was regarded as superior to previous versions. Conscious of the many textual problems that abound in the text, he consulted the epitomes of Josephus and Eusebius and noted his findings in marginal glosses. For de' Rossi's contemporaries, the appeal of the *Letter* lay in its portrayal of Ptolemy as the ideal monarch, in the sound doctrine and wisdom it propagated, and in its description of an event which was regarded by some as ratification of the Christian Scriptures. Additionally, as Arnaldo Momigliano noted, it set a good example for a king or pope patronizing translations from classical texts.[122] De' Rossi, however, cast the *Letter* in new light. Reclaiming it as

119. Ch. 50, p. 610. He refers to "three sons of pleasantness," a play on Gen. 9:19, "These three were the sons of Noah." Noah is spelled in a *plene* form and therefore can be read as the noun meaning "pleasantness."

120. Ch. 46, p. 496.

121. Jerome, *Ep.* LXIV (P.L. XXII, col. 613).

122. A. Momigliano, "The place," 17.

part of the Jewish legacy, he presented the seventy elders and Eleazar the high priest as the protagonists of the story, singling out their political astuteness, the eyewitness description of Jerusalem, the Temple, and the priestly vestments. It was additionally attractive to him because the event it described had also its parallel in rabbinic tradition. De' Rossi's claim to fame, of course, is not as a translator of ancient texts.[123] His interest in the *Letter* was also connected with his work on the origins of the Septuagint, to which he assigns three chapters of his book and about which he demonstrates familiarity with the relevant contemporary biblical scholarship. But the inclusion of the Aristean *Letter* in the body of his work as well as translations from chapters of Josephus, Eusebius, and the forged ancient texts composed by Annius of Viterbo provides another perspective on de' Rossi in the role of disseminator of the texts of antiquity for Jewish readers.

The writings of both Philo and Josephus had shared a similar fate in late antiquity. Both Jews were cited extensively by Christian writers and, as noted by de' Rossi, not even as much as mentioned in talmudic literature. By the tenth century, however, their respective *fortunae* diverged somewhat. Josephus became known to the Jews through the medieval *Josippon*. Philo, on the other hand, apart from indirect reference to his works, mostly in Karaite texts, remained a closed book to the Jews. As Momigliano wrote, "The Jews forgot Philo even before they forgot Greek. Philo was rediscovered for the Jews in a Latin translation by the Italian Jew Azariah de' Rossi."[124] De' Rossi's critique of Philo, whom he renamed Yedidyah the Alexandrian, was the first comprehensive assessment of the Alexandrian Jew to be undertaken by Jew or Christian. De' Rossi's constant oscillation between condemnation and defense of Philo is understandable. Partly it could be viewed as a token gesture on his part to demonstrate his own orthodoxy, which may have seemed suspect to some contemporary rabbis. But de' Rossi's ambivalence must also be understood as a response to the patristic interpretation of Philo. There seems to be an underlying strand to de' Rossi's critique whereby he is attempting to undermine the Christianizing process and to find the Jewish, or rather Pharisaic, elements in Philo. (He begins his critique with a discussion of the various sects of the second Temple on the basis of Josephus, the New Testament, Eusebius, and Philo himself.) Finally, however, he comes to the conclusion that Philo was an Essene, ignorant of Hebrew and Palestinian tradition. De' Rossi's emphatic description of Philo as a sectarian Jew may be contrasted with the patristic statements in which Philo is portrayed as a writer recording Christian truths and praising Christian institutions.

The genuine Josephus had been read by a few of de' Rossi's Jewish predecessors but not with the thoroughness and precision that characterize his reading. De' Rossi, like Christian scholars,[125] used Josephus as a matter of course. But he does signal a note of caution about the extant editions of Josephus,[126] suggesting that they had been tampered with. It may be that he was referring to Christian interpolations in the

123. For a discussion of his treatment of the subject, see my article "Azariah de' Rossi and Septuagint Traditions."

124. A. Momigliano, "Greek Culture," p. 343.

125. On the varied use of Josephus in the Renaissance by Catholics and Protestants, see P. Vidal-Naquet, *Du bon usage,* 30–33.

126. On the popularity of Josephus in the sixteenth century, see P. Burke, "A Survey."

text.[127] Josephus's evidence was indispensable for unraveling the historical problems in rabbinic texts and useful as a guide through the badly chartered years of the second Temple period.[128] The pitting of the historian Josephus against the authoritative rabbis is a constant feature of the book. Wherever possible de' Rossi tried to iron out the discrepancies between rabbinic accounts and Josephus, but where this would jeopardize the historian's integrity, Josephus would be given the final word (something which modern scholars would probably appreciate).

De' Rossi appears to have accepted the traditional view that the *Josippon,* the medieval compilation of Josephus written in southern Italy, was an authentic work of Josephus. Nevertheless, he draws a clear distinction between the author of the *Antiquities* and the *Jewish War,* whom he designates as the Latin Josephus (ha-Josippon la-Romiim), and the author of the *Josippon,* whom he calls the Hebrew Josephus (ha-Josippon la-Ivriim). Moreover, in contrast to his respectful attitude toward the genuine works of Josephus, de' Rossi often dismissed the *Josippon* as an "insignificant work." When he does quote it, it rarely carries much weight in the argument, and when it presents a divergent account from Josephus, he invariably dismisses it.[129] As David Flusser has demonstrated, de' Rossi was guided by Sebastian Münster in his assessment of the *Josippon.*[130] In the preface to his Latin translation of the work (Basel, 1541), Münster set out to disprove the views of those who had asserted that it was not a genuine work of Josephus by proposing that the work had been tampered with. He argued that the anachronistic references to Bulgarians, Lombards, Franks, and Goths in chapter 1 of the work were later accretions.[131] In his examination of the textual tradition of the *Josippon,* de' Rossi explicitly upheld Münster's view on the later interpolations but, surprisingly, given his generally dismissive attitude toward the work, remains silent on the question of its authenticity. It may be that de' Rossi did not want to cast aspersion on a work which had been quoted by such respectable Jews as Kimḥi and Abravanel. Alternatively, de' Rossi was showing allegiance to Münster, whose work, as shall be shown below, supplied de' Rossi with important material for his own investigations and served as a guideline for the development of his ideas.

3. The Christian Sources

De' Rossi was certainly familiar with the New Testament,[132] although he rarely quotes from it. Like the humanists before him, de' Rossi accorded considerable importance to the testimony of the Church Fathers.[133] They were enlisted even in his discussion of the priestly vestments. Augustine, "their greatest doctor," Jerome "their translator," and Eusebius "the Caesarean" are the three Fathers on whom de' Rossi most frequently

127. See his remarks at the beginning of ch. 53, which he prefaces to his translation of Josephus's enumeration of the high priests.

128. See my article "The quest."

129. When he translates from Josephus into Hebrew, however, he does occasionally use the Hebrew of the *Josippon,* which sometimes presents the material differently. See, e.g., ch. 60, n. 38.

130. D. Flusser, *The Josippon,* 2:72.

131. De' Rossi refers to the passage in ch. 19, p. 331.

132. See, e.g., his discussion of the Aramaic expressions in the Gospels in ch. 9, which is a harbinger of his extended treatment of the topic in his Italian work on the Syriac version.

133. On the humanist attitude toward the Church Fathers, see E. Rice, *St. Jerome,* 84–85.

calls. Of particular note is his adaptation of the designation "noster interpres" for Jerome. Eusebius's *Chronicle* was essential for his chronological investigations, while he foraged the *Opera Omnia* of both Jerome and Augustine for a wide range of material. On one occasion, he explicitly rejects Maimonides' somewhat convoluted view about the longevity of the ancients in preference for the more reasonable and scripturally based argument of Augustine.[134] But in a demographic study connected with the ten tribes he extrapolates the inflated figures given by Augustine for the Jewish slain during the war with the Romans without noting that Augustine's sole purpose in this context is to demonstrate that the disaster was a divinely and justly wrought punishment on the Jews.[135] Aquinas, whom he designates as "the disciple of Augustine," is the most frequently quoted medieval author, although his evidence is never crucial to his argument.

As indicated above, contemporary Christian scholarship permeates de' Rossi's work. The works of three authors play an important role.

ANNIUS OF VITERBO

Central to de' Rossi's discussions of ancient Jewish chronology and the antiquity of the Hebrew language is a collection of writings which were first published in Rome in 1498 and rapidly became a best-seller. The compilation purported to contain the works of ancient authors, including Berosus the Chaldean, Xenophon, Metasthenes the Persian, and Philo the Jew. In fact, they owed their existence to the fifteenth-century Dominican Annius of Viterbo, who not only forged the writings but supplied them with carefully constructed commentaries and introductions. With a few notable exceptions, scholars interested in ancient chronology or in the origins of peoples (particularly their own) referred to the Annian "discoveries." Written in a conspicuously anti-Greek vein, Annius's syncretistic forgeries extolling the ancient wisdom underlying Christian traditions can be seen as a tradition parallel to the Hermetic writings and the Chaldaic oracles that were similarly popular in the sixteenth century.[136] Credulous as his contemporaries, de' Rossi translated ps. Metasthenes and ps. Philo and also made thorough use of ps. Berosus on the grounds that they all shed light on Scripture, one of the reasons he offers for his study of Jewish chronology.[137] A similar view was put forward by Johannes Lucidus Samotheus, whose *Opusculum de emendationibus temporum,* frequently cited by de' Rossi, is in part a shortened form of Annian ancient history. Confident in the reliability of the Annian material—after all, Annius claimed to be publishing "reliable authorities" and even incorporated rules for gauging their reliability into his texts and his own commentaries—de' Rossi applied the relevant data to

134. See ch. 17, p. 308–9.

135. See ch. 13, p. 254, where he quotes from Augustine's *Homeliae de tempore,* Sermo CCV. Augustine states, "Ferro et fame undecies centena millia leguntur esse consumpta. Gens illa sacrilega quod merebatur excepit."

136. De' Rossi was also interested in the Hermetic texts. Struck by their similarities to the biblical text, he states in ch. 4 that he was intending to translate the *Asclepius* and *Pimander* into Hebrew. As far as I know, he never accomplished this work.

137. For a detailed discussion of this subject, see my articles "Azariah de' Rossi and the Forgeries" and "An Apocryphal Source."

disprove the rabbinic computations of the duration of the first and second Temples. The Annian products were also particularly useful for his chapters on the antiquity of the Hebrew language and script. But he is discreet in his use of the material, ignoring the more outlandish elements, while selecting the texts which were more reminiscent of the scriptural stories.

SEBASTIAN MÜNSTER (1488/9–1552)

Sebastian Münster, described as the German Ezra, was a "disciple" of Elijah Levita. In 1529 he left the Franciscan order and, following in the footsteps of his teacher and friend Konrad Pellican, became a Lutheran. He was a prolific writer, expert in astronomy, geography, mathematics, Hebrew, and Aramaic. He also made a new Latin translation of the Hebrew Bible.

De' Rossi always refers to Münster as "a scholar who shall remain anonymous," thus conforming to the papal decree of 1564 according to which the works of Protestants had to be quoted without the names of the authors being disclosed.[138] A large proportion of the subjects which Münster dealt with in separate works are represented in individual chapters of the *Light of the Eyes.* Some of the salient ideas for de' Rossi's work on the origins of the Septuagint and the antiquity of the Hebrew language and vowel points derive from Münster's introductory sections to his Aramaic grammar (Basel, 1527). De' Rossi's chronological investigations have their parallel in Münster's *Kalendarium hebraicum,* in which Münster discusses the Jewish computation of the age of the universe and translates Hebrew chronologies into Latin as well as analyzing the astronomical principles on which the Jewish calendar is based.[139] Münster's influential edition of Ptolemy's *Geographia,* which was first printed in Basel in 1540 and which contained additional maps of the New World, served as essential data for de' Rossi's discussion of the geographical notions of the rabbis, which he appraised in the light of the new discoveries. The exact location of the lost tribes of Israel and identification of the mythical country of Prester John were two more subjects of common interest to both scholars. Finally, as we have seen, Münster's evaluation of the textual tradition of the *Josippon* guided de' Rossi's own assessment of the work.

AUGUSTINUS STEUCHUS (1497/8–1548)

Augustinus Steuchus of Gubbio,[140] or Eugubino as de' Rossi called him, who served as librarian of Cardinal Grimani's library in Venice and was later appointed Vatican librarian in 1543, devoted much of his literary work to biblical studies. De' Rossi used one of Steuchus's major writings, the *Recognitio veteris testamenti ad Hebraicam veritatem collata etiam editione Septuaginta interprete cum ipsa veritate Hebraica nostraque translatione,* which was published in Venice in 1529. As the title suggests, the work is a comparative study of the various versions of the Pentateuch. Steuchus's annotations are

138. This concession was published in the seventh rule of the Tridentine Index of 1564. See F. Reusch, *Die Indices,* 248–49.

139. De' Rossi refers to the work in his *Maṣref la-Kesef* with regard to the fixed calendar.

140. The most comprehensive work on Steuchus is Th. Freudenberger, *Augustinus Steuchus.*

not exhaustive, but he chooses key verses for analysis and intersperses his commentary with references to the Church Fathers and the Targumim, and he also displays knowledge of the medieval Jewish commentators and philosophers.

Steuchus's work supplied de' Rossi with important data regarding the Septuagint and other Greek renderings of the Hebrew Bible. His superior knowledge of Greek—de' Rossi admitted his own poor knowledge of the language when he said, "I do not know the Greek language and literature as well as I should"[141]—aided him in his inquiry into Philo's knowledge of Hebrew and in his treatment of the variant readings of the Septuagint. De' Rossi himself alludes to the Bible versions of Aquila and Theodotion which Steuchus had discovered. Steuchus provided the relevant Greek passages with Latin translations. Thus, de' Rossi's philological analyses, which were based on translations, could be endorsed by the investigations of a scholar who was competent to evaluate the original Greek sources.

Catholics and Protestants alike occasionally took issue with Steuchus. Erasmus, for example, disapproved of Steuchus's denigration of the Septuagint,[142] and Sebastian Münster attacked Steuchus for claiming that Jerome was the author of the extant version of the Vulgate and for his mistranslations from Hebrew.[143] Although de' Rossi was aware of these controversies, they were not directly his concern. However, by discussing the original text of the Septuagint, which he claimed was translated from an Aramaic version, he was indirectly participating in the debate. When he commended Steuchus for perceiving that the Septuagint had not been translated from the known Hebrew text, he was as it were ratifying his own opinion, by imposing it on an unspecific and generic remark of Steuchus.

4. The Ancient Greek and Latin Sources

It is difficult to hazard a guess as to de' Rossi's knowledge of the classical texts, given their sporadic appearances in his chapters. (In his work on the New Testament [see above, p. xviii], however, he demonstrates greater familiarity with the conventions of classical scholarship.) He read the Greek texts in Latin or Italian translation. The authors needed no introduction, and for the most part de' Rossi refers to them by an italianized form of their names, such as Tullio, Livio, Plutarco. He employs standard characterizations of the writers. Thus, for example, his description of Livy's eloquence has a familiar ring when he writes,[144] "The Roman historian, the pride and glory of his esteemed native-town of Padua, Tito Livio surpassed all other gentile writers up to our own times in his creative ability[145] and in his flair for writing with the iron stylus and adamant point." He sometimes quotes authors from secondary sources. For example, although he most certainly had read Xenophon in Latin translation—he even translates parts of the *Cyropaedia* and *Anabasis*—he gives an erroneous description of Xenophon's account of the death of Cyrus by misreading a reference to the event in Mercator's

141. See the introduction to the *Light of the Eyes*.
142. *Opus epistolarum*, 9:204–24.
143. See the Praefatio to Münster's Latin translation of the Hebrew Bible, *Miqdash Adonai*.
144. Ch. 27.
145. "Creative ability," cf. Ex. 35:32.

Chronologia.[146] Ambrogio Calepino's Latin dictionary was on his work table, and he consulted it for information about many words, including place-names.

Conclusion

The high incidence of quotations from rabbinic sources gives a misleading impression. They represent de' Rossi's religious world but do not provide the key to the cultural milieu which informs his studies. His wide-ranging knowledge of non-Jewish literature and awareness of the issues of contemporary Christian scholarship infiltrate his variegated discussions and leave their imprint. That he gave prominence to the Annian forgeries does not detract from the importance of his work; rather, it highlights his involvement in current issues. He was not only receptive to the relevant scholarly studies published in his native Italy, but also had access to and took stock of those emanating from northern Europe. He was conscious of the novelty of his endeavor but nevertheless insisted, "Even those holy persons who refuse to look at a coin's effigy[147] [in case it was imprinted with an idolatrous image] will lend a listening ear to innovations in Torah studies. On seeing the crowd of foreigners cited by me, they will pronounce, like Ben Zoma on the Temple mount,[148] 'Blessed be He who has created all those to serve me.' "

THE CONTROVERSY OVER THE PUBLICATION OF THE BOOK

The *Light of the Eyes* was published by Meir ben Efraim at the press of Giacomo Rufinelli in Mantua.[149] The various stages in the printing of the book between 1573 and 1575 are bound up with the controversy which it generated.[150] The first printing was issued 18 November 1573. In Venice, Rabbi Samuel Juda Katzenellenbogen saw the letter which Isaac Foa of Reggio sent to Menahem Azariah da Fano in which Foa expressed his horror at de' Rossi's treatment of the Aggadot and took action. On 4 Nisan (April) 1574, he drew up a manifesto, headed by the words "Let the fear of heaven be upon you," which was signed by himself and other Venetian rabbis. In it, he requested that it should be agreed that no Jew should read or own the book unless he obtained written permission from the sages of his city. The resolution was subsequently ratified by some rabbis and leaders of the communities of Pesaro, Ancona, Cremona, Padua, Verona, Rome, Ferrara, and Siena.[151] Moreover, the rabbis of Ferrara and Rabbi Abraham Cohen Porto of Cremona advised their congregants not to read the book

146. In ch. 40, he states that the first books of Xenophon and Herodotus recount that Cyrus was killed by the queen of Scythia. This is a misreading of Mercator's *Chronologia,* in which it is stated, "Cyrus anno 7 imperii sui venit in Persas ubi paulo post mortuus est. Xenophon in Cyropaedia. Occisus est a Tomiri regina Scythorum Herod." Thus de' Rossi failed to see the full stop separating Xenophon's testimony from that of Herodotus.

147. This expression is based on B. Pes. 104a.

148. B. Ber. 58a.

149. The name of the publisher is not printed. See D. Friedberg, *History,* 19. There is no *haskamah* (imprimatur) at the beginning of the book. See R. Bonfil, "Some reflections."

150. For a survey and analysis of the controversy, see R. Bonfil, "Some reflections," 25–31; M. Benayahu, "The polemic."

151. The text of the manifesto, which was published in many copies, was printed by D. Kaufmann, "Contributions," 83–85.

until the Mantuan rabbis, Judah Moscato and David Provenzali, had passed their verdict on the case.[152] De' Rossi betook himself to the hostile territory of Venice "in order to discover the reason for all their outcry."[153] In an attempt to pacify his critics and to save the book, de' Rossi conceded to their stipulations. Moses Provenzali's critique (*hassagah*) of his chronological thesis had to be incorporated into the book. It should be noted, however, that Provenzali did not articulate his dissent in a polemical vein, but rather in the form of a scholarly exchange. Moreover, de' Rossi subsequently took the opportunity to reaffirm his position by writing a response (*teshuvah*) to Provenzali, and the two documents were published together at the end of the book. Rabbinic ire had also been aroused by de' Rossi's treatment of the hyperbole in chapter 20. They objected to his apparently cavalier mode of describing certain statements in the Talmud and the Zohar as metaphorical devices by means of which the performance of a precept was encouraged or the gravity of a sin accentuated. De' Rossi was requested to erase three of the various examples of hyperbole that he had cited on the grounds that they contained heavenly secrets which had to be taken literally.[154] The changes were implemented, although de' Rossi remained convinced that the rest of the chapter still proved his point.[155] In the revised edition of the book, de' Rossi also appears to have made some minor changes to the original text which were not officially requested—apparently, he wanted to make every effort to render the work palatable to the conservative members of the rabbinate. Thus, for example, his reference to the "holy order of the blessed one" [i.e. Benedictines] was changed to "the famous Benedictine brothers."

The ban was lifted. Abraham Cohen Porto publicly repealed his veto of the book and testified to having seen bundles of signatures to a statement clearing de' Rossi's name.[156] Other rabbis came to de' Rossi's defense. Isaac Cohen da Viterbo even goes so far as to say that de' Rossi deserved the highest rabbinic accolade.[157]

Bonfil has demonstrated that the rabbis who initially joined Katzenellenbogen's campaign were minor authorities.[158] Nevertheless, whatever the standing of the original detractors of the book and despite the abrogation of the ban, repercussion of the

152. Porto (1520–49), author of *Minḥah Belulah,* had not read the book but had heard rumors that it contained heretical views, particularly in regard to chronology. Eliezer Ashkenazi, however, an authority whom he respected, had praised the book. He therefore refrained from actually signing the manifesto. At the end of the letter to Menahem Azariah da Fano in which he describes the action he had taken, Porto pointedly gives the date "according to the true computation."

153. De' Rossi's negotiations with the Venetian rabbis are published in a unique copy of the *Light of the Eyes* (195–96) belonging to the Mehlmann collection in the National Library of Jerusalem, reprinted by I. Mehlmann, "Saviv Sefer Me'or Enayim," 37–39.

154. The three examples are as follows: "Anyone who spills his seed to no purpose does not deserve to see the divine presence" (Zohar, I, 187b; III, 90a); "He who takes delight in the Sabbath will be given an unbounded heritage" (B. Shabb. 118b); the description in B. B.M. 85b and Ḥag. 15a, respectively, in which Elijah and Metatron are said to have received "60 flaming lashes."

155. In the unique pages of the Mehlmann edition, de' Rossi reiterates his position on the three passages and still attempts to argue that his position can be corroborated by such authorities as Jacob ben Asher and Maimonides.

156. The text of Porto's responsum was published by S. J. Halberstam, "Sheloshah ketavim," 1–3.

157. See M. Benayahu, "The Polemic," 231, and see the other document published by Halberstam, "Sheloshah ketavim."

158. "Some Reflections," 28–29. However, Yeḥiel Nissim da Pisa, who was one of the signatories for Ferrara, was an important communal leader and erudite scholar. (See U. Cassuto, *Gli ebrei,* 351–57.)

controversy continued to be felt. On a flyleaf of a work written by Mordechai Dato, the owner of the book, Abraham Graziano, wrote a note permitting a certain Isaiah of Sezze to read the *Light of the Eyes* but counseled him to be judicious in his reading.[159] A permit of this kind was still being given in 1635.[160]

For de' Rossi's part, the battle went on. In 1576, he completed his book *Refinement of Silver* (*Maṣref la-Kesef*), yet another attempt to put forward his arguments regarding Jewish chronology. Written in both a polemical and apologetic vein, it develops the chronological and calendrical arguments with even greater attention to technical detail. The title page is telling. De' Rossi specifically states that one of his objectives is to demolish the views of the Karaites. Although he does indeed attack the Karaites for their rejection of the constant Jewish calendar, it would appear that his pronouncement was intended to demonstrate his total dissociation from heretical views. In addition, de' Rossi had to address the criticisms of Isaac Finzi of Pesaro and wrote *Everlasting Justice* (*Ṣedeq Olamim*), replies to the thirteen questions which Isaac Finzi had raised in connection with the chronological issue.[161]

The *Refinement of Silver* and *Everlasting Justice* were not published until the nineteenth century,[162] possibly because publishers were disinclined to cause further controversies. Despite the support de' Rossi received from such distinguished authorities as Judah Moscato and David Provenzali, he was deeply affected by the controversy. Although, as Bonfil has argued, the majority of de' Rossi's antagonists were people who had not read or understood the book, fear of the dissemination of such literature remained. Indeed, vestiges of the debate reverberate in an article written some sixty years ago. Speaking on the subject of comparative Jewish chronology, the late Simon Schwab wrote, "Azariah de' Rossi, a controversial figure in the annals of our people, criticized the puzzling texts of Seder Olam and the Talmud much to the righteous indignation of contemporary and later rabbinic scholars."[163]

ENGLISH TRANSLATION

My English translation of the *Me'or Enayim* is based on the first edition (there are no manuscripts of the work) with constant reference to Cassel's edition.[164] The asterisks in the text refer to de' Rossi's printed marginal glosses, which appeared in all editions of the text. De' Rossi's own copy of the text with his autograph glosses is in the Bodleian Library (Opp. 875).[165] These autograph glosses contain the revised notes (*mahadurah*

159. See my article, "Toward a New Reappraisal," 504, and D. Tamar, "Peraqim," 378–79.

160. See D. Kaufmann, "La défence," 280–81.

161. Isaac Finzi had written *Iggeret Telunah* against de' Rossi. De' Rossi never saw the *Iggeret,* but was told about the contents. On the letter de' Rossi wrote to Finzi in connection with it, see A. David, "Letoledot," 641–42.

162. The autograph manuscript in the Bodleian library (Mich. 308) was published by Filipowski in Edinburgh in 1854, and emended editions were reprinted by Benjacob and Cassel in their editions of the *Light of the Eyes.*

163. S. Schwab, "Comparative Jewish Chronology," 183.

164. There are some differences between the various prints of Cassel's edition, which I have noted.

165. Another copy containing de' Rossi's autograph glosses exists and was sold at Sotheby's, November 24, 1982. I have been unable to trace the buyer.

sheniyyah) which were later affixed to the end of the book on unnumbered pages,[166] short synopses of the subjects treated and also additional material which was never published. This additional material I have incorporated into the notes by the siglum B. I have also incorporated all the revised notes into the text, indicated between braces, {} (for the first revisions) and $\{\}^2$ (for the second revisions).

De' Rossi's Hebrew is often convoluted and obscure, with lengthy sentences, more characteristic of Italian or Latin than of Hebrew. In an effort to provide a readable translation, I have sometimes divided the sentences, while remaining as faithful as possible to the original. De' Rossi's Hebrew is impregnated with biblical and rabbinic expressions. Where these expressions are significant, I have provided the relevant references. I have generally used the new translation of the Holy Scriptures (1985) of the Jewish Publication Society but have adopted a different translation when required by the context. De' Rossi always refers to chapters in the Babylonian Talmud. In order not to adumbrate the text, I have simply given the name of the tractate and supplied the precise reference in the notes. Where standard English translations of the titles of classical patristic or Italian texts exist, I have used those translations; otherwise, I have retained the titles in the original languages. All Hebrew titles have been given in transliteration according to the prescriptions of the Yale Judaica Series (except that letter *ayin* at beginning of words has not been signalled). All references to texts have been traced, and where possible the edition which de' Rossi consulted has been indicated. Often de' Rossi quoted from works which he read in manuscript. If a modern or standard edition of the work exists, I have referred to it.

The text does not lend itself easily to the English language. I have made every effort to produce a readable translation, while preserving de' Rossi's style and imagery to enable the English reader to savor the work and appreciate the scholarship of the author.

166. There are slight differences between the printed and handwritten notes.

ABBREVIATIONS

GENERAL

Ant.	*Antiquities*
A.	*Letter of Aristeas*
B	*Light of the Eyes* (De' Rossi's autograph, Bodleian Opp. 875)
De civ. Dei	*De civitate Dei*
De ev. praep	*De evangelica praeparatione* (Eusebius)
HUCA	*Hebrew Union College Annual*
JQR	*Jewish Quarterly Review*
KS	*Kiryat Sefer*
LAB	*Liber Antiquitatum Biblicarum*
M.T.	Massoretic text
PAAJR	*Proceedings of the American Academy for Jewish Research*
P.G.	*Patrologia Graeca* (*Migne*)
P.L.	*Patrologia Latina* (*Migne*)
Tos.	*Tosafot*

ABBREVIATIONS USED FOR THE WORKS OF PHILO ACCORDING TO THE LOEB CLASSICAL LIBRARY

Abr.	*De Abrahamo*
Aet.	*De aeternitate mundi*
Agr.	*De agricultura*
Cher.	*De Cherubim*
Conf.	*De confusione linguarum*
Cont.	*De vita contemplativa*
Decal.	*De decalogo*
Det.	*Quod deterius potiori insidiari soleat*
Deus	*Quod Deus sit immutabilis*
Ebr.	*De ebriatate*
Fug.	*De fuga et inventione*
Gig.	*De gigantibus*

Her.	*Quis rerum divinarum heres sit*
Jos.	*De Josepho*
L.A. I, II, III	*Legum Allegoriarum* I, II, III
Mig.	*De migratione Abrahami*
Mos. I, II	*De vita Mosis* I, II
Op.	*De opificio mundi*
Plant.	*De plantatione*
Praem.	*De praemiis et poenis*
Prob.	*Quod omnis probus liber*
Sac.	*De sacrificiis Abelis et Caini*
Sob.	*De sobrietate*
Som. I, II	*De somniis* I, II
Spec.	*De specialibus legibus*
Virt.	*De virtutibus*

TRACTATES OF MISHNAH (M.), TOSEFTA (T.), PALESTINIAN TALMUD (P.), AND BABYLONIAN TALMUD (B.):

Arak.	Arakhin
A.Z.	Avodah Zarah
B.B.	Bava Batra
Bek.	Bekhorot
Ber.	Berakhot
Beṣ.	Beṣah
Bikk.	Bikkurim
B.Q.	Bava Qama
B.M.	Bava Meṣia
Dem.	Demai
Ed.	Eduyyot
Eruv.	Eruvin
Giṭṭ.	Giṭṭin
Ḥag.	Ḥagigah
Ḥull.	Ḥullin
Hor.	Horayot
Kel.	Kelim
Ket.	Ketubot
Maʿas.	Maʿaserot
Makk.	Makkot
Men.	Menaḥot
Midd.	Middot
Miq.	Miqvaʾot
M.Q.	Moʿed Qatan
Ned.	Nedarim
Nidd.	Niddah

Pes.	Pesaḥim
Qidd.	Qiddushin
R.H.	Rosh ha-Shanah
Sanh.	Sanhedrin
Shabb.	Shabbat
Shev.	Shevuʿot
Sheq.	Sheqalim
Sof.	Soferim
Sukk.	Sukkah
Tem.	Temurah
Ter.	Terumot
Yad.	Yadayim
Yev.	Yevamot
Zev.	Zevaḥim

OTHER RABBINIC WRITINGS

ARN	Avot d'Rabbi Nathan
B.R.	Bereshit Rabbah
Bem.R.	Bemidbar Rabbah
D.R.	Devarim Rabbah
E.R.	Ekhah Rabbah (Rabbati)
Est.R	Esther Rabbah
Meg. T.	Megillat Taʿanit
Mid.Teh.	Midrash Tehillim
Pes. d'R. Kah.	Pesikta d'Rav Kahana
PRE	Pirke d'Rabbi Eliezer
Q.R.	Qohelet Rabbah
S.R.	Shemot Rabbah
S.S.R.	Shir ha-Shirim Rabbah
V.R.	Vayiqra Rabbah

LEGENDA

* refers to de' Rossi's glosses which were printed in the margin of the first edition of the text. In the translation these passages have been inserted at the end of the paragraph in which they appear with reference to the relevant page.

{} refers to de' Rossi's first revisions of the text.

{}^{2} refers to de' Rossi's second revisions of the text.

B in notes refers to autograph glosses of the Bodleian copy (Opp.875).

THE LIGHT OF THE EYES

INTRODUCTION

In the Palestinian Talmud we read:[1] The verse, *The Lord of Hosts is with us, He is our fortress* (Ps. 46:8) should never depart from your lips. In the Zohar it is stated:[2] "When someone begins to construct a building, he should announce that the enterprise is undertaken for the worship of the Holy One blessed be He, lest it be said, *Woe to him who builds his house without righteousness* (Jer. 22:13)." Proffering a reason for the affixing of the divine name on the high priest's head, Yedidyah the Alexandrian[3] said in book 3 of the *Life of Moses:*[4] "He who from the very outset calls upon the name of God will ensure the fulfillment of his purpose." Plato, too, in the fourth part of his *Laws,* stated:[5] "Prior to any act the divine name ought to be invoked." Thus, in the name of our God will we hail this book. May He with his manifold kindness be a fortress to us.

Thus says the novice Azariah de' Rossi, may his rock and redeemer protect him, who was born in the delightful city of Mantua[6] and resides in Ferrara. For the glory of our God, His Torah and His people, after first requesting the support of His great love, I have, in His blessed name, undertaken to translate the precious book of Aristeas, the courtier of Ptolemy Philadelphus, king of Egypt, from Latin into our holy tongue. He wrote it for his brother Philocrates.[7] The purpose of his letter was to explain why and how our holy Torah was translated from the Jewish language into Greek by the seventy-two elders. They were sent to the aforementioned Ptolemy by Eleazar the high priest who officiated after the death of his elder brother Simeon the righteous. Yedidyah the Alexandrian, or Philo as he is known to Greeks and Romans, who was of Jewish stock, claimed that Jeshua son of Jehozadak was the first high priest

1. P. Ber. 5 (1) 8d.
2. Zohar, Tazria, III, 50a. De' Rossi changes the text so that it reads "lest it be said" instead of "because it is written." De' Rossi refers to both sixteenth-century editions of the Zohar, Mantua, 1558–60, Cremona, 1558.
3. De' Rossi coined the name Yedidyah the Alexandrian for Philo (see ch. 3).
4. Philo, *Mos.* II, 132. De' Rossi used Sigismund Gelenius's Latin translation of the text published in Lyons, 1555.
5. Plato, *Leges,* IV, 712 B.
6. The expression 'delightful city' is used of Jerusalem in Is. 22:2; 32:13.
7. This is a reference to the so-called *Letter of Aristeas* which purports to be a contemporary account of the translation of the Pentateuch into Greek in the time of Ptolemy Philadelphus (287–247 B.C.E.). Modern scholars agree that the work must have been written by a Jew and date it to the second century B.C.E. For a recent discussion of the text, see P. Lamarche, "La Septante."

to minister in the second Temple, may it be rebuilt speedily in our days. He was succeeded by the following high priests: his son Joiakim, Eliashib son of Joiakim, Joiada son of Joiakim, Jonathan son of Joiada and Jaddua son of Jonathan. Yedidyah made this statement in his book *De temporibus* which was recently translated from Greek into Latin.[8] If God will so help me, I shall translate the work into Hebrew in chapter 32. Yedidyah is in fact referring to the six successive generations specified by Nehemiah when he said: *And Jeshua begot Joiakim and Joiakim begot Eliashib and Eliashib begot Joiada and Joiada begot Jonathan and Jonathan begot Jaddua* (12:10–11). As Rashi, blessed be his memory, points out, all those mentioned in the verse were high priests.[9] Other statements of Nehemiah himself lead to such a conclusion.[10]

{I was overjoyed and thanked the Lord because the work *Sefer Yuḥasin* recently arrived in Italy.[11] It was printed under the aegis of the esteemed notables of the capital city of Constantinople. I came across the following statement on page 11:[12]

> It would appear that after the death of Jeshua the high priest Ezra became high priest and performed the rites of the red heifer. And yet, according to the book of Ezra[13] it appears that Joiakim son of Jeshua, his grandson Eliashib, Joiada son of Eliashib, his son Jonathan and his son Jaddua were all high priests, but not Ezra. The view expressed at the beginning of *Sefer ha-Madda*[14] that Ezra officiated as high priest before Simeon the righteous is not substantiated by historical evidence. The line of high priests descended from Jeshua, Jeshua's sons and grandsons. Rashi was also of the opinion that all six high priests were Jeshua's descendants.

This author's statement regarding the high priests who officiated from the time of Jeshua to Simeon the righteous will assist our discussion in "Days of the World" (cf. chapter 37). Since this particular chronological matter was not the central purpose of

8. This is a reference to the ps. Philonic work *Breviarium de temporibus* which the Dominican monk Annius of Viterbo forged and edited. It was first published with Annius's other forgeries of ancient writings in Rome, in 1498 and republished many times in the sixteenth century. De' Rossi used the two-volume Temporales edition (Lyons, 1554). This reference is to vol. 1, 406–7. On de' Rossi's use of Annius, see my article, "Azariah de' Rossi and the Forgeries."

9. Rashi to Neh. 12:10.

10 The siglum {}² refers to de' Rossi's second revisions (*mahadurah sheniyah*) to the text. (The siglum {} indicates the first revisions.) In the Bodleian copy (which contains de' Rossi's handwritten glosses), henceforth noted as B, these revisions are sometimes articulated differently and sometimes contain additional information. Where significant, these differences and additions will be indicated in the notes.

11. The *Sefer Yuḥasin* was written by Abraham Zacuto (1452–1515) and first published in Constantinople in 1566 under the editorship of Samuel Shullam. The work presents in chronicle form a history of rabbinic scholars and events in Jewish history with a final section on universal history. It is interesting to note that in B de' Rossi had originally written: "By my life, I was very happy about the book for I found that he agreed with my opinion in many passages, and indeed the leaders of Constantinople wrote about him in glorifying and respectful terms."

12. De' Rossi pagination of *Sefer Yuḥasin* seems to include the frontispiece. The passage is 11, col. a in Freimann's edition (Frankfurt am Main, 1924).

13. Zacuto is referring to the book of Nehemiah, perhaps because it is often considered part of the book of Ezra. Cf. B. B.B. 14b–15a.

14. The reference is to Maimonides' introduction to his code, the *Mishneh Torah*. The *Sefer ha-Madda* is the first book of the code, but the introduction serves as introduction to the whole of the code. The passage reads: "and he [i.e., Simeon the righteous] was high priest after Ezra." Maimonides may have derived his information from M. Parah 3:5.

the author's work, it is surely appropriate to explain the nature of the problem at greater length and to reach its resolution by means of correct information. We have acted thus in order to defend our rabbis rather than let the topic remain conspicuously problematic for scholars.[15]}[2]

Many other writers expressed such a view,[16] most noteworthy of whom is the Roman Josephus [i.e., Josephus Flavius][17] as will be demonstrated in the assigned chapters (33 and 37). Both Yedidyah in the aforementioned work[18] and Josephus[19] state that Jaddua begot Onias the high priest and that Onias begot Simeon the righteous. Simeon the righteous died without any successor save a little boy whose age rendered him unqualified for the office of high priest. His brother Eleazar ministered in his place, and it was with this Eleazar that Ptolemy negotiated about the translation of the Torah. The Ptolemy in question was Ptolemy Philadelphus who was third in succession to the throne of Alexander of Macedon. As Daniel[20] had predicted, the kingdom of Alexander was divided among four rulers after his death. One of those rulers, Ptolemy son of Lago, ruled thirty-six years over Egypt and its tributary towns. He was succeeded by his son who ruled thirty-nine years. He was given the epithet "Philadelphus" which signifies intimate friendship. As Vives wrote in his commentary to book 18 of the *City [of God],* this was supposed to indicate Ptolemy's passionate involvement with his sister whom he took to wife. Alternatively, it had a euphemistic implication, referring to the overwhelming hatred he ultimately bore her as happened in the case of Amnon in his relation to Tamar.[21]

In the thirty-first year of his reign, Ptolemy sent word to Eleazar who dispatched the translators to Alexandria in Egypt. The interested reader will find descriptions of the event partly in Philo's *De temporibus* and third book of the *Life of Moses,*[22] and partly in Josephus's paraphrase of the story of these elders.[23] All ancient and modern Christian scholars followed these two writers: for example, their translator [i.e., Jerome] in his

15. De' Rossi is playing here on the phrase *but if the discoloration remains stationary* (Lev. 13:23) used in relation to the leper's symptoms.

16. I.e., numerous high priests officiated between Jeshua and Simeon the righteous.

17. De' Rossi refers to Flavius Josephus as the Roman Josippon in order to distinguish between his Greek works and the Hebrew text known as the *Josippon* which was a tenth-century work but generally regarded as a genuine work of Josephus in the sixteenth century. Although de' Rossi often dismisses the reliability of the *Josippon,* and although he must have been familiar with the arguments against its genuineness, he never outrightly rejects its authenticity (see ch. 19). Henceforth, the Latin Josippon will be translated as Josephus, and the Hebrew Josippon as Josippon. De' Rossi's references are to Gelenius's Latin translation of Josephus's *Opera* (Basel, 1567) and also to the Latin translation ascribed to Ruffinus. In *Ant.* XI:120, Josephus refers to the high priest Joakeimos (i.e., Joiakim) son of Jesus (i.e., Jeshua).

18. Ps. Philo, *Breviarium,* 407.

19. *Ant.* XII:157ff.

20. See ch. 7. Jerome gives the same interpretation as does ibn Ezra in his commentary to v. 14.

21. This is a reference to the Spanish humanist Ludovico Vives whose commentary on Augustine's *De civitate Dei* was republished several times in the sixteenth century. In his commentary to bk. 18, ch. 42 the subject of which is the LXX, Vives writes: "Philadelphus est dictus vel ob amorem primum Arsinoe sororis vel ob odium postremum per antiphrasim." De' Rossi adds the example of Amnon and Tamar to Vives's statement. It is interesting to note that de' Rossi appears to ignore Vives's critical remark in which he questions the ascription of the *Letter* to Aristeas.

22. *Mos.* II, 29–44.

23. *Ant.* XII:11–118.

commentary to the book of Daniel, Eusebius the Caesarean in many passages of his works, Lucidus Samotheus in book 2,[24] and others as well. As for our sages of blessed memory, their statements on the subject somewhat contradict the accounts alluded to above. With the help of God I shall deal with the problem in the chapters designated for that purpose.[25]

On the basis of the story which recounts Alexander's obeisance before the high priest,[26] one might infer that it was during his journey from Jerusalem that Alexander went and defeated Darius. Of the wise gentiles who wrote biographies of Alexander may be cited Quintus Curtius (book 5)[27] and Plutarch (par. 37)[28] who record the approximate date of his victory as the sixth year of his reign [i.e., 330 B.C.E.]. It thus follows that Alexander who ruled twelve years in all (as is demonstrated in the last chapter of Seder Olam[29] and in the first chapter of the first book of Maccabees[30]) must have been in power for six years after that event. These are the six years which are mentioned by our rabbis of blessed memory in chapter 1 of tractate Avodah Zarah as being the period of the Greek rule of Elam.[31] These years, according to their pronouncement there, are not included in the calculation of the Seleucid era. (Further clarification of this subject will be given in chapter 23, God willing.) Thus equipped with this information, we can make the following calculation: if we deduct thirty-six years from the Seleucid era (which started after the death of Alexander) during which Ptolemy son of Lago reigned, and the thirty-one years in which his son Ptolemy Philadelphus reigned as his successor, and at which time the translation was made, the date of the current year is 5331 *anno mundi* [1570–71] and 1883 according to the Seleucid era computation (this is made clear by Rambam [Maimonides] of blessed memory).[32] In other words, it is 1816 years since the event of the translation of our Torah.

It is worth noting that the short work which explained all the details of that event, and which was written in Greek by the courtier who was one of the two royal legates sent to the high priest in Jerusalem, was translated into Latin by a certain Christian

24. This is a reference to Johannes Lucidus Samotheus who has been identified as the Dominican monk Giovanni Tolosani (d. 1549) by D. Marzi, *La questione,* 148–49. De' Rossi often consults Lucidus's *Opusculum.*

25. I.e., chs. 7 and 8.

26. De' Rossi deliberately leaves the high priest unnamed since the identity of the high priest is connected with the larger question of the length of the Persian rule. In later chapters he refutes rabbinic statements (B. Yoma 9a and parallels) that the high priest in question was Simeon the righteous.

27. There were many early editions of Quintus Curtius Rufus, *De rebus gestis.* Bk. 5 does contain the story of Alexander's defeat of Darius, but I cannot find an explicit reference to the date. De' Rossi probably derived his information from Eusebius's *Chronicon,* which contains all the relevant dates for this period, and simply assumed that the same dating was to be found in Curtius's work.

28. De' Rossi used the Paris 1558 edition of Plutarch's *Lives.* The defeat of Darius is in the *Life of Alexander,* but no dates are given here either.

29. Seder Olam Rabbah, ch. 30 (141–43). De' Rossi used the Mantua 1513 edition.

30. 1Macc. 1:7.

31. B. A.Z. 10a.

32. De' Rossi refers to Maimonides' *Mishneh Torah,* Qiddush ha-Ḥodesh XI:16 and Shemiṭṭa X:4 where Maimonides synchronizes the Seleucid and anno mundi computation. The Seleucid era (*minyan shṭarot*) was counted from the Julian year 312/311. The beginning of the Seleucid year could vary according to the calendar of particular cities. On this, see E. Bickermann, *Chronology,* 71–72.

about fifty years ago.[33] A vernacular Italian version was then made on the basis of that translation.[34] A German scholar, however, examined these translations and found them inaccurate and unliteral.[35] (The reader will confirm this view—many passages are incomprehensible.) He therefore undertook to produce a new Latin translation. This very fine version was printed about ten years ago in Basel, a city teeming with Christian sages. It is a bilingual edition with both the Greek and Latin texts, and so the scholar will be able to see that this translation is a more faithful rendering than the others.[36] As regards my humble self, I am unfortunately not well versed in the writings and language of Greece. So I translated the text from this Latin version which won praise from all those who read it. There is no doubt in my mind that even the foreigner who understands Hebrew will derive satisfaction from my rendering and regard my translation (I am perfectly aware of the calibre of the book—it is not a major work), which was accomplished in about twenty days, as no useless endeavor. Moreover, his enjoyment will be enhanced once he recognizes the greatness of those sages of old whose expertise was not confined to the legal aspects of the Torah, but who were also social and political figures worthy of being received at court. Appreciation of some of the novel information related to our Torah contained in the book would also add to his pleasure. In particular, there are two useful but different points which emerge from the account. The first regards the reasons for some of the biblical precepts as put forward to Ptolemy's envoys by Eleazar the high priest. The second point is more fundamental. Consequently, I decided to use it for the clarification of certain problematic statements about the priestly vestments made by our later sages of blessed memory. If God so wills, the matter will be clarified in the relevant chapters.

It is well known that anything which smacks of novelty reverberates loudly and is praised to excess. This is exemplified in the statement of Rabbi Ḥiyya in tractate Pe'ah in the Palestinian Talmud:[37] "Not even the whole world can equal one word of Torah." In the same passages a story is recounted about Rabbi and Artaban. [Artaban sent Rabbi a precious stone and he reciprocated by sending him a *mezuzah* on receipt of which Artaban complained that his valuable gift had been exchanged for an object of no value.] Rabbi then said: "Your values and my values cannot be compared." Therefore, the founding fathers conveyed to us an impeccable teaching:[38] "He who learns but one *halakhah* from his fellow must pay him respect." What better way to pay him respect, in this instance, than to bring his work to the attention of the general public. An

33. Matteo Palmieri's Latin translation of the *Letter* was first published in Theodorus Lelius's edition of Jerome's *Epistolae* (1468 or 1469). See A. Vaccari, "La fortuna," 8. De' Rossi appears to be referring to the Paris 1514 reprint of Palmieri's translation.

34. This is a reference to Lodovico Domenichi's Italian translation which, as Vaccari demonstrated ("La fortuna," 18–19) was plagiarized from an earlier Italian translation of the humanist Bartolomeo della Fonte (Fonzio) which was incorporated into the *Biblia uolgare* of Niccolò de' Malermi in 1471.

35. Matthias Garbitius was the author of the new translation. It was published under the editorship of Simon Schard in Basel, 1561.

36. The Latin text was printed in the second half of the book. This edition remained the standard edition until 1870 when M. Schmidt revised the text. On de' Rossi's use of Garbitius's edition, see my article, "Azariah de' Rossi and LXX Traditions."

37. P. Pe'ah 1 (1) 15d.

38. M. Avot 6:3.

a fortiori argument should be proffered here. When the author of this book labored in its production, and its non-Jewish translators, printers, and various readers sang its praises and adopted it, we are surely all the more bound not to reject it for we are the closest relatives of those elders and we all share one God and one Father. Our view of this matter is further corroborated when we see that our sages, blessed be their memory, also mentioned this incident in the Babylonian and Palestinian Talmuds and in the Midrashim and regarded it as a miracle which should not be forgotten by our descendants. It is true, however, that they do make a few statements whose purpose is solely to censure the incident, as I will show in chapter 7, God willing.

Now this entire book is the light of my eyes and the joy of my heart. With it, the Lord, my heavenly refuge, will entitle me to leave behind a blessing to posterity. Under the guidance of the blessed Lord, I have now given it the enduring name *The Light of the Eyes.* The first section of the book deals with the terrifying earthquakes which erupted in the city of Ferrara. I have designated that section by the separate title—"Voice of God"—for a reason which will be explained later. The work which the Lord prompted me to translate is known both in Greek and Latin by the name of its author Aristeas.[39] Deeming it comparable to a recently converted proselyte or to a new born babe, I have given it the new title "Splendor of the Elders." Profound reasoning went into the choice of this title. As a result of this event, the elders acquired a splendid reputation in which they shall bask for eternity. As for the section divided into chapters, its enduring name shall be "Words of Understanding" for the reason expressed in the first chapter. At the very outset of my work, in the first section of the book, I shall not refrain from relating how and when I became aroused to translate this work of Aristeas, and the translation itself shall then be followed by the third section of the book. In this detail, too, it is to the glory of God to search out the matter.[40]

Let the reader of this scroll exalt in God who shields the lives of His sacred congregation
Imagining the horror of the quakes, he is stunned, his hair stands on end.
Indeed, the hearts of all the strong and mighty, when the earth began to quake, turned to wax.
Let him pray that no disaster like it should recur as long as he may live.
Fear seizes him although he has not seen it; he shakes before its fiery wrath begins.
Blessed be He whose might fills all the world: Blessed He whose power is in His holy place.

39. The title *Letter of Aristeas* first appeared in the fourth century C.E. (See S. Jellicoe, *The Septuagint,* 30.) De' Rossi's translation *The Book of Aristeas* is more in keeping with the original title.

40. De' Rossi slightly modifies the expression in Pr. 25:2, *The glory of kings is to search out the matter.*

THE VOICE OF GOD

An account of the frightening tremors which shook Ferrara in the year 5331 [1570]. In our discourse on the earthquake we will mainly refer to holy Scripture and to what our rabbis had to say on the subject. We shall also cite some of the Christian doctors and pagan scholars of an earlier age. We tell how the event gave occasion for the writing of this book.[1]

One of the forms of worship deemed acceptable to the blessed Lord has been communicated to us by God himself in his Torah and by many of his servants the prophets. It is that all people who behold His signs and awesome works should tell of them and proclaim them to every person in each generation. Then will human beings learn good counsel and come to know deep within their hearts that it is God alone who is King of the universe. Then will they be forever firm in the knowledge that it is His great strength and manifold kindness which is present in the work of their hands, and that it is to Him they should address their supplications for the fulfillment of all their desires. Thus in the Pentateuch it is written: *that you may recount in the hearing of your sons and your sons' sons . . . that you may know that I am the Lord* (Ex. 10:2). In the Prophets it is written: *Tell your children of it* (Joel 1:3). Thirdly, in the Hagiographa, it is written: *We will not withold it from their children telling the coming generation . . . that they might put their confidence in God* (Ps. 78:4,7). There are many other such passages in Scripture. The precepts which are called "testimonies" are also assigned for this purpose, like nails hammered into our hearts.[2] It may well be true that the work of the Lord, including the natural order, instills awe and great fear into the heart of any intelligent person according to his maturity.

(The cycle of light and darkness, rainfall and the creation of living creatures, indeed

1. As Cassel notes (23–26), the earthquake of 1570 was recorded and described in great detail by many writers of different descriptions, both Jewish and Christian. Obviously, the cataclysmic event disrupted the lives of every sector of the population of Ferrara. Letters published by A. Solerti in "Il terremoto di Ferrara" describe how the event affected Alfonso II, the duke of Ferrara and his court. It was described in philosophical tracts, poems, and letters. See my article "The Voice of God." (For further bibliography, not cited in my article, see E. Guidoboni, "Riti," N. Shalem, "Una fonte ebraica," and G. Busi, "Il terremoto.") The main part of de' Rossi's account, which according to Cassel (23) excelled all others in style, structure, and understanding of the topic, was translated into Latin by Johannes Zollicofferus in 1651.

2. Cf. Deut. 6:20–22.

everything small or great which comes to our notice through His power, overawes the perceptive person and causes master and disciple alike to wonder. This is why our prophets used to cry out with the words of the Most High: *Should you not revere Me who set the sand as a boundary to the sea. . . . Let us revere the Lord our God who gives the rain, the early and late rain in season* (Jer. 5:22–24), and the psalmist proclaims: *How great, how manifold are Your works* (Ps. 92:6; 104:24). One of the gentile sages, Hermes Trismegistus, whom we shall have occasion to mention again in chapter 4 wrote in a surprisingly similar vein in the fifth part of his *Pimander* and his pronouncement should consequently be given due attention. He stated that the divine being is manifest in every existing thing; in fact, the entire world consists of the names of the blessed Lord.[3] Now our sages, blessed be their memory, said in Berakhot and in many other places, that the world was created with the letters of the Torah.[4] Hermes' statement is in fact akin to Ramban's [Nahmanides'] prefatory remark to his commentary on the Pentateuch that the whole of the Torah consists of the names of the blessed Lord.)[5]

However, it is customary for people to remain unaffected by things which occur regularly and constantly. This is evident from the way they react to a tremendous event which happens in its appointed season and to a great wonder never seen before on earth, despite their relative insignificance when compared to the natural order. We observe that when fire came down from the Lord and consumed the offerings on the day of Inauguration [of the Tabernacle], *the people saw and shouted* (Lev. 9:24); in the first book of Samuel, *the Lord sent thunder and rain and all the people stood in awe* (1Sam. 12:18), and in the sea storm described in Jonah, *the men were afraid* (1:16). Such examples can be multiplied ad infinitum. It is a fact of nature that humans are more affected by the stimulation of the senses than by the dictates of the intellect. The eye, in particular, has a special property (as Cicero the greatest gentile orator states in books 6 and 7 of his *Letters*)[6] in that it magnifies the impact made upon it more than does the ear. Consider Joseph the righteous who was not stirred to compassion for his brother until he raised his eyes and actually saw him.[7] There is also the example of the man Moses who could not summon up enough courage from the refined word of God to cast the tablets from his hands until he descended and actually saw the golden calf.[8]

3. This is a reference to the *Pimander,* one of the works of the *Corpus Hermeticum* which was probably written in Greek in the first centuries C.E. but ascribed to Hermes Trismegistus who was said to have been a contemporary of Moses and influenced by the teachings of the Bible. De' Rossi like the majority of the syncretists of his time believed in the authenticity of the work. On the subject, see F. Yates, *Giordano Bruno,* D. P. Walker, *The Ancient Theology,* B. P. Copenhaver, ed., *Hermetica,* and A. T. Grafton, *Defenders,* chs. 5–6. De' Rossi used one of the many editions of Marsilio Ficino's Latin translation of the Greek text: "Nihil enim est in omni natura quod ille ipse non sit. . . . Nomina insuper habet omnia quoniam unus est pater" (45).

4. B. Ber. 55a.

5. Nahmanides, Introduction to *Perushe ha-Torah* (6): "There is a mystical tradition that all the Torah comprises the names of the Holy One blessed be He." This is a central idea in Jewish mystical tradition.

6. De' Rossi refers in Italian fashion to Marcus Tullius Cicero as Tullio. The references appear to be to *Ep. ad fam.* VI, 1, 1: "Nam etsi quocumque in loco quisquis est, idem est ei sensus et eadem acerbitas ex interitu rerum et publicarum et suarum, tamen *oculi augent dolorem* qui ea quae ceteri audiunt intueri cogunt nec avertere a miseriis cogitationem sinunt," and VII, 30, 1: "Quamquam haec etiam auditu acerba sunt, tamen audire tolerabilius est quam videre."

7. See Gen. 43:30. Joseph sees Benjamin and is so emotionally overcome that he has to leave the room.

8. See Ex. 32:19. Previously Moses had implored God not to destroy the people.

Accordingly, on reflection, I decided that it would be both useful and correct in the opening pages of my book to leave to posterity a detailed account of what happened here in Ferrara in my lifetime. Then a contemporary of mine might corroborate my tale to his children. Naturally, I realize that from one point of view this is not a story of miracles remote from the workings of nature; this phenomenon has occurred many times in the world. And yet, surely, for the eye that beholds and the ear that hears a sudden event, one both astounding and incomprehensible, has all the appearances of a miracle. It arouses humans to recognize the divine power all the more assuredly and to reaffirm it in our heart. It might appear that the beginning of my tale is irrelevant to the subject matter of this book and bears no relation to it. Nevertheless, even before I have completed my discourse, the discerning person will realize that this new experience gave the impetus for my work; it formed and consolidated it. Whoever so desires, let him incline his ear and listen.

The memorable day was 17 Kislev (18 November) 5331 [1570] anno mundi according to our reckoning.[9] It was approaching the tenth hour of the night leading to the sixth day [Friday],[10] the time when people are usually asleep when all of a sudden a resounding and shattering noise was heard which continued for the next three minutes.[11] We had never heard the likes of it before, and as for our ancestors, it was hundreds of years since they had reported such a happening. Quite apart from the tumultous noises and threatening sounds emitted from over the skies, there was the clanging of the tiles and drains of the roofs as they collided against each other and rolled around. The ears of anyone who heard it rang—and who was so deaf not to hear it? Their hearts quivered with fear lest the earth be annihilated and the world and its inhabitants left desolate. Such were the terrors which appeared to them to be imminent. Indeed, in a state of drowsy stupefaction, they initially attributed the alarming phenomenon to an all-consuming fire or else to a thunderbolt which would engulf the earth. For during the first few moments they did not know what it was. But when the shaking and quaking was felt from underneath every bed and couch, then the truth dawned on them and they realized that this mighty storm was in actual fact a powerful earthquake which was shaking the earth from its very position.[12] Whoever had his wits about him braced himself and proceeded to bless the great God whose might fills the universe.[13] Trembling, he silently waited for Him to still the world from its raging and give us respite. And sure enough, that is what happened. Not long afterwards, the clamor ceased and for a while the earth lay dormant. But we had been wrong to suppose that God had relented from His fury. No, from then on right until daybreak, the earth reverberated time after time and its netherparts shook to and fro each and every moment. Many people took to calculating the number of minor tremors which

9. As Cassel notes ad loc., de' Rossi confused the dates. The earthquake occurred on Thursday night 16 November–Friday 17 which was 18 Kislev. This is supported by all contemporary records.

10. De' Rossi writes '10th hour', i.e., he follows "l'uso italiano" according to which the hours of the day are calculated from sunset.

11. In Christian accounts, de' Rossi's three minutes was often described as "continuò per più d'un Pater nostro."

12. Cf. Job 9:6.

13. This is a reference to the blessing which is to be said in the event of an earthquake (and also over thunder), "Blessed be He whose might and power fills the universe" (M. Ber. 9:2).

were felt during those three hours and according to their evidence there were eighteen or more. By now it was beyond any shadow of a doubt that every person had been awakened from their sleep. Father, mother, and children got up from their beds to see what was happening in the town. Terror and panic was the order of the day—it was no time for rest or relaxation. Several turrets and chimneys and anything else held high and aloft had been thrown down in the eruptions of the first quake. As soon as it was light enough for a person to recognize his fellow, the people got up and went around the city to inspect the debris. They gathered in groups to talk about the amazing spectacle. Approaching the nineteenth hour on Friday, they were still engrossed in discussion when there was another fairly violent quake and once more at the twenty-second hour, and again at the first and second hour of the holy Sabbath eve. Though these shocks lacked the virulence and fearfulness of the first quake everybody was overcome with trembling and trepidation. At the third hour on the eve of that fearful Sabbath, yet another very powerful tremor was directed at the inhabitants of the region. Like the previous one, it too lasted about three minutes. It razed buildings, tore down walls, shattered houses, and inflicted cracks and fissures. The destruction was much more devastating than that of the previous day when the noise of the quake was greater than its tremor, whereas now the tremor was far greater than the noise of the quake. Not just one area was affected; now the shaking went backwards and forwards, from east to west and from north to south as though acting on orders to produce great ruin and devastation in the land. It is indeed true that here in the great city of Ferrara clefts and fissures, destruction on a large scale, were inflicted. All the strongest and weightiest buildings, particularly those which were situated on the corners of the marketplaces and streets which lacked the cover or protection of an adjoining house to buttress them were subjected to the most devastating damage—the earth had become a terror sent from God.[14] Then the entire population of Ferrara, young and old, hastily fled in great panic from the cover of their houses and from the shelter of any rafter or wall regardless of its condition. They went out into the open, into the streets and into any garden they could find.[15] They left behind their possessions and belongings strewn and ruined, alarmed by the thought that their houses might suddenly cave in on them, as had indeed happened to more than seventy inhabitants in various parts of the town. These people had been unable to make their escape quickly enough. In a flash, their houses became their graves. How could God not forgive the iniquities of His people at a time like this? It was by then the Lord's Sabbath, but in order to save life and deliver from death those who were prepared to serve Him in perpetuity, many persons took their children on their shoulders, their clothes and other belongings on their backs, with a light or torch to illuminate their path. The difference between holy and profane was now obliterated; it was as though God had forgotten the appointed time and Sabbath.[16] So they made a hasty exodus, wandering among the gentiles through the

14. See 1Sam. 14:15: *and the earth quaked; so it grew into a terror from God.*

15. Similar descriptions are quoted by Solerti. "Il terremoto di Ferrara" (518–19): "Per il che impaurito ognuno si tirò fuori alle strade dove però dai camini cadenti molti furono oppressi, ed altri si ritirò nelle piazze larghe, altri nei sagrati delle chiese, ed altri in mezzo dei giardini" (letter from the ambassador of Urbino).

16. Cf. Lam. 2:7.

streets, preferably seeking a place which was remote from any building or enclosure. This was their salvation for which they opted:[17] Rather than sit in the shelter of their homes, they let the bitter frost and moon beat on their heads at night.[18] But this terror was insignificant in comparison with the extreme fear they suffered throughout the night when every fifteen minutes the earth shook. It seemed as though the foundations of the earth were being continually churned up in order to renew the fearful shocks.

By now they had stopped counting the minor and moderate tremors of that night which already amounted to more than fifty. The two extremely violent quakes, as travelers and inhabitants confirmed, erupted on Thursday night and on the holy Sabbath eve, and according to the calculations of reliable men of science, the sound of them could be heard for a distance of two hundred miles, from the outskirts of the city of Pesaro as far as Milan. Yet they caused no damage or destruction to any place other than Ferrara, and subsequently even the noise abated and the tremors could only really be heard in Ferrara and for about ten miles in the surrounding country. Ten frightening quakes reverberated daily, or twenty if the minor tremors be included with the major ones. They mainly occurred at about midnight—and these were the most powerful—and otherwise at the ninth hour and from then until dawn. Many of those people who had steeled themselves against the shaking had already lost more than ten successive nights' sleep. This was because without fail between the ninth and tenth hour in the morning a tremor of considerable strength would erupt, as though it had been designated by God as an appointed time for perpetuity. After the eruption of the first two mentioned quakes, the general rule was that the formidable earthquakes would occur from midnight until dawn.

In this context, I cannot refrain from mentioning Amos's prophecy about the powerful earthquake which happened in his lifetime in the year of the death of King Uzziah. With my limited intellectual faculties I may perhaps explain some of the verses of his prophecy somewhat differently from our commentators of blessed memory. In the final analysis, however, we must declare them right and accede to their interpretation. The verses under discussion read as follows: *Behold, I will make it creak under you as a cart creaks what is full of sheaves and flight shall fail the swift . . . neither shall he stand that handles the bow . . . and he that is courageous among the mighty shall flee away naked on that day* (Amos 2:13–16). According to our rabbis, blessed be their memory, all these pronouncements fortell of impending war. Yet, on the basis of the statement *two years before the prophecy* (Amos 1:1) at the outset of the prophecy, they had already agreed and proved that Amos was actually prophesying about the event of the earthquake. This view was confirmed by the following verses: *For the Lord will command and the great house shall be smashed to bits and the little house to splinters* (Amos 6:11), *and I will wreck the winter house together with the summer house . . . and the great houses shall be destroyed* (Amos 3:15). Anyone who consults the commentaries of the sages ibn Ezra,[19]

17. Cf. 2Sam. 23:5.

18. The idea of being moonstruck is taken from Ps. 121:6: *The sun shall not strike you by day nor the moon by night.*

19. Ibn Ezra to Amos 1:1: "Many commentators say that the earthquake occurred at the time when Uzziah offered incense, but there is no Scriptural proof for this . . . and the reason for mentioning the earthquake is because he prophesied before its occurrence, *For the great house shall be smitten* (Amos 6:11)."

Kimḥi[20] and the noble Don Isaac [Abravanel],[21] may their memory be for a blessing, will discover that such is their interpretation. Yet once it had occurred to them that the verses we quoted originally were a reference to war, they found it difficult to make the first verse—I *will make it creak under you*—consistent with the later verse—*and he that is courageous among the mighty shall flee naked on that day.* They therefore sought ways whereby they could impose the "war" interpretation on all these verses. It is however apparent that their interpretations are forced, as any intelligent person will realize on scrutinizing their commentaries hoping to be convinced by words of truth. They contort the verse, *I will make it creak under you as the cart creaks that is full of sheaves* in order to make it refer to war. That upright intellect, Rashi of blessed memory, however, interprets the words *under you* as signifying "your resting place." He meant that the earth itself on which they rest would shake and groan. Don Isaac gives a similar interpretation: "When the cart is overloaded, the wheels underneath it are made to creak and groan."

This all makes sense as long as the passage is taken in relation to the earthquake and understood without allegorization. In this way, the later verse, *and he that is courageous among the mighty shall flee naked on that day,* can then be understood in its proper light. If, however, the verse is referring to war, how could one reasonably infer that the warrior would flee naked? For the plain sense of "naked" is of being stripped of clothing and covering of the flesh, and not of military weapons. Moreover, why do ibn Ezra and Kimḥi suggest that his flight would be facilitated because he would not be weighed down by clothes? Surely, anyone clad in light garments would have more courage to run wheresoever he chooses than would the naked and barefooted. Natural modesty has all the characteristics of a thicket—it traps the feet and becomes a restraining entanglement. But few garments, a polished sword, or arrows in the hands of the warrior do in no way constitute an obstacle or burden. Rather, the intention of the prophet here is to convey the atmosphere of the earthquake. According to scholars, and as we ourselves know from our own experience, the earthquake occurs most often and with the greatest virulence during the night and from midnight onwards when people are sound asleep. This is particularly the case when the earthquake comes about primarily and essentially through divine intervention, as happened in the earthquake designated for the days of Uzziah. The blessed Lord knows the right moment for crushing the wicked underfoot such that they are deprived of any means of escape. When the sudden devastating event occurs, even the most courageous of warriors would not think of groping in the dark for one of his possessions or for a piece of clothing. In great haste, he would flee naked before the house or room would collapse on top of him and he be buried alive. In truth, this had already befallen many persons of high rank here in Ferrara;[22]

20. Kimḥi to Amos 1:1: "The earthquake was in the time of Uzziah as is told in Zechariah's prophecy (14:5) and he [Amos] mentions the earthquake because he prophesied about its future occurrence as he said, *And the great house shall be smitten.*"

21. Abravanel to Amos 1:1 (80, col. a). Abravanel actually disagrees with ibn Ezra (who connects the first verse of ch. 1 with ch. 3:15, *And I will wreck the winter house with the summer house,* and states that the verse should be interpreted in relation to the destruction of Samaria, and that the reason for the reference to *two years before the earthquake* (1:1) was to delineate the period of his prophecy, i.e., until and not after the occurrence of the earthquake.

22. Such stories were told of members of Alfonso's court about their flight from the Castello.

when the earth shook, overcome by fear of the night,[23] they made a hurried exit into the cold without clothing or covering.

From this perspective the following words of the prophet are to be understood: *So shall the children of Israel dwell in Samaria* (they were also affected by the earthquake) *escape with the corner of a couch and the leg of* [lit. Damascus] *a bed* (Amos 3:12). This verse alludes to the few people who were to be saved by means of providence or fate affecting the corners of their beds and corner posts of their couches at nighttime.[24] Such epithets as *the rider of the horse* or *he who handles the bow* only describe each man by his potential field of activity; for at that time, the one could not actually handle the bow nor the other ride the horse. Alternatively, the verses cover all aspects, sometimes referring to the nightly earthquake and sometimes to its occurrence during the day. For it did not erupt on one single day but continued for days on end. Thus the expression "on that day" signifies "at that time." What is meant then is that at the usual time for people to go out to work, the holder of the bow and the rider of horse would not manage to escape, while at night, the most courageous warrior would flee naked.

There is a verse in Isaiah (24:19–20): *And the earth's foundations tremble. The earth is breaking; breaking. The earth is crumbling, crumbling. The earth is tottering, tottering. The earth is swaying like a drunkard; it is rocking to and fro like a hut. Its iniquity shall weigh it down.* Seven expressions are used here which quite likely are meant to denote the seven kinds of earthquakes mentioned in the works of the natural philosophers to which we will presently refer. Whether the text is literally describing the earthquake or using figurative language to refer to war as Kimḥi would have it, the fact is that Scripture never departs from its plain meaning which in this context is the exemplification of the various types of earthquakes.[25] At the beginning of the passage, Isaiah states, *The windows from on high were opened* (v. 18). Now men of science explain that earthquakes are caused by the movements of the celestial bodies. He [i.e., the prophet] therefore says that although the cause will be absent at that particular moment, the Lord, blessed be He, by whom actions are weighed, will employ the windows of heaven as the vehicle of His wrath; they are opened, their sparks descend and affect the earth with the seven types of punitive earthquakes. In the same vein are the poet's words, *He looks at the earth and it trembles* (Ps. 104:32). In fact, the seven planets are described by the prophet Zechariah as *the seven eyes of God* (4:10), and Ezekiel refers to the sphere of the fixed stars as *rims covered all over with eyes* (1:18). Rabbi Judah known as Leon [i.e., Leone Ebreo] says this in the third part of his *Dialogue* which is called *Philone e Sophia.*[26] Such

23. 'Fear of the night.' De' Rossi uses S.S. 3:8 which refers to warriors *with sword on thigh because of terror by night.*

24. De' Rossi follows ibn Ezra, Kimḥi, and others who detect the parallelism in the verse and interpret Damascus (*Demesheq*) as an unknown word, possibly a combination of two words corresponding to the "corner" of a bed.

25. De' Rossi ignores Aristotle's definitions of the two main types of earthquakes and suggests that Isaiah's imagery is intended to conjure up the seven types of earthquakes mentioned in the *De mundo* (see n. 34). Throughout his interpretation of this passage, de' Rossi puts forward a *peshaṭ* type of interpretation, i.e., a plain reading of the verse, which is either corroborated by his own experience or by the findings of natural philosophy.

26. Judah Abravanel (Leone Ebreo, the son of Isaac Abravanel), *Dialoghi d'amore,* also referred to as *Philone e Sophia.* The reference is to bk. 3 (186): "E quali miglior occhi che'l sole e le stelle che ne la sacra scrittura si chiamano occhi di Dio per la loro visione? Dice il profeta per li sette pianeti. Quelli sette occhi di Dio . . ."

was the work's importance and beauty that Christian scholars translated it from the Italian vernacular into Latin.[27] Therefore this "looking," as we wrote, is through their [i.e., the celestial bodies] agency.[28]

Now any learned person knows that the basic discussions of the natural philosophers on the subject of earthquakes is to be found in the Greek philosopher's [i.e., Aristotle's] *Meteorologica*[29] and in book 6 of Seneca's *Quaestiones naturales*.[30] Pliny, too, treated the subject at length in chapter 79, and successive chapters of book 2.[31]

One of our own people, Rabbi Isaac Latif, relates a charming tale at the end of the first section of his book *Shaʿar ha-Shamayim*.[32] Listen to his impressive story: "In our days it happened that one of the emperor's castles which was situated close to the seashore was one night shaken by an earthquake. No trace of the place remained and a mound was seen in the midst of the sea about four miles away." Quite apart from these writers, it is of special importance to me to mention a work on the earthquake which was published in the Italian vernacular after the outbreak of the earthquakes. The author was a Christian scholar who practiced medicine here in Ferrara. His name was Buoni, and truly he was good and praiseworthy.[33] In the first book (par. 29), you will find reference to the seven types of earthquakes which I mentioned above, according to the interpretation given by the author of the ancient work *De mundo*.[34] By means of a beautifully composed dialogue, he investigates the causes and portents of the phenomenon and gives descriptions of earthquakes of the past and the incredible destruction which was caused as well as all other relevant material. The author also made a collation of the most important accounts together with their interpretation as given by the natural philosophers, the astrologers and their [Christian] theologians, thus display-

27. Leone Ebreo came to Italy after 1492. The first edition of his *Dialoghi* was printed in Rome in 1535. It is unlikely that Leone Ebreo wrote it originally in Italian. According to C. Dionisotti ("Appunti"), it is improbable that Leone wrote it in Tuscan: it was not his native tongue; it was unusual for works of that kind to be written in the *volgare* at the beginning of the sixteenth century. Dionisotti suggests that Leone may have written it in Hebrew or perhaps Latin (he was a doctor and Latin was the language of medicine), and then it was translated into the *volgare*. The Latin translation to which de' Rossi refers is that of Juan Carlos Sarrasin which was printed in Venice in 1564.

28. I.e., earthquakes occur through the movements of the celestial bodies which are called "eyes" and which are directed by *He who looks on the earth and it trembles* (Ps. 104:32).

29. Aristotle, *Met.* 2, ch. 7 (365a14–369a9).

30. Seneca, *Nat. quaest.* bk. 6, "De terrae motu."

31. Pliny, *Nat. hist.* 2, chs. 81–86. (The chapter division which de' Rossi gives is found in the early printed editions.)

32. As Cassel notes ad loc., Isaac Latif was author of a work entitled *Shaʿar ha-Shamayim,* but the work to which de' Rossi is referring was written by Gershon ben Solomon (pt. 1, ch. 7, Venice 1547). See also the English trans. and ed. of F. S. Bodenheimer, 114. The chapter is about the rainbow and the earthquake. The author came from Arles and lived in the late thirteenth century.

33. De' Rossi puns on the name of Buoni who wrote his dialogue *Del terremoto* in 1571 after the eruption of the earthquake. The work describes earthquakes from antiquity to the author's own time and philosophical and theological discussions about the phenomenon. As Cassel notes, this book was a great inspiration for de' Rossi. He derived much of his source material from the work and often agreed with Buoni's interpretations.

34. In 1, par. 29, Buoni refers to the ps. Aristotelian work *De mundo* and compares the statement there with the statement of Aristotle in his "libri legittimi." See J. Kraye, "Heinsius." The reference to *De mundo* is 4, 396a. The work classifies earthquakes not only according to the form of movement but also according to the effect each movement makes.

ing his fine understanding. Should you evince an interest to see the book, go and read it and you will find it rewarding; for what useful purpose would I serve at this point by transferring the heavy bag from one side to the other of the tired beast of burden?[35] However, I have come across a passage which he does not cite and it is also of great value. It is a synopsis of the views of the great philosophers on the subject of earthquakes. The collation was made by the wise Plutarch, teacher of Trajan, the fourteenth emperor,[36] in a treatise of his minor works entitled *De placitis philosophorum* (ch. 15). He writes as follows:[37]

> Thales and Democritus held that earthquakes are caused by water. According to the Stoic school, earthquakes occur when the vapor from the earth is dissipated in the air and then erupts. The determining factor, in Anaximenes' view, is the dryness or porosity[38] of the earth, the former occurring in time of drought, the latter in time of protracted rainfall. Anaxagoras said that the air which is trapped beneath the earth is prevented from breaking the hard concave surface above it. It then causes the quaking of that section against which it exerts pressure. Aristotle assigned the cause to the cold which envelops the earth from above and below. Heat, he said, which is light by nature, tends upwards. The dry vapor, separated in its ascent, is held back, but manages to escape through the clefts in the earth and through the crevices in its jagged places and midst all this uproar it causes the earth to quake. Metrodorus said that no body can be moved from its own particular place unless an external object exerts pressure on it or actually pushes it. Thus the earth which, of course, lies in its natural place, can in no way be moved, although certain parts on the earth's surface can change their position. Parmenides[39] said that the distance of the earth from the vault of heaven is equidistant from every point. Since its position is completely central it is impossible for it to move. When it does shake, it does so without changing its position. Anaximander[40] said that the earth quakes when its width is pushed by the air. Some people hold the opinion that the earth floats on water just like the plane tree or planks of wood, and it is the water that causes the earth's movement. Plato said that there are six types of movement: upwards, downwards, forwards, backwards, right, and left. The earth which is held compressed from all sides at the very lowest point is unable to change its position at all or to move in any of these directions for every side exerts an equal amount of pressure on it. There is, however, the view that some places on the earth quake on account of their porosity. Epicurus said that it is quite likely that the earth is disturbed into movement like the clapper of a bell[41] which rings because of the thick moist air underneath it. It is also possible that a wind entering into the circuits of the earth's parts and into its curving veins causes it to quake.

35. The expression derives from B. Ket. 110a and is particularly relevant here since de' Rossi follows Buoni in so many of his arguments and discussions.

36. Plutarch's life spans the rule of the emperors Nero, Vespasian, Titus, Domitian, Trajan, and Hadrian. The idea that Plutarch was Trajan's teacher was derived from the dedication to Trajan in the spurious *Apothegms of Kings* which later gained currency. See C. P. Jones, *Plutarch,* 30ff.

37. *De placitis* is not a genuine work of Plutarch but was regarded as such until the seventeenth century. De' Rossi consulted Budé's Latin translation of the work which was first published in Paris, 1505, and then included in his *Opuscula.* The passage is bk. 3, ch. 15.

38. 'Porosity': Latin 'raritudo.'

39. De' Rossi omits the reference to Democritus.

40. Ps. Plutarch refers to Anaximenes.

41. 'Like a clapper of a bell': this is not in the original text of ps. Plutarch.

Thus far the words of the wise Plutarch.

Whatever your mode of interpretation, you should take into account that the most important comments of the aforementioned natural philosophers which relate to the earthquake are those which deal with the time preceding its occurrence: when the air is turbulent and enveloped in darkness as happened here in Ferrara after midday on Friday before the commencement of that fearful Sabbath eve; also afterwards, when there appear to be flaming fires, swelling waters, inordinate dryness, contamination of the air, and other such phenomena which are bound to come unless the good Lord pardons and provides protection. All these things are disparately displayed throughout the prophecy of Amos whose main purpose was, in my view, to describe the earthquake and everything connected with it. This accounts for his opening statement *two years before the earthquake.* Examine those books we mentioned and compare them with the verses of holy Scripture and then see whether my assessment proves correct. But as it is, my purpose here is not to serve as an exegete.[42]

Now please be receptive and give your attention to the information I have as regards the statements of our sages, blessed be their memory, on the subject of the earthquake, its causes and portents. In Shemot Rabbah (29) Baltṣa asked Rabbi Aqiva:[43] " 'How does an earthquake occur?' He said to him: 'At the time when the Holy One blessed be He looks and sees His Temple destroyed by the nations who live in a state of peace and tranquillity, He becomes jealous as it were, He roars aloud and immediately heaven and earth quake as it is stated, *And the Lord will roar from Zion . . . so that heaven and earth tremble* (Joel 4:16).' And how do we know that this refers to Israel? It states [in the same verse] *And the Lord will protect Israel.*" There is a passage in tractate Berakhot whose subject is the Mishnah which deals with [the blessings about] "movements."[44] According to Rashi of blessed memory, the word "movements" in this context signifies earthquakes. Rav Qattina cites the words of a necromancer (i.e., one who practices sorcery with bones):

> "When the Holy One blessed be He remembers His children who are steeped in travail amid the gentiles, He lets two tears drip into the Great Sea and the sound of them can be heard from one end of the world to the other." Rav Qattina himself said: "He claps His hands together as it says, *I, too, will strike hand against hand* (Ezk. 21:22)." Rabbi Jonathan[45] said: "He emits a groan as it says, *I will vent all My anger upon them and satisfy My fury* (Ezk. 5:13)." The rabbis say: "He treads on the firmament as it says, *He utters shouts like the grape-treaders* (Jer. 25:30)." Rabbi Aḥa says: "He presses His feet together beneath the throne of glory as it says, *The heaven is My throne* (Is. 66:1)." Some say: "He roars loudly and causes the world to tremble as it says, *The Lord roars from on high* (Jer. 25:30)."

42. This disavowal is characteristic of de' Rossi when he wishes to refute rabbinic opinion. He never really retracts an opinion which he holds to be correct.

43. S.R. 29:9. This passage was often censored and de' Rossi seems to have changed the text slightly from the way it appears in most printed editions, which read: "He sees the houses of the idolators and His own house destroyed and put into the hands of the uncircumcised."

44. B. Ber. 59a.

45. 'R. Jonathan': This reading is listed in R. N. Rabinowicz, *Diqduqe Soferim,* 167, n. 8, but most editions read 'R. Nathan.'

In the Palestinian Talmud,[46] the Tanḥuma[47] and Midrash Tehillim[48] the following is related:

Elijah asked Rabbi Nehorai: "Why do earthquakes occur?" He said to him: "They occur when people fail to give the tithes correctly." He said to him: "Reason dictates as you have suggested. (In other words, the earth reels beneath its inhabitants because they transgress the law relating to the gifts which are to be allocated from the earth's produce.) But, the main reason is that when the Holy One blessed be He looks and sees the many houses which stand intact[49] while His own Sanctuary lies in ruins, He brings *apilion* (this Greek word means garment, i.e., a dark shroud)[50] to the world so that it shakes. This is why it is written, *He looks on the earth and it trembles* (Ps. 104:32)."

This explanation bears affinity to the closing passage in the Tanḥuma.[51]

One says, "I shall worship Moloch"; the other says, "I shall bow down to the sun and moon." He therefore brings an earthquake to His world in order to avenge Himself on these people and their gods. They would then say that their gods had suffered the same punishment as they themselves. Rabbi Asa [Aḥa] said that the earthquake is caused by the sin of homosexuality; according to another, the sin of contention is the cause. Rabbi Samuel bar Naḥmani said that whenever the word "earthquake" is used, it simply implies a change of government, and the prooftext is the verse, *And the earth trembled and reeled* (Jer. 41:39) which continues *for the plans of the Lord have come to pass against Babylon.*

There is a passage in the *Zohar* commenting on the verse, *And he said to his people: Look the Israelite people are much too numerous for us* (Ex. 1:9). It reads as follows:[52]

Rabbi Isaac once came to a mountain and saw a certain person sleeping beneath a tree. He sat down in that place and while sitting there saw that the earth was shaking violently. The tree was uprooted and fell to the ground. Then he noticed clefts appearing in the earth and that the ground was shaking up and down. The man woke up and cried out to Rabbi Isaac: "Jew, Jew, weep and lament for at this moment a prince is being appointed in heaven, a ruler, a divine prince, who is destined to cause you great harm. This shaking of the earth is on your account; for whenever the earth shakes, somebody is being appointed who will do you harm." Rabbi Isaac wondered and said: "Truly it is written, *For three things does the earth quake . . . for a slave who becomes king* (Pr. 30:21–22). [The earth quakes] when

46. P. Ber. 9 (2) 13c. This is probably the original source for the other passages. De' Rossi has synthesized all three texts.

47. Tanḥuma, Bereshit (Buber, 12). This passage occurs only in the Buber edition, which indicates, as Buber notes, that de' Rossi must have quoted the text from manuscript.

48. Mid. Teh. to 104:32 (447). In B, de' Rossi also refers to a parallel passage in Mid. Teh. to Ps. 18:12.

49. 'Many houses stand intact': The uncensored text reads: "The Holy One blessed be He sees the theaters and circuses." In B, de' Rossi gives an excursus here on the circuses and theaters and refers to Virgil, Aulus Gellius, and Quintilian.

50. S. Lieberman (*Greek*, 53–55) follows Ehrlich in explaining the word as a derivative of the Greek word meaning to look indignantly. De' Rossi seems to derive it from *pallium* (as does the *Arukh*). H. Orlinsky ("Studies," 499–514) compiles all the various views as to the meaning of the word and concludes that it is the Hebrew word *afilu* (even).

51. This is a synthesis of the passages quoted above from the Tanḥuma and Mid. Teh.

52. Zohar II, 17b.

somebody is appointed to replace another ruler[53] and becomes king and is given sovereign powers, and especially when he is empowered over Israel."

All these quotations from the sages must surely lead an intelligent person to conclude that the occurrence of an earthquake cannot always be attributed to the same cause. Sometimes it is due to God's jealousy of idolators or to His compassion for His people (Midrash Rabbah, Palestinian Talmud, Tanḥuma, and Berakhot); at other times, according to other sages, it is occasioned because God is angry about the sinfulness of the world (Midrash, Palestinian and Babylonian Talmuds). The phenomenon may also be a portent of change (the end of the passage in the Palestinian Talmud, Midrash, and Zohar). Diverse explanations as to how earthquakes come about are given by the other sages mentioned in Berakhot whose views are derived from the scriptural prooftexts that refer to earthquakes.

Hai Gaon, the Rashba [Solomon ben Adret], and Ran [Nissim Gaon] who are cited by Aboab all express an irrefutable opinion.[54] They say that the statements of all these Amoraim are not to be understood literally—far be it from God to behave in such a manner. Rather, they have esoteric implications and the allegorical and rhetorical nature of their enigmatic sayings are comprehensible to those with the requisite understanding. {This is clearly illustrated in the following statement of the Rashba where he is explaining the Aggadot in Berakhot:[55]

> Know that what is said in this Aggadah regarding tears, clapping of hands, pressing of feet and roaring is entirely allegorical and is intended to demonstrate sadness and distress about the destruction of the Temple and the exile of the people. We shall interpret them in respect to the scriptural verses which are cited in the Aggadah: *I will also beat My hands, the heavens are My throne, I will pour out My wrath, He roars aloud.* These are all allegories and images whose purpose is to have a shattering effect on the listener. Various other verses produce the same effect. For example, *For if you will not give heed, My inmost self must weep in secret because of your arrogance* (Jer. 13:17), and *She shall be remembered of the Lord . . . with the storm and tempest* (Is. 29:6).}

Yet on this question both Tannaim and Amoraim appear to agree that even though earthquakes might vary in the way that they are brought about and in their purpose, as was stated, they are all essentially and initially brought about by divine decree whether as chastisement or as an invocation to pious behavior. Their analysis of the problem was quite unlike that of the Greek philosophers whom we mentioned above. The latter gazed into the earth below, and the only view they held in common was that earthquakes and other such phenomena happen by chance and within the workings of nature. But as for us, to God alone do we attribute such events, who also employs natural causes as a vehicle [for His actions]. Thus, with penitence and the performance of pious acts do we react to such events in the hope of deflecting His anger away from us and ensuring that we appear righteous in His eyes. Or at least we should steer a middle

53. This is a play on the word *taḥat* which means "for" in the context of the verse, but can also mean "in place of."

54. 'Aboab': This appears to be an error. De' Rossi is more likely to be referring to the *En Ya'aqov* of Jacob ibn Ḥabib who presents all these references in his commentary to the talmudic text.

55. This is quoted in the *En Ya'aqov* to B. Ber. 59a. See discussion of Hai's opinion (more amply given by M. Lewin, *Oṣar ha-Geonim,* vol. 1, 130–32) by L. Jacobs, *Theology,* 7–9.

path and argue as follows: Since it is true that when Israel merits it, they enjoy the special providential care of the exalted God, as in the days of their exodus from Egypt and at other times more felicitous than these, it thus follows that all the various calamities, such as earthquakes which befall them, occur by divine command whether they halt or continue their journey (Num. 9:23). The same holds for the other peoples. They should not indulge in wicked acts which are bound to turn the divine countenance against them. Thus He stated that the sin of Sodom and Gomorrah was great (Gen. 18:20), and concerning Nineveh, *their wickedness has come before Me* (Jonah 1:2). Otherwise, it would have been merely fortuitous or by chance if any plague or sickness befell them. While it is true that God removes His countenance from perpetrators of transgressions and makes them suffer, it is surely reasonable that one cannot attribute the cause of such events either to God consistently or to nature consistently. Sometimes they stem from the blessed Lord, and on other occasions, as with all other natural events, they may arise purely by chance. Indeed, the rain, wind, lightning, and thunder and other such phenomena which, according to men of science, originate from the middle air are doubtlessly part of nature which is ordered by the universal creator, the blessed Lord. Nevertheless, just as He wills, these things may also happen at any undetermined moment, whether for good or for bad, as the case in the deluge, or when brimstone and fire fell on Sodom, or when Samuel brought on thunder and rain and Elijah the torrential rain. In the *Kuzari* (towards the end of section 5), the sage speaks in a similar way with regard to the individual.[56] He cites the words of David, *The Lord Himself will strike him down . . . or he shall go down in battle* (1Sam. 26:10), for premature death which is the most shattering of calamities is sometimes divinely sent and sometimes happens by chance. In tractate Shabbat,[57] our sages of blessed memory suggest that there may be death without sin and chastisement without iniquity. In the first chapter of Ḥagiga,[58] Rav Joseph tells a story of Rav Bibi as illustration of the scriptural verse, *There is that which is swept away without judgment* (Pr. 13:23). The same is true of earthquakes and other such calamities; while on many occasions they serve as a divine rebuke for transgressions, they may also happen quite fortuitously and by chance. Yedidyah the Alexandrian (Philo) tackles the problem well in the first book of *De decalogo* which is no longer extant, but which is cited by the early Christian, Eusebius of Caesarea, in the eighth book of his *Praeparatio*.[59] Speaking on the subject of divine providence, he states: "God in His wisdom decreed the existence of the four elements which would in general be of great advantage to the universe although He foresaw that in the natural process of their cycle, earthquakes, storms, and the like would be brought

56. According to Judah Halevi, *Kuzari* V, par. 20, this verse describes three types of death: divine, natural, and accidental.

57. B. Shabb. 55b. The view cited by de' Rossi contradicts that of R. Ammi.

58. B. Ḥag. 4b–5a. The story describes how the angel of death took the wrong culprit. When R. Bibi asked the angel of death whether he had permission to act in this manner, the angel replied: "Is it not written, 'There is that which is swept away without judgment'?"

59. De' Rossi used George of Trebizond's Latin translation of Eusebius's *De ev. praep.* which was criticized for its imprecision. The text reads (8, ch. 5): "Terraemotus autem et pestilentiae fulminum ictus et similia mala dicuntur et non sunt. Nullius enim mali deus causa est sed elementorum mutatione generantur neque sunt principalia naturae opera sed ad ea quae necessaria et principalia sunt consequuntur et si aliquid damnum inde habuerunt non est accusandus gubernator."

about. But the blessed Lord did not refrain from implementing His intention of producing the great good despite the fact that a slight amount of evil can also result from it. In any case, we cannot know what is for our good and what is to our detriment." It is for this reason that our sages mentioned above taught that earthquakes are of divine origin. Thus there is the statement of the psalmist, *[Then the earth rocked and quaked] . . . rocked by His indignation* (Ps. 18:8), and Isaiah's words, *And the earth shall be shaken out of her place for the wrath of the Lord of Hosts* (13:13), and Jeremiah's pronouncement, *At his wrath the earth quakes* (10:10). All these and other such verses need not always be understood as categorical statements; rather, their purpose is to underline the fact that the Lord blessed be He, acts according to His volition, and may do so, moreover, at any undetermined moment. This is demonstrated in the hyperboles used in Scripture to describe the chastisements of those who disobey the Torah which they undertook to observe.

In fact, we have noticed that our rabbis, blessed be their memory, distinguish between that which constitutes a divine visitation and that which does not.[60] In this distinction lies the root of righteousness and wickedness. The God-fearing person trembles in fear that they are divinely sent either because he is conscious of his own misdeeds or else when he sees a whole succession of calamities and takes note of their mode of occurrence. Then he repents and is forgiven. How differently does the ungodly person behave. In His wisdom, the blessed One unleashes disasters so as to enable the righteous to discern that they are discharged by God, but to entrap the wicked who regard their occurrence as merely fortuitous. For repentance is a voluntary action which is duly recompensed; it is not achieved by coercion, a response to punishment meted out hand for a hand, eye for an eye.

{In my opinion, this accounts for the hardening of the hearts of Pharaoh, Sihon, and the kings of Canaan. It is not that they agreed to listen [to the requests of the Israelites] out of their own free will and then were impeded by God. Rather, the hardening of the heart has to be measured in relation to the fear which was engendered by each new plague. Once the fear disappeared, they came under their own control with freedom of choice and it was then, of their own accord, that they refused to submit. You will observe the sequence of events. First the Lord *hardened the heart of Pharaoh* and then *he [Pharaoh] refused to let them go.*[61]}

At any rate, whenever a calamity occurs,[62] whether by divine design or pure chance, we should make swift recourse to the tower of strength, to our God. We should entreat Him to protect us against such events or, once they have happened, to deflect their course so that in all situations we may hope for assistance and help in answer to repentance and prayer. You may note that in his commentary on the Alfasi, blessed be his memory, Ran [Rabbenu Nissim] expressed the opinion that the "movements" which are the subject of the Mishnah quoted above are the gusty winds which blow when it is

60. B. Ta'anit 22a discusses the times for blowing the ram's horn and fasting when unnatural events, e.g., wild animals entering inhabited areas during the day, occur which appear to be divine visitations.

61. B has some minor differences and omits reference to the kings of Canaan. De' Rossi's opinion seems to differ from that of Maimonides in ch. 8 of *Shem. Per.* with which he was clearly familiar.

62. De' Rossi uses the euphemistic expression given in M. Ta'anit 3:8, "For any calamity that may [lit. not] occur."

raining, whereas the winds discussed in the subsequent section refer, in his opinion, to a time when there is no rain, but occasional hurricanes which can shatter mountains and so on.[63] And yet the statement of Rabbi Aḥa in the above-cited passage in the Palestinian Talmud demonstrates that these "movements" are simply earthquakes, and this is how Rashi of blessed memory understood the passage.

Now I cannot resist taking this opportunity to make reference to the passage in Josephus (book 15 [of the *Antiquities*] and book 1 of the *Jewish War* where he describes the violent war between the Jews and the Arabs in the seventh year of Herod's reign.[64] In the month of Ziv,[65] one of the two periods of the year in which such calamities tend to occur, there was a violent earthquake in their country which caused immense damage. Not only were the cattle destroyed in inordinate numbers, but more than ten thousand people were killed in their homes.[66] Only the soldiers escaped unhurt because they were encamping in the open at the time. Notwithstanding their escape they were beset by fear that the event was also a portent of crushing defeat at the hands of their enemies. Trying to dispel their fears, King Herod appealed to them in the following address: "My brothers, my people, the elements like everything else that exists under the heavens are subject to natural defects. There is no reason to fear that yet more trouble will follow in the trail of what has already happened. There may be some presages of future pestilence, destruction, famine, or earthquakes which are in themselves serious disasters and ills. But such disasters which are sufficiently calamitous in themselves should not be regarded as portents of other such events."

In truth, this speech of one who was a warrior and not a scholar was most appropriate for the occasion, particularly since the situation demanded that he should instill his army with the courage to face the impending war. Indeed the time was opportune for God came to their aid and in a short while they defeated their enemies. However, in all truth, these words of his require refinement and improvement to ensure that they correspond to the beliefs of those who uphold the Torah and do not walk contrarily with God in matters of this kind.[67] His statement that earthquakes may have natural causes can indeed be validated as we indicated above. In fact, other expressions of the harsh course of judgment, such as pestilence and famine, also have natural causes in the form of putrefaction of the air, detention of rain, and the like. Nevertheless, the upright are overcome by fear and trembling lest the source of all these ills is God who employs those natural causes in order to mete out judgment on the peoples who have committed terrible sins. Accordingly, with regard to earthquakes, we ought not dispense with critical evaluation and simply attribute the cause of the phenomenon to nature alone as did the Greek philosophers. Rather, we should be frightened and anxious that we

63. The reference should be R. Jonah Gerondi, not to R. Nissim, whose gloss is to be found on Isaac Alfasi's *Halakhot* to B. Ber. 42b.

64. De' Rossi cites *Ant.* XV:121–46; *Bellum* I:370–79 and produces a partial synthesis of the two accounts. It is interesting to note that de' Rossi ignores part of the description in *Ant.* (144ff.) which is more theological in vein.

65. De' Rossi uses the biblical expression *ziv* for 'early spring.'

66. The Greek reads '30,000 persons,' but in Sigismud Gelenius's Latin translation of the *Antiquities* which de' Rossi used, the figure of 10,000 (decem millia) is given.

67. Cf. Maimonides (*Guide* III, ch. 36) who like many other commentators understands the expression in Lev. 26:21 *And if you walk contrary* (*qeri*) *to me* to mean "if you believe that calamities are fortuitous."

ourselves are responsible for what has happened, as we stated above. Similarly, he [i.e., Herod] is also correct when he states that man is informed of impending disasters by certain portents which appear prior to the event. (This will be explained in chapter 54, if God so wills.) Adherents to Torah would have rebuked him for his statement that after the earthquake has spent itself in uprooting, razing, and destroying, the situation would then resemble other disasters which are calamities in their own right but not portents of further doom. They would insist that divinely sent earthquakes may also presage further outbreak of wrath should the sinners not have been obliterated from the earth or should His wrathful attribute not be quashed by His quality of mercy. As it says time after time, *But if despite this, you disobey Me,* and you say that it happened to us by chance,[68] *I for my part, will discipline you sevenfold for your sins* (Lev. 26:23–24). While they all seem to come about in the sphere of nature, it is as we said that nature serves as an instrument for the wrath of the Creator of all. Likewise it is also employed by Him when He wishes to reward the righteous to enable them to enjoy the fruit of their works.

Our citations from the Palestinian and Babylonian Talmuds, from Midrash Tehillim and the Zohar indicated that the earthquakes like all other plagues serves as a rebuke and also heralds further calamities. The good doctor Buoni argues in a similar vein in section 4 of his book on the basis of the statements of many distinguished Christian and ancient pagan sages. A case in point is his citation of the doctor Aquinas's interpretation of the verse in Psalms, *He will rain down upon the wicked blazing blazing coals* (11:6). Aquinas states that in the majority of cases, the earthquake demonstrates the finger of God working through the medium of nature.[69] It was for this reason that Pythagoras, the leader of those Italian philosophers who raised their eyes heavenward, used to call it the "voice of God."[70] Similar expressions are to be found in Scripture, e.g., *The voice of the Lord convulses the wilderness* (Ps. 29:8), *They perceived the thunder* (Ex. 20:18), *The whole mountain trembled violently* (Ex. 19:18). Accordingly, this section of the book was entitled "The Voice of God."

The general opinion of the aforementioned writer [i.e., Buoni] is that the earthquake not only serves to chastise humans for wrongdoing, but it is also a token of wrath and is intended as an entreaty to sinners to repent of their transgressions. Thus, there is a complete consensus of opinion among Jewish and Christ sages. Nobody disputes that it is a mark of wisdom and reveals the integrity of the upright to believe that it is the voice of God within this mighty power which rends and shatters the stalwart hearts[71] of those

68. De' Rossi is glossing the verse according to his (and Maimonides') interpretation.

69. I cannot locate this passage. Aquinas is quoted in 4, par. 343 but in connection with Ps. 18 where the same idea is being expressed.

70. De' Rossi appears to have derived this designation from Buoni 4, par. 339 in which there is a reference to Francesco Giorgio, *In Scripturam,* vol. VI, sec. VII ("De mundo et natura"): "ad Pythagoram veniamus qui pie asserit terraemotus a Deo fieri ad mortales perterrendos" and in 4, par. 340, one of the interlocutors, Padre Righini, states that like the philosopher Pythagoras, one should ascend on high to God, author of nature, and regard "il terremoto come voce del Signore." But I have been unable to find any ancient source attributing such a saying to Pythagoras. More commonly, Pythagoras is attributed with having defined the earthquake as an "assembly of the dead" (concilium mortuorum); when they quarrel among themselves vociferously, a sound of the earth quaking is heard.

71. This is an adaptation of 1K. 19:11.

in the city affected by the earthquake. He has summoned this city among all others and rouses it to acknowledge His greatness and strong hand and to fear His judgment, ready to be inflicted. For it may be, and I pray this will not be the case, that the earthquake is followed by fire or pestilence or any other such phenomenon which is usually the natural consequence as we said, unless God takes our side. In particular, the people whom He singled out as His inheritance are more likely to arouse His anger when they sin. As He said, *You alone have I singled out of all the families of the earth; that is why I will call you to account for all your iniquities* (Amos 3:2). They should examine their deeds and then repent.[72] Consequently, our sages were quite right when they said in Yevamot,[73] "There is no misfortune in the world for which Israel is not responsible." And in Shabbat they also say,[74] "If you encounter disasters . . . go and examine the judges of Israel." Similarly, in Taʿanit, Israel's transgressions are said to cause drought.[75] In the same vein, in Yevamot, they explain the verse, *All the families of the earth shall be blessed through you* (Gen. 12:3) to mean that Israel is responsible for all the blessings that the families of the earth enjoy.[76] And in tractate Sheviʿit in the Palestinian Talmud, the verse, *The blessing of the Lord be upon you* (Ps. 129:8), is said to imply that all blessings which the world enjoys are because of Israel.[77]

These maxims of our rabbis of blessed memory are provocative and meant to be an effective stimulus to repentance and righteous behavior, leaving us with the impression that the preservation or destruction of all that God made for His own sake depends entirely on our righteousness or our wickedness. These apposite turns of phrase and charming rhetoric are part of the striking methods whereby their propositions serve to implant the truth in our hearts. This is also exemplified by their statement in Qiddushin:[78] "A man should always realize that one sin of his can reduce the whole world to destruction whereas one virtuous act can deliver the guilty from transgression." Truly, this is the best attitude for a person to take in regard to any possible future disaster. In Berakhot,[79] our rabbis of blessed memory state that the clap of thunder was created solely for correcting the crookedness of the heart, which is why it says, *God has brought it to pass that men revere Him* (Eccl. 3:14). Such an argument is even more potent if applied to the eruptions of earthquakes; for from moment to moment we are overcome with the terrifying thought that the people, God forbid, will be tossed about by the tremors and disappear in a way worse than death.

With our own eyes we have seen how the men of science investigating the symptoms, causes, and effects of the earthquakes as one would try to diagnose an illness, have failed in their laborious quest for a cure. But only the religious proclaim and announce that there is indeed a savior and physician who will ensure that we are kept in

72. Cf. B. Ber. 5a where Raba says: "If a man sees that painful sufferings visit him, let him examine his conduct."

73. B. Yev. 63a.

74. B. Shabb. 139a.

75. B. Taʿanit 7b.

76. B. Yev. 63a. Note that this passage is also quoted in *En Yaʾaqov* from which de' Rossi drew his other sources (see n. 53).

77. P. Sheviʿit 4 (3) 35b.

78. B. Qidd. 40b.

79. B. Ber. 59a.

sound health, or restore it to us should it fail—that is God besides whom there is no other. Thus in this and any other situation we will fervently[80] and continually request His protection and aid. The verse, *And Jaresiah, Elijah and Zichri, the sons of Jeroham* (1Chr. 8:27) prompted the following Midrash from our rabbis (in Shemot Rabbah and Tanḥuma).[81] "When the Holy One blessed be He causes the world to quake, Elijah makes mention of the merits of the patriarchs and He is filled with compassion." Amen, may He act with His compassion which is eternal.

We will now resume the account of the earthquake which we experienced. You know, dear reader, that when it happened, many astrologers were often assuming the role of prophets declaring that at such and such a moment omens and fantastic destructive forces would be seen in the form of fire, brimstone, and scorching wind. In this way they aggravated the fears of the majority of the people whose hearts had become like melted wax. As a result, many people took to their heels before the appointed days of visitation should come to pass.[82] But when the designated time arrived, their prognostications turned out to be completely unfounded. There was neither complete nor partial fulfillment of their predictions.[83] On the contrary, these were moments of peace and quiet the likes of which had not occurred since before the onset of the tremors. *Who has stood in the council of the Lord?* (Jer. 23:18). As was explained to Job, *Do you know the laws of heaven, or impose its authority on earth?* (38:33). And His prophet said, *He annuls the omens of the imposters* (Is. 44:25). This is what Maimonides of blessed memory so beautifully expressed in chapter 10 of the Laws of the Foundations of the Torah on the basis of a statement of our sages at the end of tractate Moʿed Qatan.[84] Moreover, in our own time, there was a great Christian scholar, Giovanni Pico, prince of Mirandola, who wrote twelve volumes of diatribes against the astrologers. These books were published together with his other highly valuable works.[85]

While on the subject of earthquakes I must turn your attention to what Josephus said when he comes to describe the earthquake which happened in the time of King Uzziah.[86]

> When King Uzziah came forward to offer incense on the altar, Azariah the high priest with his band of eighty priests approached him and exclaimed: "You have no right to this

80. Lit. with all the inclinations of our heart.

81. De' Rossi refers to S.R. 40:4 and Tanḥuma, tissa 13. The four names mentioned in the biblical verse are all said to be other names of Elijah. There is a pun on the name Jaresiah which by metathesis refers to quaking (*raʿash*) and there is an implicit play on the name Yeroḥam which is connected with the root meaning to be merciful (*rḥm*). Similarly, Zichri is connected with the root meaning to remember (*zkhr*), i.e., the children of "mercy" brings to mind the merciful aspect of God.

82. According to a French translation of a letter entitled *Discours sur l'espouventable, horrible et merveilleux tremblement de terre* dated 23 November, and sent from Ferrara, Jews and Marranos were leaving the town daily. It is true that the family of Leon Modena (his mother was pregnant with him at the time) left Ferrara for Venice because of the earthquake. Modena refers to this in a marginal note in his own copy of the *Light of the Eyes.* (See n. 55 to Translator's Introduction.)

83. A similar formulation is used by Maimonides in the passage quoted by de' Rossi (see n. 83).

84. *Mishneh Torah,* Yesode ha-Torah X:3. In B, de' Rossi also refers to Maimonides' *Letter to the Sages of Marseilles,* which is a polemic against astrology.

85. Pico della Mirandola, *Disputationes adversus astrologos* was printed in his *Commentationes.* On Pico's sources and doctrines, see the edition of E. Garin.

86. *Ant.* IX:223–27. For a discussion of this passage as well as the chapters of Amos, see M. Rahmer, *Die biblische Erdbeben Theorie.*

> position. The priests of the seed of Aaron alone may offer incense to God. Now rise, go from here and forgo your place to us." The king became enraged and said: "Be silent, desist. If you refuse and rebel, you shall meet your death by the sword." Then suddenly, there was a violent earthquake which caused a small cleft in the roof of the temple. A bright ray of sun glanced through the cleft and struck the face of the ungodly man. He immediately became smitten with leprosy. (The following miracle is also related.) There was a place called Eroge near the city. Half of the mountain on the western side rolled half a mile and collided with another mountain to the east of it and was halted by it. As a result of this collision, the road on the edge of the public thoroughfare was obstructed and the king's gardens were hedged in. When the priests saw that he was leprous they urged him to leave the city as the ritual law ordained. Ashamedly, he submitted to their request and left the city. There he lived for some time divested and deprived of his royal status. Meanwhile his son Jotham maintained the realm and when he [i.e., Uzziah] died, he ascended to the throne.

This is Josephus's account of Uzziah, and it is corroborated to a certain extent in chapter 9 of Avot d'Rabbi Natan where it states:[87] "At that moment the temple was rent in two, twelve miles in each direction. The priests then urged him to leave."

Josephus mentioned that the road was obstructed. You might also note the passage in Zechariah, *And you shall flee (ve-nastem) to the valley of the mountains for the valley of the mountains shall reach unto Azel, yea you shall flee (ve-nastem) as you fled (nastem) from the earthquake in the days of Uzziah, king of Judah* (14:5). The word "fleeing" which is repeated three times in the Hebrew text is rendered as "obstructed" in the Septuagint,[88] suggesting that the verb should be understood as a passive perfect past (*nistam*). In fact, the rendering "obstructed" agrees with the account in Josephus. As Kimḥi comments on the verse in question,[89] it was patently a miracle because the earth does not usually close over the clefts caused by the tremor. Without entering into a discussion of the question whether there was vocalization in their day or not—let us grant that there was[90]—we might suppose that not only the first instance of the word *ve-nistam* was [open to different readings], as is implied by the statements of ibn Ezra and Kimḥi and Jonathan ben Uzziel's rendering, which suggests a disagreement between East and West.[91] Rather, we might assume that there was also a difference of opinion as to the reading of the other two cases where the same verb is used even though the Masorah does not mention it.[92] The sage Bar Sheshet has a similar discussion in his responsum on the correct reading of the verse in Song of Songs, *For your love is better than wine*

87. ARN, rec. A, ch. 9 (41–42).

88. De' Rossi used a Latin translation of the LXX which was printed interlinearly in the Complutensian Polyglot and then published separately by A. Cratander in 1526. The Greek and the Latin renderings have a passive sense: "Et obturabitur sicut obturata est a facie terraemotus in diebus Oziae."

89. Kimḥi to Zech. 14:5.

90. De' Rossi argues about the antiquity of the vowel points in ch. 59.

91. Ibn Ezra ad loc. reads: "And Jonathan b. Uzziel translates *and you shall flee to the valley of the mountains* and all Easterners read the word *ve-nastem* as though it reads *ve-nistam* (and it shall be closed up)." The expression 'disagreement between East and West' is used in talmudic discussions of the differences between Palestinian and Babylonian traditions regarding the division of the verses, the order of the biblical books, and the *qere* and *ketiv* (i.e., what is traditionally read as opposed to what is traditionally written).

92. This is a reference to the Massoretic notes to Zech. 14:5 and related verses, which make no mention of *ve-nastem* as a point of disagreement between Eastern and Western traditions.

which is raised in tractate Avodah Zarah.[93] Moreover, Jonathan ben Uzziel's Aramaic rendering gives many indications of different readings. This is also the case with the rabbis' comment on the last verse of Psalm 50, *To him that orders (ve-sam) his way aright will I show the salvation of Lord* (50:23): "Read not 'that orders' but, 'and there' (*ve-sham*)."[94] The Septuagint also reads "and there."[95] Another example is to be found in the discussion of the words *Dodanim* and *Rodanim* in Bereshit Rabbah (37).[96] In any case, we do not dissent from our ancestral tradition especially since in the light of our own experience, we know that there really is a connection between flight and the earthquake.

Now we will return to the original passage in Josephus. Our argument cannot be attacked on the grounds that we understood Amos's words in terms of a nightly earthquake, whereas according to Josephus, providing that his description of the sun shining in his [i.e., Uzziah's] face is authentic, it must have been daytime. The manifestations of the present earthquake demonstrate that sometimes it is protracted over a long period of time, day and night, summer and winter. But in our case, the main devastation was wrought in the first three months. We are now in the sixth month, and praised be God our helper, who until this point has not allowed it to touch us. True, it still can be heard and tremors are felt twice or three times a week, and occasionally three times a day, for He performs His act with might. The men of science, mentioned above, wrote (and it is our experience) that it may continue for forty days up until the end of the year and longer. Thus, the first quake, as we said, occurred during the day and night and could be heard at all times. At any rate, we will now set aside the holy prophecies and those of foreign stock[97]—enough has been said—and resume and complete our tale of the earthquakes of our own time.

Many people of a scientific bent observed that most of the tremors and the most violent ones came in doubles, one after the other, quake after quake. This was reminiscent of the story about Rav Qattina mentioned above in which it was stated that there were two rumblings, one after another.[98] The most powerful tremors were the fourth and seventh in the cycle. It was as though the world which is a macro-man was sick and as though in its infected part it took the course of diseases which assail man who is the microcosm. They occurred more at night than during the day so that each day when morning dawned everybody imagined that relief had come. As the rabbis of blessed memory say in Bava Batra: "When the sun rises sickness disappears."[99] But at dusk, they trembled and shook for fear of the night. As we have said, the first three months were the most devastating. Subsequently, its virulence gradually lessened and the intervening periods in which it lay dormant grew longer. Although for days on end

93. Isaac bar Sheshet Perfet (1326–1408), *She'elot,* responsum 284 discusses the question raised about the talmudic discussion in B. A.Z. 29b as to how R. Aqiva could be incorrect in the reading of the verse (S.S. 1:2) where *your* [masculine] *love* (*dodekha*) could also be read as *your* [feminine] *love* (*dodayikh*).

94. B. Sota 5b.

95. In the LXX it is listed as Ps. 49. The Latin translation reads: "et illic."

96. B.R. 37:4 (344) where Dodanim, mentioned in Gen. 10:4 as one of the sons of Yavan, is identified with the Rodanim mentioned in 1Chr. 1:7.

97. 'And those of foreign stock,' cf. Is. 2:6.

98. B. Ber. 59a.

99. B. B.B. 16b.

during those first three months, it fought the fight in fierce wrath, the main destruction was, as we said, wrought on that very first occasion on Thursday night and about the third hour on the eve of the holy Sabbath. But then, thanks be to the Lord, in like manner to a sickness, the fever dropped, became static, gradually turning, while the substance subsided and naturally disappeared. In view of this, those men of science made a good point when they said that the flaw in the earthly element is comparable to the trembling sickness. This is noted by ibn Sina [Avicenna] in book 3, fen 2, section 2, chapter 11.[100] In the course of the cure, a complete recovery does not normally take place instantaneously; apparently, the matter which causes the sickness flares up at infrequent intervals until bit by bit it recedes and disappears.

Now for the information of anyone interested in this story, let me tell how the natives escaped from the scene of destruction and where they went. When people realized that the eruption of the first two violent quakes had not put an end to this malady, they lost their nerve. Many people left the city and its suburbs and together with all members of their household went to live in villages or cities fifteen to twenty miles away which had not been affected by the earthquake. Many others who did not want to go so far looked for some shelter in large courtyards, gardens, or orchards within the city or on its outskirts. There they pitched their tents and spread out their matting as well as they were able.[101] The priest and community leader did not visit spacious rooms or exquisite places; these were the tents of Kedar for one and all, like the curtains of Solomon.[102] There they protected their young as they waited for the final plan of the Almighty. Many others went down to the riverbank south of the city where they hired ships and fishing boats, with their captains who steered at the helm. They made the boats into their lodgings and lived there with their families day and night. Any sensible person would constantly search for the security procured from joining a gathering of people on the estate of one of his friends. Truly, if a person were to find himself alone during the sudden outbreak of a tremor, there was a danger that his heart would fail and he become petrified. It had already happened that many people, even though they did not die straightaway were seized with such convulsions that they fell ill and within a few days passed away. But if one was in the company of others the catastrophe was somewhat attenuated. People would encourage each other and say, "Be strong, do not lose your nerve."

On this subject I cannot refrain from describing a memorable experience to which I and also many others were privy. The distinguished woman to whom the Lord had directed me [i.e., de' Rossi's wife] was affected by heart tremors on account of these calamities and distress. Her blood became turgid, her complexion turned yellow as a golden pillar, and anybody who set eyes on her would stare at her. After a while she was overcome by such a craving for salt that usually at mealtimes, rather than partake of broth, meat, and dessert, she would eat bread dipped in large amounts of salt regardless of whether she was in private or in the presence of others. To her, the salt tasted like royal dainties. This craving turned out to be her salvation. For praise be to God, she was

100. Avicenna, *Canon,* lib. III, fen 2, ch. 11.

101. Cf. the account cited in A. Solerti, "Il terremoto di Ferrara," 521: "e tutti i cimiteri e le piazze son piene di trabacche e di tende, sendoci valut' assai l'essere in terra di assai giardini e di fabriche basse."

102. Cf. S.S. 1:5.

restored to her former strength without recourse to any other cure and she no longer looked pallid in the face. Before one's eyes, her health improved and her features lost their emaciated appearance. At the same time, this unnatural craving gradually disappeared. It was really a miracle.

Now a sagacious person should view the work of God as one of nature's mysteries, even supposing such a cure would have occurred to Aesculapius or Hippocrates. Perhaps the toxic saline and sulphuric vapors, which rose from the earth and entered her body, were eradicated by the wholesome salt and the one thus eliminated the other, and on account of God's compassion she was saved. Who knows whether Elisha's miracle with the healing waters did not also happen in a similar way?[103]

{You should know, intelligent reader, that the sentence I wrote about Elisha raised the scruples of certain sages who claimed that I intended to associate the miracle with the workings of nature. Yet any expert in Torah knows that certain commentators of more recent times also applied that kind of interpretation to many miracles.[104] In fact, my interpretation was never meant that way. On the contrary, when I said that my wife's experience was miraculous, for such a cure had not occurred to the greatest of the natural philosophers, I was bringing nature into the sphere of the miraculous. However because I did not think that her cure was completely miraculous, I took great precaution in the way I expressed myself by saying "who knows," "in some way," and "in a similar way." This was to distinguish between what was really a miracle from that which seemed to me to have the appearances of a miracle. Moreover, one should take into account that the manner in which prophets, and Elisha in particular, implement miracles which affect individuals is to bring them into the sphere of nature, as is exemplified in the statements: *What do you have in the house?* (2K. 4:2); *And the body of the child became warm* (2K. 4:34); *Bathe and be clean* (2K. 5:13). The same is true of Elijah's miracle with the cruise of flour and when he stretched himself over the child (1K. 17) and with Isaiah's miracle with the cake of figs (Is. 38:21).}

But now we will desist from trying in our foolish manner to scrutinize the wisdom of the Lord of wonders who is exalted beyond all enquiry and praise, and we will resume our tale and keep to the main points.

Anybody who dealt in matting or boards or anything else suitable for covering was happy and so, too, his children. He could count himself rich for their worth had more than tripled for mostly they could be made into tents and dwellings. There were also many people who brought buckets and barrels out into the open. One would install himself with his dependents around the cauldron, another would do likewise with his pots. They left behind their possessions and belongings in their homes, locked up if possible, or given over to the safekeeping of guardians of cucumber fields [i.e., incapacitated persons][105] letting themselves be dependent on a miracle and the will of God on

103. This is a reference to the story of Naaman in 2K. 5.

104. De' Rossi could be referring here to a commentator such as Gersonides who propounded that miracles performed by the prophets involved knowledge of the sublunar order. Among de' Rossi's contemporaries, Abraham Farissol attempted to provide naturalistic interpretations of some of the biblical miracles. See D. Ruderman, "An Exemplary Sermon," 22–24.

105. 'Guardians of cucumber fields' is an expression in M. B.Q. 8:1 applied to somebody who is unfit for any other kind of work.

high. Indeed there is a time when one must make every effort to preserve life, and there is a time when one must consequently cast away money like stones so as to save one's skin until the fury has passed away.

Many of the elect of our people, the leaders of the holy congregation of Ferrara, will always be remembered for good. These include "the father of the poor" the princely Don Isaac Abravanel, grandson of the great writer who rests in peace;[106] the noble and distinguished Isaac da Fano and his relatives, all delightful scions, the pride of our generation; the children of the honorable Isaac Berechiah da Fano of blessed memory.[107] The names of Joseph Halevi, Aaron Degale, and Rabbi Solomon Modena also rank high among the worthy and generous; and other special individuals from the holy community of Sephardim who were among the first to distribute charity to the people of the Lord. May they all be blessed by the Lord of truth.[108] These and other such charitable people, in whose homes or estates there were large courtyards or enclosed gardens or spacious plots of land, opened up the gates of righteousness to whosoever sought refuge with them, whether poor or rich. They gave shelter and a place to stay to anyone who came among them—indeed, a hundred or more persons gathered around each one of them. Despite their agitation—for they, too, were in great distress—they saw to it that the poor and needy did not lack provisions and they provided plenty of wood to make fires to stave off the icy cold[109] and for use in baking or cooking for themselves and their children. They were always cheerful and ready with kindly words even though they had to shoulder this burden for a long time, with large numbers of fugitives looking to them for support.

In the Christian quarter too, all the streets of the city, roads, and courtyards, enclosed or open, were full of tents, huts, and booths in which precincts rich and poor lodged together. They also dispensed alms to the poor. It was a time for all people of every tongue to seek God and to demonstrate their piety before Him in order to obtain forgiveness and redemption. You would be justified in thinking that all Jews who cling to the Lord, including the women and children, followed the observance of our patriarch the elder[110] to take vows in time of trouble. Time after time, the holy community arranged fast days in keeping with the set order established by our ancestors in event of earthquakes and collapsing brickwork.[111] So too in the many nearby and distant cities people fasted and prayed that their supplication might obtain God's favor for the sake of our community here in Ferrara. They were in need of compassion, and it is the blessed One alone who can protect city and home.

It was now very dangerous to stay in the houses lest they collapsed. In fear of such a happening, anyone who valued his life refrained from prolonging his stay in his home for any length of time. Yet miraculously, not one of the ten prayer houses and

106. He was the son of Joseph Abravanel, one of the three sons of Isaac Abravanel.

107. He was the father of the kabbalist R. Menahem Azariah da Fano.

108. Cf. Is. 65:16.

109. 'Icy cold': lit. coldness of snow, cf. Pr. 25:13. De' Rossi must have had Rashi's commentary to the verse in mind.

110. A reference to Jacob, cf. Gen. 28:20.

111. This is a reference to M. Ta'anit ch. 3 which describes the order of fasts, prayer, and blowing of the ram's horn in time of natural disasters both for the inflicted and neighboring cities.

synagogues[112] devoted to God here in Ferrara fell into disuse. It is true they were damaged and suffered from cracks and fissures which had to be repaired, but this did not deter people from using them for prayer day and night. Furthermore, blessed be our God forever. Though destruction was rampant in the city such that all passers by on being sighted would be warned to watch their feet and heads, yet not one able-bodied Jew died or came to any harm. However, everybody suffered material losses and the expenses which each person actually incurred in proportion to his wealth were extremely high.

As for me, I will sing praises to the God of my salvation and give thanks to Him for His manifold kindness in accordance with all He has done for me. In the year 5327 [1567] He performed miracles for me when He delivered me from the grasp of the angel of destruction when I was staying among the holy congregation of Bologna.[113] And now again in the event of the powerful earthquake which occurred at the third hour on the eve of the Sabbath. He acted on my behalf. The roof fell in on the room in which I, my wife, and children were living. Much of the brickwork and planks were violently torn down and fell onto my bed. Had we happened to be in the room at the time as was our wont when we went to sleep at night and got up in the morning, we would have without question been crushed to pulp, God forbid, and not one of us would have survived. But thanks to Him who performs favors for the guilty, I was alerted an hour earlier when we were shaken by the previous earthquake of lesser magnitude. So I decided that we should all go downstairs to the room of my married daughter. Thank God, the blight did not reach us there and we were safe until the time came for us to join the general exodus.

The noble Isaac da Fano also [had a narrow escape]. On that fearful Sabbath eve he was seated round the fire as was his custom together with his respected wife and nine children resembling olive saplings and with other members of his household. At the first quake at nightfall, the entire roof immediately caved into the middle of the room. Only the part of the roof which was covering the place where they were sitting round the fire did not fall in because the Lord was quick to hold it in place. The uproar brought them all to their feet with distressing cries of anguish and much weeping and they made a hurried exit to another room to save their lives. They had just left when the rest of the roof fell on what remained of the room. Part of the room was even brought down into the story below. If they had stayed just one minute longer their lives would have been extinguished and no trace of them would have remained, God forbid.

These then are the words which one is bound to inscribe in one's heart and to commit to writing in order to laud the name of the Lord who is the revered object of praise and who acts wondrously. Many other brethren of ours who were at death's door experienced similar miracles and the Lord saved them, may He be blessed with heart and soul for ever and ever.

An intelligent person would not find it difficult to understand that this upheaval

112. 'Synagogue': lit. small sanctuary, from Ezk. 11:16. This expression was often used as proof of the existence of the synagogue in the time of the Babylonian exile.

113. De' Rossi lived for some time in Bologna. In 1567, Jews were expelled from the Papal States, and in 1569, the final edict of expulsion from Bologna was passed. De' Rossi like many of his coreligionists escaped to Ferrara. On the expulsion, see D. Carpi, "The Expulsion."

which continued for a long period of time brought about the destruction and annihilation of a large proportion of the property of many of the natives quite apart from the damage caused by collapsing and wrecked houses. Various parts of furniture were broken and destroyed. Astonishingly high were the wages of porters and the hire of horses and ships to bring hasty aid to fugitives with or without their possessions. I also lost much in my affliction such that when I bring it to mind I am amazed. Nevertheless, the heavenly witness will confirm[114] that I was not at all troubled and that I acknowledged that my affliction was for my good. In the light of what I have seen, I have the merit of writing contemporaneously about these mighty acts of our God who will be perpetually praised by every living being. Do not our rabbis of blessed memory say that one should extol and praise Hananiah and his group who wrote the Megillat Taʿanit because they loved the troubles from which they were redeemed?[115] They put great store by writing an account of the miracles which were enacted for them. It served as a means to praise our God.

Indeed, during this frightening time in which, as I said, I was forced to leave the ruins of my home and take up my abode wherever I could, my lot fell in with many peace-loving people south of the river Po. One of our neighbors, a Christian scholar, to pass the time and divert his mind from the distressing earthquake, was enjoying himself by reading the book which I had begun to discuss with him which relates the story of the translation of our Torah [i.e., the *Letter of Aristeas*]. It was at this time that he came up to greet me and then inquired whether by means of the Hebrew version (for he thought that we Jews possessed the book) I could clarify and elucidate some of the passages he found obscure in the Latin, a language with which he had been conversant for a long time.[116] When I informed him that we had no such thing he was utterly amazed as to how such glory could depart from Israel who could deservedly win great prestige from it. I was unoccupied at the time, being far away from my books and delightful pleasures. I lifted my eyes to the mountains to see whether they would skip like rams and to the walls should they move.[117] That man together with the distinguished persons with whom I was associated there encouraged me to produce a translation of the book in a few days. They told me it would divert my attention from the terror of the earthquake and bring solace in these distressing times, as if one were to draw honey from a goat and wheat from a thorn. So I did not refuse my heart's desire since there was a likelihood that this work would be totally acceptable to the learned of our people. In fact they were saying what sages (i.e., Cicero in his *Tusculans* which he wrote during his exile from Rome)[118] had said, namely, that there is also an admixture of evil to every good thing which happens under the sun. This is indicated by the fact

114. 'The . . . confirm,' cf. Ps. 89:38.

115. B. Shabb. 13b. Megillat Taʿanit contains a list of holidays which for the most part commemorate victorious events connected with the Hasmonean period. Fasting was prohibited on the days listed.

116. De' Rossi does not divulge the name of the Christian. The whole story has something of a literary flourish about it. He is referring to Matthias Garbitius's translation of the letter.

117. 'Skip . . . rams,' cf. Ps. 114:4.

118. Cicero fled from his home in 58 B.C.E. and subsequently Clodius passed an edict of exile on him. He returned to Rome in 57. The *Tusculan Disputations* were written in 45 B.C.E. It is a work inspired by Stoic ideas on the subject of death, pain, and virtue. In II, 27, 66, he writes that pain is not an evil and that even if the term "pain" is appropriate for it, it may be eclipsed by virtue.

that when the countenance smiles the heart can grieve. Conversely, there can be no evil thing which does not contain some good. You should take it as a sign that wherever there is sorrow there will also be profit. Wisdom then will fortify us to realize how to sustain and irradiate that one portion of good so that it should not be nullified by a thousand ills.

We had already begun to see that many of the damaged buildings of Ferrara had been impaired for their own good in order to be repaired and built more strongly and better than before.[119] Consequently, the inhabitants may still hope that she will once again be praised in the gates for her perfect beauty.[120] Then we can know that on occasions, God does not prevent evil from producing good, or a curse from being transformed into a blessing from heaven. Observe how He addressed His future worshippers as though announcing good news, *And I will put the plague of leprosy in the house of the land of your possessions* (Lev. 14:34). Our rabbis also interpreted the verse positively in the Zohar and the Vayiqra Rabbah.[121] Accordingly, I have hoped that in His compassion He will doubly replenish my loss. I will call on Him and He will answer me. May he support the one who speaks these words which the author [i.e., Aristeas][122] has written.[123]

119. It is interesting to note that the idea that natural disasters can be justified on the grounds that they make way for better living was hotly attacked by Voltaire in the light of the reactions to the Lisbon earthquake of 1756.

120. This kind of rhetoric in relation to Ferrara is also used by other contemporary writers of the event. See my article "Voice of God," 69.

121. V.R. 17:6 (384–87) and Zohar III, 50a. The verse is interpreted as promising the reward of treasure to be found in the houses uprooted according to the injunction of the Torah.

122. Here, de' Rossi is anticipating the next section of the book, i.e., his translation of the *Letter of Aristeas.*

123. The final sentence of this section rhymes.

SPLENDOR OF THE ELDERS

Great honor is bequeathed the sages; for the king's pleasure did they translate the Law.
For it is garbed in glory more resplendent, crowned with honor and distinction
Because a stranger, at extravagant cost, did lend himself unto this task.
Be strong, children of the living God, be sure to adhere to it without distraction.
By means of it shall we merit every good and in every trouble find protection.
Truly it was given us to inherit, to the Jews illumination

The *Book of Aristeas* concerning the translation of our Torah in the lifetime of Ptolemy Philadelphus: it is now renamed The *Splendor of the Elders.*[1]

A letter of the author Aristeas to Philocrates his brother

DEAR brother, it was my considered opinion that our mission to Eleazar the high priest of the Jews, and the events of our meeting with him, were worth recording for posterity. I thought you would be most appreciative of my account since I was present when certain incidents took place. Now I decided to write to you a lengthy description of the nature and purpose of the enterprise we undertook. I acted thus in the knowledge that being a man of intellectual integrity you have always yearned to acquire knowledge and understanding of events, whether belonging to documented past history or to our own life-experiences. For he who has a predilection for acquiring useful and correct knowledge must surely be fashioned with a refined and pure disposition of soul. The righteousness by which the soul aspires to apprehend and understand functions as a measure by which it regulates all its thoughts and endeavors—it is the whole man.[2]

1. De' Rossi's translation is based on Matthias Garbitius's Latin translation which was printed in the *editio princeps* of the Greek text, edited by S. Schard in Basel 1561 entitled: *Aristeae de legis divinae ex Hebraica lingua in Graecam translatione per LXX interpretes . . . historia.* By changing the title of the work, de' Rossi emphasizes the Jewish contribution to the whole episode recounted by ps. Aristeas. The seventy-two elders became the protagonists of the story. See my article, "Azariah de' Rossi and LXX Traditions." The title *Letter of Aristeas* first appeared in the fourth century C.E. (See S. Jellicoe, *The Septuagint,* 30.) De' Rossi's translation *The Book of Aristeas* is more in keeping with the original title.

A noteworthy feature of de' Rossi's translation is his careful use of biblical and rabbinic terminology, drawing out the latent Jewish elements in the text. The subtitles of the sections are de' Rossi's. He never consults the Greek text because his knowledge of Greek was inadequate. The notes to the translation are not meant to be used as explanations and annotations of the original text, but rather as a guide to de' Rossi's method of translation and to his use (like modern scholars) of the epitomes of Josephus and Eusebius for the clarification of the text. The numbers in brackets refer to the standard paragraphing of the Greek text.

2. It . . . man,' cf. Eccl. 12:13.

From my youth, I longed to become knowledgeable in matters divine. I therefore eagerly offered and made myself available for the journey to this priest. Indeed, according to his own people and all others who are acquainted with him, his pleasing behavior and reputation surpasses that of all his contemporaries. He considered that the translation of the Law[3]—which is preserved by them in Hebrew letters on parchment—would render an outstanding service to his own people and to all other nations of the world. I had another reason for wanting to undertake this mission. It would give me an opportunity to have an audience with the king and enable me to be a spokesman on behalf of the Jews who had been brought captive to Egypt by his father when he first claimed sovereign power over the country[4] and conquered it. These matters, too, should not escape your notice. I know, however, that you prefer to hear about the outstanding virtues for which upholders of the Law are famed. Our purpose here is to explain it in a way that you can see the truth for yourself. It is only recently that you came from a remote island to live among us, compelled by your longing and eagerness to gain knowledge of those things which have a beneficial effect on our souls. I have already sent you records, which, in my opinion, contain worthwhile information. I acquired them from great sages, the Jewish priests, who live in the renowned city of Egypt. You have a pronounced attraction to any knowledge that stimulates the intellectual faculties (and it is appropriate to communicate such things with all others who have the same proclivities). It is therefore even more fitting that I should share them[5] with you who are a kindred spirit in desires and judgment, and not simply because you are my brother, of the same parentage and natural disposition. Moreover, like me, you have dedicated yourself wholeheartedly to righteous behavior. Indeed, the glory and fame that accrue to the proud and vainglorious in all their quests are not of the same value as our cultivation of learning and the toil that we sustain for its sake. Now, lest we protract our discourse, thus rendering ourselves liable to the sin of verbosity, we will proceed forthwith to narrate our tale as promised.

Aristeas describes how the king was persuaded to commission the translation of our Law

When the wise[6] Demetrius of Phalerium was custodian of the library which had been founded by the king, he undertook with zeal and at great expense to assemble a collection of all books that were known to be extant. He achieved his task by purchase or transcriptions executed by ready scribes. His only aim was to fulfill the king's wish. We were present when one day the king asked him how many books there were in the collection. He answered: "There are more than 200,000, but in a few days I should be able to increase the number to 500,000. I am informed that the laws of the Jews are really worth transcribing and ought to be brought to the king's depositary." The king then asked him: "If so, what is there to prevent you from doing this? After all everything that you need for the acquisitions has been put at your disposal." Demetrius

3. A (3) is slightly obscure and is translated in a variety of ways. De' Rossi makes the high priest subject of the clause, changing the stress, and emphasizing the role of the high priest.

4. De' Rossi uses imagery from Jer. 43:10–11 about Nebuchadnezzar's conquest of Egypt.

5. Lit. 'to take sweet counsel with you.' Cf. Ps. 55:15.

6. De' Rossi usually adds the epithet 'wise' in connection with Demetrius.

answered: "My lord king, these laws have to be translated. In their lands, the Jews (just as the Egyptians have a particular mode of forming the characters [of their language]), have their own unique script and particular language. Many people claim that the script and language they use is the Syrian tongue, but they are wrong—the forms of the language and shapes of its letters are exclusive to the Jews." On receipt of this information the king said: "Well then, I shall write to their high priest and ask that he fulfill our request." On hearing those words, I was moved—for this was the day that I had hoped for. I had often spoken about it with my friends Sosibius of Tarento and Andreas, the king's chief guards. I am referring to the liberation of the Jews who had been taken into captivity from their lands[7] by the king's father. In his attack on Coele-Syria and the cities of Edom,[8] his superior strength and good fortune led him on to success. He deported some to cities which he colonized, and some he put to forced labor. He grew more powerful and gained control of nations and came to remove more than 100,000 to Egypt. He took aside about 30,000 chosen soldiers for the army and settled them in the garrison towns which they were to guard. In earlier times, however, many had come there with the kings of Persia,[9] and even before them, a great number had been dispatched into those areas to assist King Psammetichus in his campaign against the king of Ethiopia. And yet their total number was not as great as those brought by Ptolemy son of Lago, father of Ptolemy, our King Philadelphus. As we were saying, Ptolemy, father of the king, selected all those that were in their prime and who were sound of limb and had the physical strength to take to the battlefield, and he equipped the guards of the garrison with arms. He donated the troops with the remaining people, namely the elderly, the women and children, who were to serve them in perpetuity and provide what was needed for war—this is what they, too, had requested of him.

Now when we observed that the moment was opportune to plead for their freedom, we addressed the king in the following manner:

> Our lord should see to it that his request does not come to nothing and bear in mind the response that he will consequently receive.[10] For the laws which require not only transcription but also translation, pertain to the entire congregation of the Jewish community. How can we favor such a mission when, as you well know, you hold great numbers of them in captivity as slaves and bondswomen. So now, with a generous spirit and noble heart, set yourself to liberate those wretched prisoners. In particular you should bear in mind that the God who gave them this Law is the one who preserves you and your realm, as I have come to realize, and rightfully so. Do they not worship the God who created and sustains everything and in common with them do not all our peoples worship Him? I

7. 'Their lands.' Garbitius reads 'ex Iudea.'

8. A (12) refers to the conquest of Coele Syria and Phoenicia (cava Syria et Phoenicia) by Ptolemy Philadelphus's father. Josephus (*Ant.* XII:28) gives the same reading. De' Rossi strangely changes Phoenicia to 'cities of Edom.' It would seem unlikely that de' Rossi's geographical knowledge was so deficient that he confused Edom with Phoenicia. The late A. Momigliano suggested to me that de' Rossi may have deliberately used the word *Adom* for Phoenicia, having in mind the etymology of Phonicia (red) and the Hebrew word *adom* (red) or the Italian *fenico e punico-rosso purpureo* which was current usage between the fourteenth and sixteenth centuries.

9. A (13) states that many Jews had come with the king of Persia who is generally identified as Cambyses, son of Cyrus the Great. De' Rossi's translation 'kings' may have been influenced by a later passage (35) in which Ptolemy writes about the Jews who had been captured 'by the Persians.'

10. I.e., his request will be refused unless he liberates the Jews.

concede that using a barbarous tongue and another language we call him Jove.[11] This name signifies His essence—for our ancestors cleverly conceived of a name which indicates that He is Lord and a helpful* guide for all creatures and that through Him everybody lives and exists as they do. So you, my lord king, who wields power over all the nations, promulgate a decree of liberation for all their oppressed and afflicted prisoners.

(*The name Jove (Jovis) means benefit—Josephus says as much.[12])

In truth, the king did not regard that I was subverting his honor by this speech of mine. In fact, according to all indications, his reaction was favorable—perhaps, because from the very depths of our heart we had made heartfelt supplications to God concerning this matter. Given that all humanity is His handiwork, He surely has no wish to afflict any adversary and harass any person. Accordingly I brought together the various threads of my supplication in heartfelt entreaties of God that the king should be so affected as to fully accede to my request. I became optimistic that those men would be delivered because I was quite convinced of the truth of our pronouncement that it is God who answers all appeals. Moreover, when people with pure motivations become performers of charitable acts and doers of good works, it is due to Him (the director and sustainer of all) who leads and guides their steps on those paths. Turning to me, the king asked with happiness and salutary joy: "According to your assessment, how many thousands of prisoners are there?" Andreas who was present answered: "My lord king, more than ten myriads, I believe." He responded: "So let it be. In my view, Aristeas's request is trifling."** Sosibius and other bystanders came up and said: "Our lord king, it is worthy of your magnanimity that you should offer the great God the release of these people, which indeed constitutes the sacrifice of a generous spirit and pure heart. And yet, it is due to the kind mercies of God who rules over all that you reached high station. It is therefore right and proper that you should offer Him valuable gifts denoting your acknowledgment of His goodness and rendering to Him heartfelt gratitude." Consequently, when the king in company of his friends became merry at the banquet,[13] he said: "I shall do even more. As ransom for each slave, the owners will receive twenty drachmas. This edict shall be promulgated forthwith without delay, and shall be recorded in the king's registry on this very day." Such was his kindness and magnanimity (inspired by God who perpetrates everything) that he not only agreed to underwrite the ransom of those who had been brought into captivity by his father the king, but also of those who were there previously, or who came subsequently. Although he was told that the operation would amount to more than 400 talents, he did not retract on his word.

(**In Josephus's account, this statement is posed as a question: "Is not Aristeas's request but a small one?"[14])

11. Garbitius's translation preserves the connection of the name Zeus with 'life.' As Cassel notes ad loc., de' Rossi based his translation on Gelenius's translation of Josephus (*Ant.* XII:22): "Iovem . . . quod iuvet vitam omnium." In B, de' Rossi states that he had heard that some people linked the name Jove to the tetragrammaton, but that this idea was treated with contempt by Lilio Giraldi in his *De Deis* (see Syntagma I:8).

12. See n. 11.

13. De' Rossi's embellishment, using Est. 1:10 which describes Ahasuerus's banquet.

14. *Ant.* XII:24.

Now we shall not refrain from putting the text of the edict promulgated in their regard on record. For it manifests the king's many acts of generosity and his magnanimity. Indeed, in all this undertaking, he had the support of God, inspiring him to become the kind and beneficial luminary to the many communities of the world. This is the text of the document:

The king's edict concerning the liberation of the Jews

All soldiers brought by the king our father to the regions of Syria and Edom, who entered Jewish lands and took captives whom they brought with them or else sold to others here in our city or in other places in our realm, and similarly any Jews who were here previously or had been deported from their lands subsequently, we do hereby will and order that they should do nothing to impede their prompt manumission, receiving on the same day twenty drachmas for each person. Soldiers shall receive the payment in their salary, the others from the royal bank. We consider that they were seized without the knowledge of the king our father and in contravention to what is right and just. This state of affairs came about through the brazenness of the military forces who destroyed those cities and despoiled and captured the natives. The benefit that they gave in assisting the troops was certainly not inconsequential, and their enslavement of these people was accordingly illegal. We considered that every subject should receive from us his lawful right, especially those who have been wrongly subjugated by foreigners. It is our wish to maintain righteous and compassionate modes of behavior at all times and with regard to every issue. We therefore decree that every man in our kingdom who subjugated and enslaved any Jewish person or curtailed their freedom in any way, should proclaim their release on receipt of the ransom that we stipulated. No man should act fraudulently or maliciously. Three days after the promulgation of this edict, report must be made to the officers who are appointed over these matters and information given concerning the number of captives in his possession, and he must also produce the persons in question. According to our judgment, this is in our best interest and the negotiation is in itself right and proper. Whoever informs on a recalcitrant shall acquire perpetual rights over the offender and the possessions of all recalcitrants shall go to the king's treasury.

The text of this edict was read out to the king to know whether it met with his approval. He considered it to be comprehensive and adequate, but it had a clause missing, which read: "And similarly, any Jew who had been there previously or had been deported subsequently from their land." Out of the generosity of his heart and magnanimity, the king inserted these additional words. He then ordered* that the ransom money which to be sure had to be paid in different installments at different times, be taken from that already amassed in his treasuries and be divided between all the supervisors and the royal bankers.

(*On this detail, see Josephus.[15])

Thus the business involved in the ransom was completed within seven days according to royal decree. The cost of the manumissions amounted to more than 660 talents—

15. *Ant.* XII:32. In fact, de' Rossi's translation is a conflation of Aristeas and Josephus.

for included in the count of the captives were babies and infants for whom, together with their mothers, ransom was claimed by their masters. This information was conveyed to the king who was asked whether they also had to pay twenty drachmas for each of the children. He answered that they should do so to ensure the implementation of the decree.

After these transactions, he commanded Demetrius to present him with a written request for the translation of the books of the Jews. For these kings have a statute according to which nothing can be implemented without a prior written application and decree. This ensures that every matter is duly assessed and justly appraised. Accordingly, I consider it appropriate to give a transcription of the text of the application to the king and a copy of the letters which he wrote in connection with it. I also regard it appropriate to list the gifts which the king sent to Eleazar the high priest, and to describe their artistic execution—for all the items were similarly costly and of outstanding beauty.

The text of the application

My lord king, you have given me strict instructions to collect and incorporate all the books which I can procure that are missing from the library that you founded. Should any book be damaged or defective I am to take care to have them refurbished. I have always been conscientious in fulfilling your wishes. I should now like to inform you that we do not have the books of the laws of the Jews and some other works.* They are actually written in the Hebrew script and language, and those that are extant** are, in the opinion of experts, replete with errors and inaccuracies—for until today, no king or prince has been generous enough to defray the expenses which would be incurred by undertaking the necessary work.

(*The last clause is omitted in Josephus's version.)

(**This accords with the statement of Eusebius the Caesarean in his *Praeparatio* (beginning of book 8) who describes this incident in the following manner:[16] "In fact, some passage appears to have been translated negligently and with little thought, a remarkable phenomenon, which demonstrates that only the Law of the Jews is perfect and divine.")

It is surely right and proper that accurate copies of the books should be deposited in your library because these laws, by virtue of their divine nature surpass all others in wisdom and sanctity.

This being the case, all skilled poets or historians refrained from alluding to these books and the people to whom they belong. For according to Hecataeus of Abdera, they contain wise pronouncements and sacred and awesome concepts. If then it please the king, let him write to the high priest in Jerusalem that he send you six men of each of their tribes who are of outstanding moral virtue and are distinguished by reason of

16. Cassel, ad loc., was unable to locate the passage and not surprisingly, since de' Rossi was using George of Trepizond's Latin translation of the *De ev. praep.* (8, ch. 1) which, despite its wide diffusion (there were more than seven printings between 1470 and 1501), was criticized for being unliteral and paraphrastic (see J. Monfasani, *George of Trepizond*).

their seniority and understanding of the Law. We shall be able to deposit an accurate translation in our treasures. It will have been approved by the majority and tested with their discerning eye, as is appropriate given the importance of the actual subject matter and that it is your soul's desire. Long live my lord.

In response to this application, the king ordered that a letter about this matter be despatched to Eleazar the high priest, with reference to the ransom of the prisoners. He sent fifty golden talents and seventy silver talents and many precious stones for the provision of bowls, cups, a table, and libation vases. In addition, he ordered the custodians of his treasuries to allow the artisans to come and select whatever would be suitable for the artifacts they were to make. Furthermore, one hundred silver talents were provided in order to pay for the sacrifices and burnt offerings. Now I would like to give you an account of the workmanship of the gifts that the king sent Eleazar. First, however, you should be familiar with the text of the letter. It reads as follows:

The king's letter to Eleazar

Ptolemy the king to Eleazar the high priest, joyous greetings.

It has come about that a large number of Jews have been deported from their land and settled in our regions. Some of them were exiled from Jerusalem when the Persians were in power, while others were brought captive by our father the king. At that time, he selected many of their best men and appointed them as captains of his forces and as army officers on high salaries. Impressed by the valor of those chieftains, he put them in charge of his fortress cities to intimidate the Egyptians and thereby prevent them from planning a revolt against the king. Indeed, when the throne became ours, we demonstrated our sympathy and kind disposition towards all those with whom we came in contact; your people we singled out for especially humane treatment, and those of them who had been taken into exile.[17] In fact we have liberated more than 100,000 gratuitously, and allocated an appropriate sum of money to their captors. In addition, we have corrected any abuse which they may have suffered through the wickedness or folly of our people. For we have decided to act justly and properly in this matter and willingly submit ourselves with integrity of soul before the great God who has marked out peace and glory for our realm. May He preserve it forever for us, sela.[18] Furthermore, all the men who were in their prime of life and at the peak of their physical strength were drafted into our forces, while those who were more suitably engaged at court were empowered with matters of state. But our aim is not simply to gratify those Jews, but also all who are now alive as well as future generations throughout the world. We have therefore decided to translate your Law from the Jewish language into Greek so that your laws along with all the other books of the royal collection should be accessible to anyone who consults the library we founded. You would be doing the right thing and that which is worthy of your station if you send us six distinguished representatives of each tribe, men of perfect morals with expert knowledge of the Law, possessing the linguistic skills to produce a clear and accurate translation. Thereby, future

17. 'Those . . . exile,' de' Rossi's addition.
18. De' Rossi has adapted the Latin text and has given it a liturgical ring.

generations will know that it was on account of valuable learning of this nature and an undertaking of such importance that the truth became fully apprehended and approved by the majority. By such an enterprise we hope to acquire an honorable reputation for posterity. Now we are sending you two delegates, one of whom is our bodyguard, and both are respected and held in high esteem at court. They shall speak with you in person about this matter. They bring for you as well as for your Temple the first fruits of our dedication offerings and one hundred talents for sacrifices and the tasks connected with the Temple service. Should you write to us about anything you so desire, it will be our pleasure and befitting of the friendship you extend to us; we shall endeavor to fulfill whatever you request. Farewell.

Eleazar's reply

Eleazar the high priest to King Ptolemy, a faithful friend, who gives support and strength,[19] be strong and of good courage. May you and Queen Arsinoe, your sister and your children, too, be well—such is our wish. May we also have peace and tranquillity.

We were overjoyed to receive your letter with the good tidings you expressed. Once we had assembled the councillors of the community, we read it out to them so that they would be informed of your righteous devotion to our God. We also showed them the twenty golden cups, the thirty silver cups, the five bowls, and the pure[20] table on which the voluntary offerings would be displayed and the sacrifices laid out. All this was delivered by your two ambassadors, men of high morals and outstanding wisdom, suited to the duties required of king's representatives and upholder of righteousness. They communicated all your messages to us, and they, in turn, will verify our response to your letter. We shall not refrain from satisfying your every wish; whatever you deem advantageous to you, even if it overrides our capabilities.[21] This should be regarded as a token of friendship and affection on our part. For you, too, have shown us much kindness and bestowed unexpected recompense on many of our people. Therefore we have not hesitated to offer burnt offerings for you, your sister, your children, and your admirers. During the sacrifices, the entire congregation sung praises and prayed that all your endeavors would succeed to your satisfaction, and that the benign God who sustains all would preserve your realm in peace and glory, and that all your plans for the translation would be fulfilled smoothly and without mishap and in the best possible way. Then, in the presence of all assembled, we chose wise and knowledgeable men, six of each tribe whom we are now sending to you, with the book of our Law in their possession. You, my lord king, will for your part, act in accordance with that which is right and proper if, on the completion the laws that you required, you ensure their safe return to us. Farewell.

Six elders from each tribe, seventy-two persons in all are dispatched.[22]

19. 'Who . . . strength,' de' Rossi's addition based on Ps. 68:36.
20. De' Rossi uses the description of the table in Lev. 24:6.
21. Both the Greek (44) and Latin text read 'even if it is contrary to our nature.'
22. In A (47–51) there follows here a list of the names of the elders. Josephus, however (XII:57) omits the list, stating that it is unnecessary.

Exposition on the workmanship of the gifts

Now, my brother, as promised, I shall describe to you the gifts which the king sent to Eleazar the high priest, their workmanship and ornamentation. They were all made at great cost with diligence and skill. For the king was generous and unstinting in providing the craftsmen with everything they required. Moreover, he often supervised them in order to ensure that nothing wrong was done through carelessness or laziness. First, I shall give you a description of the table and its construction. Initially it was the king's intention to make it larger than what finally transpired. He had ordered his servants to ask the Jerusalemites about the measurements of the existing table in the Temple. This accomplished, he asked further whether it would be possible to construct it on a larger scale. Some of the sages and priests replied that there was nothing to prevent this. He then said that it was really his wish to make it five times as large, but hesitated, since being larger than the former table, it might therefore become unsuitable for the Temple service. It was not his intention to have the honor of providing utensils for the Temple unless they could be utilized for the purpose for which they were designed; only then, would he be satisfied. He realized that it was not for lack of gold that the existing table had been made on such a small scale. Rather, despite abundant supplies of gold, the orders for its construction on this scale had been given with good reason which suited its particular function. This being the case, he did not want to transgress or to change the measurements in any way. But no harm would be done by enhancing its decoration and design. So he ordered that the craftsmen should use all their skills to produce a beautiful masterpiece. Since the king possessed an innate gift for creating beautiful shapes and patterns, he himself devised a way of making it into an object of great excellence, containing the finest engravings. Similarly, where possible, he embellished the parts which were supposed to be left undecorated.[23] Such were his instructions to all the artisans with regard to the construction work.

(Thus says the translator: It is difficult even for skilled artists to conceptualize the construction of this table as described in some of the passages. In my opinion, Josephus's description of the table in the *Antiquities* is largely based on this account.[24] Seeking clarification, I consulted both Ruffinus's translation and the superior rendering made by Gelenius.[25] It appeared to me that Josephus's description was somewhat different. However, both accounts are useful in that they shed light on one another. One particular error of the original transcribers of the text will become clear—they mistakenly described the table as three-dimensional; after all, it was constructed on the model of the table in the Temple. Thus both versions should be taken into account. For the reader's gratification, I have amplified the description a little in certain passages, but have not done so with the rest of the book.[26])

23. In A (56) it states that where there was no prescription in Scripture, he followed aesthetic principles.

24. It should be noted that Josephus's paraphrase is written in a Greek which differs considerably from that of the Aristean text. According to A. Pelletier, *Flavius Josèphe,* Josephus's adaptation demonstrates the different ideological context in which he was writing; a Jewish-Roman one of the first century C.E. as opposed to Aristeas's Greco-Jewish audience of the second century B.C.E.

25. In the Basel 1524 edition, Ruffinus's name is given as the translator of the *Antiquities,* but it is not certain whether the attribution is correct.

26. This assertion is not completely true.

The workmanship of the table

The table was two cubits in length, one cubit wide, and one and a half cubits in height.[27] It was not overlaid with layers of gold plate but consisted of one solid piece of pure gold.[28] They made a border which was one handsbreadth in measurement, and they embellished the edges with a twisted rope and lattice design. The artistic execution included rotating three-sided ornaments that were altogether marvelous.[29] For they made them triangular in shape with an identical design engraved on each of its sides so that whichever way they were turned the onlooker would see the same design all along the border. The inner side by the border and facing the table had the appropriate embellishment. But the other part was even more beautifully decorated because it was exposed to the view of all onlookers. And because, as we said, the plaited design was triangular in every direction, the two corners—the one facing the table, the other facing the exterior—met at an acute, elevated angle. Moreover, in the other corner, various kinds of precious stones were studded in the rope design mentioned above. They were symmetrically and beautifully placed, held in their grooves by golden hooks and securely fixed. All the edges were similarly firmly affixed with fastenings which were invisible on the outside. On the exposed corners of the edge of the border was a decoration of precious stones in an egg-shaped design with a succession of engraved branches encircling the table. Under this ornamentation, they made another border of branches bearing all kinds of appetizing fruit which were actually precious stones. In their natural hue and appearance, they formed clusters of grapes, ears of corn, dates, apples, olives, pomegranates, and other fruits. The stones resembled these fruits not only in shape, but also in appearance and were hung on a golden border all around the table's circumference. Having made this frame along the diameter of the border, they made another decoration with curved branches of egg-shaped stones and with all the rope and lattice work mentioned above. The design of the table was uniform along the circumferences of the border, whichever way the table's surface was turned on its legs. For under the table's surface, on the tops of the legs, were golden plates of four fingersbreadth whose length equaled that of the table's width. The legs were fastened to these with golden hooks and clamps such that the table's surface formed a unit with them no matter which side it was put down. In view of the uniformity of the decoration of the border there was no difference between the sides. But on the surface of the table itself, they engraved a meandering river* (another version reads "labyrinth") which was iridescent; for it was entirely embellished with gems inserted within its curves: rubies, topazes, emeralds, and carbuncles which are the most brilliant of the precious stones.

(*The author [Aristeas] and Josephus[30] read "meander" which means a curving river and labyrinth. The Spanish translator[31] renders it "labyrintho" which, in my view,

27. A (57) gives only the length and height of the table. Josephus (XII:64) adds the width, thus giving the same measurements as those of the table of the tabernacle (Ex. 25:23; 37:10).

28. De' Rossi uses the vocabulary from Ex. 25:23–29; 37:10–16.

29. The artistic . . . marvelous.' This detail is only in Josephus.

30. A (66); *Ant.* XII:72.

31. This is a reference to the Castilian translation printed by the press of Martin Nucio in Antwerp,

is the correct rendering. But the Hebrew Josephus (ch. 17) renders it "Egypt's river."[32] In chapter 19, I shall demonstrate to you that it is not a reliable source.)

Next to this decoration was another which was highly embellished in branch-design. A long and rectangular shape in its center was inset with two stones of sapphire and jasper,[33] respectively, a marvelous sight for all spectators. Indeed, the legs had the shape of a bent lily stalk with its uppermost leaves supporting the table, while above it, along its stalk, they were spread out erect in the normal fashion. The base of the leg rested on the ground. It was made of carbuncle and measured a handsbreadth in every direction. The foot was placed in a cavity which was hollowed out into the shape of a well's mouth, eight fingers in width. Around each of its legs, precious shrubs[34] were budding from top to bottom, clinging to the thicket vines, and lovely foliage bearing the choicest of precious stones—all this artistic embellishment was unparalleled. All four legs had the same decoration, and the execution was such that the foliage and their fruits not only resembled the products and seemed real but were so finely wrought that when a wind blew, their branches would appear to stir and move as though they really were the artifacts of nature they represented. The edges of the table were brought together in three parts.* It was virtually tripartite, but for the fact that all the parts interlocked by means of the invisible golden pins and clamps. Thus on examination, one would think that it was all one frame, for the joinings could not be detected. And yet, the thickness of the entire table was not less than half a cubit, and was therefore very costly. Since the king had decided not to increase the measurement of the table, he wanted to spend as much as he had originally planned, and even more, on the craftsmanship. The whole endeavor was motivated by his desire to magnify its beauty and splendor; and so, by detailed ornamentation and resplendent design, a work of unparalleled craftsmanship was produced.

(*Three parts: i.e., the table, border, and the plates. The corners were almost three square for the two sides were joined there with the foot. Josephus's account reads: "The entire workmanship of the table consisted of three parts but the joints were connected.")

The workmanship of the bowls

The golden bowls were decorated with a scaly ornamentation. From the base to the middle, they were engraved with a wondrous circular design. Precious stones were interspersed between those scaly engravings. From the middle of the bowls and above a meander (labyrinth) of a cubit's height was designed. Quite apart from the beauty of its shape, the decoration of various types of pearls with which it was studded gave the artifact an iridescent effect, the likes of which had never before been seen. Above it was a pattern of intertwining branches, and from there as far as the brim was a network pattern within which were square shapes. In the middle of one of these shapes were

---

1554. The interpretation of 'meander' as labyrinth is a marginal gloss, 211v: "Meandro que corre a manera de labyrintho."

32. *Josippon,* bk. 3, ch. 17 (70).

33. De' Rossi uses the names of the stones put in the high priest's breastplate, but they do not exactly correspond to the 'crystal and amber' of the original.

34. 'Precious shrubs.' De' Rossi appeared to have no Hebrew equivalent for 'hedera' (ivy).

shields filled with different kinds of gems. Each shield was four fingersbreadth[35] and irradiated a wondrous beauty created by the varied impression produced by those stones. On the brim of the crown was a pattern of lilies, flowers, and clusters of grapes spaced here and there. Such was the form of the golden bowls both of which could hold more than the content of two clay bowls.

The brightness of the silver bowls was so dazzling that they could reflect any object with a clarity which was greater than that of bronze mirrors. An experienced orator would be at a loss for words appropriate for a description of this gift. It was simply their position, one next to the other, a silver, then a gold, followed by a third of silver and a fourth of gold which created such a pricelessly beautiful impression. Any beholder would stand there transfixed either by the encircling dazzling light or by the delight which gripped him as he took in the beauty of the workmanship. As his gaze turned from one splendid sight to the other, he would likewise be entranced as his attention turned from the delicacy of the artisanship to its dazzling light. Indeed, the greatest pleasure derived from the artisanship of the two golden bowls, particularly as one would transfer attention from one piece of delicate work to the next. Similarly, anyone gazing on the silver bowls would be dazzled by the intensity of their brightness and be unable to move from the spot, so pleasurable was the view. The splendor of the variegated artistry and craftsmanship was immeasurable.

The craftsmanship of the flagons

Now the golden flagons were decorated with a circular design. Around the middle of each flagon were fine garlands. Near the brim was a decoration of the choicest shrubs[36] and a beautiful crown of olive branches interspersed with precious stones. The remaining part of the utensil was similarly decorated with varied and fine patterns. This effect was produced by the artisans whose every consideration was to make innumerable beautiful artifacts for the honor of the realm. There were no works of comparable value and magnificence in the king's treasury nor in any other part of his realm. So great was the king's predilection for beautiful and fine objects that he personally supervised the workers and inspected everything they made. Often, he even put aside affairs of state and went to persuade the artisans to produce artifacts that were suitable for the place for which they were destined. Consequently, everything was perfectly accomplished as befitted both the king who sent [the gifts] and the high priest who presided over the place. A great number of precious stones were inset into the artifacts, and these were also the best and the most brilliant, amounting to not less than five thousand. The artisanship was of such a high standard and the stones so valuable that their worth was five times greater than the gold.

So now, my brother, I have kept you fully informed of those matters which in my view required elucidation. What follows is an account of our journey to Eleazar the high priest, preceded by a useful discourse containing relevant information about the region and other related matters.

35. The text reads 'not less than four fingers.'
36. Again, de' Rossi uses a general designation for the 'ivy' and 'myrtle.'

Concerning Jerusalem,* the curtain, the altar, and the priestly vestments

(*See book 6 (chapter 7) of Josephus's *Wars* where he provides a topography of Jerusalem.[37])

When we reached those places we saw a city centrally located on a high mountain. On its summit was a lavishly ornate temple surrounded by three walls which were more than seventy cubits high and whose width was proportionate with their height and their length appropriate for such a structure. Indeed, everything was constructed with great pomp and at sumptuous expense as was apparent from the superb gates, the beautiful joinings of the lower parts and the splendor of each threshold. There was a curtain of the same measurement which covered the gate—a pleasant sight indeed. Its folds and pleats were constantly swaying and moving, easily stirred by the wind blowing from within or without.[38] There was also an altar which was constructed in a manner commensurate with the place and the daily sacrifices that were burnt on it. The altar was approached by a slope which was highly ornate and appropriate for its functions. The priestly vestments worn during the ministrations are coats of fine linen which reach the ankles.

The view from the Temple to the rivers below

Now the front of the Temple faces east and its rear faces west and the entire pavement is marble.[39] From it, many streams and canals flow to certain places which facilitate the cleansing of the blood of the many sacrificial offerings; for during the holy days, an innumerable amount of sacrifices have to be offered. But there is an unceasing supply of water for there is a large natural spring whose waters never fail. Five-eighths of a mile beneath the ground are many marvelously constructed reservoirs which encompass all sides of the Temple, each one of which has many pipes which flow into one another on every side. All the floor and sides of these ducts are overlaid with lead and well covered with a heap of earth. On the base and foundation of the Temple are many invisible outlets which can only be seen by the priest who is engaged in the holy ministrations. The force of the water which issues from them cleanses and removes all the blood from the hundreds and thousands of sacrifices. I cannot help telling you of the great affection they showed me by explaining the structure of those streams and pipes. On one occasion, they took me about half a mile outside the city. One of them told me to incline my head and to hear the rush of water. It was then that I came to realize the magnitude of those conduits.

On the priests

Now the priests who officiate at the holy ministrations are all strong and robust. Their service is enhanced by the splendor of their garments and by the reverential silence they maintain. You could see that each one approached his work with enthusiasm despite the heavy work involved, and each one is conscientious about his duty and will not

37. *Bellum* V:136ff.

38. 'Its folds . . . outside.' This is a difficult passage to construe even in the Greek (86). De' Rossi appears to have simplified the Latin text.

39. 'Marble.' Both the Greek and Latin texts read 'stone.'

allow himself to interrupt it for the sake of some other business. One attends to the wood, another to the oil, and others to the fine flour and still others to the spices. There are also those who attend to the whole burnt offerings. Their execution of these duties demonstrates both their physical strength and laudable skill and dexterity. Sometimes you would see one of them take a calf weighing about two talents with both hands and then, by the legs, and with hand over hand, throw it effortlessly on high. In a similar fashion, they take unblemished sheep and goats which are well fatted and heavy and, holding them by the legs, throw them one to the other without hesitation. As we said, all entrusted with those duties are the best men, free of blemish and physically strong.[40] There is a chamber in the Temple where they can retire and revive themselves during the rest periods. After their repose, they then get up in an exultant and happy frame of mind. They all go about their business and have no need of any foreman to gird them into action or instruct them about their tasks. A reverential silence reigns in the Temple that you may well be deceived into thinking that not one human being was present there. And yet, sometimes you could come across more than seventy officiating priests and double the number of sacrificiants. This atmosphere was brought about by the awesome reverence which they all inevitably experienced, and it befitted the place dedicated to the sanctification of the highest God.

On the high priest and his vestments

Then afterwards we were struck with great amazement when we behold Eleazar the high priest engaged in his holy ministrations. Was he not an amazing spectacle, distinguished by the magnificent impression created by the grandeur of the coat [*meʿil*] which he wore and the precious stones with which it was studded. Behold, from this long garment which stretched to the feet, hung golden bells which produced a harmonious sound, and between each bell was placed a pomegranate adorned with flowers of various hues. He was girt with a very beautiful girdle, which was also interwoven in different colors, and on his breast he wore the ornament which they call the "breastplate of judgment" in which were set and overlaid in gold twelve precious stones of different kinds which are the most brilliant of all gems. The stones were engraved with the names of the tribes according to their original order. Now his head was covered by the so-called *sudar* [*cidaris*] and above it was the mitre which was wrought with inimitable artistry, a most splendid regal ornament and on it, brought out in relief, was a golden plate which was inscribed with the name of God in the holy letters—an awesome sight indeed—which went across his forehead as far as the eyebrows. Indeed, Eleazar himself who engaged in these ministrations appeared truly worthy of all this. The brightness which his countenance irradiated cast fear on all who beheld him. For apart from the ornaments about which we have spoken, he himself with his radiant appearance seemed to become transformed. In truth, anyone who approached him—(he would undoubtedly think that the object of contemplation was amazing)—would be gripped by trembling and wonder which was generated by the great splendor of each of those holy garments.

40. This is an incorrect translation. A (93) is referring to the animals and not to the priests.

On the citadel of Mount Zion

Afterwards, to ensure that we did not miss any of the remarkable sights, we ascended the citadel which lay adjacent to the city and we walked about it in every direction. It is situated on a high site and it has many towers which from bottom to top are constructed out of large blocks of stone. We were told that these towers were to protect all the area around the Sanctuary. Thus, in case of assault on the city, neither plunderers nor armed forces would be able to find a foothold on it; for stone slings were in position and many armaments on all the towers which would send them on their heels and prevent them from approaching. The citadel is situated on the mountain's peak and overshadows all the city's buildings. In addition, all the guards of the tower are trustworthy men who have demonstrated their unqualified and constant allegiance to the inhabitants of the city. According to a law which they do not transgress, they can leave their posts only on festive days, and then only a few at a time, and solely in turn. Moreover, not just any person could enter those gates, but only those who were known to them as irreproachable and trustworthy persons. So whenever the governor ordered them to open one of the gates,[41] as was the case when I and my friend arrived there, they would carry out a thorough inspection. Only with great reluctance on their part, after we had been stripped of our weapons, were we allowed to see those holy objects. They said that they had been entrusted with this duty and had sworn that they would give constant attention to all the matters which had been put in their charge. Although there were five hundred soldiers, only five could leave at one time. They informed us that these had been the orders of the original founder of the citadel.

On the city of Jerusalem

The city is of medium size and as far as we could judge, is about forty *ris* in circumference.* Its streets are in the form of a theater, with the lower roads leading to the thoroughfare, while there is a path leading to the upper level which runs diagonally to them. Since the city is built on mountains, its paths jut out one against the other. The paths are reached by several steps on different levels which enable the passerby to descend and ascend. The reason for this is above all to enable certain individuals, who are dedicated to the pious and holy life, to separate themselves from the rest of the people, thus ensuring that they do not touch their garments and contaminate them.[42]

(*The author uses the term "stade." In fact there is a slight difference between a *stade* and a *ris* (as can be seen in the entry for *ris* in the *Arukh*[43] and in the Latin dictionary under the entry for *stadium*[44]).)

41. 'So . . . gates,' de' Rossi's addition.

42. 'Its streets . . . contaminate them.' This passage (105) is difficult in all languages. De' Rossi's is an approximate rendering of the Latin translation.

43. In his *Arukh*, s.v. *rvs*, Nathan ben Yeḥiel refers to the use of the word in B. B.M. 33a and states that it is equivalent to two-fifteenths of a mile. He also suggests that its measurement is equivalent to the numerical value of its letters, i.e., 266 cubits.

44. Calepino, *Dictionarium*, s.v. *stadium* states that a stade is equivalent to 625 feet, i.e., an eighth of a mile.

The original founders of the city had good reason for laying it out with fitting proportions; indeed their plan was sound and wise. For this terrain was very good and ample. In fact, the area towards Samaria and that which extends as far as the outskirts of the land of Idumaea is flat for the most part, valleys mantled with grain.[45] The rest of the area is mountainous and hilly, and needs to be tilled and tended. But since the farmers and keepers of the vineyards are conscientious in their work, it unfailingly gives abundant yield. Consequently, the land which consists totally of fertile and cultivated fields yields crops of corn, wine, and other produce. However, the city dwellers live off the fat of the land and spend their lives in peace and enjoy every luxury. As a result there is a youthful population who flourish, spoilt by their life of affluence, and they despise the labor and toil of the country. They are all completely intent on pleasure and enjoyment for everybody is molded from childhood to develop such proclivities.

Now this is what happened to this city of Alexandria which supersedes all other cities of the same size and affluence. People from all corners of the region were attracted to come and settle there, without any intention of moving. They despise the pleasant surrounding country villages and as a consequence, the untended land becomes ruined. In response to this situation, our lord king issued an edict throughout his realm which stated: "Anyone who decides to immigrate to a city may take up residence there for not more than twenty days, after which he must depart and return to his family home." He passed a similar edict for those coming from the villages for business reasons. He decreed that judges should set a time limit of five days in which period any lawsuit that may arise could be dealt with. Similarly, while the sellers of produce and providers of military implements and their overseers were granted certain rights by him (for he wanted to privilege them), he nevertheless prevented the country folk and representatives of the townsmen from engaging in commerce, thus diminishing the stock and the profits from farming. We felt justified in making this truthful digression since Eleazar the priest had traced out the facts for us—the truth is their witness.

Now let us return to the subject we were treating. There is extensive cultivation of this land and they do really tend it assiduously. There are therefore many attractive plantations of vines throughout the region; all kinds of grains and vegetables as well as vineyards and swarms of bees, palm trees, and innumerable other kinds of fruit-bearing trees. There is also a huge number of sheep and cattle who graze on the fertile and rich pasture land which extends in every direction. The ancients took this all into account when they cleverly laid out the city and most of the villages so as to ensure that they all could be provided with adequate supplies and provisions. The land is not only lush and abundant, as we have said, but also very well positioned. The Arabs who live on their border import large amounts of the choicest spices and the best precious stones and gold. Indeed, the land is suited for agriculture and commerce, and the city abounds in artisans of all descriptions for there is no lack of goods imported from overseas. For ships bearing all manner of goods arrive in all its harbors, including Ashkelon, Jaffa, Gaza, and Ptolemais,[46] the city recently built by Ptolemy the king our lord. For it is located in

45. 'Valleys . . . grain,' de' Rossi's addition from Ps. 65:14.
46. In B, de' Rossi glosses Ptolemy with 'city of the Ptolemies.'

the middle of[47] all these lands and not far away from them. The place is itself blessed: it is well watered and the natives feel secure for there is nothing they lack. Indeed, the river Jordan, whose waters never fail, surrounds its borders, and from antiquity, fertilized thousands and myriads of fields which were nourished by its flow of water over the years. From nearby areas, several myriads of people immigrated into that region and each individual acquired and enjoyed the possession of one hundred acres of land. This river, like the Nile in Egypt,* overflows its banks at harvesttime and waters the land as far as Ptolemais from where it flows into another river, and from there goes into the sea.

(*A similar description of the Jordan is given in chapter 24 of Ecclesiasticus.[48] In Bereshit Rabbah[49] it states that miraculously the Jordan flows past the sea of Tiberias without intersecting it. According to the writer Solinus,[50] the river Euphrates also rises and waters the land of Mesopotamia and Babylon as does the Nile of Egypt. It is apparently for this reason that the rabbis of blessed memory state in Bereshit Rabbah[51] that the waters of the Euphrates fructify[52] and proliferate.)

In addition to this goodly river, there are many harbors[53] around it which enrich the inhabited area and provide welcome supplies of water to all the places towards Gaza and the region of the Azotus. In addition to all these admirable features, it also has naturally strong defenses because of the steepness of the surrounding mountains, the narrowness of the paths, and the difficulty of ascending them by reason of the pitholes and deep valleys which lie between them. At such a prospect, any enemy would surely take to their heels, and should they attempt to encamp there, the soldiers would be unable to get a foothold on them. I was also told that in former times there used to be metal mines of copper and iron in the nearby mountainous country of Arabia. Later, when the Persians took power, they decreed that the mining should be discontinued. The leaders persuaded the natives that it was an unprofitable expense as well as a source of danger. They argued that it could lead to the infiltration of foreigners who would fight against them and dispossess them. Their fears came true. Many foreigners did come within their gates to dig for the metals, scanned the entrances to the city, and were then in a position to raise a blockade and successfully overpower the natives.[54]

My brother, I have given you a summary of the useful information about the places. Now we shall resume the subject of the translation and the manner in which it was executed.

47. Lit. 'in the navel of these lands,' a common phrase to depict the position of the land of Israel.

48. Sirach 24:26: *He makes understanding to abound like the Euphrates and as the Jordan in the time of harvest.*

49. B.R. 4:5 (29).

50. De' Rossi is citing the *Collectanea rerum mirabilium* by the second-century geographer Solinus (which he read in Vincenzo Belprato's Italian translation, as is evident from his reference to ch. 49, 173): "Questo fiume arrichisce la Mesopotamia con inondare ciascun'anno . . . facendo lo fertile al modo dell'Egitto."

51. B.R. 16:3 (145).

52. 'Fructify,' lit. are fruitful.

53. 'Harbors.' The Latin text reads 'torrentes.' Like Cassel ad loc., I am unable to explain de' Rossi's translation.

54. The entire account of the mines (119–20) is obscure in all languages.

Eleazar's selection of the elders

Eleazar the priest chose the most prominent and erudite men of noble and distinguished lineage. They were not only well versed in the literature of the Jews, but they also took pleasure in the cultivation of Greek studies and mores. They were therefore well-qualified delegates for any mission to mighty kings and dispatched this duty whenever the occasion arose. In event of debates about the interpretation of the Law, they conferred among themselves with words imbued with spirituality, wisdom, and understanding. Similarly, as far as human behavior is concerned, they were naturally disposed to eschew extremes, which is the best position to take, and they spurned all strange conduct and odious dispositions, and pride and stubbornness in particular. Indeed, they were kindly and willing listeners and always found appropriate means of explaining any complicated matter and supplying solutions. In sum, each one of them was worthy of their priest and leader and most deserving of his upright behavior.

They all loved Eleazar with total dedication which was made manifest by their great reluctance to part from him. There was also indication that he loved them. For he not only wrote to the king requesting that they be returned to him without fail when the time came, but he also strongly urged my companion to be assiduous in implementing this matter. He also asked us both to ensure that their wishes were met and to look after their welfare as far as possible. We pledged ourselves in this regard and told him that he had no reason to fear that their stay would be prolonged. He answered: "My fears are not groundless. I know that the king is deeply engrossed in studies and that he is strongly motivated to perform just actions. He is therefore always delighted to be informed about any highly reputed sage of whatever place and then summons him to his presence and by the bonds of generosity entices him to stay. He was certainly not speaking falsely when he stated that as long as there were scholars of integrity at his court, they would serve as a bulwark and protection for his realm. For whatever they say and think is always in line with and oriented towards what is good and beneficial for the population as a whole, whose welfare is his constant preoccupation."

Such was the status and position, Eleazar said, of the men he had selected for the delegation. Moreover, with one hand raised, he took an oath that if he were to require them for a personal reason of his own, he would not allow them to leave his presence. Now, however, he would let them go since he realized that this mission of theirs would be to the advantage of all human beings. In other words, it would result in the observance of the laws, which, it is true, is achieved by listening much more than by conscientious dedication to reading. With these and other such pronouncements, he clearly demonstrated his state of mind, namely, that he regarded these men as the apple of his eye.

Questions about the Law and Eleazar's answers

Now I thought that it was wise to inform you of the main points in the valuable discourse which this sagacious man willingly gave in response to our questions. We thought it particularly important since we were aware that many people regard a considerable number of the statutes contained in the Law of the Jews as having no foundation.[55] For example, certain foods and drink are prohibited and those who touch the many animals which are unclean for them become contaminated. We enquired as to why the touching or consumption of certain animals was forbidden even though one God created all existing beings. Certainly, these and many similar prescriptions of the Law appear to be meaningless details—and, in fact, they are observed with an even greater regard to the minutiae which are but vanity of vanities. He answered in the following manner:

> Take care and realize how influential is the power of association and relationship. Do you not observe many cases of people who by association with the wicked, learn evil and render themselves obnoxious all the days of their life? But if they go among the sagacious and upright, they receive instruction, grow wise, and make their lives worthwhile forever. It was for this reason that our prophet[56] (the first of all legislators) wisely and clearly issued edicts concerning the performance of just and pious deeds. In each case, His precepts carry not only prohibitions against iniquitous deeds, but also prescriptions about right action. In addition, we are told about all the diseases and plagues which God will afflict on those who rebel against the light,[57] those workers of iniquity. In the first place, he showed us that there is but one God and that He is more powerful than all the mighty, and gives strength to the weary.[58] Nothing is withheld for Him not even if it is shrouded in cloud and darkness. Rather all our present and future decisions are divulged and known to him. All the most deep-seated secrets are not hidden from Him.

After these remarks which he developed, he then introduced and enlarged on the subject of human motivations. He said that any person who had only as much as contemplated doing a wicked act (quite apart from having already committed it), would immediately know for sure that everything is foreseen by God and that nothing is withheld from Him. In fact, by reading the Law from beginning to end, one would see that it is imbued with God's thoughts whose greatness and power is unfathomable.

After these statements, he informed us that all nations—with the exception of Israel which had been selected as His special people—seemed boorish and completely vacuous-minded. For they believe in many gods and adore them even though they themselves are more powerful and more deserving of honor. They believe that the statues which they made from wood and stone are images of the idolatrous gods which, according to their deluded ideas, can instruct them about what is useful for their living. And so it comes about that they ascribe honor to that which is palpably nothing and devoid of spirit. In their defense, one could say that they venerate them with respect to the potency which they imagine them to have from the moment that they conceive their creation and entertain the idea of their existence. But it is just in this respect that they are the most foolish of men. For the truth is that those who invented them did not create or bring into existence anything which could be described as novel. They simply showed that useful things can exist or that by imagining the amalgamation of many things that were already created, they had produced one form which they believed to be

55. De' Rossi emphasizes the negativity of the sentiment.
56. 'Our prophet,' de' Rossi's addition.
57. 'Rebel . . . light,' de' Rossi's embellishment based on Job 24:13.
58. De' Rossi prefers to give a more biblical flavor to the entire passage rather than an accurate rendering.

useful. In this respect, too, they were misguided. For they gave the name "god" to beings like themselves and no way superior to them. In fact, in every generation there have been many people of greater knowledge and inventiveness than those ancients who have conjured up things which their ancestors would never have imagined; and yet the ancients would never have revered these moderns, while the Greeks who invented these fabrications were regarded as distinguished and outstandingly knowledgeable people. And what is the point of continuing to speak of other people who are even more foolish. The Egyptians, for example, and others like them, reach the peak of madness when they revere and worship wild beasts, reptiles, and other animals and even go so far as to offer sacrifices to their carcasses. All this was patently obvious and known to our ancestors. Consequently our legislator behaved as a sage imbued by the divine spirit; with wise insight and understanding, he constructed and surrounded us with an iron battlement and a brazen wall so that we would not mix with the other nations in any respect. Instead, we remain physically pure and untainted of soul and are not contaminated by all these abominations. We do indeed revere one God alone whose power surpasses that of all existing beings—it is He whom we worship as long as we live. Therefore, the Egyptian nobles and sages who studied our Law and were greatly influenced by it called us "men of God." Such an appellation only befits those who serve the true God who is King of all the world. As for the rest of humanity, they virtually deserve the appellation "men of food, drink and precious clothes,"[59] for these are the things which absorb their attention. But our people, who regard such things as futile and senseless, turn their attention throughout their lives to the contemplation and understanding of the greatness and power of the God whose sovereignty is unfathomable. To prevent us associating and intermingling with those nations who would deflect us from the service of God and contaminate us with their idolatry and abominations, he has hedged us in with a holiness that is fitting and with purity laws regarding food that is eaten, drink that is imbibed, touch, hearing, and sight. For in general, all his precepts have one overriding reason which harmonizes with nature and is calculated by God. There is a true and wondrously excellent reason for everything from which we must abstain or towards which we are propelled. In the course of our narration, I cannot desist from providing you with one or two model examples. You should not be deluded into thinking that the great sage who gave us a praiseworthy legislation was solicitous about the weasel, mouse, and such like creatures and considered them important enough to mention in his book and to legislate about them as though they were of value. Rather, you should understand that all his commandments are distinguished by their importance and sanctity; their aim and purpose is to promote righteousness, to pave the way to virtue, and to imbue our healthy minds with holy and merciful thoughts. Indeed, all the birds, all the winged creatures, which are permitted to us are obviously domesticated, gentle, and harmless and feed on grain and pulse—in this category are the doves, turtledoves, quails, and geese.[60] But the unclean animals live solitarily among the shrubs of the forest and plantations. They are carnivores and feed on other birds of prey as well as on the domestic ones that we mentioned. These are not their only objects

59. 'Precious clothes,' cf. Ezk. 27:20.
60. De' Rossi does not give a rendering for 'partridges' and renders 'meadow birds' as 'quails.'

of prey, but some of them are rapacious enough to seize kids, lambs, and even human beings, alive or dead. For this reason, our legislator first gave us the signs and characteristics by which they can be recognized and then declared them unclean and ordered us to abstain from eating them. In so doing, he drew the attention of the people of his law to the necessity of constantly behaving in accordance with justice and righteousness and desisting from harming one another even when the oppressors have the upper hand. Similarly, we are taught not to take other people's possessions, and always to direct ourselves to that which is proper and just in like manner to the animals which feed on the produce of the ground and do not harm any other living creature by rapaciously taking prey. As such they indicate and demonstrate that right action is concerned with justice and that regardless of our strength, we should always desist from harming one another. By being prevented from touching those unclean animals with their evil and proud dispositions, we surely learn that we must be especially on our guard against emulating them in our habits and behavior. Similarly, the prescriptions regarding the clean birds and sheep give us scope for contemplation in respect to the formation of our habits and thoughts. When he commanded us to see to it that the sheep have cloven, divided hoofs, he intended to indicate and remind us that we should always examine our actions and clearly distinguish between each one. As is known, the power of the body and its focal strength is virtually entirely concentrated in the shoulders and legs. The purpose of this symbol, therefore, is to make us aware that whatever is achieved through our bodily strength and by the action of our legs should be the result of selection and discrimination between each action in accordance with the norms of justice. And there is also another reason: we should take care to remember that we ought to be separated from all other peoples who defile each other in their relationships, violating all the rules of justice. The nations and entire countries do in fact take pride in this; for according to their various laws, no crime is imputed to the man who lies with another man, and even a woman in the time of her impurity of childbirth[61] together with her daughters will seem permitted and attractive to a man. May we keep ourselves far from such things. And in the very passage in which we are exhorted to maintain this separation, he also gave us a sign whereby it becomes engraved in the memory. Intelligent people interpret the combination of ruminants and cloven-footed animals as the symbol of unfading memory. "Chewing the cud" represents memory and retention in the mind. The particular things we must commit to memory and comprehend are the wonders of our life: the construction of our limbs and the way we survive by means of the food we digest. He alludes to this notion when he says, *And you shall remember the Lord your God who gave you strength* (Deut. 8:18), and in another context he says, *He is your glory and He is your God who wrought for you those marvelous awesome deeds* (Deut. 10:21).[62] They do indeed appear great and awesome, especially when submitted to profound intellectual examination. First one should contemplate the composition of the body and the digestive system and the manner in which each limb is formed in accordance with its specific function. But even greater consideration should be given to

61. De' Rossi has added the detail about the impurity, alluding to Lev. 12:2.

62. A (155) gives a conflation of the two verses, but de' Rossi has separated the two verses without mentioning his emendation.

the disposition of the senses and the power of the intellect, its invisible movements and the adeptness with which it discerns how to act appropriately and its inventiveness in the arts. All these are doubtlessly to be regarded as wondrous matters for contemplation. He thus commanded us to set great store by them and to remember them constantly; for it is divine potency that brings them about, and it is He, their Creator, who sustains and maintains these physical functions. Besides this, he has allocated suitable periods in which we can devote ourselves to bearing this in mind, as is right, such that we impress upon ourselves that He is the guide and preserver of all creatures in heaven and on earth. Thus, at mealtimes, he has commanded us to assemble and convene for grace in order to sanctify His name and to give thanks for all that He has bestowed on us.[63] Similarly, he has us garb ourselves in clothes, which bear signs and distinctive marks so that we are constantly reminded of Him. Then again, he has commanded us to affix the words of the precepts on the doorposts of our houses and on our gates to ensure that we remember and never forget Him. It is also his wish that we should bind a manifest sign on our hands to remind us of Him, and that we ought to bear Him in mind in all our endeavors and actions. Moreover, it suggests that in all our work we must always recall that we are His creatures and should always ensure that all our deeds are governed by unsullied fear of God which we should experience every moment in regard to every matter. He has likewise ordered us to pursue this path "when we lie down" and "when we rise up," with consideration to these constant changes of state, from sleeping to awakening. Despite the limitation of the intellect of humans who weary in their attempt to grasp the nature of these functions, we should contemplate and recognize the greatness of God's works, as they come, go, and change in succession. In providing you with the reasons for the cloven hoofs and the chewing of the cud, I have shown you the value which our prophet, the legislator, attaches to our prohibitions and commandments and to the things which are always to be kept in mind. Thereby one comes to realize that His precepts were not laid down at random or by some caprice of the mind; rather, all have the express purpose of ensuring that we know and adhere to the path that brings us to truth and justice. Indeed, in like manner to the legislation about food which we mentioned, so too, and with even great insistence, are we warned about touch and hearing. For we are prevented from doing or listening to anything which is evil and abhorrent. He likewise exhorted us that we should not abuse such faculties of speech and oratory as we possess in order to act in contravention of what is right and just. Now these considerations and reasons that we have mentioned are equally valid in the case of the animals which are unclean for us. The weasel and mouse and other prohibited animals are naturally destructive and are constantly intent on causing injury. Is it not true that the mouse not only damages that which it eats and on which it feeds, but also everything in its immediate environment that it can take with its teeth and which, thus maimed, can no longer serve any purpose? The weasel, which in addition to being a major pest like the mouse, is also peculiar in its abominable trait of conceiving through the ear and giving birth through its mouth. This fact is most instructive and sheds light on the character of people who gossip about the things they

63. 'Convene for eating.' De' Rossi has omitted the reference in A (158) to the sacrifices that are offered before eating.

have heard to the detriment of others. These people suffer from a pernicious disease, and their souls are tainted with a defiling impurity. For this reason your king is publicly lauded for, according to hearsay, he metes out punishment to anyone who acts in this way. Then I said to Eleazar: "Are you alluding to informers and underhand slanderers? For these he certainly punishes with pitiless flogging and capital punishment." He answered: "Yes, I was speaking in this heated way against sinners whose lives indeed constitute the death of the guiltless. Our Law therefore commands us to be constantly wary of harming our fellows by word or deed."

In these few words, I have made every effort to enlighten you as to the truth of our discourse and to enable you to realize that everything in our Law is motivated by justice. There is nothing senseless, strange, or difficult in any of the precepts. They consist of statutes and righteous laws which teach us to preserve justice and goodness in our dealings with all people as long as we live, and never to forget for one moment that all creatures owe their origin and existence to God and that it is He who will guide us for all time.

What transpires from this priest's discourse is that the purpose of the prohibited foods and the laws regarding the unclean animals is to encourage people in the pursuit of righteousness and that all relationships and social groups should always be founded on justice. Indeed, it seemed to me that all the reasons he gave for the precepts were grounded in knowledge. He spoke in a similar vein about the sacrifices of the bullocks, rams and lambs.* He said that these were all tame animals and did not harm or assault other animals and that none of the sacrificial victims were wild or untamed. Thus the purpose of their legislator was to educate the sacrificiants in the virtues of refraining from harming others and from acting arrogantly in any way. For the person that brings a sacrifice offers that which is in keeping with the character of his soul and representative of it.

(*Yedidyah the Alexandrian (Philo) wrote similarly in the section on the sacrifices (p. 700).[64] His word are also cited by Eusebius in book 8 (chapter 3) of his *Praeparatio*[65] where he quotes from the Jewish philosopher Aristobulus.)

This is a synopsis of our discussion which, in my opinion, was worth recording. I have written to you about it, my brother, in view of your great love of all useful learning, so that you might comprehend the majesty and holiness of that Law and the inherent wisdom that lies embedded in its precepts. Now let us resume our tale.

The arrival of the elders in Alexandria

When Eleazar had completed the divine rituals and prepared a beautiful array of gifts which he was sending to the king, he let us take our leave. He gave us a security escort so that we need not be afraid of encounters with brigands. As soon as news of our arrival in Alexandria had reached the king, I and my companion were summoned to his presence. In the palace where we were cordially received, we made the appropriate obeisance and then handed him the letters which Eleazar had entrusted us with. In his

64. *Spec.* I, 163.
65. *De ev. praep.*, 8, ch. 60. See n. 16.

eagerness to receive the delegates, he ordered that all the people present who were attending to various jobs be dismissed instantly and that these others should be invited to his presence. This behavior was surprising to all present—for it was his customary routine that any of his subjects who had a petition would be given an audience on the fifth day, while it was not unusual that envoys from kings or foreign peoples had to wait a month before being given a hearing. However, his esteem for these men was very great (particularly when he considered the preeminence of the person who had sent them). Thus having dismissed all bystanders, he waited in his lobby to pay them respects in a state of great anticipation. They arrived and brought the gifts which had been sent to him as well as certain parchments in gilt lettering which contained the divine Law written in their script and language. Its leaves were put together with amazing artistry and joined so that it was impossible to detect where and how they were joined.

The king's obeisance to the Law and to the elders

On seeing these men, the king's first utterances were in the form of questions about their books. They immediately uncovered and unrolled them so that he could see the inscribed parchments. The king stood transfixed in stunned silence and then prostrated himself to the ground seven times. Then he began to speak and said: "I thank you exemplary men for coming to me, and am even more grateful to the esteemed man who sent you and, above all, to the great God whose words these are." Then, unanimously, all visitors and those who were already present, responded: "You have done well, our lord; you have indeed spoken rightly and with great refinement." Deeply moved with joy and happiness, he began to shed tears; for the soul which attains the wonderful and marvelous thing it craves, and has it in its grasp, is prone to weep. Then he restrained himself[66] and ordered them to replace the books, to bind up the testimony, and to seal the law in its cover in its proper manner.[67] He set about to greet each one of them in obeisance and with great show of friendship and then addressed them all:

> Pious men, it seemed right that my first act should be to pay my respects and homage to those exalted words for whose sake you have been brought here and only after that to extend my right hand to each of you in friendship. This is how I have acted. As long as I live, I shall commemorate this day and shall celebrate it since this was the time when I had the privilege of having you come to my presence. This happens to be the very same day on which I defeated King Antigonus* in a fierce naval battle. Therefore it is my pleasure to rejoice with you today with friendship and victuals which sustain a person's joy.

(*Perhaps this is one of the four rulers who took the throne of Alexander of Macedon after his death, as Josephus says at the beginning of book 12.[68])

Then he ordered all the king's satraps and officers in order of seniority to his presence, and for me who was one of those summoned, this was the fulfillment of all my desires.

66. The terminology derives from Gen. 45:1 when Joseph is about to reveal himself to his brothers.
67. Cf. Is. 8:16.
68. *Ant.* XII:1. This is generally considered to be a reference to the sea battle between Antigonus Gonatas and Ptolemy Philadelphus in which Ptolemy was defeated.

He commanded that a pleasant location near his palace should be prepared and bedecked as a resting and lodging place for those distinguished elders, and he said to his servants: "Dispatch all the preparations for the banquet with speed for the sages will eat with me at midday." Then Nicanor, the chief physician, summoned Dorotheus who was responsible for this and ordered him to take the greatest care to show respect and to satisfy everybody in all respects, for such were the king's orders.

The etiquettes for banquets

Now there is an etiquette that goes back to antiquity which is still observed today.* When corn, wine, and olives and anything required for the king's banquets was sent from remote cities, they would be accompanied by representatives of the states who were familiar with their neighbors and their eating habits. Thus if anyone were to come from these provinces to the king's table, he would be given the tasty food he liked; for charges were made in accordance with the customs of the guest so that he would not notice any change whatever [from his regular diet]. This practice was upheld for these elders, thus ensuring that they did not feel alienated on account of their desires.[69] Everything was arranged for them in accordance with their laws such that they could satisfy their thirst and be at ease. For Dorotheus was most conscientious in his supervision of their representatives and implemented his [the king's] wishes by providing generous and unstinting supplies of all appealing food that would rightly and understandably be acceptable to them. Nor did he fail the king in the seating arrangements. For he had ordered him to seat half of them facing him and the rest adjacent to him. Everything that they might need was provided. And thus they were regaled with honor and glory. When they were all seated at the banquet, Dorotheus, who had been instructed by the king to observe Jewish laws in their regard,** saw to it that wise heralds of the holy law and experts in the holy sacraments were summoned to make grace before the meal. But the elders entreated Eleazar, the most senior member of their group, God's priest, to make the festal blessing. He carried out this charge, and with fitting humility and with outstretched arms, he stood in prayer and said: "May the omnipotent God bless you, O King, with all the blessings He has created, and may He grant that you, your wife, children, and friends should enjoy them forever with satiety and everlasting contentment." In response, the distinguished assembly of people applauded him with rapturous cries of thanks and prolonged exultation. Afterwards, each and every one of them proceeded to enjoy the royal dainties that had been arrayed before them with great care and elegance. Under Dorotheus's supervision, the servants had put all their energy into the various tasks assigned to them to ensure that they gave pleasure with their graceful manners and thoughtfulness. Among their ranks were the king's pages and many virtuous persons who held high position at court. Everything was splendidly executed on a grandiose scale.

(*See Josephus book 12 (chapter 9) on this detail.[70])

(**According to Josephus's version, the king dispensed with the services of the

69. Cf. Ps. 78:30.
70. *Ant.* XII:94.

Egyptian sages whom he would have normally summoned.[71] In book 3 (chapter 17),[72] the Hebrew Josephus writes that the Eleazar, the priest mentioned here, is to be identified with the father of the seven brothers, the sons of Hannah, who died a martyr's death during the time of Antiochus. This incident was also described by Josephus in his work entitled *De Machabaeis* which is a Greek word meaning "fighters" (*paladini*).[73])

The king's interrogation of the ten elders during the banquet of the first day

During the time for conversation at the end of the meal, the king entertained them with the honeyed elegance of the stories which he cleverly spun. Then, when they were all seated in their allocated places, he addressed the one who in view of his age and position was to answer first.

1. "How can we ensure enduring peace and tranquillity for the realm?"

After a moment's reflection, he answered thus: "You can achieve this by following God's justice and kindness in all your activities; for should you go so far as to treat the undeserving with kindness and mercy and give due recompense to the righteous, it is likely that even sinners will repent. In this way you will attain peace and tranquillity for your realm."

He said to him, "The utterances of your lips are right."[74]

He turned to the second and asked:

2. "What should be given priority in all one's actions and thoughts?"

He answered: "You should realize that you ought to behave justly in your dealings with others, for then everything you do will go well. You yourself will indeed come to this realization once you become fully aware that even your secret thoughts are known to God. Above all, it is by fearing God that you will succeed in everything. Then you may be sure that no harm will befall you."

He said to him: "Righteousness preceded you."[75] He then asked the third:

3. "How can one acquire and retain faithful[76] friends?"

He answered: "You should behave in such a way that everybody is convinced that you are intent on the good of the entire people under your jurisdiction. You will certainly be prompted to behave thus once you have appreciated the extent to which God seeks the good of all humanity, granting them health, food and everything else they need in due season."

71. *Ant.* XII:97. Although de' Rossi follows Garbitius's rendering of A (184), he notices that Josephus's account is probably more congruent with the context in which the king is said to be respecting the customs of his Jewish guests in that the use of Egyptian priests would be inappropriate and dispensable.

72. *Josippon,* bk. 4, ch. 19 (73–78).

73. The work *De Machabaeis* was attributed to Josephus and incorporated into his *Opera Omnia* in the sixteenth century. It is usually designated 4 Maccabees. De' Rossi derived his false etymology from Johannes Lucidus's *Opusculum.* See ch. 21, n. 11.

74. Cf. Pr. 8:6. Throughout this section, de' Rossi provides his own additions for the king's responses, usually, but not exclusively, inserting a quotation (occasionally freely adapting it for the context) from the Wisdom books of the Hebrew Bible which echoes the sentiments expressed in the responses.

75. Cf. Ps. 85:14.

76. 'Faithful.' This is not an exact translation of 'consentientes' (like-minded).

He said to him: "I approve of your course of action."[77] He asked the fourth:
4. "In passing judgment and punishing offenders in the exercise of government, how can we become well reputed even in the eyes of those who complain about our actions?"
He answered: "Your wish will be fulfilled when you behave very compassionately and are neither arrogant nor irate in your dealings with offenders and do not use your power to treat them unnecessarily harshly. Instead, you should model your actions on God's benevolent ways. He fulfills the desires of all those who love him, and to those whose entreaties He does not favor, He will divulge the errors of their ways in a dream by night or by means of a sign or act. His chastisement of them will not be proportionate to their sin, nor will He use force. Rather, He treats them with compassion and mercy."
He said to him: "Your statement is most refined."[78] He then asked the fifth.
5. "How can one be assured of victory in wars against one's enemies?"
He replied: "You should not put your trust in armies or force. Instead, you should seek God; for when justice is your goal, He will ensure that your plans succeed, and He will always lead you in the paths of righteousness."
He said to him: "You have made my enemies turn tail before me."[79] He asked the sixth:
6. "How can one be sure to be a formidable foe to one's enemies?"
He answered: "You should keep a large military force and supply of arms in reserve for time of war and yet not take to the battlefield precipitously. Rather, you will disregard all those preparations once you have taken note of the extent of God's patience and how that by a mere display of His awesome power He can reduce people to fear and terror."
He said to him: "Awesome indeed is your righteous answer."[80] He asked the seventh:
7. "What is best for us in life?"
He answered: "The knowledge that God is Lord of all creatures and that there is no human being* who is self-sufficient enough to follow his own inclinations though they may lead to righteous deeds; God is King of all the universe and we should beseech Him to direct and guide our steps."

(*If this is meant as a refutation of free will you should disregard it in deference to Rambam's [Maimondes'] discussion of this subject in chapters 5 and 7 of the Laws of Repentance.[81])

He said to him: "I approve your teaching."[82] Then he asked the eighth:
8. "How can one amass riches and possessions in one's lifetime and bequeath the fortune intact to one's family for posterity?"
He answered: "You should pray to God, imploring him to ensure that your success in amassing your acquisitions is always achieved by means of right decisions. And you should instruct your children not to vaunt their wealth and fame, nor to convince

77. Cf. Ps. 5:9.
78. Cf. Ps. 18:31.
79. Cf. Ps. 18:41.
80. Cf. Ps. 65:6.
81. See *Mishneh Torah,* Teshuvah. In ch. 5, Maimonides argues that humans have free will on the basis of *Behold man is become as one of us to know good and evil* (Gen. 3:22), which, in his view, meant that the human species was unique insofar as it knows good and evil and is able to choose between the two options. In ch. 7, he argues that since every human being has free will, he should strive to repent.
82. Cf. Ps. 119:72.

themselves that their wealth was acquired by their own means and intellectual powers. Rather, they should know that the world belongs to God and everything possessed by humans derives from Him."

He said to him: "Let the rich man glory in his wealth."[83] He asked the ninth:

9. "How can one endure what happens with equanimity?"

He answered: "Once you are completely convinced that all human beings are created by God in order to be subjected to the vicissitudes of good and evil and that no one can escape from them; and yet, we should implore God who can grant us the power of endurance."

He said to him: "I shall not add to your grief."[84] Then he said: "You have all certainly given good answers. I shall pose one more question today and then we shall rest and indulge in joyful activities. For in the following six days we shall continue our pleasant camaraderie and I shall receive further instruction from those of you who remain." Then he asked the tenth:

10. "What is the goal of courage?" He answered:

"The ability to choose an inevitably correct stratagem in time of trouble. But you, my lord King, are assisted by God in all your deeds because all your plans are grounded in goodness and justice."

He said to him: "Let the brave glory in your courage."[85]

Then all present applauded and demonstrated their approval. The king addressed the many philosophers who were present and said: "I do indeed regard these men as sages of the highest rank; they surpass all their reputed and famous peers. They have given prompt and correct replies to profound questions and all have made God's just ways as their starting point." Menedemus the philosopher from Eretria answered him on this point and said: "Indeed, my lord King, their method demonstrated their outstanding wisdom; for since all existing beings are governed by God, and man is but one of them, it follows that he will extend His salvation to all those who seek His direction."[86] This explanation pleased the king. He did not ask anything more that day and everybody just returned to celebrate together until sunset.

The questions of the second day

The next day they reassembled in the banqueting hall as on the previous day. When the king decided that the time was right, he continued to seek their instruction and questioned them in order according to the seating arrangements.

He turned to the eleventh and asked:

11. "How can one retain one's wealth?"

After a pause to consider the king's question, he answered him and said:

"You should always be careful to incur only those expenses which are needed in order to maintain the prestige of your realm. You should not dissipate wealth on nonsensical

83. Cf. Jer. 9:22.

84. Cf. Pr. 10:22.

85. Cf. Jer. 9:22.

86. This is not an exact rendering of "it follows that all power and beauty of discourse come from God."

and useless things. And you should always do your utmost to make yourself loved by your people. You should seek their welfare and well-being as long as you live. By considering God's actions you will be impressed by the extent to which He is good to everybody and is Himself the origin of all blessings."

He said to him: "Riches and honor precede you."[87] He asked the twelfth:

12. "How can one be sure to cultivate the truth?"

He answered: "In the first place, you should realize how shameful it is for anybody to lie; how much more so for kings, the lords of the world, who have the power to do whatsoever they like and have no reason to lie. Furthermore, you should also understand that truth is what God desires."

He said to him: "Your teaching is true."[88] He asked the thirteenth:

13. "What constitutes useful doctrine and the fruit of wisdom?"

He answered: "To know that just as you desire protection from all evils and to receive all possible benefits, so too you should entertain the same desires for your citizens and wrongdoers; and you should take even greater pains to act kindly and patiently with the oppressed. Observe God's work—He always looks after all inhabitants of the world with compassion."

He said to him: "I will learn your precepts."[89] He asked the fourteenth:

14. "How can one motivate oneself to be kind and patient with all people?"

He answered: "You should realize that people grow up for the most part in misery and are greatly afflicted by their suffering. They therefore should not be punished hastily nor should one lightly pronounce verdict on them, particularly since life itself is the cause of much of our pain and torment. In view of these considerations, you would surely be disposed to compassion and kindness, especially when you take note of God and the great compassion He extends to all of us."

He said to him: "You are most dear to me."[90] And he asked the fifteenth:

15. "Which is the most important virtue that a king should possess?"

He answered: "He should not be blinded by bribes and should remain alert[91] most of his life, to give priority to justice, and to cling to the friendship of those who pursue righteousness; for does not God love the righteous?"

He said to him: "This shall be the king's rule."[92] He asked the sixteenth:

16. "On what does piety depend?"

He answered: "On your conviction that God's activity and knowledge affects all aspects of existence and that not one act of a human being, be it good or evil, escapes His notice. Consequently, if you learn to behave like God who, as you see, does good to everybody, you will not fail nor stumble in any respect."

He said to him: "Your piety is manifested to me."[93] He asked the seventeenth:

87. Cf. 1Chr. 29:12.
88. Cf. Ps. 119:142.
89. Cf. Ps. 119:73.
90. 2Sam. 1:26.
91. 'Alert.' De' Rossi could apparently find no Hebrew equivalent for 'sobrius' (prudent).
92. Cf. 1Sam. 8:11.
93. Cf. Ps. 26:3.

17. "What constitutes perfect kingship and how should a king behave?"
He answered: "To behave justly. Then, he should have no reason to entertain proud and improper desires. By assessing his position, he will not put his trust in glory or riches and the amassing of possessions will therefore be of no importance to him. God has no desire for extravagances, only justice; so you too, human though you are, should have similar values and should not be tempted to annex other people's lands to your realm."
He said to him: "You have spoken like Melchizedek a perfect king."[94] He asked the eighteenth:
18. "How should one think and act for the best?"
He answered: "When justice is your only concern and you convince yourself that iniquity is in fact the negation of life and the gateway to death. But God favors the righteous who will reap the rewards of their deeds."
He said to him: "All my goodwill is addressed to you."[95] He asked the nineteenth:
19. "How can we enjoy a sleep that is totally undisturbed?"
He answered: "You have asked, lord King, a difficult question, for we have no control over that which occurs during sleep. Rather, a brutish sense takes possession of us, and in such cases, it is only normal for us to be affected by them and to take heed of them. In fact, the truth is that reason has no part to play in nightly visions. Thus we imagine that we are on the sea or traveling aboard a ship or traversing the world as a merchant or carried aloft on wings or wandering from one realm to another people's dominion and other such meaningless incidents. Now although, in my opinion, such a question is difficult to answer, I am convinced that you, King, will desire that all your words and actions are motivated by peaceful and pious intentions. For insofar as you have already proved yourself, you have thought and behaved with wisdom and justice. You do not favor anybody without good reason and do not abuse your power to persecute anyone unjustly. It is therefore likely that the person who is busy in actions and thoughts during the day will experience similar things when he sleeps at night. Thus all who, in their waking moments, concentrate on actions and ideas that by virtue of their good and just objectives also give us pleasure, so too during sleep will they experience emotions and happenings that are just. Such is your situation, lord King, for God has bestowed you for life with a pure soul that bears everything with equanimity."
He said to him: "Now I can sleep peacefully."[96] He turned to the twentieth and said: "You are the last to respond today; after you have finished expressing your opinion, we shall resume our festivities. This is my question":
20. "How can we prevent ourselves from doing that which is unworthy of our station?"
He answered: "If you constantly bear in mind your prominent position and reputation and see to it that your words and actions live up to it, in the knowledge that the great masses over whom you rule will speak about your movements and discuss all your actions. Hypocrisy and simulation certainly do not befit a man of your status. In deference to the eminence of your person and your royal crown, you ought not assume

94. Cf. Ps. 110:4.
95. Cf. Ex. 33:19.
96. Cf. Job 3:13.

another personality. For your people will regard you as the embodiment of all that is good and they will all strive to emulate your ways. But you, lord King, are not of the intriguing and deceiving kind who do not reveal their true nature. You are a real king and because of your virtues have been considered worthy by God to attain a position of prominence which is continually enhanced."

He said to him: "We have listened and shall obey."[97] Joyfully and in good spirits they prolonged the banquet and festivities until the evening stars shone. The king then said: "Let the pious retire in glory." His servants then arranged for the resumption of the proceedings on the following day.

Questions of the third day

Early in the morning[98] of the third day, when they were seated in their customary places in the meeting place and the king deemed the moment opportune, he turned to the twenty-first with the following question:

21. "What is the most difficult aspect of government?"

He answered: "Self-control and not being subject to one's own desires. For all human beings possess certain innate proclivities: the masses are inclined to fill their bellies and satisfy their craving; on account of their pride and standing, kings long to subjugate the peoples under their sway. The fact is that equity should be the measure of all things, and we should endeavor to preserve that which we have been granted by God. But that which does not pertain to us and that which we have no right to possess should not come within the compass of our desires."

He said to him: "Mighty is the king who loves justice."[99] He asked the twenty-second:

22. "How can one be free of the vice of envy so that one is not jealous of others?"

He answered: "You should realize that it is God who assigns wealth and status to all kings, and that no person has sufficient power to become king through his own means. The sure indication of this is that everybody desires its benefits, but nobody attains it—for it is a gift from God."

He said to him: "This is the teaching on jealousy."[100] He asked the twenty-third:

23. "How can we despise our enemies?"

He answered: "You should constantly endeavor to win the hearts of people by demonstration of true friendship; then you will have no reason to fear any enemy. Rather, the person who is so favored and popular with all his acquaintances is endowed with the most precious of divine gifts."

He said to him: "Your consideration is right."[101] He asked the twenty-fourth:

24. "How can one maintain a good reputation and retain the respect of people?"

He answered: "By being generous and using all your powers to procure the well-being of others. But you must entreat God to ensure that you retain these qualities."

97. Cf. Deut. 5:24.
98. 'Early in the morning,' de' Rossi's embellishment.
99. Cf. Ps. 99:4.
100. Cf. Num. 5:29.
101. Cf. Job 35:2.

He said to him: "This shall be my name forever."[102] He asked the twenty-fifth:
25. "To whom ought we vaunt the superiority of our virtues?" He answered:
"Many say that we should do this only in the presence of our close friends. I think otherwise. For as long as we do not exaggerate our virtues, we can speak of them to good purpose in the presence of our antagonists who try to win fame for deeds which are diametrically opposed to our virtues. Perhaps we can help them to learn and become wise. But the best course is to pray to God that these things come to be since He controls the life of all beings."
He said to him: "Your thoughts are profound."[103] He asked the twenty-sixth:
26. "To whom must one show favor?"
He answered: "Indubitably, our parents first and foremost—this is certainly an important God-given commandment—and in second place, our friends.[104] But you, my lord King, have done well. You equally win over and make friends with all people."
He said to him: "May it be good for you and your children."[105] He asked the twenty-seventh:
27. "What deserves our greatest appreciation?"
He answered: "Piety for it is in itself beauty of the highest degree and is rooted in the divinely given attribute of mercy. This, my lord King, you certainly possess, and as a consequence, all blessings are yours."
He said to him: "Your saints shall bless you."[106] He asked the twenty-eighth:
28. "How can a person recover the respected position he lost on account of some misdemeanor on his part?"
He answered: "You, my lord King, should have no reason to fear on this count. You always insist on satisfying the desires of everybody, and because of your kind behavior you gain all people's goodwill, which is more useful than any armament. But whosoever is so foolish as to damage their prestige by committing offense against others should repent by seeing to it that they do not repeat their transgression. On the strength of acceptable deeds they should try to regain the confidence of those they angered, and their honor will be safeguarded. But the ability to take care that one's actions lead to popularity and give nobody, even friends, cause for hatred is a God-given gift."
He said to him: "It is certainly better for us to repent."[107] He asked the twenty-ninth:
29. "How can a person dispel sorrow?"
He answered: "He should take care not to harm anybody, but by loving and kind behavior always try to help. The fruits of this endeavor will be security, peace of mind, and contentment. Furthermore, we need to pray to God that He protects us from the evils which ensnare human beings quite suddenly and beyond one's control—for example, the death of relatives and sickness which infest us. But you, lord King, are pious and no such calamity will befall you."

102. Cf. Ex. 3:15.
103. Cf. Ps. 92:6.
104. 'Friends.' De' Rossi has omitted the phrase 'those equal to oneself.' In the Greek text (228) the wording is taken from the LXX, Deut. 13:6.
105. Cf. Deut. 4:40.
106. Cf. Ps. 145:10.
107. Cf. Num. 14:3.

He said to him: "These have been my aims, and sadness and misery have disappeared."[108] He asked the thirtieth:

30. "What is the highest glory that a person can deserve?"

He answered: "To serve and honor God, not with sacrifices and burnt offerings, but with a contrite and pure heart, and to bear in mind constantly that He is the creator of everything and that He controls everything according to His will. You, my lord King, have already shown that this is your attitude through the number of His servants who are totally dedicated to Him on account of all the signs and wonders that you perform daily."[109]

He said to him: "You have understood fundamental issues."[110] Then with apposite words he complimented and honored them, and all the sages who were present followed his example. They said that these distinguished men were far superior to all the wise because they drew the content of their responses from a divine source. The king then joined them again in the pleasures of the banquet and as the day drew to its close he said to them, "Prepare yourselves for the morrow."[111]

The questions of the fourth day

On the fourth day they were seated in the usual manner when the king saw that the time was opportune for pleasant discourse. He addressed those who had not yet had their turn to respond. He said to the first, namely, the thirty-first, "I shall ask you a question and you shall instruct me."

31. "Is it possible for a person to become astute and alert intellectually by intense diligent study?"

He answered: "The soul's disposition is such that only through the power of God can it be directed to acquire virtues and to repudiate vice."

He said to him: "Your words make sense."[112] He asked the thirty-second:

32. "How should one behave in order to remain in the best of health?"

He answered: "He should use restraint in speech for the sake of equity.[113] But this virtue is unattainable without God's direction."

He said to him: "No secret is withheld from you."[114] He asked the thirty-third:

33. "How can a child show his parents the gratitude they deserve?"

He answered: "A child should honor his father and mother by ensuring that he does nothing to cause them sorrow. However, this is not feasible unless he has God's helpful escort because He is the Creator of all souls and directs them wherever He wishes. His actions and attributes are their guide to good and just opinions and they will bless Him."[115]

108. Cf. Jer. 9:23 and Is. 51:11.
109. 'You, my lord . . . daily,' de' Rossi's embellishment of A (234).
110. Cf. Is. 40:21.
111. 'Prepare . . . morrow,' de' Rossi's addition from Ex. 19:10.
112. Cf. Job 34:35.
113. De' Rossi's circumlocutous way of rendering the Latin word 'temperantia' (self-control).
114. Cf. Dan. 4:6.
115. 'And they will bless Him,' de' Rossi's addition.

He said to him: "May you go in peace to your fathers."[116] He asked the thirty-fourth:
34. "How can one become an attentive listener and student?"
He answered: "When one realizes that all knowledge serves some purpose. A receptive listener is in a position to select from what has been told and apply it usefully when the occasion arises. But this is contingent on God's support; for only with His help do all actions come to a successful conclusion."
He said to him: "The wise man will listen and increase his understanding."[117] He asked the thirty-fifth:
35. "How can one be sure never to infringe the law?"
He answered: "When one realizes that the divine spirit inspired the legislators such that salvation comes to those who observe the laws."
He said to him: "Happy is he that keeps your Law."[118] He asked the thirty-sixth:
36. "What benefits ensue from familial ties?"
He answered: "We must judge the matter from the perspective of eventual occurrence of adverse times when the familial bond becomes helpful. Everybody will come together and be mutually supportive. Depending on the size of the family and frequency of such situations, glory and honor will be theirs, and the ties of the bond will be strengthened. For every family which is held together by love and kindness is indestructible. But when fortune smiles on them and there is prosperity, they will not need such help since each will be self-sufficient. Nevertheless, they ought to pray to God that they do not become dependent on each other and that they are successful in all their endeavors."
He said to him: "Your words bespeak the uprightness of my heart."[119] He asked the thirty-seventh:
37. "How does fearlessness come about?"
He answered: "When one is conscious that one has not harmed one's fellow. This comes about through the kindness of God who probes people's minds and as their spiritual guide always directs them on the path of the good."
He said to him: "You obliterate fear."[120] He asked the thirty-eighth:
38. "How can a person make instantaneous right decisions?"
He said to him: "By constantly musing on the vicissitudes of the human state. Thereby, he will come to understand that it is at God's command that some must leave the light to dwell in darkness, whereas others He raises from the dunghill to reside among world rulers."
He said to him: "Your rulings are just."[121] He asked the thirty-ninth:
39. "How can one avoid laziness and lustfulness?"
He answered: "You should understand and constantly bear in mind that you are lord over an exalted nation and are prince and sire of many peoples. Thus it is not right that your thoughts should stray. Instead, you should aim to be a good administrator. At the

116. Cf. Gen. 15:15.
117. Cf. Pr. 1:5.
118. Cf. Pr. 29:18.
119. Cf. Job 33:3.
120. Cf. Job 15:4.
121. Cf. Ps. 119:137.

same time, you should entreat God that you do not desist from discharging all your duties."

He said to him: "Your doctrine is pure."[122] He asked the fortieth:

40. "How can one detect treacherous and deceitful intriguers?"

He answered him: "You would be justified in thinking that integrity and independence befits everybody. Thus you should observe whether the people around you are true and constant in their behavior and manners by their mode of salutation and greeting, or in the way they consult with you and behave at other social events and meetings. Observe whether they transgress the customary mode of behavior in any way. However, God entreats you, king, to be mindful always that just laws are respected."

He said to him: "You have made their gestures into telltale signs [for us]."[123] He singled each one of them out for praise since all their responses provided the intelligent person with useful information. All the guests followed suit and then they all joined in the delights of all kinds of song and music of the timbrel until nightfall. Then they retired to their tents.

The questions of the fifth day

On the fifth day they took up their designated seats. When the king saw that the moment was right for desirable discourse, he turned to the forty-first and said, "Please tell me":

41. "Who are forgetful and negligent and do not attend to their duties?"

He answered: "He who abandons his children whom he wanted to bring to life, and then makes no effort to bring them up with the necessary provisions. There is surely no person who would not entreat God on behalf of himself as well as for his progeny that they should be blessed with everything. Nevertheless, they should themselves behave meritoriously so that they may benefit from temperance and discretion; but they are blessed by God who have a prudent nature which will enable them to achieve this goal."

He said to him: "You do not forsake those who appeal to you."[124] He asked the forty-second:

42. "How should a man train himself to be a patriot?"

He answered: "He should realize that it is best to live and die in one's own home, and take into account that in a foreign land the poor are despised and abased. Even the rich live abroad in an abased state because the natives will claim that their exile from their own country must have been a punishment for misdemeanors. But you, my lord King, do adhere to your own advice and behave well to everybody else for God has endowed you with a generous spirit. There is no doubt that your generosity will earn you the name 'lover of peoples' and 'father of your subjects.' "

He said to him: "Your observation is right."[125] He asked the forty-third:

43. "How can a man have a peaceful and trusting relationship with his wife?"

122. Cf. Job 11:4.
123. Cf. Ps. 74:4.
124. Cf. Ps. 9:11.
125. Cf. Jer. 1:12.

He answered: "It is well known, my lord King, that the majority of women are bold and proud and are not loathe to undertake anything they think fit. In addition, due to their feeble temperament and reasoning powers, they have a fickle nature which makes them act in a strange fashion. Therefore, whoever is wise and desires the peace of his household should always treat his opposite calmly and gently. Indeed, if he insists on dominating her, he will constantly anger her and provoke her to quarrel. But they will spend their days happily if he speaks and behaves in exactly the right manner; and if, in addition, God confers His kindness on him to this end, there will be happiness and thereby man will be blessed."

He said to him: "You have discovered wisdom."[126] He asked the forty-fourth:

44. "How can a person safeguard himself from all mishaps?"

He answered: "By acting with sound judgment and not deluding oneself into thinking that no shame or harm would ensue. Rather he should consider that he ought to assess and weigh up each and every one of his actions. Thus when he speaks to others or pays attention to what they say, he should always be concerned with standards of justice. Then all potential mishap can be avoided and all his ways directed to God."

He said to him: "Your words support him that stumbles."[127] He asked the forty-fifth:

45. "How can one eradicate a bad temper?"

He answered: "First, you should realize that since you wield power over the many, you could easily depopulate your realm through anger which would be shameful and damaging. Secondly, you should tell yourself that they in every respect bear the yoke and yet do not rebel against you. Accordingly, there would be no reason for you to vent your wrath on them. Moreover, you yourself observe God's deeds which should serve as your model; for you can appreciate how benevolent and patient He is to all those who are dependent on Him."

He said to him: "I will walk ahead and give myself rest."[128] He said to the forty-sixth:

46. "How can we be sure to make the right choices and correct decisions?"

He answered: "We should weigh every action on the scales of equity and set the harmful which is counter to that which is just on the other side; by means of comparison we will be able to determine our right course of action. In the final analysis, it is God who inspires us to make the correct deliberations."

He said to him: "Your word illuminates my path."[129] He asked the forty-seventh:

47. "What is human wisdom?"

He answered: "To make a correct evaluation of all that happens and to take care that one's passions do not lead one to be deposed from one's position, and to perform every action opportunely and with discretion—for one should realize that injuries result from those passions. But one should always seek to preserve this state of affairs by invoking God's help."

He said to him: "The wise man will exult in your wisdom."[130] He asked the forty-eighth:

126. Cf. Pr. 3:13.
127. Cf. Job 4:4.
128. Cf. Ex. 33:14.
129. Cf. Ps. 119:105.
130. Cf. Jer. 9:22.

48. "How can we be warmly received when living abroad?"
He answered: "He should guard against patronizing the natives and to behave in a way that they can feel assured that he already regards them as his equals or superiors. Indeed, God accepts the downtrodden and humble and all human beings do likewise."
He said to him: "May the stranger and sojourner live with you."[131] He asked the forty-ninth:
49. "How can we ensure that the work of our hands will endure?"
He answered: "Our goal should be to fashion them with great beauty and excellence such that all who see them will refrain from destroying them and ensure that nobody would have the audacity to make others like them or request artisans to reproduce replicas without receiving ample reward for their toil. You will be even more conscientious about this matter once you appreciate that God, whose ways we should imitate, performs innumerable and remarkable deeds and rewards all who labor in His work. So you, too, should never oppress your people because God ensures the permanence only of that which is done with justice."[132]
He said to him: "You have established equity."[133] He asked the fiftieth:
50. "How does wisdom affect us and what are its fruits?"
He answered: "A person will be conscious of having committed no evil, and will simply spend all his life as a passionate adherent to the truth. These two states, my lord King, will engender and give rise to a joyful spirit, peace of mind, and well-being which will be advantageous. For by perfecting your ways, you will indeed be able to entertain hope in God."
He said to him: "With your wisdom you have understood."[134]
Then all the assembled company applauded and demonstrated their approval. Full of goodwill and joy, the king ordered that the singers and instrumentalists be summoned. In the meantime, it became dark and drowsiness came over them, and they went to rest until the morning's effluence would bring joy.[135]

The questions of the sixth day

On the sixth day they enjoyed the king's favor. Each of them was summoned by name, and while they were eating to their full, the king turned to the fifty-first and said:
51. "How can a person deflect himself from pride and arrogance?"
He answered: "First, he should assess his position; secondly, he should take stock of the fact that he is a man as well as ruler of people; thirdly, he should understand that God humiliates the proud but elevates and saves the humble."
He answered: "With these instructions let me not be transported by pride."[136] He asked the fifty-second:

131. Cf. Lev. 25:35.
132. De' Rossi's translation of the response is a paraphrase full of appropriate biblical expressions and phrases.
133. Cf. Ps. 99:4.
134. Cf. Is. 10:13.
135. 'Morning's . . . joy,' de' Rossi's addition based on Ps. 65:9.
136. Cf. Ps. 36:12.

52. "Whom should we choose as councillors?"
He answered: "Those who are experienced and those whom you have put to the test and who have proved their loyalty to you, and who share your principles. But it befits the kings of the world to petition God to grant them the ability to recognize those who are endowed with such attributes."
He said to him: "Lead me in your counsel."[137] He asked the fifty-third:
53. "What is a king's most essential possession?"
He answered: "The submission of his people who are fond of their masters. By this means, the bond of love that ties them together is strengthened. But this mutual goodwill is due to God's kindness."
He said to him: "These are the possessions to inherit."[138] He asked the fifty-fourth:
54. "What is the aim of the orator?"
He answered: "To persuade the audience. But it is better to argue on the basis of one's opponent's statements and to prove that he is in error. Then he would influence them to accept the truth of his opinion and repudiate wickedness. However, the art of persuasion is divine."
He said to him: "Your words are sweet to my palate."[139] He asked the fifty-fifth:
55. "How can a ruler of many peoples accommodate everyone with their different religions?"
He answered: "He should make righteousness his goal and set the same condition for everybody, allowing each law-abiding subject to keep his own law. This is what you do, my lord King, for God has granted you strength and rectitude of judgment."
He said to him: "May the ruler consider your position."[140] He asked the fifty-sixth:
56. "About which things ought the living grieve?"
He answered: "When mishap persistently befalls one's friends. For there is no reason to weep for the dead who have already reached their resting place. Only those who are self-interested would grieve about such things. But God alone can guard us from all mishap."
He said to him: "You have spoken the truth and the living will take it to heart."[141] He asked the fifty-seventh:
57. "What is it that causes men to be despised and their dignity debased?"
He answered: "Arrogance stemming from self-confidence; for in the end, pride will have a fall. But it is God who is the King of Glory and He favors whosoever He wishes."
He said to him: "This is the rebuke of the accursed arrogant."[142] He asked the fifty-eighth:
58. "While I live, whom should I trust?"
He answered: "Those who associate with you out of friendship and not because they are afraid of you or show allegiance to you out of deference to your powerful position when their own self-interest is their only objective. But the former will demonstrate the bond

137. Cf. Ps. 73:24.
138. Cf. Josh. 19:51.
139. Cf. Ps. 119:103.
140. Cf. Eccl. 10:4.
141. Cf. Eccl. 7:2.
142. Cf. Ps. 119:21.

of friendship, while the latter are witnesses to their own fraudulence and will always nurture their anger. Whoever loves money and has wealth and possessions as their objective is likely to be a liar and will not keep good faith with his masters. But you, my lord king, are in a good position: you attract the good will of everybody since God has already favored your deeds."

He said to him: "Your testimonies are faithful indeed."[143] He asked the fifty-ninth:

59. "What preserves our kingdom?"

He answered: "Extensive supervision of the judges and officers you appoint in order to ensure that they do not make corrupt decisions and behave deviously to the detriment of your people. You, my lord king, have been most solicitous in this regard. With God's help, you have deliberated carefully about everything in your charge."

He said to him: "I shall stand on my guard."[144] He asked the sixtieth:

60. "What is it that conserves in us the hope to win favor and respect?"

He answered: "Righteousness which validates everything and removes all iniquity. Just as you, my lord King, have always based your government on righteousness and justice because you have found favor in the eyes of God."

He said to him: "Your speech is endowed with grace."[145] Then to the sixty-first he asked:

61. "How can one feel at peace in war?"

He answered: "When you are sure that you have made thoughtful preparations for battle and have been conscientious in providing everything that is needed.[146] The soldiers will then feel assured and do their best to please you; for they will know that you, their king, desires the well-being of his servants and that due to God's benign influence, you have the means and intention to recompense and give credit to all those who take their lives in their hands in loyalty to you."[147]

He said to him: "This gives me enduring peace of mind."[148]

Then he showed his approval to them all and treated them with honor and respect. He invited them individually to participate again in the merrymaking and jollifications. When the sun went down, each man went in glory to his bower, his bed,[149] until dawn.

The questions of the seventh day

On the seventh day, the banqueting hall was prepared and bedecked with even greater splendor and magnificence in view of the large assembly present which included many ambassadors from all corners of the world. The king's courtiers had gone posthaste to summon them all so that they could relax and participate in the festivities of that day.[150] Having waited for an opportune moment to address them, the king then turned to the sixty-second and asked:

143. Cf. Ps. 93:5.
144. Cf. Hab. 2:1.
145. Cf. Ps. 45:3.
146. This is a correct rendering of the Latin text, but it is not in the Greek (273).
147. 'The soldiers . . . you' is not a literal rendering of the Latin text.
148. Cf. Ps. 132:14.
149. 'His bower, his bed,' cf. S.S. 1:16.
150. 'The king's courtiers . . . day,' de' Rossi's addition.

62. "How can we avoid being deceived by the words of a troublemaker?"
He answered: "By careful evaluation of the speaker, the contents of his speech and the subject of his declamation. This is accomplished by various different examinations, and by going over the same ground in different ways. However, the possession of a fine mind which enables one to make instantaneous judgment on everything that is brought to one's notice is a blessing from God. Such a mind, my lord, you possess, for your intellectual faculties are as bright as the lightning in the heavens."
He said to him: "The charmer can gain no advantage with you."[151] He asked the sixty-third:
63. "Why do the majority of humans fail to embrace reason?"
He answered: "By nature, man is constantly inclined to follow his passions and they are the source of nothing but violence, destructiveness, and avarice. Reason, on the contrary, will denounce anyone who possesses those two [vices]. It dedicates all its devotees to it by imposing laws and teachings that serve to restrain them so that they pursue righteousness at all costs, in all their dealings. But even in these matters one should seek God's kindness for all our desires are under His control."
He said to him: "You pronounce reason and understanding."[152] He asked the sixty-fourth:
64. "To what matters should kings pay most attention?"
He answered: "The laws, so that as a result of their desire for justice, a good reputation and honor should be theirs. This is your position, my lord. You walk in God's ways and place all your resources in His laws and have therefore established a lasting name for yourself."
He said to him: "Your law is my delight."[153] He asked the sixty-fifth:
65. "Whom should one appoint as leaders of the people?"
He answered: "Those who hate iniquity and cultivate those norms of behavior which ensure them a good reputation. They do not deviate from the path of equity, just like you, my lord King, upon whose head God has placed a crown of justice."
He said to him: "You are provident."[154] He asked the sixty-sixth:
66. "Whom should one appoint as captains of our armies?"
He answered: "The courageous and the just and those who prefer to capture people alive rather than spill their blood in order to gain a reputation for military prowess. Indeed, just as God continually seeks the best for all people, so you, my lord King, by adhering to His ways, will tread on the right way and good path at all times."
He said to him: "You have good counsel and sound wisdom."[155] He asked the sixty-seventh:
67. "Which men should one admire?"
He answered: "Those who have acquired wealth and possessions with honor and distinction and yet find favor and gain the approval of all men. So you, my lord king,

151. Cf. Eccl. 10:11.
152. Cf. Pr. 2:6.
153. Cf. Ps. 119:174.
154. Cf. Ex. 18:21.
155. Cf. Pr. 8:14.

gain the admiration of all who set eyes on you, for you have achieved this because God recognizes the uprightness of your heart."

He said to him: "Your words utter the uprightness of my heart."[156] He asked the sixty-eighth:

68. "On what matters ought kings to spend most of their time?"

He answered: "Reading books, particularly chronicles of the reigns of various kings[157] so that they can ensure the security and safety of those who live under their aegis. By means of these studies, your caring God will set right your plans and you will attain a wondrous reputation throughout the world."

He said to him: "This is surely contained in your book."[158] He asked the sixty-ninth:

69. "How should we organize our life, and what should we do in our hours of leisure and relaxation?"

He answered: "We should concentrate on matters that require peace and quiet, and actions that are pleasing and equitable and which therefore bring honor to our name.[159] Indeed, on many occasions, insignificant and trifling things yield us a perspective on important and valuable matters. Indeed, my lord King, by virtue of your experience and maturity, you are already an expert in that which pertains to human actions. It is therefore enough that you concentrate on those matters with due regard to the dignity and prestige you have attained through God's kindness."

He said to him: "Lead me in your counsel."[160] He asked the seventieth:

70. "What is a reasonable way of behaving when we invite friends to a banquet?"

He answered: "You should choose your guests from those who have a love of learning and who are able to make appropriate suggestions about the maintenance of the realm and the government of your people. The company of such people will be sweeter than the honeycomb. For they are refined and endowed with all the best virtues and therefore find favor in the eyes of God. You, my lord King, rejoice in such a reputation, being renowned as a man instructed by God in all matters."

He said to him: "You please me very much."[161] He asked the seventy-first:

71. "Which is preferable for the people: that a commoner be elected as king or one that is of royal descent?"

He answered: "Rightfully the one who is naturally most loved and cherished should be chosen. For there have been kings of royal descent who have ruled their nations with a heavy hand and imposed a harsh rule upon them. Likewise, there have been commoners who have risen to high station and then behaved like the former. In fact, since they had already experienced and suffered the bitter grapes of poverty and other afflictions, once on the throne, they would make their subjects taste gall and wormwood and treat them more harshly than had their former masters. But as I said, the

156. Cf. Job 33:3.

157. 'Chronicles . . . Kings,' a loose translation of 'accounts of official travels.'

158. Cf. Ps. 56:9.

159. In the Greek text (228), this refers to the watching of plays; the Latin text, however, does not explicitly refer to plays although it is implied: "Contemplanda sunt illa quae sobrie et cum animi contractione adornantur."

160. Cf. Ps. 73:24.

161. Cf. 2Sam. 1:26.

person whose soul is predisposed to purity and whose humane nature flashes with sparks of kindness is the best ruler and will succeed in government. So you, my lord King, are not only renowned for your rule and your prestigious wealth, but also for the humility and honesty which God has bestowed on you. Therefore, you are preeminent among men and have won the allegiance of everybody."

He said to him: "Your righteousness belongs to the king's son."[162] He asked the seventy-second:

72. "What is the most essential aspect of government?"

He answered: "A perpetual state of peace for his subjects and the assurance that the prosecutor of justice will reach his verdicts swiftly. These conditions can be fulfilled as long as the king shuns evil and loves good and holds his people dear to him, protecting them from all mishap. Just like you, my lord King; you have always hated those who behave iniquitously. By ruling with equity you have won a distinguished reputation, for God has always stood by you, and you possess an immaculate soul which is not marred by any defect."

He said to Him: "Indeed, may the king rein in righteousness."[163]

When this speech had come to an end with applause and acclaim, the king was brimming with goodwill and joy on account of the successful outcome of his questions. He ordered that a large bowl of spiced wine should be brought to him and all the company of sages. To the elders he said: "You have brought me a divine blessing. God has graced me with the great benefit of your wisdom and knowledge; for you have taught me all I need to know about government." He said that each one of them was to be given three talents (i.e., of silver) from the king's treasury together with the slave boy who was to transfer the money to them. This arrangement met with the approval of all the nobles and assembled sages. The merriment of the banquet continued with ever-increasing intensity all that day for the king was jubilantly happy about his encounter with these sages.

My dear brother, I realize that I have been prolix in my narration, but being wise, you will not hold it against me because I found that the wisdom of those sages was truly remarkable. On the spot, they were able to give correct responses to profound questions which would normally require a considerable length of time to evaluate correctly. And I was not the only one to be amazed both by the astuteness of the interrogator whose every question contained subtle and deep ideas, and also by the intellectual faculties of the sages, all of whom, to our amazement, in succession, gave valuable responses. Not only I, but also many people of integrity, particularly the philosophers who were present, looked on with admiration.

Now I am also very well aware that in all probability, this discourse of mine will seem implausible and I might appear to be a trickster. But it should be realized that I would shame my good name if I had put falsehood and lies in writing—as soon as it had become public knowledge, my perfidy would be exposed. This would certainly be disgraceful. Indeed, it would even be shameful to truncate such precious accounts or to

162. Cf. Ps. 72:1.
163. Cf. Is. 32:1.

omit the tiniest detail. Truly, I have been totally honest and have written nothing but the truth, neither more nor less. Furthermore, my brother, it will not have escaped your notice that although I was actually involved in the event and was an eyewitness, I had the good idea of writing the entire story on the basis of the information which I procured from scholars since they never fail to examine, thoroughly investigate, and record in writing all statements and actions involving the king—even a law that might concern one of his friends. As you know, it is his custom that everything which was said or happened on the days of his public audiences is put on record. This is a truly excellent system. For before commencing on new business, all the minutes of the previous day are read out to him, and should any error be discovered, it can be swiftly rectified. As for me, as I said, I have avoided errors by transcribing everything from the books which contain faithful transcripts of all their transactions. Now I have sent it to you, my brother, since I know how much your dear soul desires all useful and valuable learning.

The segregation of the elders on an isolated island and how they chose a translation which was unanimously approved

Three days after the events hitherto described, the wise Demetrius brought the elders to an island remote from Alexandria over the jetty which was seven-eighths of a mile in length. After they had crossed the bridge, he settled them in the northern part of the island. In this beautiful and glorious place overlooking the sea, far from the madding crowd and all noise and bustle, they convened. Everything they required in the way of sustenance and other necessities was provided. He exhorted them to make every effort to produce an accurate and lucid translation of the Law. They applied themselves to the task in the following manner: Each man prepared an independent translation of each portion. The translations were then synchronized and only the most suitable version which had met with unanimous approval was then written down under the supervision of Demetrius. Such was their daily working routine which would last until the ninth hour [i.e., 3 P.M.]. Afterwards, they would go and take the afternoon air to tend to their bodily comforts. Whatever they requested was granted. In addition to these arrangements, Dorotheus also supplied them with the provisions which he prepared for the king. They would get up early in the morning, go to the king's palace to greet the king and would then return home. Having washed their hands in the sea (for it is a Jewish regulation), they would pray to God and diligently work on the reading and correct interpretation of each section. They were asked as to why they washed their hands before prayer. They replied that it served to demonstrate and prove that they were innocent of all guilt, for the hands are the perpetrators of all deeds. In this pious and holy state, they could thus bring everything to a just end. Every day, as I said, they would assemble in that idyllic place with its pure air and rich resources.[164] Far removed from all noise and the madding crowd, they could have peace of mind while they attended to their designated task. And so it came about that they completed the

164. 'Rich resources.' The Latin (and Greek) texts only speak about the peace and light of the place.

translation within seventy-two days—corresponding to the number of translators, a coincidence which seemed to have been deliberate on their part.

The ratification of the translation by the entire Jewish community

When the men had finished the translation completely, Demetrius read it out to the entire assembled Jewish community who had convened there—the elder translators were also present. The translation received the highest praise from the entire Jewish populace who acknowledged the great service the elders had performed. They also paid homage and respect to Demetrius who had supervised them, and they asked him to grant the favor of presenting their leaders with a version of their translation since it would be highly valued by them. When they had completed their reading of the volumes of the Law, the priests, the leading elders of the translators, the city leaders, and heads of the communities who were present said that since the translation had been executed with such precision and accuracy, it should remain as it was for all time and should not be changed in any way. This pronouncement met with the approval of all present. Afterwards, Demetrius ordered that they should issue a stringent decree in accordance with Jewish custom, denouncing anyone who might have the audacity to meddle with the text by means of additions, omissions, or alterations of any kind.[165] This decree was to be fully implemented in order to ensure that the translation would be preserved intact for all time.

When the king received news of all this, he was utterly delighted. He was justified in thinking that under these conditions the work in which he had been involved would be permanent. The entire text of the Law was read out to him and he marveled at the wisdom of the legislator. In this state of wonder he said to Demetrius: "How come that no historian or poet ever thought to mention this noble and wondrous work in their writings?"* Demetrius replied: "My lord King, this Law is holy and divine. It so happens that certain Jews[166] who dared to speak about it were struck down by God and therefore desisted from their endeavor. In fact, I heard that the wise Theopompus wished to insert some passages from the Law into his history; he then fell ill and became crazy and deranged for a whole month. However, when his sickness abated, he besought God to let him know the cause of this occurrence. Enlightenment came to him at night. The sickness was brought about by his sin—for he wanted to put divine words into a human text and to publicize them to all and sundry. He then desisted from his work and, according to report, he repented and was healed."[167]

(*Why did the gentile poets and historians not mention the Torah?)

As we said, after the king had heard all this, he received the copy of the complete translation of the Law from Demetrius, prostrated himself before it in pious veneration, and ordered that everybody should take great care of those revered books and

165. 'Addition . . . alterations.' Note de' Rossi's use of terminology normally applied to the Hebrew text of the Bible.

166. 'Jews.' In A (313) there is no explicit reference to Jews.

167. 'Repented and healed,' cf. Is. 6:10. De' Rossi omits A (316) which refers to another tragedy which befell Theodectes when he tried to insert 'the holy words' into his plays.

treat them with due respect for their sanctity. He also implored the translators to come and visit him often after their return to their own land. Now, he admitted, it was right for him to send them home. However, if they should once again honor him with their presence, he would welcome them with great pleasure, as was right in the case of such distinguished friends. He would also regale them with gifts which would give them pleasure. He then ordered that lavish arrangements should be made for their journey. They were all given precious gifts (presents for the translators and for Eleazar):[168] three changes of garments for each of them,[169] a cup worth a talent, and all the vestments of their ministry, magnificent finery, commensurate with their high station. To Eleazar the priest he sent, with their escort, ten couches with silver legs and all their furnishings; a cup worth thirty talents and ten changes of garments; a purple robe; a finely decorated crown; thirty pieces of fine linen; bowls, strainers, and flagons for the holy libations. He also wrote to him with the plea that he should not prevent any of the men from returning at any time should they so wish; for he always valued company such as theirs and preferred to lavish his wealth liberally on men of such stature rather than to squander it on less valuable things.

So, my brother, I have fulfilled my promise and unfolded the story of all that happened in all honesty and truth. I trust that the pleasure you gain from it will be much greater than that which you derive from engrossing yourself in the sayings of the fable-spinners. For I know that you have a passion for worthwhile studies and spend most of your time in such pursuits. If I manage to achieve anything else of worth, I shall be sure to send it to you as a gift for your perusal. Thereby you will not be deprived of the fine reward which attends all like you who cultivate knowledge.

168. 'Presents . . . Eleazar' is a gloss in the Latin translation.
169. De' Rossi omits 'two talents of gold.'

PART THREE ENTITLED WORDS OF UNDERSTANDING

I beseech thee, Lord of the universe, for whose kindness I have ever hoped to aid my work,
Be pleased with this book. Grant me strength, and the wise and tranquil heart for which I long.
With Your light enlighten the countenances of all who uphold Torah with upright heart. If I have erred,
It is precious in my eyes and of merit to them that they take pen against my wrongful suppositions
and, by the letter of truth, reduce my words to naught. To help not harm is all I have desired.
Yet do I ask of them this mark of favor,—that to this work on which I have toiled so long
They turn with good will and respond in moderation, even if they think to destroy what I have thought to build.
For through due consideration of my meaning, they will they see that I have answered all objections.
Have I not, like the best of farmers, extracted every thorn from this, my garden of delights?
The words of understanding in my book are for the wise of heart; indeed, it were my wish that it would go to the wise of heart alone.
They will judge if my feet have walked the proper path in every subject, or if I have strayed.
Dreamers, and layabouts, lovers of slumber Turn aside from me as I have turned my face from you—
Until your heart awakes; then perchance, if aught of truth I have revealed, you shall remember me for good.
But without Your help, Rock of all creation, it would be impossible to begin a praiseworthy enterprise as I have done.
Therefore, I beseech You, God great in mercy, accept my work and say to me (although I do not merit such reward),
"Commence and complete, and then rejoice, for strength and bounteous blessings have I ordained for you.
Foes and opposers all will yet embrace you, confessing that for nothing they rebelled against you."
Therefore in Your blessed name will I gird myself with valor, I shall prosper, for in You I place my trust.

Book of mine, if they ask you when you go abroad: "From whom are you and to whom you are directed?"
Say: "I am a poor man's work, one who cares not for wealth, but may your house be full.
He is of the red family,[1] Azariah is his name, and he prays to God that His help be with me.
He has sent me, an offering to all men of truth; but to all others, has he commanded: 'Stay your hands.' "

Lo, a pure soul have I planted, saplings of knowledge, as in a garden.
Come take, according to your fancy, whatever fruit or lily.
Should you make some pleasant gain, to God alone break out in joy.
For it is He who grants the power to procure wisdom and fathom WORDS OF UNDERSTANDING.

1. I.e., de' Rossi.

CHAPTER ONE

On the differences between multifaceted and homogeneous study. How we have chosen to adopt layered eclectic study in the chapters of this book. May our God bestow His graciousness upon us.

THUS speaks Azariah de' Rossi:

In the introduction to this book, I designated the third part of the book for the inclusion of certain scholarly subjects which to my mind deserved attention. Now with divine help I shall fulfill my promise. The reader will observe that the discourses do not follow one line of thought, but that their sheaves encompass different points and split into diverse offshoots.[2] Some chapters will bear some relation to the previous section, the "Splendor of the Elders," while others will have nothing in common with it. And even in the latter category, there will be no uniformity. Nevertheless, I have bound them all together for the same reason given by our rabbis of blessed memory for the grouping together of some of the minor prophets (even though their sanctity would guarantee their preservation). As they said in Bava Batra:[3] "Since it is small, it may get lost." Thus we shall speak about an assortment of subjects which will bear no relation to each other. It will be like a garden full of different plants. On every occasion the visitor to the garden will choose the flower or fruit which appeals to him because of its taste or appearance. I planned that each chapter should contain citations of many sages which are truly deserving of consideration. Accordingly, I called this part of the work which is separate from the preceding translation by the appropriate title "Words of Understanding."

Now this method of study which has many objectives, as we indicated, is often used by gentile scholars, it being highly appreciated by many erudite persons.[4] Since, however, some of our own people might regard it as an innovation which has not gained currency, I decided that my best plan would be to devote this initial chapter to an appreciative evaluation of each of the two methods of study, the one unitary and homogeneous, the other variegated and eclectic.[5] As I see it, this investigation is inextricably linked to another question; namely, is it more advantageous for those in quest

2. De' Rossi uses harvesting imagery both at the beginning and the end of this chapter which, according to stylistic requirements, I have sometimes retained, sometimes disregarded.

3. B. B.B. 14b. This is said of the book of Hosea who, according to the rabbis, lived before Isaiah, Amos, and Micah. They argued that Hosea's prophecy was placed together with the minor prophets because, due to its small size, it could not be put in a separate category lest "it get lost."

4. De' Rossi's work belongs to the genre of *miscellanea.* For a discussion of this genre, see translator's introduction.

5. For a discussion of the structure of the book, see translator's introduction.

of learning to learn from many people or to acquire for themselves one permanent teacher? Since one of these alternatives must necessarily be more commendable, the problem arises as to why our sages of blessed memory praised both methods equally, seeming to treat each of the two in a uniform manner. On two occasions in the first chapter of Avot they make the heartfelt statement:[6] "Get yourself a teacher." But in chapter 4, Ben Zoma says:[7] "Who is wise? He who learns from all people as it is written, *From all my teachers have I got understanding* (Ps. 119:99)." However, the problem is resolved when one investigates other statements of our rabbis of blessed memory on the subject in question. In tractate Eruvin, they say:[8] "The Galileans do not retain their learning because they do not study with one teacher." Similarly, in tractate Ḥullin, Rav Zera mocks at Joseph bar Ḥiyya for learning from everybody and anybody.[9] In other words, they were in favor of having one teacher. Consequently, the statement about learning from everybody must have another connotation. It appears to be a directive for us to take care to pursue learning in a spirit of humility which will indeed be a great asset to us in our endeavors. When we realize that there may be some chance of acquiring some wisdom from even an uncultivated person, we should not stand on our dignity and arrogantly spurn it. Rather, we should grasp it until it becomes ours. Then learning can issue from every place. We shall define a person of such a disposition as a sage and consider it more appropriate to learn Torah from him than from someone who is the exact opposite. This is the thrust of Rabbi Aqiva's statements in Berakhot, Avot d'Rabbi Nathan, and Bereshit Rabbah[10] which he made in reference to the verse, *If you have done foolishly in lifting up yourself* (Pr. 30:32). For in his exegesis of the verse he said: "If you debase yourself for words of Torah you shall ultimately be elevated by them." And in the same context[11] and in Yevamot,[12] he applied the verse in connection with the incident involving Levi bar Sisi and stated: "Why were you despised with regard to words of Torah? Because you were concerned with your own self-aggrandizement." Furthermore, in Taᶜanit and Makkot, Rabbi Ḥanina was not ashamed to announce:[13] "I have learnt a great deal from my teachers . . . but most of all from my students." There is also the statement of Rava in Qiddushin on the question of betrothals which cannot be consummated:[14] "Bar Ahina (who was his disciple) explained the matter to me with regard to the verse, *When a man takes a woman to be his wife and has intercourse with her* (Deut. 24:1)." Alternatively, we may resolve the contradiction which the maxims of Avot seem to present by the method indicated in the first chapter of Avodah Zarah: namely, we should learn oral traditions (*gemara*) from one teacher, but with regard to

6. M. Avot 1:6, 16.
7. Ibid. 4:1.
8. B. Eruv. 53a.
9. B. Ḥull. 18b.
10. B. Ber. 63b (where the story is told in the name of R. Jose bar Ḥanina); ARN, rec. A, ch. 11 (46); B.R. 81:2 (969).
11. I.e., B.R. 81:2.
12. B. Yev. 105a. As Cassel notes ad loc., the passage is more fully cited in P. Yeb. 12 (1) 13a. Levi b. Sisi is chosen to teach the people of Simona. He was put on a platform and asked three questions which he was unable to answer. R. Aqiva explained that his failure to answer their questions was "because you behave proudly" (i.e., let yourself be elevated and put on a platform above the people).
13. B. Taᶜanit 7a; B. Makk. 10a.
14. B. Qidd. 51a.

matters which may be logically deduced (*sevara*), many opinions are necessarily acquired from many people.[15] Accordingly, when we return to our initial consideration, we may conclude that static type of study which has a single purpose is undoubtedly far more useful in bringing us to one objective than the eclectic method which (like the manna) produces several savors.[16] Thus, the saying goes:[17] "Nobody got the better of me save the person who has one occupation." And yet there is an advantage to the variegated method; for although it may not be as useful as the static type, it is in fact more pleasurable and enjoyable. It may be compared to a varied menu where by reason of its diversity, the enjoyment is enhanced.[18] Perhaps this is one of the points the rabbis of blessed memory wanted to convey when they said in Avodah Zarah and Eruvin:[19] "A man should not study mounds of Torah at a time . . . Rava said, 'Our rabbis knew this well but disregarded it.' " In other words, they were attracted to the pleasurable activity of pursuing much knowledge, but they were unable to retain it all. Seneca the philosopher made the same point when he compared such people to a stomach stuffed full with all manner of foods which cannot be digested properly nor naturally absorbed.[20] This opinion was shared by the physician Galen in his commentary to the first book of *In morbis acutis*[21] and by Avicenna (in book 1, fen 3).[22] In any case, apart from the additional element of pleasure which the eclectic method provides, it is also commendable for another amazing benefit it confers. It is mentioned by our rabbis of blessed memory in the above-cited passage in Avodah Zarah;[23] in other words, it enables one to acquire reasoning powers and good judgment which may also be applied to any new subject which comes to our notice. When we amass observations and general information regardless of whether we reach different objectives, our eyes are opened and we are able to examine any matter which requires intellectual consideration with sharper analytical insight. Perhaps this is also what our rabbis of blessed memory meant when they said in Berakhot and Shabbat:[24] "A person should repeat his learning even though he does not understand what he says and then later he will come to understand and discuss it." For whatever method we employ, profit is to be expected from our quest for wisdom. Thus with the help of our rock we will adopt the eclectic method for these chapters. It will not be without appreciable advantage in that it enables us to strengthen our deductive

15. B. A.Z. 19a.

16. De' Rossi is alluding here to a popular Midrash that the taste of the manna varied according to the palate of the one who ate it. See, e.g., S.R. 5:9.

17. This saying is attributed to Maimonides by Simeon ben Zemaḥ Duran in *Sefer ha-Tashbeṣ*, pt. 1, responsum 72, and is directed against R. Abraham ben David (Rabad), the critic of his *Mishneh Torah*. According to I. Twersky (*Rabad of Posquières*, 195), the saying could well have been authentic since Maimonides complains elsewhere of having to expend his energies on many different disciplines instead of concentrating on study of Torah.

18. De' Rossi may have derived this analogy from Quintilian (see n. 26) who compares variegated study to a variety of foods which refreshes the stomach.

19. B. A.Z. 19a; B. Eruv. 54b.

20. Seneca, *Ad Lucilium, Ep. II*, 4–5: "Fastidientis stomachi est multa degustare: quae ubi varia sunt et diversa non alunt."

21. This is a reference to Galen's commentary, *In librum Hippocratis de acutorum victu* I, XIX (469).

22. Avicenna, *Liber canonis*, lib. 1, Fen 3, doctrina 2, ch. 7. De' Rossi consulted both the Latin and Hebrew translations of the *Canon*.

23. B. A.Z. 19a.

24. This quotation is a conflation of B. Ber. 63b and B. Shabb. 63a.

powers and, as we have already demonstrated, is by its very nature gratifying. Should you examine the works of the greatest gentile orators, you will find that they too sung its praises. In the third part of his *Rhetoric*[25] and in the fifth book of his *Letters,*[26] Cicero describes the narration of different stories as pleasing to the ear. And he claims that histories which include accounts of rises, falls, and revolutions are usually appreciated and hold the attention of the audience. In book 9 (chapter 1), Quintilian also said that it is a natural phenomenon to enjoy variety.[27] Moreover, in book 12 (chapter 11) [*sic*], he wrote that variegated study wards off lassitude and fortifies the soul.[28] To my mind, it has this special characteristic because man is himself in possession of many faculties which have different functions. A similar idea is expressed in the third section of the *Kuzari* with regard to the saintly person.[29] It is said there that each of the faculties will derive enjoyment commensurate with that which falls within its own capacity and that the one faculty will not fail as a result of variegated study, but rather that all the other faculties will come to enjoy the strength which is thereby accrued. This is undoubtedly one of the reasons for which the person who professionally occupies himself with Torah will have cause to be happy about his study of the Babylonian Talmud. For according to a statement in Sanhedrin,[30] the Babylonian Talmud is a mixture of Scripture, Mishnah, and Talmud. Thus it embraces the disciplines of physics, metaphysics, and logic. In addition, as the sage states in the *Kuzari,* the art of dialectic reaches the height of perfection in the Talmud.[31] Thus, the person who is engrossed in its study derives sustenance and enormous satisfaction. It is said in Bava Meṣia that Rav Zera undertook forty fasts when he went to the Land of Israel in order to forget the Babylonian Talmud.[32] If that is so, it was only due to his concern about the extent of the casuistry employed by the Babylonian sages. It is for this reason that in Sanhedrin the Babylonians were called *ḥovelim* (those who injure) as opposed to the Palestinian sages who on account of their congenial and civilized conduct were called *noʿam* (graciousness).[33]

In conclusion, it transpires that whatever the relative merits of the eclectic and homogeneous types of study, something appealing and satisfying is to be gained from either method. Although one method might be superior to the other in achieving a particular objective, they are both capable of imparting pleasure and benefiting the reader. God prompted me to leave for posterity the offering of a book which contains

25. The *Rhetoric* is probably a reference to the ps. Ciceronian work *Rhetorica ad Herennium* III, 12, 22: "et auditorem quidem varietas maxime delectat."

26. *Ep. ad fam.* V, 12, 4.

27. *Institutio.* The passage to which he is referring appears to be IX, IV, 59.

28. De' Rossi refers to bk. 11, ch. 12, but the passage is I, XII, 4: "We must remember that variety serves to refresh and restore the mind."

29. *Kuzari* III, par. 5. According to this passage, the saintly person is one who obeys his physical and mental faculties without exceeding the limits.

30. B. Sanh. 24a. "What does Bavel [Babylonian, i.e., the Babylonian Talmud] connote? Rabbi Johanan answered: 'That Scripture, Mishnah and Talmud is intermingled [ballul] in it.' "

31. *Kuzari* III, par. 70 (but said by the Kazar not the sage).

32. B. B.M. 85a. As Cassel notes ad loc., the text reads "a hundred fasts." Perhaps de' Rossi was confusing this passage with a preceding passage in which Rav Joseph is said to have undertaken forty fasts.

33. B. Sanh. 24a. The expression "those who injure" and "graciousness" are derived from Zech. 11:7: *And I took two staves, the one I called graciousness and the other I called binders* [or *injuries*].

some useful matters, and with good reason too, for I am about sixty years old and have no male children.[34] But good deeds may preserve the name of the deceased on his inheritance.[35] Now I found that in benefiting myself I also benefited others[36] and could sell abundant corn and bread for one type of Minnith wheat and balsam.[37] I said to myself: Let me beat that which I have gleaned from the bundles of small swathes quite apart from the larger sheaves and then I shall offer someone of like mind small amounts of parched corn, balsam, and honey.[38] Perhaps the reader will savor them and derive some enjoyment. With this "son" of mine, I hope that the God of my salvation shall, as the rabbis of blessed memory say (in Yevamot and in tractates Berakhot and Sheqalim of the Palestinian Talmud), give me the privilege of dwelling perpetually in the tent of the eternal Most High.[39] Then, as the rabbinic saying (in Sanhedrin and Berakhot) goes, my lips shall murmur in the grave.[40] Or perhaps to a greater or lesser extent I shall be remembered for good like Ben Bebai whose task as one of the guardians of the sacred watch was to prepare the wicks, as is stated in tractates Pe'ah and Sheqalim of the Palestinian Talmud.[41] For in all my endeavors I have directed myself towards truth and righteousness. It is possible that I shall make some errors in this book of mine which would displease myself no less than my reader. I therefore would like to inform any intelligent and honorable person that I am most prepared to receive his criticisms of my work and specification of my mistakes in clear terms in order to remove any stumbling block from the path of our people. But if he is magnanimous he will also not refrain from giving me credit where due, since we all deserve it. Then may he receive a complete reward from our God.

34. De' Rossi was writing in 1571–72. One would therefore assume that he was born about 1511. The expression "I am about sixty years old" is a deliberate imitation of the expression used by R. Eleazar ben Azariah in M. Ber. 1:5.

35. Cf. Ruth 4:5.

36. This is a quotation of Pr. 11:25 which is also used in B. Sanh. 92a to prove that one who teaches Torah in this world will be privileged to teach it in the world to come.

37. This is an allusion to Ezk. 27:17: *they traded for you merchandise wheat of Minnith and balsam and honey and oil and balm* and its interpretation in E.R. 3:17 that many products could be manufactured from Minnith wheat. Note how he employs harvestry imagery here as at the beginning of the chapter.

38. Cf. Ruth 2:7; 2:15.

39. B. Yev. 96b; P. Ber. 2 (1) 4b; P. Sheq. 2 (5) 47a. The word "forever" or "worlds" (*olamim*) in *O that I may dwell in your tent forever* (Ps. 61:5) is interpreted as referring to a deceased person in the "other world" whose teaching is reported in "this world."

40. B. Sanh. 90b; Bek. 31b. "If a teaching (of the deceased) is quoted in this world, his lips murmur in the grave."

41. P. Pe'ah 8 (7) 21a; P. Sheq. 5 (2) 48d.

CHAPTER TWO

That on certain issues it has been necessary for us to cite the testimony of writers who do not belong to our people.

By the very nature of the work which confronts me, it has been necessary for me to seek the help of many gentile sages for the clarification and elucidation of certain issues. Of course I would not accept their statements which hint at heresy or make light of our Torah, God forbid.[1] But merely because they are not Jews, they are regarded as aliens [lit. Kittim and Dodanim][2] whom we do not usually introduce into our community. Consequently, it might occur to some pious individual, one of those who "sits in the tents"[3] to contrive against me and make me the target for his attack on the grounds that in Sanhedrin, our rabbis of blessed memory forbade the reading of profane literature.[4] By a fortiori reasoning he would argue that if it is forbidden to discuss such texts, a more stringent prohibition would be issued against regarding them as valid support in any argument. Thus I realized that it would be in order for me to produce the following defense of my position to which the reader might refer whenever necessary.

The fact is that once he has given consideration to the statements of the scholars which I cite in this book as proof of one thing or another, he will from the very outset realize that according to the Mishnah and its gloss in the passage cited above, they are certainly not profane.[5] The truth is, as we said, you will not discover that these texts oppose or contradict any idea expressed in our Torah. Nevertheless, because it might

1. It should be noted that de' Rossi often extrapolates material from texts with an explicit anti-Jewish bias.

2. Kittim and Dodanim are listed as the sons of Yavan (Greece) in Gen. 10:4. De' Rossi probably chose the expression deliberately since the argument hinges on the rabbinic attitude towards Greek wisdom. He also may be alluding to B.R. 37:1 (344) where the word Dodanim is associated with *dodim,* i.e., kinsmen: "They are called Dodanim because they are the descendants of Israel's kinsmen."

3. 'Sits in the tents' is an expression used as an epithet of Jacob in Gen. 25:27. In Targum Onqelos ad loc. the verse is rendered: "Jacob was a man perfect in good deeds sitting in the schools." This interpretation of the verse is also found in Targum Ps. Jonathan and B.R. in which emphasis is given to Jacob's scholarly life as contrasted with Esau's idolatrous pursuits. De' Rossi is using the expression here according to its post-biblical meaning, i.e., in regard to a person who studies Torah exclusively.

4. M. Sanh. 10:1. In this context *ḥiṣonim* means heretical or extra-canonical, but I have translated 'profane' because de' Rossi is giving the term a more general application.

5. M. Sanh. 10:1 reads: "These are they who have no portion in the world to come . . . Rabbi Aqiva says: Even those who read profane books." De' Rossi is alluding to the *baraita* in B. Sanh. 100b which begins with the statement: "It is taught: he who reads profane books—this is the person who reads the books of the Sadducees."

occur to somebody to suspect the contents of a book of which they form part, I will let you hear more of my opinion on this subject in the course of the chapter.

In fact, it is appropriate to develop the critique on the basis of the passage referred to above:[6] " 'He who reads profane books.' Rav Joseph said, 'It is even forbidden to read the book of Ben Sira.' " According to Rashi,[7] the expression "profane books" refers to works like that of Ben Sira. Now there is the statement of Rambam [Maimonides].[8] "Ben Sira wrote books which contain nonsensical ideas about the human physiognomy." Nevertheless, there is no doubt that Ben Sira is to be identified with the work called *Ecclesiasticus* by the Greeks and the Romans[9] written by Jeshua ben Sirakh who is mentioned by the Hebrew Josephus [Josippon].[10] Thus it may occur to the critic to draw an analogy between some of the people cited in these chapters and Ben Sira about whom those things were said. But he should bear in mind that in the same context Rav Joseph himself also said that one may expound the valuable statements in the work of Ben Sira. Consequently, in the same passage, they proceed to cite many of his aphorisms: *Do not bring everybody into your home* (which is in chapter 11 of Ben Sira);[11] *A daughter is a vain treasure to her father* (which is in chapter 42),[12] and there are other examples. Other sayings of his are also cited here and there: e.g., in tractate Ḥagiga[13] and Bereshit Rabbah[14] *Do not investigate that which is too difficult for you* (which is in chapter 3 of Ben Sira);[15] in tractate Yevamot, *Let many people care for your well-being* (in chapter 6)[16] and *A good woman is a fine gift* (which is in chapter 16).[17] They also cite some of his aphorisms in tractates Ketubot,[18] Bava Batra,[19] and in tractate Nazir in the Palestinian Talmud,[20] and in tractate Berakhot in both the Palestinian and Babylonian Talmuds.[21]

In fact, in regard to the saying *When in trouble do not take decisions* quoted in tractate

6. B. Sanh. 100b.

7. Rashi ad loc. does not make this statement, but it is cited in his name in the *En Yaʿaqov* to B. Sanh. 100b.

8. This is a reference to Maimonides' *Perush* to M. Sanh. 10:1. It is a truncated quote which continues: "They are comparable to the works extant among the Arabs which treat chronology, the government of kings, Arab genealogies, books of songs, and similar subjects which do not contain wisdom nor have material value but are simply a waste of time." De' Rossi has ignored this part of the statement, presumably because it invalidates the value of his own studies.

9. Ecclesiasticus was the title used by the Latin Church from the fourth century onwards; see M. H. Segal, *Sefer Ben Sira,* 13. Fragments of the Hebrew original were discovered in the Cairo Geniza and at Qumran and Masada.

10. *Josippon,* bk. 3, ch. 15 (63).

11. Sirach 11:29.

12. Ibid. 42:9: *A daughter keeps her father secretly wakeful.* The talmudic quotation is closer to the Hebrew original. See Segal, *Sefer Ben Sira,* 284.

13. B. Ḥag. 13a.

14. B.R. 8:2 (58).

15. Sirach 3:21.

16. B. Yev. 63b; Sirach 6:6.

17. Sirach 26:3 (not ch. 16).

18. B. Ket. 110b.

19. B. B.B. 98b; 146a.

20. P. Nazir 5 (5) 54b.

21. P. Ber. 7 (2) 11b. In B. Ber. 48a there is no reference to Ben Sira, but Pr. 4:8 is quoted: *Hug her to you and she will exalt you; she will bring you honor if you embrace her,* which is similar to Sirach 11:1: *The wisdom of a humble man will lift up his head and will set him among the great.*

Eruvin,[22] Rashi of blessed memory states: "I looked for this text. Perhaps it is from the book of Ben Sira." Similarly, the saying cited in Bava Qama:[23] *Birds of a feather flock together and man does likewise* occasioned the comment of the Tosafist that it may have been taken from Ben Sira's work. The righteous will indeed rejoice at the Tosafist's good luck and excellent intuition which enabled him to reach the right conclusion—the saying is to be found in chapter thirteen.[24]

Some of the sayings attributed to Ben Sira by our sages of blessed memory are not to be found in Ecclesiasticus. One such example is the saying *A thin-bearded man is astute, a full-bearded man foolish.*[25] These sayings may have been taken from the work of Ben Tagla or Ben Laʿana (which we will presently discuss) both of which were classified together.[26] We may thus infer that one should not perhaps shun profane works, replete though they are with nonsensical statements, if any valuable insight regarding virtuous behavior or intellectual learning may be gleaned even from them.[27] Furthermore, the statements of our sages of blessed memory in Midrash Qohelet make it quite clear that the prohibition on the reading of profane literature was meant to be applied to habitual rather than casual or superficial study. For the person who becomes absorbed in his reading and comes to regard the books of such worth that he eagerly imbibes their words will be sure to harm himself. He will leave the fount of living water to dig for himself wells whose waters, it will be claimed, are not ours. But there is no doubt that they were not concerned about casual study, and certainly not when it was motivated by the desire to see what could be elicited from them for the clarification of some point which was somehow related to the explanations of our Torah. The formulation of the prohibition in the Midrash is as follows:[28] "*A further* (*mehema*) *word: Against them, my son, be warned* (Eccl. 12:12). Of confusion (*mehumah*) be warned. For whoever brings more than twenty four books, such as the books of Ben Sira and Ben Tagla, into his home brings confusion into his home. *And much study is a wearying of the flesh* (ibid.). These books are permitted for cursory perusal but not for fatiguing study." Now it is a known fact that the Midrashe Rabbot [i.e., including Midrash Qohelet] are Palestinian Aggadot. This is stated by Rashi, blessed be his memory, in his commentary to the verse, *And selecting a few of his brothers* (Gen. 47:2). Thus on the basis of the cited passage we will have a proper understanding of the following passage from Sanhedrin in the Palestinian Talmud:[29] "Profane literature comprises such texts as Ben Sira and Ben Laʿana but the reading of the books of Hamiros and all works which were written beyond that[30] is comparable to the reading of a secular document. What then is to be

22. B. Eruv. 65a.
23. B. B.Q. 92b.
24. Sirach 13:15.
25. B. Sanh. 100b.
26. Nothing is known of these two authors.
27. On the question of the status of Ben Sira in the talmudic period, see S. Leiman, *The Canonization,* 92–102.
28. Q.R. to Eccl. 12:12.
29. P. Sanh. 10 (1) 28a.
30. 'Beyond that.' This problematic expression is understood by Leiman (*The Canonization,* 182, n. 372) and S. Lieberman (quoted by Leiman) to signify "from the cessation of prophecy" which is equivalent to "beyond Scripture." This is also how de' Rossi understood the expression.

understood by the verse, *A further word, my son: Against them be warned . . . and much study is a wearying of the flesh* (Eccl. 12:12)? These books are permitted for cursory perusal and not for wearying study."

There is no doubt that according to its literal sense, this statement carries a prohibition of even a cursory study of the works of Ben Sira and Ben Laʿana, while all subsequently written works are permitted for superficial but not concentrated study. The problem thus arises as to how the rabbis themselves could have quoted several of Ben Sira's aphorisms in both the Babylonian and Palestinian Talmuds. One must necessarily infer that they learnt them from reading his work. Problematic, too, is their statement that all written literature beyond that time may be read as one reads a secular document. Which books were written after those of Ben Sira and Ben Laʿana and in what respect do they differ from them? The truth of the matter, however, is that the correct meaning of the passage in the Palestinian Talmud is that of the Midrash Qohelet. That is to say, profane literature comprises the works of Ben Sira, Ben Laʿana, and other works of this genre, and in any case, the books of Hamiros and all literature beyond that (i.e., apart from the twenty-four sacred books of Scripture),[31] may be read in the manner that one reads a secular document. In sum, all books excluding holy Scripture may be classified in the general category of Hamiros literature, the cursory study of which is not forbidden. In Bemidbar Rabbah,[32] the verse under discussion is also expounded in the same manner, and after the pronouncement that anyone who adds to the twenty-four books of Scripture forfeits his portion in the world to come, it is stated: "How do we know that this refers to those who make a concentrated study of the books? Scripture states, *And much study is weariness of the flesh*." Thus the sole concern was to prevent intensive study of those texts. (We shall bring this up again.) As a result, the sages of blessed memory did not refrain from studying some of these works. Whatever useful hint they discovered, they communicated to us, or else, they kept the teaching in mind until such time as we required to be instructed about it. The obscurity of the passage in the Palestinian Talmud is thus made comprehensible because of the explicitness of the midrashic texts and with it, the truth of our interpretation.[33]

Further corroboration is derived from the statement of the Ritba (Rabbi Yomtov ben Abraham) in a gloss commenting on the citation from Ben Sira: *I have weighed everything in the balance.* He writes:[34] "Although our sages of blessed memory pronounced Ben Sira to be a profane work in tractate Sanhedrin, the ban was directed against habitual but not occasional study of the text." Examine the passage in question. Similarly, the "man of ill repute" discussed in Moʿed Qatan[35] and Yoma[36] is defined by Caro as a person who is immersed in heretical literature as produced by Aristotle and his school.[37]

31. See above, n. 30.
32. Bem. R. 14:4.
33. For another solution to these contradictory texts, see Leiman, *The Canonization,* 91ff.
34. The statement of Ritba (a thirteenth-century talmudist) is given in Jacob ibn Ḥabib's *En Yaʿaqov* to B. B.B. 98b. De' Rossi may have read the *Ḥiddushe ha-Ritba* in manuscript.
35. B. M.Q. 17a.
36. De' Rossi seems to be referring to B. Yoma 86a.
37. The passage is in Joseph Caro's *Bet Yosef* on Jacob ben Asher's *Ṭur,* Yoreh Deʿah, Niddui, 334. Caro does not refer to Aristotle, but to heretics. In his *Shulḥan Arukh,* Niddui, 334:42; Caro states: "Who is a man of ill repute? One who immerses himself in the book of a heretic."

The word "immerses" doubtlessly signifies habitual study and this is also proved by the example he cites of Elishah Aḥer who is reputed to have been saturated with their works.[38]

According to our reading of the passage in the Palestinian Talmud which we recorded above, this literature was called *mirom,*[39] and the same reading is given in the Mishnah in the last chapter of tractate Yadayim.[40] You know that in his commentary on this passage, Rambam of blessed memory connects the word *miram* with the root meaning to abolish and states:[41] "The Lord will abolish them (*yarimem*) forever." But the author of the *Arukh* gives the reading *miros*[42] and I have been told that it refers to Homer the Greek poet. As far as I know, the word simply means "nonsense" in Greek.[43] (With God's help, we shall write about this in chapter 57.)

Now the critic might put forward further objections by referring to the passage in tractate Menaḥot:[44] "Ben Dama asked Rabbi Ishmael: 'May one such as I who have mastered the entire Torah study Greek wisdom?' He read to him the verse, *Let not this book of the Torah cease from your lips, but recite it day and night* (Joshua 1:8). 'Go and find a time which is neither day nor night and then study Greek wisdom.' " Such a time, as Rashi explains, does not exist. A similar statement is to be found in the Palestinian Talmud:[45] "They asked Rabbi Joshua ben Levi: 'When may a man teach his son Greek wisdom?' He said to them: 'At a time which is neither day nor night for it is stated, *but recite it day and night.*' They said to him: 'Does this also mean that you cannot teach your son a profession?' He said to them: 'No, certainly you may, for it is written, *Choose life* (Deut. 30:19).' " Thus he [i.e., his critic] in his desire to make the principles consistent, since one can hardly draw a distinction between Greek and any other language, would also ban the teachings of the foreigners cited by us. But in that same passage, various Amoraim are cited who took a different position from that of Rabbi Ishmael, in accordance with the view of Rabbi Jose. It is made clear that the prohibition was merely a restrictive measure passed by Rabbi Ishmael and Rabbi Joshua ben Levi and that, although it had scriptural support, it was not legally binding.

Furthermore you will see that in his *Responsa* the sage Ben Sheshet interprets the banned Greek wisdom as a term for symbolic and enigmatic language.[46] Examples of

38. This is a reference to Elishah ben Abuyah of whom it is related in B. Ḥag. 15b: "Greek song did not cease from his mouth. It is told of Aḥer that when he used to rise from the schoolhouse, many heretical books would fall from his lap."

39. On the manuscript reading of this word, see S. Lieberman, *Hellenism,* 106, n. 39.

40. M. Yad. 4:6.

41. This is not a precise rendering of Maimonides' statement although the meaning remains the same.

42. This is reference to the talmudic and midrashic lexicon of Nathan ben Yeḥiel (1035–1110) of Rome which was printed many times. De' Rossi consulted it frequently. The entry for *miros* reads: "He was a heretic and his name was Miros. Another explanation is that the works of Greek wisdom are called *miros* in their language."

43. Lieberman also takes the view that it is a reference to Homer. De' Rossi seems to be confusing the name with the Greek word *moros.*

44. B. Men. 99b.

45. P. Pe'ah 1 (1) 15c.

46. Isaac bar Sheshet Perfet), *She'elot,* responsum 45, 26 col. d–27 col. d. He quotes some of the same passages that de' Rossi cites including the reference to Elishah ben Abuyah and Maimonides and concludes that Greek wisdom was a type of allegorical or enigmatic language which was forbidden because it might be put to dangerous use.

these enigmas are given in the first chapter of Sanhedrin[47] and in tractate Eruvin.[48] The ban on the use of this type of code language resulted from the incident with the sinful old man during the siege of Jerusalem which is described at the end of tractate Sota and in other places.[49] Nevertheless, they permitted those who were closely associated with the ruling powers to study Greek wisdom.[50]

Similarly, according to Rabbenu Hai whose opinion is cited in the responsum mentioned above and according to Rabbi Isaiah di Trani,[51] they forbade heretical works such as those of the philosophers mentioned above because their false opinions and deceptive proofs lead to heresy and ruination. But we, here, will not call upon anybody who would in any way speak against our Torah or who might encourage you to veer towards anything wicked, God forbid. On the contrary, they will speak positively about the Torah and for its glorification. Our objective in using their texts is to find out whether the general remarks of any one of them may be put forward for the clarification of any intellectual or religious problem we might encounter. Such a procedure is well in accordance with their statement recorded above that we may expound the valuable passages contained in it [i.e., Ben Sira]. In fact, Resh Laqish [Simeon ben Laqish] defended Rabbi Meir for having gone to Elisha Aḥer in search of Torah. He found the scriptural verse, *Incline your ear and listen to the words of the sages, and apply your heart to my wisdom* (Pr. 22:17) and expounded it: "It does not say *to their wisdom* but *to my wisdom.*"[52] It was for this reason that after the dedicatory letter to his student, the author of the *Guide* [i.e., Maimonides] prefaced his work with that verse.

Indeed, we find that our rabbis had expert knowledge of philosophical concepts and were inclined to take a favorable attitude towards them as is evident from the passage of the Zohar quoted by Rav Recanati.[53] It states:[54] "*That which has no blemish* (Num. 19:2)—This is the kingdom of Greece for they drew near to the paths of truth."

47. B. Sanh. 12a: "A messenger was once sent to Rabbi: A couple of scholars have arrived from Rakat [i.e., Tiberias] who had been captured by an eagle [i.e., Rome] in possession of articles manufactured at Luz such as purple, yet through divine mercy they escaped."

48. B. Eruv. 53b: "Rabbi Jose ben Asiyan when speaking enigmatically would say: 'Prepare me a bull in judgment.' " This is a play on the Hebrew words for bull and judgment, which correspond to *tor* and *din* in Aramaic. When the letters are combined they spell the word *teradin* which means beef.

49. B. Sota 49b. "When the Hasmonean kings were fighting one another, Hyrcanus was outside and Aristobulus within. Every day they let down *denarii* in a basket and hauled up animals for the continual offerings. An old man who was learned in Greek wisdom spoke with them in Greek: 'As long as they they carry on the Temple service, they will never surrender to you.' The next day, they let down *denarii* and hauled up a pig. They declared: 'Cursed be a man who rears pigs and cursed be a man who teaches his son Greek wisdom.' " See also B. Men. 64b and B. B.Q. 82b. By using the expression 'sinful old man,' *zaqen ashmai* (cf. B. Qidd. 32b), de' Rossi may also be intending a play on the name Hasmonean (*ḥashmonai*).

50. The passage in B. Sota 49b ends: "It was different with the household of Rabban Gamaliel because he had close association with the government." (See also T. Sota 15:8.)

51. This is a reference to the commentary on ch. 10 of Sanhedrin by Isaiah b. Elijah di Trani the younger (Riaz), the thirteenth-century talmudist, which de' Rossi read in manuscript. Di Trani writes on the subject at length. See *Quntres ha-Re'iyyot,* 115–23.

52. B. Ḥag. 15b. According to the interpretation of the verse, there is a difference between the acts of the wise men who in this context are regarded to be wicked, and their words which may be listened to. Thus R. Meir could listen to and learn from Aḥer as long as he did not imitate his deeds.

53. Menahem Recanati was an Italian kabbalist and halakhic authority of the late thirteenth and early fourteenth centuries. De' Rossi quotes his kabbalistic commentary on the Pentateuch fairly frequently.

54. Recanati, *Perush* to Num. 19:2 (77, col. a).

Recanati explains that this is an allusion to the philosophers, Aristotle's predecessors, who sometimes expressed views which bear affinity to those of our rabbis. He also mentions them in laudatory terms in his comment on the verse, *and the fiery ever-turning sword to guard the way to the tree of life* (Gen. 3:24).[55] Examine the passage.

{Now in treating this subject I have not felt a pressing need to discuss the responsum of Rabbi Moses al-Ashqar[56] which was written to vindicate the author of the *Guide* who did not refrain from availing himself of secular knowledge as one might use apothecaries or cooks. He said:[57] "We do indeed find that although the holy Simeon bar Yoḥai [attributed with the authorship of the Zohar] quoted from the book of Enoch[58] which consists entirely of the ancient philosophy, we should not allege that he followed its system." But with all due respect, I must say that he [i.e., Moses al-Ashqar] misread the text. For on page 55 of the Zohar[59] (pericope *bereshit*) with regard to the verse, *This is the book of the generations of Adam* (Gen. 5:1), one finds the statement that the Holy One blessed be He indicated to Raphael that the book of Adam would be given to Adam and also be handed over to Abraham. It then states that the book was given to Enoch and served as a means of meditating on the higher resplendescence. Furthermore, on page 72, in regard to the verse, *And the sons of Noah who came out of the ark* (Gen. 9:18), Rabbi Simeon says:[60] "If I had been in the world when the Holy One blessed be He gave the book of Enoch to the the world and the book of Adam." In other words, both Enoch and his book "walked with God"[61] and his waters flow from the Holy of Holies.}[2]

Moreover, it is even permissible to read the famous heretical works in order to meet the requirements of Torah. In tractates Sanhedrin[62] and Menaḥot[63] it is explained that the members of the Sanhedrin had to be acquainted with the methods of sorcerers and the fatuities of idolatry. And there is no doubt that they acquired knowledge of these matters by reading the relevant literature. Alternatively, and even more problematic, is the fact that they sometimes received instruction in these subjects, not only by reading their writings, but also by conversing with the authors. In Berakhot,[64] in an attempt to

55. Ibid., 15, col. a: "On several occasions there have been examples of men who were burnt by the lightning of the flaming sword, all of whom were versed in the ancient philosophy which to a great extent bears affinity to the words of our sages. But they ceased to exist and Aristotle and his wicked students came and they strayed away from the Torah."

56. Moses b. Isaac al-Ashqar (1466–1542) was a talmudist and liturgical poet.

57. Al-Ashqar's critique of Shemtov ibn Shemtov's attack on Maimonides is given in his *She'elot,* 187b–188a. He quotes Maimonides' letter to Jonathan of Lunel in which he writes that the Torah was his first wife, but that foreign women, i.e., secular subjects, were taken as foreign wives, but that the Lord knows that "I took these other women initially only in order to serve as apothecaries, cooks, and bakers in order to show her beauty to the peoples for she, i.e., the Torah, is very beautiful."

58. On Enoch in the mystical tradition, see M. Idel, "Enoch," 151–70.

59. This is a reference to the first edition of the Zohar, Mantua 1558–60, 55b.

60. Zohar I, 72b. The passage continues: "I would have made an effort to prevent them from falling into the hands of humans because . . . they erred in their reading."

61. This is a play on the biblical reference to Enoch (Gen. 5:24), *Enoch walked with God, Then he was no more and God took him.*

62. B. Sanh. 17a.

63. B. Men. 65a.

64. B. Ber. 59a. The passage refers to Qattina, not to Abaye. The necromancer explained that the rumbling of the earth occurs when, in distress over the suffering of Israel, God lets two tears fall into the ocean and their sound is heard from one end of the world to the other. Qattina retorted that this is false, since according to the necromancer's explanation, there would have been one rumbling after the other. It

prevent the corruption of the entire world, Abaye denounced the necromancer publicly, calling him a liar and his words lies. And yet, Abaye himself had expounded the necromancer's statements and learnt profitably from him. In any case, it was permitted on the basis of the statement of the blessed Lord, *You shall not learn to imitate the abhorrent practices of those nations* (Deut. 18:9) which verse was traditionally interpreted in the following manner:[65] "You may not learn them to imitate them, but you may learn them in order to understand and demonstrate how correct are our own practices." Thus this permit has the same force as that which we demonstrated above concerning occasional reading of any kind which must not lead to total absorption in the subject. Quite apart from this, we have discovered that an act which is not intrinsically pure can be made pure when performed for a spiritual purpose. He who acts thus will stand firm as a mirror of cast metal[66] on the mount of the Torah of our God. This may be illustrated by the story of Rav Giddal who used to sit at the gate of the bathhouse [where women used to immerse themselves]. The rabbis said to him:[67] "Is not the master afraid that the evil inclination will get the better of him?" He said to them: "They look to me like white geese." What is more, several great Jews, eminent authorities from whose waters we imbibe decisions and interpretations of Torah, studied many profane books and referred to them by name in their works. The author of the *Guide,* the author of *Aqedat Yiṣḥaq* [Arama],[68] and others did this when embarking on an intellectual or religious discourse. After proceeding a little way with words of Torah,[69] they then proffer the offering of foreigners such as the "philosopher" [Aristotle][70] or ibn Rushd [Averroes] in the conviction that they were acting in a correct manner such as would meet with the approval of our God. Particularly striking is the knowledge of the author of the *Guide.* He describes how he studied all the Arabic books on idolatry which were known in his time. He claimed that this was advantageous for him because, in his opinion, these texts revealed many of the secrets of our Torah.[71] Thus he and all other sagacious people were confident and felt no embarrassment that some clever person might address them in the manner in which Rav Giddal was addressed. As our sages say in tractates Nazir[72] and Yevamot[73] in regard to Tamar and Jael, a transgression committed in the name of God is preferable to a precept performed with

is then stated: "There really was one rumbling after another, but he did not admit to it in order to prevent people from going astray after the necromancer."

65. B. Sanh. 68a.

66. Cf. Job 37:18.

67. B. Ber. 20a.

68. I.e., Isaac Arama (1420–94), a Spanish rabbi, philosopher, and preacher, most famous for *Aqedat Yiṣḥaq,* a collection of homilies containing philosophical and allegorical explanations of the Torah.

69. 'After . . . way,' lit. *And it was when they had walked six steps* (see 2Sam. 6:13). The verse is referring of the priests who were carrying the ark at the time of offering the sacrifices. In his interpretation of the verse, Kimḥi refers to 1Chr. 15:25 and states that because no mishap befell them while carrying the ark, this was a clear sign of God's favor. Similarly, de' Rossi is perhaps using this expression to indicate that Maimonides and Arama had divine approval for their use of non-Jewish sources.

70. De' Rossi uses the medieval designation of Aristotle which was still current usage among some sixteenth-century scholars.

71. *Guide* III, ch. 29.

72. B. Nazir 23b.

73. De' Rossi appears to be referring to B. Yev. 103a–b where a different idea is expressed in reference to Yael. It is said: "The favor of the wicked is evil for the righteous."

evil intention. Indeed, in his introduction to Avot[74] and at the end of the laws of ethics[75] Rabbi Moses [Maimonides] of blessed memory wrote that when all our actions are performed with the intention of serving God, even those acts which give us bodily gratification should be regarded as divine. Similarly, those in authority [lit. the sons of God] will realize the benefits of the external wisdom which we employ for internal purposes.[76]

Moreover, with regard to using them as support in certain problematic matters, our sages of blessed memory also instruct us that we may rely on their [i.e., gentile] sages whatever their origin even in legal matters. There is the famous and difficult law regarding grooves in a field which is based on the statement of our rabbis of blessed memory:[77] "The rabbis ascertained that five species sown within six handsbreadths do not draw sustenance from each other." The question was then raised as to the source of the rabbis' statement. Rashi of blessed memory explains the sense of the question in the following way: "They questioned the reliability of the sages' source of knowledge in order to show that the sages were experts in agricultural matters and could determine how seeds take sustenance from each other. They thus preempted your bewildered enquiry as to how human beings acquired knowledge of measurement of sustenance and how they succeeded in mastering the subject." This was their answer:

> It is written: *You shall not remove your countryman's landmarks set up by previous generations* (Deut. 19:14). The landmarks set up by the previous generations you shall not remove. What landmarks did the previous generations set up? Rabbi Johanan quoted the verse, *These were the sons of Seir the Horite the inhabitants of the land* (Gen. 36:20). Are then the whole world inhabitants of heaven? No, it merely means that they were experts in the cultivation of the land. They used to say: "This complete rod is for olives, this complete rod for vines, this complete rod for figs." Horite means they smelled (*meriḥin*) the earth. Hivite means that they tasted the earth like a serpent (*ḥivya*).

Rashi comments on this passage: "Who were the previous generations? The Amorites and Hivites who were experts in this as were the sons of Seir, and they knew how to divide the land into rods of olives or figs by means of smell and taste and presumably were thus experienced in measuring for sustenance." At this point, it seems to me that the obvious question is how anyone could entertain the idea that our sages learned anything at all from the sons of Seir the Horite, as is implied by their statement regarding the verse, *You shall not move your countryman's landmark*. Then aside from their statement that Sennacherib king of Assyria had already come up and mixed up the populace of all the nations,[78] Scripture is also explicit that before the giving of the Torah *Seir was formerly inhabited by the Horites, but the descendants of Esau dispossessed them, wiping them out and settling in their place* (Deut. 2:12). And quite apart from this,

74. This is a reference to ch. 5 of Maimonides' introduction to Avot, *Shemonah Peraqim,* in which he advises use of all faculties for the purpose of comprehending the nature of God, whether by eating, drinking, or sexual intercourse, in sleep or during waking hours.

75. *Mishneh Torah,* Deʿot III:3.

76. This is a play on Gen. 6:2.

77. B. Shabb. 85a.

78. B. Yoma 54a. Thus, the Horites and the other children of Seir no longer lived there and could not have communicated their knowledge to the sages.

one must ask what was the point of them going to Egypt to seek Torah from a nation of Keretim.[79] Indeed, among our own brethren there is King Solomon who spoke about the cedar and the hyssop. In the Tanḥuma[80] and Shir ha-Shirim Rabbah [*sic*],[81] it is said that he knew the foundation stone on which the entire world is constructed. In fact, the whole point is as follows: In subjects of this kind we do not need to rely on prophetical tradition of Sinaitic origin or an any prophet, but may also rely on the empirical knowledge of the sages in each generation. This knowledge was not recondite and was therefore accessible to our sages. In fact we may also indirectly infer that we may rely on sages of other nations in such empirical matters; and that even our sages in the question discussed above may have received their knowledge of these matters from them. For if it were to occur to you not to trust them in this matter, then you should reflect on the source of our evidence that the children of Seir, who are supposed to speak fraudulently,[82] used to taste, smell, and measure rod distances. The fact of the matter is that in all such questions we rely on them as well. Comparable is the case described in Ḥullin[83] where a decision about food was made dependent on a gentile cook tasting it.

Moreover, it was part of rabbinic procedure to accept the truth from any informant. Thus regarding the subject of a proselyte who slaughtered a cow before his conversion, Resh Laqish pointed out a contradiction to Rabbi Johanan on the basis of a *baraita*. Rabbi Johanan then replied:[84] "Do not tire me; I teach the Mishnah as the opinion of an individual." Resh Laqish retorted: "Just teach it in Ben Taddal's name [a generic term for fools]; after all, he adduces a reason for his opinion."

Thus our rabbis of blessed memory would give ear to anyone who spoke the truth, even to a fool, and even to those human beings to whom we referred above. They were not only receptive to them in regard to general matters, but also when such laws of Torah as regard forbidden foods and the ban on sowing heterogeneous plants in the same field were at issue. The same is true of other hypotheses which they advanced as absolute truths. For example they state in Eruvin:[85] "Anything that measures three handsbreadths in circumference has a diameter of one handsbreadth" and,[86] "How much does the area of a square exceed that of a circle? By a quarter." And in the first chapter of tractate Sukkah they also say:[87] "A figure of one square cubit has a diagonal of one and two-fifths cubits." In tractate Shabbat,[88] they relied on this last calculation for establishing the law regarding receptacles. Other examples regard Samuel's astronomical computations in tractate Rosh ha-Shanah[89] and his medical expertise.[90] There

79. Keretim is a name for the Philistines, cf. Zeph. 2:5.
80. Tanḥuma, qedoshim, 10 (ed. Buber, 8).
81. The passage in Q.R. to Eccl. 2:5.
82. Cf. Ps. 144:11: *Rescue me, save me from the hands of foreigners, whose mouths speak lies.*
83. B. Ḥull. 97a. The case presented regards a pot in which meat has been cooked and in which milk was then boiled. A gentile is allowed to taste the food to see whether the pot has imparted a meaty flavor to the milk and his evidence is authoritative.
84. B. Ḥull. 134a.
85. M. Eruv. 1:5.
86. B. Eruv. 14b.
87. B. Sukk. 8a.
88. B. Shabb. 8a (in regard to the Sabbath laws of carrying).
89. B. R.H. 20b.
90. De' Rossi refers here to Ketubot, but the reference is to B. B.M. 85b.

is no doubt that all or part of their information was culled from the books which the sages of other peoples had written on the subject, and that once familiar with the actual source, they also held them to be absolute truths. The author of *ha-Ḥinnukh* (pericope *qedoshim*)[91] said[92] that when they [the sages] advanced a hypothesis which was not completely accurate, this was not because it was beyond their capabilities to make the calculation. One such example is the calculation given in the passage in Sukkah quoted above, which according to theorem 27 in book 1 of Euclid is clearly not completely accurate. Rather, precision was not their concern because, as is stated in the first chapter of tractate Shabbat, the imprecision was for the sake of stringency.

Alternatively, it could be argued as did the author of the *Guide* that the basic information originated from our own people.[93] In a similar vein the author of the *Derekh Emunah*[94] wrote that once the precious volumes passed into the hands of the foreigners who had subjected us, we had no alternative but to regain all our knowledge from them. What is more, it is not just that we may pay attention to the words of their sages about whom we are taught:[95] "Whoever says something wise, even if a gentile, is called a sage for it is written, *Then Haman told his wife Zeresh . . . and his wise men said to him* (Esther 6:13)," or that we are taught in Berakhot to pronounce a blessing on seeing a gentile sage.[96] The fact is that the common man among them may also be accepted by us and for important matters of legislation of the Torah. In the last chapter of Yevamot various stories are related which demonstrate that the statements of any gentile who speaks impartially (i.e., with no intention of giving evidence) may be accepted by us even in cases regarding the question whether a woman is deemed married or not.[97] And although the subject of the passage deals with the question of the *agunah,*[98] there is sufficient proof that we may rely on his evidence in other cases involving similar prohibitions. His evidence will be considered particularly trustworthy insofar as he has no stake in the issue at hand. This is discussed in tractate Giṭṭin.[99]

Indeed anyone who studies our statements in the forthcoming chapters will discover that two conditions must be fulfilled when we call upon gentiles for their general pronouncements: their statements must be made in innocence and they must have no claims whatsoever in the issue at stake.

On reading a passage towards the end of Josephus's *Autobiography* in which he

91. *Sefer ha-Ḥinnukh* which is an enumeration of the positive and negative commandments arranged in order of the weekly pericopes has been attributed to the Spanish talmudist Aaron ben Joseph Halevi of Barcelona, but the authorship is still questioned.

92. *Sefer ha-Ḥinnukh,* qedoshim, neg. comm. 36 (341).

93. *Guide* I, ch. 71.

94. Abraham b. Shemtob Bibago (fifteenth-century Spanish theologian) *Derekh Emunah,* pt. 2, gate 3, 46 col. c. In the same context, Bibago cites many of the talmudic passages quoted by de' Rossi as evidence of the scientific knowledge of the rabbis and refers to Euclid. He also quotes Eusebius as saying that Greek wisdom originated with Israel.

95. B. Meg. 16a.

96. B. Ber. 58a.

97. B. Yev. 121b.

98. *Agunah* (lit. chained woman) is the term used of a woman who is unable to remarry because she is uncertain whether her husband is alive or not.

99. B. Giṭṭ. 28b.

compares those who write spurious history to forgers of documents,[100] I was reminded of a tradition which is also set out in the talmudic discussion in the first chapter of Giṭṭin.[101] The subject is documents which are drawn up in gentile registries. It is claimed that they have notarial authority and are therefore trustworthy, since notaries would not wish to damage their reputation. In the same chapter, there is also a reference to Rav Papa who, when summoned to deal with a Persian bill of sale, would give it to two gentiles separately so that he could get impartial evidence and then collect the sum on that basis.[102] Here, too, all the chroniclers who shall be cited in our inquiries were all concerned about their reputation for they did not want to suffer the ignominy of being proved liars. By means of truthful and acceptable writings, they sought to win a reputation and glory worthy of kings and world councillors. They are therefore to be regarded as reliable notaries.

Furthermore, the intelligent person will appreciate the fact that all the prophets of Israel also have the status of aliens when it comes to Torah and related matters. Our rabbis of blessed memory have established this point on several occasions[103] in reference to the verses: *These are the commandments that the Lord gave Moses for the Israelite people on Mount Sinai* (Lev. 27:34) and *This instruction . . . is not in the heavens* (Deut. 30:11, 12). They said: "No prophet has the authority to innovate anything from now onwards [i.e., from the time of the giving of the Torah]." Consequently, when in the first chapter of Pesaḥim [*sic*],[104] and Bava Qama,[105] our sages of blessed memory were challenged as to how Pentateuchal teachings could be deduced from post-Pentateuchal texts, they answered that in those cases the texts were not used as deductions (i.e., for purposes of obligation or exemption as the authors of *Keritut*[106] and *Haliḵhot Olam*[107] explained), but only as circumstantial evidence.

And so with due regard to the distinction between the holy and profane and to all the gradations of distinctions which a person enumerates, also our quest for merely circumstantial evidence from gentile sages will surely seem appropriate. One can adduce support for this position from a passage in tractate Qiddushin[108] and in tractate Pe᾿ah in the Palestinian Talmud[109] in which Rabbi Eliezer was asked about the extent to which the duty of filial piety should be observed. He responded: "Ask the gentile Dama ben Netina."[110]

100. *Vita* 337.
101. B. Giṭṭ. 10b.
102. Ibid. 19b.
103. De' Rossi refers to Sifra, ba-ḥuqotai, 13 (115, col. d); B. Meg. 3a; B. Tem. 16a. He also refers mistakenly to B. B.M. 59b.
104. De' Rossi may be referring to B. Pes. 7b, but there is no explicit statement on deduction from post-Pentateuchal texts in that context.
105. B. B.Q. 2b. Other parallels are B. Ḥag. 10b, B. Nidd. 23a.
106. Samson b. Isaac of Chinon (fourteenth century) wrote *Sefer Keritut,* on talmudic methodology.
107. Jeshua ben Joseph Halevi (fifteenth century) wrote *Halihḵot Olam* on the formation and methodology of the Talmud.
108. B. Qidd. 31a.
109. P. Pe᾿ah 1 (1) 15c.
110. Dama ben Netina was prepared to lose a large financial profit rather than disturb his father who was asleep.

Generally speaking, the judicious person should bear in mind that by His holy utterance regarding words of Torah, *Ask your father* (Deut. 32:7) and only him in order that you should not go astray, God also saw fit to permit the evidence of gentiles in general matters when He said: *You have but to inquire about bygone ages* (Deut. 4:32) and *Ask the generation past* (Job 8:8); *Stand by the roads and consider, Inquire about ancient paths* (Jer. 6:16); *You must have consulted the wayfarers* (Job 21:29). And if you protest that these are all references to the children of Israel or their ancestors, then come and hear what Jeremiah has to say: *Assuredly, thus said the Lord, Inquire among the nations: Who has heard anything like this?* (18:13).

In general then we have proceeded on the principle[111] that wherever there is no denial of the Written and Oral Torah, it is not a vain endeavor, as I see it, to comprehend that which is obscure in our texts by means of the explicit statements of the gentile sages. This will be the method especially when they cannot be suspected of favoring each other—each witness stands in a different corner, and yet their evidence concurs. We do indeed find in tractate Ketubot[112] that our sages of blessed memory carried out the same kind of procedure for a case in which a deposit was left with a man who died intestate and the depositor came to claim the goods. In this case, Rabbi Ammi, Rav Naḥman, and Rabbi Abba arrived at the same decision independently. [They ruled that the decision rests to the advantage of the person who can produce tokens of ownership.] and according to Alfasi's comment on this passage, their decision became a widely accepted law.

Now you should examine the book *Nofet Ṣufim* written by the great sage Rabbi Judah known as Messer Leon of Mantua.[113] In the chapter on memory, he states that the awareness of the beauty of oratory which we derive from the pagan sages facilitates our appreciation of the far greater beauties and niceties of holy Scripture. This is what he writes:[114] "This exposes the magnitude of the error and misunderstanding which has been fostered in the minds of some self-opinionated members of our people who say nowadays: 'Do not look for truths from Assyria or Egypt. . . .' For although their intention is to exalt the Torah and promote it, they do in fact debase it. . . . Woe to those who say of evil that it is good." Now you are already acquainted with the statement of the author of the *Guide:*[115] "Hear how we have benefited from the study of mathematics and what great value we have derived from it." I hope that the reader will make a similar pronouncement about some of these chapters. The prudent person will therefore at that time fall silent, give praise, be struck with surprise and confusion all at

111. 'We . . . principle,' lit. 'with this we go down and with this we go up.' Cf. B. Pes. 87b.

112. B. Ket. 85b. Three stories are related here in which people come to recover a deposit which has been left with a person who died intestate. On each occasion, the rabbi consulted ruled that as long as the collector of the deposit was not a habitual visitor to the deceased's house and could produce tokens of ownership, he could be considered as a genuine depositor.

113. Judah b. Yeḥiel Messer Leon was an Italian rabbi, physician, educator, and scholar of the fifteenth century. His work *Nofet Ṣufim* is a treatise on the rhetoric of the Bible, which was printed in the author's lifetime in Mantua, 1475. See the introduction of R. Bonfil to the facsimile edition of the work, Jerusalem, 1981.

114. *Nofet Ṣufim,* bk. 1, ch. 13 (145).

115. *Guide* I, ch. 73 (Pines trans., 210).

once.[116] But anyone who has a brain in his head should not think of this method of ours as alien because of that part in which we happen to apply it. Rather, he should accept the truth from whatever source—this was the opinion of Rabbi Moses in his introduction to his commentary on Avot[117] and in his long and beautiful discourse at the end of chapter 17 of the Laws on Sanctification of the Moon.[118] And he [i.e., the reader] would be correct in thinking that if the material for my immediate purpose could have been drawn entirely from Jewish writings, I would have most certainly and with great pleasure invoked beloved members of my own people and in such a case would not have brought foreigners within these gates. And if these words of mine do not adequately establish a rule which may be applied to all other cognate studies (and this was not in fact my purpose), I nevertheless deem them sufficient for the defense of the task which I was, as it were, forced to undertake. I shall also repeat the pronouncement which I uttered at the end of the previous chapter in the manner in which witnesses repeat the word "yes" when being sworn in:[119] I hereby attest to all intelligent men of integrity that I shall always value and prize their criticism of me and my work. And if I am in the wrong (and may that not be the case), I shall remove my error. Yet in any case, I should have no cause for embarrassment when I consider Galen's statement in the last chapter of *De facultatibus naturalibus*[120] that books are always subject to criticism. But as for the simpleton or hypocrite whose sole aim is to libel me for his own self-aggrandizement or to exploit my work, he should keep his hands off my book for it is not intended for him. Now in all probability, there will be many such critics. There is therefore some grounds in applying the author's statement in the preface to the *Guide* to my own case. He said: "I am the type of man who when dealing with an intractable subject and have no other means [of teaching the truth] except by satisfying one worthy person and displeasing ten thousand boors, I prefer to address myself to that one person while disregarding the censure of the masses." A similar statement cited from a letter of Rabad [Rabbi Abraham ben David] of blessed memory to the sages of Béziers is quoted by the author of the *Sefer ha-Hashlamah* regarding the rule about forbidden wine.[121] He wrote:[122] "I would like to answer the enquiries of who those who ask with a genuine desire of receiving knowledge, but not those who ask in order to get the better of me. One citizen can reflect credit on an entire city. It cannot be that there is not one among you who cannot listen."

Finally, I cannot desist from using the statement of one wise gentile, namely, Plutarch, which he said in regard to his work on the *Lives of the Kings*. In it he had collated many different opinions from various sources. He therefore prefaced it by saying that

116. This is a conflation of Amos 5:13 and Is. 42:14.

117. *Shem. Per.,* Introduction.

118. *Mishneh Torah,* Qiddush ha-Ḥodesh XVII:25.

119. Cf. B. Shev. 36a where it is stated that the witness must repeat the word "yes" if his statement is to be regarded as an oath.

120. Galen, *De nat. fac.* 2:9. Galen speaks of those who are so ambitious that they unscrupulously attack other people "as does Erasistratus and many of the more recent authorities."

121. Meshullam b. Moses of Béziers (1175–1250) wrote the *Sefer ha-Hashlamah* in order to complete and expand Alfasi's *Halakhot.* De' Rossi appears to have read the work in manuscript.

122. The letter is published as an appendix to the rule on forbidden wine (28a).

his book should be read by benevolent and indulgent people who would appreciate the nature of the subject matter and the complexities involved in obtaining the true facts and would not be undermined by those who sought pretexts to libel him because he had aimed at providing them with pleasure and amusement.[123]

At any rate, as far as this is concerned, I have trusted to meet with your approval, wise reader. From beginning to end, you will notice the clarity of my pronouncements and how that I have said nothing which after a judicious reading you might reject. From now on, I will invoke God and entreat His kindness that He should strengthen my resistance and deliver me from a libelous tongue. May it be His will to lead me in the paths of righteousness.

123. De' Rossi is referring (a little loosely) to the beginning of the Life of Theseus where Plutarch speaks of his attempt to make fables conform to reason, but where that was not possible would seek the indulgence of his readers who should listen to the tales of antiquity with forbearance.

CHAPTER THREE

Our assessment of Yedidyah the Alexandrian who has also been summoned to speak on some of these questions. The Jewish sects of the second Temple period will feature in the discussion.

You should also know, dear reader, whoever you are, that it is my wish that among those invoked by me to enter the portals of these chapters should also be Yedidyah the Alexandrian called Philo by the Greeks and Romans.[1] Following the method of certain distinguished contemporaries of mine, I have from the very outset called him "Yedidyah," a Hebrew equivalent for his name Philo, and "the Alexandrian" because he was an inhabitant of Alexandria in Egypt.[2] I have turned to him, even calling on him by name, because his works contain invaluable information for my purposes which are unobtainable from other such sources. He had a preeminent position among our people slightly prior to the destruction of the second Temple,[3] and he witnessed and recorded many things which ought to be publicized. The truth of the matter is that however much I suspect the integrity of this man as regards God and the holy people, I cannot pass an immediate and absolute verdict on him. At any rate, I do not wish to beguile you by dyeing your clothes with an imitation rather than the genuine purple,[4] nor claim to give you wine to drink about which you will ultimately protest, "You have given me vinegar to quench my thirst."[5] I think it best to provide you with the true facts that I know about him. Then, in direct relation to his wisdom and righteousness he may be praised or censured by informed people. In their assessment of him, they will determine whether he is to be given a hearing whenever he speaks regarding the laws of the Jews[6] as other interpreters of our Torah, or whether he is to be regarded as one of those who babble and chirp as the spirit takes them.[7] And without doubt, it is impossible to

1. On de' Rossi's critique of Philo, see R. Marcus, "A Sixteenth-Century Critique" and my article, "The Quest."

2. 'Yedidyah' like the name Philo signifies friendship. De' Rossi hebraizes his name in the way that contemporary writers latinized their names, e.g., Melanchthon (Schwarzerd).

3. Philo was born about 20 B.C.E. and died after 40 C.E.

4. De' Rossi is using an expression from B. B.M. 61b which speaks of God taking vengeance on people who are fraudulent in one way or another. One of the examples given there, to which he alludes, refers to the purple dye which had to be extracted from a rare fish with which the fringes were to be colored. Cf. Num. 15:38.

5. Cf. Ps. 69:22.

6. Cf. Dan. 3:12.

7. Cf. Is. 8:19.

investigate these matters without breaking new ground which, as I think, you will not deem lightly.[8]

Now before I elaborate on the subject of Yedidyah, I must first cite Josephus on the subject of the different sects which during the time of the second Temple, hundreds of years before its destruction, disgraced our people in respect to the Torah and the one precept which one God, the Lord our God, wrote for one people. Josephus describes at length how from very early times, the Jewish sages were split into three groups: the Pharisees, the Sadducees and the Essenes.[9] By means of identifiable evidence, I have come to the conclusion (as will be clarified later) that the Essenes were none other than the Boethusians who receive unfavorable mention by our rabbis. In some of the passages, Josephus also refers to a fourth sect, that of Judah the Gaulonite[10] from Galilee,[11] which is also mentioned by the Christians at the end of chapter 5 of the Acts of the Apostles.[12] This man upheld the doctrines of the Pharisees but took upon himself the additional charge of not submitting to the yoke of any kingdom (and this was contrary to the concept of the holy Torah and that of all the Pharisaic sages who, as is well known, abided by the authority of the government and encouraged obedience to it and observance of its laws),[13] save that of heaven. It was for this reason that all his followers would submit themselves to death, extermination, or any form of self-immolation, rather than bear the yoke of any powerful king or ruler who happened to be governing the country. My feelings lead me to think that it was in an attempt to eradicate such beliefs that our sages of blessed memory state: "[Ha]-Gavlan will be devastated and Galilee destroyed."[14] They are alluding here to a time when people would be forcibly enslaved and those who yearned for freedom like that man associated with the place called Gavlan, which is in Galilee, would be devastated and their country destroyed.[15] This contradicts Rashi's opinion that ha-Gavlan refers to a place-name[16] [and not to a person]. If Rashi's view was correct, the word should have been spelled without the definite article [*ha*]. Moreover, one would have to question why the author of the statement under discussion singled out the devastation of Gavlan when many other

8. De' Rossi's critique of Philo was the first comprehensive assessment to be undertaken by Jew or Christian. He refers to certain Jews, including his friend David Provenzali "who thirstily imbibe Philo's words." De' Rossi's familiarity with Christian readings of Philo determined his ambivalent stance towards the philosopher. On this question, see my article, "The Quest."

9. De' Rossi refers to Josephus's *Ant.* XIII:171–73; 297–98; XVIII:11–25, *Bellum* II:119–66.

10. Judas the Gaulonite is first mentioned by Josephus in *Ant.* XVIII:4; although the other references to Judah the Galilean cited do not designate him "the Gaulonite," it is quite plausible that Judah the Gaulonite and Judah the Galilean are one and the same person. In de' Rossi's Latin text of Josephus, the name Judas Gaulonites is used; thus the term Judah ha-Gavlani which he uses is a straightforward translation from the Latin. T. Fishman's argument (*Shaking the Pillars,* 167–68) therefore with regard to de' Rossi's use of Eusebius's *Hist. Eccl.* in this context is not convincing.

11. *Ant.* XVIII:23–25.

12. Acts 5:37: *After this man [Theudas] rose up Judas of Galilee in the days of the taxing and drew away much people after him.*

13. The passage in parentheses is a marginal gloss of most printings of the first edition of the work. On Judah the Gablonite, see M. Stern, "Sicarii and Zealots."

14. He refers to the addendum to M. Sota 9:15; B. Sanh. 97a; S.S.R. to S.S. 2:13 where the statement is made in reference to the period preceding the messianic age.

15. In other words, de' Rossi understands the name ha-Gavlan as a reference to the Gavlonite.

16. Rashi to B. Sanh. 97a.

places suffered the same fate at that time, culminating in the erasure of the whole area? At the beginning of his *Autobiography,* Josephus himself also mentions another sect whose adherents dwelt in the desert scorched by the blazing sun, picking berries for sustenance, and clothing themselves with mallows, the foliage of bushes.[17] But these two sects [i.e., the Gaulonites and the desert sect] did not earn a lasting name, for their adherents were few and, like the snail, they disappeared into oblivion. This was particularly the case with the Galilean. Josephus describes how that when Alexander was the Roman governor of the Holy Land, the sons of the Galilean—namely, Judah, Jacob, and Simon—were exterminated because they had been inciting the people to revolt against the Roman rule.[18]

Now let us return to the subject of the three sects. It is well known that the Pharisees were a community of our sages. Josephus always refers to them in laudatory terms. At the beginning of his *Autobiography,* he wrote that in his youth he had wanted to examine and experiment with all the various sects, including the one whose adherents led a solitary life in the forests. Finally, arriving at the best option as it were, he espoused the Pharisees whose style of life he compared to the Greek philosophical school of the Stoics.[19] He declared that they understood the truth of the Torah and the laws according to the tradition, and that the general populace followed their sway. There were occasions, however, when some of the Sadducees were appointed as members of the Sanhedrin. This emerges from the account at the end of Megillat Taʿanit,[20] Bava Batra,[21] and other passages. Yet wherever the people could be under the leadership of the Pharisees, the teachers of righteousness, they never swayed from their path. Then it happened that Herod of Ashkelon who was of Edomite origin had intermingled[22] [by marriage] with the Jews in order to strengthen his rule over them, which position he had been granted by Octavian the emperor. He proceeded to put several thousands of Jews to death who had rejected him because he was not our brother. Hillel and Shammai who realized that it was better to choose the lesser evil, successfully persuaded the people to capitulate to him. As a result, Herod favored them and held them in high esteem as long as he lived. This is described by Josephus in the *Antiquities.*[23]

In fact, we can identify and trace the origins of the two sects whom our sages called Sadducees and Boethusians from various statements made by our rabbis of blessed memory in Avot d'Rabbi Nathan[24] which are cited by some of the commentators of tractate Avot and by Rashi blessed be his memory.[25] They [Ṣadoq and Boethus] were

17. *Vita* 10–12.
18. *Ant.* XX:102.
19. *Vita* 9–13.
20. *Meg. T.* 10 (342). This passage describes how Simeon b. Sheṭah expelled the Sadducees from the Sanhedrin. See the discussion of B. Luria, Megillat Taʿanit, 181–84. De' Rossi used the first edition of Meg. T., Mantua, 1513.
21. B. B.B. 115b.
22. 'Intermingled,' '*hi ṭamʿao*' (not '*hi ṭaʿamo*' as in Cassel), cf. Deut. 24:4. This is an allusion to Herod's marriage to Mariamme, daughter of Alexander.
23. *Ant.* XV:3; 370. De' Rossi identifies Pollion and Sameas mentioned in Josephus with Hillel and Shammai. They are usually identified with Shemaiah and Avtalion.
24. ARN, rec. A, ch. 5, 26. For a recent discussion of this passage, see L. Finkelstein, *The Pharisees,* 762–69 and J. Le Moyne, *Les Sadducéens,* 113–17.
25. Rashi to B. B.B. 115b.

disciples of Antigonus who stumbled and caused others of like disposition to stumble in regard to the teaching which he [i.e., Antigonus] publicly preached:[26] "Be not as servants who serve their master for the sake of a reward, but be like servants who serve their master without the condition of receiving a reward." And I saw that one of the early Christians called Epiphanius put forward the view in his work *Against the Heretics* that their objectives [i.e., the Sadducees] from the very start were not righteous ones [*ṣadoq*]; they were merely a wicked group of people who had come together and given themselves that name in order to lend the impression that their aim was the pursuit of righteousness.[27] However that may be, we do know from various sources that these two opposing sects denied the Oral Torah for which they were both pronounced to be disqualified.[28] In tractate Yoma[29] it is described how they used to make the high priest vow not to arrange the incense in the manner of the Sadducees which was contrary to the traditional teaching based on the verse, *I shall appear in the cloud over the cover* (Lev. 16:2). At the beginning of chapter 4 of *Megillat Taʿanit,* it refers to the abolition of the book of decrees deposited by the Sadducees.[30] And in chapter 10[31] and in Bava Batra,[32] the Sadducees are also said to have permitted a daughter to inherit with the daughter of the son, and in Taʿanit and Menaḥot, to have allowed any individual voluntarily to offer the daily offering.[33] Similarly, regarding the Boethusians, it is said that they used to say that Aṣeret [i.e., Pentecost] must always occur on a Sunday.[34] The Boethusians are also reported to have understood many verses of the Torah literally, e.g., *But if damage ensues the penalty shall be life for life, eye for eye* (Ex. 21:24); *and they shall spread out the cloth before the elders of the town* (Deut. 22:17); *His brother's widow shall . . . spit in his face* (Deut. 25:9); and there are many other such examples.[35]

26. M. Avot 1:3. According to the passage in ARN Antigonus's disciples misinterpreted Antigonus's saying and understood it to mean that there was no reward in the afterlife nor resurrection of the dead. They formed two sects after the names of their leaders Ṣadoq and Boethus. De' Rossi does not refer to the last part of the passage which refers to Boethus as leader of the Boethusians, presumably because it contradicted his theory that the Boethusians were a Greek sect and did believe in the immortality of the soul.

27. Epiphanius, *Contra haereses,* lib. 1, haeres XIV (*P.G.* XLI, col. 239). Epiphanius states that the Sadducees had chosen a name which in Hebrew signifies righteousness [*ṣedeq*], but that they turned away from the teaching of their leader, Ṣadoq. Many Christian historians of de' Rossi's time discussed the etymologies of the names of the sects and often quoted Epiphanius's conjectural etymologies.

28. Lit. 'burnt in the ash heap.' The expression occurs in M. Zev. 5:2 in reference to the burning of disqualified sacrifices.

29. B. Yoma 19b; 53a.

30. Meg. T., 331. The Sadducees seem to have deposited this book in the temple archives and it would have been consulted on questions of law. See S. Lieberman, *Hellenism,* 86.

31. The passage is in ch. 5 (234) and not ch. 10.

32. B. B.B. 115b.

33. B. Taʿanit 18a; Men. 65a. According to the Pharisees, the daily offering could only be bought out of Temple funds, but the Sadducees maintained that it could be bought from private funds.

34. B. Men. 65a; Meg. T. 1 (324). The Pharisees and Sadducees disputed the meaning of the verse, *He shall elevate the sheaf . . . on the day after the Sabbath* (Lev. 23:11). The Pharisees understood the word Sabbath to refer to the Passover day and that consequently the sheaf had to be elevated on the day after the first day of Passover; the Sadducees maintained that the word Sabbath referred to the first Sabbath day after the Passover week.

35. See Meg. T. 4 (331).

Now I discovered that the Sadducees were indicted with one particular charge which was not leveled against the Boethusians, namely, the denial of the resurrection of the dead. The subject is first brought to our notice in the Mishnah:[36] "These have no share in the world to come: who say that resurrection of the dead is not a tenet of the Torah." This is Rashi's reading,[37] but in the Turkish edition of Alfasi,[38] in the laws of repentance of Rabbi Moses [Maimonides],[39] in his treatise on resurrection[40] and in the Tosefta[41] the words "of the Torah"[42] appears to be lacking. The same reading appears in the last letter of Rabbi Meir bar Todros Halevi addressed to the sages of Lunel regarding the apologia of Maimonides for his treatment of this fundamental issue.[43]

{In reference to this subject I have some information, sagacious reader, which I cannot withhold from you. Among the books which I purchased from the estate of Rabbi Yeḥiel Nissim of Pisa[44] of blessed memory, I found a very old copy of the commentary to Mishnah Ḥeleq by Rabbi Moses of blessed memory. I noticed that the passage which refers to the thirteen principles of the Torah reads as follows:[45]

> The thirteenth principle is the resurrection of the dead which is famous and well known among our people and agreed by all sections of our community. It is frequently mentioned in the prayers, stories, and supplications which prophets and great sages composed and the Gemara and Midrashim abound with references to it. It concerns the return of the soul to the body after they have been separated one from the other. It has never been the subject of dispute among the people. It must be understood literally, and it is forbidden to suspect any religious person of holding a contrary belief. In the same way, resurrection of the dead which signifies the return of the soul to the body, as has been said, belongs to the miraculous. It is completely self-evident, its meaning is clear, and there is no other way of believing in it but in the way we have explained the true tradition. It is already mentioned by Daniel in a way which defies refutation when he states, *Many of those that sleep in the dust of the earth will awake* (12:2) and when the angel says to him, *But you, go on to the end;*

36. M. Sanh. 10:1.
37. Rashi to B. Sanh. 90a.
38. Alfasi, *Halakhot,* Constantinople, 1509, vol. 3, to Sanh. 90a.
39. *Mishneh Torah,* Teshuvah III:6.
40. *Ma'amar Teḥ. ha-Met.* (350).
41. T. Sanh. 13:5.
42. 'Of the Torah' is not in Cassel or in the printed first editions, but is in B.
43. Meir b. Todros Halevi Abulafia (1165–1244) was an opponent of Maimonides and attacked him for his apparent denial of physical resurrection. Abulafia did finally qualify his position as is shown by B. Septimus, *Hispano-Jewish Culture.* Regarding de' Rossi's rather strange statement, Septimus writes (54): "Perhaps de' Rossi had a letter in which Ramah [Abulafia] had communicated his modified position to Lunel." Abulafia's modified position is clear from his commentary to B. Sanh. which he wrote after his exchange of letters with the sages of Lunel.
44. Yeḥiel Nissim da Pisa, grandson of the famous banker of the same name, possessed a valuable library of books. He was author of the *Minḥat Qena'ot,* a critique of Yediah Bedersi's defense of philosophy. On Yeḥiel, see D. Kaufmann, "La famille."
45. At the end of his introduction to his *Perush,* Ḥeleq (M. Sanh. 10), Maimonides lists and explains his thirteen principles of faith. On the thirteenth principle which is the resurrection of the dead, he simply states: "The thirteenth principle is the resurrection of the dead and we have already explained it." This lapidary statement was understood by some of his critics to imply that he did not really believe in resurrection.

you shall rest and arise (12:13).[46] And when these principles are perfected in the heart of man. . . .[47]

Thus Rambam of blessed memory presents here a synopsis of his lengthy treatise on resurrection. I therefore came to the conclusion that because he had been censured for the brevity of his statement in his commentary on the Mishnah, namely: "The thirteenth fundament is the resurrection of the dead; we have already explained it," he went and added those words that we cited for the purpose of his apologia which is also the view expressed by the sage al-Ashqar in his responsum 117.[48] Thus should somebody reprint it, he would be duty bound to use the wording of the later version. Moreover it looks very probable to me that the reading "we have already explained it" is an error of the translator or a scribal error, since the explanation alluded to is not to be found anywhere and he was not the kind of person to lie. I wish we had his own Arabic text. I believe that it would read, "and it is evident" or "and it is already clear," meaning that it is self-explanatory and that one must simply believe in it.[49]}[2]

Now this sin of the Sadducees comes to light in the passage in the Gemara in which they challenge our sages to produce explicit evidence that resurrection of the dead is mentioned somewhere in the Bible.[50] Similarly, both the first and third apostles[51] describe an incident in which the Sadducees ridicule the idea by demanding as to which of seven brothers would marry a widow in the afterlife. And in their Acts, they [the Sadducees] are said to have rejected the idea of the resurrection of the dead, the existence of angels, and all spiritual, nonmaterial being.[52] Josephus also wrote that the Sadducees denied the immortality of the soul since they thought that both body and soul perish simultaneously.[53] Thus even further from their purview was the belief that the soul would return at the end of days to receive its allotted portion. However, no such allegation was made about the Boethusians. The Essenes, too, while clearly not subscribing to the basic tenet that the Oral Law was transmitted to our ancestors, did, according to written report, believe in the immortality of the soul, its transmigration,

46. This entire passage is to be found in Maimonides' Treatise on Resurrection. (See J. Finkel, "Maimonides," 63–64.) It appears to have been added to Yeḥiel Nissim da Pisa's text. According to L. N. Goldfeld, *Moses Maimonides' Treatise,* 107–11, this passage which is also found in the *Yad Ramah* ascribed to Meir Abulafia, presents opinions which are not consistent with those of Maimonides and should be judged as additions made by the pro-Maimonidean party. Although he notices its correspondence to what Maimonides later wrote in his treatise on resurrection, de' Rossi seems to be intent on taking up Maimonides' defense by regarding the text as original.

47. This last sentence is the continuation of Maimonides' text which is found in all editions of his Introduction.

48. Moses al-Ashqar, *She'elot,* responsum 117, 181b–82. Al-Ashqar defends Maimonides against Shemtob ibn Shemtov's attack on Maimonides. (His critique was also appended to the Ferrara 1556 edition of Shemtov's critique *Sefer ha-Emunot.*) Al-Ashqar argues that Maimonides includes those who reject resurrection among those who forfeit the world to come and produces other evidence to prove that Maimonides believed in physical resurrection.

49. As Cassel notes ad loc., the Hebrew text reflects the Arabic original exactly.

50. B. Sanh. 90b refers to 'heretics' (*minim*) and does not specify Sadducees.

51. Mat. 22:23–33; Mark 12:18–27. De' Rossi wrongly calls Mark the third Apostle. There is also a parallel passage in Luke 20:27–36.

52. Acts 23:8.

53. *Ant.* XVIII:16.

and reward in the afterlife. One finds that Josephus, Yedidyah the Alexandrian (in part of book 6 and all of book 37 entitled *On the Contemplative Life*) and Eusebius of Caesarea the Christian had the following to say of them:[54]

> The Essenes (according to Eusebius the name means "the holy ones" in Greek, and "healers of the soul" according to Yedidyah) numbered about four thousand in all. They came from Greek cities,[55] and Alexandria in Egypt served as their capital. All their adherents were men who had repudiated the world of flux and had come together in order to learn and teach and serve God in communal dwellings outside the towns, particularly in the region of Alexandria, away from the madding crowd. They observed all the same regulations which as we see nowadays are maintained by the Christian orders of brothers and which affect all aspects of the maintenance of their community. One could thus infer that these Christian orders followed in their footsteps and took their [i.e., the Essene] lifestyle as their model. Nobody claimed "what is mine is mine and what is yours is yours," for homes belonged to them all equally. The wealthy were not differentiated from the poor neither by clothing nor food; for all conducted themselves according to one system as dictated by the elder, their leader. Early morning and evening were spent in study and recitation of rhymed prayers which had either been written by some of their predecessors or were their own compositions that had met with the approval of the experts. In keeping with this lifestyle they kept themselves away from women whom they described as "snares and nets to the desires." But they were not all subject to the same manner of living. Some were obliged to remain totally celibate, just like those brothers mentioned before, while others were allowed conjugal relations for the purpose of procreation, and as soon as the woman was found to be pregnant she was kept at a distance.

{According to Philo, these Essenes who were assigned the name "the holy ones," as was said, devoted themselves to the active life. He spoke about them in chapter 36 [i.e., *That Every Good Man Is Free*]. But from what he says at the beginning of chapter 37 [i.e., *On the Contemplative Life*], it seems that those devoted to the contemplative life were called healers, i.e., healers of the soul [*therapeutae*]. In any case, there is no reason to assume that they did not belong to the Essene sects, for Josephus and Eusebius apply that which is said about the one group to the other.[56]}[2]

While I am engaged with the subject of the Essenes, I do not wish to omit to touch on any essential detail of the topic which is provided by those writers mentioned above. I must therefore also refer to their description of some members of the sect who were gifted with divine prescience. There was Menahem for example, a contemporary of

54. This is a conflation of Josephus, *Bellum* II:119–61, *Ant.* XVIII:18–23, Philo, *Prob.* 175–91; *Cont.;* Eusebius, *De ev. praep.,* 8, ch. 12 (*P.G.* XXI, col. 643–666). De' Rossi used George of Trebizond's translation where the reference is to bk. 8, ch. 4.

55. In his second revision of the book, de' Rossi substituted the passage in brackets until 'Greek cities' with the following: "According to Yedidyah in ch. 36 (i.e., *Prob.*) and Eusebius in the aforementioned passage, this designation means 'the holy.' For *hosia* means 'holiness' in Greek and *hosios* 'holy.' Although many of them came from many cities, the best of them numbered about four thousand and came from Greek cities."

56. De' Rossi attempts here to gloss over the discrepancies between the various accounts. He does not acknowledge that Josephus makes no reference to Greek Jews in his description of the Essenes. He does not mention that the Therapeutae are not described as sharing their homes and clothing as are the Essenes.

Hillel and Shammai, who is perhaps to be identified with the Menahem of whom our sages of blessed memory state in Mishnah Ḥagigah:[57] "Menahem went forth, Shammi entered." In other words, he left the community of the Pharisees to lead a solitary life among this sect at which point Shammai replaced him.[58] {This interpretation does not concur with Rava's view that he went forth for the service of the king, but with Abaye's view. Study this and the ensuing passage.[59]} According to Josephus, Menahem observed Herod, then still a boy, playing with other children of his own age and predicted that he would become king. When Menahem's prophecy came true, Herod inquired of Menahem as to whether he would retain his power for as long as ten years. Menahem replied that he would reign thirty years or more. And so it was, for he ruled thirty-seven years.[60] Josephus also refers to a certain Judah of the same sect who, on seeing Antigonus the high priest pass through the royal palace,[61] prophesied that he would die the same day. His prediction came to pass.[62] In a similar vein, he writes about a certain member of the sect called Simeon who correctly interpreted a dream of Archelaus as a presage of disaster.[63] And if all these stories which are also related in his Hebrew work [i.e., the *Josippon*] are true,[64] they may have been caused by malign influences[65] seeing that it is acknowledged that they sinned against God.[66]

According to Essene doctrine, all events in human life are determined by decree of the celestial angels. A person cannot injure his finger down here on earth without it having been decreed from above. The Sadducees held the opposite belief and declared that everything which happens to a person is brought about by his own free will and by his own decision; neither good nor bad events could be attributed to divine agency. The Pharisees steered a middle path when they said that some things were held under divine control, while other things were dependent on man's wish to bring them to actuality. The members of this sect, I mean the Essenes, were eager to understand the Torah and strove to use it as a means to penetrate the wonderful secrets of natural existence. For this task they were aided by the ideas which they had received from their ancestors. But unlike the Pharisees, they did not hold the tenet that the [Oral] Tradition was also enjoined on us together with the Written Torah. Josephus describes their beliefs concerning the soul in the following manner:[67]

57. M. Ḥag. 2:2. L. Ginzberg, *On Jewish Law* (101) interpreted this passage as a reference to a certain Menahem, a conservative Pharisee, who was removed from office when he went over to the Essenes.

58. De' Rossi originally wrote: "This interpretation is proffered on the grounds that it is possible to differ from our rabbis of blessed memory who explained that he [i.e., Menahem] went forth for the service of the king." He then emended it as given in the text.

59. This is a reference to B. Ḥag. 16b: "Whither did he go forth? Abaye said: 'He went forth into evil courses.' Raba said: 'He went forth to the king's service.' "

60. *Ant.* XV:373–79.

61. Josephus—'Temple.'

62. *Bellum* I:78–80.

63. Ibid. II:113.

64. The story of Menahem, e.g., is given in *Josippon,* bk. 6, ch. 55 (189).

65. 'Malign influences.' This expression (*mi-siṭra dimesa'ava*) is kabbalistic and is used in the Zohar.

66. This is a somewhat paradoxical statement. On one hand, de' Rossi appears to be questioning the authenticity of these stories, and on the other hand, he uses terminology which expresses a belief in satanic powers. It should be remembered that he is a fierce opponent of astrology. It may be, then, that he is using the kabbalistic expression tongue in cheek.

67. *Bellum* II:154–57.

> They hold the firm belief that the bodies perish because they are made of impermanent matter. The souls, however, survive; death cannot reach them. They are fashioned from the rarified fiery element, becoming imprisoned in the body as though drawn into them through a bond and natural desire. When they reject the bodily fetters, they rejoice, liberated as it were from a long term of bondage, and return to dwell on high. They claim that the virtuous souls go to dwell in a place beyond the ocean where wondrous pleasure awaits them. For this region is not subject to heavy rains, snow, or deadly pestilence, but the unceasing breezes of the bright north wind keeps it perpetually pleasant. But the wicked souls are expelled to a stormy place, overladen with trouble and fraught with sorrow and distress which is unending (Sela). They think that primarily, the souls are immortal since they are naturally drawn to righteousness and eschew iniquity. Thus on arriving in this world, the virtuous souls become even more virtuous in anticipation of the good to which they will again return. But the wicked ones are restrained from their wicked desire; for although during their lifetime they appear to be hidden under the cover of the body, after death, they will suffer perpetual afflictions.

Indeed, on many occasions I wondered how it came about that not one of our teachers ever alluded to this sect that was renowned among the gentiles. On the other hand, I examined the works of our sages in order to ascertain whether they made any distinction between the Sadducees and Boethusians. It seemed to me that although they were indistinguishable insofar as both denied the Oral Law, the Boethusians were not incriminated, as had been the Sadducees, for rejecting the immortality of the soul and its recompense after death. I also pondered over the similarity of the names Boethusians and Essenes which would be obvious to the expert who knows how that in antiquity, names were interchangeable. It was easy to see that the name Boethusians was formed from a combination of *bayit* (i.e., "house" because of their unique mode of sharing their houses in common) and Essene.[68] Then I also considered the passage in tractate Shabbat which is also cited in tractate Soferim which reads as follows: "A Boethusian asked Rabbi Joshua ha-Garsi: 'How do we know that the skin of an unclean animal may not be used for the writing of the phylacteries. . . .' Then he [i.e., the Boethusian] said to him: 'Kalos.' "[69] As Rashi of blessed memory explains, the word *ḳalos* means "fine" in Greek. One might conclude from this that the Boethusian in question was a Greek. And on the basis of what we have already been told by Yedidyah and Josephus, one might conclude that all these Essenes were Greeks, that is, Greeks of Jewish parentage from the neighbourhood of Alexandria. The passage from tractate Shabbat also brought to our notice something in the Boethusian's favor; for he did not insist in opposing the Pharisee on a halakhic issue regarding the precept of the phylacteries, as the more stubborn Sadducees were wont to do.

In view of all this I was confident enough to make certain assertions. The Boethusians, that is the Essenes, differed from the Sadducees on many issues and particularly as regards the soul and reward and punishment in the afterlife. Thus they were regarded as two distinct sects as Rambam states.[70] For if they had shared all the same

68. The name "Boethusian" is separated into two words in the T. Sukk. 3:1. See S. Lieberman, *Tosefta,* 870 for citation of other passages in which the two words *bet sen* occur.

69. B. Shabb. 108a; Sof. 1:2 (but there is no reference to the Boethusian in Soferim).

70. *Perush,* M. Avot 1:3; Ḥull. 1:2.

doctrines, even if their population was more numerous than locusts, they would have been considered one sect. In fact, they were united in this wickedness—they did not believe that the true Oral Torah had been given to us together with the Written Torah. Indeed, on consultation of the *Kuzari,* you will find that a distinction is drawn between the Karaites and those two sects.[71] For the author traces the origins of Karaism to the incident which occurred in the days of Simeon ben Sheṭaḥ involving the sages and King Jannai. And he dates the formation of the Sadducean and Boethusian sects a long time before this during the lifetime of Antigonus.[72] In his commentary on tractate Avot, Don Isaac [Abravanel] also was inclined to accept his opinion.[73] But Rambam seems closer to the truth in regarding them all as one undifferentiated heresy. This is what the sage of blessed memory writes: "In the land of Egypt they are called Karaites, but the sages named them Sadducees and Boethusians and they were the first to challenge the tradition of our sages."[74] Actually, the story about Jannai as related by our sages in Qiddushin[75] lends more support to the view put forward in the *Kuzari.* But the realization that the denial of the Oral Tradition is a single heresy, which explanation is corroborated by the talmudic discussion of the subject, eradicates the need to find nonexistent differences between the sects. This position is all the more justifiable in view of Josephus's account of the story about King Jannaeus which makes it quite clear that it was the Sadducees who drew him away from the paths of the Pharisees in order to deny the Tradition.[76] There are, however, discrepancies between his version of the story and that of our rabbis. If God so wills it, we shall discuss this matter further in chapter 21.

We shall now leave these investigations and reassert once more that the Boethusians and Essenes were one and the same sect. Indeed, regardless of whether this evaluation of mine is correct or complete nonsense (for when all is said and done I cannot be too dogmatic), please give me your attention, sagacious reader, and hear me on the subject of Yedidyah the Alexandrian on which I have already embarked.

71. Judah Halevi, *Kuzari* III, par. 65. "At this period arose the doctrine of the Karaites in consequence of an incident between the sages and King Jannai who was a priest. His mother was under suspicion of being a profane woman. One of the sages alluded to this, saying to him: 'Be satisfied, O King Jannai with the royal crown but leave the priestly crown to the seed of Aaron.' His friends prejudiced him against the sages. He replied: 'If I destroy the sages, what will become of our Law?' They replied: 'There is the written law; whoever wishes to study it may come and do so; take no heed of the oral law'" (trans. H. Hirschfeld).

72. Ibid. "He was followed by Antigonus of great fame. His disciples were Ṣadoq and Boethus who were the originators of the sects called after them Sadduceans and Boethusians."

73. Abravanel, *Naḥalat Avot,* 1:6: "Joshua ben Peraḥia was the teacher of Jesus the Christian and the Karaite sect originated in his time as a consequence of the incident involving the sages in Jerusalem and King Hyrcanus who is called Jannai the king by the rabbis of blessed memory."

74. *Perush,* M. Avot 1:3.

75. B. Qidd. 66a.

76. *Ant.* XIII:372–98 describes the people's rejection of Alexander Jannaeus from the priesthood and how on his deathbed, Alexander Jannaeus counsels Alexandra to succumb to the Pharisees.

CHAPTER FOUR

On the commendable aspects of Yedidyah's works which are compatible with our Torah.

This man Yedidyah the Alexandrian had expert knowledge of Greek and expressed himself fluently and lucidly in the language with a mastery equal to that of all those who put pen to paper. Writers have praised him, declaring that his methods bear such great affinity to those of Plato that one cannot judge which one influenced the other.[1] Among his forty-three works which were published together, there are some allusions to other writings of his which have not come down to us.[2] The majority are commentaries on the Written Torah on which he bestows great praise. He also extols our lord Moses who was sent to give the Torah to us. He [i.e., Yedidyah] was a great philosopher, well versed in the works of Plato and Aristotle and all other scholars who won a reputation for themselves in the gentile world.[3] He also puts forward his own original ideas, sometimes as a follower of their systems, while at other times he dissents from them to forge a contrary path. And yet, despite all his wisdom, he does on various occasions admit that the knowledge of the earthly and higher elements of the perceptible world leads to the conclusion that all the thoughts and ideas of men are vanity and a striving after the wind. In his book entitled *On Dreams* he has the following to say on the subject of the heavens:[4]

> Who knows whether they are formed of frozen water, pure fire or a fifth circulating substance? Is there any density to the outermost sphere of the fixed stars? (At the beginning of his book *On the Eternity of the World*[5] he also writes that it encircles everything, which statement is similar to that of ibn Ezra who said that there is no corporeal existence above the sphere of the planets.[6]) Or does it merely resemble a plane marked out by a

1. De' Rossi is referring to the popular Greek saying quoted by Jerome in his profile of Philo: "Either Philo is like Plato or Plato is like Philo." De' Rossi used Sigismund Gelenius's Latin translation of Philo which contained Jerome's *testimonium* on Philo.

2. This figure is given in Gelenius's edition of Philo. It does not include the *Quaestiones et solutiones* on Genesis and Exodus but subdivides parts of the *De specialibus legibus* into separate books.

3. H. A. Wolfson (*Philo,* 100) compares this statement to Eusebius, *Hist. eccl.* 11:42: "Vir a plurimis non modo nostrorum verum etiam gentilium maximo in pretio habitus."

4. *Som.* I, 21–24 (486–87). De' Rossi refers to page numbers in the Lyons 1555 edition of Philo. These page numbers are put in brackets here.

5. *Aet.* 4 (785).

6. Ibn Ezra to Gen. 1:14. In B, de' Rossi also refers to ch. 5 of Samuel ibn Tibbon's work *Yiqqavu ha-Mayim* (19) in which he states that the heavenly sphere comprises all the other spheres including the ninth sphere.

> stylus? As for the stars themselves, are they fiery masses of earth or compressed globes of fire? Are they animate rational beings or are they devoid of intelligent life? Are their motions voluntary or necessary? Does the moon have its own light or is it incidental?[7] Do its rays of light emanate from itself or from the sun or do they emanate from both sources simultaneously?

Similarly, regarding the soul he says:[8] "Who can boast knowledge of it? Does it come into being as a result of the formation of the body or does it descend into it from without?[9] Is it located in the heart or in the brain? At death, does it perish with the body or does it survive for a subsequent period, or is it immortal? Such opinions have been expressed with regard to all the questions we have raised." On the basis of this premise, in book 1, he resolves the problem as to why Adam who named all the species of living creatures did not name himself.[10] The solution lay in the fact that he did not know the nature of his own soul, let alone the nature of the Creator who is the soul of the entire universe. (This is not, however, in accordance with what our rabbis of blessed memory say in Bereshit Rabbah.[11]) The gentile orator Cicero raises similar doubts in the first of his *Tusculans,*[12] where like Rabbi Meir (in Bereshit Rabbah), he declares that death is good.[13] Indeed, one should not suppress the fact that Yedidyah poses all these questions that we have mentioned, and particularly those related to the immortality of the soul from the perspective of human wisdom alone.[14] In the same manner, the preacher [Ecclesiastes], speaking as a man divested of divine illumination, asks: *Who knows if a man's lifebreath does rise upward and if a beast's breath does sink down into the earth?* (Eccl. 3:21). But as regards our Torah, the books of Yedidyah do in fact occasionally ennunciate the right doctrine that the soul definitely survives after death. Look at his book *On the Unchangeableness of God* in reference to the blessed Lord's statement, *But you remain here with Me* (Deut. 5:28);[15] his book *On Abraham* regarding the verse, *And the lifebreath returns to God* (Eccl. 12:7);[16] his book *On Dreams* with regard to the verse, *I . . . will bring you back to this land* (Gen. 28:15); and at the end of the same work

7. The Latin reads: "Nativone an mutuaticio luce luminet?" (Does it shine with its own or borrowed light?)
8. *Som.* I, 30–32 (488).
9. *Som.* I, 31: "At our birth is it at once introduced into us from without? Or does the air which envelops it impart intense hardness to the warm nature within us . . . ? The name of 'soul' would seem to have been given it owing to the cooling which it thus undergoes" (R. Marcus, Loeb trans.).
10. De' Rossi is not referring to book 1 which is *De opificio mundi,* but to *Legum allegoriae* 1, 91.
11. B.R. 17:4 (156). "He [God] said to Adam: 'What is your name?' He said to Him: 'I ought to be called Adam because I was created from the earth.' He said: 'And what is My name?' He replied: 'You ought to be called Lord for You are Lord of all your creation.' "
12. Cicero, *Tusc. Disp.,* 1, VIII, 16: "quoniam post mortem mali nihil est ne mors quidem est malum."
13. B. R. 9:5 (70): "In the Torah [scroll] of Rabbi Meir they found it written, *behold it was very good* (Gen. 1:31)—behold death is good." This is a play on the word "very" (*me'od*) and the word "death" (*mavet*).
14. Cf. Petrarch's statement in his *De sui ipsius . . . ignorantia,* 24–25: "Num quid, oro, naturas beluarum et volucrum et piscium et serpentum nosse profuerit, et naturam hominum ad quod nati sumus unde et quo pergimus [vel nescire vel] spernere?"
15. *Deus* 23–24 (258).
16. *Abr.* 258 (333–34). Philo does not refer to the verse from Ecclesiastes, but he uses similar language: "mortem non extinctionem animae sed separationem disiunctionemque a corpore illa redeunte retro unde venerat, venerat autem a deo sicut in opificio mundi declaratum est."

in regard to the verse, *I will dedicate him to the Lord* (1Sam. 1:11).[17] Of especial note is his statement in *On Flight.* For despite Rabbi Eleazar ben Azariah's fine saying that a woman's wisdom extends only as far as the distaff,[18] Yedidyah extends great praise here to the statement of a wise woman who in like manner to the rabbis of blessed memory[19] declared that even in death the righteous are called living.[20] The prooftexts for this view are the verses, *While you, who held fast to the Lord your God, are all alive today* (Deut. 4:4); *and they died before the Lord* (Lev. 10:2) which describes the death of the ministering priests Nadav and Abihu. He thus solves the problem as to why the Torah employs double terminology in decreeing the death of the sinner for it states, *If a man smite another and he die, he shall surely die* (*mot yamut*) (Ex. 21:12). The sinner is thus threatened with death of both the body and soul because notwithstanding that he is still alive, he is virtually dead.

Now in chapter 8 of his seventh book, the Christian sage Lactantius Firmianus claims that while Plato believed in the immortality of the soul, he did not believe that it reached a blessed estate;[21] and there is a great difference between a mere existence and a blessed one. Now it will become clear to you that Yedidyah believed not only that the soul survives, but that it enjoys a blessed estate in its immortality. Among the passages in which he puts forward this opinion is the discussion about Abraham our father at the beginning of his book *On the Sacrifice of Abel:* "When Abraham left mortal life, he was gathered to the people of God and enjoyed eternal life like the angels who are the divine host and unembodied souls whose lot is eternal happiness."[22] He also believed that the soul once separated from carnal existence eventually returns to it. This is shown in a lengthy passage from his book entitled *On Dreams* which I will quote in translation in a successive chapter if God so wills.[23] It contains the following statement: "There are some souls which enjoy the company of the living and will therefore return to them once more."[24] If you examine the entry for "soul" in the index to his works you can acquaint yourself with his apposite remarks on any aspect of the subject which interests you.[25]

Nevertheless, you should know that the idea of the blessedness of the souls in the afterlife is also to be found in Plato's *Phaedo.* At the conclusion of his discussion following the description of the souls' bliss in the Elysian fields which corresponds to our Garden of Eden and their attachment to the saints in the firmament of heaven, he writes: "Now a thinking person ought not to believe all this literally. But in a general way, a

17. *Som.* I, 180; 1, 254.

18. P. Sota 3 (4) 19a; B. Yoma 66b; Bem. R. 9:48: "A wise woman asked R. Eliezer [*sic*], 'Since with regard to the offense with the golden calf, everybody was equally associated, why was the penalty of death not equally apportioned to them all?' He answered, 'There is no wisdom in woman except with the distaff.' "

19. P. Ber. 2(3) 4d; B. Ber. 18a.

20. *Fug.* 54–57 (396 and not 386 as de' Rossi writes). As Cassel notes ad loc., Philo's metaphorical woman is understood by de' Rossi as a real woman.

21. Lactantius Firmianus, *Divinarum institutionum lib,* 7: 8 (*P.L.* VI, col. 762): "Nam licet verum de animae immortalitate sentiret [i.e., Plato] tamen non ita de illa tanquam de summo bono disserebat."

22. *Sac.* 5 (115).

23. I.e., ch. 6.

24. *Som.* I, 139 (501).

25. He is referring to the entry for *anima* which is in the index at the end of the second volume.

wonderful future is assured the virtuous in the manner that I have described or something very like it."[26] It thus transpires that the writer Lactantius, whom we cited above about Plato not believing in the soul's blessed immortality, could not have read this text of the *Phaedo.*[27]

Yedidyah also poses the question as to whether the heavenly hosts are rational bodies or not and argues in the affirmative in his book *On the Giants.*[28] He speaks on several occasions and in particular in his work *On the Confusion of Tongues* about the existence of angels who, in his view, dwell in the upper region of the air under the heavens.[29] His discussion of the verse, *And the sons of God saw the daughters of man* (Gen. 6:2) in his work *On Giants*[30] is reminiscent of the passage in *Midrash Ruth ha-Neʿelam* regarding the psalmist's words, *He makes the winds His messengers* (Ps. 104:4).[31] We will mention it again in chapter 6, God willing, with reference to its citation by the sage Recanati in his commentary on the verse, *And the sons of God.*

The existence of the blessed God, the only completely unified being without admixture of corporeality, is a tenet of his which he upholds as clearly as the rising sun throughout his works. In his works *On the Confusion of Tongues* and *On Flight* he raises the problem of the plural used in the statements: *Let us make man* (Gen. 1:26); *Come, let us go down* (Gen. 11:7); *If man was one of us* (Gen. 3:22).[32] He propounds the view as expressed by the Greek bard Homer that for sovereignty, plurality is harmful and oneness desirable. He then asserts the view that no distinction should be drawn in this matter between the heavenly and earthly kingdoms; it thus follows that our God is unquestionably one. He resolves the problem by asserting that the plural form refers to the potencies of the blessed Lord which emanate from Him either in the form of loving-kindness or castigation. And even the implementation of the attribute of judgment which puts an end to evil actions is in itself a form of loving-kindness. In his works *On the Cherubim, On the Life of Moses,* and *On Abraham,*[33] he states that Abraham's vision of the three men standing before him signifies the three names of the blessed Lord—i.e., the tetragrammaton which denotes true existence because there is none comparable to Him; Elohim, the name of Godship which denotes that He is the propagator of all created beings; Adonai, the name of Lordship which denotes that it is He who oversees their existence. He makes it very clear, however, that we must believe

26. *Phaedo* 114b–c. Plato does not use the term "Elysian fields." De' Rossi appears to have derived his use of the term in this connection from Marsilio Ficino who in the *argumentum* to the tenth book of the *Republic* (which de' Rossi quotes in another context) states that the Elysian fields are located in the terrestial paradise of the good souls as described by Plato (see *Opera omnia,* 656).

27. De' Rossi's criticism of Lactantius is a good example of his syncretistic approach to Plato. Plato and his follower Philo had a notion of the paradise of virtuous souls, the pagan counterpart to the Jewish Garden of Eden.

28. *Gig.* 8 (248).

29. *Conf.* 174 (300) and passim.

30. *Gig.* 6–11 (249).

31. Midrash ha-Neʿelam, Ruth, 81 col. b: "Rabbi Qisma bar Rabbi Jannai opened his discourse with the verse, *He makes the winds his messengers, fiery flames His servants.* Some angels are made of wind, some of fire. . . . Those who descend are made of these two elements. When they descend they are more robed in the air of this world and they become embodied in matter."

32. *Conf.* 168–70 (299); *Fug.* 68–70 (397).

33. *Cher.* 27–28 (99); *Mos.* II, 99–100 (111, 567); *Abr.* 119ff (318–19).

in the blessed Lord as a complete unity dissociated from any form of corporeality which is what all the children of Israel believe whose ways are perfect.

In Bereshit Rabbah, our rabbis of blessed memory state with regard to the first verse of Genesis:[34] "Just as the architect builds on the basis of plans and diagrams, so the Holy One blessed be He looked into the Torah and created the world as it says, *The Lord created me at the beginning of His course* (Pr. 8:22)." Corresponding to this passage is his [i.e., Yedidyah's] statement in his work entitled *On the Creation of the World:*[35] "He resembles a skilled craftsman who first conceives the model of the entire building and transforms his mental image and likeness into concrete existence. . . . Thus in the beginning, understanding beginning not in a temporal sense for time was created with the creation, but in a numerical sense, God blessed be He caused the world of the intellect (I believe that the kabbalists call it the world of emanations and *sefirot*) to emanate through, but not independent of, His intellect, and from it was established the whole of the sensible world in its time and part by part." Here as in his *On Agriculture, On the Confusion of Tongues,* and *On the Unchangeableness of God,*[36] he calls the intelligible world of emanations the "firstborn of God" or alternatively, the "incorporeal light"; whereas the sensible world is called "His simple and material son." In his *Life of Moses,* he writes that the high priest's vestments represent all parts of the entire realm of existence. He said that when he [i.e., the high priest] presented himself before the blessed Lord robed in these garments, it was as though he was evoking His love and compassion for the whole world which is His only son and requesting Him not to desist from extending His loving-kindness towards it.[37]

Now in treating this subject, I shall not refrain from drawing your attention, intelligent reader, to the statement of Marsilio Ficino, a great contemporary Christian philosopher, in his preface to his Latin translation of the Greek text of the *Pimander.*[38] Ficino first states that the great astronomer Atlas and his brother Prometheus, the greatest physicist, lived in Egypt in the time of Moses. It could be inferred that it was because of their wisdom along with the other clever magicians that God selected Egypt as the iron blast furnace for testing. Moreover, there is also the verse that states, *Solomon's wisdom was greater . . . than all the wisdom of the Egyptians* (1K. 5:10).[39] {There may also be a reference to them in the Zohar when it states that the heads of all the Egyptian magicians were Jannus and Jambres[40] and alternative names Johanne and

34. B.R. 1:1.

35. This is a synopsis of *Op.* 16–18, 26 (3–4).

36. *Agr.* 51 (172); *Con.* 145–49 (286); *Deus* 31–32 (259).

37. *Mos.* II, 135 (11, 570).

38. This is a reference to one of the Hermetic writings which according to most writers in the sixteenth century were written by Hermes Trismegistus, a contemporary (or, according to Ficino, a great grandson of a contemporary) of Moses. Isaac Casaubon detected the apocryphal nature of the Hermetic texts in 1614. On this subject, see F. A. Yates, *Giordano Bruno,* D. P. Walker, *The Ancient Theology,* B. P. Copenhaver, ed., *Hermetica,* and A. T. Grafton, *Defenders,* chs. 5 and 6. Marsilio Ficino translated the Asclepius and Pimander into Latin in 1463. It was first printed in Treviso in 1471.

39. De' Rossi omits the first part of the verse that states that Solomon's wisdom was greater than the wisdom of all the Kedemites.

40. Zohar I, 191a. On the tradition about Jannes and Jambres, see A. Pietersma and R. T. Lutz, Introduction to the fragments of Jannes and Jambres, *The Old Testament Pseudepigrapha,* ed. J. H. Charlesworth, vol. 2, 421–26.

Mamre are mentioned in Shemot Rabbah[41] and tractate Menaḥot.[42] For any name suffices for these kind of stories.[43]} Ficino then states that four generations after Prometheus, an outstanding sage, whose name was Hermes in Greek and Mercurius in Latin, won a reputation. He was given the designation Trismegistus which means thrice great, because he was regarded in Egypt as a great philosopher and consequently as a great priest and thus also as a great king.[44] This Hermes promoted himself[45] from the natural sciences and astronomy to the study of theology. He wrote two works which specifically deal with theology in the Egyptian language for his Egyptian readers and in Greek for his Greek readers: the *Pimander,* the subject of which is the wisdom and potency of the deity, and the *Asclepius,* which treats divine will. All readers of these books will certainly admit that although he was of foreign stock, he wrote in a manner which closely follows that of the Mosaic Torah. It is likely that he knew about the great wonders performed by our God in Egypt and came to hear of the giving of His Torah at the holy convocation. Awed, he tried to understand its meaning by means of books and writers and although he was a foreigner, applied it to his own works. In view of my attraction to ancient works which contain certain comments which bear affinity to aspects of our Torah, I was moved to undertake—with the permission of "He who dwells in the bush,"[46] and assuming my kind God grants me the years, and once this book of mine had a favorable reception in Jewish circles—for the glorification of His blessed and exalted name, a translation of those Hermetic texts accompanied by introductions and notes which I regarded appropriate for making the necessary distinction between the holy and profane. In this way, any intelligent person would remain unscathed and more likely to derive benefit.[47]

Now what I should like to convey to you in this discourse of mine is information about chapter 1 of the *Pimander* where he speaks about creation. You will discover that he writes about the "darkness over the surface of the deep" and about "the spirit of God hovering over the water."[48] You will also observe that like Yedidyah as mentioned above, he describes the light of emanation as the son of God, who is yet removed from all corporeality and sensation.[49] In this respect he is like all others who endeavor to describe the Lord.[50] In view of the statements of these two sages [i.e., Philo and Hermes], I was encouraged to think that provided it is indeed true that the kabbalists

41. S.R. 9:4.
42. B. Men. 85a.
43. De' Rossi seems to be implying here that he is sceptical about the veracity of these stories.
44. This sentence would have been clearer had de' Rossi quoted the following sentence of Ficino's statement (Hermes, 4). He states that it was an Egyptian custom to elect priests from the best of the philosophers and kings from the best of the priests. Mercurius's career followed this pattern.
45. 'Promoted himself.' The Latin simply reads "se contulit."
46. 'He who dwells in the bush,' cf. Deut. 33:16.
47. As far as I know, de' Rossi never made these translations.
48. Ficino points out the same parallels in his Argumentum [or Commentaria] to the first dialogue of the *Pimander:* "In primo dialogo, videtur Mercurius Mosaica mysteria tractare. Moses enim tenebras vidit super faciem abyssi et spiritum domini ferri super aquas" (9).
49. This, too, is stated by Ficino: "Ille [Hermes] potenti verbo domini cunctà creata nuntiat, hic vero verbum illud lucens, quod omnia illuminet, germen mentis, filium dei esse asseverat, et mentem patrem et verbum mentis filium natura non distare" (9).
50. Cf. Is. 44:5.

wrote the passage known as Qaddisha Abba etc.,[51] there is no reason for surprise when one takes into account that the sage Recanati and others made statements of a similar kind.[52] The enlightened will correctly gauge their meaning. This is valid as long as you do not overstep the limit in ascribing corporeality. Realize that in every question the intellectual concept is divided in our perception but unified in the blessed Lord. It is merely a matter of terminology whether it is called son or emanation or light or *sefirah* or idea as Plato cleverly puts it.[53] The sage Galen has said on several occasions in his medical writings that once scholars are agreed about concepts, differences in terminology may be disregarded.[54]

All these words of mine are only proffered on the specific condition that judicious people will admit that they are correct in every respect; otherwise, their validity is completely undermined and they are rendered worthless. You should also certainly know that according to the greatest Christian doctor [i.e., Augustine] whose statements are cited by Champier of Lyons in his introduction to his explanation of the Hermetic texts, Hermes uses the expression "son" as if he were a foreseer of their religion.[55] Gelenius the Christian scholar who translated Yedidyah's works into Latin expressed the same view with regard to Yedidyah's terminology in his introduction.[56] And truly, the upright will deem them worthy of praise for this, inasmuch as the more a person can transform something to the merit of his religion, the more deserving is he of praise.[57]

Now let us resume our discussion of Yedidyah with which we began. He writes at length about the perfection of the Torah, and its justice, likening the ten commandments to mothers and all their offspring to the other precepts. This view which he expresses in many passages, the most noteworthy of which is in *On the Decalogue,*[58]

51. The "Qaddisha Abba" quotation is an allusion to a Christian interpretation of the *trishagion Holy holy holy is the Lord of Hosts* (Is. 6:3). The passage does not occur in any extant Jewish kabbalistic text. It is cited in the *Zelus Christi* of 1450 by Pedro della Caballeria. In book 2 of his anti-Jewish tract *Opus de arcanis* (XXXI^r), Petrus Galatinus claims that the trinitarian interpretation of Is. 6:3 is confirmed by Simeon bar Yoḥai and Jonathan ben Uzziel. He writes: "For Rabbi Simeon says in Hebrew . . . 'Holy'—this is the father; 'holy'—this is the son; 'holy'—this is the Holy Spirit." De' Rossi knew Galatinus's work and may have been alluding to this passage. For further discussion of this subject, see my article, "Philo," 171.

52. Recanati, *Perush,* aḥare mot, 63 col. b. I assume that de' Rossi is referring to the passage about forbidden sexual unions where Recanati speaks about the *sefirot* in terms of familial relationships.

53. M. Idel ("The Magical and Neoplatonic Interpretation," 227) has pointed out that his passage also betrays the mark of Ficino and Pico. The comparison between *sefira* and *idea* implies that the ideas are to be found in God himself and not only in the *logos.*

54. Galen's distaste for terminological disputes is manifested throughout his works. See, e.g. *Methodus medendi* I, 5, 9.

55. Symphorien Champier (1470?–1537), *De triplici disciplina,* hh1111r–v.

56. De' Rossi is referring to Gelenius's "epistola nuncupatoria" to Joannes a Balma Peranus (Basel, 1554). He appears to be referring to the Prisca Theologia notion used by Gelenius when he quotes the Greek saying, "Either Philo is like Plato or Plato is like Philo" and then states: "I believe that it is rather Plato who is like Philo, because he emulated Moses whose disciple Philo was. After all, it is agreed that Plato traveled to Egypt where he received instruction from both Jewish and Egyptian priestly tribes."

57. The use of the expression "the more deserving is he of praise" is provocative. To Jewish readers this expression would be associated with the Seder liturgy. In the Haggadah it is expressly stated, "The more he relates the story of the exodus from Egypt, the more deserving is he of praise."

58. *Decal.* 154, 175 (447, 381). In the second part of the book, Philo describes how the ten commandments are summaries of the entire body of legislation. But from the page numbers, it is clear that he is referring to *De congressu quaerendae eruditionis gratia,* 120.

bears affinity to our sages's statements in Bemidbar Rabbah[59] and Shir Rabbah.[60] In the second book of the *Life of Moses* he speaks in the most sublime language about the perpetuity of the Torah, its indestructibility and immutability.[61] He mentions Moses' four positions as king, lawgiver, priest, and prophet, and the four attitudes which any legislator must necessarily possess, namely, compassion for humanity, practice of justice, love of virtue, and hatred of evil. And he says that the laws which are enacted by any philosopher, whoever he is, will, in the course of time, be changed and ultimately, disintegrate entirely either when the circumstances of the people change very much for the worse and their leadership falls away, or when the change is so beneficial for them that they are led to cast off the yoke and stamp against their former leaders. He then writes:[62] "Indeed, only our Torah[63] remains for it can never be brought to an end nor be subject to change. It is eternal, imprinted as it were with the seals of nature. This is the way it has been from the very first day of its enactment until the present day (i.e., about twenty-five years before the destruction of the second Temple). It is anticipated that it will remain thus eternal forever as long as the sun, moon, and heavens exist above the earth. Whatever vicissitudes or changes have befallen our people, the abrogation of even the most insignificant precept has never been countenanced." Thus far his words which resemble Josephus's statement:[64] "Is not our Torah controlled by God who ensures that it is not anulled nor subject to any change. God forbid that a time should come when there is any innovation or it is transformed in any manner." He says that all the stories and precepts of the Torah contain hints and allusions to wondrous matters which are connected to the perfection of the soul. Yet while we comprehend those intellectual concepts we may not uproot the practice of the precepts which the Torah ordains for us. We must be careful to preserve them all intact. He has lengthy discourses on this subject in many places. Of particular note is his discussion in *That Every Good Man Is Free,*[65] in *On the Contemplative Life,*[66] and *On the Migration of Abraham.*[67] He writes:

> There are some people who, having come to the conclusion that the written laws symbolize intellectual concepts, set themselves the task of understanding these forms while neglecting the actual observance of the laws. We do not approve of this negligence of theirs since it is necessary to be attentive to both aspects at one and the same time: the comprehension of the esoteric truths as well as the observance of the revealed aspects with which we have been commanded. Man is most certainly a social animal and because he is not an immaterial being, it is all the more appropriate that he should not dismiss practical observance and devote himself entirely to conceptualizing. Indeed, the Torah teaches us not to neglect our duty nor to repudiate the divine teachings which our ancestors explained

59. Bem. R. 13:15 to Num. 7:14. "Between each commandment that was inscribed on the tablets and the next were written out the ramifications and niceties of the Torah."

60. S.S. R. 5:12 to S.S. 5:14.

61. *Mos.* II, 12ff. (II, 556).

62. Ibid. 14–16.

63. The Greek text reads "Moses is alone in this."

64. *Ant.* IV: 181. De' Rossi changes the emphasis of the text which is part of Moses' address to the people before his death.

65. *Prob.* 69 (732–33).

66. *Cont.* 78 (754).

67. *Mig.* 89–93 (348).

> to us. Although we understand and know that the Sabbath is a commemoration of the power of the Creator[68] and of the inertness of the creation (in the following chapter you will get to understand what is meant by "the inertness of the creation"), we are nevertheless not able to transgress the laws pertaining to it: light fires, till the soil, do business, press legal proceedings on somebody, demand restitution of deposits, receive loans, and other such acts which are forbidden on days of rest. While the day of the Festival [i.e., Tabernacles] stimulates in us spiritual enjoyment and gratitude to God, we should not therefore absent ourselves from joining the gatherings of people who are assembled for the glorification of the sacrosanct. Although the commandment of circumcision provokes in us a repugnance of all excesses and a desire to excise the seeds of thoughts which breed useless ideas in us, we may not desist from the actual circumcision of our flesh. For otherwise, if we consider it sufficient to pay attention to the form and symbolic meaning alone, we will eradicate all the precepts one by one. Rather, we should regard the comprehension of the esoteric meanings of the precepts like the soul and compare the actual observances to the body. Just as we care for the upkeep of the body because it is the soul's sanctuary, so together with the preservation of the esoteric we should be conscientious in preserving the revealed commandments of our Torah. In fact, by observing them, we ensure a better understanding of their symbolic meaning and when our conduct becomes known, we will be cleared of all suspicion and reproach.

Thus far his words which bear affinity to what the author of the *Aqedah* [Isaac Arama] wrote in gate 7.[69]

In his work *On Abraham,* he wrote beautiful allegories on the binding of Isaac,[70] the stories about Abraham, Lot and the four and five kings, and on the five cities of Sodom.[71] In his work *On Dreams,* he gives a long and delightful account of the vision of the ladder, proffering his own allegorical interpretation of the story.[72] There are many other examples of allegorical interpretation in his work. In his work *On the Unchangeableness of God,* he composed a beautiful discourse on the subject of free will, saying that man is given free will even though God has prior knowledge of all his actions.[73] He devotes two works specifically to the subject of sacrifices[74] and the reward which is to be meted out for our actions.[75] They are certainly worthy of consideration. At the beginning of his last work, entitled *On the Embassy to Gaius,* he describes in beautiful terms how the blessed Lord cares for individual human beings, and the children of Israel in particular.[76] He also wrote on other subjects relating to the Torah and to other topics such that one is able to pick whichever of his intellectual products appeals to the intellect. Generally speaking, as one passes from gate to gate of his forty-three works (and they are readily accessible from the indices which give lists of subject

68. 'Creator.' The Latin reads "ingenitus" (unborn).

69. Isaac Arama, *Aqedat Yiṣḥaq,* gate 7, bereshit (54b–60a). Arama is more concerned to explain that notwithstanding the duty to accept the literal meaning of the stories of the Torah, one should also realize their esoteric significance.

70. *Abr.* 167ff. (327).

71. Ibid. 133ff. (330).

72. *Som.* I, 133ff. (500 ff.).

73. *Deus* 47–48 (261).

74. In the Latin translation the work is entitled *De animalibus idoneis sacrificio deque victimarum generibus.* In the Greek text, it is included in *Spec.* I, 162ff.

75. *Praem.* 162ff. (762).

76. *Leg.* 3.

matter), you will come to the realization that as regards the divine, the exaltation of our perfect Torah, the panegyrics of Moses the chosen of God, and the blessedness which awaits all who keep the commandments, he speaks as a man of exalted station who may be called by the name of Israel. By constant repetition, those pure statements of his become firmly established and fixed such that they cannot be dislodged.

Now enlightened reader, it seems to me appropriate that I should meet with your approval by disclosing yet further thoughts of mine concerning this man. You should know that in addition to his forty-three works which were published in one printing, he is also attributed with the authorship of two works which are not part of the collection. These works were translated from Greek into Latin. One is entitled *On the Times* and is published together with the works of Berosus the Chaldean, Metasthenes the Persian, and other chroniclers. In view of their brevity, all these works, being of the same genre, were preserved together.[77] I have translated the work in chapter 32 in the third section of this book of mine because I had some use for it in the chapters on chronology. The other work entitled *Book of Biblical Antiquities* begins its account with Adam and ends with the death of Saul. Either he did not write about the subsequent period or else that section of the work is no longer extant. It is actually full of errors because it was translated from a very old version from which words and sentences were missing.[78] In any case, the righteous person will be overjoyed to observe that it contains various passages which are also found in diverse rabbinic Midrashim.[79] Now an intelligent person might regard them as dubious stories and think to himself, "These matters and stories belong to remote antiquity: Who could have been their informant? What are these fantasies?" But on discovering that the same or similar accounts are to be found in a book like this which was written (if Yedidyah was indeed the author)[80] in the second Temple period, in a barbarous tongue, in another language,[81] he would rightly check his tongue and bite back his words and say, "There must be some basis to what they say." We may take this as an indication that these stories were transmitted to the people through the medium of the tradition and were related to us by our wise ancestors insofar as they were remembered by the former generations and their accounts were completely or at least partially correct. And even if you argue that the Yedidyah who composed the work is not be identified with the Alexandrian, it will surely be beneficial for us. This is because we will not have to admit that the opposite was the case: namely, that our sages derived these traditions from the gentile masses, took a liking to them, and then imparted them to us.

It recounts how Abraham our father was cast into the fiery furnace for his attempt to

77. De' Rossi is referring to the ps. Philonic work, which, like the other works mentioned by him, was forged by Annius of Viterbo.

78. The work was first published in Basel in 1527. The editor Sichardus also states that the work was corrupt. He based his edition on two manuscripts. See D. Harrington, *Ps.-Philon,* vol. 2; L. Feldman, *The Biblical Antiquities;* G. Kisch, *Pseudo-Philo's Liber.* For a recent discussion of the printing history of the work, see F. Parente, "Il *Liber.*"

79. De' Rossi was the first scholar to point out the parallels between the rabbinic texts and the *LAB.*

80. The work is not genuine. In his preface to the work (a2r), Sichardus notes that Guillaume Budé had questioned the authenticity of the work, but Sichardus himself thought the work authentic.

81. The work is only extant in Latin and scholars are divided as to whether it had originally been written in Hebrew.

challenge the idolators.[82] The same story is related by our rabbis of blessed memory in Bava Batra, Bereshit Rabbah, and Midrash Tehillim.[83] It also contains the story mentioned by Rabbi Johanan in Bereshit Rabbah in connection with the verse, *Look toward heaven and count the stars* (Gen. 15:5) that God lifted Abraham above the dome of heaven.[84] That the land of Israel was not affected by the fury of the flood[85] is also the opinion expressed by Rabbi Johanan to Resh Laqish in Taʿanit, Zevaḥim and Shir ha-Shirim Rabbah.[86] The view that Dinah the daughter of Jacob was married to Job[87] is also held by some anonymous rabbis in the Babylonian Talmud[88] and by Rabbi Abba in the Palestinian Talmud[89] and in Bereshit Rabbah.[90] Their opinions are also corroborated by a great Christian doctor called Origen who was a contemporary of our holy Rabbi,[91] as is noted by the wise Christian Pico prince of Mirandola in his seventh discourse which is an apologia for the said Origen,[92] and also by the bishop Eugubinus in his introduction to his *Recognitio* on the translation of the Torah.[93] Origen said that he found an ancient scroll which described how our master Moses, on him be peace, would present the book of Job to each of the elders of Israel during the bondage of Egypt. His purpose was to let them know and learn that all those who trust in God could hope that after having suffered evil times they would be the recipients of His kindness and goodness. A supporting statement is found in chapter 3 of Seder Olam to the effect that Job was born in the time when our ancestors went down to Egypt and died during their exodus.[94] Like the rabbis of blessed memory in Ḥullin,[95] Yedidyah accounts for the words of the angel, *Let me go for dawn is breaking* (Gen. 32:27) as inferring "Let me go because dawn is breaking and I must sing praises [to the Lord]."[96] He says that the children of Israel went down to Egypt and stayed there 210 years[97] as do the rabbis in Pirqe d'Rabbi Eliezer and Bemidbar Rabbah in relation to the verse, *Now I hear that*

82. *LAB* VI:16–18.

83. B. B.B. 91a; B.R. 38:13 (363–64); Mid. Teh. 118:11 to Ps. 118:8. For a discussion of these parallels with *LAB*, see G. Vermes, *Scripture and Tradition*, 83–91.

84. B.R. 44:12 (432). *LAB* XVIII:5.

85. *LAB* VII:4.

86. B. Zev. 113a; S.S.R. to S.S. 1:15. De' Rossi also refers to a passage in Taʿanit, but I was unable to trace it.

87. *LAB* VIII:8.

88. B. B.B. 15b.

89. P Sota 5 (7) 20c.

90. B.R. 57:4 (615).

91. The reference here is to a spurious work of Origen which was regarded as authentic in the Renaissance: ps. Origen, *Super Job* (*P.G.* XVII, col. 374).

92. De' Rossi is referring to the Quaestio septima of Pico della Mirandola's *Apologia* which is entitled "De salute Origenis." There is no reference to Rabbi (i.e., Judah the Patriarch, the compiler of the Mishnah), although it is true that he was a contemporary of Origen.

93. Augustinus Steuchus, *Recognitio*, 5r. This work influenced de' Rossi, particularly in his critique of Philo. The passage is not in the introduction, but in his commentary to Gen. 1: "De Job testatur Origenes in antiquissimis monumentis se reperisse Moysen cum Hebraei in Aegypto gravissima servitute premerentur, librum Job circumferre solitum ut illius viri exemplo fortius ad eas calamitates perferrendas omnes animaret. Credimus igitur cum hebraeis eum librum a Mose esse conscriptum."

94. Seder Olam, ch. 3 (14).

95. B. Ḥull, 91b.

96. *LAB* XVIII:6.

97. Ibid. VIII:14.

there are rations to be had in Egypt. Go down (Gen. 42:10).[98] According to Yedidyah, Moses was born circumcised,[99] and this is also stated by some [lit. other] rabbis in tractate Sota.[100] In like manner to our rabbis of blessed memory in Shemot Rabbah,[101] he says that the darkness in Egypt was actually tangible.[102] He says that "in fifties" in the verse *In fifties* [or *armed—ḥamushim*] *they went up out of Egypt* (Ex. 12:51) signifies that one-fiftieth of the people went up because forty-nine parts of the people had died during the plague of darkness, and that when the people of Israel cried out on seeing the sea were divided into three groups. Similar statements are found in the Midrash of our rabbis of blessed memory in the Mekhilta.[103] God said to Moses: "I shall entrust you with an everlasting Law with which I shall judge the entire world. It will be used as a testimony. If the nations say, 'We have not served You because we did not know You,' I will bring them to judgment for not having known my Law."[104] This bears affinity to what our rabbis of blessed memory say in tractate Avodah Zarah: "In the future, the Holy One blessed be He will bring a scroll of the Law in His arm and pronounce, 'Whoever has occupied himself with this, let him come and get his reward.' "[105] The expression *God visits the iniquity of the fathers on the children* (Ex. 20:5) is taken to refer to children who persist in behaving like their fathers.[106] A similar interpretation is given in the Targum Onqelos and by our rabbis of blessed memory in Sanhedrin.[107] Moses broke the tablets when he saw that they were not imprinted with lettering.[108] A similar statement is made in Pesaḥim and tractate Taʿanit of the Palestinian Talmud: "The tablets were broken and the letters flew away in the air."[109] Moses also made the Israelites drink the waters [into which the golden calf had been cast] in order to put them through the same kind of investigation as is given the suspected adultress.[110] This is said in tractate Avodah Zarah in the Palestinian Talmud.[111] On the festival of Pentecost, two loaves of bread are brought for the purpose of blessing the produce of the fields, and the festival of the New Year is a commemoration of the beginning of the work of creation.[112] A similar statement is made by Rabbi Eliezer in tractate Rosh ha-Shanah and in Jonathan ben Uzziel's Targum on the scriptural expression "the month of

98. PRE 48; Bem. R. 13:20. This is a play on the word *redu* (go down) which has the numerical value of 210.

99. *LAB* IX:13.

100. B. Sota 12a.

101. S.R. 14:1.

102. *LAB* X:I.

103. Mekhilta d'Rabbi Ishmael, beshalaḥ, 1 (1, 175). In Mekhilta, beshalaḥ, 3 (1, 214), it is stated that the Israelites were divided into four not three groups. However, the threefold division is found in other Midrashim. De' Rossi may have confused the passage with Mekhilta, shirata 7 (2, 57) in which it is stated that the Egyptians were divided into three groups.

104. *LAB* XI:2.

105. B. A.Z. 2a.

106. *LAB* XI:6.

107. Targum Onqelos to Ex. 20:5; B. Sanh. 27b.

108. *LAB* XII:5.

109. B. Pes. 87b; P. Taʿanit 4 (5) 68c.

110. *LAB* XII:7.

111. P.A.Z. 3 (3) 42d.

112. *LAB* XIII:6.

Etanim."[113] As in the first chapter of Rosh ha-Shanah, Tabernacles is described as the festival in which judgment is made regarding water.[114] The statement that the sons of Korah were assigned a place in hell[115] is also said in Sanhedrin.[116] In regard to the verse, *For I know that he whom you bless is blessed indeed, and he whom you curse is cursed* (Num. 22:6), he says that Balaam and his father cursed Moab at the request of Sihon.[117] A similar statement is found in Midrash Rabbah.[118] That Balaam advised Balak to free the daughters of Moab [in order to entice the Israelites][119] is also asserted by our rabbis of blessed memory in Sanhedrin.[120] That Israel was given the well, the pillars of cloud, and the manna through the merit of Miriam, Aaron, and Moses, respectively, and that on their death all three gifts were removed[121] is in the first chapter of Taʿanit.[122] That the Holy One blessed be He buried Moses in the valley and that the ministering angels did not sing the hymn of the day [on the day of his death][123] is stated in Sota.[124] His lengthy account of Othniel, Kenaz, and Achsah his wife[125] bears great resemblance to what our rabbis of blessed memory write in tractate Temurah.[126] As regards the daughter of Jeptha, he wrote that after having run about the mountains wailing she returned to the house of her father to be cut into pieces like an animal for a burnt offering.[127] He understands the [scriptural] statement that God was to deliver Sisera into the hands of a woman as an allusion to Jael.[128] He offers an explanation for King Saul's question to David, *Who are you young man* (1Sam. 17:58) although he was already acquainted with him. He suggests that when David approached Goliath, the angel changed his appearance[129] by making his face shine with a brilliant effulgence. Israel sinned by asking for a king because the institution of monarchy had been reserved for the time of David, as the Holy One blessed be He said, *Go, anoint him* (1Sam. 16:12).[130] You know what the rabbis of blessed memory said on this subject in Sifre[131] and in tractate Sanhedrin.[132]

113. B. R.H. 10b; Targum Jonathan to 1K. 8:2.
114. *LAB* XIII:7; B. R.H. 16a.
115. *LAB* XVI:3.
116. B. Sanh. 109b.
117. *LAB* XVIII:2. De' Rossi slightly misreads the text. Balaq says to Balaam: "Behold I know that in the reign of *my father Sefor,* when the Amorites fought against him, you cursed them."
118. Bem. R. 19:30; 20:7.
119. *LAB* XVIII:13.
120. B. Sanh. 106a.
121. *LAB* XX:8.
122. B. Taʿanit 9a (and see other parallels cited by Feldman, *The Biblical Antiquities,* 135).
123. *LAB* XIX:16. *LAB* reads 'highplaces' not 'valley.' ". . . et sepelevit eum per manus suas super excelsa terrae."
124. B. Sota 13b.
125. *LAB* XXV–XXIX.
126. B. Tem. 16a.
127. *LAB* XL:5–8.
128. Ibid. XXXI:1.
129. *LAB* LXI:9, 'changed.' The Latin reads 'lifted up' (erexit). In his *Legends* (vol. 6, 252, n. 44) L. Ginzberg suggests that the original Hebrew text of *LAB* may have read, *shanah* (changed) rather than *nasa* (lifted up).
130. *LAB* LIX:2.
131. Sifre Deut. par. 156 (208).
132. B. Sanh. 20b.

They are cited by Rambam [Maimonides] at the beginning of the Laws of the Kings.[133] "Their sin lay in the perverse manner in which they requested a king. It was not motivated by the desire to fulfill the commandment, but in order to vent their anger on Samuel as it is said, *for they have not rejected you* (1Sam. 8:7)." This is indeed the correct explanation and that great Mantuan Rabbi Judah Moscato,[134] may his shield and redeemer protect him, clarified the matter to me by referring to the scriptural passage about the spies in which it is written, *And the Lord heard the voice of your words and He was angry* (Deut. 1:34). This statement implies that it was not the request itself that was the main reason for His anger but rather their tone of voice and the querulous manner of presenting their request. Another case may be cited which is the obverse of the preceding example: *And the Lord heard the voice of your words and the Lord said to me: I have heard the words of this people . . . , they have spoken well* (Deut. 5:25). Because their refusal to listen to the voice of God was expressed in a submissive and unaggressive manner, their speech was accepted. The sages of blessed memory deal with these two opposite tones of voice in Midrash Qohelet with regard to the verse, *For a bird of the air shall carry the voice* (Eccl. 10:20).[135] Similarly, in tractate Qiddushin regarding the way a son honors his father, they say:[136] "One son may give him pheasants to eat [and yet drive him from the world]; another may make him grind in a mill [and this brings him to the world to come]."

Since the sin of Israel in requesting a king has been mentioned, I shall not refrain from adducing Josephus's statements on the subject in book 6 (chapter 4) in addition to what he writes in book 4 (chapter 8).[137] Previously, I told you about Homer the Greek's statement in the second book of the *Iliad* in which he says that sovereignty is, for all occasions and all purposes, adverse to plurality and welcomes unity.[138] This is also the opinion of Yedidyah the Alexandrian (in *On the Confusion of Tongues*[139] and *On the Embassy to Gaius*)[140] and Justin Martyr (in his first book).[141] Both writers cite the Homeric saying in approval. In a similar vein on the subject of Alexander of Macedon's absolute monarchy, Curtius states in book 4 that there ought to be one sun in the universe and one king on earth.[142] Towards the end of the sixteenth book of the *Statesman,* Plato mentions seven forms of government, and he also appears to have

133. *Mishneh Torah,* Melakhim, I:2.

134. Judah Moscato was an important Rabbi and philosopher. He wrote a commentary to Judah Halevi's *Kuzari,* the *Qol Yehudah,* and a volume of sermons entitled *Nefuṣot Yehudah.*

135. Qoh. R. to Eccl. 10:20. "There are reports for good and reports for evil."

136. B. Qidd. 31a–b.

137. Josephus, *Ant.* IV:223–24; VI:60–61.

138. *Iliad* II, 204–5.

139. *Conf. 170.*

140. *Leg.* 149.

141. Justin Martyr, *Cohortatio ad Graecos* (*P.G.* VI, col. 273). De' Rossi must be referring to the Basel 1565 edition containing Joannes Langus Silesus's Latin translation in which the *Cohortatio* appears as the first work in the first of the three volumes.

142. Quintus Curtius Rufus's work had a complicated manuscript tradition. The passage to which de' Rossi is referring is not in bk. 4 of the standard edition. It is in bk. 4 of the reconstructed Latin and Italian editions of the sixteenth century, at the end of Alexander's response to Darius. The reconstructed text reads: "Caeterum nec mundus duobus solibus potest regi; nec duo summa regna salvo statu terrarum potest habere" (*De rebus gestis,* 46).

shared the view stated above, but he adds the following proviso:[143] "Monarchy is the best form of government when it is administered according to a constitution, but there can be nothing worse than a monarchy without a constitution." And yet, the upshot of Josephus's statement quoted above is that we should not always eschew plurality and approve monarchism. Rather, we should take into account that the aims of government are two: arbitration in civil strife and protection of the people from their enemies at times when "their foes misjudge."[144] Thus in regard to questions of legislation, the rule of the many is most expedient because there will be no unanimous decision to pursue a course of injustice. But in case of war, monarchy is desirable for when plans have to be made, they will not be foiled for lack of secrecy.[145] It is however true that Israel who is saved from its enemies by the Lord our God has no cause to request the rule of one monarch unless it is made in the realization that they do not deserve divine providential care. It is for this reason that the precept regarding the king is expressed in the Torah in these words: *If after you have entered the land that the Lord your God has assigned to you . . . you decide, I will set a king over me as do all the nations about me* (Deut. 17:14). The implication of this verse is that you yourselves will come to the knowledge that you deserve to be deprived of providential care and be in the same position as all the other nations. Yet, whatever the case, the king is not to be put in the position of judge in matters of civil strife because these laws have already been assigned to us by the Lord of all the earth. It is thus understandable that Samuel's anger was provoked when they said, *Give us a king to judge us* (1Sam. 8:7) and that the blessed Lord went on to say, *It is not you that they have rejected; it is Me they have rejected* (ibid.). By these words, He indicated that not only were they indifferent to His providential care which is needed for the elimination of the enemy and avenger, but that they were rejecting His rule and his laws which are totally just.

Now we shall resume our discussion of Yedidyah's *Book of Biblical Antiquities.* Yedidyah speaks about the resurrection of the dead in several places and with particular attention in regard to the story of the flood. You know how our rabbis of blessed memory deal with the generation of the flood and their deprivation of a portion in eternal life in Sanhedrin. Yedidyah himself writes:[146]

> As long as the world exists, seedtime and harvest . . . will not cease until such time as I remember the inhabitants of the earth and the times be fulfilled. For it shall be that when the years of the universe are completed, the light shall cease and the darkness disappear. Then will I resurrect the dead and awaken those who sleep from the dust. Hell[147] will restore that with which it was entrusted and I will recompense every person according to their actions and inventions even until I judge between the soul and the body. Then the world will cease and death be extinguished and Hell shall shut its mouth. But the earth will not fail to produce its fruits and be unfertile for those who dwell on it. Whoever has

143. Plato, *Politicus,* 302e.
144. 'Their foes misjudge'—this is de' Rossi's addition, which is a reference to Deut. 32:27.
145. As S. Leiman indicated to me, de' Rossi is using the Targum to Pr. 15; 22 where the expression: *Plans are foiled for want of counsel* is rendered "for want of secrecy."
146. *LAB* III:9–10.
147. De' Rossi substitutes the expression 'Sheol and Abbadon' (Pr. 15:11) for the Latin 'infernus' (hell).

proved his innocence to Me shall not be put to shame. There will be another earth and new heavens as an eternal habitation.

He also wrote about the designated time for the resurrection of the dead in connection with Korah's quarrel. He wrote that Korah and his company would never die but pine away in Hell until that proscribed time at which moment they would not live, but be totally exterminated together with the generation of the flood and the Egyptians who had been drowned in the [Red] Sea.[148]

Concerning the incident in which the sorceress accuses Saul of having deceived her, he mentions that when Samuel was raised from the dead appearing in divine guise, he was seen by the sorceress accompanied by Saul and two angels.[149] He also says that Saul realized that Samuel was robed in the same cloak which he rent at the time when he reprimanded Saul because of his treatment of Agag. And Samuel complained about being raised from the dead because he had thought that the moment for resurrection and recompense had come. He said to the sorceress and Saul: "Do not take pride in imagining that it was you who raised me from the dead; for it was the Lord who decreed to me while still alive that when dead[150] I was to tell you, Saul, that you flouted his word on two occasions. Thus, after my soul's return, my bones have been agitated such that being dead I would tell you that which I heard while still alive." This passage bears affinity to the statements of Rabbenu Saadya and Rabbenu Hai, blessed be their memory, which have been collated by Kimḥi in his commentary on the story of the sorceress.[151] Examine the passage for yourselves.

There are also other topics treated by the author of this work in which he touches on statements which are to be found in the Aggadot of our rabbis of blessed memory or else proffers novel ideas of a similar nature. I have left them at the disposal of anyone who wishes to consult the book.

I raised the question as to whether the author of this work is to be identified with the Yedidyah who was author of the forty-three works and of the aforementioned book *On the Times*. I cannot desist from presenting you, reader, with three pieces of evidence which have led me to believe that he is the same person. First, in his discussion of the ten commandments, he places the prohibition on adultery before that of murder. He also follows this order in the previously mentioned works, namely, in *On the Decalogue, On the Special Laws* and *Who Is the Heir.*[152] I know of only one other writer who reverses the order in this way, i.e., their chief apostle [i.e., Paul] in his Letter to the Romans.[153]

148. *LAB* XVI:3.
149. *LAB* LXIV:5–7.
150. De' Rossi's translation is slightly erroneous. The Latin reads: "mortuusque audirer vivens," i.e., "being dead I should be heard as one living."
151. David Kimḥi to 1Sam. 28:25: "But the Geonim Rav Saadya and Rav Hai of blessed memory say that it is unlikely that the woman would have known the future and that she could have resurrected the dead by witchcraft. Rather, it was the blessed Lord who resurrected Samuel that Saul should get informed as to what would happen to him in the future. And the woman did not know any of this and was astounded as it is said, *and she shrieked loudly* (1Sam. 28:12)." As Cassel notes, this was not Kimḥi's own opinion.
152. *Spec.* III:8; *Decal.* 121–22; *Her.* 173.
153. Romans 13:9. In his notes to *LAB* XI:10–11, Feldman states that this version is also found in the Hebrew Nash Papyrus; he also points out that in *LAB* itself (XLIV:6–7), the Massoretic order is given.

Secondly, in his account of the verse, *And she put him in an ark (tevet) of bulrushes* (Ex. 2:3), he follows the Septuagint version, as was his practice, and renders the word *tevet* by *thibbin.*[154] In his *Recognitio,* the bishop Eugubinus also expressed surprise at such a rendering since *thibbin* is not a Greek word.[155] It would seem that he retained the Hebrew or Aramaic form of the word in transliteration. The reason for my words "or Aramaic" will be disclosed in one of these chapters.[156]

Thirdly, he has the blessed Lord say with regard to Moses: "In former times I made this calculation when I said that his life span shall be 120 years."[157] This statement is found in similar wording in his book *On the Giants.*[158]

At any rate, I believe that I have gained some value from this study. It is as follows. According to the translation which is nowadays attributed to the seventy elders [i.e., the Septuagint], both in the Greek version and its Latin translation, 2,242 years are accounted for the period from Adam to the flood. As the Christian translator [i.e., Jerome] writes in his introduction to his translation of Eusebius's chronological tables, this calculation is not in accordance with that of our Torah which gives the figure of merely 1,656 years.[159] Many great Christian doctors were astounded by this fact, and Augustine in particular, for whom it was unusual to attribute errors to the Septuagint.[160] In fact, he would not entertain the idea that our Torah was corrupt.[161] We shall raise this subject again in chapter 8. Now it must be plainly acknowledged that Yedidyah never deviated from the Septuagint in the thousand passages which he quotes throughout his forty-three works. (You will hear more on this presently.) Nevertheless, in the two works *On the Times* and *The Biblical Antiquities,* he appears to calculate 1,656 years which is the correct figure that we uphold. The problem is dissipated, and we may conclude that the greatest Christian doctor [i.e., Augustine] was justified in regarding the larger figure as a scribal error rather than an actual mistake on the part of the Seventy and that our holy Scriptures preserve the correct reading.

This discussion will suffice for now, but we will give the subject further consideration in some chapters of this book. The fact is that nothing distorted or perverse in regard to our Torah has appeared to emerge from our treatment of Yedidyah the Alexandrian. Now let him approach, and in the following chapter we will scrutinize and probe him in order to ascertain whether he is suspect on any count.

154. *LAB* IX:12: "Et accepit infantem suum et fecit ei thibin de cortice arboris pini et posuit thibin in os fluminis."

155. It should be noted that Steuchus is not referring to *LAB* but to the genuine *Mos.* (I, 14) where Philo omits the word altogether. Steuchus (*Recognitio,* 104r) deduces that Philo deviated from the LXX in his citation of the verse because he was unable to recognize the graecized form of a Hebrew word: "Usi sunt hoc loco LXX vocabulo hebraico arcam exprimere volentes. . . . Quae vox nusquam apud alios authores reperitur atque hinc factum suspicor quod Philon Judaeus hebraicae linguae imperitus ut ex multis fit manifestum totam hanc rem de fiscella scirpea omisit."

156. See ch. 9 in which de' Rossi proposes that the LXX was translated from an Aramaic original.

157. *LAB* IX:8.

158. *Gig.* 55 (254). Feldman (XXIII) points out correctly that this connection may easily be made by anyone recalling Gen. 6:3.

159. Jerome does not state this explicitly in this context.

160. Augustine, *De civ. Dei,* 15, ch. 13.

161. Ibid. "And I myself should in no way doubt that credence is rightly given rather to the original language from a rendering which was made by translators into another tongue" (trans. P. Levine, Loeb).

CHAPTER FIVE

There appear to be four defects[1] with which Yedidyah may be charged that are not in accordance with our Torah.

There is the other side to the argument. It is in fact possible to charge this Alexandrian with four apparent defects for which on high[2] he shall be proclaimed defiled. They are as follows. When he cites holy Writ in his works (and there are innumerable cases), he does not follow the genuine text which we have, but the Septuagint which contains many divergent readings.[3] We shall have more to say on this subject. Although this [i.e., the use of the Septuagint] is inconsequential as regards the tenets of the religion, it is in fact something which renders a man of such standing worthy of contempt. It provoked comment from the bishop Eugubinus in his discussion of the verse, *But a mist went up from the ground* (Gen. 2:6).[4] Following the Septuagint rendering, Yedidyah gave a lengthy interpretation of the verse as though it read, "And a spring went up from the earth." This is evident from his citations of the verse in his works *On the Allegorical Interpretation of the Law*[5] and *On Flight.*[6] The translation of this verse as well as other evidence led Eugubinus to conclude that Yedidyah had never set eyes on the holy tongue. In supporting and clarifying his view, I will make my own contribution to the discussion.

In some of the following chapters it will be demonstrated that the Jews of the second Temple period possessed two written Torah [scrolls]. The one scroll was written in the Assyrian script and in the holy tongue which is the format of our scrolls that we consider valid for use. This was the scroll which Ezra the scribe corrected and revised when he realized that the texts had become corrupt. The reason for this state of affairs may have been due to the sinful negligence of our ancestors during the first Temple period about whom it was said, *And you forgot the Torah of your God* (Hos. 4:6); alternatively, it

1. 'Defects,' lit. skin diseases/afflictions. De' Rossi is using imagery from Lev. 13 which describes the priest examining people for such diseases as leprosy.

2. 'On high.' This expression occurs in Hos. 11:7, *For my people persists in its defection from Me; when it is summoned on high, it does not rise at all.*

3. For a detailed analysis of Philo's use of Scripture, see P. Katz, *Philo's Bible.*

4. Steuchus, *Recognitio,* 21v: "Philon autem iudaeus videtur suas litteras ignorasse quod cum ex multis licet cognoscere, tum ex hoc [i.e., Gen. 2:6] praesertim. Exponit enim de fontibus qui e terrae visceribus surgunt non de vaporibus. Videtur certe codices hebraeos non legisse."

5. *L.A.* 1, 28 (39).

6. *Fug.* 178ff. (411).

may have come about through the many vicissitudes of fortune they suffered during the Babylonian exile. Once he had written down the corrected text, he gave the scroll to the priests and Sanhedrin, the upholders of the Torah, in order to instruct us about it.

The other scroll which was interspersed with different readings and widely disseminated among the people was written in the Hebrew script (i.e., the characters of those who lived "beyond (*ever*) the river") was left for the use of common folk.[7] It was in Aramaic, which was their language and vernacular at that time. This translation may have been composed before Ezra's time during the Babylonian exile, or else it could have been made in Ezra's lifetime as is implied by the comment of the sages blessed be their memory on the verse, *And they read in the book of the Torah distinctly* (Neh. 8:8): "*distinctly*—this means 'translated.'"[8]

Whatever the case, that Aramaic translation was made without careful supervision. It also contained variant readings and an explanatory amplification of the text in order to illuminate the understanding of the common people as far as is possible. That is why they use the vernacular for those who do not understand Hebrew.[9] Moreover, many errors arose because the interpreter mistook similar-looking characters of the Assyrian script and interchanged one for the other, and also because the text was neither vocalized nor accented, resulting in further error. It so happened that as a result of the sinful negligence of the leaders of the generations and because the ignorant, always being the majority, will always gain the upper hand over the group of the intellectuals, this Aramaic version became widely circulated and world famous. Consequently, the elders who were summoned to Ptolemy felt justified and considered that they were acting in Ptolemy's interest when they translated the Torah from that version. I shall elucidate this matter further in the designated chapters, but only on the condition that for the time being you simulate ignorance of what you have just been told.

Now Yedidyah grew up in the Greek world and despite all his wisdom and fluency in their language never saw nor knew the actual original text of Torah. It was not just a question of the holy tongue, but he was even ignorant of Aramaic, the language that was widely used in the Land of Israel. The Torah which he studied and wrote about throughout his works was entirely based on his reading of the translation of those elders. Since he accepted the view that they translated the Torah from an Aramaic version which they brought to the king, he consequently also believed that Moses had been given the Torah in Aramaic at Sinai. This is evident from his description of the story of the elders and Ptolemy in the second book of *On the Life of Moses*. He writes: "In former times, our Torah was written in Aramaic[10] and remained in that language for a long time until the moment came when the nations also desired to acquire its beauty and Ptolemy came."[11] The Christian translator [i.e., Jerome] took him to task for this and told the truth when he said that it was given in the holy tongue.[12]

7. Cf. B. Sanh. 21b and de' Rossi's discussion of the passage in ch. 9.

8. B. Ned. 37b.

9. Cf. M. Meg. 2:1.

10. In B, the word "Aramaic" is crossed out and substituted by the word "Chaldaic" which corresponds more closely to the Greek and Latin.

11. *Mos.* II, 25–29 (558).

12. Jerome, *Comm. in Danielem,* lib. 1, (*P.L.* XXV, col. 496).

Similarly, in his discourse on the perfect man in his book *On Reward and Punishment,* he states:[13] "The Chaldeans call such a man *enosh* which means 'man.'" He continues (and the same remark is found in his *On the Embassay to Gaius*):[14] "This kind of person is called Israel by the Chaldeans which means 'he who sees God.'" This interpretation also aroused the Christian translator's derision. In his *Hebraicae Quaestiones* he declared that such an interpretation indicated acceptance of the Septuagint, whereas one should not deviate from Scripture which accounts for the name Israel when it states, *Your name shall be called no more Jacob, but Israel for you strove with God* (Gen. 32:29).[15] It is true that both etymologies [i.e., Philo's and that of the biblical text] use the holy tongue and you shall hear more on this subject in chapter 9.[16] However, even if it is assumed that Yedidyah was aware that the Torah was given to Moses in the holy tongue, we cannot suppress the fact that he declares that it was promulgated in the Aramaic language and that the elders translated from that version. This fact can also be gleaned from his book *On the Times* which is reproduced in chapter 32 where he states that Chaldeans and Egyptians regard the names Eli, Eliyakim, and Jehoiakim as synonomous.[17]

In fact, there can be no doubt that he derived all his knowledge of the Torah from their translation. By comparing all the divergent readings of Scripture which Yedidyah gives throughout his works with the readings of the Septuagint, you will find that they are in each case identical and in the light of examination have the same form. For example, the word "created" as in *In the beginning God created the heaven and the earth* (Gen. 1:1) is rendered "made," and in every case where a form of the word "create" is found, it is rendered "made." He writes, *And He finished on the sixth and rested on the seventh* (Gen. 2:2).[18] He puts *When the Lord God made heaven and earth* (Gen. 2:4) and *when no shrub of the field and no grasses of the field had yet sprouted* (ibid. 2:5) in the same verse.[19] He writes, *And the two will be one flesh* (ibid. 2:24).[20] He writes, *He drove the man out and made him dwell east of the Garden of Eden and put the Chrerubim there and the flaming sword* (ibid. 3:24).[21] He writes, *And Cain said to his brother Abel: Let us go out into the field* (ibid. 4:8).[22] Instead of *And the Lord regretted* (Gen. 6:6), he wrote, *And God thought.*[23] He writes, *And Noah found favor with the Lord God* (Gen. 6:8) and then puts

13. *Praem.* 14 (763): "Hunc Chaldaei nominant Enos quod interpretatur homo."

14. *Leg.* 4 (829).

15. Jerome, *Heb. quaest.* to Gen. 32:27–28: "Illud autem quod in libro nominum [he is referring here to the ps. Philonic work *De nominibus hebraicis*] interpretatur Israel vir videns Deum, sive mens videns Deum omnium pene sermone detritum tam vere quam violenter mihi interpretatum videtur. Hic enim Israel per has litteras scribitur Iod Sin Res Aleph Lamed, quod interpretatur princeps dei sive directus Dei." (*P.L.* III, col. 988).

16. For a modern discussion of Philo's etymologies, see L. Grabbe, *Etymology.*

17. This is a reference to the ps. Philonic work *Breviarium de temporibus* forged by Annius of Viterbo (392): "Nam synonyma sunt Syris et Aegyptiis Elyh, qui et Eliakin, Ioakin."

18. *L.A.* I, 2 (36). "Et complevit die sexto opus suum quod fecerat." M.T. *seventh* not 'sixth.'

19. *Op.* 129 (26): "Hic est liber generationis . . . die quo fecit deus caelum et terram et omne virgultum agri antequam orietur in terra."

20. *Gig.* 65 (255): "Facti sunt duo in carnem unam." M.T. *and they will be one flesh.*

21. *Cher.* 1 (95): "Et expulit Adamum et collocavit ante paradisum voluptatis." De' Rossi does not note that the Latin reads 'before paradise.'

22. *Det.* 1 (137). In M.T., the words of Cain are missing.

23. *Deus* 20 (258): "recogitavit deus."

forward an argument to prove the necessity of using both names of God.[24] He writes, *And the son of Masek my servant is Damascus* (Gen. 15:2).[25] {On the verse, *Birds of prey came down upon the carcasses, and Abram drove them away* (Gen. 15:11), he substitutes the word "cut-up pieces" for "carcasses" and interprets the expression *and he drove them away* (*va-yashev*) in the sense of "sitting."[26] He expresses the idea that everything good is attracted to the soul, and everything bad to the body such that what is loved by the one is repugnant to the other. He then explains that the purpose of this vision is to make us aware of the struggles within our souls. For this reason the birds are described as sweeping down onto the bodies, gnawing at them and glutting themselves with the flesh. However, the wise person who is desirous of curbing these vices is depicted as sitting among them, as though standing like a sentinel over his house to protect it from any evil which might assail it from within or from outside.[27]}

He makes a distinction between the words "his people" and "his race" in connection with the verse which he renders, *And Isaac expired and died and was gathered to his race* (Gen. 35:29).[28] He states, *He and his shepherd Hirah* (Gen. 38:20).[29] He quotes, *And Israel bowed down at the top of his staff* (Gen. 47:31).[30] *Issachar is the achievement of good deeds* (Gen. 49:14).[31] He says, *The total number of persons that were of Jacob's issue came to seventy-five* (Ex. 1:5).[32] He says, *And they made houses for them* (Ex. 1:21).[33] Instead of the expression, *I will be that which I will be* (Ex. 3:14), he renders, *the existing being which is the existing being.*[34] Such an interpretation anticipates the explanation of the expression given in the first part of the *Guide* when the author renders *I Am has sent me to you* (Ex. 3:15) as *The existing being sent me to you.*[35] He translates *swarm of locusts* (Ex. 8:17) as "dog-flies."[36] He renders, *as it were coriander seed, white as hoar-frost on the ground* instead of *a fine and flaky substance as fine as frost on the ground* (Ex. 16:14).[37] He renders,

24. Ibid. 86ff. (268): "apud dominum deum."

25. *Her.* 2 (416): "Filius meus iste susceptus ex ancilla, haeres meus erit, Damascus Eliezer." M.T. *The one in charge of my household is Damascus Eliezer.*

26. Ibid., 237 (442): "Et descenderunt aves in corpora divisa bifariam."

27. According to Cassel, the original text of this passage reads (it is not in B): "*And the birds came down . . . and Abram settled them* (443), and he [i.e., Philo] explains that the descent of the birds on the pieces which were in Abraham's possession symbolized the external cause of controversy in his home. However, when he sat with them, as it were supervising those who were attached to him, he could prevent controversy. Rabbi David Provenzali, may his shield and redeemer protect him, the defender of Yedidyah, reproved me for jumping to such an interpretation, and happily I accepted his reproof."

28. *Sac.* 6 (116).

29. *Fug.* 149 (407) to Gen. 38:20: "pastorem suum odolamitam." M.T. *He and his friend Hirah.*

30. M.T. *On the top of his bed.* I cannot find this verse quoted by Philo. However, Steuchus (*Recognitio,* 96v) notes that this reading is found in the LXX. De' Rossi may have inferred that Philo also used that reading.

31. *Plant.* 134 (205); *L.A.* I, 80 M.T. *Issachar is a strong-boned ass.*

32. *Mig.* 199 (362). In M.T. the number is 70.

33. Ibid. 215 (365): "fecerunt sibiipsis domos." M.T. *He* [i.e., God] *made houses for them.*

34. *Det.* 160 (162): "Ego sum Qui sum."

35. *Guide* I, ch. 63: "Accordingly, God made known to Moses the knowledge that he was to convey to them and through which they would acquire a true notion of the existence of God, this knowledge being: I am that I am. This is a name deriving from the verb to be which signifies existence" (Pines trans.).

36. *Mos.* I, 130 (530), "cynomyia."

37. *L.A.* III, 169 (80): "et ecce in superficie terrae in solitudine tanquam corianum album in similitudinem pruinae."

galbanum of spices i.e., "sweet-smelling galbanum" (Ex. 30:34).[38] He substitutes *Make known yourself* for *Make known to me Your ways* (Ex. 33:13).[39] Where it states *And he who blasphemes [noqev] the name of the Lord . . .* (Lev. 24:16) he translates, *And he who utters the name of the Lord.*[40] By such a rendering he seems to have adhered to the system of the ancient Egyptians who not only refrained from pronouncing the name of their mother or father, but also that of any being they revered such as Hermes whom we mentioned in the previous chapter. In his introduction to the work, Ficino wrote that they would not take his [i.e., Hermes'] name in vain.[41]

He writes, *I have not taken one valuable from them* (Num. 16:15) [instead of *one ass*].[42] He renders the verse, *We will go up by the highway* (Num. 20:19) by *We will go up by the mountain,*[43] and he states that the expression suggests the idea that they were expert in elevating their thoughts. He writes, *This thing is in your mouth, your heart and in your hand to do it* (Deut. 30:14).[44] In his work *On the Migration of Abraham,* he says that Moses, like the Seventy, called the books of the Pentateuch: Genesis, Exodus, etc.[45] Go and read for yourself all the numerous passages in which Yedidyah's rendering of Scripture is the same as the Septuagint's.

Similarly, there are passages in the Septuagint where, for some reason or other, the words of one speaker are put into the mouth of somebody else. This is noted by the bishop Eugubinus in his *Recognitio.* The same variations in the text are straightaway to be found in Yedidyah's works. Consider the dream of Jacob in which God states, *I am the Lord, the God of your father Abraham and the God of Isaac* (Gen. 28:13). To this statement, Yedidyah adds the words "Do not fear," which were said to Isaac, *I am the God of your father Abraham. Do not fear* (Gen. 26:24). He then explains the words "Do not fear" in relation to Jacob.[46]

I have discovered only three passages in which he independently gives a divergent reading which is not to be found in the Septuagint: (1) *He caused rest on the seventh day* (Gen. 2:2).[47] He thereby applies the "resting" to the creation, a subject which he treats at length throughout his second book entitled *The Allegorical Interpretation of the Torah.* This can also be inferred from the passage I quoted in the previous chapter in which he states that the Sabbath commemorates the power of the Creator and the repose of the created beings. It is true, however, that a similar interpretation of a homiletic nature is also made by Rabbi Jose at the end of section nine of Bereshit Rabbah.[48] Examine the

38. *Her.* 198 (437): "galbanum suaveolens."
39. *Spec.* I, 41 (685): "Ostende mihi teipsum."
40. *Mos.* II, 203–4 (575).
41. Marsilio Ficino, Hermes, 9: "Nomen eius proprium ob reverentiam quandam pronuntiare vulgo ac temere non licebat."
42. *Conf.* 50 (284): "rem concupitam accepi ab illorum nemine." M.T. *I have not taken one ass.*
43. *Deus* 145 (276): "praeter montem."
44. *Prob.* 68 (733): "In ore tuo, in corde tuo, in manibus tuis." M.T. has no reference to "hands."
45. *Mig.* 14 (337): "Recte igitur sacer vates unum integrum legis librum Exodum intitulavit." The reference to Genesis is in *Abr.* 1.
46. *Som.* I, 159 (503): "Ego sum dominus Deus Abrahami patris tui et Deus Isaaci, noli timere."
47. *L.A.* I, 16 (36): "Quiescere fecit." M.T. *He rested on the seventh day.*
48. B.R. 10:9 (86): "Rabbi Levi said in the name of Rabbi Jose bar Nehorai: As long as the hands of the owner handle them, they are bent on going. But when the hands of their owner cease to move, they are given rest: *And he gave [his world] rest on the seventh day* (Ex. 20:11)."

passage for yourself. (2) *And the servant of Isaac came and told him about the well which they had dug and said: We found no water* (Gen. 26:32).[49] He then proceeds to explain the reason for the absence of water in that fourth well. (3) He lists the commandment regarding adultery before that of murder, as I noted at the end of chapter 4. Thus the bishop [i.e., Steuchus] was justified in holding the view that Yedidyah did not read the Torah in the Hebrew text.

I can also produce evidence of his inability to read the Aramaic version. You should look at his book *On the Confusion of Tongues* where he cites Zechariah, *Behold a man called the Branch shall branch out from the place where he is* (6:12). His quotation and explanation of the verse implies that it read, *Rising is his name and from his place will he rise.*[50] I have noticed that this is also the reading of the Septuagint. However, the Greek word *anatole* as well as the Latin word *orior* connote both "rising" and "growing." This is not the case with the Aramaic word.[51] Yedidyah had no knowledge of Aramaic and therefore translated the word with the sense of "rising" and then proceeded to construct, on the basis of this translation, allegorical castles in the air which were completely unfounded both as regards the words as well as the subject matter. Moreover, you should look at the passage where he speaks about the tetragrammaton which was engraved on the golden plate. He writes: "Theologians say that the name has four letters."[52] Similarly, two pages later, he says of this holy name: "Theologians say that it denotes existence."[53] Observe how even in regard to the number of its letters and its well-known meaning, he was like a dreamer, acquiring his knowledge from hearsay because his only source of information was the Greek version of the Septuagint. There are in fact occasions when the names are explained according to their meaning in our language; but I am convinced that he had no knowledge of these matters, but necessarily had to derive it from secondary sources. This is actually the opinion of a Christian scholar who published various worthless studies on the book of Genesis which are ascribed to Philo and which include explanations of the etymologies of several biblical names.[54] In his introduction, he writes that they are certainly not written by the renowned Philo of Alexandria. In fact, in his book of *Synonyms,* [ps.] Xenophon lists five people with the name Philo.[55] But

49. *Plant.* 78 (198): "Non invenimus aquam." M.T. *They said to him: We found water.*

50. *Conf.* 62 (246): "Ecce homo cui nomen Oriens."

51. De' Rossi appears to be arguing on the basis of the hypothesis he is to put forward in ch. 9, namely, that the LXX was translated from Aramaic. Presupposing that the LXX used an Aramaic equivalent to *ṣamaḥ,* de' Rossi claimed that Philo simply perpetuated the error already existing in the LXX because of his ignorance of Aramaic. But the argument is strange since it follows that the translators of the LXX did not know Aramaic.

52. *Mos.* II, 115 (bk. III, 568).

53. Ibid. II, 132 (670). He is probably assuming that Philo thought that the Greek word *kurios* (Lord) was a literal translation of the Hebrew tetragrammaton. For a modern discussion of this question, see V. Nikiprowetzky, *Le Commentaire,* 58–62.

54. This is a reference to the *Quaestiones et solutiones in Genesin* which is generally considered to be authentic, and the passage corresponds to the old Latin version, IV, 154. The work was published in Sichard's volume which also contained the *Liber biblicarum antiquitatum, De essaeis, De nominibus hebraicis,* and *De mundo.* De' Rossi appears to be referring to Sichard's statement in the preface about the works published in the volume: "Nisi in ea simus opinione ut credamus alterum quendam Philonem fuisse nonnullorum auctorem."

55. This is a reference to another forgery of Annius of Viterbo, ps. Xenophon, *De Aequivocis.* I cannot find the passage.

how is it conceivable that he would have fallen into the debris of all those variants and confusions had he been able to understand the correct text of Scripture? The fact is that he was enshrouded in darkness because he had no access to the modes of the holy tongue. Thus it was that when I pondered over the anomalous nature of such a person, I considered that he was certainly raised at the feet of many of the great gentile sages and philosophers that lived in his Greek city of Alexandria in Egypt. And while he cultivated those vineyards, he neglected his own precious vineyard which would have enabled him to gain the joy of drawing the holy waters from the fountains of salvation. As a result, these [limitations] befell him. Moreover, when we turn our attention to the verse at the end of Nehemiah which speaks of the children who did not know how to speak the Jews' language, but only the language of the various peoples (13:24), we are able to judge that he was far from being an exception among our people.

The second defect is as follows: in his first book entitled *On the Creation of the World* he writes in a manner which would lead the reader to conclude that he believed in primordial matter. This is what he says:[56]

> Indeed, anyone who wants a reason for the creation of the world would not be far from the mark if he were to say as did one of the sages of old that it was due to the manifold goodness of the Creator, Father of all existence. {He speaks in a similar vein in his book entitled *On the Unchangeableness of God.*[57]} For in His great goodness, He did not begrudge matter which by its nature lacks all virtues but is capable of becoming anything which is desired. In itself it lacked quality, it was turgid, inorganic, unformed, unordered, and full of discord. But it was capable of change and mutation such that all its deficiencies could be reversed as would be appropriate for the divine design.[58] Of His own free will and specific bounty (for there is no God besides Him),[59] the blessed Lord conferred some of His bounties on that nature which is itself has no capabilities of reception unless it finds itself the object of His bounty. He did not bestow this bounty in proportion to his own power which is limitless, but in proportion to His material recipient. For indeed, no creature is capable of receiving all that the blessed Lord is capable of giving. Thus, in His fine wisdom, he measured out a limited amount of the bounty which accorded with the capabilities of the recipient.

Thus far his words are such that an intelligent person will regard as an endorsement of our previous statement. Furthermore, in his twelfth observation of his preface to his translation of Plato's *Timaeus,* the Christian scholar Ficino cites another passage which he alleges is in book 2 of Yedidyah's *On the Creation of the World.* It is missing in our text. It reads thus: "When the Creator began to form the matter which was unordered and intermingled with its own nature, He accomplished the necessary separation and ordering by forming earth and water in the middle of it."[60] Similarly, at the beginning

56. *Op.* 21–23 (4).

57. *Deus* 108 (269).

58. 'As would be appropriate for the divine design.' De' Rossi glosses over the more philosophical language of Philo: "quae ad potiorem ideam attinent" (which is more fitting of the better model).

59. The Latin (and Greek) are in the form of a question: "quis enim erat alius?"

60. Marsilio Ficino, *Omnia . . . opera,* 677: "[Philo] in secundo eius libri volumine, Cum inquit creator substantiam inordinatam et natura sua confusam in ordinem ex inordinatione et in discretionem ex confusione traductam formare coepisset terram atque aquam, medio loco firmavit."

of his work *That the World Is Indestructible,* he sets down an axiom on this topic which he articulates in a strange fashion.[61] He proposes that no thing can issue from no thing and that something can only be dissolved into something. And he cites the gentile poet who said, "That which is born cannot die; rather its consitutent parts become changed and in the process its original form is transformed into another." One is inclined to believe that it was this belief of his which demonstrated that he was a follower of Plato. According to the majority of scholars, Plato as well as many other Greek philosophers are said to have held this belief, namely, that matter is uncreated. This is stated in part two of the *Guide.*[62] However, you should know that one of the Christian doctors called Justin Martyr who was a contemporary of Antoninus and Rabbi cites proofs from the prophecies of the astute woman Sibyl and other such ancient sages regarding the unity of God and the creation of the world in the first section of his work.[63] {The same passages are cited by Lactantius Firmianus in his first work in the name of the Eritrean Sibyl.}[64] Justin was convinced that Plato's divine words did not constitute a departure from the teaching of Moses our teacher, and he produced a profound and far-reaching apologia on his behalf. His purpose was to use the evidence of Plato's statements dispersed throughout his works in order to demonstrate to peoples and sages that he [i.e., Plato] was truly convinced about creation ex nihilo. He argues that Plato had learnt from the example of the murder of his teacher Socrates. He had been found guilty for turning from idolatry to belief in the God of heaven and was put to death by the tribunal of the Areopagi as is known from Xenophon's defence of Socrates[65] and from the second part of Josephus's *Against Apion.*[66] Consequently, Plato was afraid that he would suffer a similar fate if he publicized his true belief about creation ex nihilo which was unacceptable to those Greeks. He thus adopted a deliberately confusing and ambiguous style of speaking in order to protect himself from his enemies who were lying in wait for his blood. In the second part of his dialogue between Philone and Sophia, the wise Rabbi Judah goes even further than Justin.[67] According to his interpretation, all Plato's statements irrefutably demonstrate that the primordial matter was undoubtedly created at the time of the creation.[68] Examine the passage.

Now I saw that the bishop Eugubinus calls to task the great teacher Ramban

61. *Aet.* 5 (789).

62. Maimonides, *Guide* II, ch. 13.

63. Justin Martyr, *Cohortatio ad graecos, P.G.* VI, col. 271–74.

64. This is a reference to Lactantius, *Divinarum institutionum lib.* I, ch. 6 (*P.L.* VI, col. 146–47): "Omnes igitur hae Sibyllae unum deum praedicant, maxime tamen Erythraea . . . In his ergo versibus . . . de uno deo haec sunt testimonia hunc esse solum summum deum qui caelum fecerit luminibusque distinxerit."

65. This is a reference to Xenophon's *Memorabilia.*

66. *Contra Apionem* II, 263.

67. This is a reference to Judah Abrabanel (Leone Ebreo). De' Rossi may have wanted to cite Leone Ebreo in order to give a Jewish Platonist's view in addition to those of the Christian Platonists.

68. *Dialoghi* 2 (109): "perché essendo Iddio produttore di tutte le cose bisogna ancora che habbi produtto la materia de la quale sono generate, ma si debbe intendere che essi significano che per essere stato il Chaos in compagnia di Dio ne la eternità, essere da Lui produtto ab eterno e che Dio producesse tutte l'altre cose di esso Chaos di nuovo in principio di tempo (secondo l'oppinione platonica) e chiamanla compagna non ostante che sia produtta, per esser produtto esso Chaos ab eterno e trovarsi sempre mai in compagnia di Dio."

[Nahmanides] of blessed memory who in his opinion nonsensically confuses the Greek notion of *hyle* in his explanation of the expression "dull and void" (*tohu va-vohu*).[69] The bishop argued that the ways of our divine Torah are superior to their perverted paths. Rabbi Judah's statement, which I quoted above, provoked me to come to Ramban's defense and to pronounce on the falsity of the bishop's criticism. For Ramban of blessed memory had also not intended to identify the primordial matter with the first cause as had those philosophers. Rather, he was alluding to the matter which was created from nothing by the Creator prior to the creation of His individual works.[70] From that matter, He then subsequently brought the world into being, each part according to its shape. Moreover, it is obvious that when the concept of before or after are used, it does not have a temporal sense since time was part of the creation. Rather, it signifies priority in number and order. This is stated by the Christian sage Ficino, as you will see in the next chapter. And even if the concept of *hyle* as used by the Greeks does not always have this connotation, there is no question that this is what was meant by the Rav of blessed memory who is innocent of all guilt or transgression. Thus, rather than regard the righteous Plato as the author of the pernicious notion of primordial matter, I would approve the statement of the Christian translator [Jerome]. For in his commentary to the eleventh chapter of the Letter to the Hebrews, he wrote that the Chaldeans were the first to propagate such a notion.[71] It was regarding this matter that Abraham our ancestor dared to challenge them. Our rabbis of blessed memory wrote about this in the Aggadah in Ḥeleq[72] as does the author of the *Guide* in regard to the verses, *and [Abraham] invoked there the name of the Lord, the everlasting God* (Gen. 21:33) and *I swear to the Lord God most high Creator of heaven and earth* (ibid. 14:22).[73] But let us resume our discussion of Yedidyah and his treatment of matter. There is no doubt that it lays him open to castigation. No discussion is required[74] since it is a known fact that all

69. De' Rossi has misrepresented Steuchus who does not actually mention Nahmanides, but refers to "certain Jews" (*quidam hebraei*). (Steuchus may have also had Gersonides in mind who explicitly reduced the world to a formless substratum out of which all existence derived.) Steuchus's statement is confusing and is not consistent with either Aristotelian or Platonic ideas. The passage reads (*Recognitio,* 10r): "Quod autem quidam hebraei *thou* et *bou* [i.e., *tohu va-vohu*] ad materiam primam referunt ut thou sit ipsa privatio materiae, bou desiderium eius et aptitudo ad formas non tam est mosaicum quam peripateticum. . . . Hyle enim i. prima materia inventum est philosophorum quam ne somniavit quidem Moses."

70. In his commentary to Gen. 1:2, Nahmanides wrote: "This matter which they call the *hyle* is *tohu* in the holy tongue . . . and the form with which the matter is clothed is called *vohu* in the holy tongue." On the use of the concept of *hyle* and form, see G. Scholem, *The Origins,* 425–27.

71. Jerome did not write a Commentary to the Letter to the Hebrews. De' Rossi appears to have derived this statement from Annius of Viterbo. In his praefatio to ps. Philo, *Breviarium* (379), Annius writes: "Hoc loco admonendos existimo lectores ut initio utamur beati Hieronymi in commentario super illud Apostoli ad Hebraeos dicentis, 'Fide credimus aptata fuisse secula ut ex invisibilibus visibilia fierent' (11:2) ubi divus Hieronymus sic ait Chaldaeorum veterum traditio est, huius visibilis et formati mundi fuisse invisibilem et informem praeiacentem naturam sempiternam a nullo productam quam posteriores Graeci hylen, Chaosque vocaverunt, Moyses vero abyssum." This spurious passage which seems to have been Annius's invention was obviously popular among ecclesiastical writers. It was quoted, e.g., by the Dominican Sisto Senese in his *Bibliotheca Sancta.* See my note, "An Apocryphal Source," 280–84.

72. B. Sanh. 93a. This passage only refers to the Aggadah about Abraham in the furnace. A more apposite reference would be B.R. 38:13 (363–64).

73. *Guide* II, ch. 13; III, ch. 29.

74. 'No discussion is required,' cf. B. B.M. 16a.

those who keep the Torah testify and pronounce whether on the basis of Scripture or tradition that the creation was totally and absolutely new and was not preceded by any matter.

The third defect appears to be the following evil matter: several stories are recounted in the Torah which absolutely and certainly happened and saw the light of day. Even those who expound the underlying meaning of the texts and uncover the hidden and veiled allusions and symbols for whatever intellectual[75] consideration will assert that all the stories happened as described and are not simply parables or allegories. But I have caught this Yedidyah several times like a thief divesting the word of the Lord of its true meaning, asserting that the real essence of the story is simply some philosophy or intellectual consideration. However true and correct is his conception, evil and bitter is his rejection of the truth of the written word. It is as though the perfect Torah is a piece of poetry, the best part of which is its lie[76] which draws attention to the falsity of its apparent meaning, and that its essential character can only be elicited by the initiates. Thus, in *On the Creation of the World*[77] and in the first book of the *Allegories of the Law,*[78] he writes that the belief in the literal account of the creation extended over six separate days is popular and unfounded. For since days and time were part of the things which were created and God's purpose cannot be thwarted, He created everything simultaneously. Thus he explains the number six in geometrical terms: it is a perfect* number. He says that it denotes order and has a specific connotation of the dimensions of both the male and female bodies.[79] The blessed Lord desired to demonstrate that He had retained their specific order and perfection in creating them. For this reason He wrote in his Torah that He had created them on six separate days.

(*This is not ibn Ezra's opinion. With regard to the verse, *Balaam said to Balaḳ: Build me seven altars here and have seven bulls and seven rams ready here for me* (Num. 23:1), he calls the number seven perfect, and likewise in his comment to the verse, *See, this is what I found, said Koheleth, one to one in order to find the account* (Eccl. 7:27). For he says that by adding one to one it becomes the first of the numbers [2] and when one is added to the first number it becomes "endlike" [3].[80] When one is added to the end number it becomes a square [4].[81] When one is added to the square it becomes circular [5].[82] [And

75. 'Intellectual.' Cassel (but not in all editions) reads incorrectly 'unimportant' (*shiflit* instead of *siḳhlit*).

76. This is a common saying used by theoreticians of poetry. See ch. 60, n. 5.

77. *Op.* 13 (2).

78. *L.A.* I, 2–4 (36).

79. Philo states: "We may say that it is in its nature both male and female and is a result of the distinctive power of either. For among things that are, it is the odd that is male and the even, female. Now of odd numbers, 3 is the starting point, and of even numbers 2, and the product of these two is 6."

80. Ibn Ezra is using neo-Pythagorean and neo-Platonic notions. The use of the expression "endlike" is probably equivalent to the Greek term *teleios* which is used as a symbol for the number 3. See M. Olitzki, "Die Zahlensmbolik," n. 85, 117 where he refers to use to this expression in Nicomachus, *Theologoumena Arithmeticae* and explains that the name indicates that everything is divided into a beginning, middle, and end. According to H. Maccoby who unraveled the meaning of the entire passage for me, the expression "endlike" is used because it concludes the first occurrence of both an odd and an even number (1 is separate from the other numbers within the decade).

81. Ibn Ezra uses the expression "bounded." According to Olitzki (105), 4 is the first bounded number because all other numbers are built on it.

82. It is called 5 because it always rebounds on itself. Ibn Ezra explains this in his *Sefer ha-Mispar,* 2.

when one is added] it becomes complete [6].[83] [When one is added,] it becomes perfect [7]. [When one is added] it becomes a body [8].[84] And study the super commentaries on this passage, and in particular, that of Rabbi Samuel Biba. In his commentary to the pericope Balak [Num. 23:1], he says that the number seven is called perfect because if you take the lowest number of the even numbers and the highest number of the odd numbers it will come to seven. Similarly, if you take the largest of the even and add it to the lowest of the odd numbers you reach seven, e.g., 2 + 5; 4 + 3.[85] But your thirst will be even more quenched if you were to read chapters 5 and 6 of Macrobius's commentary on Cicero's *Dream of Scipio*[86] as well as the introduction of Marsilio Ficino to the tenth dialogue in Plato's *Republic.*[87] In any case, you will find that from different perspectives, the opinions of both writers are equally meritorious.)

As regards the number seven, he writes in a delightful manner in his first work.[88] And then at the beginning of book 2,[89] he also says that seven is the only number in the decade which has neither sum nor factor. For example, two multiplied by two produces four, and four doubled produces eight, and three tripled produces nine. These sums are derived from their factors such that all numbers below ten are either sums or factors with the exception of seven which is found in neither category. The Pythagoreans therefore call it virgin because it is motherless; indeed, that which is not subject to generation must exist naturally. Thus Torah gives it a special significance in order to denote the creation of the holy things which have perpetual rest. This is what he has to say. Indeed, it is obvious how easily refutable is such an opinion. The holy verses proclaim, indeed cry out, "one day," "second day," "third day." The author of the *Aqedah* elaborates on this when he takes as his subject the Mishnah of our sages[90] that the creation could have been accomplished by one utterance.[91] Examine the passage.

Similarly, in the closing section of his first work,[92] and in the first book on the *Allegories of the Law,*[93] and near the beginning of his book *On the Planting of Noah,*[94] Yedidyah deals with the garden which God planted in Eden. He writes: "Do not imagine that that garden was like the gardens and orchards we have, the fruit of which is for eating and their foliage for medicine as is well known. For God has no need of it nor do human beings live there. Rather, it signifies a garden of wisdom and intellect

83. The number 6 is regarded as perfect in Pythagorean arithmetic because it is the sum of its factors.

84. It is called "body" because it is the first cube, i.e., it is three-dimensional. Cf. N. Krochmal, *Moreh,* gate 17, 306.

85. Cassel assumed that this was a reference to Samuel Ṣarṣa. However, the supercommentary on ibn Ezra's commentary to the Bible written by Samuel Biba (Bodleian, Opp. Add 4 to 134) contains the exact passage (67a) de' Rossi quotes.

86. Macrobius's commentary to the *Somnium Scipionis* which was written at the end of the fourth or beginning of the fifth century was very popular and published in many editions. Ch. 2 to which de' Rossi refers deals with Pythagorean arithmetic and the virtue of the numbers within the decade.

87. "Argumentum Marsilii Ficini . . . in dialogum decimum de iusto," *Opera . . . omnia,* 652–60.

88. *Op.* 89 ff. (18).

89. *L.A.* I, 8–15 (37).

90. M. Avot 5:1.

91. Arama, *Aqedat Yiṣḥaq,* gate 3, 20b ff.

92. *Op.* 154 (31).

93. *L.A.* I, 43 (42).

94. *Plant.* 36–37 (192).

that instructs us regarding the soul and all the parts of its faculties." If you should so desire, you can look at the passage for yourself—it is very lengthy.

But in his *Shaʿar ha-Gemul,* Ramban of blessed memory adduces various arguments and rabbinic statements to prove that that garden actually existed.[95] Moreover, Rambam of blessed memory also wrote:

> The Garden of Eden is a fertile and lush place, with the choicest produce of the earth, many rivers and fruit-bearing trees. In the future, the blessed Lord will reveal its location to human beings and indicate the path which leads to the Garden so that they may derive pleasure from it. It is possible that besides the plants which are known and familiar to us, it may also contain fantastic plants which yield rich produce of the greatest pleasantness and sweetness. All this is not beyond the bounds of credibility and not far-fetched; but it is quite likely that it would have existed even if it had not been described in the Torah. The fact that it is depicted there and publicized gives even greater confirmation that it exists.[96]

He also writes about the generation of the tower of Babel in his book *On the Confusion of Tongues.*[97] He admits that there is no harm in anyone believing that the story happened as described. Nevertheless, he demonstrates how, in his opinion, the main point of the story is to teach about matters related to confused conceptions and moral turpitude.

His treatment of the verse, *The divine beings saw how beautiful were the daughters of men* (Gen. 6:2) in his work *On the Giants* is in a similar fashion.[98] We shall mention it presently. He writes that the purpose of that passage is that the souls which are naturally pure and untainted are inclined to cleave to the desires alluded to in the expression "daughters of men" which is material existence. Many other stories mentioned or recounted in Scripture are, in his view, not meant to be taken in their literal sense; rather, their main purpose is their underlying meaning which can be studied through one's intellectual faculties. And if this is indeed what he meant, then it is actually forbidden to listen or even pronounce[99] his views. For this is Ramban's ruling in regard to other views similar to his.[100] We ought to praise the wise author of the *Aqedah* who devoted his book (*Ḥazut Qashah*) to this subject[101] and also discussed it at length in gate 7 in his commentary on the Torah.[102] He condemns anyone who holds that the literal text of Scripture and its propositions are merely philosophical concepts couched in the form of parables or metaphors. This is what he states in gate eight of *Ḥazut Qashah.*[103]

95. *Shaʿar ha-Gemul* which forms the last part of his larger work *Torat ha-Adam* was first published separately in Naples, 1494. See *Kitve Ramban,* 298.

96. Maimonides, *Perush,* Introduction to Sanh. ch. 10 (Ḥeleq).

97. *Conf.* 190–91 (302).

98. *Gig.* 6–7 (249).

99. 'Pronounce.' Ramban states 'believe,' not 'pronounce.'

100. De' Rossi is referring here to Nahmanides' critique of Maimonides in his commentary to Gen. 18:1. Nahmanides gives a long discourse in which he attacks Maimonides for interpreting the visit of the three angels to Abraham as a prophetic vision. It is significant that in his desire to find arguments against Philo, de' Rossi even resorts to using a passage of Nahmanides in which the object of attack is usually Maimonides.

101. Arama's *Ḥazut Qashah* was first published in Sabbioneta, 1551.

102. *Aqedat Yiṣḥaq,* gate 7, 55ff.

103. *Ḥazut Qashah,* 13a–15b.

Indeed, there is no doubt that once having accepted the reality of the literal meaning of the stories as they are, we can (and even should) apply metaphorical and allegorical interpretation to them. This was demonstrated even by the sage himself who was mentioned before [i.e., Arama], quoting the words of the divine Rabbi Simeon bar Yoḥai in the Midrash ha-Neʿelam.[104] He writes: "Woe to the man who says that the Torah is just a story book . . . but all the words of Torah belong to the upper and lower worlds."[105] This quotation is given at the beginning of gate 7 [of *Aqedat Yiṣḥaq*]. Look at the passage. Thus the author of the *Aqedat Yiṣḥaq* himself applies the allegorical method to holy Scripture. One such case is his lengthy discourse in his commentary on the Torah [i.e., the *Aqedat Yiṣḥaq*] and in gates 10 and 11 of *Ḥazut Qashah* on the general and particular symbolism of Eden, the Garden, its trees, rivers and everything else pertaining to it. In similar fashion, in his introduction to his commentary on the Torah, ibn Ezra wrote: "And the tree of knowledge is a sweet secret although the words [used to describe it] are meant to be taken literally."[106] He also wrote: "Know that everything which was written regarding the garden and the rivers is true and existed in that way and it cannot be called into doubt, but it also has an esoteric meaning."[107] The sage Recanati also wrote in this fashion in regard to the verse, *and the fiery ever-turning sword to guard the way to the tree of life* (Gen. 3:24).[108] Thus, two things have to be borne in mind when dealing with such questions. First, our acceptance of the plain sense of Scripture must never waver—this is what the sage [i.e., Arama] said in his two works mentioned above. Likewise, our sages of blessed memory articulated an important principle in this regard in tractate Shabbat. Notwithstanding Midrash and Aggadah and the seventy faces of Torah, they declared that Scripture never departs from its plain meaning.[109] The other point is as follows: the symbolism which we apply to Scripture must in some way have been transmitted to us by a sage who is "better than a prophet."[110] Not just anyone who wishes to show off and devise his own explanations may interpret Scripture in this way. The divine Simeon bar Yoḥai opposed such practices. In the Zohar, he comments on the verse, *You shall not make for yourself a sculptured image or any likeness of what is in the heavens above* (Ex. 20:4), and says: "Do not make for yourself another Torah which you do not know and have not been told about by your teacher."[111] Study the passage for yourself. The reason is that the statements of such people who allegorize resemble a sculptured image of human workmanship which is vain and useless. And if Yedidyah can be charged with these two crimes, he must surely be humiliated and held guilty of a mortal sin.

This man may be accounted with yet another defect, a fundamental shortcoming. This last charge is weighty enough to sink him like lead into bottomless waters. It is as follows: reading from beginning to end of his works you will not come across any

104. *Aqedat Yiṣḥaq,* gate 7, 55ff., and *Ḥazut Qashah,* gate 10, 17b, and gate 11, 22b.
105. Zohar III, 152a.
106. Abraham ibn Ezra, haqdamah to *Perush al Ha-Torah* (7).
107. Ibn Ezra to Gen. 3:24.
108. Recanati, *Perush* to Gen. 3:24 (15a–b).
109. B. Shabb. 63a; B. Yev. 24a. For a recent discussion of these passages, see D. Weiss Halivni, *Peshat and Derash,* 56–61.
110. 'Better than a prophet' is a talmudic expression. Cf. B. B.B. 12a.
111. Zohar II, 87b.

indication that he took upon himself the Oral Tradition alongside the Written Torah. As the primary example, you should take his work *On the Special Laws.* You will notice that whenever our sages of blessed memory have in accordance with their traditional reading slightly deviated from the plain sense of the verse in order to elicit a particular law, his interpretation follows Scripture to the letter, and his translation retains the structure of the verse without alteration. He does this with the expression "eye for an eye" (Ex. 21:24) which the sages of blessed memory traditionally interpret as signifying monetary compensation.[112] In the Sifre, the rabbis proffer a similar type of interpretation of the verse, *If two men get into a fight with each other and the wife of one comes to save her husband from his antagonist and puts out her hand and seizes him by the genitals, you shall cut off her hand; show no pity* (Deut. 25:11–12). On the basis of a verbal analogy [*gezerah shavah*], they interpret the verse to mean that she is forced to pay compensation in proportion to the shame she caused the man.[113] In all cases of this kind, Yedidyah explains the verses literally as did the Boethusians. In chapter 3, we quoted the statements of our rabbis, blessed be their memory, regarding the Boethusians.

When men quarrel and one strikes the other and he does not die but has to take to his bed, if he then gets up and walks outdoors upon his staff, his assailant shall go unpunished except that he must pay for his idleness and his cure (Ex. 21:17). In the Mekhilta, the rabbis explain the expression "upon his staff" as referring to the man's health and strength,[114] and this interpretation is cited by Rambam of blessed memory in chapter 4 of his laws concerning murder.[115] Yedidyah, however, takes the expression "upon his staff" literally.

The verse, *If he did not do it by design* [i.e., kill a man], *but it came about by an act of God, I will assign you a place to which he can flee* (Ex. 21:13) is discussed by the rabbis in Makkot.[116] As Rambam states, this means that if somebody intends to kill one person and kills somebody else, he is not liable to the death penalty implemented by the law court, nor is he liable to pay damages or to be exiled.[117] The same applies to one who fails to carry out his premeditated murder, or as the sages of blessed memory say, "Do you really think that such a person is put to death?"[118] But in all these cases, Yedidyah claims that the death penalty is passed.[119]

The expression "but no damage ensues" in the verse, *When men fight and one them pushes a pregnant woman and a miscarriage results, but no damage ensues, the one responsible shall be fined* (Ex. 21:22) is understood according to the teaching in the Mekhilta as a reference to the woman.[120] So too, the fine is understood to be for the loss of the fetus. But Yedidyah in his sixteenth book[121] as well as the Septuagint interpret it as though it refers to a case when the fetus is not fully formed for when damage does ensue, life must be exchanged for life.

112. B. B.Q. 83b.
113. Sifre Devarim par. 292.
114. Mekhilta d'Rabbi Ishmael, neziqin 9 (3, 53).
115. *Mishneh Torah,* Roṣeaḥ IV:4.
116. B. Makk. 7b.
117. *Mishneh Torah,* Roṣeaḥ IV:1.
118. This is an inexact quotation from B. Makk. 7b.
119. *Spec.* III, 120 (664).
120. Mekhilta d'Rabbi Ishmael, neziqin 8 (3, 65).
121. I.e., *De congressu quaerendae eruditionis gratia,* 137 (384).

In the Mekhilta, our sages explain the verse, *You shall not revile God* (Ex. 22:27) as a warning not to curse the Lord and not to curse the judge.[122] But in his book *On Government,* Yedidyah interprets it in reference to the gentile deities, which is the way the Septuagint translates it.[123] According to Yedidyah's understanding of the verse, when you provoke the idolator by cursing his god, he might be roused to anger and revile God. Now abide with me, dear reader,[124] and I shall inform you of something which you should reflect on. For Josephus gives a similar interpretation of the verse.[125] He states: "We are not allowed to pay attention to the laws of other nations for our sole obligation is the observance of our Torah. And yet, this does not give us the license to despise the laws of others. On the contrary, we are cautioned not to curse the object of their worship for the name god is ascribed to it." This is indeed a moral lesson which scholars could indirectly derive from Scripture, namely, the realization that it is best to keep silent on potentially dangerous issues. *And they looked after Moses* (Ex. 33:8) is an expression which the sages understood figuratively as the author of the *Guide* states [i.e., they regarded Moses as their model].[126] It was he who wisely said, *If we sacrifice that which is untouchable to the Egyptians, before their very eyes will they not stone us* (Ex. 8:22).[127]

But we should give credit to Yedidyah. He discusses the enormity of the sin of those who lie with a woman during the time of her menstruation.[128] He says that such an act is destructive and is comparable to one who sows in a field which is inundated with water. He also says that one who copulates with a barren woman is like one who ploughs and shatters his seed on rocky ground. But he has nothing to say about the period following menstruation.[129] In Sanhedrin, they discuss the law, *If a man is guilty of a capital offense and is put to death and you impale him on a stake* (Deut. 21:22). Rabbi Eliezer's opinion that all people who are stoned are also hanged is not accepted. The law is in accordance with those who said that hanging is only reserved for the blasphemer and idolator.[130] But Yedidyah explains the verse according to its literal meaning that all who commit a capital offence are to be hanged.[131] In the Mekhilta, the sages give the traditional interpretation of the verse, *And you shall not seethe a kid in its mother's milk* (Ex. 23:19).[132] They rule that it is prohibited to eat, cook, or derive any benefit from a mixture of meat and milk. In his work *On Kindness,* he interprets the verse according to its literal meaning, and he tendentiously rebukes hedonists when he says: "If you so

122. Mekhilta d'Rabbi Ishmael, kaspa 1 (3, 151).
123. *Spec.* I, 53 (686).
124. In B, de' Rossi calls this passage "an essential note."
125. *Ant.* IV:207; *Contra Apionem* II, 237.
126. *Guide* I, ch. 4. "Similarly it says, 'And they looked after Moses of which words the Sages may their memory be blessed have said that they too have this figurative meaning, as they inform us that the Israelites watched his actions and words and scrutinized them" (Pines trans.).
127. I.e., Moses was careful not to offend the religious sensibilities of the Egyptians: thus the moral lesson can be derived from Scripture, but not from its citation by Philo and Josephus.
128. *Spec.* III, 32–33 (657).
129. According to rabbinic law, intercourse is forbidden for seven days after the end of menstruation.
130. M. Sanh. 6:4.
131. *Spec.* III, 151 (672).
132. Mekhilta d'Rabbi Ishmael, kaspa, 5 (3, 187–96); B. Ḥull. 115b.

relish a kid cooked in milk, could you not obtain the milk of another animal to avoid the use of the milk that nature provided for the rearing of the kid, instead of destroying its flesh on account of lust?"[133]

In a similar vein, he interprets various verses as expressions of the merciful and compassionate attributes of the Holy One blessed be He. They are: *However, no animal from the herd or from the flock shall be slaughtered on the same day with its young* (Lev. 22:28); *You shall not plough with an ox and ass together* (Deut. 22:10); *When in your war against a city you have to beseige it a long time in order to capture it, you must not destroy its trees, wielding the axe against them* (Deut. 20:19).[134] Our rabbis, however, in Berakhot, simply describe these verses as royal enactments.[135]

{In the third book of *On the Life of Moses*[136] and in his work *On Sacrifices,*[137] he wrote that it is the priest who does the ritual slaughter. This runs counter to the tradition of our rabbis of blessed memory in Torat Kohanim and Zevaḥim that even the slaughtering of a layman is valid.[138] And in the same context in *On the Life of Moses*} and in *On the Decalogue,*[139] he wrote that all the Israelites would slaughter and sacrifice their Paschal offerings without waiting for the priests because the Torah had assigned that annually on the day before Passover, every Israelite should assume the role of the priest. Perhaps he derived this idea from the verse, *You shall keep watch over it until the fourteenth day of this month and all the assembled congregation of the Israelites shall slaughter it at twilight* (Ex. 12:6). According to our sages' interpretation of this verse in Pesaḥim, the Passover offerings of the community were sacrificed in three groups.[140] In his work *On Government,* he wrote that the high priest could only marry a priest's daughter.[141] Perhaps he derived this interpretation from the verse, *A widow or divorced woman, or one who is degraded by harlotry—such he may not marry. Only a virgin of his own kin may he take to wife* (Lev. 21:14). {But in Torat Kohanim our rabbis say that the expression "of his own kin" includes the daughter of an Ammonite proselyte woman; she too is eligible to marry a priest.[142] This statement is also cited in Yevamot[143] and in the Pesiqta in Emor[144] as well as by Rambam.[145] And in Bereshit Rabbah, citing *Women will deem me fortunate* (Gen. 30:13) and also with reference to the verse, *Malchiel who was the father of Birzaith* (1Chr. 7:31), they explicitly state that the daughters of the tribe of Asher were comely and married to priests who were annointed with olive oil.[146]}

{After writing this chapter, I happened to come across in Venice two commentaries

133. *Virt.,* 142–44 (*De charitate* 601).
134. Ibid., 134–51 (*De charitate* 601ff.).
135. B. Ber. 33b.
136. *Mos.* II, 224 (581).
137. *Spec.* I, 255 (*De victimis* 703).
138. Sifra, vayiqra 4, 6, col. a; M. Zev. 3:1.
139. *Decal.* 159 (645).
140. M. Pes. 5:5; but priests could do the slaughtering.
141. *Spec.* I, 110 (*De monarchia* 694).
142. Sifra to Lev. 21:14 (95 col. a).
143. B. Yev. 77b.
144. Pesiqta Zutarta (or Leqaḥ Ṭov), (118).
145. *Mishneh Torah,* Issure Bi'ah XIX:13.
146. B.R. 71:10 (835). This passage is crossed out in B.

on the Torah written by two Karaites. The one called The *Sefer ha-Mivḥar* was written by Rabbi Aaron bar Joseph in the year 5054 [1294];[147] the other called *Keter Torah* was written in 5122 [1362] by Rabbi Aaron bar Elijah,[148] may all their names, fathers and sons, be cursed.[149] Indeed, the first mentioned commentator says that the words "but a virgin" are added to remind one that she should be a daughter of a priest from his people. The second writes as follows: "The statement 'from his kin' possibly signifies that she should be a daughter of a priest." Thus, in this matter, Yedidyah is a fellow traveler with these evil people.[150]][2]

In *On the Special Laws,* he writes that one who rapes a widow or divorcee should be punished either by stripes or by a fine.[151] He may have deduced this from his interpretation of the injunction against adultery, which he understood as referring to all kinds of adultery, while our sages define adultery only in connection with a married woman.

In fact, all these discourses of his are worthless for they are not formulated according to the tradition. Occasionally, it is true, he does say, "This is the tradition I received from our ancestors." One occurrence is in his work *On Compassion* where he gives some explanations of the concept. The context in which he uses this particular expression demonstrates that he is referring to cocksure people who make up their own explanations for the precepts of our God. Similarly, he writes about the ancestral tradition of those who led a contemplative life.[152] From his discussion, you realize that he is referring only to a certain type of allegory which he applies to some of the precepts and which, in truth, is of inferior quality. A prime example is to be found at the end of his work *On the Special Laws* in which he explains that the law regarding the impurity of the dead is intended as a deterrent against murder. By "tradition," he did not mean the interpretation of the practical laws which was how our rabbis understood the term. Rather, it referred to their custom pertaining to their own needs. As Rambam of blessed memory says in his commentary on Avot: "They sought for themselves those things which were acceptable to just a few people."[153]

These then are the four main defects in such a man which make him liable to four serious charges, particularly since they reveal that his heart was not upright in the way that any member of our people is and that he was possessed by an alien spirit as regards the Torah which Moses received face-to-face on Sinai and transmitted to us. It is true that we cannot claim that he was an adherent of the Sadducean sect. As we noted before, they denied resurrection of the dead, reward and punishment, and the existence of spirits which dwell without attachment to the body. In contradistinction to them, he acknowledged all these things and declaimed on them, producing many demonstra-

147. Aaron ben Joseph (1250–1320), *ha-Mivḥar,* III, 39a. De' Rossi read the work in manuscript.

148. Aaron ben Elijah (1328?–1369), *Keter Torah,* 2, 59a–60d. De' Rossi read the work in manuscript.

149. Cf. Pr. 10:7.

150. This passage is crossed out in B and in its place de' Rossi quotes from Abraham ibn Ezra's *Yesod Morah,* gate 7, which deals with the question of how traditional interpretations cannot be derived from a simple reading of the biblical text.

151. *Spec.* III, 64 (661).

152. *Cont.* 28–29 (748): "dant operam philosophiae per manus acceptae a maioribus."

153. *Perush,* M. Avot 1:3. Maimonides refers to the Sadducees and Boethusians who rejected the tradition and then links their heresy to that of the Karaites.

tions and examples from holy Writ. Thus, in my opinion, when somebody attacks him by issuing an evil report about him, he would be justified in identifying him as one of the other heretics, that is, the Boethusians, as we said before. However, in the following chapter we shall hear whether an angel serving as his advocate may find a way of resuscitating his case.

CHAPTER SIX

A plausible defense of Yedidyah on all charges leveled against him and our final verdict concerning him.

It is true that the person who proposes some means of exonerating Yedidyah and defending him against the criticisms we raised will not find all the gates of repentance closed nor all tongues rendered dumb. In fact, a case can be presented in his favor, and a line of defense can be taken whereby he may be cleared of all these charges.

Now Yedidyah's citation and interpretation of Scripture was based on the Septuagint version and not on our correct text. This was because everything he wrote about in all his works was not intended for his own people the Jews, but for the Greeks and Romans to whom he wished to demonstrate the many merits of the Torah of our God. He therefore realized that it was in his best interest to instruct them according to their own system and to conduct his studies along the lines of the version which they possessed. In order to avoid confusing and bewildering them, he refrained from emending the script, writing methods, and texts[1] in which they had been trained from childhood. In fact, the Christian translator [Jerome] discusses this question in his *Hebraicae Quaestiones* with regard to their statement in Acts 7 (v.14) that our ancestors went down to Egypt with seventy-five persons.[2] This was an error which, as I have already demonstrated, also occurs in Yedidyah's *On the Migration of Abraham.*[3] He [i.e., Jerome] wrote that the speaker made that error intentionally so that while he was making every effort to achieve other ends, he would not disturb the beliefs of the common people. For they took on trust the reliability of the figure given in the translation which had been promulgated among them for the number of Israelites who went to Egypt.[4]

Now, why should I derive my proof from extraneous sources when the Palestinian Talmud claims that the prophetical books contain stories which are not strictly accurate

1. This expression is taken from M. Avot 5:6 where the "[Hebrew] script, writing, and tablets" are enumerated among those things which were created on the eve before the Sabbath of creation.

2. Jerome, *Heb. quaest.* to Gen. 46:26 (*P.L.* XXIII, col. 1051–53). In Gen. 46:27, the number given is 70 and not 75. In a gloss, omitted from Cassel's edition, de' Rossi writes: "Moreover, Josephus numbers Jacob, his sons and grandsons together with Joseph and his sons, and like us arrives at the figure of 70 inclusive of Jacob. This is also the opinion of ibn Ezra, Abravanel, and Gersonides."

3. *Mig.* 199 (362).

4. This argument was known as the *Lex Hieronymiana* and was severely denounced by the Spanish theologian Melchior Cano (*De locis,* bk. 11, ch. 5) who described it as a potential source of scepticism which deprived historical sources of all historical value.

but are written with respect to popular views? It is as though the prophets thought it permitted to manipulate the true facts in order to avoid controversy. And so, in the last chapter of Taʿanit in the Palestinian Talmud, they say, "This is a case of incorrect computations."[5] I shall discuss this statement in chapter 42[6] together with the Rashba's [Rabbi Solomon ben Adret] and the Tosafists' discussion of the subject in Rosh ha-Shanah and with a passage from the end of the *Kuzari*.

And so, Yedidyah, who was so careful not to alter the literal meaning of the stories, would have been even more conscientious not to contort Scripture with regard to such precepts as relate to the seething of a kid in its mother's milk and to the postmenstrual period. He did not wish to add to or detract from their given text on the basis of a midrash or a traditional interpretation. For these testimonies could not be obtained merely by crossing the sea, but lay out of reach in the heavenly regions.[7] Thus nobody who would make the effort to reach for them would be regarded as clever or meet with divine approval; it could be that he would appear to be a trickster in the eyes of those peoples. Indeed, you should look at the passage where the author of the *Guide* [Maimonides] gives a reason for the precept about giving eye for an eye based on the literal meaning of the text. He states: "Do not trouble yourself by thinking about the fact that we impose a monetary fine in such a case (i.e., as shown in his *Yad Ḥazaqah*);[8] for the purpose here (i.e., in the *Guide*) is to give the reason for the biblical pronouncement and not to explain the words of the Gemara."[9] Discussing the subject of the four rivers [of Eden], the sage ibn Ezra defended the Gaon Rav Saadiah who was criticized on similar grounds [i.e., for his Arabic translation of the Bible]. He writes: "Perhaps it was in order to glorify the blessed Lord that he acted in this way; for he translated the Torah into the Arabic language and script so that they should not complain that it contained precepts which were unfamiliar to them."[10] This all bears relation to what the author of the *Guide* says when he gives the fifth reason to account for the phenomenon of contradictory statements. He says that sometimes, when a certain idea cannot be fully comprehended by the audience, it is simply stated but not explained.[11] We could thus articulate our defense of Yedidyah regarding this particular sin with the words of our rabbis of blessed memory in Menaḥot: "Sometimes the obliteration of Torah becomes its very foundation, as it says, *and I will inscribe upon the tablets the words that were on the first tablets which you shattered* (Ex. 34:1). The Holy One blessed be He said to Moses, 'You did well to break them.' "[12]

5. P. Taʿanit 4 (5) 68c.
6. Ch. 42 and not 40 as in Cassel.
7. This passage is a play on Deut. 30:11–14: *Surely this Torah which I enjoin upon you this day is not too baffling for you, nor is it beyond reach. It is not in the heavens that you should say, Who among us can go up to the heavens and get for us and impart it to us that we may observe it. Neither is it beyond the sea that you should say, Who among us can cross to the other side of the sea and get it for us and impart it to us that we may observe it.*
8. This is another name for Maimonides' code of Jewish law, the *Mishneh Torah*.
9. *Guide* III, ch. 41.
10. Ibn Ezra to Gen. 1:11. Saadiah's (882–942) translation of the Bible into Arabic, the Tafsir, is both translation and commentary. Ibn Ezra is referring to Saadiah's identification of the four rivers (e.g., he says that Pishon is the Nile). He states that it is all a figment of Saadiah's imagination but excuses him on the grounds that he wanted to render the rivers by names familiar to his readers.
11. Maimonides, *Guide*, Introduction (17–18).
12. B. Men. 99b.

Similarly, we should also give him credit when he quotes the theologians' opinion that the tetragrammaton is the name of four letters which connotes being. He speaks evasively, even quoting the authority of the theologians since if the truth be known, that is the sum total of what we know about the name of the blessed Lord. In fact, despite all the knowledge that has been divulged to our people, all that is known is that it is composed of four letters which recognizably connote being; but the pronunciation of the letters has not been disclosed to us. Indeed, the vocalization marks under the letters do not pertain to that name, but merely indicate how the name is to be read. For example, when there is a verse such as *Lord God you have begun* (Deut. 3:24), they indicate whether the tetragrammaton is to be read as Elohim (God) or as Adonai (Lord) which is the usual pronunciation of the tetragrammaton when it occurs in the Bible. For it is characteristic of the holy tongue to indicate the vowels of the letters which are to be read [but are missing from the text] on the written word. This occurs in cases of obscenity as in, *who will have to eat their dung and drink their urine with you* (Is. 36:12),[13] or it may be to augment holiness as with this awful, glorious name of the blessed Lord selah.[14] Thus, when the word Lord (Adonai) is spelt with a *sheva* under the *yod* instead of a *ḥataf pataḥ* as is correct for the *alef,* this is to ensure, according to the true kabbalists, that the numerical value of the letters and vowels of the actual name amount only to seventy-two regardless of whether the computation is done by *millui* or by *ṣiruf.*[15] Moreover, since the singular name of God (*elo'ah*) is vocalized with a *ḥataf segol* [so too, the plural form]. But since the singular form of the name Lord (*adon*) is not vocalized with *ḥataf pataḥ,* neither is the plural form. Or perhaps there is another reason for this of which I am ignorant. However, there is no doubt that if the *sheva* is actually intended for the *yod* when it is joined to any of the letters *bet, vav, kaf, lamed,* it must be pointed with a *ḥireq* as is exemplified in the expression *Let us go up into Judah* (biy-hudah) (Is. 7:6) or *Levi and Judah* (Viy-hudah) (Ex. 1:2). It is already made obvious that this mode of reading [the tetragrammaton] was not just an innovation made by us in the time of our exile, but was also in use by the ancients.[16] Look at the Septuagint which renders the tetragrammaton by the Greek word *kurios* [Lord]. The Christian [i.e, Jesus] and his disciples using Aramaic which was the vernacular during the second Temple period (as will be explained in chapters 9 and 57) used the word *maran* which was translated into Latin as *dominus* (Lord). Moreover, reading brother Theseo Pavese's *Introduction to the Languages,* I noticed that the Aramean gentiles of Syria translate *The Lord said to my lord* (Ps. 110:1) by "Amar morio limori"; likewise they translate, *I cry out with my voice to the Lord* (Ps. 142:2) by "Be qoli morio qerit."[17] (Similarly, in the Turkish edition of the

13. I.e., the vowels for the words "dung" and "urine" are indicated in the text, but not the consonants.

14. I.e., with the exception of the vowel given to the first *yod* in the YHWH, the vowels pertain to the name Adonai.

15. *Millui* is the term given to the calculation of the numerical values of all the letters that make up the name (in this case, God's name of 72 letters). *Ṣiruf* is calculated by adding the numerical value of each letter to the numerical value of the next letter. The name of 72 letters derives from three verses in Ex. 14:19–21, each of which contains 72 letters. On the kabbalistic use of *gematria,* see G. Scholem, *Kabbalah,* 337–43.

16. The pronunciation of the tetragrammaton as Adonai seems to have been in use from about the third century B.C.E.

17. Theseo Ambrogio (Albonesius), *Introductio,* 109. Theseo Ambrogio was one of the first Western

Pentateuch which contains Rabbenu Saadiah's Arabic translation as well as a Persian translation, the tetragrammaton is always rendered *Allah* in Arabic and *Kuddah* in Persian, and the same word is used when translating the expression *my lord Moses* [Num. 11:28] or *my lord is old* [Gen. 18:12].[18] And this is the case for all languages—the tetragrammaton is expressed by a word meaning "lordship.") {And I also learnt from that text [i.e., the Arabic translation of the Pentateuch] that when ibn Ezra refers to the Gaon's [i.e., Saadiah's] translation of the Torah into the language of the Ishmaelites, he is not referring to Turkish, but to Arabic. And in the Arabic translation I saw confirmation of what he [i.e., ibn Ezra] says about the additional *vav* functioning as an embellishment as does the *fa* in the Arabic language.[19] Moreover the word "Ishmaelites" is translated as "Arabs" in the Targum.[20]} Thus in all the examples given, the word used for the tetragrammaton has the meaning of lord and does not connote being. This is due to the fact that although the tetragrammaton is written, its letters are not pointed with the vowels requisite for its proper pronunciation. Thus in his letter to Marcella, the translator [i.e., Jerome] speaks of "the four-lettered name which is ineffable."[21] It is not simply as a sign of respect that the name is not pronounced—this is the view of the Christian scholar Pagninus in his *Thesaurus of the Holy Tongue*[22]—but also because the actual vocalization is not known. Thus the sin of he who "pronounces the letters of the Name" is twofold:[23] he articulates a name which does not exist; and according to his own view, would be behaving disrespectfully regarding something which is even forbidden for human beings, for it is not allowed to call one's parents by their own name. Thus the ban is not placed on the one who simply reads, which would mean reading in its usual sense, but on the one who meditates. For meditation conveys the sense of something which is veiled or hidden as is demonstrated by the expressions *consider my meditation* (Ps. 5:2) and *May the meditation of my heart be acceptable to You* (Ps. 19:15). However, you should known that even certain gentile sages who lived near to the time of our prophet Moses called the blessed God by the specific designation "the one that is" or one might say "the existing being," namely, He who alone has true being. This may be corroborated by the bishop Eugubinus's comment on the expression *I am that I am* (Ex. 3:14). He specifically refers to the fact that it was on authority of Hermes, who was mentioned by us in chapter 4, that a designation of God was written in the temple in Egypt which read, "I am he who was and is and shall be for always and no living person shall ever uncover my veil." He also quotes Plato's words in the *Timaeus* in which he

---

scholars to learn Syriac and did so at the time of the fifth Lateran council of 1512 when three Maronite clergymen asked permission to say mass in Syriac. De' Rossi also speaks about Theseo in ch. 59.

18. This is a reference to the polyglot Pentateuch published in Constantinople (1546) which contained Saadiah's Arabic version and the Judaeo-Persian version in Hebrew characters.

19. Ibn Ezra to Lev. 11:44. Ibn Ezra actually states that the *fa* is used in Arabic at the beginning of a section (as the *vav* in Hebrew).

20. This is the case in all the Aramaic Targumim.

21. Jerome, *Epistolae* (*P.L.* XXII, 25, col. 429).

22. Xantes Pagninus was the author of a new Latin translation of the Hebrew and Greek Bible (1528). His *Thesaurus linguae sanctae,* Lyons 1529 was reprinted in the sixth volume of the Plantin Polyglot. He writes: "Nomen est dei ineffabile divinum significans essentiam . . . ob cuius reverentiam non profertur ab hebraeis ut scribitur. Sed legunt Adonai quod dominum sonat."

23. This is a reference to M. Sanh. 10:1: "The following have no portion in the world to come . . . one who pronounces the divine name as it is spelled."

declares that past and future are categories of time which we in our foolishness inappropriately attribute to Him who exists forever. However, the truth of the matter is that only the present tense is applicable to Him, for past and future imply subjection to time in nature.[24] Yedidyah, too, following the Septuagint version often expatiated on the truth of this name. In his work *On Dreams*[25] and in the first book of *On the Life of Moses,*[26] he said that the point of the response "I am that I am" is to imply: "It is impossible for Me to have a proper name." Rather, it indicates true existence.[27]

One might also take up this line of defense with regard to the question of primordial matter. After all, it was regarded as an axiom by some of their philosophers, and the expression *the earth was void* when not understood correctly may give an erroneous impression of signifying primordial matter. Thus he [Philo] may have chosen not to dissent from them entirely. This is even more justifiable when we take into account the statement of the divine author of the *Kuzari:* "If an upholder of the Torah is bound to profess a belief in the primordial *hyle* and in the existence of many worlds prior to this one, it should not be accounted as a flaw in his belief. It is enough that he believes that this world was created at a specific moment in time and that Adam and Eve were the first human beings."[28] The author of the *Guide* offers a similar point of view and puts the case even more strongly: "He who believes in the eternity of the universe according to the second of the theories expounded above—i.e., the Platonic view that the heavens both come into being and disintegrate—does not contravert the principles of the Torah, nor does it lead to the negation of miracles; it is in fact possible to interpret Scripture in accordance with this notion and there are many analogies in the verses of the Torah and other places which corroborate and even testify to the phenomenon."[29] He was doubtlessly alluding to the statement of Rabbi Judah bar Samuel and Rabbi Abbahu in Bereshit Rabbah regarding the verse, *And it was evening* (Gen. 1:5).[30] This is apparent from the explanation he gives in part 2 [of the *Guide*].[31] You should know, however, that in his twelfth note on the *Timaeus* (to which I referred in the previous chapter), the Christian sage Ficino defended Plato for his views on the eternity of matter. He said that this view did not imply temporal precedence in any way, but priority in beginning and order. And he adds that the statement of Moses our teacher that the earth was null

24. Steuchus, *Recognitio,* 106v–108r. See the discussion of this passage by D. P. Walker, *The Ancient Theology,* 38.

25. *Som.* I, 230 (511).

26. *Mos.* I, 75: "First tell them that I am he who is that they may learn the difference between what is and what is not and also the further lesson that no name at all can properly be used of Me to whom alone existence belongs."

27. De' Rossi's digression on the subject of the tetragrammaton and his emphasis on the fact it is an unpronounceable name is perhaps to be understood in the context of the expositions of Christian kabbalists such as Reuchlin, Galatino, and Pico della Mirandola, who interpreted the tetragrammaton as signifying the mysteries of the trinity. It was also claimed that the name of Jesus was contained within the Name.

28. *Kuzari* I, par. 67.

29. *Guide* II, ch. 25.

30. B.R. 3:7 (23): "*And there was evening.* Rabbi Judah ben Simon said: 'Let there be evening' is not written here, but *And there was evening.* Hence we know that a time-order existed before this. Rabbi Abbahu said: This proves that the Holy One blessed be He went on creating worlds and destroying them until he created this one."

31. *Guide* II, ch. 30.

and void does not signify precedence in time since matter was also created with the other parts of the creation; rather, it means priority in beginning and order. He further supports his apologia for Plato with a citation from Yedidyah's first two books *On the Creation of the World* which we quoted in the previous chapter. And he says that although Yedidyah was a religious Jew, his statements were nevertheless similar to those of Plato. Consequently, the position of both men should be vindicated in the manner demonstrated.[32] Accordingly, the passage we quoted from *That the World Is Indestructible* which was used to incriminate Yedidyah should not be regarded as his own opinion, but that of the philosophers to whom he refers. This argument becomes all the more plausible in the light of the statement of Eusebius the Caesarean in his *Praeparatio evangelica.* He first cites clear proofs in the name of the early Christians Dionysius and Origen. They had argued against the doctrine of the eternity of matter and in favor of the truth of the view of the Torah, namely, that the primordial matter, the *hyle,* as the Greeks called it, was created completely new by the Creator and that there was no reason to deduce from the scriptural statement "the earth was null and void" that it had already existed. Among the various sources he quotes to substantiate this correct notion, he cites from a work of Yedidyah which is no longer extant. It reads as follows:

> We should believe that the blessed Lord created a sufficient amount of matter to produce all the created things. It is evident that a skillful human craftsman sees to it that he has the exact amount of material necessary for his task. This is even more true of the Creator of everything who knows all numbers and measurements without misjudging the quantity at all. And speaking boldly one would claim[33] that He did not need either more or less matter for the creation of the world. But while it is right that any skillful person should prepare the material he needs for his work, it is likely that afterwards, a human will need to make adjustment either by supplementing the material or by removing some of it. But the blessed Lord for whom nothing is too difficult and who can do anything He wishes, doubtlessly supplied Himself with the requisite amount of *hyle* with absolute precision.[34]

Thus far his words which clarify our point.

{I found another passage which corroborates this. It is in the second book of the *Allegorization of the Law.* He writes: "He created everything from nothing."[35] And in the third book of *On the Life of Moses,* he also wrote: "The world was created and completed from nothing."[36] One should indeed register approval of these statements. However, one has no alternative but to admit that his other statements that I mentioned allows a sage such as Ficino to raise doubts about him. It is therefore not surprising that I have a similar understanding of those passages.[37]}[2]

32. Plato, *Omnia . . . opera,* Compendium in Timaeum, 677.
33. 'And speaking boldly' (ausim exclamare).
34. Eusebius, *De ev. praep.,* 7, ch. 8. De' Rossi used George of Trebizond's imprecise Latin translation which was published several times in the sixteenth century.
35. *L.A.* III, 10 (55).
36. *Mos.* II, 267 (587).
37. I.e., de' Rossi seems inclined to think that Philo believed in the eternity of matter. De' Rossi's ambivalence on this issue seems justifiable. After all, modern scholars such as H. A. Wolfson argue that Philo believed in creatio ex nihilo as against Drummond, Neumark, and Bréhier who propose that he believed in the eternity of matter.

Similarly, there may perhaps be grounds for defending him for his allegorization of some of the stories narrated in the Torah. For while he considers that the essence of the stories lies in their esoteric meaning, he does ultimately admit that the revealed text is for us and our children,[38] and that we must believe in them in the manner described by our sages in the Mekhilta when it says, "The Torah was given with all its tittles," that is to say, it is to be understood according to the written text.[39] Such was his view which we mentioned above concerning such commandments as Sabbath and circumcision: they have esoteric meaning and implications, but he opposes those who nullify them completely and warns against desisting from actually fulfilling the precepts.

As for the Garden of Eden, you should know that there are no lack of Jews as well as Christians who on various counts found it problematic to take the story literally; they therefore stumbled in judgment just like Yedidyah. This can be illustrated by statements made by the great Christian doctor Augustine in his commentary to Genesis[40] and by his disciple Aquinas, who in the first book of his *Quaestiones* indicates the controversies, problems, and solutions.[41] In the final analysis, they both reach a valid conclusion. They state that all events related in the Torah as having happened must be taken at face value and cannot be refuted in any way even though some allegorical interpretation is also desirable. {I will now show my approval in the fashion of Rabbi Tarfon with "a knop and a flower"[42] for something on a similar subject that I was told by that giant of our generation Rabbi Eliezer Ashkenazi, may his shield and redeemer protect him, the son of Rabbi Elijah the physician.[43] It is as follows: "Anyone who wishes to convey a complicated intellectual concept to his audience and wants to compare it to a simple concept, but does not know of a similar example, will describe it by means of a parable. The truth of the matter is that the blessed Lord, whose will alone suffices to actualize everything at its appropriate time, uses all His parables to signify certain teachings. But it is also undoubtedly true that they all come to pass. Thus it necessarily follows that we should say that the stories of the Torah which He meant as allegories required but His volition to ensure that they come to pass. In no way can their actuality be denied."[44] But we should return to Yedidyah's defense.} It seems that there is some way of defending him for his statement that the world was not created over the

38. 'The revealed text for us and our children.' This expression occurs in Deut. 29:28 and there are dots above these words. De' Rossi appears to be alluding to the explanation of the dots as given in B. Sanh. 43b which states that they indicate that God would not punish Israel for that which was hidden from them.

39. Mekhilta d'Rabbi Ishmael, neziqin, 17 (3, 136–37). De' Rossi gives a rather free interpretation of this somewhat obscure passage.

40. *De Genesi ad litteram* 8:1 (*P.L.* XXXIV, col. 371). Augustine puts forward three different ways of interpreting the story including a literal one.

41. Aquinas, *Summa theologica* I, quaestio 102, articulus 1: "Respondeo dicendum quod sicut Augustinus dicit. . . . Ea enim quae de paradiso in scriptura per modum narrationis historicae proponuntur. In omnibus autem quae sic Scriptura tradit, est pro fundamento tenenda veritas historiae et desuper spirituales expositiones fabricandae."

42. B.R. 91:9 (1133): "When one made a sound observation before Rabbi Tarfon he would remark, 'A knop and a flower' " (cf. Ex. 25:33).

43. Eliezer b. Elijah Ashkenazi (1533–86) lived in Egypt, Famagusta, Prague, Venice, Cremona, Gniezno, and Cracow. He was a rabbi of great standing but, like de' Rossi, became the target of attack by the Maharal of Prague for his interpretation of the Aggadot. De' Rossi must have met him during his stay in Venice.

44. This idea was developed by Ashkenazi in the introduction to his *Maʿase Adonai,* Venice, 1583.

course of time. His opinion is similar to that of Rabbi Nehemiah in Bereshit Rabbah. On being challenged by Rabbi Judah on the grounds that Scripture refers to one day, a second, a third day, he replied with the parable of the fig-gatherer who picks each fig as it appears in its own time. And he supported his view with the verse, *Let the earth sprout vegetation: seed-bearing plants, fruit trees of every kind on earth that bear fruit with the seed in it* (Gen. 1:11) which implies that the stock of the earth was stored within it.[45] This can be compared to the parable of the gardener mentioned by our rabbis of blessed memory who plants various different types of seeds in one fell swoop, but which sprout forth one after another. The author of the *Guide* has a lengthy discussion of this subject.[46] One of the great Christian doctors who express this same opinion is Augustine. In his commentary to Genesis and in the second book of his *City [of God],* he adduces one proof from the aphorisms of Ben Sira, or Ecclesiasticus as they call him, who stated, *He who lives forever created everything simultaneously* (18:1).[47] It is true however, that his disciple, the philosopher Aquinas, disagreed with him on this point as did many of their sages who gave rationalistic interpretations. The passage is readily accessible in the first part of his *Quaestiones* where he gives a lengthy survey of all the various opinions, proofs, and solutions of the question.[48]

Equally defensible is his statement that the attributes of the Holy One blessed be He are [expressions of His] compassion whereas our sages of blessed memory called them "decrees." His opinion may easily be justified on the basis of what was stated by the author of the *Guide*[49] and by Ramban of blessed memory.[50] Examine those passages.

{I discovered a passage in Rabbi David bar Samuel d'Estella's work *Migdal David* (on positive commandment n. 141) in which he writes: "Although the commandments regarding the sending away of the mother bird and not killing a cow or ewe with their young on the same day are intended to make us compassionate and to eschew cruelty, we are told to silence one who says, 'To a bird's nest Your mercy extends.'[51] This is because it would imply that divine providence is given to individual animals as it is to individual human beings whereas in the case of the latter, it is related to the intellect."[52] He follows the Maimonidean system regarding providence as expounded in part 3 of the *Guide.* Examine the passage.[53]}

At any rate, all these points enable one to suspect the legitimacy of his position. Moreover, in chapter 3, I also put forward the hypothesis that the Boethusians and the

45. B.R. 12:4 (100).

46. *Guide* II, ch. 30.

47. *De civ. Dei,* 2, ch. 17; *De Genesi ad litteram* 5:3 (*P.L.* XXXIV, col. 322–23).

48. Aquinas, *Summa theologica* I, quaestio 74, articulus 2: "Utrum omnes isti dies sint unus dies."

49. *Guide* III, ch. 48. Commenting on Deut. 22:6–7, Maimonides states that the eggs over which the bird has sat and the young that need their mother are not fit to be eaten. Thus, if the mother is allowed to leave her young, she will not be pained by seeing her young taken away, and this, in most cases, would lead most people to refrain from eating unsuitable food.

50. Nahmanides to Deut. 22:6: "The reason for this precept is that a person should not be cruel and unmerciful."

51. B. Ber. 33b.

52. David b. Samuel d'Estella (Kokhavi) was probably from Navarra. The ms. of *Migdal David* is in the Biblioteca Palatina of Parma (Parmense 3540–42), (ed. Hershler, p. 209).

53. De' Rossi correctly connects d'Estella's statement to the Maimonidean definition of providence (cf. *Guide* III, ch. 17).

Essenes partook of the same heresy and were one and the same sect. I am therefore now in the position to prove that Yedidyah, whose case we are presently examining was affiliated with their sect. Even if he was not actually one of the chosen four-thousand-member congregations and did not join in their wanderings and emigration from the cities, he was a fellow traveler [lit. one of those who came at their rear] as far as some of their opinions are concerned, and he did uphold some of their teachings. This has all the more credence in view of his laudatory assessment of them in his thirty-sixth and thirty-seventh books which we discussed [i.e., *That Every Good Man Is Free* and *On the Contemplative Life*]. The origins of my thesis and how I came to be apprized of this, I will unfold and reveal to you, intelligent reader, if only you would give me a hearing.

Go and read the passage in his work *On the Giants* where he discusses the verse, *And the sons of God saw the daughters of man* (Gen. 6:2). He translates the expression *sons of God* as though it read "angels of God." He writes as follows:[54]

> The creatures which other philosophers call "genii" (i.e., the created beings [*yeṣarim*] because they are formed [*noṣeru*] when we are formed) are called angels by Moses. These are spirits which hover in the air. There is no reason to suppose that this is a false fabrication. Animate spirits must certainly exist in all parts of the universe. We ourselves see that each of its principal parts, namely, the elements, contain forms of life appropriate to it. The element earth contains terrestial beings; the element water, aquatic creatures; the element fire, too, contains creatures produced from fire which, according to report, abound in the environs of Macedonia. Similarly, all the heavenly regions contain the stars which are doubtlessly endowed with an eternal and divine soul. This is why their motion is circular, for it is the natural movement for an intelligent soul. And each star possesses a perfect soul. It thus necessarily follows that the element air is also filled with living creatures compatible to it, although they are not actually perceptible to our senses. But the fact that we are unable to perceive the form of the souls visually should not lead us to infer that they are not present in the air. Rather, we must ascertain their existence by means of our intellectual faculties for we can come to an understanding of existence by comparing like with like. We surely cannot deny that all living creatures whether terrestial or aquatic are sustained by air and breath. When you investigate what pestilence is, it will become evident to you that it is merely polluted air which enters bodies that are animated by breath. Thus when the air is pure and untainted, as happens when the north wind blows and is inhaled, we realize how greatly it benefits our health. How then can it be imagined that the air which is the source of life for all creatures of the earth and water should itself lack its own beings. No, the contrary is the case. For even if the other elements cease to propagate living creatures, the element air would in no way be lacking since it has been endowed by the Creator in such a way that it should be the source of the vital forces which animate all living creatures. In fact, some of these animate beings that we have mentioned descend into the bodies, while others remain perpetually dissociated from all parts of the earth. The highest God who produces everything uses the service of those holy beings to administer temporal affairs. But the others which descend into the bodies plunge, as it were, into the depths of a river. Sometimes, waves and torrents engulf them, and sometimes, resisting the torrent, they initially float on the crest and then proceed upwards and return to their former place. These are in fact the souls which have perfected their

54. *Gig.* 6–15 (248).

knowledge of the higher philosophy.[55] They have a prior perception of the destiny of the body which is assigned to death and they acquire for themselves eternal life in the company of God who is Himself eternal. But those which sink in the waters are the souls of the rest of mankind who, in their contempt of wisdom and righteous behavior, subject themselves to the buffeting of the prevailing wind. Not one of them will be borne to the good essential part of us (namely, the intellect), but they will be driven towards the mortal body which is born with us or to even less spiritual things as riches, glory, power, honor, and the like. These are invented and fabricated in the minds of those who have never recognized the true good and result from self-deception based on false opinions. Thus when you come to the realization that there is no essential difference between souls, inclinations, and angels but that they are distinguishable only in name, you will save yourself from more than a little foolishness. In common parlance, one speaks of good and bad inclinations and good and bad souls. Similarly, one might speak of good and bad angels. The so-called good angels are those sent to and fro and serve as intermediaries between God and human beings. They earn this noble and pure title from the nobility and purity of their mission. The others are their antithesis, profane and wicked. One would not be misrepresenting them by calling them abominations. The psalmist testified to this when he said, *He inflicted His burning anger upon them, wrath, indignation, trouble, and a band of deadly angels* (Ps. 78:49). These evil ones which flaunt the name angel have never known the daughters of reason, the offspring of wisdom and virtuous behavior. Instead, they pursue the daughters and offspring of man who are doomed to death and who are stripped and void of any natural and true beauty which is only discernable by means of intellectual conceptualization. All they have is a dissembling appearance which deceives our senses. They take their choice from these women and they do not all follow the same criterion. Each one will make his selection according to the sensual pleasure he might derive from it; one will enjoy visual gratification, another aural, and yet others food, sex, and other such pleasures.

He writes in a similar vein in his book entitled *On the Planting of Noah*:[56]

Indeed, there exist two species of living creatures in the element air: one consists of all the birds and winged creatures visible to the eye and the other the potencies which cannot be detected by the senses. These latter form a contingent of bodiless souls which are actually divided according to rank. Some of these are said to be united in their adherence to bodies which are subject to death; after a period of time, they are released and revert to their former state. Other souls which are endowed with a divine constitution despise all aspects of earthly life. The purest of them all are those which the Greek philosophers call "sons of the gods" or "created beings" which dwell in the upper region near the heavens. Moses called them "angels," a name which reflects their vocation—for they act as mediators between the great God and his lowly creatures. They bring them good tidings, while also, when required, they go on missions for them up to the God in heaven.

In his work *On the Confusion of Tongues,* he writes:[57]

There is in the air a sacred contingent of immaterial souls and they minister to the heavenly souls. In holy Scripture, these souls of the air are actually called "angels." They are separated into individual categories according to rank and their duty is to carry out the missions

55. 'Higher philosophy' (supernam philosophiam).
56. *Plant.* 14 (190).
57. *Conf.* 174–75 (300).

of God. Him alone do they serve and among all their myriads there is not[58] one that transgresses the command of the King. He, the Almighty God, who presides over these servants employs them for only such jobs that ought not be done by God alone. Given that He is the Creator of all, He does not require the help of any created being to lighten the burden of whatever task He wishes to undertake. But He considers what is appropriate to Him in view of His own nature and what is appropriate to created beings in view of their own nature. Accordingly, he delegates some tasks to those officials. Yet He does not invest them with total autonomy lest they make mistakes in the course of implementing their tasks.

Then there is his work *On Dreams* in which he gives some allegorical interpretations of the dream about the ladder (Gen. 28:12ff.). He proposes that the air which extends from the earth to the moon's arc is filled with souls and angels as numerous as the heavenly stars. He then states:[59]

Many of these souls descend in order to attach themselves to mortal bodies, and they live rather near to earth and have a rather pronounced propensity for material things. Many of these souls will return to the supernal place once they have detached themselves from the bodies when the cycle of times fixed in nature has been fulfilled. But there are also many souls which attracted to the pleasures of this life will retrace their steps. And some of them, fearful[60] of the vanities of the world, will consequently flee the bodies as one would the prison or grave and, rising heavenward, will set down their light wings and remain there forever. There are also some which surpass all the others in purity and virtue—these will ascend to the most elevated and divine region; for they spurn base and earthly things and serve God, and acting as it were as the ears and eyes of the King of the entire world, they see and hear everything. The philosophers call them *genii* (i.e., created beings), but holy Writ gives them the name angels [or messengers], a particularly apposite name in that they act as intermediaries, announcing God's command to His children and bringing their requests to His notice. This is why he [i.e., Jacob] saw the angels ascending and descending. It is not that God is in need of ambassadors for He is omniscient. Rather, it is to the benefit of us mortals for these are our intermediaries and advocates and in this way, we acquire even greater reverence for the great God and His might and limitless power. It is a known fact that it was because we feared His might that we requested a mediator, saying, *You speak to us* [they said to Moses], *and we will obey, but let not God speak to us lest we die* (Ex. 20:19). See if we can withstand His power when His anger is directed at us, when even His bounties we are unable to withstand unless they are given through an intermediary. There is therefore profound wisdom[61] contained in this analogy between the whole of the etherial region and a ladder, the foot of which rested on earth and whose top reached heaven. For the vapors which exude from the earth are rarefied and rise into the air with the earth functioning as its root and the heavens, its head and peak. Some sages claim that the body of the moon is not a rarified globe of ether like the other stars, but a compound of air and ether and that the dark patches visible on it which is generally called "the face of the moon" are simply compounded air that extends to the heavens and is naturally black.

Here then is a summary of his statements. In order to facilitate your comprehension of his view and to enable you to see how firmly convinced he is, I did not refrain from collating

58. 'There is not.' The Latin reads 'non licet,' i.e., there must not be.
59. *Som.* I, 138–46 (501).
60. 'Fearful.' The Latin reads 'pertaesae' i.e., disgusted.
61. 'Profound wisdom.' The Latin simply reads 'pulchre.'

disparate passages and presenting them in order to extract new ideas. You thus have a very clear picture, intelligent reader, of his belief that the souls and angels belong to one order of existence. They all bear the common name, souls, although, as we are told by him, they are distinguished by rank. The habitation and resting place of them all is the manifold strata of the air. When the souls, which tend to attach themselves to the bodies, sever that connection, they fly like a cloud through the aerial windows as in former times.

Now the fact is that some of these statements of his are alien to rabbinic opinion. This will become clear to you on examining the passage in Ḥagigah (and there are other examples): "Resh Laqish said, The heavens and heaven of heavens are seven, namely, Vilon, Raqia, [Sheḥaqin, Zevul, Maʿon, Maqom, and Aravot]. Aravot holds the treasuries of peace, the treasuries of blessing, the souls of the righteous, and the spirits and souls of those who are yet to be born. There, too, are the Ofanim, Seraphim, the holy creatures, the ministering angels and the throne of glory of the high and exalted King who dwells above them as it says, *Extol Him who rides the Aravot* (Ps. 68:5)."[62] Thus they distinguished between souls and angels by name and species and also concluded that unlike the winged creatures of the sky, the heavens and heaven of the heavens sustain them and serve as their resting place near the throne of glory and the Lord of the entire world. Another passage which is not in accordance with rabbinic opinion is his statement in *On the Confusion of Tongues* that the angels serve the etherial souls, for it implies that the level of the spheres is higher than their own level.

As regards the various species of spirits, our rabbis of blessed memory state that the only inhabitants of the air are the demons and harmful spirits. According to the their description, they are more numerous and more powerful than humans and are to be found in ruins, underneath gutters and in rivers. This is made clear from their statements in Berakhot, Pesaḥim, and Ḥullin[63] and from Ramban's comment on *And that they may offer their sacrifices no more to the goat-demons after whom they stray* (Lev. 17:7). But it is also true that the sage ibn Ezra wrote: "Do not think that the angels are made of fire and wind simply because it is stated, *Who makes the winds His messengers* (Ps. 104:4). The meaning of the verse is that both the air and the fire are His ministering emissaries who carry out all His wishes."[64] This scriptural verse seems to endorse Yedidyah's view and contains an explanation of the designation angel or Seraph. His view is further corroborated by the statement in Bereshit Rabbah[65] and Midrash Tehillim:[66] "Rabbi Johanan said, 'The angels were created on the second day as it is written, *Who makes the winds His messengers.*' " It is also a well-known fact that there is no difference between the expression *And the angel of the Lord called to him from heaven* (Gen. 22:11) and *Then the Lord caused brimstone and fire to rain from heaven* (Gen. 19:24). The term "heavens" as used in the holy Scriptures embraces the entire area which extends upwards from these nether parts. When Yedidyah speaks about Moses in his work *On the Planting of Noah*[67] and elsewhere, he writes regarding those elect souls who

62. B. Ḥag. 12b.
63. B. Ber. 3a; B. Pes. 110a; B. Ḥull. 105b.
64. Ibn Ezra to Gen. 1:1.
65. B.R. 3:8 (24).
66. Mid. Teh. 104:7.
67. *Plant.* 25–26 (191).

are summoned to the Creator of all, one such example being Moses to whom it was said, *Come up to me on the mountain* (Ex. 24:12) and, *But you remain with me* (Deut. 5:28). He says that once these souls are separated from material existence they soar to the heights beyond the heaven of heavens and penetrate the innermost parts of the Most High, who dwells there from of old Selah.[68]

Nevertheless, his statements about souls and angels as described above do not demonstrate convictions which are consistent with those of our sages. As on other issues, he holds neither a Pharisaic nor a Sadducean position. All the indications that we have noted point to the fact that he held different views from them. And you, intelligent reader, must have come to the realization that each of his opinions are identical to that of the Essenes. This was what I had in mind when I first gave an exposition of Essene doctrine in chapter 3 which was based on various passages in Josephus. In the course of that passage, I spoke of their firm belief in the mortality of the body, that the souls are immortal, fashioned from the rarified ether, and that they are released from the fetters of the body. It is a lengthy passage and you should examine and assess it for yourselves. Such then is the case regarding souls and angels. Then again, the fact that his interpretation of such laws as "eye for an eye" agrees with that of the Boethusians, as we demonstrated at the end of chapter 5, is proof to me that Yedidyah belonged to their group and was one of their adherents and followed their views in respect to the basic beliefs they held. Nevertheless, while giving due consideration to the case I had put forward, I also realized—as I have set out in this chapter—that it is possible to judge him favorably and to protect him from any incriminating offense. My effort to exonerate him has all the more justification because I know that there are learned and upright contemporaries of mine who thirstily imbibe his words and set a golden crown on his head, regarding him as a noteworthy member of our people.[69] And I had even more reason given that both the Hebrew Josephus [Josippon][70] and the Latin Josephus[71] refer to him in a favorable light and extol his wisdom and virtue. It is also known that the great community of Alexandria appointed him as their spokesman and sent him to plead their cause so that they could be freed from the evil decree of the emperor Gaius who had ordered his statue to be placed in the holy Temple. In that same passage, it is related that when he realized that disaster was imminent, he called for fasting and prayers.[72] And miraculously for him, on the very day when all hope was lost, the emperor was killed by his own men and his plans immediately came to nothing. Thus

68. 'Who dwells there from of old Selah,' cf. Ps. 55:20.

69. One such contemporary was David Provenzali who had also written about Philo and to whose work de' Rossi was intending to reply once it had been published. At the end of his response (*Teshuvah*) (Cassel ed., 506) to Moses Provenzali's critique (*Hassagah*), de' Rossi writes about Provenzali: "It is indeed fitting that he should defend Philo since he was the first to promulgate his name among our people by means of his learned studies. He is indeed justified in not giving the appearance of introducing an alien among the holy." Judah Moscato, another Mantuan and friend of de' Rossi, also read and used Philo's works, particularly in his *Qol Yehudah,* a commentary on the *Kuzari.*

70. *Josippon,* bk. 6, ch. 63 (227).

71. *Ant.* XVIII:259.

72. The reference to fasting and prayer (cf. Joel 2:15) is only in the Josippon. According to D. Flusser, *Sefer Josippon,* vol. 1, 273, n. 29, these details were invented by the author of the Josippon.

this was a man who, in my opinion, fell between two stools on whom no decision, as it were, can be reached.

In view of all that has been written in this chapter, I say to the Jewish people that I cannot pass an unconditional verdict on this Yedidyah or Philo, to use his Greek name, or indeed any other name or surname he has been given. I cannot absolutely absolve or convict him. I shall call him neither Rav nor sage,[73] heretic nor sceptic. My only name for him shall be Yedidyah the Alexandrian. Whenever he is mentioned in these chapters, it will not be as an intimate member of my people, but as any other sage of the world to whom a hearing will be given when he makes general statements and has no vested interest in the subject. But as for his other statements and works, the reader should judge for himself and use his discretion in each case. If they are iniquitous, they should be kept at a distance, but if he speaks with the truth of the Torah, he should be brought near like a prince. My attitude towards him shall remain neutral. I have had all my say concerning him. But I cannot desist from clarifying my position. Everything I said about those four thousand Greeks is dependent on the fact that their form of Judaism was a variety of the Sadducean type. However, if they were imbued with a different spirit,[74] I have no quarrel against them.

73. This is an allusion to B. B.M. 85b–86a about Samuel Yarḥina who was "to be called sage but not Rabbi."

74. 'A different spirit.' Cf. Num. 14:24 where this is said of Caleb who is contrasted with the other spies who brought back a false report.

CHAPTER SEVEN

On the story of the elders' translation of Scripture as recorded by our rabbis and by several secular writers other than Aristeas whose book we have already translated. On the differences and similarities in their accounts.

In tractate Megillah,[1] our rabbis of blessed memory tell the story of the translation[2] of our Torah which was related in the "Splendor of the Elders," the work we translated. It reads as follows:

> It is taught: it is told of King Ptolemy that he assembled seventy-two elders and put them in seventy-two rooms without disclosing to them the reason for his conduct. He went in to each one of them and said, "Write out the Torah of Moses your teacher for me." The Holy One blessed be He instilled each one of them with wisdom and they all gave identical renderings of the text and wrote: *God created in the beginning* (Gen. 1:1); *I will make man in image and likeness* (Gen. 1:26); *And he finished on the sixth and rested on the seventh* (Gen. 2:2); *Male and female He created him* (Gen. 5:2); *Come, let me go down and confound their tongues* (Gen. 11:7); *And Sarah laughed among her relatives* (Gen. 18:12); *For in anger they slew an ox and in their wrath they dug up a stall* (Gen. 49:6); *And Moses took his wife and sons and made them ride on a carrier of men* (Ex. 4:20); *And the abode of the children of Israel which they stayed in Egypt and other lands was four hundred years* (Ex. 12:40); *And he sent the elect of the children of Israel* (Ex. 24:5); *And against the elect of the children of Israel he put forth his hand* (Ex. 24:11); *I have not taken a valuable of theirs* (Num. 16:15); *which the Lord your God distributed to provide light to all the peoples* (Deut. 4:19); *And he went and served other gods which I commanded should not be served* (Deut. 13:3). And they substituted the word the "beast with short legs" for the word "hare" (Lev. 11:6) because Ptolemy's wife was called "hare." The reason for the emendation was to prevent him from saying, "The Jews are deriding me; they have put the name of my wife in the Torah."

This entire passage is also in the Mekhilta,[3] and it was actually to the Mekhilta they were alluding when they said, "It is taught."[4] However, according to the Mekhilta and

1. B. Meg. 9a–b.
2. De' Rossi uses various Hebrew words—*targum, hataqah, pitron*—to signify translation. The usual meaning of *pitron* is interpretation. He appears to be using it in the same way as the Latin *interpretatio* can signify either interpretation or translation.
3. Mekhilta d'Rabbi Ishmael, bo, 14 (1, 111–12).
4. The Mekhilta is usually regarded as a Tannaitic work (and thus predates the Talmud). The phrase "it is taught" as used in the Talmud implies that the ensuing passage is a *baraita,* i.e., it dates from the Tannaitic period.

Bereshit Rabbah,[5] the fourth variant reads, "A male with its female parts did He create him." The passage is reproduced in the Palestinian Talmud but without the preliminaries. It simply begins: "Thirteen passages were changed for Ptolemy the king: *God created in the beginning.*" It continues exactly like the Babylonian version apart from the conclusion where Ptolemy's mother and not his wife is said to have been called "hare."[6] There is also a passage in the Midrash Rabbah which reads "his mother."[7] [This corroborates] Rashi's statement quoted before[8] that the compilations of the Midrash Rabbah are Palestinian in origin.[9] The story is also related in tractate Soferim in the following manner:[10] "It happened that five elders wrote the Torah in Greek for King Ptolemy. That day was as calamitous for Israel as when the golden calf was made because it was impossible to make an adequate translation of the Torah. There is also the story of the seventy-two elders whom Ptolemy assembled and put in seventy-two rooms without disclosing . . ." The rest of the passage is identical to that given in the Babylonian Talmud, the only difference occurring in relation to the verse, *And the abode of the children of Israel . . . in Egypt and other lands.* Instead of *in other lands,* it reads: "in Egypt and the land of Canaan." The same reading is found in the Greek Septuagint. No explanation is proffered in regard to the matter of the hare.

At the end of the printed version of the *Megillat Taʿanit,* there is a list of the days on which fasting is ordained according to the Torah. (What is actually meant, is the Torah of our sages.)[11] The eighth of Tevet is classified as one such day because "on that day, the Torah was translated into Greek in the time of Ptolemy the king and the world was engulfed in darkness for three days." I must admit that this passage is missing from a manuscript copy of the work dated 105 (i.e., 1345 C.E.].[12] But I did notice that the entire passage is reproduced in the Siddur of Rav Amram Gaon[13] and in the *Halakhot Gedolot.*[14] The fast is also alluded to in the *Ṭur.*[15]

This comprises all my knowledge of rabbinic references to the story of these elders. It is true that there is the passage in Bereshit Rabbah in which Ptolemy asks the elders in

5. B.R. 8:11 (64). Most mss. and the printed editions read: "A male with its female parts did He create them."

6. P. Meg. 1(9) 71d. This is probably a reference to the word *lagos,* the name of Ptolemy's father. But at the end of the chapter, de' Rossi explains this variant reading in conjunction with the version given in the Palestinian Talmud where the word "hare" is given in Aramaic form *arnavta.* He considers that this is the closest equivalent to the name of Ptolemy's wife "Arsinoa" [Arsinoe].

7. V.R. 13:5 (290): " 'The hare'—this alludes to Greece. Ptolemy's mother was called 'hare.' "

8. I.e., in ch. 2.

9. Rashi to Gen. 47:2.

10. Sof. 1:7.

11. De' Rossi used the Mantuan edition of 1513. The list of fasts which is not part of the Scroll was compiled, probably in Palestine, in the Gaonic period. (See M. Margolioth, "Moʿadim," 215–16.) The fast of 8 Tevet could not have been scripturally ordained since the event alluded to happened in the post-biblical age.

12. The ms. to which de' Rossi refers may be identified with the ms. dated 1344 and described by H. Lichtenstein in "Die Fastenrolle," 261.

13. *Seder Rav Amram Gaon,* Seder taʿaniyot (91, par. 49). De' Rossi must have consulted one of the many manuscripts of the prayer book.

14. *Halakhot Gedolot,* Tisha b'Av ve-Taʿanit (38a).

15. This is a reference to the code of Jacob ben Asher, *Arbaʿah Ṭurim,* Oraḥ Ḥayyim, Taʿanit, par. 580.

Rome as to the number of days the Holy One blessed be He took to create the world, and was given the answer "six days."[16] But it would appear that this Ptolemy defies all identification with the Ptolemy, king of Egypt, who is listed as one of the kings of Greece; nor could those elders be identified with the elders under discussion who had not yet become subjugated to the Romans. Furthermore, there is no mention of any Ptolemy among the 120 emperors and 238 popes who governed Rome until the present day. I therefore concluded that there was an error in that text.[17] This is probably also the case for the passage about circumcision in Bereshit Rabbah where another Ptolemy the king is mentioned.[18] I shall discuss it in chapter 52. In his *Sefer ha-Qabbalah,* Rabad [Abraham ibn Daud] cites the passage from the Babylonian Talmud and proffers his own interpretations.[19] In my opinion, one should not delve too deeply into that work which does not always correspond to rabbinic opinion and is interspersed with stories from the Josippon. As will be demonstrated in chapter 19, there is reason to be suspicious of that work.[20] He also tries to account for the word change, "God created in the beginning." He suggests that since the sentence structure in Greek is such that the subject is placed first and followed by the object, they changed the order. In this way, they precluded the possibility that *bereshit* (in the beginning) would be taken to mean the Creator and that God was created. But even beginners in that language know that this is far from the truth. In fact, Rashi of blessed memory and the Tosafists give the purely rational explanation that the change in word order was intended for heretics who might believe that the Creator was mentioned first in the verse.[21] And he [Rabad] wrote: "The Torah was written in Greek for Ptolemy because he was persecuting and oppressing Israel and trying to find grounds against them in their Torah in order to expel them from the community,[22] as it says, *since my youth they have often assailed me* (Ps. 129:1)." But all the accounts of Aristeas, Yedidyah the Alexandrian, Josephus, and other narrators of the event under discussion refute his view. In fact, there are various indications to prove that Ptolemy and his servants were well disposed towards us and our Torah. Rabad's statement led the distinguished author of the *Kimḥa d'avishuna* to explain a line in the penitential prayer for the eighth of Tevet, which reads "My spirit is overcome as when the Law was written in Greek." He explained the text, which was written by a mere poet,[23] as referring to Ptolemy's intention of distorting the words of

16. B.R. 10:9 (85).

17. De' Rossi is probably correct. According to the editors of Bereshit Rabbah, the reading may have been "a certain philosopher." It is possible that the scribe might have confused this passage with the immediately foregoing one in which "one of the changes made for Ptolemy" is mentioned.

18. B.R. 46:10 (467–68): "Monobaz and Izates, the sons of Ptolemy were sitting and reading the book of Genesis . . . they both went and circumcised themselves."

19. Abraham ibn Daud (twelfth century). This is a reference to the third part of the *Sefer ha-Qabbalah* on the history of the kings of the second Temple period, entitled *Ve-eleh Divre Malkhe Yisrael be-Bayit Sheni.*

20. In ch. 19, de' Rossi examines the various editions of the Josippon and concludes that there must have been interpolations to the text printed in Constantinople in 1510. Ibn Daud did use the Josippon extensively, particularly for information regarding the second Temple period. According to G. Cohen (*Sefer ha-Qabbalah,* XXXV), ibn Daud utilized the recension on which the Constantinople edition was based.

21. Rashi and Tosafists to B. Meg. 9a.

22. Lit. 'to make an exception of them.'

23. I.e., the poet did not necessarily have Ptolemy in mind when he wrote that line.

the living God into heresy.[24] But such a statement would be sheer ingratitude on our part and does not accord with Scripture, *the remnant of Israel speaks no falsehood* (Zeph. 3:13). As for the fast and darkness, we will speak further about these matters in chapter 8, if God so wills.

In any case, you should know that the Rabad mentioned here is not to be confused with the Rabad of Posquières who was the author of the *Hassagot.*[25] He is Abraham ben Daud Halevi of Toledo mentioned by the author of the *Yesod Olam*[26] and by the scholar Don Isaac in his introduction to the book of Kings and in his commentary to Zechariah's prophecy about the beauty and the bands.[27] Now before proceeding to a discussion of our topic in secular writings, I thought it appropriate not to relinquish our treatment of the rabbinic material without raising a problem which occurs in the Palestinian Talmud[28] and tractate Soferim.[29] The passage in question is also discussed in the Responsa of Ramban [Nahmanides][30] and by the sage Bar Sheshet.[31] "Rabbi Simeon ben Laqish said: 'Three Torah scrolls were found in the Temple court: the *Maʿon* scroll, the *Zaʿaṭuṭe* scroll and the *Hi* scroll.' One scroll read, *And he sent the zaʿaṭuṭe [elect] of the children of Israel* (Ex. 24:5) and the other two read, *And he sent the naʿare (young men).* So they adopted the reading of the two scrolls and discarded that of the one scroll." Now if one follows the opinion [expressed in tractate Megillah],[32] namely, that these elders substituted the word "elect" for "young men," it would not have been necessary for [Rabbi Simeon ben Laqish][33] to claim that the version which read "elect" had been discarded because they followed the majority reading "young men." He should have said that they discarded it on the grounds that the reading had been changed at that time as a result of a temporary flaw in the text. It is possible that the rabbis knew that the three scrolls in question predated the time of the elders and that they [i.e., the elders] had preferred the reading "elect" for the reasons given by Rashi, the Tosafists, and Rabbi Abraham ibn Daud.[34] Alternatively, we could say that the passages about the thirteen variants and the three scrolls belong to mutually exclusive corpora of Midrashim. This is how the Tosafists account for the statement which

24. This is a reference to the Festival prayer book according to the Italian rite which was edited with a commentary by Johanan ben Joseph Treves (1490?–1555).

25. Abraham b. David (1125–98), a talmudic authority who wrote *Hassagot* on Maimonides' *Mishneh Torah.*

26. Isaac Israeli (fourteenth century), *Yesod Olam* (written in Toledo, 1310), 4, ch. 18, 86a: "Rabbi Abraham Halevi b. David of blessed memory, a wise and sagacious man, expert in all fields of wisdom . . . wrote many works, one of which is entitled *Sefer ha-Qabbalah.*"

27. Abravanel, Introduction to Kings (427 col. b); to Zech. 11:10 (232, col. b).

28. P. Taʿanit 4 (2) 68a.

29. Sof. 6:4.

30. Responsum 232. The Responsa which were published in Venice in 1519 are for the most part written by Rabbi Solomon ben Adret and not by Nahmanides. On the basis of the passage in the Palestinian Talmud, ps. Nahmanides explains that in cases of variant readings, the majority reading is normally accepted.

31. Isaac b. Sheshet Perfet [Barfat], *She'elot,* responsum 284. Bar Sheshet's interpretation of the talmudic passage is like that of ps. Nahmanides.

32. De' Rossi writes 'Rabbi Simeon Laqish' here, but is really referring to the passage in Megillah quoted at the beginning of the chapter.

33. He writes 'the author of the other statement' when he is really referring to Rabbi Simeon b. Laqish.

34. Rashi and the Tosafists to B. Meg. 9a explain that 'elect' was used instead of 'young men' because it was a more prestigious term and therefore more appropriate in the context.

identifies Enoch with Metatron.[35] A similar argument is put forward by Rashi with regard to the verse, *And selecting a few of his brothers* (Gen. 47:2)[36] and by Mizraḥi with regard to the verse, *Jacob left Beer-Sheba and set out for Haran* (Gen. 28:10).[37]

Now there is reason for the intelligent person to feel perplexed. On the basis of the book [i.e., the *Letter of Aristeas*], the translation of which was given in the previous section, one would infer that the elders' translation of the Torah was merely a human accomplishment and had nothing of the miraculous about it. For towards the end of the book, he wrote: "They followed a system whereby each man translated every part of the text by himself, after which all the translations were collated and only the best version that gained unanimous approval was inserted into the text by Demetrius."[38] And yet our sages explicitly wrote that they were divinely inspired when they said: "The Holy One blessed be He instilled each elder with wisdom and they gave identical readings of the text."

As I said, I will enlighten you on this question. Many writers of antiquity described the event, although not in the lengthy and detailed manner of Aristeas, and gave a general and brief synopsis. Many of those writers confirm our rabbis' view that the event took place with divine guidance. Similarly, while there are some differences regarding other details between the account of the rabbis and those of the other writers, there are also those who report corroborating traditions. Now every writer regards his own method of selecting from transmitted traditions as correct. Such stories as these are not precepts or laws which are eternally bound by Sinaitic *halakhah* and the Holy Spirit. Thus, the narrator is dependent on the information he receives from hearsay. And we are aware that as a general rule, anything which is poured from one vessel to another loses its essential flavor. Even in the case of events to which we are eyewitnesses, different writers will give different reports of it, either adding or omitting points. In the *Lives* (par. 33), the gentile writer Plutarch proposes a particularly convincing reason to account for this phenomenon. He states that bias of writers makes it difficult to determine the truth of accounts. There is the enemy and the revengeful, and there is the admirer and the encomiast. Each person slants the story to his own standpoint.[39] The author of the *Guide* [Maimonides] makes the same point when he discusses the causes of controversy.[40]

35. Tos. to B. Yev. 16b, s.v. *pasuq*. But in Tos. to B. Ḥull, 60a, the problem is also raised that, Metatron is said to have lived at the time of the creation, whereas Enoch did not yet exist.

36. Rashi to Gen. 47:2 raises the problem of the discrepancy between Bereshit Rabbah (a Palestinian Midrash) in which those brothers of Joseph whose names Moses did not repeat in his blessing (Deut. 37:7) are said to have been the weaker and B. B.Q. 92a where the reverse is said to have been the case.

37. This is a reference to the supercommentary on Rashi by Elijah Mizraḥi to Gen. 28:11. Mizraḥi is commenting on the passage which describes Jacob's journey from Bethel to Haran. The expression *And he lighted upon the place* (Gen. 28:11) is taken to mean that the distance between the two places became contracted. According to Mizraḥi, there are contradictory accounts of this "contraction of distance" in different Aggadot.

38. *Aristeas*, 302.

39. De' Rossi appears to have used the Paris 1558 edition of the Latin translation of the *Vitae* (based on the Campano edition of 1470) in which the paragraphs are indicated by numerals rather than by the more usual letter divisions. The passage is in the Life of Pericles (par. 33, 88r): "Sic perdifficile valdeque laboriosum videtur veritatem ipsam historia consequi quandoquidem et posteris ex antiquitatis memoria rerum cognitio repetenda est et hi quibus contigit praesentibus res ipsas gestas intueri, partim odio et invidia, partim gratia et assentione veritatem corrumpunt ac pervertunt."

40. *Guide* I, ch. 31. He quotes Alexander of Aphrodisias who gives three reasons for controversy: (1)

There is the account of Yedidyah the Alexandrian who was a native of Alexandria, the very city in which the translation was made. He lived about three hundred years after those elders. In his *On the Life of Moses,* he pays tribute to the Law of Moses our teacher and demonstrates that even foreigners were attracted to the Torah. He describes this event. He relates how seventy-two elders were put in separate cells, and how their translations tallied not only in the overall content, but also in all nuances of language and turns of phrase, appearing to be the work of one craftsman.[41] But he says nothing about the thirteen divergent readings.

Then there is also the account of the Christian sage named Justin Martyr who was a contemporary of Antoninus and Rabbi [Judah ha-Nasi].[42] The printed collection of his completed works contains a fine work, a polemic against idolatry which he dedicated to Antoninus.[43] It may have been under the influence of this work and Rabbi's teaching that Antoninus converted.[44] The subject of his conversion is raised in the Palestinian Talmud.[45] Justin gives a brief description of the event in one of his works entitled *Oratio ad gentes.*[46] To summarize, he wrote that Ptolemy placed these seventy-two elders on an island that was situated less than a mile from Alexandria. Each of them was placed in solitary isolation to ensure that they would produce independent translations. In this way, the basic accuracy of each translation could be ascertained. When he saw that all the translations not only tallied in meaning but also were linguistically identical, he was completely amazed and realized that it must have come about through divine agency. He bestowed great honors and glory on them all and dispatched them, laden with many gifts, back to Jerusalem. And he placed the books they had translated in his library like wondrous objects in the glorious Sanctuary.[47] Justin continues his narrative in the following way:[48] "These words of mine are no mere fables or lies but are the honest truth. I have seen for myself the traces of the cells on that island which is not far from the city of Alexandria. Moreover, elderly inhabitants of that country informed me of this tradition which they had all preserved from the remote past." A similar description of the event was given by a certain Christian, one of their first sages, Irenaeus by name, who lived in the time of Trajan the fourteenth emperor.[49] He said that they were

---

love of domination or strife; (2) the obscurity of the subject; (3) ignorance of the one who is trying to understand the subject. Maimonides adds a fourth reason: a person's fondness of that which is familiar to him will lead him to ignore the truth of the matter.

41. *Mos.* II, 31–44 (558–559).

42. The Talmud records many discussions between Rabbi and Antoninus. De' Rossi takes for granted that the Antoninus in question is the emperor Antoninus Pius (138–161 C.E.).

43. This is a reference to Justin Martyr's *Apologia secunda pro Christianis ad Antoninum Pium Imperatorem.*

44. Antoninus is normally depicted as a righteous gentile in talmudic literature. There are, however, a few passages which suggest that he did convert.

45. P. Meg. 1 (13) 72b; 3 (2) 74a. See S. Lieberman's discussion of these passages in *Greek,* 78–81.

46. This is a reference to *Oratio paraenitica id est Admonitio sive Adhortatio ad gentes.* It is not a genuine work of Justin but was regarded as such in the sixteenth century.

47. *Oratio* (*P.G.* VI, col. 265–68).

48. *Oratio* (*P.G.* VI, col. 268).

49. Trajan lived 52/3–117 C.E., Irenaeus in the latter part of the second century. De' Rossi followed the chronology of the Roman emperors as presented in Pedro Mexía's *Le vite degl'imperadori* which begins with the life of Julius Caesar, in which case Trajan could be counted as the fourteenth (and not, as is the more usual computation, the thirteenth) emperor.

segregated one from the other, and that their translations were identical in every respect as though there was one pen to them all. This was proof that God had directed the entire event from heaven. The event bore comparison with the way Ezra the scribe had been divinely inspired to correct the Mosaic Torah in the language of the Jews which had become obliterated from their mind during the years of the exile. Similarly, in this subsequent period, the translation had been made by those noble men for the universal good. This account is to be found in the work of that writer.[50] {It is also quoted in the Caesarean's [i.e., Eusebius's] *History*}[51] and also in the introduction to the Latin version of the translation attributed to the Seventy.[52]

Isidore who lived in the time of Pope Damasus also wrote a description of the event in his *Etymologies*.[53] He states:[54] "Each in his separate cell translated all the words under the influence of the Holy Spirit. Consequently, it transpired that there were no divergencies either in meaning or in phraseology."

Augustine, the greatest Christian doctor, who also lived during the papacy of Damasus gave a lengthy description of the event in his *City [of God]*.[55] In the course of his eulogy of the elders, he mentions that they were put in separate cells so that the reliability of their translations could be ascertained. Their renderings were identical to a word since, so it would seem, the Divine Spirit rested equally on them all. As a consequence, the Christian community decided to use their translation exclusively and this was in fact its status until his own day. At a later date, as we shall discuss again in chapter 45, they selected the Jericho version—this is the view of the bishop of Mondognedo.[56] Others claim that it was another rendering which is their current version.

Thus the accounts of these five esteemed men concur with that of our sages. In other words, God was acting in the interests of those noble Jews, guiding their lips so that in

50. Irenaeus, *Contra haereses* 3 (*P.G.* VII, 1, col. 947–49). The Greek text is preserved in Eusebius. De' Rossi used a secondary source for his citation of Irenaeus, see n. 52.

51. Eusebius, *Hist. eccl.* 5:8 (*P.G.* XX, col. 451–54).

52. This was a reprint of the Latin interlinear translation of the LXX printed in the Complutensian Polyglot. Andreas Cratander (Hartmann) reprinted the Latin translation in Basel in 1526 and prefaced it with an introduction entitled "De authoritate LXX interpretum." He discusses the development of the legend about the translation and pours scorn on those who embellished and elaborated the account of the origins of the translation of the Bible which Paul and other early Christians used. De' Rossi clearly used the sources he cites. Cratander's quotation of Irenaeus is in the introduction, 3r: "Omnes enim eadem iisdem verbis, iisdem nominibus ac sententiis scripserant ab initio usque ad finem ita ut ipsi qui aderant gentiles agnoscerent, quia dei nutu scripturae tunc interpretatae sint. Et nihil mirum si divina providentia hoc ita fieri procuravit quam et in ea captivitate quae populo accideret sub Nabuchodnozor rege corruptis scripturis . . . inspiraverit deus Esdram . . . ut omnium priorum volumina et verba repararet et restitueret populo legem quae per Moysen data fuerat."

53. Isidore lived 560–636 and not during the papacy of Damasus 366–84.

54. *Liber Etymologiarum* 6:4 (*P.L.* LXXXII, col. 236).

55. *De civ. Dei* 18, ch. 42, 43 (*P.L.* XL–XLI, col. 602–5).

56. Antonio de Guevara (1480–1545) was Bishop of Mondognedo. His works were very popular and translated into many languages including Italian. De' Rossi is referring to the second book of his *Littere* and to the letter entitled "Seguita l'auttore e dichiara qualmente gli hebrei falsificarono le scritture sacre" (Venice, 1559, 403). Guevara discusses the Greek translation called the "Quinta editio" or the "editio Hierochontina" which was given that name because it was allegedly found in a jar in Jericho. According to Eusebius (*Hist. eccl.* 6:3), it was the fifth version put into Origen's Hexapla; Origen himself refers to it as the sixth version of the Hexapla. On the Hexapla, see S. Jellicoe, *The Septuagint*, 118–24.

prophetical manner they came up with the same oracle[57] even though each man accomplished his work independently.

But there were those who followed Aristeas, whose book we translated, in asserting that their translation was a human accomplishment without divine guidance. They are: Josephus who lived at the time of the destruction of the Temple;[58] and two hundred years later, Eusebius the Caesarean;[59] the translator for the Christians [i.e., Jerome] who lived in the time of Damasus, the thirty-ninth pope, about three hundred years after the destruction of the Temple;[60] another sage called Clement of Alexandria who lived in the generation before Justin and was actually an inhabitant of Alexandria;[61] and another early father of the Church, Epiphanius.[62] In fact, the translator [Jerome] avers that the original fabricator of the fictitious story about the elders who were put into solitary confinement to ensure that each translation was independently executed, deserved to be the object of contempt and fury: after all, Aristeas who was a reliable envoy, one of the participants in this event, and had heaped praises on them, had not written anything of the kind.[63]

Another detail connected with this subject should also be divulged. There is a distinct divergency of opinion among the fore-mentioned writers as to whether it was only the Torah [Pentateuch] which was translated, as is implied by our sages of blessed memory, or the entire text of Scripture. From a literal reading of Aristeas's account one would realize that he always refers to the translation of the Torah alone. It is true that from one point of view, the word "Torah" in its wider sense can be used as a generic term for all holy Writ. That this is indeed what was implied gains greater credence when one considers that the reason which motivated Ptolemy to request the translation of the Torah should also, according to all logic, have caused him to request a translation of the entire text of the Prophets and Hagiographa. For his purpose in acquiring them was to enrich and complete his library from which no book was to be missing. In fact, there are many passages in which our sages, blessed be their memory, use the term "Torah" to signify the Prophets and Hagiographa as well as the Pentateuch. There is the passage in Sanhedrin where they seek proof-texts for resurrection "from the Torah." Various proofs are proffered on the basis of verses in the Torah and the passage then continues:[64]

57. Cf. B. Sanh. 89a: "The same signal [oracle] is passed to many prophets."

58. *Ant.* XII:86–119.

59. *De ev. praep.* 8:1 (in George of Trepizond's translation which de' Rossi used); (*P.G.* XXI, cols. 587–88).

60. Jerome, Praefatio in Pentateucho Moysi (*P.L.* XXVIII, cols. 150–52).

61. De' Rossi should have written "a generation after Justin." Clement of Alexandria lived 150–215. In his *Stromata* 1, ch. 22 (*P.G.* VIII, col. 148), Clement of Alexandria does admit the divine element in the translation: "neque vero ab inspiratione dei erat alienum qui prophetiam dederat ut interpretationem quoque tanquam Graecam efficeret prophetiam."

62. Epiphanius's account is the most embellished of all the mentioned writers. It is true that in the initial account of the event *De mensuris* 3 (*P.G.* XLII, cols. 241–44), he gives a straightforward account, but in a later part of the book (cols. 315–403), he certainly stresses its miraculous aspect.

63. Jerome, Praefatio: "Et nescio quis primus auctor septuaginta cellulas Alexandriae mendacio suo extruxerit quibus divisi eadem scriptitarent cum Aristeas eiusdem Ptolemai *hyperaspistes* et multo post tempore Josephus nihil tale retulerint, sed in una basilica congregatos contulisse scribant, non prophetasse."

64. B. Sanh. 91b–92a.

> Rabbi Joshua ben Levi said: "[Resurrection] may be derived from, *Happy are those who dwell in Your house; they will forever praise You* (Ps. 84:5). It does not state 'praised,' but 'will praise.' This is proof that resurrection is derived from the Torah. *Your watchmen have raised their voices, as one they shall shout for joy* (Is. 52:8). It does not state 'shouted,' but 'shall shout.' This is proof that resurrection is derived from the Torah." Ravina said: "It is derived from the verse, *Many of those that sleep in the dust of the earth will awake* (Dan. 12:2)." Rav Ashi said: "It is derived from the verse, *But you go on to the end; you shall rest, and arise to your destiny at the end of days* (Dan. 12:12)."

This passage has bearing on the statement at the beginning of Mishnah chapter Ḥeleq [in Sanhedrin] which according to Rashi's reading states: "He has no portion in the world to come . . . He who says that resurrection cannot be derived from the Torah."[65] It becomes evident that the phrase "from the Torah" does not refer exclusively to the written Mosaic Torah or to the Oral Torah. In fact, in his treatise on resurrection [and in his explanation of Mishnah Ḥeleq as I mentioned in chapter 3], Rambam wrote that irrefutable evidence of resurrection is contained in the two verses in Daniel cited above, which were not said at Sinai.[66] Moreover, at the beginning of this chapter, we noted that the same expression was used when they spoke of "the fasts ordained according to the Torah." In that context, the word Torah simply meant the Torah of our ancestors.

Nevertheless, a balanced and accurate assessment of Aristeas's words leads to the obvious conclusion that he was only alluding to the Mosaic Torah. This is also how Yedidyah's statements in *On the Life of Moses* should be understood. Apart from his description in book 12 of the *Antiquities,*[67] Josephus explicitly writes in his preface to that work that they translated only the Mosaic Torah.[68] And do not quote to me from the Hebrew Josephus [Josippon]—in my opinion the text is corrupt in many places.[69] (You shall hear more about this from me.) The translator for the Christians [i.e., Jerome] expressed the same opinion in many of his introductions to the books of Scripture and specifically in his commentary on Ezekiel.[70] He asserts that the erudite sages who described this event believed that only the Pentateuch was translated. He also states that any discriminating person would necessarily judge on the basis of style and language that the translator of the Pentateuch which is attributed to the seventy elders was not the translator of the remaining books of Scripture since they share no common characteristics.[71] The translations are their own testimony. Moreover, if it is true, as Aristeas and Josephus say, that the elders completed their task in seventy-two

65. In ch. 3, de' Rossi discusses the reading of M. Sanh. 10:1: "These have no portion in the world to come . . . those that say that resurrection cannot be derived from the Torah."

66. *Ma'amar Teḥ. ha-Met.,* 4 (363–64).

67. *Ant.* XII:11.

68. Ibid. I:12: "But those translators only rendered the Law."

69. The passage in the *Josippon,* bk. 3, ch. 17 (69–70) refers to priests or sages interpreting or translating the Pentateuch together with the rest of Scripture.

70. *Comm. in Ez.* 2, ch. 5 (*P.L.* XXV, col. 55); 4, ch. 16 (col. 159).

71. The passage beginning 'any discriminating person' is not by Jerome but taken directly from Cratander's preface (see n. 52): "Et confirmat plane diligentior amplior et phrasis purior, si quis utranque linguam conferat, ab aliis interpretibus prophetos versos et ab aliis legem."

days, there is no doubt that it would not have been humanly possible to translate more than the Mosaic Torah.

The opinion of the Caesarean [i.e., Eusebius] and other sages have been cited as men of integrity in regard to this particular detail. There is, however, the statement of Epiphanius who wrote in the fore-mentioned work: "The books of the Jews are divided into two categories: the Pentateuch and the Prophets. Eleazar sent them all to Ptolemy and so they were translated." The bishop Eugubinus also wrote on this matter in his *Recognitio,* taking issue with our sages.[72] His strongest proof is based on his idea that the existence of a Septuagint translation of all Scripture has been vouchsafed throughout the centuries.[73] He argues that even in our own time, a full translation of all books of Scripture which is attributed to their authorship is extant in the Greek language and script and has been translated into Latin. The fact is that although this bishop is a distinguished scholar, I am constrained to bring a case against him on behalf of our rabbis. In his hatred for them, he distorted his own argument by citing the statements of the Jews Yedidyah and Josephus to ratify his opinion.[74] In fact, he sets alight his arrows against himself, for the witnesses he uses to uphold his thesis actually testify against him as I have shown, while the consensus of opinion was not as universal as he describes.[75]

And so you see, reader, that there is support for our sages of blessed memory in regard to these two particular issues. Many of the writers who share their view relate both that the spirit of God rested on those elders who like prophets inspired, produced the translation, and that only the Mosaic Torah was translated. Our sages state that Ptolemy assembled them without informing them of the reason for his action. According to all those other writers, however, he informed them of the reason for his summons from the outset, when he first wrote to Eleazar the high priest requesting their presence. This discrepancy should not prove problematic. When our sages, blessed be their memory, wished to be concise, they rightly concentrated on the main point of the narrative. In this case, the description of Ptolemy separating the elders on their arrival to ensure that they could not confer together gives the impression that they had not been told the reason for their summons. And one should recall the passage in tractate Megillah in the Palestinian Talmud where the event is described without preliminary observations. The list of the thirteen variant readings is given, and the passage concludes with the reference to Ptolemy's mother who was called "hare" [*arnavta*]. This reading [i.e., *arnavta*] would make more sense, given that the name of his wife,

72. *Recognitio,* 144r: "Mentiri autem in Talmud Hebraeos in his quae de hac aeditione scribunt illud argumento est quod asserunt solum pentateuchum a LXX esse translatum quod falsum esse tota aeditio proclamat."

73. Ibid.: "Totus etiam antiquitatis consensus refragatur et omnes qui eruditissime scripsere ex nostris."

74. Steuchus does admit that Josephus clearly speaks of a translation of the Pentateuch but argues that Philo refers to a translation of the Pentateuch and Prophets, although he does not give a prooftext for this view.

75. The subject of the contents of the Seventy's translation was a contemporary issue. It would come to de' Rossi's notice from his reading of the dedicatory letter in Garbitias's translation of *Aristeas* on which his own translation was based, as well as from Cratander's preface to his edition of the Latin translation of the LXX.

according to the fore-mentioned writers, was Arsinoe. But none of those writers recount the story of the thirteen variants told by our sages of blessed memory. On the contrary, as we demonstrated in our citations of their writings, they all explicitly testify to the fact that not one word of Scripture was omitted. Now you who are blessed of the Lord[76] apply your mind to the additional comments which I shall give. In order to give respite to the student, I have allocated them a separate chapter.

76. 'Now you . . . Lord,' cf. Gen. 26:29.

CHAPTER EIGHT

As to how the various differences arose between the translations of the Seventy and their followers and the correct text of holy Writ.

You should know that the translation which is currently attributed to the seventy elders contains only four of the thirteen divergent readings mentioned in the previous chapter.[1] They are as follows: (1) *And he finished on the sixth and rested on the seventh* (Gen. 2:2); (2) *And he made them ride on a carrier of men* (Ex. 4:20); (3) *And the abode of the children of Israel which they and their fathers stayed in the land of Egypt and Canaan* (Ex. 12:40); (4) *I have not taken one valuable of theirs* (Num. 16:15). But on examination, you will find countless examples of other variant readings or additions and omissions in other parts of the Pentateuch as well as the Prophets and Hagiographa. This is due to the extensive variation in vocalization, letters, and words. The most striking discrepancies occur in the division of verses according to meaning such that the end of one verse is put at the beginning of the following verse. This happens with the verses (Deut. 25:2) *and be given lashes in his presence as his guilt warrants with the number* (ibid. v.3) *forty lashes he may beat him.*[2] Another example is prayer of Moses (Ps. 90:2), *from eternity to eternity You are God* (ibid. v. 3), *You return man to dust.*[3] This was a frequent occurrence, and consequently the meaning of the verses became corrupt because of the fusion of verses.[4] Some Christian translators of our own time decided therefore to arrange the verses according to letters and numbers to ensure that the structure of the Holy Scripture which we possess would be retained.[5] In their version for Psalm 145 [which follows alphabetical order], they relegated the verse *God is faithful in all words and upright in all His deeds* to the letter *nun.* [In the Hebrew text, there is no verse for the letter *nun.*] They may have understood the verse as referring to

1. Cf. this statement with that of Augustinus Steuchus (*Recognitio,* 144r) who argued that the Jews falsely claimed that only four changes were made in the LXX translation.

2. The LXX begins v.3, "with the number."

3. This is Ps. 89 in the LXX. The LXX reads the word *El* (God), as *al* (not) and thus renders the two verses (in the Latin translation used by de' Rossi): "Priusque montes fierent et formaretur terra . . . a seculo et usque in seculum tu es. Ne avertas hominem in humilitatem."

4. 'The meaning . . . corrupt.' This is a pun on Ex. 8:20.

5. In 1509, Henri Estienne (Stephanus) published Lefèvre d'Etaples's *Quincumplex Psalterium* which was the first printed edition of any part of the Hebrew Bible to be given verse division. In 1528, Xantes Pagninus's new Latin translation of the Hebrew Bible divided the text into numbered verses. The numeration of the verses was introduced into Bomberg's Bible of 1547/48 in which every fifth verse was designated by a Hebrew numeral. On this subject, see G. F. Moore, "The Vulgate Chapters," 815–20.

future time which would be consonant with the tradition of Rabbi Ezra as reported by the sage Recanati in his commentary to the verse, *So early next morning Abraham saddled his ass* (Gen. 22:3); namely, that these words are ultimately to be said at the time of redemption.[6] It is indeed true that these words would be apposite at that time.

What struck me as the strangest aspect of the whole matter emerged from my perusal of all forty-three works of Yedidyah the Alexandrian which were published in one collection.[7] He lived before the destruction of the Temple and was an inhabitant of Alexandria, the city in which the translation was executed, as we indicated in the previous chapter. In more than fifty passages he availed himself of the divergent version contained in the translation attributed to the Seventy (this was my complaint about him before). He then applied his own method of interpretation to those texts as though in that form it had been written before God in heaven. Josephus is another case. He was an honorable Jew. At the beginning of his *Autobiography,* he actually says that although four sects existed in his time—the Sadducees, the Boethusians [*sic*], the Gablanites, and the Pharisees—he became a loyal adherent of the Pharisaic sect.[8] (They were our sages.) And yet he makes no mention of holy Scripture in the context of his writings apart from a few casual references at the beginning of his *Antiquities* which he wrote for the Romans. There he refers to the duration of the period spanning the ten generations from Adam to Noah and his calculation is made according to the Septuagint translation, for he increases the total from 1656 to more than two thousand years.[9]

With regard to this, you should also know and be cognizant of the fact that in the first generations after the Septuagint was produced, Greek Jews made many other translations. The translator of the Christians [Jerome] testifies to this fact in his introduction to the chronological tables of the Caesarean [Eusebius]. He writes:[10] "The books which were translated by the seventy elders did not retain their true meaning in the Greek language. And so Aquila, Symmachus, and Theodotion made other translations which were different from it. One endeavored to produce a completely literal translation; another gave more consideration to the meaning of the text; the third produced a translation which did not differ much from that of the elders; a fifth, sixth, and seventh translation were made. Although the names of these translators are not known, they are also praiseworthy and were therefore also taken into account." Were I not restrained by certain scruples, I would say that it was perhaps to these three elders that the author of tractate Soferim was alluding when he spoke of the story of the five elders who wrote the Torah in Greek. I cited the text at the beginning of chapter 7. There is a difference between three and five; but there is no doubt in my mind that the passage is not exact. In fact, according to the evaluation of Rosh [Asher ben Yeḥiel] of blessed memory (which we shall discuss again in chapter 19 if God so wills), the entire text of tractate Soferim does not have the same authority for us as do the other works of

6. Recanati, *Perush,* 25, col. d.: "The *nun* will be said at the end of days at the moment of redemption for then night will have the light of day."

7. I.e., Gelenius's Latin translation of Philo's *Opera Omnia.*

8. *Vita* 9–12. Josephus only mentions three sects in this context.

9. *Ant.* I:82: "The time of this event [i.e., the deluge] was 2,262 years after the birth of Adam."

10. Jerome, *Praefatio in librum chronicorum Eusebii* (*P.L.* XXVII, cols. 35–36).

our ancients.[11] This seems all the more credible in view of our present problem as to why, if those five had translated the Torah for Ptolemy, he required another seventy-two. Furthermore, the statement that the Torah could not be adequately translated into Greek is in distinct contradiction to the statement in the Palestinian Talmud declaring that Greek is the only language into which the Torah can be translated.[12] You should not be surprised that the author of Soferim first relates the story of the translation of the five and then tells about the seventy-two. One might compare it to the story told by our sages of a divine voice that issued from the Holy of Holies which they relate as having happened in the time of Johanan the high priest, and then go on to relate a similar story occurring in the time of Simeon the righteous.[13] Now Simeon the righteous must have lived a long time before the high priest Johanan, because he was the leader of our sages after the period of the Great Synagogue. But the fact is that sometimes there is no chronological order to their statements. The Aquila mentioned above is to be identified with Akylas the proselyte—he together with the two translators who followed him shall be the subject of our discussion in chapter 45, if God so helps us.[14] Then after all those translators, twelve hundred years ago, in the time of Damasus, the thirty-ninth pope, the Christian mentioned before [i.e., Jerome] also undertook a translation of the entire text of Scripture. But I am not aware that this translation of his is actually extant.[15] The Christian doctor Augustine, who was a contemporary of the translator [Jerome], used two versions: the one ascribed to the Seventy and another one as is indicated by his use of the expression "another version" in his commentaries. You will notice that in his *City [of God]* he also mentions the six translations, including the translator's [Jerome's] among the six.[16]

Now, as one might think, we have firmly established the fact that the translation of the seventy-two elders was based on a Jewish source, namely, a scroll of the Torah possessed by us which was written in our script and language and brought to King Ptolemy. According to Aristeas, Yedidyah, and other narrators of the event, their translation won the approval and approbation of all Jewish scholars who saw it on the day of its completion. This brings us to a very difficult question. What happened to that version or to our own one that it now appears to diverge from our own text to such an

11. Asher ben Yeḥiel (Rosh) (1250–1337), Sefer Torah 13. Rosh argued that Soferim was written after the completion of the Talmud. It is generally held that it was written in about the middle of the eighth century.

12. P. Meg. 1 (9) 71c.

13. B. Sota 33a: "Johanan the high priest heard a divine voice issue from within the Holy of Holies announcing: 'The young men who went to wage war against Antioch have been victorious.' It also happened with Simeon the righteous that he heard a divine voice issue from within the Holy of Holies announcing: 'Annulled is the decree which the enemy intended to introduce into the Temple.'"

14. See ch. 45 where he identifies Aquila with Akylas but distinguishes him from the Aquila mentioned in Acts 18:2 who was a Jew converted to Christianity in the time of Claudius (41–45 C.E.).

15. This is an allusion to the controversy about Jerome's authorship of the extant edition of the Vulgate which was hotly debated at the beginning of the sixteenth century. Erasmus, Xantes Pagninus, and Sebastian Münster were convinced that the extant edition of the Vulgate (with the exception of the Psalter, according to Münster) could not be attributed to Jerome. Steuchus, however, argued the case for Jerome's authorship.

16. *De civ. Dei,* 18, ch. 43.

extent? And why did the ancients require the other translations mentioned above? We should not desist from pointing out that the greatest Christian doctor raised this particular question in his *City [of God]*.[17] He divides his reply under two headings. He first establishes that our version is right and correct. Then, with regard to some of the variants, he states that the spirit with which the prophets of old were imbued such that they wrote what they wrote was subsequently invested on the seventy translators such that they changed what they changed. For he believed that the variant text contained support for their faith. Thus it was his opinion that both versions should be regarded as the words of the living God.[18] But he realized that this thesis of his was not borne out in respect to the duration of the period from Adam to the deluge.

It is indeed our duty to praise him for he defended us all. He discredited the belief that the Jews who were a dispersed and scattered nation could have made the decision to corrupt the text of their books which were all written in the same style. And if it were assumed that they could do such a thing, it was surely far-fetched to imagine that zealotry of foreigners would have impelled them to perpetrate the corruption of such sacred books. Similarly, one could not claim that those seventy men, who had been selected for their sagacity and who were honored with every possible distinction, would have changed the sense of the text and written completely unfounded things. It is however right to conclude that in the period following the execution of the authentic translation, Greeks and Egyptians, out of malice or foolhardiness, falsified the number of years and some other passages of the first published version; this tampered text infected all other books of its kind. This is a synopsis of his discussion for which he produces further corroboration in his treatment of the subject of the alteration of Methuselah's age.[19] And similarly, in book 18 (chapter 43), he says that second in place to the Hebrew version which retains its distinction forever is the Septuagint which is more praiseworthy than all other translations. Given that this was his view, he also tried in chapter 44 to resolve the discrepancy between the two versions with regard to the statement of Jonah. For the Hebrew text reads, *Yet forty days and Nineveh shall be overthrown* (3:4), whereas they write, *Yet three days*.[20] And his view of us remained consistent, for in his *Commentary to the Psalms* which is in the eighth volume of his *Opera omnia,* he gives us the designation "a chest of books."[21] The wise Aquinas, who followed his methods, also called the Jews by the same designation in his *Commentary* to

17. Ibid., 15, ch. 13.

18. From 'the spirit with which the prophets' to 'living God' is in bk. 18, ch. 43.

19. *De civ. Dei,* 15, ch. 11 (*P.L.* XLI, cols. 449–50). According to the LXX, Methuselah survived the flood, whereas according to the Hebrew Bible, he died in the year of the flood. Augustine follows the text of the Hebrew Bible.

20. Ibid., 18, ch. 44 (col. 605). Augustine justifies both readings. He says that "forty" refers to the number of days Jesus spent with his disciples after the resurrection and before ascension, while "three" refers to his resurrection on the third day.

21. This is a reference to Augustine's *Enarrationes,* "In psalmum quadragesimum enarratio" which was contained in the eighth volume of most editions of his *Opera omnia* (*P.L.* XXXVI, col. 463): "modo, fratres, nobis serviunt Iudaei, tanquam *capsarii* nostri sunt, studentibus nobis codices portant." This is Augustine's interpretation of Gen. 25:23, *And the older shall serve the younger* in which he defines Israel as "the elder" and the despised nation, serving the Christians, "the younger," but chosen people. De' Rossi's citation does not bring out Augustine's conception of the Jews as a subservient people.

the Letter to the Romans (9:13).[22] They used this designation to indicate that it is by means of the traditional annotations and notations that we preserve the texts undamaged and unflawed. And it was one of the passages studied by the expert in Roman law, Alexander of Imola, for his Consilium (n.233) in the sixth volume of his works which he wrote in order to defend the Jews against the charge that their book contained blasphemous material.[23] According to his verdict, there were no grounds for holding us or the Seventy responsible for those changes.[24] Of particular note is the sage Samotheus [Johannes Lucidus] who adduces proofs to demonstrate that the figure 1656 years which he culls from chronological works of remote antiquity is correct and precise. His authorities include Berosus the Chaldean and others who wrote on the origins of nations and kingdoms, all of whose calculations are in accordance with our Torah.[25] He cites Josephus as a support for his view. For at the beginning of *Against Apion,* he writes that when different writers agree on one point, this is sure proof that its veracity is unquestionable.[26] Thus, having conceived this premise, he [i.e., Lucidus] drew its conclusion; namely, that the figure for the number of years for the period from Adam to the flood as given in the translation of the Seventy and by the Greeks which contraverts that given in our Torah must necessarily be erroneous.[27] He explains why scholars adhered to the Greek method in two ways: either, it was to maintain the good will of the peoples of the time by not inciting disagreements—this was what Josephus did on many occasions and specifically in book 10; alternatively, writers like Eusebius, Clement of Alexandria, Justin, and Isidore followed the Greek system in order to preserve their ancestral customs.[28] But he considered the statements of all these writers to be incorrect because they were based on an invalid computation. In this connection, he also cites with approval, the statements of the greatest doctor of their religion [Augustine] which we mentioned before. The bishop Eugubinus expressed a similar view in his *Recognitio.* You can see what he says if you are so disposed.[29] Then there are also the statements of the Christians' translator [Jerome]. Perusing his introductions to the books of Genesis, Samuel, Chronicles, and Job, as well as his commentaries to chapter 5 and 16 of Ezekiel, you will come across his statements on the Septuagint to which we referred in the previous chapter. In the course of his discussion, he defends himself

22. *In omnes . . . epistolas Commentaria,* Rom., lectio 2, ch. 9 (138): "Maior ergo populus serviet minori inquantum Iudaei sunt nostri *capsarii* custodientes libros ex quibus nostrae fidei testimonium perhibetur."

23. Alexander Tartagni (1423/4–72) taught jurisprudence at Pavia, Ferrara, Padua, and Bologna. This is a reference to bk. 6 of his *Consiliorum . . . libri.* Consilium 233 is entitled "Pro excusatione Iudaeorum a poena blasphemiae."

24. Tartagni does not make any explicit reference to the LXX. He argues (*Consiliorum . . . lib.,* 147, col. a) that since the Jewish books were written before the time of Jesus, the Jews could not be accused of blaspheming against the Christian religion.

25. Johannes Lucidus, *Opusculum,* bk. 1, ch. 7. Lucidus relied heavily on Annius of Viterbo's forgeries of Berosus and other ancient authors.

26. *Contra Apionem* I, 26; Lucidus, *Opusculum,* 9v: "et teste Josepho de antiquitate iudaica veritatis historiae signum illud est ut de eisdem rebus eadem omnes conscribant."

27. Ibid., 12r–12v: "Ex praedictis rationibus patet solam hebraicam computationem esse veram, graecanicam vero falsam."

28. Lucidus does not explicitly refer to Justin and Clement of Alexandria, but he does refer to Prosper.

29. Steuchus, *Recognitio* (to Num. 24:14), 170v.

against those who derided his translation of holy Writ on the grounds that our scholarly sages, those renowned seventy elders, had already preceded him with their translation which was correct. While firstly admitting that they were indeed sages, he said that they were not prophets by whose words we must all live. Even though it might be conceded that they were honest and told the truth, the only extant version of their translation was actually interspersed with all manner of errors. This had been caused either in antiquity by people who were living close to the time of its composition, or else by copyists since in the course of its transmission it did not remain free of errors and flaws. In his introduction to Chronicles he specifically refers to the Alexandrians who followed the version of the translation of one of their sages called Hesychius. He also refers to three other countries, each of which followed the version of a specific sage and they all differed from each other. He also claimed that Origen had interpolated Theodotion's version into the Septuagint. In view of the disarray of the text, he decided with his friends' encouragement that the time was ripe for a completely new translation of the original source which we have. And he always submitted all problems regarding the readings of the text to the Jews who are, as it were, the ancient custodians of the authentic text.[30] Thus you are confronted, reader, with the plain fact that he agrees with the greatest doctor of their religion [Augustine] that our extant copies of the translation which is attributed to the Seventy is not the original text which they produced, but a tampered version of it. As to the question of the persons responsible for this situation, one might infer as did their greatest sage, that one should hold mainly responsible the Greek inhabitants of Alexandria of that time and the other inhabitants of the Egyptian lands who were arrogant and innately and willfully wicked. And we might suspect that they would have said that they had meddled with the text in order to prevent the root growing to its full dimensions. Reliable evidence will be advanced to show that the Greeks who were living in Alexandria at the time were contrivers and liars by nature, and that they bore a heartfelt hatred for the Jews who had been the target for their hatred ever since they had left Egypt. So all the honors which Alexander of Macedon and Ptolemy the king bestowed on our ancestors must have been like coals heaped on the heads of the Alexandrians. It is therefore most plausible that in an attempt to deprive them of their protection[31] and to eradicate fear of them, they immediately set out to discomfort and humiliate them. They achieved this by [symbolically] plucking out the right eye of each one of them which is what Nahash the Ammonite did according to rabbinic opinion.[32] Go and examine Yedidyah the Alexandrian's final work[33] and Josephus's *Against Apion the Alexandrian.*[34] They said that the hatred of one nation for another never reached the proportions of the enmity which the Alexandrians bore towards our people who continually sought every means in their power to vituperate them. One could therefore easily deduce that in their hatred and jealousy they had

30. "Ad Hebraeos igitur revertendum est unde et Dominus loquitur et discipuli exempla praesumunt."

31. 'To deprive them of their protection,' cf. Num. 14:9.

32. He is alluding here to the interpretation of 1Sam. 11:2, *And Nahash the Ammonite answered them: I will make a pact with you on this condition, that everyone's right eye be gouged out; I will make this a humiliation for all Israel.* The right eye is understood as a figurative expression for a scroll of the Torah.

33. *Leg.* 170.

34. *Contra Apionem* II, 31–32.

no rest or peace of mind until they had falsified and destroyed that translation which was internationally renowned for its perfect beauty. In fact, this was also the way they treated the works of one of the great Christian sages, Origen by name, who was actually a native of Alexandria and lived in the time of Urban the eighteenth pope. Even in his lifetime, they seized his work and ascribed ideas to him which were alien to his thought. He retaliated with a sharp rebuttal as is evident from the seventh *Apologia* of Gian Pico prince of Mirandola. In his treatment of this subject, Pico also referred to other wise men who had suffered similar experiences, particularly at the hands of the Alexandrians.[35] And now you should keep silent and listen to the great monarch's assessment of them, who swore that his words were not fraudulent. I refer to Caesar Augustus[36] who made the following statement in the fourth volume of his notebooks:[37] "If I were to come forward in defense of the Alexandrians and claim that they were not liars and arrogant, my words would be in vain. For as a race and by temperament they have been known as a people prone to perfidy, and there is nobody who thinks otherwise." In the light of this evidence, the statement of the Christian doctor that the Greeks and Egyptians tampered with the text of the Septuagint becomes more plausible. And the other sage who approved his opinion must be said to have been correct and reasonable in following that view.

Now aside from all this, it should be borne in mind that the immense building constructed by Ptolemy to house the library of Alexandria, in which the actual translation of the Seventy was kept, was completely burnt down. The fire occurred during the assault of the emperor Augustus when he was in pursuit of Pompey who had taken refuge with Cleopatra. The writer Aulus Gellius supplies evidence of this event. He says that the library contained more than seven hundred thousand volumes and that during the first war, when the city was taken by assault, the soldiers without having being given orders, set fire to that building.[38] The writer Orosius[39] corroborates his account as do other historians of Rome.

Thus two reasons might be given for the damage to the text. Either the translation was falsified by malicious gentiles. Alternatively, it was destroyed during the great fire. And so there is no reason to think it curious that several of those Greeks applied themselves to the making of a new translation of holy Scripture. You are aware of the fact that Baḥur the Levite[40] claims in his *Massoret ha-Massoret* that there were no vowels or accents to the letters in those days because they had not yet been invented.[41] The bishop

35. Pico della Mirandola, *Apologia,* Quaestio septima "De salute Origenis disputatio." Pico mentions Clement of Alexandria and Dionysius of Alexandria, but he does not specifically refer to the Alexandrians as their persecutors.

36. The reason that de' Rossi wrongly calls Caesar "Augustus" must be due to his consultation of Pedro Mexía's *Historia imperial y Cesárea* which begins with the life of Caesar.

37. This is a reference to the *De bello Alexandrino* (7) which is counted as the fourth book in Caesar's *Bellum Civile* in his *Commentaria* (439). The work is of uncertain authorship.

38. Aulus Gellius (second century), *Noctes Atticae* 7 (6): 17, 3.

39. Orosius (fifth century, a pupil of Augustine), *Adversus paganos* (6:15). Orosius states that the library contained more than four hundred thousand volumes.

40. This is a reference to Elijah Levita who also called himself and entitled his grammar of 1518 *Baḥur* (the "chosen" or the "young man").

41. Levita claimed that the vocalization of Scripture was first instituted by the Tiberian Massoretes (sixth or seventh century). De' Rossi discusses this subject in ch. 59.

who is author of the *Recognitio* [i.e., Augustinus Steuchus] makes the same assertion in his commentary on several passages in the Pentateuch. Alternatively, one might at least propose, and this is our opinion which will be elucidated in chapter 59, that as a rule, the majority of the texts were unvocalized and unaccented. Those translators took on a heavy task[42] because they based their translation on a plain reading of the text unaided by the appropriate tradition. It is very likely, therefore, that they tripped up and became susceptible to error because there was nobody to give them the correct reading. Now you should bear in mind the solution I have proposed to the question under discussion until the next chapter where I shall approach the subject in a different way.

Nevertheless, I consider it worthwhile to expose those falsifiers and to prove the point by means of the opinion of the greatest Christian sages. This is because there are some people who accuse us of sacrilege by making additions and subtractions to our texts. But you reader, being sensible and intelligent, like servants addressing your masters will produce your proof regarding our books in the manner of Rabbi Abbahu when I said, "I shall bring you proofs from your own language."[43] Then the word of our God will be preserved in its sanctity; the hooks of the pillars will be preserved just as everything which is contained in our holy Writ.[44] The Lord would not impute iniquity to any one of us, even though there are grounds for casting suspicion on some of the statements falsely attributed to our sages. This is a subject which will concern us in chapter 19. As soon as you understand it, intelligent reader, you will acclaim it in gratitude to me.

The foregoing information implies that the sages' tradition concerning the thirteen variants can be regarded as highly plausible only as far as the original translation is concerned. One cannot pit any contrary evidence against them because the version which is now attributed to them appears to contain countless divergent readings—the text bears no resemblance to the original one. There is also support for the statements of our sages of blessed memory, noted in the previous chapter, that they completed their work in seventy-two days. It was beyond human capabilities to translate all twenty-four books in such a limited time correctly, and, in fact, it was no mean achievement to have translated the Mosaic Torah within that time. The conclusion to be drawn from this is that the translation which contains all the books can certainly not be the version with which we are concerned. And consequently our perplexity about the man Yedidyah and others like him who followed the variant translation which was in the past attributed to the Seventy becomes irrelevant. From the chronological tables of Samotheus,[45] one can easily see that there was an interval of many years between the time that the Alex-

42. 'Took on a heavy task,' lit. they entered into the thick end of the beam. Cf. B. Ber. 64a.

43. B.R. 14:2 (127). This is a phonetic play on Greek words: "Rabbi Abbahu was asked: How do you know that a child born at seven months can live? He replied: From your own language I will prove it to you—*zeta epta, eita octo.* I.e., *zeto* in Greek means 'let it live' and *hepta* is 7, *eito* is 'let it go,' i.e., die at *octo* which is 8."

44. This is an allusion to the discussion about the script in B. Sanh. 22a: "The writing was never changed for it is written *The vave [hooks] of the pillars* (Ex. 27:10)" The word *vav* means hook and it is also the sixth letter in the Hebrew alphabet. The meaning is that the shape of the letter *vav* must have been the same in Moses' time as now. De' Rossi uses this allusion to emphasize the idea that the Masorah is the original and authentic text of Scripture.

45. This is a reference to Lucidus, *Opusculum:* "Secunda pars annalium quae tabularis dicitur in qua continentur tempora annales tabulae ab orbe condito."

andrians falsified the text, or even the event of the fire and Yedidyah's lifetime. Almost three hundred years elapsed between the lifetime of the Seventy and that of Yedidyah, and during that period, another or other translations, as we said, came into circulation. And you should bear in mind and not forget what we noted about him at the end of chapter 4. For two of Yedidyah's works which we mentioned provide proof that the Seventy's version of the passage about the number of years between Adam and Noah was tampered with by other people.[46]

In the passages cited in the previous chapter, both Yedidyah and Justin state that still in their own time many of the inhabitants of the cities in the vicinity of Alexandria held annual gatherings on the island of Pharos which was where the translators had stayed. The purpose of the gatherings was to celebrate and commemorate the event in perpetuity—they took delight in the island's stones and cherished its dust.[47] One should not infer from this that their translation was in its original state at that time. Whether it was changed or not, the people had decided to accept the fact that those nobles had been divinely inspired, and they believed that the site was an awesome camp of God which was potentially a constant source of divine bounty. Comparable to this is the way all three nations [Jews, Christians, and Muslims] according to the *Kuzari,* believe that the divine presence rests on Jerusalem.[48] One might add that the leaders of Alexandria were justified in upholding that custom; there is no doubt that they profited from the foreigners who gathered there, with purses in their hands.[49] Moreover, Yedidyah and Josephus may be defended on the specific grounds mentioned before. Since their works were intended for the Greeks of their own time they realized that to avoid disputes, it was expedient not to make any changes. The Christian translator [Jerome] argued in a similar way in the passage noted previously regarding the seventy-five persons who went down to Egypt. In that context he went on to say that in addressing the nations, any apostle would adduce his proofs from that text of Scripture which was currently in use. This all goes to prove that our books contain the true text.

By now I would imagine that one would be amazed to discover that our sages of blessed memory loved the Greek language. For in Megillah, they said that the Bible could be written only in the Greek language, a view based on the verse, *May God enlarge Japhet and let him dwell in the tents of Shem* (Gen. 9:27).[50] And in tractate Megillah in the Palestinian Talmud it is stated that on examination they decided that Greek was the only language into which the Torah could be translated adequately.[51] Then there is the statement of Rabbi: "Why use Syriac when either the holy tongue or Greek can be used?"[52] And Rabbi Abbahu said in the name of Rabbi Johanan: "A man may teach his daughter Greek wisdom for it is an ornament for her."[53] Moreover, we

46. He is referring to the two ps. Philonic works: *Breviarium de temporibus* and *Antiquitatum biblicarum liber* which follow the Hebrew computation of the period.

47. 'Islands' stones,' cf. Ps. 102:15.

48. Judah Halevi, *Kuzari* II, par. 23.

49. These comments demonstrate de' Rossi's somewhat cynical but also sympathetic attitude towards folk traditions.

50. B. Meg. 9b. Japhet, in this context, symbolizes Greece and Shem, Israel.

51. P. Meg. 1 (9) 71c.

52. B. B.Q. 83a.

53. P. Pe'ah 1 (1) 15c.

find that our sages single out the event of the translation for praise. In their view, it brought prestige to the Jews—this is apparent from their account: "When they permitted Greek, they only permitted it for a scroll of the Law. This was because of the episode with Ptolemy the king."[54] And they also say that they received divine guidance. Given these views, what significance should given to the passage in tractate Soferim: "There is the story of the five elders who wrote the Torah in Greek for King Ptolemy, and that day was as calamitous for Israel as when the golden calf was made because it was impossible to translate it adequately"? And there is also the passage at the end of the Megillat Taʿanit proclaiming the eighth of Tevet a fast day in commemoration of the writing of the Torah in Greek in the time of Ptolemy when three days of darkness came to the world. We referred to this in chapter 7.

Now at the beginning of this chapter we did cast aspersions on the above-quoted passage of tractate Soferim and dismissed it as a corrupt Mishnah. And we also noted that they only speak of the calamity in regard to the five elders but not about the story of the seventy-two. Discounting all these questions, it does appear that at least one of two explanations might be given. Either the sages who had been elected for the task imposed a fast and solemn assembly for the whole community in like manner to Esther before she presented herself to the king, or to Yedidyah the Alexandrian when he went to Emperor Gaius to plead the case of his people (Yedidyah describes it in book 43).[55] This was why the faces of the Jews were clouded in darkness at that time; they were frightened that their envoys would be humiliated and our people held to be transgressors. Thus, for many years until the abrogation of the Megillat Taʿanit, some people upheld the custom [of fasting].[56] Similarly, from antiquity they had observed the fast of Esther with lamentation. Alternatively, one might suggest that they feared that Ptolemy's kindness and goodness would highlight Israel's sin, as our sages say in Shir ha-Shirim Rabbah.[57] This is also the way they interpreted the verse about Mesha, king of Moab, *So he took his firstborn son, who was to succeed him as king, and offered him up on the wall as a burnt offering. A great wrath came upon Israel* (2K. 3:27). This sacrifice indicated, according to their interpretation, that they did not behave like the upright of the idolators.[58] The true judge saw that in the course of the second Temple period, His very own people were becoming more negligent about observing the commandments than those on whom this obligation did not devolve. In fact, they resorted to heresy, forming the Sadducean and Boethusian sects. This was the reason for all the calamities which befell them and the conversion of the gentiles which is as intolerable to us as a running sore.[59]

54. B. Meg. 9a.

55. I.e., *Legatio ad Gaium.*

56. The point is that the fast of Esther is still observed (see Est. 9:31) despite the happy outcome. The memorial holidays mentioned in Megillat Taʿanit were observed until the third century, but then rescinded. See B. R.H. 18b. The fast days, however, were later additions. De' Rossi's statement is thus unfounded.

57. I cannot find the passage in Shir Ha-Shirim Rabbah. But he might be referring to another Midrash, Aggadat Shir ha-Shirim 1:15 (and also Pes. d' R. Kah. 2:5 and other parallels) where this comment is made with regard to one of the interpretations of Pr. 14:34, *Righteousness exalts a nation, but the kindness of a people is sin,* i.e., the kindness shown by gentiles makes the sins of Israel conspicuous.

58. B. Sanh. 39b.

59. The statement "Proselytes are as intolerable for Israel as a running sore" is attributed to the fourth-century Amora R. Ḥelbo. See B. Yev. 47b, Qidd. 70b, and Nidd. 13b. As B. Bamberger notes (*Proselytism,*

Indeed, it seems that Ptolemy's actions won divine approbation. The Ptolemaic dynasty lasted the reigns of ten rulers as is evident from the chronological tables of the Caesarean [Eusebius] and Samotheus.[60] If filial piety could earn Dama ben Netina all the riches and honor mentioned by our rabbis of blessed memory in Qiddushin[61] (we will bring this up again in chapter 38), the Holy One blessed be He was all the more justified in not witholding reward from Ptolemy who had bestowed such honor on His Sanctuary, Torah, and people through this event.

The main point of the chapter may be summed up in the following manner: what our sages of blessed memory said about the thirteen variant readings and nothing further is in the realm of possibility. From the comments of the great Christian sages, it is obvious that notwithstanding all the versions of holy Scripture which exist in translation, and particularly as regards the number of years from the creation until the flood, the true and correct reading is preserved in our holy Writ.

163–64) both Rashi and the Tosafists give seven different explanations of the saying. They include the explanation that proselytes make Israel's negligence all the more conspicuous, or that proselytes lower Israel's standards. The ambiguity of R. Ḥelbo's statement parallels the ambiguity with which the story of the Greek translation was received according to tractate Soferim.

60. Eusebius, *Chronicon*, lib. 1, ch. 22 (*P.G.* XIX, col. 208); Lucidus, *Opusculum*, 107b–112r. Both Eusebius and Lucidus list twelve Ptolemies including Cleopatra. The Ptolemaic dynasty is usually counted from Ptolemy Soter (305–282) to Ptolemy XV (44–30).

61. B. Qidd. 31a.

CHAPTER NINE

Another valid solution to the problem under discussion.

THERE is indeed another way, and I alluded to it above, of resolving the problem of the variant readings in the Septuagint. Now give it a hearing, for in my opinion, it is valid, but realize that the approbation of scholars both Jewish and Christian is essential for its ratification; otherwise it loses all validity.[1]

The answer lies in a well-known fact; namely, that in Ezra's day, the Torah was promulgated among the common people in the Aramaic language. This is indicated by the way our rabbis of blessed memory expound the verse, *They read from the scroll of the Torah of God distinctly* (Neh. 8:8). "*The scroll of the Torah of God*—this is Scripture; *distinctly*—this is translation [Targum]."[2] Aramaic had become their vernacular since their stay in Babylon. (This point shall be elaborated further.) It was probably not a literal interpretation but a fuller elucidation of the text like Themistius's translation of the works of the "philosopher" [Aristotle], the *Paraphrases,* as it was called by the Greeks and Romans.[3] Such a rendering was particularly necessary when explaining the text to non-Hebrew speakers in their vernacular,[4] and especially in the case of this people to whom the precept of sitting in a booth[5] and the prohibition about the Ammonites and Moabites had become a novelty.[6] Even from the time of their ancestors, it had been said,

1. De' Rossi's cautious manner in introducing his original solution to the problem is entirely consistent with the self-effacing style with which the whole of his work is written. Whereas the Vulgate was declared the authoritative Bible version of the Church in 1546, the LXX was still regarded as the version used by Paul and the apostles. He might have been concerned that his idea that the LXX was translated from a faulty Aramaic version would be regarded as offensive to Christian tradition. Later seventeenth-century scholars such as Anthony Van Dale, Johannes Buxtorf, and Jean Morin, while rejecting his theory, submitted his arguments to careful analysis and translated some of the relevant passages into Latin. See my article, "Azariah de' Rossi and LXX Traditions," 23–35.

2. B. Ned. 37b.

3. Themistius (b. 317 C.E.) wrote explanatory paraphrases of many of Aristotle's works of which those on the *De anima* and the *De caelo* are still extant. Moses Amram Alatino (b. 1529) made a Latin translation of a Hebrew translation of Themistius's *Paraphrases* on the *De caelo* which was published in Venice in 1574.

4. This is an allusion to M. Meg. 2:1 in which it is stated that the scroll of Esther may be read to non-Hebrew speaking Jews in their vernacular.

5. *They found written in the Torah that the Lord had commanded Moses that the Israelites must dwell in booths during the festival of the seventh month* (Neh. 8:14).

6. *At that time they read to the people from the book of Moses, and it was found written that no Ammonite or Moabite might ever enter the congregation of God* (Neh. 13:1).

And you forgot the Torah of your God (Hos. 4:6). There is no doubt that they required an even fuller elucidation of the text than that provided by the *Paraphrases* which we mentioned above. Consequently, they retained this method of translating the Torah into Aramaic for the general populace throughout the period of the second Temple; for that language remained the vernacular of the common people up until the exile from Jerusalem. (With God's help, we shall elaborate on this subject in chapter 57.) However, it is beyond all doubt that their translation became like a city under siege; errors began to appear in the text after the death of Ezra because there was no Massoretic text to serve as a fence around the Torah. Thus, as the Aramaic version was transmitted orally through the ages, it progressively diverged more and more from the written text of holy Writ. This was the situation until Onqelos the proselyte discovered the extensive corruption of the text and undertook a new translation of the Torah, which enterprise had the approval of the two distinguished rabbis Eliezer and Joshua, as is explained in chapter 1 of Megillah.[7] Thus, Onqelos was not the first person to transpose the words of the Torah into the Aramaic language. Rather, he examined, investigated, and emended the passages which had become corrupt. It was for this reason that they said that the Aramaic Targum is numbered among those items which had been "forgotten and then reconstructed."[8] If this had not been the case, one would be hard pressed to understand the use of the word "forgotten" in this context given that Aramaic was their language at that time. Rather, what is meant is that the Targum implied by the word *distinctly* [as used in the verse (Neh. 8:8)] remained corrupt until Onqelos undertook its revision.

With regard to this subject, my dear reader, you should also be aware that we have clear proof that Jonathan ben Uzziel, who is known for his Targum on the prophetical books, also wrote a Targum of the whole of Scripture.[9] The evidence is provided by the sage Recanati who mentions the Targum on several verses: for example, Genesis 2:3, 2:7, 3:21, 4:1, 5:22, 6:4; Exodus 15:17; Leviticus 14:7; Deuteronomy 29:14; and there are other examples.[10] But I also noticed that he [Recanati] also refers to a Palestinian Targum [Targum Yerushalmi] in regard to some verses such as Genesis 2:1 and 11:7.[11] It was with hesitation that I assumed that he regarded both Targums of the same authorship. My suspicion was reinforced on seeing two identical Targums on the entire Pentateuch. The Targum which belonged to the distinguished Foa family of Reggio was ascribed to Jonathan ben Uzziel on its margins;[12] while the other, the property of

7. B. Meg. 3a.

8. Ibid.

9. According to B. Meg. 3a, Jonathan b. Uzziel wrote the Targum to the Prophets "at the dictation of Haggai, Zechariah, and Malachi." Jonathan was reported to have been Hillel's most prominent pupil. In his *Meturgeman,* Elijah Levita raises the question as to why Jonathan who was older than Onqelos should have written his Targum on the Prophets rather than on the Pentateuch. Like de' Rossi, he noticed the linguistic similarity between the two Targums.

10. The attribution of the Targum to Jonathan ben Uzziel was first made by Menahem Recanati in his *Perush al ha-Torah* who mistook the abbreviation *tav yod* as a reference to the Targum of Jonathan ben Uzziel. In view of this misattribution, the Targum is often called Targum ps. Jonathan. Levita also refers to Recanati in his discussion of the Targum.

11. This is the Targum Yerushalmi 2, which is a fragmentary Targum containing about 850 verses. In some places, the text is identical to that of ps. Jonathan.

12. The editio princeps of the Targum (Venice 1590–91) was based on this manuscript. The sons of Isaac Foa defrayed the costs of the publication. See A. Yaari, *Studies,* 334–45.

Samuel Cases of Mantua, was designated Targum Yerushalmi on its margins.[13] Both texts begin by translating the word *bereshit* (in the beginning) "from the beginning" and not "in wisdom."[14] We shall discuss this again in chapter 25. Both Targums give the same renderings of the verses which were cited by Recanati.

{I also came across a passage near the beginning of Midrash Ruth ha-Neʿelam in which Rabbi Jose ben Kisma states: [15] "*For him will I accept that I do not do to you anything unseemly [nevalah]* (Job 42:8). What is *unseemly?* Leprosy, for it is written [in connection with Miriam's leprosy], *If your father had spat in her face, would she not bear her shame for seven days* (Num. 12:14). Jonathan translates the verse, 'He shall surely put her to shame' (*minbal yinbal*)." It is true that I saw another version of this text which read, "Rav Joseph translated,"[16] but this is obviously an error. How could Rabbi Jose cite somebody who lived after him?}[17]

Now as I went through all that Targum, I discovered that the text was often expanded sometimes by way of elucidation and sometimes by way of exegesis—you shall be given examples of this in some of the later chapters. This was the method of the Targum Yerushalmi which has been printed at the end of the Rabbinic Bible.[18] However, although both Targums often give identical renderings, there are also many divergencies between the two texts. One must therefore conclude that either they are of different authorship or, alternatively, that one author translated the same passage in different ways. A case in point is the Targum on the verse, *So Zipporah took a flint and cut off the foreskin of her son and touched his legs with it* (Ex. 4:25). Some transcribers designate it Targum Jonathan ben Uzziel, others Targum Yerushalmi.[19] Discussing the subject of someone who finds coins in an unordered pile (*meshalḥafe*), Alfasi of blessed memory states: "The Targum of the Land of Israel renders the verse, *And he guided his hands wittingly* (Gen. 48:14), as 'And he placed his hands crosswise (*shalḥafineho*).' "[20] Similarly, under the entry *shalḥaf,* the compiler of the *Arukh* states that the Targum on the verse renders it, "And he placed his hands crosswise." In the Cases and Foa versions, the verse is rendered, "He changed (*perag*) his hands," and that is the way it is rendered in the Targum Yerushalmi printed at the end of the Rabbinic Bible mentioned above. Under the entry for *perag* in the *Arukh,*[21] the Targum for the expression,

13. This manuscript is in the British Library (Add. 27031) and has also been described by R. Le. Déaut, *Targum du Pentateuch,* 30–31. According to Le Déaut, the words *Targum Yerushalmi al ha-Torah* appear on the back of the last rebinding. The words Targum Jonathan ben Uzziel are found on the top of the first flyleaf.

14. This is the reading of the fragmentary Targum Yerushalmi.

15. *Midrash ha-Neʿelam al Megillat Ruth* (75 col. d). The work is a kabbalistic interpretation of the book of Ruth. It was first printed as an independent work in Thiengen in 1560.

16. The confusion would have occurred because Rav Joseph bar Ḥiyya, a fourth century Babylonian Amora, was described in the Babylonian Talmud as having written an Aramaic Targum.

17. Rabbi Jose was a Tanna of the first century C.E. and would therefore have been unable to quote the interpretation of the fourth century Rav Joseph. The standard edition (75 col. d) reads "Rabbi Jose translated."

18. This is a reference to the two-volume Bomberg Rabbinic Bible of 1517 in which the fragmentary Targum was printed at the end of vol. 2.

19. For a discussion of the targumic traditions of this verse, see G. Vermes, *Scripture and Tradition,* 178–92.

20. Isaac Alfasi, to B. B.M. 25a (13b). Alfasi's reading is also found in the Neofiti Targum to Gen. 48:14.

21. This is a reference to the tenth-century talmudic and midrashic lexicon of Nathan ben Yeḥiel of Rome, s.v. *shalḥaf.* There were many early printed editions of the lexicon.

He shall not change (Lev. 27:10) is given as *la yifrag* (he shall not change) and this is also the reading of the Targum Yerushalmi mentioned above.

In any case, all the above-mentioned Targums never retain the structure of the verse but often expand the text as we noted. It is also quite possible that there was yet another Targum. If God so wills, I shall inform you about this in section 4 just before the end of chapter 45. I therefore deduced that Onqelos, though a contemporary of Jonathan, was his junior (as we shall prove in chapter 45) and thus must have seen Jonathan's Targum which had already been completed as well as the entire text of any earlier Targum. With the aim of providing the Jews with a literal Targum which exactly conformed to the written text of Scripture, Onqelos thus undertook to produce a new Targum of Scripture which was accepted and achieved renown among our people. In fact, over a period of time, even before Onkelos had written his Targum, many Targums had been in existence which contained divergent readings—for this inevitably happens to anything which is disseminated among the people without being regulated.

Similarly, we know that from Ezra's time, the Aramaic text was not written in Ashuri (Assyrian) characters as is the case with our text, but in the *ever hanahar* (Hebrew) script. The tradition is given in tractate Sanhedrin:[22] "Mar Zuṭra or according to another opinion, Mar Ukba said: 'Initially the Torah was given to Israel in the Hebrew (*Ivri*) script and in the holy tongue. The Torah was restored to them again in the time of Ezra in the Assyrian script and the Aramaic language. They selected the Assyrian script and the holy tongue for Israel and the Hebrew script and the Aramaic language were left for the *hedyotot.*' " Many people were confused as to how the passage fitted together. This is evident from the comments of Rashi, Ritba [Yomtov ben Abraham],[23] and the author of the *Iqqarim.*[24] At any rate, one ought to acclaim those sages and eminent authorities who said that the Torah was [initially] written in the Assyrian script. (With God's help, we shall discuss all this in section 4, chapter 58.) Nevertheless, one must necessarily conclude that the passage refers to the fact that Ezra made a clean sweep, emending the errors which he discovered in the text of Scripture. He then replaced the Hebrew script (i.e., the script of those who were "on the other side of the River" [*ever hanahar*]) by the Assyrian script which is what we use nowadays. At the end of this chapter, I shall supply you with some novel information about his holy scroll. I hope you will approve.

Finally then, the Jews who agreed to Ezra's recommendation to use the Assyrian script selected for themselves the holy tongue. Thus the language and script which became the special preserve of their leaders and sages was once again as it had been at Sinai, and the Hebrew script and the Aramaic language was left for the *hedyotot,* namely, the common people. The Sanhedrin passage quoted above ends with the

22. B. Sanh. 21b.

23. *Ḥiddushe ha-Ritba* to B. Meg. 2b (23 col. a). De' Rossi either read the work in manuscript or used the citation in the *En Yaʿaḳov* of Jacob ibn Ḥabib. The Ritba argues that the Assyrian script was used only for the Tablets and thus merited the epithet "holy," while the Hebrew script was used for the scrolls. When the ark was despoiled by the Babylonians and the Jews were taken into captivity, the form of certain characters of the Assyrian script was forgotten and had to be learned from the Babylonians. Thus when Ezra changed the script, he reinstated the Assyrian script, but he did not invent it, since it had already been used for the Tablets in the ark.

24. Joseph Albo, *Sefer ha-Iqqarim,* bk. 3, ch. 16 (144).

question "Who were the *hedyotot?*" Mar Ḥisdai said, "The Cutheans'." But this really cannot be the case; for there was no reason for Mar Zuṭra to be so terse in his language as to refrain from explicit reference to the Cutheans. In any case, we have already established that Aramaic was the vernacular of the Jews at that time. Moreover, I saw a holy sheqel imprinted with Hebrew characters. (I shall show [a picture of] it in chapter 56 God willing.)[25] Although the latest date for its issue must have been the second Temple period, it was minted for Jews and not for the Cutheans who were living in the land. Rather, the point of Rav Ḥisdai's statement was to demonstrate that among the ranks of our people there was no lack of outstanding individuals who possessed a fine knowledge of the holy tongue and the holy script as opposed to the Cutheans, an uneducated people, who had all adopted the Hebrew script and Aramaic language exclusively.[26] According to Josephus[27] and the Pirqe d'Rabbi Eliezer,[28] the Cutheans under discussion are to be identified with the Samaritans.

Now I was delighted to discover that the change of script which was the subject of our rabbis' discussion was also treated by two great Christian doctors who lived before the author of the statement in question. This will be demonstrated at the end of the chapter. One is Eusebius the Caesarean who wrote as follows in the tables to his *Chronicle:*[29] "It is known that Ezra examined and emended the holy Scriptures and that he reinforced the schism by changing the script so that Jew would not mix with Samaritan." The other is their translator [Jerome] who wrote the following in his introduction to the book of Samuel:[30] "It is a fact that after the construction of the Temple in Zerubbabel's time, Ezra the scribe discovered other characters which are currently used by the Jews. In the past, however, Jews and Samaritans used an identical script." And he also makes the point that there were scriptural texts extant in his day in which the numbers for the census described in the book of Numbers were indicated by a figure which differed from that of our own texts.[31] He also says that the tetragrammaton was written in those original characters in these texts and that they also preserved the alphabetical order of the verses of the Psalms, Lamentations, and the last

25. In ch. 56, he describes a sheqel inscribed with Samaritan letters which can be identified as a sheqel minted in the fourth year of the first revolt. He believed that the letters *shin dalet* signify Shekel David rather than Shanah Dalet (year four). A reproduction of the same coin was published in 1538 by the sixteenth-century scholar Guillaume Postel in his *Linguarum duodecim Alphabetum.* See my discussion of this interesting coincidence in "Azariah de' Rossi and LXX Traditions," 26–28.

26. According to J. Purvis, *The Samaritan Pentateuch,* 85, n. 150, the rabbinic tradition that the old Hebrew script was rejected in favor of the Assyrian script in the time of Ezra must be revised in the light of the Qumram discoveries. He states that palaeo-Hebrew continued to be used as a script for biblical texts long after the time of Ezra.

27. Josephus, *Ant.* IX:290: "They are called Cutheans by the Jews and Samaritans by the Greeks."

28. PRE 38: "And the Samaritans came against them with 180,000 men. Were they Samaritans? Were they not called Cutheans? But they were called Samaritans because of the city of Samaria." Cf. 2Kings 17:24.

29. Eusebius, *Chronicon* II (*P.G.* XIX, cols. 475–76): "affirmaturque divinas Scripturas memoriter condidisse et ut Samaritanis non commiscerentur, litteras Judaicas commutasse." According to S. D. Luzzatto (in his appendix "De scriptura Samaritana" to R. Kirchheim's *Karme Shomron,* 109–10), de' Rossi misunderstood the statement. He states that the purpose was to avoid the intermingling of Samaritan and Jewish scrolls and not, as de' Rossi said, the intermingling of Jews and Samaritans.

30. Praefatio in libros Samuel et Malekim (*P.L.* XXVIII, cols. 548–54).

31. De' Rossi's translation is not exact. Jerome writes that the number for the census was indicated in an esoteric way ("mystice ostenditur").

part of Proverbs.[32] Thus it is generally claimed that when Ezra corrected the corruptions in the text of the Torah, he also altered the script in an effort to unite the Jewish people with a Torah which was perfect both in language and script. The Aramaic language and the profane script that they had previously used were relegated for the *hedyotot,* the Cutheans and the common people. The latter text became more widely circulated than the version which was authentic both as regards language and script because it was known only to a few people.[33] We made the same point in chapter 5. Thus the problem of the variant readings disappears completely. One might justifiably believe that with the approval of the high priest who had dispatched them, those elders decided to bring the Aramaic version which was popular at the time and to translate it for Ptolemy. This version was undoubtedly replete with errors due both to the occasional expansion of the text and to corruptions in the text which had occurred in the period subsequent to Ezra. They produced a rendering of this version which was so accurate and correct that it gained the approval and was praised by all those who read it—there were many people living in the Egyptian city of Alexandria at the time. By this means, they upheld the system of Ezra and his court; for they ensured that the sacred text would remain the sole possession of the holy people. It is also conceivable that they thought that this behavior would win them the approval of Ptolemy. For all the people and particularly the Jewish population would bring him report of the linguistic and textual precision of their rendering; it was not the case that their [i.e., the elders'] translation contained different readings to those found in the texts of the other peoples. You must notice that they brought him a scroll of the Law inscribed with gilt lettering and whose sheets of parchment were glued together, which is not permitted for our own scrolls. One might reasonably assume that the text brought to him for translation was one of the ancient versions which was still extant. Perhaps it was a gift of a foreigner, like the candelabrum made by Queen Helena, which is described in tractate Yoma.[34] In tractate Soferim, the use of gold for the writing of a scroll is forbidden. This prohibition is mentioned in connection with Alexander's scroll (in my opinion, he was Alexander Jannaeus, the father of Hyrcanus, who was one of the Hasmonean kings), throughout which the divine name was engraved in gold. When the matter was brought to the notice of the sages, they ordered the scroll to be stored away.[35] As is well known, our rabbis of blessed memory relate that at the time when the Targums were written, there was an earth tremor in the Land of Israel—for there

32. He was referring to those Psalms, chapters of Lamentations, and the last part of ch. 31 of Proverbs which follow alphabetical order.

33. S. D. Luzzatto attacks de' Rossi on this point in his introduction to *Philoxenus.* He says that the Targum was never in the hands of the people, and they were dependent on the teacher's explanations because Scripture was unvocalized. He also argues that there was no fixed Targum until the time of Onqelos and that each *meturgeman* followed his own style of interpretation.

34. M. Yoma 3:10. Helena, the mother of Monobaz, king of Adiabene is said to have made a golden candlestick for the door of the Sanctuary and a golden plate on which the biblical section regarding the adulterous woman was inscribed. Both Helena and her son are said to have become converts.

35. Sof. 1:9. Another reading (which is also in the minor tractate Sefer Torah 1:10) states: "It is related that all the divine names were written in gold in an Alexandrian scroll." If the variant reading "Alexandrian" is correct, the allusion may be to a LXX scroll. According to H. Graetz, "Notes," 102–4), the Alexander mentioned in Soferim is to be identified with Tiberius Alexander, the brother of Philo, who was reputed to have been very wealthy.

ought to be one holy text for the holy people.[36] Moreover, in many passages in his *Recognitio* and specifically in regard to the verse, *No, my lord, listen to me* (Gen. 23:15), the bishop Eugubinus states that the elders must have translated from a version which was different from our present text and which was circulating among the peoples at that time.[37]

We may therefore assume that from Ezra's day until the time of the translation, a period of more than one hundred years, the Aramaic version suffered additional changes and errors. One case, for example, is the calculation for the duration of the period from Adam to the flood. In any case, the text on which they based their translation must have been the one which was regarded as suitable and acceptable by the general populace. Thus it is not surprising that their rendering, which had been extracted from various recipients and which were themselves faulty, did not retain its character nor preserve its sweet aroma. Whether they knew the true text of the Torah or not, Yedidyah and Josephus, both Jews, also kept to the Greek version when addressing Greek readers. Moreover, there may be justification for the statement of our sages about the thirteen variant readings. For the elders might have thought it right to make those changes even if initially all or the majority of the passages had been written correctly. Indeed, they did not claim that the only changes [i.e., between the translation of the elders and the Hebrew text] made were those indicated. However, you should know that the words of Torah were translated into gentile languages and specifically into Greek even before the Septuagint was produced. Aristobulus the Jew, according to Vives, the commentator of Augustine's *City [of God]* is a witness to this fact. He [i.e., Vives] writes:[38] "Eusebius of Caesarea notes that in his first book, Aristobulus the Jew wrote to Ptolemy Philometer stating that Plato often adhered to the method of our Torah. It is quite apparent that his understanding of many of its details was derived from the Mosaic books which had been translated even prior to the Alexandrian era, and prior to the Persian dynasty. He, and likewise the philosopher Pythagoras, gained many ideas from it." This quotation from Aristobulus's first book concurs, in my opinion, with the passage which I discovered in the *Supplement to the Chronicles.*[39]

36. B. Meg. 3a. At the time of the tremor, a heavenly voice proclaimed, "Who has revealed My secrets to mankind?" Jonathan responds, "I, but I have acted so for Your honor and to prevent dissension."

37. Steuchus, *Recognitio,* 73v–74r to Gen. 23:15. He discusses the difference between the Hebrew text which reads, *And Ephron answered Abraham saying to him* (*lo*) [spelled with a *vav*], *my lord, listen to me* whereas the LXX reads, *No* (*lo*) [spelled with an *alef*], *my lord, listen to me.* He insists that LXX must have had a different text since the error arising from a confusion between the Hebrew word *lo* (to him) and *lo* (no) was inexcusable, and one "which even Jewish children, despite their ignorance of grammar, would have been unlikely to make."

38. Vives, *Augustini de Civitate Dei* (to bk. 8, ch. 11, 246–47): "Et Aristobolus Iudaeus ad Philometora libro primo, sicut Eusebius citat: Legem, inquit, nostram in multis Plato sequutus est aperte nanque in multis diligenter examinasse singula videtur Mosaica enim volumina ante Alexandrum, et ante Persarum imperium traducta fuerant unde plurima, sicut et Pythagoras philosophus ille accepit."

39. There were many editions of the *Supplementum Supplementi Chronicarum* by Jacobus Philippus Bergomatus (Foresti). De' Rossi appears to have used an Italian translation of the text. (The Latin texts do not refer to a "hundred commentaries.") The translation of F. Fiorentino (114v) reads: "Aristobolo per natione iudaeo peripatetico filosofo fu in questi tempi secondo Eusebio molto honorato el quale fra gli altre sue opere degne scrisse a Filopatre re cento commentarii sopra Moyse." De' Rossi seems to have failed to see that Foresti refers to Ptolemy Philopator, and Eusebius, to Ptolemy Philometor. On the likelihood that Aristobulus wrote for Ptolemy Philometor, see E. Bickerman, "The Septuagint," 168, n. 2.

There Aristobulus is said to have written a book of one hundred chapters on the Mosaic Torah for that same Ptolemy. And I have been told that the wonderful library of the city of Florence possesses a large work in Greek of his authorship.[40] The renowned brothers of the Benedictine order whose monastery is situated on the outskirts of Mantua also possess a copy of it.[41] One of their order told me that it is far superior to the works of Yedidyah. And it is quite likely that other distinguished fellow countrymen also possess the work. I wish I could procure it and study it. Then God might prompt a scholar to translate it into Latin or Italian, which honor and prestige was bestowed on the works of Josephus and Yedidyah.[42] You should realize that there was also another Jew called Aristobulus who was a historian. We shall have reason to speak about him at the end of chapter 10. The Aristobulus who wrote the treatise on the Torah is mentioned by Eusebius in his *Praeparatio evangelica.* He speaks of the correct views expressed by Aristobulus in his letter to Ptolemy Philometor concerning the meaning of the anthropomorphisms used by the prophets when speaking of the blessed Lord.[43] Similarly, the formulation of Demetrius's request to Ptolemy Philadelphus at the beginning of the *Splendor of the Elders* demonstrates that some parts of the Torah had previously been translated. But it also makes apparent that all the translations made before the Septuagint were for the most part erroneous for reasons given at the beginning and end of the book.[44]

Now for the ratification and confirmation of our claim that the seventy [elders] translated from an Aramaic source alone, intelligent reader, would you please go back to the beginning and bring to mind what we said about Yedidyah in chapter 5. In the second book of *On the Life of Moses,* he explicitly states that from olden times, the Torah was written in the Chaldaic language, namely, Aramaic.[45] This was its state when Ptolemy conceived the desire to have it translated. Yedidyah also gives the etymologies of some names, commenting on their meaning in Chaldean. We can take this as clear proof that the elders only translated from the Aramaic text. Nevertheless, it is true that the learned Provenzali brothers, who uphold the Torah in Mantua, criticized this opinion of mine, being loathe to hear that Yedidyah was ignorant of the Hebrew tongue. They argued: "What is the Chaldean language? The language, spoken by

40. De' Rossi is referring to the Laurenziana library. There is no extant text of Aristobulus, and the work is known only through fragments quoted by the church fathers, Clement of Alexandria, Anatolius, and Eusebius. See N. Walter, *Der Thoraausleger Aristobulos.*

41. This is the Abbazia di Polirone at S. Benedetto Po, near Mantova which was said to have been founded by Count Teobaldo in 1007. Benedetto Bacchini wrote a history of the monastery, *Dell' istoria.* He refers to the "buona e copiosa libreria" of the monastery and to the monks' transcription of manuscripts. The final dissolution of the monastery occurred in 1797 by order of Napoleon at which time a large part of the library was transferred to the Biblioteca comunale of Mantua. See B. Benedini, *I manoscritti polironiani.* Few Greek items are listed, and there is no reference to the work of Aristobulus.

42. In the first draft, de' Rossi had articulated this in a somewhat different way: "Then God would accept that I should procure the agreement of his majesty the duke to sanction a translation of the text as though legislated from time immemorial for the purpose of the greater glory of the Torah."

43. *De ev. praep.* 8:3 (*P.G.* XXI, cols. 636–42).

44. *Aristeas* 30: "Certain books of the Jewish law have been interpreted somewhat carelessly." Ibid., 314: "He said that he had heard Theopompus say that when he was on the point of introducing into his history certain matters which had previously been translated from the Law too rashly, he suffered a derangement of the mind."

45. *Mos.* II, 26.

Abraham and his household who were raised in the land of the Chaldees, which was then transmitted from them to us." I was unable to defer to their superiority with regard to this matter in view of all the other indications discernable in his works which I mentioned in that chapter. The strongest objection to their view is the specific problem as to why, if he did know the holy tongue, he should have made those confusions with the text (which we mentioned in chapter 5) as though another Torah was on his lips. {We could argue along the lines of the defense we brought on his behalf in chapter 6 and say that in addressing the Greeks, he chose not to confuse them with regard to the text they used. But then the question arises as to who led him to expand the text and necessitated[46] the use of strange words and ideas which we discussed in chapter 5. Moreover, why did he feel constrained to speak about the acceptance and ratification of the translation by all the Jews who read it in his narration of the incident. For he says that it was so precise and accurate that even a scholar was unable to discern which of the two texts was the original. Is this how a sage behaves? In his altruism, he did not want to be negative in case recognition of its flaws would lead to its neglect and ultimate disappearance. Surely, it would have been better for him to pass over all this in silence, rather than incidentally impairing the holiness of his Torah while acting in the interests of all those peoples? This is all the more valid given that we must believe that he used the word Chaldean to denote Aramaic.} It is a fact that by his time, the word "Chaldean" simply meant Aramaic. After all, Daniel who lived before him said, *and teach them the writing and the language of the Chaldeans* (1:4). And the point may be taken further. For Aramaic was used by our people until the end of the second Temple period. Speaking about the priests and their vestments, Josephus states: "In our language they are called *ḳahane, ḳahana raba, ḳetina, hemiyya, maṣnefta.*"[47] God willing, we shall elaborate this further in chapter 57. Similarly, he says that the Torah was translated by the elders "from our language into Greek."[48] In view of his own statements, it is evident that he means that they simply translated from Aramaic. With such proof you are not in a position to challenge me on the basis of the letter Ptolemy wrote Eleazar the priest which reads: "We have decided to translate your Torah from Hebrew into Greek."[49] For the word "Hebrew" in this context simply refers to their vernacular which was, as we said, Aramaic. A similar argument might be made to a Christian scholar were he to challenge you on the basis of the statements of the writers mentioned in chapter 7, and in particular Augustine, who wrote that Eleazar sent Ptolemy a text of the Torah which was written in the "language of the Hebrews."[50] But you could also put forward admissable proof from their fourth Gospel which according to their translator [Jerome] was written in Greek.[51] In chapter 19 (v.13), it reads, *He sat down on the judgment seat which is called Gabbata in Hebrew.* And later, in the same chapter (v.18), it states that they crucified him in a place called *Calvaria which means Golgotha in*

46. 'Necessitated.' I have emended the text slightly.

47. *Ant.* III:153.

48. Ibid. XII:14. Josephus does not specifically say that the translation was made "from our language," although he does say that the texts were written "in the script and language of this people."

49. *Aristeas* 38.

50. *De civ. Dei,* bk. 18, ch. 42 (*P.L.* XLI, col. 602).

51. Jerome, Praefatio in Evangelio (*P.L.* XXIX, col. 527). According to Jerome, all the Gospels, with the exception of Matthew, were originally written in Greek.

the language of the Jews. And in the first chapter of Acts (v.19), which was written in Greek, a reference is made to *a certain field called Hakel Dama in the language of the Jews.* Now there is no question that all three expressions are in Aramaic and not in the holy tongue; and yet they are Hebrew when seen from the perspective that we have given.[52]

I have provided testimony from two Jews, the Christians, and the bishop. I shall now adduce yet another clear proof from the celebrated Christian texts [i.e., the New Testament] that the elders did not translate from Ezra's Hebrew emended text, but from the popular Aramaic text which was disseminated among the people at that time. It is as follows. Obviously, their apostles and evangelists were Jews living in the Land of Israel. When they quoted a verse, they most certainly cited it in the language used by them at the time which was Aramaic, and not in Greek based on the Septuagint, which was intended for a Greek people. The Greek version could hardly have had any relevance for either spokesmen or their audience.[53] In the second chapter of Acts they speak of their Savior bestowing his apostles with the gift of the languages of all the nations to whom their witnesses had come.[54] But even they would surely have admitted that they would have spoken to the Jews in the language known to them and not in a foreign tongue. Nonetheless, if you look up the verses [i.e., from the Hebrew Bible] which they cite where the readings are divergent—this is easily done by consulting the index which was published at the end of the Latin Bible[55]—you will discover that the variant readings are the same as those in the Greek translation, which implies, therefore, that the Seventy actually translated from the Aramaic. They read, for example, *male and female He made them; and the two shall be as one flesh; and all the souls who came from the thigh of Jacob were seventy-five.* All these verses are rendered in exactly the same way in the Septuagint.

Should you desire to have demonstration that Aramaic and not Greek was the vernacular language of the Christian himself and his apostles, you should examine the text of the four Gospels. On the twelve occasions when they wish to give the *ipsissima verba* of the speaker, all the words in question are actually in Aramaic: e.g., *bariona,*

52. De' Rossi was not the first scholar to differentiate between Hebrew and the Jewish vernacular. In his *Chaldaica grammatica* of 1527, Sebastian Münster draws a distinction between "lingua Hebraeorum" and "lingua Hebraica" and also discusses the Aramaic expressions of the New Testament. See my article, "Azariah de' Rossi and LXX Traditions," 30–32. De' Rossi's discussion here can be viewed as his preliminary investigation into the subject to which he was to devote his work *Osservazioni di Buonaiuto de' Rossi ebreo sopra diversi luoghi degli Evangelisti novamente esposti secondo la vera lezione siriaca* which is still in manuscript. See my article, "Towards a Reappraisal."

53. This was also Jerome's view. In his Commentary to Is. 38:10, he writes that the Evangelists, and particularly Luke, did not follow the LXX, "sed iuxta Hebraicum ponere, nullius sequentes interpretationem sed sensum Hebraicum cum suo sermone vertentes." The subject of the citations of the Old Testament in the New Testament is discussed by scholars from the mid-sixteenth century. See Richard Simon's treatment in his *Histoire critique du Nouveau Testament,* ch. 20. He claims against the Protestants that the evangelists and apostles must have used the LXX because the majority of people did not know Hebrew.

54. Acts 2:1–13.

55. This is probably a reference to the "Index testimoniorum a Christo et Apostolis in novo testamento citatorum ex veteri quae ad huc in id congesta sunt ut pii lectores nativam quorundam intelligentiam facile assequi valeant quae ab ipso Christo vero interprete et spiritu eius per Apostolos sit tradita perspiciantque in quem usum ea adduxerint Apostoli et Evangelistae." It was inserted at the end of R. Stephanus's *Biblia Regia* of 1538, but in later printings it is usually at the beginning of the Bible.

golgota, sabactani, hakeldama, talita qumi, maran ata.[56] Given that both groups [i.e., the Septuagint and the New Testament] give absolutely identical variant readings, the Seventy must obviously have translated from the Aramaic version alone which, as we said, was being circulated at the time.

In comparing the one text with the other, wise reader, you should also apply Yedidyah's proven criterion; namely, that insignificant clues often demonstrate the truth of matters which are important and valuable to informed people.[57] In his *Hebraicae Quaestiones,* the Christian translator [Jerome] commented on the verse, *And Cain said to Abel his brother. And it came to pass when they were in the field* (Gen. 4:8) and wrote:[58] "One can infer from the context that he addressed him with words of God. The words 'Let us go out into the field' which are given in both the Samaritan and our Scriptures are therefore redundant." Such a statement enables one to deduce that their popular version [i.e., the Vulgate] is not his translation, as many would suppose.[59] In fact, the same reading of the verse is found in the Septuagint, in Yedidyah's work *That the Worse Attacks the Better*[60] as well as in the Vulgate.[61] It will thus become evident to you that all the texts which include the interpolated words "let us go out into the field" based their reading on the Samaritan version, that is to say, the Aramaic text, which was popular at the time of the elders and which was ultimately to remain extant in the Hebrew script among the Samaritans.

The best test for the confirmation of my opinion is the Targum [ps.] Jonathan ben Uzziel. For he renders the verse in question, "And Cain said to Abel his brother: Let us both go out into the field. And it was when they both had gone out into the field." The Targum Yerushalmi printed at the end of the Rabbinic Bible similarly renders the verse, "And Cain said to his brother Abel: Come, let us go out to the field." The verse, *And they shall be as one flesh* (Gen. 2:24) is rendered "And the two shall be as one flesh" in the Targum Jonathan. Yedidyah also adds the word "two,"[62] and this is the reading of the Septuagint.

Now you are familiar with the statement of the author of the *Guide* [Maimonides] that one man can be regarded as representative of the entire human species.[63] Similarly, one can assess every Bible text on the basis of those two additional words. Thus completely justified are the reports we received from Aristeas, Yedidyah, Clement of Alexandria, and those others who testified to the approval and approbation with which the translation of the Seventy was received by all their contemporaries who read it. They gained this acclamation because their rendering was textually and linguistically precise. And this was right, for there was in fact no discrepancy whatsoever between

56. He discusses these Aramaic expression in his *Osservazioni.* See n. 53.

57. *Abr.* 71 (312).

58. *Heb. Quaest. in Genesim* (*P.L.* XXIII, col. 945): " 'Et dixit Cain ad Abel fratrem suum.' Subauditur ea quae locutus est Dominus reperitur, 'Transeamus in campum.' "

59. This remark indicates that de' Rossi was aware of the contemporary debates regarding the authorship of the extant version of the Vulgate.

60. *Det.* 1 (137).

61. In the Vulgate, Gen. 4:8 contains the words "egrediamur foras" and this reading appears in all mss. See *Biblia Sacra* (ed. Quentin), Rome, 1926, vol. 1, 154, n. 8.

62. *Gig.* 65 (255).

63. *Guide* II, ch. 46.

the texts. The two doctors, Augustine and the translator [Jerome], who expressed surprise at the discrepancies between the Septuagint and our sacred text had every reason to be surprised. But had it occurred to them that the translation was derived from the popular Aramaic version, they would have had no cause for bewilderment. In their pleasure at knowing the truth of the matter, they would have kept silent. As for the bishop, the author of the *Recognitio,* who insisted that they must have used a different version from ours, while he said this in an accusing fashion, as is evident from several of his statements, he actually possessed fine judgment, and his evaluation was correct.

There are Christians who are attached to the famous Jericho version of the Bible as is explained in the *Epistles* of the bishop of Mondognedo. We shall refer to this again in section 4, chapter 45.[64] It contained some of the variant readings which were in the Aramaic version at that time. They wanted to retain this version in preference to all other translations new or old which concurred with our own holy text. And they were right and deserve praise. For they desired to revere and preserve the very version that had been used by the founders of their faith as well as by other Jews who lived in those days. This was the only version they valued and rightly so. As their translator [Jerome] wrote in his introduction to their first Gospel: "We have no reason to pay attention to any other translation whether it be that of the Septuagint, Aquila, Symmachus, or Theodotion. We only follow the version which was approved by the Apostles." They all acted meritoriously by adopting that language, given that it was used by all the inhabitants at that time. And they were particularly justified in view of their greatest doctor's opinion [Augustine] that the Seventy were also inspired by the Holy Spirit, as we noted in the previous chapter. If the claim that they translated from the holy tongue is correct, then there are also grounds for our claim that they translated from Aramaic.[65] I should, however, inform you that the Provenzali brothers, whom I mentioned previously, also criticized me on this point. They argued that both Yedidyah, and before him Aristeas, give us the account of the elders looking for a clean and unpolluted site outside the city in order to segregate themselves from its defiled inhabitants with their vulgar habits. Such behavior, they argued, indicated that the Torah from which they translated was sacred both in script and language. An Aramaic version would not have necessitated such behavior. However, in view of the proofs which I have adduced, we need not be concerned by this argument. The elders acted astutely, giving the impression that their words were as authoritative as the perfect divine Torah. Moreover, according to that event, the holiness of the Torah was established as being greater than the laws of all other nations, and continues to have this status whatever the language. Previously we mentioned that Onqelos produced a new Aramaic translation with the purpose of giving an exact rendering of the holy text. Similarly, one might say that Aquila saw the Septuagint which had been changed to conform to the needs of the Greeks for the

64. De' Rossi gives a page number for his citation from the *Littere* of Antonio de Guevara, but it does not correspond to the page number in the sixteenth-century editions that I consulted. The text was cited in ch. 7.

65. This assertion makes more sense when read with the sentence which originally followed it: "But I have not come to attack any of their opinions in any part of my book." This was deleted in the later printings, presumably because of pressure from the Venetian Rabbinate.

reasons we gave. Acting out of kindness to the speakers of his native tongue, he chose to translate the whole of Scripture from the true text. If God so wills, we shall elaborate on this subject in chapter 45 which we have assigned for this purpose.

Now the truth of our previous assertion that both Eusebius the Caesarean and the Christians' translator [Jerome] lived before Mar Zuṭra shall be demonstrated for you. It is proved by the translator's statement in his introduction to Eusebius's *Chronicle.* He writes that Eusebius lived in the time of Constantine, the thirty-ninth emperor during the papacy of Silvester, the thirty-fourth pope in 311 C.E., that is 238 years since the destruction of the Temple, the year 618 according to the Seleucid era.[66] From the autobiographical remarks in his works, it is evident that the translator [Jerome] was living in the time of Pope Damasus the thirty-ninth pope, in the year 370 C.E. or 680 according to the Seleucid era.[67] Mar Zuṭra was a contemporary of Rav Ashi for both rabbis are described in tractate Shabbat and Pesaḥim as partaking of a meal together.[68] Now from the *Epistle* of Rav Sherira Gaon of blessed memory which was addressed to the holy community of Kairwan[69] (we shall mention it again in chapter 14 [24] with the Creator's help) and Rabad's *Sefer ha-Qabbalah,* we know that Rav Ashi died in the year 738 according to the Seleucid era and that Amemar and Mar Zuṭra survived him. For Rabad wrote that Amemar was one of the last sages of the Gemara in 4265 anno mundi, seventy-three years after Rav Ashi died.[70] And Rav Sherira wrote that he was killed in the year 781 according to the Seleucid era.[71] Thus, the two Christians mentioned above must have lived many years earlier, even before Rav Ashi. And if the author of the statement mentioned above was Mar Uqba[72] who was appointed head of the court of law during Samuel's day, as is evident from tractate Shabbat,[73] he might have been a contemporary of one of the two. But he was in Babylon, and they far away in Caesarea or Italy. Each individual happened to be addressing his own people in his own way and therefore their statements, when elucidated and clarified throughout the world, would be regarded as particularly reliable.

Now I promised that at the end of the chapter, I would give you novel information about the scroll of the Law written by Ezra. To ensure that it does not become forgotten, I have spoken about it to everybody and so it is firmly riveted.[74] It is as follows. At

66. This is not exactly what Jerome says in his preface to his translation of Eusebius's *Chronicon.* He explains that the first part is pure translation of Eusebius's text; the period up to the twentieth year of Constantine contains additions from other writers, while the period from the twentieth year of Constantine onwards contains his [Jerome's] own additions. Eusebius lived 265–340 C.E.

67. Jerome lived 347–419 C.E.

68. B. Shabb. 50b; B. Pes. 103b.

69. *Iggeret,* 94. This is the important *Epistle* by the tenth-century head of the academy of Pumpeditha which deals with the question of how the corpus of talmudic literature came into being and also contains a history of the Geonic period. De' Rossi appears to have owned a ms. of the *Epistle.* Zacuto's *Sefer Yuḥasin,* which he read while he was writing the revisions of his work, contains Sherira's *Epistle.*

70. *Sefer ha-Qabbalah* (41). Amemar succeeded Rav Dimi as head of the academy in Nehardea and officiated from 390 to 423.

71. *Iggeret,* 96.

72. The passage in B. Sanh. 21b reads: "Mar Zuṭra, or according to others, Mar Uqba said."

73. B. Shabb. 55a. Mar Uqba was the exilarch in Nehardea and a contemporary of Samuel who died in 257.

74. 'Firmly riveted,' cf. Is. 41:7.

the end of an ancient manuscript copy of a Pentateuch which was in the bequest of the deceased Rabbi Solomon Sasson here in Ferrara, I came across the following statement:

> I, Moses ben Maimon, have been most zealous for the Lord God of Israel. I saw scrolls of the Law in Egypt in which the open and closed paragraphs and divisions were not written according to the regulations. I considered that the time had come for me to act for the Lord. So I put aside my studies in order to write out a scroll of the Torah of our God, the five books of the Pentateuch bound together by quires from which other texts could be corrected and transcribed. The scroll that I transcribed was the famous Egyptian text which included the twenty-four books. It had been in Jerusalem from the time of the Tannaim and Amoraim. When King Charles captured Jerusalem,[75] the scroll was removed from there and brought captive to the land of Egypt and we use it as the exemplar for our texts. When I had completed the transcription of my scroll, thanks to my God's benevolent care of me, I decided to leave Egypt and to go to the city of Chalon sur Saône in the duchy of Burgundy in France. Having made thorough inquiries and investigations, I discovered that a scroll of the Torah of our God, written in the sacred hand of the ready scribe, Ezra the high priest, existed in that place. I had taken a scribe's manual with me which indicated the open and closed paragraphs and the divisions according to the text which I had transcribed from the Bible brought from Jerusalem. I discovered a parchment which contained the same division of paragraphs as found in the text which I had brought with me. I was overjoyed and took upon myself to celebrate that day, that is the twenty-eighth of the month of Ziv [i.e., the month of Iyyar] every year. I labored for the glory of my Rock and transcribed the entire text, including the defective and plene letters, the maiuscules, miniscules, the changed and reversed letters. My purpose was to have a scroll of the Law of the Lord in which there were neither additions nor omissions. On return to my land, I wrote out a Torah of our God correctly and everybody copies from it. May my God remember me for good and pay me my due reward. Regarding one who is meticulous about such matters and does not make any changes, Scripture says, *How abundant is the good that You have in store for those that fear You* (Ps. 31:20).

Now, I have no doubt that these words at the end of the Pentateuch were not written in Rambam's hand, but must have been transcribed from another source. How much benefit and pleasure scholars would derive from knowing the text. And yet I cannot refrain from admitting that I find it surprising as to why, if the passage is authentic, he does not allude to it in chapter 8 of the Laws of the Scroll of the Torah where he mentions Ben Asher.[76] Perhaps this event occurred at the end of his life after the publication of his work [i.e., the *Mishneh Torah*] which has come down to us.[77] However, if we do claim that it is authentic, given that he was not a person to lie, it follows

75. There are many legendary accounts of Charlemagne's visit to Jerusalem. An early version is found in *Il Chronicon di Benedetto.* For a discussion of the Jewish sources, see A. Grabois, 'The legendary figure,' 22–58.

76. This is the Ben Asher codex to which Maimonides refers in the *Mishneh Torah,* Sefer Torah VIII:4: "And the scroll on which we rely in these matters is the one renowned in Egypt which contains all twenty-four books. It was kept in Jerusalem many years ago so that all scrolls could be corrected according to it. Everyone is accustomed to rely on it because it was corrected by Ben Asher who, over the course of years, corrected it many times." The codex in question has been identified as the Aleppo codex. It had been bequeathed to the Karaites in Jerusalem and appears to have been transferred to Old Cairo during the Crusaders' assault on Jerusalem in 1099.

77. This passage is undoubtedly a forgery. Maimonides was never in France.

that on hearing this evidence, all critics of the passage in the Laws of the Scroll of the Torah [from the *Mishneh Torah*] would have to accede unanimously that he was in the right. Moreover, if the outstanding authority of his time, Rabbi Judah Minz of blessed memory, could have heard such evidence, he may have perhaps changed the opinion he expressed in his eighth responsum.[78] You should study the passage.

78. Judah Minz (1408–1506), *She'elot,* 15b–16a. In responsum 8, Minz pronounces that a Sefer Torah which is not arranged according to Maimonides' prescription is not invalid. He argues that there had been no unanimity of opinion on the subject of the closed and open paragraphs, and that the Ben Asher school of Massoretes did not always agree with that of Ben Naftali in regard to the reading of certain letters and vowels.

CHAPTER TEN

The questions which Alexander of Macedon put to the elders of the South as recounted by our rabbis in tractate Tamid. How the ancient gentile writer Plutarch wrote about them.

When I saw the story about those elders who were so astute in responding to the questions put to them that they were honored by the king,[1] I was reminded[2] of a similar story. It must surely be something of a novelty and therefore welcome to the listener. My thoughts, then, led me to the idea of writing about it in this book, particularly since it is a rabbinic method to collate all analogous matters so that they remain associated in our mind.[3] I shall first reproduce the account of the rabbis of blessed memory. It is as follows:[4]

It is taught: Alexander of Macedon put ten questions to the elders of the South. (1) He said to them, "Which distance is greater, from heaven to earth, or from east to west?" They answered, "From east to west; for when the sun is in the east, and likewise when it is in the west, it is completely visible.[a] But when it is in the center of the sky, nobody can see it."[b] But the sages say that the two distances are equal, for it is said, *For as the heaven is high above the earth, so great is His mercy towards them that fear Him. As far as the east is from the west, so far has He removed our transgressions from us* (Ps. 103:11–12). If one distance had been greater than the other,[c] the two should not have been mentioned in the same context. And why is the sun invisible when it is in the center of the sky? Because of its brightness, for there is nothing to obscure it from view.[d] (2) He said to them, "Which was created first, the heavens or the earth?" They answered, "The heavens were created first, for it is said, *In the beginning, God created the heavens and the earth.* (3) He said to them, "Was the light created first or the darkness?" They said to him, "This question has no answer." They could have said that the darkness was created first because it is written, *And the earth was dull and void and there was darkness on the face of the earth,* after which it is then written, *And God said, Let there be light.* But they reasoned that he might then proceed to inquire as to what is above,[e] below,[f] before,[g] and after.[h5] If that were the case, they should not have answered his question about the heavens. Initially, they had thought that he was asking the questions randomly, but when they realized that he was continuing to ask these kind of questions, they decided not to give him an answer in case he persisted in this line of

1. He is referring to the account in *Aristeas* 187–294 ("Splendor of the Elders" pp. 58–74).
2. 'Reminded.' He uses the talmudic expression, "I saw the practice and recalled the tradition."
3. L. Wallach follows in de' Rossi's footsteps in his article, "Alexander the Great."
4. B. Tamid 31b–32a.
5. This is a reference to M. Ḥag. 2:1: "Whoever speculates on four things, he is regarded as though he had not come into the world, namely, what is above, what is beneath, what is before, what is after."

inquiry. (4) He said to them, "Who is called wise?" They said to him, "He who forsees what will come to pass." (5) He said to them, "Who is called a mighty man?" They said to him, "He who subdues his inclination." (6) He said to them, "Who is called rich?" They said to him, "He who is happy with his lot." (7) He said to them, "What should a man do in order to live?" They said to him, "He should mortify himself."[i] "What should a man do in order to kill himself?" "He should keep himself alive." (8) He said to them, "How should a man behave in order to be liked by others?" They said to him, "He should hate power and sovereignty." He said to them, "I have a better answer: he should love power and sovereignty and thereby confer favors on people." (9) He said to them, "Should one live on sea or on land?" They said to him, "On land, for there is no peace of mind to seafarers until they have returned to land." (10) He said to them, "Which of you is the wisest?" They said to him, "We are all equally wise for we have responded to your questions as one man." He said to them, "Why do you persist[j] in your refusal to accept me?" They said to him, "Satan[k] wins." He said to them, "I will have you put to death by royal decree." They said to him, "Power is in the hand of the ruler and he ought not prove himself a liar."[l] He immediately had them clothed in purple and hung golden chains around their necks.

Commentary of Rashi[6]

a. Because it is far away and cannot harm the eyes.
b. Because it is near and its light is too bright to withstand.
c. Both actually have the same measurement and that is why they are put together.
d. Because nothing obscures it; as a result its light irradiates and hurts the eyes of those who look at it. But in the evening and morning, it stands at the lowest point of the universe. There are mountains which obscure the view of those who look at the sun.
e. The sky stretching over the heads of the "living creatures" [of Ezekiel's vision].
f. Below the deep.
g. Before the creation of the world.
h. What will happen when the world is has run its course.
i. He would eat more delicacies than he could stomach; once they were finished, he would go and steal them and they would then kill him.
j. Why do you fight against us and refuse to adopt our faith. After all, are we not greater than you?
k. Satan wins by leading you astray and by putting us to the test.
l. Because he promised that he would not punish them if they could respond to his questions.

The language used by our rabbis of blessed memory in this passage makes it apparent that those elders were Jewish.

Now this story is told by the writer Plutarch in his *Life of Alexander* (par. 137)[7] as well as by Clement of Alexandria in the sixth book of his *Stromata*.[8] But they relate that the event took place with the sages of India who incited Sabbas their king to revolt against Alexander. Their version of the story is different. I have therefore translated the Latin text and put it before you.

6. The passages from Rashi's commentary are not taken from the text published with the Babylonian Talmud, but correspond to Rashi's text printed in Jacob ibn Ḥabib's compilation of Aggadot (with commentaries), *En Yaʿaqov,* Venice, 1566, 184, col. d.

7. Plutarch, *Graecorum . . . Vitae,* Alexander (64). De' Rossi used the Paris 1558 Latin translation which is divided into numbered paragraphs.

8. Clement of Alexandria, *Stromata* VI, cap. 4 (*P.G.* IX, cols. 255–58).

> Alexander of Macedon arrested ten sages who were inciting King Sabbas to revolt against him. They gave astute and terse responses to complex questions. He put ambiguous questions to them and warned them that the first person unable to respond correctly would be put to death, and then the others, following the designated order. He appointed the eldest as referee and then asked the first one, "Who do you think are more numerous, the dead or the living?" He answered, "The living, for the dead no longer count." He asked the second, "Which produces larger animals, the sea or the land?" He answered, "The land, because the sea forms part of the land." He asked the third, "Which is the most cunning of all creatures?" He answered, "That which man has yet to discover." He asked the fourth, "Why did you incite King Sabbas to revolt against me." He answered that he preferred him to live in freedom than die in subjection.[9] He asked the fifth, "Which do you think is older, the day or the night?" He replied, "The day, by one day." On noticing that the king looked contemptuous, he said to him, "Subtle questions require such replies."[10] The king then changed the tenor of his questions and asked the sixth, "How can the ruler of a great empire gain the support of all his subjects?" He answered that he should be fair to everybody and not inspire fear. To one of the three remaining, he asked, "How can a man reach the rank of the divine?" He answered, "By performing superhuman acts." He asked the other, "Which do you regard as stronger, life or death?" He answered, "Life because it endures considerable suffering and troubles." To the ninth and last, he asked, "What is the optimum duration of a human life?" He answered, "Until such time as one would prefer death to life." The king then addressed the man who had been appointed as referee and told him to pass a verdict on them. He answered, "But the fact is that each one has answered worse than the next." He said to him, "In that case, you shall be the first to die." He replied, "My lord King, if you do keep to your word, then this is not fair. For you said that you would kill the first person who was unable to respond correctly." Alexander then paid homage to them, showered them with gifts and dismissed them in peace.

This is the interpretation: he safeguarded all those who preceded him by saying that each one had answered well in comparison to his successor. And he safeguarded himself for the king had said that he would kill the first one and there was nobody to follow on from him.

There is, however, no mention of these questions in the *Life of Alexander* by the Egyptian magicians which I have in a Hebrew translation,[11] nor in the book of Alexander written by the ancient Roman historian Curtius. They are not even mentioned by Arrian the Greek whom I regard as the most reliable of all historians. My assessment is based on his own statement in the introduction to his work that his essential information was derived from the works of King Ptolemy, son of Lago, who had served as captain of Alexander's forces, and from the writings of Aristobulus son of Aristobulus who, according to the Latin lexicon, was a Jew.[12] But he is not be identified with the

9. The Latin text reads: "se illum egregie vivere quam ignavum mori maluisse."

10. The Latin text reads: "Cum rex admiraretur, Frivola persecrutanti, frivola quoque referri oportere dixit."

11. This is a reference to the popular Alexander Romance which exists in many languages and many versions. De' Rossi had a manuscript of a Hebrew translation of the Arabic version of the Alexander Romance, the text of which was used in one of the interpolations of the *Josippon.* The attribution of the work to Egyptian magicians was also found in the Mantuan edition of the *Josippon.* On this, see D. Flusser, *Sefer Josippon,* vol. 2, 221.

12. Calepino, *Dictionarium,* s.v. Aristobulus: "Aristobulus alter historicus item Iudaeus qui res gestas

Aristobulus mentioned in the previous chapter who wrote on the Mosaic law. The other Aristobulus was also a captain of Alexander's armies. Arrian mentions the Gymnosophists (i.e., the Indian sages) in his eighth book, but he makes no reference to these questions.[13] Josephus is also silent on this matter. It is true that the Hebrew Josephus refers to them in book 2, chapter 11 as the sages of India.[14] But that account (whoever its author)[15] bears no resemblance to either of the two accounts given above. Since our people possess the book, I thought it unnecessary to reproduce the passage here. It is also possible that both the story of our sages and that of Plutarch is true, the one took place with the Jewish sages, the other with the Indian sages.[16]

Alexandri Magni conscripsit comesque peregrinationis fuit." The entry for Aristobulus is found only in the later editions of the *Dictionarium* (e.g., Venice, 1557, 43, col. a.).

13. This is Arrian's *De Indica* which was published as bk. 8 of the *Anabasis.*

14. *Josippon,* bk. 2, ch. 11 (51–52).

15. He casts aspersions on the authenticity of the *Josippon,* although he never explicitly denies that it is a genuine work of Josephus.

16. De' Rossi's scepticism about the authenticity of the story is obvious. The episode of the interrogation was very popular among ancient writers. Plutarch's description is regarded as unhistorical. For a discussion of the passage, see N. Hammond, *Sources,* 119–20.

CHAPTER ELEVEN

Our sages' glorious reputation will last forever.[1] In these days, however, intelligent and experienced people disagree with some of the statements they have put forward about the essence and accidents of some parts of existence. In fact, the sages did not treat these matters as they did the laws of Torah according to the prescriptions transmitted from Sinai and the prophetic tradition to which everyone must defer without hesitation or prior investigation. Rather, they proceeded on the basis of human wisdom and evaluation which was the scholarly approach prevalent in their time and in those parts of the world. It is also quite possible that their pronouncements were either wholly or partially superior to those of the others. And yet, we should not constrict them by the bonds of love and press them to make statements which we palpably know were never their intention. It would simply be a case of letting the emotions take the line of least resistance. And then we would put ourselves in the fraudulent position of Job's friends who "did not speak the truth." In fact, they themselves informed us that *flatterers cherish anger* (Job 36:13).

THE *baraita* from tractate Tamid which we quoted above raised the question as to which is the greater distance: from east to west or from heaven to earth. I therefore thought it appropriate in this context to mention a similar passage which is in tractates Ḥagiga[2] and Sanhedrin,[3] and then discuss both passages together. It reads as follows:[4]

"Rabbi Eleazar said, 'The first man extended from earth to heaven as it says, *ever since God created man on earth, from one end of heaven to the other* (Deut. 4:32). [But as soon as he sinned, the Holy One blessed be He placed his hand on him.]' Rav said, 'He extended from one end of the world to the other as it is said, *ever since God created man on earth . . . from one end of heaven to the other* (ibid.).' But are these verses contradictory? 'No,' they replied, 'both distances have the same measurement.' "

The Tosafists gloss this passage and write:[5]

The anonymous conclusion of this talmudic statement (i.e., both distances are the same) agrees with the view expressed by the sages in tractate Tamid, but it is at variance with that of the elders of the South [also given in tractate Tamid]. For if you would not make such an assertion, then (speaking in the manner of that Aggadah)[6] one would have to raise the question as to where Adam could have stood since it is written that he extended from one end of the heaven to the other.[7] Or indeed, one could maintain that their opinion is not at variance with that of the elders of the South and propose that he was in the Garden of Eden until he sinned from which moment his stature was diminished.

1. Pr. 3:35.
2. B. Ḥag. 12a.
3. B. Sanh. 38b.
4. In the Ḥagiga passage, the order of the opinions is reversed.
5. This passage is only found in the Tos. to B. Ḥag. 12a.
6. I.e., the Aggadah in the passage quoted from Ḥag.
7. The elders of the South said that the distance from east to west is further than from heaven to earth, and therefore Adam would have been unable to stand upright.

They are alluding here to the *baraita* in tractates Taʿanit and Pesaḥim that the world is one sixtieth part of the Garden of Eden.[8] In fact, these two passages present a problem. For according to the Zohar, the Palestinian Talmud, and Bereshit Rabbah (and we shall need to discuss these texts presently), as well as on the authority of the expert men of science, the earth is spherical and the heavens revolve about it as the wheel around its pivot. The problem thus arises (and we shall mention it again, God willing, in chapter 28 of this book) as to how one can imagine that the distance from heaven to earth is equivalent to that from east to west. Surely, the diameter which begins at one side of the circumference and passes through the center to the other side of the circumference is twice the length of that part which ends at the center. You should know that this problem was raised by the sage Mizraḥi in his *Novellae* on Rashi's commentary.[9] He proposed his own interpretation of the statement that the distances from east to west and from heaven to earth are equal. He argued that they were not referring to the distance extending from one side of the circumference to the other. Rather, they had in mind the distance from the circumference to the center, for the center itself has both an eastern and western extremity. And similarly, there are two extremities to the heavens: the higher point at the circumference and the lower point on earth, for even the other extremity of the circumference is high in respect to the lower point opposite it on earth. This is what he says. However, I am not convinced that this was what our rabbis of blessed memory had in mind. The literal meaning of the phrases *from one end of the world to the other* and *from one end of the heavens to the other* is unquestionably from one side to the other of both extremities of the heavens, which is how the Tosafists understood the passage. If we were to agree to take up Mizraḥi's line of reasoning, then it would be more appropriate to present the equality of those distances in another way. The passage would be interpreted in the light of the law of the globality of the earth. In other words, the meaning of the expression used in tractate Tamid about the height of the heavens over the earth (Ps. 103:11) and the statement in tractates Ḥagigah and Sanhedrin that both distances are equal is not exactly the measurement of the distance from one side of the center to the heavens, but the height of both sides taken together. For although half of the globe is below our feet, it is also above for those who dwell down there. We shall discuss this again in the course of the chapter. Thus, their statement about the sun being completely visible (Tamid) refers to the inhabitants in both hemispheres. When the sun is in the east or in the west, its light is seen by half the globe as the early morning light and in the other as twilight. But even this explanation is unsatisfactory in view of the continuation of the passage in Tamid which explains that when the sun is in the center of the sky it cannot be seen by anybody. It is also untenable in view of Rabbi Eleazar's proof in tractates Ḥagiga and Sanhedrin based on the proof-text, *Since the day that God created man on the earth . . . from one end to the other* from which it is evident that it was impossible for Adam to have been on one side of the earth alone. These passages do not support his [Mizraḥi's] view. The truth of the matter is, in my opinion, that the problem can be solved once one realizes that the notion of a spherical earth which is set in the center like the pivot of a wheel was not accepted by all

8. B. Taʿanit 10a; B. Pes. 94a.
9. Elijah Mizraḥi, *Perush Rashi* to Deut. 4:32 (286v). De' Rossi gives a synopsis of the passage.

our rabbis. And in this enquiry one authority shall not be pitted against another. In fact, the gentile sages had different views on this subject. When the "philosopher" [Aristotle] discusses the subject of the earthquake in the second book of the *Meteorologica,* he cites and then disproves Anaxagoras's view that the earth is flat.[10] And among the many opinions of the philosophers as to the cause of earthquakes which we cited at the beginning of the book,[11] you will find the view that the earth is wide and flat. In addition, there is also the passage in chapter 10 of [ps.] Plutarch's *De placitis philosophorum* in which he cites many of their views on this subject. He writes as follows:[12] "Thales and the Stoic school said that the earth is round. Anaximander said that it is in the form of a pillar. Anaximenes said that it is like a table. Leucippus said that it is like a drum (*tamburo*). Democritus said that it is like a flat implement which is slightly hollowed out in the middle." You will find that many of the statements of some of our sages of blessed memory may be assessed by intelligent people as being equivalent to the notion of those gentile sages who believed that the earth was flat. You are familiar with the statement of the author of the *Guide:*[13] "Do not expect me to demonstrate that everything our rabbis said about astronomy conforms to the actual truth of the matter. In those days, they had an imperfect knowledge of the mathematical disciplines. They did not speak of these subjects as transmitters of a prophetic tradition, but only because they were the authorities of their time or because they had heard about these matters from the sages of those generations." He speaks in a similar vein with regard to the belief of the sages blessed be their memory that the spheres produce sounds. He writes:[14] "This opinion stems from their belief that the sphere is fixed and that the stars rotate. You know that they rejected their own view in favor of the opinion of the gentiles on these astronomical questions. They explicitly state: 'The gentile sages prevailed over the Jewish sages.' And this is correct—for the person who speaks about philosophical matters does so according to the results of his consideration of the matter and thus believes that which is proven from his demonstration." The wise author of the *Aqedat Yiṣḥaq* [Arama] also speaks in the same way in section 37.[15] Study the passage for yourself. Nevertheless, I was surprised at them both, for they only cite the beginning of the *baraita* which states:[16] "The Jewish sages say that the sphere is fixed and the stars rotate [while the gentile sages say that the sphere rotates and the stars are fixed] and the gentile sages prevailed and the sages conceded to their view." In fact, the passage concludes with the statement of Rabbi who says: "Our view seems more correct than theirs for we have never seen the Great Bear in the north or the Scorpion in the south." In fact Rami bar Ḥama [Aḥa bar Jacob] objected to this when he said: "Perhaps it is like the axle of a millstone or like the hinges of a door socket." You should consult Rashi's interpretation of this passage. The fact remains that Rabbi's opinion is upheld. It is right

10. *Met.* 365a15ff.
11. I.e., in "Voice of God."
12. Ps. Plutarch, *De placitis,* lib. III, ch. 10: "Thales et Stoici eorumque studiosi globosam terram. Anaximander columnarem. Anaximenes mensae similem. Leucippus tympani. Democritus latitudine disco assimilem, in medio autem cavat."
13. *Guide* III, ch. 14.
14. Ibid. II, ch. 8.
15. Arama, *Aqedat Yiṣḥaq* 37, bo (38b–39a).
16. B. Pes. 94b.

that they did not completely concede to them that the stars are stationary. It is true that the "philosopher" held that the star is implanted in its sphere which rotates round the earth like a knot in a board.[17] But according to the greatest astronomer Ptolemy, the star is put into a small sphere called the epicycle which is set within the revolving sphere and it [i.e., the star] together with the epicycle have their own motion quite apart from the fact that it is moved by the revolving sphere and the deferent. The views of these two philosophers are readily accessible in the Christian Aquinas's commentary on book 2 of *De caelo*[18] and in book 1 of the *Quaestiones* where he responds to question three concerning the creation of the fourth day.[19] For according to the view of the "philosopher," it should follow that the lights should have been created on the second day [and not on the fourth] together with the firmament since it says, *And God put them in the firmament* (Gen. 1:17), implying the placing of a matter within matter. Similar expressions are given in the verses, *And God took Adam and put him in the Garden of Eden* (Gen. 2:15) and *And he put their gods through fire* (Is. 37:19). Consult the passage. So if those two rabbis [i.e., Maimonides and Arama] had wished to prove that our rabbis themselves acknowledged their limited grasp of astronomy, it would have been more appropriate for them to quote the latter part of the passage which states: "The Jewish sages say that the sun travels below the firmament during the day and above it during the night. The gentile sages say that the sun travels below the firmament during the day and goes below the earth at night and their view seems more plausible than ours because the springs are cold by day but warm at night." It is logical that they should concede to them on this point. For the statement that the sun travels above the firmament at night is an offshoot of the belief of the rabbis, blessed be their memory, that the earth is flat and that the firmament is above it like a tent into which the sun enters from behind as it becomes evening. According to the later authorities, this view is not correct. And I shall also cite the view of the Geonim Rav Sherira and Hai of blessed memory in chapters 14 and 28 who rightly proved that our sages conceded this point to the gentile sages on the basis of the last part of this *baraita.* But you should know that the specific purpose of the author of the *Guide* was to repudiate the notion of the music of the spheres; and similarly, the purpose of the author of the *Aqedat Yiṣḥaq* was to prove that the stars are stationary bodies which was originally explained as being the position of the gentiles sages. But had they cited the proof correctly they would not have succeeded in their argument. Bestir yourself to look for the passages in the works of those people—for it is not right to digress from the subject of the chapter—and you will find that my statement will be endorsed. The expression "and the gentile sages prevailed" seems to me to be Maimonides' statement which the author of the *Aqedat Yiṣḥaq* adopted, for I could not find it either in the *baraita* in Pesaḥim nor in the Tosefta.[20]

17. Cf. *De caelo* II, 289b32–34.

18. Thomas Aquinas, *In Aristotelis libris De caelo,* II, lectio XVII, par. 454.

19. De' Rossi always refers to Aquinas's *Summa theologica* as *Derushim,* i.e., Quaestiones. This passage is I, quaestio 70, "De opere ornatus quantum ad quartam diem in tres articulos divisa," articulus 1, "Utrum luminaria debuerint produci quarta die."

20. De' Rossi is right—the passage is not in any extant text of Pesaḥim. Some commentators (cf. J. Even Shemuel's edition of the *Guide,* Jerusalem, 1959, ad loc.) attempt to justify Rambam's position on the basis of the continuation of the passage, while others claim that he was working from a corrupt Talmud text. But S. Leiman pointed out to me that in the Shiṭah Mequbeṣet to Ket. 13b, s.v. *mai,* R. Tam cites the same

Now let us resume the main point of the investigation. It is true that the best men of science, in particular "the philosopher" in his *De caelo*[21] and Ptolemy in the book of the *Almagest*[22] prove that the earth is spherical and placed in the center of the heavens on the basis of the eclipses, the setting and rising of the stars, and other such evidence. Nevertheless, there were gentile sages before them who held different opinions including the notion that the earth is flat as we said, and some of our rabbis either agreed with them or derived their opinion from them. Thus we learn in chapter 2 of Bava Batra:[23] "It is taught: Rabbi Eliezer said: 'The world is like an exedra[24] and the northern side is not closed. When the sun reaches the northwestern side, it bends back and goes above the firmament.' But Rabbi Joshua said: 'It is like a tent and when the sun reaches the northwestern corner it goes round at the back of the tent as it says, *It goes towards the south and turns northwards* (Eccl. 1:6).' *It goes towards the south* always by day; *and turns northwards* always by night. *It turns about continually in its course and the wind returns again to its circuits* (ibid.)—this refers to the eastern and western sides which the sun sometimes goes round and sometimes traverses." Rashi explains the passage as follows:

> "Like an exedra"—for it does not have a fourth side. "It is not enclosed"—by a partition; "It goes above the firmament"—it goes northwards into the roof of the firmament. "Like a tent"—like a tent which is totally enclosed. "To the northwestern side at night"—for the sun always travels northwards at night and from the west it turns to the north, for its course is from east to south and from south to west and from west to north, and then it goes behind the vault as through a window. "It goes to the south"—its daily circuit is called "traversing" and its nightly circuit is called "going around"; for it goes around from outside and during the day it always goes southwards. Even on a short day, it travels at least as far as the southern side. "And goes round to the north at night"—even on the short summer nights, it goes round at least as far as the northern side. "Sometimes it traverses"—on the long days of the summer solstice for it goes out from the northeastern side and sets in the northwestern side. "And sometimes it goes around"—on a short day, for the sun goes out into the southeastern corner as far as the southwestern side and traverses the three sides during the night.

Now anybody who understands this passage correctly realizes that although the covering of the north side is a matter of dispute, both agree that the sun's circuit is not from above to below, as is the rotation of the wheel of the whetstone for example. And they agree that the nightly darkness is not caused by the sun being at that time below the horizon. Rather, its circuit is always above the earth's surface from one side to the other like a millstone, and the night's darkness is a consequence of it being behind the vault of heaven. This is all calculated on the basis that the earth is flat and that the heavens only cover it like a roof of the exedra or like a tent which encloses the floor of the house with its wall-like sides. Similarly, in many of his Chapters, Rabbi Eliezer follows this notion.

---

phrase. Leiman suggested that this was a legitimate reading which was still circulating in the twelfth century.

21. *De caelo* II, 297a2ff.
22. Ptolemy, *Almagest,* bk. 1, ch. 4.
23. B. B.B. 25b.
24. I.e., closed on three sides and open on the fourth.

In the fifth chapter he writes:[25] "On the third day [of creation], the earth was flat like a plain." Later in the same chapter he writes: "The earth is spread on the depths like a ship which floats on the sea as it is said, *Who spread the earth over the water* (Ps. 136:6)." And at the end of chapter 3 he says: "The *qurqesim* of the heavens are fixed in the waters of the ocean. The waters of the ocean are situated between the ends of the earth and the ends of the heavens and the ends of the heavens are spread out over the waters of the ocean as it says, *He sets the beams of his chambers in the waters* (Ps. 104:3). The inside of the heavens ascends upwards; it is round like a tent which is spread out with its extremities downwards and its inside stretching upwards." (According to the *Arukh, qurqesim* means the hooks [*qarse*] of heaven.[26] I think the word *qurqos* is of Greek origin for the word for a tail is *kirkos,* i.e., the extremity of a thing,[27] which is how the passage is cited by ibn Ezra when he speaks about the extremities of the heavens.[28] The word also occurs at the end of Zevaḥim in the expression *iza d'qurqesa* ["goat with hooks," i.e., a threshing sledge].[29] And even the expression *qurqesin shel zahav* [golden curtain rings] used in Bereshit Rabbah[30] and Ekhah Rabbah[31] is related in meaning). Although he [in Pirqe d'Rabbi Eliezer] refers to the shape of the heavens as an exedra [i.e., the roof of an exedra], he also describes them as a tent since their arch hangs over us like a tent." He continues with the description of an exedra when he writes: "He created but did not complete the quarter facing north for [God said], 'Let anyone who says that he is a god come and complete the side.' " Likewise, in this passage and in chapter 2 of [Bava] Batra mentioned above,[32] it says: "*and from the scatterers cold* (Job 37:9)—this is the north wind. For it scatters and spreads snow and hail and rain comes to the world. There [in the north] is the abode of the demons and earthquakes . . . for it says, *From the north shall disaster break loose* (Jer. 1:14)." Both follow the same line of thinking that the sun's circuit is from one side to the other as was mentioned above. He discusses this at length in the sixth chapter [of *Pirqe d'Rabbi Eliezer*]. This was undoubtedly the source of the statement of Rashi[33] and Rabbenu Tam and Rabbenu Nissim[34] about the windows that are open for the sun to enter its vault on the eastern side and to go out behind it on the western side. We shall refer to this again in chapters 14 and 28.

Now the nature of these statements is also such that a person of intellectual integrity could not accommodate them with the notion of a spherical heaven and earth. And likewise, the concluding part of the *baraita* cited above is unquestionably based on the

25. PRE ch. 5.
26. *Arukh,* s.v. *qrqs* (second entry).
27. The Greek word *kirkos* means "ring." De' Rossi is confusing *kirkos* with *kerkos.*
28. Ibn Ezra to Gen. 1:6: "How precious are the words of the one who said that the extremities of the [circuit of the] sun are coextensive with the extremities of the waters of the ocean. The firmament is the air because when the light shone very strongly on the earth and the air over the earth dried, the rays were reflected and the firmament was formed." The Vat. Ebr. ms. 38 reads "extremities of the heavens" (as de' Rossi) and not "extremities of the sun."
29. B. Zev. 116b.
30. B.R. 18:1 (162). According to Theodor, the word derives from the Greek *krikos* meaning a ring or peg.
31. E.R. to Lam. 4:18. Here the expression is *qurqesin abin* (thick slippers).
32. B. B.B. 25b.
33. Rashi to B. B.B. 25b.
34. Rabbenu Nissim to Alfasi, Shabb. 15a to B. Shabb. 35a.

idea of a flat earth. For it reads:[35] "The Jewish sages say that the sun goes below the firmament during the day and above it during the night." And it may be that the exedra and the tent as posited by either authority would have a width from wall to wall that measured the same as the height from the earth to the roof [of heaven]. In that case, the expressions "from one end of heaven to the other," "from one end of the world to the other," "from east to west," as used in the Midrashim would fit with both notions [of the tent and exedra] such that we would have no need to distort and contort the writings of the rabbis of blessed memory in a dishonest manner.

Moreover, there are also some other statements that demonstrate this view of theirs, namely, that the earth is flat and that the vault of heaven does not fold back under the earth. This is taught in the *baraita* cited above: Rabbi Nathan says:[36] "In the summer time, the sun goes into the highest part of the sky and consequently all the world is warm and the springs are cold; in the rainy season, the sun goes into the lower part of the sky and consequently the whole world is cold and the springs are warm." Rashi explains that "the lower part of the sky" refers to the part near to the earth at the lowest parts of the vault. And he explains that the statement "consequently all the world is cold" implies that it only reaches the lowest parts of the world. When he uses the expression "lowest parts of the world," he is undoubtedly referring to the horizon which is close to the earth as Rashi says. There is an analogous passage in Bereshit Rabbah:[37] "How do the sun and moon set? Rabbi Judah said: behind the vault and above it. The rabbis said: behind the vault and below it. Rabbi Johanan[38] said: "The opinion of Rabbi Judah is more correct as far as the summer season is concerned when the whole world is hot . . . while the rabbis' statement is correct in respect of the rainy season." When the rabbis describe the setting of the sun "behind the vault and below," the word "below" has the same meaning as "the lowest part of the sky" as used by Rabbi Nathan. The same idea is expressed in the fifth chapter of Eruvin when they say:[39] "When the sun reaches the northwestern corner, it turns back behind the vault." All this stems from their belief that the sun's circuit is always from one to the other side of the horizon in an upward movement since the earth is flat and the spheres do not rotate beneath it. There are also other statements that express the same ideas. In tractates Pesaḥim and Ḥagigah it is stated:[40] "Our rabbis taught: Egypt is four hundred parasangs square; Egypt is a sixtieth part of Ethiopia; Ethiopia is a sixtieth part of the world; the world is a sixtieth part of the Garden; the Garden is a sixtieth part of Eden; Eden is a sixtieth part of Gehinnom. Accordingly, the whole world in respect to Gehinnom is as a lid to a pot." Thus, they compared the earth in its entirety to a lid which is laid over a pot which is Gehinnom. Apparently they conceived Gehinnom underneath the earth and lower, for they said in Bereshit Rabbah:[41] "*He reveals deep and hidden things*

35. B. Pes. 94b.
36. Ibid.
37. B.R. 6:8 (48).
38. This is the reading in the edition of Venice, 1545, but other editions read "Rabbi Jonathan."
39. B. Eruv. 56a.
40. B. Pes. 94a. De' Rossi also refers to Ḥagigah, but the parallel passage is in B. Taʿanit 10a.
41. B.R. 1:6 (3).

(Dan. 2:22). This is Gehinnom for it is said, *His firepit has been made both wide and deep* (Is. 30:33); . . . *that her guests are in the depths of Sheol* (Pr. 9:18)."

And on the verse, *And Jacob was exceedingly afraid* (Gen. 27:33), they say that he saw Gehinnom open up beneath him.[42] And it also states in Bava Batra:[43] "Come and I will show you where Korah's set were swallowed. I saw two cracks that emitted smoke." And there are many other such statements since this idea appears also to be derived from such verses as, *They went down alive into Sheol* (Num. 16:33) and *For you, God, will bring them down to the nethermost pit* (Ps. 55:24). Thus on the basis of all these statements of theirs one might imagine that if one were to bore a hole through all the places under the earth's surface, they would lead to the entrances to Gehinnom. However, there is the statement, "Gehinnom has three entrances: one in the desert, one in the sea, and one in Jerusalem."[44] It would appear that it was with the entrance in the sea in mind that they said in Bava Batra that Gehinnom is in the west.[45] Similarly, their idea that the Garden of Eden is in the east is perhaps based on the verse, *And the Lord God planted a garden in Eden in the east* (Gen. 2:8). For when they discuss the reason for the ruddiness of the sun in the morning and evening, they state: "[It is red] at sunrise because it passes the roses [*varde*] of the Garden of Eden (according to Rashi, *varde* are lilies]; at sunset [it is red] because it passes the gate of Gehinnom."[46] Consult Rashi's commentary on the passage.

Furthermore, if I did not have certain qualms, I would suggest that the concept of the flatness of the earth which was disseminated among some of our sages with the idea that the heavens do not extend below the horizon may have given rise to Jonathan ben Uzziel's rendering of the verse, *And God made the firmament* (Gen. 1:7). For he translates: "And the Lord made the firmament of three-fingers thickness between the sides of the heavens and the waters of the ocean and He separated the upper waters of the firmament from the lower waters by the arch of the firmament, and it was so." Now in his comment on *let there be a firmament in the heavens* (Gen. 1:6), ibn Ezra refers to the statement that the extremities of the heavens touch the ocean—this is a reference to the passage from Pirqe d'Rabbi Eliezer that we cited above about the hooks of the heavens. The sage Israeli derides this notion in his work *Yesod Olam,* but to no purpose as shall be explained presently. Nevertheless, it would appear that the translator [i.e., Jonathan ben Uzziel] intended to refer to the arch of heaven which covers the earth like a tent (or one might say, like the arch of the oven over the base below it such that the extremities of the heavens meet the waters of the ocean which are comparable to the earth's base). Thus the firmament which has three-fingers thickness separated and divided off the lower waters that are real water from the substance of the holy upper waters. This can be understood to be in accordance with the statement of Rabbi Eliezer that the hooks of heaven are fixed in the waters of the ocean, as we cited before. And similarly in his sixth chapter [i.e., of Pirqe d'Rabbi Eliezer] he writes that the sun goes on its course in the

42. This is not in Bereshit Rabbah, but the passage is found in Tanḥuma, zot ha-berakhah (Buber 1) and in other Midrashim, usually in reference to Esau.

43. B. B.B. 74a.

44. B. Eruv. 19a.

45. B. B.B. 84a: "at sunset, it passes the gate of Gehinnom."

46. Ibid.

waters of the ocean which are between the ends of the heavens and the end of the earth where it sets. As regards the thickness of the firmament, his statement agrees with that of Rabbi Joshua ben Nehemiah who states in Bereshit Rabbah that the thickness of the firmament is two or three fingersbreadths.[47] His opinion is likewise in agreement with that of Rabbi Joshua ben Hananiah who in tractate Ḥagigah[48] in the Palestinian Talmud puts forward a dissenting view against the rabbis who said that the thickness of the firmament is a journey of five hundred years. However, should these words of mine about Jonathan ben Uzziel, of whom it is said that any bird that passed over him when he was studying was burnt,[49] not be regarded as correct by intelligent people, I would annul them and they will be as though never said. But you should know that the topic of the sun's setting in the waters of the ocean is also found among pagan sages of antiquity. A noteworthy occurrence is in the first book of Ovid's *Metamorphoses.* He describes it being borne by a four-horsed chariot throughout the day, and at the onset of night it submerges them into the ocean and there they remain until dawn when they are brought back to it by Aurora.[50] The rabbis, too, at the end of chapter 6 of Pirqe d'Rabbi Eliezer speak of the sun riding on a chariot and rising crowned like a groom. Similarly, in Bemidbar Rabbah[51] they comment on the expression, *its chariot is of purple* (S.S. 3:10)—this is the sun which is carried upwards and rides on a chariot and gives light to the world as it says, *as a bridgroom coming out of his chamber* (Ps. 19:6). The fact is, as the gentile sages have explained, these descriptions of theirs are a rhetorical way of representing reality.[52] One might say that the four horses are the four seasons and likewise it is true that in this matter our perfect Torah is like them and even superior.

It is true, as we said, that some of our sages did have a notion of the sphericity of the earth. The passage is actually to be found in the Zohar with regard to the verse, *If his sacrifice is a peace offering* (Lev. 3:1).[53] Having described the layers of the seven firmaments in terms of onion skins,[54] it states as follows:[55] "Parallel to these are the seven earthly lands that are all inhabited with the exception of the uppermost and nethermost ones, and the Land of Israel is the highest of them all, and Jerusalem, the highest point of the inhabited world. And our friends who live in the South read the book of Adam, one of the ancient books, which divided all these lands that are in the lower world in proportion to those upper firmaments, in layers, one above the other." And because this

47. B.R. 4:5 (29).
48. De' Rossi refers to Ḥagiga, but the passage is actually in P. Ber. 1 (1) 2c.
49. See B. Sukk. 28a.
50. The reference to the sun's four horses is in bk. 2 of the *Metamorphoses* and de' Rossi's description is not at all accurate.
51. Bem. R. 12:4.
52. In the sixteenth century, many editions of Ovid's poetry were printed with allegorical commentaries. However, I have been unable to trace de' Rossi's suggestion that the four horses represent the four seasons.
53. According to Baron ("Azariah de' Rossi's Attitude," 410, n. 35), the only implication of this passage is that the earth rotates around its axis.
54. It is interesting to note that in ch. 1 of his *Iggeret Orḥot Olam* (written in 1525 and published in 1586), the first geographical treatise by a Jew to include an account of the discoveries of the New World, Abraham Farissol describes the spheres circulating one above the other like onion skins. De' Rossi does not seem to have read the work, although he does refer to Farissol's commentary on Job which contained many geographical descriptions.
55. Zohar III, 10a.

text is abstruse implying that the seven lands are also one within the other like onion skins, it continues with the statement:

> And in the book of Rav Hammuna Saba it further explains that all the inhabited world rotates like a circular globe, some below and some above and all these creatures differ in appearance because of the variation in air in each place and they have the same stature as other human beings. Therefore when it is light in some parts of the inhabited world, it is dark for others, day for the one part and night for the others. And there is a place where it is always day, and night never falls except for one brief moment. This is what is said in the books of the ancients and in the book of Adam, and that is why it is written, *Your work is wonderful* (Ps. 139:14), *How many things have You made* (Ps. 104:24).

Thus far the statements of our rabbis of blessed memory, the truth of which is certainly known to those who are expert in geography. In similar fashion, it is written in Bemidbar Rabbah:[56] "*One silver dish* (Num. 7:13)—this symbolizes the world which is shaped like a ball that is thrown from hand to hand." And further on it is written: "How do we know that the sea is made like a dish and the world like a ball? This accords with what has been taught (in tractate Avodah Zarah):[57] 'Any image where there is an orb, a dish . . . in the hand [is forbidden].' Rabbi Jonah said: 'When Alexander of Macedon wanted to go up in the air, he went up and up until he saw the whole world like a ball and the sea like a dish. On account of this they depicted him with an orb in his hand.' " This entire Midrash together with Rabbi Jonah's statement is also to be found in the Palestinian Talmud in its comments on the Mishnah, "Forbidden are only those statues that are depicted with a staff or an orb in the hand."[58] Thus, diverse opinions regarding the shape of the earth were held both by our rabbis of blessed memory and by the gentile sages as we said. The reason for this is that the topic was treated by them and promulgated without the prophetic tradition; instead each individual used the wisdom that he had amassed through experience or from what he had heard from others. However, you should know that this Midrash and Rabbi Jonah's statement about the world being a ball and the sea a dish is only superficially but not absolutely correct in the view of cosmographers. For they only describe a perfect globe when the earth and sea are depicted together with the gaps and clefts in its corners filled in. Alfraganus is one of the sages who demonstrates this in the third part of his *Astronomy*.[59] Moreover, it can be easily demonstrated should you cast your eyes on the solid globe on which are represented the climates with the seas and rivers and all the other sections that are related to the elements earth and water which by reason of their heavy nature tend downwards by the will of the Creator. And yet, one thousand years ago, Rabbi Jonah heard from a secondary source that Alexander alone, like a bird, raised himself above the firmament of the sky and saw the world in the shape of a ball. He believed it and rightly accepted that it was spherical. If this was the case with Rabbi Jonah, how much

56. Bem. R. 13:14 to Num. 7:13.
57. M. A.Z. 3:1.
58. P. A.Z. 3 (1) 42c.
59. This is a reference to Al-Farghani or Aḥmad ibn Muhammad ibn Kathir (d. after 861) whose work on astronomy was translated into Latin by John of Spain and Gerard of Cremona and published several times in the fifteenth and sixteenth centuries, and translated into Hebrew by Jacob Anatoli.

more so would the sages of blessed memory who believed that the world was flat have come to the same belief had they been informed of what has become known in our times, namely, how the Spaniards, who wield the oar, discovered the New World in the Northern Hemisphere where the inhabitants have their rest opposite the place where we put our feet. And the same is true of the place under the equator and also beyond it to the south above and below. With one voice they would have acknowledged that the earth was spherical. Particularly convincing would have been the report in the book on the life of the great emperor Charles V written by the wise Ulloa.[60] He wrote that the sea captain Sebastian del Cano[61] in the course of three years "like the years of a hired laborer"[62] accompanied by about four hundred men traversed the globe of the world in his ship called the *Vittoria* like the belt that encapsulates the loins of a man.[63] This is why he added a motto to his banner, as though the sphere of the earth were speaking to him, "You are the first to have traversed me." He departed to the west, and then turned and sailed until he had gone round the eastern side and he went through the whole of Asia and Africa and then, on the wings of the wind, returned to the land of Seville in Europe, the point of his departure.[64] However there is no doubt that the recently discovered place only justified its designation "New World" in respect of those who did not previously know of it. It is indeed true that Ptolemy the Greek, the greatest geographer who lived in the time of the emperors Hadrian and Antoninus Pius, the friend of Rabbi, and who lived in Alexandria as is recorded by gentile historians (as well as by the astronomer Israeli in his work *Yesod Olam*[65]), did not depict it in his maps. For over the many preceding centuries, its existence had disappeared from human memory. But according to the wisest of all men, *is there anything of which it is said: See this is new* (Eccl. 1:10). It is therefore really feasible that in the time of King Solomon, that part of the inhabited world was well known and that even at scheduled times, travelers would come and go from that part of the world to the other for trade and every kind of necessity. From the land of Ophir and Parvaim, as is written in the book of Kings (1, 10:22) and Chronicles (2, 9:21), a fleet would go out every three years, bringing gold, silver, spices, ivory, and other things.[66] All these objects were also brought by the ship *Vittoria* within a similar space of time, taking into account the unavoidable

60. Alfonso de Ulloa, *La vita*. Alfonso de Ulloa was the son of a Spanish captain who went with the expedition of Charles V into Africa. He spent most of his life in Italy. Apart from his historical work, Ulloa also translated Spanish works into Italian. He died in Venice in 1580.

61. Sebastian del Cano, a Basque navigator, was Magellan's subordinate who completed Magellan's enterprise of finding a passage to the Orient around South America after Magellan died. He returned to Seville in September 1522.

62. 'Like the years of a hired laborer,' cf. Is. 16:14.

63. 'Like . . . man,' cf. Jer. 13:11.

64. *La vita,* 182: "Et la nave Vittoria si volteggiò attorno tutto il mondo et lo cinse come il centurino cinge l'huomo. Percio che navigando al Ponente, ritornò per l'Oriente per la navigatione che fanno i Portoghesi e circondò intorno tutta Asia e Africa e ritornò in Siviglia in Europa dove s'era partita. Per la qual cosa Sebastian Cano, capitano di quella mise nella sua arma il motto che diceva PRIMUS CIRCUNDEDISTI ME."

65. Isaac ben Joseph Israeli (fourteenth century) was a Spanish astronomer and is best known for his *Yesod Olam* which he wrote in 1310 in Toledo. De' Rossi read the work in manuscript. The reference is to bk. 1, ch. 1 (5b).

66. The items listed in Kings and Chronicles are gold and silver, ivory, apes, and peacocks.

delays on the journey. There is no doubt that the land of Ophir and Parvaim is the land of Peru which has been discovered in the New World.[67] We shall speak about this further in chapter 51. For nowadays, just as with all the things that the ancients forgot and the moderns reestablished, so, too, this place with its adjacent areas deserves to be once again recognized by us. Moreover, they are daily perfecting their skills such that they can now complete in one week a journey which in the captain's day, and perhaps also in the time of Solomon, required one month. And your scholarly colleagues, intelligent reader, would confirm this for you since it can be demonstrated that Tarshish lies west of the land of Israel as it is written, *as the Tarshish fleet* (that were coming to attack our land) *was wrecked in an easterly gale* (Ps. 48:8). And there is the expression in Jonah, *and he found a ship going to Tarshish and he paid and he went to go with them to Tarshish* (1:3). This signifies that the direction of the journey was to the west and the conclusive proof of this is the statement, *And he went down to Jaffa and he found a ship going to Tarshish* (ibid.). And in Ptolemy's *Geography,*[68] (book 5, chapter 16) the fourth map of Asia indicates that Jerusalem is located on the sixty-sixth longitude that extends from the Canary Islands in the western corner to the east. And on the previous page of the same chapter you will notice that the coast of Jaffa which is called Ioppe in Latin and Zapha in the vernacular [i.e., Italian],[69] is on a longitude of 65° 40′, in other words, 20′ west of Jerusalem. Accordingly, one must necessarily say that when Jonah went down to Jaffa which is in the west in order to set out for Tarshish, Tarshish must have been located even further to the west. Furthermore, the Christian translator [Jerome] (and he was also wise) translates *Tarshish was your merchant* in Ezekiel (27:12) as Carthage,[70] referring to old Carthage[71] which was in Africa Minor in the time of Solomon and Ezekiel. Subsequently, in the time of the Roman consuls, when it was at its zenith, it was devastated and razed to the ground by the warrior Scipio Aemilianus. It undoubtedly lay to the west of the land of Israel; for in the additions to the maps of Ptolemy, in the second map of Africa (in book 4, chapter 3), it is clear that it lies on the longitude 34° 50′[72] and as we said, Jerusalem is on the sixty-sixth longitude. Thus Carthage lay to the west of it. You will also notice that the journey from Jerusalem to Jaffa and from Jaffa to Carthage is virtually a straight line. Now on those maps, Jerusalem is situated on the latitude that extends from the equator to the Pole at 31° 40′ and Jaffa is situated at 32° 6′ and Carthage at 32° 20′. Thus, the diagonal line that runs through them only veers slightly from the straight line. On studying the map of the world, you will see that on its voyage through the Mediterranean Sea which is on the

67. It is interesting to note that this view is also argued by Arias Montanus in his *Phaleg* which was printed in the eighth volume of the Antwerp Polyglot in 1572. He argues that the New World was known to the ancient Israelites although there is no reference to it in Greek and Latin writings. He also refers to Ophir and identifies the biblical Parvaim as Peru.

68. Ptolemy's *Geographia* was translated, edited, and interpreted extensively during the Renaissance. De' Rossi used Sebastian Münster's edition which was first printed in Basel in 1540 and which also contained maps related to the recent discoveries.

69. *Geographia,* 102, col. b: "Ioppe, Iaphet Iapha portus peregrinis, barbaris Zapha." Ptolemy is probably referring to non-Greeks when he speaks of "barbari." I have been informed by G. Lepschy that Zapfa or Zapho was the name given to Jaffa in Italian, particularly in Venetian texts.

70. In the Vulgate, Ezk. 27:12, "Carthaginienses negotiatores tui."

71. Carthago vetus (Old Carthage) is mentioned in Ptolemy's *Geographia* (bk. 2, cap. 6, 15, col. a).

72. *Geographia,* 63, col. b.

eastern side of the coast of Jaffa towards the Ocean, that is to its west, Solomon's fleet would undoubtedly have traversed the islands of Crete, Malta, and Sardinia. Thus Tarshish, too, which is Carthage, was situated in one of the places between Malta and Tripoli in Barbary opposite Jerba. When it approached the exit for the Ocean, the fleet would necessarily have had to pass Seville, the place from which the ship *Vittoria* began its voyage. For at that point there is a convergence of the Mediterranean with the Ocean, although Seville is situated further towards the Pole at a latitude of 37° 50′ and Jerusalem is at 31° 40′, as we said. Now the ship *Vittoria* would have left the Mediterranean for the Ocean at an earlier point than Solomon's ship, since Seville is closer to it, being situated more to the west than Jerusalem—for its latitude is only 7° 15′; both its longitude and latitude are shown on the second map of Europe. Consequently, the return journey to Seville, after it had turned around from the eastern point, would have taken proportionally longer and the reverse would have been the case for Solomon's ship.

Now if you read the gentile histories of the wars of Carthage, when at the zenith of its power it crushed the nations of the world, you will come to approve our statements about the verse, *as the ships of Tarshish were crushed in an easterly gale* (Ps. 48:8). And you will also discover that in Kings (1, 22:49) and Chronicles (2, 20:36,37) the ships which Jehoshaphat assembled in preparation for his journey to Tarshish and from there to Ophir for gold were built and wrecked in Ezion-geber. From the verse, *We then moved on, away from our kinsmen, the desendants of Esau who live in Seir, away from the road of the Arabah, away from Elath and Ezion-geber* (Deut. 2:8), it would appear that Ezion-geber was south of Jerusalem. It therefore makes complete sense that the woodcutters of Ezion lived near to that sea [i.e., the Mediterranean] or lived by rivers that flowed into it; their job was to prepare the wood (perhaps that is why it was called Ezion)[73] and they possessed consummate skill in constructing good ships for the travelers to Tarshish. But when an alliance was established with a wicked person [i.e., Ahaziah, king of Israel], they were broken up in their moorings (as is written) and were prevented from making the journey to Tarshish.[74] The identification of Tarshish with Carthage of Africa may be supported by the fact that Jonathan ben Uzziel translates every occurrence of the name Tarshish in Scripture by the word "sea." And he translates the verse in Kings, *And Jehoshaphat made ships of Tarshish* (1K. 22:49) by "He made ships of Africa." This should make you beware not to confuse the city of Tarsus on the mainland which is located close to the northeastern side of that sea [the Mediterranean] with Tarshish, the subject of our enquiry. For Tarsus is in Asia Minor, one of the cities of Cilicia, as is demonstrated on the first map of Asia (book 5, chapter 8).[75] Tarshish, however, is in Africa, and is an island and not a land, as is stated, *To Tarshish, Pul and Lud . . . the distant islands* (Is. 66:19)—this is also evident from the map. From study of the gentile historians, you will discover that Carthage was built by Dido, the daughter of one of the kings of Tyre, after she had fled from her father's house to Africa. It was called Carthage because *carta* means city in the Tyrian and Aramaic languages while

73. *Eṣ* means "wood."
74. See 2Chr. 20:35–37.
75. *Geographia,* 93, col. a.

gyne means woman [in Greek].[76] Likewise, the word "androgynous" means and, according to our calculation,[77] is equivalent to male and female. Similarly, on the map of Palestine, Tyre and Sidon are located on the sea coast of Philistia about which it is said, *I will set your borders from the Sea of Reeds* (which is southeast of the land of Israel) *to the Sea of Philistia* (which is northwest of it) (Ex. 23:31). As I will mention again in the course of this chapter, the reference here is to the Mediterranean Sea. It was to Tarshish that Hiram, king of Tyre sent Solomon's fleet. And of the destruction of Tyre, Isaiah said, *Be ashamed, O Tyre* (Is. 23:4), *Howl o ships of Tarshish* (ibid. v.14) for they made regular journeys there. Thus Tarshish must lie to the west of the land of Israel. This is not the case with Nineveh which from the fifth map of Asia (book 6, chapter 1)[78] is seen to the east of it. As was said, it is remotely situated at a latitude of 78 degrees and even more minutes—this was the path of Jonah's flight which was revealed [in Scripture] when he turned his back on Nineveh. According to our statements on this subject, Solomon's fleet must have followed the same course as the ship *Vittoria,* traveling in the manner described, from one side to the other. Accordingly, that world is only new in our own perception, and the statement of the captain of the ship, "You are the first to have traversed me," is only correct insofar as those lands have been rediscovered in these times. But the truth of the matter is that he did have a predecessor in the time of Solomon, as we have said. Now a statement may be put forward that would cause you problems with regard to the saying of our sages of blessed memory in tractate Menaḥot.[79] "From Tyre to Carthage they know Israel and their Father who is in heaven; but from Tyre westwards and from Carthage eastwards, they do not know them." This statement would imply that Carthage is east of the land of Israel. However, you must retort that they were not referring to the well-known Carthage, and the remark would make sense since it no longer existed in the time of our rabbis as was said. It was for this reason that Ptolemy himself did not insert it into the tables, but rather the person who compiled the additions to his work.[80] It is also certainly not a reference to New Carthage that is situated on the extreme west of Spain. It must have been another Carthage in the east that was known in their day. Alternatively, there may have been a spelling mistake. One might suggest that it ought to have read Carthara which is on the latitude 79 as is demonstrated on the fourth map of Asia (book 5, chapter 18).[81] Similarly, the place called Carthigna mentioned in tractate Tamid,[82] Tanḥuma,[83] and Vayiqra Rabbah[84] in relation to the story of Alexander of Macedon's journey to the kingdom of Casia and the Amazons, who are said to have lived beyond the mountains of darkness, should not be transferred to any of the places under discus-

76. De' Rossi derived this etymology from a marginal note (cited by Buber ad loc.) to the Tanḥuma text (cited below n. 81). See also *Arukh,* s.v. *antropos.*

77. According to Cassel, de' Rossi is implying that the numerical value of the word *androgynus* is equivalent to that of *zakhar u-neqevah* (male and female).

78. *Geographia,* 108.

79. B. Men. 110a.

80. I.e., Sebastian Münster.

81. *Geographia,* 105, col. a.

82. In B. Tamid 32a there is no reference to Carthage, but only to "the country of Africa."

83. Tanḥuma, Emor 6 (Buber, 9).

84. V.R. 27:1 (618–19).

sion. For, according to the context, it was situated far from human habitation near the North Pole.

Now you should not be displeased if we have digressed slightly from the subject in the course of our discourse. You have in fact gained understanding of the underlying meaning of certain verses and certain rabbinic statements. Come what may, we should resume the question of the globality of the earth. Regarding the rabbis of blessed memory whether it be all or some of them who considered any matters related to this question and anything else of a similar nature that belong to the category of speculative thought and not of Torah, we would make the following claim. If they came to incorrect conclusions in the opinion of the moderns, we would not hold them culpable in any respect given that in matters such as these their position was that of any other person of their generations. In general terms of a defense, one would say that a judge can only evaluate things on the basis of his intellectual perception. Ptolemy, too, in fact explained and admitted in section 1 of his *Geography* that in all subjects of this nature it is better to concede to the moderns who for several reasons come day by day closer to the truth.[85] We, too, have witnessed this come true in an amazing and noteworthy way—for all the ancients until these days over thousands of years claimed that the area from the tropic of Cancer to the tropic of Capricorn was not habitable due to the extreme heat, and similarly uninhabitable due to the cold was the area from the northern and southern tropics to the Poles. This is what was written by Sacrobosco, the author of the book *De sphaera,* who also cites the great pagan poets Virgil[86] and Ovid[87] to this effect.[88] Experience has shown that even in the area opposite the Zodiac, the chill of night tempers and distills the heat of the day and the sun's potency is greatly dispersed from that area to the circle around the Pole. Consequently, there is no lack of food and human beings live there along with all the requisite matters needed for a healthy life and the maintenance of a place. Thus nowadays, scientists do not divide up the habitable world into three main sections, Asia, Africa, and Europe, all of which are located in the northern quarter of the globe as described by the wise Israeli.[89] But now they divide it into four parts by joining the New World to the three zones which were known from antiquity. May He who always knew all the secrets be praised; all human wisdom is but foolishness in respect of His wisdom and power that are beyond comparison.

You should have no doubts that the same method, I mean that of putting forward an appropriate defense of the rabbis of blessed memory for any error or anomaly that resulted from their use of human wisdom, should also be applied to their statements about the substance of the stars and the heavens. There is a *baraita* in the name of Rabbi

85. *Geographia,* bk. 1, cap. 5: "Quod historiis novissimis magis sit adhaerendum, propter mutationes quae per tempora accidunt in terra."

86. *Georgica* I, 233–34: "Quinque tenent coelum zonae, quarum una corusco / semper sole rubens et torrida semper ab igne."

87. *Metamorphoses* 1, 48–51: "Totidem plagae tellure premuntur in orbem / quarum quae media est non est habitabile aestu. Nix tegit alta duas, tot inter utrasque locavit, / temperiemque dedit mixta cum frigore flamma."

88. Johannes de Sacrobosco (thirteenth century), *The Sphere,* bk. 2, "De quinque Zonis." There were many editions of Sacrobosco's work which was used extensively from the thirteenth to the seventeenth centuries as a textbook of astronomy and cosmology.

89. *Yesod Olam* II, ch. 3 (22v).

Simeon bar Yoḥai in the Palestinian Talmud, tractate Rosh ha-Shanah,[90] and also in Bemidbar Rabbah[91] and Shir Rabbah[92] in which it is stated: "Rabbi Johanan said: 'The firmament is of water and the stars are of fire'." And in Bereshit Rabbah and in Ḥagiga[93] it is stated: "What does heavens (*shamayim*) mean? Rav said: 'Fire (*esh*) and water (*mayim*)'. Rabbi Abba said in the name of Rav: 'The Holy One blessed be He took fire and water and mixed them together out of which the heavens were made. . . '. Rabbi Isaac said: '*Sa-mayim*—be laden with water, *sham mayim*—there is water'." Now although certain people who uphold the Torah find it feasible to believe in these statements, the secrets belong to the Lord our God and they ought not be taken literally. For the philosopher [i.e., Aristotle] demonstrated that they are simply made of a fifth substance. In fact, there are those philosophers who have been mentioned in regard to this subject who held different opinions which also agree with those of our rabbis of blessed memory as is demonstrated from the synopsis given by the wise Plutarch in book 2. He writes:[94] "Anaximenes said that the outer part of the heavenly circle is made of earth. Empedocles said that their substance is air which becomes solidified into crystal by the heat of the fire. Aristotle said that it is a fifth substance or fire or else a mixture of heat and cold." In chapter 13, Plutarch also gives the views of different philosophers regarding the substance of the stars, the majority of whom say that they are made of fire or of fiery spherical stones.[95] Moreover, in the second part of his fine dialogue of Philone e Sophia, the wise Rabbi Judah [Leone Ebreo] records the view of Plato and many philosophers who said that the heavens and stars are made of fire and water.[96] In the fourth section of his work *On the Sayings of Socrates*,[97] the Greek Xenophon wrote that the philosopher Anaxagoras who thought that the sun is fire, was troubled by the following points: we can look at fire, but not at the sun; moreover, the sun's rays darken the countenance which the fire does not, and while the earth's products give their yield by means of the sun, they are burnt by fire; and while the fiery sun irradiates its light, this is not the case with the stone that is whitened by fire; and whereas the sun remains, the fire is consumed and disappears. Indeed by investing so much thought on these questions, he [Anaxagoras] lost his mind. And in chapter 4 I referred to the doubts raised by Yedidyah the Alexandrian [Philo] about the heavens when he states: "We do not know whether they are frozen water or rarified fire or a fifth substance. . . . All these opinions are held in regard to this question." Similarly, one finds that the sages of blessed memory put forward views about the number and order of the spheres which were also upheld by other sages of a later generation who were men of experience. At any rate, their position is clearly justifiable on the grounds that

90. P. R.H. 2 (3) 58a.
91. Bem. R. 12:8.
92. S.S.R. to S.S. 3:11.
93. B.R. 4:7 (31); B. Ḥag. 12a. De' Rossi has conflated these two passages.
94. Ps. Plutarch, *De placitis*, bk. II, ch. 11: "Anaximenes circunferentiam, coeli extremam terream. Empedocles solidum esse coelum ex aereque constans, in crystalli duritiam ab igne compacto, igneam aereamque immensitatem in utroque hemisphaerio continens. Aristoteles ex quinto corpore vel ex igne vel ex caloris rigorisque mixtura."
95. Ibid., bk. II ch. 13.
96. Leone Ebreo (Judah Abravanel), *Dialoghi*, 2 (111).
97. Xenophon, *De factis et dictis Socratis* (*Memorabilia*) IV, VII, 7.

we put forward before. You must surely know the statement of the author of the *Guide* in part 2, chapter 9. He writes: "It is evident that the number of spheres was not known exactly in the time of Aristotle. . . . Thus, we need not reject the view of certain sages who held that there are two firmaments for it is said, *Behold the heaven and the heaven of the heavens are the Lord's* (Deut. 10:14). For I would say that they count the whole globe of the stars—that is to say, the spheres in which there are stars—as one globe and also count the globe of the all-encompassing sphere in which there are stars [*sic*][98] as the second globe." His statement that only certain sages held the view about the two firmaments may perhaps be ratified by the statement in the Zohar that we cited previously which gives the number of spheres as seven. But when, with reference to the opinion about the two firmaments, he [Maimonides] states that the one is the globe of all the stars and the other the all-encompassing sphere, one should, with all due respect to his greatness, note that this is in explicit contradiction to what is stated in Bereshit Rabbah. There it is stated:[99] "How do we know that the sphere of the sun and moon were put in the second firmament? For it says, *And God put them in the firmament of the heavens* (Gen. 1:17). Rabbi Abbahu said: 'Scripture is explicit and the Men of the Great Synagogue explained it, *You have made the heaven, the heaven of heavens with all their hosts* (Neh. 9:6). Where were all their hosts put? In the second firmament which is above the heavens'." I have seen the passage in Pesiqta d'Rav Kahana in the Midrash for Tabernacles which expresses this notion even more explicitly.[100] Consult the passage. However, this error of his should be overlooked and should not be regarded as so momentous that it cannot be covered up. For in the same chapter, he expounds on the controversy of the sages over the generations with regard to the order of the spheres: the ancients located Venus and Mercury above the sun, whereas the later sages [i.e., Ptolemy] said that they were below the sun. He himself, blessed be his memory, explicitly states in the Laws on the Foundations of the Torah[101] that they are below it as does Yedidyah [Philo] in his work entitled *Who Is the Heir of Divine Things* (page 440).[102] Then in the same context, although the Guide of blessed memory conceals twice as much as he reveals (according to the view of the commentators on his work which indeed seems to be correct), he attributes the view which he regards as false to the prophet before whom the heavens were opened [i.e., Ezekiel].[103] For his desire was to interpret the four Hayyot [living beings] as the four spheres, namely, the sphere of the fixed stars, the sphere of the five planets which are contained one within the other, the sphere of the sun, and the sphere of the moon. In the same way, according to the commentators on his work, in the previous chapter, he had ascribed to him the belief in a fixed sphere and that the star revolves which is consequent on the view that the heavenly bodies produce sounds, which the Guide of blessed memory explicitly refutes in absolute terms. Would that he had kept his silence and not only on this subject, but

98. Maimonides writes, "the all-encompassing sphere in which there are *no* stars."

99. B.R. 6:6 (45).

100. Pes. d' R. Kah. (452). It was Leopold Zunz who reconstructed the text of this Midrash from fragments quoted in the Yalqut and the Arukh. Buber then discovered various manuscripts of the Midrash.

101. *Mishneh Torah,* Yesode ha-Torah III:1.

102. *Her.* 224.

103. See the commentaries of Profayt Duran (Efodi) and Shem Tov ben Joseph ibn Shem Tov ad loc.

also with regard to the deep secrets of Ezekiel's chariot to which in the first chapters of part 3 he applies ideas that, in his opinion, are divulged and known to men of science. In fact, already in chapter 21 of part 1 [of the *Guide*], and in chapter 10 of part 2 and in other earlier chapters, he had explained them and took pride in his exposition.

Similarly, one can augment the preceding discussion about our sages by citing the rather anomalous view that some of them held concerning the setting and rising of the sun. For they do not say that it rotates above and below the globe of the earth such that night falls when it goes below the horizon. Rather, they hold that it only rotates upwards from its flat surface from side to side. In other words, that it rises within the dome in a southwesterly direction and then exits through the window behind the dome such that it cannot be seen by us. It then rotates northwards throughout the night until it reaches the east by morning, when it enters through the window to give us light. In their view, this is its course throughout the year. However, when the days are short, it remains longer in the east before entering into the vault and setting in the west opposite the point of its rising in the east. And when the days become longer, it remains there for a shorter period of time. As was shown above, these were their statements and their explanation with regard to the flatness of the earth. And just as there is a variation in the length of the days according to whether it remains a long or short period of time in the east as we said, so, too, there is a variation in its altitude depending on whether it is winter or summer. As Rabbi Nathan said as quoted above, "In the summer the sun travels high in the sky and therefore the world is hot while the springs are cold and in the rainy season it travels in the lower part of the sky."

This view of the way the sun sets and rises is one that the major gentile scientists would reject and that the later Geonim of blessed memory have also ruled out of court, as shall be shown in chapters 14 and 28. And yet, there is no doubt that this was the view of some of the ancient philosophers who accepted the notion of a flat earth. This opinion must have come to the notice of one or another of our sages; alternatively, one of them may have come to this belief independently, which some of them then accepted, after which it was also put into writing. On the basis of all these observations, a general conclusion may be drawn. You might take our sages' statements on the subject of the heavens, their constellations, their shapes and movements in a literal way and likewise, their treatment of the earth's shape and all related matters. You then might notice that their view is contradicted by the philosophers whose views were promulgated at a later date. However, even if one were to regard the opinions of the gentile sages as having a firmer foundation, and that proof could possibly be adduced to verify the truth of their contentions, this should not be accounted as an inherent defect in the teachings of the rabbis of blessed memory or in the other traditions they transmitted to us. For they were not speaking on matters such as these through prophetic tradition, but rather as ordinary human beings who evaluate the evidence as they see it or argue on the basis of what they come to hear. In regard to all such matters did not the sweet singer say, *All men are liars* (Ps. 116:11)? And his wise son [i.e., Solomon], a man of experience, corroborated this statement when he said, *There is no man that does not go wrong* (Eccl. 7:20). This applies equally to physical and sensory actions as to notions that stem from the soul and its faculties.

Now in dealing with the topic of the contradictions between rabbinic statements and those of men of science regarding this kind of question, I thought it appropriate to speak in a similar vein about another basic subject. It is relevant to a topic that will be discussed at the end of this discussion and to an observation which will be necessary in chapter 40, section 3, when we discuss the controversies of the later authorities of blessed memory concerning the fixing of the calendar. Now the matter that you should consider is as follows: I have already rightly indicated to you as to how the ancients, who were not imbued by divine illumination, and who did not range over the ends of remote lands and seas, put into writing their belief that the globe of the earth, which is 360 degrees all around in proportion to the degrees of the sphere, is only inhabited in one-quarter. That is to say, it is 180 degrees longitude from the east which begins close to the coast of China to the western side where are located the Fortunate Islands or Canaries and 42 degrees latitude from the tropic of Cancer which is 24 degrees distant from the equator as far as the Arctic Circle which is the place of the seven stars called the Great Bear. For the atmosphere of the 24 degrees that extend from the equator to the tropic of Cancer, according to their belief, was not tolerable due to the extreme heat; and, likewise intolerable, were the 24 degrees adjoining the Pole due to the cold and biting frost. Within the area of 180 degrees longitude and 42 degrees latitude, they depicted the seven climates as seven long strips, which were separated from each other, such that as one approaches the east, there is an increase of half an hour's daylight between one and the other. But in the quarter of the globe that extends from the equator towards the South Pole (although some did hold that its 16 middle degrees are inhabited), and likewise the entire hemisphere that is opposite the other hemisphere, was universally agreed to be uninhabited. Their view is given in the synopsis written by the sage Israeli in his *Yesod Olam*. He writes:[104] "Indeed it is clear and proved to us that when the blessed Lord stated, *Let the waters be gathered to one place* (Gen. 1:9), the globe of the earth was divided into two halves; the one half was exposed to the air—the part known to us which is widely inhabited—and the second half was covered by the waters of the great sea and submerged by them. This is what is meant by the expression, *Who spread forth the earth above the waters* (Ps. 136:6) and *founded it upon the seas* (Ps. 24:2)." Similarly, with regard to the beginning of the Psalm, *The earth is the Lord's and all that it holds* (Ps. 24:1), the wise ibn Ezra[105] and Kimḥi,[106] blessed be their memory, state that the upper hemisphere is exposed, while the lower hemisphere is submerged in water. Moreover in the parable which he gives in part 1, the author of the *Guide* depicts the shape of the globe by imagining two men standing on the two extremities of the diameter which is parallel to the horizon, i.e., one standing in the east, the other in the west.[107] Had he not believed this, he would have gone beyond the said measurements and spoken about all the inhabitants of the lower hemisphere. It is well known that all

104. *Yesod Olam* II, ch. 2 (21v).

105. Ibn Ezra to Ps. 24:2.

106. Kimḥi to Ps. 24:1. The commentary was first printed separately in 1477 and then in the Rabbinic Bible, Venice, 1517.

107. *Guide* I, ch. 73: "Imagine further a diameter passing through the center of the sphere; and thereupon imagine the two human individuals standing upon the two extremities of the diameter so that their feet are put in a straight line with respect to the diameter so that their feet and the diameter form one and the same straight line—then one of two possibilities must be true; either the diameter is parallel to the horizon or it is not. Now if it is parallel, both individuals should fall" (Pines trans., 210).

these statements accord with the ancient opinion that our sages also held that we described in the passage cited above which depicts the world as a ball and the sea as a dish. Now it is true that the main part of the inhabited world is in the north. As is stated in Job, *He it is who stretched out the north over chaos* (Job 26:7). This is how the verse is interpreted by all commentators and by Farissol in particular.[108] However, since that time, we have become informed through actual observation and not by means of parables. For the seafarers of our time have discovered that the inhabited area includes not only the part parallel to the latitude of the Zodiac which is called Torrid Zone, i.e., the scorching and burning zone in the middle of the equator that we mentioned, as well as the area from there to the Arctic Circle, 10 degrees from the North Pole, but also the other hemisphere that is beneath our feet. Thus, it turned out that those ancients, whether Jewish or gentile, were in error and were incorrect in much of what they said on this subject. Now when the sage Israeli quoted those verses, *Who spread forth the earth* and *and founded it upon the seas* as referring to the hemisphere that is submerged in the sea, he was taking to task the sage ibn Ezra in regard to the statement about the extremities of heaven touching the ocean as we indicated above.[109] He [Israeli] did not realize that he was taking a risk,[110] and that the explanation of the phrase *on the waters* and *on the seas* (Ps. 24:2) is equivalent to that of *and founded it upon the seas.* For he [i.e., ibn Ezra] also held that the meaning of the word "on" is "coextensive."[111]

However, we may not desist from admitting that all those sages, ancients and moderns, nonetheless deserve defense for their inadequacies. For in their time they did not have the benefit of the experience that we have had. Moreover, they are praiseworthy for what they began to divulge to us. Since we already discussed the main thrust of this in the first half of the chapter, it was not necessary to come back to it now. However, we have reverted to this topic and expanded somewhat the explanation of it in order to connect to it the subject we are about to discuss. In other words, in dispensing with the error concerning the inhabited world, whatever its magnitude, you should realize, intelligent reader, that the points raised in our discourse demonstrate that the true navel of the world and its true center in relation to the upper hemisphere is from a given point on its circumference, from which you could imagine diagonal lines drawn to the eastern and western extremities and to the two poles, North and South. This is the point at which the celestial equator, that goes from pole to pole, intersects the equator which is from the eastern to the western point, dividing each section into two. And correspondingly, it goes through the globe in a straight line and descends to the depths which is the point called the navel of the sea[112] since the ancients imagined that half the globe that is under the foot is entirely submerged by the sea as we related. Go and read about the truth of all this in the wise Israeli's *Yesod Olam.*[113] As to the true position of the navel of the earth, it has already been explained as to how the ancients thought it

108. Abraham Farissol's commentary to Job was first printed in the Rabbinic Bible, Venice, 1517.

109. I.e., ibn Ezra's passing reference to this idea in his commentary to Gen. 1:6.

110. 'Taking a risk,' cf. Pr. 7:23.

111. Cf. Ibn Ezra's commentary to Ps. 24:2 in which he expresses the same idea about the lower hemisphere being submerged in water.

112. Cassel reads *yom* instead of *yam*.

113. *Yesod Olam* II, ch. 3.

uninhabitable due to the extreme heat since it is situated under the Torrid Zone. Accordingly you will find that many rabbinic statements refute this correct proposition as to the location of the navel of the earth when they take it for granted that the land of Israel which is in the northern zone of the *oikoumene* is called the navel of the earth. There is the statement in Bereshit Rabbah that states that the first man was created in the place from which his sin could be expiated, in other words, the Temple.[114] But then there is the statement in the eleventh chapter of Pirqe d'Rabbi Eliezer: "He formed his dust into a mass in a clean place on the navel of the earth." Then there is the statement in Tanḥuma:[115]

> Just as the navel is in the middle of the human being, so too, the land of Israel is in the center of the world as it says, *those who live at the navel of the earth* (Ezk. 38:12) and from there is the foundation stone of the world as it says, *From Zion, perfect in beauty God appeared* (Ps. 50:2). The Land of Israel is in the middle of the world and Jerusalem is in the middle of the Land of Israel and the Temple is in the middle of Jerusalem and the sanctuary is in the middle of the Temple and the ark is in the middle of the sanctuary and the foundation stone is in front of the ark from which the world was founded. And Solomon had knowledge of the roots from which the entire world was produced.

This passage is also cited in Midrash Qohelet.[116] Similarly, in tractate Yoma it is stated:[117] "The world was created from its center as is stated, *From Zion, perfect in beauty.* And in the Zohar pericope Terumah (p. 157)[118] they say:[119] "The Holy Land is in the middle of the world and Jerusalem is in the middle of the Holy Land." And they also say, as is cited by Rabbi Recanati,[120] that Jerusalem is the focal point of the entire world. In addition, there is the statement that it is higher than all the lands as is evident from the text cited above:[121] "The seven lands of the lower world are all inhabited except that there are the higher ones and the lower ones and the Land of Israel is the highest of all of them and Jerusalem is the highest point of the inhabited world." So, too, in the Sifra [*sic*][122] and Qiddushin,[123] they state that the verse, *you shall arise and go up* (Deut. 17:8) teaches that the Temple is higher than the rest of the land of Israel and the land of Israel is higher than all [other] countries.

Now, intelligent reader, it should not escape your notice that the noted Christian sages also depicted the Land of Israel as the navel of the earth. Their major commentators, the translator [Jerome] and the Valencian [Perez de Valencia][124] advance this view in their commentary on the verses, *who brings deliverance in the midst of the land*

114. B.R. 14:8 (132).
115. Tanḥuma, Qedoshim, 8 (Buber, 10).
116. Q.R. to Eccl. 2:5.
117. B. Yoma 54b.
118. This is a reference to the Zohar published in Mantua 1558–60.
119. Zohar II, 157a.
120. Recanati, *Perush,* Terumah (49, col. a).
121. Zohar, Vayiqra, III, 9b–10a.
122. Sifre Deut., eqev, par. 37.
123. B. Qidd. 69a.
124. The "Valencian" is the Augustinian Jacob Perez (or Pharez) de Valencia (1409–90). His *Expositiones* was first printed in Valencia, 1484, and was reprinted in 1518 together with other works of Perez including a specifically anti-Jewish work, *Quaestiones et earum subtilissimae resolutiones contra Iudaeos fidei nostrae adversarios.*

(Ps. 74:12), *till there is room for none but you to dwell in the midst of the world* (Is. 5:8).[125] This notion is specifically mentioned by the translator with regard to the verse, *I set this Jerusalem in the midst of the nations and the countries round about her* (Ezk. 5:5).[126] This verse is similarly interpreted by our commentators Kimḥi[127] and Don Isaac [Abravanel],[128] may they rest in peace. Finally, in the last chapter of the first section of his work, the Italian poet, the wise Dante, describes Inferno as adjoining the center of the earth and states that it is situated opposite Jerusalem which is in the zenith of the hemisphere of dry land.[129] This location is corroborated by the Midrash in Eruvin which states that it produces light in Jerusalem.[130] Moreover, he [Dante] prefaces the second chapter of the second part of his work [*Purgatorio*] by writing that at its highest point the meridian covers the city of Jerusalem.[131] According to the commentators on his work, these words indicate that it is located right in the center of the world[132] and it is also higher than all other lands, in the same way as the curved part of the globe is the highest point from every side. Here, then, is presented the unanimous view of theologians of two nations which contradicts the facts that have become clear to the men of science mentioned above not only through proof, but also from perception and by use of the astrolabe. By their examination, they discovered the truth of what Ptolemy wrote in his *Geography* (section 5, chapter 16)[133] in the fourth map of Asia, namely, that Jerusalem is located within the 180 degrees that extend from the western to the eastern extremity of the northern quarter of the globe at the sixty-sixth degree [longitude] and within the 90 degrees that extend from the equator to the North Pole at 32 degrees

125. See Perez's commentary to Ps. 73:12 (according to the Vulgate numbering of the Psalms), clxix col. c. It is interesting to note that both Perez and Jerome (cited below) discuss the centrality of Jerusalem with reference to the crucifixion of Jesus, which point is totally disregarded by de' Rossi.

126. Jerome, *Commentarius in Ez.*, lib. 2, cap. 5 (*P.L.* XXV, col. 52): "Jerusalem in medio mundi sitam, hic idem Propheta testatur umbilicam terrae eam esse demonstrans. Et psalmista navitatem exprimens Domini. . . . Ac deinceps passionem, operatus est, inquit, salutem in medio terrae (73:12). A partibus enim Orientis cingitur plaga quae appellatur Asia, a partibus Occidentis, eius quae vocatur Europa. A meridie et austro, Libya et Africa. A Septentrione, Scythis, Armenia atque Perside et cunctis Ponti nationibus. In medio igitur gentium posita est ut qui erat natus in Iudaea Deus et in Israel magnum nomen eius, omnes in circuitu nationes illius sequerentur exempla."

127. David Kimḥi to Ezk. 5:5: "for it is in the center of the inhabited world."

128. Abravanel to Ezk. 5:5 (475, col. a): "Just as the heart is in the middle of the body and the rest of the limbs surround it, so too, Jerusalem is in the center of the inhabited world with the countries surrounding it."

129. *La Commedia, Inferno,* canto XXXIV, 110–13: "quand'io mi volsi, tu passasti 'l punto / al qual si traggon d'ogni parte i pesi / E se' or sotto l'emisperio giunto / ch'è contraposto a quel che la gran secca / coverchia, e sotto 'l cui colmo consunto." In other words, Jerusalem is the central point of the northern hemisphere and the exact antipodes of the Mount of Purgatory which is the central point of the southern hemisphere.

130. B. Eruv. 19a: "Gehinnom has three gates: one in the wilderness, one in the sea, and one in Jerusalem. . . . In Jerusalem since it is written in Scripture, *Said the Lord whose fire is in Zion and His furnace in Jerusalem* (Is. 31:9). And the school of Ishmael taught, *Whose fire is in Zion*—this refers to Gehinnom, *And his furnace in Jerusalem*—this refers to the gate of Gehinnom."

131. *La Commedia, Purgatorio,* canto II, 1–3: "Già era 'l sole all'orizzonte giunto / lo cui meridian cerchio coverchia / Jerusalem col suo più alto punto."

132. See, e.g., the commentary of Christoforo Landino (1424–98), whose 1481 edition of the *Commedia* contained his accompanying commentary which was republished many times: "'coverchia'—cioe sta sopra ad Hierusalem col suo più alto punto . . . quando è nella sua maggior alteza. Il che se e seguita che Hierusalem sia nel mezo del mondo."

133. *Geographia,* 103, col. a.

[latitude], as we said above. This is also what the sage ibn Ezra wrote with regard to the verse, *get up into the Negev* (Num. 13:17).[134] There is a scribal error in his text for he writes 33 degrees instead of 32. This then means that Jerusalem's location is remote from the real center as we said. Now you are already familiar with the author of the *Guide*'s statement: "The truth is not wanting nor undermined when people challenge it." On the basis of the true notion of the location of the navel of the earth, the wise Israeli deemed it right to castigate the wise sage of the *Kuzari*[135] and the author of *ha-Ma'or*.[136] He took them to task for their statement that our sages' calculation of the new moon days and the solstices was based according to the centrality of the land of Israel.[137] For according to his view, it was based solely on the true center of the earth. And so when the author of the *Ma'or* attempted to resolve in his way the strange astronomical sayings of our rabbis in the first chapter of tractate Rosh ha-Shanah, the Israelite boasted that he could provide a better justification. Study the fourth section of his work, chapter 8. We will need to go through the same channels again in chapter 40 of the third section.

Moreover, as we proceed to the next question related to this subject, you should consider ibn Ezra's statement on the verse mentioned above and on the verse, *And Judah went down* (Gen. 38:1) and *They took some of the fruit of the land and they brought it down to us* (Deut. 1:25). He writes: "One who goes from the north to the south is said to descend." In this light then, the expressions, *I myself will go down with you to Egypt* (Gen. 46:4), *while Jacob and his sons went down to Egypt* (Joshua 24:4), *and I myself will also bring you up* (Gen. 46:4), and *They went up into the Negev* (Num. 13:22) all make sense. Now you could object to his statement by saying that all the area northeast of the land of Israel is called west by the Babylonians. And in the first [*sic*] chapter of Bava Batra,[138] Rabbi Ḥanina said to Rav Ashi, "You that are to the north of the land of Israel should go to the south.[139] How do we know that Babylon is north of the land of Israel? For it says, *Out of the north the evil shall break forth on all the inhabitants of the earth* (Jer. 1:14)." Moreover Persia is also northeast of Babylon according to Jeremiah, *For see, I am rousing and leading an assemblage of great nations against Babylon from the lands of the North* (50:9) which is a reference to Cyrus, king of Persia, as is evident from Isaiah (45). Furthermore, Isaiah, also refers to this in *I have roused him from the north and he has come, from the sunrise, on who invokes My name* (41:25). Now if one looks up the relevant places on Ptolemy's maps, one will see quite distinctly that those lands are located in the northeast, one adjacent to the other. This is on the condition that you do not mistake the city of Babylon which is mentioned in book 4, chapter 5 located in the south at a longitude of 62 degrees and at a latitude of 30 degrees—for the name Babilonia was also given to the city of Cairo as can be seen there.[140] But old Babylon which is to be seen at

134. Ibn Ezra to Num. 13:17: "And it is known that Egypt is south of the land of Israel . . . for the latitude of Egypt is less than 30 degrees and the latitude of Jerusalem is 33."

135. Judah Halevi, *Kuzari* II, par. 20.

136. This is a reference to Zechariah b. Isaac Halevi Gerondi (twelfth century) who wrote *ha-Ma'or ha-Qatan,* a critical commentary on Alfasi. The reference is to Alfasi, Rosh ha-Shanah 5a (to R.H. 20b).

137. *Yesod Olam* II, ch. 17; IV, chs. 3, 7.

138. Ch. 2 of B. B.B. (25b).

139. Rav Ashi was in Babylon.

140. *Geographia* 72, col. a: "Babylon Babulis. Alcayrum sive Cayro nunc vocant."

the end of book 5 is at a longitude of 69 degrees [*sic*] and at a latitude of 35 degrees.[141] Despite the fact that it is located north of the land of Israel, one finds that one speaks of going up from Babylon to the land of Israel. Apart from rabbinic statements that refer to people going up [to the land of Israel] and going down [to Babylon], it is said in Jeremiah, *As the Lord lives that brought up the children of Israel from the land of the North* (Jer. 16:15) which is equivalent to the statement in the same verse, *who brought up the children of Israel out of the land of Egypt* which is south of it. In the same manner, the expression "going up" is used in connection with going from Persia to Babylon as in his statement, *For see I am rousing . . . an assemblage of great nations against Babylon from the land of the North* (Jer. 50:9). And in the same passage *for there has gone up against Babylon a nation from the north* (ibid. v.3) *from the kingdom of Ararat, Minni, and Ashkenaz, designate a marshal against her, Bring up horses like swarming locusts* (ibid. 51:27). Both Onqelos and Jonathan translate Ararat as "the mountains of Kardu"; Minni is translated by Jonathan as Armenia and Ashkenaz, all located in the north, which *bring up horses like swarming locusts* (ibid.). One cannot say that ibn Ezra's statement only refers to the land of Israel in relation to Egypt which is south of the land of Israel, that is towards the north. For he says in absolute terms "from the northern part of the world."[142] Indeed when he states that men of science would realize that this is correct, he was undoubtedly not alluding to what Moṭoṭ,[143] who wrote a supercommentary on his work, dreamt up—look at the passage.[144] Rather, he was referring to the view of all cosmographers, namely, that in its elevation above the earth, the North Pole is 24 degrees above the sphere of the Zodiac and on the opposite side the South Pole is plunged 24 degrees below the band [Zodiac] of the earth.[145] On this account, in the first book of the *Georgics,* the great Roman poet Virgil said, "The North Pole is always high above us, while the South Pole is only seen by those who live in the land of deepest gloom and by the souls who go down to the Netherworld."[146] A similar view is given by the writer Justin[147] in his description of the quarrels between the natives of Scythia where the Amazons live and the Egyptians as to which of the two nations was of greater antiquity and importance. He states that the Scythians who live closer to the Arctic Circle confuted the Egyptians by their claim that their land had dried up after the flood prior to Egypt and, consequently, was built and settled at an earlier date since

141. Ibid. bk. 5, cap. 20, 107, col. a. The longitude given is 79° not 69°.

142. Ibn Ezra to Gen. 38:1 "One who goes down from the north of the world to its south descends and men of science would realize that this is true."

143. Samuel Moṭoṭ or Mutad (lived in Guadalajara in the second half of the fourteenth century) wrote *Megillat Setarim* (Venice, 1554), a supercommentary on Ibn Ezra's commentary on the Pentateuch.

144. Ibn Moṭoṭ to Gen. 38:1 (f. 15, col. d): "The meaning is that above the sphere one goes to the left which is where the hills and mountains are, and the earth juts out above the waters because of the power of the heavens which affect it more as a result of its inclination, as it says 'He who spoke and the world came into existence.' The whole of the inhabited world is to the north and one who goes into the inhabited part from the north to the south is said to descend."

145. 'Band of the earth,' cf. Job 18:10.

146. *Georgica* I, 242–43, "Hic vertex nobis semper sublimis at illum / sub pedibus Styx atra videt Manesque profundi." These verses are also quoted by Sacrobosco.

147. This is a reference to Justin's *Epitome* of Pompeius Trogus's *Historiae Philippicae* (ed. pr. Venice, 1470) which was printed many times. The reference is to II, 1, 1–21.

it was on a higher position than Egypt. The proof put forward was that the rivers that flow from that area course through Armenia and Pontus and then overflow into the Egyptian sea. Accordingly, all these sages apply the expression of ascent from the south not only in going up to the land of Israel which is at the midpoint between Egypt and the Arctic Circle, but even beyond it, as far as the Arctic Circle. But in holy Scripture, as we said, ascent is applied in reference to going from the Pole to the land of Israel, as well as from Egypt to the land of Israel while Egypt is south of it.

As for me, I have not insisted on proffering proof that there is a descent from the land of Israel to Babylon, since the land of Israel is located to its south. But this is the view given by the rabbis of blessed memory in connection with the topic of [ritual] immersion in rivers:[148] "When it rains in the west, the Euphrates is an important witness." This is explained by Rashi of blessed memory who writes:[149] "In the west—in the land of Israel. For the Euphrates descends from the land of Israel to Babylon and swells from the rains such that the Babylonians know that rain has fallen in the land of Israel." And yet, I do not believe that the expression "west" as used in that context bears any reference to the land of Israel even though Ran [Rabbenu Nissim] of blessed memory writes with reference to this statement in tractate Shabbat[150] and in his Tosafot to tractate Nedarim[151] as follows: "When it rains in the land of Israel, the Euphrates in Babylon due to its swelling bears witness to it." Rather, the expression "west" refers to other lands which are also west of Babylon in a northerly direction. The river Euphrates flows through the middle of Babylon as is also explicitly shown by Jeremiah at the end of chapter 51 who sent a scroll by the hand of Seraiah to Babylon and said to him, *You shall bind a stone to it and cast it into the Euphrates* (v.63).[152] From the map of the world one can easily see that it descends from the north obliquely in an easterly direction and traverses far above the northeastern tip of the land of Israel such that in its course at no point does it flow through the land of Israel. One should not raise the objection as how it is possible that it flows from northern parts when it was one of the four rivers that issued from Eden about which it is said, *And the Lord God planted a garden in Eden mi-qedem* (Gen. 2:8). The word *mi-qedem* is to be interpreted "from the East of the world." But in Pirqe d'Rabbi Eliezer[153] and in Bereshit Rabbah,[154] *mi-qedem* is understood as an expression signifying priority in time, i.e., prior to the creation of Adam. Likewise, Onqelos translated the word as "from the beginning" and his translation was approved by Ramban [Nahmanides].[155] Furthermore Aquila who will receive favorable mention in chapter 45 and Theodotion both of whom translated our Torah,

148. B. Ned. 40a, B. Shabb. 65b.
149. Rashi to B. Shabb. 65b.
150. Rabbenu Nissim to Alfasi 29b to Shabb. 65b.
151. Rabbenu Nissim to B. Ned. 40a, s.v. *amar.*
152. The scroll contained prediction of the downfall of Babylon. Seraiah was to read it out when he reached Babylon and then cast it into the Euphrates.
153. PRE, ch. 3: "*And the Lord God planted a garden mi-qedem* (Gen. 2:8). *Miq-edem,* as yet the world had not been created."
154. B.R. 15:3 (137): "*Mi-qedem* . . . rather it means before Adam for Adam was created on the sixth day, whereas the garden of Eden was created on the third."
155. Nahmanides to Gen. 2:8.

rendered the word, according to the bishop Eugubinus, with an expression denoting priority in time.[156] The Septuagint and later Yedidyah the Alexandrian [Philo], however, translated it with the expression "east." Now you may agree with their translation and that of Rashi and ibn Ezra and say that it means east; but they meant that it was east of Eden even though it may have been located in the west of the world. There is the verse in Ezekiel (27:23), *Haran, Canneh, and Eden the merchants of Sheba, Assyria.* Should then it occur to somebody to claim that the place Eden mentioned here is the location of the Garden, his colleagues would surely inform him that its location is in the north and its rivers splash onto its shore.[157] Helpful in this would be the passage in Pirqe d'Rabbi Eliezer that reads:[158] "Adam was expelled from the Garden of Eden and settled on Mount Moriah which is next to the gate of the Garden of Eden." Study the passage. In addition, according to the ancient writers Solinus (chapter 49),[159] Strabo,[160] and Ptolemy, the Euphrates, as we said, flows from the north and continues on a diagonal line towards the east above the northeastern side of the land of Israel far from this Holy Land that is located in Palestine and via two tributaries falls into the Persian Gulf to the east. This, in my opinion is referred to in the blessed Lord's statement, *I will set your borders from the Sea of Reeds to the Sea of Philistia* (Ex. 23:31) which is the diagonal of the land of Israel from the southeastern corner to the northwestern corner and *from the wilderness (of the peoples) to the river* (ibid.), i.e., the great river Euphrates, which is its diagonal from the southwestern corner to the northeastern corner. As is seen on the map of the world, the city of Jerusalem would be on this diagonal. And with the purpose of delineating the border that passes in a straight line from east to west of the land of Israel, that sea is also designated *the latter sea* as when it states at the end of pericope Eqev, *from the river Euphrates even to the latter sea shall be your border* (Deut. 11:24). To this corresponds Isaiah's statement *Aram on the East and Philistia behind* (9:11). However, these borders that are encompassed by the Euphrates, as was said, would only be given on the condition articulated at the end of pericope Eqev, *If then you faithfully keep all this instruction that I command you* (Deut. 11:22). If that were the case, He would extend their border as is written at the end of pericope Tissa[161] and give them as inheritance all the ten nations which He had sworn to Abraham.[162] Ramban of blessed memory also writes in this fashion.[163] In the Targum Yerushalmi, one of the nations, the Kadmonites, is rendered as "all the people of the east." But in the pericope Masse[164] there is no reference to the border of the Euphrates for they had not yet earned such an extension of their territory. In fact, due to the many sins of our ancestors, they

156. Steuchus, *Recognitio,* 28v–29r.

157. This is a play on Ps. 98:8 *and the rivers clap the hand* (*kaf*), substituting *kef* (shore) for *kaf.*

158. PRE ch. 20.

159. Gaius Iulius Solinus, *Delle cose,* ch. 49.

160. Strabo, *Geographia* XI, 14, 2. De' Rossi used the Latin translation of Guarino and Tifernas entitled *De situ orbis.*

161. *I will drive out nations from your path and enlarge your territory* (Ex. 34:24).

162. *On that day the Lord made a covenant with Abram saying, To your offspring I assign this land, from the river of Egypt to the great river, the river Euphrates; the Kenites, the Kenizzites, the Kadmonites, the Hittites, the Perizzites, the Rephaim, the Amorites, the Canaanites, the Girgashites, and the Jebusites* (Gen. 15:18–21).

163. Nahmanides to Deut. 2:23; 11:24.

164. I.e., Num. 33–35 which describes the journeys from Egypt and the apportioning of the land of Canaan among the tribes.

never reached that point. Similarly, in the Laws of the Heave-Offerings, Rambam of blessed memory, on the basis of Mishnah Demai and Mishnah Shevi'it, treats the precepts that are only performed in the Land of Israel. He divides the world between the Land and that which is outside the Land and Syria. Having delineated the boundaries of the Land in relation to those who came out of Egypt, the sanctity of which areas were only temporary, and according to those who came up from Babylon, the sanctity of which areas were also for posterity, he discusses Syria which is not part of the Land of Israel. He writes:[165] "What is the extent of Syria? From the Land of Israel and outwards in the direction of Aram Naharaim and Aram Zovah. The entire basin of the Euphrates up to Babylon, including such places as Damascus and Ahalav. . . ." The author of the Semag[166] gives the same delineation under the entry for positive commandment 133.[167] In other words, the entire Euphrates basin is outside the Land. Similarly in his book, the author of the *Guide* speaks about Jeremiah's prophecy of the girdle which was given to him in the Land of Israel, *[Take the loincloth which you bought which is about your loins] and go at once to the Euphrates and cover it up there* (13:3, 4) and he writes: "Jeremiah did not leave the Land of Israel for Babylon and did not see the Euphrates."[168] In his opinion, it was all a prophetic vision and the disintegration of the girdle in the Euphrates signified the future disintegration of Israel in Babylon through which the Euphrates flows.[169] Accordingly, we have learned that Rashi, with all due deference to his stature as an authority on Torah, was not correct when he said that the Euphrates flows down from the Land of Israel to Babylon. How much more incorrect is the statement of the Tosafists who uphold that the Euphrates is in the Land of Israel, but who reverse its course, stating that it flows down from Babylon to the Land of Israel. They take Rashi to task, and after citing his statement that west refers to the Land of Israel as we mentioned above, they write: "It is not clear, for Babylon is east of the Land of Israel and all rivers flow from east to west; rather, they [in Babylon] would realize that it was raining in the Land of Israel when they saw the Euphrates reverse its course due to it becoming swollen in the Land of Israel as a result of the rains." You must notice that with all the brevity of the comment, it contains a great many problems. First, how is it possible that the Euphrates should flow down from Babylon which is in a lower position than the Land of Israel which is on higher ground as is well known? Furthermore, how could they conceive that due to the heavy rains, the Euphrates would reverse its course from the Land of Israel to Babylon which is hundreds of miles away. Thirdly, one should unquestionably not accept the general principle that they enunciated that all rivers flow from east to west. Looking at the map of the world you will notice that most rivers go out into the plain and hill country from the west and course into the seas to the east. We ourselves are in sight of the Po which with its various tributaries sets its surging waves into the eastern sea in its course—this is the Venetian sea called the Adriatic. For the statement, *all rivers flow into the sea* (Eccl. 1:7) is not the same as *the very strong sea wind* (Ex. 10:19) i.e., a west wind; rather, it refers to one of the

165. *Mishneh Torah,* Terumot, I:9.
166. Moses of Coucy, author of *Sefer Miṣvot ha-Gadol.*
167. *Sefer Miṣvot ha-Gadol,* positive commandment 133 (122 cols. c–d).
168. *Guide* II, ch. 46.
169. Maimonides does not actually give this extended interpretation.

many seas of the world. Now certain scholars* and in particular Cardinal Contarino in his work *De elementis*[170] have by means of much experience come to understand the movements of the sea. The fact is that in their opinion, apart from the specific movement of every sea whose tide goes in and out every six hours, as is known, the ocean as well as all seas that flow between countries, all of which, it is true, flow into it, have an inconspicuous movement from east to west such that from the perspective of the person who is on its shore one sea would be going to the east while from the other shore (since it goes round) it goes to the west. This is its characteristic because nature directs it such that both in its six-hourly movement as well as in this other movement it is comparable to the diurnal rotation of the all-embracing sphere.[171] This is also confirmed by the author of the *Guide* who wrote that the sphere of the moon has a specific effect on the element water.[172] The Christian scholar Guicciardini[173] gave a good explanation of this phenomenon in the chapter on the sea (p. 17) in his book *On Lower Germany.*[174] Given that this is the case, one must surely say that all rivers flow from east to west. But you should realize that this only pertains once they have flowed into the seas, at which time they acquire the characteristics that we described and take on that course. However, as far as rivers are concerned, they undoubtedly flow in all directions according to the way the land lies. In fact, for the purpose of our topic, we do not have to consider what happens to the waters once the seas have retreated; only to what occurs when the river's flood waters sweep into them. Since that statement [of the Tosafists] is permeated with implausible assertions, I do not believe that they, who were imbued with wisdom and understanding, could have propounded it.

(*The author of the *Conciliator* touches on the subject,[175] and it is explicitly treated in the Italian dialogue *Del flusso e reflusso del mare* which was published in Lucca. Examine page 42.[176])

{My refusal to ascribe such a view [to the Tosafists] appears to be corroborated in two statements of the Tosafists, one in chapter 7 of Bekhorot,[177] and a much longer passage in chapter 9[178] which were brought to my attention by my friend Rabbi Abraham ben David Provenzali. Examine the passages.}

However, let us resume our treatment of the Euphrates. In the light of everything

170. Gaspar Contarini, Cardinal (1482–1542), *De elementis libri quinque,* lib. II, 33r–v: "Eius motus qui in Oceano conspicitur perpetuus esse ad occidentem solem, nullam aliam esse posse causam existimavimus praeter motum diurnum coelorum, cuius, vi sphaerae etiam ignis aerisque bona pars circunducitur. Fieri etiam non potest ut naturaliter aqua hoc motu moveatur."

171. This description is entirely taken from the *Dialogo del flusso,* 42. See below, n. 176.

172. *Guide* II, ch. 10.

173. Lodovico Guicciardini (1521–89) was the nephew of the historian Francesco Guicciardini.

174. M. Ludovico Guicciardini, *Descrittione* (17–23): "Discorso sopra il mare."

175. This is a reference to Pietro d'Abano (1250–1315), physician, philosopher, and astrologer. The reference is to Differentia XVI of his work *Conciliator,* 24, col. b.

176. This is a reference to the *Dialogo del flusso e reflusso del mare* written by Girolamo Borro (under the pseudonym of Alseforo Talascopio) which was printed in Lucca in 1561. Borro (b. 1512 in Arezzo) was an Aristotelian who was accused of heresy. He puts forward a meccanistic explanation for the movement of the seas in relation to light, heat, and the rays of the moon. (I am grateful to Denis Rhodes of the British Library who helped me to locate this work.)

177. Tos. to Bek. 44b, s.v. *lo.*

178. Ibid. 55b, s.v. *matra.*

that has been put forward, I believed that the reference to the west in the passage cited above could apply with the exception of the Land of Israel to numerous lands which are likewise to the west of Babylon in the north. We would say that the Babylonians knew that the rain had fallen into the Euphrates in those countries because its waters have swollen there [in Babylon]. The fact is that the land from which the rains fall into the river has no bearing on the law of [ritual] immersion. In this context I cannot refrain from commenting on a statement of Rambam of blessed memory in his commentary on the first chapter of Rosh ha-Shanah that appears surprising—we shall mention it again at the end of chapter 25. It is also cited in his name by the wise commentator[179] of chapter 7 of the Laws of the Sanctification of the New Moon.[180] He writes: "You ought to know that the land of Israel is situated in a more westerly position than all other lands as is indicated by the expression used in several passages 'They say in the west.' And Rabbi Aqiva said that the Divine Presence is in the west." One can only be surprised as to how he could have made such a comment. There are surely countries that are farther to the west. Is not the whole of Europe and a large part of Asia and Africa located not only west of Babylon, but also of the whole of the Land of Israel, as is obvious from one glance at the world map? As for us Italians, we bow and prostrate ourselves towards the east in order to fulfill the injunction, *and they shall pray to You in the direction of the land [which You gave to their fathers]* (1K 8:48). When Rabbi Aqiva who was actually in the Land of Israel said that the Divine Presence was in the west, he must surely have simply meant that the blessed Lord stands behind our Western Wall, as is said in Bemidbar Rabbah[181] and in Bava Batra[182] with regard to the verse, *and the host of heavens prostrate themselves before You* (Neh. 9:6). Now one might say that according to the promise, *If you faithfully keep all the Instruction that I command you* (Deut. 11:22), the territory of the Land of Israel would extend as far as the "latter sea." Now although there are all those lands mentioned above, on either side of its borders as well as islands that are west of it, it was correct to say that the Land of Israel was in the west since no dry land or mainland interposes between it and the sea. Moreover, on a careful examination of the end of chapter 18 of the Laws of the Sanctification of the New Moon, you will find a solution to this problem.[183] Whatever the case, it does seem, as I said before, that west, as used in that context, does not refer to the Land of Israel. For this reason I did not deal with that statement in our treatment of this subject which is to prove that when one speaks of an ascent from south to north as ibn Ezra said, the journey does not come to a halt in the Land of Israel. And thus, the problem which he and his fellows raised on the basis of the verses that we cited is removed.

The fact is, in my opinion, that in resolving the problem one should take into account

179. This is a reference to Obadiah ben David, whose commentary (written in 1310) on Maimonides' Qiddush ha-Ḥodesh is simply designated Perush in standard editions.

180. *Perush to Mishneh Torah,* Qiddush ha-Ḥodesh VII:1.

181. Bem. R. 11:2 "*Behold he stands behind our wall* (S.S. 2:9). *Wall* alludes to the Western Wall of the Temple which will never be destroyed. Why? Because the Divine Presence is in the west."

182. The passage that he appears to be referring to is B. B.B. 25a: "Let us be grateful to our ancestors for showing us the place of prayer, as it is written, *And the host of heaven prostrate themselves before You.*"

183. *Mishneh Torah,* Qiddush ha-Ḥodesh XVIII:14. Maimonides acknowledges here that there are countries to the west of the land of Israel, but that with regard to the calculation of the new moon day, only those countries that are on the same latitude as Palestine may be taken into account.

the truth, namely, that the earth has two set circles: the upright and oblique sphere.[184] As regards the upright sphere, you should depict and imagine the two Poles of the world, one in the north the other in the south, that are placed at the two extremities of the straight axis. This is in fact the case when the sphere is set uprightly between the eastern and western point and the southern and northern point. Then, the true navel of the earth which is on its curve will be the point that we mentioned. In relation to such a sphere, encompassed by the heavens in all directions, one cannot speak about above and below and people going up and down on it. For on all its sides, the heads of the inhabitants are towards the sky and their feet are upright on the earth. This is what was meant by the passage in the Zohar, pericope Vayiqra, mentioned above in the name of Rav Hammuna Saba, which are all, in their detail, correct, that the inhabitants of all places have the same stature as the rest of mankind. But ibn Ezra and his colleagues were not speaking of this upright sphere, but of the one set on the oblique, i.e., which is set in relation to those who live on it on which a dividing line called the horizontal inclines below the pole. Consequently, we, the inhabitants of the world, which is in the north, are, as it were, walking obliquely on the earth although we attribute the obliqueness to the sphere and regard ourselves as being upright. For we would say that the North Pole is turned in an upwards direction. This would pertain to one who lives in one of the climates or goes towards it more than any other, according to the latitude which is from the equator to that place, because in proportion to its distance from the equator and its proximity to the North Pole, it would be imagined that the Pole is high above the earth and that the South Pole according to this image would tend downwards. Accordingly, we would estimate the words of those sages as a reference to those who dwell in the north of the world. For one who goes from the equator which is our south side facing north would be said to be going up since its horizon tends below the Pole. And going from north to south would be called "descending" since its horizon would be above it from the north and below in relation to the south in the way that we wrote. However, even if this is correct according to the notion of the mathematicians mentioned by ibn Ezra, we would not agree with him that the words of our Torah and our sages are following this system. For according to them, there is ascent and descent in every direction. But the reasoning is as follows. In every part of the northern inhabited region of the world, there are various places, that is to say, different countries whose position are on high mountains one higher than the other, while others are in the valleys and plains, one lower than the other. Jerusalem in particular is surrounded by mountains, while in the lowland of Babylon, all the corpses of the flood were deposited.[185] Indeed, only according to this perspective is ascent and descent applied to countries in holy Scripture and in rabbinic statements. Apart from this, we know that semantically these two verbs have other functions, as the author of the *Guide* wrote.[186] Sometimes, the idea of ascent is applied to a person of lowly stature who approaches a person of high station as in the case of Dathan and Abiram who said concerning our

184. It would seem that de' Rossi derived his definition and exposition of the upright and oblique spheres from ch. 1 of Sacrobosco's *The Sphere* which he quotes on several occasions.

185. This is a reference to the oft-quoted Aggadah which is a play on the name Shinar. See, e.g., B. Shabb. 113b.

186. *Guide* I, ch. 10.

master Moses, *We shall not go up.*[187] And although the standard of the division of Reuben[188] was on the south,[189] the Israelites were, in fact, at that time all in the same valley,[190] and Moses would take the tent and place it in different directions. Likewise, one might speak of ascending to an important place. Among other usages, the term is also used in relation to those going out of exile and to those making an assault on a city. From this perspective, then, given that some cities and countries are on high ground and some in the valleys, we might resume our discussion regarding the Land of Israel being on a higher level than all other lands. It would then be plausible to speak of going [down] both north and south from the Land of Israel. This is all the more feasible when you take into account that in such matters as these, one cannot draw conclusions from general rules in a dogmatic way and that the method of our sages was to speak about the majority of cases as when they said in tractate Niddah[191] and Bereshit Rabbah:[192] "The fetus emerges from the womb in the position that it assumes during intercourse: the male with his face downwards, the female with her face upwards." But Jewish midwives say that this is only true of the majority of cases. Similarly, if one were to suggest that there are cities and countries on mountains with high peaks, it will not affect the statement about the Land of Israel. And although the main point is to refer to countries of note that deserve praise as is also the case with regard to the statement of the rabbis of blessed memory that the Land of Israel is in the center of the world, one should realize as Yedidyah the Alexandrian [Philo] wrote at the beginning of his work entitled *On the Eternity of the World*[193] that the word "world" is used in both a general and a specific sense. And going from the particular to the particular, you can see the rabbis of blessed memory make the general assertion "By ten sayings was the world created,"[194] while in a specific statement they say [that Adam extended] from one end of the world to the other. And specifying even further, it is stated: "Sennaherib came and mixed up the entire world."[195] Even more specific are the sayings, "retribution comes to the world"[196] and "he brings redemption to the world."[197] The meaning of such statements is that even one country or one city will, if innocent, be saved, even if it is as small as the city of Zoar.[198] So, firstly it is sufficient that we realize that the statement about the center of the world refers to the northern inhabited part as we said. Moreover, it was in order to encourage the possessors of the Land to cherish it, to enhance her reputation and to justify her important status that they said that the land of Israel was in the

187. *Moses sent for Dathan and Abiram, sons of Eliab, but they said, We shall not go up* (Numb. 16:12).

188. According to Num. 26:5, 8, Dathan and Abiram were the sons of Eliab, who was son of Pallu, son of Reuben. I.e., they belonged to the tribe of Reuben.

189. Cf. Num. 2:10, *On the south, the standard of the division of Reuben.*

190. 'Same valley' (*emeq shaveh*). This is a play on Gen. 14:17, *in the valley of Shaveh.*

191. B. Nidd. 31a.

192. B.R. 17:8 (158–59): "Why does a man come forth with his face downwards, while a woman comes forth with her face turned upwards? The man looks towards the place of his creation [the earth], while the woman looks towards the place of her creation [the rib]."

193. *Aet.* 4.

194. M. Avot 5:1.

195. B. Ber. 28a; B. Yoma 54a.

196. M. Avot 5:8.

197. B. Meg. 15a.

198. Cf. Gen. 19:20 which describes Zoar, the town to which Lot fled as *such a little place.*

center—but one should not measure its distance from the surrounding countries with the compass or a rope. For our purpose it is sufficient to know that it is situated in the fourth climate, and the middle one of all the seven. For this reason with its temperate climate, its air makes its inhabitants wise.[199] This must certainly be what they meant, as is made explicit in the statement of the rabbis of blessed memory in the Zohar with regard to the verse, *Therefore, I pray, let my Lord's forbearance be great* (Num. 14:17). Here they describe the Temple as the heart of the entire world, located in its center from which all its other parts are sustained, just as the heart is in the middle of the body which is the source of all its sustenance. Although everybody has been informed that the heart is not literally in a central position, they said as follows:[200] "The Holy One blessed be He gave human beings strength in the middle of the body for there is the seat of the heart and from it all the body is nourished. . . . Similarly, the oceanic sea surrounds the inhabited areas of all seven nations; it surrounds Jerusalem, and Jerusalem is in the center of all the inhabited area . . . and the Temple surrounds the Holy of Holies . . . for this is the heart of the entire earth." Look at the passage yourself for it is lengthy and exquisitely beautiful.[201] Moreover, when you have comprehended the statements of the Christians scholars cited above, you will realize that this is also what they meant. The Valencian [Perez de Valencia] brings proof of Jerusalem's centrality from the fact that it is located in the fourth climate. And in his commentary on the verse, *I set this Jerusalem in the midst of the nations with countries round about her* (Ezk. 5:5),[202] the translator [Jerome] states: "Jerusalem is in the navel of the world since to her east are all the regions of Asia, and to her west is Europe, and to the south, Libya and Africa, and to her north, Scythia and Armenia and Persia and all the regions of the Pontus. Thus she is situated in the midst of them all." It is true that Dante is in an indefensible position and is a fellow traveler of the author of *ha-Ma'or.* The fact that the rivers of Scythia flow into the Egyptian sea, according to Justin's statement quoted above, does not necessitate that the entire side adjacent to the polar circle is on high ground. For according to the said way of viewing the matter, it is possible that only the land of Scythia is on high ground, while the adjoining countries are in the valley. And concerning the question of the true center of the earth, we might wish to join the wise Israeli in apprehending the author of *ha-Ma'or* (we shall mention this again in chapter 40) for entertaining the idea that our rabbis said that the Land of Israel is exactly in the middle of the universe when in fact they only meant it in a metaphorical manner, as was said. And yet we cannot fail to praise the sage of the *Kuzari* who said that which the intellect would embrace and adopt. For he said that while the course of the planets and their path go through all parts of the world, the Sabbaths and divinely appointed times could only be measured according to the rising and setting of the great luminaries in the Lord's inheritance regardless as to whether it [Land of Israel] was located in the true center of the universe or not.[203] In fact, there are many verses that demonstrate that the basic purpose of all the precepts is that they should be observed in the Land as was

199. See B. B.B. 158b.
200. Zohar III, 161b.
201. 'Exquisitely beautiful' lit. 'perfection in beauty,' expression used of the Land of Israel.
202. See n. 125.
203. *Kuzari* II, pars. 18, 20. He does state that Palestine is in the center of the world.

stated by Ramban of blessed memory in his commentary on pericope *aḥare mot* and at the beginning of pericope *va-etḥanan*[204] and Rashba [Solomon ben Adret] in his responsum 134.[205] (We shall mention this again in chapter 43.) However, one should not remain silent as to the fact that regarding personal duties, it is said that they may be observed *in all your dwelling places,* as Ramban himself writes in the passage indicated above, and in his commentary on the verse, *Therefore impress these My words* (Deut. 11:18). And now you have come to appreciate that the word "world" does not actually always refer to the whole, but that, according to the context, it may signify part of it, you should keep it in mind so that our beloved sages of blessed memory should be protected from the accusation that some of their statements give reason for wonder. For example, the passage quoted above in which the world's relation to Gehinnom is compared to the lid of a pot, should be explained as follows. The northern part of the inhabited world is, as it were, a lid over the other parts of the globe, since, according to the belief of those days, they were all *an empty howling waste*[206] and *a land of deep gloom*[207] which was in the shape of a pot with a closely fitting lid which is the inhabited part of the globe. According to our way of thinking, they called this lower part Gehinnom, in keeping with their belief which is comparable to that of the Christian scholars, as we mentioned above, that the *Tofeth that has long been ready for him*[208] and Sheol below is situated close to the center of the earth and is covered by the earth and the *oikoumene.*

Furthermore, it should not displease you that the existence of the Antipodes—this refers to those who live opposite our feet—is denied in some of their statements. Even the great Christian doctor Augustine vehemently denied their existence in his *City [of God].*[209] He put forward the following argument, to which our rabbis in the first passage that we cited from the Zohar clearly touch upon. He said that there was evidently only one man created in the beginning. Since it was unfeasible that a human being should dare to pass below the Zodiac and to traverse from the exposed hemisphere of dry land to the other hemisphere that is through the water, one must surely claim that no human being exists beyond the northern *oikoumene.* Similarly, with regard to the other statements of the rabbis of blessed memory regarding the heavens and their constellations, scholars might come to the idea that the Greek philosophers were superior to them. However, we would say in their defense, as is proper, one of two things. Either we lack the prerequisite knowledge for understanding their method, or alternatively, a veil covered the eyes of the elite who were inclined to speculative thinking in those generations and countries. We are then safe[210] for not everybody can study everything. In addition, even in relation to those things in which we would claim to be more correct than they, one should realize how poor is the dough that the bakers themselves declare to be bad.[211] I mean that on their own admission, they (that is to say

204. Nahmanides to Lev. 18:25; Deut. 4:3.
205. Solomon ben Adret, *She'elot,* responsum 134 (vol. 1, 54, col. b–55, col. a).
206. Cf. Deut. 32:10.
207. Cf. Jer. 2:31.
208. Cf. Is. 30:33.
209. *De civ. Dei,* 16, ch. 9.
210. Cf. Jer. 7:10.
211. Cf. B.R. 34:10 (320).

the natural philosophers) let us know as to how it is very likely that the truth of the matter is somewhat different to what they taught us. You will indeed see that in his discussion of astronomy the author of the *Guide* said that although we cannot deny its conformity to the times of the eclipses and the new moons, it is in some way unsustainable according to the principles of natural science on which that astronomy is based and should be refuted.[212] In particular, as he explained in chapter 11 of part 2, there is no conclusive proof of this matter. Rather, it is possible that an expert might conjecture conversely. Ptolemy himself, the greatest of the astronomers, having posited the existence of the epicycle and the eccentric sphere in his *Almagest* wrote in book 3: "Whether this is true or not, God only knows. But for us it suffices that we find a means by which it is possible to account for everything that is demonstrated to us by way of the movements of the heavenly stars." {And in section 11 [*sic*],[213] speaking of the declination posited for the latitude of Venus and Mercury the existence of which we are unable to conceive in those bodies, Ptolemy wrote that which was cited by the author of the *Guide* in part 2, chapter 24. Judging from the abstruse and convoluted Hebrew translation of Rabbi Jacob bar Abba Mari which I read, one could well assume that the Arabic text was also confused.[214] Thus, the author of the *Guide* of blessed memory who did not see the text in the original Greek, but only in its Arabic translation, hoping to give us the actual words of the author in addition to his desire to be brief, was forced in the end to reproduce only the bare essentials, as is demonstrated in his text. That is to say, he states that in regard to certain aspects of astronomy, the revolutions of the heavenly bodies cannot be represented in the same way as one does for things obtained by artifice since human matters cannot be compared to those that are divine.[215]

Now in order to win favor with scholars and the soul of the author of the *Guide,* blessed be his memory, I thought it appropriate in this context to translate the entire passage from the Latin version of the *Almagest* which is much clearer.[216] Should somebody compare the Hebrew translation with this text, he would realize the benefit that would result from emending the Hebrew version. He wrote as follows:[217]

> On considering the multiplicity and difficulty of the instruments and devices used for our considerations, let nobody regard our hypotheses as strange and difficult. For it is not right to compare things of human artifice to those that are divine. Nor should you make any evaluation between things which are of such a different nature. For you cannot evaluate things which are not eternal in the same way as things that are eternal and do not change their nature, and what is more unlike than those which may be impeded by any accidental cause and those things which are not even impeded by themselves in any way? But it is

212. *Guide* II, ch. 24.

213. *Almagest* XIII, ch. 2.

214. Jacob ben Abba Mari ben Samson Anatoli (thirteenth century) translated several works on astronomy and logic from their Arabic version into Hebrew. The first Arabic translation of the *Almagest* was produced by Ishaq ibn Hunain (d. 910/11) and later revised by Thabit ibn Qurra. De' Rossi read the Hebrew translation in manuscript.

215. *Guide* II, ch. 24.

216. De' Rossi used George of Trepizond's Latin translation of the *Almagest* which was first published in 1451 and republished several times in the sixteenth century. It is regarded as inferior to the translation of Peurbach and Regiomontanus. See O. Pedersen, *A Survey.*

217. *Almagest* XIII, ch. 2.

right for us to endeavor to put forward the most simple hypotheses possible for the heavenly movements; and if this does not succeed with all the hypotheses, then we will be satisfied with whatever is possible. For once it is confirmed that one of the heavenly phenomena exactly preserves the order that is required according to our hypotheses, why should one be surprised that this variation in the heavenly movements is possible, particularly when we know that they do not have any nature which impedes. Rather, its nature is totally conceding to the natural movements of each one of them even if they were to appear to us to be contrary so that they can all penetrate fluidly and widely and freely act through those simple bodies. And this free action takes place not only about the circles but also about the spheres themselves and the axes of revolution. Moreover, the variation and sequence which occurs to them in their different movements seems so strange and difficult in the images that we construct that one would judge that it is unfeasible that there is unimpeded movement. And yet, in heavenly things, this variation and sequence does not cause any impediment. Therefore, in our evaluation of the simplicity of the heavenly beings one should not do so by comparing them with those that we know as simple, when the fact is that to all people the same thing does not seem likewise simple. And one who would direct his thinking along these lines would imagine that it is impossible to have anything simple in the heavens, not even the stable and simple nature of the first motion for since it is always the same, it is not only difficult but impossible for us to conceive. Therefore we should not use examples from the lower world, but from the nature of the heavenly beings themselves and since they always maintain the same order and progression in their movements, we could judge them all as simple, even simpler than everything that is regarded as simple by us since one could not conjecture any anomaly or difficulty with regard to them.}[2]

Indeed, this is all proof that as far as human understanding of the heavenly ordinances is concerned, one cannot say categorically that there is only one truth. This view is further strengthened when one augments it with the information put forward by Ralbag [Rabbi Levi ben Gershon, Gersonides] in his commentary on the Torah and in the fifth section of his work *Milḥamot.*[218] For he conceived the idea of accounting for all heavenly phenomena by means of a new astronomy which refuted the concept of the epicycle and the eccentric sphere which are the basis of Ptolemaic astronomy. Likewise, the wise Israeli wrote about a certain Arab of the twelfth century whom he describes as "the man who shook [the world],"[219] who thought that all the elements of Ptolemaic astronomy should be changed.[220] It had already occurred to me that I should defend our sages for their notion of the rotation of the luminaries to the sides of the world in the same way that the *Guide* defended the astronomers from the position taken by the rabbis of blessed memory with regard to the times of the new moons and the equinoxes. However, in truth, we must admit that we cannot claim that our perception corroborates any one of their statements, just as he [Maimonides] testifies to the deficiency

218. Levi ben Gerson, Gersonides (Provence 1288–1344) was a philosopher, biblical exegete, mathematician, and astronomer. Book 5 of part 1 of his *Milḥamot ha-Shem* deals with astronomy. It only survives in manuscript and was omitted from the printed editions. See the edition of B. R. Goldstein, *The Astronomy.*

219. This is a reference to the astronomer Al-Bitruji (Alpetragius), a contemporary of Averroes, whose astronomical work *De Motibus Caelorum* written in Arabic was translated into Hebrew by Moses ibn Tibbon who expanded the system of his teacher ibn Tufayl that challenged the Ptolemaic system.

220. Isaac Israeli, *Yesod Olam* II, ch. 9, f. 29r.

described above. Rabbi Moses does in fact write in chapter 6 of his Laws on the Sanctification of the New Moon: "The calculation of the new moon that is used nowadays to ascertain the conjunction of the sun and the moon is according to their mean and not true motion."[221] And in chapter 10 he writes: "The fact is that the calculation of both cycles that we have explained (i.e., that of Samuel and of Rav Ada) are only approximate, based on the mean motion of the sun and not on its true position. For the vernal equinox in our times will occur about two days before."[222] Study the passage. As we shall mention again in chapter 40 of the third section also in connection with our idea that we are ten times better than the gentile sages in natural sciences, go and look at the statement of the divine sage, the author of the book of the *Kuzari.* For he made a great effort to demonstrate in a similar way the inadequacy of the hypotheses of the "philosopher" not only in metaphysics, but also in the natural sciences. He goes even further than the author of the *Guide* who said:[223] "I say by way of rhetoric, *The heavens are the heavens of the Lord.* Thus, as is demonstrated in that passage,[224] he [i.e., the author of the *Kuzari*] even raises questions regarding the well-known theory that the sublunar world is composed of a combination of the four elements. Thus, on the basis of the foregoing, I would say by way of a general principle that wherever one can incline in our sages' favor even in matters of speculation in which their opinion was only based on human wisdom (for in matters transmitted by tradition there is no need for consistency—they have their own defense) every person according to his capacity will be praised for this and gain eternal blessing. And insofar as we have the impediment that experience and reason does not agree with it, we must find a way of defending them from a perspective that is appropriate according to one of the methods that we have given in this chapter. For in this manner, the rabbis of blessed memory would, as lovers of the truth, agree with us and be honored by having been honored in a just and correct manner. But whoever, for whatever reason would speak falsely and hypocritically should be alienated; and let nobody deceive himself into pressing their statements by force of hand in order to make them conform to his own idea in a way that had never occurred to them. It must surely be the case that by upholding falsehood or by daubing plaster, God forbid, they would become an object of derision for those who oppose them. And flatterers, as it states in Sota "nurture anger."[225] In the final analysis, man is not God that he does not lie. To God, the Lord, should praise, honor, and greatness be attributed on account of everything that exists apart from Him—the Lord is a God of truth. For the sake of His loving-kindness, He will direct and instruct us in His truth. He will make His face shine upon us and we shall be saved.

Now I cannot conceal from the reader that having with God's help reached the end of this chapter, a book entitled *Torat ha-Olah* just came to my notice.[226] It is composed by one of the leading figures in the city of Cracow and was published in Prague in the year

221. *Mishneh Torah,* Qiddush ha-Ḥodesh VI:1. This is not an exact quotation.

222. Ibid. X:7.

223. *Guide* II, ch. 24: "I mean thereby that the deity alone fully knows the true reality, the nature, the substance, the form, the motions and the causes of the heavens" (Pines trans., 327).

224. Judah Halevi, *Kuzari* V, par. 4.

225. B. Sota 41b.

226. The work was written by Moses Isserles (d. 1572), known by his acronym Rema, who was born in Cracow. He was a great halakhic authority as well as a philosopher and kabbalist.

1569. On the title page of the book he is described as being endowed with all the seven qualities that our sages apply to a man of distinction.[227] Indeed, it has actually been reported to me that he is a saintly man of God and one of the outstanding talmudists of our generation. Perusing the tables of content, I discovered that he treated some of the statements of the rabbis of blessed memory that we discussed in this chapter, in an effort to make them consistent with what he believed to be the prevailing doctrines of our time. It was thus with feelings of great affection that I turned to see what essential matter he would inform us about. Indeed, beforehand, I noticed that he raised the problems about their statements that we mentioned, and he reinforced them most strongly. However, in his responses, I realized that he was interpreting the passages in a far-fetched manner both in respect to the contents and the language. He covered them with plaster such that one could not believe that our sages' statements could be described in the manner he suggested. And if they had intended to say that which he claims, they undoubtedly would not have used those words. One example is in chapter 2 of part 1. He writes that the meaning of their statement that the northern side is spread out like an exedra refers to the orbs of the sun that the gentile sages call "parallels,"[228] whose rotation is from east to west; and their dispersion, which in his view, is the point at which they intersect at the horizon, occurs in the south. {But in our view, it is more appropriate to understand the statement of the rabbis of blessed memory as a reference to the elevation of the North Pole above the horizon according to the notion of the oblique sphere, as we mentioned above. For if one were to posit an upright sphere, the distance between the Pole and the horizon would surely seem enclosed and submerged from the horizon and below. And when he showed it to us high and disclosed, it would be exposed as it were, and imperfect was this emendation which he deemed necessary. And in chapter 4, this leading figure} says that the meaning of the phrases "from one end of the world to the other" and "from one side of the world to the other" is from the east as far as the middle of the heavens. And in chapters 27 of section 3,[229] he says that the firmament is the earth, and the waters that are underneath it are above the heavens insofar as they [the heavens] go round the earth with us from beneath.[230] {And is not this explanation contradicted by the statement in chapter 4 of Pirqe d'Rabbi Eliezer: "Which firmament did He create on the second day? The firmament that is above the heads of the Hayyot . . . which divides between the upper and lower waters."} And he adduces certain verses and statements to uphold his position, while from the many verses that contradict his statements, he closed his eye. And he utters other such implausible propositions that can be seen in the above-mentioned passages. Then the statement of the Lord to Eliphaz and his friends crossed my mind: *Now take seven bulls and seven rams and go to My servant Job and sacrifice a burnt offering*

227. I.e., Rav, erudite scholar (*ḥakham kollel*), kabbalist, master (*aluf*), outstanding authority (*gaon*), our master, Rav (*morenu ha-Rav*). See Bonfil, *Rabbis,* p. 90.

228. 'Which the gentile sages call parallels'—this is de' Rossi's addition. He is referring to a common term "parallel circles" or simply "parallels" used by such classical authors as Pliny to denote the parallel circles of the celestial sphere.

229. *Torat ha-Olah* III, ch. 27, 94 col. a–c.

230. According to Isserles' exposition, firmament refers to both earth and heaven which were created on the waters. As the heavens rotate, the waters below the earth become the waters above the heavens.

for yourselves (42:8).[231] And I would say concerning him: "If you would offer up a burnt offering to the Lord, you should offer it up to truth." For it is certainly the best course to be silent rather than to justify the righteous with arguments that are not correct. And I could not refrain myself from putting this on record in case somebody informed about the text of this chapter would exclaim against me, "the ruler shall be the one to supply provisions."[232] And I would trust that even the Ashkenazim, a wise and knowledgeable people who are attached to him, would proclaim that my words are not false.[233] Of this I am convinced: well intentioned though he is in his attempt to substantiate at all costs the words of our sages, he has not disproved me. In any case, his intention was acceptable and his portion is with them in an eternal life of pleasantness.[234]

231. As S. Leiman pointed out, de' Rossi is actually referring to the end of the verse: *And let Job, my servant, pray for you; for to him I will show favor and treat you vilely.* In this context, de' Rossi is identifying himself with Job.

232. Cf. Gen. 42:6 where these epithets are applied to Joseph. Here they are applied to Isserles who provided the "tablecloth" (*mappah*) to Joseph Caro's "set table" (*shulḥan arukh*).

233. This statement probably reflects the inner tensions which existed between the various communities of different origin which was a feature of Italian cities such as Ferrara which had a considerably large Jewish population.

234. On Isserles' contribution to astronomy, see Ruderman, *Jewish Thought,* 69–77. De' Rossi's position seems partly confirmed by those who argue that Isserles work is simply an extension of talmudic scholarship, "an act of rabbinic piety." Ruderman, however, argues that Isserles must have been influenced by the new focus of astronomy in his own environment of Cracow.

CHAPTER TWELVE

There appears to be a contradiction in the statements of our rabbis of blessed memory when they endeavor to inform us as to the identity of the person who extirpated the Jews from Alexandria in Egypt. The solution of Don Isaac of blessed memory and our own view of the matter.

It was in the city of Alexandria in Egypt that the distinguished elders were honored. The entire event is described in the book which I translated, the *Splendor of the Elders*. The subject inspired me to raise certain problems regarding our sages' statements about the adversary and enemy who annihilated the glory of the Jews from that same city. I shall also report the opinions of others and give my own view of the truth of the matter.

In tractate Sukkah in the Palestinian Talmud it is stated:[1]

> Rabbi Juda taught: Whoever has not set eyes on the double portico of Alexandria never saw the glory of Israel. They said it was built in the style of a large basilica, colonnade within colonnade. On occasions it held twice the number of people who went out of Egypt. There were seventy gilt chairs studded with precious stones and pearls for the seventy elders. Each chair was placed on a base worth twenty-five myriad golden dinars. The sexton of the synagoge would stand on a wooden platform placed in the center. When a person would come up to read from the Torah, the official would wave a scarf and they would respond Amen. After each benediction the official would wave his scarf and they would respond Amen. The seating was not, however, haphazard, but arranged according to trades. In this way, any stranger could, on arrival, join his guild from which he would receive maintenance. Who destroyed it? Traginus [Trajan] the wicked. Rabbi Simeon ben Yoḥai taught: There are three passages in which Israel was warned not to return to Egypt: *For the Egyptians whom you see today you will never see again* (Ex. 14:13); *Moreover he shall not . . . send people back to Egypt . . . since the Lord has warned you: You must not go back that way again* (Deut. 17:16); *The Lord will send you back to Egypt in galleys by a route which I told you you should not see again* (ibid. 28:68). Three times they returned and three times they fell. Once during the days of Sennacherib as it is stated, *Those who go down to Egypt for help* (Is. 31:1), which then continues, *For the Egyptians are man, not God . . . [and both shall perish together]* (ibid. v.3). Once during the days of Jonathan ben Kareah for it is written, *The sword that you fear shall overtake you there in the land of Egypt* (Jer. 42:16). Once during the days of Trajan [Traginus] the wicked. A son was born to Traginus on the ninth of Av when the Jews were fasting [because of the destruction of the Temple]. His daughter died on Hanukkah when they were kindling the lights. His wife sent a message to him: "Instead of

1. P. Sukk. 5 (1) 55a–b.

> subjugating the barbarians, go and subjugate the Jews who are rebelling against you." He thought that the journey would take ten days, but it took him five days. He found them studying the verse in the Torah which states, *The Lord will bring a nation against you from afar, from the end of the earth* (Deut. 28:49). He asked them what they were studying and they told him this and that. He said to them: "I thought that the journey would take ten days, but it took me five days." He surrounded them with his legions and killed them. He said to their wives: "If you surrender yourselves to my legions, I will not kill you." They said to him: "That which you did to those who are above [the earth], do to those that are below [on earth]." Their blood intermingled with the blood of their husbands and the blood flowed as far as Cyprus. At that moment, the glory of Israel was extirpated and it shall not be restored until the son of David comes.

This is the version of the incident given in the Palestinian Talmud which names Trajan as responsible for the massacre for those Jews. The story is also related in the Mekhilta,[2] and in Midrash Ekhah,[3] where the birth and death of the child is mentioned, but there Tarkinus is held responsible. Similarly, the "gall" and "travail" mentioned in the verse, *All round me He has built gall and travail* (Lam. 3:5) are said to represent respectively Vespasian and Tarkinus. And the "bear" and "lion" mentioned in the verse, *He is a lurking bear to me, A lion in hiding* (ibid. v.10) are likewise said to represent Vespasian and Tarkinus respectively.[4] The same attributions are made at the beginning of Midrash Esther.[5] In fact, the Palestinian Talmud and the works of the Midrash Rabbah do concur in the majority of cases. This is because, in the words of Rashi which we quoted previously, the works of the Midrash Rabbah are actually Palestinian Aggadot. The passage about the grandeur of Alexandria in all its details is cited in the Babylonian Talmud in tractate Sukkah.[6] It also begins with the teaching of Rabbi Judah and describes the double portico. However, its conclusion is different. It ends: "Abaye said: Alexander of Macedon killed them all." Moreover, in tractate Giṭṭin, we find that the Babylonian Talmud actually recounts the story in an other manner. Expounding the verse, *The voice is the voice of Jacob, yet the hands are the hands of Esau* (Gen. 27:22), they state: "*The voice*—this is Hadrian the emperor who killed sixty plus sixty myriads in Alexandria in Egypt, which is twice the number of those who came out of Egypt." It continues: "*The voice of Jacob*—this is Vespasian the emperor who killed four hundred thousand myriads in the city of Bethar, or four myriads according to another opinion."[7] A complete account of the story of Bethar and Ben Koziba is related at length both in tractate Taʿanit in the Palestinian Talmud[8] and in Midrash Ekhah.[9] In those passages as well as in Bereshit Rabbah,[10] the responsibility for the destruction of Bethar is rightly attributed to the emperor Hadrian. They say: "Bethar* stood for fifty-two years after

2. Mekhilta d'Rabbi Ishmael, Beshalaḥ 3 (I, 213–14).
3. E.R. to Lam. 1:16.
4. Ibid. to Lam 3:5; Lam. 3:10.
5. Est.R., Proem 3.
6. B. Sukk. 51b.
7. B. Giṭṭ. 57b.
8. P. Taʿanit 4 (5) 68b–69a.
9. E.R. 2:4 to Lam. 2:2.
10. B.R. 65:21 (740).

the destruction of the Temple." Moreover, in Midrash Shir ha-Shirim, Rabbi Johanan states: "Hadrian the emperor killed one [four] thousand myriad people in Bethar."[11]

(*The place Bethar is often spelled with a double *tav* (Be*tt*ar) in the Palestinian Talmud and in Shir ha-Shirim Rabbah, and likewise in Latin it is spelled Bettar.)

Now let us put aside the story of Bethar with its contradictions, and let us return to the city of Alexandria. We are confronted with three different accounts. The wicked murderer is identified as Trajan in the Palestinian Talmud, Tarkinus in the Midrash Rabbah texts, and Alexander of Macedon in tractate Sukkah in the Babylonian Talmud, while in tractate Giṭṭin, they change their opinion, and the name of Hadrian is proffered. Now we have undertaken to investigate the truth of all this, although we are not really concerned with the actual event, for whatever happened, happened.[12] Rather, our aim is to ensure that our rabbis are not found to be giving contradictory accounts of well-known events. So, in the first place, I should like to disclose to you, reader, that the source of the *baraita* cited in the name of Rabbi Judah, "Anyone who did not set eyes . . ." is in the last chapter of tractate Sukkah in the Tosefta.[13] The passage begins, "Rabbi Judah said: Whoever did not set eyes on the double portico of Alexandria" and ends "from which he would receive maintenance." There is no reference to the person who destroyed it, neither to Trajan nor to Alexander. Apparently, the question about who destroyed the city did not form part of the original statement of Rabbi Judah but was an anonymous addition to the talmudic text both in the Palestinian and Babylonian Talmuds.

Furthermore, there is a problem about the correct reading of the name Traginus, for since it is unvocalized it can be read in different ways. Particularly problematic is the passage which is close to the beginning of Midrash Esther. It states: "I did not loathe them in the days of Tarquinius."[14] We must therefore make clear that the reference to Tarquinius is completely untenable and that the reading of the Midrash is unquestionably erroneous. This name is applied by all gentile historians to two Roman kings alone: Tarquinius Priscus, i.e., the elder, who lived before the destruction of the [first] Temple, and Tarquinius Superbus (i.e., the insolent, the proud), who was third in succession after the other Tarquinius and lived during the Babylonian exile. Yet in the following pages it will become clear that the city of Alexandria only came into being a long time after the construction of the second Temple. The reader of the last two treatises of Yedidyah the Alexandrian, *Against Flaccus* and *On the Embassy to Gaius,* will find descriptions of the many calamities and troubles which happened to the Jews during his lifetime. This was due to the levies and per capita taxes which were collected by the Roman governor and because the emperor [i.e., Gaius Caligula] wanted to erect his statue in the holy places. From those descriptions it emerges that at that time, which

11. S.S.R. to S.S. 2:17.

12. 'Whatever happened, happened.' This is a talmudic expression which is used in various ways. Here, de' Rossi is using the expression according to its meaning in B. Yoma 5b that antiquarian study has no implication or practical significance for the present.

13. T. Sukk. 4:6.

14. Est.R., Proem 4.

was slightly before the destruction of the second Temple, there were more than one million Jewish inhabitants in Alexandria, and they had their own law courts and innumerable study houses. This means that it is incorrect to deduce that there is an allusion to any Tarquinius in the Palestinian Talmud or Midrash Rabbah texts. In their commentary to the passage in tractate Giṭṭin, the Tosafists show awareness of the contradiction implicit in the Babylonian Talmud. They write: "In tractate Sukkah they say that Alexander of Macedon destroyed it; perhaps we should assume that Alexandria was resettled a second time."

Now if, as we said in chapter 2, we are to believe the incidental statements of the gentile sages when they have no vested interests in the subject, it would certainly appear that Abaye's statement (granted that this was what he actually said), and the Tosafists' solution have no basis whatsoever. In fact, it was Alexander of Macedon who laid the foundations of Alexandria which had not existed previously, and he called it by his name. He also populated it with a mixed multitude from many countries in order to accelerate its settlement and enhance its prestige. It stands to reason therefore that he could hardly have been the cause of its destruction. All this is made clear by Plutarch in his *Life of Alexander* (par. 56):[15] Alexander selected a wide plain, set all the thorns and brambles on the site on fire, and built a great city which he called Alexandria after his own name. In his long work on Alexander of Macedon, Curtius also writes in book 4 that he was the founder and builder of Alexandria and gave it his own name.[16] The ancient Greek historian Arrian, whom we mentioned above in chapter 10, tells the same story at the beginning of book 3.[17] In the course of his discourse on people who frequent magicians, Valerius Maximus also relates the event treated by the other three writers.[18] He says that Alexander of Macedon ordered Demetrius [Dinocrates], an outstanding architect, to draw him a plan of the site of the city. For this purpose, the architect made clay mingled with rice flour. It so happened that swarms of birds were aroused from the nearby pools and they came and devoured all the clay. The report of this incident astounded Alexander, but his magicians interpreted it as a good omen, auguring the settlement of the city by many peoples who would have more than enough for their needs. In book 8 of the first of the *Decades,* the famous historian Livy writes about the consuls who governed Rome in the days of Lucius Aemilius in the time of the second Temple, 430 years after the foundation of Rome [326 B.C.E.]. He writes: "According to a report transmitted directly from our ancestors, Alexandria in Egypt was founded in the year of his [i.e., Lucius Aemilius] consulate."[19] As you shall be shown in subsequent chapters (24 and 42), this was the time when Alexander was in power. And even the compiler of the Latin lexicon gives a lengthy entry for Alexandria, explaining that the city was founded by Alexander of Macedon and

15. Plutarch, *Graecorum . . . Vitae, Alexander,* 36. De' Rossi used the Paris, 1558 edition of the *Vitae* which has numbered paragraphs. De' Rossi corrects the number of the paragraph in B to 56 (and not 137 as printed).

16. Curtius Rufus, *De rebus gestis,* bk. 4, VIII.

17. Arrian, *De rebus gestis* (*Anabasis*), bk. III, 1, 5.

18. Valerius Maximus, *Factorum . . . memorabilium libri,* 1, IV, 7.

19. Titus Livius, *Decades* (VIII, 24, 1).

adduces the writer Justin as a witness to this fact.[20] I actually saw the relevant passage at the beginning of chapter 2 and in other parts of his work.[21] Then there is Contractus who wrote: "Alexander of Macedon built Alexandria in Egypt in the seventh year of his reign."[22] Finally, you should heed the words of the king as they are given by Plutarch in the second part of his *Moralia* in the chapter on government.[23] He writes that when Caesar Augustus captured Alexandria, he entered the city holding the hand of one of his friends, who was a native Alexandrian. The leaders of the people entreated him not to make them captives of the army. He replied: "I willing accede to your entreaties for the sake of this great city, out of respect for the king Alexander of Macedon, its founder, and as a token of my friendship for this man who is one of its inhabitants."

So here we have seven shepherds and eight princely men[24] who do not speak falsely in such matters. They testify to the fact that Alexander of Macedon obviously did not destroy the city nor even overhaul its streets in order to populate it. But rather, he brought it into existence and founded it. Now it is obvious that when the Palestinian Talmud and the Tosafists referred to its destruction, they were not referring to the destruction of the city, but merely to the slaughter of its Jewish inhabitants. Nevertheless, it would still be rather difficult for you to claim that in the six years he reigned after establishing the city, he found an excuse for massacring the Jews who had come to settle there. Thus Abaye's words "and they were all killed" can easily be proved to be untenable. In fact, the contrary was the case. For we know how much Alexander of Macedon esteemed and showed favor to the Jerusalemite Jews when he was leaving Jerusalem to march against Darius during the high priesthood of Jaddua. And at the request of the high priest Jaddua, he also granted many favors to all the other Jews of his empire. This is described by our rabbis of blessed memory in tractate Yoma[25] and at the end of Shemini Rabbah[26] and by the Hebrew[27] and Roman[28] Josephus. And in the second book about our wars, Josephus states that he bestowed greater honors and respect on the Jewish inhabitants of Alexandria than on the rest of the Greek population of the city.[29] Thus the sage Don Isaac [Abravanel], who rightly believed that Alexander of Macedon laid the foundation stone of Alexandria and that one could not find a means of claiming that he had done any harm to the Jews, decided that the word "Macedon" in Abaye's statement was a scribal error and had been interpolated into the

20. Calepino, *Dictionarium,* s.v. Alexandria.

21. This is a reference to Justin's epitome of the history of Trogus Pompeius, the Roman historian who lived in the time of Augustus.

22. Hermannus Contractus, *Chronicon,* 173r.

23. Plutarch, *Moralia,* "Praecepta gerendae reipublicae," 814d. De' Rossi refers to the second part of the *Moralia.* It would therefore appear that he was consulting the Italian translation of Giovanni Tarchagnota entitled *Alcuni opusculetti de le cose morali,* in which this section ("Politica o de le cose civili") is placed as the second part of the *Moralia.* The passage is 24v.

24. Cf. Micah 5:4.

25. B. Yoma 69a.

26. V.R. 13:5 (294).

27. *Josippon,* bk. 1, ch. 5 (31).

28. *Ant.* XI:329.

29. *Bellum* II:488. He says that they were given equal rights with the Greek population.

text.[30] Supporting his argument with a statement from the end of *Sefer ha-Qabbalah* by Rabad [Abraham ibn Daud] of blessed memory,[31] he came to the conclusion that Abaye was referring to Alexander [Severus], the twenty-fourth emperor of Rome. He thought that in this way he could correct all the corruptions contained in the statements of our sages which relate to this subject. He was faced with the problem of the identification of No Amon with Alexandria in Jonathan ben Uzziel's translation [Targum] of Jeremiah's prophecy about Egypt, *Behold I will punish Amon of No and Pharaoh of Egypt* (46:25), of Ezekiel's prophecy, *And I will execute judgment on No* (30:14), and of Nahum's prophecy, *Are you better than No Amon* (3:8). Our sages of blessed memory make the same identification at the beginning of Bereshit Rabbah.[32] And similarly, at the end of the Midrash Rabbah they explain the verse, *And when they shall be afraid of that which is high* (Eccl. 12:5) in connection with Nebuchadnezzar who shook arrows in the name of Alexandria but without success.[33] Rashi,[34] Kimḥi,[35] as well as the philosopher ibn Tibbon in his *Ketav ha-Moreh*[36] follows this interpretation which seemed to imply that Alexandria had already been built in the time of the prophets of the first Temple period. Don Isaac, who relied on the well-known facts which I mentioned before, dissented from their view. His explanation of No Amon appears to agree with that of ibn Ezra, namely, that it was another large Egyptian city.[37] He states that from childhood, their monarchs were brought up in that city which was therefore called Amon, a name derived from the word *omen* as in the verse, *And he brought up [omen] Esther* (Est. 2:7). Rashi of blessed memory used the same wording which he must have derived from a Midrash when he writes, "It was a city in which monarchs are raised."[38] However, I do not know what purpose was served by the sage Don Isaac's emendation of the text when he deleted the word "Macedon." How could a man of his knowledge not realize that these words of his were even more unreasonable and untenable than that which was actually written in the text? The fact is that the passage in the Tosefta and the two Talmuds about the glory of Israel in Alexandria was a *baraita* taught in the name of Rabbi Judah. He was lamenting the former times which had been happier for Jews than his own time. The elders had said that the Alexandrian synagogue was like a large basilica, which is the Greek word for a royal palace. Both Rabbi Judah as well as Rabbi Simeon bar Yoḥai who assented to his view were, as we know, Tannaim of the generation of Rabbi Jose and Rabbi Meir and their associates, a generation after Rabbi Aqiva

30. Abravanel, Introduction to *Perush al Melakhim* (425 col. a).

31. This is a reference to the second part of *Sefer ha-Qabbalah* entitled "Zikhron Divre Romi" (no pagination). There is a short reference to the rule of Alexander (Severus).

32. B.R. 1 (1): "*Are you better than No Amon?* which is translated: 'Are you better than Alexandria the Great?' "

33. Q.R. to Eccl. 12:7. Nebuchadnezzar was afraid of God when he set out to destroy Jerusalem and was only successful in *shaking the arrows to and fro* (Ezk. 21:26) when he did so in the name of Jerusalem.

34. Rashi to Nahum 3:8.

35. David Kimḥi to Nahum 3:8.

36. This appears to be a reference to Samuel ibn Tibbon's Hebrew translation of Maimonides' *Guide.* I have been unable to find this use of No Amon, although there are many letters addressed to Maimonides in which No Amon is used as a designation of Alexandria. See e.g., J. Blau's edition of Maimonides' *Teshuvot* (vol. 1, 143; vol. 2. 412).

37. Ibn Ezra to Nahum 3:8.

38. Rashi to Nahum 3:8. The citation is in Aramaic.

and a generation before our holy Rabbi [Judah ha-Nasi]. Now according to our sages of blessed memory, Rabbi was born on the day on which Rabbi Aqiva died.[39] And yet there is no doubt that the chronographers of those times referred to the days when those Tannaim were in office, and thus Rabbi Judah and Rabbi Simeon would be listed in the period between Rabbi Aqiba and Rabbi. We know that Rabbi who, according to Raba,[40] compiled the Mishnah, lived in the time of Antoninus, that is Antoninus Pius as he was called by the gentiles who was the sixteenth emperor. There is a consensus of opinion as to the date of Rabbi's compilation of the Mishnah: it could not have been later than the date given by Rav Sherira Gaon of blessed memory in his *Epistle* to the holy community of Kairwan. With God's help, favorable mention will be made of his *Epistle* in these chapters.[41] His view also concurs with that of the sage in the *Kuzari,* namely, that the *terminus ad quem* for Rabbi's compilation was the year 530 according to the Seleucid era, which is 150 years after the destruction of the Temple [220 C.E.].[42] Following Don Isaac's theory, one is confronted with the untenable position that Abaye was explaining that those two Tannaim, Rabbi Judah and Rabbi Simeon, were referring to the time of [Severus] Alexander, the twenty-fourth Roman emperor who was ninth in succession after Antoninus and fourteenth in succession after Titus. In other words, Alexander was in office more than 170 years after the destruction of the Temple, long after the death of the Tannaim who were the spokesmen in the *baraita* under discussion. All this is historically true and is attested in the chronologies of the Roman emperors. Thus, while according to the reading of the text, Abaye missed the mark by antedating the event, Don Isaac's conjectural emendation overstepped the mark by postdating it. Besides all this, the books are open for anyone who cares to look. Go and examine the histories of the wise gentiles. Special attention should be given to book 8 of *On the Deeds of the Romans* by the ancient historian Eutropius[43] and to chapter 19 of Platina's lengthy work on the lives of the popes and emperors.[44] In the description of the power and might of Alexander the twenty-fourth emperor, there is only reference to hostilities against one Persian king and that was not conducted with military force. But nothing is related regarding the Jews, the city of Alexandria, or the realm of Egypt.

Now I feel that there is a resolution to some of these problems whereby the statements in the Palestinian Talmud and the Midrash Rabbah texts can actually be ratified and upheld. For we must first know the correct reading of the name of the emperor to whom they referred when they said that Jewish inhabitants of Alexandria were massacred by Traginus or Tarkinus. It must be read as Trajan who was the fourteenth emperor and the uncle of Hadrian, his successor to the imperial throne. Messia's

39. B. Qidd. 72b; Q.R. to Eccl. 1:5.

40. B. Yev. 64b. The same passage is cited by Sherira Gaon.

41. *Iggeret* (78): "And in the time of Rabbi, Rav went down to Babylon, in the year 530 according to the Seleucid era."

42. *Kuzari* III, par. 67.

43. This is a reference to Eutropius (fourth century), *Breviarium ab urbe condita libri* X, bk. 8 (2), 23 (56). The title of the work appears in some sixteenth-century editions (e.g., Paris, 1539) as *De Gestis Romanorum libri decem* which would conform to de' Rossi's designation of the book.

44. Bartolomeo de' Sacchi (Platina), *De vitis.* There were various Latin and Italian editions of the work. I have consulted the 1913 reprint of the 1734 edition of L. Muratori published in the series *Rerum Italicarum Scriptores.* The reference to the emperor Alexander occurs in the life of Pope Urban (35–36).

[Mexía's] *History of All the Emperors,* which was recently published in Spanish,[45] gives an explicit description of the rebellion of the Jewish inhabitants of Alexandria against the Roman government. More than two hundred thousand Jews were killed by the Roman armies and troops. Trajan the emperor had despatched a large army against them which slaughtered all Jews it could find. All writers are agreed that this was the greatest massacre in history. Similarly, you should read the two writers mentioned before, Eutropius (book 1)[46] and Platina (chapter 6),[47] as well as the more detailed account in the chapter on Emperor Trajan in book 7 of Orosius.[48] You will notice that although they do not actually refer to the Jews by name, they give a general account of his battles and the extensive devastation he wrought in many places, particularly in the Egyptian city of Alexandria. What sage is there who does not realize that he trod the Jews underfoot and ground them to dust, particularly in view of the fact that this evidence concurs with the statements of our sages and the other writer whom we recorded? Now anyone who knows the function of the letter *gimel,* as used in the recording of the name in the Palestinian Talmud, and the function of the *kaf* as used in the Midrash Rabbah texts, will realize that they were unquestionably referring to the Latin name Traianus. Don Isaac similarly understood the passage in the Palestinian Talmud as referring to Trajan, the fourteenth emperor, an interpretation which was also derived from his reading of the final section of Rabad's *Sefer ha-Qabbalah.*[49] We could also retain Abaye's statement by adopting Don Isaac's emendation and deleting "Macedon" and letting it be a reference to another Alexander. But on no account could it be a reference to the twenty-fourth emperor who, as was said, lived about one hundred years after the author of the *baraita.* It could only have been a reference to Alexander, the general of the Roman army, who was procurator of Alexandria in Egypt during the reign of the emperor Nero before the destruction of the Temple. The incident is clearly described in book 2 of Josephus's *Wars.*[50] He writes that all the Jewish inhabitants of Alexandria lived in one quarter of the city. One day, a fierce quarrel broke out between the Jews and the Greek community in Alexandria. (Ever since the exodus from Egypt, anybody who identified themselves with Egypt became hostile towards us.) The Roman general, who served there as viceroy and procurator, was called Alexander, as we said. In reasonable terms, he ordered the Jews to withdraw and to put down their arms for the sake of peace; otherwise, it could appear that they were inciting rebellion against the Roman government. But they rebelled and disregarding his advice, made trouble.[51] He then turned hostile towards them. With a contingent of

45. This is the *Historia imperial y Cesarea en la qual en suma se contiene las vidas y vechos e lodos los Cesares Emperadores de Roma.* Seville, 1547. It is quite likely that de' Rossi read one of the Italian translations of the work, particularly since his translation of the title would concur with the Italian translation, *Le vite di tutti gl'imperadori composte dal nobile cavaliere Pietro Messia.* In the Italian translation of Lodovico Dolce, the passage under discussion (190) reads: "dove trovarono Giudei fecero di essi generale uccisione e affirmano gli scrittori, che questo fu la maggior giustizia e gastigo che giamai fosse fatto al mondo."

46. The reference should be to bk. 10.

47. Platina, *De vitis,* 19–20.

48. Orosius, *Adversus paganos,* bk. VII, ch. 12, 474 (bk. VII, 12, 6). He does refer to the Jews. "In Alexandria autem commisso praelio, victi et attriti sunt Iudaei."

49. I.e., the *Zikhron Divre Romi.*

50. *Bellum* II:487–98.

51. 'They rebelled . . . trouble,' cf. Is. 63:10.

Greek inhabitants of the city, he surrounded them with his legions and slaughtered more than fifty thousand men. Blood gushed forth like overflowing rivers and they burnt down their houses and appropriated and plundered all their possessions. The truth is that the number of the victims was negligible in respect to the large numbers of Jews who, according to the sages of blessed memory and Yedidyah the Alexandrian, were living there. And one can believe that over the course of time, the community as far as was possible regained its former strength as was stated by the Tosafists. It thus makes sense that in the time of Trajan the emperor, subsequent to Alexander's assault, the utter annihilation[52] which we mentioned took place. It is to this event that the closing words of the passage in the Palestinian Talmud refer. For it states: "At that moment the glory of Israel was extirpated and it shall not be restored until the son of David comes." But these words were not appropriate for the Babylonian Talmud and Abaye because there the allusion is only to the first stages of the destruction, and in any case, the beginning as "the philosopher" [Aristotle] states in the *Ethics* is like half of the whole.[53] But their final end only came in the time of the emperor Trajan after the destruction of the Temple, while the destruction of Bethar, which we shall presently discuss, only came about in the time of his nephew Hadrian. In fact, both the Palestinian and Babylonian Talmuds mention that the inhabitants of Alexandria were punished for their transgression of the commandment, *For whereas you have seen the Egyptians today, you shall see them again no more* (Ex. 14:13). For it is certainly forbidden to live in Egypt. This is what Ritba [Yom Tov ben Abraham] wrote on the basis of the Sifre quoted in tractate Yoma.[54] And according to Midrash Ekhah, the inhabitants of Bethar were punished because they celebrated the fall of Jerusalem by lighting lamps. This was because in the time of their prosperity, they [i.e., the Jerusalemites] lorded over them; but the fact is *he that is glad over calamity shall not go unpunished* (Pr. 17:5).[55] And another reason for the destruction is given both in Midrash Ekhah and the Palestinian Talmud. They say that it was because they used to play with a ball on the Sabbath.[56] While there is no doubt that such statements would be made on God's behalf concerning other such serious transgressions, they also demonstrate our rabbis' outstandingly clever way of dissuading Jews from committing even these kind of sins which are not taken seriously. This is illustrated by their statement that one transgression is sufficient in itself to raze a great city to its foundations. We shall elucidate this matter further in chapter 20.

Now I hold the Tosafists dear to my heart and am going to turn my discussion in

52. This is an allusion to Is. 10:22, *Even if your people, O Israel, should be as the sands of the sea only a remnant of it shall return. Destruction is decreed, retribution comes like a flood.*

53. De' Rossi quotes the popular saying which appears in Plato and other classical authors. The passage from *Nicomachean Ethics* I, 1098b7 which is a play on the maxim reads: "The beginning is more than half the whole."

54. *Ḥiddushe ha-Ritba* (cols. 236–37). De' Rossi must have seen a manuscript of the work. The Ritba discusses the prohibition on living in Egypt and states that it only applies to the time when all Israel is living in the land of Israel or for those who willingly leave the land of Israel to live in Egypt.

55. E.R. to Lam. 2:2. The Midrash describes how the Jerusalemites exploited the people of Bethar who then rejoiced at Jerusalem's downfall. The moral of the story is to demonstrate that *Schadenfreude* even in this situation is not to be encouraged.

56. Ibid.

their favor. For I cannot refrain from admitting that there is a possibility of upholding their statement that there was some kind of settlement on the site of Alexandria in Egypt in remote antiquity. You will then come to understand that they were illuminated by some special intuition. You should take into consideration the following passage I discovered in the commentary of the Christian Annius to the *Synonyms* by Xenophon the Greek.[57] Speaking of four floods that occurred in specific places after the universal deluge he writes: "The fifth flood was that of Faros; namely, the site on which Alexander of Macedon built Alexandria in Egypt was in antiquity the island of Faros which had been populated by a foreign people who had been sent there by Pharaoh. At about the time of the destruction of Troy, it was inundated by water and sank, just as the priest Proteus had predicted." This statement yields confirmation of what we said. For during the period from the destruction of Troy, which occurred in the time of David, until Alexander of Macedon, that site lay desolate. Thus one cannot claim that it was the place called No Amon by Jeremiah. The statement also slightly vindicates the Tosafists who said that it was populated before the time of Alexander of Macedon. But as far as our own inquiry is concerned, that settlement happened too far back in remote antiquity to have any significance. And I tried to make it fit the statement in tractate Giṭṭin, but was unsuccessful. Thus it seems that we have no alternative but to believe that it was undoubtedly a scribal error, particularly since another examination on the subject will necessarily bring us to the same conclusion. I refer to the statement about Vespasian in Bethar which is completely untenable. For we have the explicit testimony of historians and specifically Josephus (towards the end of book 6) and the author of the *Lives of the Emperors* that within a few days of beginning the assault on Jerusalem, Vespasian was recalled to Rome to be enthroned as emperor. He then entrusted the siege to his eldest son Titus and the duration of the reigns of both men only lasted about twelve years. And in tractate Taʿanit in both the Palestinian and Babylonian Talmuds it is affirmed that fifty-two years elapsed after the destruction of the Temple before the war against Bethar occurred, and that would synchronize exactly with the dates of Hadrian who was unquestionably responsible for the destruction of Bethar. He also put Ben Koziba to death. This is stated in the rabbinic passages quoted above, and the same account is given by many historians, and specifically Platina[58] and Orosius.[59] In his *History,* Eusebius also states that Ben Koziba's name was originally Bar Kochba.[60] This statement bears affinity to the way the rabbis of blessed memory expound the verse, *A star rises from Jacob, a scepter comes forth from Israel* (Num. 24:17) in Ekhah Rabbati[61] and in the Palestinian Talmud.[62] But in the war of Hadrian he turned out to be a pretender, a liar [*akhzav*], as it were, and so they called him Ben Koziba [son of a lie]. A

57. This is a reference to ps. Xenophon, *De Aequivocis,* which was one of Annius of Viterbo's forgeries. The passage reads (31) "Ultima vero quae notatur ab autoribus fuit Pharaonica i. Alexandrina Aegypti. Ubi enim nunc Alexandria a magno Alexandro condita, olim erant insula Pharon, habitata coloniis Pharaonicis, ubi inundatio fuit tempore vatis Protei sacerdotis."

58. Platina, *De vitis,* 21. According to Platina, Bar Kokhba persecuted Christians before being killed by Hadrian.

59. Orosius, *Adversus paganos,* bk. VII, 13, ch. 4.

60. Eusebius, *Hist. eccl.* bk. 4, ch. 6 (*P.G.* XX, col. 311–12).

61. E.R. to Lam. 2:2.

62. P. Taʿanit 4 (5) 68d.

clear description of all these events is also to be found in the life of Hadrian in the book *Lives of all the Caesars.* In my opinion, the rabbis of blessed memory were alluding to this at the end of tractate Sota in the Gemara and the Tosefta[63] when they said, "In the last war they decreed." For after the utter annihilation which took place in his day, the Jews did not hold their heads high[64] nor take up arms against any nation.

Now we had no alternative but to dismiss the last clause in the statement in tractate Giṭṭin about "Vespasian who killed in Bethar" as corrupt. We should therefore adopt talmudic methods and say, "This is a corrupt statement and cannot be used as a basis for argument." In fact, even the first clause which speaks of Hadrian killing in Alexandria in Egypt is totally erroneous. And with regard to this passage, we should not pay attention to the Tosafist whose text was unquestionably faulty, particularly since the texts of the Palestinian Talmud and the Midrash Rabbah concur with what we have said. There is also a passage in the Tanḥuma which is cited by the compiler of the *Arukh* under the entry for *da*ʿ. It reads: "Rabban Simeon ben Yoḥai said: When Hadrian entered the Temple, and was blaspheming and reviling. . . ."[65] And in Devarim Rabbah it states: "Rabbi Tanḥuma said: What is the meaning of the expression, *A time for throwing stones* (Eccl. 3:5)? It refers to the time when Hadrian would come up and shatter the stones of the Temple."[66] It might occur to one that this is a scribal error since the Temple had already been destroyed in the time of Titus, and Hadrian was the fourth emperor in succession after Titus. Nevertheless, I have some means of justifying these statements. All historians who describe the life of Hadrian mention that he rebuilt Jerusalem and called it Aelia after his own name.[67] He then expelled the Jews from the city, promulgating an edict that any Jew who set foot in the city would be put to death. It is therefore possible that he did come into the site of the Temple which had been destroyed in the past, blasphemed as described and ordered them to take some of the stacks of demolished stones and to use them for some other purpose. But I did see a passage in the Tanḥuma commenting on the verse, *See, I begin by placing Sihon and his land at your disposal* (Deut. 2:31) which states: "When Hadrian the wicked subjugated Jerusalem, he boasted and said, 'I have subjugated the city by my own power.' Rabban Johanan ben Zakkai said to him . . ."[68] Study the passage. We must necessarily conclude that it is erroneous. The Roman subjugation of Jerusalem was perpetrated by Titus, and according to the account in Ekhah Rabbati, it would appear that it was with Vespasian that Rabban Yohanan ben Zakkai held his discussions.[69] Now having unraveled this story for you, I cannot refrain from informing you, intelligent reader, that I had already got some gratification from Don Isaac's comment on the verse in Zechariah, *And Jerusalem shall continue on its site in Jerusalem* (12:6). He said that Hadrian completely rebuilt the city of Jerusalem some miles away from its original site, and for

63. This passage is also in the Mishnah Sota 9:14 (B. Sota 49b) and comes after a reference to the wars of Vespasian and Titus: "In the last war they decreed that a bride should not go out in a palanquin."
64. 'Hold . . . high,' cf. Ps. 110:7.
65. Tanḥuma, 'pequde' 4 (Buber, 3).
66. D.R. 3:13.
67. The building of Aelia Capitolina by Hadrian has been the subject of much scholarly investigation. See G. Alon, *The Jews,* 435–52.
68. Tanḥuma, Devarim (Buber, 7). See "Voice of God," n. 47.
69. E.R. to Lam. 1:5.

this reason the promise is given that she would in the future be restored to the real site of Jerusalem.[70] This gains greater plausibility in the light of the verse in 2 Chronicles (3:1), *Then Solomon began to build the House of the Lord in Jerusalem on Mount Moriah.* I have been told that the present site of Mount Moriah is about five miles away from Jerusalem. This signifies that we should not deprive ourselves of all satisfaction[71] given that our holy site has not been transformed into a house of prayer for any other people, as our rabbis of blessed memory say in their Midrash on the verse, *I will make the land desolate so that your enemies who settle in it shall be appalled by it* (Lev. 26:32).[72] Yet on due consideration, I realize that this is remote from the truth. There are two reasons. First, the gentile historians, whose evidence he cites for the life of Hadrian and restoration of Jerusalem, simply state that he destroyed it and then enlarged it. In their commentaries to the end of the first and fourth Gospels, the Christian scholars also write that they enlarged it to the north to ensure that the cemeteries which had been an arrow's shot outside the city came within the walls.[73] And when Rambam says that the cemeteries were about six miles outside the city, he puts his view as conjectural when he says "it seems to me."[74] Study the passage.

The second reason is derived from Rabbi Eliezer's statement: "On seeing Jerusalem, one is obliged to rend one's garment and to make another rent on seeing [the site of] the Temple."[75] He was probably speaking of the Jerusalem known in his own time and of the site of the Temple as identified throughout the centuries. This was what Ramban did on arrival in the city as is made clear in the appendix printed at the end of his commentary on the Torah.[76] For he would have given indications or spoken of the original Jerusalem or something of that kind had he been referring to the Jerusalem and Temple in which even in his own time, as nowadays, no Arab would pitch his tent.[77] Thus it is my opinion that this statement of Don Isaac has no foundation and that the verses under discussion should be explained according to the manner of our other commentators.

But let us resume our discussion of Alexandria. There is further reliable proof that

70. Abravanel to Zechariah 12:6 (239 col. a).

71. Play on *Satisfaction shall be hidden from My eyes* (Hosea 13:14).

72. Sifra, *beḥuqotai* 1 (110 col. c). They interpret the verse to signify that on finding the land desolate without inhabitants, the enemy would therefore abandon it.

73. De' Rossi is referring to the site of Golgotha which has been a question of discussion among modern archaeologists. See, e.g., C. Coüasnon, *The Church.* The site of Golgotha could have already been inside the walls from the time of Herod Agrippa who built a third outer wall on the northern side of the city. I do not know to which commentators de' Rossi is referring, although medieval Christian pilgrims do make the same assertion. Jacques of Vitry (1226), e.g., states that when Hadrian rebuilt Jerusalem and enlarged it, he enclosed Golgotha and the Holy Sepulchre which had previously been outside the walls. See C. W. Wilson, *Golgotha,* 104.

74. De' Rossi is referring to and implicitly attacking Abravanel who based his argument on this quotation from *Mishneh Torah,* Sanhedrin 12:3: "The place of execution was outside the court. . . . It seems to me that it was approximately six miles from the court."

75. B. M.Q. 26a.

76. This is a reference to Nahmanides' poetic prayer which he wrote on his arrival in Jerusalem in 1267 which was published at the end of his *Perush al ha-Torah* in the edition Rome, 1490, and in subsequent editions. He refers to rending his garment the two statutory times: "Near the city, in front of the gate, I rent my clothes over her, and when I came in sight of the great and sacred Temple . . . we then rent our garments a second time" (vol. 1, 429).

77. 'No Arab would pitch his tent,' cf. Is. 13:20.

Hadrian did not murder its Jews, but not out of kindness on his part. Rather they had already been totally obliterated in the previous disasters of the time of Alexander, Nero's captain, and subsequently in Trajan's day. In his account of the papacy of Sixtus the eighth pope, the writer Platina, who had in the previous chapter described Hadrian's destruction of Bethar and murder of Ben Koziba, then praises him for some of his fine qualities and describes how he built Jerusalem at his own expense as was said, and also that he built Alexandria in Egypt which had been destroyed by the Romans.[78] About its Jews, however, he has nothing good or bad to say, for they had perished for their sins in days gone by. And in the words of the Palestinian Talmud quoted before, their glory will be held back and not reach its summit until the hope of Israel, the Lord, will speedily cause the sprout of David to blossom forth.

I have dealt with this subject so far to the best of my limited knowledge. Subsequently I was happy to come across a passage in Midrash Tehillim on the verse, *The enemy is no more* (Ps. 9:7) which reads: "Constantine built Constantinople, Antiochus built Antiochia, Alexander built Alexandria, Seleucus built Seleucia (and another version) Siculus built Sicily."[79] One must necessarily conclude that different Midrashim treat the subject of Alexandria in different ways. Yet while we are ready to admit that certain stories came to the notice of our sages in a somewhat corrupt state, and that was how they then transmitted them to us, this should not detract at all from their honor. We shall speak of this again in subsequent chapters. Now the greater part of this chapter has been devoted to inconsequential investigations which one could dismiss by saying "what happened, happened" or on the grounds that it has no bearing on any law or precept. Nevertheless, the beautiful soul[80] yearns to know the truth of every matter and the way of man in the world even when such issues are not directly relevant to it. There is, at any rate, the advantage that the texts cited by us are not fraudulent but tell the truth and are authentic documents.[81]

78. Platina, *De vitis,* 22.

79. Mid. Teh. to Ps. 9:7.

80. De' Rossi uses the expression 'beautiful soul' in its Neoplatonic sense. (The expression does occur in M. Ḥull. 4:7, but in a euphemistic meaning of one whose appetite is robust.

81. This apologetic conclusion to the chapter is, as de' Rossi himself insinuates, a kind of leitmotiv which runs throughout the book. Conscious of his challenging stance on rabbinic knowledge of history, he must necessarily separate his investigations from the domain of practical *halakhah,* while at the same time justify his endeavor to set the historical record right.

CHAPTER THIRTEEN

As to how one can account for the extraordinarily large numbers of people, noted by our rabbis, who perished or were exiled from Jerusalem, Alexandria, and Bethar since these figures do not include the tribe of Judah and Benjamin. And whether it is plausible that the ten tribes returned in the time of Josiah.

THE stories related in the preceding chapter opened our eyes to an amazing fact. In our estimation every noble-minded person would wish to know how such a thing can be entertained on rational grounds. It concerns the well-known fact that the ten tribes were exiled from Samaria to Halah and Habor at the time of the rule of Hoshea.[1] This is evident from the account in the books of 2 Kings (17:6) and 1 Chronicles (5:26).[2] One hundred and thirty-three years later, in the time of Zedekiah, Judah was exiled to Babylon. According to the accounts in 1 Ezra (2:64)[3] and Nehemiah (7:66), the Jews who returned with Zerubbabel and Jeshua after the seventy years of the Babylonian exile only numbered forty-two thousand [42,360]. For the moment we will disregard the problem which was also raised by the author of Seder Olam (ch. 29) that the individual figures given do not add up to the total[4] and that in the book of Ezra itself there is a surprising discrepancy between the individual figures which really needs to be resolved. The commentators Rashi and ibn Ezra raised this problem and if God so wills it, we may perhaps speak about it on another occasion.

Furthermore, when Ezra came up to Jerusalem he brought with him not more than one thousand and six hundred persons. This fact is made evident in 1 Ezra (ch. 8). And in tractate Qiddushin, our rabbis say that the "pure sifted flour" remained in Babylon.[5] Moreover, in his introduction to the book of Kings, the wise Don Isaac [Abravanel] wrote that many Jews who were exiled to Egypt at the time of the destruction of the first Temple remained there until Alexander built Alexandria. They then went and made their homes in Alexandria, became numerous and sufficiently comfortable there that they did not think of transferring themselves to Jerusalem even though it was the

1. There is a large bibliography on the subject of the lost ten tribes. For a general survey of the subject, see A. Neubauer, "Where Are the Ten Tribes?" See also, D. Ruderman's discussion of Abraham Farissol's treatment of the ten tribes in his *Iggeret Orḥot Olam* in *The World,* ch. 11.

2. The book of Chronicles refers to the deportation of the Reubenites, Gadites, and the half-tribe of Manasseh, whereas Kings simply refers to the deportation of the Israelites.

3. Here (and elsewhere in the book, depending on the context) de' Rossi uses the non-Massoretic designation for the book of Ezra.

4. Seder Olam (131).

5. B. Qidd. 69b. The idea is that Ezra intentionally left the people of pure stock who would certainly not assimilate with the Babylonians and went up with those of inferior rank.

site of the Temple and the place where the greater part of the people lived. Many of the Jews of Amon, Moab, and the Greek lands acted in the same manner. So too, the Jews of the entire Sephardic diaspora were unwilling to leave their well-decked homes in order to go up to the Holy Land.[6] Perhaps this was their sin and the sin of all Jews who settle on their lees. For they thereby showed contempt for the word of the Holy One of Israel when He stretched out His hands towards them by means of His three servants, the latter prophets,[7] to bring them peace and inheritance. For He promised them that if they magnified the glory of the Temple, He, the blessed Lord, would also magnify it and magnify them, and they would settle in the land for eternity and in security. But they refused to return and as a consequence, the reverse happened. Surely it must have been with regard to the promises of future happiness that Zechariah said, *If only you will listen to the voice of the Lord your God* (6:15). In other words, although the blessed Lord is patient, He was not indulgent and therefore decreed that they would be uprooted from the land in which they had installed themselves.

In any case, let us resume the subject of the chapter. For we cannot fail to see that although it was said that subsequently in the course of time, many would be stirred to go up to Jerusalem, these all (whether they went up or not) belonged to the exiled tribes of Judah and Benjamin who had lived together from their childhood. They did not include members of the ten tribes who had been cast out into another land in bygone times. Herein lies the source of our wonder and bewilderment. For when you make a thorough investigation and count the great numbers of people and enormous figures for the Jews mentioned in regard to the various disasters, whether you include those who died in the war of Titus in Jerusalem or that of Trajan in Alexandria or that of Hadrian in Bethar, or those who were taken in to captivity by the enemy, and those who survived and were scattered to the four winds, you will find that they actually come to more than four million which is seven times the number of those who came out of Egypt. How can one intellectually entertain the idea that these two tribes were so prolific that they could come to be so amazingly numerous? And this is not counting the several thousands and myriads who had previously disappeared while the Temple was still standing.

Consider what our rabbis said about the Jerusalemites in tractate Pesaḥim. "On one occasion, Agrippa the king wanted to set eyes on [i.e., count] the crowds of the Jews. He said to the high priest, 'Set eyes on the Paschal offerings.' " It transpired that there were countless offerings.[8] The very same statement in practically identical language is to be found in book 6 of Josephus.[9] Then, in his narration of the war, he also gives in book 7 an amazingly inflated figure for the number of those who were taken captive and fell by the sword.[10] In the tenth volume of his works, the sage Augustine also mentions that all historians agree the figure of a hundred and one thousand for those

6. Abravanel, Kings (425, col. a).
7. I.e., Haggai, Zechariah, and Malachi.
8. B. Pes. 64b.
9. *Bellum* VI:422–26. Josephus describes the census taken by Cestius on Passover. The figure comes to 2,700,000 (or 2,556,000).
10. *Bellum* VI:420: "The total number of prisoners taken throughout the entire war amounted to 97,000 and those who perished . . . 1,100,000." (In the Latin text, the passage is in bk. VII.)

who were killed in Jerusalem, and one hundred thousand for those who were taken into captivity.[11]

Similarly, you have seen that the number of the inhabitants of Alexandria is variously given by the rabbis of blessed memory as either sixty or one hundred and twenty myriads.[12] Then in Ekhah Rabbati they write that eighty thousand myriads of the inhabitants of Bethar were killed.[13] In tractate Giṭṭin, they inflate the figure even more to four hundred myriads or according to another opinion, four thousand myriads,[14] and they go to the point of saying that several hundreds of phylactery boxes and several kavs of brain were found on one stone.[15] These figures are nonsensical and hyperbolic and are not intended to be taken literally. But anybody who is versed in the rabbinic manner of speech knows that they were accustomed to use this mode in all kinds of stories, and not only in those three passages which they themselves listed.[16] For example, there is the passage in which it is said that Og went and uprooted a mountain of three parasangs[17] and the evidence of Ben Satriel in tractate Bekhorot[18] and the like. Despite all this, we must surely come to the conclusion that something of reality is indicated by exorbitant figures. You can even find corroboration for what the rabbis of blessed memory say in the work entitled *Lives of the Emperors* which we mentioned before. With regard to Hadrian's reign and his wars against the Jews, it is stated that chroniclers unanimously pronounce that no war between nations is known to have brought about such extensive destruction as was wrought on our people by Hadrian.[19] And you know how our rabbis of blessed memory inflate the figures for the many cities and enormous population which were under the sway of King Jannai.[20] Finally, I shall ensure that you are completely convinced that the returnees from the Babylonian exile were numerous and had become like the stars of the heaven. You should contemplate the authentic infor-

11. This is an unusual way for de' Rossi to refer to Augustine. He abbreviates the name to Augo and fails to call him by the more usual designation "the greatest Christian sage." Here de' Rossi is referring to the tenth volume of Augustine's *Opera omnia* which contains his *Homeliae de tempore.* In sermo CCV (col. 1044). He writes: "In historiis legimus quod tunc tricies centena milia hominum ex Iudaeis Hierosolymis fuerint congregata, ex quibus ferro et fame undecies centena millia [*sic*] leguntur esse consumpta et centum millia iuvenum Romam perducti sunt in triumphum." The author (the passage appears to be spurious) makes this statement in the context of speaking of the well-deserved divine punishment of the Jews. It may be that de' Rossi gives a particularly obscure reference here in order to gloss over Augustine's purpose in citing the historians.

12. B. Sukk. 51b.

13. E.R. to Lam. 2:2.

14. B. Giṭṭ. 57b.

15. Ibid. 58a.

16. B. Ḥull. 90b: "In three places the sages spoke in exaggerated terms: about the ash-heap, the vine, and the curtain."

17. B. Ber. 54b.

18. B. Bek. 57b. He testified to the fact that "the lettuce in our place (i.e., Arca Caesarea) has six hundred thousand peelings of small leaves round the core."

19. This is a reference to Pedro Mexía's *Le vite di tutti gl'imperadori.* The passage is found in the Life of Trajan (not Hadrian) "mandò Capitano [i.e., Hadrian] con bastante numero di soldati per diverse parti i quali nelle dette terre e in altre dove trovarono Giudei, fecero di essi generale uccisione et affirmano gli scrittori che questo fu la maggior giustizia e gastigo che giamai fosse fatto al mondo permettendolo Dio per la malvagità et ostination loro."

20. B. Giṭṭ. 57a: "King Jannai had sixty myriads of cities in the king's mountain and in each of them was a population as large as that of the exodus, save in three of them which had double as many."

mation[21] which I am setting before you, i.e., the letter of Agippa the king to Emperor Gaius as it is cited by Yedidyah the Alexandrian [Philo] in his last work called *The Embassy to Gaius.* Gaius the wicked had devised a plan to be worshipped as a deity by all his subjects. The reason for such behavior was pathetic. He argued that just as the shepherd is naturally on a higher level than his flock, so too it follows that the ruler of men must be elevated above the human level and be called god.[22] He therefore commanded that all the Jews should also put his despicable statue in the holy places. As a consequence, the great community, the inhabitants of Alexandria in Egypt, were stirred to action. They sent Yedidyah and four colleagues to plead their common cause before him in Rome. There they met Agrippa the king of Israel who was Gaius's favorite as far as that was possible and requested his help, thinking that his words may be persuasive. Agrippa fell ill because of his distress about the calamity and was unable to speak face-to-face with him, as would have been appropriate in such a moment of crisis.[23] From his sickbed he fulfilled his promise and wrote a fine supplicatory letter in which he wrote the following in defense of the holy city:[24]

> It is my native city, but I may tell your majesty, it is the metropolis not just of one country of the Jews, but of many countries which were colonized by her. They include the nearby neighboring lands like Egypt, Edom,[25] Syria, and that part of Syria called the Hollow [Coele-Syria] and the rest of its territories, as well as outlying countries, such as Pamphylia, Cilicia, most of Asia as far as Bithynia and the borders of Pontus as well as of Europe, Thessaly, Boeotia, Macedonia, Aetolia, Attica,[26] Corinth, and the best parts of the Peloponnese. And not only are the mainlands full of Jews, but also the important islands of Nigropontis [Euboea],[27] Cyprus, and Crete. I say nothing of those which are to be found beyond the river Euphrates for with the exception of a small part in Babylon and of its other satrapies, every prestigious city and good land has Jewish inhabitants.

He wrote all this to let him know how much it was logically in his interest to retain the loving reverence of all that great multitude and how he would at some juncture regret and be aghast at the evil he was planning against them. Moreover, Josephus quotes the great gentile historian Strabo to the effect that at that time [about 87 B.C.E.] the world was filled with people of Jewish origin.[28] Thus if one were to collate all these stories, one might think that the prophecy of the barren woman whose children shall outnumber those of the espoused (Is. 54), and other such prophecies have already been fulfilled. In fact, that writer [Strabo] actually says:

> There were four classes of men in the city of Cyrene: citizens, agriculturists, resident-aliens, and Jews. This fourth class has infiltrated all cities and there is hardly a place in the inhabited world in which they have not got a foothold and taken possession of. For Egypt

21. Cf. Ps. 17:2.
22. *Leg.* 76.
23. 'Crisis.' Cf. Esther 3:15 where the same word is used to describe the state of the Jewish community in the city of Shushan when the king had agreed to Haman's request for the extermination of all the Jews.
24. *Leg.* 281–83.
25. De' Rossi always translates Phoenicia as Edom. See n. 8 to "Splendor of the Elders."
26. De' Rossi has omitted Argos from the list.
27. Both the Greek and the Latin translation read 'Euboea.' De' Rossi uses the medieval name for the region.
28. *Ant.* XIV:114–18.

> and Cyrene were lands which were accustomed to accept their domination[29] and many other such lands have allowed them to practice their laws and they have established large communities within these countries so that over the course of time they have ruled with them and passed legislation as they would any organized country. In fact, in Egypt, this nation has been regarded as native except that in Alexandria, a large section of the city has been allocated for them.[30] And they have their own magistrates who administer all juridical matters of the people in accordance with the institutions of a city which has its own sovereignty. And so this people flourished in Egypt because from ancient times they put their roots there.[31] Furthermore, it was nearby and therefore easily accessible. And similarly [they could migrate to] Cyrene because it was on their border and in former years, to the land of Judaea also, or rather, it once formed part of the Egyptian kingdom.

These are his words. The reference to Cyrene reminded me of the designation *siraniyyot* used in tractate Bekhorot with regard to eye blemishes. Rabbi Moses [Maimonides] of blessed memory explains the word as signifying corners of the eyes which are watery.[32] Given that it is not spelt *siriyyot* [but *siraniyyot*], I thought it may perhaps refer to watery eyes which is a trait of the inhabitants of the city of Cyrene. After all we find that people have native physical characteristics, for it states in chapter 2 of Shabbat: "The heads of the Babylonians are round, the eyes of the Palmyreans are half closed, the feet of the Africans are broad."[33]

But let us go back to the main point of the chapter. For every reader will wonder as to how it was feasible that the two tribes of Judah and Benjamin could have become so fertile that they actually came to be as numerous as we said. After all, they alone remained in their own place after the ten tribes were exiled to an inaccessible and confined land, and their numbers also became diminished and depleted because of the pressures of the wars at the time of the destruction of the first Temple. In fact, when David was incited to count all the tribes (2 Sam. 24), at the end of the book of Kings,[34] Israel only amounted to 800,000 and Judah 500,000. It is true, however, that in 1 Chronicles (21:5) it is stated that Israel numbered 1,100,000 and Judah 470,000, all of whom were of military age, that is to say, twenty years and above, and these figures excluded [the tribes of] Levi and Benjamin. The author of *Aqedat Yiṣhaq* (gate 98) suggests a reason for this discrepancy,[35] or else another appropriate reason might be proffered. Nevertheless, it is all a question of the situation and time; for at that period they were in

29. This passage is also obscure in the Greek. Colson's translation (Loeb) reads: "And it has come about that Cyrene which had the same rulers as Egypt, has imitated it in many respects, particularly in notably encouraging and aiding the expansion of the organized groups of Jews which observe the national Jewish laws."

30. The text has been slightly emended: "In Egypt, for example, territory has been set apart for a Jewish settlement."

31. The text reads: "because the Jews were originally Egyptians."

32. Maimonides, *Perush* to M. Bek. 7:3.

33. B. Shabb. 31a.

34. Once again, de' Rossi follows the Christian Scriptures whereby the second book of Samuel is called the second book of Kings.

35. Isaac Arama, *Aqedat Yiṣhaq*, gate 98, ki tavo (85b). According to Arama, Joab questioned the reason for making the census and was reluctant to carry it out. He therefore did not take sufficient care in making the census and even omitted to count the tribes of Levi and Benjamin.

God's favor which was not the case when the massacres which we were discussing took place. Our problem thus remains unsolved.

I noticed that after relating the story of the flood in his third book, Berosus the Chaldean has the following to say: "The blessed God saw that the world was at that time depleted and empty of human beings. And since He never deprives it of anything which it needs, He blessed the fruit of the womb of all those who conceived such that for many years every time they gave birth they produced both a male and female and due to His benevolence, the same thing happened to their children when they grew up."[36] Thus far his words which in my opinion completely concur with that which is written in our Torah when God once again spoke to Noah saying, *Be fruitful and multiply* (Gen. 9:7).[37] This statement incorporated both a commandment and a blessing. We have also noted similarly miraculous procreation which occurred under an apple tree during the bondage in Egypt.[38] But one has no reason to wonder that at those two moments in time [i.e., during the Egyptian bondage and the first Temple period], in order to supply the world's needs, God desired to benefit our ancestors. However, the truth is that the generations of the second commonwealth did not gain favor because of their righteousness. On the contrary, the destiny of those who were delivered from the womb was to be sent to the slaughter. It was therefore appropriate that for these people there should be a diminuition and closing of the womb rather than fruitfulness and increase. And, in fact, in Yevamot, our rabbis of blessed memory wrote of a tradition that the women of that generation were "torn apart" [*istedu*][39] which according to the compiler of the *Arukh* means that the women of the generation of the destruction of the Temple became sterile and could not conceive.[40] Now someone might try to mislead you by claiming that this increase in numbers came about when the ten tribes returned after a short while to their own borders. As evidence, the statement of Rabbi Johanan in chapter 1 of tractate Megillah would be put forward where he justifies the fact that Josiah sought the advice of Huldah the prophetess instead of Jeremiah:[41] "This was because he [i.e., Jeremiah] had gone to bring back the ten tribes. How do we know that they returned? The prooftext is, *For the seller shall not return to that which is sold* (Ezk. 7:13)."[42] But there are two reasons for not being persuaded by such an argument. First, this is an Aggadah and we do not draw conclusions from it. Alternatively, one might say as does Rav Sherira Gaon (who will be discussed in the subsequent chapters) that it is merely a conjectural statement and does not have the weight of the tradition.

36. This is a reference to ps. Berosus, one of the forgeries of Annius of Viterbo. The passage is in ch. 3 (117).

37. De' Rossi refers to the fact that the statement *Be fruitful and multiply* is repeated in Gen 9:1 and 9:7.

38. This is a reference to the aggadah in B. Sota 11b which speaks of the miraculous ways the people survived in Egypt including the way they gave birth: "When the time came for them to give birth, they would go and give birth in a field under the apple tree as it says, *Under the apple tree I roused you, it was there your mother conceived you, there she bore you who conceived you*" (S.S. 8:5).

39. B. Yev. 17a.

40. Nathan ben Yeḥiel, *Arukh,* s.v. *aṣṭdyy.*

41. Hulda the prophetess was a contemporary of Jeremiah. When Josiah was told about the discovery of the scroll of the Torah, he sent Hilkiah the priest and others to get advice, and they went to Huldah (2K. 22:13–14).

42. B. Meg. 14b.

Furthermore, we might also say (as do many of our commentators who reject the Midrashim of the sages of blessed memory—we shall also deal with this in the subsequent chapters), if it is a tradition, we must accept it; if, however, it is simply an inference, it is open to rebuttal.[43] Now, according to the evidence given in tractate Bava Batra, the book of Chronicle was written down by Ezra.[44] When Ezra who lived a long time after Jeremiah mentions the exile to Halah and Habor, he adds *to this day* as a gloss: *So the God of Israel roused the spirit of Pul of Assyria . . . and he carried them away, namely the Reubenites, the Gadites, and the half-tribe of Manasseh and brought them to Halah, Habor, Hara, and the river Gozan to this day* (1Chr. 5:26). If in his [i.e., Ezra's] lifetime they were still in exile, then it is certain that in the time of Josiah and Jeremiah they had not yet returned. Moreover, if you were to make such a claim, then you would be disproving several prophecies of several prophets who promised us that Israel and Judah would return to live in their land together, something which has not yet happened. In particular, there is the famous and explicit prophecy of Ezekiel 37, *Take a stick, one for Judah and one for Ephraim.* No conditions are attached to the entire prophecy. In no uncertain terms it is sworn[45] that this will ultimately occur to Judah which is the kingdom of the two tribes and to all the house of Israel its companions, in other words, the exiled ten tribes. There is an authoritative Mishnah that Rabbi Aqiva and Rabbi Eliezer who lived in the time of the massacres and were among the greatest sages familiar with local matters disputed with one another as to whether the ten tribes would return in the future.[46] This then implies that in their time the situation was still unchanged. Then there is the passage in Torat Kohanim. First with regard to the verse, *But you shall perish among the nations* (Lev. 26:38). Rabbi Aqiva says: "These are the ten tribes who were exiled to Media."[47] Then towards the end of the chapter, they state: "I did not reject them in the time of Vespasian. . . . How do we know that the covenant was made with the tribes? Because it is said, *I will remember in their favor the covenant with the ancients* (Lev. 26:45)."[48]

In view of all this, there is no doubt that in his commentary, Rashi of blessed memory was forced to find a way of accommodating Rabbi Johanan's statement.[49] He therefore came up with the suggestion that the statement in Megillah meant that Jeremiah went to bring back some, but not all of the tribes. This method of his is commendable whereby he reconciles every sage's statement, justifying it as far as possible so that it cannot be refuted on the basis of Scripture or the statements of our great rabbis.

43. Cf. M. Yev. 8:3; Ker. 3:9.

44. B. B.B. 15a.

45. 'Sworn,' lit. hand put on the throne of the Lord. Cf. Ex. 17:16.

46. M. Sanh. 10:3: "The ten tribes will not return as it says, *and He cast them out into another land as is still the case* (Deut. 29:27). Rabbi Aqiva said: As the day goes and does not return, so, too, the ten tribes have gone and will not return. Rabbi Eliezer said: As the day becomes dark and then light, so, too, the ten tribes who are now in the dark will have light in the time to come."

47. Sifra, beḥuqotai, 8:1 (112, col. b).

48. Ibid., 8:10 (112, col. c). The verse ends *whom I freed from Egypt.* The meaning of the midrashic comment is that God made His covenant with the ancestors of the tribes, the twelve sons of Jacob.

49. Rashi to B. Sanh. 110b: "And yet it is stated [in B. Meg. 14b] that Jeremiah brought them back. He did not bring them all back, but only some of them for it is said, *The Lord uprooted them . . . and cast them into another land as is still the case* (Deut. 29:27).

Nevertheless, one can say that the manifest meaning of Rabbi Johanan's actual words does not allow for such an apologia. Rather, Rashi is simply being generous, since the literal meaning of Rabbi Johanan's words and the prooftexts he gives indicate that he meant that they all returned. Moreover his opinion is corroborated by Rav Naḥman on the basis of the verse, *Also, O Judah, there is a harvest appointed for you, when I would restore the captivity of My people* (Hos. 6:11). If so, their words are certainly repudiated by Scripture and the words of the Tannaim quoted above [i.e., Rabbi Aqiva and Rabbi Eliezer]. Furthermore, with due deference to Rashi, it seems that one perhaps ought to say that both Rabbi Johanan himself and Rav Naḥman did not make that statement dogmatically. After all, he did not receive this opinion as a tradition transmitted by earlier sages. Rather it was, as Rav Sherira would say, a conjectural statement whereby he judged that by examining those verses it was possible to resolve the problem of Josiah, saying that such and such is also evidence to prove that he brought them back and that Josiah ruled over them.[50] This would all be said on the basis of the statement of the sages of blessed memory, "I am expounding Scripture." We will enlarge on the question of such exegesis in chapter 15. Who would not admit that if Jeremiah had really done this, it would have been celebrated in writing and enshrined in many historical works both of the Jews and other peoples? And if, with God's help, he had brought some of them back, he could have also brought them all back, particularly since the object of bringing them back was to enable them to fulfill the precept of the Jubilee which cannot be observed until all the Jews are living in their land. This is made clear by Rambam of blessed memory.[51] So there would have been no point in bringing back just a few of them. In the final analysis, such Aggadot and all contrived solutions do not dissuade us from accepting the literal meaning of the verses and facts which are as clear as the light of the sun.

In addition to the scriptural passages we cited, you should also consider the statement of Josephus who wrote: "Only two tribes which are dispersed throughout Asia and Europe live under the domination of the kingdom of Rome; but the ten tribes still in these times live beyond the river Euphrates. They are innumerable, in fact too numerous to count."[52] An allusion to those who live beyond the river Euphrates, as we noted before, was also made in King Agrippa's letter to Gaius. In chapter 13 of 4 Ezra, which is part of the Greek canon but not ours,[53] there is also the passage in which the angel interprets Ezra's dream about another angel:[54]

50. After quoting Ezk. 7:13, it is stated (B. Meg. 14b): "Now is it possible that after the Jubilee had ceased the prophet should prophesy that it will cease? The fact is that it teaches that Jeremiah brought them back. Josiah the son of Amon ruled over them, as it says, *He [Josiah] asked, 'What is the marker I see there?' And the men of the city replied, 'That is the grave of the man of God who foretold these things that you have done to the altar of Bethel'* (2K. 23:17). Now what connection is there between Josiah and the altar in Bethel? It teaches therefore that Josiah reigned over them."

51. Maimonides, *Mishneh Torah,* Shemiṭṭah X:8.

52. Josephus, *Ant.* XI:133.

53. This is a strange statement. Although 4 Ezra was included in the Apocrypha of the majority of Bibles, it was excluded from the canon of the Greek Church. De' Rossi may have reached such a conclusion because Jerome translated the work from a Greek version. On the reception of the work in the Renaissance, see A. Hamilton, "The Book," 45–62.

54. The vision refers to a "man" which is understood to be a reference to an angelic being.

> And whereas you saw him gathering to himself another multitude which was peaceful, these are the ten tribes which were led away captive out of their own land in the days of Hosea ben of Ela[55] who was exiled by Salmannassar the king of the Assyrians. And he carried them across the river to another land. But they decided that they would leave the rest of the peoples and wander far away from them to a place where no human being has ever dwelt, where they would keep their Torah which they had not kept when they lived in their own land. Did they not enter by the narrow straits of the river Euphrates and the Most High God then performed miracles for them and stayed the springs of that river until they had reached their goal? For the journey to that country which was called Arsaret took a year and a half. They then settled themselves there until the end of days (vv.39–46).[56]

A great geographer of our own time who shall remain nameless[57] made additions to Ptolemy's maps. In his note to the map of New Africa he wrote: "This part of Africa was unknown to the ancients for they were not acquainted with the source of the river Nile which springs from the mountains that the ancients called the Mountains of the Moon and are nowadays called the Mountains of Bet. A great number of Jews live in these mountains, paying taxes to the king of Ethiopia called Prester John."[58]

{This part of Africa is in the south as is evident from map 22 of New Africa in the section of new maps of Ptolemy's *Cosmography* which was translated by Ruscello.[59] One might therefore infer that these were not the ten tribes since they were exiled to northern parts by the king of Assyria. They must be identified as other Jews, perhaps the "sons of Moses"[60] or a section of the tribes which got dispersed to that place in their flight from Samaria. The existence of the tribes is also attested in the cosmography entitled *Theatrum mundi* written by the Christian scholar Abraham Ortelius which was printed in Antwerp in 1572 according to their [i.e., Christian] era.[61] In map 47 of Tartary, there is a place called Horda (i.e., expulsion or descent) Danorum and adjacent to it another place called Horda Nephalitorum. The description reads: "They were called Nephaliti after Naphtali, one of the ten tribes of Israel and they are located adjacent to the Danites and they are called Ethiopians or Jews and 476 years after the birth [of Jesus], they conquered the kingdom of Perosa." You will observe that the fore-

55. According to Charles, this is an error and should read "Josiah."

56. This text was cited by all those involved in the contemporary debates on the ten tribes. A. Hamilton ("The Book," 50) notes the existence of a Hebrew translation of ch. 13 of 2 Esdras, which bears the date 1487.

57. This is a reference to the Protestant scholar Sebastian Münster. In compliance with the Tridentine decree of 1564, de' Rossi refers to Protestant writers anonymously.

58. This passage occurs in the revised edition of Münster's *Geographia,* which was issued in 1545 in Latin and in 1548 in Italian (with subsequent printings). The quoted passage is 34 in the Italian translation (Venice, 1548). On the printing history of Münster's work, see the introduction of R. A. Skelton to the facsimile edition of the Basel 1540 edition (Amsterdam, 1966). The legend of Prester John, the Christian ruler and priest of the East, who was to mount an attack on the Muslims, was much disseminated from the twelfth century onwards and particularly popular in the fifteenth and sixteenth centuries.

59. Ruscello's *La geografia* was printed in Venice, 1561.

60. The "sons of Moses" are mentioned by the ninth-century traveler Eldad ha-Dani in his description of the kingdom of the tribes of Dan, Naphtali, Gad, and Asher in Havilah near Ethiopia. He refers to their neighbors "the sons of Moses" who live cut off from the world by the impassable river Sambation.

61. The work was first published in 1570. It contains all the elements of the modern atlas and fifty-three of the best maps of the world produced by the most renowned geographers.

mentioned places are depicted as being located adjacent to the Scythian region which is the kingdom of the Amazons on the edge of the northernmost point, i.e., the Scythians are located near the [North] Pole and below them and closeby are the Danites and the Naphtalites are next to them as we said. Moreover, in the middle of the map you will come across a place called Tabor or Tybur which is also mentioned by Solinus. He says that it is a very large mountain which is divided over two separate climates by the river Euphrates.[62] There is no question that this mountain should not be identified with that of the same name located in the land of Israel as in, *Go and march up to Mount Tabor* (Jud. 4:6). [In the gloss on the map] it is written: "Although the people of this place lost the holy writings in former times, they are now united under one king who in 1530 came to France and spoke with Francis the first. Afterwards, by edict of the emperor Charles V, he was burnt in the city of Mantua because he was secretly trying to convert Christian kings to Judaism and made the king himself a particular object of persuasion." Yet this account of his is confused and he did not give an accurate description of the event. The person who was burnt in Mantua in the year 1533 [1532] was Rabbi Solomon Molcho of Portugal, a companion of Rabbi David Reuveni who came from Tartary.[63] It is true that the emperor then carried the Reuvenite to Spain in chains where, as report has it, he suffered the bitterness of death.[64] While speaking of the novelties of this map, I cannot resist from informing you of a place not far from Tabor which according to the description is called Tangut and reportedly possessed the art of printing a thousand years ago.[65] The entire area of this map is under the sway of Chan the great. According to the explanation given there the word "Chan" means "king" in the Tartaric language.}

In view of all this, we are therefore perfectly justified in saying that the ten tribes did not return to join the Jewish exiles of the Jerusalem area and our quandary remains. Now I know that the book of 4 Ezra was not accepted by our sages and was rejected for some reason.[66] However, as the sages of blessed memory say in Niddah, "Even though one should not accept evil rumors, one should take note of them."[67] Perhaps then we should also apply this to a good rumor which is not contrary to Scripture. Although it does not supply absolute proof, it may contain a partial allusion; and do not react to its blessing lightly, particularly since it is corroborated by the miraculous events mentioned in the Targum [ps.] Jonathan ben Uzziel on the verse, *before all our people I will work such wonders as have not been wrought on all the earth* (Ex. 34:10). The Targum reads: "For all your people will I do wondrous things at the time when they go into captivity

62. Gaius Iulius Solinus, *Delle cose,* ch. 49. Solinus refers to Mt. Taurus not Mt. Tabor.

63. Solomon Molcho was a kabbalist with messianic pretensions who was born in Lisbon of Marrano parents. He is said to have circumcised himself. Together with Reuveni, he is said to have gone on a mission to Charles V, but Molcho was brought to Mantua in 1532 and burned at the stake for refusing to convert to Christianity.

64. 'He suffered the bitterness of death.' This is a play on 1Sam. 15:32. A. Z. Aescoly in *Sippur,* 179 mentions de' Rossi's statement and then argues that Reuveni may have been subsequently freed from prison.

65. "TANGUT Hic artem imprimendi ante mille ut ferunt, annos habuerunt."

66. According to most scholars, 4 Ezra was a Jewish work written circa 100 C.E. It was probably originally written in Hebrew and then translated into Greek. In the third century, Christian additions were inserted into the text.

67. B. Nidd. 61a.

by the rivers of Babylon and I will bring them up from there and I will bring them to dwell on the other side of the river Sambation and such wonders shall not have been created for all the inhabitants of the earth and all peoples." Moreover one need not disprove this for the reason suggested to me by a wise person who said: "If the ten tribes had been there, surely some time later, one of them would have been released to go into our part of the world, especially since the Median cities are actually in the realm of the living; moreover, word from those living at other end of the world is brought to our notice from time to time. And if it is true that they are now trapped because of the hazards of the journey, then they should not have been able to go there in the first place." Now anyone who reflects on the passage we quoted from 4 Ezra will find that it contains an answer to all these queries of his. And even more convincing is the blessed Lord's statement, *I will scatter them* (i.e., I will set them at the corner) which means that they still exist; and the verse continues *and made their memory naught among men* (Deut. 32:26). In other words, He thus decreed that they should cease to be among us because of the magnitude of iniquities for He was not concerned *should their enemies misjudge* (ibid. 32:27). In addition to the fact that their [return] journey was rendered impossible because the path was tortuous and beset by obstacles, it may be that they did not want to undertake the journey. After all, they live alone there in security and there is no reason for them to have anything to do with us. They had already, as is right, selected a place for the sacred service—just as the Alexandrians had done when they were enjoying times of peace—and for that reason did not think of going up to Jerusalem.

All this while, we have neglected to speak of something which may contain a grain of truth in it. For in our own time, Rabbi David the Reuvenite came to Italy declaring that he was an ambassador sent from those regions.[68] Similarly, from earlier times, there is the record of Eldad the Danite who wrote about some of their practices.[69] Then there is also the continuous rumor, namely, the river Sambation, which is proof.[70]

Consequently, the problem returns to where we left it. How is it feasible that out of the two tribes alone, all those thousands and myriads of people could emerge? True, we could answer that this incredible multiplication of numbers was one of the things which our God promised with regard to their prosperity in the time of the second Temple as pronounced by Ezekiel at the end of chapter 36, *I will multiply their people like sheep* (v.37) and by Isaiah in his prophecy, *Shout, O barren one you who bore no child* (54) and by Zechariah *Shout for joy, fair Zion* (2:14). But the commentators of blessed memory are in agreement as to the fact that these promises all refer to the third Temple, may it be built speedily in our days. This solution is therefore completely untenable and we must seek another which will satisfy us. I therefore would like to say that in my opinion there is a correct way of solving this problem; we can give a reasonable

68. David Reuveni claimed to be the son of a King Solomon and brother of a King Joseph who ruled the lost tribes of Reuben, Gad, and half Manasseh in Habor in the Arabian peninsula. On arrival in Italy in 1523, Reuveni said that he had come to propose an alliance with the pope against the Moslems. See D. Ruderman, *The World,* 137–40.

69. On Eldad, who claimed to have communicated with four of the ten tribes in Abyssinia, see Neubauer, "Where Are the Ten Tribes," 98–114.

70. This is an allusion to the discussion between Aqiva and Turnus Rufus in B.R. 11:5 (93) in which Aqiva tells Turnus Rufus about the river Sambation which has a mighty torrent during the week but comes to a standstill on the Sabbath.

explanation for the existence of such large numbers. First of all we should articulate the proven principle which is accepted by all thoughtful people, namely, that things are designated by that part which is predominant in their makeup. Thus the name Adam is derived from earth (*adamah*) which is heavier than the other elements. Now we do indeed know that the tribe of Benjamin was allied with the tribe of Judah and that the two were ruled by one king. Nevertheless, holy Writ only refers to the king of Judah as though this tribe was the only nation in the land. Then we have it confirmed that from the time of King Asa, a large part of the rest of Israel joined the two tribes for it is written in Chronicles, *He assembled all the people of Judah and Benjamin and the people of Ephraim, Manasseh, and Simeon who sojourned among them, for many in Israel had thrown in their lot with him when they saw that the Lord was with him* (2Chr. 15:9). With regard to Hezekiah's Passover it is also written in Chronicles, *For most of the people—many from Ephraim and Manasseh, Issachar and Zebulun* (2Chr. 30:18) and in chapter 34 in regard to Josiah, *They delivered to him the silver brought to the House of God which the Levites, the guards of the threshold had collected from Manasseh and Ephraim and from all the remnant of Israel and from all Judah and Benjamin* (2Chr. 34:9). And in an earlier passage, it first states, *Judah was taken into exile in Babylon because of their trespass* (1Chr. 9:1) and then, *and some of the Judahites and some of the Benjamites and some of the Ephraimites and Manassehites settled in Jerusalem* (v.3). Thus, despite our claim that the ten tribes went away and did not return, we cannot suppress the feeling that Judah was also joined by many crowds of people from the other tribes of God and that they all went under the name of Judah because Judah was greater than this brothers and their leader. To these, one might also add the many proselytes who in the time of the second Temple attached themselves to the House of Jacob as it said, *In that day, many nations will attach themselves* (Zech. 2:15). It is all the more plausible seeing that we know that they were intrinsically connected with the various liberations of Israel ever since they came up out of Egypt accompanied by the mixed multitude. And on account of the miracle of Purim, many peoples of the land converted to Judaism.[71] And the law is, as Rambam of blessed memory states at the end of his *Yad Ḥazaqah,* that a family which becomes intermingled with Israelites retains that status [i.e., remains Israelite).[72]

Now at the beginning of this chapter we mentioned that many communities did not uproot themselves in order to go up to the Holy Land. This was the case with the most renowned of all those communities, Alexandria, where they increased greatly but also where the enemy assaulted them depleting them time after time. Thus we can come to the conclusion that the inhabitants of Bethar were as numerous as the heavenly hosts because the city from its very foundation was interspersed with many of the tribes as well as foreigners who joined their ranks; therefore in that place, too, the enemy encountered them in their myriads.

Finally, we may also be receptive to Rabbi Johanan's statement and judge that some of the tribes who had been exiled to Media did gradually, over the course of time, return to the holy precincts. In this way we may make a general assessment on the basis of the true principle that we articulated. In other words, since people are designated by the

71. Cf. Est. 8:17.
72. Maimonides, *Mishneh Torah,* Melakhim XII:3. (Maimonides is speaking of the time of the Messiah.)

name of the dominant sector, every stranger is included in the count; thereby, every problem is mitigated and becomes intellectually tenable. And when Ptolemy the king wrote for a despatch of six representatives from every tribe, he may not have had in mind the exiled ten tribes, while Eleazar, for his part, decided not to be put to shame by informing him about something which was a source of shame for us. Alternatively, there may have been at least some vestiges of the tribes, and he sent some of these people in fulfillment of the king's request. And now, may the good Lord behold our affliction—we the few who are left of those many—and may he gather the dispersed of all His people and may they find favor before His splendid majesty as long as the earth endures.[73]

END OF SECTION ONE

73. De' Rossi's discussion of this subject which focuses on demography rather than on the exact location of the ten tribes is of a different order from other tracts of the time. Unlike most Jewish and Christian writers, he is not intent on proving or disproving the existence of the tribes by means of the new geographical knowledge. He remains somewhat sceptical about the various reports from distant lands, while reaching a reasonable conclusion about the absorption of peoples into the Jewish nation.

SECTION TWO

CHAPTER FOURTEEN

As to how the sages' interpretations of certain passages in holy Scripture were disputed in subsequent centuries by many of our commentators of blessed memory. The question is raised as to how it can be presumed that their perception was greater than that of the sages.

THERE can be no doubt that everything relating to the precepts of the Torah in all their ramifications,[1] which was transmitted to us by our sages, is the word of God. In love and reverence we should set it as a crown upon our heads. With God's help, we shall expand on this matter in chapter 28.

We may surely take it for granted that the authoritative teachers[2] would not have bequeathed any falsehood to their descendants and still less promulgate it in the assemblies of the law courts or among the religious leaders. As the sage states in the *Kuzari,* it is inconceivable that preeminent individuals would have refrained from speaking out should there have been any conspiracy, God forbid, to suppress the truth.[3] And he should beware who would stoop[4] to cast any aspersions on the Sinaitic tradition received by our rabbis; for thereby a person might have the effrontery to question the Mosaic Torah itself, God forbid, which they have also handed down to us. It was in this vein that Hillel the elder[5] and Samuel Yarḥina'ah[6] spoke to the two proselytes who approached them. You should observe that a similar view is found among the Christians who were taught the obligation to believe in matters transmitted by word of mouth by their lawgiver [Paul] in the second of his fifth and sixth letter.[7] In his book

1. Lit. 'their roots, branches as far as the uppermost branch.' Cf. Is. 17:6.

2. 'Authoritative teachers,' lit. 'fathers of the world.' The expression is used in M. Ed. 1:4 with reference to Hillel and Shammai.

3. Judah Halevi, *Kuzari* III, par. 41: "For they have divine assistance and would never, on account of their large number, concur in anything which contradicts the Torah. They could not have erred because they had inherited vast learning, for the reception of which they were naturally endowed."

4. This is a play on Eccl. 4:10, *For should they fall, one can raise the other; but woe betide him who is alone and falls with no companion to raise him.*

5. B. Shabb. 31a: "When he went to Hillel, he accepted him as a proselyte. On the first day, he taught him *alef, bet, gimel.* The following day, he reversed the order [of the letters]. 'But yesterday you did not teach them to me in this way,' he protested. 'Must you then not rely on me with respect to the Oral Torah too?' "

6. Q.R. to Eccl. 7:8: "He went to Samuel and said to him, 'Teach me the Torah.' He said to him, 'Say *alef,* say *bet.*' He said to him, 'Who says that this is an *alef?* The teacher took hold of his ear and the man exclaimed, 'My ear, my ear.' He said, 'Who says that this is your ear?' He said, 'Everybody knows it.' 'In the same way, everybody knows that this is *alef* and this is *bet.*' "

7. He must be referring to 2Thess. 2:15: *So then, brothers, stand firm and hold to the traditions which you were taught by us, either by word of mouth or by letter.* The letters to the Thessalonians are the eighth and ninth in the standard order of the N.T.

against the letter of the Manichean, their greatest doctor [Augustine] wrote that if he did not believe in the accepted traditions of their congregation, he would thereby also be denying the written Gospel.[8]

Then there is also a second point which is quite obvious to all thinking people: Our sages, blessed be their memory, treated such scientific subjects as astronomy and cosmology from a completely human perspective; each sage addressed those subjects according to his intellectual ability or else by means of the knowledge he had acquired from the recognized scholars of whatsoever nationality. Prophetic inspiration did not aid their endeavor in any way. With their good will, we may therefore give a hearing to the later sages who wrote against them and evaluate the disputants according to our intellectual capacity. But we shall not do this presuming equality between the two sides as is implied by the favorite saying of the rabbis of Yavneh, "I am a human being and my fellow is a human being."[9] According to the Tosafists, this meant, "He like me has the capacity to distinguish between good and evil." The fact is that they said: "The hearts of the ancients were like the door of the Ulam [the hall leading to the interior of the Temple which was two hundred cubits in width], and that of the later generations like the eye of a needle."[10] In a similar vein is a passage quoted in several places:[11] "If the ancients were the offspring of men, we are the offspring of asses." And it is also said:[12] "The nails of the ancients were superior to the belly of the moderns." The fact is that once the later generations had become recipients of what the ancients had comprehended, quite apart from what they themselves had grasped, their situation seems to have become like that of the proverbial dwarf who rides on the shoulders of the giant.[13] The author of the *Shibbole ha-Leqeṭ* quotes this proverb in the name of one of the ancient sages in the introduction to his work.[14] One might justifiably conclude that the superiority of the ancient over the modern consists in matters that are dependent on prophecy since he would have been closer in time to those who were prophetically

8. Augustine, *Contra epistolam Manichaei:* "Ego vero Evangelio non crederem nisi me catholicae Ecclesiae commoveret auctoritas" (*P.L.* XLII, col. 176). At first glance, it appears surprising that de' Rossi refers to Paul and Augustine to corroborate the rabbinic view of Oral Tradition. But it should be remembered that the question of the relation between Oral Tradition and the revealed truth of the Bible was an important issue debated by Protestants and Catholics. At the Council of Trent, it was decreed that the Christian faith was based both on the revealed truth of the holy Writ and unwritten tradition. See *Histoire,* ed. C. J. Hefele, 24.

9. B. Ber. 17a.

10. This is not an exact citation of B. Eruv. 53a: "The hearts of the ancients were like the door of the *Ulam,* the words of the later generation like the door of the *hekhal,* while our hearts are as wide open as the eye of a fine needle."

11. B. Shabb. 112b; P. Demai I (3) 21d; P. Sheq. 5 (1) 48c–d; B.R. 60:8 (650).

12. B. Yoma 9b.

13. The proverb is attributed to Bernard of Chartres (d. 1126) by his pupil John of Salisbury. See R. Klibansky, "Standing," 147–49, R. Merton, *On the Shoulders,* 37, 40ff., 177ff., 193ff., and S. Leiman, "Dwarfs," 90–94.

14. *Shibbole ha-Leqeṭ* (18a). The author was Zedekiah ben Abraham Anav (thirteenth century). It is probable that de' Rossi was quoting from a manuscript since the introduction is missing from the first editions of the work. Anav quotes the proverb from Isaiah ben Mali di Trani (d. 1250) who cites it in the name of a "gentile philosopher." "We are dwarfs astride the necks of giants because we have seen their wisdom and through their wisdom we have become wise and are in a position to say all that we say; but that does not imply that we are greater than they." The original text is in the *Teshuvot* of Isaiah di Trani (ed. A. Wertheimer, Jerusalem, 1967, 302–3).

inspired; the modern, on the other hand, is in a more advantageous position in matters which stem from speculative thinking and empirical investigation. For he is engaged in a perpetual process of adding rope to rope and thong to thong. Finally, therefore, with the help of the ancients themselves who struggled to no avail by the river bank to draw water, the latter digger could ultimately proclaim, "It is I who have dug and I who have drunk."[15] Now you are familiar with the statement of the great teacher Rambam [Maimonides] who wrote in the introduction to his commentary on the Mishnah: "The achievement of Joshua and Phineas in speculative thought and reasoning is equal to that of Ravina and Rav Ashi."[16] Thus, while the difference between the ancient sages and ourselves should be measured according to the yardstick which distinguished them from those prophets, where speculative capacity is concerned, the ancients and moderns are surely equal. Indeed, already in chapter 11, I began to give you some inkling of this in regard to certain astronomical questions on the basis of several passages in the *Guide* of Rambam and in the commentaries of the author of the *Aqedah* [Isaac Arama] who would not show partiality to their elders. Now in this context, I shall reinforce my position in a way appropriate for my purpose. Give due consideration to the citations of Rabbi Moses al-Ashqar which he brings in his responsum about the exact moment of twilight.[17] He mentions Rabbenu Tam who was guided by our sages on the subject of the rising and setting of the sun and by their belief that the sphere is fixed and that the planets revolve, and he comments on Midrashim and many of the codifiers who dispute their statements. He makes the specific point:

> Rabbenu Sherira Gaon and his son Rabbenu Hai Gaon, blessed be their memory, have already refuted the opinion of the sages of blessed memory on this question and overwhelmingly defeated them in the argument. They wrote: "You should know that although the *baraita* [of Rabbi Judah] in Pesaḥim serves as a refutation of the opinion of Ulla and Raba, neither this *baraita* [nor that quoted by Rabba bar bar Ḥanah] is acceptable since there is no real difference between the views of Rabbi Judah or Rabbah.[18] Both are of the opinion that the sky is like a vault and that the sphere is fixed and that the sun itself travels during the day below the firmament and at night enters its thickness. . . . But this opinion

15. According to L. Segal, *Historical Consciousness,* 159, n. 159, de' Rossi's image here "suggests a qualitative distinction between the somewhat muddied waters with which the ancients had to work as opposed to the clear spring water that the modern discovers." While correctly alluding to the biblical images (Is. 37:24ff.), Segal disregards the talmudic allusion (B. B.Q. 51a) which is concerned with the case of a pit dug by several people, where the last person to dig the pit should be liable if it causes any harm to anybody. The image thus suggests not only the progress of the modern over the ancient, but the modern's responsibility to acknowledge the results of his investigations. For another discussion of de' Rossi's concept of progress, see J. Teicher, "Il principio," 268–75; E. Jeauneau, *Nani;* G. Veltri, "The Humanist Sense," 372–93.

16. "Know that prophecy does not aid understanding of the explanations of the Torah and the study of the laws by means of the hermeneutical principles; rather, whatever was achieved by Joshua and Phineas [biblical leaders] in matters relating to understanding and logical thinking is on a par with what was achieved by Ravina and Rav Ashi [who were traditionally regarded as the compilers of the Talmud]." (3, col. a).

17. Moses ben Isaac Al-Ashqar, *She'elot,* responsum 96, 155b–156a (Jerusalem, 1959, 258b–269a).

18. B. Pes. 94a. According to Rabbi Judah, the thickness of the sky through which the sun has to traverse from sunset until the stars appear is four mils (one-tenth the average distance a man walks in a day, which is forty mils). Rabbah quotes a *baraita* in the name of Rabbi Johanan in which the daily journey of a man is said to be thirty mils and the journey from sunset until the appearance of the stars is five mils and therefore the thickness of the firmament is a sixth of an average day's journey.

> cannot stand for various reasons; for there is not just one firmament. . . . If the sun would go above the firmament at night, it could still be seen on earth and the firmament would not obstruct vision of it; for there are several firmaments between us and the sun, but they do not partition it off and even its own firmament does not create a partition such that one cannot see what is above it. . . . It transpires that the sphere has one orbit, but that the stars are fixed.

Study this responsum for yourself.

In other words, these leading Geonim, father and son, who were familiar with astronomy,[19] taught us as did many others as we mentioned, that it is not beneficial to give precedence to the ancients in speculative matters. They seemed to be implying that they knew and acknowledged that permission for this had been granted by our rabbis themselves who were fonder of the truth than their own honor, which thereby becomes enhanced.

After these preliminary remarks, our task is to discover whether the blameless person, who is faithful to God and the holy, may doubt or challenge the sages' interpretations of those verses in Scripture which have no bearing on its precepts. Regarding the stories they narrate or the historical events they describe, may we bring evidence (we shall mention this again) to prove that the event did not take place in the way described nor at the time suggested? Or may we simply completely repudiate their statement and claim that it was a fabrication made with some useful purpose in mind? For example, it could be instructive or some moral lesson might be gained from it.

Now beginning with the first question, we could say that we are certainly not subject to them in this matter and we have no reason for scruples should we challenge them since we are not intending to contravert them in any of three fundamental areas about which we shall speak further in chapter 28. Rather, each person, depending on his intellectual gift and the strength of the proofs he adduces for his argument, certainly has freedom of speech provided his intent is for the sake of the truth and heaven. If you are uncertain about applying this way of thinking, go and examine the statement in the Palestinian Talmud in which the practices of the people are taken into account.[20] It is not simply that our ancient sages themselves argued about the interpretation of thousands of verses and the description of several incidents, with different people presenting different accounts. But in addition, we are also confronted with the fact that the later commentators of blessed memory threw off all restraint in relation to the sages on countless occasions, and these people were all unquestionably men of integrity, righteous and upright.

Now our rabbis took it as a matter of course that Samuel of Rama died at the age of fifty-two.[21] Yet Scripture states, *When Samuel was old* (1Sam. 8:1), *Behold you are old* (ibid. v.5).[22] In tractate Taʿanit, the problem is resolved by the claim that he was

19. 'Who were familiar with astronomy,' lit. who saw the new moon. Cf. M. R.H. 1:7.

20. P. Yev. VII (1) 8a: "If you are uncertain about the application of any *halakhah,* go and see how the people are accustomed to behave."

21. De' Rossi refers to B. Taʿanit 5b; B. M.Q. 28a; P. Bikk. II (1) 64c; Seder Olam, ch. 13 (58). He also refers to Tanḥuma, *tissa,* but the statement is not given there.

22. De' Rossi adds: *And you are grey-haired,* possibly conflating the text with 1Sam. 12:2 where Samuel himself says, *As for me, I have grown old and gray-haired.*

prematurely overcome by old age. But the wise Don Isaac [Abravanel] refused to accept their opinion and came to the conclusion that Samuel did indeed live to old age. In his desire to show the reader that he was not speaking heretically, he drew support from other commentators. He said:

> Do not be surprised that I have dissented from the opinion of the Seder Olam. (For dissembling motives,[23] he refrained from mentioning the other passages where they all give the same view in that the Seder Olam was in fact highly estimated in its own right as is clear from their statement that the anonymous compiler of Seder Olam was Rabbi Jose,[24] and in this particular case, they all derived their opinion from him.) It so happens that Redaq [Kimḥi] already had the courage to refute their statements with regard to the time of the incident of the concubine in Gibeah, while Ralbag [Gersonides] refuted them in other matters.[25]

Again, according to the Seder Olam, Saul reigned for two years,[26] whereas in his commentary on Samuel and in his introduction to the book of Kings, Don Isaac claims that he reigned seventeen or twenty years.[27] There is a similar case regarding the interpretation of several verses in the book of Kings which concern the duration of the reigns of the kings of Israel and kings of Judah and which are crucial for the correct calculation of the duration of the first Temple. According to the rabbis of blessed memory, its duration was 410 years.[28] Now Kimḥi blessed be his memory rejects their interpretations and calculations out of hand on the grounds that they cannot be supported on the basis of the plain meaning of Scripture. For every passage he works out another method of interpretation. Look at his commentary on the verses 1K. 15:28; 2K. 8:16,26, 14:17, 15:1, and there are other examples. Finally in his comment on the verse, *In the fifteenth year of Amaziah* (2K. 14:23), he states that the first Temple stood for 429 and a half years.[29] And yet Rabad [Abraham ben David] the Levite writes that it stood for 430 years,[30] while Ralbag [Levi ben Gershom][31] gives 419 and a half years. Then there is the statement of the sages of blessed memory in Sanhedrin that the first generations of men were able to beget at the age of eight, an opinion derived from the verse about Caleb, *I was forty years old when Moses sent me* (Jos. 14:7). Yet in his commentary to 1 Chronicles (2:18), *Caleb son of Hezron had children by is wife,* Kimḥi of blessed memory writes that the rabbis' opinion is not substantiated by the plain meaning of the verses nor by logical deduction. Ibn Ezra, too, in regard to this subject writes:

23. 'Dissembling motives,' lit. for stately clothing. De' Rossi is implicitly referring to the interpretation of this expression in B. Pes. 119a: "What does the expression and *for stately clothing* (*li-mekhasseh atiq;* Is. 23:8) mean? It refers to him who conceals (*mekhasse*) the things which the Ancient (*atiq*) of Days concealed."

24. B. Nidd. 46b.

25. Abravanel to 1Sam. 8:1 (202, col. a).

26. Seder Olam, ch. 13 (56).

27. Abravanel, to 1Sam. 13 (230, col. a–240 col. a) and to Kings (426, col. b).

28. Seder Olam, ch. 28 (130); B. Yoma 9a; B. Arak. 12a.

29. The printed editions of Kimḥi ad loc. give the figure 409 and 6 months (not 429 and 6 months). This clearly appears to be a printer's error.

30. In *Sefer ha-Qabbalah* (6), he writes that the Temple stood for 433 years, but that "only 410 years were reckoned for it, since the kingship was not taken into account after the exile of Jehoiakim." Later (10), however, he writes that the first Temple stood for 427 years.

31. Gersonides to Daniel 7.

"According to the literal interpretation of the text, the verse is referring to Caleb ben Hezron not to Caleb ben Yefuneh and the proofs are conclusive—the wise will comprehend."[32] Then with regard to the subject of Er and Onan, the author of the Seder Olam states that Er reached puberty at the age of seven and got married.[33] Again, ibn Ezra states that it is impossible to procreate within the short time indicated by our rabbis.[34] Then again, the juxtaposition of the sections narrating the binding of Isaac, the birth of Rebecca, and the death of Sarah, prompted the rabbis of blessed memory to claim that all these events occurred simultaneously. Consequently, the author of the Seder Olam concluded that Rebecca was three years and Isaac thirty-seven years at the time.[35] Ibn Ezra wrote: "Our ancestors said that Isaac was thirty-seven years at the time of his binding. If this is a tradition we should accept it, but if it was simply an inference, it would have been appropriate."[36] Then there is a similar case where the close proximity of the passages dealing with the graven image of Micah, the children of Dan and the concubine in Gibeah led the rabbis of blessed memory to claim that all the episodes occurred simultaneously in the days of Cushan Rishatayim. The commentators Kimḥi and Don Isaac [Abravanel], however, basing themselves on the verse *And there was a man from the hill country of Ephraim* (Jud. 17:1), assert that the literal sense of Scripture does not allow for such an interpretation. And in his commentary on the passage which begins, *And when Samuel was old* (1Sam. 8:1), Kimḥi first quotes many opinions on the subject of the necromancer and then cites the view of Rabbenu Samuel ben Ḥofni the priest. He writes: "The final words of the Gaon are as follows: 'Even though the statements of our sages of blessed memory in the Gemara signify that she did truly resurrect Samuel, the statements as they stand are unacceptable in that they contain elements which defy the laws of reason."[37] In Rabad's *Sefer ha-Qabbalah,* this Samuel ben Ḥofni is listed in the period of the Geonim as head of an academy famous in the time of Hai Gaon of blessed memory.[38] With regard to the verse in Jeremiah, *And the word of the Lord came to me a second time* (1:13), Kimḥi mentions the verse, *The word of the Lord came to Jonah a second time* (Jonah 3:1) and then refutes the claim of the exegete [i.e., the rabbis] that "second" implies that He did not speak to him a third time.[39] Concerning the acacia wood [used for the building of the Tabernacle] which according to our rabbis of blessed memory was brought from Egypt,[40] ibn Ezra first asserts the

32. Ibn Ezra to Ex. 31:2.

33. Seder Olam, ch. 2 (12).

34. Ibn Ezra to Gen. 38:1: "And Onan was born who was Judah's second son and when he had matured such that he could produce sperm which cannot happen below the age of twelve years."

35. Seder Olam, ch. 1 (7). In most of the printed editions, the passage states that Rebecca was fourteen years, but as Ratner notes (n. 41, ad loc.), this is a scribal error and de' Rossi's reading is correct.

36. Ibn Ezra to Gen. 22:4: "If this is tradition we should accept it, but if merely an inference, this cannot be correct. For it would have been appropriate that the righteousness of Isaac should have been made explicit and his reward double that of his father because he willingly offered himself for the slaughter."

37. This statement is found in his *Commentary* to 1Sam. 28:25.

38. *Sefer ha-Qabbalah* (60). The academy was in Matha Mehasia. According to Rabad, Samuel was Hai's father-in-law. Samuel ben Ḥofni (d. 1013) appears to have been the first to give priority to the *peshaṭ* (the plain or simple sense of Scripture).

39. Kimḥi to Jer. 1:13. Kimḥi compares the two verses because in both cases, in his opinion, the word "second" is used to signify that God was speaking on the same subject in both cases.

40. Tanḥuma, *terumah* 9.

correct proviso that if it is a tradition we should accept it, and then challenges their opinion by an argument based on common sense.[41] The author of the *Guide* [Maimonides] wrote: "You should not find it incongruous that I mention the interpretation of Jonathan ben Uzziel whereas my interpretation differs from his. You will find that many sages and even some of the commentators dissent from his interpretation with regard to certain words and many concepts used by our prophets."[42] And he also disputes the view of Rabbi Judah son of Rabbi Simon in Bereshit Rabbah regarding the expression *And it was evening.* According to Rabbi Judah, the formulation of the verse, *And it was evening* as opposed to *let there be evening* signifies that an order of time existed previously. On similar grounds, Rambam also disputes Rabbi Abbahu's view that the expression signifies that He used to build worlds and destroy them.[43] Moreover, with regard to the meaning of some of the precepts, he writes: "Do not object that the sages blessed be their memory silence those who use the expression, 'Your mercy extends to young birds,' for we are following the other opinion."[44] And yet, in his *Yad Ḥazaqah* in which he brings all his statements in line with those of the sages of the Gemara, he does not dissent from them on this point as is evident from his Laws of Prayer.[45] I shall mention this again at the end of chapter 37. Then there is the noted statement of Rabbi Jose in Seder Olam which is also affirmed in the anonymous talmudic statement:[46] "The [second] Temple stood for 34 years of the Persian Empire, 180 years of the Greek Empire; 103 years of the Hasmonean dynasty; 103 years of the Herodian dynasty." Don Isaac demolishes three-quarters of this statement when he says regarding the Greek Empire: "According to the accurate numbers I have at my disposal, it lasted 145 years, the Hasmonean dynasty lasted 142 years, and the Herodian dynasty, 99 years."[47] He reinforced his position by claiming that his was the correct reckoning. He also brandished his sword against the first part of the statement. This shall be elucidated further in chapter 36 of the third section of the book, if God so wills. In regard to Isaiah's pronouncement on Tyre (ch. 23), he writes:[48] "In Bereshit Rabbah, Yelammedenu, and the Pesiqta, our sages of blessed memory say that whenever the place name Tyre is spelled *plene,* it refers to Tyre in Sidon; but when it is spelled defectively, it refers to another place. If this is a tradition, we must accept it, although we should not dissent

41. Ibn Ezra to Ex. 25:5. He suggests that they got the acacia wood from a forest which was close to Mount Sinai.

42. *Guide* III, ch. 4.

43. Ibid. II, ch. 30.

44. Ibid. III, ch. 48. Maimonides is explaining the reason for the law in Deut. 22:6–7, which forbids taking the mother with her eggs. He claims that taking away the eggs when the mother is present causes her much pain, and that the eggs are not fit to be eaten. If the mother is sent away, she will not suffer from seeing her young taken away. Such a law encourages people to refrain from unsuitable food. Maimonides' interpretation is at variance with M. Ber. 5:3.

45. *Yad Ḥazaqah* is an alternative title of Maimonides' code *Mishneh Torah.* See Tefillah 9:7: "Whoever says in his supplications, 'May He who has dealt mercifully with the nest of birds have mercy on us' or offers a petition of a similar nature, should be silenced; for these precepts are divine decrees and are not given for compassionate reasons. Were this the motive, the slaughtering of all animals would have been prohibited."

46. Seder Olam, ch. 30 (141–43); B. A.Z. 9a.

47. Abravanel, *Mayyene ha-Yeshuʿah,* 2, 3 (289, col. a).

48. Abravanel to Isaiah 22 (131). He states that the prophecy regards the downfall of Tyre by Sennacherib.

from what the literal sense of the verses teaches us regarding the true meaning of the prophecy and its promises." And why should I cite further examples of great later commentators who protest against the stories and explanations of the sages of blessed memory, when those distinguished guides, Rashi and the Tosafists, write in a manner which annuls the sages' statements that Sihon Canaan and Arad are one and the same person and that Cyrus, Darius, and Artaxerxes are similarly one and the same person. I shall discuss this further in chapter 18. Similarly their identification of Sheshbazzar with Daniel who witnessed six calamities in his lifetime[49] is rejected as inconceivable by Ramban of blessed memory. Likewise, Rambam of blessed memory apparently did not support their identification of Malachi with Ezra. For in the introduction to his *Yad Ḥazaqah,* he mentions both men as separate members of the Great Synagogue.[50] Then there is the statement of Ramban [Nahmanides]:[51] "Rashi wrote that the ark was submerged in eleven cubits of water—this reckoning is found in his commentaries as well as in Bereshit Rabbah. Since, however, he elsewhere shows great precision in his use of the Aggadot of the Midrashim and makes great effort to provide the plain sense of Scripture, we are therefore granted the license to do the same. For Scripture has seventy facets and many Midrashim give differing interpretations of the same point. It is my contention that the calculation they give does not tally with the language of the verse."

There are numerous other such examples where Geonim, codifiers, and commentators dissent from the sages' interpretations of the verses, each individual employing his own independent method of interpretation. In fact, having raised several questions in regard to the rabbis' interpretations of many of those verses, Rashi then makes the general statement:[52] "So it is my contention that Scripture should be explained according to its plain sense and that each statement should fit into its context, while any midrashic exposition that is given is to regarded as the verse, *Is not My word like fire, says the Lord and like a hammer which shatters the rock* (Jer. 23:29)." He seems to imply that for a correct understanding of the verses, one should not have recourse to our rabbis' Midrashim.

Thus, the problem we put forward at the beginning of the chapter has been clarified by means of concrete examples to the extent that an intelligent person might express surprise at us and say: "This question was unnecessarily brought to attention. Why did he raise the question in the first place and must he go on like a peddlar continually hawking his wares?" Now although this question does in fact require a satisfactory answer, I have chosen to disregard it for the time being. But when, with the Almighty's help, I reach chapter 28, I shall indirectly show the reader how I was forced into this position by the enmity of scholars who attacked me for no good reason. Under pressure

49. Sheshbazzar was a prince of Judah (see Ezra 1:8, 5:16). The identification with Daniel is facilitated by a play on Sheshbazzar's name: *Shesh* (6); *ba* (came); *ṣar* (trouble). These six troubles are associated with six events that happened in Daniel's lifetime. De' Rossi refers to B. Meg. 15a in which other such conflations are given; the identification of Daniel with Sheshbazzar, however, is not in Megillah, but in Pesiqta Rabbati 6:3 and Yalqut Shimoni II, par. 1068, 5.

50. In his list of tradents at the beginning of the *Mishneh Torah,* Maimonides lists Malachi as one of the members of the law court of Ezra (who were called Men of the Great Synagogue).

51. Nahmanides to Gen. 8:4.

52. Rashi to Ex. 6:9.

from them, I had no alternative[53] but to present here a compilation of the disparate controversies of the moderns with the ancients of blessed memory in the awareness that in this corner of the field, the forgotten sheaves still outnumber those that are actually collected. And I did not shirk from presenting this compilation at the beginning of the section. The chapters relevant to this subject will refer back to it and so, in my opinion, will become understandable. Thus keep these words of mine in mind until you reach the designated chapter, for then you will retrospectively understand and see the point of what I am putting before you.

And yet, the contents of this chapter do arouse wonder. It is very problematic as to how our leading sages of former time, blessed be their memory, who were members of the academies and great assemblies, each individual sharpening the wit of the other, who lived closer to the time of prophecy than us and who taught us knowledge and the way of understanding could say anything in their explanation of Scripture which could be questioned by the later sages of blessed memory. The question gains all the more urgency and becomes even more pressing when one realizes that out of every fifty of their interpretations, barely ten were accepted. This might give the impression, God forbid, that they would be recounting false dreams. How could one imagine that they did not see the light as did those later disputants, when they, the sages, were endowed with wisdom? And how is it that we who are [blind as] bats should see more than they? The fact is that in the forthcoming chapters, I shall, with God's help, show you a holy man of God who briefly raised this same question and who in a few words raised the axe and cut down the problem from its very roots. And you will see that while presenting his reply, I shall expand on the matter in like manner to a good physician who widens the wound for the purpose of administering the medicine and the requisite cure.

53. 'I had no alternative,' lit. I was taken by the hairs of my head. Cf. Ezk. 8:3.

CHAPTER FIFTEEN

Our rabbis have expounded many verses in the Midrashim for various purposes, but not because they believed that their interpretation was [literally] correct. Rather, their purpose was to provide instruction on many matters and also to make the verses memorable, but always with the valid proviso that they are never divested of their plain sense. Thus, anybody who objects to a Midrash on the basis of the plain meaning of the text (*peshaṭ*) or believes that the Midrash constitutes the plain meaning of the text is misrepresenting their [i.e., the rabbis] view. And the problem regarding the statements of the sages of blessed memory, in praise of the Aggadot, will be resolved.

At the end of section three, the divine sage Rabbi Judah Halevi, may he rest in paradise, has the king of the Kazars raise a question about the people of the second Temple period. He gets him to express surprise that they were not even cognizant of the revealed parts of the Torah until, as emerges from Nehemiah's narrative, *they found it written in the Torah* (8:14) and *therein was found written* (13:1).[1] Similarly, he has him wonder as to how the sages of the Gemara could so often divest scriptural verses of their plain meaning in ways which would be instantaneously refuted on rational grounds.[2] The response which he puts into the mouth of the sage, the king's disputant, is irrefutable. It is that we have decisive evidence, which we can glean by examination of passages other than those quoted, that the people of the second Temple period knew the Torah better than us.[3] Similarly, the sages of the Gemara had precise understanding of very obscure matters; intelligently and reasonably they divulged wonderful and correct interpretations of these matters for those who have understanding.[4] Consequently, on the basis of those other passages, we must acknowledge the wisdom of both groups of people [i.e., the people of the second Temple period and the sages of the Gemara] in no uncertain terms—for what was disclosed to us was not hidden from their purview.

It is therefore our task to endeavor to discover on which crux the resolution of the apparent problems will depend. The question is whether everything can be dealt with uniformly, or whether a multifaceted approach is required which takes into account the nature of the varied subject matter. This is regardless of the possibility that we may have to acknowledge that their methods in learning are in some cases beyond our ken. This approach is certainly appropriate and praiseworthy. It was already demonstrated to all thinking people by the God of knowledge, the Lord, through the agency of Moses, our chief prophet, when he invented the dialogue which is so fundamental to the Torah

1. *Kuzari* III, par. 54. In Neh. 8:14, it is demonstrated that the people had become ignorant of the festival of booths, and in 13:1, that they had forgotten about the prohibition regarding Ammonites and Moabites.

2. *Kuzari* III, par. 68.

3. Ibid. III, pars. 57, 59, 61. He argues that the men of the second Temple knew how to sacrifice and were acquainted with regulations of the Day of Atonement which required the detailed instruction of a teacher.

4. Ibid. III, par. 73.

He commanded us.[5] By that means we are assured of providence and recompense without which the striving of all who keep the Torah is to no purpose. It was indeed ascribed to a man who was known in his time to be deserving of it—Job is his name. For Job raised the momentous problem of theodicy, and despite all the endeavors of his friends, they could not with their human wisdom find the correct answer as was indicated by the true God when He said concerning them, *You have not spoken correctly concerning Me* (Job 42:7). In fact, when Job was alone, and He appeared to him from the storm wind, He did not even debate the question with him since He had already demonstrated and clarified that His providential care is extended to the individual and to the entire human species. The fact is that in order to compel him to acknowledge that also all his complaints and quests were of no effect since, lacking the sufficient knowledge or understanding of the profundity of His wisdom, he was not in a position to submit it to scrutiny, He directed him away from that question to different issues. In the first reply to the question, *Who is this who darkens counsel by words without knowledge?* (38:2), He brings him to acknowledge that His wisdom is too great for any intellect to apprehend. In the second reply when He says, *Have you an arm like God's?* (40:9), He brings him to make the same admission with regard to His incomparable power. On the basis of these two replies, even the person who cherishes resentment [against God] would realize that such divine behavior, which is amazing in our view, is not by virtue that the blessed Lord does not know or is incapable of acting differently—for we have already had various other examples in which He has shown Himself to be wise and powerful.[6] But given that we are unable to have a clear perception of things, we must necessarily admit that all His ways are just and wise beyond human evaluation. This is what is meant by their statement in the Palestinian Talmud, "If the word of God appears to be void of significance, it is your fault."[7] Indeed, this particular method was the one which the wisest of all men adopted in the book of Ecclesiastes. In that book, he does not speak with divine and inspired wisdom as in his other books, but like a man who speaks by means of human wisdom alone. It was for this reason that he did not use his famous name, Solomon, but rather a new name which derived from the wisdom which was publicly endorsed by the assemblies [*Maqhellot*-Qohelet-Ecclesiastes] of people.[8] For when knowledge of first causes of the subjects under consideration was withheld from them, they were forced in each case to proceed from the apparent posterior event to what they imagined to be the first cause. This is why he called it Qohelet, a book whose inquiries move in the same direction as that of the book of Job. And it was also because of the beauty of such a method of inquiry that he did not refrain

5. He is referring to the dialogue between the friends and Job and between God and Job. He appears to be following the rabbinic notion (B. B.B. 15a) that Moses wrote the book of Job. It is interesting to note that de' Rossi's friend, the dramatist and theater-theoretician, Judah de' Sommi Portaleone, put forward a similar view in his *Quattro Dialoghi* (13). He writes that the ancient Greeks and Romans had learned from the Hebrew Scriptures, "il modo da introdur varie persone a ragionare insieme, imitato poi da Platone." He also refers to the book of Job written by Moses (14) "descritta in modo di colloquio o ragionamento trattato da più persone."

6. Cf. Job. 9:4, *Wise of heart and mighty in power, who ever challenged Him and came out whole?*

7. P. Pe'ah I (1) 15b; P. Shevi'it, I (7) 33b; P. Sukk. 4 (1) 54b.

8. Cf. Q.R. to Eccl. 1:1: "Why was Solomon called Qohelet? Because his words were said in the assemblies."

from adopting it for himself. It is true that the speculative content of his work is comprehensive and that he examines more specific issues than does Job. While Job speaks exclusively about the question of providence and retribution, Qohelet goes over and over[9] all the futile[10] questions which are engendered by the affairs of the world and its routine.[11] In all human disciplines he was the greatest of all ancient sages. And through each of his inquiries, he demonstrates that human beings are so foolish that they are unable to know the nature and reason of the universal matters which he describes in chapter 1 ending with the words, *I Qohelet was king in Jerusalem over Israel* (1:12) as well as of the specific events to which he alludes in the course of the book. The intelligent person will consequently come to the realization and admit that we have indeed no means or possibility of fathoming the truth of anything. As the ancient adage goes, "The blind is no judge of color, nor the deaf person of song." He will realize that his meditations and arguments are not objectively correct, but only due to his self-delusion. Nevertheless, once he has acknowledged [God's] absolute wisdom and power, he will proceed to dispel his thoughts from his mind on the grounds that his best course is to heed and obey His precepts and for everybody to revere Him and hold Him in awe.[12] For this is the conclusion that is finally reached, and it is to the good of every person.[13] Whoever would take an opposing view will receive his due payment from the God of justice.

In the light of this, when we undertake a consideration and examination of our sages' statements, we should similarly recognize the profundity of their intellect for which we have various irrefutable examples and illustrations. The sage of the *Kuzari* alludes to some of them in his treatment of this question at the end of section 3. There, he provides evidence of the correctness and precision of their explanations in the Mishnah and Baraita.[14] Likewise, he comes to this conclusion with regard to that part of their statements that happen by chance to deal with astronomy which, as is well known, is needed for the development of several disciplines. He gives a similar evaluation of their knowledge of all natural sciences, which is all quite astonishing and remarkable.[15] We thus come to the certitude that we may not apply the term "foolish" to the rabbis in regard to their handling of the literal sense of Scripture which is evident to anyone who gives it attention. On the contrary, we should know and let it be known that they understood and comprehended it as we do and better.

On the basis of this introduction, we should necessarily state along the lines of the method stated above that the apparent strangeness of the blessed sages' interpretations of Scripture, some of their homilies and other pronouncements, are nothing but demonstration of their great and marvelous wisdom which is proportionate to the strange impression they make on us. The thoughtful person will reflect and be commended for

9. 'Goes over and over'—the expression is used in Eccl. 1:6.

10. 'Futile,' cf. Eccl. 4:16.

11. A similar comparison between Job and Ecclesiastes is made by David de Pomis in the introduction to his Italian translation of Ecclesiastes. He also states that they both speak "di un'istessa cosa, dico della mirabil divina providenza e reggimento e parimente dell'humana gran merce."

12. Cf. Is. 8:12.

13. Here, too, de' Rossi's prose echoes Ecclesiastes, cf. Eccl. 12:13–14.

14. *Kuzari* III, par. 69.

15. Ibid. IV, par. 29.

his intellect when he investigates and reveals its mysteries, particularly when he follows the guidelines transmitted by the author of the *Kuzari,* may he rest in paradise, in the third section of the work, and applies his correct methods which he demonstrated to us. This, in fact, was also done by many respected people such as Rabbenu Nissim Gaon, Rashba [Solomon ben Adret], and other similarly sagacious people. They confronted those Aggadot and stories of the sages of blessed memory, which appeared to be problematic, on rational grounds, and attempted to accommodate them like putting golden apples in silver lockets.[16]

Now I noted that the wise Rabbi Isaiah di Trani the younger, blessed be his memory, put forward a defense of our rabbis for their strange interpretations of Scripture which is precisely the subject of our present inquiry.[17] While he was generally expressing the same view as that of the *Kuzari,* he elucidated and developed the subject more extensively. Since his opinion agrees more than any other's with mine, I thought it a good idea to present his statement *verbatim* and then to let you know my opinion about it. As a consequence, all the critical remarks and bewilderment expressed by some of the later codifiers and commentators with regard to our sages' statements that were cited in the previous chapter will vanish like smoke and automatically be annulled. This is how Riaz (Isaiah di Trani the younger) formulates his opinion in his *Decisions* on tractate Sanhedrin.[18] It is also cited in the *Shilṭe ha-Gibborim* in chapter 1 of tractate Elilim:[19]

> Know that there are three categories of Midrashim. There is the hyperbole. As is said in Ḥullin: "The sages spoke in exaggerated terms"[20]; likewise is Scripture in the verse, *large cities with walls sky high* (Deut. 1:28). There is the hyperbole used in speech, exemplified in the sayings of Rabbah bar Bar Ḥanah in Bava Batra.[21] There are those Midrashim which recount miraculous occurrences as in the stories about Rabbi Bena'ah in Bava Batra.[22] Then there are those Midrashim where our rabbis of blessed memory aim to interpret Scripture in every possible way. They drew support for such an interpretation from the verses, *One thing God has spoken; two things have I heard.* (Ps. 62:12), *Behold My word is like fire, declares the Lord* (Jer. 23:29). On the basis of these verses, they deduced that one verse may be broken up into several layers of meaning.[23] Accordingly, they interpreted Scripture in every possible way, although they did say that Scripture never loses its plain sense, which remains paramount. Some Midrashim are closer to the literal meaning while others retain scant allusion to it. This is exemplified by their statement:[24] "Jacob our patriarch never died. An objection was raised, 'Was it for nothing that they mourned for him.' The other

16. *Golden apples in silver lockets* (Pr. 25:11). This verse is used by Maimonides in his introduction to the *Guide* to explain the nature of prophetic parables, in terms of their external and internal meaning. "When looked at from a distance or with imperfect attention, it is deemed to be an apple of silver; but when a keen-sighted observer looks at it with full attention, its interior becomes clear to him and he knows that it is of gold."

17. For a critique of de' Rossi's treatment of the Aggadah, see L. Segal, *Historical Consciousness,* ch. 6.

18. De' Rossi must have seen the work in manuscript. The commentaries of Isaiah di Trani (both the elder and the younger) were often consulted by Italian Jews although few of them were printed. See M. Perani, "Due biblioteche," 255–60.

19. Joshua Boaz, *Shilṭe ha-Gibborim* (Glosses on Alfasi), to A.Z. 15b (6a).

20. B. Ḥull. 90b.

21. B. B.B. 73b: "I saw a frog the size of the fort of Hagronia."

22. Ibid. 58a.

23. B. Sanh. 34a.

24. B. Taʿanit 5b.

replied, 'I am interpreting Scripture.' [*Fear not Jacob for I will save you from afar and your seed from captivity* (Jer. 30:10). The verse compares Jacob to his seed. Just as his seed will live, so too, he will live.]" In other words, although I know that he died, my purpose is to interpret Scripture in every way that is appropriate. If the Midrash cannot be understood literally, it does contain a hint of the idea that he did not die as expressed in the saying, "the righteous even when they are dead are called living." In a similar vein is the statement in the Palestinian Talmud,[25] "The Land of Israel will in the future produce cakes and cloaks of fine wool." This means that the Holy One blessed be He will restore the world in the future and endow it with extraordinary boons. And again in the Gemara of the Land of Israel [i.e., the Palestinian Talmud] they say,[26] "But are the Midrashim fundamental truths (*amana*)? No, but rather, expound Scripture and receive reward for it." It is thus clear to you that the Midrashim are not meant to express truths and fundamental propositions, but to convey many meanings of Scripture by expounding it in all manner of ways.

Before I proceed, it is only right that I should make known my reading of the Palestinian Talmud even though there is good reason to believe that the reading he had before him which was corroborated in the *Shilṭe Ha-Gibborim* is the only correct one. My text reads as follows: "Rabbi Judan asked, 'Does a corpse impart impurity when its bulk is less than an olive's. After all, Rabbi Johanan said that a fetus is included even if it is smaller than an olive's bulk; and a carcass the size of a bean imparts impurity.' Rabbi Ḥanina said, 'I saw the embryo of a calf which was the size of a bean.' 'What does this all mean then?' 'I am just giving [*amena*] Midrashim so that you should expound and receive reward.' " Thus the reading, "But are the Midrashim fundamental truths?" is either a variant or erroneous, whereas the meaning of the version that reads, "I am giving midrashim" would be as follows. The questioner says in surprise, "What is all this"—that is to say, how is it possible that a carrion of a calf can be as small as a bean, or an aborted fetus be smaller than an olive? And the author of the statement replies, "My words are not meant to be taken literally, but are Midrashim." In other words, a corpse imparts impurity if the fetus, which is fully developed, is less than an olive's bulk; or in the case of a carcass, if the embryo of the calf is as small as a bean. For a fully developed creature imparts impurity, regardless of whether its bulk is smaller than a bean or an olive. But all this is by way of midrashic exegesis which one should undertake and receive due reward.

Now, in truth,[27] we should return to the subject. The statement of our master Moses (which we mentioned previously), *Show me your ways that I may know You* (Ex. 33:13) serves as an illuminating example for every intelligent person. It enables one to realize that in order to understand anything which is difficult or obscure in the meaning or statements of the other, one must become acquainted with his methods and characteristics. Surely, even the physician, politician, or person who wants to read a foreign script must in each case immediately apply himself to understanding the humors, human character, and the practice of one who forms the shapes of the letters? Then he will attain the expertise needed to reach the truth. We should act in the same way with our

25. B. Shabb. 30b.

26. P. Nazir 7 (2) 56b. On the reading of the passage, see S. Lieberman, *Shkiin*, 82 (Hebrew) who refers to de' Rossi's discussion and ratifies the reading in the *Shilṭe ha-Gibborim.*

27. 'In truth' (*amana*). This is a pun on the previous statement.

sages to ensure that we gain deep insight into their thought,[28] and then we and they will be untouched by folly or sin. We should attain knowledge and understanding of their methods. In commenting on Scripture they were not using the methods of the literalists who were intent on understanding the actual words in the light of their context and would take into account the entire scope of what is being communicated in the narrative. Rather, external considerations determined their statements and teaching. These may comprise praise of our God for His good ways and His might, or extolling a certain virtue and censuring a particular vice. Their purpose may be to give instruction about a particular concept or to encourage avoidance of a particular folly or other matters of a similar nature. This all has its own truth, but it has no bearing on the sense of the verses which serve their purpose as pointers and as a frame of reference. You should see what the author of the *Guide* wrote:[29]

> With regard to the Midrashim,[30] there are two classes of people: The one class imagines that they are an explanation of the meaning of the verse in question, and they fight and strive to prove the truth of the Midrashim and to uphold them and to give them the same status as the accepted legal decisions. The second class is contemptuous of the Midrashim and regards them as derisory since it is obvious and manifest that they do not convey the meaning of the verse. But neither of the two categories realize that poetic rhetoric, which was generally known at that time, is used in the Midrashim. This may be illustrated by their Midrash on the verse, *And you shall have a paddle on your weapon* (*azenekha*) (Deut. 23:14) which, by means of figurative language, simply admonishes the one who would even listen to reprehensible things.[31]

Similarly, in his explanation of the Aggadot on Berakhot and Bava Batra,[32] cited by Aboab,[33] Rashba [Solomon ben Adret] of blessed memory speaks of the Midrash on the verse, *Therefore those who make parables* (these are they that master their inclination) *would recite: Come to Heshbon* (come and give account of the soul) (Num. 21:27).[34] He writes: "In Midrashim such as these, the point of our sages is to provide support from Scripture by using expressions which render them memorable; but they had no intention whatsoever of interpreting the verses as such." Moreover, with regard to the verse, *Gather to me seventy men* (Num. 11:16), the sage Recanati writes:[35] "You should realize that our rabbis sometimes make a true pronouncement based on tradition or clear-cut evidence and then cite a verse as a mnemonical allusion to it or simply as a support." This method is even applied to the precepts. For example, ibn Ezra discusses the

28. 'To gain deep insight into their thought,' lit. that we should understand their end. Cf. Deut. 32:29.

29. *Guide* III, ch. 43.

30. De' Rossi uses the word *derashot* interchangeably with *Midrashim.*

31. The passage is B. Ket. 5a–b: "Bar Kappara teaches: . . . Do not read *azenekha* but *aznekha* [your ear]. This teaches us that whenever a man hears a reprehensible thing, he should put his finger into his ear."

32. Solomon ben Adret, *Ḥiddushe ha-Rashba* (49; 58–59). De' Rossi may have seen the work in manuscript, although the quotation is taken *verbatim* from Jacob ibn Ḥabib (see following note).

33. De' Rossi refers to Aboab, the author of *Menorat ha-Ma'or.* However, it would appear that his citation of the Rashba is taken from Jacob ibn Ḥabib who quotes it in his *En Jacob* in his commentary to B. B.B. 78b.

34. B. B.B. 78b. The Aggadah plays on the word *ha-moshelim* which either means "those who make parables" or "those who rule," and on *ḥeshbon* (in the verse, a name of a place) which may also mean "reckoning."

35. Recanati, *Perush* to Num. 11:16 (74 col. c).

precept of procreation linked to the verse, *Be fruitful and multiply* (Gen. 1:28) and writes: "This precept was transmitted by our ancestors and they used the verse as an aide-memoire and as a support."[36] Likewise, there is the statement of the rabbis of blessed memory in tractate Eruvin:[37] "The laws relating to minimum quantities, interpositions, and partitions fall into the category of laws transmitted from Sinai. They objected: 'But are they not scriptural for it is written, *a land of wheat and barley* (Deut. 8:8)?' Rabbi Isaac [Hanan] said, 'The entire verse refers to measures and sizes.' They responded, 'Yes, it does fall into the category of *halakhah* transmitted [orally] from Sinai, and the scriptural verse is used simply as a support.' " In a similar vein is Rav Ashi's statement:[38] "A divorce given by a levir is a rabbinic enactment for which Scripture is used as a mere support." In other words, since we are fully conversant with the verses of Scripture, we should similarly commit to memory the words of wisdom which they [i.e., the sages] linked to them. This method is particularly beneficial for beginners, as is illustrated by their statement in Midrash Qohelet with reference to the verse, *I constructed pools of water, enough to irrigate a forest shooting up with trees* (Eccl. 2:6):[39] "*I constructed pools of water*—these are the homilies; *to irrigate a forest shooting up with trees*—these are the children." This is undoubtedly applicable to some of the Midrashim, but they do not all have the same purpose. Note that it is for this reason that they are called Midrashim and not *perushim* (explanations). For on investigating the basic notion of the designation Midrash, you will realize that it suggests the idea of removing the intended literal sense[40] and investing it with a meaning remote from it. Thus, with regard to the word *bereshit* (in the beginning), they say, "This scriptural verse is asking to be expounded (*derashani*) . . . God created the world for the sake of Israel . . . for the sake of the Torah."[41] In Bereshit Rabbah, it is stated:[42] "The book of Chronicles was only given in order to be expounded [*li-daresh*] as when it reads, *The sons of Shela, the son of Judah, . . . the father (av) of Lecah . . . the father of Maresha* (1Chr. 4:21–23). *The father of Lecah*—this refers to the head (*av*) of the court of Leca; *the father of Maresha*—this refers to the head of the court of Maresha." Moreover, in Vayiqra Rabbah, it states with regard to the verse, *And his Judahite wife bore Jered* (1Chr. 4:18): "The book of Chronicles was only given in order to be expounded. *His Judahite wife* refers to Jochebed."[43] With regard to Ben Sirach's maxim, "Do not strip the skin [of a fish] from its ear," they say in Sanhedrin:[44] "If its literal meaning appears to be problematic, you should consider the verse in Torah which also states, *You must not destroy its*

36. Ibn Ezra to Gen. 1:28. (De' Rossi's reading of ibn Ezra agrees with the French recension of the text printed by M. Friedlander, London, 1877, vol. 4, 32.) The idea is that the expression *be fruitful and multiply* appears to be in the form of a blessing. The rabbis, however, classified procreation as one of the commandments on the basis of the biblical expression.

37. B. Eruv. 4a (ch. 1 and not ch. 3, as de' Rossi writes).

38. B. Yev. 52b.

39. Q.R. to Eccl. 2:8.

40. Cassel reads *mishpaṭ* instead of *mi-peshaṭ*.

41. See Rashi to Gen. 1:1. He quotes from Midrashim which use verses that contain the word "beginning" in order to compose homilies stressing that the world was created on behalf of the Torah and Israel, etc.

42. B.R. 61:4 (662). The beginning of the quotation is taken from V.R.

43. V.R. 1:3 (8).

44. B. Sanh. 100b.

trees (Deut. 20:19). If you expound it midrashically, it teaches normal behavior, namely, that one should not indulge in unnatural intercourse." Similarly, in Bereshit Rabbah, they comment on the verse, *and he [man] shall rule over you [woman]* (Gen. 3:16): "You might think that he is dominant in all situations, and so Scripture states, *A handmill or an upper millstone shall not be taken as a pledge for that would be taking someone's life as a pledge* (Deut. 24:6)."[45] Rambam also gives a fine treatment of this subject in chapter 21 of the laws on forbidden sexual intercourse.[46] Study the passage for yourself. In addition there is another passage in Bereshit Rabbah in which it is said:[47] "If a Noachide has unnatural intercourse with his wife, he is liable to the death penalty as it says, *Hence a man leaves his father and mother and clings to his wife so that they become one flesh* (Gen. 2:24)—in the place where both form one flesh." Josephus's reference to this prohibition in his *Against Apion* may indicate that he derived his information from one of these homilies.[48] Then again, they describe the list of names between Azel (1Chr. 8:38) and Azel (1Chr. 9:44) in the book of genealogies [i.e., Chronicles] as "laden with four hundred camel-loads of homiletical interpretations."[49] The author of the *Arukh* did not give the correct interpretation of this statement. He writes:[50] "The section in Chronicles begins with the word Azel and ends with Azel; and despite the fact that they are in close proximity to one another, it is stated that the section is laden with four hundred camel-loads of homiletical interpretations." According to his explanation, there was no reason to divest the verses of their literal meaning. But the correct understanding of the statement was given by Rashi and we will mention his comment again in chapter 28. At the end of chapter 8, the verses begin, *The father of Gibeon dwelt in Gibeon* (vv.29ff.) and these are all repeated at the end of chapter 9 (vv.35ff.), although there are some difference between the two passages. Then again, the verses at the beginning of chapter 9 which begin, *The first to settle in their towns* (v.2) and later, *Of the priests* (v.10) are mentioned in the book of Ezra in the chapter which begins, *These are the people of the province who came up from among the captive exiles* (ch. 2), although there is a great difference between the two versions. Thus, what emerges from this is that there are two kinds of problems: substantial redundancy and extensive divergencies which all occur between the passage referring to Azel at the end of chapter 8 and the reference to Azel at the end of chapter 9. As a consequence, our sages of blessed memory proposed that every word [in the section] lent itself to homiletical expositions that divested the text of its literal meaning. Likewise, there are many other passages in which the sages of blessed memory clearly demonstrate that an explanation of the verse according to its plain sense cannot in any way be called a Midrash. Thus, with regard to some expositions which are very close to the plain sense of the text, Rashi expounds,[51] "I heard a

45. B.R. 20:7 (191).

46. *Mishneh Torah,* Issure Bi'ah.

47. B.R. 18:5 (167). The verse is understood to refer to a female debtor and therefore implies that a man may not seize a pledge from a woman.

48. *Contra Apionem* II, 199: "The Law recognizes no sexual connection except the natural union of man and wife and that only for the procreation of children."

49. B. Pes. 62b.

50. Arukh, s.v. *Aṣl.*

51. The midrashic source of Rashi's comment is not known. According to Cassel (ad loc.), Rashi may have been quoting a scribal gloss. Cf. B.R. 63:9 (692): "A Roman prefect asked a member of the family of

Midrash Aggadah which explains the verse, *Then his brother emerged holding on to the heel of Esau* (Gen. 25:26) according to its plain sense. It was right that he should have grasped the heel of Jacob."

The gentile sages called these methods of exposition metaphor, symbol and allegory. Thus, if you raise a question which is not germane to the topic in hand, the respondent might object in surprise, "Lord of Abraham, he bases his teaching on that which was not taught."[52] In the same way, the commentators and later authorities mentioned previously[53] disputed our sages' statements in their commentaries and questioned the expositions from the perspective of the plain meaning of the verses as for example in the case of the interpretation of the three passages linked to the episode of the binding of Isaac.[54] These and all such statements are surely rendered null and void[55] since each person follows his own method. One will adhere to the plain meaning of the text, while another will expound it with an extraneous purpose in mind, as we have stated, and these are both "the words of God." This is the truth of the matter and requisite knowledge. The fact is that not all their Midrashim on Scripture can be evaluated by us in one fell swoop since they produced them by means of those devices that we mentioned, and are a product of their own wisdom. However, as Rabbenu Samson said in his *Keritut,* we must distinguish the thirteen hermeneutical principles (which Rabbi Ishmael taught)[56] by which the Torah is expounded from which we deduce lenient and stringent decisions and laws, from the thirty-two paths by which (according to the pronouncement of Rabbi Eliezer bar Rabbi Yose the Galilean),[57] the Aggadah is expounded but which cannot be used to deduce any of the main aspects of Torah.[58] The fact is that anything which is deduced by means of any of the thirteen principles, although it is called Midrash, is a completely literal interpretation of the text which one may not question nor transform into allegory in any way. Consequently, in their classification of learning, the sages of blessed memory state[59] (and the statement is cited by Rambam):[60] "If cases are brought forward of which one is midrashic and the other aggadic, the midrashic case is taken up." Then with regard to the statement, "Be married to me on condition that I am learned" Hezekiah states:[61] "This refers to *halakhot*" (while Rashi and Alfasi interpret it as a reference to the study

Sallu: 'Who will enjoy power after us?' He brought a blank piece of paper, took a quill and wrote, 'Then his brother emerged holding on to Jacob's heel.' "

52. This expression occurs in B. Shabb. 22a.

53. I.e., in ch. 14.

54. See ch. 14.

55. This expression is taken from the liturgy for the abrogation of vows in the Kol Nidre service for the Day of Atonement.

56. The thirteen hermeneutical rules ascribed to R. Ishmael are an expansion of the seven attributed to Hillel.

57. These thirty-two hermeneutical rules are ascribed to R. Eliezer ben Yose the Galilean (second century), although the list of rules is not mentioned in its entirety in the Talmud.

58. Samson of Chinon *Sefer Keritut,* pt. 3, Netivot Olam (115).

59. T. Sanh. 7:7. De' Rossi also refers to ch. 8 of tractate Berakhot in this regard, but there is no such reference.

60. *Mishneh Torah,* Talmud Torah IV:8.

61. B. Qidd. 49a–b.

of Mishnah).[62] Rabbi Johanan said, "This means Torah," which is explained in the Gemara as referring to the Midrash on the Torah, i.e., the Midrash through which the main areas of the Torah are taught, while according to the author of the *Oṣar ha-Kavod,* Torah refers to the esoteric meanings of the Torah.[63] This topic is discussed in the Avot d'Rabbi Nathan:[64] "Whoever has a grasp of Midrash but not *halakhot* has not savored the taste of wisdom; whoever has a grasp of *halakhot* but not Midrash has not savored the taste of the fear of sin. Again, if he has Midrash but not *halakhot,* he is a warrior without arms; while the one who has *halakhot* but not Midrash is weak although armed. If he is in possession of both Midrash and *halakhot,* he is a warrior and armed." Under no circumstances should we confuse this term "Midrash" on the Torah with the auxiliary terms "Midrash Aggadah" or simply "Aggadah." The former designation constitutes Torah according to its textual and written form which is ours and our descendants's legacy.

While we were roaming the paths of Aggadah, we became aware of a matter which required examination that was surprisingly anomalous and was certainly worthy of discussion, namely, that the rabbis of blessed memory spoke about the subject of Aggadah in greatly contradictory terms. This is particularly conspicuous in the statements of Rabbi Joshua ben Levi. Sometimes he appears to detest and debase the Aggadot in no uncertain terms, while on other occasions he appears to embrace the Aggadot and exhort study of them, singing their praises to the sky. Now in tractate Shabbat of the Palestinian Talmud and in tractate Soferim, it is stated:[65] "Rabbi Joshua ben Levi said, 'Anyone who commits Aggadah to writing forfeits his share (i.e., will have no benefit from it) [in the world to come]; whoever uses it for exposition, will get burnt (i.e., his words will become shriveled up even on his own person); and whoever listens to Aggadah receives no reward (i.e., as would the one who studies Torah)." Then it is also stated in the same passage in the Palestinian Talmud:[66]

> Rabbi Joshua ben Levi said: "I have never looked at aggadic sayings save the time I discovered a text in which it was written that the 175 sections of the Pentateuch[67] corresponded to the years of the life of Abraham and that the 148 Psalms[68] corresponded to the years of Jacob *who sits enthroned on the praises of Israel* (Ps. 22:4)[69] and that the 123 responses

62. Alfasi does understand the term as a reference to Mishnah, but Rashi (ad loc.) interprets it as a reference to Sinaitic *halakhah.*

63. Todros Halevi Abulafia (1221–98) was the author of *Oṣar ha-Kavod,* a kabbalistic interpretation of the Aggadot of the Talmud. De' Rossi must have read the work in manuscript. De' Rossi is referring to Abulafia's comment on B. Qidd. 49a (60, col. a) in which he claims that whenever the sages of the Talmud use the word Torah in an absolute form, it refers to the secret wisdom by which the secrets of the Torah are explained.

64. ARN, rec. A 29:7 (89).

65. P. Shabb. 16:1 (15c); Sof. 16:2. The word *mitharekh* (burnt up) is problematic. See Z. H. Chayes, *The Student's Guide,* 246, who suggests a different reading, "banned."

66. Ibid. In B., he also refers to Mid. Teh. 22:19 to Ps. 22:4.

67. This appears to be a reference to the 154 weekly readings of Pentateuch read according to the triennial cycle and the 21 sections read for special occasions.

68. There are 150 Psalms in our present Psalter, but in these instances the rabbis counted the adjacent Psalms as one. See S. Buber's note to Mid. Teh. 22:19 (190).

69. Israel is taken as a reference to Jacob.

> of Hallelujah[70] corresponds to the years of Aaron[71] (that is why Rambam refers to Aaron in this way).[72] Nevertheless I am still frightened about this at night (i.e., despite a certain delight and aesthetic pleasure that this Aggadah conveys, I pronounce that it ought to be obliterated and expunged).

In contrast, the passage which treats the question of the omission of an allusion to a good life[73] in the first occurrence of the ten commandments (Ex. 20:12)[74] contains the statement that Rabbi Tanḥum used to go to Rabbi Joshua ben Levi who was an expert in Aggadah.[75] And it is stated that Rav Simi ben Uqba would visit Rabbi Simeon ben Pazzi to hear legal decisions, while coming to Rabbi Joshua ben Levi to hear Aggadot.[76] And the expression *the Lord's deeds* in the verse, *For they do not consider the Lord's deeds* (Ps. 28:5) is expounded by Rabbi Joshua ben Levi as a reference to the Aggadot.[77] On the verse, *He who strives to do good and kind deeds attains life, success, and honor* (Pr. 21:21), Rabbi Joshua ben Levi states: "He will be worthy of having children who are wise [wealthy] and Aggadists."[78]

The contradiction is thus quite apparent. It is true that in the specific case of Rabbi Joshua ben Levi, one of two possible solutions may be proffered. The first possibility is that there were two people of the name Rabbi Joshua ben Levi whose teaching differed one from the other. After all, the Tosafists suggest that there were two people named Rabbi Ishmael ben Elisha[79] and that there were two called Rav Ada bar Ahava[80] and there are many other such examples. Alternatively, he might have retracted his opinion in like manner to Rabbi Zera who said:[81] "At first, when I saw the scholars running to the lecture on the Sabbath, I thought that they were desecrating the Sabbath. . . . But since I heard the sayings of Rabbi Tanḥum . . . , I also run." There is a similar case of Rav Joseph:[82] "Formerly, if someone would say to me [in accordance with the ruling of Rabbi Judah] that a blind person is exempt from fulfilling the commandments, I would celebrate. . . . But now having heard the statement of Rabbi Ḥanina, should I be told that a blind person is obliged to fulfill the precepts, I would celebrate." Similarly, it may be that Rabbi Joshua ben Levi initially detested the Aggadot. His opposition may

70. This is a reference to the Hallel Psalms (113–18).

71. In Ps. 106:16 Aaron is called a *holy one of the Lord;* in Ps. 34:10 it states, *Fear the Lord, O you holy ones,* and in Ps. 22:24 it states, *Praise Him, all you who fear the Lord.* By juxtaposition of these three passages, it is inferred that Aaron is the subject of Ps. 22:4.

72. *Mishneh Torah,* Ḥanukkah III:12: "The custom of the ancients in reading the Hallel was that they responded with Halleluyah 123 times which has as its mnemonic the years of Aaron."

73. I.e., in connection with the commandment of honoring one's parents.

74. I.e., as opposed to the second occurrence in Deut. 5:16.

75. B. B.Q. 55a.

76. B. Ber. 10a. De' Rossi has a different reading from the standard text. His reading is noted by Rabbinovicz in his *Diqduqe Soferim.* De' Rossi gives the same reading as is found in the introduction to the *Menorat ha-Ma'or.*

77. Mid. Teh. to Ps. 28:5.

78. B. B.B. 9b.

79. Tos to B. Yev. 104a, s.v. *amar.*

80. Tos to B. Taʿanit 20b, s.v. *amar.*

81. B. Ber. 6b.

82. B. Qidd. 31a.

have been similar to that of Yedidyah the Alexandrian [Philo]. For in his books, *The Worse Attacks the Better* (p. 157),[83] *On Compassion* (p. 605),[84] *On Reward and Punishment* (p. 763)[85] and *That the World Is Indestructible* (p. 789),[86] he forcefully rejects the fictitious inventions of the poets, which are undoubtedly their kind of Aggadah, on the grounds that natural philosophers would reject any fiction[87] that has its existence only in the imagination. They would not even tolerate its use for conveying a philosophical notion. However, when Rabbi Joshua ben Levi heard rabbinic pronouncements in praise of the Aggadot which we shall presently mention, he did not shun them but rather acclaimed them. In any case, the problem has not been eradicated since we have noticed that this particular contradiction is not exclusive to Rabbi Joshua ben Levi, but it is also manifested among the community of sages of blessed memory. Indeed, there is a statement in tractate Shabbat in the Palestinian Talmud mentioned before which reads:[88] "Rabbi Ḥiyya saw a book of Aggadot and said: 'If that which is written is good, let the hand of the one who wrote it be cut off.' [Someone said, 'It was your father who wrote it.' He said, 'I still maintain that it should be cut off.] It is *as great as an error committed by a ruler* (Eccl. 10:5).'" And in tractate Maʿaserot in the Palestinian Talmud, Rabbi Zeʿera, rebuking the propagators of Aggadah, dubbed their books sorcery.[89] And in tractate Soferim they say that Aggadah must not be put down in writing.[90] The fact that Rabbi Johanan used to study a book of Aggadot on the Sabbath is presented as a novelty in Giṭṭin.[91] In Shevuʿot, they refer to a book of Aggadot belonging to orphans as falling into the category of things which may be lent and hired out.[92] According to Rashi, this implies that these kinds of books were not used for continuous study. In contrast to all these statements is he comment on the expression, *every prop of water* (Is. 3:1): "These are the masters of Aggadah who attract the attention of people like water."[93] And in the Sifre they comment on the verse, *And foaming grape blood was your drink* (Deut. 32:14), ["These are the Aggadot which attract the attention of people] like wine."[94] In the Mekhilta, they comment on the verse, *It* [i.e., the manna] *was like the seed of Gad* (Num. 11:7): "[It was like the words of Aggadah which attract the attention of people] like the manna."[95] In Midrash Qohelet, they comment on the expression *the delights of the sons of men* (Eccl. 2:8): "These are the Aggadot that are the delightful part of Scripture." And in the Sifre, they comment on the verse, *But that man may live on everything that comes forth from the mouth of the Lord* (Deut. 8:3): "These are the *halakhot* and Aggadot. If you desire to know Him who spoke and the world came into being, study Aggadah for

83. *Det.* 125.
84. *Virt. (De humanitate),* 65: "For no created being is God in reality, but only in men's fancies."
85. *Praem.* 8.
86. *Aet.* 56.
87. Cassel reads "ha-domeh." It should read "ha-medumeh."
88. P. Shabb. 16 (1) 15c.
89. P. Maʿas. 3 (10) 51a.
90. Sof. 16:2.
91. B. Giṭṭ. 60a.
92. B. Shev. 46b.
93. B. Ḥag. 14a.
94. Sifre Deut. par. 317.
95. Mekhilta d'Rabbi Ishmael, vayassa beshalaḥ 6 (II, 123).

through it you will come to know Him and cling to His ways."[96] And they say,[97] "Rich in goods, rich in pomp—that is the preachers of Aggadot." And in Bava Batra they say:[98] "Whenever you encounter Rabbi Eliezer bar Yose the Galilean's statements about Aggadah, make your ear like a funnel." There are many other examples of this kind. Anyone who really takes account of the contradiction, will exclaim in amazement, "What is the meaning of this?"[99]

Now the fact is that the person who will extricate us from this predicament will be the truly noble Gaon, Rav Sherira of blessed memory, together with his son Rav Hai of blessed memory, who followed in his ways. The author of the *Menorah* cited their statements in the introduction to his work.[100] He writes that in his *Megillat Setarim,* Rav Sherira has the following to say about the Aggadot: "Those statements which are derived from verses and are called Midrash and Aggadah are conjectural."[101] When Rav Hai Gaon his son was asked about the difference between the Midrash and Aggadah of the Gemara and that contained in other writings, he responded that the passages fixed in the Gemara were clearer than the others. From this we may gather that the Aggadot are undoubtedly not to be regarded as authentic and received *halakhah,* but merely conjecture on the part of their inventor. Some of the passages are apposite, precious, admired, and delightful, while others fall into the opposite category, for not everybody has the privilege of excelling in this sphere, as is also the case with other areas of wisdom. Take the example of Rabbi Aqiva of whose great stature we are cognizant. Nevertheless, when he gave an aggadic explanation, identifying the gatherer of wood on the Sabbath with Zelophehad,[102] and Elihu ben Barakhel with Balaam,[103] Rabbi Eleazar retorted with regard to both interpretations, "You shall in the future have to give account of yourself." In fact, with regard to the interpretation of *Thrones were set in place* (Dan. 7:9), Rabbi Eleazar said to him, "Aqiva, what do you have to do with Aggadot; cease your talk and go and deal with the laws of leprosy and impurities."[104]

Thus, despite our praise of the sages' statements that we articulated above, we cannot help but say that the purpose of the Aggadot corresponds to the meaning of their designation, namely, from the expression *naged ve-nafeq* (to flow and to come forth),[105]

96. Sifre Deut. to Deut. 11:20, par. 49.

97. B. B.B. 145b.

98. B. Ḥull. 89a.

99. The contradictory attitudes towards the Aggadot was noted by David ibn Zimra (1479–1559) in his Responsa. In his attack on de' Rossi (*Be'er,* 134, cols. a–b), the Maharal of Prague states that Joshua ben Levi's negative appraisal of the Aggadot was related to his opposition to having the Aggadot committed to writing.

100. Isaac Aboab (born at the end of the fourteenth century in Castille), *Menorat ha-Ma'or* (17). The book is a compilation of Aggadah divided into different topics. The first edition was printed in Constantinople, 1541.

101. De' Rossi truncates Aboab's quotation from Sherira who limits the application of the term conjectural only to "some of the Midrashim of the later Rabbis such as Tanḥuma and Oshaiah, and only in regard to a few of the Aggadot in the Talmud . . . but most of them are secrets, the highest of wisdoms. . . . Thus it is not right to dispense with the majority because of those few."

102. B. Shabb. 96b.

103. P. Sota V (7) 20d.

104. B. Ḥag. 14a.

105. The expression occurs in Dan. 7:10. De' Rossi appears to be claiming that the word "Aggadah" derives from the Aramaic expression "to flow and to come forth" which used transitively signifies "to cause to flow," i.e., to draw or attract.

namely, to attract people's attention to the meaning of our words. In fact, it is not just a question of listening, as was the case in the story related in the Mekhilta and Shir ha-Shirim Rabbah about the preacher who on seeing the community falling asleep, tried to arouse them by saying, "In Egypt one woman would give birth to sixty myriads at one delivery."[106] Rather, compliance is what is essential, to ensure that they are receptive to the teaching and by their instruction are drawn away from vices to virtues, and particularly to the love of God. This is analogous to the objectives of rhetoric which according to the gentile sages is intended to delight and to attract attention to whatever meaningful and knowledgeable statements of theirs may be acceptable to the listeners. This gives confirmation to the saying from the Sifre, "If you wish to know the Creator of all, study Aggadah." For it is indeed true that the one who employs parables and rhetoric in an effort to inspire people to attain knowledge of the blessed Lord, must surely himself have been previously inspired in exactly the same way. It is in reference to such commendable Aggadot that the sayings in praise of Aggadot pertained. However, there may be the case of the one who does not have the natural gift of speech (since we do say that the spirit is in man).[107] And there are those who would make pronouncements of the type we shall mention in chapter 19 with regard to the eighteen scribal emendations and the ten points in the Torah and other such matters that are found in some of the passages in the Pesiqta, the Yelammedenu and Midrash Avkir and the like, which according to Rav Hai Gaon of blessed memory were not fixed in the Gemara. It would seem appropriate that if someone were to mention one such statement, a person might respond in all honesty, "My brother, you embrace it as one would a babe, but I have no justification in giving it a stamp of approval in my teaching." Likewise, we have heard that in his disputation in the presence of the king, Ramban of blessed memory said to his opponent with regard to one Midrash, "Let he who so wishes believe in it."[108] But this should not lead us to suspect that his [i.e., Ramban's] purpose was anything but for the sake of heaven.[109] Similarly, when he deals with the question of the discrepancies between the Massoretic text and [the Scriptural citations in the] Gemara—this is also treated sensibly by ibn Adonijah in his introductions to the Venetian edition of the Rabbinic Bible[110]—Ramban lays down a principle in his *Responsa.* He writes:[111] "If it has a legal implication, we do not dissent from the Gemara;

106. Mekhilta d'Rabbi Ishmael, Beshalaḥ, 9 (II, 69); S.S.R. to I:15.

107. Cf. Job 32:8: *But truly it is the spirit in men, the breath of the Almighty that gives them understanding.* The point is that people's skills and abilities are a divine gift.

108. This is a reference to the Barcelona disputation of 1263 in which Nahmanides was one of the main disputants. In response to questions regarding the Aggadah in E.R. 1:16 according to which the Messiah was born on the day that the Temple was destroyed, Nahmanides states with regard to Midrash in general: "Whoever believes in it, fine, but no harm is done if one does not believe in it." (*Vikkuaḥ* in *Kitve Ramban,* vol. 1, 308).

109. De' Rossi's remark here is most interesting when seen in the light of modern scholars who have given different interpretations of Nahmanides' statement. Baer, e.g., did not take the statement at face value. On this, see H. Maccoby, *Judaism,* 44–46.

110. Jacob ben Hayyim ibn Adonijah worked on the second edition of the Rabbinic Bible published by Bomberg in Venice in 1524–25. He noted the discrepancies between the Massoretic text and citations in the Talmud. See the introduction published by C. D. Ginzburg, *Jacob ibn Adonijah,* 42, 57ff.

111. Ps. Nahmanides, *Teshuvot,* responsum 232. The responsum is actually written by Rashba (Solomon ben Adret).

otherwise, we follow the majority reading."[112] Moreover, since, as Rav Sherira stated, each Aggadah is simply conjectural and is intended to propel one's mind to any of the entire range of learned disciplines, you will notice that even with regard to those Aggadot canonized in the Gemara, there is total consensus that one does not learn from them or raise objections because of them. In other words, one does not raise objections about something else on the basis of the Aggadot nor question the Aggadot on the basis of something else. There is the statement of the sage in the *Kuzari* who says: "I acknowledge, king of the Kazars, that there are matters in the Gemara for which I cannot give you satisfactory explanations nor link them with the subject matter. These things were introduced through the conscientiousness of the disciples."[113] Quite apart from this pronouncement, there is the statement of the sages themselves, blessed be their memory, that we mentioned above, who said, "But are the Midrashim fundamental truths?" And there is the statement in tractate Ḥagigah and Pe'ah in the Palestinian Talmud where they say that no halakhic inferences may be deduced from Aggadot.[114] And in tractate Horayot in the Palestinian Talmud[115] and in Midrash Qohelet[116] they comment on the verse, *God sometimes grants a man riches, property, and wealth . . . but God does not permit him to enjoy it* (Eccl. 6:2), "This is the Aggadist who may issue neither permits nor prohibitions." And they say: "No questions should be asked about Aggadah." This is quoted at the end of the introduction to the *Guide*. And he also discusses this question at length in his commentary on Mishnah (chapter Ḥeleq) and in several places in the *Guide* in the formulation that I quoted previously from part 3 (chapter 43) of the work and even more specifically in section 2 (chapter 6) where he derides those who believe in the literal meaning of the homilies. A similar attitude is shown by Ritba [Yomtov ben Abraham] in regard to the Aggadah about Adam's reaction to the gradual disappearance of daylight.[117] And concerning the story of the necromancer, Rabbenu Nissim Gaon writes: "This is an aggadic tale and about all such tales our rabbis have stated that one does not rely on the words of Aggadah."[118]

Consequently, you should not find it problematic should you come across mutually contradictory Aggadot as mentioned by the Tosafists,[119] Rashi,[120] and Mizraḥi with regard to the vision of the ladder and other such passages.[121] Each Aggadah is said according to the requirements of its compiler, namely, to propel people to one idea or another. And the author of the statement himself may not use it as an established truth. Rather, as is stated in the Palestinian Talmud, it shrivels away.[122] And you will notice that in Bereshit Rabbah, the question as to how we know that ritual slaughter must be

112. I.e., the majority reading of biblical manuscripts against the reading in talmudic Aggadot.

113. *Kuzari* III, par. 73.

114. P. Pe'ah 2 (4) 17a; P. Ḥag. 1 (8) 76d.

115. P. Hor. III (5) 48c.

116. Q.R. to Eccl. 6:2.

117. *Ḥiddushe ha-Ritba* (col. 29 to B. A.Z. 8a). The passage is also cited in *En Ya'aqov* to B. A.Z. 8a: "But one does not make objections with regard to Aggadah."

118. Rabbenu Nissim Gaon is quoted by Jacob ibn Ḥabib (ha-Kotev) in *En Ya'aqov* to B. Ber. 59a.

119. Tos. to B. Yev. 16b s.v. *pasuq zeh*.

120. Rashi to Gen. 47:2; Num. 11:20.

121. Elijah Mizraḥi (1450–1526), *Perush Rashi* to Gen. 28:11 Mizraḥi speaks of Rashi's conflation of two "contradictory Aggadot."

122. I.e., the Aggadah has no permanent value.

done with a movable object is answered with reference to a verse from the section dealing with the binding of Isaac.[123] This is followed by the statement: "If he said this as a tradition, it cannot be retracted, but if it was as an Aggadah it may be retracted." Accordingly, it would appear that there are some Aggadot that bear a certain affinity to the angels created from the river of fire mentioned in several places by our sages of blessed memory;[124] once they have sung their song, they depart never to return. In the same way there are some Aggadot which, once the expositor has used them to achieve his desired purpose, are no longer referred to nor enlisted as proof of events that really happened or as substantiation of matters that are rationally implausible. For example, one should not adduce proof of the statement about the sixty myriads born in one delivery. All this approximates to the principle laid down in tractates Peʾah and Ḥagigah in the Palestinian Talmud that one must not deduce *halakhah* on the basis of Aggadot.

In conjunction with Rav Sherira's statements that the Midrashim are conjecture and Rabbi Moses' [Maimonides] designation of the Aggadot as allegory as stated above, we might also evaluate some of them as a simple device intended to arouse our attention and instruct us in a variety of matters. One Aggadah does not necessarily contain instruction on just one single matter, but very often one Aggadah may comprise many teachings. This may be illustrated by the famous passage in Ḥullin:[125] ["Rabbi Simeon ben Pazzi pointed out a contradiction between, *And God made two great lights* (Gen. 1:16) and, *and the greater light and the lesser light* (Gen. 1:14). The moon said, 'Is it possible for two kings to wear one crown?' He answered, 'Go and make yourself smaller. . . . Israel shall reckon days and years by you.' On seeing that it would not be consoled, the Holy One blessed be He said, 'Bring an atonement for Me for having made the moon smaller.' This is what is meant by Resh Laqish. . . . The Holy One blessed be He said, 'Let this he-goat be an atonement for Me for making the moon smaller.' "] As you know, Rav Alfasi made a forced interpretation in order to bring Resh Laqish's statement in line with that of Rabbi Simeon ben Pazzi, as is clear from his reading of the passage and from everything he states with regard to that *halakhah*.[126] Moreover, there is lack of clarity in his final statement: "The purpose of the atonement offering [every new-moon day] is that you should keep the peace for me[127] [by maintaining the glory which I said I would give to the moon because I diminished it"]. However, a sage would not be contemptuous of your words, should you say that all this is simply a device to make us wary of the inappropriateness of appointing two people to minister with the same crown; of deterring us from contention and jealousy among our peers; how that commensurate punishment is meted out for such behavior so that one becomes reduced to size; that all the homilies about pacifying the moon are appropriate for the righteous as for the world;[128] that one should not be too hasty in punishing a

123. B.R. 56:6 (602).
124. He refers to B. Ḥag. 14a; B.R. 78:1 (916); E.R. to Lam. 3:22.
125. B. Ḥull. 60b.
126. Alfasi Shev. 1a–b to B. Shev. 2a.
127. 'Keep the peace for me.' The text is unclear.
128. Cf. M. Avot 6:8: "Beauty, strength, riches, glory, wisdom, old age, grey hair, and children are fitting for the righteous and fitting for the world."

person of high station. This is the method commended by the rabbis—that one should not punish a colleague with stripes;[129] that every sinner, even somebody of high station, ought to seek atonement. And the passage contains other such ideas.

Then there is the statement of the great Rav Meir of Toledo in his book of *Pesaqim* [decisions] on tractate Bava Batra which in my opinion should be showered with praises.*[130] He cites (par. 61) the exposition of the verse, *For Joab and all Israel stayed there for six months and killed every male [zakhar] in Edom* (1K. 11:16). In Bava Batra, it is stated:[131] "[When Joab came before David, he said, 'Why did you act like this?' 'Because it is written, *You shall blot out the males [zekhar] of Amalek* (Deut. 25:19).' David said, 'But we read *zekher* (remembrance).' He replied, 'I was taught to read *zekhar*].' " In that context they cite the verses from Jeremiah, *Cursed is he who is slack in doing the Lord's work. Cursed be he who withholds his sword from blood* (Jer. 48:10). Meir then writes:[132] "Even though those verses of Jeremiah were said several generations after David and Joab, they [i.e., these teachings] were all traditionally transmitted as Mosaic *halakhah* from Sinai. Jeremiah came and attached them to the verse, using them as a support for the purpose of teaching us how grave is the sin of scribes, teachers of children, and others like them who are negligent in the Lord's work. As a result they become deserving of the curse and liable to a divinely ordained death." It is certainly evident that there are no grounds for either his question or solution. The author of the passage did not intend to refer to an actual event. Rather he simply invented the story in order to teach us the gravity of the kind of sin described by Rabbi Meir of blessed memory. On the contrary, should there have been any vestige of a problem, the author of the statement would have been pleased that it had alerted the reader not to take the story at face value, as we shall mention again at the end of the next chapter. In this way, many other statements of a similar nature can be resolved. Indeed instruction by means of imaginary tales was a mode very much current among the gentile sages of antiquity. (I shall speak about this again in chapter 40.) But they were accustomed to associate their teachings with stories about animals and mundane matters. Our sages, however, derived their teachings from the stories of the Torah, according to their axiom that everything is contained in it,[133] although it was obvious to them that they were not conveying the literal meaning of the text.

(*I saw the work which was in possession of my brother-in-law Rabbi Hayyim Massaran.[134] It was transcribed in the year 5066 [1306] in the city of Toledo. It is far longer than the *Pesaqim* of Rabbenu Nissim and is written in an extremely beautiful style. He gives decisions derived from the Mishnah separately from those based on the Gemara. I did not notice that he referred to any of the later authorities of blessed

129. Cf. B. M.Q. 17a. De' Rossi has misquoted the passage, in which they suggest that stripes are preferable to the ban.

130. This is a reference to Meir Halevi Abulafia (1165–1244), the Ramah, who was renowned for his talmudic expertise. De' Rossi's adulation of Ramah reflects a common view. Cf., e.g., Judah Alḥarizi's view: "None compared to him in wisdom." On Ramah, see B. Septimus, *Hispano-Jewish Culture.*

131. B. B.B. 21a–b.

132. *Yad Ramah,* par. 61, f. 59b. See n. 136.

133. Cf. M. Avot 5:22, "Turn it around, turn it around for everything is in it [i.e., the Torah]."

134. According to S. Simonsohn (*History,* 217), de' Rossi's brother-in-law was Vita (Hayyim) Massaran, a Mantuan banker.

memory.[135] But in a comment on Bava Batra, he writes (par. 40): "From the passage given by Rabbenu Hananel . . ."[136] This was undoubtedly the method he used in all the other tractates of laws which is similar to the method of Alfasi of blessed memory. Would that we could find the texts. As far as I can glean from the final words of Rabad the Levite in his *Sefer ha-Qabbalah,* the fore-mentioned Rabbi Meir was the son or nephew of Rabbenu Joseph son of Meir Halevi ibn Megash with whom he fled from Granada to Toledo because of the calamities.[137])

However, while we are speaking on the subject of the Aggadot, we may offer a further observation on and confirmation of the words of Riaz [Isaiah di Trani the younger]. While it is not my intention to explain all their methods, I cannot refrain from mentioning one specific feature that is crucial for understanding one of their methods, and which is frequently applied by the sages of blessed memory. It is as follows. The rabbis knew that the specific semantic formulation of the text conveyed its meaning in an individual manner. This may be illustrated by the expression *And you shall circumcise the foreskin of your hearts* (Deut. 10:16), which is certainly not to be understood literally but is intended to encourage submission and obedience. Nevertheless, for the sake of a laudable purpose and precious teaching, the sages of blessed memory were in the habit of reading certain verses exactly as written as though they were meant to be the actual truth. This may be exemplified by a passage in the Mekhilta:[138] "It is written, *And the Lord came down on Mount Sinai* (Ex. 19:20) and it is also written, *I have talked with you from heaven* (Ex. 20:22). This teaches you that He bent down the upper and lower heavens and spread them on Mount Sinai as a person spreads a mattress on a bed, and the Throne of Glory descended." A thinking person should not be concerned about taking this and countless other statements of a similar nature literally. Rather he should declare them to be a rhetorical way of demonstrating the blessed Lord's manifold goodness to the house of Israel; that He as it were lowers the level of His glory for the sake of cleaving to them. This purpose was achieved by the author of the statement because he interpreted the text exactly as it was written. Rabbi Johanan's statement mentioned before is in this vein.[139] When he was asked, "Let our master tell us words of Aggadah," he said, "Jacob our father is not dead." When his questioner replied in surprise, "But was he not embalmed?" he answered, "I am expounding Scripture." The point of the comment is that Scripture states, *And he expired and was gathered to his people* (Gen. 49:33) without mentioning death. In other words, such an assertion, it would appear, is feasible from the basis of Scripture itself and through the efforts of the person who wishes to understand the actual configuration of the text. Similarly with regard to his statement that suffering is precious, Rabbi Aqiva [when questioned by a sick man] answered, "I am expounding Scripture."[140]

135. Abulafia does not mention teachers and rarely, predecessors, but does sometimes draw upon the works of early Spanish Rabbis.

136. De' Rossi read the *Pesaqim* (also known as *Peraṭim*) in manuscript. His text agrees exactly with the reading in the Salonica 1790 edition of the work (par. 40, f. 130, col. b) entitled *Yad Ramah.*

137. *Sefer ha-Qabbalah* 7 (87). The 'calamities' refer to the Almohad persecution. De' Rossi's identification is not correct. Ramah was the son of the Nasi R. Todros Halevi Abulafia.

138. Mekhilta d'Rabbi Ishmael, baḥodesh 4 (II, 224).

139. B. Taʿanit 5b.

140. B. Sanh. 101a; Sifre to Deut. 6:5, par. 32.

And when Rabbi Eleazar said,[141] "The dead outside the Land of Israel will not be resurrected," Rabbi Abba objected. Then he answered, "My teacher I am expounding the verse, *Thus says God the Lord . . . who gave breath to the people upon it and life to those who walk thereon* (Is. 42:5)." Then further in the same context,[142] when the statement, "The illiterate will not be resurrected" was challenged, the response is given, "I am expounding Scripture which states, *For your dew is the dew of light* (Is. 26:19). The light of Torah revives all who use the light of Torah."

The juxtaposition of the sections [in Scripture] was treated in a similar fashion. It offered the possibility of claiming that all those stories were sequential, which led them to make such amazing statements as discussed above in relation to the story of Rebecca and to Micah's idol. One may assuredly say that in all cases, our rabbis, blessed be their memory, made those statements with a view of giving instruction for worthwhile purposes. Each passage should be examined in its own context in relation to its own setting.

{On the basis of this comment, it would appear that even more problematic is the sages' statement with regard to the verse, *There was no thing in his palace or realm that Hezekiah did not show them* [i.e., the Babylonians] (2K. 20:13). For in Pirqe d'Rabbi Eliezer it states that Hezekiah opened up the Ark and showed them the tablets of the Law.[143] And in his commentary on Kings, Rashi uses the rabbinic Midrashim when he states that he [i.e., Hezekiah] showed them the Ark, the tablets, and the scroll of the Torah. You might say that this was done by instigation of the high priest, just as in the beginning of Midrash Mishle, Solomon motioned to the high priest that he should open up the Ark of the Covenant for the Queen of Sheba.[144] Nevertheless, there is a problem with both passages. How was such an act possible given that it was prohibited according to the command, *Thus only Aaron shall enter the Shrine* (Lev. 16:3)? Moreover, according to Torat Kohanim, he was not even then allowed to enter at all times.[145] However, you could interpret the statement in line with the proposition "I am expounding Scripture." In other words, it would be actually tenable in the light of our other examinations to describe it as conjectural according to Sherira's definition. Then one might say that the expression "There was no thing that he did not show them" even includes the tablets and the scroll of the Torah which are called "things." In this way, our question is resolved.}

Now we have shown how our rabbis of blessed memory were deeply engaged in the realm of Aggadot. Nevertheless, in order to display their nobility to the peoples and royalty,[146] notwithstanding their method of linking Midrashim and Aggadah to Scripture, they themselves claimed that the true meaning was only to be found in the correct plain sense of Scripture, and that no Midrash or Aggadah should lead us to dispute in

141. B. Ket. 111a.
142. B. Ket. 111b.
143. PRE, ch. 52.
144. Midrash Mishle to Pr. 1:1: "The Queen of Sheba brought circumcised and uncircumcised men before him, all of the same height, all clothed the same. Then she said to him, "Distinguish between the circumcised and uncircumcised. He motioned at once to the high priest to open the Ark of the Covenant" (trans. B. L. Vizotsky, 19).
145. Sifra to Lev. 16:2, par. 8 (80, col. a).
146. Cf. Est. 1:11.

any way the plain meaning of the verses and rational interpretation. Thus they enunciated the important principle in tractate Shabbat[147] which is also cited in Yevamot,[148] "Scripture can never be divested of its plain meaning." When Rav Kahana heard this useful and notable teaching, he was so overjoyed that he virtually became like the gazelle mentioned by our rabbis[149] whose skin cannot contain its flesh, and he learnt it from his teacher forty times.[150]

Thus we have elucidated the point that we set out to communicate. The language of Torah according to its plain sense is completely distinct from the language of the sages in their Midrashim. The one does not encompass the other, and one may not learn from one to the other or raise questions from one to the other. Each category functions according to its own system.[151] Consequently, anyone who boasts of gifts not given, and claims that he understands the plain meaning of Scripture better than they, who in their own time were certainly the wisest of the wise, is simply wandering from the path of reason and will have his rest in the company of the shades.[152] As for me, I have expanded and extended the area for my research[153] of this subject to the extent that you, wise reader, will see for yourself that half of it would be more than enough for its corroboration required for many of these chapters. It will, I hope, suffice. And now, let us turn to the other part of the designated investigation. It is related to the events and historical episodes put in writing by our sages of blessed memory. Since they are strange by reason of their content or because of information gleaned from other sources, one might be induced not to believe them. This is the subject of the next chapter.

147. B. Shabb. 63a.
148. B. Yev. 24a.
149. B. Gitt. 57a.
150. In his second revisions not printed by Cassel but by Jaffe (Berlin, 1899), and with slight modifications in B, de' Rossi gives a long note in which he discusses examples from Talmud that indicate that the rabbis are aware of the *peshaṭ* of the verse, but derive *halakhah* from nonliteral exposition of the verses. He traces the acceptance of these interpretations among later authorities including Jonah ibn Janaḥ, Maimonides, Rashi, and Nahmanides.
151. 'Each category . . . system,' cf. B. Ber. 16a.
152. 'Company of the shades,' cf. Pr. 21:16.
153. 'Extended the area of research,' lit. I have extended my ploughing-ground. Cf. Ps. 129:3.

CHAPTER SIXTEEN

Concerning the story about the gnat that went into Titus's nostril as related by our rabbis.

In chapter 49 of Pirqe d'Rabbi Eliezer which is of greater antiquity than most of the other Tannaitic works known to us,[1] the following story is told: "Titus the wicked entered the Holy of Holies and said, 'There is no adversary or enemy that can get the better of me.' What did the Holy One blessed be He do? He dispatched a gnat against him; it entered his nostril and made its way to his brain; it became as a young pigeon weighing two selahs. This was to make him aware that his power was of no consequence." You can read a longer version of the story in Bereshit Rabbah,[2] Vayiqra Rabbah,[3] as well as in the Gemara in tractate Giṭṭin.[4] There is a marked divergency between the midrashic accounts and the passage in the Gemara, but this much may be abstracted from both versions. During his sea voyage on his way to Rome after the destruction of the Temple, he [Titus] blasphemed and uttered profanities. Then, a gnat went into his nostril and pecked at his brain for seven years. He cried out, "Break open my brain so that you can know how the God of the Jews has punished me." It is taught: Rabbi Eleazar bar Rabbi Jose said, "I was with the nobles of Rome and when he died, they broke open his brain and found something resembling a sparrow weighing two selahs." According to a mishnaic text, it was like a one-year-old pigeon weighing two pounds. Abbaye said, "We have a tradition that its beak was of copper, its claws of iron. They put it into a bowl and whatever mutation happened to the one [the gnat] happened also to the other [Titus]—the gnat flew away and so, too, the life of Titus."

You will find an account in the Tanḥuma which differs greatly both as regards the details and incidents of the event and its duration.[5] I did not care to make an exact transcription of all the various passages since the books are available. On comparing all the texts, one cannot fail to notice that there are many points on which they do not agree. Indeed, quite apart from this extensive divergency, the intelligent person is alerted into thinking that it cannot be taken literally—for if the story had been true, the

1. The authorship of the *Pirqe d'Rabbi Eliezer* is traditionally attributed to R. Eliezer ben Hyrcanus who lived in the first century C.E. It is usually dated to the ninth century C.E., although much of its material is of earlier origin.

2. B.R. 10:7 (82–83).

3. V.R. 22:3 (499–502).

4. B. Giṭṭ. 56b.

5. Tanḥuma, ḥuqqat 1.

narrators would have tended to produce more consistent accounts. Moreover, the thinking person would surely come to reflect on various matters. First of all, the tale is replete with matters contrary to nature. While they are certainly feasible by means of God's decree, their combination is, in truth, so extraordinary that one would have expected some outcome or publicity which would have been appropriate for a miracle of such magnitude. Now one may suppose that when the gnat entered the nostril, it would have ascended and placed itself above the meninges for, according to the anatomists, this is indeed an open channel. Of particular note is the statement of the scholar Fernelius[6] in his work *The Methods of Healing* (p. 49). He says that the correct method of unclogging the cerebral cortex is not by means of taking medicine orally, but by draining it through the nostril, ears, or neck or through the sutures of the skull.[7] And if one also supposes that it did not perforate his brain which is the opinion of the Tosafists when they solve the question as to whether he would have become *ṭerefah,*[8] had it torn the meninges,[9] one must surely wonder as to how there could have been sufficient space between the brain and the skull to contain a young bird of such a size? And surely it must have weighed upon the brain and wittled it away even more? For it is clearly stated in the passage in Bereshit Rabbah that it pecked at his brain and, what is more, for a long time. And in tractate Ḥullin, it is clearly stated that creatures without backbones cannot survive for more than twelve months.[10] And what of its beak being of copper and its claws of iron? According to the naturalists, these metals are produced in the bowels of the earth by the action of the primary qualities and the heat of the sun. Iron, in particular, is formed from turgid sulphur burnt with an admixture of a small amount of unrefined particles of mercury. And copper is formed from mercury that is in a process of becoming refined with red turgid sulphur. This information is readily accessible in ibn Latif's *Shaʿar ha-Shamayim*[11] and in the *Margarita.*[12] Thus if he did not

6. Jean Fernel (Ambianus) 1497–1558 was one of the most important sixteenth-century medical writers and physicians. He introduced the term "physiology" to describe the science of the functions of the body. He rejected the use of magic and sorcery for the understanding of medicine. He was a prolific writer and his works were frequently republished. See C. S. Sherrington, *The Endeavour.*

7. *Medicina,* "De purgandi ratione," lib. 3, ch. 9, 75–76. Here, Fernel refers to the draining of the skull through the nostrils and the ears. As for the remainder of the quote, I am indebted to Nancy Siraisi who has informed me that the idea that the function of the sutures of the skull are to allow harmful vapors to leave the head goes back to Galen (*De usu partium,* 9), and this idea was generally accepted in the sixteenth century by Vesalius and others. Galen also claimed that liquid residues from the brain flow out both through the nostrils and another pair of channels that led to the sphenoid bone. Vesalius rejected this route and postulated (see Singer's translation of Vesalius, *On the Human Brain,* 53, and n. 81) a channel adjacent to the carotid artery, which according to Siraisi may be a reference to the neck. De' Rossi may thus have conflated his quotation from Fernel with an interpretation of Vesalius. Alternatively, Siraisi suggests that the reference to draining through the neck is simply an allusion to some form of bloodletting.

8. *'Ṭerefah'* is a technical term to signify a human or an animal with a fatal disease, i.e., it cannot survive for more than a year.

9. Tos. to B. Giṭṭ. 56b, s.v. *ve-niqqer.* The Tosafists' question starts from the assumption that if the gnat had perforated Titus's brain, Titus, being a *ṭerefah,* could not have survived for more than one year.

10. B. Ḥull. 58a.

11. *Shaʿar ha-Shamayim* II, gate 2. De' Rossi wrongly attributed its authorship to ibn Latif, possibly because the author's name is not displayed on the title page of the ed. pr. Venice, 1547. The author was Gershon ben Solomon of Arles. The work is a compendium of natural history.

12. This is a reference to the fifteenth-century encyclopedic work of Gregorius Reisch entitled *Margarita Philosophica,* bk. 9, ch. 24. It was first printed in 1496, and there were many subsequent editions.

perforate the brain with his beak and claws, we must then consider the controversy of Rambam [Maimonides] and Ramban [Nahmanides] concerning the existence of the body in the world to come where all the body's appurtenances are of no consequence since there is no eating as is explained by Rambam in the laws of repentance[13] and by Ramban in the *Shaʿar ha-Gemul.*[14] And why were they of iron and copper when even if they had been of bones and sinews they would not have had any effect on it? And how come that in a sickness of this kind, which is comparable to that described in Ḥullin where there is softening and dissipation of the brain,[15] could his mind have remained unimpaired? After all this defies the usual and necessary course of sicknesses of the brain. For according to their account, Titus uttered rational statements. Furthermore, there is also a considerable problem as regards the date of the event. Go and read the chronicles of the emperors or more specifically Rabad's *Sefer ha-Qabbalah.*[16] You will find that the destruction of the Temple occurred in the second year of Vespasian's reign, and that he ruled for about ten years. He was succeeded by his son Titus who reigned less than three years. This means that at the end of the seven years when, according to the rabbis of blessed memory, Titus's life came to an end, he actually came to power. Furthermore, in some of my leisure moments, I looked through all the famous chronicles. For on a matter such as this I invoke the words of Jeremiah, *Assuredly, thus said the Lord: Inquire among the nations* (Jer. 18:13). My purpose was to find out what they had written about Titus's death and the nature of his illness. I found eight notable writers on the subject who all agree that the illness which caused his death was the fever. They are as follows: the Caesarean [Eusebius] in his chronological tables, Cassiodorus, and Contractus (all three were printed in the same volume);[17] Suetonius,[18] Eutropius,[19] Platina,[20] Mexía's *Lives of the Emperors,*[21] and Petrarch.[22] In each case, the relevant passage can be consulted by means of the index. There are also two others who provide additional evidence and clarification. There is the writer Dio who records that at the point of death, Titus said that he was unhappy that he had failed to accomplish one thing at the moment which was opportune for him. Dio then expresses the opinion that Titus was regretting that he had not killed his brother Domitian, since Titus believed that he had poisoned him in order to take over the throne, which was in fact the case.[23] In his *Life of Apollonius,* Philostratus the Greek writes that Domitian killed him by pricking his flesh with a spine from the tail of a fish called *pastinaca* (the stingray) which

13. Maimonides, *Mishneh Torah,* Teshuvah VIII:3, 4.

14. Nahmanides, *Shaʿar ha-Gemul,* 309–11. Ramban differs from Rambam in positing the existence of the body in a higher form for an interminable era in the world to come.

15. B. Ḥull. 45b.

16. This is a reference to the second section of Abraham ibn Daud's, *Sefer ha-Qabbalah* entitled *Zikhron Divre Romi.* Rabad speaks positively of Titus: "He was a great sage and forced to destroy the Temple."

17. This is a reference to the work entitled *En Damus Chronicon divinum plane opus eruditissimorum autorum* edited by Joannes Sichardus. The reference to Eusebius is 74v; Hermannus Contractus, 177r; Aelius Cassiodorus, 160v.

18. Suetonius, *Caesarum XII libri,* Titus X.

19. Eutropius, *De gestis Romanorum* VII, 22.

20. Platina (Bartolomeo de' Sacchi), *De vitis,* 16.

21. Mexía (Messia), *Le vite di tutti gl'imperadori,* 164.

22. Ps. Petrarch, *Chronica,* IXv. This work was translated into Latin and published in Petrarch's *Opera.*

23. Dio Cassius, *Romanae historiae libri,* LXXVI, 26, 4.

emits poisonous cold humors. This was also the means by which valiant warrior Ulysses, king of the island of Ithaca, was killed by his son Telemachus.[24]

Here, then, are ten men from nations of every tongue[25] who in their innocence speak wantonly[26] against the account of our blessed rabbis. It would seem that those who acknowledge the truth will have to admit that they knew the specific details of such stories better than our sages. On the other hand, I noticed that in his works on the kings of Greece, the contemporary writer called Ferentilla alleged that the person who died by means of a gnat entering the nostril was Antiochus Epiphanes, the enemy of the Jews, in the time of the Hasmoneans.[27] Consequently, the Lord delivered us from his power and that is why, as is well known, we celebrate Hanukkah. It is true, however, that he did not recount the incident in the miraculous fashion as did our rabbis. Now in 2 Maccabees, there is mention of the fact that Antiochus blasphemed and uttered profanities and behaved arrogantly. While the words were still in his mouth, he was gripped by pains and a severe and wasting sickness, his flesh was covered by worms, and he died in the grip of these diseases.[28] The event is described at length there, but there is no reference to the gnat as described by Ferentilla. I have no idea what his source was. The fact is that all this information makes it quite clear that our rabbis' story about Titus never happened neither in its entirety nor in part.

Now it is not my intention to be a wiseacre when I show people that some rabbinic statements should not be taken literally. Belonging to this genre, is the story of Og uprooting a mountain the size of three parasangs in Berakhot[29] and the stories about Rabbah bar bar Ḥana in Bava Batra.[30] These have long been acknowledged to be parables and riddles by all except fools as is noted by the author of the *Guide*.[31] However, with regard to this subject, I have been told specifically by people whom I regard as highly versed in Torah that they believe that the statements should be taken on face value, and they vehemently attack those who do not believe them. So I have put forward an opinion for the one who thirstily imbibes the words of our sages and who, as the fore-mentioned sage says, is drawn by the human intellect and thus led to dwell within its province.[32] For on hearing the story of the curse[33] of Titus or other such matters, he might be overcome and become perplexed because he is unable to bring himself to believe it. I spoke about the subject with integrity and in all honesty, in deference to the ruling of all those who possess knowledge. I would therefore make an analogy between the gentile sages and the rabbis. The poems and rhetoric of the gentile

24. De' Rossi refers to bk. 7 of Philostratus, but the quotation (which he does not quote precisely—Philostratus refers to the stingray, but then states that Titus was finally killed by eating the sea hare) is in bk. 6, 32.

25. Cf. Zech 8:23.

26. 'Speak wantonly,' cf. Ps. 94:4.

27. Agostino Ferentilli, *Discorso universale*, 110–11: "Morì Antiocho Epifane nell'ultima impresa . . . venne a morte per un grandissimo tormento che pativa d'una mosca che sendogli entrata dentro alle narici per solo guiditio di Dio." (The work was first published in 1570.)

28. 2 Macc. 9:5–10.

29. B. Ber. 54b.

30. B. B.B. 73a–b.

31. Maimonides, *Guide*, Introduction; II, ch. 6.

32. This is a quotation from Maimonides's Introduction to the *Guide*.

33. Cf. Deut. 29:18.

sages are replete with representations of events which never took place. They invented imaginary events for the moment so that those who "saw those sounds"[34] or imagined them would be inspired to acquire wise counsel and knowledge. This was the way many of them wrote and in particular their gifted orator, Cicero, in the first *Philippics*[35] and in his oration *Pro Roscio.*[36] In a similar fashion, our sages who were truly wise, were perfectly aware that even a story such as this had no foundation, or at least not in the way they described it. And yet, it did not prevent them from representing and embellishing it with such conspicuous detail as if it had really happened in the way they had enunciated. Their aim was to instill and infuse the people with knowledge of the goodness and justice to which they should aspire, and to impress upon their souls the purpose of morals and instruction which are requisite for us. For the sake of the glorification of God's name, they could even speak rhetorically as in the following passage from Sanhedrin: "*After these things [Jeroboam did not return from his evil way*] (1K. 13:33). What is meant by 'after'? Rabbi Abba said that the Holy One blessed be He seized Jeroboam by his garment and said, 'Repent and I, you, and the son of Jesse will walk in the Garden of Eden.' He said to him, 'Who will be at the head?' He replied, 'The son of Jesse will be at the head.' He said to him, 'If so, I do not want it.' "[37] The apparent purpose of this statement of our sages of blessed memory is to indicate how the Divine Presence takes pains to make the wicked relinquish their ways, and to show how some of them are so stubborn that they reject incomparable bounty for fatuous reasons. Similarly there is a passage about Sennacherib with regard to the verse, *In that day my Lord will cut away with the razor that is hired beyond the Euphrates—with the king of Assyria—the hair of the head and the hair of the legs and it shall clip off the beard as well* (Is. 7:20). It states: "The Holy One blessed be He went and appeared before Sennacherib as an old man."[38] The picture conjured up here demonstrates the extent to which His attribute of mercy functions for our salvation. Such stories as these clearly negate their literal sense and were put in writing, therefore, in order to inspire one to achieve the goal of the desired good. As the divine author of the *Kuzari* wrote, this praiseworthy and wonderful method was adopted from the prophets of blessed memory. This is illustrated by Micaiah's statement, *I saw the Lord seated upon His throne with all the host of heaven standing in attendance . . . and the Lord asked, Who will entice Ahab . . . until a certain spirit came forward* (1K. 22:19ff.). He states that this entire narration is rhetorically rendered in order to press home the intended point.[39]

Thus, with regard to the story of Titus you may, and have the right, to assert that the tale is simply an invention and a way of instruction used by those of perfect knowledge. Their purpose was to ensure that the people were convinced of the greatness of our

34. 'Saw those sounds,' an expression from Ex. 20:18 describing the revelation at Sinai.

35. The first book of the *Philippics* contains no such statement.

36. *Pro Sexto Roscio Amerino* XVI:47: "I think in fact that those fictions of the poets are intended to give us a representation of our manners in the characters of others and a vivid picture of our daily life" (Loeb trans.).

37. B. Sanh. 102a.

38. B. Sanh. 95b–96a. God tricks Sennacherib by appearing to him as an old man, and finally Sennacherib is killed by his sons who release the Jewish captives.

39. *Kuzari* III, par. 73.

Lord and His mighty power by which He requites Himself on those who rise up against Him, particularly the haughty and insolent, who receive their due punishment by means of the smallest of His creatures. With great wisdom did they appropriately apply their invented tale of the wicked man to Titus who had devised evil against us. {In my opinion, the intelligent person will be receptive to these words of mine when he realizes that this type of instruction on the part of our sages of blessed memory is contained in all the amazing things they describe about Hiram, king of Tyre, which give the impression that they were telling a story that actually happened. He is said to have made himself seven firmaments, a throne, Hayyot [living beings], and thunder and lightning in the midst of the sea on forty pillars of iron. There, he suspended himself in the air and boasted that he was God. Finally, the Holy One blessed be He raised a wind through the locks of Ezekiel's hair which brought him [i.e., Ezekiel] up to him [Hiram]. After they had argued about his overweaning pride and arrogance, Hiram died an unnatural death. The story is recorded at length by the compiler of the Yalqut.[40] Any rational person will undoubtedly declare and admit that this was all simply an invention intended to reprove all those born of woman who are infected by the impurity of pride. They applied the story to Hiram because it corresponded and conformed to what is related about him in Scripture. The story of Hiram about pride is analogous to that of Titus about rebelliousness and reproachfulness towards God. The point that these and all such stories have in common is that they are recounted as though reflecting reality although in fact they are simply riddles and parables.} Surely it is permissable to modify the truth in this way in the interest of bringing peace between us and our Father in heaven.[41]

And if you should still be interested in verifying that this mode of wisdom was also employed by scholars of all nations whereby matters are invented and imagined because they are regarded as valuable for religious purposes, go and read the story recounted by our rabbis of blessed memory in Bereshit Rabbah. It took place in the time of Rabbi Joshua ben Ḥanina and Lulianus and Pappus when the rebuilding of the Temple was impeded because the Samaritans informed on them to the emperor of the time. Rabbi Joshua being the sage he was, and a man of temperate speech, pacified and calmed the assembled people who had decided to rebel, by telling them the parable of the lion and the heron[42] which corresponds to the fable about the wolf told by Aesop in his famous book.[43] The acts of Julian the forty-sixth emperor, who lived in the time of Damasus, the thirty-ninth pope, are described in Nicephorus Callistus's *Chronicle* and in the work of Socrates the Christian—they are cited by Buoni in his book on the

40. Yalqut Shimoni II Ezk. par. 367. On this story, see L. Ginzberg, *Legends,* vol. 6, 424–26.

41. Cf. B. Yev. 65b.

42. B.R. 64:10 (710–12). "Rabbi Joshua expounded the parable: Once a lion ate his prey and got a bone stuck in his throat. Said the lion: 'If anyone can get the bone out of my throat, he will get a reward.' There came an Egyptian heron, who stuck his head into the lion's throat and pulled out the bone. Said the heron: 'Give me my reward.' Said the lion: 'Be off with you. Go and boast you entered the lion's mouth and got out of there safely.' So it is with us Jews. We ought to be satisfied that even though we got entangled with the Romans, we got disentangled without coming to harm."

43. De' Rossi states that the fable of the wolf [and the heron] is n. 6 of the fables. It is numbered 161 ed. Hausrath, vol. 1, 187.

earthquake,[44] Platina,[45] and in the *Lives of the Caesars.*[46] In the course of their account, they also relate the incidents associated with the rebuilding of the Temple. But they succeed in describing it to our detriment. For they say that when they embarked on the construction, an earthquake occurred that threw the whole edifice to the ground. This, they say, was due to the curse uttered by their savior that stone would not remain on stone.[47] It is likely that the event did not happen as they describe for I cannot find any ancient source which refers to that earthquake. Nevertheless, one should not reproach them for this, since their intention was to inspire people to their belief.[48]

Incidentally, you should realize that the Rabbi Joshua ben Ḥanina who is mentioned here and also in tractate Niddah in connection with the twelve questions put by the men of Alexandria[49] is to be distinguished from Rabbi Joshua ben Hananiah, the disciple of Rabbi Johanan ben Zakkai.[50] The latter [i.e., Rabbi Joshua] lived in Temple times and was present at the festivities of the drawing of water,[51] and he also redeemed Rabbi Ishmael ben Elishah from prison.[52] Similarly, one should distinguish the Trajan who murdered Lulianus and Pappus in Laodicea from the fourteenth emperor Trajan who massacred the Jewish population of Alexandria in Egypt. The former Trajan was merely a Roman governor. This is apparent from the final statement in tractate Taʿanit describing the murder: "Hardly had they moved from there when two *diyuple* (according to the *Arukh,* the word means two messengers) from Rome arrived and split open his skull with *gezirin* (according to Rashi, the word *gezirin* means clubs).[53] The other Trajan, according to all biographers of the emperors, died from a bowel sickness on his return from battle with the Parthians, near the city of Seleucia.

Now let us resume our discussion of Titus. All the elaborate, implausible and unnatural disquisitions of our rabbis on the subject of the gnat was simply amazing wisdom on their part. Two things they achieved by this means. They magnified the wonder and amazement of the common people, while they succeeded in getting scholars to consider the inner meaning of the tale, as the author of the *Guide* says in his introduction, in reference to the verse, *A word fitly spoken is like apples of gold in settings of silver* (Pr. 25:11). For the tale is simply an invented representation. This wisdom was employed by the divine poet when he used the expressions, *your belly is like a heap of*

44. Antonio Buoni, *Del terremoto,* II, 26r, par. 239.
45. Platina, *De vitis,* 64.
46. Mexía, *Le vite di tutti gl'Imperadori,* 156.
47. Cf. Luke 19:44.
48. This statement is deleted by censors in some of the first editions.
49. B. Nidd. 69b.
50. M. Avot 2:8 describes him as one of the five disciples of R. Johanan ben Zakkai. Ḥanina is a variant spelling of the name Hananiah. However, de' Rossi has correctly discerned the difficulty in regard to the dating of the incident. Rabbi Joshua ben Hananiah could have been present if the story reflects an incident in the time of Hadrian. However, if, as some suppose, the event refers to the rebuilding of the Temple in Julian the Apostate's time, as de' Rossi is clearly suggesting, Rabbi Joshua would have been long dead. For a discussion of the passages, see G. Alon, *The Jews,* 436–41.
51. B. Sukk. 53a; T. Sukk. 4:5.
52. B. Giṭṭ. 58a.
53. B. Taʿanit 18b. De' Rossi is probably correct. According to Alon (*The Jews,* 421), the governor was probably Lusius Quietus who was executed by order of the Senate in the early days of Hadrian's reign.

wheat (S.S. 7:3), *your nose is like the Lebanon tower* (ibid. 7:5). Such unusual adulations immediately arouse one to reflect that their true meaning is different from their apparent meaning. I shall speak further about this, God willing, in chapter 22. And when the Tosafists endeavor to make the passage [about the gnat] somehow conform to nature, this was not because they believed it in its literal formulation, but to justify the words of the author of the Aggadah. A similar method was used by the author of *ha-Ma᾿or*[54] in connection with the statement that Cyrus Artaxerxes and Darius were one and the same person. This will be demonstrated at the end of chapter 18.

Now, reader, I hope that this explanation of mine will be acceptable to you. But you must be careful to apply it, as well as any other explanation of a similar nature you will hear from me, only where it may be beneficial. Otherwise, my desire to help you will result in you harming both yourself and me. For not all the statements of the sages of blessed memory can be interpreted in a uniform way. In a general vein, you should realize that it was this that the righteous teacher[55] explained in his introduction with regard to the *Book of Correspondence* which he intended to write. He writes: "In this book we promised to explain all the problems of the Midrashim where their apparent meaning is remote from the truth and departs from the rational—they are all parables."[56] Further on in the same context, he states: "Know that the key to the understanding of all that the prophets of blessed memory said and the knowledge of its truth is an understanding of the parables and their meaning."[57] His entire book may be summed up by the words "they are all parables." And if our sages were not prophets, they were at least sons of prophets and, indeed, did no wrong in following their methods.[58]

Now I shall not refrain from informing you, dear reader, that when some learned members of our people came to hear what I had written about Titus's gnat, they spoke out against me claiming that I had, as it were, impaired the holy words of our sages. They insisted that God was so powerful that He could inflict a more than fitting punishment on enemies such as him [i.e., Titus].[59] Nevertheless, I did not hold myself back from recording their statement in the book. In addition to what I set out at the beginning of the chapter, I may pronounce in the same vein as the author of the *Guide* as follows:[60] There are two possibilities: either the reader will, despite what I have said, believe everything that our sages wrote at face value—imagining thereby that the act of

54. I.e., Zeraḥiah ben Isaac Halevi Gerondi (thirteenth-century Spanish rabbi) who first justifies the rabbinic statements and then gives his own opinion.

55. I.e., Maimonides. He is punning on the word *Moreh* (guide).

56. *Guide,* Introduction (trans. Pines, 9).

57. Ibid., 10.

58. Cf. Ps. 119:3.

59. I.e., since God is capable of acting beyond the bounds of nature, the account of the gnat should be taken literally.

60. *Guide,* Introduction, 6: "However, even when one who truly possesses knowledge considers these parables and interprets them according to their external meaning, he, too, is overcome by great perplexity. But if we explain these parables to him or if we draw his attention to their being parables he will take the right road and be delivered from this perplexity." Ibid. I, ch. 5: "If however an individual of insufficient capacity should not wish to reach the rank to which we desire him to ascend and should he consider that all the words are indicative of sensual perception . . . there is no harm in his thinking this."

making accessible every remote matter is for the sake of the glory of heaven. In that case, this chapter of mine would be regarded as though never written, either for good or for bad. Alternatively, should he try to accommodate it intellectually and fail, then in my opinion, he would do wisely in approving the method I put forward. Blessed be He who imparted His wisdom to our sages of blessed memory,[61] and he, too, [i.e., the reader] will be blessed by their lips which murmur in the grave.[62]

61. Cf. B. Ber. 58a: "On seeing sages of Israel one should say, 'Blessed be He who has imparted of His wisdom to them that fear Him.'"

62. Cf. B. Yev. 97a. "As soon as a traditional saying is cited in the name of the sages in this world, their lips murmur in the grave."

CHAPTER SEVENTEEN

Concerning the statement of our rabbis, blessed be their memory, that the primevals used to procreate at the age of eight.[1]

It is my concern that you should comprehend the nature of one of those statements of our rabbis blessed be their memory that belong to the category of pronouncements that are not derived from ancient tradition and was not held by them to constitute a necessary deduction from the scriptural verse. Rather, the statement was made according to the useful principle they divulged to us through the phrase, "I am expounding Scripture." Discussing this principle in a previous chapter[2] we also cited Riaz [Isaiah di Trani the younger]. In the forthcoming discussion, you should bear it in mind for reasons that you will come to ascertain. In Sanhedrin, they say:[3]

> The primevals begat at the age of eight. How do we know this? Shall we say since it is written, *Is this not Bathsheba, daughter of Eliam, the wife of Uriah the Hittite?* (2S. 11:3). But it is deduced from, *Now these are the generations of Terach* (Gen. 11:27) . . . Perhaps it is derived from, *Now Bezalel son of Uri, son of Hur of the tribe of Judah* (Ex. 35:30). [And it is written, *And when Azubah was dead, Caleb took Ephat who bore him Hur* (1Chr. 2:19). Now, how old was Bezalel when he made the Tabernacle? Thirteen years, for it is written, *And all the wise men who were engaged in the tasks of the Sanctuary came, each from the task upon which he was engaged* (Ex. 36:4). And it has been taught. On the first year after the exodus, Moses made the Tabernacle; in the second he erected it and sent out the spies. And it is written, *And Caleb said . . . forty years old was I when Moses sent me from Kadesh Barnea to spy out the land . . . and here I am today four score and five years old* (Joshua 14:7). Now, how old was he when he was sent as a spy? Forty. Deduct fourteen, Bezalel's age at the time and this leaves twenty-six. Now deduct two years for the three pregnancies; hence each must have begotten at the age of eight.]

From the very outset, you can see that the author of this passage is continually searching for verses that prove his case. It was a difficult task for him to connect those verses to the story of Bezalel, the great-grandson of Caleb. In chapter 14, I informed you as to how all the literalists treated this subject. So now give your attention to what they [i.e., the

1. The subject of the age of the ancients was a topic that interested Renaissance writers. See, e.g., the first two chapters of Pedro Mexía's *Silva de varia leçion.* The quotations from Augustine and Pliny are also cited by Mexía.

2. Ch. 15.

3. B. Sanh. 69b.

rabbis] said. Apparently, their purpose was to demonstrate that the ancients were stronger than us and of a tougher constitution. The evidence they cite actually disproves their claim[4] and the fraudulent position can be reversed.[5] The stories of the Torah make it quite clear that those who die prematurely, procreate at a young age and vice versa. Consider the ten generations from Adam to Noah and then (since, according to Ramban, the flood caused rarefaction of the atmosphere and those who grew up in it were consequently weaker)[6] progress to the ten generations from Noah to Abraham, and you can hardly fail to see the truth of our claim. Furthermore, with regard to the anticipated time in which God will renew His world to its former state, it is written, *He who dies at a hundred years shall be reckoned a youth* (Is. 65:20). This point is also elucidated by Rashi in his comment on the verse, *Can a child be born to a man a hundred years old?* (Gen. 17:17). He writes: "Although the primevals procreated children at the age of five hundred, the life span was reduced by Abraham's time; people became feebler and they procreated at an earlier age." We can also prove our case by means of Rav's statement on the Mishnah:[7] "If a man married a woman and lived with her for ten years and she bore him no child, he may not abstain [i.e., he must divorce her]." According to Rav,[8] this Mishnah applied to the primevals who were long-lived (and delayed the time of procreation); later generations, however, whose life span was shorter (and who procreated at an earlier age) needed wait only two and a half years. It is true that in that context, Rava claims that such rules are inapplicable. He argued that even in the lifetime of Rabbi, the compiler of the Mishnah, the life span was reduced and that Rabbi himself did not differentiate between the two periods. Nevertheless, Rav's statement is well founded and correct and he pronounces the truth. Furthermore, there is the comment of the Tosafists in tractate Bekhorot with regard to a three-year-old cow that gives birth[9] and in tractate Avodah Zarah with regard to a three-year-old cow and ass[10] which provides us with proof even from the animal species that there is a correlation between early procreation and debility.

You should also consider my next point. By stating that the primevals could begat at the age of eight, they were implying that it was an unnatural phenomenon. In fact, our sages of blessed memory make other statements that demonstrate that even an eleven-year-old male is incapable of procreating naturally or unnaturally. There is the discussion in the Gemara of the law relating to minor boys and girls and their age of puberty[11] which is also recorded by Rambam [Maimonides].[12] From the discussion in tractate

4. De' Rossi uses phraseology from B. Beṣ. 24a.
5. Lit. *and the bow of deceit be overturned.* Cf. Ps. 78:57.
6. Nahmanides to Gen. 5:4.
7. M. Yev. 6:6.
8. B. Yev. 64b.
9. Tos. to Bek. 19b, s.v. *parah.* According to the talmudic passage, the offspring of a cow that gives birth at the age of three may be regarded as a firstling (and therefore belongs to the priest).
10. Tos. to A.Z. 24b, s.v. *parah.* According to the Talmud, the offspring of a three-year-old cow or ass definitely belongs to the priest (i.e., they are regarded as firstlings). The Tosafists comment: "For they cannot give birth before that age. And although one might be surprised because it is a normal occurrence for a two-year-old to give birth, the fact is that times have changed from what they were in the first generations."
11. B. Nidd. 47b; B. B.B. 156a.
12. *Mishneh Torah,* Ishut, ch. 2.

Yoma about children fasting on the Day of Atonement, we learn that a girl is regarded as a minor until the age of twelve years and one day, and a boy until his thirteenth year.[13] According to Rabbi Moses [Maimonides],[14] the discrepancy between the ages is because the male is of a hotter temperament and physically fragile whereas the female becomes fully developed at an earlier stage. But neither the male nor the female are regarded as having reached their majority until the two hairs which signify the onset of puberty have appeared. The matter is elucidated from another perspective in the *baraita* cited by Rav Bibi:[15] "Three women may use an absorbent for intercourse. . . . [A minor because she may become pregnant and die. . . . And what is the age of a minor? From eleven years and a day to twelve years and a day.]" This statement is interpreted by Rashi and Ran [Rabbenu Nissim] of blessed memory as signifying that it is impossible for a female under the age of eleven years and one day to become pregnant even in abnormal circumstances, while the life of a girl of eleven years and one day would be put at risk if she became pregnant—as we said before, this is the natural consequence when girls give birth before reaching puberty. This corresponds to the following passage from tractate Niddah:[16]

> Our rabbis taught. It is related that Justinia, the daughter of Aseverus appeared before Rabbi and said to him: "Rabbi, at what age may a woman marry?" He said to her, "At three years and one day." "When is she capable of conception?" He said to her, "At twelve years and one day." She said to him, "I married at six and gave birth at seven. Alas for the three years I wasted in my father's house." Then they asked: "How is it possible to become pregnant at such an age? Did not Rav Bibi recite the *baraita?* Three women may use an absorbant in intercourse: a minor, an expectant mother, and a nursing mother. A minor because otherwise she may become pregnant and die; an expectant mother because otherwise she might cause her fetus to degenerate into a flat-fish-shaped abortion; a nursing mother because otherwise she might have to wean her child and this would result in its death. And what is the age of such a minor? From eleven years and one day until twelve years and one day. One who is under or over this age must carry on intercourse in the normal way. This is the opinion of Rabbi Meir. But the sages ruled: in every case there should be normal intercourse and may heaven protect them. If you wish, I could reply, *the flesh of bulls is their flesh*[17] (and a Jewish girl would not become pregnant in that way). Alternatively, you could say that the girl spoke falsely.[18]

Thus, on the basis of these two premises, it transpires that the male who matures later than the female cannot procreate at the age of eleven years and one day even in freak circumstances. And the sage ibn Ezra states that Onan had reached an age that he was able to produce sperm; namely, at least twelve years.[19] Furthermore, relevant to our

13. B. Yoma 82a.
14. Maimonides, *Perush* to M. Yoma 8:2.
15. B. Yev. 12b.
16. B. Nidd. 45a.
17. In the standard editions the quotation is *whose flesh is the flesh of asses* (Ezk. 23:20). De' Rossi appears to have conflated the quotation with Ps. 50:13, *Do I eat the flesh of bulls.*
18. The talmudic text reads: "And if you prefer I might reply, *Whose mouth speaks falsehood and their right hand is a right hand of lying* (Ps. 144:8). De' Rossi puts part of the quotation from the Psalm in relation to the girl in order to strengthen his case.
19. Ibn Ezra to Gen. 38:1.

inquiry is Mizraḥi's statement in his *Novellae* about Hur, the son of Miriam. He states that we cannot make deductions about minor boys from what is known about minor girls, since, as our rabbis of blessed memory said, the female has a stronger constitution.[20] It is true that they state that a minor of nine years who cohabits with his childless brother's widow acquires her thereby.[21] The grounds on which such a levirate marriage is regarded as valid even when the intercourse cannot be productive is the verse, *Her husband's brother shall unite with her; take her as his wife and perform the levir's duty* (Deut. 25:5). But, in relation to any other woman, they rule that the intercourse of a minor has no validity unless he has reached his majority.[22] In other words, a boy under the age of twelve years and one day cannot procreate even in abnormal circumstances. And if he does procreate when he is thirteen years and one day, it is regarded as a freak occurrence and an unlikely phenomenon. For normally, the generative power does not begin to throb in him until he reaches the age of fourteen and has already produced the tokens of puberty. Even then, as we shall mention again, he cannot procreate easily. The passage quoted [at the beginning of the chapter] thus appears anomalous on two counts. Moreover, it is not based on tradition nor does the precise meaning of the verses lead one to the incontrovertible conclusion that it really[23] did happen. Rather, as we said, it was stated in the manner suggested by the phrase, "I am expounding Scripture."

Now if a scholar were also to procure the works of the gentile sages, whose evidence is impartial, in order to ascertain whether a boy can really procreate at such a young age, he would certainly find considerable evidence in favor of our claim. To begin with, you should examine the *City [of God]* written by the greatest Christian sage [Augustine]. In book 15 (chapter 15),[24] he raises the question as to whether one should assume that because the ancients are only described as having procreated at the age of one hundred or two hundred, they were incapable of procreating at an earlier age. He suggests that because they lived to a great age, they may have reached puberty and attained the capacity of procreation at a proportionally later age. He also gives an alternative solution and proposes that Scripture is only concerned with recording the children who were in the line of succession to Noah and our patriarch Abraham. A similar view is also expressed by Ramban.[25] Since we are dealing with this subject we might say that we regard this view as actually more apposite than that of the author of the *Guide* who writes:[26] "I say that the only individuals who enjoyed longevity were those mentioned; but the other men lived the normal life span." With all due respect to his eminence, I must say that in regard to this subject, the other opinion is consistent

20. Elijah Mizraḥi (1450–1526), *Perush Rashi* to Ex. 35:30. Rashi identifies the Hur mentioned in the verse, *Bezalel son of Uri son of Hur* as the son of Miriam. De' Rossi gives a partial quote. Mizraḥi actually affirms the statement about the earliest generations begetting at eight, while rejecting the idea that minor girls are able to give birth.

21. B. Nidd. 45a.

22. M. Yev. 10:9.

23. 'Really.' He uses the expression *hin ṣedeq* from Lev. 9:36 which is homiletically interpreted to mean "that your yes (*hen*) be true" (see, e.g., B. B.M. 49a).

24. Augustine, *De civ. Dei,* bk. 15, ch. 15 (*P.L.* XLI, col. 456). In the earliest printed version, de' Rossi had actually referred to Augustine by name.

25. Nahmanides to Gen. 5:4, where he rejects Maimonides' view which is cited by de' Rossi below.

26. Maimonides, *Guide* II, ch. 47.

with the Torah and more acceptable. In any case, you can surely see that the first answer given by the Christian is relevant to our enquiry. Similarly, in proposing a solution to the problem he raised about the ages of Nimrod and Peleg, he [Augustine] states that those who beget prolifically at a young age are short-lived, while the reverse is also true.[27] You could also find support for this view by observation of plants—for whatever grows over night perishes over night.[28] As for the long-lived phoenix, it is, according to their statement in Bereshit Rabbah,[29] unique of its kind. In book 15 (chapter 12), he [i.e., Augustine] derides those who hold that one of our years is equivalent to ten of the years of the ancients. He states:[30]

> If that had been the case, the first man who was 130 years when he beget Seth would have actually been 13 years. And previously when he begot Cain and Abel, he would have been only 12 years old. What person is there who according to the norm and natural law could procreate at such an age? If you argue that it was feasible in the case of Adam who was created as a fully grown man and according to his choice,[31] how can you account for his son who was born like any other child and who was 105 years old when he begot Enosh? According to your reckoning, he would have not yet reached his eleventh year. How much more so in the case of Kenan who was 70 years old when he begat Mahalalel; in other words, he would have been 7 years old. Is this not complete nonsense?

The law of nature that dictates that those who procreate prematurely, die prematurely is discussed by the great writer Pliny in book 7 of his *Natural History.*[32] Quoting the philosopher Clitarchus, he states that in a remote corner of the world there is a certain place where women give birth to daughters at the age of seven, but are already approaching the end of their lives by the time they are thirty.[33] He also quotes Artemidorus as saying that in a certain region of India, women give birth to daughters at the age of five, but do not survive beyond their eighth year.[34] The ancient writer Solinus also mentions this fact in chapter 64 of his book of *Memorabilia.*[35] It is comparable to the fore-mentioned passage in tractate Yevamot which states that a girl of eleven years and a day could die if she becomes pregnant[36]—her tender years bring her close to death's door. In the *Politics,*[37] the "philosopher" [Aristotle] states that those who oversee the well-being of the children they are rearing, see to it that men do not marry before the age of thirty-six and women until they are eighteen. And in the fourth part of his *History of Animals,*[38] he writes that the male is thrice seven years before his sperm reaches it full generative capacity, and that the male sperm begins to develop when he is

27. *De civ. Dei,* bk. 16, ch. 11 (*P.L.* XLI, col. 491).
28. Cf. Jonah 4:10.
29. B.R. 19:5 (174–75).
30. *De civ. Dei,* bk. 15, ch. 12 (*P.L.* XLI, cols. 450–52).
31. Augustine writes: "Non enim eum tam parvum quam infantes nostri sunt factum fuisse credibile est." De' Rossi uses the rabbinic phrase from B. Ḥull. 60a: "All the animals were created fully grown and *according to the shape of their own choice.*"
32. Pliny, *Nat. hist.* VII, II, 29.
33. Pliny reads 'forty.'
34. Ibid, 30.
35. This is a reference to ch. 65 of Solinus, *Delle cose,* 205.
36. B. Yev. 12b.
37. Aristotle, *Politica* VII, 1335a25.
38. Idem, *Historia animalium* V, 544b25.

fourteen. That this is all correct will easily become clear and apparent to the intelligent person once he understands that the generative sperm according to the definition of the "philosopher" is the ultimate residue of digested food. In his work *Medical Definitions,*[39] Galen also concurs with this view.[40] Ibn Sina [Avicenna] writes as follows:[41] "The sperm is the residue of the fourth stage of digestion and is formed from the distribution of food through the limbs. It issues like sweat from the veins once the third stage of digestion has been completed." Thus, an adult only requires food in order to replenish that which has been dissipated. He therefore ought to have a sufficient surplus for the formation of the seed since nature provides him with a sufficient quantity for that purpose. But a minor, who still needs to develop, is not in possession of the physical capacity to provide the surplus needed to produce the sperm. Consequently, should somebody rush into the act prematurely, his progeny will be of a weaker constitution. It was for this reason that in his discussion of the causes of sterility and infertility, the wise physician Fernelius who is the greatest expert of our time, basing himself on the authority of the eminent natural scientists quoted above, made the following statement in section 2 of his works:[42] "Minors whose genital hair has not grown are sterile and infertile, and likewise the elderly for their sperm is thin, liquid, and flaccid and unsuitable for procreation." And in his work *Shaʿar ha-Shamayim,* the wise Rabbi Isaac Latif[43] wrote:[44] "The initial period for the production of the male seed and the female menses is normally after the completion of the fourteenth year. At that time, his pubic hair will grow, the process being comparable to the way a tree produces blossoms before the fruit has grown." He then writes:[45] "The age of procreation for males is from the age of twenty when the sperm is fully developed; should he procreate at an earlier age, the offspring will be weak and of an unsound constitution." This view corresponds to that of the "philosopher" quoted above. On consultation of the imperial jurists you will come across Modestinus's law on adoption called *adrogatio.*[46] It states that if the adoptive parent cannot be called a major because his pubic hair has not grown, the adoption is without validity. Modestinus explains that pubic hair begins to sprout at the end of the fourteenth year and are fully-grown by the eighteenth year.[47] One might well make

39. De' Rossi appears to be referring to the ps. Galenic work *Definitiones Medicae.* However, this particular definition of the sperma is not given. It is interesting to note that Gershom ben Shelomo whose work de' Rossi quotes here also cites these authorities in bk. 8: "According to Aristotle the semen is a surplus of the body. . . . This is also the opinion of Galen, namely, that the semen is a surplus like the other surpluses of the body."

40. According to Galen, there are three stages of digestion: through the stomach, through the liver when the nutriments are converted into blood, and through the target organs to which blood and nutriment are supplied. The view goes back to Hippocrates.

41. Avicenna, *Liber canonis,* bk. 3, fen 20, tract. 1, ch. 3.

42. Jean Fernel, *Medicina, Pathologiae Libri,* lib. VI, cap. XVII, 207: "Steriles enim et infoecundi sunt impuberes et senio confecti quod his tenue et aquosum languidumque sit semen . . . viri enim ita affecti [i.e., old men with or without disease] aut semen non proferunt aut prorsus evanidum et infoecundum utpote nec ex utili materia productum nec spirituum benignitate perfusum."

43. The author of the work was Gershon ben Shelomo (see ch. 16, n. 9).

44. *Shaʿar ha-Shamayim,* gate 8, 36, col. a.

45. Ibid.

46. *Adrogatio* unlike *adoptio* which can only be applicable to somebody "alieni iuris" is only applicable to a person who is *sui iuris* such that the child's family merges with that of the "adrogator."

47. The reference is to Justinian's *Digest* (*Corpus iuris civilis,* I, VII, n. 40): "Non tantum cum quis

the assumption that because this is a fact grounded in nature, our sages of blessed memory also had it in mind when they said in Avot,[48] "At eighteen to the marriage canopy." The reason for this is, as we said, that before this time, a man is not sufficiently ready for procreation. The statement of Rav Ḥisda has a similar thrust:[49] "I am superior to my colleagues because I married at sixteen. Had I married at fourteen, I would declare it an arrow in the eye of Satan." For a person who copulates at too young an age weakens the reproductive organs, and then his desire for even the most beautiful woman shall be extinguished.[50] (This is similar to the statement of Rabbi Moses of blessed memory in his introduction to the order Ṭoharot.)[51] On this account he said, "Had I married at fourteen." But before the age of fourteen, a man is not physically capable of producing semen; and it still takes some time after that before he can procreate. The analogy of the tree is again relevant—there will be a lapse of time between the growth of the blossom and the seed.

In our discourse on the premature procreation of the primevals our intention was to console, but instead we caused distress;[52] the less stringent decision turned out to be more stringent and the favor turned to their disadvantage. We can certainly conclude that the passage under discussion was simply an Aggadah and was not meant to be understood as an accepted fact. Rather, the purpose was to expound Scripture in any way that it could sustain. Thereby they could attain the objective summed up in their statement "expound and receive reward."

I have already demonstrated that all the literalist interpreters denied that those verses could sustain the meaning given to them by the sages of blessed memory. Further clarification of this matter may be provided. The author of the Seder Olam asserts that Haran was physically mature at the age of eight when he begat Yiskah who is identified as Sarah.[53] This statement [which assumes that in Scripture the progeny of persons are mentioned in order of age] is refuted in the passage under discussion from tractate Sanhedrin. It is objected there that the order is determined by the relative wisdom of the persons mentioned.[54] Examine the passage for yourself.

Now despite everything we have written so far, I cannot refrain from admitting that there is a verse in the book of Kings which implies that Ahaz was eleven years old when

---

adoptat sed et cum adrogat, maior esse debet eo quem sibi per adrogationem vel per adoptionem filium facit et utique plenae pubertatis: id est decem et octo annis eum praecedere debet. [Spado adrogando suum heredem sibi adsciscere potest nec ei corporale vitium impedimento est."]

48. M. Avot 5:21.

49. B. Qidd. 29b–30a.

50. 'Desire shall fail.' Cf. Eccl. 12:5.

51. Maimonides, *Perush,* Ṭoharot (Introduction): "When a person indulges in intercourse many times in succession within a short period, the blood comes out before its has been transformed into seed."

52. 'Console . . . distress.' Cf. B. Ket. 8b.

53. Seder Olam, ch. 2 (13).

54. B. Sanh. 69b. The deduction is based on Gen. 11:29, *Now these are the generations of Terach: Terach begot Abraham, Nahor and Haran.* "Now Abraham must have been one year older than Nahor and Nahor one year older than Haran. Thus Abraham was two years older than Haran. And it is written, *Abram and Nahor tooḳ to themselves wives, the name of Abram's wife being Sarai and that of Nahor's wife Milcah, the daughter of Haran, the father of Milḳah and Iscah.* Therefore Abraham was ten years older than Sarah and two years older than her father. Therefore Haran was eight when he begot Isacah. But why? Perhaps Abraham was the youngest and was mentioned first because the names were mentioned in order of wisdom."

he begat Hezekiah. It states: *Ahaz was twenty years old when he became king and he reigned sixteen years in Jerusalem* (2K. 16:2 and 2Chr. 28:1). Then in the same book (2K. 18:2) and in 2 Chronicles (29:1), it states that Hezekiah was twenty-five years old when he ruled. I did not come across any Jewish sage who had any comment to make on this passage. However, you should know that there was a certain Christian scholar called Tostado,[55] acknowledged by Christians as a great commentator on holy Writ, who was struck by this anomaly and discussed it in his commentary on the book of Kings.[56] Having established that it is against the law of nature for a man to procreate at the age of eleven, he then presented somebody else's solution to the problem: namely, it had been suggested that one could well believe that Hezekiah had not come to the throne directly after the death of his father. It had somehow transpired that there was an interregnum or that he was not comfortably installed on the throne for a number of years. According to this reckoning, then, one must add the said number of years to Ahaz's eleven years. But he [Tostado] dismissed this solution on the grounds that it was impossible that nothing about this would have been mentioned either in the book of Kings or in the book of Chronicles. His own answer to the problem was to take into account the way in Scripture that half years are sometimes counted as whole years, or sometimes, not taken into account at all. A similar view is expressed by Rashi of blessed memory in his comment on the verse, *Ahaziah son of Arab had become king of Israel in Samaria in the seventeenth year of King Jehoshaphat of Judah* (1K. 22:52). We shall discuss this statement of his further in chapter 35. Thus it may well be that the twenty years of Ahaz were in fact twenty-one incomplete years, and similarly the sixteen years [of his rule], seventeen. Conversely, Hezekiah's twenty-five years were only twenty-four complete years and a few days.[57] You can thus add three truncated years to [Ahaz's] eleven years which gives a total of more than thirteen. Even the imperial jurists would hold that it is feasible to procreate at the age of thirteen, although it still constitutes something of a deviation from nature.[58] This is what Tostado had to say. In fact, it may even be possible to uphold the first solution. Moreover, it does appear that Ahaz's progeny were born providentially, and that their birth was heralded with portents or rather that the prophet warned him of untimely births. In any case, any anomaly in nature's domain is regarded as a novelty and, according to the sages' statements, one does not make decisions on the basis of novelties.

When I had written thus far, I was overjoyed to find that my opinion was confirmed by Rabbi Isaiah [di Trani] the elder. For in his *Sefer ha-Mahadurot,*[59] he discusses the passage about Bat Sheba from which it is deduced that a man is called a major at the age of eight and a woman at the age of seven. He writes:

55. Alonso Tostado (1400–55) was Bishop of Avila.

56. Alonso Tostado, *Commentaria in lib. III Regum,* in *Opera,* cap. XVIII, quaestio III, 174, col. b–c.

57. "Ezechias viginti quatuor annorum et paucorum dierum quando coepit regnare. Subtrahuntur ergo viginti quatuor de triginta octo et manebunt quatuordecim et sic esset Achaz quasi quatuordecim annorum quando gigneret Ezechiam."

58. Tostado actually states "istud non est admirabile, . . . nec contra communem cursum." De' Rossi makes the statement more circumspect.

59. See B. Sanh. 69b. This work of Isaiah ben Mali di Trani (ha-Rid; 1200–1260) to which de' Rossi refers is also called *Pesaqim.* De' Rossi must have read the text in manuscript.

> I find it problematic that they could put forward such a view in conjunction with the statement that Bezalel constructed the Tabernacle at thirteen years because it is written, *all the men were engaged in the task of the Sanctuary.* This implies that even among the primevals, a male was not considered a major until he had reached his thirteenth year. We may therefore claim that they were only considered majors once they were thirteen although they did beget at the age of eight—for this was considered a miraculous phenomenon and we do not make rulings on the basis of miracles. It was for this reason that the school of Hillel said that we do not derive our traditions from the primevals—for they procreated at the age of eight and this was a phenomenon of a miraculous nature.

Here, then, he expresses the view we wished to communicate.

CHAPTER EIGHTEEN

Concerning the saying of the rabbis of blessed memory that Cyrus, Darius, and Artaxerxes are one and the same person.[1]

There is yet another saying which ought not be regarded as a dogmatic assertion, but was said by way of exegesis. (This also had its reason as you shall be informed.) It was said by the author of the Seder Olam in regard to the verse, *So the elders of the Jews progressed in the building . . . by the order of Cyrus, Darius, and Artaxerxes [Artahshasta] king of Persia* (Ezra 6:14). He writes:[2] "Cyrus, Darius, and Artaxerxes are one and the same person because all monarchs are given the title Artaxerxes." This statement is cited by Rashi in his commentary on the verse in question. He writes:[3] "All Persian monarchs are given the royal title Artaxerxes just as Egyptian monarchs are called Pharaoh." Now Berosus the Chaldean proffers information which I can use as corroboration of his view. For in book 5, he refers to the eighth Babylonian king called Baleus Xerxes—their designation Xerxes is equivalent to Hshasta—and he then explains:[4] "This designation Hshasta [Xerxes] means fighter and Art means great; thus when the two designations are combined to form the name Artaxerxes [Artahshasta], it means great fighter. The additional word [Art] was added to the name of one of their monarchs because his might surpassed that of all his predecessors." So too, in the Gemara on Rosh ha-Shanah, they raise the question as to why the text speaks in one case of Darius, but of Cyrus in another, and they respond by quoting the *baraita* (in other words, the statement in the Seder Olam):[5] "Cyrus, Darius, and Artaxerxes are one and the same person. He was called Cyrus [*koresh*] because he was worthy [*kasher*], Artaxerxes after his realm, while Darius was his own name." According to Rashi, even the Darius who reigned after Ahasuerus was called Cyrus.[6] However, from the very outset, you should know that in his commentary on the book of Ezra, Rabbenu Isaiah

1. On the aggadic theme of the merging of different people into one identity, see Z. H. Chayes, *The Student's Guide,* ch. 21.

2. Seder Olam, ch. 30 (136–37).

3. Rashi to Ezra 6:14. He does not refer explicitly to the Seder Olam.

4. This is a reference to ps. Berosus forged by Annius of Viterbo. The quotation is from Annius's commentary to Berosus (vol. 1, 221–22): "Xerxes est bellator, Artaxerxes, maximus bellator. Verum tamen non absolute bellatorem significat sed ut significantius exprimit Berosus significat debellatorem atque in bello victorem."

5. B. R.H. 3b.

6. Rashi to R.H. 3b.

[di Trani] of blessed memory cites the passage from Seder Olam Rabbah quoted above with regard to the verse under discussion, and then writes:[7] "But it is demonstrated in Seder Olam Zuṭa that Artaxerxes and Darius were two different kings and that Artaxerxes ruled thirty-two years, while his successor Darius the Persian ruled two years. This *baraita* from Seder Olam is at variance with the other." Thus far his words for what they are worth.[8]

Next, my brother, you should pay close attention to everything I have to say. You should know that this Midrash is simply one of the many examples given by our rabbis of blessed memory which in the words of Riaz quoted above are not to be understood as fundamental truths, but are for the purpose of "expounding and receiving reward." This contention is based on the fact that another Midrash of the same type is given in the same context in Rosh ha-Shanah.[9] It is written, *After he had defeated Sihon king of the Amorites* (Deut. 1:4) and when Aaron died, Sihon was still alive for it is written, *And the Canaanite, the king of Arad heard* (Num. 33:40). An objection is raised that the one verse refers to Canaan and the other to Sihon. [In other words, the verses do not refer to the same person.] The problem is resolved by means of the *baraita:* "Sihon, Arad, and Canaan are one and the same person. He was called Sihon because he resembled a foal of the wilderness, Canaan after his kingdom, while his real name was Arad. Some say that he was called Arad because he resembled a wild ass in the wilderness, Canaan after his kingdom, while Sihon was his real name." And the Tosafists comment on that passage with regard to the verse, *And the Canaanite, the king of Arad heard* and write: "In a Midrash, he is identified as Amalek and this is also established by the poet in his liturgical poem for the pericope Zakhor:[10] 'He changed his clothing and language in order to assume the identity of the king of Arad.' In any case, it is precise insofar as Sihon was alive when he assumed his identity." And they also write: "Arad—according to the literal meaning of Scripture, Arad is the name of a place or the name of his town." Similarly, in his Scripture commentary, Rashi of blessed memory comments on the verse, *When the Canaanite, the king of Arad, who dwelt in the Negeb, heard [that Israel was coming by way of Atharim]* (Num. 21:1), and writes: "*who dwelt in the Negeb*—this is Amalek for it is written, *Amalek dwelt in the Negeb* (Num. 13:29). But he changed his language and spoke in the language of Canaan." The source used by both authorities [i.e., Rashi and the Tosafists] of blessed memory is Midrash Bemidbar Sinai (sec. 19).[11] Thus, the rabbis themselves in this Midrash, and later, those two great talmudists Rashi

7. De' Rossi read the work in manuscript. It was published by A. Schächter, from the mss. in the Angelica Library, Rome and the Bodleian Library, Oxford. (It was republished by A. Wertheimer, Jerusalem, 1978, who claimed that he was printing the text for the first time.)

8. De' Rossi truncates a crucial part of the comment of Isaiah di Trani. Di Trani writes that the Seder Olam Zuṭa is not reliable and that one should rather accept the statement in Seder Olam Rabbah that Cyrus, Darius, and Artaxerxes are one and the same person.

9. B. R.H. 2b–3a.

10. The pericope Zakhor (Deut. 25:17–19) which commands remembrance of the assault of Amalek on the Israelites after the exodus from Egypt is read on the special Sabbath before Purim. The poem was written by Kallir and is read in the additional service. See Baer, *Avodat Yisrael,* 668.

11. Bem. R. 19:20: "If he was in reality Amalek why was he called by the name of Canaan? Israel was forbidden to fight against the children of Esau. . . . Now when Amalek came and waged war against them a first and a second time, the Holy One blessed be He said to them, 'This nation is not forbidden to you as the children of Esau. They are like Canaanites to you.' "

and the Tosafist, deviated without much ado[12] from the statement identifying Sihon with Arad. The passage in which many persons are merged into one identity is a *baraita* and is also an alternative interpretation as indicated by the expression "according to others." And yet, it was simply with one of the purposes of Midrash in mind that the sages of blessed memory made this statement, and they did not assume that it would be taken literally. This assertion is further strengthened by reason of their other pronouncements about Sihon that contradict the fore-mentioned statement. In tractate Niddah, they say that Sihon and Og were brothers.[13] And in the Tanḥuma,[14] they identify the fugitive in the verse, *A fugitive brought the news to Abram* (Gen. 14:13) as Og, who was apparently younger than him [Abraham]. And Rabbenu Baḥya cites another Midrash:[15] "Shemhazael, one of the children of God, had intercourse with Ham's wife just before she entered the ark and Sihon was born [from that union]; as a consequence, Ham had intercourse in the ark [which was forbidden] in order to protect his wife." Put all these Midrashim together and consider whether one should believe that the sages of blessed memory intended to give us a factually correct and literal account of Sihon and to divert us from what is explicitly said about him in holy Writ.

Furthermore, in order to elicit even greater wonder about the said statement, I would direct your attention to another passage. Indeed, by demonstrating that the rabbis of blessed memory applied this method in relation to many individuals, the shutters may perhaps be opened and we may catch a glimpse of their true purpose. So consider the following statement. In Bereshit Rabbah they say:[16] "*And he [Judah] turned to a certain Adullamite and his name was Hirah* (Gen. 38:1). The Rabbis said: 'The Hirah mentioned here is Hiram who lived in David's time as it is said, *for Hiram had always been a friend of David* (1K. 5:15). This teaches that he had always been a friend of this tribe [i.e., Judah].' Rabbi Judah ben Rabbi Simon said: 'Hiram was another person.' According to the opinion of the rabbis, he would have lived nearly twelve hundred years while in Rabbi Judah's view, he lived nearly five hundred years." Rashi explains:[17]

> "This teaches"—He was a friend of Judah and later of David and Solomon, a period of nearly thirteen hundred years. The teacher gives the precise figure of nearly twelve hundred years. That calculation is reached by reckoning from the period when Joseph was sold until the exodus from Egypt, their entry into the land, the building of the Temple, and the exile. In the fourth year of the exile, Nebuchadnezzar captured Tyre and killed Hiram, as is stated in Seder Olam. But according to the view of Rabbi Judah, he lived almost five hundred years. Such a figure is reached by calculating from David's time until he was killed after the exile.

12. 'Deviated without much ado,' cf. Ex. 32:8.
13. B. Nidd. 61a.
14. Tanḥuma, Ḥuqqat 25. The assumption is that Og was a contemporary of Abraham because he was five hundred years old when he died, i.e., in the last year of the wandering through the wilderness. Abraham was born 1948 A.M. and the forty years of wandering ended in 2488 and therefore Og would be fifty years younger than Abraham.
15. Baḥya ben Asher, *Perush ha-Torah* to Num. 41:30. Cf. Ginzberg's discussion, *Legends,* vol. 5, 188, n. 54.
16. B.R. 85:4 (1036).
17. This is a reference to a spurious commentary on Bereshit Rabbah attributed to Rashi, *Sefer Or ha-Sekhel,* 167b.

This is Rashi's explanation. Since he extends the calculation to the time of the exile, one might plausibly believe that there is an omission in the Midrash: the rabbis must have held the view that the Hirah mentioned in connection with Judah is to be identified with the Hiram mentioned in connection with David, Solomon, and Nebuchadnezzar, whereas Rabbi Judah distinguishes between Hirah and Hiram and only includes the Hiram mentioned in connection with David and Nebuchadnezzar in his calculation.

However, reader, you know how intellectually troublesome it is to believe in the longevity of the generation of men who lived from Adam to Noah were it not for the fact that Moses wrote it all down from the mouth of the Lord. The author of the *Guide* was therefore forced to declare that only the individuals who were singled out in Scripture lived so long. We quoted his statement in the previous chapter. You should also know that with regard to the decreed human life span of one hundred and twenty years (Gen. 6:3), there are no lack of people (as ibn Ezra states)[18] who hold that from then onwards,[19] such was to be the circumscribed age, when with the failure of their powers most people would die. It is obvious that you should neither pursue the notion nor fall into the trap of believing that Hirah reached the age of twelve hundred. A similar example may be taken from the Palestinian Talmud in tractate Sota.[20] "Rabbi Aqiva expounded: *Then Elihu son of Barachel the Buzite of the family of Ram was angry* (Job 32:2). Elihu is to be identified with Balaam. He was the *son of Barachel* because he came to curse Israel but blessed them (*bere*ḵ*h*); *from the family of Ram* because Balaam said, *From Aram has Bala*ḵ *brought me* (Num. 23:7). Rabbi Eliezer said to him: No, Elihu is to be identified with Isaac, *from the family of Ram*—this is Abraham." And there are many cases in which the sages merge separate individual righteous people into one identity. In Midrash Tanḥuma it states regarding the verse, *And Moses was (hayah) a shepherd* (Ex. 3:1):[21] "Anyone about whom Scripture applies the word *hayah,* that person saw a new world." The wise Recanati comments on this statement: "I mentioned the esoteric element in this statement when I spoke about the verse, *And Abel was a shepherd* (Gen. 4:2)."[22] This was because the sages of blessed memory had a tradition identifying Abel with Moses.[23] They also say that Phineas is Elijah. And in tractate Megillah,[24] it is stated that Malachi is Mordechai while Rabbi Joshua says that Malachi is Ezra. Sheshbasar is Daniel who witnessed six [*shesh*] calamities [*ṣarot*] in his lifetime;[25] Hatach is Daniel because they degraded him [*ḥata*ḵ*hu-hu*] from his position.[26] And they also

18. Ibn Ezra to Gen. 6:3. Ibn Ezra reports this view, but then rejects it on the grounds that subsequent to the decree of 120 years, many biblical figures lived longer.

19. I.e., from the time that the human lifespan was declared to be 120 years (as given in Gen. 6:3).

20. P. Sota 5 (6) 20d.

21. Tanḥuma, Shemot 13 (also B.R. 30:8 [274]; Est. R. 6:3).

22. Recanati, *Perush* to Ex. 3:1 (39 col. b). Recanati is alluding to the doctrine of transmigration. On this, see G. Scholem, "Gilgul," ch. 5.

23. The idea that Abel was reborn in Moses is found in early Kabbalah (see Scholem "Gilgul," n. 22) in order to account for his seeming unjustified murder at the hands of Cain. According to this tradition Abel had experienced an impure and confused vision of the Shechinah when he made his sacrifice. This defect was corrected by means of the transmigration of his soul into Moses who also had a vision of the Shechinah at the burning bush.

24. B. Meg. 15a.

25. The identification of Sheshbaṣar is not in Megillah, but in Pesiqta Rabbati 6, 23b.

26. B. Meg. 15a.

identify Petahiah with Mordechai because he was able to open [*pataḥ*] matters and interpret them.[27] And they also say that Mordechai is Bilshhan who was one those appointed to go up with Zerubbabel to build the Temple.[28] As regards the statement about Petahiah, the Tosafists first raise the question, "you may wonder as to how he could have lived so long," and then solve the question by suggesting,[29] "Apparently all Mordechai's successors were given his name." And even more amazing than all the foregoing examples is the passage in Shemot Rabbah on the verse, *See I have called him by the name Bezalel* (Ex. 31:2):[30] "He was one of the seven men who were given many names: Elijah was given four names; Bezalel, six; Joshua, six; Moses, seven." And in that context, there is their statement that all souls are one.[31]

All these statements are surely most astounding and as we have seen, there are many commentators who would reject some of them with the builder's measure[32] and in no uncertain terms.[33] The fact is that in the course of the argument it will become clear that the real meaning of all such cases may be understood in one of three ways. The wise Recanati writes:[34] "You should know that the sages of blessed memory state that Phineas is Elijah while they also say that he was of the tribe of Gad, while yet others say that he was Rachel's offspring. Then Elijah himself sometimes traces his lineage to one side and sometimes to another. However, everything can be resolved when one understands the secret of impregnation. This is why in Midrash Ruth they identify the subject of the verse, *Who has ascended heaven and come down?* (Pr. 30:4) both as Phineas and Elijah."[35] Thus from his words, we are given the idea as to how the sages' transformation of certain beings and particularly the heavenly righteous into one identity may be understood from the perspective of "impregnation." Similarly we are given a second insight from the Tosafists that in many of the cases under discussion, the sages did not mean that they were really physically one body, but that the name and lineage was preserved. And then there is the concluding statement of that passage in the first chapter of tractate Megillah:[36] "Rav Naḥman said: There is good reason for upholding the view that Malachi was Ezra. For it is written in Malachi, *for Judah has profaned the holiness of the Lord . . . and has married the daughter of a strange god* (2:11). But in Ezra, it is written, *And Shechaniah . . . said to Ezra: We have broken faith with our God and have married foreign women* (10:2)." This gives you a third insight, namely, that by such

27. This statement is not in Megillah, but in B. Men. 65a.

28. In Ezra 2:2. Bilshan is mentioned after Mordechai in the list of those who came up with Zerubbabel. Cf. B. Men. 65a: "Mordechai used to mix together expressions [*ballal* means to mix and *lashon* means language] and explain them; and therefore it is said of Mordechai, Bilshan."

29. Tos. to B. Men. 64b, s.v. *amar.*

30. S.R. 40:4.

31. Ibid. 40:3. The verse, *See I have called him by the name Bezalel* is expounded with regard to *Whatever happens, its name was given long ago* (Eccl. 6:10), and the idea is put forward that all living beings were *in potentia* even before the creation of Adam.

32. Lit. 'builder's cubit,' cf. B. Shabb. 31a.

33. 'In no uncertain terms,' lit. by extending the hands and the feet.

34. This is a kabbalistic term akin to the doctrine of transmigration of souls which from the thirteenth century acquired a particular meaning. It denotes the phenomenon of impregnation after birth by means of which an additional soul enters the body. See G. Scholem, "Gilgul," 302, n. 19.

35. Recanati, *Perush* to Num. 25:10, 79 col. d.

36. B. Meg. 15a.

examples, the sages of blessed memory are intending to point out the similarity and compatability that may be detected between different persons whether in respect of their acts or words. The author of the *Guide* writes in a similar manner with regard to the creatures [depicted by Ezekiel] when he says that the names given to the forms fit with the shapes they resemble.[37] But more persuasive is Don Isaac's interpretation of the forms [seen in the vision of Ezekiel] for which he was guided by the sage of the *Kuzari*.[38]

Now before we make our concluding remarks concerning the statement that Cyrus, Darius, and Artaxerxes are one and the same person, it seems right to lend some support to our foregoing remarks by citing the Tosafists of blessed memory yet again on the same subject, but where they give a contradictory explanation of the saying. That is to say, according to their view, the three names do not belong to one king, but rather, there were two people called King Artaxerxes. They state:[39]

> *In the twentieth year of King Artaxerxes, wine was set before him: I [Nehemiah] took the wine and gave it to the king.* (Neh. 2:1). According to the literal meaning of Scripture, that act of Nehemiah took place before Artaxerxes the king who was Darius son of Esther[40] in whose lifetime the Temple was built. However, this is not tenable given that the Temple was built in the sixth year of Darius's rule[41] while that event took place in the twentieth year. One must therefore explain it as referring to the twentieth year of Artaxerxes, Cyrus the first, who issued the decree.[42] The King Darius[43] to whom Nehemiah brought wine is to be identified as Darius son of Esther and this event took place in the third year of his rule as it is written, *At that time work on the House of God in Jerusalem stopped and remained in abeyance until the second year of Darius* (Ezra 4:24). And in the third year of his reign, Nehemiah spoke to him about the wall of Jerusalem, and this was in the twentieth year after the accession of Cyrus the first as is stated in Megillah,[44] "Three years of Cyrus, fourteen of Ahasuerus, and two [three] of Darius." And in the third, Nehemiah made his request for the rebuilding of the city.

Accordingly, the Tosafists of blessed memory, in encountering a problem which they thought of no account, as is seen from the continuation of their statement, opposed the Midrash equating Cyrus, Darius, and Artaxerxes. In fact, as we have seen, they made two persons out of the one. However, when they finally realized the extent to which both their question and answer were equally futile, they continued as though on the right path when they say: "However, one should explain Scripture according to its literal meaning. In the second year of Darius, they began to build the Temple and in the sixth year of his rule, the building was completed, and they did not build the wall of the city and its gates, but only the Temple. They were in a difficult situation because the

37. *Guide* III, ch. 1.

38. De' Rossi is referring to Abravanel, *Mayyene ha-Yeshu'ah* II:2 (286 col. a) who quotes *Kuzari* IV, par. 3. Abravanel takes issue with Maimonides' interpretation of Ezekiel's vision.

39. Tos. to B. R.H. 3b s.v. *shenat*.

40. According to midrashic tradition (Est. R. 8:3 and V.R. 13:5), the Darius referred to in Dan. 9:1 was Darius son of Esther "who was pure from his mother's side and impure from his father's."

41. Cf. Ezra 6:15.

42. I.e., Cyrus I was also called Artaxerxes and the verse in Nehemiah should read, "twenty years after the accession of Cyrus I who also had the title Artaxerxes."

43. I.e., Darius II was also called Artaxerxes.

44. B. Meg. 11b. This is not a precise quotation but rather an inference from the text.

nations were obstructing the work and this continued until the twentieth year of Darius when the wall was built as Scripture shows. But they were not occupied with the building of the Temple because it had already been built." Now we should resume the discussion of their statement that Cyrus, Darius, and Artaxerxes are one and the same person. The fact is that the companion passage about Sihon and the other statements which we examined shed light on it,[45] and one can therefore conclude that the rabbis of blessed memory did not posit it as a true fact but had some other consideration in mind. One might say that the three were alike and were regarded as one because they showed great kindness towards Israel. In this respect they are to be distinguished from the other kings who wrote decrees of indictment against us, and particularly the kings of the other peoples who were hostile to us. It was Cyrus who first passed the decree to send them free with the permit of building the Temple although he did not see its completion. Following Cyrus's example, Darius completed the construction of the Temple, and Artaxerxes built the walls of Jerusalem. In any case, we cannot fail to uphold such a view given that the literal meaning of Scripture also militates against transforming the three individuals into one person.[46] Indeed any intelligent person would take into account all the problems that are raised by this Midrash. Even without the complementary evidence of Sihon which is convincing and everything that had been said, he would finally reject it in the same way that several commentators rejected many of the Midrashim of the sages of blessed memory as we stated in chapter 14. In the first place, after the indictment was drawn up,[47] the name of Cyrus does not appear again as a king of Persia. This was why, with regard to the statement Cyrus, Darius, and Artaxerxes are one and the same person, Rashi of blessed memory was forced to write as follows: "Even the Darius who succeeded Ahasuerus was called Cyrus." Further, it is written, *So the elders of the Jews . . . brought the building to completion . . . by the order of Cyrus and Darius and Artaxerxes* (Ezra 6:14). Here, the copula does not function as though it were written on wood[48] where it does not serve any purpose, but like a rudder on the river Libruth,[49] which, according to their statement in Bava Batra, is like a sharp knife which divides off the biblical verses.[50] This demonstrates that they were undoubtedly three separate individuals. A similar view is expressed by the sage ibn Ezra in his commentary on chapter 11 of Daniel regarding the number of the kings of Persia. He cites the verse from Ezra and writes:[51] "Had the verse been referring to one king, according to the dictates of the language it would have literally read, 'Cyrus who is Darius who is Artaxerxes'." And he also cites the view of Rabbi Moses Hakohen[52] that the Darius who built the Temple and the Artaxerxes who built the

45. 'Companion . . . . illuminating,' lit. His companion Sihon . . . does tell concerning it. Cf. *His neighbor tells concerning him* (Job 36:33) used in B. B.B. 19a to mean that the companion passage sheds light on the other passage.

46. Cf. Ezk. 37:17 *so that they become one stick joined together in your hand.*

47. Cf. Ezra 4:5.

48. B. Ḥull. 16a., i.e., it is unintelligible and has no function.

49. Cf. B. Meg. 16b.

50. Cf. B. B.B. 111b.

51. Ibn Ezra to Daniel 11:2.

52. This is a reference to the eleventh-century liturgical poet and grammarian Moses Hakohen ha-Sefardi Gikatilla. Ibn Ezra cites him frequently. He is noted for his literal interpretation of Scripture.

walls were two different people, for you cannot say David and the king when you mean to say David the king. Then there is the statement of Kimḥi of blessed memory in his commentary on the verse, *I am going to shake the heaven and the earth* (Haggai 2:21): "These wars took place in the days of Darius or in the lifetime of Artaxerxes his successor to the throne." And at the beginning of his commentary to Haggai, he explains that the fore-mentioned Darius who ruled before Artaxerxes was the son of Esther. Furthermore, any thinking person would realize at a mere glance that the verse in Ezra (7:1), *And after these events, in the reign of Artaxerxes king of Persia, Ezra,* signifies that Artaxerxes was a new king, a successor to Darius who is mentioned earlier in the same section. It is comparable to the statement in chapter 4, *all the years of King Cyrus of Persia and until the reign of Darius of Persia. And in the reign of Ahasuerus* (vv.5–6). This is the way the author indicates the advent of one king succeeding another. And Ezra the scribe recognized the kindness and faithfulness which this Artaxerxes had shown to Israel in no small degree—for in his time the Temple was erected and he aided Nehemiah in the building of walls, not to speak of the favor he granted through the agency of Ezra himself. Accordingly, it pleased Ezra to accord him favorable mention in the verse which puts together the three Persian kings who, as we said before, acted with great kindness towards us.

Thus in the light of all that has been said, our objective has been made clear. That is to say, the Midrash identifying Cyrus, Darius, and Artaxerxes as one and the same person belongs to the category of statements of a specific genre; this is how the author of the *Guide* categorizes the statement about the six thousand years.[53] Expound and receive reward and comprehend it.

As for me, I must exult in the Lord. For having reached this juncture in the chapter, I subsequently[54] came across the comment of Rabbenu Zeraḥiah Halevi of blessed memory in *ha-Ma'or ha-Gadol*[55] concerning the statement in tractate Rosh ha-Shanah:[56] "[The first of Nisan is the new year for kings.] 'For kings'—what is the point of this law?" After he had endeavored to square the statement of Rabbi Abbahu and the objection of Rav Joseph with the *baraita* that Cyrus, Darius, and Artaxerxes are one and the same person, he writes:

> This is what we derive from the Midrash of the sages and their specific mode of interpretation. However, the correct interpretation according to the plain meaning is that the verse, *and by decree of Cyrus, Darius, and Artaxerxes, the king of Persia* (Ezra 6:14) refers to three kings. The verse, as it were, reads "kings of Persia" [and not king of Persia], for each of them was a king of Persia. The first two are mentioned in connection with the building of the Temple, since Cyrus was the initiator of the project and Darius completed it. And the last king, Artaxerxes, is included for he, too, built the walls of Jerusalem as is shown in

53. *Guide* II, ch. 29. Concerning the statement in B. R.H. 31a, "The world lasts six thousand years and will lay waste for a thousand years." Maimonides states that it does not signify that there will be total extinction, but that it is the saying of an individual that "has a certain form."

54. 'Subsequently,' lit. many days later. De' Rossi appears to be intent on demonstrating that he was not plagiarising from Zeraḥiah Halevi.

55. Zeraḥiah ben Isaac Halevi Gerondi wrote *ha-Ma'or* which is divided into two parts: *ha-Ma'or ha-Gadol* is a commentary on orders Nashim and Neziqin; *ha-Ma'or-Qatan* is on Berakhot, and sections of Moed and Ḥullin.

56. Ha-Ma'or to Alfasi, R.H. to B. R.H. 3a.

> Nehemiah. By means of all three, Isaiah's prophecy *Aliens shall rebuild your walls, Their kings shall wait upon you* (60:10) was fulfilled. But the said Artaxerxes is not the first Artaxerxes who ordered the cessation of the work on the Lord's Temple. These three kings are thus put together in the verse, the formulation of which is intended to indicate their association on account of their praiseworthy and meritorious behavior.

Thus far the words of a sage which bring him favor[57] and embrace my view in its entirety. In fact, this is one of the chapters which by reason of adding the words of the *Light* to it, I tasted the sweet honied words[58] with which my beloved friend, the wise, experienced, and talented writer Judah de' Sommi addressed me.[59] For when I was in Mantua, trying to get this book of mine printed, I was detained longer than expected.[60] I was distressed and looked downcast. On seeing me, that distinguished man [i.e., Judah de' Sommi] asked, "Why do you look like that." In my reply, I told him what had happened to me. Then he beamed and said: "This news will certainly have an invigorating effect[61]—for this book of yours on which you have worked so far only for a short while, will be like the fruit of a goodly tree which remains on the tree until it becomes ripe and then is sweet to the palate. For in this adverse time,[62] you will revise it and as a result of your immense effort you shall produce not silver but rather gold and precious stones."

57. 'Brings him favor,' cf. Eccl. 10:12.

58. Lit. honey and drippings of the honeycomb.

59. Judah Leone ben Isaac de' Sommi Portaleone (1527–92), born in Mantua was dramatist, theater director, and poet.

60. De' Rossi must be referring here to the opposition to his book that he received in some rabbinic circles. See my introduction.

61. Lit. 'This news will fatten the bone,' cf. Pr. 15:30.

62. 'Adverse time,' lit. 'at this time of indictment.' De' Rossi deliberately uses the expression "indictment" which is used in Ezra 4:6 with regard to the indictment sent to the Persian king to obstruct the inhabitants of Judah and Jerusalem from building the Temple. The reference is clearly both relevant to the subject of the chapter and to de' Rossi's sense of being persecuted by the rabbis who were opposing the publication of his book.

CHAPTER NINETEEN

Observation on the ancient work Seder Olam into which additional material was interpolated by somebody at a later date; and that other books were also tampered with.[1]

Our sages, may they rest in peace, attached their precious words to holy Writ in order to enhance the prestige of the Torah. This may be exemplified by the statement in the second chapter of tractate Ketubot.[2] "Rabbi Jose said: It is not right to be in possession of an uncorrected book [of the Bible] for it is written, *Do not let iniquity reside in your home* (Job 11:14)." This is a truly just ruling. For if somebody acts dishonestly in general or financial matters, he is abhorrent to our God; how much more so, if the matters concern Torah which no desired object can equal.[3]

Now many times in the course of this work of mine, there has been occasion to refer to the *baraita* called Seder Olam which is often quoted in the Gemara. I noticed that it contained stories that are undoubtedly anachronistic, which somebody must have inserted into the text. I thought it right to draw your attention to the passages—this example would prove to you that other books could suffer a similar fate. You will not fail to notice that Rabbi Jose's statement,[4] "The Persian Empire lasted 34 years after the building of the Temple, the Greek Empire 180 years" ends with the statement, "from then on, one should count 762 years from the destruction of the Temple [830/832 C.E.], and, 1,117 years according to the Greek era [805 C.E.].[5] Then it continues: "From the war of Aseverus until the Roman war of Vespasian is 80 years; from Vespasian's war until Qitos's war is 52 years.[6] From Qitos's war until the rule of Ben Kosiba is 16 years and Ben Kosiba's rule lasted 3 and a half years. From then on, calculate 616 years and a half."

I discovered that the wording of this statement in the printed text differs from that of the manuscript. Similarly, the Turkish and Venetian printed editions of the Yalqut of

1. This entire chapter was translated into Latin by Johannes Meyer in the preface to his Latin translation of the Seder Olam.

2. B. Ket. 19b. Here the statement is given in the name of R. Ammi, but in the Yalqut Shimoni (II, par. 906) to Job 11:14 it is said in the name of R. Yose. The change of name may be explained by the fact that de' Rossi is dealing with R. Jose's authorship of the Seder Olam.

3. Cf. Pr. 8:11.

4. Seder Olam, ch. 30 (141–46).

5. According to Ratner (Introduction, 47–48), de' Rossi's figures are corrupt; and should read 768 (not 762) which would correspond to 1147 Seleucid era (given in Yalqut and ms. Bodleian of Seder Olam). This would yield the figure 4596 a.m. (836 C.E.), the date of the scribe who transcribed the Seder Olam.

6. This is usually understood to be a reference to Lusius Quietus, a Moorish general of Trajan's forces.

Rabbi Simeon ha-Darshan give different readings of the above-cited passage from Seder Olam—it is cited in connection with the verse, *and the buck, the he-goat, the king of Greece* (Dan. 8:21).[7] So I transcribed the passage from a manuscript copy of the Yalqut dated 5070 [1310] which belonged to the distinguished brothers of the Montelbodo family. At any rate, if those figures[8] were given by the author himself, it necessarily follows that he must have lived after our Gemara was closed.[9] For as we said before in chapter 9, Rav Ashi who is known to have been the editor [of the Gemara] died in 738 of the Seleucid era [427 C.E.] and Amemar who was one of the last teachers died 73 years after him which comes to a total of 811 [500 C.E.]. Those calculations, conflicting though they are, come to more than a thousand years. Now we see that Rabbi Jose's statement is cited as a *baraita* in the first chapter of tractate Avodah Zarah in connection with the duration of the second Temple. Rashi comments here that the *baraita* is taken from the Seder Olam.[10] In the concluding remarks it states: "From then on, one should go on counting the years as from the destruction of the Temple." We shall discuss this again together with Rashi's comment in chapter 25. There is no doubt that the Seder Olam is an ancient *baraita,* particularly since they unambiguously state in tractate Niddah that the anonymous compiler of the Seder Olam was Rabbi Jose.[11] But the text is certainly corrupt. I mean that some later sage who was not "superior to a prophet"[12] interpolated the text in some places. It was not to no purpose that Rabbi Jose himself, as though predicting the future, warned about this in his interpretation of the verse, *Do not let iniquity reside in your home.* In this connection, one should incidentally be alerted to the fact that a similar situation pertains to our printed editions of the Pesiqta Rabbati or Zuṭarti [Zuṭarta] in that more recent material of a later date was inserted into the text.[13] This is particularly evident in the statement of Tobiah ben Eliezer when he speaks about something[14] "which occurred 1,427 years after the city was hit in the time of Zedekiah which is 1,417 years after the cessation of prophecy[15] and 1,027 years after the destruction of the Second Temple which is 4866 anno mundi [1106 C.E.]." On due consideration, one would come to the realization that these figures and those given at the end of Seder Olam cited above have the same source. And in the pericope Emor, the text reads:[16] "It happened that the saintly congregation of Mainz consecrated itself to the Lord in the preparatory period before[17] the festival of Pentecost in the year 4856

7. Yalqut Shimoni II, par. 1064 to Dan. 8:21, Salonika, 1521 (183b) and Venice, 1566 (156 col. d).
8. There is a scribal error in Cassel's edition. He reads *shinuye* instead of *sakhe.*
9. Rabbi Jose who is attributed with the authorship of Seder Olam lived in the second century C.E.
10. B. A.Z. 9a.
11. B. Nidd. 46b.
12. Cf. B. B.B. 12a, "A sage is superior to a prophet."
13. In the Venice 1565 edition (containing only Midrash on Leviticus, Numbers, and Deuteronomy), the work is entitled Pesiqta Zuṭarta o Rabbata, but its more usual title is *Leqaḥ Ṭov.* It was written by Tobiah ben Eliezer in Kastoria in Bulgaria in 1097. Thus the dates to which de' Rossi refers are authentic, being the author's reference to contemporary events.
14. *Leqaḥ Ṭov* to Num. 15:18 (vol. 2, 219).
15. 'Cessation of prophecy.' This is one of the terms used to denote the beginning of the Seleucid era.
16. *Leqaḥ Ṭov,* to Lev. 22:33 (vol. 2, 123). This is a contemporary allusion to events of the first Crusade.
17. 'In the preparatory period before,' lit. at half the period, cf. M. Sheq. 3:1. The expression is used to denote the days before a festival during which the laws relating to the festival are expounded. The detail

anno mundi." According to the minor computation,[18] it was a year in which they were "totally eliminated." Now there is no doubt that this was all added by somebody at a later date. However, one might also plausibly suggest that the entire work was written after the compilation of the Gemara.[19] Rosh [Asher ben Yeḥiel] expresses such a view with regard to tractate Soferim. Speaking about the section on the open paragraphs, he writes:[20] "The Palestinian Talmud gives the essential ruling as against that given in tractate Soferim; for tractate Soferim was written at a later date and is therefore not cited in the Gemara." Such a claim is all the more applicable to the Pesiqta since as I noticed, it contains some material which does not accord with the Midrash of our rabbis. In particular, the issues raised concerning the interpretation of Isaiah 60 (v.1) which are also cited by the author of the Yalqut must undoubtedly have been added by one of those who undertake to adjudicate a matter of contemporary relevance.[21] This is mentioned by the author of *Magen Avraham.*[22] Search and examine the passage. And in the work *Meshare Qitrin* of Abraham Halevi which was printed in Turkey,[23] I came across the explicit statement:[24] "A person should not become confused by the passage in the Zohar on the verse, *When the ark was to set out* (Num. 10:35) and the following passage, in which the end of time is calculated and a reason given for the two inverted *nuns.*[25] For I am convinced that the passage is not to be found in any ancient text but that it was fabricated in this generation. May the Lord forgive its author for I know the man and his talk." Then indeed, it is clear as daylight that Mordechai's dream, his prayer, and that of Esther which are written in the holy tongue in Midrash Esther are taken word for word from chapter 3 of the Hebrew Josephus [Josippon].[26]

Now the time has come[27] for me to fulfill the obligation I took upon myself in

---

given here corresponds to the account of the martyrdom of the community of Mainz as given in the chronicle of Solomon bar Simson.

18. I.e., if one omits the thousand and hundred digits from the date, the remainder (56) is numerically equivalent to "totally" and "eliminated."

19. De' Rossi's intuition was correct. See n. 14.

20. *Pisqe ha-Rosh* to Sefer Torah I, rule 13.

21. De' Rossi is referring to the passage in the Yalqut Shimoni II, par. 499 (also in Pesiqta Rabbati 36, 162a) which refers to the kings of Persia, Arabia, and Edom [i.e., Byzantium] in connection with the revelation of the Messiah. See B. Bamberger, "A Messianic Document," 425–31.

22. This work by the fifteenth-century writer Abraham Farissol was read in manuscript by de' Rossi. He is referring to ch. 74 which was published by Löwinger, "Recherches," in which Farissol is attacking contemporary messianic predictions based on Is. 60:1.

23. Abraham ben Eliezer Halevi (1460–1528?) was a Spanish kabbalist who after the 1492 expulsion went to Italy, Greece, Turkey, and Egypt and finally moved to Jerusalem. The *Meshare Qitrin* is an apocalyptic interpretation of the book of Daniel.

24. 'I know . . . talk,' cf. 2K. 9:11. G. Scholem tentatively suggests that the anonymous author is Joseph ibn Shraga (see "The Cabbalist" and "The Author").

25. In the massoretic text, the marks which appear before and after the verses (Num. 10:35–36) are known as "inverted Nuns." The Rabbis attempted to explain the reasons for those signs. According to modern scholars, they are comparable to the critical marks employed by the Alexandrian grammarians. See S. Lieberman, *Hellenism,* 38–43.

26. This is a reference to the Greek additions to the book of Esther which are also in the Vulgate. The author of the *Josippon* translated the text into Hebrew in chapter 4 (not 3), 25–30.

27. Since there is a reference to Esther at the end of the preceding paragraph, de' Rossi may have decided to begin here with an expression from Esther 2:12.

chapter 8 to discuss the anomalous statements that are attributed to our rabbis—such matters should be completely disassociated from them given their wisdom and righteousness.[28] In all extant printed editions of the Midrash Yelammedenu,[29] they list every verse for which a scribal emendation (*Tiqqun Soferim*) is given.[30] The following passage was inserted into the text: "But the Men of the Great Synagogue modified those verses and that is why they were called scribes—for they used to count the letters in the Torah and expound them and so they modified the verse, *they provoke Me still further and thrust the branch to My nostril* (Ezk. 8:17) to *and thrust the branch to their nostril.*" And under the entry for *kbd* in the *Arukh,* the eighteen scribal emendations are listed, and in relation to *whoever touches you, touches the pupil of his own eye* (Zech. 2:12) he states: "In ancient texts, the verse reads *the pupil of My eye.*" Surely all this runs contrary to the prescription of the sages of blessed memory set down in Sanhedrin,[31] "Anyone who says that even one letter of the Torah is not from heaven has despised the word of the Lord?" And in tractate Megillah, they state:[32] "Any verse that Moses did not divide, we may not divide." Similarly, as the author of the *Arukh* himself also points out under the entry for *kn,* it is stated in Megillah that if somebody introduces euphemisms into the passage dealing with forbidden marriages by saying *his father and his mother* (Lev. 18:7) instead of *your father and your mother,* he is told: "Read the verse as it is written.[33] How can you sift the words which Moses our teacher did not sift?" And this is true of all the rest of holy Writ. Who can tamper with it and remain guiltless?[34] However, the correct formulation is essentially given in the Mekhilta which is known to have been the composition of Rabbi Ishmael, a great and esteemed Tanna.[35] And with regard to all those verses [which contain scribal emendations] cited in reference to the verse, *In your great triumph, You break Your opponents* (Ex. 15:7), it is stated:[36] "Scripture, however, modified the expression." According to Rashba [Solomon ben Adret] whose opinion is

28. De' Rossi may also have been tempted to discuss this issue because it was treated in the anti-Jewish tract of Petrus Galatinus's *Opus de arcanis catholicae veritatis* which he had read. (See lib. I, cap. VIII, which is entitled "Quod per Talmudicas traditiones sacrae scripturae depravationes optime corriguntur, quae tam in nostra sive Graeca sive Latina editione, quam in textu Hebraico passim inveniuntur.")

29. De' Rossi could have read the editions of the Midrash Yelammedenu or Tanḥuma published in Constantinople 1520/22, Venice 1545, and Mantua 1563. The text is found in the standard editions of the Tanḥuma, Beshalaḥ 16.

30. The term *Tiqqun Soferim* (emendation of the scribes) was used in connection with certain euphemisms in which single letters were said to have been altered in order to avoid blasphemy. Some scholars (like de' Rossi) held that the scribes never changed the text of Scripture but that the Bible itself employed euphemistic expressions. Others maintained that the "corrections" were a later invention and maintained that the later rabbis continued to emend the text of Scripture. See S. Lieberman, *Hellenism,* 28–37.

31. B. Sanh. 99a.

32. B. Meg. 22a. This is a reference to the reading of the scriptural pericope and the question of the division of the verses.

33. M. Meg. 4:9: "And one who renders the portions concerning the forbidden sexual unions . . . must be silenced." In B. Meg. 25a it states: "If, for example, he says 'the shame of his father, the shame of his mother' in connection with *Your father's nakedness and the nakedness of your mother you shall not uncover* (Lev. 18:7). The quotation in the *Arukh* agrees with Maimonides' comment on the Mishnah.

34. This remark echoes the statement by Galatinus in *Opus de arcanis catholicae veritatis* (XXIIIv): "Quam ob rem tantum nefas ausi sunt ut quae Deus dictaverat, ipsi mutarent?"

35. The work was named after Rabbi Ishmael probably because the Midrash begins in Pisḥa 2 with the mention of Ishmael.

36. Mekhilta d'Rabbi Ishmael, shirata 6 (2, 42–45).

cited by the author of the *Halikhot Olam*[37] and the author of the *Iqqarim*[38] and the sage Mizraḥi,[39] this expression denotes that Scripture was originally modified according to the method of the emendations of the scribes which are indicated in an ancient text of the Bible to which Mizraḥi refers. Study the passage. There is no question that if Rabbi Tanḥuma, the author of Midrash Yelammedenu, did write that section on the scribal emendations, he must have transcribed it from the passage in the Mekhilta. Heaven forbid that he added that explanation [cited above] to their words which are as clear as crystal. That I may be trusted in this matter is certain, for I am in possession of two copies of the Midrash Yelammedenu which are more than three hundred years old and they contain no trace of that passage; moreover, they are undoubtedly not the only exemplars in the world.[40] I therefore came to the conclusion that some impetuous person, as I think, wanting to honor the Men of the Great Synagogue, wrote those words in the margin of his copy of the Yelammedenu. His colleague, the printer, then inserted his words into the body of the text for the sake of clarity. A similar occurrence befell certain versions of the commentary of Rashi of blessed memory on the verse, *The men went on from there to Sodom while Abraham remained standing before the Lord* (Gen. 18:22) which reads:[41] "Our Rabbis reversed the text, writing it thus." It is also cited by Mizraḥi on that verse.[42] It is unquestionably an error—God forbid that such a statement would issue from the mouth of such a saintly man.[43] The witnesses against this reading are the other versions of the commentary which do not contain that statement. In this matter we must surely show our approbation of the Septuagint which was composed before the time of our rabbis and testifies, as is demonstrated by both the Greek and Latin text,[44] that the verses originally read: *Abraham remained standing before the Lord* (Gen. 18:22); *And if You would deal thus with me . . . and let me see no more of my wretchedness* (Num. 11:15); *Whoever touches you, touches the apple of his own eye* (Zech. 2:12), and this is true for all the verses [in which a scribal emendation is given]. So how

37. Jeshua ben Joseph Halevi, *Halikhot Olam* II, ch. 1 (18): "The term 'emendation of the scribes' does not, God forbid, signify that they made any additions whatsoever to what was written in the Torah; rather by careful examination of the context of each verse, they found that the basic meaning was not that which would appear from the written text but another, and that therefore the reading should only be according to that other meaning."

38. Isaac Albo, *Iqqarim* III, ch. 22: "The reason for the changed reading . . . is like a correction which a scribe makes out of respect to God. . . . Moses changed the expression by divine order as a scribe changes an expression by way of euphemism."

39. Elijah Mizraḥi, *Perush Rashi* to Gen. 11:15 (245, col. c).

40. As Lieberman states (*Hellenism,* 30), it is probable that the passage was deliberately eliminated.

41. Rashi to Gen. 18:22: "But surely it was not Abraham who had gone to stand before Him, but it was the Holy One blessed be He who had come to see him and had said to him, *Because the cry of Sodom and Gomorrah is great.* And it should therefore have written here, *And the Lord stood yet before Abraham.* But it is a scribal emendation." Cf. B.R. 49:7 (505).

42. Elijah Mizraḥi, *Perush Rashi,* to Gen. 18:22, 32b–c. Mizraḥi refutes Rashi's statement, "The rabbis reversed the verse," and reasserts his opinion given in the previous passage.

43. In his edition of Rashi, A. Berliner ad loc. claims, like de' Rossi, that this was an interpolation of the text which was put into the Munich ms. dated 1233. However, it is difficult to substantiate his claim, given that there are more than two hundred mss. of Rashi's commentary (and no two identical) on the Pentateuch which have yet to be submitted to critical examination.

44. I.e., the text of the Septuagint and the Latin translation of the Septuagint which he had read in Andreas Cratander's 1526 reprint of the Latin interlinear translation of the LXX given in the Complutensian Polyglot.

could the nations not take the opportunity to abuse us and to open their mouths wide against us.[45] Furthermore, if I did not have qualms,[46] it would occur to me to add yet another passage to the one mentioned from the Tanḥuma. It is given in Avot d'Rabbi Nathan[47] and Bemidbar Sinai Rabbah[48] and in Aggadat Mishle on the verse, *An enemy dissembles with his speech* (Pr. 26:24).[49] It is cited by the compiler of the *Arukh* under the entry *nqd* where he discusses the ten passages in the Torah in which diacritical dots are placed above the letters: "Ezra said: If Elijah would come (another version reads Moses), and would say to me, 'Why have you written them?' [i.e., Why have you included the suspect passages?], I would say to him, 'I have already placed the dots above the letters.' And if he were to say to me, 'What you have written is fine, I would remove the dots from above them.' "[50]

And was Ezra great enough to have the capacity to add to or detract from the divine script in any way? God forbid that he or we should do such a thing. The responsibility may perhaps be laid on some pupil who wrote the passage without permission of his teacher, as was said in the *Kuzari* quoted above.[51] Alternatively, one must necessarily account for it in terms of the statement of Rabbenu Hai Gaon of blessed memory that we may disregard those Midrashim and Aggadot which were not fixed in the Gemara. Alternatively, it may be understood in the manner of the author of the *Guide* that we mentioned previously, namely, that it is a statement of an individual according to a certain manner of thinking.[52] This implies that it is not to be taken literally but has some artificial reason. It is as if one were to say that the sage adopted that turn of phrase in order to demonstrate that those verses were inherently capable of being either in a written or unwritten form. However, although his intention was acceptable, his action and his turn of phrase could have been articulated in a manner more consonant with reason. We should lay down the following rule: if you are able to endorse that which is written in such Midrashim and Aggadot, simultaneously preserving the honor of Torah and the prophets and all related matters, you should do so, and you should make every effort to present them in a favorable light; such an action will earn you a good reputation. But God forbid that you should be involved in any sinful matter or anything that appears harmful which might affect holy Scripture. Say to the artisan who

45. I.e., if it is said that the text was deliberately altered, the gentiles would be able to accuse the Jews of tampering with the text. This was a standard accusation in anti-Jewish writings. De' Rossi may in fact be referring to the treatment of the subject of *Tiqqun Soferim* in anti-Jewish tracts.

46. De' Rossi's 'qualms' are described more fully at the end of the original version of ch. 20, which was omitted in subsequent versions. (See my discussion in ch. 20. The passage will be translated in the notes.) There he encourages the reader to evaluate the passages with care. He may have also had in mind Christian discussions of this subject. In *Opus de arcanis catholicae veritatis,* XXIIIv, Jews are attacked for their attributions of emendations to Ezra's pen: "Tanta est quorundam Iudaeorum iuniorum impudentia, ut eas sancto Ezrae imponere non erubescant. Sed eos impie mentiri."

47. ARN, ch. 34 (A 51a; B 49b).

48. Bem. R. 3:13.

49. Midrash Mishle 26:24.

50. On certain words in the Pentateuch there are dots above the letters. According to Lieberman (*Hellenism,* 43–46), this passage indicates that some rabbis understood the dots as signifying doubtful passages, a system used by the Alexandrian grammarians. See also the discussion of D. Weiss Halivini, *Peshat and Derash,* 138–54.

51. It is not clear to which passage de' Rossi is referring here.

52. *Guide* II, ch. 29.

printed them, "Bury them in the earth[53] together with yourself, for it is a law for Israel, a ruling of the God of Jacob."[54] The Gaon Rav Hai and Rosh mentioned above would both lend you their support. Ramban [Nahmanides], too, of blessed memory would also endorse your position.[55] We mentioned all their views in chapter 15. Go and study the relevant passages. You should also know that you will be confronted by such anomalous passages not only in those Midrashim referred to, but also in the works of the kabbalists as well as in those attributed to the saintly Rabbi Simeon bar Yoḥai. For anyone who is sensitive to language will sense when expressions that are not characteristic of the manner and style of Rabbi Simeon bar Yoḥai are used in certain passages. And I was amazed to find that the Midrash ha-Neʿelam Zohar on the pericope Toledot (p. 139) contained quotations from Rav Naḥman, Rava, and Rav Joseph which would imply that it is not as ancient as we thought.[56] {And in the Zohar itself and in Midrash Ruth ha-Neʿelam and the text called Raya Mehemna there are not a few references to Amoraim. In particular, in Raya Mehemna, on the verse, *And as a meal offering there shall be a tenth of an ephah of choice flour* (Num. 28:5), it states:[57] "Our rabbis of the Mishnah and the Amoraim arranged all their teaching according to the secrets of the Torah." Now I had spoken about this matter with various sagacious persons who were likewise amazed on seeing these passages. Everybody agreed that the most plausible explanation was that some disciple whose passion was greater than his grasp of the matter found glosses in the margins of the text which he inserted into it. It is also possible that the entire texts of Midrash ha-Neʿelam and Raya Mehemna were originally written by the Amoraim, although the greater part of their sayings were actually derived from the sages of antiquity. And there is some semblance of evidence for this. For in the Zohar, there is a Midrash on the verse, *I have come to my garden* (S.S. 5:1) which is also cited in the Raya Mehemna in the fore-mentioned passage as deriving from the "first book."[58] Study the passage. Now in the *Sefer Yuḥasin* of Rabbi Abraham Zacut which was printed in Constantinople by the noble Rabbi Samuel Shullam,[59] may God protect and redeem him, he refers among other later authorities to Rabbi Moses de Leon who was in Spain in about 5050 [1290].[60] In the name of the judge of Acre[61] he makes false allegations with regard to some of the "words of truth" [i.e., the Zohar]. He claims that through the power of the holy Name,[62] this Rabbi Moses inserted his own

53. Cf. Job 40:13.

54. Cf. Ps. 81:5.

55. 'Endorse your position,' lit. take hold of your strength. Cf. Is. 27:5 *Or let him take hold of my strength that he may make peace with me and he shall make peace with me.*

56. De' Rossi is referring to the Mantua 1558 edition of the Zohar. The rabbis mentioned were Amoraim and thus lived after Simeon bar Yoḥai.

57. Zohar III, 244b.

58. In the Raye Mehemna, the main body of the Zohar is designated as the "first book." The phrase does not, as de' Rossi implies, refer to an ancient source.

59. Abraham Zacuto (or Zacut), *Sefer Yuḥasin.* This story is discussed by I. Tishby, *The Wisdom,* 13–17.

60. The passage (141b–142a) was omitted from other editions of the *Sefer Yuḥasin* because of its controversial nature. It was printed again in Filipowski's edition (88–89).

61. Isaac of Acre was a well-known kabbalist who went from Acre to Spain after the conquest of the Muslims in 1291.

62. The idea is that Rabbi Moses was a medium for automatic writing and was not an intentional forger.

fabrications into the text at great pains in order to get wealthy from the monied, and that he brought the work to two frivolous and unhappy women.[63] I must therefore praise the printer of the work who added the following note in the margins of the text: "You see the foolishness of those who speak arrogantly about the righteous. They do not know nor realize that they are distorting into bitterness words that constitute the secret of the world and they regard the esoteric work as strange and make it worthless, but their proofs and arguments are useless and are of no benefit." This is how he makes amends for having consented to the publication of that passage, while actually, he would have gained more praise had he omitted it. For while his gloss has some value, it would have been much more laudable had he passed over the entire story in silence.[64] As for me, I would corroborate his fine statement and clinch the matter on the following grounds. For although it may be supposed that there are people who write through the medium of the powerful Name, this power is reliable only within its own constraints, namely, it has the capacity to direct the hand of the pen of the ready scribe such that he is able to accomplish a lengthy task within a short period of time. Likewise, it is said by our sages of blessed memory in the Sifre (according to the Mordechai),[65] but the passage is to be found in Devarim Rabbah, that our master Moses under divine inspiration wrote thirteen scrolls of Torah on the day of his death.[66] It is however possible that the author of that statement would allude to the verse, *And Moses wrote* (Deut. 31:22) and claim, "I am expounding Scripture." In other words, no mental illumination was bestowed on him such that he could divulge and produce the secrets of the divine and the sacred esoteric mysteries. As for those talkative women,[67] it is a known fact that women are classified first in the list of the ten persons who are disqualified from giving evidence.[68] And they were further disqualified in that they were relatives, and mother and daughter alike had been corrupted by poverty.[69] In any case, since the story has been published—if it has no significance in itself—it may have bearing on certain statements which may be found in specific writings; namely, that the reader should only be receptive to them if they accord with correct reason and are attached to the known texts of our ancestors. In particular, one should hold these qualms with regard to some writers of amulets and not reject the statement of the "teacher of righteousness"[70] who in the introduction to his work writes:[71] "They would be led to recognize the falseness

63. This is an allusion to the story told by Zacuto that Isaac of Acre was brought to the wife and daughter of Moses de Leon who both independently stated that Moses had no text of the Zohar but wrote it "out of his own head and heart."

64. 'For while . . . silence.' He uses here an expression from B. Meg. 18a: "A word is worth one sela; silence two selas."

65. Mordechai ben Hillel ha-Kohen (1240?–1298), *Sefer Mordechai* to B. Pes. 105b (37, col. a). Mordechai's reference to the Sifre has not been discovered.

66. D.R. 9:9: "He wrote thirteen scrolls: twelve for the twelve tribes and one he placed in the Ark. Thus, should somebody wish to make any fabrications, they could produce the scroll of the Ark."

67. A reference to the story of Isaac of Acre's discussion with Moses de Leon's wife and daughter.

68. See *Mishneh Torah,* Edut IX:1.

69. Cf. M. Ned. 9:10.

70. 'Teacher of righteousness,' a play on the title of Maimonides' *Guide* (*Moreh*—teacher) *of the Perplexed.*

71. *Guide,* Introduction (trans. Pines, 16). Maimonides is not explicitly referring to amulet writers in this context.

of the forgeries in their hands." Moreover, he writes further on this subject in part 1:[72] "You should not take into account the vain imaginings of the writers of amulets." For in such matters one ought to be suspicious until such time that both the person and the amulet[73] are approved by experts in magic and divination.}[2]

Similarly, it is only to one's own good to be circumspect with regard to the texts of our law books and codes. In fact, this was actually borne out by my own present experience in the study house of the esteemed Yeshivah which was founded by those people of the Lord, the Sephardim, who live here in Ferrara.[74] The members of the gathering appoint one leader for each day who serves in rotation. It was the turn of Avtalion of Modena[75] to discuss the well-known *halakhah* in tractate Shabbat [which states that anything which issues from trees is not subject to the law] of three fingersbreadth square.[76] In the course of his lecture in which he presented a profound and extensive interpretation of the passage, he produced reliable proof from manuscript copies of Alfasi that in relation to this particular *halakhah,* the printed edition contained extensive additions to the original text of the author. And for a reason of which you will be apprised in a later chapter, it also seemed to me appropriate in this context to draw your attention to another point. In our opinion, certain passages in Josephus are fabrications;[77] and this is also the case with the Hebrew Josephus [Josippon]. For certain scholars who set eyes on any of the printed editions of the Hebrew Josephus which were extant realized that it contains fabrications.[78] In other words, many people in successive generations had the audacity to tamper with the text either by inserting glosses or by adding stories from another source—this should not be done. In particular, those scholars realized that the names of the nations in chapter 1—the Franks, Goths, Lombards, and Bulgarians—must have been fabricated.[79] After all, in the time of Josephus, those clans had not yet come to be. The entire passage is not in the version of the Josippon published in Germany.[80] Similarly, it contains no mention of the episode of Nektanebus and his witchcraft, which is however to be found in the *History of Alexander* written by the Egyptian magicians. I saw the text; indeed, it is in my possession in

72. Ibid. I, ch. 61.

73. 'Both the person and the amulet get approval.' Cf. B. Shabb. 61a.

74. Many Sephardi Jews came to live in Ferrara after the expulsions from Spain, Portugal, and Sicily. In 1559 they were accorded permission from Alfonso d'Este to live and trade in the city.

75. Avtalion Modena (1529–1611), uncle of Leon Modena, lived in Ferrara and was renowned as a talmudist and scholar.

76. B. Shabb. 26a. Cloth which has a minimum measurement of three fingersbreadth square is liable to impurity.

77. De' Rossi discusses these corruptions of Josephus in ch. 53.

78. De' Rossi seemed to accept the traditional view that the *Josippon,* the medieval compilation of Josephus written in southern Italy in the tenth century, was an authentic work of Flavius Josephus. Nevertheless, he always draws a clear distinction between Josephus's works and the Josippon by adopting the designations "the Roman Josippon" and the "Hebrew Josippon."

79. De' Rossi is referring to Münster's edition, Basel, 1541 (see n. 80): "Caeterum quod quarundam graecarum vocum fit mentio et citantur quaedam gentes quae longe post Iosephi tempora in mundo surrexunt ut sunt: Franci, Gothi, Lombardi, Bulgari, etc. haec plane arguunt Iosepho quaedam accessisse per posteros Iudaeos expositionis et praefationis gratia."

80. This is a reference to Sebastian Münster's edition of the *Josippon.* In his preface, Münster discusses whether the work was a genuine work of Josephus. He states that he had purposely omitted the interpolated passages because most of them were fictitious. "Nos propterea consulto omisimus ea quae ab initio huic auctori sunt adiecta, eo quod pleraque sunt fabulosa."

a Hebrew translation.[81] The writer Justin also refers to it in his histories of foreign monarchs.[82] The story of Nektabenus recounted in the work of the magicians is given in an identical version in the Josippon which our people possess. The fact is, as Curtius writes,[83] the priest of the god Ammon incurred much guilt by ingratiating himself to Alexander when he called him the son of the god who went by the name of Jupiter. The entire story was a piece of flattery invented by the priests of the shrine. But [the Hebrew] Josephus himself was certainly not the inventor of the story. Some weaver of tales bent on engaging his readers' attention chose to insert that confused account into the text. You will notice that Josephus makes no mention of it. For all truthful people hold that Alexander was the son of Philip. Similarly, the account of the translation of our Torah in the Hebrew Josephus[84] is most certainly corrupt and is different from the other versions of the story which I have seen, and this is evident to anyone who makes an intelligent comparison between the text of the Hebrew and Roman Josephus.[85] Moreover, the story of the enthronement of Vespasian in Rome in the presence of Josephus is only to be found in the Turkish edition from which the Venetian print was transcribed.[86] But there is no trace of it in the German edition and in the first prints of Abraham Conat.[87] On this matter, I had previously consulted certain Christian scholars who have expert knowledge of Roman history, and they told me that the story is completely nonsensical. There are more examples of this kind, particularly on the subject of the high priest before whom Alexander prostrated himself. We shall mention this again, God willing.[88] Thus, while it is not a basic text, the beautiful soul still desires to know the truth of every matter. You should bear in mind everything I have told you in this chapter; then you, too, will be protected from any harm for our God will command His angels to protect you.[89] May His name be blessed, for the holy Writ, His Torah, and His prophets, according to universal consensus, are preserved in the tradition which serves as a fence around them all as I mentioned in chapter 8. Now, enough has been said on this subject.

81. This is a reference to a Hebrew translation of the Arabic version of the Alexander Romance, the text of which was used in one of the interpolations of the *Josippon.* The attribution of the work to Egyptian magicians is also found in the Mantuan edition of the *Josippon.* See D. Flusser, *Sefer Josippon,* vol. 2, 221.

82. Justin, *Epitoma,* XI, 11, 6–8.

83. Curtius Rufus, *De rebus gestis* IV, 7.

84. *Josippon,* bk. 3, ch. 17 (69–70).

85. See de' Rossi's discussion in ch. 7.

86. Constantinople, 1510; Venice, 1544, bk. VI, ch. 77 (288). On this story, see D. Flusser, *Sefer Josippon,* 33–34.

87. Abraham Conat was the printer of the first edition of the *Josippon* (Mantua, 1480?). They were not two separate editions but various exemplars of the work, some on vellum and some on paper. See A. M. Habermann, *Peraqim,* 5–6.

88. See ch. 22.

89. Cf. Ps. 91:11.

CHAPTER TWENTY

Solution to the problem that arises from the statements of the rabbis, blessed be their memory, regarding the number of high priests who served in the second Temple, and a refutation of the views of Rabbenu Tam and Rabbi Isaac regarding the number of high priests who served in the first Temple.[1]

When one becomes acquainted with the rabbinic mode of teaching, the many doubts that obscure our understanding are removed. One should realize that this is likewise true of one of their methods to which the author of the *Kuzari* and Riaz (Isaiah di Trani) also alluded in their statements cited above. I am referring here to the way our sages employed exaggeration and hyperbole in many of their refined[2] sayings. For it is characteristic of human beings to make inflated assertions both about ideas as well as numerical figures. The point is not to present the actual truth or even to approximate it, but rather to demonstrate that something is greater than we might suppose. Accordingly, they note in Ḥullin,[3] "The sages spoke in hyperboles." Furthermore, there are several passages in which they say that a teaching has been expressed through hyperbole. As regards numerical sayings, you should look at their statements that we mentioned in chapter 13 in which the Jewish population of Alexandria in Egypt is said to have numbered twice 400 myriads, or according to another view, 80,000 myriads.[4] Then there is the statement in Yoma that Rabbi Eleazar ben Ḥarsom possessed a thousand towns and as many ships.[5] And it is said in Ḥullin that [Samuel sent Rabbi Johanan] thirteen parchments (or camel-loads, according to Rashi's reading) dealing with problems of *ṭerefah*.[6] They state that between the word "Azel" [mentioned in 1Chr. 8:38] and "Azel" [1Chr. 9:44] 400 camel-loads of exegetical interpretations are

1. It was this chapter which provoked some of the most violent criticism from certain rabbis. De' Rossi was forced to remove three examples of the hyperbole from the first version. The original text of the chapter is printed in Z. H. Jaffe's edition as well as by Y. Mehlman, "Saviv Sefer Me'or Enayim," who published all the pages from the exemplar of 28 Ellul 5334 (September 1574) which contains the original text as well as two pages in which de' Rossi describes his negotiations with the Venetian rabbis. There he claims that the omission of these three examples does not substantially change the basic argument of the chapter. The original text will be given here in the notes.

2. In the original text, this sentence is phrased slightly differently. The word "refined" is added here, presumably to stress that no depreciation of the rabbis is meant.

3. B. Ḥull. 90b.

4. De' Rossi is confusing two figures here. He is actually referring to the passages in B. Giṭṭ. 57b and E.R. 2:4 to Lam. 2:2, which give various figures for the number of inhabitants of Bethar who were killed. In B. Sukk. 51b the inhabitants of Alexandria are said to have numbered 60 or 120 myriads.

5. B. Yoma 35b.

6. B. Ḥull. 95b.

borne.[7] There is the explicit statement in tractate Eruvin[8] in which figures of a hundred and more appear not to be taken as precise figures. For they say that Bar Qappara's figure of a hundred cubits [for the height of a cross beam spanning the entrance to a blind alley] may well be regarded as a hyperbole, whereas it is questioned as to how Rabbi Judah's figure [of forty cubits] can be postulated as a hyperbole. In particular, the figure 80 or 80,000 is frequently used as a hyperbole in tractate Taʿanit in the Palestinian Talmud.[9] Likewise, the figure 60 is predominantly used in the Babylonian Talmud. There is the statement about five things that are one-sixtieth part of something else in tractate Berakhot,[10] and there are similar statements in Pesaḥim,[11] Nedarim,[12] and elsewhere. In addition, you should consider the passage which describes Rabbi Eleazar's penance in Bava Meṣia:[13] "[Every morning they spread 60 sheets for him; every morning 60 basins of blood were removed from under him. . . . Every morning his wife prepared 60 kinds of pap."} The number 60 is utilized extensively in this context. There is the statement in Bava Qama:[14] "Sixty men can run after the one who takes meals early in the morning, but they will not succeed in overtaking him." Commenting on this passage, the Tosafists explicitly say: "In this passage of the Gemara, the same method is employed as in tractate Ḥullin[15] where they speak of 60 *minas* [weights] of iron. In the same context, they refer to 60 bereavements occurring in one family. Rashi comments: "It is a general statement, a colloquial idiom, and not precise."[16]

7. B. Pes. 62b.
8. B. Eruv. 2b.
9. P. Taʿanit 4 (2) 69a–b.
10. B. Ber. 57b.
11. B. Pes. 94a: e.g., "The world is a sixtieth part of the Garden of Eden."
12. B. Ned. 39b: "He who visits an invalid, takes away one-sixtieth part of his pain."
13. B. B.M. 84b.
14. B. B.Q. 92b.
15. This is a reference to B. Ḥull. 58b: "As the popular saying goes, 60 minas of iron are suspended on the gnat's proboscis."
16. The original text reads: "Similarly the number 60 [is a hyperbole] . . . 60 fiery lashes . . . They also say (B. Shabb. 119b) that Jerusalem was destroyed because they were not ashamed of one another. R. Ḥidka said it was because they put small and great on equal terms. And other such reasons are given which are not in themselves sufficient grounds for our compassionate God to have brought about such a destruction. Similarly they say in the Palestinian Talmud (Taʿanit 4 (5) 69a) that the great city of Betar was destroyed because they used to play with a ball on the Sabbath, and the same assertion is made E.R. (to Lam. 2:2) of several cities on the Mount of Olives. And in chapter three of Avot (3:11), it is stated: "He who shames another in public . . . even though he possesses Torah and good deeds, has no portion in the world to come." And to these examples, one might even add the statement in the Zohar (pericope Emor), "He who spills his seed for no purpose does not deserve to see the Divine Presence." And in pericope Vayeḥi they add that such a person cannot get repentance. And in Niddah (13a) they say that such a person, like the murderer and idolator, is liable to the death penalty. This is comparable to their hyperbolic statement in Arakhin (15b) that one who speaks ill of others commits a sin that is commensurate with the three cardinal sins. And there are innumerable other sayings in which they use the hyperbole to warn people away from transgression. This is also made clear by Rambam in his commentary on Sanhedrin (7:4) where he says: "They went to great lengths to warn and to frighten the person who causes an erection willfully and thus spills his seed for no purpose." This statement should be applied to all other matters of a similar nature. . . . And in Shabbat (118b) they say: "All who take delight in the Sabbath (according to Rambam this means one who, for example, prepares his cooked food with large amounts of oil or with balsam wine) deserves an unbounded heritage." In the same category are all their exaggerated statements about acts of charity in Sukkah (49b) and Bava Batra (9b)."

{I did not include the passage in Sanhedrin that states:[17] "When love was strong, we could make our bed on the blade of a sword, but now that love has diminished, a bed of 60 cubits is not large enough for us." For one might well suggest that it alludes to the well-known passage in the first book of Kings (6:2) which gives the length of the first Temple as 60 cubits. Similarly, I heard that the statements that Elijah,[18] Gabriel,[19] and Metatron[20] were given 60 fiery lashes are taken as a precise statement by the kabbalists, and I discovered a similar view expressed by by the author of *Maʿarekhet Elohut,*[21] in the "gate of destruction"[22] where he writes:[23] "Why were there 60 lashes? It is an esoteric allusion to the six directions [Sefirot],[24] each of which embraces the ten [Sefirot]."[25]}[2]

But it is the number 300 that is most frequently utilized by our sages of blessed memory. We shall mention this again in the course of the chapter. The hyperbole is likewise adopted for express purposes. For example, when they wish by means of analogies to exhort people to avoid transgression, they exaggerate the harm that will ensue from committing it. Thus they say:[26] "One who speaks ill of others, commits a sin that is commensurate to the three cardinal sins for which it is stated that one should let himself be killed rather than commit the transgression. It is stated in tractate Nedarim:[27] "Rabbi Aqiva says: Whosoever does not visit the sick is like a murderer." It is also stated:[28] "One who breaks his possessions in a moment of anger is like an idolator." The wise Bar Sheshet cites these last three passages in his responsum (171) as proof of the view that he expresses as follows:[29] "The sages' method is to magnify the gravity of sins in an effort to protect people from stumbling therein. Similarly, with regard to certain transgressions, Rambam [Maimonides] states:[30] "They went to great lengths to warn and to instill fear."[31] In fact, in some cases, they went to the extent of issuing the crushing pronouncement that there could be no repentance, although in tractate Rosh ha-Shanah they do affirm their salutary principle that nothing can stand in the way of repentance.[32] One can also propose an additional interpretation of their

17. B. Sanh. 7a.
18. B. B.M. 85b.
19. B. Yoma 77a. Gabriel is given 40 (not 60) fiery lashes.
20. B. Ḥag. 15a.
21. This work which became one of the classical texts of kabbalah. It is sometimes ascribed to Perez of Barcelona and was written at the end of the thirteenth or beginning of the fourteenth century.
22. This section of the book deals with the nature of sin.
23. *Maʿarekhet Elohut,* ch. 9, 129a.
24. The six directions correspond to the six lower Sefirot (excluding the lowest Sefirah of *malkhut*).
25. This passage which belongs to de' Rossi's second revisions on the text is clearly an attempt to pacify his critics. In the original text (see n. 16), de' Rossi clearly tends to the view that the "60 fiery lashes" are a hyperbole.
26. B. Arak. 15b.
27. B. Ned. 40a.
28. B. Shabb. 105b.
29. Isaac Bar Sheshet, *She'elot,* 39, col. b.
30. Maimonides, *Perush,* Sanh. ch. 7:4. The passage is dealing with sexual sins.
31. De' Rossi does not complete the quotation as he did in the original version (see n. 16) which reads: "They went to great lengths to warn and to frighten the person who causes an erection willfully and thus spills his seed for no purpose."
32. In B. R.H. 17b it is stated: "Great is repentance that it rescinds the final sentence." De' Rossi's quotation is actually from P. Pe'ah 1 (1) 16b which is also used by Maimonides in *Mishneh Torah,* Teshuvah III:14.

statement that there can be no repentance: the nature of the sin is such that repentance is for certain reasons out of reach or unattainable as Rabbi Moses [Maimonides] of blessed memory states at length in chapter 4 of the Laws of Repentance.[33] Conversely, when they wish to encourage and promote a certain commendable act, they exaggerate its value. Thus, in tractate Bava Batra, they state:[34] "One who gives charity in secret is greater than Moses our teacher"; while in tractate Ketubot, it states:[35] "One who closes his eye to charity is like an idolator. In tractate Megillah, it is stated:[36] "One who quotes something in the name of his informant brings redemption to the world." However, they do bring this statement in line with reason by stating that this has a practical application. For it was as a result of such virtuous behavior that Israel was the beneficiary of great salvation in the past;[37] it is thus likewise feasible that a comparable act can be achieved by anybody who adheres to the same standard of behavior. And there are many other examples of this kind on a variety of topics. This is indeed (I refer to hyperbole in speech) the wisdom of the subtle and an appropriate method of communicating our message. From the passage in tractate Ḥullin you know that it [i.e., the hyperbole] was used in the holy Scriptures which undoubtedly serves as an illuminating model for all speakers and rhetoricians. It was likewise extolled and adopted by the gentile orators, for example, by their leading orator Cicero in the fourth book of the *Topics*[38] and by Quintilian in the eighth book of his work on rhetoric.[39] These were the sources used by the Jewish rhetorician in gate 4 of his *Nofet ṣufim.*[40] Although it is not the purpose of our work to explain the methods of the Gemara and the specific characteristics of the Midrashim, it is important, in my opinion, to follow up this line of thinking which is certainly of fundamental importance in drawing such statements as these into the realm of the rational. The purpose will be to resolve a specific problem that arises from a story told by our sages. You will then be in a position to draw the analogy between this example and all other similar cases. After all, an evaluation of the stories recounted by the sages is our designated task.

The specific problem occurs in our [i.e., the Babylonian] Gemara in tractate Yoma:[41] "Rabbi Johanan said: What is the meaning of the verse, *The years of the wicked will be shortened* (Pr. 10:27)? This refers to the second Temple which stood for 420 years and in which more than 300 high priests served." But in tractate Yoma in the Palestinian

33. *Mishneh Torah,* Teshuvah IV.

34. B. B.B. 9b.

35. B. Ket. 68a.

36. B. Meg. 15a. This statement is made in relation to Esther who told King Ahasuerus about the plot against the king's life in the name of Mordechai, *Mordechai learned of it and told it to Queen Esther, and Esther reported it to the kings in Mordechai's name* (Est. 2:22).

37. I.e., in the time of Esther and Mordechai.

38. *Topica* X:45: "Under the topic of similarity, orators and philosophers have license to cause dumb things to talk . . . in order to add force to an argument or lessen it—this is called hyperbole." Cf. *Rhet. ad Herennium* IV, xxxiii, 44.

39. *Institutio* VIII, 6, 67–76.

40. This is a reference to Judah Messer Leon's *Nofet Ṣufim* (gate 4, ch. 43). The purpose of the work was to demonstrate that classical rules of rhetoric were embodied in the biblical writings. On de' Rossi's use of these rhetorical ideas, see Altmann, "Ars Rhetorica," 13–15.

41. B. Yoma 9a. This passage assumes that there were 300 or more high priests in second Temple times.

Talmud,[42] they state that the high priests of the second Temple bought their appointments with money, or killed each other by witchcraft. Eighty high priests are said to have served, while alternative figures of 81, 82, 83, 84, and 85 are also given. There is surely then a significant discrepancy between the two Gemaras. What is particularly problematic is that the author of the statement in the Babylonian Gemara is Rabbi Johanan who was actually the editor of the Palestinian Gemara.[43] One would have at least expected him to have given the alternative view that there were more than 300 high priests. In fact, according to the hypothesis we put forward, it may be possible to resolve the problem by defining the statement in the Babylonian Gemara as an imprecise statement that was articulated in the form of a hyperbole, while the Palestinian text, in their view, gave the more accurate figure. Evidence that this is so [i.e., that the Palestinian text is more accurate] is provided by the list of alternative opinions, each one claiming to be more accurate than the others. As you shall see, the same version is given in Vayiqra Rabbah and in the Sifre. And you should disregard the fact that the Babylonian Gemara presents the figure in the following statement:[44] "Subtract from this figure 40 years during which Simeon the righteous served, 80 years of Johanan the high-priest. . . . Count the high priests from then onwards, and you will find that not one of them completed his year of office." Hyperbole as we said, constitutes the basis of this entire statement. It is comparable to the method applied to the story of Titus which we discussed in chapter 16, and to the mode discussed in the introduction to the *Guide*[45] of reading the proverb, *From the window of my house, through my lattice, I looked out* (Pr. 7:6). Here, there are many additional details that are not given corresponding signification, but whose purpose is simply for the embellishment of the parable, and to provide the requisite completeness to meet the objectives of the one who invented it. This, then, is surely the way you should understand the above-quoted statement, "some say, there were 80 thousand myriads." For although they appear to be claiming that the latter figure is more accurate than the former one, both are in fact inflated figures that have no basis in reality.[46] From the ranks of the Christians is the wise Ficino who in his commentary to Plato's *Symposium* expressed exactly the same view as the author of the *Guide* in the name of their greatest doctor [i.e., Augustine].[47]

The truth of the matter is that the figure 300 was frequently used as a hyperbole by our sages. There is, for example, their statement,[48] "The great city of Rome measures 300 parasangs by 300." And in tractate Sanhedrin[49] and in Avot d'Rabbi Nathan[50] it is

42. P. Yoma 1 (1) 38c.
43. Maimonides designates R. Johanan bar Nappaḥa (d. 279) as the author of the Palestinian Talmud in his introduction to his Commentary on the Mishnah.
44. B. Yoma 9a.
45. Maimonides, *Guide* (trans. Pines, 13).
46. This statement does not appear in the original version.
47. Marsilio Ficino's commentary on Plato's *Symposium* was written in 1469 and published with Latin translation in Florence in 1544. The passage is Oratio Quarta, cap. 2 (383): "Nos autem quae in figuris superiorum et aliis describuntur, singula exacte ad sensum pertinere non arbitramur. Nam Aurelius Augustinus non omnia inquit quae in figuris finguntur significare aliquid putanda sunt. Multa enim propter illa quae significant ordinis et connexionis gratia sunt adiuncta."
48. B. Meg. 6b.
49. B. Sanh. 68a.
50. ARN, ch. 25 (rec. A, 81).

stated: "Rabbi Eliezer used to study 300 laws about the deep bright spot[51] and the same number of laws about the planting of cucumbers." And it is also stated:[52] "Rabbi Meir knew 300 parables about foxes." And in Temurah,[53] "300 laws were forgotten during the period of mourning for Moses." And in tractates Ḥagigah and Sanhedrin,[54] they speak of "300 laws on a tower flying in the air." And in tractate Yevamot,[55] "Jonathan has 300 answers regarding a daughter's rival." And in Pesaḥim,[56] "Yohanan ben ben Nadbai ate 300 calves and drank 300 barrels of wine." And again in Pesaḥim,[57] they speak of Beruriah wife of Rabbi Meir who studied 300 laws from the Book of Genealogies[58] in one day. And in tractate Shabbat,[59] "300 barrels of oil were taken up to him [Hananiah ben Garon] and he sat in an upper chamber and expounded them [i.e., reconciled the contradictions in the book of Ezekiel]." And in tractate Bekhorot,[60] "Once the egg of a Bar Yokhani [a fabulous bird of the ostrich family] fell and swamped 60 [16] cities and destroyed 300 cedars." And in Midrash Ekhah,[61] "Simeon used to distribute 300 barrels of wafers." And with regard to the verse, *The Lord is righteous* (Lam. 1:18) it is stated:[62] "Three hundred arrows were shot into Josiah." A similar story is told of Rabbi Judah ben Bava.[63] And in Tanḥuma, it is stated,[64] "Three hundred priests used to immerse the curtain." The figure 300 is also used by the kabbalists in connection with the verse, *For in seven days' time, I will make it rain upon the earth* (Gen. 7:4). It is stated in the Zohar:[65] "Rabbi Ḥiyya and Rabbi Judah walked 300 steps on the bone of one of those [who died in] the deluge." A similar statement is made without exaggeration by the greatest Christian doctor in his *City [of God]* about the enormous bodily stature of the giants. He says that he saw a tooth of a human being which if divided up into pieces according to the dimension of our teeth, would have made one hundred of them.[66] Then again in the Zohar, on the verse, *But I have made him master over you* (Gen. 27:37) it states:[67] "Rabbi Simeon taught 300 rulings on the secret of the sublime wisdom contained in the verse, *And his wife's name was Mehetebel* (Gen. 36:39).

51. One of the symptoms of leprosy, cf. Lev. 12:2.
52. B. Sanh. 38b.
53. B. Tem. 16a.
54. B. Ḥag. 15b; B. Sanh. 106b.
55. B. Yev. 16a.
56. B. Pes. 57a.
57. B. Pes. 62b.
58. The exact passage reads: "R. Simlai came before R. Johanan: 'Let the master teach me the Book of Genealogies.' He said to him . . . 'let us learn it in three months.' He took a clod and threw it at him saying, 'If Beruriah wife of R. Meir and daughter of R. Hanina b. Teradion, who studied 300 laws from 300 teachers in one day, could nevertheless not do her duty in three years, yet you propose to do it in three months."
59. B. Shabb. 13b.
60. B. Bek. 57b.
61. E.R. to Lam. 2:2.
62. E.R. to Lam. 1:18.
63. B. Sanh. 14a; B. A.Z. 8b: "It was said that the enemy did not move from the spot until they had driven three hundred iron spearheads into his body."
64. Tanḥuma, Vayaqhel, 7 (Buber, 10). The passage is also in M. Sheq. 8:5.
65. Zohar I, 62a.
66. Augustine, *De civ. Dei,* bk. 15, ch. 9 (*P.L.* XLI, col. 448).
67. Zohar I, 145b.

And there are many other such examples. This is all similar to what Rashi wrote in the name of Rabbenu Halevi[68] with regard to the pearl that was sold by the "one who honored Sabbath" for 13 roomfuls of gold dinars.[69] Rashi states that the 13 roomfuls is simply a hyperbole signifying great wealth, and he refers to other examples such as the "13 camel-loads of questions" regarding *ṭerefah* and the passage about the 13 butchers.[70] And Rava said that the statement,[71] "Sometimes there was as much as 300 *kor* of ashes [on the altar]" is an exaggeration.[72] Thus all these examples reveal that the problem of the discrepancy which we raised has been correctly resolved.

As to the number of high priests, it should be known that in the final chapter of his last work, Josephus gives the figure 83 for the number of high priests from Aaron the priest to the end of the line of high priests of the second Temple. That is to say, there were 13 from Aaron until the erection of Solomon's Temple, another 18 served in the first Temple and 52 in the second Temple.[73] This information will also be presented, if God so wills, when I translate the passage in chapter 53 in the fourth section of the book. And although the sum total given by Josephus is different from that given in the Babylonian and Palestinian Talmuds as indicated above, I thought it important to mention it for the following reason. The statement in tractate Yoma that 18 high priests served in the first Temple is discussed by the Tosafists.[74] On the basis of the problem which he raises, Rabbenu Tam reads 8 [rather than 18] while Rabbi Isaac rejects his view and emends the text to 12. Yet both views may be simultaneously refuted twice over.[75] For in tractate Yoma in the Palestinian Talmud, the reading is also 18. It reads:[76] "In the first Temple in which a man [Aaron]; his son and his grandson served there were 18 high priests." The same reading is given in Vayiqra Rabbah[77] and as you know from Rashi, the Midrash Rabbah texts are Palestinian Aggadot. There is a similar passage in the Sifre which is at the end of the pericope Balaq,[78] or, in the exact versions, at the beginning of the pericope Phineas:[79] "*Say therefore, grant him My pact of peace, it shall be for him and his descendants after him a pact of priesthood for all time* (Num. 25:12, 13). This teaches you that from his [i.e., Phineas's] line there were 18 priest prophets, but in the latter Temple, there were 80 prophet priests from his line, but because they sold the office for money their years began to be shortened." This is the correct reading

68. Rashi to B. Shabb. 119a.

69. B. Shabb. 119a.

70. Ibid.: "R. Abba bought meat for 13 half zuz from 13 butchers."

71. M. Tamid 2:2.

72. B. Tamid 29a.

73. De' Rossi is referring to bk. XX:220 of the *Antiquitates,* and here is referring to Ruffinus's translation of the work in which ch. XVIII is the last chapter of the twentieth book (whereas it is ch. 8, the penultimate chapter in Gelenius's translation).

74. As Cassel notes, this is not the reading in the Tosafists to B. Yoma 9a. He is probably correct in his conjecture that de' Rossi is referring to the Ritba. (See *Ḥiddushe ha-Ritba* to Yoma [cols. 41–42] who cites the views of Rabbenu Tam and Rabbi Isaac as cited by de' Rossi.)

75. 'Twice over,' lit. height of two men.

76. P. Yoma 1 (1) 38c.

77. V.R. 21:9 (487–89).

78. The verse under discussion is in pericope Phineas and not in Balaq. This division of the text which, according to de' Rossi, is more correct, is to be found in Midrash Ḥakhamim.

79. Sifre Bemidbar, Balaq, par. 131.

which I found in two very old manuscript versions of the work. Then there is also the Sifre Zuṭa[80] which is called Midrash Panim by the compiler of the *Arukh* in the entry for *ṭg*,[81] and Baraita shel Panim Sheni by Rashi in his commentary to pericope Shemini.[82] It reads:[83] "In the first Temple 18 high priests from his line served and in the second Temple 80 high priests because they reverted to selling the office for money." Josephus, too, who was a priest and an expert in local matters wrote, as we said, that there were 18 high priests in the first Temple. Thus Rabbenu Tam and Rabbi Isaac would have gone and put together another solution to their problem. After all, one of those who have dealt with this matter that we have seen, was a secular writer, namely, Josephus, is in agreement with the reports we have received from four of the most ancient of the works of our ancestors: the Palestinian Talmud, the Babylonian Talmud, the Sifre, and the Midrash Rabbah. They all say that there were 18 high priests, and it is not logical that we should invalidate five valid witnesses. But we should not conceal from you, reader, the statement of the Tosafists in tractate Zevaḥim which reads:[84] "In Chronicles we find that the high priests are only counted from Phineas and in the Sifre, it is derived from the time [when God states] *I grant him [Phineas] my pact of peace* (Num. 25:12). From his line, 8 high priests served in the first Temple and 300 in the second Temple and all of them are listed in the Sifre." And yet, the Pisqe ha-Tosafot[85] which derive from that statement [in the Tosafot], reads 18 high priests. But you have trustworthy evidence from all versions of the Sifre Rabbah and Zuṭa that this was not the figure that they gave. Accordingly it would appear that one should not use that statement since the reading was corrupt. And if they really intended to posit the figure 300 for the number of high priests of the second Temple, it was because they needed to make their own solution to the problem of the discrepancy that we raised. And do not content yourself with Rashi's comment on the verse in Chronicles, *And Johanan begot Azariah who served as priest in the house that Solomon built in Jerusalem* (1Chr. 5:36) in which he invalidates the figure 18 and 8, and states that the correct figure is 12. The fact is that the printed commentary on Chronicles attributed to Rashi is not entirely authentic.[86] For had that been the case, he would have referred to this statement in his comment on the passage in tractate Yoma, while Rabbenu Tam and Rabbi Isaac would have made some reference to it in their discussion. Anyone familiar with his style would have no difficulty in concluding that the language used in that passage is not characteristic of Rashi. Rather, one must necessarily deduce that some wiseacre interpolated it into the text after having read Rabbi Isaac's emendation. As for me I have reason to rejoice in the Lord because having written down this opinion on the basis of

80. Sifre Zuṭa [the Small Sifre] as opposed to Sifre to Num, as de' Rossi shows, was variously designated by medieval authorities. The text which probably began with Num. 5 is only fragmentarily preserved in medieval quotations in the Yalqut, Midrash ha-Gadol, and Bem. R.

81. Nathan ben Yehiel, *Arukh*, s.v. *ṭag*.

82. See Rashi to Lev. 10:19.

83. De' Rossi must have read a manuscript of the Sifre Zuṭa. See S. Lieberman, *Sifre Zuṭa*, 10.

84. Tos. to B. Zev. 101b, s.v. *ve-idakh*.

85. The *Pisqe ha-Tosafot* is the compilation of rulings derived from the Tosafot and is printed in most standard editions of the Talmud.

86. De' Rossi is correct. In fact, the entire printed commentary to Chronicles under the name of Rashi is not authentic.

reasoned calculation, I discovered, after much effort, that Morenu Rabbi Moses Shalit of Mantua[87] owned a copy of Rashi's commentary on the whole of Scripture. It is a very beautiful gilt text written in the year of mercy (ḥsd), i.e., 5072 [1312]. In the commentary on Chronicles there was no trace of the text contained in the printed edition. Instead, the text read:

> *Azariah who served as priest in the House.* It is possible that he alone served as priest, accompanied by no other priest. You might say that Zadok must have been priest when he began to serve as priest. Or you might say Zadok died and they gave him the priesthood, and yet surely Ahimaaz his son should have been given the office of priest? My opinion is that in all cases, after the death of a priest, they gave the office of priesthood to the priest's son, and Ahimaaz was Zadok's son. However, it is explicitly stated in the Palestinian Talmud that anyone who devotes himself to sanctifying God's name or to the Temple service is given the title [of priest], and he [Azariah] devoted himself to the purification of the Temple as is written in the subsequent passage about Uzziah the king, *when he grew strong he grew so arrogant he acted corruptly, he trespassed against God . . . and the priest Azariah . . . followed him [and said to him, It is not for you, Uzziah to offer incense to the Lord, but for the Aaronite priests who have been consecrated to offer incense]* (2Chr. 26:16–18). Azariah, then, had devoted himself to the Sanctuary and that is why he told the king that the priesthood had been designated for him.

At this juncture I had indeed to congratulate myself; after all evidence has emerged which demonstrates that my statements in the previous chapter on the detection of forgeries have not been proved false. The thoughtful person knows and is a witness of the extent to which deceit contributes and increases[88] the confusion in the beautiful soul[89] whose place of rest is truth and righteousness.[90]

87. This is probably Moses Shalit who served as the agent of the Jewish community of Mantua in 1578–79 in a lawsuit between the Jewish community and the duke. See S. Simonsohn, *History,* 356.

88. 'Deceit . . . increase,' cf. Ps. 120:3.

89. The text printed in Ellul 5374 (September 1574) ended here.

90. In the Ellul 5374 text, de' Rossi added the following: "Now dear reader, if I erred in the foregoing discourse, I saw to it that you should not be left with my error. Thus I said that I would inform you, as is my way, regarding the fact that distinguished scholars of our people entreated me to remove the quotations from our sages which I gave as examples of exaggeration and hyperbole at the beginning of the chapter. They are: 'He who takes delight in the Sabbath'; 'He who spills his seed for no purpose.' For they insisted that they are to be taken literally. Consequently I reflected on my methods, and after having given you this information, it was a question whether those two passages would be omitted or remain in the text as was the case with the passage about the diacritical points in the Torah given in Avot d'Rabbi Nathan and discussed in that passage, Bemidbar Rabbah and Aggadat Mishle. In chapter 19, I warned you to have a correct understanding of the passage which states, 'Ezra said: "If Elijah would come (another version reads Moses), and would say to me: Why have you written them? [i.e., Why have you included the suspect passages?]" ' I would say to him, 'I have already placed the dots above the letters.' So if one were to say to me, 'What you have written is fine,' I would remove the dots from above them. So you, too, with regard to those two passages, should neither pay too much attention to them, nor completely disregard them until you have continued to weigh them in the just balance."

CHAPTER TWENTY-ONE

On the differences between our sages and the Christian and gentile writers in their narration of certain stories. And new information regarding the sanctuary erected on Mount Gerizim and the figure of a dove that was found there. And as to how many people called King Jannai lived in Temple times.

In the first chapter of tractate Eduyot in the Mishnah[1] and Tosefta,[2] it is taught: "Why is the rejected view of an individual recorded with the majority view? So that if somebody were to say to you, 'I have learned the tradition in this way,' one might say to him, 'You have learned the opinion of so and so [whose opinion has been refuted.']" So it was that when I saw that Josephus related many stories somewhat differently from our rabbis, I thought it in order to put some of them on record, both in this and subsequent chapters, and it was important, in my opinion, to inform you about any novel findings that I might have on the topic.

The subject of my present discourse is the altar which was built in Alexandria in Egypt, the sanctuary that was erected on Mount Gerizim, and the figure of a dove that was found there, and I shall also deal with the question of the number of people called King Jannai who lived in Temple times. Indeed, my observations on this and allied subjects which I hope to pursue should God in His kindness give me His support, will clarify for you the source and implications of the facts that you can read in *Sefer ha-Qabbalah* of Rabad (Abraham ibn Daud) the Levite or other later sages of blessed memory which do not accord with the teaching of our sages.

But let us take first things first. Everybody is familiar with the story recounted by our sages of blessed memory in tractate Yoma of the Palestinian Talmud and at the end of tractate Menaḥot about Onias son of Simeon the righteous who built the altar in Alexandria in Egypt.[3] They relate that when Simeon was about to die he said, "My son Onias shall be my successor." A quarrel then erupted between Onias and his [elder] brother Shimei. Rabbi Meir and Rabbi Judah disagree about the actual course of events. Study the passage for yourself. Onias was ultimately forced to flee to Alexandria in Egypt where he built an altar. Further on in the same context, they record Rabbi Meir's view that princes had already built another altar there in the time of Hezekiah.[4] Now if

1. M. Ed. 1:6.
2. T. Ed. 1:4.
3. P. Yoma 6 (3) 43c–d; B. Men. 109b.
4. B. Men. 109b–110a. Hezekiah is said to have encouraged the princes not to serve idols. They went to Alexandria and built an altar to God. The prooftext adduced to support this view is Is. 19:19, *In that day there shall be an altar to the Lord in the land of Egypt.*

you turn your attention to Josephus's version of the same story, you will notice that there are considerable divergencies between the two accounts. Rather than translate all his statements on the subject in extenso, I thought it sufficient to give a full transcription of the basic passages which are divergent. In book 12 (chapter 3),[5] he writes that after the death of Simeon the righteous, Eleazar his brother, in whose lifetime our Torah was translated [into Greek], became high priest. He was succeeded by Manasseh, uncle of the brothers Simeon and Eleazar. Manasseh was succeeded by Onias son of Simeon the righteous. Then at the beginning of chapter 6,[6] he writes that when this Onias died, his descendant, also called Onias, was unable to officiate as high priest because he was a minor. So Jeshua, brother of the father of Onias and son of Simeon the righteous, officiated in his place. A quarrel broke out between this Jeshua and his third brother also named Onias, but who chose to call himself Menelaus, all three being sons of Simeon the righteous. In an effort to gain the position of high priest, this Menelaus made a vow to Antiochus, who was the ruler of their country at that time, that he would make the majority of the Jewish populace submit to the law of the Greeks. In chapter 15,[7] he writes that Antiochus finally realized that Menelaus was a troublemaker, stirring up a great deal of contention among his Jewish subjects. So he put him to death and appointed a certain Joakim of another family to the high priesthood. This man was a totally disreputable person—he is depicted in the same manner in book 2 of Maccabees.[8] When Onias, son of the fore-mentioned Onias, saw that his uncle had been killed, that his family had been divested of the high priesthood, and that also the rest of the Jews were in an extremely bad situation, he betook himself to Ptolemy the fourth surnamed Philometor,[9] the husband and brother of Cleopatra who was coregent with him over Egypt. In chapter 17,[10] he writes that when Joiakim was resolving to pull down the wall around the Sanctuary that had been built by order of the ancient prophets, he was struck by a sudden divinely ordained death. The people then gave the high priesthood to Judah the Hasmonean who was called the Maccabee.*

(*According to Samotheus, "Maccabee" is a Greek word that is translated as *paladino* (fighter) in Italian.[11] But I have been told by others that he received the designation Maccabee because it was inscribed on his banner and derived from the acrostic based on the words *Mi Kamokha Ba-elim Adonai* (Who is like You among the gods O Lord).[12] But this interpretation is not consistent with the fact that *On the Maccabees* is the title Josephus gave to the work in which he describes the sufferings of

5. *Ant.* XII:156–58.
6. Ibid., 237–41.
7. Ibid., 385–87.
8. 2Macc. 14:3ff.
9. Ptolemy Philometor was the sixth (not the fourth) Ptolemy.
10. *Ant.* XII:413.
11. Johannes Lucidus Samotheus, *Opusculum,* bk. 2, ch. 10, 25v "ad Judam Maccabeum qui ab ipso Philone dicitur Asmonai id est pugnax latine et vulgo palladinus ab armata Pallade, Graece vero Machabeus." This etymology was derived from Annius of Viterbo's interpretation in his ps. Philo, *Breviarium* (414). Annius appears to be saying that Asmnonai [i.e., Hasmonean] is a Hebrew word that signifies fighter corresponding to the word "Maccabeus" in Greek.
12. Ex. 15:11. I do not know the source for this explanation.

Eleazar and Hannah and her seven sons,[13] and this episode predated the rise of the Hasmonean dynasty. But the first explanation would fit, since they, too, [i.e., Eleazar and Hannah who suffered martyrdom] were heroes.[14])

In book 13 (chapter 6),[15] he relates how Onias son of Onias son of Simeon the righteous who, as we recounted above, went to Egypt where he cleverly ingratiated himself with the king and queen, made a petition to them. He asked them to grant him permission to erect an altar[16] to the Lord in Egyptian territory, a request which was all the more justified given that it was the subject of the prophet Isaiah's prophecy, *In that day there shall be an altar to the Lord inside the land of Egypt* (19:19). They replied that they had no desire whatsoever to accede to his request if it entailed transgression of the law of our God; but if they could be totally assured that it was permitted, they would comply fully with his request. He then built a replica of the Jerusalem Temple in Alexandria in Egypt. Josephus mentions this briefly in the first book of the *War,*[17] and in book 7, he gives a longer account describing the reasons for its construction, the troubles attendant on its erection, and the length of its duration.[18] Here we have dealt with the episode regarding Onias in Alexandria. Verily, scholar and disciple alike will easily see to what extent the essential elements in these stories are at variance with our rabbis' statements.[19]

However, according to the citations in tractate Yoma[20] and chapter 9 of Megillat Taʿanit,[21] it would appear that the sanctuary erected on Mount Gerizim by the Cutheans [Samaritans] was already standing in the time of Alexander of Macedon, having been built in earlier times. It is stated that when the Cutheans requested Alexander to destroy the House of our God in Jerusalem, Alexander was met by Simeon the righteous and a retinue of priests who secured the death of those Cutheans, and Mount Gerizim was ploughed up and sown with vetch and salt. Another story is related in tractate Ḥullin that in the time of Rabbi Meir they discovered that the Cutheans had placed a figure of a dove on the summit of Mount Gerizim. It was thus decreed that they were henceforth to be regarded as heathens in every respect.[22]

Now there does appear to be a certain discrepancy between the two stories. According to the first account, the sanctuary was destroyed in the lifetime of Simeon the righteous and Alexander, while according to the second account, it was still standing in

13. The work *De Machabaeis* was attributed to Josephus and incorporated into the *Opera omnia* of Josephus in the sixteenth century. It is usually designated 4 Maccabees.

14. There is no adequate etymology for the word Maccabee. According to Joseph Justus Scaliger (*De emendatione temporum*), the word only applied to Judah, but was later used to describe the other Hasmoneans and became a term to denote all those who had been persecuted for their religion. For a short survey on the etymology, see E. Schürer, *The History,* vol. 1, 158, n. 49.

15. *Ant.* XIII: 62–72.

16. De' Rossi translates the Latin word "templum" as "mizbeaḥ," i.e., altar, possibly to express his disapproval about its erection, or else because the word occurs in the verse from Isaiah cited in the context.

17. *Bellum* I:33.

18. Ibid. VII:426–32.

19. De' Rossi does not inform the reader of the divergencies between the versions of the story as given in the *Wars* and the *Antiquities* which complicates the matter further.

20. B. Yoma 69a.

21. Meg. T. 339–40.

22. B. Ḥull. 6a.

the days of Rabbi Meir.[23] Now Ritba [Yom tov ben Abraham] of blessed memory resolves the problem on the grounds that the Cutheans were forced converts, and that while it is a fact that they were regarded as true Jews in the time of Simeon the righteous, they reverted [to paganism] in the time of Rabbi Meir and were discounted as Jews.[24] On reading Josephus's account in book 11 (chapter 8),[25] you will notice that according to his view this episode is similar to what happened in Alexandria in Egypt as related above. In other words, the sanctuary on Mount Gerizim was actually first erected by command and sanction of Alexander of Macedon and had never been in existence previously. It was Alexander, too, who granted permission for its erection to Manasseh the brother of Jaddua the high priest, the son-in-law of Sanballat the Cuthean. He did this in friendship for Sanballat who had won the favor of Alexander. And the sanctuary was pulled down by Hyrcanus the high priest two hundred years after its erection. Rabad the Levite [Abraham ibn Daud] does not hesitate to follow Josephus in his *Sefer ha-Qabbalah*[26] and does so even more explicitly in his discussion of the kings of Israel of the second Temple in which he mentions Hyrcanus and the entire episode in full.[27] In book 13, chapter 6,[28] Josephus relates that the Cutheans filed a complaint against the Jerusalemites to Ptolemy the fourth (Philometor) claiming that the holiness of Mount Gerizim was greater than that of the Temple.[29] The representatives of both sides made an agreement among themselves that the party who lost the case should be put to death by the king. And so it came about that the foolish Samaritans who had persisted in the case had to pay the penalty.[30] Who knows whether this is not the incident referred to as the Day of Mount Gerizim in tractate Yoma and Megillat Taʿanit which we mentioned previously?[31] Now in connection with this subject I cannot refrain from averting the reader to the statement of the Tosafist of blessed memory regarding the figure of the dove that was found on the summit of Mount Gerizim. He states:[32] "There is a Midrash that it [i.e., the figure of the dove] was the idol which Jacob buried under the oak tree that was near Shechem."[33] It is my view, however, that scholars will also beam with approval[34] when they hear the following words of mine. From the accounts of Berosus the Chaldean it would appear, and certain scriptural

23. Rabbi Meir lived in the second century C.E.

24. 'Forced converts,' lit. lion-proselytes. Cf. 2K. 17:26ff. where lions are sent against the peoples settled in Samaria by the king of Assyria to force them to acknowledge the God of the land. The comment of the Ritba is in *Ḥiddushe ha-Ritba,* to Yoma 69a (col. 379) and in the *En Yaʿaḵov* of Jacob ibn Ḥabib to B. Yoma 69a.

25. *Ant.* XI:309–11.

26. *Sefer ha-Qabbalah* 2 (17).

27. I.e., in the third part of the work printed in Mantua in 1513 which was entitled *Ve-eleh Divre Malḵhe Yisrael be-Bayit Sheni.*

28. *Ant.* XIII:74–79.

29. This is a free translation. Josephus states that they claimed that the temple had been built "according to the laws of Moses."

30. 'The foolish . . . penalty,' cf. Pr. 27:12. Cf. also Sirach 50:25: *Two nations I detest and the third is no nation at all: the inhabitants of Mt. Seir, the Philistines, and the foolish people that live in Shechem.*

31. For a recent discussion of the subject, see J. A. Goldstein, "Alexander."

32. Tos. to B. Ḥull. 6a, s.v. *be-rosh.*

33. See Gen. 35:4, *They gave to Jacob all the alien gods that they had . . . and he buried them under the terebinth that was near Shechem,* and cf. P. A.Z. 5 (4) 44d and B.R. 81:3 (974).

34. 'Scholars will beam with approval.' De' Rossi is using an expression from Dan. 12:3.

verses support his view (we shall mention this again in chapter 38), that the Babylonian and Assyrian Empires were unified from the time of Nimrod until their third ruler called Sardanapalus.[35] While it is true that according to the account of Metasthenes the Persian, of which you shall hear more from us later, they were subsequently divided into two kingdoms, during the reigns of Darius and Cyrus over Babylon, they reunited as in the past and similarly they maintained one entity even under Alexander of Macedon whose dominion was universal as is well known. Now it is a known fact that Semiramis was one of the rulers in remote antiquity. She was the fourth to rule after Nimrod. Several historians, and noteworthy among these Diodorus Siculus, relate that she was brought food by the birds of the sky and in particular, by doves.[36] For this reason she was called Semiramis which (according to Diodorus) signifies the chirping of birds[37] in the Aramaic language. In my opinion, the name derives from the expression *the time of singing* [*zamir*] *has come* (S.S. 2:12) by substituting the letter *samekh* [of the *S* in Semiramis] with the letter *zayin* [of the *Z* in *zamir*]. There is also the Aramaic expression *zimra d'mana* (instrumental songs) and *zimra d'fuma* (vocal songs).[38] Consequently, the dove became her emblem. Since this queen, according to Berosus, was more renowned and esteemed than any other ruler, the dove continued to be used as the Babylonian emblem even after her death. This is all described at length by the Christian scholar Annius in his commentaries on Berosus[39] and on Xenophon's book on synonyms[40] and by the Christian Samotheus.[41] And on authority of the Christian doctors, Jerome the translator and Thomas Aquinas, they say that all this is indicated in Jeremiah's statement, *Like a lion he has gone forth from his lair . . . because of the wrath of the Dove* (25:38). In other words, every king and his people have fled and forsaken their home on account of the wrath of the Babylonians. The expression *because of the sword of the dove* also occurs in Jeremiah's prophecy about Egypt (46:16). He says that the foreigners in Egypt or the mercenaries who had come to her aid from other lands would say one to the other, *Up and let us return to our people because of the sword of Babylon.* And in his prophecy on Babylon, Jeremiah also states: *Make an end in Babylon of sowers, and of the wielders of the sickle at harvest time because of the sword of the dove, each man shall turn his back to his people, they shall flee every one to his land* (50:16). The meaning of the verse is that the foreign sowers and harvesters who had come to help the farmers, as is the widespread custom in many parts of Italy, where there is much work to be done in gathering in the harvest, would then flee because of the assailing sword. For according to grammarians, the word can refer either to that which proceeds from it or to that which comes to it, as is exemplified by two verses: *And I will let them rejoice in the House of My prayer* (Is. 56:7) and, *I have heard your prayer* (Is. 38:5).[42]

35. This information is derived from the forgeries of Annius of Viterbo discussed above.

36. Diodorus Siculus, *Bibliothecae historiae libri* II:4–20. De' Rossi (like Annius) refers to bk. III since the ancient versions of the book (and the Latin and Italian sixteenth-century editions of the work) divide the first book into two separate books.

37. Diodorus actually states that the name Semiramis means dove.

38. B. Giṭṭ. 7a.

39. Annius to *Berosus,* ch. 4 (vol. 1, 186).

40. Annius to Xenophon, *De aequivocis,* vol. 1, 36–37.

41. Johannes Lucidus Samotheus, *Opusculum,* bk. 4, ch. 1, f. 35r–v.

42. De' Rossi is distinguishing here between the subjective and objective genitive. The expression *the*

Accordingly we could claim that Zephaniah's statement about Jerusalem, *Ah sullied polluted city of the dove* (3:1) is meant to compare Jerusalem's behavior with that of Babylon whose emblem is the dove, as we said. In fact, certain peoples were so devoted to the memory of Semiramis and her emblem that they pledged not to eat doves. This is noted by the pagan poet Tibullus[43] and by Yedidyah the Alexandrian [Philo] in his fine work of which only fragments are extant that are preserved by Eusebius.[44] Yedidyah writes that on his journey from Alexandria in Egypt to Jerusalem, he passed through the land of Ashkelon (according to Rambam, it takes eight days to travel from Egypt to Jerusalem via Ashkelon)[45] where he noticed that doves accompanied and attached themselves to human beings without fear and trepidation on account of the age-old local custom not to kill the birds. Annius also mentions their fictitious lies that Semiramis was the daughter of the god Dagon who had the form of a fish and that she was also given the designation Semiramis Ascolanita [of Ashkelon].[46] In the light of all this, it seems to me plausible that the Samaritans who were settled in Samaria by the king of Assyria and Babylon demonstrated and attested their devotion to that ruler. His emblem was the dove which they adored and placed as object of their worship on the summit of Mount Gerizim near Shechem which was the capital of Samaria in those days[47] as Josephus writes at the end of book 11.[48]

Now we shall discuss the subject of Jannai. We find that our sages of blessed memory mention three people called Jannai the king living in Temple times. One is said to have lived in the time of Jose ben Joezer. They say in Bava Batra[49] that the son of Jose ben Joezer married the daughter of the crown-plaiter of Jannai the king. According to Rashi, "crown-plaiter" signifies one who made wreaths of crowns for King Jannai.

Another Jannai is mentioned in tractates Berakhot,[50] Sota,[51] and Sanhedrin[52] and in Bereshit Rabbah[53] and Midrash Qohelet[54] as living in the time of Simeon ben Shetaḥ who was his brother-in-law. Now according to the first chapter of Avot, Simeon ben

---

sword of the dove can either refer to the sword that is coming against the dove (i.e., Babylon) which would explain Jer. 50:16. This is exemplified by *I have heard your prayer,* i.e., the prayer that comes from you to Me, or it can refer to the dove's (i.e., Babylon's) sword that is assailing others, as is exemplified in the verse, *in the house of My prayer.*

43. Tibullus, Elegiae I, 7, 17–18: "Quid referam, ut volitet crebras intacta per urbes / alba Palaestino sancta columba Syro."

44. Eusebius quotes from Philo's work *On Providence* in his *De ev. praep.,* bk. 8 (*P.G.* XXI, col. 675).

45. *Mishneh Torah,* Qiddush ha-Ḥodesh V:10.

46. Annius, *Berosus,* 186. In Ashkelon there was a famous temple to the goddess Atargatis (or Derceto) which was linked to the male deity Dagon who was represented as part fish. According to the legend alluded to by Annius, Aphrodite took offense at the goddess and had intercourse with a youth. She gave birth to Semiramis, exposed her daughter (who was then fed by the doves), and threw herself into a lake where she became a fish.

47. Thus Annius's forgeries enable de' Rossi to give some credence to the talmudic account which reported traces of idol worship on Mt. Gerizim before and after the time of Alexander of Macedon. Annius's information served as a link between Scripture and Talmud.

48. *Ant.* XI:340.

49. B. B.B. 133b.

50. B. Ber. 29a, 48a.

51. B. Sota 47a.

52. B. Sanh. 107b. This passage only occurs in uncensored editions of the Talmud.

53. B.R. 91:3 (1115).

54. Q.R. to Eccl. 7:12.

Shetaḥ was of the third generation after Jose ben Joezer.[55] If, then, he [Simeon ben Shetaḥ] had lived in the time of Jose, he could not have received his teaching from Joshua and Nittai, the disciples of Jose,[56] but rather they would have received their teaching from him. The Jannai mentioned in tractate Berakhot is in my opinion also referred to in another passage in Berakhot,[57] in Qiddushin,[58] and in chapter 11 of Megillat Taʿanit.[59]

There is another Jannai who lived a few years before the destruction of the second Temple as is evident from tractate Yoma[60] and Yevamot.[61] It states that Martha, daughter of Boethus (but according to tractate Giṭṭin[62] and Ekhah Rabbati[63] she lived at the time of the destruction of the Temple), brought an amount of dinars to King Jannai in order to get him to appoint Joshua ben Gamla as one of the high priests. Ritba comments on this passage as follows:[64] "This Jannai cannot be identified with the Jannai mentioned in tractate Qiddushin, for the latter was a high priest and did not confer his office on others. Accordingly, there must have been two persons named Jannai." Thus, inclusive of the Jannai mentioned in tractate Bava Batra whom Ritba had no reason to discuss there are three people whom the sages call Jannai.

Now the only reference to Jannai[65] in the histories of Josephus is the one mentioned by our sages of blessed memory in tractate Qiddushin. In that context, Eleazar ben Poirah tells Jannai the king and high priest, "The Pharisees are opposed to you." This was because a false rumor had circulated that his mother had been taken captive in Mount Modiim, a situation which would have rendered him ineligible for the high priesthood. The same story is narrated by Josephus in book 13 (chapter 18)[66] with the one difference that the sages of blessed memory associate the incident with Jannai, whereas Josephus associates it with his father Hyrcanus. You should notice that in tractate Berakhot,[67] there is uncertainty as to the identity of Jannai. According to Abaye, Jannai and Johanan [i.e., John Hyrcanus] were one and the same person, whereas Rava regarded the two as separate individuals. Now in Yedidyah's work *De temporibus*[68] (which you will read in chapter 32) and in book 13 (chapter 20) of Josephus,[69] there is reference to Jannaeus Alexander. It is stated that of the Hasmoneans, Johanan the first, also called Hyrcanus, was the father of Jannaeus Alexander,

55. M. Avot 1:8: "Judah ben Tabbai and Simeon ben Shetaḥ received from them [i.e., Joshua ben Peraḥyah and Nittai the Arbelite]."

56. Ibid. 1:6: "Joshua ben Peraḥyah and Nittai the Arbelite received from them [i.e., Jose ben Joezer and Jose ben Johanan]."

57. B. Ber. 44a: "When R. Dimi came, he stated that King Jannai had a city in the king's mountain."

58. B. Qidd. 66a: "It once happened that King Jannai went to Kohalit in the wilderness and conquered sixty towns there."

59. Meg. T. 343.

60. B. Yoma 18a.

61. B. Yev. 61a.

62. B. Giṭṭ. 56a.

63. E.R. to Lam. 1:16.

64. *Ḥiddushe ha-Ritba,* to B. Yoma 18a (col. 104).

65. It should be noted, as de' Rossi states subsequently, that Hyrcanus and not Jannai is the subject of Josephus's account.

66. *Ant.* XIII:288–92.

67. B. Ber. 29a.

68. Ps. Philo, *Breviarium,* 415.

69. *Ant.* XIII:320.

the husband of Queen Alexandra.[70] On his deathbed, he advised her to transfer her allegiance from the Sadducees to the Pharisees who would be supportive of her rule. This is described by Josephus in book 13 (chapter 23)[71] and by Rabad in his *Sefer ha-Qabbalah.*[72] It would seem that it is to these stories about the man and his wife which the sages' statement in tractate Sota refer:[73] "Jannai the king said to his wife, 'Do not fear the Pharisees or the non-Pharisees, but rather the hypocrites.' " These are, in my opinion, the same Jannai and his wife who are mentioned in chapter 11 of Megillat Taᶜanit. There, before his death, Jannai is said to have ordered the prison warden to put the elders of Israel to death in order to ensure that the entire population would mourn and not rejoice at his death. His wife who is called Salmenon is none other than Salome Alexandra, for, as Josephus writes in book 13 (chapter 20), Alexandra is the Greek name for Salome.[74] However, in book 17 (chapter 8), Josephus attributes this cruel decree to Hyrcanus[75] who just before his death made such an order to Salome his sister who was also called Alexandra. It is true that in his list of the princes of the House of David in his work *De temporibus,*[76] Yedidyah names a certain Jannaeus called Hyrcanus the second to distinguish him from Judah the first who was also called Hyrcanus. In my view, this Jannaeus is to be identified with the one mentioned in tractate Bava Batra who was not a high priest but simply prince (or one might say noble), fourth in line from Zerubbabel. His lifetime would coincide with that of Jose ben Joezer. In his enumeration of the high priests, Yedidyah further mentions Jannaeus Alexander as was mentioned before. In other words, there must have been two people called Jannai. That is to say, there was the king from the Davidic dynasty who lived in the time of Jose ben Joezer, and there was the high priest from the Hasmonean dynasty who lived in the time of Simeon ben Shetaḥ. But the Jannai who according to tractate Yoma lived just before the destruction of the Temple is not mentioned by any of the gossip writers of the kings of the Herodian dynasty who were in power at the time,[77] and neither do they refer to any Hyrcanus or Johanan and Alexander. And one cannot claim that the Jannai mentioned in Yoma can only be identified with the Jannai mentioned in connection with Simeon ben Shetaḥ, and that there was another Marta daughter of Boethus, for her husband Joshua ben Gamla lived at the time of the destruction of the Temple.[78] In book 20 (chapter 8),[79] Josephus writes that Agrippa the king who lived in the days of the emperor Nero appointed Joshua ben Gamla to the high priesthood after Jeshua ben Dana. Concerning this Agrippa they write in tractate Sota[80] that the Jewish multitude

70. This statement is only in ps. Philo, *Breviarium:* "Iohannes Hyrcanus priscus praefuit ex Asmonaim annis XXVI. Aristobulus uno, Iannaeus Alexander XXXVII. Eius uxor Alexandra IX."

71. Ibid., 398–404.

72. Abraham ibn Daud, *Sefer ha-Qabbalah* (19).

73. B. Sota 22b.

74. *Ant.* XIII:320.

75. *Ant.* XVII:175–79. As Cassel notes, ad loc., de' Rossi wrongly refers to Hyrcanus instead of Herod.

76. Ps. Philo, *Breviarium,* 407: "Duces vero ex domo David usque ad dictum Iudam fuere. . . . Iannaeus secundus Hyrcanus praefuit."

77. 'Gossip-writers' (*ḳotve paṭaṭaya*). The identity of these writers is not clear. De' Rossi may have been referring to a writer such as Suetonius who tended to include personal anecdotes in his Biographies.

78. See B. Yoma 18a.

79. *Ant.* XX:213.

80. B. Sota 41a (M. Sota 7:8).

pandered to him by saying, "Do not fear Agrippa—you are our brother." Rashi of blessed memory writes: "Agrippa, king of Israel, was a Herodian and the Temple was destroyed in his lifetime."[81] In the light of this, I would claim that Marta brought the coins not to Jannai but to Agrippa. The reference to Jannai here is an error which undoubtedly must be attributed to some ancient scribe. The same reason would account for the many confusions contained in some of the statements of our rabbis of blessed memory with regard to historical events. And reliable evidence of the truth is that it satisfies the dictates of reason.

81. Rashi is referring to Agrippa II, but it is more likely that the incident occurred in the time of his father, Agrippa the Great.

CHAPTER TWENTY-TWO

Criticisms of Rabad the Levite and the noble Don Isaac on the topic of Simeon the righteous—whether more than one person went by that name.[1]

THERE is yet another story of which the version recounted by our sages differs from that told by Yedidyah the Alexandrian [Philo] and Josephus. The account of the latter two was adopted by Christian sages. The rabbis of blessed memory say that Simeon the righteous was high priest in the time of Alexander of Macedon and that it was Simeon's image that Alexander saw whenever he was victorious in battle. This is evident from tractate Sheqalim in the Palestinian Talmud,[2] chapter 9 of Megillat Taʿanit, Yoma,[3] Menaḥot,[4] and Vayiqra Rabbah[5] and other passages.[6] They place Simeon, who was one of the last members of the Men of the Great Synagogue[7] in the second generation, after that of Jeshua ben Jozadak, the first priest to serve in the second Temple. According to the sages, all the Men of the Great Synagogue were contemporaries.[8] This is also made clear by their statement in Bereshit Rabbah that the generation of Hezekiah and the generation of the Men of the Great Synagogue [had no need of the sign of the rainbow because they were completely righteous],[9] and in Midrash Tehillim in which they say that two generations used the Ineffable Name: the Men of the Great Synagogue and the generation that suffered persecution* (*shemad*).[10] This point [i.e., that the Men of the Great Synagogue were of the same generation] is also to

1. This is a subject over which much scholarly ink has been spilt. De' Rossi was correct in identifying two Simeons, although scholars usually give the designation "righteous" to only Simeon II.

2. I could find no reference to the story in Sheqalim, although Simeon is mentioned in P. Sheq. 4 (2) 48a.

3. De' Rossi refers to B. Yoma 9a and 39a in which the name of Simeon the righteous appears; the actual story to which he is referring, however, is in 69a.

4. B. Men. 109b. Here, too, there is only a reference to Simeon the righteous.

5. V.R. 13:5 (294).

6. E.g., Mid. Teh. 18:11 to Ps. 18:7.

7. The nature and origin of the institution of the Men of the Great Synagogue is obscure. Traditionally it is dated to the period following Ezra. The idea of a Synagogue (or Assembly) of leaders of the community is based on Neh. 9 and 10.

8. Since rabbinic chronology telescoped the Persian period of the second Temple into thirty-four years (which de' Rossi challenges), the institution of the Men of the Great Synagogue had consequently to be limited to one generation.

9. B.R. 35:2 (328).

10. Mid. Teh. to Ps. 36:11. The term *shemad* is usually used of the persecutions of the Hadrianic period.

be inferred from the work entitled *Seder Tannaim ve-Amoraim*[11] which gives evidence of having been written in the year 4647 a.m. [887 C.E.].[12] There it is written:[13] "Haggai, Zechariah, and Malachi transmitted it to Ezra, Ezra to the Men of the Great Synagogue among whom were Zerubbabel, Jeshua, and Nehemiah, and the Men of the Great Synagogue handed it over to Simeon the righteous." In my opinion, this information was taken up by all later writers such as Samson of Chinon, Rabad, Rambam, Bertinoro, and many others besides. On the basis of the facts which with God's help we shall elucidate further, and taking on trust that the generations of Jeshua and Simeon were successive, our rabbis' statement in Seder Olam[14] and in tractate Avodah Zarah[15] fits into place. I refer to Rabbi Jose's statement that the Persian Empire which was annihilated by Alexander of Macedon lasted only thirty-four years during the second Commonwealth and that when the years of the Greek Empire and the Hasmonean and Herodian dynasties are added together, the sum total of 420 is reached which is equivalent to the length of the second Temple period.

(*[see p. 351] This refers to the terrible persecution which occurred under the Greek government that prohibited the observances of Sabbath, New Moon, and circumcision and made them write on their garments and on the horn of every ox with which they ploughed, "We have no portion in the God of Israel."[16] Rabbi Moses [Maimonides] of blessed memory also refers to it in his admirable *Epistle to Yemen*[17] which begins with the words "Strengthen the hands that are weak."[18])

The other school of thought places Simeon the righteous in the eighth generation after Jeshua. In their opinion, there were six generations of high priests separating those two individuals as is indicated in Nehemiah: *Jeshua begot Joiakim; Joaiakim begot Eliashib; Eliashib begot Joiada; Joiada begot Jonathan; Jonathan begot Jaddua* (Neh. 12:10–11). And according to their tradition, Jaddua begot Onias and Onias begot Simeon the high priest. And they state that Alexander was a contemporary of Jaddua of the sixth generation, and that it was to Jaddua that he prostrated himself and showed respect, which is all attributed to Simeon by the sages of blessed memory. This means that the duration of the Persian Empire according to these others was longer, which further implies that the Temple stood for more years than was stated by our rabbis. Now the purpose of this chapter is not to discuss this general point which, with God's help, we shall discuss in detail in the appropriate place. Rather, by raising the issue of the discrepancy between Jaddua and Simeon the righteous, my intention was to inform you that Rabad, either knowingly or not, muddled up different passages. This is also true of his follower, the wise Don Isaac [Abravanel], who by association with him formed

11. The *Seder Tannaim ve-Amoraim* is in two parts, giving a history and methodology of mishnaic and talmudic literature. De' Rossi's text corresponds to that inserted in the *Maḥzor Vitry* which is found in the ms. of the British Library Add. 27200, but differs slightly from the majority of mss. of the text.

12. The anonymous author of *Seder Tannaim* writes (7): "We are presently in the year 1644 [i.e., 884] from creation."

13. *Seder Tannaim,* 1.

14. Seder Olam, ch. 30.

15. B. A.Z. 9a.

16. Cf. B.R. 2:4 (16) and the scroll of Antiochus.

17. *Iggeret Teman,* 127.

18. Is. 35:3.

inferior dough about which Nehemiah the prefect[19] had given evidence. For at the beginning of his work Rabad writes:[20] "The second generation of the Men of the Great Synagogue was that of Simeon the righteous and his name was Iddo son of Jeshua son of Jehozadak." Similarly, Rabbi Isaac Israeli, author of *Yesod Olam,* accepted his view and wrote that Simeon the righteous is identical to Iddo ben Jeshua ben Jehozadak.[21] The wise Don Isaac, who also relied on him [i.e., Rabad], wrote at the beginning of [his commentary] on the book of Haggai:[22] "The first high priest to serve in the second Temple was Jeshua ben Jehozadak, and Jeshua's successor was Iddo his son as is written in the book of Ezra." And in his introduction to tractate Avot he writes:[23] "Simeon the high priest was the son of Jeshua son of Jozadak the high priest who was the brother of Ezra the scribe." And in his commentary on the Mishnah dealing with Simeon the high priest he writes:[24] "He was also called Hananiah according to Josephus." Now if you search throughout the book of Ezra and Nehemiah you will find no reference to anyone of the name Iddo, the high priest. Only the name Jaddua is mentioned whom Yedidyah the Alexandrian in his book *De temporibus*[25] and Josephus and the others in their group call Iaddo in Greek and Latin. Similarly, the Hebrew Josephus [Josippon], according to the German edition[26] and the two early prints of Abraham Conat,[27] in his narration of the story of Alexander and the high priest, simply refers to the high priest without giving his personal name. However, later in the account which deals with Manasseh who erected the sanctuary on Mount Gerizim, he writes:[28] "Manasseh was the brother of Iddo the high priest of Jerusalem." Indeed Iddo was high priest at that time, or rather not Iddo but Jaddua. In fact I believe that the name Iddo was not actually given by Josephus who would have written Jaddua, but by someone who tampered with the text. On seeing that all the sages of that group had written the name Iaddo, he believed that it would be transcribed as Iddo in our language and put it down thus in the text. Rabad and Don Isaac would have also discovered that the Turkish version [of the Josippon][29] from which the Venetian print was transcribed gives the name Hananiah or Onias as the name of the high priest who met with Alexander,[30] and later in the story about the sanctuary he is called Iddo.[31] Thus, these passages were the source of their confusion and they were made to ride on two horses;[32] they did not follow the view of the Jewish sages nor that of the other group. As a result, they upheld

19. The expression "Nehemiah the prefect" occurs in Neh. 12:26. De' Rossi is referring in a rather convoluted manner to the verse in Nehemiah which gives the list of the high priests. He is also punning on a passage in B.R. 34:10 (320) which speaks of the "inferior dough about which the baker *naḥtom* testifies to its bad quality."

20. *Sefer ha-Qabbalah* (16).

21. *Yesod Olam,* 4, ch. 18, 84r.

22. Abravanel to *Haggai* 1 (186, col. a).

23. Abravanel, *Naḥalat Avot,* 21, col. b.

24. Ibid. (51 col. b).

25. Ps. Philo, *Breviarium,* 406. The name is given as Iaddua.

26. I.e., the edition of Sebastian Münster.

27. These were printed in Mantua.

28. *Josippon,* bk. 1, ch. 5 (32).

29. I.e., the edition of Constantinople, 1510.

30. *Josippon,* Venice, 1544, bk. 2, ch. 5, col. 51.

31. Ibid., col. 53.

32. Cf. B. Ket. 55b.

neither position—this situation is described by the author of *Halikhot Olam* in his treatment of the rule that one follows him who adopts a balanced view.[33] It is certainly unbelievable that our sages refrained from calling him Jaddua, the name known from holy Writ, or even Hananiah or Iddo according to whichever of the versions of the Josippon is consulted. Instead, they gave him the new name, Simeon the rightous, without an express reason for doing so such that from the name Jaddua [jaddua = is known] he became a non-jaddua [i.e., unknown]. This is aside from taking into account the fundamental differences which must be considered as to whether there were two or six or eight generations.

Now I noticed that in his commentary on the mishnah dealing with Simeon the righteous, the wise Don Isaac claims that Aristotle who was the teacher of Alexander of Macedon describes in one of his letters how he spoke with the said Simeon in Jerusalem whom he discovered to be a man inspired by the Lord with knowledge of the divine.[34] He also alleges that in many of his letters he refers to the responses of the said Simeon on matters of common interest. Now when I saw this, I thought it right to give you the benefit of my knowledge. In his introduction to his commentary on the *Ethics,* Rabbi Joseph ibn Shem Tov makes an even more exaggerated claim than did Don Isaac.[35] He asserts that he saw a book in Egypt which described how, at the end of his life, Aristotle had no embarrassment in acknowledging the truth of all that was written in the Mosaic Law, and became a righteous proselyte. And a similar account, if my memory does not play me false, is given by the wise Farissol in his work, the *Magen Avraham.*[36] It is true that when I was investigating the sources of the story, I came across the biography of the "philosopher" [Aristotle] written by Diogenes Laertius,[37] as well as the work of Caelius Rhodiginus.[38] They described how that at the end of his life, Aristotle ran away to the city of Chalcis because a slanderous rumor had circulated that he had shown disrespect to the worship of the renowned goddess Ceres of Eleusis, who was highly revered by his Athenian compatriots. According to the allegations, Aristotle fell in love with a certain

33. Jeshua Halevi, *Halikhot Olam,* gate 5, 109–10. According to Halevi, the statement in B. Shabb. 39b that the *halakhah* follows the view of the "compromiser" or "balancer" of two opinions does not apply when the "balancer" does not effect a real compromise but contradicts both opinions. I am grateful to Louis Jacobs for having clarified this passage for me.

34. Abravanel, *Naḥalat Avot,* 51.

35. According to M. Schmidman ("The Avot Commentary"), the author of the Commentary on Avot, is the fifteenth-century Spanish philosopher Shem Tov b. Joseph ibn Shem Tov. The work, which has not yet been printed in its entirety, compares Aristotelian and Jewish concepts.

36. *Magen Avraham,* ch. 23. See D. Ruderman, *The World,* 49.

37. Diogenes Laertius, *De vita . . . philosophorum,* bk. V, 23: "He departed to Hermias the eunuch; according to another, Hermias bound him by ties of kinship, giving him his daughter in marriage. . . . Aristippus says that Aristotle fell in love with a concubine of Hermias and married her with his consent and in an excess of delight sacrificed to a weak woman as the Athenians did to Demeter of Eleusis. . . . He then withdrew to Chalchis because he was indicted for impiety . . . the ground of the charge being the hymn he composed to the aforesaid Hermias."

38. Caelius Rhodiginus (Ricchieri), *Lectionum antiquarum libri,* lib. 2, cap. 2, 36: "Ut praeteream, quod Graeci scribunt et repetit Seneca, Athenis raptim Aristotelem profugisse, veritum ne impietatis nomine in vincula coniectus ultimo afficeretur supplicio." Ricchieri was born in Rovigo in 1469. His *Lectiones antiquae* was first printed in Venice in 1516. He produced an amplified version of the text which was posthumously printed in Basel in 1542. This was the text used by de' Rossi, as is evident from his reference to bk. 2, ch. 2 of the work which is the correct reference for the Basel, but not the Venice edition in which the passage is placed in the first book of the work.

concubine belonging to his friend Irenaeus [Hermias] and had offered to her the sacrifice which is specially designated by the high priests for that goddess. {I had already seen the entire story described by the author of *Me'irat Enayim* which is an explanation of the esoteric parts in Ramban's commentary on the Torah.[39] However, there are some variants in his account. He states that the woman with whom [he wanted to commit] adultery was the wife of Alexander of Macedon, his pupil. This is a phenomenon which I have discussed on many occasions, namely, that when the sages speak of mundane stories, they are not particular about details because their purpose is to convey a general point; but the person who is particular about knowing the actual reality of the matter will place his trust in those who have expert information regarding the character of the person about whom these matters were written.}[2] This was taken as an indication about the nature of women as described by King Solomon in Israel and likewise Zerubbabel in his first speech to Darius.* He [Zerubbabel] stated that there is no power greater than a woman's; even to the wise-hearted, her hand is a fetter and her heart snares.[40] However, as regards their claim that he converted to the true faith, there is no evidence nor would such a claim be reasonable. If it were they who made the error, it must have resulted, in my judgment, from their reading of the report in Josephus's *Against Apion*[41] which is also cited by Eusebius in his *Praeparatio*[42] and later by Pico della Mirandola in his work *On the Study of Philosophy.*[43] Ibn Bibago also gives a thoroughly erroneous version of the story in his *Derekh Emunah.*[44] But whoever used that account to report that he became a Jew, is, in my judgment, a liar and completely misinformed. Alternatively, if they did read the [original story], they did not study the passage in sufficient depth. The story is told at length, but the jist of it is simply as follows: Aristotle told his friend Clearchus how he happened to spend a long time on one of the Greek islands in the company of a great sage who spoke Greek. He concluded that he was a Jew because he had arrived there from the land of the Jews. He said that he really imparted more wisdom to him than he, Aristotle, gave him. Josephus describes all this as part of his rebuttal of the lies of Apion who said that the Jews are a lost nation that right from the beginning were neither known nor acknowledged by the prominent people of the time. To counter the claim, he cites many ancients of high status who referred to us in laudatory terms including the "philosopher" of our story. If the spirit takes you, go and examine the said passage, and you will find confirmation of my account. Moreover, from a careful examination, you will be able to discover how they fell into the error of Aristotle's conversion. When the words are separated correctly, it is obvious that the word "Jew" in the passage refers to the Jew of the story and not to Aristotle.[45]

39. *Me'irat Enayim,* 77. The work was written by Isaac ben Samuel of Acre (late thirteenth century). De' Rossi read the work in manuscript.

40. Cf. Eccl. 7:26.

41. *Contra Apionem* I, 177–81.

42. *De ev. praep.,* 9:5–6. De' Rossi used George of Trepizond's Latin translation bk. IX, ch. 3.

43. Pico della Mirandola, *De studio,* lib. 2, cap. 2: "Scribit peripateticus Clearchus . . . Aristotelem ipsum a Iudaeo quodam multa didicisse celebratum illud dogma nosse se quemque nonne ex Mosi Deuteronomio sumpsit exordium."

44. Abraham ben Shem tov Bibago, *Derekh Emunah,* 46c. He quotes the story in the name of Eusebius.

45. De' Rossi is correct. The error arose because of misleading punctuation both in the Latin translation of Josephus: "Tum ille. Genere igitur Iudaeus erat . . ." and in George of Trepizond's translation of

(*[see p. 355] This is recorded by Josephus[46] whose source was 3 Ezra which is not part of our canon.[47])

But now let us resume our discussion of the issue raised by the wise Don Isaac. I questioned all those who are fully conversant with Aristotle's works. Not one of them could provide me with any reference to Simeon in the corpus of his writings. It is very likely that whatever snippet of information he had heard about him derived in some way from the story described above. It may be that such a Jew really existed and that his name was Simeon. After all, in tractates Bava Meṣia[48] and Giṭṭin[49] they describe a case of a little town with a small population in which doubts arise [about the validity of the divorce bond] because there are two people named Joseph ben Simeon; in the wide world, then, how many more must there be—go and see how many people called Simeon without the designation "the righteous" are to be found in the marketplace. In particular, you should take note of the philosopher's statement when he said that the Jew gave him the impression of being a Greek by reason of the language he spoke.[50]

The fact is that you should at least be aware of the conspicuously problematic nature of the statements of our rabbis of blessed memory regarding Simeon the righteous, the subject with which we commenced this chapter. For it is known that he was one of the last members of the Great Synagogue, living many years before the translation was made in the time of his brother Eleazar and Ptolemy Philadelphus, the third successor to Alexander's throne. Now in chapter 11 of Megillat Taʿanit,[51] in tractate Sota in the Palestinian Talmud[52] and in the same tractate in our [i.e., the Babylonian] Gemara,[53] in the Tosefta tractate Sota,[54] and in Midrash Shir ha-Shirim,[55] it is stated that Simeon the righteous heard a voice issue forth from the Holy of Holies announcing, "Cascalgus [Caius Caligula] is killed and his decrees annulled." This Cascalgus is listed in Seder Olam as the last of the eight Greek monarchs. It reads:[56] "These are the kings of Greece: Alexander of Macedon, Piratus, Telemon, Seleucus, Psanterus, Antion, Antiochus, Casacalgus." The last was apparently reigning at the beginning of the dynasty of the Hasmoneans who are renowned for their fight against the Greeks. One cannot say that they all reigned simultaneously at the beginning of the Greek Empire since Alexander, who is included in the list, was the sole ruler of his time; subsequently, his kingdom was divided into four as is indicated by the famous prophecy of Daniel. My

---

Eusebius: "Ille, igitur subiunxit. Aristotles iudaeus erat . . ." See C. Wirszubski in the appendix to his edition of Flavius Mithridates (73–75) where he discusses the legend of Aristotle the Jew.

46. *Ant.* XI (ch. 4) 49.

47. 1Esdras 4:13ff.

48. B. B.M. 18b.

49. B. Giṭṭ. 24b.

50. In fact, according to Josephus's account, Aristotle said that the Jew not only spoke Greek, "but had the soul of a Greek."

51. Meg. T., 345.

52. P. Sota 9 (13) 24b. Here the reading is Golikom.

53. B. Sota 33a.

54. T. Sota 13:6: "Simeon the righteous heard: '. . . and Casagalgas [Caligula] is killed and his decrees anulled' and he heard this in the Aramaic language."

55. S.S.R. to S.S. 8:9. "The intention of the enemy is frustrated and Caius Caligula is slain and his decrees are annulled."

56. Seder Olam, ch. 30 (144).

solution to the problem is to propose that there were two people called Simeon the righteous. In fact, according to *De temporibus* by Yedidyah the Alexandrian, Simeon the righteous the second was the son of Onias the second, both of whom were the descendants of Onias the first and Simeon the first.[57] Accordingly, it is feasible that the name Cascalgus is erroneous and should read Gallinicus, since the chronological tables of Eusebius[58] and Samotheus[59] list Seleucus Gallinicus in about the seventieth year of the Greek Empire, and another Simeon the righteous is mentioned as living in the same period. Moreover, at the end of the book of Ben Sira [Ecclesiasticus], which, as you know, was not wholeheartedly rejected by our sages,[60] this Simeon appears in the list of heroic prophets and sages on whom he bestows praise.[61] He describes Simeon the righteous son of Onias as the morning star of Israel who brought them salvation and magnified the glory of our God.[62] As Eusebius wrote in his *Chronicle,*[63] Ben Sira the author of the book was a contemporary of that Simeon, and both lived subsequent to the time of the composition of the translation [of the Septuagint]. I deliberately used the designation "Ben Sira the author" in order to avoid the impression that I was referring to Ben Sira his grandson who, as he writes in the preface, published the work.[64] Indeed the incidence of two people bearing this distinguished appellation has an honorable parallel in the person of our holy Rabbi [Judah ha-Nasi].[65] As you know, there is the saying in Qiddushin[66] and in Midrash Qohelet with regard to the verse, *The sun rises and the sun sets* (Eccl. 1:5):[67] "When Rabbi Aqiva died, Rabbi (who was also called our holy Rabbi) was born." And yet in the Mekhilta, one finds a passage which reads: "Rabbi Aqiva said: 'The following was told me by our holy Rabbi.' "[68] Thus there are two given the designation "holy."[69] However, I cannot conceal the fact that it is likely

57. Ps. Philo, *Breviarium,* 407: "Ab Alexandro vero ad Asmonaim pontifices usque ad Judam, *Onias priscus* annis XXVII, *Simon priscus* XIII. Eleazarus Antiochi Theos inimicus XX. Manasses Seleuco Gallinico amicus XXVII. *Simon justus* honoratus a Magno Antiocho XXVIII. *Onias huius filius* a Seleucho spoliatus templo XXXIX." Ps. Philo appears to be saying that Onias II was the son of Simeon the righteous and not vice versa as de' Rossi states. In fact, according to Josephus (*Ant.* XII:224), Simeon II was the son of Onias II, and Simeon the righteous son of Onias I (*Ant.* XII:43).

58. Eusebius, *Chronicon* (*P.G.* XIX, lib. II, col. 499).

59. Johannes Lucidus Samotheus, *Opusculum,* 108v–109r.

60. This is a reference to the discussion in B. Sanh. 100b about the ban on reading Ben Sira which is presented in detail by de' Rossi in ch. 2.

61. I.e., the section from ch. 44 to ch. 50 that begins, *Let us now praise famous men and our fathers in their generations.*

62. See ch. 50.

63. Eusebius, *Chronicon,* col. 501: "Iudaeorum Pontifex maximus Simon Oniae filius clarus habetur sub quo Iesus filius Sirach sapientiae librum componens."

64. "My grandfather Jesus, after devoting himself to the reading of the law and the prophets, . . . was himself led to write something pertaining to instruction. . . . It seemed that I should myself devote some pains and labor to the translation of the following book."

65. The editor of the Mishnah.

66. B. Qidd. 72b.

67. Qoh. R. to Eccl. 1:5.

68. This is the reading in the early printed editions of the Mekhilta d'Rabbi Ishmael (Constantinople, 1515; Venice, 1545). But the correct reading as given in the editions of Horovitz and Rabin (Vayassa, 154) and Lauterbach (II, 88) is: "R. Abba said: The following was told me by our *great teacher.*"

69. This would imply that there were two rabbis called "holy" because Rabbi Judah ha-Nasi lived after the time of Rabbi Aqiva.

that there is an error in the Mekhilta. For in Shemot Rabbah the same statement is cited but it reads:[70] "Rabbi Abba related before our Rabbi."

Alternatively, we could say that Cascalgus is the correct reading and that the Simeon in question is to be identified with Simeon, the son of Mattathias the high priest. It is in fact the case that in our [the Babylonian] Gemara in tractate Sota and in the Tosefta of Sota cited above, there is a *baraita* about Johanan the high priest, followed by a story about Simeon the righteous. Had they been referring to the Simeon who was one of the last members of the Men of the Great Synagogue, he should have been placed in chronological order before Johanan. However, I must admit that in the Palestinian Talmud, at the end of tractate Sota, Simeon is placed before Johanan in these stories.[71] And in tractate Megillah there is the statement of the rabbis of blessed memory:[72] "*I did not reject them, neither did I abhor them to destroy them utterly* (Lev. 26:44)—in the days of the Greeks when I raised for them Simeon the righteous and Mattathias the high priest." This refers to the Simeon the righteous who deserved a greater reputation than his brothers Judah and Jonathan, the sons of Mattathias, because of the mighty feats that he performed for Israel as is described in chapters 14 and 15 of the first book of Maccabees. In the end, all his achievements were engraved on a bronze tablet which they erected on Mount Zion.[73] We shall mention this again in chapter 25. He lived at a later date than those two other Simeons, at the end of period of the government of the Greeks whom, with his sword and bow, he ejected from our land.

70. S.R. 24:4 to Ex. 15:22.
71. P. Sota 9 (13) 24b.
72. B. Meg. 11a.
73. 1Macc. 14:27.

CHAPTER TWENTY-THREE

Further criticism of the two sages mentioned previously, as well as Rabbenu Saadiah, Rambam, and the authors of *Yesod Olam* and *Kaftor va-Feraḥ*. They said that the era of documents [Seleucid era] which according to the rabbis blessed be their memory, began 380 years before the destruction of the second Temple, started at the beginning of the reign of Alexander of Macedon. In fact, it was first adopted only after his kingdom was divided between his four ministers since "the six years in which the Greeks reigned in Elam are not counted."

There is yet another issue on which I must take the two sages, Rabad [Abraham ben David] and Don Isaac [Abravanel], to task. However, I must first apprise you of an incontrovertible fact which is also of fundamental importance for the chapter. The era of documents or the Greek [Seleucid] era about which we are informed from ecclesiastical tables did not begin in the lifetime of Alexander of Macedon, but after his death when his kingdom was divided between his four ministers. Indeed, in tractate Avodah Zarah our rabbis claim that the duration of the period from the exodus of Egypt until the beginning of the Seleucid era, from which time the era of documents was adopted was one thousand years.[1] Rashi elucidates this as follows: "From the exodus from Egypt to the destruction of the second Temple is 1,380 years: 480 years to the construction of the first Temple; it stood for 410 years which comes to a total of 890 years; 70 years of the Babylonian exile; the second Temple stood for 420 years; this comes to a total of 1,380 years." And in another passage in the same context he writes:[2] "The Greeks came to power after the Temple had been standing for 34 years. To this figure should be added the 6 years which are not counted. Accordingly, their era begins 40 years after the Temple had been standing, namely, 380 years before the destruction of the Temple." The "6 years which are not counted" refers to Rav Naḥman's statement about a document that the rabbis regard as postdated because 6 years are added to its date. Rashi explains that there can be no legal seizure [by a creditor] until the said date.[3] This is cited by the wise Caro in his comments on the Tur, Ḥoshen Mishpaṭ:[4] "Rav Naḥman [who was of the opinion that it is not considered a postdated document] said to them [the rabbis]: 'The scribe in question wrote with precision for he was counting the 6 years in which the Greeks ruled in Elam that are not ordinarily counted.' As Rabbi Jose said: The Greeks ruled 6 years in Elam and subsequently their dominion extended universally." The question is as to whether the reckoning should perhaps be counted from the exodus, omitting the one thousand years. The response given in the

1. B. A.Z. 10a.
2. Rashi, ad loc.
3. This is actually part of the Talmud.
4. Ḥoshen Mishpaṭ, Halvaʿot 43:12, i.e., the creditor cannot take the debt owed to him until the date specified in the document.

Talmud is "We only count from the Greek era." Rashi explains: "One does not count from the beginning of their dominion which are the 6 fragmented years[5] in which they only ruled in Elam, but after those 6 years when their dominion extended universally." It is clear then that although the Greeks seized power after the Temple had been standing for 34 years of Persian rule at which time Darius fell into the hands of Alexander, the era of documents was not initiated during that 6- year period which corresponds to the last 6 years of Alexander's rule that was 12 in total as is clear from the Seder Olam[6] and the first book of the Maccabees.[7] He captured Darius in his sixth year of rule. This is documented in the third book of Arrian the Greek,[8] the fifth book of Curtius,[9] in Plutarch's *Lives of the Kings* (par. 37),[10] in the chronological tables written by the Christians Eusebius[11] and Samotheus[12] as well as by all other biographers of Alexander. But the Greek era was first adopted only after his death as we said. This fact is given further support in a statement by Abraham the Prince[13] in his work *Sefer ha-Ibbur* where he records Ptolemy's opinion of a gentile sage whose calculation for the length of the lunar year was the same as that of our sages. He writes:[14] "Ptolemy who praised this sage Hipparchus wrote that he lived 80 years after the death of Alexander of Macedon who reigned for 6 years." According to Ptolemy's statement, the era began after Alexander's death subsequent to the time that he had been monarch, namely, a universal ruler, for 6 years. Likewise, in the first book of Maccabees, it is stated that in the year 137 of the Greek era, a sinful root came forth,[15] Antiochus Epiphanes, and he began to assail the Jews in the year 143 and intensified his attacks on them in the years 145 to 148, but in the year 149 he was destroyed by nonhuman hands,[16] as is related in chapter 6 of the first book and chapter 9 of book 2. Now the account given in the opening section of book 1 of Maccabees indicates that the Greek reign, to which the calculation of the Greek era is linked, began after the death of Alexander when there was a government of many Greeks.[17] The same facts are also explicitly given by Josephus in his treatment of Antiochus. He writes that the calculation of the Greek era began from the reign of Seleucus Nikanor [Nikator] who, as he writes at the beginning of book 12, was one of the four rulers who came to the throne after Alexander.[18] Accordingly, the statement of our sages of blessed memory is confirmed, and we have verification of our proposition that the 6 years they reigned in Elam correspond to the

5. The expression 'which are fragmented years' is de' Rossi's addition.

6. Seder Olam, ch. 30 (140).

7. 1Macc. 1:7.

8. Arrian, *De rebus gestis* III, 21, 2: "So ended Darius in the archonship at Athens of Aristopon and in the month Pyanopsum" (i.e., October 331 B.C.E.).

9. Quintus Curtius Rufus, *De rebus gestis,* bk. V does describe the final downfall of Darius, but no date is given.

10. Plutarch does not explicitly refer to 'the sixth year.'

11. *Chronicon,* lib. I (*P.G.* XIX, cols. 177–78).

12. Johannes Lucidus Somotheus, *Opusculum,* 107r.

13. Abraham ha-Nasi (the Prince) or Abraham bar Ḥiyya, of Barcelona, eleventh-century author of astronomical and philosophical works.

14. *Sefer ha-Ibbur* II, 2 (37–38).

15. 1Macc. 1:10.

16. 'Broken by nonhuman hands,' cf. Dan. 8:24.

17. 1Macc. 1:6–8.

18. *Ant.* XII:119.

last years of Alexander's reign that are not counted. Therefore, as regards the statements of the two distinguished authorities Rabad and Don Isaac, the appropriate response is that they are necessarily erroneous. For after describing the event of Alexander's meeting with the high priest when he was on his way to fight Darius, Rabad writes:[19] "The high priest swore to Alexander that they would begin the dating of their documents from that year, namely, one thousand years after their exodus from Egypt." Similarly, Don Isaac who adopts Rabad's line of thinking in his commentary on Avot in the mishnah on Simeon the righteous, writes on the subject in the following manner:[20] "The high priest swore to Alexander that from that day onwards, they would date the years from the time of his arrival in their country, namely, they would adopt the era of documents. This was one thousand years after the exodus from Egypt which corresponds to the year 3448 anno mundi." But the fact is that the year 1000 to which they refer, as we demonstrated above, corresponds to the year after the period of 6 years subsequent to his victory; thus the era of documents does not begin from his time. Indeed, according to their accounts, we are told that the incident which they described occurred before the victory [of Alexander]. This was why, as is well known, he was happy about Daniel's prophecy that predicted his destiny.[21] And according to their statements, the thousand years that the rabbis count from the exodus from Egypt to the beginning of the Greek era do not include the 6 years under discussion. Moreover, according to their view [i.e., Rabad and Abravanel], one would have to claim that the 6 years that they reigned in Elam, which are clearly not counted as part of the era, must have occurred before his overthrow of Darius; but this cannot be correct. After all, Elam was the metropolis of the Persian kings and the seat of their government was in Shushan [Susa] the capital as is shown in the scroll of Esther and in chapter 9 of Daniel, and it was situated in the province of Elam [Susiana].[22] Likewise, it is written in Jeremiah, *And I will set my throne in Elam and wipe out from there king and officials* (49:38). The rabbis of blessed memory interpret "king" as a reference to Vashti, and "officials" as a reference to Haman and his sons.[23] But how can one justify the statement that the Greeks ruled in Elam before the overthrow of Darius, especially when at the time of that war the Persians were in full power and control? As is stated in Daniel 11 (v.2), *Persia will have three more kings . . . by the power he obtains through his wealth he will stir everyone against the kingdom of Greece.* Should you wish to entertain the idea that the Greeks possessed another Elam over which they ruled for six years before the capture of Darius, and if you will permit me to make a humorous comment, then you may wish to fantasize that the Elam mentioned in Jeremiah (49:36) that is written[24] with an extended *vav* indicates that there were two places called Elam.[25] This would be

19. *Sefer ha-Qabbalah* II (16–17).
20. Abravanel, *Naḥalat Avot* to M. Avot 1:2, 51.
21. This is a reference to Josephus *Ant.* XI, 337: "and when the book of Daniel was shown to Alexander in which Daniel declared that one of the Greeks would destroy the empire of the Persians [probably a reference to Dan. 8:4], he supposed that he was the person intended; and he was glad."
22. Alexander captured Babylon and Susa in 331 and Persepolis in 330, i.e., about seven years before his death in 323.
23. B. Meg. 10b.
24. De' Rossi writes 'read,' but must mean 'written.' See next note.
25. The word is written (*ketiv*) EVLM, but is read (*qere*) as EYLM, i.e., Elam.

comparable to Rav Ashi's statement that there were two places called Jerusalem which were encompassed by walls from the time of Joshua.[26] In that case I would then inform you of the validity of such a proposition. For when Yedidyah the Alexandrian [Philo] proposes five principles at the end of his first book on creation, he explains that our Lord God is one and created only one world.[27] The wise Christian Aquinas brings the same proof in the first of his *Quaestiones.*[28] And so in truth and with reasoned argument I would respond to you that your proposed emendation does not help you.[29] Indeed, if you examine the list of Greek kings compiled by the annalists, you will notice that they reigned in the domain of Macedonia and its provinces for decades and not just in the six years prior to Darius's death. Indeed, on examining Eusebius's chronological tables you will have no difficulty in seeing that he lists Philip the father of Alexander as the twenty-second king of Macedon; Curtius, however, at the end of book 1,[30] counts him as the twenty-third king. Now I tried to discover the source of their statement that the high priest swore to Alexander that the era of documents would be counted from his time. But in all my investigations, I could find no mention of it at all, neither in the first chapter of Rosh ha-Shanah where they discuss the regnal eras nor in the first chapter of Avodah Zarah in the discussion of the era of documents. Nor is it mentioned in Josephus's discussion of the incident of the meeting between Alexander and the high priest.[31] He simply states that he [Alexander] offered a burnt offering and sacrifices to our God, and that it was agreed that all Jews in every part of his kingdom would be permitted to observe all the laws of their Torah, and that they would be exempt from paying the royal tax on produce in the sabbatical year. An identical statement is to found in the *Life of Alexander* composed by the Egyptian magicians.[32] The Hebrew Josephus [Josippon] also makes no mention of that fact. He simply says that the high priest swore to Alexander, "All the priests born in this year will be given your name."[33] And you should realize that if the high priest had sworn to bestow such honor on his name, it would have been a mark for perpetuity. If this had been the case, they would have dated years by referring to the kingdom of the unique Alexander, rather than to the reign of the Greeks. On the contrary the expression, "reign of the Greeks," indicates a time when there were numerous kings, and such a situation only pertained after the death of Alexander.[34]

What I found particularly strange was that besides the two sages mentioned above,

26. B. Arak. 32b.

27. Philo, *Op.,* 171.

28. *Summa theologiae* I, quaestio 47, articulus 1: "Sed Deus est maxime unus. . . . Ergo non producit nisi unum effectum."

29. De' Rossi has cited Philo and Aquinas simply to stress the absurdity of the idea that there could have been two places called Elam or Jerusalem.

30. The first two books of the work of Quintus Curtius Rufus are lost. De' Rossi is referring to a supplement of the lost books which was compiled on the basis of other sources by Christopherus Bruno: "Vixit annos XLVII; regnavit XXV fuitque vigesimus tertius Macedonum rex" (bk. 1, 5).

31. *Ant.* XI:333–35.

32. On this reference to the Alexander Romance, see ch. 19, n. 72.

33. *Josippon,* bk. 1, ch. 5 (32).

34. This is also explicitly stated in Eusebius's *Chronicon,* lib. II (*P.L.* XXVII, cols. 399–400): "Alexander . . . in Babylone moritur post quem *translato in multos imperio* diversi regnaverunt."

many respected people, some of them, Rabad's predecessors, some living after him, wrote in the same vein. Thus I saw that in his *Sefer ha-Ibbur,* Abraham the prince quoted Rabbenu Saadiah as saying, "We are in the year 1238 from the reign of Alexander, that is, 4686 from the creation."[35] Rambam [Maimonides], too, of blessed memory, writes at the end of chapter 1 of the Laws of Divorce:[36] "All Israel are accustomed to date divorce documents either from creation or from the reign of Alexander of Macedon which is the era of documents." Now it is true that the era of documents is equivalent to the reign of the Greeks that according to our rabbis began in the fortieth year of the second Temple period. Rambam also gives this calculation in one of his responsa regarding the question as to when the era of documents began.[37] But this cannot be connected with the reign of Alexander, for according to this calculation the era would begin in the thirty-fourth[38] year when the Persian Empire was obliterated, and then there would be no question of the 6 years that they reigned in Elam that are not counted. For during the first 6 years when Alexander reigned in the land of Macedon and other areas of Greece, he actually did not reign in Elam which was the Persian metropolis at that time, as we said. Now I examined the inspired work of the great sage our teacher Rabbi Joseph Caro, may he have eternal life. I am referring to his comments on the *Yad Ḥazaqah*[39] of Rambam of blessed memory. Recently, they sent the work from the city of Safed, may it be rebuilt speedily in our days, to Mantua to the great authority Rabbi Moses Provenzali, may the Lord preserve him, to arrange for its [i.e., Caro's work] publication which would be to the benefit of all Israel.[40] As for me, I was successful, thanks be to God, in raising the funds to defray the costs of publication. Now Caro, who is a worthy and wise man, passed over the passage under discussion without raising any of the points that we have indicated. Likewise Rabad of blessed memory[41] and Rabbi Moses ha-Kohen of Lunel[42] whose animadversions on his [Maimonides'] work were polemically motivated, had neither negative nor positive remarks to make on the passage. Their silence would lead one to believe that they were in agreement. The author of *Kaftor va-Feraḥ*[43] who according to what he wrote in chapter 51 was exiled from France in the year 5066 [1306] was a fellow traveler with those sages.[44]

35. *Sefer ha-Ibbur* III, 7 (97).

36. *Mishneh Torah,* Gerushin I:27.

37. The Responsum was first published in Venice in 1544, but there is an error in the text since it reads, "the era of documents began in the forty-first year after the destruction of the Temple" (vol. 2, n. 389, 662).

38. Cassel reads 'lamed,' i.e., 30, but it should be 34.

39. Another name for the *Mishneh Torah.*

40. Caro's commentary on the *Mishneh Torah* called *Kesef Mishneh,* was printed in Venice in 1574 by Meir Parenzo for the publishing house of Alvisio Bragadini. The name of Moses Provenzali appears in the list of those who assisted in the publication.

41. Abraham ben David [Rabad] of Posquières, a contemporary of Maimonides wrote *Hassagot* [*Animadversiones*] on the *Mishneh Torah.*

42. As Steinschneider writes (*Catalogus Librorum Hebraicorum,* col. 1704), de' Rossi is actually referring to the glosses of Meir ha-Kohen which were confused with those of Moses ha-Kohen (which are only extant in one manuscript—Bodleian 617, 2) and those of Jonathan ha-Cohen of Lunel. These glosses (*Haggahot Maimoniyot*) were published anonymously in the Venice 1550 edition.

43. Estori (Isaac ben Moses) ha-Farḥi (1280–1355) wrote *Kaftor va-Feraḥ,* a topography of the Land of Israel in 1322.

44. *Kaftor va-Feraḥ* (vol. 2, 902).

For in chapters 6[45] and 51,[46] he wrote: "Know that the era of documents which marks the beginning of the reign of Alexander of Macedon and end of prophecy and is equivalent to the fortieth year of the second Temple and the beginning of the period of the Men of the Great Synagogue was the year 3449 anno mundi. In other words, the era of documents began 379 years before the destruction of the Temple." Then there is the wise Rabbi Isaac Israeli of Toledo who wrote a learned work, the *Yesod Olam,* for his teacher Rosh [Asher ben Yeḥiel] in the year 5070 [1310]. At the end of the fourth section of his work,[47] he gives the same information as these others, although he does admit that he had derived his information from the *Sefer ha-Qabbalah* of Rabad who like him was from Toledo. It is true that I have information which I cannot refrain from communicating to those ignorant of it. I saw a statement in the Hebrew translation—it is not in the Latin translation—of the Arabic astronomical work of al-Farghani[48] in which he wrote in gate 1: "The Egyptian era starts from the year in which Nebuchadnezzar the Babylonian came to the throne; the era of the Romans and Syrians starts from the reign of Alexander." Likewise, in the section on the origin of the Greek [and Roman] computation,[49] Rabbi Abraham the prince who was living in the year 4865 [1105], as is apparent from his work *Ḥeshbon ha-Mahalakhot,*[50] wrote "The ancients used to count the reigns of the kings and all the documents pertaining to them from the beginning of the reign of Alexander of Macedon, that is the year 3450 anno mundi according to those who calculate according to *baharad,*[51] that is 310 years before the Christian era, and we date the era of documents from that year." One must surely say that all later sages depend on the view of these two witnesses, particularly if you also take into account another consideration which is as follows. In the passage discussed above about the postdated document, Rav Naḥman spoke of a scribe who wrote with precision. According to Rashi's explanation, he was referring to "one who is precise in calculations and does not follow our method." In his statement Rav Naḥman is acknowledging that the figure calculated by that scribe was more accurate and correct than that of our rabbis. But you also heard the opinions of other witnesses, namely, Josephus and Ptolemy, that we cited at the beginning of this chapter. Accordingly, rather than state that there are two mutually contradictory sets of witnesses, you must necessarily uphold the opinions of them all and state that different situations pertain in different places: there are those who are accustomed to count from the beginning of Alexander's reign, while others count from the reign of his four ministers who came to

45. Ibid., ch. 6 (vol. 1, 243).

46. Ibid. (vol. 2, 901). The figure given here is 380.

47. *Yesod Olam,* 4, ch. 18 (84a).

48. This is a reference to Al-Farghani or Ahmad ibn Muhammad ibn Kathir (d. after 861) whose work on astronomy was translated into Latin by John of Spain and Gerard of Cremona and published several times in the fifteenth and sixteenth centuries and translated into Hebrew from Arabic and with recourse to the Arabic by Jacob Anatoli. De' Rossi read the Hebrew translation in manuscript. The Hebrew text was transcribed by Jacob Christmann (Frankfurt on Main, 1590). On the various versions of the text, see R. Campani, *Alfragano.*

49. *Ḥeshbon,* gate 8 (54).

50. De' Rossi saw this work in manuscript The work was edited and translated into Spanish by J. M. Millás-Vallicrosa.

51. *Baharad* is a mnemonic symbol (2, 5, 204) that expresses the idea that the first conjuction of the sun and moon in the year of creation occurred on a Monday (2), at the fifth hour (5), and 204 parts (of an hour).

power after his death. This should serve as corroboration of the act of the scribe who wrote that the document was drawn up 386 years before the destruction of the Temple according to the Greek era, rather than 380 years in line with our rabbis. Undoubtedly the scribe did not imagine that he was the only person in the world using that computation; rather he must have been following a view that was also widespread in those days. Nevertheless, the sages of blessed memory had agreed to adopt Rav Naḥman's view cited at the beginning of this chapter, according to which the era begins after the Greeks had reigned in Elam for 6 years, namely, after the second Temple had been standing for 40 years, 6 years after the 34-year rule of the Persians after the second Temple had been built. According to this reckoning, 380 years would have elapsed by the time of the destruction of the Temple. There is every indication then that all those sages should not have dissented from our rabbis. And if on account of Rav Naḥman's admission they had agreed with the view of the scribe who wrote with precision, and had begun the computation from Alexander's time, they would then have had to calculate not 380 years until the destruction of the Temple, but 386 years, as he had done. And as is explained by the authors of *ha-Keritut*[52] and *Halikhot Olam,*[53] the rule that the *halakhah* follows the view of the balancer implies that there can be no third opinion.[54] Study the texts. In this case, a third opinion surfaced[55] which agreed with neither the one or the other view. Now my only way of defending them is to propose the following suggestion: Rav Saadiah was the first to use that date in that specific way, possibly because he was adopting an opinion current in his own time. His successors, who did not care to scrutinize the source he offered, did not digress from his position. It is a known fact that when a great man, such as he was, says something, particularly when it is only related to chronology, no further examination is required, and everybody will follow it. In any case, while it is possible that this fact escaped the memory[56] of those esteemed authorities that we mentioned, their defense is evident—for people who are engrossed in the study of the essentials of Torah need not be conscientious about errors of this kind.

52. Samson of Chinon, *Sefer ha-Keritut,* pt. IV, gate 3 (180).
53. Joshua Halevi of Tlemçen, *Halikhot Olam,* gate V, ch. 3 (109). See ch. 22, n. 34.
54. In other words, the person who arbitrates between two opinions.
55. 'Opened up . . . ,' lit. broke open its door frame. Cf. B. B.B. 12a.
56. 'This fact escaped the memory,' lit. the *halakhah* escaped the memory.

CHAPTER TWENTY-FOUR

As to how there is no significant disagreement among all scholars, both Jewish and gentile, regarding the time which has elapsed since the beginning of the Greek Empire, that is, the era of documents, until the present day.

While treating the subject of the era of documents, it seems right—for a reason that will be disclosed to you in the course of these chapters—that we should provide verification that our computation of the era of documents is correct and universally accepted. In other words, there is no gentile or Jewish sage who would propose a significantly greater or smaller figure for the computation of the epoch. Thus, it will come to your notice that in his chronological tables, the Christian Samotheus writes that the astronomers reckon that Alexander's reign began in the first year of the one hundred and fourteenth Olympiad which is 430 years after the foundation of Rome and 323 years before the Christian era, and that in the sixth year of his rule, he captured Darius.[1] According to this calculation, it would appear that 318 years elapsed from his universal rule until the beginning of the Christian era. If [1]571 years that they count to the present year are added to this figure, a total of 1,889 is reached. If the 6 last years of Alexander which correspond to their rule in Elam "that are not counted"[2] is subtracted from the figure, a total of 1,883 remains which corresponds to the figure that is used for the era of documents in our calendar. Accordingly, there are two calculations: 1,889 years which proceeds from the beginning of the Greek Empire, i.e., from the year of Alexander's universal rule that commences in his sixth year of government when he overthrew Darius; the other figure is 1883 of the era of documents which corresponds to the Greek rule mentioned by our rabbis that begins with the government of Alexander's four ministers who succeeded him, as we said. And we see that this calculation is so exact[3] that although Eusebius[4] and Aulus Gellius[5] and other writers date the Alexandrian Empire from the first year of the one hundred and eleventh Olympiad

1. Johannes Lucidus, *Opusculum,* 107v: "Anni Alexandri secundum astronomos sumunt initium anno 1 Olympiadis 114." In fact, the year 323 B.C.E. is the year of Alexander's death. In ch. 26, de Rossi corrects this error.

2. This is a reference to his discussion in ch. 23 of the talmudic passage about the scribe who added those years in his calculation of the date.

3. 'Exact,' lit. slings [the stone] at a hair, cf. Jud. 20:16.

4. This is a reference to Jerome's translation of Eusebius's *Chronicion* (*P.L.* XXVII, cols. 471–74): "Olymp. 114. Alexander . . . moritur in Babylone postquam translato in multis imperio, diversi regnaverunt."

5. This appears to be a reference to Aulus Gellius's *Noctes Atticae* XVII in which Alexander's dates are given. But there is no mention of the dating according to the Olympiads.

[i.e., 336/5 B.C.E.], the one date [i.e., the one hundred fourteenth Olympiad] will therefore begin when the other [i.e., the one hundred eleventh Olympiad] is in full course with a difference of twelve years between them. From this it is evident that our calculation is based on the astronomical reckoning. If the astronomical reckoning can stand, our calculation will stand and if the astronomical reckoning must be brought back those few years, then our calculation will also be brought back in line with it. In any case, the difference of 12 years is not our present concern.

Now I was pleased that the Lord let fall into my hands at this time a version of the *Epistle* which the Gaon Rav Sherira of blessed memory wrote to the holy community of Kairwan.[6] It is not the version mentioned by the compiler of the *Arukh* under the entry for Abbaye,[7] but another seven times as long. He begins by answering the question as to why Rabbi composed the Mishnah, and tackles[8] the laws governing the precepts, as though motivated to relieve future generations from the greater part of this task. This is followed by information about the transmission of the tradition from its beginning until his own times. It contains the following statement:[9] "In the lifetime of Rabbi, Rav went down to Babylon in the year 530 of the Greek era that we are accustomed to use." And he also states:[10] "In the year 570, Rabbi Johanan died." He gives many dates according to the Greek era, including those of certain Amoraim, and then writes that Rav Ashi died in the year 738. In the same way, he goes through the list of the Saboraim and the generations of the Geonim, blessed be their memory, and he relates that Rabbenu Saadiah was appointed Gaon in year 1239 of that era. His closing words are as follows: "And in the year 1279, I was appointed as Gaon and we ordained my son Hai to the position of head of the law court about two years ago. . . . May it be the will [of the Holy One blessed be He to include us among the living]." It was written in year 1299 of the era of documents in Firuz Shabur which, according to Sherira, was situated on the border of Nehardea in the country of Babylon and had a population of about ninety thousand Jews excluding the gentile natives.[11] The dates of the Amoraim, as recorded by Rabbenu Samson of Chinon in his *Sefer Keritut* are computed according to the era of documents[12] and were undoubtedly transcribed from the text of this *Epistle*.

The date of Sherira's ordination, 1279 of the era of documents, corresponds to 4728 anno mundi. It is discussed by Rabad the Levite in his *Sefer ha-Qabbalah,* in the section dealing with the seventh generation of Geonim, may they rest in peace.[13] Similarly, the

6. Sherira was the Gaon of Pumpedita (tenth century). His *Epistle* written in response to the questions about the origin of the Mishnah and related topics is an important historiographical source, particularly for the post-talmudic and geonic period.

7. The entry for Abbaye in the *Arukh* is certainly much abbreviated and deals specifically with the question of the various titles of the rabbis (Rav, Rabbi) and as to why certain sages did not have a title but were simply called by their names.

8. 'Tackles,' lit. climbs up and down.

9. *Iggeret,* 78.

10. Ibid., 84. Lewin's text reads "590." The figure 570 is found in Ms. Parma (cod. 117). See G. B. de Rossi, *Mss,* vol. 1, 74–76.

11. The Jews were in favorable circumstances in Firuz Shabur.

12. Samson of Chinon, *Sefer Keritut,* pt. IV, gate 2.

13. *Sefer ha-Qabbalah* (58): "He [R. Nehemiah] was succeeded by R. Sherira who lived a very long life. . . . When he saw that his life was prolonged, and that his son R. Hai was worthy of being head of the academy, he stepped down in favor of his son."

date 530 of the era of documents for Rabbi's compilation of the Mishnah is agreed upon by the sage of the *Kuzari* who states:[14] "Rabbi compiled the Mishnah in year 530 of the era of documents, that is 150 years after the destruction of the second Temple, 530 years after the cessation of prophecy." And likewise, the great light Rambam wrote in a way that corroborates the dating of the era of documents when he says:[15] "It is 1,107 years since the destruction of the Temple, that is 1487 era of documents which corresponds to 4936 anno mundi [i.e., 1176 C.E.]." Similarly, Rabbi Levi ibn Ḥabib[16] discusses the dates of the years since creation in his responsum. He writes:[17] "The era of documents began 40 years after the Temple had been standing." In other words, on the subject of the era of documents, there is complete unanimity on the part of both Jews and gentiles—the discrepancy such as it is could not be written by a child.[18]

14. Judah Halevi, *Kuzari* III, par. 67.
15. *Mishneh Torah,* Qiddush ha-Ḥodesh XI:16; Shemiṭṭah X:4.
16. Levi ibn Ḥabib (1483–1545) was born in Spain and was rabbi in Jerusalem.
17. *She'elot,* 257, col. b.
18. As Z. H. Jaffe writes on this passage, de' Rossi is alluding to B. Sanh. 95b which comments on the verse, *What trees remain of it shall be so few that a child may write them* (Is. 10:19): "What figure can a child write? Ten [i.e., the letter *yod*]." He may have also had in mind Mid. Teh. to Ps. 79:1 commenting on the same verse, "And what character does a child write most easily? The *yod* which stands for ten. Six, for the *vav* stands for six." As Jaffe writes, de' Rossi implies that the discrepancy is not a matter of six or ten or more years according to the views that he cites in the previous chapter; rather, his intention is to demonstrate that the Seleucid era begins after the death of Alexander. In fact, the discrepancy is a matter of one year: the Macedonians counted the Seleucid era from the autumn of 311, whereas the Babylonians counted from 22 April 310.

CHAPTER TWENTY-FIVE

As to how the anno mundi computation was scarcely used by our people before the close of the Babylonian Talmud

MANY are my opponents[1] who would debate with me regarding the number of years which we count from creation and who dogmatically assert the belief that Israel used that computation from antiquity, from the very day on which we became a peculiar people to our God. Now, therefore, I shall present to you matters related to the previous chapter, as well as anything else relevant to our inquiry. So brother reader, pay attention to me.

I have observed that research into the past reveals that our custom of calculating according to the anno mundi computation was adopted at the earliest, at the time of the close of the Babylonian Talmud, if not a long time subsequent to that date. Originally, they used to seek other epochs of different types corresponding to the revolutions of time, to the happy or adverse periods in our people's history. In the first place, you should realize that although the number of years that elapsed from the creation until the giving of the Torah can be ascertained from the narrations in the Torah, the only specific era to which any episode is related (as is about to be demonstrated) is Israel's exodus from Egypt, and not the creation as might have been the case. Even in the actual account of creation it does not state, "2,448 years ago, God created the heavens."[2] Rather it simply states, *In the beginning.* This expression is translated by Onqelos as *beqadmin* (in the beginning); in the Targum of [ps.] Jonathan ben Uzziel, it is rendered *min-avvila* (from the beginning). He uses the same word for his translation of *ba-teḥillah* (at first) in the verse, *the place where his tent had been at first* (Gen. 13:3); for *ke-barishona* (as at first) in the verse, *I will restore your magistrates as at first* (Is. 1:26); and for *le-qadmatan* (to their former state) in the verse, *they shall return to their former state* (Ezk. 16:55). From these examples, it is clear that both Targumists understood the literal meaning of the word *bereshit* (in the beginning) (disregarding its esoteric meaning inherent in the scriptural text) as corresponding to all those expressions used to denote former times. The meaning of the verse is therefore, "In former times, in days of old when there was a beginning of existence, God created." {This is analagous to the poet's statement, *In former times (lefanim), You founded the earth* (Ps. 102:26). This is translated by Jonathan

1. 'Many are my opponents.' This expression from Ps. 55:19 is unclear. De' Rossi appears to have followed David Kimḥi's interpretation of the verse who understood it in this negative sense.

2. This is the traditional date for the period from creation to the revelation at Sinai. Cf. B. A.Z. 9a.

ben Uzziel as *min sheruya* (from the beginning) implying that the expression had the same meaning as when it occurs in the verse, *Now this was formerly (lefanim) done in Israel* (Ruth 4:7).}[2] We therefore have no need for the interpretation of the author of the *Guide* who rendered the word *bereshit* as "in principle"[3] or for the wise Sforno's specification "in the first indivisible moment of time."[4] To my great joy, God let fall into my hands the work copy of the *Guide of the Perplexed* which had belonged to that distinguished man of his time, Baruch of Peschera [Peschiera].[5] I noticed that in his gloss to the fore-mentioned passage in the *Guide* he refers to the Targum of [ps.] Jonathan ben Uzziel and his rendering which I discussed above. He seemed to be indicating that he was more convinced by the rendering in the Targum than by what was written in the text.

The next point for consideration is the passage in tractate Rosh ha-Shanah in the Palestinian Talmud.[6]

> How do we know that one should reckon from the exodus from Egypt? The prooftext is the verse, *In the third month after the children of Israel had gone forth from the land of Israel* (Ex. 19:1). This text only gives information about that specific period. What do we know about the subsequent period? Scripture states: *In the fortieth year after the Israelites had left the land of Egypt* (Num. 33:38). This text is only informative about that time. What do we know about the subsequent centuries? Scripture states: *In the four hundred and eightieth year after the Israelites left the land of Egypt* (1K. 6:1). After the Temple had been built, they began to reckon from the time of its erection as it is stated: *At the end of twenty years during which Solomon constructed the House of the Lord* (2Chr. 8:1). When they were no longer worthy of counting from the time of the Temple's erection, they began to count from its destruction as is stated, *In the twenty-fifth year of our exile, the fourteenth year after the city had fallen, at the beginning of the year* (Ezk. 40:1). When they were no longer worthy of reckoning according to their own era, they began to count according to the eras of the foreign powers as it is said, *In the second year of King Darius* (Hag. 1:1) and *In the second year of the reign of Nebuchadnezzar* (Dan. 2:1).

In the Mekhilta it states:[7] "They did not want to reckon from the erection of the Temple and so they had to count from its destruction as is said, *the fourteenth year after the city had fallen* (Ezk. 40:1). They did not want to count according to their own era, so they had to count according to the era of others as is said, *In the second year of the reign of Nebuchadnezzar* (Dan. 2:1), *In the second year of Darius* (Hag. 1:1)." In the Sifre, they

3. *Guide* II, ch. 30. Maimonides distinguished between first (*teḥillah*) and principle (*reshit*). He argues that a principle exists in the thing whose principle it is even if it does not precede it in time; whereas first is only used in connection with something which is prior in time. Since the world was not created in a temporal beginning, the word *bereshit* signifies "in the principle" or "in the origin." (See Pines's trans., 348–49.)

4. Obadiah Sforno (b. Cesena 1470, d. Bologna 1550), *Bi'ur* to Gen. 1:1; see also, his philosophical work *Or Ammim* 4, proposition 25 in which he explains that the "first indivisible moment" is not part of time itself since time is part of creation.

5. This manuscript is in the de' Rossi collection in the Biblioteca Palatina, Parma, cod. 660. It was written in 1472. It had several owners. On the first folio, it reads: "Ad me pertinet Baruch filium Samuelis de Peschera felicis memoriae, Describendum eum curavi in mei usum anno 232 min. sup. [i.e., 1472] hic Mantuae."

6. P. R.H. 1 (1) 56a–b.

7. Mekhilta d'Rabbi Ishmael, baḥodesh, 1 (II, 193).

state:[8] "*In the first month of the second year from the exodus from the land of Egypt* (Num. 9:1). This teaches you that they counted from the exodus from Egypt. They came to the land. . . . The Temple was built. . . . The Temple was destroyed.[9] From the moment they were subjugated they began to reckon from the time of their subjugation as it says, *In the second year of Nebuchadnezzar, in the second year of Darius.* The months were also reckoned in this fashion." The meaning of this closing remark is to be understood in the light of their statement in the Palestinian Talmud in which it is stated that they imported the names of the months and angels, such as Nisan, Iyyar, Michael, and Gabriel, when they came up from Babylon.[10] The mishnah that the first of Nisan is the New Year for kings[11] is interpreted [in the Gemara] as a practical guideline for the dating of documents since it is taught in a *baraita* that "antedated bonds are invalid."[12] Furthermore, there is a passage in tractate Avodah Zarah that appears to imply that for a long time after the destruction of the Temple, the Palestinians would reckon from the date of the destruction of the Temple, whereas the rest of the Jews of the Diaspora would use the Greek era. Nowadays, the same kind of division pertains between them, for Jews of the Diaspora observe a second festival day. Now Rabbi Jose Berribi[13] taught:[14] "Persian rule lasted 34 years after the building of the Temple . . . the Herodian dynasty 103 years. From then onwards one should calculate dates from the destruction of the Temple." Rashi interprets this passage as indicating that all chronological references to the sages and their lives, documents or any event occurring after the destruction were henceforth to be dated from the destruction of the Temple.[15] Further on in the same passage, Rav Naḥman states:[16] "In the Diaspora only the Greek era is used . . . for it is indeed taught, 'One only uses the Greek era of dating in the Diaspora.' Ravina said, 'Our Mishnah also proves this.' " It is also stated:[17] "If a Tanna does not know the exact figures . . . let him ask a notary." A notary, as Rashi explains, is somebody who writes bills of divorce and bonds which he dates according to the Greek era. Similarly, the figures of 762 years from the destruction of the Temple, or 1017 according to the Greek era are given at the end of the Seder Olam.[18] This figure is, however, incorrect and one should certainly not ascribe it to the author of the work. This was what we wrote in chapter 19 in which we gave a similar judgment on the figures given in the Pesiqta. Examine the passage. As we have seen, the various chronological lists

8. Sifre Bemidbar par. 64 (60–61).

9. De' Rossi omits the material dealing with counting of the eras according to the entry into the Land of Israel, the erection of the Temple and destruction, since it is basically identical to the other passages quoted previously.

10. This is certainly not the literal meaning of the Sifre. De' Rossi omits to say that the statement about the months in the Sifre is followed by the prooftext, *In the third month after the children of Israel had left Egypt.* This simply means that they reckoned not only the years but also the months which related to a specific era.

11. M. R.H. 1:1.

12. B. R.H. 2a.

13. I.e., R. Jose b. Ḥalafta.

14. B. A.Z. 9a.

15. Rashi ad loc.

16. B. A.Z. 10a.

17. Ibid. 9a.

18. See ch. 19.

extending to the year 1298 of the Greek era given in the *Epistle* of Sherira Gaon, which we cited in the previous chapter, are prefaced by the statement: "These are dated according to the Greek era which we are accustomed to use." Clarification of this matter is also given in the gloss of the Tosafists on the passage from Avodah Zarah which speaks of a "precise scribe." It is given in the name of Rabbenu Tam: "It does not matter if the scribe omits the words 'anno mundi' or the thousand digit; for in those days they dated documents according to the Seleucid era. . . . Nowadays [it also does not matter] since we only use the anno mundi computation."

The matter is further elucidated on the basis of statements partly in the Mishnah and partly in the Gemara of tractate Giṭṭin.[19] It concerns a bill of divorce drawn up in the name of "an unsuitable government." According to Rambam, this apparently refers to a government which has no jurisdiction over the place in which the bill of divorce was drafted.[20] The bill of divorce is also rendered invalid if drafted in the name of the Median kingdom or the Greek Empire, or dated from the building of the Temple, or from its destruction, or from the exodus from Egypt. The reason for this is, in Rabbi Meir's view, to ensure good relations with the appropriate government by signing the document in its name. It is true that Rabbenu Nissim makes a specific qualification in this regard when he writes:[21] "But the anno mundi dating is [always] valid because any king would forgo his own honor for the sake of heaven." Nevertheless, one can observe that this was not always the practice for he writes: "Nowadays they are accustomed to count from the creation. And they account for this legislation [i.e., counting according to the foreign era] that it was only implemented at the time when the gentiles were accustomed to dating with reference to their own rulers and they insisted on it. But the legislation was only applied to bills of divorce and not to other documents on the grounds that the welfare of the state is affected by divorces* for it is important that they should pay due attention to the relations between man and wife." But the same care was not taken with other documents since as it is stated in chapter 1 of Avodah Zarah,[22] "Only the Greek era is used in the Diaspora." The same view of the matter is expressed by Rambam,[23] the Ṭur [Jacob ben Asher] in Even ha-Ezer with the comments of Caro[24] and by the compiler of the *Arukh*. From chapter 7 of Megillat Taʿanit,[25] it would appear that they also used to give dates pertaining to the Hasmonean priesthood in the name of the Highest God until the sages decreed that the divine name should be omitted from the documents. The reason for the decree was that the documents would ultimately be consigned to the rubbish dump, and no disrespect should be shown to God. Thus, from the evidence of Scripture, the sages of the Mishnah and Gemara, and the codifiers, it is apparent that the anno mundi computation was not used by the ancients but was recently introduced among our community.

19. B. Giṭṭ. 79b–80a.
20. Maimonides, *Mishneh Torah,* Gerushin I:27.
21. Nissim Gaon to Isaac Alfasi, 42a to B. Giṭṭ. 80a.
22. B. A.Z. 10a.
23. *Mishneh Torah,* Gerushin I:27.
24. Jacob ben Asher, *Even Ha-Ezer,* par. 127; Joseph Caro, *Bet Yosef* to Even ha-Ezer 127.
25. Meg. T., 337.

(*[see p. 372] In the Tosafot, it is stated:[26] "They pay due attention since it is a matter of great consequence when they implement a separation between husband and wife.")

Now I have already told you about the passages in the books of the Maccabees which demonstrate that everybody reckoned according to the Greek era in Temple times. This is true of both books which according to the Christian translator [Jerome] may have been written by different authors, the first book having been written in Hebrew and the second in Greek.[27] And the Greek era was not only used during the period in which they governed us and when the peace of their realm was sought. For even when their yoke had been removed from our necks, the earlier custom persisted, as was demonstrated by the quotations of the sages mentioned above. A particularly cogent piece of evidence is provided in chapter 14 of book 1 of the Maccabees (v.27). It refers to bronze tablets engraved on Mount Zion by the Sanhedrin as a memorial in order to celebrate the feats of Mattathias the high priest and his good works on behalf of Israel—with divine guidance he extricated his people in joy from the "brazen pot" of Greek domination. We alluded to this at the end of chapter 22. In the same chapter [of Maccabees] it is clearly stated that those words were inscribed on the tablets on the eighth of Ellul[28] in the year 172 of the Greek era. Examine the passage.

We are therefore in a position to state that our people began to use the anno mundi computation, so it would seem, from after the time of Rav Sherira Gaon, less than six hundred years ago. This [innovation] occurred, in my opinion, when later authorities took into account the fact that the Greek Empire had been obliterated and that we were no longer subjugated to one kingdom, united in our perseverance in seeking its welfare alone. Rather, we are constantly wandering from one nation to another. Consequently, they preferred to relinquish the former practice and to link the epoch to the beginning, thus ensuring that we are mindful of the kingdom of heaven; after all, as Rabbenu Nissim said, any great monarch or ruler would be prepared to relinquish his own honor for the sake of heaven. Alternatively, we might suggest that this mode of reckoning was introduced at the earliest, at the end of the period in which the sages of the Babylonian Gemara were active, which coincided with the introduction of the fixed calendar for the use of our people. For according to Rambam, our ancestors had always sanctified the new month by observation of the new crescent and intercalated the years according to the season, and the dictates of expediency, and this practice continued until the time of Abbaye and Rava.[29] At that time, in view of the suffering and widespread destruction of the land of Israel, the Jews feared the possible removal [from the Land of Israel] of the established law court on whom this task [i.e., the fixing of the calendar] devolved; for as is stated in Pirqe d'Rabbi Eliezer,[30] at the end of Berakhot,[31] and in the

26. Tos. to B. Giṭṭ. 80a s.v. *mipne.*
27. Praefatio in libros Samuel et Malachim (*P.L.* XXVIII, cols. 556–57).
28. The text reads "18 Ellul."
29. *Mishneh Torah,* Qiddush ha-Ḥodesh V:3.
30. PRE, ch. 8: "The Israelites were wont to intercalate the years in the Holy Land. When they were exiled to Babylon, they intercalated the year through those who were left in the Land."
31. B. Ber. 63a.

first chapter of Sanhedrin[32] as well as by Rambam of blessed memory in his *Sefer ha-Miṣvot,*[33] it is the place that makes the act legal. So the Lord inspired the leaders of the exile to equip us with a calendar in which the calculations and intercalations were fixed. This is the calendar that we use nowadays, and so it is that all the days of our exile have been fixed and intercalated by decision of the law court which was authoritative in the [Holy] Land. Now according to the opinion expressed by Ramban [Nahmanides] in his *Hassagot*[34] and by Isaac Israeli in his *Yesod Olam* (which you will come across in chapter 40), the person who established the calendar for the reason given above was Rabbi Hillel son of Rabbi Judah the patriarch with his court of law towards the end of the period in which the sages of the Babylonian Gemara were active. Now it is true that Israeli contradicts himself with regard to his dates. In chapter 5 of section 4 of his book,[35] he writes that it occurred in the year 4260 anno mundi (i.e., 810 e.d.),[36] whereas in chapter 9 he writes that it occurred about three hundred years after the destruction of the Temple[37]—this makes a difference of more than 102 years. The figure given in chapter 9 is the correct one since, according to Rambam as you have been informed, the calculation of the calendar, according to the observation of the new moon, continued until the time of Abbaye and Rava. And both Rav Sherira Gaon and Rabad [Abraham ben David] write that Abbaye died in 629 e.d. and Rava in 663. Furthermore, Rabbi Abraham bar Ḥiyya refers to Rabbenu Hai in his *Sefer ha-Ibbur* and writes:[38] "In his responum, he [i.e., Hai] writes that from the year 670 e.d. which was 290 years after the destruction of the Temple, the Sanhedrin and ordination were abolished in the Land of Israel. The same information was given by the author of *ha-Terumot,*[39] blessed be his memory, on the authority of Ramban who himself was quoting Rabbenu Hai in his *Sefer ha-Zekhut* on which we have not had the privilege of setting our eyes.[40] However, you should not be misled by the matter of the abolition of the Sanhedrin into thinking that the Great Sanhedrin of seventy-one members and that of twenty-three continued to function for our people until that time. Rather you should pay due attention to the explanation already given by Rambam of blessed memory based on the statement in tractate Avodah Zarah. He writes:[41] "The Sanhedrin were exiled to ten places, the last of which was Tiberias. From then until the present time there was no Great Sanhedrin." Then there is the explicit statement in Mishnah Sanhedrin:[42] "The Great Sanhedrin used to be composed of seventy-one members . . . [Rabbi Judah says, there were seventy]." In other words, it refers to an event in the past. Moreover, if it had

32. B. Sanh. 11a.
33. *Sefer ha-Miṣvot,* positive commandment 153.
34. Nahmanides, *Hassagot ha-Ramban,* 222.
35. Isaac Israeli, *Yesod Olam* IV, ch. 5 (67b).
36. E.d. = era of documents.
37. Isaac Israeli, Yesod Olam IV, ch. 9 (73b).
38. *Sefer ha-Ibbur,* sec. 3, gate 7 (97).
39. The author of *Sefer ha-Terumot,* a code of civil and commercial law, was Samuel b. Isaac Sardi (1185/90–1255/56), a pupil of Nahmanides.
40. Nahmanides' *Sefer ha-Zekhut* is a critique of Abraham ibn Daud's criticisms of Alfasi. It was first printed in *Shiva Enayim,* Livorno, 1745. The reference is 43, col. b.
41. *Mishneh Torah,* Sanhedrin XIV:12.
42. M. Sanh. 1:6.

existed in the time of those Tannaim, Rabbi Judah would have had no reason to put forward his dissenting view that there were seventy [not seventy-one] members. They could have ascertained how many there were simply by entering their chamber. Rather, Rabbenu Hai was not just referring to the abolition of the Sanhedrin from that point in time; he was also implying that every law court in the land of Israel, which consisted of ordained rabbis who received their ordination from an uninterrupted line of ordained members of the Sanhedrin, was abolished in those days. And we know that the intercalation of the years was done either by the Sanhedrin or by a Palestinian court of judges who had been ordained on the authority of the previous Sanhedrin through the successive generations. This information is also provided by Rambam of blessed memory in his Laws on the Sanctification of the New Moon.[43]

Now it might stretch your credibility too far to accept that there is a reference to Rabbi Judah the patriarch, father of the said Rabbi Hillel, when it is stated,[44] "Rabbi Judah the patriarch asked Rabbi Ammi." You could claim that he [Rabbi Judah] and Rabbi Ammi were first generation Amoraim, and his son Hillel of the second generation whereas Abbaye and Rava were both fourth generation Amoraim, as is evident from Rabad's *Sefer ha-Qabbalah.* However, one could argue that Rabbi Judah was given his grandfather's name since the title of patriarch was used for all members of that lineage. This becomes all the more plausible in the light of the *Epistle* of Rav Sherira in which it is stated that certain sages bore this title even in the time of Rabbenu Saadiah Gaon of blessed memory.[45] And if it were not for the statements of Rabbenu Hai and Rambam, we would have ratified the other figure [given by Israeli] of 4260 [500 C.E.]. For it was then, also due to the succession of national disasters, that the Babylonian Talmud was closed as is stated by Rav Sherira in his *Epistle*[46] and by Rabad at the beginning of the section on the succession of the Saboraim.[47] It would appear even more anomalous had Rabbi Hillel's enactment been implemented before the close of the Gemara, given that neither Rav Ashi nor his successor Amemar make any reference to it. After all, it was an important basis for the preservation of our religion. Moreover, it would not be too far-fetched to explain the purpose of the above-cited statements of Rabbenu Hai and Rambam in the following way: After the story recounted about Rava and his fasts from which we gather that there was an ordained law court in his time in the Land of Israel[48] (as we shall discuss in section 3, chapter 40), the Gemara gives no other indication that there was still an ordained law court in the Land, but neither is there any authoritative tradition that refers to its abolition from that time. It is thus in the realm of possibility that an ordained law court continued to function until 4260 [500 C.E.]. Accordingly, the problem raised by Ran [Rabbenu Nissim] regarding the lenient ruling of those who say that the remittance of financial debts [during the sabbatical

43. *Mishneh Torah,* Qiddush ha-Ḥodesh V:1.
44. B. A.Z. 33b; B. Men. 29b. The Judah in question is Judah the Patriarch II.
45. *Iggeret,* 117.
46. Ibid., 61.
47. *Sefer ha-Qabbalah* (43).
48. See B. R.H. 21a where it is recounted that Rava used to fast two days for the Day of Atonement because he was uncertain as to whether the law court had prolonged the month of Ellul or not.

year] is not current practice could undisputably be resolved.[49] Look at the passage for yourself, but for my intimation you would not have reached such a conclusion, and see that I have not taken the wrong path now.

In any case, the ordinance came into being approximately before or after the time of Rav Ashi. It is thus a plausible assumption that in view of the change of guard and upheaval of the established order, Rabbi Hillel and his law court realized that that they should no longer date documents according to the Greek reign or era of documents as in the past, but to count from the creation for the reasons given above. They were aware that with the exception of the problem of the duration of the Egyptian bondage which is explained by our sages, the computation of the years from Adam to the building of the Solomonic Temple was explicitly given in the Pentateuch and Prophets. They also came across the tradition that the first Temple stood for 410 years and Rabbi Jose's statement in the Seder Olam and tractate Avodah Zarah according to which the second Temple stood for 420 years—all this will be explained, God willing, in chapter 35 and subsequent chapters. On the basis of these figures, they then fixed and grounded the aera mundi computation. Thus, from that time onwards, each successive generation preserved that custom and will continue to do so until, as Ramban and Israeli said, the teacher of righteousness shall come. But it does seem, that for a long time after Rabbi Hillel (given that he was indeed the first to implement the aera mundi computation), the era of documents continued to be used in certain places. Indeed, Rav Sherira Gaon who was active on Babylonian soil charted the line of several generations according to that computation. And the entry for *sḥ,* by the compiler of the *Arukh* of blessed memory, who was a Roman, reads: "It is reported that Mar Abraham Gaon who lived in 1140 e.d. understood the speech of palm trees." For my part, I was shown, and even held in my hands, an old volume of Rashi's commentary on tractate Pesaḥim. At the end of chapter Arve Pesaḥim at which point the commentary of Rashbam [Solomon ben Meir] takes over, a French scribe had written:[50] "Here has been presented Arve Pesaḥim with the commentary of Rashi of blessed memory completed on the eve of the Sabbath, Adar, 1501 e.d." Now Rambam blessed be his memory, came from the city of Cordoba which lies on the extremity of Spain and spent the end of his life in Egypt. In his treatise of resurrection, he writes:[51] "In the year 1500 e.d. [1189 C.E.], a letter from the Yemen reached me." And further on,[52] "And in this year 1500 e.d., letters arrived from Babylon." And at the end of chapter 1 of the Laws on Divorce, he writes:[53] "Nowadays, all Jews are accustomed to date their bills of divorce from creation or from the reign of Alexander of Macedon, namely, the era of documents." I saw the precious collection of books belonging to the scholar Rabbi Ezra da Fano the Mantuan[54] which contained the

49. Rabbenu Nissim, to Alfasi Giṭṭ. 20a (to Giṭṭ. 37b).

50. Rashbam, the grandson of Rashi was an important Tosafist who completed Rashi's commentary on ch. 10 of Pesaḥim and on most of Bava Batra. On his commentary, see E. E. Urbach, *Baʿale ha-Tosafot,* vol. 1, 49.

51. *Maʾamar Teḥ. ha-Met.,* 358.

52. Ibid., 359.

53. *Mishneh Torah,* Gerushim I:27.

54. Ezra da Fano was known for his valuable collection of Hebrew manuscripts, some of which he annotated and published.

commentary of Rambam of blessed memory on tractate Rosh ha-Shanah,[55] in which particular attention was paid to the astronomical parts of the text—he used much of this material for his commentary on the Laws of the Sanctification of the New Moon. At the end of the commentary, there was a colophon in the hand of the blessed Rambam's grandson. He writes:[56] "Rabbenu Moses, on him be peace, author of this work was born to his father on the fourteenth of the month of Nisan in the year 1446 e.d. in the city of Cordoba and died in the year 1516 e.d. on Monday the twentieth of Tevet. In other words, he illuminated the Diaspora for seventy years less eighty-three days. And my father, my teacher, his son, was born 1496 e.d. and died in 1566 e.d. And I David, son of the son of the Rav, my grandfather Rabbi Moses was born to my father in Egypt in 1534."

Now one should not be surprised at this use of the era of documents for dating which continued for several generations after Rabbi Hillel and Rav Sherira. The fact is surely that the displacement of an old for a new custom is difficult to implement, especially in the case of a dispersed nation, unless a long period of time has elapsed. However, over the course of time, the dispersed communities of Israel gradually came to adopt and accept that change. And since there is no remembrance of former times,[57] many people think that the aera mundi computation is Sinaitic and originates from time immemorial. In reality, as we have said, it is merely a recent innovation.

55. On the question of the authenticity of this commentary, see M. Steinschneider, *Die Arabische Literatur,* 203. For a bibliography of other writings on the subject of the commentary, see J. Dienstag, "Perush," 353–66.

56. This date for the birth of David Maimuni (i.e., David ben Abraham ben Moses) is confirmed in various documents. See E. Ashtor, *Toledot,* vol. 1, 117–18.

57. Eccl. 1:11.

CHAPTER TWENTY-SIX

Questions regarding two statements of Rabbi Jose and their resolution.

In this present context there will be two occasions for me to call upon Rabbi Jose Be-Ribbi[1] the great man among the towering personalities who are our adornment.[2] Indeed, I shall not relinquish this subject until, with God's help, his evidence has been confirmed in the eyes of all discerning people and I have given a just presentation of his statements.

As a preliminary to the first question, it should be known that according to the accounts of all gentile historians as well as Josephus and Rabad [Abraham ben David], the first Roman to attack the Jews and reduce them to submission was their great general Pompey. This was our own doing; for the priest Hyrcanus summoned him to come to his aid against his brother Aristobulus—they were both the sons of Alexander Jannaeus. Ramban [Nahmanides] of blessed memory also writes about this in relation to the voluntary descent of Joseph's brothers into Egypt. He states that this event was a presage of what was to happen to their descendants since our brothers also made a pact with the Romans of their own free will. Here he is referring to the story of Hyrcanus and Pompey. He also writes that subsequently, not long before the destruction of the Temple, Agrippa, the last king, fled to them in Rome.[3] All this information is repeated at greater length in his commentary on the verse, *The Lord will drive you, and the king you have set over you* (Deut. 28:36).[4] The same information is also given by the historian Dio in his account of the deeds of Pompey,[5] and with greater elaboration by the ancient historian Tacitus in his twenty-first book. I became acquainted with this last source from Vives's commentary on Augustine's *City [of God]* in the passage describing the troubles that befell the Jews in Temple times. Tacitus states explicitly that Pompey was the first Roman to attack us.[6] The same information can be gathered from the *Antiq-*

1. I.e., Yose ben Ḥalafta. BeRibbi is an honorific title, referring to one who belongs to a school of an eminent teacher.

2. This is a play on Josh. 14:15, *Arba was the great man among the giants* (*anaqim*) and Pr. 1:9, *necklaces (anaqim) around our throats.*

3. Nahmanides to Gen. 47:28.

4. Nahmanides to Deut. 28:42.

5. Dio Cassius, bk. 37, 15–17.

6. Vives, *De civ. Dei,* bk. 18, ch. 45: "Tacitus vero lib. 21 Romanorum inquit primus Gn. Pompeius Iudaeos domuit templumque iure victoriae ingressus est." The passage is in Tacitus, *Historiae* V, 9, 3.

uities of Josephus (book 14, chapter 5),[7] his *Wars* (book 1, chapter 5)[8] and from the Hebrew Josephus [i.e., Josippon],[9] and more specifically from book 2 of his *Against Apion* (p. 883) where he writes:[10] "When the Greeks were in power, we were independent and wielded power over the neighboring peoples for about 120 years until the arrival of Pompey the Great." Moreover, not one of the well-known chronicles contains reference to any Roman before Pompey's time who caused us harm. On the contrary, examination of chapters 8 and 12 and the three following chapters in the first book of Maccabees and book 12 of Josephus's *Antiquities* (chapter 17)[11] proves that throughout the lifetimes of Judah, Jonathan, and Simon, the sons of Mattathias—a span of thirty-two years—they were at peace with each other and that ambassadors went to and fro between the peoples exchanging precious gifts with a show of great affection and sweet assurances. And they gave each other mutual help in their fight against the Greeks as is stated by the sages of blessed memory:[12] "[Thirty-two battles did the Romans fight against the Greeks and they could not prevail against them until the Romans made an alliance with the Jews, and these were the conditions]: if the kings are chosen from among us, the princes should be chosen from among you." Even subsequent to this time, there is no evidence whatsoever that they ever damaged or destroyed any part of Jerusalem [lit. the Temple Mount]. For until the outbreak of the quarrel between the two brothers, all military activity on the part of the Jews was directed against the Greeks. It was specifically Hyrcanus who brought about Pompey's entry into Jerusalem. The bishop of Mondognedo's book, the *Dial* (*Orologio*) on the work of Marcus Aurelius,[13] contains a beautiful speech made by a Jewish elder before the Roman Senate in which he complains about the four wicked Roman judges who had been despatched to the Holy Land.[14] On examination of this speech, it will become clear to you that before the incident with Pompey, there was nothing but goodwill between Romans and Jews.[15] Now this disgraceful episode involving Pompey could not have occurred at the earliest more than 140 years before the destruction of the Temple. Hyrcanus who was appointed at that time as high priest by his [i.e., Pompey's] mandate was the last of the Hasmonean dynasty, and as is shown in the chronological tables of Eusebius, Samotheus, and other writers, he held the office for thirty-four years. The Hasmonean dynasty was succeeded by the House of Herod which according to rabbinic opinion

7. *Ant.* XIV:40ff.
8. *Bellum* I:138ff.
9. *Josippon,* bk. 5, ch. 39 (136–38).
10. *Contra Apionem* II, 134: "Nos autem liberi consistentes, etiam civitatum in circuitu positarum tenuimus principatum, annis viginti et centum usque ad Pompeium magnum." De' Rossi's reference to page numbers clearly indicates that he used Gelenius's translation, printed in Basel, 1567.
11. *Ant.* XII:413ff.
12. B. A.Z. 8b.
13. Antonio de Guevara (1480?–1545), the bishop of Mondognedo, was Charles V's historiographer. He wrote the *Libro aureo de Marco Aurelio* which first appeared in 1528 without his name. He then revised his text and published the *Relox de Principes* (*The Dial of Princes*) in Valladolid in 1529 which contained a great part of the material from the *Libro aureo.* De' Rossi read the work in Italian translation, *Aureo libro de Marco Aurelio con l'horologio de principi.* The work was republished many times.
14. *Aureo libro* III, ch. 10.
15. Ibid. (22r) "che voi sapete bene che dall'immemorabil tempo in qua Roma sempre ha tenuto pace con la Giudea e Giudea sempre ha conservato amicitia con Roma." This passage was often cited by authors. See I. Zinguer, "Historiographes juifs," 286ff.

lasted 103 years. The matter is further clarified by means of statements of Josephus. In book 12, chapter 11, he writes that the victory of the Hasmoneans and the miracle of Hanukkah occurred at the beginning of the one hundred and fifty-third Olympiad; and in book 14, chapter 8, he writes that the Pompey incident occurred in the one hundred and seventy-ninth Olympiad during the consulship of Marcus Antonius and Marcus Tullius in Rome. In other words, twenty-seven Olympiads or 108 years elapsed between the two events. If the 34 years of Hyrcanus are added to this figure, a total of 142 years is reached which is exactly the same figure given by Don Isaac [Abravanel][16] for the reign of the eleven Hasmoneans who held both priestly and royal office concurrently. Investigating the treatment of the Pompey incident in the works of the chroniclers, particularly that of Rabad, you will discover that Pompey returned to Rome at that time holding Aristobulus as a prisoner.[17] A little later, Pompey was forced to protect himself from the wrath of his oppressor, Julius Caesar, and fled to Cleopatra and Ptolemy, the rulers of Egypt. Julius then campaigned against them and took them captive. This was one of the coups referred to by the sages of blessed memory in their statement that Rome seized power, once in the time of the Greeks, and once in the time of Cleopatra.[18] Whichever source you turn to for information regarding the dates of these people and these events and the years of the Roman emperors subsequent to the three and a half years of Julius Caesar's reign up until Titus, you will find irrefutable corroboration of the historicity of the event and that it took place not more than 140 years before the destruction of the Temple.

In the light of these considerations, a question thus emerges with regard to Rabbi Jose's statement which is recorded by his son Ishmael.[19] For he said that Roman rule extended over Israel for 180 years during the period of the second Temple. Rashi understands the word "extended" as signifying "ruled" in line with the subsequent statement in the Gemara "that they enslaved them." But as we have seen, Pompey was the first Roman to make trouble for us and the incident in question must have occurred less than 140 years [before the destruction of the Temple]. Now it already occurred to me that it would be acceptable should a reliable authority emend the figure of 180 to 140. This was the case with the statement in Yoma:[20] "Our rabbis taught: Eighteen high priests officiated in the first Temple." For in the light of his objection to this statement, Rabbenu Tam emended the figure to eight, and his opinion was rejected by Rabbi Isaac who emended the figure to twelve. In fact, as we showed at the end of chapter twenty, both views should be rejected. Thus the change from 140 to 180 would be merely due to a mental lapse by the scribe, a slip of the pen. However, I realized that in the passage under discussion,[21] there is extensive debate regarding that calculation. Indeed, with regard to the 206 years of the Hasmonean and Herodian dynasties, it is said that the Romans kept faith with Israel for 26 years of this period and subjugated them for 180

16. Abravanel, *Mayyane ha-Yeshuʿah,* 2, Tamar 3 (289, col. a).

17. This is a reference to the second section of the *Sefer ha-Qabbalah.*

18. B. A.Z. 8b; De' Rossi also refers to B. Nidd. 30b in which Cleopatra is mentioned but not in relation to the rule of the Romans.

19. B. Shabb. 15a; B. A.Z. 8b.

20. B. Yoma 9a.

21. B. A.Z. 8b.

years. In view of this, I decided that the [proposed] emendation was not the solution to the problem.

Then there is another statement of Rabbi Jose which is cited in the first chapter of Avodah Zarah that we mentioned in chapter 23 which appears to be problematic. He states: "The Greeks reigned six years in Elam and subsequently, their dominion extended throughout the world." On the basis of these words, Rashi of blessed memory writes with regard to the statement, "In the Diaspora only the Greek era is used"[22] as follows: "The beginning of their dominion is not counted because those six years were incomplete for they only ruled in Elam, but subsequent to the six years, their dominion extended universally." Now this information about the six years of Alexander's universal rule after his overthrow of Darius, indicating that it was a sovereignty of lesser magnitude than that of his successors, contradicts that which is evident from Scripture and from other statements of the rabbis of blessed memory and from the testimony of all expert gentile writers of all times. For they demonstrate the reverse, namely, that those who replaced Alexander would continually diminish and be swept away, as Daniel said, king after king.[23] But Alexander ruled over sea and land and, according to the statement of our sages of blessed memory in tractate Tamid and several other passages,[24] his dominion extended as far as the mountains of darkness. Indeed, we have it on record that the king of Persia boasted *The Lord God of heaven has given me all the kingdoms of earth* (2Chr. 36:23). And the angel said, *By the power he obtains through his wealth he will stir everyone up against the kingdom of Greece* (Dan. 11:2). Nevertheless, it was the kingdom of Alexander that prevailed over him and spread to the ends of the earth. Scripture is explicit. It states in Daniel, *Four kingdoms will arise out of a nation but without its power* (8:22), and in chapter 11, *His kingdom will be broken up and scattered to the four winds of heaven, but not for any of his posterity, nor with dominion like that which he had* (v.4).

Now I undertook to resolve these questions and find a solution that favors the position of Rabbi Jose. With regard to the question that the Romans attacked and subjugated Israel in the 180-year period before the destruction of the Temple, I believe that the following response could be submitted. All the gentile sages who dealt with this subject, even were they to be twice as numerous, are to be regarded as those who claim that they have not been privy to the matter nor received information in that regard. For in Eduyot[25] and Zevaḥim,[26] the sages say that the statement "we have not seen" is no proof. They even use this reasoning with regard to two witnesses who say "we have not seen that she has been betrothed" to which it is objected, "This is obvious. After all 'we have not seen' is no evidence."[27] Moreover, in tractate Yoma,[28] on the basis of the verse, *The heart alone knows its bitterness* (Pr. 14:10), they state that one should pay heed to the patient as opposed to the entire assembly of doctors in everything that relates to

22. B. A.Z. 10a.
23. Cf. Dan. ch. 11.
24. B. Tamid 32a.
25. M. Ed. 2:2.
26. M. Zev. 12:4.
27. B. Ket. 23a.
28. B. Yoma 83a.

self-mortification. Similarly, one might claim that those writers did not pay attention to the first wars that the Romans waged against us and were not concerned about our ruination[29] and therefore did not object to it. The Jews, however, who were afflicted repeatedly, felt the pain of their flesh; their evidence is therefore highly trustworthy.

As regards the second question where we expressed surprise as to how the empire of Alexander could be regarded as inferior to that of those who succeeded him, we should say that our complaint is not directed against Rabbi Jose, but against Rashi of blessed memory who in his additional comment to Rabbi Jose's statement actually detracted from it. Now Rabbi Jose's statement is as follows: "The Greeks ruled six years in Elam, and subsequently their dominion extended universally." In his comment on the passage about the scribe, Rashi writes:[30] "The six years were incomplete for they only reigned in Elam, but subsequently, their empire extended." The purpose of his statement is undoubtedly to indicate that the latter period of the empire was better than its beginning. This is how the said problem was created for us. But Rabbi Jose himself did not think in this fashion. Rather, the point of his statement is simply that the dating according to the many Greeks who reigned concurrently only commenced after the death of Alexander. For Alexander reigned for six years in Elam which was the seat of his empire as is indicated by the prophet, *And I will set my throne in Elam* (Jer. 49:38), and from there he was the shepherd, the bulwark[31] of the entire world.[32] But the six years were not included in the dating of the empire of the many Greeks. This is the truth and it is well founded. And as we also proved in chapter 23, the dating of the Greek era only commences after the death of Alexander. But it is not correct to say that they only ruled in Elam and that subsequently their empire extended by means of additional conquests as appears to be the literal meaning of Rashi's statement. By God, we are also able to justify Rashi by explaining that the meaning of his statement that they only ruled in Elam is that the seat of the empire was in Elam only during Alexander's government. However, he was unique and his sovereignty was greater than that of all the Greeks who subsequently extended their power in the world. You should know, however, intelligent reader, that Samotheus says that Seleucus the Greek—about whom we wrote previously in chapter 23—from whose reign the Greek era is dated, did not come to the throne until eight years after Alexander's death.[33] Both the Christian translator [Jerome] in his commentary on Daniel[34] and the writer Otto (in book 2, chapter 42)[35]

29. 'Were not concerned about our ruination,' cf. Amos 6:6.

30. See ch. 23.

31. 'From there he was the shepherd, the bulwark,' cf. Gen. 49:24.

32. In his *Chronologia,* in which he translated David Gans's *Ṣemaḥ David,* H. Vorstius also translates chs. 23 and 25 of de' Rossi's work. While he is clearly appreciative of de' Rossi, he criticizes him (and other Jews) for the statement about Alexander's seat of government in Elam: "Altum de hoc Alexandri regno silentium est apud omnes historiographos, nullus illorum meminit ante vel post devictum Darium imperii sedem fuisse Elami. Sed hoc solemne Iudaeorum magistris est, quaelibet pro lubitu exoticis historiis assuere" (254).

33. Johannes Lucidus, *Opusculum,* bk. 4, ch. 3 (39r): "In Syria vero et Babylonia transactis octo annis post mortem Alexandri magni primus regnavit Seleucus Nicanor anno primo Olympiadis 117."

34. Jerome to Dan. 9:24 (*P.L.* XXV, col. 545).

35. This is a reference to Otto Bishop of Friesing (1114?–58), *Rerum ab origine Mundi . . . libri octo,* lib. III, ch. 42, "Supputatio diversa quo tempore Machabei fuerunt" (XXIIr–XXIIIr): "Quod enim a Seleuco regni Graecorum supputatio iuxta Machabaeos incipiat, Hieronymus in Daniele velle videtur, ubi ait Post

state that the Greek era only commenced twelve years after the death of Alexander. Arrhidaeus his brother ruled for some of the eight or twelve years. Since Alexander's wife Roxane[36] was pregnant when Alexander died, many of his servants said that the throne should be kept for his son. However, in the end, the four princes who initially were mere leaders, took the royal throne, and by means of these people, Greek sovereignty extended throughout the world, i.e., they divided the universal empire which had belonged to Alexander among themselves. All this information is to be found partly in Curtius's work[37] and partly in Plutarch's *Life of Alexander.* In view of the fact that the beginning of the Greek era was deferred for some years after the death of Alexander, there is until today, as I indicated at the beginning of chapter 24, a negligible discrepancy in the counting of the era of documents. In the light of this observation, it does appear that we are able to consider a solution to the question we raised both in regard to Rabbi Jose and to Rashi. We could say that those six years they reigned in Elam that are not counted and whose sovereignty was of lesser magnitude do not refer to Alexander's reign; rather, these were the years immediately after his death in the intervening period between his reign and that of Seleucus. And the dating of the Greek era was only initiated at the end of that period of eight or twelve years.[38]

However, my brother, you should known that in the forthcoming chapters of "Days of the World" another weighty problem will be considered regarding a third statement of Rabbi Jose, namely, that the Persian Empire lasted only thirty-four years of the second Temple period. Some people say that its duration was longer, and these additional years would necessarily have to be added to the figure of 5,331 that we count today from creation. This shall be shown in the forthcoming chapters. And if the solution of the second problem is acceptable, and you say that the Greek Empire together with the era of documents only began after the eight or twelve years mentioned above, the profit that ensues from this will then have a disadvantageous effect on the other figure. For then, quite apart from the thirty-four years and the question we raised about them as will be shown, you will have to add and count the last six years of Alexander and also the years that followed his death until the beginning of the Greek era. Accordingly, the correct figure for the period before the 380 years of the Greek Empire during the second Temple period will be greater. Consequently, the figure for the years from creation will necessarily be greater as well. However, in the chapters of "Days of the World," we shall attempt to present the arguments in favor of the date that we currently count. Consequently, we shall not accept the second solution presented here in order to prevent the proliferation of our enemies in that section. Rather, we shall remain content with a solution to the second problem in a manner similar to the way that we dealt with the first question as described above.

---

mortem Iaddi sacerdotis qui sub Alexandro templo praefuit, suscepit pontificatum Onias, quo tempore Seleucus subiugata Babylone, diadema totius Asiae capiti suo imposuit anno XII mortis Alexandri."

36. De' Rossi transliterates her name as Rasamo.

37. See bk. X, 7.

38. Finally, de' Rossi reaches the correct date for the initiation of the Seleucid era, i.e., 312 in the Macedonian calendar from Nisanu 1 = 3 April 311 in the Babylonian calendar. The confusion about the dating is discussed by E. Mahler, *Handbuch,* 143–47.

CHAPTER TWENTY-SEVEN

An apologia on behalf of our sages even though it is suggested that as regards their account of certain events that have no bearing on the laws of the Torah, they neither knew nor transmitted to us the true facts.

THE Roman historian, the pride and glory of his esteemed native town of Padua, Titius Livius surpassed all other gentile writers up to our own times in his creative ability[1] and in his flair for writing with the iron stylus and adamant point.[2] He wrote 140 books on the great city of Rome and on the causes of the various vicissitudes it underwent from the day of its foundation until his own time, a period of more than seven hundred years. At the outset of his work, he wished to demonstrate the benefit that the intellectual could derive from his histories and to what end the reader should expend effort on them. He thus writes as follows:[3] "Indeed, we may reap great benefit from knowledge of the past derived from written documents; for we become informed about teachings that are embedded in all manner of examples which lead us to recognize that which is useful for ourselves and our people, to avoid what is harmful and to promote what is beneficial." Certainly, his words are not false as far as concerns the nations who have not set eyes on the light of the perfect Torah and the other parts of holy Writ and who proceed unenlightened by their human studies. By the sweat of their brow and intellectual endeavor, they must needs winnow and fan all that happens on earth to man and to beast alike. They must discover how to proceed in order to ensure that the number of the days of their service under the sun are spent well. But we, the people of the God of Abraham, and the stock devoted to His worship (Blessed be He whose mercy prevails over us) have already been liberated and extricated from this labor such that we are relieved from the need to exert our skills to no purpose.[4] For it is indeed true that by means of his Torah and His precepts He has illuminated all that we would find obscure and opened up the gates of righteousness for us, pointing to the path that each individual or community of people should take in order to ward off the offensive of the oppressor and in order to facilitate success, as much as the soul would desire. The blessed Lord foresaw that in view of the limitation of the human intellect

1. 'Creative ability,' cf. Ex. 35:32.
2. 'Iron . . . point,' cf. Jer. 17:1.
3. *Decades* (praefatio, 10) "Hoc illud est praecipue in cognitione rerum salubre ac frugiferum, omnis te exempli documenta in inlustri posita monumento intueri inde tibi tuaeque rei publicae quod imitere capias, inde foedum inceptu, foedum exitu, quod vites." De' Rossi's translation is an adaptation of the text rather than a literal translation.
4. Cf. Eccl. 4:4.

and its weak and flaccid constitution, there would be a need for signs and examples that would be seen or known through experience which would help to preserve the teaching that is engraved in the mind. As we said in chapter 16, it was for this reason that when there was a dearth of true events to recount, the gentiles sages invented and made certain representations of stories to serve as illustrations for the audience. We see that the blessed Lord did not desist from juxtaposing the one with the other in writing that we should gain adequate demonstration of the best and correct path to pursue and thereby to imbue us with His illumination. For His perfect Torah and the books of His servants, the prophets, contain several stories which describe experiences and indications about events that both preceded and followed the giving of the Torah. It is therefore through the intellect and sensory perception rather than by enigmas that we come to know the truth of all things that should be pursued for our own good. Consequently there is no longer any need for excessive study that wearies the flesh or for the texts that issue from the pen of writers who, in the plethora of their words, do not cease from destroying one another. Everything is constituted before us all in the just balance and scales of the Lord.[5] There can be no teaching or intellectual instruction that those of foreign stock can offer us whether it concerns an oral communication or an event that might occur about which it would be said among us, "Look, this is something new which has never been known before." For we are in possession of the word of our God, and with it we do not lack for anything. As the sage says in Avot,[6] "Turn it around for it contains all . . . do not digress from it." If they say in Taʿanit,[7] "Is there anything in the Hagiographa which is not alluded to in the Pentateuch," one might with even greater justification state, "Is there anything contained in the nonsense of the secular domain that is not in the Mosaic Torah and its associated holy Scriptures." According to all commentators, exclusive of the precepts and laws which He put before us, each and every story related to human actions and events as described in His Torah, His Prophets, and His holy Writings are not meant for our enjoyment to be perused in our leisure moments. Rather, they should be the object of study and we are to gain practical knowledge from them: to know what the future has in store for us and how, as it comes to pass, we should conduct ourselves with God and humans. For, indeed, there should be parity between all men, for all souls are equal in the eyes of God. In this connection, we should not fail to mention the statement of the sages of blessed memory in the Zohar: "Woe to the man who says that the Torah is simply a story-book."[8] Now those with limited capacity for speculative thought are unable to detect its most intimate secrets[9] and to distinguish between its different garments as was Rabbi Simeon. For, as is stated in the Zohar,[10] he told his son Rabbi Eleazar three hundred (it was meant as hyperbole) rulings about the secret of the sublime wisdom contained in the verse, *and his wife's name was Mehetebel* (Gen. 36:39). But we, without this capacity, may

5. 'Just . . . Lord,' cf. Pr. 16:11.
6. M. Avot 5:22.
7. B. Taʿanit 9a.
8. Zohar, Behaʿalotekha, III, 152a.
9. 'Its intimate secrets,' lit. the curves of its secrets. Cf. S.S. 7:2, *the curves of your thighs* and see the comment of Obadiah Sforno ad loc., "*the curves of your thighs*—these are the secrets of the Torah."
10. Zohar, Toledot, I, 145b (in the standard text, the statement is in the name of R. Johanan ben Zakkai who transmits the rulings to R. Eliezer); Zohar, ha'azinu, III, 292b.

expect our reward and recompense from our God when we take counsel and instruction appropriate for our needs from the plain meaning of the stories and happenings told in the Torah and, according to our capacity, attain favor and approbation from His splendid majesty. Consider how the author of the *Guide,*[11] the Ralbag [Gersonides] in his *To'aliyyot*[12] and Yedidyah the Alexandrian [Philo] in his *Life of Moses* produced extensive and fine disquisitions on this question along the lines that we indicated.

Given the truth of the foregoing pronouncements, it is not difficult to understand the attitude of the sages towards all occurrences in the world and to events that happen over the course of time to rich and poor alike[13] that have no connection with Torah, but are simply of a general nature and cases about which one would pronounce, "It makes no difference whichever way one looks at them." Thus our sages saw no reason to divert themselves from the study of the Torah to which they were completely committed and to waste part of their time in giving mental application to detailed investigation of the facts either for their own edification or for our instruction. If they did want to give us any information about these things, they were content to extract for the purposes of the moment anything valuable they could take from the dross. When they would happen to relate some aspect of these matters, they, as it were, set their sights on attaining[14] the worthwhile purpose to which they were aspiring. Such is the way the author of the *Guide* accounts for the fifth cause [of contradictory statements] in his introduction.[15] This method may also be applied to certain subjects related to the understanding of the Torah itself. For in whatever way you extract the pearl from the sand, there is no harm nor reason for fear should one grope and turn it around to one's heart's content.

There is in fact a matter which is crucial for our understanding of this topic. Our sages of blessed memory have already demonstrated that our holy Torah is like an unlimited supply of water, while human life as the saying of the (father of physicians)[16] goes is short, not giving us adequate time to master even a single discipline. One is pierced to the heart by the divine statement, *Let not this Book of the Torah cease from your lips, but recite it day and night* (Josh. 1:8). The sages of blessed memory used to make their study of Torah fixed and were careful not to waste even a minute of their time on extraneous matters. Such was their concern that they even went as far as pronouncing on those who prolonged their prayers, diminishing thereby their time spent on the study of Torah: "They forsake eternal life and occupy themselves in temporal

11. *Guide* III, ch. 50. Maimonides uses the designation "mysteries of the Torah" for those passages such as lists of the names and places of Noah's descendants which are regarded by the "uninitiated" as of no value.

12. The *To'aliyyot* (ed. pr. Riva di Trento, 1550) drawn from his larger commentary on the Bible explains the ethical teachings of the biblical narrative that can be usefully applied in order to attain "true happiness."

13. 'To rich and poor alike,' cf. Ps. 49:3.

14. 'They as it were . . . attaining,' cf. B. B.B. 11b.

15. *Guide,* Introduction: "The fifth cause arises from the necessity of teaching. . . . For a certain obscure matter . . . has to be taken as a premise in explaining something that is easy to conceive. . . . He will not undertake to state the matter as it truly is in exact terms . . . but rather will leave it so in accord with the listener's imagination that the latter will understand only what he wants him to understand" (trans. Pines, 17–18).

16. This is a reference to Hippocrates' aphorism "Life is short and art is long."

matters."[17] In a similar vein is their statement in Yoma:[18] "*And you shall speak of them* [i.e., the words of Torah] (Deut. 6:7), but not words of prayer; 'of them,' but not of other things; 'of them,' make the study of the Torah fixed." This was the reason for the prohibition on the reading of profane works enunciated in Sanhedrin.[19] Moreover, to the question [as to when one may study Greek] put by Ben Dama to Rabbi Ishmael[20] which was also asked of Rabbi Joshua by his students,[21] they both replied that one may only study Greek in a time that is neither day nor night. On being questioned [about spending time on astrology], Samuel Yarḥinaʾah, who was himself an astrologer, replied that he only engaged in the science of astrology when he was relaxing.[22] With this concern of theirs not to expend their time on the study of history which had no value for them, they stated in Ketubot:[23] "Whatever pertained before the time of Ezra's enactment [is irrelevant] because what was in the past, is past." And they state that speculation on what is above and below may be acceptable, but as regards that which was before creation and after, when the world is finished, "what is past is past."[24] And in tractate Sukkah,[25] praise is bestowed on Rabbi Johanan ben Zakkai and his disciple Rabbi Eliezer as well as on Rav, the disciple of Rabbi Ḥiyya for having never engaged in idle talk. And in Yoma[26] they state that one who engages in idle talk transgresses a negative commandment. And in tractates Ḥagigah and Avodah Zarah,[27] the verse, *They pluck salt-wort with wormwood and the roots of juniper are their food* (Job 30:4)[28] is applied to anyone who interrupts his study of Torah and engages in idle gossip. Once again in their preoccupation that the study of Torah might become neglected, they forbad visits to the stadiums and circuses. The only exceptions to the rule, as Rabbi Nathan states, occur when by shouting, one might fulfill the precept of the saving of life, or when one is in a position to give evidence [of the death of a victim] and thus enable the victim's wife to remarry.[29] They also enjoined that school children should not be made to neglect their studies even for the building of the Temple.[30] The fact is that since the Torah is our life and length of our days, nothing should stand in its way.

We thought it worthwhile to expatiate on the truth of these matters. For since the

17. B. Shabb. 10a.
18. B. Yoma 19b.
19. M. Sanh. 10:1.
20. B. Men. 99b.
21. P. Peʾah I (1) 15c.
22. De' Rossi erroneously gives the source for this passage as tractate Eruvin. As Cassel states, the passage is in D.R. 8:6 to Deut. 30:11.
23. B. Ket. 3a. According to tradition, Ezra passed an enactment that girls should marry on the fourth day of the week (since the courts sit on the second and fifth day of the week), whereas previously they could marry on any day.
24. B. Ḥag. 16a. De' Rossi appears to have changed the talmudic statement which reads: "What is above, what is beneath, what is after, that is well. But as regards what was before—what happened, happened." He appears to be including the idea of both pre-creation and post-world history in the sense of the past.
25. B. Sukk. 28a.
26. B. Yoma 19b.
27. B. A.Z. 3b; B. Ḥag. 12b.
28. By a slight alteration of the vocalization of the verse, it is read, "They who break away from the table to idle gossip will have roots of juniper for their food."
29. B. A.Z. 18b.
30. B. Shabb. 119b.

sages of blessed memory were exclusively devoted to and immersed in the study of Torah and did not distract themselves by the conceit[31] of idle talk or read documents about the remote past, it will not come as a surprise to us should they make some mistakes or give a shortened account of any of those stories. For when people are not interested in a subject, they do not normally engage in investigation of all its facets. They simply transmit the version that they themselves were given. A similar opinion is expressed by the wise author of the *Aqedah* when he accounts for certain errors that our rabbis made in the field of astronomy. He writes:[32] "The rabbis of blessed memory only had recourse to that science in order to inform themselves about the intercalation of the calendar and the calculation of the equinoxes and new moons in accordance with the precepts of the Torah. As for the rest, they regarded it as alien and as a waste of time spent on extraneous matters that they were only permitted to study casually and at a time 'that is neither day nor night.' " And yet, the truth of the matter is that we may not take the license of removing the restriction [on telling the truth] even in regard to matters of a secular nature, proceeding right from the outset to utter falsehood. For he who utters lies shall not stand.[33] Rather we would say that any error that they should happen to make—without having to resort to an examination of the truth of what we are told—ought to be defended. And should any of the sagacious ancient and modern authorities offer whatever came to hand regardless of its defect,[34] his contribution would not be regarded as disqualified, for this is a profane matter, external to the sanctuary and not consecrated for use in the holy enclosure. Moreover, on many occasions, they will contain confused ideas and imperfections, but this should not mislead us such that we would ignore the important statements that underlie the nonsensical.

Now there is the known fact to which we also alluded above that on various occasions throughout the second Temple period they used an oracular voice (Bat Qol) as is stated in tractate Sota in the Palestinian Talmud[35] and Babylonian Talmud[36] as well as in tractate Sanhedrin[37] and at greater length in the Tosefta[38] and at the end of Midrash Shir ha-Shirim.[39] Even in the Amoraic period, "a certain old man" talked with them and Elijah himself appeared to them as is stated in Ketubot[40] in the story about Rav Ḥanan and in the parallel passage about Rav Judah[41] and there are several other passages. Moreover, the same phenomenon is even recorded for the time of Mar Rav

31. 'And did not distract themselves by the conceit of idle talk.' This expression is difficult to translate. He is playing on Ps. 40:5, *who turns not to the arrogant.*

32. Isaac Arama, *Aqedat Yiṣḥaq,* gate 37, bo (39a).

33. 'He who utters . . . stand,' cf. Ps. 101:7.

34. The passage is highly intricate and rhetorical with use of imagery pertaining to the sacrificial cult. De' Rossi refers to a *sarua* (an animal one of whose legs is longer than the others) and a *qaluṭ* (an animal whose feet are uncloven).

35. P. Sota 9 (13) 24b.

36. B. Sota 33a (and 45a).

37. B. Sanh. 11a.

38. T. Sota 13:2–6.

39. S.S.R. to S.S. 8:9.

40. B. Ket. 106a. The story is about R. Anan (not Ḥanan) who used to receive frequent visits from Elijah.

41. B. B.M. 114a. The story is told of Rabbah bar Abbahu, not Rav Judah.

Joseph a righteous and perfect Gaon; for according to Sherira's *Epistle* mentioned above, Elijah is said to have frequented his esteemed academy.[42] Nevertheless, in all these passages they acknowledge that the Holy Spirit departed from Israel after the death of the last three prophets. And the sage of the *Kuzari*[43] and Rabad the Levite in his *Sefer ha-Qabbalah*[44] likewise state that forty years after the building of the second Temple, the Holy Spirit departed from our people. And concerning the five things that were missing in the second Temple, Rashi gives the following explanation:[45] "From the second year of Darius's reign, the Holy Spirit no longer rested on the prophets." Now there may be a scribal error in the reading of Rashi's comment; if not, he must have overlooked the verse in Zechariah 7 (v.1) that explicitly states, *In the fourth year of King Darius . . . the word of the Lord came to Zechariah.* However, it could be said in his defense that he was alluding to the statement at the end of chapter 20 of Seder Olam: "Mordechai the Jew and Haggai, Zechariah, and Malachi all prophesied in the second year of Darius."[46] If, then, those sages of ours erred in their narration of some mundane matters and did not tell (because they had not been told) the real truth about them, they should nevertheless not be caught in the intrigues[47] of those who would criticize them. This argument has all the more force when one considers that even the chosen prophets in the moment of divine inspiration neither knew nor had self-awareness of the truth of the concealed matters unless it had been divulged to them from on high. As the prophet Elisha said, *For the Lord has hidden it from me and has not told me* (2K. 4:27). Now you might immediately think of the statement of the sages of blessed memory in Bava Batra,[48] "A sage is better than a prophet." But you should not be misled into believing that the meaning of their statement was that a sage knows what a prophet knows and more. For this is nonsense. After all, one of the three preconditions for the occurrence of prophetic inspiration is that the recipient should be a sage.[49] How can it be that the thing which is defective should be more perfect unless the element that brings it to perfection is connected to it. Rather, their intention is to consider a specific perfection that pertains to the sage but not to the prophet. One might say that extraordinary knowledge comes to the prophet from without which requires no concerted effort on his part to grasp. It is as though he comes into amazing wealth through inheritance or through finding. The sage, in contrast, comes to acquire all his knowledge of whatever degree by himself and through his own effort, like one who, by means of intellectual endeavor and painstaking labor, will gain more than sufficient profit for himself. Such a person is regarded by some as more praiseworthy than the other.[50] The fact is, however, that those who love the rich for their wealth which they use to good purpose are indifferent as to how it came to be acquired. You certainly know that they juxtapose

42. *Iggeret,* 109.
43. Judah Halevi, *Kuzari* III, par. 65.
44. Abraham ibn Daud, *Sefer ha-Qabbalah* (13).
45. Rashi to B. Yoma 21b.
46. Seder Olam, ch. 20 (88).
47. 'Caught in the the intrigues,' cf. Ps. 10:2.
48. B. B.B. 12a.
49. Cf. B. Shabb. 92a, "The Divine Presence only rests on one who is a sage, strong and rich."
50. De' Rossi may be referring here to Aristotle's discussion of wealth in bk. 4 of the *Nicomachean Ethics.*

the statement,[51] "Since the Temple was destroyed prophecy has been given to the wise," with the further comment that it has been given to fools and children.[52] When they wished to give us an example of a sage being superior to a prophet, they mention something which happens to be coincidental. For they say,[53] "The proof is that a great man makes a statement . . . and then the same is reported in the name of Aqiva ben Joseph." But the truth of the matter is that this statement of theirs is consistent with the fine method they adopt in their other sayings and rhetorical expressions that we discussed in chapter 20. That is, when they wish to exhort or warn about a shameful or praiseworthy matter, they use hyperbole such that the shade of the gourd appears to us like a high mountain. Likewise, when they say that a sage is superior to a prophet, the purpose is to encourage and inspire us to acquire wisdom by reason of its supreme value. There may also be other reasons for the statement as the wise author of the *Aqedah* writes in gates 35 and 39. Study the passages. Nevertheless, just as they follow any Midrash they give on Scripture by the words, "Scripture is never divested of its plain sense," as we have mentioned several times, so, too, one might comment on the weird statements they make about the natural world, "The world does not digress from its natural and normal course." And even the most inferior of the prophets is certainly superior to all the sages that ever lived on earth because he is imbued with "a supernatural spirit."[54] In tractates Megillah[55] and Bava Batra[56] they say that Haggai, Zechariah, and Malachi were superior prophets to Daniel who was the recipient of divine knowledge and proficient in all wisdom, and who was imbued with the supernatural spirit to which we referred. Furthermore, it is clearly apparent and absolutely certain and true that commensurate to the neglect for which they are not culpable that may be discerned in the way the sages of blessed memory treat the area of the mundane, is the powerful superiority and amazing skill with which they were proficient in the words of Torah—in this their understanding and communication was perfect. There is no way that the two areas can be compared. For there are no grounds for comparison between breath in which there is sin,[57] as when error in teaching is accounted as an intentional sin,[58] to a mistake in history for which no expiation is required. But wherever the teaching of laws or *halakhot* would be required, their decisions were undoubtedly precise and they were in each case careful to be exact to the last minutia, as is apparent from tractate Eduyot and chapter 3 of Keritot and several other passages. They also obligated themselves, as is stated in chapter 1 of Eduyot,[59] to transmit each tradition in the very words of its teacher. And when they had not heard a certain tradition they said

51. B. B.B. 12a.
52. Ibid. 12b.
53. Ibid. 12a–b.
54. Cf. Dan. 6:4.
55. B. Meg. 3a: "They were superior to him because they were prophets and he was not a prophet. He was superior to them, because he saw and they did not see."
56. B. B.B. 4a. Daniel is mentioned here but not in comparison with Haggai, Zechariah, and Malachi.
57. Cf. B. Shabb. 119b: "The world endures only for the sake of school children. Said R. Papa to Abbaye. 'What about mine and yours? Breath in which there is sin is not like the breath in which there is no sin.' "
58. Cf. M. Avot 4:13.
59. M. Ed. 1:3.

so as for example in Sukkah:[60] "They asked him for thirty decisions. . . . Of twelve of these he said, 'I heard them'; of eighteen he said, 'I have not heard them.' " According to another opinion, it was the reverse [i.e., he said of eighteen that he had heard them and of twelve that he had not heard them]. Likewise, many of the later authorities and specifically the Gaon Sherira of blessed memory in his *Epistle* and Rambam in his introductions[61] went to great lengths to prove the truth of the Sinaitic tradition and to identify the distinguished authorities who transmitted it to us. But as regards other matters that do not entail meritorious or wrongful acts, whatever their source, if they agree with *halakhah* all well and good, and if not, the content of dreams has no bearing on anything. If you would understand, listen to this. Even in the disciplines on which laws and the main aspects of the Torah do not hinge, the author of the *Guide* wrote (as I mentioned in chapter 11),[62] "Do not expect me to demonstrate that everything our rabbis said on astronomy conforms to the actual truth of the matter." Therefore many of the later authorities challenged them by means of explanations and reasons that did not spring from Sinaitic tradition which all living beings acknowledge with Selah. Rather, they were transmitting the opinion of certain contemporary sages or were basing themselves on common sense and intellectual probity, as I demonstrated at length in chapter 14 and other chapters. And the religious author of the *Kuzari* who expatiated in their defense at the end of sections 3 and 4 of the book, and demonstrated their considerable wisdom, as I showed above, concluded as follows:[63] "We should not be concerned with anything that is not related to the permitted and forbidden and does not detract from their stature in any way." Indeed, in their treatment of the incident of Jeroboam, they say overtly about Ahijah the prophet,[64] "He too signed and erred." And in Megillah,[65] it is stated of Daniel that he made an error in his calculation. And it is also stated of Joab (although he was not in the same category as those others mentioned) that he made three errors.[66] And why should one be surprised at the error of individuals even if they are special. After all, the true God states, *If it is the anointed priest who has incurred guilt* (Lev. 4:3), *In case it is a leader who incurs guilt* (Lev. 4:22), and then we hear Him not desist from stating, *If it is the whole community of Israel that has erred* (Lev. 4:13) which in the Mekhilta [*sic*] is explained as a reference to the Great Sanhedrin.[67] Accordingly, all people, as David on him be peace, states, *tell lies*[68] on occasions, and yet, as the apologia has verified, not in a rebellious fashion or in a willful act of transgression. Respect for the person who inadvertently errs should be upheld and the crowns of the righteous will remain forever on their heads.

60. B. Sukk. 28a.

61. I.e., his introduction to his *Mishneh Torah* and to his commentary on the Mishnah.

62. *Guide* III, ch. 14.

63. *Kuzari* III, par. 73. De' Rossi is not precise in his quotation which reads: "For the whole of this relates to topics which are not related to the permitted and forbidden and the book will lose nothing if we consider the points discussed here."

64. B. Sanh. 102a.

65. B. Meg. 12a.

66. B. Makk. 12a.

67. Sifra 4:4 (19 col. a). By means of an analogy with the use of the word "community" in Num. 24 and 25 where it refers to the judges (the small Sanhedrin), the term "the whole community of Israel" here is interpreted as referring to the Great Sanhedrin, implying that it represents all Israel.

68. Cf. Ps. 116:11.

CHAPTER TWENTY-EIGHT

As to how the sages of blessed memory did not put obstacles in the way of future generations from challenging them with reasonable arguments on any matters beyond the three types of study which are the foundations of the Oral Torah. And further defense of the [sages] for any errors that they may have made in matters of a nonreligious nature. And that one cannot in any way use this as grounds for claiming that they made any errors whatsoever with regard to the Torah, God forbid.

We are indeed honor-bound to praise these divinely inspired men, perfect and many,[1] our sages, blessed be their memory, and on account of them give praise to our God who is eternally blessed. For during our servitude and throughout the period in which He has turned His face away from us, He has through them not failed to bestow on us consolations and the preventitive remedy to preempt our spiritual castigation. The following fact is surely patently obvious to all those who sincerely acknowledge the truth. Were it not for their [i.e., the sages] efforts and zeal to control lawlessness and to hold up our collapsing tabernacle through the transmission of the Sinaitic traditions and their correct teachings and appropriate enactments that they innovated for us (as is eloquently described by the noble of Coucy in his noted introduction),[2] we would no longer have food prepared according to the correct observance of ritual purity and we would have become, God forbid, like all the gentiles. But they (and may they receive full recompense from our God) joined and healed our breaches and caused the remnant of Israel to cleave as far as it is possible to the Creator of all. Thus, through their merit and with their protection, we can speak of our life of joyous contentment both in this desolate world and in the land of eternal life.

We should always keep in mind the principle that the rabbis of blessed memory transmitted with regard to the verse, *According to the Torah which they shall teach you* (Deut. 17:11)[3] and which was articulated by Rambam of blessed memory.[4] It is that we may not, God forbid, tender any criticism of any minor or major matter that they transmitted as a tradition handed down from Moses our teacher, or through one of the hermeneutical principles by which the Torah is expounded, or when they made precautionary enactments with regard to the Torah. We may neither undertake our own examination into these matters, nor take issue with them in that regard as though their testimony was not of unimpeachable trustworthiness, or that our methods are superior

1. 'Perfect and many,' cf. Nahum 1:12.

2. This is a reference to the introduction to the *Sefer Miṣvot ha-Gadol* written by Moses ben Jacob of Coucy (thirteenth century) which orders the positive and negative commandments following Maimonides' arrangement to give the essence of Oral Torah. The work was first published before 1480 and republished many times subsequently.

3. B. Sanh. 87a.

4. *Mishneh Torah,* Mamrim I:2.

to theirs, or even that we are their equals. Far be it from us to behave in this manner. For the arrogant person who has the gall to act thus will not see any good emerge from it but will be like a shrub in the wilderness, smoke from the lattice, chaff before the wind.

The fact is that not only is the truth of the Written Torah clear to us as the light of the sun, but also the Oral Torah of Sinaitic origin is known to us to be firmly established and true. As the great authority mentioned above [Maimonides] wrote, it is a matter of general consensus and has not been the subject of any controversy.[5] This chain of tradition both reliable and wonderful, which "has passed between the holy pieces,"[6] is mentioned by the founding fathers in tractate Avot and by the subsequent Geonim and codifiers may they rest in peace.

And when we study their righteous ordinances and appreciate their methods, God will grant us the privilege of understanding the underlying principles and the meaning of the matters transmitted to them and by them. Then we will certainly rejoice and give thanks to our God wholeheartedly. But when we encounter a problematic matter in these areas and fail to grasp it for one reason or another, one should not feel or act aggressively against them, God forbid, nor should it lead one to transgress the statutes of the Torah. As the fore-mentioned great authority said:[7] "It is fitting for every person to understand the laws of the holy Torah and according to their capabilities delve into its meaning. If he cannot find a reason for it, he should not invent fictions about it. Let him not break through lest He break out against him."[8] Rather he should remain blameless and take the laws upon himself. As the divine poet said both as regards Scripture and the tradition, the teachings and enactments mentioned above, the servant who is faithful to our God would surely say, *But with all my heart I will keep your precepts* (Ps. 119:69).

However, there is the case of those issues that by their very nature cannot be claimed to derive from Sinai. In this category are stories about events that happened subsequent to that time [i.e., after Sinai], or matters that are clearly stated on the basis of reason without the support of holy Scripture. Should it be possible to explain these matters in a manner that agrees with the clarification of the later authorities, any person of standing, as the author of the *Guide* wrote, ought to do so.[9] But when this option is not possible, you should consider what the same authority wrote in the very same chapter. For he said that one should not be concerned if their statements are not consistent with the actual truth. After all, they did not discuss the subject as transmitters of the prophetic tradition, but rather because in those times they were the experts in the subject or had heard about it from the sages of those generations. Aside from this teacher's statements, you have seen the citations from other later authorities of blessed memory quoted in chapter 14 which challenged our sages' views. For why should we be hypocritical

5. Ibid. I:3.
6. This is a play on the expression *covenant of the pieces* in Gen. 15:9–10. De' Rossi appears to be saying that God's covenant with Israel is based on the Oral Torah which has been transmitted through the holy authorities of successive generations.
7. Maimonides, *Mishneh Torah,* Temurah IV:13; Meʿilah VIII:8.
8. 'Let him . . . him,' adaptation of Ex. 19:24.
9. *Guide* III, 14.

against their wishes and utter things that we do not believe in our heart. As we said at the end of chapter 11, our blessed Lord was angry with the three friends of Job for trying to justify His decisions with false and misleading pronouncements. In his [i.e., Maimonides'] Laws of the Rebellious, you must surely see that the same authority, basing his position on that of our sages of blessed memory themselves, only confined himself to true *halakhah,* in other words, one may not contravert the judgments of the supreme law court in any of the three main categories which, as he states, comprise Sinaitic tradition, the deductions from Torah made on the basis of the hermeneutical principles, and the precautionary measures. But in all other areas, there is no higher deciding authority[10] and there is no restriction.

Furthermore, I have no need at this moment to defend those who challenge our rabbis by means of their own reasoning and common sense. I have no issue to make regarding this type of controversy. On the contrary, in chapter 15, I endeavored to demonstrate that those who adhere to interpretation based on the plain sense of Scripture and challenge the sages for their interpretation of Scripture ought to have desisted from this behavior. After all, each area of interpretation [i.e., both the literal and nonliteral] is valid each in its own way, and the characteristic of Midrash is not comparable to that of the *peshaṭ* which was the aim of their exegesis. But I was brought to this now because of the matter that I began to discuss in chapter 14. It regards the chapters of the third section [of this book]. With no intention of establishing a deviant *halakhah* or showing myself to be cleverer than my teachers, but as part of the thrust and parry of the arguments and like one who desires to enlighten his teachers, I was aroused to pass judgment on the dating we use from the creation of the world. There were confusions about the duration of the bondage in Egypt and the length of the period of the two holy Temples according to many esteemed authorities who gave a different opinion to that of our sages of blessed memory. We put ourselves into the position of advocates for both sides, providing explanation of the sources of their views as seemed right to us. In sum, we let it be known that it is likely and reasonable that after considering all the possible ways that others had treated the subject, our rabbis of blessed memory would finally come to the conclusion that in all matters that are by their very nature impossible to clarify in their entirety, it is only right and proper to uphold the most plausible position, particularly when they know that in any case this would not result in any harm or nullification of any matter related to our Torah, God forbid.

All this is put forward by me with the declaration that I shall annul my opinion in favor of that of true scholars and with regard to the instructive point taught us by Rabbi Aqiva in chapter 3 of tractate Keritot[11] which was also adopted by the sages in their dispute with Rabbi Simeon:[12] "If this is an authentic tradition we shall accept it; but if it is only a logical deduction, there is a rebuttal." At these words, Rabbi Joshua gave him permission and said to him, "Rebut it." Everything, as will be shown, is to be clarified and elucidated by us in the specified chapters.

10. Lit. 'there is no justice and no judge.' This expression is used in Targum ps. Jonathan to Gen. 4:8 in which Cain is described as denying the concept of reward and punishment.
11. M. Ker. 3:9.
12. M. Yev. 8:3.

When rumor of this research of mine came to the notice of certain people in office[13] who are taking positions to oppose me, smoke signals began to rise, and without testing or reading my words and what elements of justification they contained, may our Lord forgive them, they proceeded to use the mouth before having first used their eyes. And they complained vociferously against me, and claimed that any public articulation of controversy or dispute regarding anything transmitted by our rabbis whether its source be Sinaitic or any other in time or origin, particularly if it was combined with interpretation of certain verses in Scripture that did not accord with that of our rabbis of blessed memory, constituted undermining of the religion and heresy, God forbid.[14] Consequently I saw that if not wise, it was necessary and opportune for me to demonstrate at the beginning of this second section how that several later authorities who were righteous and worthy took the freedom to challenge our sages of blessed memory without any restraint. (It is true, however, that we did take them to task about this in some ways as was shown in the following chapter.[15]) The purpose was to defend ourselves even should you say that in the course of our discussion we are manifestly coming into dispute with our sages, blessed be their memory. How much more so then, should we not be put to shame, particularly since our purpose in dealing with this subject is to explain and not to contravert as was said, and that we have tended to make every effort within our means to justify the rabbis of blessed memory. And there is even greater reason [not to be treated so], since this investigation that is set before the one who would examine it with due consideration regards secular matters alone and does not give scope for doubting any of the precepts of the Torah as shall be elucidated. Consequently, anyone who makes a concerted effort to attack us, brings a charge of sin for no reason; in the eyes of the public he makes a mountain out of a molehill[16] and a wagon rope from a single hair.

And indeed now, on the day of action, may my words penetrate the ears of every reader. For in those chapters, you will see me explaining and clarifying as to how our wise ancestors did not err in any matter, and that we today are not privy to anything to which they were not privy. And you may be able to say that wherever one disputes anything said by them in relation to this subject, many objections will be raised against the author of the statement and the proofs he adduces for his statements. But ultimately the response of that scholar, "this is the tradition that I have received," will surely be regarded as correct defense and there will be no further grounds for criticizing him.

You should give careful consideration to the passage in tractate Ḥullin where even with regard to words of Torah it is stated:[17]

> Rabbi Eliezer taught: "I have heard that a limb severed from a living body is unclean." Rabbi Joshua said to him: "Do you mean from a living body and not from a corpse? Surely it is all the more so; for if a limb taken from a living body that is clean is unclean, how

13. Lit. those who wear the robe. Cf. B. Ber. 28a, where the expression is used to indicate those in office.
14. This was indeed one of the central issues of the controversy over the book which protestations such as these failed to preempt.
15. I.e., ch. 15.
16. Lit. a *yod* turned into a town. Cf. B. Qidd. 16b: "The *yod,* a small letter, has grown into a town."
17. B. Ḥull. 129b.

> much more so is a limb from a corpse that is unclean, unclean. It is written in the Scroll of Fasts that no mourning is allowed on the minor Passover. What about mourning on the major festival?[18] Surely if it is not allowed on a minor festival, how much more so is it not allowed on the major festival. Similarly, in this case, it is all the more true that a limb from a corpse is unclean." He replied to him, "This is what I have heard" [namely, that a limb from a corpse is not unclean].

There is a similar case in Pesaḥim:[19] "Rabbi Joshua said: 'I have heard that the substitution of a Passover offering is offered [and also that a substitute for the Passover offering cannot be offered] and I cannot explain it.' Said Rabbi Aqiva: 'I will explain it.'" And in chapter 1 of tractate Parah,[20] there is the discussion about the three-year-old heifer. ["Rabbi Eliezer ruled: 'The heifer must be no more than one year old and the red heifer no more than two years old.' But the sages ruled: 'The heifer must be even two years old and the red heifer even three or four years old. . . .' Rabbi Joshua stated: 'I only heard of a cow that was *shelashit.*' He replied: 'Thus I have heard it without explanation.'] When Rabbi Eliezer and Rabbi Joshua, about whose stature we are fully aware were questioned with regard to an anomalous statement, all that they were required to say in their own defense were the words, "Thus I heard." Such is the use of this expression that on many occasions in which there is no proof for a *halakhah,* even before they are made aware of the thorn of the problem, justification of their position is anticipated by the use of this expression as is the cases cited before and in the passage in Sanhedrin[21] and in the Palestinian Talmud:[22] "I have heard that the law court may impose flagellation and pronounce sentences." And in tractate Eruvin it is stated:[23] "I have heard that hills are treated as though they were pierced." And there are other similar examples. Such a statement precludes any legal objection to what is about to be said.

Now in connection with this subject, I shall mention a most apposite matter that I already touched on in chapter 15. It should serve as a model for our inquiry. It pertains to the commentary of the great light of Rashi of blessed memory on Chronicles regarding the verses: *And Shuppim and Huppim were the sons of Ir, Hushim the sons of Aher* (1Chr. 7:12); *The sons of Naphtali: Jahziel, Guni, Jezer, and Shallum, the descendants of Bilhah* (1Chr. 7:13); *The father of Gibeon dwelt in Gibeon and the name of his wife was Maacah* (1Chr. 8:29). It also pertains to his commentary on the verses in Chronicles that deal with the cities of the Levites. In view of the problem of the redundancies and many variants that are contained in those verses, he makes the explicit pronouncement that Ezra had transcribed the verses from different texts, and that because he was doubtful as to which text preserved the correct reading, he wrote down both versions. And in a similar vein he writes that when Ezra found the text different from that written down in other parts of holy Scripture, he did not desist from transcribing the text as he found it. I have not quoted Rashi's comments which are prolix, but since you know where

18. This refers to the seven-day festival of Passover as opposed to the one-day Passover in the month of Iyyar. Cf. Num. 9:11.
19. M. Pes. 9:6.
20. M. Parah 1:1.
21. B. Sanh. 46a.
22. P. Ḥag. 2 (2) 78a.
23. M. Eruv. 5:4. This is a metaphorical statement used for indicating net horizontal distance.

they are to be found, it would not be too difficult for you to examine them *in loco*. In my opinion, there is support for what he says from the verse in Nehemiah 7 (v.5), *I found the genealogical register of those were the first to come up, and there I found written.* And if we do not accept the commentators' solution to the problem of the divergencies between these words of Nehemiah [who states in the following verse], *These are the people of the province* and Ezra's version,[24] one might therefore suggest that Nehemiah did not transcribe from Ezra's text. It is true, however, that Ezra who came up from Babylon, and Nehemiah who came from Shushan at a later date, saw each other. For, as is clear from Nehemiah 12, both went to the thanksgiving rites for the dedication of the walls of Jerusalem. In any case, it is clear from Rashi's statements that the most recent recorders of the times, even those who recorded our holy Writ, were transcribing from ancient texts. Now you have heard from him that when they found discrepancies in the texts such as in 1 Chronicles (8:29) where it speaks of *Maacah his wife* whereas in 7:15 it reads, *Maacah his sister,* they did not refrain from setting down the two mutually contradictory versions. Consequently, you will have all the more reason to believe that this also occurred with vowels and individual letters, particularly those that resemble each other; for example, with the names Rodanim and Dodanim[25] and Jehoadah and Jarah[26] which are duplicated in the list of the descendants of Saul.

This can serve as one of the explanations for the phenomenon of *ketiv-qeri*[27] which has more than one explanation and one reason. The examples of *ketiv-qeri* in the Pentateuch in the verses, *The Lord will strike you with inflammation with hemorrhoids* (Deut. 28:27) and *If you pay the bride price for a wife, another man shall sleep with her* (ibid. v.30) are certainly not, God forbid, due to any doubt, but were right from the outset used as euphemisms. And there is the case [in Gen. 24:16] in which Rebecca is described as a *naʿar* (young boy) rather than (*naʿarah*) young girl. Perhaps this was because she was regarded as having the agility of a boy. But the word *naʿar* in regard to a betrothed woman [in Deut. 22:23] is used as a derogatory term because she left [her home].[28] An alternative reason was proposed in a *Collectanea* that I came across. It reads: "In the *Shorashim* written by Dunash ben Labrat [*sic*],[29] he writes under the root for *naʿar* as follows: 'In the Pentateuch, the word *naʿar* refers to any girl that has not reached puberty, but it is pronounced as *naʿarah.*'" Thus in each case, the most legitimate reason for the *ketiv-qeri* will be sought.

Now the statement of the great guide, Rashi of blessed memory, has directed us such

24. I.e., the parallel passage in Ezra 2:1, *These are the people of the province who came up from among the captive exiles.*

25. 1Chr. 1:7 reads, *The sons of Yavan: Elishah, Tarshish, Kittim, and Rodanim,* whereas Gen. 10:4: *The descendants of Javan: Elishah and Tarshish, the Kittim, and Dodanim.*

26. 1Chr. 8:36: *Ahaz begot Jehoadah* and 1Chr. 9:42: *Ahaz begot Jarah.*

27. Ketiv-Qeri is a technical term to denote passages in the Bible that are written in one way in the text but are read out in another.

28. *If a young girl (naʿar) that is a virgin is betrothed to a man and a man find her in the city and lie with her* (Deut. 22:23). As Rashi writes, quoting the Sifre, the girl is culpable because she went out rather than remain chastely at home.

29. The reference here is to the *Maḥberet he-Arukh* of Solomon b. Abraham Parḥon of Aragon (twelfth century) which was a compilation based on the works of the grammarians Ḥayyug and ibn Janaḥ. The passage in question is s.v. *naʿar* (42, col. a). I am grateful to S. Leiman who indicated to me the correct reference.

that we can now say that divergencies in descriptions of events and genealogical lists are due to the variation in versions from which they were transcribed.[30] We should therefore not pay attention to the statement of the wise Don Isaac [Abravanel] who, in his introduction to the book of Jeremiah,[31] expresses surprise that Kimḥi put forward a similar view about the *qeri-ḳetiv* in his introduction to the former prophets, as did the wise Ephodi in his work on grammar.[32] In sum, the statement of our sages, "this is what I heard" will be an acceptable defense since men of inspiration, including the writers of records discussed above[33] would say, "This is what I found."

But let us resume our discussion of the statements of the rabbis of blessed memory. Chapter 9 of tractate Pesaḥim contains a most notable and educative statement of one of the blessed sages which did not derive from Sinaitic tradition, but from his teacher. The members of the academy arrayed themselves against him, putting forward many rebuttals until they finally rejected and completely undermined it. And yet, the great teacher Rambam of blessed memory brings the weight of evidence to prove that it was correct. It is taught as follows:[34] "Rava said: The world is six thousand parasangs and the thickness of the heavens is one thousand parasangs. The first statement is a tradition and the second is based on reason. Then they objected to the statement based on tradition on the grounds of four *beraitot.* They said: Come and hear. Egypt is four hundred parasangs square. . . .[35] Come and hear. The whole of the inhabited world is situated under one star. . . .[36] Come and hear. The Wain is in the north and Scorpio is in the south. . . .[37] Come and hear. What answer did the oracular voice give him?"[38] With regard to each of these rebuttals, Rashi explains:[39] "The world is consequently several thousand parasangs. The rebuttal of Rava's view stands." And you know Rashi's statement in Sanhedrin:[40] "There is a difference between an objection and a rebuttal. A rebuttal cannot be further challenged even under pressure." This is also the line taken

30. The question of the *ḳetiv-qeri* is also treated by Jacob ben Hayyim ibn Adonijah in the introduction to the *Rabbinic Bible* of 1524–25 who also gives the same citations from Abravanel and Efodi. See the edition of C. D. Ginsburg, 42–48.

31. Abravanel, Introduction to Jeremiah (298 col. b–300 col. b). Abravanel argues against the view that Ezra found the text of the Bible in a confused state and proposes that when phrases were anomalous, he left them in the text as they were written and put the *qeri* in the margin as explanation of the anomaly according to the idiom of the language, and to indicate that the gloss was his own.

32. Profayt Duran (Ephodi), *Sefer Ma'aseh Efod,* ch. 7 (40). De' Rossi read the work in manuscript.

33. E.g., the authors of Chronicles.

34. B. Pes. 94a.

35. "Egypt is 400 parasangs square. Now Egypt is one-sixtieth of Ethiopia, Ethiopia is one-sixtieth of the world." According to this calculation, the world is 576,000,00 square parasangs.

36. Since there are countless stars, the sky must be immeasurably greater than the earth and not, as Rava says, only one-sixth greater.

37. "The Wain is in the north and Scorpio is in the south and the whole of the inhabited world lies between the Wain and Scorpio, and the whole of the inhabited world represents but one hour of the day for the sun enters the inhabited world only for one hour in the day. The proof is that at the fifth hour, the sun is in the east, while at the seventh, the sun is in the west: during half of the sixth and half of the seventh the sun stands overhead all people." This also proves that the sky is infinitely larger than the earth.

38. "Now from earth to heaven is a 500-year-journey, and between the first heaven and the next lies a 500-year-journey and similarly between each [of the seven] heavens." Here, too, Rava's view is refuted.

39. De' Rossi does not appear to be representing Rashi's comment who finally does state: "Consequently, the world is more than 6,000 parasangs."

40. Rashi to B. Sanh. 72b.

by Rabbenu Samson in his *Sefer Keritut*[41] and by the compiler of the *Arukh,* blessed be his memory, under the entry for "rebuttal": "The rabbis say that whenever the Gemara uses the expression, 'the rebuttal of somebody is a rebuttal' this signifies that the view of the one against whom the rebuttal is brought is completely rejected." Thus although there are grounds for saying that Rava's tradition was put forward as an anonymous tradition which is regarded as Sinaitic (this was why Rashi of blessed memory who knew what he was doing took up the pitchfork [to repudiate it] and says that it was a tradition from his teacher), it was regarded by them as false and was therefore rejected. And yet Rava should not be regarded as propounding defective teaching since he would be able to defend himself with the words, "This is what I heard." Moreover it is stated:[42] "Rav Naḥman said to Rav Huna: Is the *halakhah* according to us or according to you? He said to him: The *halakhah* is according to you." With regard to this passage, Rabbenu Samson wrote: "Rav Naḥman raised doubts about his own view and Rav Huna himself acknowledged that the *halakhah* was not according to his [i.e., Rav Huna's] view and nevertheless, each one put forward his tradition.[43] Moreover, in tractates Shevu'ot[44] and Zevaḥim[45] there is an anonymous talmudic statement which discusses two Tannaim each of whom is said to give traditions of what they heard from their teachers. Accordingly, you should not find it problematic that one specific story is told by the rabbis of blessed memory in different ways. This discrepancy was demonstrated to you in the two stories that we discussed in chapters 12 and 16. Similarly, there is the story recounted in tractate Yevamot both in the Palestinian and Babylonian Talmuds[46] about the four elders who came to Rabbi Dosa to discuss the question of a daughter's rival in which each participant could have said, "I recounted that which I heard." You should know, however, as I rightly indicated, that the other tradition stated by Rava—that the world is six thousand parasangs—which according to our rabbis was rejected out of court, when understood properly, is correct and upheld by astronomers and principally by Ptolemy. In the fifth book of the *Almagest,* he speaks about the magnitudes of the sun, moon and earth. Rambam of blessed memory alludes to the passage when he says in the Laws of Oaths:[47] "It is well known to intelligent and learned scholars that the sun is 170 times larger the earth." In the introduction to the Order of Zera'im, he states with more precision that it is 166 and three-eighths larger than the earth.[48] Ptolemy states that the circumference of the earth is 5,650 parasangs—these are German miles which equal 22,600 Italian miles according to the version given by some of the commentators on his works.* According to Rambam's statement in the introduction cited above, both he and Ptolemy consider that the earth has a circumference of 24,000 miles that is equivalent to 6,000 parasangs exactly—there are four miles to the parasang as is known. Thus Rava's tradition is completely accurate in the view of those whom Rambam of blessed memory designated as "men of knowledge."

41. Samson of Chinon, *Sefer Keritut,* V, gate 3 (317).
42. B. B.B. 65a.
43. *Sefer Keritut* (367).
44. B. Shev. 16a.
45. B. Zev. 107b.
46. P. Yev. 1 (6) 3a.; B. Yev. 16a.
47. *Mishneh Torah,* Shev. V:22.
48. Introduction to *Perush* (68).

And even if you were to say that Rava was espousing the rabbinic view that the earth is flat, it does not matter in this case since he simply applied this tradition to a flat, rather than a circular surface. Then there is his other statement that the thickness of the heavens is 1,000 parasangs. Rava deduced this by his own reasoning from the first statement based on tradition,[49] and on the basis of the sages' hypotheses that the heavens are formed like a vault over the earth's surface, that the sphere is fixed, that the sun moves during the day below the heavens from east to west in a southerly direction and in the evening enters the thickness of the heavens as through a window, which on the basis of chapter 6 of Pirqe d'Rabbi Eliezer,[50] Rashi, and Rabbenu Tam cut out[51] for it[52] [i.e., the sun]. This is apparent from the passage in Pesaḥim with Rashi's explanation,[53] chapter 2 of Bava Batra,[54] and the end of chapter 2 of Shabbat which are cited by Ran [Rabbenu Nissim] of blessed memory.[55] All these notions are entirely foreign to the system of the fore-mentioned astronomers. You will certainly notice that in the first book of his work, Ptolemy provides proofs of the globality of the earth and of the sun's circuit during the day around one-half of the globe of the heavens above the earth and at night around the half of the globe beneath it. And you know that the author of the *Guide* upholds the view of the globality of the earth and thus has no need of opening up the windows of the heavens for the sun.[56] But although, according to the rabbis of blessed memory, the heavens are made out of the substance of water, they also state in Bereshit Rabbah:[57] "The [middle layer] of water solidified . . . [and on the second day] they congealed." And so you hear those commentators piercing the copper elevations of the heavens[58] and proliferating the arched windows of the sun as many as the days through which uninterruptedly, moving from position to position, it comes out and goes in, to give light to the world. They derive these ideas from Pirqe d'Rabbi Eliezer. Indeed, the author of the *Guide* writes: "Our sages certainly gave precedence to the view of the gentiles over their own opinion in matters of astronomy, for everyone who speaks of speculative matters does so [according to the conclusions to which he was led by his speculation]."[59] I discussed this in chapters 11 and 14. The two great luminaries, Rabbenu Sherira and his son Rabbenu Hai, world authorities, and other later sages, blessed be their memory, also rejected out of court the rabbinic statement that the heavens are like a vault, that the sphere is fixed, that the star revolves, and that the sun sinks and rises through the thickness of the heavens. This is discussed at length by Rabbi Moses al-Ashqar blessed be his memory in his responsum on twilight which I

49. I.e., the world is 6,000 parasangs.

50. In ch. 6 of PRE, there is a detailed description of the movements of the sun through the windows of the sky which are as numerous as the days of the solar year.

51. Cassel reads *qadmu* instead of *qar'u* as in the ed. pr.

52. 'Provided for it.' This is a play on Jer. 22:14: *I will build me a vast palace with spacious upper chambers cut out with windows.*

53. I.e., Rashi to B. Pes. 94a.

54. B. B.B. 25a–b.

55. Rabbenu Nissim to Alfasi Shabb.15a (to B. Shabb. 35b).

56. *Guide* I, ch. 73: "Now it has been demonstrated that the earth is spherical in form and that portions of the inhabited part of it lie at both extremities of its diameter."

57. B.R. 4:2 (26).

58. 'Copper elevations,' lit. copper mountains. Cf. Zech. 6:1.

59. *Guide* II, ch. 8.

also mentioned in chapter 11.[60] These considerations provide the intelligent person with proof as to how in secular matters, our rabbis could be made to change their opinion, even though they could defend themselves with the statement, "this is what we heard" when challenged by a convincing argument. For it does not constitute undermining and abrogation of the law of the Torah, God forbid. Thoughtful people would pay attention to their words for the sake of the requisite truth. The whole enterprise is for the honor of the Lord, the true, forever blessed, and eternal God.

(*[see p. 399] Examine Mauro's comments on the *Book of the Sphere*[61] and the *Margarita Philosophica*[62] and the *Silva de varia leçion*[63] which was translated into Italian from Spanish (part 3, chapter 20).[64])

END OF SECTION TWO

60. Moses ben Isaac al-Ashqar, *She'elot,* 96, 155b.

61. This is a reference to Johannes de Sacrobosco's *The Sphere.* Here he is referring to the commentary of Marco Mauro Fiorentino (1493–1556) with "una nuova e fedele traduttione" (a new and faithful translation) of the work entitled *Annotationi sopra la lettione della spera del Sacro Bosco,* 44–49. The author's dedicatory preface to Cosimo de' Medici is dated 1547.

62. Gregor Reisch, *Margarita Philosophica,* bk. VII, tract. 1, ch. 44, "De terrae rotunditate."

63. This is a reference to Pedro Mexía's *Selva di varia lettione (Silva de varia leçion),* which was translated several times into Italian.

64. In all the Italian versions that I consulted, the passage is to be found in pt. III, ch. 19.

SECTION THREE: DAYS OF THE WORLD

CHAPTER TWENTY-NINE

An investigation into the number of years that we count from creation: whether there should be any addition or subtraction of years.

Now if my kind God will come to my aid, I should like to examine and investigate the number of years that we count from the time of the creation. The chapters devoted to this subject have been assigned a separate section entitled "Days of the World." The object of this study is to get to the underlying truth of the matter and to discover whether there are well-defined proofs that provide us with grounds for adding to or subtracting from the computation. Now some of the figures for the period extending from remote antiquity to the second Temple period are clearly given in the Pentateuch and Prophets and are therefore undisputable. But because there is inadequate clarification with regard to some of the figures, many distinguished commentators of later generations were led to write on the subject, adducing opinions that were at variance with those of our rabbis. With God's help, this shall be clarified in chapter 35 and in the successive chapters. We have nothing new to say regarding the figures about which we are certain; and likewise, for the questionable figures, we are not going to make a fundamental contribution to the discussion, but simply state and briefly elucidate the views of the sages who preceded us. Alongside those commentators of blessed memory who were held to have been observers of the Torah and from whose waters we continually drink, we shall not desist from citing the opinions of two sages of antiquity who lived in the time of the second Temple: they were also members of our nation and originated from the source of Judah even though many of our own people had no knowledge of them. Thus, the sole object of this discourse is to cite the statements of others and not to adduce any original opinion of our own. Indeed, whatever criterion a person might wish to use in judging those participating in this debate[1] may undoubtedly be deemed appropriate. Now you shall hear from me, intelligent reader, the scope of their controversy, and where possible, I shall try to justify the views of all parties, particularly those of our rabbis. In any event, regardless of whatever increases or subtractions that will be made to the aera mundi computation, we shall always retain it: the custom of the ancestors of Israel has the status of Torah as in bygone days. Indeed there will be justification of the said disputants, and even justification of the disputant whose position, according to speculative thinkers, is of the lowest consideration. Opposition to anything related to the

1. This is a play on Is. 65:7.

laws of the Torah is far from the object of this investigation, nor will anything be proposed that would mar the honor of our rabbis, may they rest in peace. This has already been demonstrated in the previous chapters, and with God's help, a sun of truth will shine upon it in the forthcoming chapters.[2] Before the close of this section, there will be clarification and elucidation as to how the method adopted by our rabbis of blessed memory for the computation of the years was based on outstanding wisdom, the magnitude of which any intelligent person would know and acknowledge. The fact is that from the very outset I can imagine you saying to yourself, kind reader, that this investigation is a type of *halakhah* suitable for messianic times or of an even lesser significance. For what relevance does it hold for us; after all, what happened, happened thousands of years ago or seven times again. But you could answer your own objection once you take into consideration the following points. First, the truth itself which is the quest of thousands of sages in investigations more obscure than this one is in fact like a seal of the true God,[3] the characteristic of the beautiful soul, and the good to which all aspire.[4] Secondly, and more important is that in the course of this investigation we shall happen to gain understanding of the meaning of certain passages in holy Writ. You are already aware as to how the rabbis of blessed memory regarded messianic *halakhah*. For in their discussion of the validity of sacrifices,[5] a priest's daughter who transgresses the sexual laws,[6] and about the order in which Moses clothed Aaron in his vestments[7] which nowadays has no relevance to us and is of no importance, they encourage such study and investigation either for the purpose of clarifying Scripture or for the purpose of "expounding and receiving reward." We shall illustrate this further, if the Lord is pleased with us, in our discussion of the priestly vestments in chapter 46 in section 4. The third reason for undertaking the investigation is not devoid of importance—for in the process of the debate, *halakhah* relevant to the time of the Messiah will be explained correctly, and according to many distinguished persons, this time is imminent.[8] It seems to us that the subject is profitable and worthy of discussion today, as will be shown, God willing, in chapter 43, inasmuch as we will be able to remove a stumbling block from the path of our people. In view of these three points in particular (quite apart from the other things that will emerge in the course of this study), I evaluate this subject not only permissible and open for discussion, but also a religious duty that deserves a reward from our bountiful God.

2. Cf. Mal. 3:20.

3. Cf. B. Shabb. 55a; Yoma 69b; Sanh. 64a: "The seal of the Holy One blessed be He is truth."

4. R. Bonfil ("How Golden," 98) has described this statement as revolutionary in that "de' Rossi in his own way was affirming the relevance of history to the definition of the cultural identity of the self." I would stress that by combining the Neoplatonic idea of the beautiful soul with the rabbinic concept of the divine nature of truth, de' Rossi is enhancing the significance of his work despite all his protestations that Torah study is of paramount importance. On this, see also translator's introduction.

5. B. Zev. 44b–45a. The discussion regards a priest who intended to eat the flesh of a sacrifice in the Temple court at the wrong time. The issue, according to one view, is described as "messianic halakhah," but it is nevertheless justified by the slogan "study and receive reward."

6. B. Sanh. 51b. The passage regards the type of capital punishment meted out to the priest's daughter who transgresses the sexual laws. Since the Sanhedrin had no powers of implementing capital punishment, the discussion was regarded as having no practical relevance and only applicable in messianic times.

7. B. Yoma 5b. The discussion pertains to the order in which Moses clothed Aaron in the priestly vestments. It was regarded as of only academic value since "what is past is past." In the messianic era, however, Moses would know how to perform this duty.

8. He is alluding to Jewish messianic speculation regarding the year 1575 which he combats in ch. 43.

As we demonstrated at length in chapter 2, it is evident that the testimony of any gentile writer may be used in secular matters, particularly in an investigation such as this which has already been declared to have no bearing on the observance of any law or precept. And we consider it appropriate to rely on their testimony, particularly when they speak impartially, having no vested interests in the issue at stake. If, therefore, we come across an account of an event of the past relevant to this study, the testimony of various writers among the scholars of all the various nationalities and tongues who, in order to attain fame, studied, elaborated, and recorded these events as they happened with no ulterior motive but to inform the world about these events, it would occur to one that an intelligent person may allow their evidence be disseminated among the array of the reports and establish our position on the basis of their statements. If, as when an opportunity is given to fulfill a religious precept, their purpose was also to fulfill to the best of their ability the words of the saints who though dead still live on,[9] there would be no disgrace in giving the words of these writers some consideration; for the intelligent person would notice that they contain most attractive features which strike the eye. However, we should draw a distinction between these people and the sages of blessed memory to whom we ought to give priority because, for us, their position is paramount. Thus we shall refuse to listen to them when they are sole propounders of an opinion. When we embark on an investigation based primarily on our holy Writ, their statements ought to be taken into account. They would be regarded as an ally in Judea,[10] for, as is discussed in the first chapter of Qiddushin, they will be in the category of a practice based primarily on Scripture.[11] We shall adopt this method particularly when by means of such a comparison, we shall receive illumination and therefore be able to clarify and elucidate certain problematic passages that we encounter in regard to the true and righteous prophets. In his second [first] book of *Against Apion,*[12] Josephus already wrote that we are shown weighty indication of the truth of a story when different writers of various nationalities and writing in diverse languages give a unanimous and identical report. In the seventh book of the *Ethics,* the "philosopher" [i.e., Aristotle] puts forward a similar view. He writes that the voice which is heard by various assemblies of people does not completely disappear.[13] Consequently, while the entire investigation is based on the mountains of holy Writ and the words of our prophets,[14] as will become evident to every reader, I have assembled a band of world

9. This is an allusion to the passage (B. Ber. 18a) cited earlier: "The righteous though dead are called living."

10. 'Ally in Judah.' This expression occurs in Zech. 9:7 in regard to the inclusion of the neighbouring gentiles within Judah.

11. De' Rossi's rhetoric combines the verse from Zechariah in which Judah is mentioned and B. Qidd. 6a in which the expression occurs: "And [may the local custom of] Judea be used to add to Scripture?" His purpose is to demonstrate that the evidence of gentiles or those outside rabbinic tradition may only be adduced in support of Scripture (or a rabbinic view), but not when it reflects an independent opinion.

12. *Contra Apionem* I, 26. The Latin translation of Gelenius which de' Rossi used reads: "Verae siquidem historiae indicium est si de eisdem rebus omnes eadem dicant atque conscribant."

13. De' Rossi appears to be referring to the *Nicomachean Ethics* 7, 1153b25–30 where Aristotle quotes Hesiod: "The rumor that flies through all people from man to man, is a thing divine and never wholly dies." De' Rossi has taken the passage out of context. Aristotle is using the quotation to prove that pleasure is sought by all men and animals, which is an indication that pleasure is the highest good.

14. 'Based on . . . mountains,' an allusion to Ps. 87:1.

historians before engaging in the main body of the subject.[15] These also include two ancient writers of Jewish origin, who wrote in Greek. It may be that this was the reason that there is no reference to them by our Babylonian rabbis.[16] I have started my discourse with these writers because they have a separate status.[17] They are five in number and will be given either a brief or prominent part in this study. They lived in antiquity, not in modern times, in the Temple period or close to the time of its destruction. Listed in chronological order they are: Xenophon the Greek[18] who, according to the *Chronicle* of Eusebius of Caesarea, lived in the lifetime of Artaxerxes Memonon, one of the eleven Persian kings—this shall be elucidated further at a later stage; Metasthenes the Persian[19] who lived in the time of Seleuco the Greek whom scholars call Seleucus, one of the four rulers who came to the throne after Alexander; Yedidyah the Alexandrian (Philo) who was of Jewish stock—we gave a description of the man previously. He defended the Jews before the Emperor Gaius [Caligula]; Josephus the Jew who saw our affliction[20] and the Christian Eusebius of Caesarea who lived in the time of the emperor Constantine. These were all renowned writers. You will be informed as to their relevance to our investigation. As regards the conclusions and general points that emerge from their statements, wherever a fundamental view is a bone of contention among them or contraverts one letter of holy Writ, it shall be suppressed and we shall not pay any attention to it. But where there is unanimity of opinion such that it cannot be disproved on the basis of the works of the prophets, or if one of them happens to provide us with adequate clarification such that we can resolve a problematic passage, you, reader, being a man of intelligence, should be prepared to accept it. For although we do not rely on them, their accounts most certainly contain something of substance, as we said from the very outset. It is known that many of our commentators, including the compiler of the *Arukh,* under the entry for *sv*ʿ[21] Rabbenu Saadiah, ibn Ezra, Ramban [Nahmanides], Kimḥi, and Don Isaac [Abravanel] cited Josephus and other non-Jewish writers as support for their views particularly on the subject of the second Temple with regard to the prophecies of Haggai, Zechariah, Malachi, Daniel, and Ezra. Thus reasonable people would have no justification in despising our enterprise, given that we have also devised a system by which we approve or reject the views of those people, and particularly since it is undertaken in the quest of truth and for the sake of heaven.

Now it is an accepted and established fact that the number of years reckoned from creation according to the Pentateuch, and likewise that which is explicitly shown in the post-Mosaic works of the prophets, Moses' successors, who recorded historical events,

15. 'Main body of the subject,' lit. with the thick bossed of its shields. Cf. Job 15:26.

16. Cf. his statement in ch. 40 that the rabbis of the Talmud had not read Philo and Josephus either because they were unable to read Greek or because "they did not believe in them."

17. De' Rossi appears to be forced to justify that he has given precedence to the historians over the scriptural and rabbinic material.

18. Xenophon d. 359 B.C.E.

19. Metasthenes is one of the forgeries of Annius of Viterbo. See ch. 31, n. 1.

20. He deliberately uses the expression in Lam. 3:1 *I am the man who saw affliction* which refers to the destruction of the first Temple, and he uses it with regard to Josephus who lived in the time of the destruction of the second Temple.

21. *Arukh,* s.v. *sw*ʿ. He refers to Joseph ben Gorion who writes about the many battles the Jews fought in the time of the second Temple.

may not be submitted to any examination or investigation. All this is true and correct and how can an inferior human being question the King our God?[22] But this does not pertain to the period of years which was not recorded under divine inspiration. Rather, individual sages throughout the ages, who were not eyewitnesses of the events, informed and set out for us that which they had heard from the ancients. We have already justified their case and will do so further. But in addition, it is recognized that in times of upheaval and when differences of opinion become a matter of concern, certain errors and disorder may arise. Thus experts would have good reason to work in this area; one would set about to refine and correct[23] in the knowledge that a colleague would also come to investigate his research. Such must be the case with all human study and research until it please God to fill the world with knowledge so that the truth is not a matter for doubt or wanting. Of course, as was said, if some of the figures reckoned from creation as proposed by our rabbis were actually in the category of orally transmitted Sinaitic tradition, we would not allow an alien to enter the discussion, while the sinner who would vainly pontificate on the matter would harm himself. Any member of our people would be justified and have the right to force him to bow his head like a bulrush[24] in submission to them and their verdict. Cursed is he who would not support them or regard their behavior as iniquitous. But as regards the number of years recorded in the Pentateuch, the Prophets, and later texts, the only means capable people had at their disposal for the computation was as human chronologers since the Holy Spirit had ceased to function in the time of the second Temple. Thus Rabbi Simeon ben Gamaliel as is stated in Bereshit Rabbah lamented the fact that they were unable to make use of it in his lifetime.[25] Now should we wish, as is appropriate, to allocate part of the glory of our God to those that fear Him [i.e., the rabbis], one might claim that if all the gentile sages were on one side of the balance and one of them were on the other, he would outweigh them all. And yet the gate [of this chapter] is not closed; the righteous may enter and see whether the prophetical books contain anything which would call into question that which they had received and had transmitted to us. For then it would be our duty to investigate and search out a solution, applying correct methods and not useless tools[26] in order to ensure that faithfulness and truth are met.

But now let us resume our presentation of the five aforementioned sages. You, reader, will correctly notice that since the texts of Metasthenes and Yedidyah are short, I have not refrained from translating them in the form that they are. In fact, some of the details that are not relevant to this study may have relevance for some other topic in the rest of the book, or for another subject that might occur to you. But I found it sufficient to use the grapes of the other three sages as data for this study[27] and to press them into a synopsis as I thought appropriate. Now you, who are blessed of the Lord, incline your ear and listen to what they have to say.

22. 'What . . . king,' lit. what is man that comes after the king. Cf. Eccl. 2:12.
23. 'One would set . . . correct,' lit. he shall sit like a smelter and purger. Cf. Mal. 3:3.
24. 'Like a bulrush,' cf. Is. 58:5.
25. B.R. 37:7 (349).
26. 'Useless tools,' lit. empty vessels. Cf. B. A.Z. 37b.
27. 'Grapes . . . study.' This is a play on Deut. 32:32 *Anavemo inve rosh—their grapes are grapes of poison* which is transformed by de' Rossi into *Anavemo inve derush.*

CHAPTER THIRTY

Data from the works of Xenophon the Greek regarding the two kings of Persia called Cyrus.

XENOPHON the Greek wrote two long works which were recently translated into Latin.[1] The first book deals with Cyrus the first who captured Babylon;[2] the other book concerns Cyrus the second.[3] At the beginning of the first book, he wrote that Cyrus the first was son of Cambyses, the king of Persia, and that his mother, called Mandane, was daughter of Astyages, king of Media.[4] Throughout the eight books of this work he is highly complimentary about Cyrus. He describes how he captured Babylon in one night when the king had become drunk during the celebration of a Babylonian feast day, and speaks about his conquest of many other countries. At the end of book 8, he wrote that the borders of Cyrus's realm extended from the Persian Sea in the east to the Pontus Euxinus in the north, to Cyprus and Egypt in the west, and to Ethiopia in the south.[5] He describes how Cyrus would spend the seven winter months in Babylon because of its salubrious climate, the three spring months in Susa, and the two summer months in Ectabana. In his old age he returned to the cities of Persia[6] where his parents had been buried. One night, in the seventh year of his reign, a form of more than human proportions appeared to him while he was still asleep and called to him by name and said: "Prepare yourself, for in a short while you shall go to the gods." When he awoke from his sleep, he summoned his children and friends and addressed them in fine and appropriate terms on the subject of the vicissitudes of time, right action, the immortality of the soul, and on the benefits and pleasure that ensue when brothers live together in peace.[7] He had two sons—the elder was called Cambyses, the younger Tanaozares [Tanaoxares]. He decreed that the first-born son was to be his successor and he gave gifts and incomes to the second son as was appropriate to his station. He then expired and died. According to Xenophon, his sons did not emulate

1. The Latin translation of Xenophon's *Opera omnia* (undertaken by humanists such as Francesco Filelfo) was first published in Basel, 1534.

2. I.e., the *Cyropaedia.*

3. I.e., the *Anabasis.*

4. *Cyropaedia* I, II, 1.

5. Ibid. VIII, VIII, 1.

6. The Latin translation reads "in Persas." It may be that de' Rossi's translation 'cities of Persia' is a reference to Persepolis.

7. This is a brief synopsis of the contents of the long speech of Cyrus.

the ways of their father. Quarrels broke out between them and there was a gradual decline in all the virtuous standards of behavior which had characterized the Persian nation during Cyrus's lifetime. In the final chapter of the book, he occasionally calls the son who was on the throne by the name of Artaxerxes, which was a royal title as we wrote at the beginning of chapter 18. Thus he says that in the time of Artaxerxes, the people had become addicted to pleasures and wine.[8]

In his other work on Cyrus the second, he wrote that Darius had two sons from his wife Parysatis: the elder was called Artaxerxes, the second, Cyrus.[9] Realizing that his death was imminent, he decreed that Artaxerxes should take the throne. Some time after he [i.e., Artaxerxes] had come to the throne, one of his courtiers brought him a slanderous report about his brother Cyrus, alleging that he wanted to take his life. He imprisoned Cyrus and would have had him put to death were it not for the intervention of his mother who saved him. When Cyrus came out of prison, he endeavored to gain the favor of the people. He killed the king his brother and ruled in peace and quiet.[10] This is what Xenophon had to say.

The essential part of my translation regards the Persian kings and will be used in the discussion of the problems related to their number and sequence. It also supplies information that the Artaxerxes mentioned in Ezra (4:7) *And in the time of Artaxerxes [Bishlam, Mithredath, Tabeel, and the rest of their colleagues wrote to King Artaxerxes of Persia],* who wrote a letter of indictment at the request of his courtiers, ought to be identified with Artaxerxes, the base son of Cyrus the first, whom he mentioned. This Artaxerxes and the Ahasuerus mentioned in the preceding verse [v.6) ruled between the reigns of Cyrus the first and Darius who is mentioned in verse 5. These then are the four kings. Furthermore, on the basis of his account, one must give consideration to Artaxerxes, the son of King Darius, and to his successor, Cyrus the second. It may be that he is to be identified with the Cyrus king of Persia mentioned at the beginning of chapter 10 of Daniel.[11] Thus, even according to a plain reading of Scripture, and discounting the Darius who built the Temple and any other king who may have succeeded him, there must have been more than four kings of Persia. And the statement, *Persia will have three more kings* (Dan. 11:2) can sustain the interpretation which will be applied to it, as you shall discover in chapter 38. Nevertheless, as was said, it shall not constitute the basis of our proof. As for the conclusions that may possibly be drawn from the next four writers, these should be sought in chapters 35 following.

8. *Cyropaedia* VIII, VIII, 12–15.
9. *Anabasis* I, 1.
10. Ibid. I, 1, 1–6.
11. *In the third year of King Cyrus of Persia, an oracle was revealed to Daniel who was called Belteshazzar.*

CHAPTER THIRTY-ONE

Metasthenes the Persian: *On the Order of the Times*[1]

METASTHENES the Persian wrote a short work *On the Order of the Times* which together with the works of Berosus the Chaldean was recently translated into Latin and annotated by the Christian scholar Annius.[2] Metasthenes writes as follows:

> Whoever wishes to write about chronology ought not to follow popular hearsay or the opinion of one of the ancients. For when they, in like fashion to the Greeks, write from such a perspective, they must surely deceive both themselves and others, and remain unenlightened all their life.[3] But we would avoid all error if we familiarize ourselves with and follow the annals of the world-ruling kingdoms[4] and ban all the other written documents on the grounds that they are unreliable.[5] For these chronicles contain such truthful and clear exposition of the course of history and the succession of kings such that the facts of their rule are well known.[6] Furthermore, not all the chroniclers of the kingdoms are acceptable.[a] The only trustworthy writers are the priests of the kingdoms who were privy to the true facts, both public and secret, of all events in their history. Such a person was Berosus. He was Chaldean and wrote an entire history of the Assyrians according to the arrangement set out in the ancient annals. It is for this reason that we Persians follow him exclusively.[7]
>
> He wrote that prior to Ninus, three kings who were called gods[b] ruled in the world over a period of 249 years. The first to rule over the universe was Ogyges (their name for Noah).

1. This is de' Rossi's translation of the forgery of the Annius of Viterbo. De' Rossi does not give an exact translation for Annius's title for the work *De Iudicio Temporum* (*On the Appraisal of the Times*). I can find no reason for his translation. Perhaps he was unable to find an equivalent Hebrew word to express the sense of "iudicium." In his commentary to his Metasthenes, Annius asserts that *De Censura Temporum* would be a more appropriate title for the work since it is above all an emendation of incorrect chronology. For a discussion of the principles articulated in the first part of the text, see A. Grafton, *Forgers,* 104–7.

2. Annius framed his forgeries with commentaries which corroborated the fictitious material. Annius claimed to have acquired the Berosus texts from two Armenians and to have discovered the other texts in Mantua. With surprising uniformity, all these texts were preserved in Latin.

3. The Latin reads: "et per omnem vitam aberrent" (they are in error all their life).

4. 'World-ruling kingdoms.' Annius reads: "duarum monarchiarum" (of the two kingdoms).

5. 'Unreliable.' Annius writes "ut fabulatores" (as fable-spinners).

6. Annius writes: "Vere digesta sunt tempora Reges et nomina quam apud eos splendissime regnatum est." (For these contain the dates, kings, and names set out as clearly and truthfully as their kings ruled splendidly.)

7. Annius writes "solum vel maxime" (exclusively or above all).

He was in power at the time of the deluge. He was succeeded by Saturn (their name for Nimrod) who founded the land of Babylon and he reigned there for 56 years. He was succeeded by his son Belus Jove who ruled 62 years. He was succeeded by his son Ninus, the first monarch, who ruled for 52 years. Then Semirames ruled for 42 years; Sameis, 38 years; Arius, 30 years; Aralius, 40 years; Xerxes Baleus, 30 years; Armatrites, 38 years; Bel Ochus the first, 35 years; Baleus the second, 42 years;[8] Altadas, 32 years; Mamitus, 30 years; Mancaleus, 30 years; Spherus, 20 years; Mamelus, 30 years; Sparetus, 40 years; Ascatades, 40 years; Amyntes, 45 years; Bel Ochus the second, 25 years; Bellepares, 30 years; Lamprides, 32 years;[9] Teuteus, 40 years; Tineus, 30 years; Dercylus, 40 years; Eupales, 38 years; Laosthenes, 45 years; Prythydias, 30 years; Ofrateus, 20 years; Ofraganeus, 50 years; Ascrazapes, 42 years; Tonosconcoleros, 15 years. He was called Sardanapalus by the Greeks.

This is the information supplied by Berosus whose authority we follow, and we do not rely on any other writer—only the public records found in the archives of Susa. From Persian annals it is evident that there was a Bel Ochus the third, captain of Sardanapalus's army, who secretly plotted against Sardanapalus. This Bel Ochus divided up the entire kingdom with Arbace who was king of the Medes at the time. He set the condition that he Bel Ochus should rule over Babylon and Arbace over Media and Persia. Thus, when Sardanapalus had been killed—his body flung into the flames[10]—the kingdom was divided in two.

The following kings ruled Media over a period of 304 years: Arbaces, 28 years; Mandanes, 50 years; Sosarmon, 30 years; Arti Carmin, 50 years; Arbianes, 22 years; Arceus, 40 years; Artines [Attines], 22 years; Astybarus with his son Apanda, 20 years; Apanda as sole ruler, 30 years. After defeating Apanda, Cyrus and Darius ruled 36 years. Before the reunification of the kingdom, they reigned together for 6 years over Persia. They then appointed the son Cambyses over Persia for a further 6 years while they waged war against Tamyra queen of the Scythians.[c] In the sixth year, they were summoned by the Babylonians and they killed Belshazar [Baltassar] and the reunited kingdom was restored to the Persians.

For the duration of the period of the partition of the kingdom, the Babylonians also had their own dynasty:

First Bel Ochus, 48 years; Phul Assar, 25 years; Salman Assar, 17 years; Sennacherib, 7 years; Assar Adon, 10 years; Merodach, 52 years; Ben Merodach, 21 years; Nebuchadnezzar [Nabuchodnozor] the first,[d] 35 years; Nebuchadnezzar the Great, 45 years; Amilinus Evil Merodach, 30 years; his eldest son Regassar, 3 years; his second son Lab Assar Dach, 6 years; his third son Belshazar [Baltassar], 5 years. After Belshazar had been killed, Cyrus and Darius ruled together for 2 years. Cyrus then ruled alone for 22 years. Ahasuerus Artaxerxes, the elder son of Darius, ruled 20 years. He wreaked vengeance on the Tamyrican people for treacherously handing over his uncle into the power of the queen of Tamyra. Ahasuerus had two sons, Cyrus Artabanus and Darius Longimanus.[e] They contended for the kingdom for seven months, and in the seventh month, Darius Longimanus overpowered his brother and then ruled for 37 years. He was succeeded by his son Darius Nothus who ruled for 19 years. He was succeeded by Darius Menon, that is, Artaxerxes the Great, who ruled for 55 years. He was succeeded by Artaxerxes Ochus who ruled for 26 years. In our own time, Arses ruled 4 years; Darius the last, 6 years; Alexander of Macedon who transferred the empire into the hands of the Greeks ruled for 12 years;

8. Fifty-three years (not forty-two).
9. Here he omits Panias 45 years; Sofarmis 19 years; Mytreus 24 years; Tautanius 32 years.
10. The Latin reads: "Itque interfecto et ex ipso [i.e., Belochus] flammis iniecto Sardanapalo."

Seleucus Nicanor who is presently in the thirtieth year of his reign is king of the whole of Asia and Syria.

This is the text of Metasthenes.

[De' Rossi's notes to text of Metasthenes]

a. Josephus makes a similar statement with regard to Jewish records pertaining to the time of the Sanhedrin,[11] and this may also be gathered from the statement of Yedidyah the Alexandrian in his work *On the Times* which is translated in the following chapter.

b. This may help to explain the expression *And the sons of God saw* (Gen. 6:2).

c. They are the Amazons.

d. In the first book of *Against Apion,* Josephus calls Nebuchadnezzar the first, Nabulassar.[12] It was Nebuchadnezzar the second who destroyed the Temple. In book 10 (towards the end of chapter 11) of the *Antiquities,*[13] he also refers to both Nebuchadnezzars and he, too, derived his information from Berosus and other writers.[14]

e. His hand was long, thus the appellation, Longimanus.

11. *Ant.* XX:261. Josephus speaks of preserving accurate records, but does not refer to the Sanhedrin.

12. *Contra Apionem* I, 131ff. The Greek text reads "Nabopalassar."

13. *Ant.* X:220–21.

14. Indeed, Josephus's praise of Berosus for following the most ancient records guided Annius in his invention of Metasthenes' statement on rules for evaluating the authenticity of documents.

CHAPTER THIRTY-TWO

The Book of the Times by Yedidyah the Alexandrian [Philo] which was translated from Greek into Latin and from the Latin version it is now translated into the holy tongue[1]

HERE is presented the text of Yedidyah the Alexandrian's work entitled *On the Times.*

From Adam to the flood is 1,652 years.

From the flood to Abraham is 292 years.

From Abraham to Moses is 425 years.

From Moses to the exodus of Israel from Egypt and the initiation of the wooden Tabernacle[2] is 80 years.

From the Tabernacle to the initiation of the stone Temple in the fourth year of Solomon's reign and to David's mandate concerning the succession of his sons is 480 years. When quarrels broke out among the sons born to David by Bathsheba as to who should be his successor (their names are listed in 2Sam. 5[3] and 1Chr. 3), he [David] decreed that the youngest should rule first and should the youngest die without offspring, the brother nearest to him in age should reign in his stead. Thus Solomon, the youngest, was the first to reign. The crown was then to have been transferred to Nathan who, by reason of age, was next in the line of succession. He was called Ahiasar [brother of the prince] and Mathat[4] (1K. 4:6), and his sons were called Ahiasarim and Mathatim because they were all brothers of the prince and destined to rule. Subsequently, until the time of Jehoshaphat and Ahaziah, the descendants of Nathan were always designated Ahiasarim The men who were murdered by Jehoram were descendants of Nathan (*He [Jehoram] had brothers, sons of Jehoshaphat: Azariah, Jehiel, Zechariah, Azariahu, Michael, and Shephatiah; all these were sons of King Jehoshaphat of Israel* [2Chr. 21:1]). They had been honored by Jehoshaphat the father of Jehoram in excess of the mandate of his father, and they were called the "sons of Jehoshaphat" and "brothers of Jehoram." Similarly, the children of those[a] whom Jehoram had allowed to remain part of the tribe of Judah, while withholding their right to an income, were called "sons and brothers of Ahaziah," despite the fact that Ahaziah was Jehoram's only son and the sole remaining descendant of Solomon. Thus after his murder,

1. This is also a forgery of Annius of Viterbo. The work was entitled *Breviarium de Temporibus* and purports to give a complete chronology of all four monarchies of Persia, Babylon, Greece, and Rome.

2. The Latin reads: "Inchoatum templum ligneum."

3. De' Rossi gives the reference as 2 Kings; he is actually following the LXX's titles of the books whereby 2 Samuel is called 2 Kings.

4. The name Mathat does not appear in the Hebrew Bible but does appear in Luke 3:24, *Joseph son of Heli, son of Mathat, son of Levi.*

Athaliah attempted to extirpate all the Ahiasarim who were in line to the throne. But due to the deliberations of Jehoshabat, Ahaziah's sister, the youngest of the Ahiasarim who was called Eli or Eliakim, was saved—the names Eli, Eliakim, and Jehoiakim are interchangeable in the language of the Arameans[b] and Egyptians. Called Eli in his youth, he was Joash the first, of Davidic stock, and a surviving descendant of Nathan. For him, the choristers of the right and left groups sung the psalm indicated as number 74 in the Septuagint (it is 75 in our text). It was arranged at the behest of Jehoiada[c] as a plea to God not to exterminate the descendants of the Davidic dynasty once Solomon's line had come to an end. From the time of Joash onwards, kings were designated by two or even three names. Accordingly, the first was called Eli, Joash, and Simeon. Likewise Er was called Manasseh and Hezekiah, Jeshua, and there are other such examples. From the fourth year of Solomon's reign until the end of his line and the succession of the first of the Ahaiasarim called Joash, was a period of 138 years. Indeed, from Joash until the voluntary exile of Jehoram was a period of 291 years. These include the 10 years when Amon reigned while his father Er Manasseh had been taken captive.[5]

From the exile of Jehoiachin until the destruction of the Temple was a period of 11 years. Twenty years elapsed from the destruction of the Temple until the imprisonment of Joiachin, and 31 years from the time of his exile. In the course of the next 6 years, Psalm 87 was published (it is 88 in our text), and at the end of the seventh year, Evil Merodach released Joiachin from prison and paid him respect. The people called him Neri [my light] because he had kindled the lamp of David whose extinction they had feared.[6] Psalm 88 (89 in our text) was then published as thanksgiving to God and as a prayer for the welfare of the people and the triumphant ascendacy of their Messiah. Soon after Neri had been liberated, he was given a son by divine grace, Meshezebal called Shealtiel, who, 17 years prior to the end of the Babylonian exile, begot Berechiah. Seventeen years after the end of the Babylonian exile, this Berechiah became leader of the people. In deference to his position, he was renamed Zerubbabel (i.e., "this one who is great in Babylon") in the eighty-first year since the Babylonian exile, 70 years after the destruction [of the Temple]. There were two systems of government of the people: there were the princes of the Houses of David and there were the priests from the tribe of Levi who each wielded separate powers until the Hasmonean period. This was recorded in writing by seventy of our elders in the following manner: Jeshua son of Jehozadak the high priest with Berechiah Zerubbabel son of Meshezebel son of Neri, that is, Joiachin, came to Jerusalem in the first year of Cyrus's reign. In the second year they laid the foundations [of the Temple] by dictate of the prophets Haggai and Zechariah, but its erection was delayed as a result of the death of Darius Hystaspes, and he was unable to come to Darius[7] because he was engaged in the war with the Tamyricans. After Cyrus had been killed, Ahasuerus Artaxerxes the first came to the throne. He was waging war against Artaxat, who had come to the aid of the Tamyricans and who was inciting the Assyrians, Medes, and Persians to revolt. Ahasuerus's seat of government was in Babylon. When the leaders of the land of Syria filed a document of indictment against the Jews, Jeshua entrusted the high priesthood to his son Joiakim Eli—this was in the twelfth year of Ahasuerus's reign—and betook himself to

5. The first book of the *Breviarium* ends here.

6. De' Rossi seems to have emended the Latin text in order to make sense of the etymology. The text reads "Heri" (not Neri) which is not a Hebrew word. But the names Neri and Er do appear in the list of Joseph's lineage in Luke 3:27ff. which is mentioned by Annius in his commentary who himself refers to Neri and not to Heri.

7. De' Rossi's translation is confusing. The text reads (405): "nec adiri potuit Cyrus."

Ahasuerus who, however, refused to give him a hearing because he was engaged in warfare. Having won the battle, he was informed of the beheading of Holofernes, the captain of the army,[d] by the Jews and issued a decree forbidding the rebuilding of the Temple. After his death he was survived by his two sons who jockeyed for power. In the seventh month, Darius the Longhanded who had sworn to abrogate the edict of his father won the struggle by divine agency[8] and became king. In the first year of his reign, Jeshua the high priest returned to Jerusalem and by dictate of the prophets Haggai and Zechariah undertook to build the Temple. Thus Jeshua served his first term as high priest and he remained in this office 36 years.[9] He wrote about the exploits[e] of Judith and instituted an annual commemoration of the liberation. After his return in the twentieth year of the reign of Darius the longhanded, he once again served as high priest and remained in office for 20 years. He was 130 years old at the time when the high priesthood reverted to his son Joiakim who officiated for 48 years until the twelfth year of the reign of Ahasuerus Artaxerxes the Great. It was he who wrote the scroll of Esther and instituted Purim at the exhortation of Mordechai who sent him letters to that effect. Mordechai lived 18 years longer than Isaac.[f] The third incumbent of the high priesthood was Eliashib who ministered for 21 years up to the thirty-third year of the reign of Artaxerxes the Great. He was the first to conceive the idea of building the sheep gate (2Ezra, 3)[10] in Jerusalem. The fourth high priest was Joiada who ministered 23 years (another version reads 24). Jonathan also officiated 23 years and his office lasted until the end of the reign of Ochus Artaxerxes. The sixth and last high priest to serve under the Persians was Jaddua who officiated for 10 years.

These were the princes of the dynasty of the House of Nathan: Simeon also called Joash was the first to govern He was succeeded by Levi also called Amaziah. He was succeeded by Jeshua also called Hezekiah. He was succeeded by Er also called Manasseh. These princes reigned before the exile. After the exile, the first to rule was Zerubbabel whose reign lasted for 58 years. He was succeeded by Resa Meshullam for 66 years. After him Johanan son of Resa Meshullam reigned for 53 years. He was succeeded by Judah called Hyrcanus the first for 14 years.

These were the high priests who officiated from the time of Alexander until the Hasmoneans, namely, until Judah: Onias the first ministered 27 years; Simeon the first ministered 13 years;[g] Eleazar the enemy of Antiochus Theos[h] ministered 20 years; Manasseh the friend of Seleucus Gallinicus ministered 27 years. Simeon the righteous who was honored by Antiochus the Great ministered 28 years. Onias his son in whose lifetime Seleucus[i] plundered the Temple, ministered 39 years. He was succeeded by Judah the Maccabee.

The princes of the House of David who governed until the time of the aforementioned Judah were as follows: Joseph the first, 7 years; Avner Shammai, 11 years; Eli Mattatiah, 12 years; Asar Maat, 9 years; Nagid Artaxat, 10 years; Haggai Eli, 8 years; Maslut Nahum, 7 years; Amos Sirach, 14 years; Mattatiah Siloah, 10 years; Joseph the second Arses who was honored by Ptolemy, 60 years; Jannaeus, that is, Hyrcanus the second, 16 years. The Hasmoneans then came to power and took over both the government of the House of David as well as the high priesthood—this action aroused jealousy and enmity. Judah the

8. 'Won the struggle by divine agency.' The Latin reads "victoria cessit." De' Rossi has given the text a theological overtone using a phrase from Is. 45:17.

9. De' Rossi omits the statement "Ioakin filius in eius absentia annis VIII."

10. By 2 Ezra, de' Rossi is referring to the book of Nehemiah, once again using Christian designations of the books of the Bible.

Hasmonean who took up the sword against Antiochus the illustrious (i.e., Epiphanes which is rendered *illuster* in Latin), his son Eupator and also Demetrius ruled for 5 years. His brother Jonathan ruled for 19 years; and Simeon who was granted tax immunity by Antiochus Sidetes ruled for 8 years. Johanan Hyrcanus the first ruled for 26 years; Aristobulus for 1 year; Jannaeus Alexander for 27 years; his wife Alexandra for 9 years; Hyrcanus the last for 34 years. The latter Hyrcanus was captured by the Parthians while his wife, daughter, and his son Aristobulus were left behind. Then the Romans decreed against the wishes of the Jews that Herod should rule as tyrant.[11] Herod married the daughter of Hyrcanus who had been taken captive by the Parthians and in an effort to win over the Jews declared that Aristobulus, Hyrcanus's son, should officiate as high priest. His wife, Hyrcanus's daughter, bore him two sons. In the twenty-sixth year of his tyranny, he came to hear that his father-in-law had returned to his people and that the Jews were greeting him in the manner appropriate to one who had formerly been their ruler. So he killed his father-in-law, mother-in-law, their daughter (his wife), and the two sons she had born him. He also killed Aristobulus the high priest and persecuted the Jews excessively in the subsequent two years. In the thirtieth year of his tyranny, he murdered the Sanhedrin who belonged to the House of David and selected a recorder and Sanhedrin from the remnant of the people,[12] who appeared to possess very great learning. He also murdered Salome, his sister, and her husband who was of the tribe of Judah.[13] At this point the Jews who were weary from their struggle against him, voluntarily offered him the kingdom and swore allegiance not only to him but also to his successors. This Herod of Ashkelon[14] ruled tyrannically for 31 years and with permission of the Jews, for a further 6 years. He was succeeded by his son Archelaus who reigned 9 years. He was succeeded by Herod Tetrarch[j] who ruled for 24 years. In the twenty-first year of his rule I, Yedidyah the Alexandrian, a mere youth, was despatched from Alexandria to plead the cause of my Jewish brethren.[k] Agrippa the first succeeded this Herod for 7 years. He was succeeded by Agrippa the second for 27 years. He was succeeded by Agrippinus who was the last Agrippa who has ruled for 30 years up to this year of my old age.

This is the text of Yedidyah.

[De' Rossi's notes to Yedidyah's text]

a. In 4 Kings[15] (10:14) it is Jehu who kills forty [forty-two] kinsmen [lit. brothers] of Ahaziah and in 2 Chronicles (22:8), it is said that they were the princes of Judah and nephews of Ahaziah.

b. You are aware that the author of this work did not know the holy tongue and believed that our language was Aramaic; alternatively he called it Aramaic because Abraham came from Aram.

c. According to Rashi, the sages of blessed memory refer to this incident. In his commentary on the verse, *The son of Solomon* (1Chr. 3:10), he writes: "There were eight generations from Solomon to Joash. When David realized that his seed would be exterminated in the time of

11. De' Rossi renders "regnum tyrannicum" as 'rule by might.'

12. 'From the remnant of the people.' The Latin text reads "ex proselytis," i.e., from converts.

13. Here de' Rossi omits the sentence: "Itemque, proprium filium quem ex uxore eiusdem tribus susceperat interfecit quod diceretur iam in lege promissus CHRISTUS natus." (He killed his son from his wife of the same tribe because in the law he was predicted to be the Christ.)

14. It was Justin Martyr, followed by Eusebius, who claimed that Herod was from Ashkelon, i.e., from the hated Philistine people.

15. I.e., 2 Kings.

Joash by Athaliah about whom it is said, *she promptly did away (va-tedaber) with all who were of royal stock* (2Chr. 22:10)—the expression *va-tedaber* means to plot to kill by poison[16]—he stood in prayer and said, A Psalm on the *sheminit*[17] *[A psalm of David] Help, O Lord for the faithful are no more* (Ps. 12:1–2), i.e., eight strings (*nimin*) for the eighth generation. Thus Joash was saved. And there were eight generations from Joash to Josaiah and when he saw that Josiah and his sons were doomed for destruction—one would be killed, the other would have his eyes gouged—he prayed yet again on the *sheminit* [*O Lord, do not punish me in anger* (Ps. 6:2)]. These are the only occurrences of the phrase *on the sheminit* in the entire book of Psalms."

d. As is described in the scroll of Judith, he was the captain of the army of Nebuchadnezzar the first. It was to him that the adversaries addressed the letter in which they wrote, *and know that this city is a rebellious city* (Ezra 4:15).

e. There is no doubt that Hanukkah which commemorates the incident with Antiochus, several years after the beginning of the Hasmonean period, is different from the commemoration [of Judith]. I shall discuss this in chapter 51.[18]

f. I.e., Isaac our father was 180 years and, accordingly, Mordechai was 198. Moreover, our rabbis of blessed memory hold that he was extremely long-lived. This emerges from the story told in tractate Menaḥot[19] and in tractate Sheqalim in the Palestinian Talmud,[20] cited in the Yalqut on Ezra,[21] which describes how in the time of the second Temple, Mordechai interpreted the sign language of a deaf-mute with regard to the *omer* and two loaves. According to Rashi, Mordechai lived in the time of Ahasuerus. Now the Tosafists of blessed memory raise the question as to how he could have lived so long and resolve the problem by suggesting that Mordechai's successors were given his name.[22] This solution must however be rejected since in the talmudic passages about the deaf-mute they call Mordechai by the names Bilshan and Petachiah, and in tractate Megillah,[23] they interpret these names with reference to the Mordechai who lived in the time of Ahasuerus.

g. Our sages' tradition that Simeon the righteous ministered for 40 years may perhaps be based on these two figures of 27 and 13.

h. This is the Theos mentioned by Josephus in book 2 of his *Against Apion* (p. 880),[24] one of the despoilers of the Temple excluding Antiochus Epiphanes.

i. This is the Seleucus Nikanor mentioned by Josephus in his work *On the Maccabees* who was father of Antiochus Epiphanes.

j. Tetrarch refers to one who rules over a quarter of the realm.

k. Calculating the dates of the emperors in the period until the destruction of the Temple in relation to these kings of the Herodian dynasty, one must conclude that this is not a reference to the embassy to Gaius [Caligula].[25]

---

16. De' Rossi rightly realizes the anomalous form *va-tedabber* which may be a scribal error for *va-teabbed*—to kill.

17. The word *sheminit* is understood to be connected to the word *shemini,* i.e., eighth, and the word *nimin,* i.e., strings.

18. De' Rossi is referring to the statement of Rabbenu Nissim who stated that the episode with Judith occurred on Hanukkah. In chapter 51, he demonstrates that Rabbenu Nissim's account is confused.

19. B. Men. 65b.

20. P. Sheq. 5 (2) 48d.

21. Yalqut Shimoni, Ezra, par. 1067, 2.

22. Tos. to Men. 64b, s.v. "amar."

23. B. Meg. 15a.

24. *Contra Apionem* II, 82. Yet another precise reference to the Basel 1567 edition of Josephus.

25. Herod tetrarch ruled from 4 B.C.E. to 34 C.E. and the embassy to Caligula took place in 39 or 40 C.E.

CHAPTER THIRTY-THREE

A synopsis of the statements of Josephus concerning the number of Persian kings and the high priests who held office at the beginning of the second Temple period.

THE following is a synopsis of the statements of Josephus from his *Antiquities,* which was written for a Roman readership, regarding the royal dynasties of Media and Persia from the time of Darius, the conqueror of Babylon, until the kingdom passed into the hands of Alexander of Macedon. It is also a synopsis of his statements that relate to the line of high priests who held office from the beginning of the second Temple period until the days of the said Alexander, and even later, until the time of Ptolemy, who arranged for the translation of the Torah.

In the last chapter of his tenth book[1] he wrote that Darius and Cyrus captured Babylon. At the beginning of book 11, he wrote that after the death of Darius,[2] Cyrus ruled alone, and that in the first year of his reign, which was seventy years after the destruction of the Temple (unlike our sages he does not date it from the exile of Jehoiakin),[3] he freed the Jews so that they could rebuild the Temple. In chapter 2, he writes that while the work on the Temple was in progress, the Cutheans, the enemies of Judah and Benjamin, bribed the princes of Persia and Media who were governing the Holy Land, thus obstructing work on the building. This was perpetrated without the knowledge of Cyrus because he was involved in the Massagetican war in the course of which he died. His son Cambyses succeeded to the throne and reigned for six years. Acceding to the pressure from those adversaries mentioned above, he issued a ban to the effect that work on the building of the Temple ceased. At the end of the chapter,[4] he wrote that the family of the Magi held sway over those peoples, thus deferring the crowning of a new king for one year. The seven princes of Persia and Media[5] unanimously agreed to crown Darius the Persian, son of Hystaspes. At the beginning of chapter 4,[6] he wrote that this Darius had vowed to God that were he to become king, he would see to the rebuilding of the Temple. He kept his vow, and on the authority of Darius's written permit, Zerubbabel the prince and Jeshua the high priest brought it to completion in the second year of his reign

1. *Ant.* X:248.
2. This phrase is not in Josephus.
3. Cf. B. Meg. 11b.
4. *Ant.* XI:31.
5. Josephus writes, "the seven so-called houses of Persia and Media."
6. *Ant.* XI:31.

nine years after the letter of indictment had been written, i.e., from the edict of Cyrus [to rebuild the Temple] until the second year of Darius. At the beginning of chapter 5,[7] he writes that after the death of Darius, Xerxes his son succeeded to the throne, and in his day, Joiakin son of Jeshua officiated as high priest in Jerusalem in place of his father who had died. Ezra the scribe served as chief priest[8] for the Jews who remained in Babylon. In the seventh year of his reign, Xerxes also called Artaxerxes, granted written permission[a] for Ezra, accompanied by many of the exiles, to go up to Jerusalem. Ezra acted in the interests of the Jews in several ways, notably by segregating the foreign women and by reading the Torah on the festival of Tabernacles. He died at a ripe old age and they buried him with great pomp near Jerusalem. Joiakim the high priest also died at that time, and Eliashib his son officiated in his stead. It was the period in which Nehemiah son of Hacaliah came to Jerusalem. He was the butler of King Xerxes Artaxerxes who had given him written authorization to build the walls of Jerusalem. Nehemiah also acted in the interests of the Jews and died at a ripe old age, as is described at the end of the chapter.[9] At the beginning of chapter 6,[10] he writes that after the death of Xerxes Artaxerxes, Ahasuerus Artaxerxes succeeded to the throne; it was in his lifetime that the episode with Haman occurred.[b] In chapter 7, he refers to the last Darius who was defeated by Alexander.[11] However, he does not specify as to whether another king ruled between the reigns of Xerxes and Darius, since his only purpose in enumerating the Persian kings was insofar as they were relevant to the history of Israel. In the same chapter,[12] he also writes that after the death of Eliashib the high priest, Joiada his son officiated in his stead. After the death of Joiada, Jonathan his son succeeded to the high priesthood. He killed his brother Jeshua in the Temple precincts. The incident occurred when Jeshua who was a friend of Bagoses, captain of the king's army in Jerusalem, vaunted himself, pronouncing, "I shall be high priest." A quarrel broke out in the holy precincts and Jonathan assailed his brother Jeshua and killed him. The captain was greatly infuriated with Israel for this incident and punished the natives, persecuting them for seven years. After the death of Jonathan, Jaddua his son officiated. Jaddua had a brother called Manasseh who had married the daughter of Sanballat the Horonite of Samaria. In chapter 8,[13] he writes that after Darius had been killed and the kingdom fell to the hands of Alexander, Sanballat curried favor with Alexander. He came to meet him at a night encampment, presenting him with precious gifts. Alexander then granted his request to allow Manasseh his son-in-law set up a shrine on Mount Gerizim which is situated near Shechem and is the highest point in Samaria. For the priests and people had coerced Jaddua the high priest to expel his brother and to sever his connection with the Jerusalemite priesthood. Infuriated by this action, Sanballat then appointed him as high priest over that shrine. He was joined by all the people who were in troubled circumstances[14]

7. *Ant.* XI:120.
8. The Latin translation reads, "primarius sacerdos erat Esdras vir iustus." Cf. Ezra 7:21: *Ezra the priest, scholar in the law.*
9. *Ant.* XI:183.
10. *Ant.* XI:184ff.
11. *Ant.* XI:313.
12. *Ant.* XI:297.
13. *Ant.* XI:321.
14. According to Josephus, these were people who, like Manasseh, were involved in mixed marriages.

and had fled from the Sanhedrin in the Holy Land and by the Cutheans, that is the Samaritans—these were the people whom the king of Assyria had brought out of Cutha and settled in Samaria after the expulsion of the ten tribes from the area. At the end of book 11[15] he wrote that after the death of Jaddua, his son Onias officiated. And in chapter 2 of book 12,[16] he wrote that after the death of Onias, his son Simeon the righteous ministered. When Simeon died he was survived by a small son who, being a minor, was unqualified to officiate as high priest. Thus his brother Eleazar ministered in his stead. It was to this Eleazar that Ptolemy king of Egypt sent letters and presents at the time of the translation of our Torah by the elders. And at the end of chapter 13 of book 12,[17] he wrote that Eleazar was succeeded by his uncle Manasseh. He is not to be identified with Manasseh, brother of Jaddua and son-in-law of Sanballat, but with Manasseh, the son of Jaddua, brother of Onias the first and uncle of Simeon the righteous and his brother Eleazar. When Manasseh died, Onias, son of Simeon the righteous officiated.

This is what Josephus had to say. Now dear reader, it is only right that you should know that his works which were written in Greek were translated in antiquity into Latin by Ruffinus of Aquila.[18] The Italian translation is based on his rendering of the text.[19] However, Gelenius, who possessed great mastery of both languages and was a great scholar in all fields of learning, and who had translated the forty-three works of Yedidyah the Alexandrian [Philo], set himself the task of translating the works of Josephus. His rendering superseded the earlier versions. Indeed, scholars of the world regard him as one who conveys the truth.[20] This is why I delved into his text and derived my information from him.[21] And so you should not turn to me in bewilderment when you come across some passages in this book in which my citation of Josephus is somewhat different from the older renderings whether in chapter numbering or in the actual subject matter. For I only availed myself of their texts when I encountered problems in Gelenius's version. As I already informed you concerning the translation of the book of Aristeas presented above, I regard the later version as being of greater value.[22]

[De' Rossi's notes to Josephus]

a. According to this statement of his, the king who supported Ezra is not to be identified with the one who built the Temple.

b. From this, one must necessarily deduce that Mordechai who went into exile with Jeconiah survived up until this time. Previously we wrote about the rabbinic view of his longevity.

---

15. *Ant.* XI:347.

16. *Ant.* XII:43.

17. *Ant.* XII:157.

18. Ruffinus was a contemporary of Jerome. According to F. Blatt (*The Latin Josephus,* 17–24), it is not certain that this translation was composed by Ruffinus. It was first published under Ruffinus's name in Augsburg, 1470. On the editions of Josephus, see Heinz Schreckenberg, *Bibliographie.*

19. The first printed Italian translation of the *Antiquitates* rendered by Pietro Lauro was published in Venice, 1544, and the first printed Italian translation of the *Bellum* rendered by Bartolomeo Presbitero was published in Florence, 1493.

20. Sigismund Gelenius was born in Prague and died in 1555. He worked in the press of Froben in Basel and was highly regarded by Erasmus.

21. 'I delved . . . him,' lit. I dug and drank his waters. Cf. 2K. 19:24.

22. This is a play on the popular saying, "last is best" derived from B.R. 78:8 (925).

CHAPTER THIRTY-FOUR

A synopsis of the statements of Eusebius the Caesarean on the number of Persian kings and high priests at the beginning of the second Temple period, as well as extracts from Curtius and the Christian translator [Jerome] concerning the number of Persian kings.

Now in his *Chronicle* (f. 52 of the tables),[1] Eusebius the Christian from the city of Caesarea wrote that fourteen kings reigned in Persia from the fifty-fifth Olympiad onwards. They are as follows:

1. Cyrus the Persian who reigned 30 years.
2. Cambyses who ruled 8 years.
   He writes that some people claim that Cambyses was also called Nebuchadnezzar by the Jews, and that it was in his lifetime that the episode with Judith occurred.
3. The two Magi brothers who ruled 7 months which are counted as 1 year.
4. Darius who ruled 33 years. In the second year of his reign, Zerubbabel returned to build the Temple, and its construction was completed in the sixth[2] year of his reign. They had started to build it in the first year of Cyrus's reign, but their adversaries impeded the work for a period of 40 years.
5. Xerxes son of Cambyses ruled for 20 years.
6. Artabanus the Persian ruled for 7 months that are counted as 1 year.
7. Artaxerxes surnamed Longimanus, i.e., the longhanded, ruled 40 years.
   There are many people who claim that the episode involving Esther occurred in his lifetime, but I (that is, Eusebius) am disposed to think that this is not the case since Ezra and Nehemiah who wrote about his reign are silent on that subject.
8. Artaxerxes the Persian ruled 2 months.
9. Sogdianus ruled 8 months.
10. Darius surnamed Nothus ruled 19 years.
11. Artaxerxes the Persian surnamed Memnon, son of Darius and Parysatis, ruled 40 years. The episode involving Esther occurred in his time.
12. Artaxerxes surnamed Ochus ruled 26 years.
13. Arses son of Ochus ruled 4 years.
14. Darius the last, son of Arsamus, ruled 6 years.

1. De' Rossi used Joannes Sichardus's compilation of chronicles which included Eusebius, Jerome, Prosper of Aquitaine, Cassiodorus, Contractus, Mattheo Palmieri the Florentine, and Mattheo Palmieri the Pisan.

2. Most texts read "fourth year," although de' Rossi's rendering, 'sixth year' could be justified on the basis of the layout of Eusebius's table.

His account of the number and dynasties of the high priest tallies with that of Yedidyah (Philo) and Josephus, namely: Jeshua, Joiakim, Eliashib, Joiada, Jonathan, Jaddua, Onias, Simeon the righteous, Eleazar his brother, Manasseh, uncle of Eleazar.

All these data are culled from Eusebius. I cannot desist from providing you with additional authorities. In the second part of his work devoted to the deeds of Alexander of Macedon, the ancient historian Quintus Curtius wrote: "Darius son of Arsamus who was defeated by Alexander was the fourteenth king after Cyrus."[3] Likewise, in his commentary to the verse, *Persia will have have three more kings* from the book of Daniel (11:2), the Christian translator [Jerome] writes: "It is a well-known fact which requires no proof that from Cyrus to Darius there were fourteen kings of Media and Persia."[4] This constitutes the data which I saw fit to cull from those writers. From now on, kind reader, be silent and pay attention to what I have to tell you in the forthcoming chapters. May our God be with us.

3. The first two books of Quintus Curtius's work are lost. De' Rossi is quoting from the supplement compiled by Christopher Bruno (24).

4. Jerome, *Commentaria in Dan.* 11:2 (*P.L.* XXV, col. 558).

CHAPTER THIRTY-FIVE

The age of the world as computed by us on the basis of that which is recorded in holy Writ is open to doubt in respect to the duration of the bondage in Egypt, the middle period of the first Temple and the first years of the second Temple. Despite their frequent assertion that the duration of the first Temple period was 410 years, our rabbis themselves taught us that it lasted for at least 418 years.[1] In view of this specific fact, it necessarily follows—without undermining anything that pertains to the Torah—(and the sages of blessed memory were themselves aware of it) that the age of the universe must also in all truth be greater than that which we reckon. In any case, even our customary computation and the discussions of the rabbis of blessed memory on this subject, given their wise method of procedure, appear reasonable to intelligent people.[2]

It is an indisputable fact (as we proposed in chapters 8 and 29) that the number of years from creation as computed on the basis of holy Writ is universally approved and accepted. All the nations walk in accordance with that computation, in the reflection of our light—blessed be He who showed us grace. Indeed, the duration of the period from Adam to the deluge, to Abraham, and from the exodus from Egypt until the erection of the first Temple as well as the greater part of its duration, cannot be challenged nowadays since Scripture is clear as the rising sun as far as these years are concerned. Similarly, the number of years computed from the beginning of the era of documents of the Greek Empire—according to our rabbis of blessed memory as stated in tractate Elilim,[3] it was first implemented 380 years before the destruction of the second Temple, 6 years after the establishment of the Alexandrian Empire—is neither increased nor diminished by any scholar of any nation, as we explained in chapter 24. It is true that in the Septuagint, the figure for some of the ten generations from Adam to Noah is greater than that given in our own correct text. But in chapter 8 we cited the statements of the bishop Eugubinus and the wise Christian Samotheus who is held in great esteem by the moderns and who was particularly aided by the opinions of the greatest Christian doctor [i.e., Augustine] as adduced in book 15, chapter 13 of the *City [of God].* Thereby we demonstrated that their scholars had reached the conclusion that besides the innate trust in whatsoever figure is found in our holy books which from time immemorial were disseminated throughout the world, anyone who took it into his head to count the years according to the Septuagint or the other Greek versions based on it, and likewise anyone who disregarded the figures given in the Pentateuch and Prophets for the period from Noah onwards, was not speaking correctly. For the truth will emerge from every corner, to be found in the works of the various scholars who

1. Cassel's text reads 415, but in the Italian text (see below, n. 2) and in the Hebrew ed. pr. the figure 418 is given.

2. This chapter was translated by de' Rossi into Italian (Bodleian Ms. Mich 308, 133r–115v) at the request of Giacomo Boncompagno, governatore generale della chiesa. It is significant that this chapter which met with considerable antagonism from certain rabbis of the time was the one that de' Rossi translated for a Christian readership. See my article, "Towards a Reappraisal," 499–500.

3. B. A.Z. 9a.

wrote the histories of the world empires. This, according to Metasthenes the Persian whose work we translated in chapter 31, is the correct method by which to ascertain the truth. Thus, by means of comparing and contrasting, it becomes palpably evident that all versions are corrupt and all figures false save those which are in our sacred books. It was for this reason that the Christian translator [Jerome] invariably followed our text both in his translation of the Pentateuch and Prophets as well as in the introduction to his translation of Eusebius's *Chronicle.* It is true, however, that although we take the veracity of holy Writ for granted, this did not prevent the adoption of different opinions as regards the meaning of certain passages that concern the number of years. I allude to three main areas: the duration of the bondage in Egypt, the middle period of the first Temple, and the first years of the second Temple.

As regards the length of the Egyptian exile, Scripture states, *The length of time that the Israelites lived in Egypt was four hundred and thirty years* (Ex. 12:40). In the Seder Olam,[5] the Mekhilta,[6] Shemot Rabbah,[7] Tanhuma,[8] and above all in the Targum of [ps.] Jonathan ben Uzziel[9] regarding the verses, *The length of time.* (Ex. 12:40) and *At the end of the four hundred and thirtieth year . . . all the ranks of the Lord departed from the land of Egypt* (Ex. 12:41), our rabbis state that the Egyptian exile began in the seventieth year of Abraham, from which time thirty years elapsed until the birth of Isaac, and from then, 400 years until the exodus from Egypt. According to rabbinic calculation, the exodus occurred in the year 2448 anno mundi as is shown in the Seder Olam cited above and in the Pesiqta which is cited by the author of the Yalqut on the verse, *the wonders You have devised for us* (Ps. 40:6).[10] And yet, there were many of our well-reputed sages of later times who disregarded their arguments and challenged them on this count, although they, too, were not of one opinion. Indeed, the Gaon Rabbenu Hananel of blessed memory whose view is cited by Rabbenu Baḥya in his commentary on the verse, *The length of time that the Israelites lived in Egypt was four hundred and thirty years* (Ex. 12:40) wrote: "The 430 years are calculated from the birth of Isaac."[11] Accordingly, the exodus from Egypt should be postdated and 30 years added to the figure 2448 proposed by our rabbis. The same opinion is expressed by the wise Don Isaac [Abravanel] in his commentary on the Torah[12] and in his work entitled *Zevaḥ Pesaḥ* with regard to the paragraph, "Blessed be He who keeps His promise to Israel."[13] He said that the 400 years intimated to Abraham by the Holy One blessed be He were reckoned from the

4. 'Histories,' lit. the other events, an expression taken from a phrase used frequently in the books of Kings, e.g., *The other events of Solomon's reign* (1K. 11:41).

5. Seder Olam, ch. 1 (4–6).

6. Mekhilta d'Rabbi Ishmael, bo 14 (I, 111).

7. S.R. 18:11.

8. Tanhuma, bo 9.

9. On Ex. 12:40, ps. Jonathan amplifies the verse by stating that it was 430 years from the "covenant between the pieces" until the exodus and he renders v.41 "And it was at the end of 30 years from the making of the covenant that Isaac was born."

10. Yalqut Shimoni to Ps. 40:6, par. 738.

11. Baḥya ben Asher to Ex. 12:40 (97). He gives three calculations for the period: 400 years which marks the beginning of the wandering of Abraham's descendants; 430 years that are counted from Isaac's birth; 210 years for the period in Egypt.

12. Abravanel to Gen. 15 (204, col. b); to Ex. 12:40 (89, col. b).

13. *Zevaḥ Pesaḥ* (Haggadah). The ed. pr. was printed in Constantinople 1505.

birth of Isaac, but that 30 more years were added to this figure because of Israel's sins; similarly, the wandering in the desert was prolonged by 40 years because of the sin of the spies. In the same vein Ramban [Nahmanides] writes that the bondage in Egypt was prolonged by thirty years because of Israel's sin. Don Isaac may have derived his opinion from Ramban.[14] But as is evident from his two explanations of the verse, *The length of time that the Israelites lived in Egypt was four hundred and thirty years* (Ex. 12:40), Ramban reckons the 400 years from the time of the "convenant between the pieces" which he dates long after the time when Abraham left Haran at the age of seventy-five.[15] Thus according to his view, the redemption would have taken place 8 or 10 years after 2248. Furthermore, there is the opinion of Rabbi Moses Latif[16] of Jerusalem[17] expressed in his public sermons which he later put into writing. I, together with certain reliable persons, came across these sermons among the books belonging to Rabbi Jehoseph Ḥazaq [Joseph de Forti],[18] may his shield and redeemer protect him. He discusses the fact that the age of the world cannot be known for certain and that certain trustworthy writers increase the number of years that our people reckon. Then, in like manner to Ramban, he adds 8 years to the bondage in Egypt according to which calculation the redemption would have occurred not in the year 2448, but 2456. For this calculation he adopts the symbol *and we will take our daughter* (bitenu) *and go* (Gen. 34:17).[19] For he objected to the use of the figure 210[20] on the grounds that it was not a prophetic tradition. It is indeed the subject of controversy in chapter 48 of Pirqe d'Rabbi Eliezer. Rabbi Eleazar ben Azariah said that the [bondage in Egypt] was *redu,* i.e., 210 years, whereas Rabbi Eleazar ben Arakh states that it was 215 years which figure through God's kind mercies is counted as doubled.[21] Study the passage for yourself.[22] In the *Chronicle of Moses*[23] our teacher, may he rest in peace, a work which is often cited by the author of the Yalqut, the figure of 216 is given. This is the figure that Latif is inclined to accept, and he clinches his opinion by means of three prophetic omens which in his view are connected with this figure: i.e., in the verse, *And the fourth generation shall return* (Gen. 15:16), the sum of the first letters of each word, and likewise the final letters of each word, amount to 216. The sum of the letters in the individual word *ve-dor* (and the generation) also amounts to 216. He is also of the

14. Abravanel does refer to Ramban explicitly.

15. Ramban (to Ex. 12:42) disagrees with Rashi who states that the 430 years begin from the birth of Isaac since "all the days of Abraham cannot be counted as exile with respect to his seed." Instead he argues that the 430 years begin from the time of the "covenant between the pieces" when it was said, *your seed shall be a stranger in a land that is not theirs* (Gen. 15:13), which took place "a long time" after his exit from Haran at the age of 75.

16. In his Italian translation, de' Rossi spells the name as Latef. Normally, it is spelled Latif.

17. This may be a reference to Moses ben Isaac ibn Latif, son of the thirteenth-century Spanish philosopher and kabbalist.

18. Joseph son of Solomon de Forti lived in S. Martino dall'Argine which is in the province of Mantua.

19. Each letter of the word *bitenu* respectively represents the numerals 2456.

20. This is derived from Jacob's command to his sons, *Go down (redu) to Egypt* (Gen. 42:2). The numerical value of the word *redu* is 210.

21. I.e., both the days and nights are counted.

22. The idea is that the Egyptians oppressed the Israelites at night as well as by day.

23. This is a life of Moses, belonging to the genre of the "rewritten Bible," probably written in the tenth century. It was a popular work, first published in Constantinople in 1516. De' Rossi appears to have known the work only through the citations in the Yalqut.

opinion that the 430 years are reckoned from the seventy-sixth year of Abraham—this is the year that he went down to live in Egypt after leaving Haran—and are completed in the given year 2456. He further corroborates this evidence by using the well-known fact as demonstrated in Seder Olam[24] that the Israelites left Egypt on a Thursday. Calculating the new-moon days by means of the mean motion which occur every 29 days, 12 hours, and 793 parts from the very first new-moon day (which occurred on a Monday at the fifth hour, 204 parts), until the year 2448 or 2449, it would be impossible for the Nisan new-moon day [the month of the exodus] to have occurred on a Thursday such that the fifteenth of the month would also have been a Thursday. But this could have been the case had the exodus occurred in the year 2456. Latif defended himself for his culpable effrontery in contraverting the Seder Olam on this matter in several ways, above all by the fact that *justice is the Lord's*.[25] This is all to be found in the two passages in his sermons, and I and the wise Ḥazaq are trustees in this matter since we are both alive and thus in a position to demonstrate the opinion of Latif to whosoever is interested. {For the reader's satisfaction, I shall not desist from quoting from the actual text of Latif of blessed memory such that he can be apprised of the firm basis of his argument. After mentioning the two views as to the date of our exodus, namely, 2448 or 2456, he writes as follows:

> I studied the calculation of our fixed calendar which was transmitted to us by the sages in order to see which date was correct. Now the Torah makes it clear that they left on a Thursday on the fifteenth of Nisan from which it would follow that the next new moon of the month of Iyyar would have occurred on a Saturday. Accordingly, the fifteenth of Iyyar would also have been a Saturday—this was the day on which they asked for bread—and thus the next day on which the manna fell, the sixteenth, would have been a Sunday. Now if we calculate that 2456 years had elapsed since the creation, it would be correct that the year 2456 in which they left Egypt would have been the sixth year in the one hundred and thirtieth lunar cycle.[26] It would have been a leap year with the months of Ḥeshvan and Kislev being defective months [i.e., only 29 days] and the new-moon day for Tishri of that year would have occurred on a Sunday at 13 hours, and 52 parts and the New Year would have been on a Monday. The new-moon day for the month of Nisan would have been a Thursday and so, too, the fifteenth of Nisan, as is evident from the Torah and this is also what Rashi writes on the verse, *And they journeyed from Elim* (Ex. 16:1) in accordance with our rabbis' statement in tractate Shabbat.[27] But if one follows the *baraita* as given in Seder Olam which calculates 2448, then it would not fit at all with the calculation of the fixed calendar. For if they left Egypt in the year 2448, it would have been the sixteenth year of the one hundred and twenty-ninth lunar cycle, and an ordinary year, and the new-moon day for Tishri in that year would have on a Friday and 16 hours and 579 parts. The New Year would been on a Saturday and Ḥeshvan and Kislev would have been full months and the new-moon day for Nisan would have been on a Tuesday and likewise the fifteenth of Nisan. Accordingly, they did not go out on a Thursday. And if they left in the following year such that 2448 years had already elapsed, the new-moon day for Tishri for the year 2449 would have been on a Tuesday evening at 385 parts of an hour and New Year would

24. Seder Olam, ch. 5 (22).
25. Deut. 1:17.
26. A lunar cycle consists of 19 years of which 12 have 12 months and seven have 13 months.
27. B. Shabb. 87b.

> have been on a Thursday and it would have been the seventeenth year in the one hundred and twenty-ninth lunar cycle It would have been a leap year and Ḥeshvan and Kislev would have been defective and the new-moon day for Nisan of that year would have been on a Sunday as would the fifteenth of Nisan. Accordingly it ought to be the case that they left Egypt on a Thursday on the fifteenth of Nisan in the year 2456."

This is what he says, and according to what he writes in another passage in his papers, he is of the opinion that his arguments are favored.}[2]

However, given that his proof is based on the calculation of the new-moon days, I can only ratify it by adding a point of clarification—for it is well attested that the fixing of the calendar according to the mean motion was only initiated in the lifetime of Rabbi Hillel when the circumstances of the exile necessitated its establishment, as will be explained in chapter 40. Originally, however, they used to sanctify the new-moon day on the basis of the observation of the moon as we indicated in chapter 25.—we shall discuss this matter further in chapter 40. And when the Holy One blessed be He said to Moses, "When you see the moon in such a shape you shall sanctify it,"[28] this referred to the observation of the moon in the evening in the west about one day after its conjunction with the sun according to their true motion, as Rabbi Moses writes in chapter 1 of his Laws on the Sanctification of the New Moon.[29] But since the day established by calculation according to the mean motion may occur before or after the day in which the moon becomes visible, as the teacher wrote in chapter 5[30] and as is explained by the commentator[31] on the two chapters in question, the only means of establishing the new-moon day for Nisan is according to the calculation of the new-moon days, by the true, and not the mean, motion. We shall discuss this further in chapter 40 in connection with our critique of Rabbenu Hananel. It is true that the real new-moon day may only be deduced from that calculated according to the mean motion, as Rambam [Maimonides] explains[32] once the calculation according to the mean motion is known. This fact alone gives credence to his [i.e., Latif's] argument, despite his statement about the additional eight years calculated according to the symbol *bitenu* (our daughter, i.e., 2456).

Now Ralbag [Gersonides] proposes a figure that exceeds those given by the other four commentators.[33] He deemed it possible to reckon the 400 years from the birth of Jacob; consequently, about 45 years would be added to the date in which the period of 400 years would be completed. And so I have presented you with a band of celebrated members of our tribe but have omitted the author of the *Sefer Toledot Yiṣḥaq*[34] who adheres to the approach taken by Ramban [Nahmanides] and Rabbenu Baḥya who by citing the opinion of Rabbenu Hananel is, as it were, giving it his approval. The common feature in all their approaches is that they postdate the redemption to after the year 2448, some extending it to 2458, others to 2478, either more or less, as is demonstrated

28. This is an explanation of the verse, *This shall be to you the beginning of months* (Ex. 12:2) as given in B. R.H. 20a.

29. *Mishneh Torah,* Qiddush ha-Ḥodesh I:3.

30. Ibid. V:2.

31. I.e., the commentator of Qiddush ha-Ḥodesh, Obadiah ben David.

32. *Mishneh Torah,* Qiddush ha-Ḥodesh VI:1; XV:1.

33. Gersonides to Gen. 15:13; Ex. 12:40. Gersonides argues that the 400 years of exile commenced from the period of uninterrupted wandering, i.e., from the period of Jacob's stay in Egypt.

34. Isaac ben Joseph Caro, *Toledot Yiṣḥaq,* to Ex. 12:40 (36, col. b–f, 37, col. a).

from their statements. The very fact that they all challenge the authority of the Seder Olam is indicative that they did not hold its view on this question as in any way a prophetic tradition—for who would be so rash as to have a desire to challenge a prophetic tradition? Rather, it simply presents an evaluation of the scriptural verses, and the person who does not incline to subscribe to its view, should not be regarded as a sinner. Indeed the fact of the matter is as follows: by increasing the years of the bondage in Egypt, it necessarily follows that the sum of the years of the world must also be greater.

Now in order to enhance your understanding of the topic, I cannot desist from imparting to you some novel information. It concerns the fact that Christian doctors, Bible exegetes, are also divided on this question, although the difference in their various calculations does not amount to more than five years. Acquaintance with their views is facilitated by consultation of the *Catena* of Lippomano[35] which presents the view expressed by Eusebius the Caesarean in his *Chronicle* which was also adopted by their greatest Christian doctor [Augustine] in his *Questions on Exodus.*[36] The same view is also expressed by Tostatus[37] and Hugo.[38] All these held that the 400 years are reckoned from the seventy-fifth year of Abraham. And they claim that from this it follows that 405 years must be counted from the birth of Isaac to reach the total of 430, even though Scripture does not record precise details about these years. However, other Christian sages including the modern Gaetanus [Cajetan], whom they hold in high esteem,[39] agree with out rabbis, and consequently also with Rashi and Ibn Ezra, in commencing the calculation from the seventieth year of Abraham. But the reason they proffer for their view is not grounded in the same exegesis of Scripture as given by the rabbis. For in the first chapter of Seder Olam, the duplication of scriptural verses is taken into account such that the "vision of the parts"[40] is said to have occurred while Abraham was still in Ur of the Chaldees. The Christians, however, following the apparent course of the narrative, say that it occurred subsequent to the time indicated in the statement, *And Abraham was seventy-five when he left Haran* (Gen. 12:4). And yet, the wandering of the same Abraham is regarded to have begun from the time, aged seventy, he left his homeland, Ur of the Chaldees. And when Scripture states, *The length of time that the Israelites lived in Egypt was four hundred and thirty years,* it comprises the beginning of Abraham's wandering and also the greater part of the period which was designated for the wandering of our forefathers. {And if you count the figures given by Yedidyah which I gave in translation at the beginning of chapter 32, i.e., 1656, 292, 425, 80, they

35. This is a reference to the *Catena in Exodum* written by Aloysio Lippomano (1500–1559) who was Bishop of Modena and other places in Italy and who was involved in the Council of Trent.

36. See *Catena,* 94r. (The *Questions on Exodus* is not a genuine work of Augustine.) De' Rossi does not refer to the way in which the author also discusses the chronology in the light of Galatians 3:17, *a covenant had already been validated by God; it cannot be invalidated and its promises rendered ineffective by a law made 430 years later.*

37. Alfonso de Madrigal El Tostado (b. in Madrigal de las Altas Terras in about 1410) was a theologian, moral philosopher, and biblical exegete. This is a reference to his *Commentaria ad Genesin,* 254v.ff.

38. This is a reference to the theologian and biblical scholar, the Cardinal Hugo of St. Cher (1200–1263) who is quoted in Tostado's *Commentaria.*

39. Cardinal Cajetan (1469–1534) was a philosopher, theologian and exegete, and critic of early reformation doctrines. He tended to give literal interpretations in his commentaries on the Bible.

40. Gen. 15.

come to a total of 2453, which tallies with the figure proposed by those who increase the figure given by our rabbis by counting those 5 years.}

Now it is also true that there is also uncertainty about the duration of the periods of the two holy Temples. As regards the second Temple, the prophetic narratives are only partial and lack the requisite clarification of the events related to it. Their account of the first Temple, whose entire history is covered, contains a manifest contradiction and, as is usually the case with human opinion, there are a variety of interpretations and different calculations are proffered without any final arbitration in the matter being reached. We shall relegate our treatment of the second Temple period to subsequent chapters. This chapter will be devoted to that which pertains to the first Temple and we shall point out the source and cause of the controversy to which we referred.

On the basis of various talmudic passages, we said from the very outset of our work that our rabbis were of the opinion that the first Temple stood for 410 years.[41] However, sages of our people held opposing views. Thus, Yedidyah the Alexandrian, as is evident from his work *On the Times* which we translated in chapter 31, counted 440 years from the fourth year of Solomon's reign, when the work on the construction of the Temple was begun, until its final destruction. When Josephus gives a chronology of the world (in book 10, chapter 11) for the period from Adam to Noah, he followed the Septuagint which was the version used by the gentiles of that time—he reckons 470 years for the duration of the first Temple period.[42] In chapter 8 of book 20, however, he gives the more precise figure of 466 and a half years.[43] In the opening section of *Sefer ha-Qabbalah* which begins with the exodus from Egypt, Rabad the Levite [Abraham ben David] reaches a total of 430 years, which figure is calculated on the basis of the reigns of the kings of Judah. But one must suspect that his text became corrupt in some passages. This is particularly apparent with the figure of 28 years given for the reign of Jehoshapahat, whereas it is explicitly stated in the books of Kings and Chronicles that his reign only lasted 25 years. That is why he gives then the total of 433 years instead of 430.[44] Again, he continues with the statement that the Temple stood for 427 years and was destroyed after it had been under storm for 7 years. It is obvious that he meant to write 3 years in conformity to what is written at the end of the book of Kings which would bring the total to 430.[45] (As clarification, we shall cite this opinion of his in our treatment of his statements in the fourth section of this chapter.) In his introduction to the book of Kings, the wise Don Isaac also refers to the fact that Rabad of blessed memory held that the first Temple stood for 430 years. In his commentary on Daniel[46] and in the eighth and last section of his To'aliyyot, Ralbag [Gersonides] writes that it stood for 419 and a half years. The sage Kimḥi, whose flour was reputed to be of the best quality,[47] stated that it stood for 429 and a half years. With regard to the verse, *In the fifteenth year*

41. B. Yoma 9a; A.Z. 9a; Arak. 12b; Zev. 118b et al.
42. *Ant.* X:147.
43. Ibid. XX:231.
44. Abraham ibn Daud, *Sefer ha-Qabbalah* (7), and see Cohen, 9, n. 52 in which he says that the error is not ibn Daud's but one of transmission.
45. Cf. 2K. 25:1–3.
46. Gersonides to Dan. 7:24; 8:14. The commentary was first printed in Ferrara 1477 (?) with the *To'aliyyot* and subsequently published in the Rabbinic Bible, Venice, 1517.
47. This is a pun on the name Kimḥi and the word *qemaḥ* (flour).

of Amaziah the son of Joash king of Judah (2K. 14:23), he criticizes Rashi who had written: "The duration of the Temple, when calculated according to the reigns of the kings without omitting these 15 years of Amaziah and Uzziah, comes to a total of 425 years." But Kimḥi of blessed memory writes:[48] "The proof he adduces for the duration of the Temple is no proof. There are two methods of calculating the duration of the Temple period: either to count 410 years and three months from the initial building of the Temple until the assault of Nebuchadnezzar in the third year of the reign of Jehoiakim; alternatively, to count 429 and a half years, extending the reckoning to the final destruction of the Temple which would include the 11 years of Zedekiah's reign." This is what he says, and, indeed, his view may be confirmed by consultation of the scriptural accounts in Kings and Chronicles (i.e., by collating all the years of the reigns of the kings of Judah from the fourth year of Solomon to the exile of Zedekiah). Now if you follow my example and consult all printed copies of Kimḥi's commentary, ancient and modern,[49] you will be able to deduce that the reading of 409 years [i.e., instead of 429] is corrupt. For it is certainly impossible that the total of the unabridged calculation should be less than the total of the abridged calculation. I know this to be a fact. For here in Ferrara there is the library belonging to the study house of the distinguished authority of his time Isaac da Fano, which contains the bequest of Don Judah Abravanel. I discovered there four manuscripts of Kimḥi's commentaries. These texts of varying degrees of antiquity all being of greater reliability, gave the figure of 429 and a half.[50] Doubtlessly, many other testimonies to this correct reading are to be found in other parts of the world.[51] In fact, Scripture reckons 20 years exactly from the third year of Jehoiachim until the eleventh year of Zedekiah.

The wise Don Isaac calculates 430 years. In the introduction to his commentary on Kings, he sets out a table of the kings of Judah and then writes:[52] "I would have you know that I arranged this table on the basis of the literal text of Scripture from which it necessarily follows that the destruction of Jerusalem and the burning of the House of our God occurred in the year 3358 anno mundi. This was also the calculation of Rabbi Abraham ibn Dior [Daud] in his *Sefer ha-Qabbalah* which was followed by later sages. However, according to the author of the Seder Olam, the final destruction occurred in the year 3338. This figure was reached because the rabbis of blessed memory subtracted 20 years from the reigns of Jehoram son of Jehoshaphat and Uzziah. If the Lord will consider me worthy, I shall investigate this matter in my book *The Days of the World*[53] which I intend to compose." At the top of the table he writes that the Temple was erected in the year 2928 which corresponds to Solomon's fourth year. Accordingly, he was of the view that the Temple stood for 430 years. In his first introduction, he writes as follows:

48. Kimḥi to 2K. 14:22.

49. The commentary was first printed separately in Soncino in 1485 and then published in the Rabbinic Bible of 1517 and later editions.

50. De' Rossi's claim can be substantiated. A manuscript of Kimḥi's commentary in the Bodleian Library (Opp. Add. fol. 37) gives the figure 429 and 6 months.

51. 'Other parts of the world,' lit. witnesses are in the North. Cf. B. Qidd. 12b.

52. Abravanel, Introduction to Kings (427, col. b).

53. In his Italian rendering de' Rossi translates the title of Abravanel's work, a biblical phrase *yemot olam,* with the Latin phrase *de diebus mundi.*

> The reigns of the three righteous kings, Saul, David, and Solomon, come to a total of 100 years. The mnemonic for this is contained in the expression *The kings [of the House of Israel] are merciful* (1K. 20:31).[54] Excluding Athaliah whose reign should not be counted, there were nineteen kings of Judah, some righteous, others wicked, whose reigns amounted to total of 393 years. The mnemonic for this figure is contained in the expression *The eyes of the Lord . . . observing the wicked and the good* (Pr. 15:3).[55] Likewise, from Jeroboam until the exile of Hoshea there were nineteen kings of Israel, all of whom were wicked sinners. The sum total of their years is 241 and their mnemonic is contained in the expression *And to the wicked God said* (Ps. 50:16).[56]

So Abravanel. He likewise gives further ratification and corroboration of all this at the end of that section[57] when he notes the astonishing fact that the reigns of the nineteen kings of Judah amounted to 393 years, whereas nineteen kings of Israel covered only a period of 241 years—for *the fear of the Lord prolongs life* (Pr. 10:27). He also expresses wonder at the divine plan according to which an equal number of kings was assigned to Judah as to Israel. This is what he says. Now anyone capable of counting, who adds the 37 remaining years of Solomon's reign (that is from the fourth to the end of the fortieth year) to the figure of 393 will necessarily arrive at the figure of 430 which tallies with the figure given by Kimḥi and his fellow companions. We spoke of 37 years because we count the fourth year itself. Since work on the Temple was begun in the second month of the fourth year, the eleven months of the year are included. In the passage indicated above, Rabad also wrote: "Four hundred and thirty years cover the period from the end of the third year of Solomon's reign until the destruction of the Temple."[58] Now in the course of his discussion of this subject, the wise Don Isaac indirectly informed us that investigation into the age of the world is an activity sanctioned by many writers of high repute. Even if you were to increase or deduct a thousand years from the figure customarily reckoned by us, your computation would not be rendered invalid nor reflect a heretical standpoint. And so, he and that group of distinguished authorities stood their ground[59] and explicitly increased the figure for the duration of the first Temple to 430 years. And it is manifestly clear that the requisite testimony from the aera mundi reckoning that the world was created *ab novo,* as the sage of the *Kuzari*[60] states in section 1,[61] is not refuted in any way by the positing of a lesser or greater figure. We shall clarify this matter further in chapter 42. When Don Isaac came to comment on the verse, *In the twenty-seventh year of King Jeroboam of Israel, Azariah son of King Amaziah of Judah became king* (2K. 15:1), he cites the Seder Olam together with statements of our sages of blessed memory in the Gemara which accord with those of the Seder Olam. He then states: "This opinion of theirs is not reliable. . . . Kimḥi has

54. The numerical value of the word *malkhe* (kings) is 100.
55. The numerical value of the words *ra'im ve-ṭovim* (good and evil) amounts to 393.
56. The numerical value of the word *amar* (said) amounts to 241.
57. Introduction to Kings (424, col. a).
58. *Sefer ha-Qabbalah* (6). The text actually reads 433 years. See Cohen's discussion of this figure (194–95) in which he argues that ibn Daud contrived a method for finding three additional years over the total of 430.
59. 'Stood their ground,' lit. sat on their saddlebags. Cf. Jud. 5:10.
60. In his Italian version, de' Rossi does not refer to the *Kuzari* but adds the statement that the notion of *creatio ex nihilo* is "important according to the holy law."
61. *Kuzari* I, par. 67.

already adduced other arguments against them which are based on Scripture and which appear correct to those who understand." At the end of that discussion, he cites Rashi's statement which refers to the verse, *It was he [Azariah] who rebuilt Elath and restored it to Judah after King Amaziah slept with his fathers* (2K. 14:22), "The duration of the Temple when calculated according to the reigns of the kings without omitting these fifteen years of Amaziah and Uzziah comes to a total of 425 years." He then concludes: "It thus transpires, as I wrote in the introduction to my book, that there are a variety of opinions regarding the duration of the first Temple." In that section he refutes Rashi's view of the verse quoted above. And although we have not had the merit of setting eyes on his book *The Days of the World,* it is unquestionably evident that he posited a greater figure for the anno mundi date than is customarily reckoned by us. For he adds 30 years to the period of the bondage in Egypt, as we indicated in the first part of this chapter, and increased the length of the first Temple period to 430 years. There are also other passages in which he puts forward this opinion as shall be demonstrated in the course of our discussion. Thus in his work *Zevaḥ Pesaḥ* he comments on the paragraph "Blessed be He who keeps His promise" and writes: "Take note of the marvels of Him whose understanding is perfect. For the Egyptian exile lasted 430 years. Before the erection of the Temple, they lived in the Land for 440 years; and the first Temple stood for 427 years (this figure does not include the three war years to which Rabad referred); and the second Temple stood for 428 years. In other words, all these figures more or less correspond to the number of years intimated in the 'covenant of the parts.' " Here then, I have presented you, wise reader, with four modern experts of our people who challenge our sages of blessed memory with regard to their assignation of 410 years for the duration of the first Temple. I have placed Yedidyah and Josephus in a separate category and also all the Christian doctors who followed their example as we demonstrated before. Now while the view of the wise Don Isaac is still on my lips, I cannot forgo the opportunity of informing you of his statement that from the beginning of Saul's reign until the end of Zedekiah's, the kings of Israel ruled 493 years. You should take note of this figure which with God's help I shall discuss further at the end of chapter 41. I believed that you would approve of my view regarding this matter and think likewise.

Now let us resume our discussion of the length of the first Temple period. I am not prepared to exert myself with an investigation into the source of Josephus's computation, particularly in view of the fact that even the Christian doctors rejected it. However, it would not be unreasonable to excuse him on the grounds that one of the transcribers had introduced an error into the text. There is the figure of 429 and a half years which the Ralbag clearly gives on three occasions. It appeared surprising that he saw fit to dissent from the view of his three colleagues mentioned above who counted 430 years. But when one takes his method into account, this criticism becomes unnecessary. For one could argue that he reckoned 410 years, which was the figure promulgated by our rabbis, to which he added the first 9 years of Hoshea son of Ela—you shall be given more information about this in the course of the chapter. But I cannot desist from evaluating Yedidyah's chronological calculations which are taken on trust by Christian scholars. Indeed, if the truth be known, his opinion accords with that of Rabad, Kimḥi, and Don Isaac, may they rest in peace. That he adds 10 more years to the reckoning is because he followed the Septuagint in regard to the reign of Amon. For our text reads: *Amon was twenty-two years old when he became king, and he reigned two years in Jerusalem* (2K. 21:19; 2Chr. 33:21), whereas the Septuagint renders, *He reigned twelve years.* This is noted by the Christian Samotheus.[62] Once this erroneous figure is removed, Yedidyah's reckoning is exactly 430 years. There is no doubt (as we said regarding the additional years for the bondage in Egypt) that when it is affirmed that the length of the first Temple period was more than 410 years, it necessarily follows that our aera mundi reckoning has a deficit of those additional years. To no avail would be the response of certain upright persons that these 20 years do not affect the total sum on the grounds that according to those commentators, the years were incorporated either into the period prior to the building of the first Temple, or into the period following its destruction. Such a statement would be invalidated since it is impossible to detach those years from the figure of which they are part. In addition, the figure of 480 years which cover the period from the exodus until the building of the Temple, and likewise the 70-year period between the first and second Temples pose no difficulties. Rather, Scripture gives an explicit and precise record of these years such that no addition or subtraction can be entertained. But according to these persons, 480 years would become 500 or 70 years, 90. Moreover, in his commentary on the first chapter of Avodah Zarah (which we also mentioned in chapter 23), Rashi of blessed memory enumerates the 1,380 years which according to rabbinic opinion span the period from the exodus to the destruction of the second Temple according to the following specification: "Four hundred eighty years until the building of the first Temple which stood for 410 years, a total of 890 years. The Babylonian exile lasted 70 years and the second Temple stood for 420 years. This comes to a total of 1,380 years." The additional years would then bring the total to 1,400 years. And you might set yourself the task of investigating as to whether there was scope for proposing a lower figure for any section of the years from creation until the destruction of the Temple. Thus you might say that the accumulation of those 20 years would disappear when the gap in the years would be filled such that the figure would come to the correct amount. You will discover, however, that the contrary is true; whatever changes are made will be to increase the figure whether by a small or great amount. This, as was demonstrated, was the unanimous view of the five sages who lengthened the period of the bondage in Egypt. Similarly, this fact about the bondage in Egypt is instructive and so, too, this response which is of a similar nature to those who add to the length of the first Temple. In regard to all this, you are justified in claiming, both in regard to the general and the specific, that most people would add to the figure, and that none decrease it. This implies that the number of years of the duration of the first Temple which was disseminated by our rabbis as coming to a total of 410 must be more. And likewise there must have been more than seventeen Jubilees which they count from the time of the entry into the Land until the destruction of the first Temple.[63] This calculation, as Rashi[64] and Rabbi Moses [Maimonides][65] write, is based on the assumption that the first Temple stood for 410 years; it is in any case defective in

62. Johannes Lucidus Samotheus, *Opusculum,* bk. II, ch. 9, 24v.
63. B. Arak. 12b; B. Zev. 118b.
64. Rashi to B. Arak. 12b.
65. *Mishneh Torah,* Shemiṭṭah X:3.

that it requires the additional years posited by these later authorities. Moreover, it is quite evident from a study of the chronological tables of the sage ibn Ḥabib which he inserts into his responsum (143) that those twenty additional years will necessarily increase the aera mundi computation.[66] What is problematic is to understand how such a controversy arose and the reasons for each position. Incline your ear and I shall tell you.

Know that when the length of the reigns of the kings of Israel is reckoned from the beginning of the reign of Jeroboam son of Nebat to the exile of Hoshea, on the basis of the scriptural exposition, a figure of 241 is reached, as we mentioned above. The corresponding period for the kings of Judah reckoned from the reign of Rehoboam to the sixth year of Hezekiah's reign, which was when Hoshea and Israel were exiled from their land, amounts to 261 years. Accordingly, when the years are reckoned on the basis of the reigns of the kings of Israel from the fourth year of Solomon until the destruction, there is a total of 410 years, but 430 when reckoned on the basis of the reigns of the kings of Judah. Go and read the books of Kings and Chronicles where all this information is made available. The wise Don Isaac composed two tables in his introduction to the book of Kings, one for the kings of Israel, the other for the kings of Judah, in which he records the names of the kings, the length of their reigns, and the total figures for either category which accord with my description. Here, indeed, the commentators were hard pressed to equalize the totals. According to the view of Kimḥi and his associates, when one wants to follow the course of Scripture, as is proper, one cannot avoid arriving at the figure of 430. This was the way he challenged our sages with regard to the six verses which I demonstrated in chapter 14. And in his commentary on the verse, *In the third year of King Asa of Judah* (1K. 15:33), he suggests one of the reasons for the shortness of the reigns of the kings of Israel. In his view, the 8 years of the reign of Nadab, during which he was not tending affairs of state on account of being engaged in warfare, were not included in the count. And we shall also discuss the first 9 years of the reign of Hoshea son of Ela which, according to unanimous opinion, are not counted for the same or a similar reason. Thus the length of the reigns of the kings of Israel falls short of that of the kings of Judah, although they both span the same period of time. The discerning person will realize that substantial proof is provided by Rashi in his statement recorded by us concerning the reign of Uzziah. For struggling to fit the foot to the shoe, as the popular saying goes, he states as follows: "If those 15 years are not omitted, it transpires that the Temple stood for 425 years." So even this man of integrity is shown to manipulate Scripture in an effort to uphold the view of our rabbis. Kimḥi had already apprehended him for this act. Don Isaac, too, who upholds Kimḥi's position with regard to the 430 years, disassociated himself from Rashi's method and castigated him in the same way as his fellow.[67] But there are also some sages who believe that the simpler way to account for the shorter period of the reigns of the kings of Israel is to assume that occasionally there was an interregnum, since the line of succession was not always passed from father to son as was the case with the kings of Judah. Instead, there was no direct transmission; the crown passing to the one who could muster the

66. Levi ben Jacob ibn Ḥabib, *She'elot,* Responsum 143 (257).
67. 'Castigated him,' a play on Is. 27:7.

greatest power, while the reigns of the kings of Judah can be said to have been counted twice. This is particularly evident given that the figure of 261 years for the kings of Judah as given in the book of Kings is also given by another prophet, the author of the book of Chronicles. You would be justified in saying that all alike were divinely inspired and that the years counted by the one are no more valid than that of the other. However, it is right to judge that the author of the book of Chronicles was solely concerned with the history of the kings of Judah and took every precaution not to recount the years which had already been included. As regards the author of the book of Kings, please take note of the following statement of Rashi of blessed memory concerning the kings of Israel on the verse, *[Meanwhile Azaziah son of Ahab had become king of Israel] in the seventeenth year of King Jehoshaphat of Judah* (1K. 22:52). He writes: "Some are surprised at this. . . . But after due investigation, I discovered that for the most part, precise figures are not given for the reigns of the kings of Israel." Indeed, you will discover sure proof that some of the years for the reigns of the kings of Israel are missing from the count (I alluded to this above). For in the second book of Kings (15:27), it is written that Pekah son of Remaliah ruled Israel for 20 years and that Ahaz ruled over Judah in the seventeenth year of Pekah (16:1). Thus the twentieth year of Pekah would correspond to the fourth of Ahaz. It should thus follow that the reign of Hoshea son of Ela, who was Pekah's successor to the throne, ought to have commenced in the fourth year of Ahaz. And yet it is written: *In the twelfth year of King Ahaz of Judah, Hoshea son of Ela became king over Israel in Samaria and reigned nine years* (2K. 7:1). And you will find that his reign and that of Hezekiah are also calculated on the basis that he began to rule in the twelfth year of Ahaz. Thus 8 or 9 years of the reigns of the kings of Israel are skipped over such that Hoshea's reign is said to have lasted 9 rather than 17 or 18 years. Our rabbis explained this matter, and indeed provided a conclusive interpretation which they submitted to us in chapter 22 of Seder Olam. With regard to the verse, *In the twelfth year of King Ahaz of Judah, Hoshea son of Ela reigned,* they raise the following question:[68] "How is this possible? Is it not written that he reigned from the fourth year of Ahaz? Why does Scripture state that there were 9 years? These are the nine years in which he [Hoshea] rebelled against him [i.e., the kings of Assyria]." In connecting the reign of Hezekiah to that of Hoshea, they also explain [the discrepancy] in relation to Hoshea's rebellion. Again, in chapter 23,[69] they ratify the explanation of the omission of the first 9 years of the reign of Hoshea with reference to the verse, *In the fourteenth year of King Hezekiah, King Sennacherib of Assyria marched against all the fortified towns of Judah and seized them* (2K. 18:13): "There is a period of 8 years between the first and second exiles, a further 8-year interval between the third exile and Sennacherib's assault of Judah, a fulfillment of the prediction, *Now the former has lightly afflited the land of Zebulun and the land of Naphtali, but the latter has dealt a more grievous blow by way of the sea beyond the Jordan in the district of the nations* (Is. 8:23). All this is approved by all our commentators, Rashi, Kimḥi, Ralbag, and Don Isaac, blessed be their memory, as may be seen from each commentator's interpretation of the verses under discussion. From Rashi's words, in particular, it

68. Seder Olam, ch. 22 (98–99).
69. Ibid., ch. 23 (99–100).

is made clear that the first exile corresponds to that which is described in the book of Kings, *In the days of King Pekah of Israel, King Tiglath-pileser of Assyria came and captured Ijon, . . . the entire region of Naphtali and he deported the inhabitants to Assyria* (2K. 15:29). This accords with Rabbi Samuel bar Naḥmani's statement in [one of] the proems to Ekhah Rabbati.[70] This event occurred in Pekah's twentieth year which was the fourth of Ahaz's reign. The second exile occurred in the twelfth year of Ahaz when the tribes of Reuben and Gad were taken into captivity. At this time, Hoshea son of Ela enlisted the support of So, king of Egypt, for his revolt against Assyria. The third exile occurred in the seventh year of Hoshea's reign when [the king of Assyria] beseiged Samaria and captured it after three years; and in the fourteenth year of Hezekiah, he attacked the cities of Judah and came upon Jerusalem. Thus the first nine years of Hoshea's reign are accounted for in two passages in the Seder Olam, as we noted.

In his commentary on chapter 16,[71] of the second book of Kings, one of the Christian sages, the great commentator Tostatus, also affirms that the first nine years of Hoshea's reign were omitted.[72] He, too, tried to account for the omission, but he refutes the rabbinic view[73] that only the years of liberty are counted on the grounds that if this were the case, the same would hold good for the equivalent years of Ahaz's reign. For it is explicitly stated in chapter 22 of the Seder Olam that both Ahaz and Hoshea were subject to the king of Assyria for 8 years.[74] He offers the alternative reason that Hoshea could not attend to affairs of state during those years because he was waging war against Pekah's relatives and popular following.[75] A similar view, as we stated above, was put forward by Kimḥi of blessed memory in relation to the reign of Nadab. He adduces proof of his view from the account of Omri's reign in chapter 17 of the first book of Kings. Omri reigned from Asa's seventeenth year in which he killed Ela son of Baasha his master, until Asa's thirty-eighth year in which Omri died and was succeeded by his son Ahab. And yet, because he was engaged in war with Tibni and the people, Scripture states, *In the thirty-first year of King Asa of Judah, Omri became king over Israel—for twelve years he reigned in Tirzah six years* (1K. 16:23). In other words, of his 12-year reign which began in the twenty-seventh year of Asa, only the years between the thirty-first and thirty-eighth of Asa's reign are counted since the first years were in disorder. Such is the view of the above-cited Christian. Come what may, it is patently evident to everybody that the first years of Hoshea's reign, whether 8 or 9, were not included in the count and that only the last 9 years of his reign are reckoned, which according to the two fore-mentioned solutions correspond to the time when he had liberated himself after the rebellion or after he had seized the throne. Now I can assure you that the question as to whether he was a vassal of the king of Assyria or involved in warfare during those first 9 years is irrelevant to our topic of the computation of the years from creation. Whatever the case, we ought to reckon all his 18 years from the

70. E.R., proem 5: "In what order were they exiled? . . . R. Samuel bar Naḥmani says: The tribes of Zebulun and Naphtali went into exile first and so it is written."

71. The reference is to ch. 17 not ch. 16.

72. *Commentaria in lib. IV Regum* (162–63), XVII quaestio 2: "Osee Rex Israel quo anno Achaz regnare coepit."

73. Tostatus does not refer explicitly to the rabbinic view.

74. Seder Olam, ch. 22 (96).

75. The Latin text reads "amicos," and de' Rossi's Italian version "heredi" (heirs).

death of Pekah until his exile, which correspond to the period from the fourth year of Ahaz who reigned 16 years, until Hezekiah's sixth year. And yet you have noticed that the figure of 241 years for the reigns of the kings of Israel only include the last 9 years of Hoshea's reign. In my opinion, the first 9 years, which are not counted, were included by Ralbag in the total of 419 and a half years for the duration of the Temple, as we have already noted in this chapter. And I was astonished to see Don Isaac's commentary on the verse in question [i.e., 2K. 17:1] and on the verse, *In the third year of King Hoshea son of Ela of Israel, Hezekiah son of Ahaz of Judah became king* (2K. 18:1). For there, he sustains the view that the first 9 years of Hoshea's reign were counted together with the last years.[76] And in his table of the kings of Israel which he inserted at the beginning of the book of Kings, he forgot them and only reckoned 9 years for the reign of Hoshea. Thus in view of this, the period extending from the beginning of Jeroboam's reign until the exile of Hoshea ought to amount to 250 and not 241 years. We could say in his defense that his sole aim was to count the regnal years of all the kings. We shall discuss this idea in the course of the chapter. For our investigation, it is sufficient to note that the first 9 years of Hoshea's reign became absorbed and that we have no option but to add them to the figure for the duration of the Temple, and, of necessity, to the computation of the age of the world. Now with regard to Kimḥi's view about the 8 years of Nadab which were discounted, I showed less concern than with these 9 years of Hoshea. This was because I found his opinion inconclusive. In fact, the commentators Rashi, Rabbi Levi ben Gershon [Ralbag], and Don Isaac did not agree with him, while they did accept the argument regarding Hoshea's years. There is the explicit statement of Rashi of blessed memory on the verse, *In the twelfth year of King Ahaz of Judah, Hoshea son of Ela became king over Israel in Samaria and reigned nine years* (2K. 17:1). He writes: "There is absolutely no basis for saying that Hoshea reigned only 9 years. For he reigned from the fourth year of Ahaz until the sixth of Hezekiah, a period of more than 16 years. When Scripture refers to nine years, it applies to the years subsequent to his revolt against the kings of Assyria—this is the way the matter is expounded in the Seder Olam." The wise Ralbag writes that during the first 9 years in which he was merely a vassal of the kings of Assyria, his sovereignty was not recognized. Now you might have problems regarding Kimḥi's view. For occasionally he asserts that the first Temple stood for 410 years, as for example, in his comment on the verse, *The glory of this latter House shall be greater than that of the former one* (Hag. 2:9). To this I would answer that in all such cases, Kimḥi is deferring to rabbinic opinion and specifically using their own criteria in order to solve the problem inherent in the verse. We shall discuss this further in chapter 51. But we have heard his own view regarding the duration of the Temple directly from his mouth and his writings, and recorded it. You will find that the Christian Samotheus writes that many Christian sages endeavored to harmonize the years of the reigns of the kings of Israel with that of the kings of Judah, but without success.[77]

76. Abravanel to 2K. 17:1 (645–46): "These years pose great problems. . . . To resolve this, they state in Seder Olam that these were the nine years in which he was in revolt. For he ruled from the fourth year of Ahaz until the sixth of Hezekiah. And in the twelfth year of Ahaz which was the eighth year of Hoshea's reign, he rebelled against the king of Assyria. From the time of his revolt until the end of his reign there were nine years as Scripture states."

77. Johannes Lucidus Samotheus, *Opusculum,* bk. VI, ch. 11: "De intiio et fine Regum Israel."

Finally he cites their translator [Jerome] who, in one of his letters to his friend Vitalis, describes the effort of solving the considerable discrepancies which are difficult to reconcile as a waste of time and an activity suitable for somebody who has nothing to do.[78] This statement of his is in line with that expressed in chapter 3 of the Letter to Titus[79] and its interpretation as given by the wise Aquinas.[80] It is therefore clear that even in the time of the second Temple, this question was a subject of debate in certain Jewish circles. Nevertheless, for all the reasons indicated, all Christian doctors, Yedidyah as well as Josephus (whose statements comprise their views), agreed to leave the computation of the reigns of the kings of Israel incomplete, while following the line of the kings of Judah as did Kimḥi and his companions in the manner that we have described.

Now it is fitting that I should speak out on this matter in favor of the sages, blessed be their memory, who are like a golden crown perpetually adorning our heads. I should give some explanation as to why they counted only 410 years for the duration of the first Temple. There are two reasons which I shall regard as satisfactory until I am supplied with further information from a judicious scholar who, like me, feels duty bound to justify their position. The one reason can be demonstrated by means of our statement in chapter 15 in which we heard the momentous comment of our righteous teacher, our master Moses, *Pray let me ḳnow Your ways that I may ḳnow you* (Ex. 33:13). Likewise, you, reader, for the purposes of this study, must comprehend and acquaint yourselves with the methods of the sages and thus profit from being all the wiser. This is my point. It is stated in Torat Kohanim on the verse, *When a woman has a discharge of blood for many days* (Lev. 15:25)[81] (and the *baraita* is cited in tractate Yoma of the Palestinian Talmud[82] and in the first chapter of Shevuʿot concerning the woman who has an issue)[83] as follows:

> "Days" signifies two days. One might say that it signifies many days. Rabbi Aqiva said: "Anything that can signify a large or small number and you take it as a large amount, you have taken nothing; but if you take the smallest amount, you have taken something." Rabbi Judah ben Betera said: "When two measurements are given of which the one is limited, the other not, the unlimited measurement is not used." Rabbi Nehemiah said: "Is the object of Scripture to open up or to close? Surely the object of Scripture is to open up. If you were to say that "days" signifies ten days, you could also claim that it signifies one hundred, or two hundred or a thousand. But when it is interpreted as signifying two days, a definite limit is given."

78. Jerome, *Epistolae,* Ep. LXXII (*P.L.* XXII, col. 676): "Relege omnes et veteris et novi Testamenti libros et tantam annorum reperies dissonantiam et numerum inter Iudam et Israel, id est, inter regnum utrumque confusum, ut huiusmodi haerere quaestionibus, non tam studiosi, quam otiosi hominis esse videatur."

79. Titus 3:9: *But avoid stupid controversies, genealogies, dissensions, and quarrels over the law, for they are unprofitable and futile.*

80. Thomas Aquinas, *Super Epistolas . . . ad Titum,* cap. 3, lectio II: "Dicendum est in Scriptura sacra secundum veritatem nihil est contrarium. Sed si aliquid apparet contrarium, vel est quia non intelligitur vel quia corrupta sunt vitio scriptorum quod patet specialiter in numeris et genealogiis. Et hic ideo quia determinari non possunt, vult quod vitentur."

81. Sifra, Meṣora, 7, 5 (76, col. c).

82. P. Yoma 2 (5) 40a.

83. Although the tractate deals with the subject, the passage in question is not given.

Here then we are presented with three witnesses where even one would have sufficed to demonstrate that this is the rabbinic rule. In all cases when calculations or other subjects are open to doubt such that different suggestions are put forward, they always use the minimum or the part which all opponents have no option but to accept. This limitation takes the ground from under the feet of all who would come with the intention of opposing their measurement. The use of this principle is also demonstrated in chapter 1 of Ḥagigah[84] and in Ḥullin,[85] and a lengthy exposition of the rule is given by Rashi in his commentary on those passages. Tostatus, however, interprets the phrase "many days" as signifying a long period of time, but he does acknowledge that such an interpretation poses the problem of the unknown and undetermined quantity.[86] However I happened to converse on this subject with experts in jurisprudence who indicated to me a passage in the Liber Sextus of the papal *Decretals*[87] and the section "ubi numerus" in the *Old Digest*[88] in which this principle, "The plural consists of the number two" is ratified. Moreover you will correctly judge that our sages used this method in tractate Ḥullin when they raised the problem regarding the length of office of the Levites.[89] One verse states, *From twenty-five years of age they shall participate in the service of the Tent of Meeting* (Num. 8:24). The other verse states, *From thirty years of age up to the age of fifty, all who are subject to service in the performance of the duties for the Tent of Meeting* (Num. 4:23). They reconciled the discrepancy by stating that at the age of twenty-five, the Levite begins his training for the Levirate, and at the age of thirty assumes office, and at the age of fifty he retires. For they preferred the minimum period from thirty to fifty, to the maximum period from twenty-five. We therefore see that there are two approaches based on Scripture for gauging the length of the Temple period, involving the positing of two figures, one larger than the other. Since there is no way of ascertaining which is the correct one, our rabbis and leaders were content to agree to the proposition that the person who upholds the smallest figure is praiseworthy. In any case, we need the Modite[90] for synchronizing the various verses and to draw them together such that the righteous might retain their method of taking the minimum figure which is 410 in this case. Secondly, when they were contemplating the synchronization of the two figures, they had to adopt one of two methods. Either one should propose that there were interregna amounting to twenty years during the course of the reigns of the kings of Israel or else to reckon that 20 years of the reigns of the kings of Judah were counted twice. Now in this matter which involves mere reasoned and balanced judgment, they showed a preference for the second reason. Indeed, it

84. B. Ḥag. 7a.

85. B. Ḥull. 137b.

86. Tostado, *Commentaria in Leviticum* to Lev. 15, quaestio X, 149–50.

87. The Decretales are rescripts containing papal rulings. The Liber Sextus, together with the Constitutiones Clementinae and the Decretales of Gregory IX comprise the official *Corpus Iuris Canonici.* The reference is to the section "De regulis iuris" (vol. 2, col. 1123): "Pluralis locutio duorum numero est contenta."

88. This is a reference to Ulpian's ruling "Ubi numerus testium non adicitur, etiam duo sufficient: pluralis enim elocutio duorum numero contenta est" (*Corpus iuris civilis. Digesta,* 328).

89. B. Ḥull. 24a.

90. 'We need the Modite,' an expression from B. Meg. 15b and B. B.B. 10b referring to Eliezer the Modite's exegesis of Scripture to which deference was shown.

would appear—and this without slighting our commentators who took pride in their exposition based on the plain meaning of Scripture, which is not our present concern—that we should praise our rabbis of blessed memory for whose opinion we have practical evidence. Even recourse to the past is unnecessary. For in our own time, there have been no lack of great renowned rulers who in quest for spiritual perfection by means of withdrawal from the vanities of the world, or in order to relieve themselves from the troubles of old age or sickness, or in order to instruct their successors in their view of correct government, robed their sons in the regal finery and in their lifetime invested them with either full or partial sovereignty.[91] The fathers lived a long time after this event; and thus it was possible for historians to count both the years of the fathers until their death, as well as those years from the time in which their sons came to power. In this way, many of the years which pertained to the sons were also incorporated in the years of the fathers.

Our rabbis of blessed memory thought that such a situation had arisen in the case of certain kings of Judah, for certain patent proofs[92] from the number of years of the kings of Israel led them to this view. In their opinion, this observation could be supported from the scriptural description of the kings of Judah with regard to Jehoram son of Jehoshaphat and Uzziah. Accordingly, the rabbis of blessed memory decided to make their calculations according to the reigns of the kings of Israel. And they did not intend that their calculation should have any bearing on the figure for the years from creation to which, as we showed in chapter 25, had never been their practice to assign a date. Moreover, as we indicated, the teaching of *creatio ab novo* is not affected by the positing of a smaller or larger figure. Thus they opted to count only the regnal years expressly recorded in Scripture for each king. This is the method used by the author of the Seder Olam who did not deviate from counting the years of the kings of Israel, including those of Hoshea, according to Scripture which, as is apparent to the one who wishes to count them, come to the correct and clear figure of 241. With the 36 or 37 years which cover the period from the fourth year of Solomon, and the 133 years which cover the period from the exile of Hoshea in the sixth year of Hezekiah until the destruction of the Temple, there is a total of 410 years discounting the one-month reign of Shalom son of Yabesh and the six months of Zechariah's reign. On account of this, they refrained from adding the first years of Hoshea's reign to their calculation, although they themselves (I refer to the author of the Seder Olam whose view represents that of our rabbis) acknowledged them, as was noted, not on one but on two occasions. And if it were proposed even by the rabbis themselves, that there had been various interregna, there would have been no place for them according to their method of reckoning, given that such is the course of the scriptural narrative, as we stated above. Although it is evident that the length of Hoshea's reign subsequent to the death of Pekah until his exile was 17 or 18 years, for one of the two fore-mentioned reasons, it is stated in chapter 17 of the second book of Kings that he only reigned 9 years over Israel. Our rabbis of blessed

91. As Cassel notes, the case of the Holy Roman Emperor Charles V illustrates de' Rossi's point. In 1556, he retired to a monastery and abdicated his claim to the Netherlands and Spain in favor of his son Philip II.

92. 'Certain patent proofs,' lit. certain proof of an ox slaughtered before you. The expression is based on B. Nidd. 15a.

memory regarded this as indicative of the wisdom of retaining the course of the narrative as given in holy Writ. This is the implication of the above-cited comment of Rashi: "The duration of the Temple when calculated according to the reigns of the kings without omitting these 15 years of Amaziah and Uzziah comes to a total of 425 years."

Once having put the figure of 410 years on record as the duration of the Temple period calculated according to the regnal years, when they happened to discuss the duration of the Temple period in its own right, which according to the true reckoning was 418 years, they were loathe to dislodge the established computation and to publicize the figures given according to different standpoints. Throughout all their discussions, they always retained the figure of 410 which was also the first figure yielded by a simple reading of Scripture. This accorded with the principle formulated in tractates Shevu'ot[93] and Qiddushin,[94] "The first teaching is not removed from its place."[95] You see the statement of our trustworthy master Moses regarding the gluttonously craving people There were several thousand more present in addition to the soldiers, but once the assembly had been announced as numbering six hundred thousand persons, he kept to that figure and addressed them thus: *The people who are with me number six hundred thousand men* (Num. 11:21). Perhaps it may be desirable to posit a second reason as to why they retained the figure of 410 which had already been disseminated. For they were not concerned to include the years of Hoshea's subjection to Shalmaneser, since they did not amount to a complete decade. Similarly, our master Moses did not include the 3,550 members of the military in his statement in addition to the six hundred thousand. The kabbalists also disregarded that additional figure when they said the number six hundred thousand comprises all types of human physiognomies.[96] Similarly, on the verse, *One generation goes* (Eccl. 1:4) they state in Midrash Qohelet that a generation numbers sixty myriads on the basis of the verse, *Not one of these men, this evil generation shall see the good land that I swore to give to your fathers* (Deut. 1:35). And in Pirqe d'Rabbi Eliezer,[97] tractate Shabbat,[98] Bereshit Rabbah,[99] and Shir ha-Shirim Rabbah,[100] they refer to sixty myriads of ministering angels, crown-wreathers, whose

93. B. Shev. 4a.

94. B. Qidd. 25a.

95. In other words, although the second or later teaching may be more authentic, once the first teaching was disseminated, it could not be removed.

96. See, e.g., Nahmanides, *Torat Adonai (Kitve Ramban,* 162): "A person's knowledge is reflected in his facial features. Only 60 myriad different faces have been created. This figure represents the sum total of all minds."

97. PRE, ch. 47: "When the Holy One blessed be he descended on Mt. Sinai to give the Torah to Israel, 60 myriads of the ministering angels descended with Him, corresponding to the 60 myriads of the mighty men of Israel and in their hands were swords and crowns, and they crowned the Israelites with the crown of the Ineffable Name."

98. B. Shabb. 88a: "When the Israelites gave precedence to *we will do* over *we will listen,* 600,000 ministering angels came and set two crowns upon each man of Israel, one as a reward for *we will do,* and the other as a reward for *we will listen.*"

99. B.R. 74:17 (877) to Gen. 32:2: "The Shechinah does not rest upon less than 60,000 myriads."

100. S.S.R. to S.S. 7:1: "60 myriads of angels danced and leapt before Jacob our father when he went out from the house of Laban. The rabbis say: 120 myriads *as it says And Jacob said when he saw them This is God's camp* (Gen. 32:3);—this accounts for 60 myriads: *And he called the name of that place Mahanyim* [two camps]—this is 120 myriads."

number was equivalent to that of the camp of Israel. And yet, there were several thousand more, quite apart from the fact that all the rest of the people who said, *We will do and we will hear* also deserved that crown. In the book of Kings (1, ch. 6) it is shown that Solomon began the building of the Temple in the fourth year of his reign in the month of Ziv, which is the second month, and completed the construction in his eleventh year in the month of Bul which is the eighth month. This was a period of 7 years and 7 months. Nevertheless, at the end of the verse, it states, *It took him seven years to build it* (1K. 6:38), omitting all reference to those months. In fact, this is logical as may also be demonstrated from the question posed by our rabbis of blessed memory in tractate Rosh ha-Shanah of the Palestinian Talmud[101] with regard to the reign of David. In the second book of Samuel it is written, *In Hebron he reigned over Judah seven years and six months, and in Jerusalem he reigned over all Israel and Judah thirty-three years* (2Sam. 5:5). This is a period of 40 and a half years. And yet in several other passages, it is written that he reigned a mere 40 years. They resolve the problem by asserting that the larger figure incorporates the smaller. We shall consider this matter further in chapter 40, God willing. In a similar way, they disregarded these few years which ought to have been mentioned in addition to the 410 years, and with all the more reason, given that the literal text of Scripture does not disclose whether the precise amount was actually 8 or 9 years. We are of the opinion that this was one of the reasons which led our sages to disseminate the figure of 410 years for the period extending from the building of the Temple until its destruction despite their own belief that it lasted a few more years. However, there is a third reason given by Rabad at the beginning of his *Sefer ha-Qabbalah* which ought to be mentioned in this context, but with a difference as you shall observe. He writes:[102] "From the building of the Temple until its destruction is 430 years. (The figure of 433 is an error, as we demonstrated at the beginning of the chapter.) However our sages reckoned 410 years since the kingship was not taken into account after the exile of Jehoiakim." This was alluded to by Kimḥi in his critique of Rashi which we cited above. Thus, for one of those reasons or any other one which might seem appropriate, our rabbis of blessed memory established the figure of 410. This figure is therefore symbolically derived from scriptural verses, such as, *With this shall Aaron enter the Sanctuary* (Lev. 16:3),[103] *And let them make Me a sanctuary that I may dwell among them* (Ex. 25:8),[104] and *clear oil of beaten olives for lighting* (Ex. 27:20)[105] which alludes to the first Temple of 410 years and the second of 420 years. In the Midrash of Nahum ben ha-Qanah[106] the word *bereshit* is divided into *be-rosh* (at the

101. P. R.H. 1 (1) 56b.

102. *Sefer ha-Qabbalah* (6).

103. The word *with this* [*be-zot*] has the numerical value of 410. See V.R. 21:9 (416).

104. As Cassel notes, this interpretation is found in Baḥya ben Asher's commentary to Ex. 25:8 in which he states that the expression *that I may dwell* (*ve-shakhanti*) and the expression in Ex. 29:46 *that I might abide* (*le-shokhni*) refer respectively to the first and second Temple. The numerical value of *ti* in *ve-shakhanti* is 410, while the numerical value of *le-shokhni* is 420.

105. This interpretation is also from Baḥya ben Asher's interpretation to Ex. 27:20 where he cites a Midrash (source unknown) in which the word *beaten* (*katit*) is divided up such that the first part *kat* has a numerical value of 420 and the second part *it* a numerical value of 410.

106. There is, as far as I know, no such Midrash. It may be that de' Rossi meant to refer to Nehuniah ben ha-Qanah, the alleged author of the *Bahir,* but the passage is not to be found there.

beginning of) *it* (410).[107] There are other such examples in which the purpose was not to give an exact figure. Rather, they were simply following their own line of thinking and conforming to the system that they had initiated. Thus their statement in Arakhin,[108] "They counted seventeen Jubilees from the time that they entered the Land until their departure from it" means, as ibn Ḥabib states in his responsum,[109] that such was the number of Jubilees they ought to have counted. Moreover, according to their statement in the last chapter of tractate Zevaḥim,[110] the rabbis of blessed memory admit that they did not actually have evidence for the 7-year allocation which is one of their basic presumptions in calculating the Jubilees, but that it was conjectured thus. For they state that since the conquest of the Land took seven years (which they prove from Scripture), the allocation of the Land also took seven years. Rashi comments here: "The seven years of allocation is a mere deduction." In any case, whether the figure, which is a thing of the past, was more or less, is of no consequence. A similar way of reasoning is made by the author of *ha-Terumah*.[111] Having raised the problem that from one point of view the second Temple stood for 419 years, while 421 according to another view, he states: "They adopted the figure of 420 because it is a whole number; or else, because they were following the 70 weeks [of years] (Dan. 9:24) of Scripture which refer to the 70 years of exile and the 420 years of the Temple." Now you reader, should pay great attention to these considerations, and particularly, to the reasons for their claim that the Temple did not stand for more than 410 years. Otherwise, one would find a discrepancy between the various rabbinic statements and particularly between those of Rabbi Jose and Rabbi Jose. For how could they count 410 years when on two occasions in the Seder Olam they count 418 years on account of the eight first years of Hoshea. You should bear this all in mind in case we happen to review this subject in subsequent chapters. I deliberately used the phrase "Rabbi Jose and Rabbi Jose" for I wanted you to know that the statement in the Seder Olam about the eight years of Hoshea, which we also cited in the name of Rashi of blessed memory, is also cited in the Yalqut Shimoni on the book of Kings in the name of Rabbi Jose himself.[112] Moreover, in tractates Yevamot[113] and Niddah[114] they state that the anonymous author of the Seder Olam is Rabbi Jose. In fact I also found the citation in the name of Rabbi Jose in the ancient copy of the Yalqut to which I referred in chapter 19. In the light of this discussion, you cannot accept the statement of Don Isaac to which we referred earlier in the chapter who wrote: "According to the author of the Seder Olam, the final destruction of the Temple occurred in the year 3338," but rather 8 more years must be added which brings the total to 3346.

107. A similar statement is also found in Baḥya ben Asher's commentary to Gen. 1:2: "The word *bereshit* alludes to the building of the first Temple which stood for 410 years." A similar statement is also found in ibn Ezra's description of the fourth method of exegesis in his introduction to his Bible commentary: "Why is the word *bereshit* made up of the letters *bet* followed by *resh, alef, shin,* and then *yod* and *tav*? It alludes to the fact that first Temple would stand for 410 years."

108. B. Arak. 12a.

109. Levi ibn Ḥabib, *Teshuvot* (258, col. b).

110. B. Zev. 118b.

111. Baruch ben Isaac of Worms, *Sefer ha-Terumah* (on Avodah Zarah, par. 135).

112. Yalqut Shimoni 2, par. 236.

113. B. Yev. 82b.

114. B. Nidd. 46b.

You will also disagree with his statement that the rabbis of blessed memory counted 410 years because they followed the reigns of the kings of Judah with the deduction of the twenty years of Jehoram son of Jehoshaphat and Uzziah. The problem would still remain. Quite apart from the fact that none of the 241 years for the reigns of the kings of Israel were duplicated, there remain the first eight years of Hoshea which increase the length of the period from the beginning of the division of the kingdom until the exile of Hoshea in respect to both the kings of Israel and the kings of Judah. With the addition of the 37 years of Solomon and the 133 years of the period from Hoshea's exile until the destruction, the total comes to 418. If you say that they counted according to the reigns of the kings of Israel, as was said, there is nothing to prevent you from adding the 8 years of Hoshea's subjection or wars which would also accord with their view. But if you insist that they followed the reigns of the kings of Judah and subtract those 20 years, you are deprived of the means of adding these 8 years which have to be counted whatever method is employed.

Now despite all that has been said in defense of our blessed rabbis for their calculation of a mere 410 years, there is no doubt that any critic of their position as, for example, the four commentators mentioned above, would not have been regarded by them as a heretic or as spurning their teachers' authority; nor would they have considered it an act of wickedness in any way. In fact, had they been living today, they would not have refrained from examining his [R. Jose's] statements—which is perhaps contrary to what one of the crowd of pedantic scholars might imagine who, as he passes by, becomes embroiled in the dispute[115] for no good reason. For in the final analysis, this computation is not a tenet of the faith and its refutation is not to the detriment of any law or precept nor does it form an integral part of the ancient tradition transmitted to them by Moses our teacher. Even were a stranger to offer convincing evidence from the other monarchies, as we demonstrated above, and prove that the Temple stood for 430 years which was the opinion of Kimḥi and fellow travelers, they would not refuse him a hearing. Now, my intelligent reader, pay attention to the reproof which I received from one of the Christian scholars. He said as follows: "On examination of the tables of Eusebius the Caesarean and those of Samotheus and other chronologers, it is clear that Rehoboam ruled in the thirty-fourth year of Alba, the king of the Latins, which was the thirty-third year of the reign of Laosthenes, king of Assyria, and the ninth of Sheshak, the king of Egypt. It is therefore evident that from that year until the twentieth year of the reign of Romulus, king of Rome, and the seventeenth year of Shalmaneser, king of Assyria, and the first year of Sabacon, king of Egypt, which was the sixth year of Hezekiah's reign and Hoshea's last year was a period of 261 years. Clearly, from Rehoboam and Jeroboam until the ninth year of Hezekiah, 261 years elapsed. It is therefore obvious that we should adopt the computation of the reigns of the kings of Judah according to the literal text without claiming that any years were ascribed simultaneously to two different kings, father and son. We should not follow the line of the kings of Israel which are less, but rather increase them on the supposition that for some reason or other there were some interregna. In my response in defense of our sages I did not adduce the proofs given above which I judged to be of little authority for

115. Cf. Pr. 26:17.

us. I preferred to reply with the words of the sage of the *Kuzari* which he used in his exoneration of the "philosopher" [Aristotle] who was indicted for his belief in the eternity of the universe. When he realized that he found convincing proofs both for the eternity of the universe and for creation with no overwhelming proof to decide the issue, he opted to take the line which, according to his reasoning, posed the least serious problems. But if he had been the recipient of a tradition or an experience of some other kind, which would have necessarily led him to a belief in the creation, he would have certainly endeavored to uphold that belief while refuting any contrary view. The teacher of the *Guide* gave a similar exoneration [of Aristotle] in chapter 16 and successive chapters of part 20. Likewise, this explanation can be put forward for our sages' computation of these years, and for their interpretation of the relevant verses which we have recorded. Nevertheless, all other Jews and the Christians mentioned above were inclined to take the other view, which, as Kimḥi and others wrote, was demonstrated by the course of the scriptural narrative, while the rabbinic exegesis of this topic was somewhat disassociated from the literal text of holy Writ. Now if we dismiss any external consideration as something which is excluded from our purview, I would make the general statement that the difference between 410 and 430 should not be regarded as an authoritative doctrine which later became the subject of controversy by the later challenging authorities. On the contrary, it was first the subject of controversy and then became an authoritative doctrine in that the ancients[116] had initiated the controversy. The rule is explicitly formulated in the Palestinian Talmud;[117] practice follows the authoritative opinion which represents the view of our rabbis. At any rate, I believe that even they would hold that there is no option but to add Hoshea's first years to the total since there is explicit reference to them in Scripture, and the author of the Seder Olam and all Jewish and Christian commentators agree to it. These years necessarily augment the number of years which are counted from creation, for they cannot be regarded as overlapping years between father and sons, as appears to be the case with some of the kings of Judah according to the sages' view. But there was no direct line of succession among the kings of Israel; the crown was transferred from family to family and from tribe to tribe. Each reign is clearly counted in its own right and poses no difficulties or problems which would cause us to confuse the various sections, and to say in their regard that which our sages only asserted in relation to the kings of Judah. The sum total of their reigns thus amounts to 418 years, as we explained. Nevertheless, once the rabbis of blessed memory had made their first declaration with regard to the details of the years of those who reigned in Israel that their reigns amounted to 410 years as is stated in the Seder Olam, which has implications for the duration of the Temple and the age of the world, they did not change their position. After all, from the time of the destruction of the Temple, this fact can have no legal repercussion—I shall clarify this matter further with God's help.

Now there is also another point, intelligent reader, which I cannot refrain from communicating. We cannot make the forced assertion that our rabbis omitted the seven years during which the Temple was constructed, and began their enumeration of the

116. In the Italian translation, de' Rossi refers here to Philo and Josephus.
117. P. Taʿanit 2 (14) 66a.

410 years from the time of its completion, and counted the years of Hoshea's subjection in lieu of those years. One would first have to raise the question as to why they did not treat the second Temple in the same way. For they state that 7 years after Ezra had come up to the Land was 8 years after its completion and the thirteenth year of the second Temple period—this is plainly evident in the tenth chapter of the Laws of the Sabbatical year written by Rambam of blessed memory.[118] Thus it is obvious that such was not their method of delineating these periods. Then a further objection could be raised on the basis of the verse in the first book of Kings (6:1) in which the beginning of the construction of the Temple is related to the fourth year of Solomon's reign, 480 years after the exodus from Egypt. Most important is the fact that we have clear evidence that our rabbis of blessed memory began their computation from the time in which they embarked on the construction of the Temple. For in tractate Avodah Zarah,[119] they count 1,000 years which in their view spans the period from the exodus until the Greek Empire, or 1,380 years if the period is extended to the destruction of the second Temple. According to that computation, the figure of 410 follows consecutively from the figure of 480 without the interposition of any years between the two periods. I brought this to your attention earlier in the chapter with my citation of Rashi of blessed memory and, more explicitly, in chapter 23. We could still propose to disregard these arguments and maintain that the Temple stood for only 410 years. But it is true that as far as the aera mundi computation is concerned, which is the subject of our inquiry, we would gain nothing. For it would in any case be necessary to count 480 years, and 7 for the period of the construction of the Temple and 410 such that the total would be increased by 7 years. It would be impossible to incorporate or assimilate these years into the subsequent or preceding periods for the reason provided by us in this chapter regarding the 20-year figure posited by our commentators. We shall mention it again in chapter 38 in our treatment of the second Temple, may it be built and erected speedily in our days.[120] Similarly, if Rabad's statement is true, namely, that our rabbis computation of 410 years only extended until the third year of the reign of Jehoiakim, the 20 years from that time until the destruction of the Temple would undoubtedly have to be added to the aera mundi computation. Apart from these years, it is common knowledge that 70 years separated the period of the two Temples.

Now, my brother, having confronted you with all this, you should not speak out rashly regarding the fixing of the new-moon days and festivals and object in the following manner. Surely anyone who adds or subtracts just one month from all the years which are counted from creation, dismantles and refutes the formula *baharad*[121] such that it no longer denotes the very first new-moon day, computed according to the mean motion. In that case one would have to add or deduct 1 day, 12 hours, and 793 parts of an hour to every month. As a result one would imagine that all the fixed computations would revert to chaos. Now, as my shield and armor, I could muster the five commentators, Rabbenu Hananel, Ramban, Ralbag, Don Isaac, and Latif, who

118. *Mishneh Torah,* Shemiṭṭah X:3.

119. B. A.Z. 9a.

120. Not surprisingly, the prayer about the rebuilding of the Temple is omitted in the Italian version.

121. *Baharad* is a mnemonic symbol used to denote the first conjunction in the month of Tishri, six months before the creation of the world on a Monday (*b*) at the fifth hour (*h*) and 204 parts of an hour (*rd*).

added 30 years or so to the 400-year period of the exodus; and likewise the four commentators, Rabad, Kimḥi, Ralbag, and Don Isaac, who added 20 years to the first Temple period. And I could tell you that you should first address them on this matter in order to know that their protector would respond to your reproof. For they were all leading authorities of recent times. Their statements merit examination, and if they prove problematic, attempts should be made to resolve them. And if I have bent over backwards to uphold the 410 years posited by our sages, I have not thereby disqualified, nor do I have definite proof by which to disqualify the interpretation of the four commentators who claim that the literal text of Scripture proves and justifies their view. The fact is that while I make no pretension to wearing their cloak, against this criticism—from which they certainly merit being defended—I will, God willing, rise to the defense, not in this chapter but in chapter 40. For in the forthcoming chapters, we shall also treat the subject of the second Temple, after which in chapter 40, we shall bring this specific topic and other related matters to rest. In that chapter you will come to an understanding of the fundamental formula *baharad* and its scientific working as well as the related formulas[122] which represent different views, indicating the new-moon days for the first three years of creation which are a logical consequence of each other if one adds or subtracts 4 days, 8 hours, and 876 parts of an hour to the ordinary year in order. These calculations were not obtained by a priori reckoning as occurs in prophecy or in an instantaneous moment as when the windows of heaven are opened. Rather it was based on a posteriori reckoning which is the human mode of understanding, as is described by the teacher of the *Guide* in part 3, chapter 21, and by the "philosopher" in the second chapter of the first book of the *Physics*[123] and in the first book of the *Metaphysics.* These scientific facts were applied discriminately to the calculation of the years of creation which was then decided and established sensibly and intelligently by the formulator of our calendar. Thus you will come to the realization that addition or subtraction of years does not change, disrupt, or defer any of the fixed dates of our calendar in any respect. Then indeed there will be exultation in the seventh day[124] for you will understand the origin of all these rules and the basis on which they were established. From now on you can rightly judge that not all the years collated by us from the books of the prophets were precise insofar as they began on the first of the year and ended at the end. You will also realize that if the *baharad* had been part of the prophetical tradition, no doubts would have been raised in connection with it and they would not have had recourse to alternative formulas. The controversy about this matter is discussed at length by the commentator on Rambam's Laws of the Sanctification of the New Moon. Moreover, if this were not true, there would have been no reason for the statement of Rabbenu Hai Gaon who wrote: "The computation that should be used is that which posits the new-moon day on Friday at the fourteenth hour and not *baharad.* The formula *baharad* was only instituted for pedagogical reasons." This is

122. I.e., *Vayad,* the mnemonic symbol used to denote that the first new-moon day was on a Friday (creation of Adam) at the fourteenth hour, or *Geyavtatu* which denotes the first new-moon day after the creation of man on a Tuesday at the tenth hour and 876 parts of an hour.

123. De' Rossi refers to the Physics as *On hearing,* an abbreviated form of the full title of the work, *Physica Akroaseos,* which signifies that the work consisted of Aristotle's lecture notes.

124. 'Exultation . . . day,' cf. Ps. 119:164.

mentioned by Rabbi Abraham the prince in his *Sefer ha-Ibbur*[125] whose words are also cited by the wise ibn Ḥabib in his responsum on the sabbatical year.[126]

Now we shall leave the elucidation of this matter for treatment in chapter 40. Whatever the case, we can reassert that the contents of this chapter would not give a judicious person any justification for attributing any error to our sages, or to say that they were ignorant of anything which was disclosed to us. For aside from the justification of their case which we shall put forward in chapter 40, it is a fact, as we explained in chapter 25 and will mention again in the forthcoming chapters, that there is no passage in which they assert that the aera mundi computation is a basic tenet of *halakhah.* As for the duration of the Temple period, I have indeed demonstrated that they informed us on two occasions in the Seder Olam that the Temple stood for more than 410 years. And yet when they began to count the regnal years according to the characteristic mode of Scripture, the figure first posited by them was not dislocated. Consequently, should any one of us say that our rabbis of blessed memory erred, it is in fact he who has gone astray due to his misunderstanding of their methods.

125. *Sefer ha-Ibbur* III, gate 7 (97).
126. Levi ibn Ḥabib, *Teshuvot* (254, col. a–b).

CHAPTER THIRTY-SIX

The views of those who dispute our rabbis' computation of the duration of the second Temple period.

Now our rabbis of blessed memory stated that the second Temple stood for 420 years. However, as we mentioned in chapter 24, it is universally accepted by both Jews and Christians that from the time of the Greek Empire, according to which the era of documents is reckoned, until the destruction of the second Temple was a period of 380 years, and 386 years from the establishment of the universal Alexandrian Empire, when Darius, and with him the entire Persian Empire, was conquered. As has already been communicated, it is accepted without qualification[1] that there were 70 years between the destruction of the first Temple and the building of the second Temple. This was the computation used by Rashi of blessed memory in his interpretation of the statement in Avodah Zarah[2] that 1,380 years elapsed from the time of the exodus until the destruction of the second Temple, as we mentioned at the beginning of chapter 23. Now according to the rabbinic computation of 420 years, it would transpire that there were 34 years from the time when the construction of the Temple was begun until the Alexandrian Empire. As is stated by Rabbi Jose in the Seder Olam[3] and in Avodah Zarah:[4] "Persian rule lasted 34 years of the Temple period; the Greek Empire 180 years; the Hasmonean dynasty 103 years, and the Herodian dynasty 103 years." It is noteworthy that in his commentary on Daniel, the wise Don Isaac [Abravanel] skillfully contradicts Rabbi Jose's statement in regard to the last three of the four figures.[5] Concerning the Greeks, he wrote: "In my opinion, the exact figure for the years of their domination is 145 years." He said that eleven kings ruled for 142 years during the Hasmonean dynasty. Concerning the Herodian dynasty, he wrote: "The Hasmoneans were succeeded by the Herodian dynasty—there were six kings who ruled over 99 years. This is the correct figure." The fact that he does not dispute the figure of 34 years for the Persian reign in this context should not be taken as sign of his approval. The appropriate place for an investigation into this matter would have been his work *The Days of the World* which he designated in his introduction to the book of Kings. But

1. 'Accepted without qualification,' cf. Lev. 22:21.
2. B. A.Z. 9a.
3. Seder Olam, ch. 30 (141–42).
4. Ibid.
5. *Mayyene ha-Yeshuʿah,* 2, tamar 3 (288, col. a–289).

either he never wrote it, or else it was destroyed during his expulsions from place to place[6] and is no longer extant. In any case, as I indicated in the previous chapter, it is evident that he also disputed this figure since in his work *Zevaḥ Pesaḥ,* he states that the second Temple stood for 428 years. I agree with him regarding the figure for the reign of the Greeks, but only with the proviso that it is granted that there is a printing error in the text—it should read 148 not 145 years. For in the first book of Maccabees[7] and in book 12 of Josephus's *Antiquities,*[8] it is stated that the miracle of Hanukkah which occurred during the last years of Greek domination and at the beginning of Hasmonean rule on holy soil was in year 148, of the Greek era. In other words, the wicked Antiochus Epiphanes began to harass the Israelites in year 143 of the Greek era, and the persecution became intensified when he put his desecrating abomination in the Sanctuary in 145. Three years later, God saw the affliction of His people and drove him out and he departed in great wrath. And in 149, he died from a disease, the likes of which had never been seen before.

Now although according to rabbinic opinion, the era of documents was used from 380 years before the destruction of the Temple, Don Isaac counted 386 years since he began the computation, as had the scribe mentioned in Avodah Zarah, from the time of Alexander's victory over Darius, as we wrote in chapter 23. He likewise disputed their statement that Daniel's computation was faulty.[9] As ibn Ezra writes in his commentary on Daniel,[10] the wise Rabbi Judah Halevi, author of the *Kuzari,* also dissented from this view. Study the passage. Now although he [i.e., Abravanel] does not actually spell out his refutation of the first part of Rabbi Jose's statement about the 34 years, he does write that the individual figures which complete the total were more or less accurate.[11] It would appear that he did have some reservations and defended them, for the manner in which he expresses himself implies that even if the figure is not really precise, being more or less too little or too great, it is approximately correct. In truth, even an unthinking person would be able to work out that if, for example, it were proposed that the figure of 5,331 is not exact,[12] but an approximate figure, give or take 4 or 5 years, or even 1 year, the opponent would have the right to augment it to 5,351 or to some other such figure. Ratification for this could be supplied from the statement of Tullio [Cicero], the greatest pagan orator. For in the third of his chapters called *Paradoxes* (i.e., extraordinary things), he states that the gravity of a sin, be it major or minor, is the same since once you have crossed over the dividing line of what is lawful, the extent of the

6. Abravanel had to flee from Portugal to Spain in 1483, and then from Spain to Naples in 1492.

7. 1Macc. 4:52. (De' Rossi refers to ch. 1—perhaps he was referring to v.54 where the desecration of the temple is dated to the year 145.)

8. *Ant.* XII:321.

9. Abravanel, *Mayyene ha-Yeshuʿah,* 10, tamar 1 (364, col. b). He is referring to the statement in B. Meg. 12a.

10. Ibn Ezra to Dan. 9:2. He cites Halevi's view as the exception since "all the Geonim" accept the rabbinic view that Daniel's computation was faulty.

11. *Mayyene ha-Yeshuʿah,* 10, tamar 7 (376, col. a). In this passage, Abravanel is presenting a critique of the Christian position. With regard to this specific point, he writes: "The view of the sages of blessed memory is correct, for only five Persian kings ruled from the time of Belshazzar until Alexander, and the length of their dominion was more or less 54 years."

12. I.e., the year (1571) in which de' Rossi was writing his book.

infringement becomes of no consequence.[13] Furthermore, the Tosafists raise a problem with regard to the statement of Rashbam [Samuel ben Meir] who claimed that the Temple had been standing for 421 years when it was destroyed. They state as follows:[14] "There is another problem for according to his view, the customary aera mundi computation would be proved erroneous since it would be necessary to add one more year to the count."

Now let us relinquish this examination and turn our attention to those who add to the figure of 420 years. There is no question of being right or wrong with regard to the figure computed for the period from the establishment of the universal Alexandrian empire until the destruction of the Temple and from then until today. But what still remains a point of contention is the duration of the Persian Empire which, according to the disputants, was longer than 34 years. This view gains greater significance when it is not implied but rather explicitly stated that the Persian Empire lasted more than 34 years after the erection of the Temple. Now there are very few opponents to this view among the later sages whose works have so far come to my notice, and I do not know what was said outrightly to dispute the views of the rabbis of blessed memory. The exceptions are Ralbag [Gersonides] who wrote that the second Temple stood for 437 and a half years in his commentary to Daniel[15] and Don Isaac, who, as I informed you, held that it stood for 428 years. Even the sage of the *Kuzari* who is generally considered to be one of the few who scrutinize their statements appears to have changed his mind on this issue. For he writes:[16] "Prophecy lasted for forty years among the people of the second Temple period. For after their return, Haggai, Zechariah, Ezra, and others were still present. Forty years later, there was the assembly of sages called the Men of the Great Synagogue, and they were succeeded by the generation of Simeon the righteous." The author of *Kaftor va-Feraḥ* which we cited at the end of chapter 23 puts forward a similar view when he said: "Know that the era of documents which marks the beginning of the reign of Alexander of Macedon and the end of prophecy which is equivalent to the fortieth year of the second Temple and the beginning of the period of the Men of the Great Synagogue began 380 years before the destruction of the Temple." In other words, according to their dating, Simeon the righteous lived a long time after the first 40 years of the second Temple period, since they say that he was the successor to the Men of the Great Synagogue who began their office after the 40 years had elapsed. Now from various statements of our sages we know, as shall be clarified later, that Alexander's victory over Darius occurred in the lifetime of Simeon. According to their view, then, it necessarily follows that many more than 34 years had elapsed before the Persian Empire came to an end during the time of the second Temple. But since all the other esteemed authorities follow our rabbis in computing 420 years, as shall be explained presently, I must honestly suspect that the translator of the *Kuzari* was not

13. Cicero, *Paradoxa,* III, 1, 20: "Peccavit vero nihilominus, siquidem est peccare tamquam transire lineas, quod cum feceris, culpa commissa est quam longe progrediare cum semel transieris, ad augendam transeundi culpam nihil pertinet."

14. Tos. to B. A.Z. 9b, s.v. *hai man.*

15. Gersonides to Dan. 7:25; 12:13.

16. *Kuzari* III, par. 65.

reliable in conveying this point. If the translator was one of the Tibbonides, he was definitely not Samuel who was a literal and faithful translator.[17] Consider his statement about the precepts that are observed in the Land where he says:[18] "At present you are in great confusion regarding these duties." This statement is completely out of context, and the commentator Kaspi was unsuccessful in his attempts to make it fit.[19] Then I remembered that I had seen the partial translation of Judah ben Kardinal[20] who had rendered the passage: "At present you enjoy peace and tranquillity."[21] By this inversion, he restored the sense of the text as would become evident to anyone who studies the passage. Now this is an inspired book, replete with true beliefs in which every Jew, who is faithful to his covenant, should instruct himself and endeavor to inculcate his children and students with the command and injunction: "Take care not to forsake the Levite."[22] Yet also in the rest of the book, Moses ibn Tibbon[23] misconstrued the text and did not make it comprehensible for us in a way which is compatible with the recognizable features and upright nature of the author Rabbi Judah Halevi—for he is known for his clear and unsullied doctrine. If only he could have spoken to us himself.[24] Nevertheless, I must truly acknowledge our gratitude to ibn Tibbon and praise him for the kindness he has done by providing us with the text. However, I cannot make the same plea on behalf of the author of *Kaftor va-Feraḥ* since we have his own words, and particularly because he wrote that the Persian Empire lasted for not more than 34 years during the second Temple period. After all, we do know that Alexander was the assailant who brought about the downfall of the Persians.

But let us give priority to the subject of the chapter. Of the Jews of antiquity whose views regarding the duration of the second Temple period oppose that of our sages are Yedidyah the Alexandrian whose work *On the Times* we presented before, and Josephus whose statements on the subject we collated next to it.[25] They both lengthened the Persian domination during the second Temple period to more than 103 years. Josephus wrote explicitly that the second Temple stood for 639 and a half years.[26] Similarly, it is evident from the works of Eusebius the Caesarean and the entire community of Christian doctors whether mentioned or not by us that they all approximately arrive at the same point, with slight differences either above or below that

17. The translator was Judah ibn Tibbon who translated the *Kuzari* in 1147, about thirty years after the work had been written.

18. *Kuzari* II, par. 57.

19. This is a reference to Nethanel ben Nehemiah Kaspi (fifteenth century) whose commentary on the *Kuzari* de' Rossi read in manuscript. As Cassel notes (ad loc.), Kaspi's comment does not given any indication that he found the text problematic. He simply explains that people would be burdened by the precepts since they would be frightened in cases they were unable to observe them correctly.

20. Only the preface and fragments of the translation of Judah ben Isaac Cardinal are extant.

21. As Cassel notes (ad loc.), the word "confusion" (*mevukhah*) was changed into "rest" (*menuḥah*), but the Arabic original reads "confusion."

22. A play on the name of Judah Halevi based on Deut. 12:19.

23. The translator was Judah not Moses.

24. 'Clear . . . himself.' This is an adaptation of Job 11:4–5. The text is slightly ambiguous, and it is not clear whether de' Rossi is referring to Halevi's clarity of style or to his doctrinal integrity.

25. I.e., he translated ps. Philo in ch. 31 and selections from Josephus in ch. 33.

26. *Bellum* VI:270. There is a wrong reference to the 10th book of Bellum in the text.

figure. In fact, Samotheus calculated a total of 587 years for the duration of the second Temple period.[27] Now before we proceed with a presentation of the proofs for each side and draw up the battle lines, it is particularly appropriate that we should continue our explanation of the reasons and origin of these discrepancies. Since from our point of view, the birthright belongs to our rabbis of blessed memory, we shall let them initiate the discussion.

Open your eyes, intelligent reader, and see that our sages, one by one, bring the generation of Simeon the righteous the high priest in close proximity to that of Jeshua ben Jehozadak who was the first high priest after the return of the exiles to Jerusalem. You may trace this piece of information from the later texts to the earlier ones, when you study the words of the great teacher Rambam of blessed memory in the introduction to his commentary on the Mishnah. He writes: "The Men of the Great Synagogue were Haggai, Zechariah, Malachi, Daniel, Hananiah, Mishael, Azariah, Ezra, Nehemiah, Mordechai, and Zerubbabel, and included with these prophets are the craftsmen and smiths[28] which come to a total of 120 elders. The last member of that unsullied group who was the first of the mishnaic sages is Simeon the righteous who served as high priest in that generation." Then he continues: "Simeon the righteous who was one of the last members of the Great Synagogue received the tradition from Ezra." And in his *Yad Ḥazaqah* [i.e., the *Mishneh Torah*] he writes: "The members of Ezra's law court were called Men of the Great Synagogue—these are Haggai, Zechariah. . . . They come to a total of 120 elders, the last of whom was Simeon the righteous. He was one of the 120 and he received the Oral Torah from them all and he was high priest after Ezra." At the beginning of his *Sefer ha-Qabbalah,* Rabad wrote:[29] "The second generation of the Men of the Great Synagogue was that of Simeon the righteous, known as Iddo ben Jeshua ben Jehozadak. In his days, the Persian Empire was destroyed by Alexander." Rabbenu Samson, author of *Sefer Keritut* wrote:[30] "Simeon the righteous was one of the last of the Men of the Great Synagogue who were members of Ezra's law court." In his introduction to *Naḥalat Avot,* the wise Don Isaac mentions the Men of the Great Synagogue and then writes: "The last of them was Simeon the righteous the high priest who was the son of Jeshua ben Yehozadak who was the brother of Ezra." In his commentary on the first chapter of Avot, Rav Bertinoro wrote:[31] "The Men of the Great Synagogue comprised 120 elders: Zerubbabel, Sheraiah, Raaliah, Mordechai, Bilshan. They came up to the second Temple in the time of Ezra." He then continues: "Simeon the righteous was one of the last of the Men of the Great Synagogue. He remained the holder of the tradition after they had all died and he was high priest after Ezra."

27. De' Rossi refers to bk. 2, ch. 14 (29v) of Johannes Lucidus's *Opusculum,* which gives the figure of 586 for the period from the destruction of the Temple to the birth of Jesus: "A desolatione ad Christi conceptionem anni 586." Since the second Temple was erected 70 years after the destruction of the first Temple, and the second Temple destroyed 70 years after the birth of Jesus, the figure 586/7 is also valid for the length of the second Temple period, although Lucidus is not actually writing about the second Temple as such.

28. Cf. 2K. 24:16.

29. *Sefer ha-Qabbalah* (16).

30. Samson of Chinon, *Sefer Keritut,* Yemot Olam 1 (151).

31. Obadiah Bertinoro (b. 1450) to M. Avot 1:1.

These quotations facilitate comprehension of the following rabbinic statements: "The Men of the Great Synagogue instituted for Israel."[32] "Why were they called the Men of the Great Synagogue?"[33] "The generation of the Men of the Great Synagogue."[34] Whenever this distinguished community is mentioned, the implication is that they all belonged to the same generation including Simeon the righteous who, as the youngest, survived into the second generation. For they describe him as "one of the last of the Men of the Great Synagogue." Rashi explains this designation in the following manner: "He was living at the very end of that generation; he was not with them from the outset at the beginning of Temple times as was Ezra and he ministered as high priest after Jeshua because no one else officiated in the intervening period." Thus, in their view, 34 years was ample time to encapsulate the two high priesthoods. And having accepted the fact that Alexander who had defeated Darius was a contemporary of Simeon the high priest, the rabbis of blessed memory could accommodate the view that the duration of Persian domination in Temple times was not longer than 34 years and that after the conquest of Babylon, both before and after the building of the Temple, there were no more than four kings who are listed in chapter 30 of the Seder Olam; or alternatively three kings as listed in Bereshit Rabbah:[35] "*And a three-year-old she-goat* (Gen. 15:9)—this alludes to Media which produced three kings: Cyrus, Darius, and Ahasuerus." Yet they had to account for the fact that Scripture refers to many more Persian kings. About one alone it is stated, *for in the thirty-second year of King Artaxerxes . . . and only after a while did I ask leave of the king* (Neh. 13:6). Thus they identified all three kings as one and the same person. As is stated in Seder Olam[36] and in tractate Rosh ha-Shanah:[37] "Cyrus is Darius is Artaxerxes." Here we have presented the view of our rabbis. As for the opposing party whom we have mentioned above, it is clear that each contestant, under his own banner, counts in different ways seven high priests before Simeon, the line of succession being handed down from father to son over an ample period of time, i.e., Jeshua, Joiakim, Eliashib, Joiada, Jonathan (also designated as Johanan, according to Josephus[38] and the Christian Honorius Augusta),[39] Jaddua, Onias who fathered Simeon the righteous. And they relate that Alexander's meeting was with Jaddua, the sixth high priest, whom they called Iaddo. The number of Persian kings who reigned during Temple times which they reckon is likewise greater than that calculated by our rabbis. The smallest figure is given by Josephus. He lists Darius, who built the Temple, succeeded by his son Xerxes Artaxerxes, who wrote a recommendation for Ezra and later for Nehemiah concerning the building of the walls. He was succeeded by Ahasuerus Artaxerxes in whose lifetime the incident with Haman occurred, and he also mentions Darius who was captured by Alexander.

Here then we have presented the views of each of the two sides and their dispute. Now in the following chapter we shall see whether holy Writ can lend them any support.

32. B. Ber. 33a (Meg. 17b, 18a—the Men of the Great Synagogue are not designated in Megillah).
33. B. Yoma 69b.
34. B.R. 35:2 (328); Mid. Teh. to Ps. 36:11.
35. B.R. 44:15 (437).
36. Seder Olam, ch. 30 (136–37).
37. B. R.H. 3b.
38. *Ant.* XI:297.
39. Honorius of Autun or Augustodunensis (1080–1156), *De aetatibus mundi,* bk. V (*P.L.* 172, col. 180).

CHAPTER THIRTY-SEVEN

An apparent problem regarding our rabbis' reckoning of the succession of high priests.

It does appear that the three lines of succession mentioned in holy Writ support the views of the opponents which we described above. I refer to the line of high priests, Persian kings, and descendants of Jechoniah, all of whom were living at the beginning of the second Temple period before the rise of Alexander who extirpated Darius. Proceeding from the beginning, it is a fact that in chapter 12, Nehemiah records the succession of the same six high priests mentioned by the opponents, which at the outset was an uninterrupted line, passed directly from father to son. Thus at the beginning of chapter 12, Nehemiah undertakes to tell us the names of the heads of the priestly clans and Levites who went up with Zerubbabel the prince and Jeshua the high priest. He gives separate lists of the heads of the priestly clans which included Seraiah and Jeremiah (vv.1–7) and of the heads of the Levites who included Jeshua, Binnui, and Kadmiel (vv.8–9) and then refers again to Jeshua the high priest when he writes: *Jeshua begot Joiakim; Joiakim begot Eliashib; Eliashib begot Joiada; Joiada begot Jonathan; Jonathan begot Jaddua* (vv.10–11). It is impossible to identify the Jeshua who begot Joiakim with Jeshua the Levite (v.8) who is mentioned by him since he adds the clarifying comment, *These were in the time of Joiakim son of Jeshua son of Jehozadak* (v.26). Rashi similarly remarks [to v.10]: "All these mentioned in the scriptural text were high priests." He [Nehemiah] does not specifically refer to each individual as a high priest. However the expression *It was in the time of such and such a person, they were heads of the clans* indicates that the person was a distinguished member of the high priest hierarchy as is illustrated by his statement at the beginning of the account, *These were the heads . . . in the time of Jeshua* (v.6). This also becomes obvious from the rest of Nehemiah's narrative. For he describes the heads of the priests and Levites who were also of the time of Joiakim when he further states, *And in the time of Joiakim the priestly clans were . . .* (v.12) and *the heads of the Levites . . .* (v.24) *These were in the time of Joiakim* (v.26). Similarly, when he enumerates the Levites, he states that they were in the days of Eliashib, Joiada, Johanan, and Jaddua (v.22), and each of these four lived out his own span of days. The same style is used in the verse, *The prophecies of Isaiah . . . in the days of Uzziah, Jothan, Ahaz, and Hezekiah* (Is. 1:1). And Johanan son of Eliashib is undoubtedly to be identified with Jonathan as we wrote. Rashi of blessed memory explains that Johanan was high priest, and he also said this of Joiakim in the preceding passage. At the beginning of chapter 3,

Nehemiah describes the building of the wall and writes that Eliashib the high priest built the sheep gate. At the end of the book (13:28), he writes that one of the sons of Joiada the high priest was a son-in-law of Sanballat. This information relates to the story of Manasseh the brother of Jaddua the high priest who was expelled by his priestly brothers and dissociated from the Temple inheritance. As Josephus writes in book 11 and 13,[1] he then built an altar for himself on Mt. Gerizim. This Jaddua was the son of Jonathan who was the son of the Jaddua mentioned [by Nehemiah]. Thus we can see how Nehemiah classified these six high priests with the succession passing to the son after the death of the father in accordance with the dictates of the Torah. In Torat Kohanim,[2] our rabbis of blessed memory derived this fact from the statement of the blessed Lord *[The priest who has been anointed and ordained] to serve as priest in place of his father* (Lev. 16:32), whereas in tractate Sanhedrin,[3] it is derived from the verse applied to all Israelite rulers in general, *to the end that he and his descendants may reign long in the midst of Israel* (Deut. 17:20). Thus the disputant would have every justification in saying that the plain text of Scripture does lend him[4] most authoritative support and provides a convincing rejoinder against our sages on two counts. First, we learn here that Simeon was not of the second generation, nor served as high priest after Jeshua since Joiakim was the second high priest who ministered after his father. Simeon the righteous belonged only to the generation after that of Jaddua. The outlandish idea might come into your mind that Simeon is to be identified with Joiakim. Not only is there the problem as to why the rabbis of blessed memory should have taken into their minds to alter the celebrated scriptural name, it would also necessarily follow that after the victory of Alexander which, in their view, took place in his [i.e., Simeon's] time, Artaxerxes king of Persia, who built the walls of Jerusalem, would still have been in full power as in the past, and this is manifestly untrue. Furthermore, you might even take the license of making a forced interpretation and claim that their designation of the generation of Jeshua and Ezra is not exact, but refers to all six generations all of whom were called the Men of the Great Synagogue. In that case, my brother, wonder at yourself when you come to understand the following elucidation. It is as follows. Those six generations were not comparable to the seven children of Qimḥit who are praised in several passages. As the saying goes: "All flours are flour, but the flour of Qimḥit is fine flour."[5] For it was feasible for them all to officiate at the same time since they were brothers. One could substitute for the other as was the case with Judah who took the place of his brother Simeon who had become unclean on the eve of the Day of Atonement as night fell—this is explained in tractate Megillah of the Palestinian Talmud.[6] Or

1. *Ant.* XI:322–24; XIII:256.
2. Sifra, Aḥare Mot 6:8 (83a).
3. The passage in question is not in Sanhedrin, but in B. Hor. 11b.
4. 'Him'; Cassel reads incorrectly, *lo,* "not," instead of *lo,* "to him."
5. De' Rossi adds the references in the margin, i.e., P. Yoma 1 (1) 38d; P. Meg. 1 (10) 72a; P. Hor. 3 (2) 47d; B. Yoma 47a; T. Yom ha-Kipp. 3:19; V.R. 20:11 (471). The story recounted in these passages is that Simeon the son of Qimḥit was defiled when saliva from an Arabian king spurted onto his priestly garments. His brother Judah officiated in his stead and thus their mother Qimḥit had the merit of seeing two of her sons officiating as high priests. There is a play on the word *qimḥa* (flour) and Qimḥit, the name of the mother.
6. P. Meg. 1 (10) 72a.

the one could substitute if the other was still absent, or he could serve in his stead after his death even if he officiated for only one or two days. In my opinion, these are the same brothers mentioned by Josephus although he only refers to five.[7] But the six high priests that are the subject of our inquiry were of successive generations, one coming, the other going as is the way of the world. Thus the total number of the years of their office was very great. This conclusion is necessitated by the fact that in each case the formula *in the days of Jeshua, in the days of Joiakim . . . such and such persons were the heads of the priestly clans and the Levites.* The use of the word "days" in this context does not have the same sense as "many days" used in connection with the woman with a flux, which term is expounded in Torat Kohanim as signifying two days.[8] This would lead one to think that their lifetime, and that of all the family clans mentioned by him, would have come to an abrupt end. And if you would continue to object that there was only a negligible period of time separating their respective tenures of office, you should go and read. For it is clear from Scripture that Eliashib, the third in office, built the sheep gate in the twentieth year of the reign of Artaxerxes and that his ministry extended far beyond the thirty-second year of this same Artaxerxes in Temple times. For after Nehemiah had left Jerusalem to return to Shushan in the thirty-second year of Artaxerxes' reign, as is clear from chapter 13 of Nehemiah, Eliashib built the chamber for the use of his relative Tobiah. He did not have the audacity to build it while Nehemiah was still in Jerusalem. When after a time Nehemiah returned to the Land of Israel, he found the erected chamber filled with Tobiah's equipment and threw it out. It is out of the question that these happenings and events could have occurred over a few days; a considerable amount of time[9] was required. It is also probable that Eliashib, who was third in the line of the six high priests, and who was still officiating after the thirty-second year [of Artaxerxes], must have survived for some time subsequently since his death is not recorded. Herein lies the problem. For this example only illustrates the case of one high priest of one time. And if we were follow Rabbi Jose and claim that the Persian Empire lasted for 34 years of Temple times, only a few hours would remain to encompass all the days of Joiada and Jonathan and some of the days of Jaddua who, according to our supposition, lived at the time when the episode with Alexander occurred. Such a position is completely untenable on intellectual grounds. On the contrary, according to Yedidyah, Josephus and their followers, as far as they are to be trusted, each one of these three held a long tenure of office and they experienced several vicissitudes. In Yoma,[10] our rabbis of blessed memory interpret the verse, *But the years of the wicked shall be shortened* (Pr. 10:27) as a reference to the high priests of the second Temple. Such an interpretation should not confound you into claiming that times were also troubled on account of these three [priests], since there are two correct responses which may be put forward. First, the reason given by our rabbis of blessed memory to account for the reduction of their years is certainly only applicable to those subsequent to Simeon the righteous. For in the first chapter of Yoma in the Palestinian Talmud,[11] they state that

7. *Ant.* XX:235–41.
8. Sifra, Meṣora, 7, 5 (79, col. a). See de' Rossi's discussion of the passage in ch. 35.
9. 'A considerable amount of time,' lit. a time, times, and half a time. Cf. Dan. 12:7.
10. B. Yoma 9a.
11. P. Yoma 1 (1) 38c.

eighty high priests officiated in the second Temple because some sold the office, and according to one opinion they used magic to kill each other. And in Sifre[12] they state that because they sold the high priesthood for money, their years began to be shortened. There is no doubt that this sin was not committed by the generations from Jeshua to Simeon the righteous since there was a direct line of succession from father to son, and their inheritance was never transferred from one clan to another. In fact, the reverse is the case and we should rather apply to them the verse, *The fear of the Lord prolongs life* (Pr. 10:27). After all, in Bereshit Rabbah,[13] there is the statement of the rabbis of blessed memory that the rainbow was never seen in the time of the Men of the Great Synagogue of whom Simeon was the last in the priestly succession, since their merit was on a par with that of the generation of Hezekiah. Similarly in Midrash Tehillim[14] on the verse, *Bestow Your faithful care on those devoted to You* (Ps. 36:11), they compare the generation of the Great Synagogue with that of Hezekiah in regard to their knowledge of the Tetragrammaton. (We shall refer to this again in chapter 46 of the fourth section of the book.) As a consequence of the righteousness for which they were renowned, the structure of ordination was retained, and a son would succeed his father in office. Subsequently, however, this was not the case. For over the course of time priests and Levites became corrupt in the fulfillment of their ministry and office[15] and acquired their positions for money. This is described by Josephus in chapter 8 of book 20.[16] Just prior to the destruction of the Temple, in return for money pledges, kings gave the Levites permission and the right to don the linen garb worn by the priest in the holy ministry, and in like manner, priests who were unqualified for the priesthood used to buy the office. Similarly, our sages of blessed memory state in the Palestinian Talmud and Sifre quoted above as well as in our Gemara[17] that Martha daughter of Boethus brought Jannai the king an amount of dinars in order to get him to appoint Joshua ben Gamla to the high priesthood. As I indicated at the end of chapter 21, Josephus also refers to this incident. Thus there is every reason for us to believe that those first six generations who did not behave like the others had a long life and did not take wings unto themselves.[18]

The problem becomes all the more exacerbated when, intelligent reader, you turn to another consideration. It is that there is no doubt that the overthrow of Persia was achieved by Alexander of Macedon when he extirpated Darius, or if you like Artaxerxes, for the name is not our present concern. Now the unanimous view expressed in both the Palestinian and Babylonian Talmud and all the Midrashim and specifically chapter 9 of Megillat Taʿanit[19] is that Simeon the righteous was high priest at that time, and that it was his image that he [Alexander] saw whenever he was victorious in battle. Now according to the information conveyed to us by our sages of blessed memory, Simeon officiated as high priest for 40 years. It is therefore a fair supposition that the

12. Sifre, Balaq, par. 131.
13. B.R. 35:2 (328).
14. Mid. Teh. to Ps. 36:11.
15. Cf. B. Yoma 53a.
16. *Ant.* XX:180–81.
17. B. Yoma 18a.
18. Cf. Pr. 23:5. I.e., their years were not truncated on account of their behavior.
19. Meg. T., 339–40.

incident with Alexander occurred in about the fourth or fifth of the 40 years, or you might even stretch the point and claim that it occurred in his first year. We might even ignore the view of those who say that Simeon was the son of Onias who was son of Jaddua and consider him to be the son of Jaddua himself. The fact is that after the thirty-second year of Artaxerxes, some time had already passed during the office of the third priest Eliashib about whom it is said, *or in the thirty-second year of King Artaxerxes . . . and only after a while did I ask leave* (Neh. 13:6). If this is the case, where can we find the time which ought to remain in order to encompass the the last days of Eliashib, all the days of Joiada, Johanan, Jaddua, and the first days of Simeon who, it was conceded, was not Jaddua's grandson as the writers relate, but his actual son. The remaining time is not more than a year thereabouts in which to squeeze the time alluded to in the expression "after a while" until the end of the thirty-fourth year [of Artaxerxes]. How then can one speak of the long term of office of these people? Should we regard them like Jews, whom we turn into kings during the Purim games,[20] who are allowed to reign one or two weeks and then in an instant revert to their former state frustrated?[21] Not only is there the prediction of Zechariah to the people in general, *There shall yet be old men and women in the squares of Jerusalem, each with staff in hand because of their great age* (8:4). But also about Jeshua ben Jozadak, in particular, it is said, *you in turn will rule My house and guard My courts and I will permit you to move about among these attendants* (ibid. 3:7). All these are promises of a long life in this world after the completion of the building of the Temple. Moreover, the rendering of the verse according to the Targum of Jonathan ben Uzziel also alludes to his being "among these Seraphim," namely, in the world to come.[22] And if the statement of Yedidyah in his book *On the Times* is to be trusted, he [Jeshua] lived 130 years and officiated as high priest for 56 years. This figure is alluded to in the letters *vav* and *nun* the first two letters in the words of truth, which state, *and I will permit you [ve-natati] to move about among the attendants.* Indeed this covenant of life and peace was undoubtedly intended for him and his descendants who walked in His ways. And as we have already mentioned, our rabbis of blessed memory stated that the Men of the Great Assembly lived meritoriously and deserved a blessed and sated long life.

Now I know that the intelligent person would inveigh against me exclaiming, "Open your eyes and see that Eliashib who built the chamber as you noted is designated merely as an ordinary priest in Scripture and is not to be identified as the high priest who built the gate." He would meet with the response that although Eliashib is described as high priest in several scriptural passages, there are also many references to him as well as to Jeshua which omit the honorific appellation—for it is the writer's prerogative either to enlarge on the explanation or to rely on the understanding of the reader. Indeed, the impression conveyed by the story of this Eliashib proves that

20. 'Games played on Purim,' cf. B. Sanh. 64b. De' Rossi is referring here to the Purim parody described in the *Megillat Setarim.* A master of ceremonies called King is appointed on the first day of Adar. All the townsmen come to his house. He then hands over his staff to another who in turn hands it to another until it has been handed round the whole of the community by the 16th of Adar.

21. 'Revert . . . frustrated,' cf. Ps. 6:11. In other words, they enjoy a brief spell of power which comes to an abrupt end as they return to reality.

22. Targum Jonathan to Zech. 3:7: "And at the resurrection of the dead I will raise you to life and will give you feet to walk among these Seraphin."

certainly no other than he was the high priest. Who else would have taken such liberty to build wide chambers in that holy place and to turn them into a wardrobe for personal use unless he was the priest who is appointed above his fellows?[23] Would you imagine that a common priest would have enough authority to act in such a manner? This becomes all the more convincing when one understands the statement of Rashi who wrote that Eliashib was a relative of Tobiah, the son-in-law of Sanballat, and that he, out of affection for him, put Tobiah's furniture into the chamber. How could one imagine that at the request of Tobiah, an Ammonite slave and enemy of the Jews, any common priest would have the gall to devise such a thing? Consequently, the problem becomes reinstated. For it is unimaginable that the lifetimes of all the high priests mentioned by us could be absorbed into the short period of time which remained until Darius met his end. And even if one were to assume that this Eliashib was somebody else, we still see that Eliashib the high priest was alive and active in the twentieth year of Artaxerxes' reign. How could one reasonably hold that a mere 14 years could encompass the lifetimes of Joiada, Jonathan, Jaddua, and Onias and some of the days of Simeon the righteous, all in a direct line of succession from father to son? You will observe that in his critique of ibn Ezra regarding Jochebed, Ramban of blessed memory mentions that 370 years—encompassing four generations—elapsed from their entry into the Land until the birth of King David.[24] It is true that they were righteous men, but as we have already noted, these too [i.e., the six high priests] were not muddled by wine.[25] My spirit of inquiry led me to probe further in the book which is a catalogue of all the kings of France, Spain, Portugal, England, Mauretania, and all parts of the world known to chroniclers in regard to the reigning kings and their descendants.[26] I excluded the kings of Israel, the popes, and emperors who came from different dynastic houses such that there could easily be a frequent number of rulers within a short period of time. I did not discover a succession of generations of equal number to that of these high priests which did not last at least 70 years. If one was short-lived, another would compensate for all of them. On studying the kings of Judah which, with the exception of Athaliah, were a succession of twenty generations, you will discover that the shortest span of time for six successive generations was 95 years. Moreover, from the chronicle of the fifteen Ottoman kings,[27] you will notice that the succession of the six kings whose rule lasted the shortest period of time, exceeded 80 years. How then could one think that more than all the noble[28] these remnants[29] rolled up their lives like

23. Cf. Lev. 21:10: *The priest who is appointed above his fellows on whose head the anointing oil has been poured.*

24. Nahmanides to Gen. 46:15.

25. Cf. Is. 28:7: *Priest and prophet are muddled by by liquor, they are dazed by wine.*

26. There were many chronicles of this kind written and published in the sixteenth century. One chronicle which fits de' Rossi's description and to which he may well be referring is the *Chronicon Regum regnorumque omnium Catalogum, et perpetuum ab exordio mundi temporum seculorumque series complectens ex optimis quibusque Hebraeis, Graecis et Latinis congestum* written by Paulus Constantinus Phrygio and published in Basel in 1534.

27. De' Rossi is most probably referring to *Gli annali turcheschi overo le vite de' principi et signori della casa othomana* written by Francesco Sansovino, Venice, 1571, which was published several times. The last chapter of the work is about Suleiman, the fourteenth Ottoman emperor and only mentions his successor.

28. 'All the noble,' cf. Job 41:26.

29. 'Remnants,' i.e., these virtuous high priests continued the line of succession after the destruction of

a web[30] and departed with but a few years.[31] And in chapter 22, I already gave my critique of Rabad, Rabbi Isaac Israeli, and Don Isaac who confused Simeon the righteous with Hananiah and Iddo, calling him, like Jethro, by seven names.[32] Go back to the passage if it so pleases you.

Furthermore, with regard to the successive line of high priests, we should consider the teaching in Ḥullin[33] which is cited by Rambam in the Laws of the Temple Furniture:[34] "When a priest grows up and comes of age, he is qualified for service, but his fellow priests would not allow him to minister in the Sanctuary until he had reached the age of twenty." Similarly, in the Palestinian Talmud,[35] it is stated that he may not act as prayer-leader or give the priestly benediction or officiate until his pubic hair is fully grown. And Rabbi says that they all must be twenty years or older as it says in Ezra, *and they appointed Levites from the age of twenty and upward* (3:8). If this pertained even to the Levites and lay priests, how much more so must it have been applied to the high priest about whom it is said: "A high priest must surpass his brother priests in comeliness, strength and appearance." This is cited by Rambam in the chapter referred to above.[36] The fact is that strength and looks only come to perfection with the fullness of years such that at the sight of his shining countenance the young conceal themselves.[37] We may surely regard this as correct when we consider that the ancient gentile orders also chose their high priest from the old and grey-headed. And as we learn from the statements of our rabbis of blessed memory, it was the custom of those days that not only he, but also his attendants in his inner circle, should be of a venerable age. This was the reason for the appellation "elder" as is apparent from the story recounted in Midrash Tehillim on the verse, *The enemy is no more—ruins everlasting* (Ps. 9:7) in which the verse from Malachi is quoted, *They may build but I will tear down* (1:4): "A philosopher[38] said to Rabbi Elasah: 'As you live it is so. Every year we sit down to devise a plan for destroying you and then a venerable old man comes and blocks it (another version reads "us").'" Thus, we have no reason to believe that Joiada and his colleagues, who succeeded Eliashib at the end of the reign of Artaxerxes, were young boys when they officiated in the place of their fathers who had died prematurely.

All these facts strengthen the position of the opponents who argue that the meager 34 years, which, according to rabbinic opinion, were completed with Alexander's defeat of Darius in the time of Simeon the righteous or even in the time of Jaddua, were not enough to accommodate the lifetimes of all the high priests who are mentioned in

---

the first Temple although it had been said (Jer. 44:14) *No survivor or fugitive shall be left to return to the land of Judah.*

30. 'Rolled . . . web,' cf. Is. 38:12.

31. 'Departed . . . years,' cf. Job 16:22.

32. This is a playful reference to the midrashic statement that Jethro had seven names. See Mekhilta d' Rabbi Ishmael, amalek 3 (2, 164).

33. B. Ḥull. 24b.

34. *Mishneh Torah,* Kele ha-Miqdash V:15.

35. P. Sukk. 3 (12) 54a.

36. Kele ha-Miqdash V:1.

37. Cf. Job 29:8 and its application in P. Ber. 2 (1) 4b: "That is their custom there. The lesser does not greet the greater, for they fulfill the verse *The young men saw me and hid themselves* (Job 29:8).

38. The text actually read Polipos, but Buber (ad loc., 86) emends the text to "a philosopher."

connection with Persian rule. Consequently it is necessary to widen their sphere of action and insert an interval of time between the incumbents, either from the time of Darius the builder of the Temple until the Artaxerxes who lived in the time of Ezra and Nehemiah, or else from Artaxerxes until the Darius who was captured by Alexander. The same examination may also be made retrospectively for their predecessors, Jeshua, Joiakim, and Eliashib. Now that we know that Eliashib built the sheep gate in the twentieth year of Artaxerxes' reign, it necessarily follows that Jeshua, Joiakim, and partly Eliashib only ministered as high priests for 14 years from his [i.e., Darius's] sixth year in which the construction of the Temple was completed. Indeed, the prophet predicted that Jeshua would live for a long time after the Temple had been built when he said, *you in turn will rule My house and guard My courts . . . among these attendants* (Zech. 3:7). In the course of his narrative, Nehemiah wrote, *in the days of Joiaḳim the heads of such and such priest clans,* the Levites *in the time of Eliashib were* so and so and similarly in the time of Joiada and his colleagues. It is unfeasible, as we indicated above, that they all expired and died in such rapidity. It would therefore appear that there were Persian kings who ruled in the intervening period, but the truth regarding their number and length of their reigns has been withheld from us. Now, as we indicated above, according to Rambam of blessed memory and Bertinoro, Simeon the righteous was the high priest after Ezra. So before leaving this subject, it is certainly worthwhile to mention that if it is indeed true that the six mentioned by Nehemiah were high priests after Jeshua, one is led to judge the rabbis in two ways. First, even if Ezra was really a priest and distinguished leader of his people in a city of Babylon as well as in Jerusalem, he never ministered as high priest in the Lord's Sanctuary. Read out his words for they provide the evidence. Moreover, Rashi of blessed memory comments on chapter 5 of book 1 of Chronicles in the following way: "How come that Ezra the son of Seraiah was not high priest, but rather his nephew, the son of Jozadak his brother. In my opinion, the reason is that Jeshua went up with Zerubbabel a few years before Ezra." The second point is that although Simeon the righteous was high priest, he was not close enough in time to Ezra to warrant being placed after him, that is to say, next to him. For on examination of Scripture one would necessarily say that he could only have succeeded Jaddua who was the last of the six priests. Simeon was either Jaddua's own son or else his grandson as is indicated by Yedidyah and Josephus and their group when they say that Jaddua was the father of Onias and Onias the father of Simeon. And according to Josephus, Simeon was given the designation righteous because he was intent on righteousness and piety.[39] As for the view of Rabad and Don Isaac that Simeon the righteous was the son of Jeshua ben Jozadak, which I discussed in chapter 22, it is clearly beyond the pale. And there is no reason for expressing wonder at Rashi who diverges from the path of our rabbis when he comments on those six persons in chapter 12 of Nehemiah, "All these mentioned in the scriptural text were high priests." For in that context he was providing a literal commentary on the verses. Already at the beginning of his commentary on the pericope *va-era* he had written: "So I say that Scripture should be explained according to its plain sense, but the midrashic exposition

39. *Ant.* XII:43.

may be given."[40] I cited this statement towards the end of chapter 14, as well as a similar comment by our teacher in the *Guide,* on the commandment to let the mother go from the nest.[41] Another case in point is his discussion of the question as to whether the righteous gentiles have a portion in the world to come which emerges when the content of his response as recorded by one of his disciples to Rabbi Ḥasdai Halevi[42] is compared with his statement at the end of chapter 8 of his Laws of the Kings. Study the passages with due consideration. At any rate, Nehemiah's words appear to support the opponents' position, which was the objective of the chapter.

40. Rashi to Ex. 6:11.
41. *Guide* II, ch. 48.
42. This is a reference to a letter written by a disciple of Maimonides to Ḥasdai Halevi who claims that he had been faithful to the content of Maimonides' text but had changed the language. He claims that Maimonides had made him promise not to show it to anybody. According to I. Shailat (vol. 2, 673), the letter is not authentic. It was published in the ed. pr. of Maimonides' *Teshuvot.* In this letter, he explicitly states that the righteous gentiles have a share in the world to come if "they have acquired what can be acquired of the knowledge of God and if they ennoble their souls with worthy qualities." In contrast, the passage in *Mishneh Torah* (Melakhim VIII:11) states that they will have a portion in the world to come provided that they accept and observe the Noahide commandments because God commanded them in the Torah. He then states: "But if his observances are based upon a reasoned conclusion, he is not deemed . . . one of the pious gentiles but one of their wise men."

CHAPTER THIRTY-EIGHT

An apparent problem regarding our rabbis' account of the succession of the kings of Persia.

Now when considered from the perspective of the succession of Persian kings, it is also surprising that Persian rule could have lasted only 34 years during Temple times. For one might assume that this period of 34 years only began after the building of the Temple had been completed in the sixth year of Darius's reign as is written in chapter 6 of Ezra (v.15); but then there is no information as to how long Darius lived subsequently. Nor do we know whether there was another king between his reign and that of Artaxerxes who is the next king to be mentioned (7:1). From our reading of chapter 13 of Nehemiah, we observe that Artaxerxes alone reigned 32 years, as well as for a significant period of time subsequently as shall be clarified. It is also possible that he lived even longer after that period; but Nehemiah had no need to mention it for there was nothing new to record.

Our investigation also has to take into account the aera mundi computation. The 70 years during which Jerusalem lay in ruins came to an end in the second year of Darius's reign, as is indicated by Zechariah who prophesied in his second year. In the name of the angel he raised the complaint, *How long will You withhold pardon . . . seventy years ago* (1:12). And at the end of chapter 4 of the first book of Ezra, it is explicitly written, *[At that time work on the House of God stopped] and remained in abeyance until the second year of the reign of King Darius* (v.24) and *Thereupon, they set to . . . and began rebuilding* (5:2). Thus, 4 or 5 years remain during which time the work on the building of the Temple was carried out, and these years must be added to the number of years counted from creation. Our current year is 5331. Included in this figure are 490 years which comprise 70 years of the Babylonian exile and 420 years for the duration of the Temple period, i.e., according to chapter 30 of the Seder Olam, 34 years of Persian rule, 180 years of Greek rule, 103 years of the Hasmonean dynasty, and 103 years of the Herodian dynasty. One has no option but to add the excluded years to the total amount which means that it is now the year 5335 or 5336 and not 5331. And if we say that the Persian period of 34 years began in the second year of Darius's reign which is in fact the case as shall be clarified later, the problem of the 34 years must have become patent, just by adding the 5 given years of Darius and the 32 given years of Artaxerxes which comes to a total of 37. The problem becomes exacerbated when a certain amount of time is added to these years indicated in chapter 13 of Nehemiah, *in the thirty-second year of*

King Artxerxes . . . and only after some time had gone by did I ask leave of the king. It is true, however, that in chapter 30 of Seder Olam it is stated that this Artaxerxes is identical with Darius who is also called Artaxerxes. But my revered reader, perhaps you have forgotten or perhaps you did not read what I wrote in chapter 18. Go and look—you only need to turn the pages back—there you will find a convincing response with regard to this matter. And if you still maintain that this Artaxerxes is identical with Darius, then we must probe further into that subject. It is written that Nehemiah's first stay in Jerusalem lasted from the twentieth until the thirty-second year of Artaxerxes' reign. He then returned to the king and remained in his service *for some time* which could not reasonably have been less than two or three years. This is all the more probable given that he had already protracted his stay abroad when he asked leave of the king to return again to Jerusalem. Clearly, Artaxerxes must have reigned for at least 35 years. Then if it is assumed that he was actually Darius in the second year of whose reign the reckoning of Rabbi Jose's 34 years begin, then for his time alone, there are 34 years to be reckoned with. Now there is no doubt that in their view, the Artaxerxes under discussion is the one who built the Temple. Consequently, it necessarily follows that the reckoning of the 34 years begins in the second year of his reign and not in the sixth, the year of the completion of the Temple's construction. Otherwise, as we mentioned above, we are left with the years in which the work on the Temple was undertaken. From the statements of the rabbis of blessed memory, it is also apparent that they always calculate 70 years for the Babylonian exile and attach the years of the duration of the Temple to that figure. Now Rambam of blessed memory writes in the tenth chapter of the Laws of the Sabbatical Year as follows:[1] "In the seventh year after its erection, Ezra went up [to the Land]. From that year they began a new count and declared the thirteenth year after the building of the second Temple a sabbatical year." In my opinion, he based this view on the statement in tractate Arakhin.[2] "In the 6 years before Ezra came up and dedicated the Sanctuary, they did not count Jubilee years." Consequently, one must admit that the Temple period does not commence from the second year, but from the beginning of his reign which was in the previous year. Although it is written that they began to rebuild the Temple in the second year, it is possible that the rabbis of blessed memory added the 1 year of Cyrus's reign in which they began to build the Temple before the indictment document was drafted—this would bring the total to 7 years. Accordingly, the problem becomes even greater. For of the 34 years reckoned by Rabbi Jose, 32 were during the time of Artaxerxes alone and even more, for there is the time implied in the expression *and after some time had gone by I asked leave of the king.* Since this king reigned more than 32 years during Temple times, where can one accommodate the period of time which should be allocated to the other Darius who was captured and who, according to the commentators Kimḥi and his colleagues, as I wrote in chapter 18, was another king? Moreover, all the chroniclers mentioned above record that other kings ruled in the intervening period and that before his capture, the last one was sovereign of the whole world for 6 years. And if, in the face of all this evidence, we wish to confine ourselves to the law and assert that it was this Artaxerxes himself who,

1. *Mishneh Torah,* Shmiṭṭah X:3.
2. B. Arak. 13a.

in the last year which is the thirty-fourth year of the Persian Empire, suffered defeat in the war with Alexander, then, my brother, wonder and be astonished on two counts.

The first matter concerns Cyrus who merely by word of mouth authorized the Jews to build the Temple, and it was in his days that they were forced to discontinue the building. We hear one saint, the prophet Isaiah, speak of wonders and promises of success in his regard when he said: *Thus says the Lord to Cyrus his anointed one—Whose right hand He has grasped treading down nations before him* (45:1). Such was all the bounty and victory promised him in that chapter. And this (unfortunate man) in the face of the wrath of our enemies and persecutors decreed that the Temple should be built in the time of Zerubbabel, giving remissions and presents as is well known. He then wrote those precious letters in which he authorized Ezra, and then, adding kindness to kindness, he gave authorization to Nehemiah. It was thus due to his mediation and help that the Temple was rebuilt on its mound and the palace in its proper place.[3] How then can we account for the fact that the God of justice, the Lord, suddenly turned away from him, brought about his undoing, and delivered him into the hands of the enemy in great wrath. Are these the commandments and this their reward?[4] Is it not the case, as they say in Pesaḥim, that He does not withhold reward from any creature.[5] Go and learn from the passage in Shemot Rabbah dealing with the commandment, *You shall not eat any flesh that is torn of beasts in the field; you shall cast it to the dogs* (Ex.22:30).[6] There is also the case of Dama ben Netina in the first chapter of Qiddushin[7] and the four steps which Nebuchanezzar ran, mentioned in Sanhedrin.[8] And in the first section of the *Kuzari,* the sage states:[9] "We do not deny that the good actions of any person of whatever nationality are rewarded." And in his commentary on the Mishnah, Rabbi Moses [Maimonides] of blessed memory comments on the passage in tractate Terumot in which it is declared that the heave-offering given by the gentile or Samaritan is valid,[10] and writes: "Although the gentiles are not obliged to perform the precepts, should they happen to do so in any way, they receive some reward, and this is one of our principles." Now you might argue on the basis of the example of Josiah. For directly after the words, *there was no king like him* (2K. 23:25) are applied to him, it is written *Pharaoh Neco came up . . . and slew him* (v.29). In that case, it would be right to say that the Lord wreaks justice on Israel in this world, but in the world to come, they are altogether righteous.[11] But as for the nations of the world, that is to say, the righteous among them, they have a portion in the world to come as the rabbis of blessed memory

3. Cf. Jer. 30:18.

4. Cf. B. Men. 29b.

5. B. Pes. 118a.

6. S.R. 31:9. According to this passage, on the night of the killing of the Egyptian firstborn, the dogs barked at the Egyptians, but not at the Israelites. As a reward, the dogs are given the flesh of the animals that the Israelites are forbidden to eat.

7. In B. Qidd. 31a, the gentile Dama ben Netina receives reward from God for his exemplary behavior in fulfilling the precept of honoring parents.

8. In B. Sanh. 96a, Nebuchadnezzar is said to have been victorious because he ran four steps in order to recall the messenger and emend the letter he was carrying so that the name of God would be given priority.

9. *Kuzari* I, par. 111.

10. M. Ter. 3:9.

11. A play on Ps. 19:10.

remark in tractate Sanhedrin.[12] Rabbi Moses writes similarly in the Laws of Repentance,[13] the Laws of Forbidden Unions,[14] the Laws of Testimony,[15] and particularly in the Laws of the Kings[16] and in the text to which I alluded in chapter 37.[17] But certain it is that for idolators their judgment is that expressed by Rabbi Eliezer in the Tosefta in tractate Sanhedrin,[18] Midrash Tehillim,[19] and the Pesiqta which is given in the Yalqut,[20] namely, that for them, death is final. It is therefore proper to believe that the blessed Lord will reward them instantly as is expressed in the saying of Rabban Johanan ben Zakkai in Bava Batra:[21] "The righteousness of the gentile nations makes atonement for them in this world." Moreover, one should not respond by referring to their statement in Rosh ha-Shanah that Cyrus degenerated.[22] For even if it were supposed that it was a reference to the king under discussion who was also called Cyrus, they could nevertheless find no proof of his degeneration, nor did they know the reason for his undoing; rather it was simply a rumor which they had received.[23] And one can only wonder as to the nature of this gentile's degeneration. After all, when Nehemiah returned in the thirty-second year of his reign to serve him in the usual way, he gave him permission after some time to return to supervise the affairs in Jerusalem. And taking the period [of the Persian Empire in Temple times] to have lasted 34 years, he could not have survived in the world long enough after this act of righteousness in order to leaven[24] the dough that had been kneaded. Alternatively, it was known that this had happened to him because he had committed a mortal sin. But there is still reason to wonder at the opinion of our commentators and the Tosafists[25] who claim that he was Darius, the son of Esther. How could the Judge of the entire world have allowed such a thing to come to pass? How come that the righteous queen who effected great salvation for Israel was not sustained by the merit she had earned, but rather went into exile, and suffered subjugation? In fact all the gentile historians, and specifically Arrian the Greek, who based his work on the testimony of Ptolemy son of Lago, and Aristobulus the Jew to whom we referred in chapter 10, described how Darius fell into the hands of the enemy, and his mother, wife, and sister taken captive—the account is to be found in the second book of Arrian.[26] And according to Curtius, a reliable historian, his mother was called Sisigambes. He wrote that overcome by the death of Alexander who had taken great pains to look after her and the rest of her household, she took her own life by refraining

12. B. Sanh. 105a.
13. *Mishneh Torah,* Teshuvah III:5.
14. Ibid., Issure Bi'ah XIV:7. Here Maimonides speaks of the righteous of the nations, but makes no reference to their portion in the world to come.
15. Ibid., Edut XI:10.
16. Ibid., Melakhim VIII:11.
17. He is referring to the letter written by Maimonides' disciple to Ḥasdai ha-Levi. See ch. 37, n. 42.
18. T. Sanh. 13:2.
19. Mid. Teh. 9 to Ps. 9:18.
20. Yalqut Shimoni II, par. 300 to Jer. 20:7: "I would be like one the nations for whom there is no reward and no punishment."
21. B. B.B. 10b. The words "in this world" are not in the text, but are implied from the context.
22. B. R.H. 3b.
23. In the passage, the rabbis are hard-pressed to find a reason for Cyrus's degeneration.
24. The verb "degenerate" (*heḥemiṣ*) literally means to leaven.
25. Tos. to B. R.H. 3b, s.v. *shenat.*
26. Arrian, *De rebus gestis,* II, 2ff.

from eating for five days.[27] Now you should not pass judgment on this chapter by raising an objection on the basis of the statement of Josephus whom we cited in chapter 33 from which it transpires that Darius the last succeeded Esther's Ahasuerus which therefore implies that he was her son. There are two responses to this. Firstly, on close examination of Josephus's text, it emerges that he does not state explicitly that there was no other king ruling between their two reigns. For his objective was not to enumerate the kings of Persia, but simply to narrate the noteworthy events which happened to our people under the rule of the governing power, as I indicated. This view gains greater credibility in the light of the statement of the Hebrew Josephus who after referring to the story of Haman wrote:[28] "And our ancestors served all the Persian kings in peace and quiet until the reign of Darius the second." In relation to our rabbis' figure of 34 years, these words of his constitute both honey and thorns. For if he is to be trusted, the implication of his statement must be that the Temple stood for 7 years of Darius' reign which was followed by that of Xerxes Artaxerxes who gave authorization to Ezra and Nehemiah and who ruled at least 32 years and for some time after that. He was succeeded by Ahasuerus about whom it is written, *In the twelfth year of King Ahasuerus, pur—which means the lot—was cast* (Est. 3:7), and the last of them all was Darius who was captured.

The second point is as follows. The purpose of Nehemiah's account was to inform us of the events of his lifetime which related to the Jews. How then could it be possible that he kept silent about the notable events that had happened. He did not describe how Alexander passed through Jerusalem on his way to engage this Darius in battle nor did he extol Daniel for the fulfillment of his vision, nor did he promulgate news of the kindness which our God had shown us. For although Alexander was ruler then of all regions of the nations and the object of their worship, he, contrary to the expectations of his servants, prostrated himself before the high priest who had come out to meet him and did not harm our people, but rather treated us kindly and mercifully. These facts must surely convince every perceptive being that this person could not have been the Darius who was captured during the rampage of Alexander, and that Nehemiah, and still less Ezra, did not survive until his time and were completely unaware of the things that had happened to him. This is also made clear by Josephus in chapter 5 of his eleventh book.[29] We are thus in a position to conjecture that many years passed between the reign of Darius, who built the Temple, and that of Artaxerxes, who built the walls, and that of Darius, who was subjugated. Now I do not suspect any thinking person who reads Nehemiah's description of this Artaxerxes king of Babylon in chapter 13 of entertaining any doubts that he was one of the kings of Persia; for thereby he would give us a distorted rendering of the authentic texts. There is no doubt that the Babylonian kingdom did not become reinstated after the rise of Persia. Rather, the Persians seized both Babylon and Assyria as part of their universal empire. This is a well-known fact to which we referred in chapter 21. The same person who is called Artaxerxes, king of Persia (Ezra 7:1), is also called Artaxerxes, king of Babylon, in chapter 13 of Nehe-

27. Curtius Rufus, *De rebus gestis,* 10, 5, 24–25.
28. *Josippon,* bk. 1, ch. 4 (30).
29. *Ant.* XI:120ff.

miah (v.6) and also designated thus in the earlier passage, *who came up with me in the reign of Artaxerxes the king from Babylon* (Ezra 8:1). He is also called king of Assyria at the end of chapter 6 where speaking of Darius it is stated that *our God inclined the heart of the king of Assyria towards them* (Ezra 6:22). On the subject of Manasseh and his people, it is also written in the second book of Chronicles, *so the Lord brought against them the officers of the army of the king of Assyria who took Manasseh captive in manacles, bound him in fetters, and led him off to Babylon* (2Chr. 33:11). And at the beginning of his text, Nehemiah himself discloses that this king was in Shushan,[30] which is known to have been the capital city of the Persian kings. From Josephus, you may gather that the incumbent ruler was designated by one of three names king of Persia, or Babylon, or Assyria according to the country of his abode.[31] A study of the end of book 5 and the beginning of book 6 of Ptolemy's *Geography* makes this point easily comprehensible for you. In the fourth and fifth tables of Asia, as well as on the representation of the map of the world, these three countries are located adjacently to one another to the northeast of the Land of Israel and Assyria, that is to say, the land of Ashur, which has Mesopotamia and Babylon to the west of it and to the south the entire area of Susiana which is Shushan, the royal city of the Persians, as we said. In his treatment of Babylon, the writer Solinus has the following to say:[32] "Babylon was built by Semiramis, and due to her great reputation, the lands of Assyria and Mesopotamia were also called Babylon."

However, while we are still speaking in favor of the group of the opponents I can see that a clever person might raise an objection against them and say: "How could you be right in claiming that there were several more Persian kings than the three or four counted by our rabbis of blessed memory in chapter 30 of Seder Olam and in Bereshit Rabbah. After all, in the first year of Cyrus's reign, the angel said to Daniel, *Persia will have three more kings* (Dan. 11:2)". I would give a legitimate response and say as follows. First of all, a superficial examination of the scriptural narrative demonstrates that there were at least six kings, and this view is also put forward by the wise Don Isaac.[33] They were Darius the Mede, the fore-mentioned Cyrus, the three kings mentioned [by Daniel], and the wealthy[34] fourth which must amount to six. And if Xenophon the Greek is to be trusted whose work we cited in chapter 30, there were two kings called Cyrus—he wrote a long work about each of them. We surely have grounds for suggesting the possibility that the Cyrus who is mentioned at the beginning of chapter 10 [of Daniel] is Cyrus the second which would imply that the number of kings was possibly even greater. Aside from this, understand and pay attention to Daniel's vision of the Persian kingdom in chapter 7 (v.5). He said that it had *three fangs in its mouth between its*

30. *In the month of Kislev of the twentieth year [of King Artaxerxes] when I was in the capital of Shushan* (Neh. 1:1).

31. De' Rossi refers to *Ant.* XI ch. 6 which is about Artaxerxes and the reign of Ahasuerus, but does not contain the information to which he alludes.

32. De' Rossi writes that the forty-ninth chapter of the book is on Babylon. In fact, there is an error in the Italian version that he read. There is a heading C. 49, but it is clearly ch. 69 (in other editions, ch. 70): "Babilonia . . . edificata da Semiramis, tanto eccellente che per la sua nobiltà l'Assiria e la Mesopotamia furon trasferite nel nome di Babilonia."

33. *Mayyene ha-Yesuhu'ah,* 2, tamar 3 (288, col. b–289, col. a).

34. A reference to the verse, *Persia will have three more kings and the fourth will be wealthier than them all* (Dan. 11:2).

teeth. Now if his intention was to infer that Persia would only have a total of three fangs, namely, kings, he would not have added the words *between its teeth.* Rather it would appear that he meant that Persia would have many kings, powerful and weak, famous and insignificant, just as there are incisors and molars, and among them all there would be three powerful kings and the fourth who would be greater than all his predecessors would fall into the hands of his enemies. Now the kings were not all of equal stature nor individually enumerated. It may have been the case that they were short-lived and therefore not individually counted—for according to the accounts of the writers mentioned above, there were some who only reigned seven or eight months—or else they did not distinguish themselves in any significant way. You will therefore see that some of them were not called Artaxerxes which means "great fighter" as we mentioned in chapter 18. Due to Ahasuerus's greatness, Scripture refers to *all his mighty and powerful acts* (Est. 10:2). And it may be that because he defeated kings who bore this designation that Alexander of Macedon merited and desired to be given the epithet "the Great." Similarly, when subsequently Romans performed outstanding feats, they were given that designation as was the case with Pompey the Great.

Now returning to our topic, it would appear that it is not impossible that according to Scripture there were other kings apart from the three or four that are mentioned. In fact after expounding on this subject, the wise Don Isaac writes:[35] "Accordingly I say that our sages did not deny that there were more than three Persian kings but they did not list them. Rather, they only referred to those who had treated Israel either well or badly, namely, Cyrus, Ahasuerus, and Darius. The remaining kings did not have any dealings with them. Alternatively, Cambyses son of Cyrus had no hold on the kingdom after his father since Ahasuerus gained power over the kingdom." His statement can also be supported by the passage in chapter 49 of Pirqe d'Rabbi Eliezer: "Come and see how that Ahasuerus was wealthier than all the kings of Media and Persia and concerning him Scripture says, *And the fourth shall be wealthier than them all* (Dan. 11:2)." For this sage thought that Ahasuerus was the fourth, and yet it is universally agreed that there were other Persian kings who also reigned afterwards, and specifically the one who fell into the hands of Alexander. But I was surprised at the wise Don Isaac whose view was mentioned above. It was he of all the commentators of blessed memory whose interpretation required reference to additional kings of Persia; and yet he was not roused to make a precise interpretation of those (two) leading words *between his teeth*. Instead, as is apparent from his text, he focused on the three fangs signifying the three kingdoms of Babylon, Persia, and Media which were subjugated by the Persians.[36] However, you should know that this method of interpretation was actually taken from our rabbis who said:[37] "*And three fangs were in his mouth between his teeth*—this refers to Hulwan, Adiabene, and Nisibis which it sometimes swallowed and sometimes regurgitated." But it would appear that Don Isaac pilfered the specific details of those kingdoms from the Christian translator's [Jerome's] commentary on Daniel. Go and study it if so it pleases you.[38] The truth is that while the "three fangs" refer to what is said in the

35. Abravanel, *Mayyane ha-Yeshu'ah,* 11, tamar 3 (384, col. b). The quotation is not exact.
36. Ibid., 8, tamar 3 (331, col. b–333 col. a).
37. B. Qidd. 72a.
38. He is referring to Jerome's commentary to Dan. 11:2.

second prophecy about Persia having three more kings, the phrase "between his teeth," that is to say, the princes of the world and the high of stature, quite apart from the insignificant ones, can be explained in reference to both [prophecies]. In any case, in resuming the topic of the subject on the basis of the literal text of Scripture it appears that Rabbi Jose's span of 34 years is too short for accommodating all the kings of Persia who ought to be counted from the time of the building of the Temple until their defeat at the hands of Alexander.

CHAPTER THIRTY-NINE

An apparent problem regarding our rabbis' account of the genealogy of Jeconiah's descendants.[1]

Now there also appears to be support for the opponents on the question of the genealogy of Jeconiah's descendants, whereas the rabbinic view is problematic. In chapter 3 of the first book of Chronicles (vv.17–24) the descendants of Jeconiah are listed again: Jeconiah begot Assir and Shealtiel, Shealtiel Pedaiah, and Pedaiah Zerubbabel, and Zerubbabel Hananiah, and Hanaiah Shecaniah, and Shecaniah Neariah, and Neariah Elioenai, and Elioenai Anani. These comprise nine generations after Jeconiah. On the verse, *And Malchiram* (v.18)[2] Rav Kimḥi writes as follows: "Malchiram and Pedaiah these are all the sons of Shealtiel, but for the sake of brevity it does not state *and the children of Shealtiel*; for it is taken for granted that the reference is to a father and all his sons. And Haggai,[3] Zechariah,[4] and Ezra[5] refer to Zerubbabel as the son of Shealtiel although he was his grandson, since Pedaiah was the son of Shealtiel and Zerubbabel son of Pedaiah.[6] It is therefore evident that in several passages, grandsons are referred to as sons." Similarly, in his commentary on Haggai, Kimḥi of blessed memory writes:[7] "Zerubbabel was not the son of Shealtiel, but rather the son of Pedaiah, and Pedaiah was the son of Shealtiel for as was said in our commentary on Chronicles, grandsons are referred to as sons. It may be that mention was made of Shealtiel because he was more distinguished than Pedaiah. The same is true of the designation Zechariah son of Iddo[8] who was actually the son of Berechiah son of Iddo." Indeed, it would appear that one has to take this position, for if Pedaiah was not the son, but rather the brother of Shealtiel, it would imply that Zerubbabel was a collateral and not a direct descendant of Shealtiel. Rashi of blessed memory, too, in his comment on the verse, [*The sons of Judah, Perez, Hezron, and Carmi and Hur and Shobal*] *And Reaiah*

1. Jeconiah is another name for Jehoiachin, king of Judah, who was brought into exile by Nebuchadnezzar.

2. *And the sons of Jeconiah Assir, Shealtiel his son Malchiram and Pedaiah and Shenazar, Jecamiah, Hoshama, and Nedabiah. And the sons of Pedaiah: Zerubbabel and Shimei* (vv.17–19).

3. Hag. 1:1; 1:12; 1:14; 2:2; 2:23.

4. Zechariah only refers to Zerubbabel without mentioning the name of his father (4:6, 7, 9).

5. Ezra 3:8; 5:2.

6. In 1Chr. 3:19 it states: *And the sons of Pedaiah were Zerubbabel and Shimei.*

7. Kimḥi to Hag. 1:1.

8. Ezra 5:1.

son of Shobal (1Chr. 4:1–2) writes: "This is the convention for this genealogy; Reaiah had not yet been mentioned, but the list is according to generation. The same is true of *Koz was the father of Anub* (v.8), for Koz had not yet been mentioned, but his sons are mentioned." Now in tractate Sanhedrin[9] and Vayiqra Rabbah[10] they say: "He was called Assir[11] because his mother conceived him in prison; Shealtiel because God did not plant him in the way that others are planted.[12] We have a tradition that a woman cannot conceive in a standing position, but this woman did." From these words, we may deduce that the period allocated for those generations does not begin until the time of Jeconiah's imprisonment. Moreover, it is a reasonable assumption that the dating did not begin immediately from the time he was imprisoned. We need only believe that his two sons mentioned above would have been born during the fourth or fifth of the 37 years in which he was in prison. And it is indeed probable that Ezra, who was the author of Chronicles, as the rabbis of blessed memory state in Bava Batra,[13] wrote the book and particularly these first chapters, during the domination of Persia, before any Greek king ruled the universe. Accordingly, all these generations must have lived in the time of Persian rule. Now Nehemiah lived a long time subsequently, as is clear from the narratives and from Josephus's statement in chapter 5 of book 11.[14] According to the view of the rabbis of blessed memory as expressed in Bava Batra[15] and Sanhedrin,[16] Nehemiah completed the book of Ezra and Chronicles. But even he did not live to see the defeat of Darius at the hands of Alexander as we suggested in the previous chapter. And although we would agree that Ezra was virtually a contemporary of Nehemiah, one should not think that Ezra wrote the section of the book of Chronicles which was of his authorship exactly within a hairsbreadth of the time of its occurrence. Rather we would apply our rabbis' dictum in tractates Shabbat[17] and Taʿanit[18] that one kingdom must not overlap another. It is a fair estimation that he wrote it at the most three or four years before the kingdom was secured by Alexander. And if one supposes that Jeconiah's imprisonment lasted 37 years,[19] this period could only have begun 11 years before the destruction of the Temple in the reign of Zedekiah.[20] By adding the 70 years of the exile and Rabbi Jose's 34 years, the total must amount to not more than 115 years. And by subtracting about 8 years which should be deducted partly from the beginning of the 115-year period and partly from the end of the period as we said, and further subtract about 7 years on account of the nine pregnancies, there must remain only about 100 years for the duration of those nine generations. This is what is puzzling. For how is it possible that nine successive generations could be born within such a limited

9. B. Sanh. 37b.
10. V.R. 19:6 (440). The passage is slightly different from Sanhedrin 37b which he is quoting.
11. The word *assir* means imprisoned.
12. This is a play on *shatal* (to plant) and *el* (God).
13. B. B.B. 15a.
14. *Ant.* XI:183.
15. B. B.B. 15a.
16. B. Sanh. 93b.
17. B. Shabb. 30a.
18. B. Taʿanit 5b.
19. In 2K. 25:27 (and Jer. 52:31), it is stated that Jehoiachin was released from prison in the thirty-seventh year of his exile.
20. Jehoiachin was succeeded by Zedekiah who reigned eleven years (2K. 24:18).

period? Is it not the way of the world and in accordance with rabbinic opinion as expressed in the words of Avot that even the person who is eager to fulfill his duty should be at least eighteen years old when he goes under the marriage canopy?[21] Thus, even if we suppose that Anani, who is the last of the list, was only one or two years old, it logically follows that the span of their lifetime comes to a total of more than 130 years, while the maximum number of years at our disposal is only 100. And you might oppose the interpretation of Kimḥi, blessed be his memory, and argue that Malchiram and Pedaiah were Jeconiah's sons and that Zerubbabel was in the generation after that of Shealtiel—for although he was the son of Pedaiah, Shealtiel may have adopted him as a son. Consequently there would have only been eight generations, and each of them must have procreated a son at exactly the age of fifteen. Nevertheless, there would still be a total of at least 105 years. Moreover, it is possible to complicate the problem further. For according to Yedidyah the Alexandrian [Philo], Shealtiel was born only after Jeconiah had come out of prison. This view is also tenable according to our rabbis. In other words, it could be said that he was conceived in prison but born outside. In this case, one would have to deduct 37 of the 100 years that we calculated. Alternatively, you might turn the argument along the following lines. For Yedidyah wrote that Jeconiah was put in prison only 6 years before he was set free, and the verses at the end of the book of Kings and Jeremiah[22] do not contradict this fact. For when they refer to his exile, they do not say that it was at this point that he was put in prison; nor is this fact repudiated by our rabbis. Consequently only 6 of the 37 years need be counted in relation to the 100 years, and what remains is about 70 years for the entire span of those generations, which would also imply that each one procreated at the age of ten years or less. Now the 11 years of Jeoconiah's exile which preceded the destruction of the Temple and likewise the 70 years in which Jerusalem lay in ruins is correct and clearly shown in Scripture. So we must calculate the years that must be added to the duration of the Persian Empire in Temple times and say that their empire and the equivalent Temple period lasted more than 34 years before the rise of the universal Greek Empire.

And you who are an intelligent reader should not give perverse testimony in the dispute by referring to our rabbis' statement in Sanhedrin that the primevals used to procreate at the age of eight.[23] For I have already showed you in chapter 17 how to demolish such a rejoinder. So you do not need to take the trouble to go back and study it and apply the arguments to this case—for you should realize that it is an Aggadah on the basis of which no questions may be raised. Moreover, in that passage, the rabbis of blessed memory were referring to the generation of Bezalel for whom the procreative faculty was still in full vigor. For the Lord desired to make the descendants of the seventy persons[24] like the stars of heaven. As Berosus the Chaldean wrote in his third book,[25]

21. Cf. M. Avot 5:21.

22. 2K. 25:27–30 and Jer. 52:31–34. In these verses it simply states that in the thirty-seventh year of Jehoiachin's exile, Evil Merodach released him from prison, thus giving no indication as to the length of his imprisonment.

23. B. Sanh. 69b.

24. This is a reference to Ex. 1:5: *The total number of persons that were of Jacob's issue came to seventy persons.*

25. This is a reference to ps. Berosus, bk. 3, "De antiquitate Iani patris" (vol. 1, 117): "congressi vero coniugibus, perpetuo geminos edebant, marem et foeminam qui adulti et coniuges effecti et ipsi binos

the flood was a kindness on the part of God and a blessing for the offspring that they should become as prolific as the plants of the field; [twins] male and female, were in every womb generation after generation. And yet in tractate Ḥullin,[26] they conclude that one cannot make deductions on the basis of miraculous events, and in Pesaḥim[27] and Ḥullin[28] they comment that one cannot draw inferences from an anomaly. Furthermore, while the rabbis of blessed memory refer to this twofold anomaly in respect to one or two generations, they would not make the same claim for eight or ten successive generations when we know that it is difficult for the minor to procreate and that his progeny is weak and frail and the more licentious they are, the more difficulty they encounter in procreation. And we have already seen the case of the young girl Justinia.[29] Even in respect to the first solution which was disproved by the second one, they say that even if her claim may have been true, one should not use her as an example for the seed of the House of Israel who are superior to such peoples.[30]

With regard to this topic of the nine generations, I cannot refrain from expressing my surprise at Rabad the Levite who does not keep to the sense of the scriptural text in his list of their genealogy at the beginning of his *Sefer ha-Qabbalah.* For he classifies one father with many children,[31] as is apparent when one reads his words together with the scriptural text.[32] Then there is a second important point. With regard to Hezekiah son of Neariah, he writes: "Some say that Hillel was the brother of Hezekiah, son of Neariah. . . . Hillel came up from Babylon."[33] Now we know from the statement in tractate Shabbat that Hillel lived about 100 years before the destruction of the Temple.[34] How could he come to the notion that Ezra, the author of Chronicles, or we could say Nehemiah who, according to our rabbis of blessed memory, completed the book,[35] lived more than 300 years during the period of the second Temple? He would have had to survive all these generations. According to his view, Hillel and his law court ought to have received the tradition from Ezra and his law court, and not from the various sages who transmitted the tradition in the intervening period. Even more bizarre to my mind is the fact that the wise Rabbi Isaac Israeli, author of the *Yesod Olam,* cites these words of his as though they were the true ruling on the issue.[36] Now there is a strange verse in the section on that genealogy, namely, *And the son of Hananiah: Pelatiah and Jeshaiah; the*

---

partu liberos semper edebant. Neque enim unquam Deus vel natura defuit necessitati quae ad universi orbis spectat opulentiam."

26. B. Ḥull. 43a.
27. B. Pes. 44b.
28. B. Ḥull. 98b.
29. See ch. 17 where the example is taken from B. Nidd. 45a.
30. Justinia claims that she gave birth at the age of seven. The rabbis discuss the question as to whether this is possible and whether action should be taken to prevent pregnancy. (See p. 307.)
31. I.e., as father, son, and grandson. Brothers have become father and son.
32. *Sefer ha-Qabbalah* (8): "Jehoiachin his son Shealtiel, his son Zerubbabel, his son Meshullam, his son Hananiah, his son Berechiah, his son Hasadiah, his son Isaiah, his son Obadiah, his son Shechaniah, his son Neariah, his son Hezekiah."
33. According to G. Cohen (*Sefer ha-Qabbalah* [109, n. 74]), this opinion reflects the rabbinic tradition that Hillel was a descendant of the House of David.
34. B. Shabb. 15a.
35. B. B.B. 15a.
36. *Yesod Olam* IV, ch. 18 (84a).

sons of Rephaiah, the sons of Arnan, the sons of Obadiah, the sons of Shecaniah (1Chr. 3:21). I cannot deprive the reader from knowing how this verse was interpreted by a wise commentator called Rabbi Benjamin Haba bar Judah, may he rest in peace. I saw his work in the collection belonging to Rabbi Avtalion of Modena.[37] He wrote as follows: "*The sons of Rephaiah, the sons of Arnan*—this means the son of Jeshaiah, Rephaiah, and the son of Rephaiah, Arnan, and the son of Arnan, Obadiah, and the son of Obadiah, Shecaniah, and so on. The expression 'and the sons of' signifies 'and his son' who are listed in successive generations." Although there is no proof for his view, there is an allusion to it in that the Septuagint renders the text according to his understanding.[38] If it is indeed correct, one has all the more reason for accentuating and aggrandizing the problem under discussion since the number of those generations will become increased to thirteen. The fact is that this would stretch one's credibility too far. One would wonder as to how the prophets Ezra or Nehemiah could have lived so long[39] that they could survive all those generations. By God, the only explanation appears to be that a great person of later times was imbued with an overweening spirit[40] and made additions to the sacred text. The wise ibn Ezra was brazen enough to write in this way at the beginning of Deuteronomy with regard to those who were more righteous and better [i.e., Moses and Joshua] than they [i.e., Ezra and Nehemiah] when he said:[41] "If you understand the secret of the twelve verses." Study the passage. But as for me, God forbid that I should associate myself with that rejected view. Even Yedidyah the Alexandrian, who was so castigated in chapter 5, spoke more piously than he. At the end of his *Life of Moses,* like our sages, he expressed the view that the twelve verses beginning, *And Moses went up* (Deut. 34:1) to the end of the Pentateuch were also written by Moses when he was divinely inspired into a state of prophecy.[42]

But the problem that we raised regarding the nine generations, which are telescoped into about 100 years, is sufficiently great in itself. For if one were to suppose that they all begot children at the exact age of 13 years and 1 day, one would need 104 years for eight generations and another 6 years to accommodate nine pregnancies which comes to a total of at least 110 years. And should just one of them had not married until the age of eighteen or twenty, or if one allows for 12 months as in the case of a virgin, we would necessarily have to increase the figure of 34 years [of Persian rule during second Temple times]. Then there is yet another consideration to take into account. For in the description of the building of the walls during the twentieth year of Artaxerxes' reign, we find that one of the repairers of the walls was Shemaiah son of Shechaniah (Neh. 3:29), but according to the third chapter of Chronicles, this Shemaiah son of Shechaniah was of

37. The author of the commentary was from Rome. The passage in question is in Bodleian Ms. Opp. 25, 173a.

38. This is correct. The LXX renders: *And the sons of Hananiah: Pelatiah and Jeshaiah his son, Rephaiah his son.*"

39. Cf. Zech. 1:5.

40. This expression taken from Dan. 6:4 is used by Rabad in his critique of Maimonides (introduction to the *Mishneh Torah*) for having omitted all his source references.

41. Ibn Ezra to Deut. 1:2. In this passage, ibn Ezra is implying that the last twelve verses of Deuteronomy 34:1–12, Deut. 31:22, Gen. 12:6, Gen. 22:14, and Deut. 3:11 were not written by Moses. In his comment on Deut. 34:1, he explicitly writes that the last verses were written by Joshua.

42. Philo, *Mos.* II, 290–92.

the sixth of the nine generations. For Shemaiah begot Neariah and Neariah, Elioenai and Elioenai, Anani. Accordingly, even if one were to assume that this Artaxerxes is to be identified with Darius and that the twentieth year of his reign was the nineteenth of the 34-year period of the Persian Empire during Temple times, how could it be that in the limited number of allotted years between these generations, three generations could have been born in swift succession during the 15 years that remained of the 34. This does indeed have all the same features as the problem which is apparent regarding the latter generations of the high priests and is even more anomalous.

These then are the three kinds of evidence which one might put forward in regard to holy Writ in order to favor the position of the opponents. Furthermore, when Yedidyah the Alexandrian lists the high priests from the beginning of the second Temple until the war of Alexander—according to his view, the length of their ministry came to 191 years—he also gives a concurrent list of the princes of the House of David of their time with the corresponding dates. All gentile chronologers used his data. It is therefore appropriate to connect the question regarding the reigns of those princes to the three examinations that have been undertaken. Similarly, it appears feasible to follow through the question raised at the end of chapter 35 regarding the duration of the first Temple by a study of the reigns of the other kingdoms recounted by gentile historians for the period just before the second Temple until the reign of Alexander. One should pay particular attention to the words of the noted writer Metasthenes the Persian whose work we translated in chapter 31, namely, that there were also 191 years from the fall of Belshazzar until the rise of Alexander. Study the text. There is also corroborating evidence for his view that from the destruction of the Temple which occurred in the eighteenth year of Nebuchadnezzar's reign until the murder of Belshazzar was 70 years since this is also the figure explicitly given in the holy Writ. And similarly, the figure of 137 years which he gives for the period from the fall of Sennacherib that occurred in the fourteenth year of Hezekiah's reign until the eighteenth year of Nebuchadnezzar's reign comes close to the number explicitly given in the Septuagint and by Yedidyah who count 12 and not 2 years for the reign of Amon. The fact is that if it would be necessary to rely on foreigners for all these data without the evidence of holy Writ, then their statements would be invalid and we would not pay attention to them.

CHAPTER FORTY

Responses on behalf of our rabbis with regard to the criticisms that were discussed.

We shall now take the other side and turn the argument in favor of our sages. Beginning with the minor criticisms,[1] we shall speak about the evidence which appeared to support the view of the opponents regarding Jeconiah's descendants as explained in the previous chapter. Notwithstanding the other arguments which ought to be raised against it, we can easily cut away its twigs with the prongs[2] of the following response.

The anomalous verse which is in the middle of that chapter, *And the son of Hananiah: Pelatiah and Jeshaiah, the sons of Rephaiah, Arnan* (1Chr. 3:21) interrupts the thread of those generations, such that we become confused with regard to the line of their descendants. One cannot therefore explain that which is obscure by that which is even more obscure.[3] And although the problem can be set along the lines of Kimḥi's explanation of those verses, as we said, an individual's view may not be pitted against the traditional teaching. Everything cannot depend on his view when he says "accept my opinion" since there are also other views which could be sustained in that context. Then there is the apparent proof with regard to the enumeration of the Persian kings which was elucidated in chapter 38. The rabbis of blessed memory did not accept the view that there was a large number of kings as indicated by the writers whom we cited—in any case, they too did not reach consensus. Then we have heard the angel's words to Daniel, *Persia will have three more kings and the fourth will be wealthier than them all* (Dan. 11:2). It is possible that the "fourth" refers to the fourth king from [and including] Cyrus which would make him the third and final king [after Cyrus].[4] Indeed, they thought it right to bring the matter into the realm of the feasible and maintain that those kings were small in number. They therefore identified Cyrus Darius and Artaxerxes as one and the same person, with all the greater reason given that the name Artaxerxes is the

1. Lit. 'beginning from the side,' an expression taken from M. Sanh. 4:2 where it refers to eliciting the opinion of the minor judges who sat on the side benches.

2. Cf. Is. 18:5.

3. I.e., the verse cannot be used as evidence for unraveling the complexities of the chronological problem.

4. Modern scholars are also divided as to whether the verse refers to the four kings after or including Cyrus. See, e.g., H. H. Rowley, *Darius the Mede,* 93.

honorific title of all Persian kings, as we said. However, the proof that was put forward in favor of the opponents with regard to the six high priests mentioned in chapter 12 of Nehemiah as was delineated in chapter 37, does indeed, according to my limited understanding, pose a problem with regard to the view of our sages who placed the generation of Simeon the righteous immediately after that of Jeshua without any intervening time between the two ministries. And those who say that the verse, *Jeshua begot Joiakim* (Neh 12:10) should be interpreted with reference to Jeshua whom he mentioned earlier[5] are certainly not right. Firstly, even if they were Levites, a long period of time was needed to encapsulate the long line of their generations during that Persian rule which extended from Jeshua the high priest until Simeon the righteous who was born at the end of their line in the seventh or eighth generation from Jeshua after the death of Nehemiah. They would further observe that the verse is repeated within the very same chapter, *These were in the time of Joiakim son of Jeshua son of Jehozadak* (Neh 12:26). We discussed all this in chapter 37. Moreover, one cannot say that the rabbis of blessed memory were recipients of a tradition that all those six high priests were of one and the same generation since Jeshua reached a venerable old age, and all those descendants of his officiated in his lifetime. For each one is singled out in the chapter under discussion, respectively referred to by the expression, *in the days of Jeshua, in the days of Joiakim, in the days of Eliashib, in the days of Joiada, Johanan, and Jaddua.* As we said in chapter 38, these expressions are comparable to the phrase *in the days of Uzziah, Jotam, Ahaz, and Hezekiah* (Is. 1:1.) As you know, the teacher of the *Guide* criticized those who rely on forced arguments. He argued that when it is clearly demonstrated that proofs have been demolished, the soul becomes less receptive to what we wish to prove.[6] Now it is true that a Tosafist does say that on occasion, some of our sages demonstrated lack of expertise in holy Writ.[7] He exemplifies his claim by the passage in Bava Qama.[8] There [Ḥiyya bar Abba] replies to the question as to why the first text of the Decalogue [i.e., in Ex. 20:12][9] makes no reference to the fact that all will be well [with the one who performs the commandment of honoring one's parents]. In his response he states that he did not know whether it was mentioned or not. Then there is also the passage in which Rabbi Abbahu says of Rav Safra.[10] "[I may have told you that he was learned in Tannaitic teaching]; did I tell you that he was learned in Scripture?" It is obvious that such a view cannot be taken of Rabbi Jose Berribi, author of the statement about the 34 years, and still less of all the sages who followed him. Moreover, there is all the more reason for this claim when we see that many of the verses in the book of Ezra are explained in disparate places quite adequately.[11] But the

5. Neh. 12:8.
6. *Guide* II, ch. 16.
7. Tos. to B. B.B. 113a, s.v. *tarvehu.*
8. B. B.Q. 54b–55a.
9. The Exodus version of the Decalogue does not contain the words *that you may fare well,* which are in Deut. 5:16.
10. B. A.Z. 4a. The passage describes heretics who had exempted R. Safra from paying taxes because, according to R. Abbahu, he was a learned man. When the heretics discover that R. Safra is unable to interpret a scriptural verse, they torture him. When they explain the reason for torturing him, R. Abbahu responds that he had never said that he was learned in Scripture.
11. 'Explained . . . adequately.' This is a play on Ps. 111:2.

correct way of considering this matter, and I shall uphold this view until I hear something better, is that this notion of the rabbis of blessed memory, which to all appearances was an error on their part, was produced by them right from the start and with wise discretion which one cannot deny. In other words, they acted as though Jeshua and Simeon the righteous were the only priests of those generations known to them, omitting all references to the priests of the intervening period. Indeed, all that we need to know about it is that either out of necessity or for the sake of perfection or for some other reason that we are unable to fathom, it constitutes wisdom, not an error, by means of which consensus is achieved from which everything can proceed. Now our sages realized that it was appropriate to set a limit to the duration of the second Temple as was done for the first Temple. It is a known fact that from Greek rule until the destruction of the Temple, reckoned according to the widely adopted era of documents, was a period of 380 years, excluding their 6-year rule in Elam as we mentioned in chapter 23. However, our rabbis saw that Nehemiah does not give explicit information regarding the whole of the period preceding the Greek era relating to the six high priests. Moreover, they did not set eyes on the Greek writings of the Jewish writers Yedidyah [Philo] and Josephus or else they did not believe in them. They gave the impression that they were ignorant of those priests, or as though they all belonged to one generation; so they decided to reckon the Persian kings within that time when they said that Persian rule lasted 34 years during Temple times. And yet, it is of itself quite obvious that all the eight priestly generations would have had to be incorporated into those years, which is intellectually untenable as we wrote in chapter 37. And if you were to say that the duration of the reigns of the Persian kings was also longer as was elucidated in chapter 38, two responses may be put forward.

Firstly, when the rabbis of blessed memory noticed that the greater number of the years [of the Persian kings] was not clearly given in Scripture, they took into account only that section of years which was given explicitly, namely, the 32 years of Artaxerxes and about 2 years which are estimated to have elapsed between the time in which it is stated, *and when some time had gone by I asked permission from the king* (Neh 13:6) and the year of the war during which he was captured by Alexander. This was in line with their well-known method of adhering to the smallest possible figure. The second response is based on the reason given by Rabad [Abraham ben David] of blessed memory as to why their computation of 410 years for the duration of the first Temple extends until the third year of Jehoiakim's reign. For he argued that since the kingdom of Judah was in such a debased and troubled state from that time until the destruction of the Temple, they thought it right not to take its kingship into account. And you know that although with the help of God, the Persians defeated the kingdom of Babylon, many years went by before they were able to secure the kingdom. Rather, they were constantly involved in foreign wars with other world powers or in internal strife with those factions jockeying for power by force of might and the sword. A reading of the first books of the writers Xenophon[12] and He-

12. There is no reference to Cyrus's death in the first book of the *Cyropaedia,* which is usually listed as the first of Xenophon's works in the first editions of his *Opera omnia*. In fact, in *Cyropaedia* 8, 7 the account of Cyrus's death is unlike that of other Greek sources, describing Cyrus as dying peacefully in bed. It is

rodotus,[13] respectively, makes this all quite evident. They recount how Cyrus killed the son of the queen of Scythia in battle, and as a result the queen amassed a strong army and made him suffer defeat after defeat.[14] When Cyrus fell into her hands, she cut off his head and put it in a receptacle full of the blood of the slain and exclaimed, "See, you were thirsty for blood, blood you shall drink to your fill." I acknowledge that this event occurred before the Temple was built. But both writers, and Xenophon's account is lengthy, recount that for many years afterwards, there was an unceasing succession of numerous wars among the Persians themselves, since each of them wanted to be the heir to the throne. We gave a synopsis of Xenophon's treatment of this subject in chapter 30. Now in whatever way these notions were accepted by the rabbis of blessed memory whose method it was to take into account only the years of a secured and well-established kingdom, they only counted 34 years which were demonstrated by the verses of Scripture. However this does not imply that they were unaware that the unsettled years bring the total to a larger figure. Don Isaac whom I cited towards the end of chapter 38, followed a similar reasoning when he said that our sages did not deny that there were more than three kings of Persia. Study the passage and draw the parallel. In fact, this is clearly demonstrated by the way they refer to Temple times in relation to the Persian Empire, Greek Empire, the Hasmonean dynasty, and the Herodian dynasty. Implied in their statement is that they were referring to the section of years which were known for certain, while admitting that there were other years which were open to doubt and which were not the subject of their discussion. That statement led to the notion that the duration of the second Temple was 420 years, being the sum of the reigns of those four kingdoms. Now Scripture refers to the 6 years in which the Temple was built in Darius's time before mentioning Artaxerxes; and yet since there is question as to whether Artaxerxes is a personal name or simply a title, they thought it best to regard it as the title of Darius. Thus, here too, they were using the principle that it is best to apply the smallest figure. Having resolved the question in this way, they used midrashic exegesis to apply the title to Cyrus since he was an upright ruler and identified all three as one and the same person. In addition, there may have also been another factor which necessitated this conclusion. For in chapter 29 of Seder Olam it is established that the 70 weeks include the 70 years of exile which means that only 420 years remain for the duration of the Temple. In any case, it was a wise act on the part of our rabbis of blessed memory to establish a fixed computation also for the duration of the second Temple, giving peace of mind to future generations, such that the sum total of years tallied with the traditional figure that we had received. It became the commendable legal convention that scribes of every generation drafted all manner of documents with the formula, "It is such and such a year according to the era that we count." Thereby, everybody followed ancient practice. In any case, it is obvious that given that what is past is past, the fixing of the months and festivals and the intercalation of the

---

clear that de' Rossi culled his information from Mercator's *Chronologia* (70) which he quotes in ch. 42. But he misread Mercator who states: "Cyrus anno 7 imperii sui venit in Persas ubi paulo post mortuus est. Xenophon in Cyropaedia. Occisus est a Tomyri regina Scythorum. Herod." In other words, the information about the murder of Cyrus by the queen derived from Herodotus alone.

13. Herodotus 1, 213–14. But the battle was against the Massagetae not the Scythians.

14. Lit. broke him with breach upon breach, cf. Job 16:14.

years is not affected by whether the figure is actually more or less, as shall be demonstrated further in the course of this chapter. In particular, even if one were to prove that this would disarrange all the fixed times which is in fact not the case, our God, who is eternally blessed, desired to make Israel meritorious, and He showed us abundant grace when He said, *This month shall mark for you the beginning of the months* (Ex. 12:2), *These are My fixed times, the fixed times of the Lord which you shall proclaim as sacred occasions* (Lev. 23:2, 4, 37). The true tradition on this is given in the Palestinian Talmud[15] and in the Babylonian Talmud tractate Rosh ha-Shanah.[16] [The text says "you" three times to indicate that you may fix the festivals] even if you err deliberately, err inadvertantly, or are led astray. Regarding this point, Rabbi Joshua said to Rabbi Aqiva: "You have comforted me." Now, similarly, the divinely inspired author of the *Kuzari*[17] stated that knowledge of the Sabbaths of the Lord and festivals of the Lord depends on the Land which is the inheritance of the Lord. But due to the globality of the earth, the inhabitants of the other climates are not in line with the Land of Israel at the time of the rising and setting of the sun as the author of the *Ma'or*[18] writes on the verse, *And it was evening and it was morning one day* which refers to the duration of day. Ibn Ezra states likewise with reference to the verse, *And the sun rose upon him* (Gen. 32:32).[19] Nevertheless, in order to prevent the banishment of His people, the blessed Lord wrote *in all your dwelling places* in reference to those sacred times, thus indicating that He was referring to every person wherever he was. This is also made clear by the wise ibn Ezra.[20]

Apart from all these issues, one must also consider the following. Now in his Laws on the Sanctification of the New Moon, Rabbi Moses [Maimonides] explained how the sanctification of the months according to the observation of the moon and the intercalation of the years according to the formulae which he elucidated in chapter 4, continued in use among Jews until the time of the last sages of the Gemara. He writes:[21]

> Since when did Israel begin to employ this method of calculation which we use nowadays? Since the time of the last sages of the Gemara; namely, from the time when the Land of Israel was destroyed and no regularly established court of law remained. (This refers to ordained rabbis in the Land of Israel, for the Sanhedrin had already been abolished. We quoted his statement on this issue in chapter 25.) But in the time of the sages of the Mishnah and likewise, in the time of the sages of the Gemara, up until the days of Abbaye and Rava, the people depended on the Palestinian courts for the fixing of the calendar.

He derived this view from the passage at the end of chapter 1 of Rosh ha-Shanah:[22] "Rava was accustomed to fast two days [on the Day of Atonement]. On one occasion he was found to be right." This means that he used to fast two days and nights for the Day

15. P. R.H. 1 (3) 57b. The passage here is slightly different from that of the Babylonian Talmud, expressing the idea that the phrase *you shall proclaim* indicates that from now on, it will be the task of subsequent generations to proclaim and fix the appointed times of the Lord.
16. B. R.H. 25a.
17. *Kuzari* II, par. 18.
18. Zerachiah Halevi, *ha-Ma'or ha-Qatan* to Alfasi R.H. 5a (to B. R.H. 20b).
19. Ibn Ezra to Gen. 33:10.
20. Ibn Ezra to Ex. 12:2.
21. *Mishneh Torah,* Qiddush ha-Ḥodesh V:3.
22. B. R.H. 21a.

of Atonement in case they declared the month full.[23] He [i.e., Maimonides], may his memory be blessed, did not inform us as to who introduced this calculation, but this information was given us by the Gaon Rabbenu Hai of blessed memory whose view is recorded by the Prince Rabbi Abraham of blessed memory in his *Sefer ha-Ibbur,*[24] and by Ramban in his *Animadversions* who wrote:[25] "Nowadays there is no ordained law court in all Israel; but the person who solved this difficulty was Rabbi Hillel the patriarch, son of Rabbi Judah the patriarch, who established a calculation of the *ibbur,*[26] that is the sanctification of the months and the intercalation of the years which must be intercalated according to our reckoning until Elijah comes and we revert to the practice of observing the moon." And at the end of that section he writes:[27] "This is the current method of establishing the months and the fixed times which will continue until he comes and teaches us what is right." In his work *Yesod Olam,* the great astronomer Rabbi Isaac Israeli (as we described in chapter 25—examine the passage) also wrote:[28]

> Rabbi Hillel son of Rabbi Judah the patriarch and his law court who were ordained and lived close to the time of the last sages of the Gemara established and fixed for us the beginnings of the months and appointed times and intercalated the years for all times from then until the righteous teacher comes. Their objective was to ensure that the law regarding the regulation of the months would not be eradicated as a result of the abolition of ordination. For once he and his law court had agreed that the expression, *when you shall proclaim them* [the appointed times] was to be applied for all times, it was first agreed by Rabbi Hillel and his law court to establish a lunar cycle of 19 years for us and to fix the years that were to be leap years such that the sixteenth of Nisan would always fall in the new season.[29]

In his work *Shaʿar Shamayim,*[30] he also writes: "Throughout the ancient period, the sanctification of the moon and the intercalation of the years was always performed by the ordained law court as they saw fit, whether according to the computation, or the dictates of the moment. However, they were conscientious in their intercalation of exactly 7 out of all the 19 years, thereby ensuring the equality of the solar and lunar years at all times and that the festivals would always occur in their appropriate season." Now, thoughtful reader, if you delve into the first gate of the work on astronomy by the Arab Alfraganus whether in the Latin or Hebrew translation,[31] you will discover that all the Arabic nations who live in the beautiful land[32] were accustomed to use the same calculation, and it is to be believed that they still reckon lunar months according to the mean motion as Rabbi Hillel had established, namely, one month full, the next month

23. I.e., in case the law court proclaimed the month of Elul to be 30 and not 29 days.

24. Abraham bar Ḥiyya, *Sefer ha-Ibbur,* 3, gate 7 (97). He refers to Rabbi Hillel bar Judah in whose time the fixed calendar was adopted.

25. Nahmanides, *Hassagot* (on Maimonides' *Sefer-ha Miṣvot* [223]).

26. The term *ibbur* (which will be retained in the translation) is used to refer to (1) the intercalation of a month or year; (2) the regulation of the calendar; (3) the science of the fixed calendar.

27. *Hassagot,* 226.

28. *Yesod Olam* IV, ch. 9 (73b–74a).

29. 'Season.' The term used is *tequfah* which refers here to the vernal equinox.

30. The work is still in manuscript.

31. Al-Farghani, *Compendium,* Differentia 1, 5.

32. This expression, based on Dan. 11:16, is usually applied to the land of Israel. Here it would appear that de' Rossi is using it to denote the expression *Arabia felix.*

defective with some months full in order to make up for the fractions of hours, for they, too, count whole days. He says that it is for this reason that they begin their day from the setting of the sun since at that point the moon rises. Thus, given that this arrangement was initiated among our people by Rabbi Hillel, and as long as no error occurred since that time—and in fact there has been no error—then they are without doubt constant in their order and correctly enacted. The proof is the calculation of documents, the beginnings of our months and the intercalation of our years and all the days of the appointed times which are according to our established calculation in accordance with the Secret of the Calendar. The essential facts of the calendar is that there is 1d 12h 793p between one *molad*[33] and another[34] and seven embolismic years within every 19 years. And one has no reason to have any scruples because in the earlier period they used to sanctify the new-moon day on the basis of observing the moon. For although the rabbis of blessed memory claim that the law court would work out whether the evidence was acceptable, their calculation, as Rabbi Moses states (in chapters 1, 2, 5, 6, and 7 and the end of chapter 18), was only reckoned according to the conjunction of the two luminaries [sun and moon] according to their true motion which is dictated by the rotation of the planets, as he explains at the end of chapter 11.[35] And as he says in the aforementioned passages, the calculation was precisely reckoned by the method of the astronomers who are familiar with the positions of the stars. This tallies with the teaching in chapter 2 of Rosh ha-Shanah which describes the examination of the witness who is questioned among other things as to whether he saw the moon facing the sun or turned away from it, and as to how high or broad it was. It also describes how Rabban Gamaliel had pictures of the shapes of the moon on a tablet and on the wall of his upper chamber.[36] This is not Rabbi Hillel's calculation which is called *ibbur,* and which is according to the uniform motion of the star in its own sphere, called the mean motion, as Rabbi Moses says at the end of chapter 11,[37] and which does not require the same kind of investigation. The only necessary information for Rabban Gamaliel's tradition[38] is that for the purpose of fixing the calendar, the duration of a synodical month is 29d 12h 793p. This is explained by Rabbi Moses in chapter 6.[39] And we shall not discard this calculation until Elijah comes as Ramban said, when we shall revert to calculation based on visual observation, or as Israeli said, until the teacher of righteousness comes. Similarly ibn Ezra wrote:[40] "Our sages transmitted to us the practice followed in the Diaspora of relying on the *ibbur* which is constructed according to the mean motion, and we can do nothing better." Now according to Rabbenu Hananel whose opinion is

33. *Molad* is the term denoting the mean conjunction of the sun and the moon.

34. I.e., an average lunation is 29d 12h 793p. This is equivalent to 1d 12h 793p since the day after an event will occur on the same day of the week as the first day after the event.

35. Qiddush ha-Ḥodesh XI:15.

36. M. R.H. 2:6, 8.

37. Qiddush ha-Ḥodesh XI:15.

38. This is a reference to the passage in B. R.H. 25a: "Rabban Gamaliel said to them: 'I have it on authority of the house of my father's father that the renewal of the moon takes place after not less than 29 and a half days and two-thirds of an hour and 73 parts.' "

39. Qiddush ha-Ḥodesh VI:3.

40. Ibn Ezra to Lev. 23:2.

cited by Rabbenu Baḥya,[41] that calculation of theirs [in the biblical period] was the same as that of Rabbi Hillel. But you will realize that it was not for nothing that the great sage Rambam of later times dissented from his view. We also demonstrated this in chapter 35 in our citation of Latif of blessed memory. In my opinion this can be shown by using ibn Ezra's view to challenge his claim:[42] "Sometimes the difference between the mean conjunction (i.e., according to Rabbi Hillel's calculation) and the true conjunction is such that sometimes one must add, sometimes subtract about 14 hours." This corroborates the statement of the wise Alfraganus who wrote in his *Astronomy*[43] that it is often the case that the new-moon day calculated according to the mean motion (i.e., according to the *ibbur*) will occur on one day, while the calculation based on observation will fall on another day. Accordingly, why did they need the calculation of the *ibbur* when, according to the divine statement, they were to sanctify the new-moon day when they saw the moon in such and such a shape. Moreover the proof that he [Baḥya] cites on the basis of the prooftext, *[Jonathan arose . . .] on the second day of the new moon* (1Sam. 20:34) is refuted by the authorities Rashi and Kimḥi, blessed be their memory.[44] {Clarification of this issue is provided by the wise ibn Ezra's comment:

> During the days of the Temple, the appointed times were in the hands of the law court as it states with regard to Hezekiah's Passover, *And the king had taken counsel [and his princes and all the congregation in Jerusalem to keep the Passover in the second month]* (2Chr. 30:2), and there is no proof in all Scripture as to how the Israelites used to fix the times of the new moons and appointed times. The statement of the Gaon that they used to rely on the calculation of the *ibbur* is not true for there is evidence both in the Mishnah and the Talmud. . . .

Examine the passage in which he expatiates at length, providing a fine treatment of the subject, particularly on the intercalation of the years according to the *baharad* formula.}[2] We know that even after the destruction of the first Temple they did not observe the Jubilee year, and nowadays, the scant commemoration of the sabbatical year is not based on scriptural law as Rabbi Moses of blessed memory explains in the Laws of the Sabbatical Year.[45] Moreover, in his *Responsa,* Rabbi Levi ibn Ḥabib who calculated as to which year we should observe as a sabbatical year, prefaced his words with the following statement.[46] "The sabbatical year is one of the divine precepts which cannot be observed among this exiled force,[47] for the release of land can only be performed in the Land of Israel—this is rabbinic law. And even though we have been obliged to observe the release of money debts outside the Land of Israel according to rabbinic law, it has

41. Baḥya ben Asher to Ex. 12:2 (86); to Ex. 13:10 (102).

42. Ibn Ezra to Ex. 12:2.

43. Al-Fargani, *Compendium,* Differentia 1, 6: "Accidit enim ut non semper sit primus dies mensis per numerum medium et per visionem idem, id est, per motum verum vel visum."

44. According to Baḥya's citation of Hananel, the view is put forward that the verses in Samuel demonstrate that in the time of Jonathan and David, two new-moon days were observed as was the case with the fixed calendar. However Rashi and Kimḥi understand the phrase *on the second day of the new-moon* as referring simply to the second day of the month.

45. *Mishneh Torah,* Shemiṭṭa X:6.

46. Levi ibn Habib, *She'elot,* 249 col. b.

47. 'This exiled force,' cf. Ob. 1:20.

been the practice in our places of residence to exact the debt when the sabbatical year has ended, whether it is proper legal practice by way of conferring authority on documents, or a custom which has arisen out of error." He then writes:[48] "There is a controversy among codifiers as to whether the sabbatical year falls in the eighty-sixth, eighty-seventh, eighty-eighth, or eighty-ninth year of the sixth millennium." Then at the end of the responsum, he writes:[49] "Are we obliged to observe all the years about which there is doubt or not? I would say that since the obligation to observe the sabbatical year after the destruction of the Temple is only a rabbinic enactment, we should accept the principle that a doubtful case in which a rabbinical enactment is under discussion is decided in favor of the more lenient practice. We should therefore only observe one year in commemoration of the sabbatical year." Given our lack of knowledge about this matter it is only natural to say "either take it or leave it"; but in addition, there are so many questions with regard to the precept which is a rabbinic enactment such that if we wish to keep the sabbatical year according to our customary reckoning, our only option is to select one year out of respect for the Torah which shall be observed until the teacher of righteousness comes.

Now I can see that somebody might object on astronomical grounds, and raise a weak and false argument against me[50] and say: "We surely see that Rabbi Moses of blessed memory in chapter 6 of the Laws of Sanctification of the New Moon, the *Semag* [of Moses of Coucy], (par. 47), the *Ṭur* [of Jacob ben Asher], Oraḥ Ḥayyim (par. 428), and all the best sages of recent times, teach us how to calculate the new-moon days on the basis of the computation of the years and cycles from *baharad* which they claim to be the new-moon day of the first year of creation. If then the number of years reckoned from creation is less or greater, then *baharad* cannot be the true formula which would mean that all of us, ourselves and they, have all wandered like sheep in regard to the fixed calendar." My response to you, my brother, would be to single out the words of the Semag [i.e., Moses of Coucy] whose statement on the subject is the most lucid of them all. He wrote: "With regard to the seasons [solstices and equinoxes], we accept the view of Rabbi Joshua who stated that the world was created on the first day of Nisan, and that the luminaries were suspended at the beginning of the eve of the fourth day. Due to the accusation of the moon and its reprimand, there was a delay of 7d 9h 642p. When one adds 2d 4h 435p[51] retrospectively you will find that the *molad* for the Tishri of Chaos [*Tohu*] before Nisan was on a Monday at 5h 204p which corresponds to the formula *baharad.*" Now consider the following point. Not only is it well known that the *molad* is imaginary and set in Tishri of the year preceding the creation of the world which never occurred—that is why it is called chaos [Tohu]. But you have also reason to wonder with regard to the first axiom that the world was created in Nisan which is concluded in the statements of the rabbis of blessed memory in Seder Olam[52] and Rosh

48. *She'elot,* 249 col. a.
49. Ibid., 256, col. c–d.
50. 'Raise . . . me,' a play on Job 16:8.
51. This is half of 4d 8h 876p which is the character of an ordinary year of twelve lunations and there are six months between Nisan and Tishri.
52. Seder Olam, ch. 4 (18–19).

ha-Shanah[53] that Rabbi Eliezer's view is followed for the dating from the flood and Rabbi Joshua's for the seasons. If they meant by this that the world was created in Nisan, how then can they testify to a woman that she has given birth when the next day her belly is between her teeth.[54] In other words, subsequently they claim that it is dated from the flood, which implies that the beginnings of the years are dated on the basis that the world was created in Tishri. These are mutually contradictory datings and it is impossible that both systems are correct. One problematic ruling leads to another; for our rabbis of blessed memory make the general pronouncement that the world was created in Tishri. We are given this enactment in tractate Rosh ha-Shanah[55] and in the [additional service] prayer for New Year which states, "This day is the beginning of your works."[56] This is the truth as is demonstrated by ibn Ezra[57] and Ramban[58] who put forward correct proofs which can also be corroborated and confirmed by the Targum of Jonathan ben Uzziel on the verse, *[All the men gathered . . . at the feast] . . . in the month of Ethanim* (1K. 8:2) which he rendered: "The month which the men of old called the first month (i.e., before the exodus of Egypt, as Kimḥi of blessed memory explains[59]) and which is now the seventh." This means that the month became the seventh after the precept was given that *this month* [i.e., Nisan] *shall be to you the first of the months.* This proof is also mentioned by Ramban in a beautiful sermon he wrote on the festival of New Year of about twelve pages which I have in my possession.[60] He also refers to it in his commentary on the flood[61] in which he also cites proof from the Mekhilta[62] derived from the verse, *This month shall be to you the first of the months* that Adam did not reckon by this dating. He thus felt no need to mention it again in the appropriate place, namely, in Exodus (12:2). This view is also supported by the anonymous tannaitic teaching cited in Avodah Zarah:[63] "When Adam saw the day getting gradually shorter he said, 'Woe is me.' But when he observed the day getting gradually longer he said, ['This is the world's course.'] . . . This is right according to the view that the world was created in Tishri, but according to the view that the world was created in Nisan, Adam must have seen the days getting longer." This also supports their unanimous view[64]

53. In B. R.H. 12a it states: "The wise men of Israel follow R. Eliezer in dating the flood [i.e., that the dating begins in the month of Tishri], and R. Joshua in dating the annual cycles [i.e., from the month of Nisan], while the scholars of other peoples also follow R. Joshua in dating the flood."

54. This expression is taken from M. R.H. 2:8.

55. B. R.H. 27a.

56. I.e., this is said on Rosh ha-Shanah which is observed on the first day of Tishri, therefore indicating that the world was created in Tishri.

57. Ibn Ezra to Lev. 25:9.

58. Nahmanides to Ex. 12:2.

59. David Kimḥi to 1K. 8:2. He explains that before the exodus, Tishri was the first month and subsequently became the seventh month while Nisan became the first month.

60. De' Rossi read the sermon in manuscript. The passage with the reference to the Targum is in *Kitve Ramban,* vol. 1, 216.

61. Nahmanides to Gen. 8:5.

62. Mekhilta d'Rabbi Ishmael, pisḥa, 2 (I, 18). The expression *to you* is taken to indicate that this dating could not have been used by Adam.

63. B. A.Z. 8a.

64. B. Ḥull. 60a. De' Rossi also refers to B. Sanh. 38b which contains the idea that Adam's stature extended from one end of the world to the other.

which is also expressed by the greatest of the Christian doctors[65] as we mentioned in chapter 17 that all the works of the creation were created in their full-grown stature. Similarly in Bereshit Rabbah,[66] Bemidbar Rabbah,[67] and Shir ha-Shirim Rabbah,[68] it is stated that Adam and Eve were created as twenty-year olds. The meaning of their statement is that they were not created as one-day-old babies, but as adults of fully grown stature. Then again there is their statement[69] that the bullock that Adam sacrificed produced horns before hoofs. This means, as Rashi's interpretation also suggests, that it was created fully developed such that when it was brought from the ground (Gen. 1:24), its head with its horns was seen first and then its hoofs. Similarly, the other parts of creation, and specifically the products of the earth, were created in a complete state as is implied by the phrase *every tree that has seed-bearing fruit* (Gen. 1:11, 12). This then would have occurred in the month of Tishri in which the festival of the ingathering is celebrated, and not in the month of Nisan. Moreover, according to the statements of the rabbis, blessed be their memory, in the Palestinian Talmud, tractate Rosh ha-Shanah, the names of the months were imported with them from Babylon.[70] You might deduce from this that Tishri signifies "beginning" for the verse, *See, I began* (Deut. 2:31) is rendered in the Targum, "See, I have begun [*shareti*]." This is also mentioned by Rabbi Maimon of blessed memory at the beginning of his commentary on the Alfraganus's Digest of the *Almagest.*[71] But, indeed, the statement of the rabbis of blessed memory that they follow Rabbi Joshua in dating the seasons[72] is simply an agreed and selected hypothesis which may have been chosen in order to begin the year in felicitous circumstances, as the commentator of the Laws of the Sanctification of the New Moon writes. He states:[73] "Why was the new year for the seasons set in the month of Nisan and not in Tishri? Because one should make a beginning only in a propitious and pleasant period and that is [in Nisan] when the sun is at the beginning of Aries." Alternatively there may have been another reason which means that they had no intention of corroborating the view that the world was created in Nisan. Accordingly, it would appear that both the Semag and the wise Abudarham did not follow the right path. For the Semag elaborated that view at length in the passage about the suspension of the luminaries of the eve of the fourth day, and the wise Abudarham wrote:[74] "We have an ancestral tradition that the sun and moon were created at the end of the month

65. Augustine, *De civ. Dei,* bk. 15, ch. 12 (*P.L.* XLI, cols. 450–51).
66. B.R. 14:7 (130).
67. Bem. R. 12:8.
68. S.S.R. to S.S. 3:11.
69. B. A.Z. 8a; B. Ḥull. 60a.
70. P. R.H. 1 (2) 56d.
71. This is a reference to the commentary of a certain Maimon of Montpellier which de' Rossi must have read in manuscript. A manuscript of the work is in the Biblioteca Comunale of Mantua (Ms. ebr. 10) and the reference is 60r. On Maimon, see M. Steinschneider, *Die Heb. Übersetzungen,* 556.
72. B. R.H. 12a, i.e. the solar year begins in Nisan.
73. Obadiah ben David to Qiddush ha-Ḥodesh IX:2.
74. *Abudarham ha-Shalem,* Shaʿar ha-Moladot, 378. David ben Joseph Abudarham was a Spanish liturgical commentator. His work contained a commentary on the prayers and discussion of different rites and the rules of the calendar. As Cassel notes, Abudarham's statement is a quotation from Abraham bar Ḥiyya.

of Adar."[75] This is explained by Ran [Rabbenu Nissim][76] of blessed memory in connection with the passage that describes all creatures passing before God like sheep.[77] And the wise Abudarham was not right in ascribing his view to an ancestral tradition, still less if what he meant was Sinaitic tradition. For as Rabbi Moses says[78] and Rabad the Levite at the beginning of his *Sefer ha-Qabbalah*[79] {and the Tosafist in the passage in Yevamot about Rabbi Simeon[80]}[2], the content of the tradition was never in principle subject to controversy; only its ramifications could be disputed. But here on a basic issue of *halakhah* and a real case, Rabbi Eliezer was disputing with Rabbi Joshua. Furthermore, you would again have reason to wonder at the statement of the Semag about the claim of the moon and its reprimand which lasted 7d 9h 642p. Surely one could say that it would have been sufficient that the divine reprimand, like that of a father,[81] last 7 days. What then was the function of the 9h and 642p? Moreover, the passage about the claim of the moon is simply a wonderful invention in order to alert us to various teachings, as I wrote in chapter 15. By this means, they were able to harmonize the verses which from a superficial consideration pose a problem. For it states, *And God made two great lights* (Gen. 1:16) and then continues, *the greater light . . . and the lesser light* (ibid). And their reference to the sin offering to the Lord[82] was because they were using their well-known method expressed in the dictum "I am expounding Scripture." One should not believe that the rabbis of blessed memory meant the story to be taken literally and that the reason for the moon's delay in appearing was because it was ashamed and vanished into nothing. If we propose, as the teacher of the *Guide* states, that the planets are living rational beings,[83] we must surely know that there can be no quarrels among them as is written, *He makes peace among His upper beings* (Job 25:2). Accordingly this idea which was expressed openly was not held to be true; God forbid that the Rav [i.e., the Semag] would set it before us as a true fact. Moreover the rabbis do not make any reference to the *molad* of *baharad,* and in his elaborate chapters on the courses of the luminaries,[84] Rabbi Eliezer only refers to 1d 12h and 793p [the difference between one *molad* and another] and the calculations which ensue from it, namely, 4d 8h and 876p [the difference between one *molad* and the corresponding *molad* of the ensuing year] and 10d 21h 204p [the excess of the days of the solar year over those of the

75. I.e., just before the beginning of the month of Nisan when Adam was created.

76. Rabbenu Nissim to Alfasi R.H. 3a (to B. R.H. 16a). He states that the world was created on 25 Ellul and Adam on 1 Tishri.

77. M. R.H. 1:2. "On New Year's day [on 1 Tishri], all that come into the world pass before Him like sheep." The rendering "in single file" is sometimes suggested instead of "like sheep."

78. *Mishneh Torah,* Mamrim I:3.

79. *Sefer ha-Qabbalah* (3).

80. Tos. to B. Yev. 77b, s.v. *halakhah.* In the context of a debate, Rabbi Simeon states: "I am reporting a *halakhah.*" According to the Tosafist, this saying could not belong to the category of Sinaitic *halakhah* which is never subject to controversy.

81. Cf. B. M.Q. 16a in which the duration of a "reprimand" is said to be not less than seven days. (Cf. Num. 12:14).

82. According to B. Ḥull. 60b, the he-goat which is offered on new-moon days as *a sin offering to the Lord* (Num. 28:15) is an atonement for God because the moon was made smaller than the sun.

83. *Guide* II, ch. 5.

84. PRE, chs. 6, 7, 8.

lunar year]. For even in his time, when they were sanctifying the new-moon day on the basis of observation, they used this kind of data. Now Rabbi Moses of blessed memory writes in the Laws of Sanctification of the New Moon as follows:[85] "It is a Mosaic tradition from Sinai that . . . in times when there was no Sanhedrin, the fixing of the times was based on the calculation that we use nowadays." Ramban of blessed memory challenged this statement when he wrote:[86] "The Rav sets this down as a tradition and as a Mosaic *halakhah* from Sinai, but it was not described as such in the Gemara or in any other passage." It is also true that the commentators on Maimonides' [Code] who note the sources of his laws do not give us indication of the derivation of this particular statement of his. But we would say in his defense that his purpose was to obligate us to obey the law court in times of emergency, as occurred in the time of Rabbi Hillel. However Rabbi Eliezer makes no allusion to *baharad* and the formulae which logically emanate from it. On the contrary, there is controversy over the *baharad* formula which would not have arisen had it been a transmitted prophetic tradition. And there are those who count from the *molad* of *vayad,*[87] that is, in Tishri from the day that Adam was created, and there are those who count from the *molad* of 3d 10h 876p, that is, from the Tishri in the year after Adam's creation—you shall hear more on this from us. But from thorough study, it will become clear to you that both the *baharad* formula and the two others that we mentioned, whichever of the three one adopts, was simply an invention of the formulator of the calculations, which is also true for the other formulae used for the fixing of the calendar. For example, the division of the hour into 1,080 parts is because it is easily divisible,[88] although there is allusion to it in the verse, *who have understanding of the times* (1Chr. 12:32).[89] In other words, that sage calculated from his own time retrospectively to the creation of the world according to the figure which he proposed, just as we, too, calculate retrospectively from our own time in order to know the *moladot* of the past. Indeed, the last formula he produced was that of the second Tishri on a Tuesday at 10h 876p and the formula *vayad* corresponding to the Tishri in which Adam was created and *baharad* the imaginary *molad*. Each of these formulae would emerge likewise for any one of us who investigate retrospectively from whichever year one happens to count. Thus, by fixing the established calendar by means of one of those formulae according to any one of the three given opinions and on that basis according to the agreed figure of the aera mundi computation, the *moladot* would always be in order. And if the formulator of the calendar were to think that the years of the world were greater even to the extent of ten thousand years, he would still proceed to calculate with the excess cycles retrospectively until the end point of the calculation. And if this would result in reaching, for example, Tuesday at 5h 250p, instead of Monday at 5h 204p (*baharad*), that calculation would become our current guide. Similarly, if he thought that the figure was smaller than that which we count, he would

85. Qiddush ha-Ḥodesh V:2.
86. *Hassagot,* 221–22.
87. *Vayad* is the symbol for the sixth day (i.e., Friday) at 14h.
88. Cf. Maimonides, Qiddush ha-Ḥodesh VI:2.
89. This expression from Chronicles is often used to denote experts in the calendar. De' Rossi is using *gematria* with regard to the word "times" which comes to a total of 1,080 when the final *mem* of the word is reckoned as 600.

complete his procedure and fix the formula from the final point of the time as calculated by him. In fact you can see that the sage Abudarham who made the effort of listing each "character" over one thousand cycles of years which is equivalent to nineteen thousand years said that for one thousand cycles the "character" is 1d 14h 1,000p. By means of the many formulae he gives there one can know every future *molad* for several thousands of years as long as one adds the "character" calculated by him for every *molad* of your time. And thus according to that procedure of his, one can calculate and know retrospectively thousands of imaginary years before creation by means of subtraction. By this method which is indeed simple for those who understand the way the experts make the divisions with regard to the principles of the formulae, addition or subtraction of years of the aera mundi computation would not bring the fixed calendar into disrepute in any way, as I shall proceed to clarify further.

Now an honest sage should not imagine with regard to those who abide by the fixed formula of *baharad* or either of the two other formulae, that the formulators reached their calculation by proceeding a posteriori; in other words, that it was through prophecy or Sinaitic tradition that they came to the knowledge that this was indeed the first *molad,* and that on that basis they proceeded to calculate all past or future *moladot.* For then one would have to say that the addition of one month alone would dislodge the *baharad* formula and result in the annulment of prophetic declarations from which it derived. Such a notion is most certainly intellectually implausible, and particularly when consideration is given to my following observations. Firstly, my brother, you should realize that the statement that the years counted from the Pentateuch or Prophets which are collated with the purpose of establishing the aera mundi computation are all invariably precise and complete periods of time is not an acceptable proposition. For then you might say that all the generations counted from Adam, to Noah, and to Abraham, and to the exodus from Egypt and the 480 years up until the building of the Temple, and the regnal years of the first Temple which are approximately fifty figures in all begin exactly at the beginning of the year and end right at its end. On the contrary, we have reliable proof that many of the years were truncated. First you should consider the statement of the rabbis of blessed memory in relation to the verse, *I am one hundred and twenty years old this day* (Deut. 31:2). They state:[90] "*This day* are my days and years completed This teaches you that the Holy One blessed be He completes the years of the righteous from day to day and from month to month as it says, *The number of your days will I complete* (Ex. 23:26). This then could not have been the case for the ten generations from Adam to Noah since they were wicked as is well known. Moreover, the point of the statement is to refer to the delimited period of their lives even when the end comes in the middle of the year.

{From this you can also understand that when they count the years until death, this does not mean that they are counted precisely to the end of the years. So too, when age is given in connection with birth as for example, "And so and so was this number of years and begot so and so" from which data we collate the aera mundi computation, calculation precisely to the end of the year is not implied. Rather, they subtract or add months which were of no concern to the Holy Spirit. And should you argue that these months

90. B. Sota 13b.

are equalized, either by being taken with the last year of the father or the first of the son, you must surely realize that this has a detrimental effect on the literal meaning of the verse whether in relation to the years of the fathers or those of the sons. For these additions and subtractions are new in respect of the figure written in the text of Scripture. Furthermore, you should take into consideration} that in tractate Rosh ha-Shanah[91] all agree[92] that Isaac was born on Passover and that the exodus from Egypt took place in the middle of the year; and yet it is written, *At the end of the four hundred and thirtieth year [on the very day, all the ranks of the Lord departed from the land of Egypt]* (Ex. 12:41). Their entry into the Land in the days of Joshua was also at the time of Passover and yet in Joshua it is written, *For the Israelites had traveled in the wilderness forty years* (Josh. 5:6). And the construction of the Temple was begun in the second month about which it is written, *In the four hundred and eightieth year after the Israelites had left the land of Egypt [in the month of Ziv, that is, the second month. . . . Solomon began to build the House of the Lord]* (1K. 6:1). And according to our rabbis of blessed memory, the destruction of both Temples took place in the tenth month [Av] from Tishri[93] and they number the years of their duration 410 and 420 years, respectively. And with regard to the regnal years during the First Temple, it is said of Ahaziah, *he reigned over Israel two years* (1K. 22:52). With regard to this verse, Kimḥi wrote: "The two years were not complete. . . . Rather, since the second year of Ahaziah's reign was not completed, it was counted for his reign, his brother's, and that of his father."[94] And Rashi of blessed memory writes in the same context: "On examination, I discovered that in the majority of cases, the computation of the regnal years of the kings of Israel is not precise. If a king came to the throne at the end of a year, it is counted as the first year of his reign and it is not included in the computation of his reign in any other place." Similarly, in the book of Ezra with regard to the discrepancies in numbers between the section beginning *These are the people of the province* (2:1) and the repeated section in the book itself (Neh 7:6), Rashi writes: "Scripture is not exact in enumerating these figures."* But this should not appear strange to us since similarly the seventy souls who went down to Egypt were in effect only sixty-nine and yet they are described as numbering seventy. Then Benjamin was born in the land of Israel, and yet with regard to all the sons of Jacob it is written that they were born in Paddan-Aram (Gen. 35:26). Then Ephraim and Manasseh were born in Egypt, and yet it states, *Your ancestors went down to Egypt seventy persons in all* (Deut. 10:22). And the murdered sons of Gideon numbered only sixty-nine, for Jotham escaped and yet in three places they are said to have numbered seventy.[95] This is explained by ibn Ezra.[96] In his *Animadversions,* Ram-

91. B. R.H. 10b–11a.

92. I.e., both R. Eliezer and R. Joshua, who hold different views about the month in which the world was created.

93. As Cassel notes, it is actually the eleventh month from Tishri.

94. Ahaziah's rule begins in the seventeenth year of Jehoshaphat's reign, which began in the fourth year of Ahab who reigned for 22 years. Thus Ahaziah's reign lasted less than 2 years. It also states that Jehoram, brother of Ahaziah ruled (after the death of Ahaziah) in the eighteenth year of Jehoshaphat (2K. 3:1).

95. [Abimelech] . . . *killed his brothers, the sons of Jerubbaal [Gideon] seventy men on one stone* (Jud. 9:5) and also Jud. 9:18, 24; 9:56.

96. Ibn Ezra to Gen. 46:23.

ban of blessed memory also goes to great length to demonstrate that this is the method of the Pentateuch, our prophets, and our rabbis. In his explanatory notes on the Torah, Rabbi Isaiah di Trani of blessed memory also writes with regard to the period of the flood.[97] "The scriptural method is to use whole figures even if individual numbers are omitted or added." Apart from this, it is made clear in Scripture that in addition to the whole years which were counted for the kings of Israel during the first Temple, another month ought to be added to the reign of Shallum son of Jabesh and six months for Ahaziah. In any case, there is no cause for concern since it is a juridical rule that one need not take specific figures into account since, according to the statement in tractate Rosh ha-Shanah of the Palestinian Talmud,[98] which we mentioned in chapter 35, the larger figure incorporates the smaller and is thus of no account. This is also elucidated in chapter 4 of Seder Olam:[99] "We learn from Scripture that whenever one day of a month has occurred, it is reckoned as a month and when one month of the year has occurred, it is reckoned as a complete year for part of the month is regarded as the whole month and part of the year is regarded as the whole of the year." Furthermore, according to Scripture, the four hundred and eightieth year from the exodus is actually the fourth year of Solomon's reign and the first year of the construction of the Temple. And yet in his comment on the passage in Avodah Zarah about the 1380 years that we mentioned in chapters 23 and 35, Rashi counts the years preceding the building of the Temple and the subsequent years, allotting a total of 410 years for the duration of the [first] Temple.[100] This corresponds to the way the year of the flood is reckoned about which there is controversy in Bereshit Rabbah[101] according to Rashi's explanation.[102] Examine the passage. And in chapter 35 I cited the words of the author of *Terumah* that from one perspective one should count 419 years for the duration of the second Temple, and from another, 421. Thus it necessarily follows that if one were to think that one must add to the number of all the years that have elapsed since the very beginning of the creation until this day—disregarding the years mentioned by the commentators with regard to the exodus mentioned above in chapter 35, and the 20 years which according to the commentators mentioned in chapter 35 increase the duration of the first Temple, or the 8 first years of Hoshea's reign for which we also gave evidence in the same chapter and yet are counted by everybody as part of the 410 years—just one month omitted from the beginning of the year or subtracted on account of a truncated year that was counted as a whole year would surely and patently result in the need to subtract 1d 12h 793p from *baharad* or to add to it as many times as there were months.

97. Isaiah di Trani, *Nimmuke Ḥumash,* to Gen. 7:12 (11). The work is essentially a collection of remarks and criticisms of Rashi's commentary. De' Rossi read the work in manuscript.

98. P. R.H. 1 (1) 56b.

99. Seder Olam, ch. 4 (21).

100. Rashi to B. A.Z. 9a: "From the exodus from Egypt to the destruction of the second Temple is 1,380 years: 480 years to the construction of the first Temple; it stood for 410 years."

101. B.R. 32:6 (293): *And Noah was six hundred years old* (Gen. 7:6). "Rabbi Judah said: 'The year of the flood is not counted in the number of Noah's years.' [For he was 600 years old when the flood began and the flood lasted one year and he lived 350 years after the flood and therefore the total of his years should be 951 and not 950 as stated in Gen. 9:29.] R. Nehemiah said: 'The year is counted in the reckoning of the seasons and calculations [from the creation].' "

102. Rashi's commentary on B.R. is not authentic. It was first published under his name in Venice, 1556.

The necessary consequence would be that *baharad* would be dislodged such that it could not constitute the starting point of the reckoning counted by us. But when we say that this *baharad* was the agreed figure laid down by the formulators of the computation, everything is established and synchronized; we are not confronted with any gap or anomaly. Now when Rabbi Hillel and his law court undertook to define the beginning of the number of years and to establish their calculations on that basis, they wished to link it with the creation of the world as we mentioned in chapter 25, and not with the Greek era or to the destruction of the Temple to any other epoch used in the past. When they undertook to compute the number of years from creation until their own time, they certainly knew and took cognizance of all the possible doubts regarding the number of years given in the Torah on the basis of whether there are fewer or more months to be reckoned with, both as regards the length of the Egyptian exile and the duration of the first and second Temples as was said. They would have also realized and acknowledged that it was impossible to reach the actual truth—for who could step back for us into time gone by and clarify it for us? Indeed, the verses could sustain the various views which were applied to them given that we do not possess a prophetic tradition to give the decisive interpretation. After all, controversies cannot occur in connection with prophetic tradition; in that case, then, the Gaon Rabbenu Hananel and the pious Ramban of blessed memory and the others would not have had the gall to contravert the Seder Olam with regard to the figure of 2,448, nor Rabad the Levite and Kimḥi and their colleagues dispute the figure of 410. Indeed Rabbi Hillel acted like a sage who knew the interpretation of the matter and, for his calculation, decided to use all the figures as propagated among the people without being concerned as to whether one or another figure should be augmented or diminished. He decided that this figure, which he computed on the basis of them all, should be the basis of all his calculations with regard to the past and to the future after his own time until the righteous teacher will come. Accordingly, one could say that this decision with regard to the sum of the years was indicative of Rabbi Hillel's wise discretion, which was also displayed when he chose to use the calculation based on the mean conjunction rather than that based on observation which is according to the true conjunction, since this cannot be done without an ordained law court in the Land of Israel. In the same way, he decided to calculate the seasons from Nisan, and the *moladot* from Tishri, although the world could only have been created in one of these two times, and to follow our customary calculation of the seasons although it was known that it could be questioned as shall be shown. When something cannot be ascertained with certainty, we must do the best we can; and if it is inherently questionable, we should not speak of it as fact, but rather as reflecting convention. And it stands to reason that had Rabbi Hillel and his court thought it right to establish the anno mundi computation on the basis of a lesser or greater figure, they would have established for us another set point which proceeded backwards from their computation. The passage about the reprimand of the moon, which was conceived by its authors with the purpose of alerting us to a variety of teachings, as we mentioned above in chapter 15, and was also mentioned by some of the later authorities, specifically in the commentaries of Rashba [Solomon ben Adret] of blessed memory and Rabbi Reuben bar

Ḥayyim Zevi[103] in connection with other passages, fitted in with the calculations of the formulators of the calendar according to the statements of the Semag mentioned above. For to all appearances it seemed to offer a reason and support for proceeding from the *baharad* of Tishri of Tohu 7d 9h 642p of the next Nisan by adding 2d 4h 438p with the preceding period of 7d 9h 642p which was the duration of the moon's reprimand.

(*[see p. 494] A similar point is made by ibn Ezra at the beginning of his commentary on the book of Daniel. He writes:[104] "No king reigns from the beginning of the civil year; there will therefore be a difference of about one year between each computation. This should not cause surprise since the Torah states that a boy should be circumcised at eight days but no boy is circumcised exactly eight days after his birth. It can even happen that a boy is circumcised when he is seven and a half days old.")

There is a second proof on good authority that the *baharad* formula or any other is a scientific tradition deduced retrospectively from the figure of the anno mundi computation which was a convention accepted by the formulators of the computation unrelated to prophecy and Sinaitic tradition. It is demonstrated by the wise commentator on Rabbi Moses' Laws of the Sanctification of the New Moon.[105] He writes that there are three views concerning the beginning of the years of the world. The western [Palestinian] Jews begin from *baharad,* the *molad* of the Tishri of Tohu which was before the creation of man whether one follows Rabbi Joshua's view that he was created in the following Nisan or, according to Rabbi Eliezer, in the following Tishri. According to this computation, the seven intercalated years would occur in the third, sixth, eighth, eleventh, fourteenth, seventeenth, and nineteenth years of each cycle. The eastern [Babylonian] Jews begin from the *molad* of the Tishri in which man was created. According to the statement which the commentator attributes to our rabbis, both the *molad* and the creation [of man] would have occurred on Friday at the end of the fourteenth hour, the formula being *vayad,* or one might say *yov,* namely, on the sixth day at the second hour of the day, which comes to the same thing. According to this computation, the intercalated years would fall in the second, fifth, seventh, tenth, thirteenth, sixteenth, and eighteenth years of the cycle. The latter computation was held by Rabbenu Saadiah and Rabbenu Hai of blessed memory, as is shown in *Sefer ha-Ibbur* of Rabbi Abraham the prince[106] and the author of the *Ma'or*[107] and in ibn Ḥabib's responsum on the sabbatical year. Moreover, according to the author of *Ḥeshev-ha-Efod,*[108] (chapter 22) one must count the 2,448 years as posited in Seder Olam[109] from the formula *vayad,* and not from *baharad.* There are also those who begin the count from the *molad* of the year after the creation of the first man which was on the third day at

103. Reuben b. Ḥayyim was a thirteenth-century-Provençal talmudist who also wrote philosophical explanations of the Aggadot.
104. Ibn Ezra to Dan. 1:1.
105. *Perush* to Qiddush ha-Ḥodesh VI:8.
106. *Sefer ha-Ibbur* III, gate 7 (96–97).
107. Zerachiah ben Isaac Halevi, *ha-Ma'or ha-Gadol* to Alfasi, A.Z. 2v.
108. Profayt Duran (d. circa 1414). De' Rossi read *Ḥeshev ha-Efod* (or *Sefer ha-Ibbur*) on the Hebrew calendar in manuscript.
109. I.e., the date of the exodus from Egypt.

10h 876p. The intercalated years, according to this computation, would fall in the first, fourth, sixth, ninth, twelfth, fifteenth, and seventeenth years of the cycle. And he [the commentator] writes: "Each of these three views is true. It is simply that each counts one more year from creation than the other. (In a similar way, in the responsum cited above, Rabbenu Saadiah gives the figure 1,238 according to the Alexandrian era, 4,686 from creation, while others count 4,687 years.) The majority of experts in the calendar, however, chose to fix the beginning from *baharad* in order not to deduct the five days preceding the creation of man."

So now intelligent reader you are in a position to judge that if *baharad* had a Sinaitic origin or had somehow been a prophetic tradition, the two other views would never have been mentioned, nor would they have occurred to any of the early or late authorities. For in that case, what reason would they have had to alter it[110] when it served its purpose and was adopted by us not because the majority had opted for it, but as a fixed law for all generations and assemblies of our ancestors. And in chapter 35, I cited Rav Hai Gaon of blessed memory who said that the computation that should be used is the *molad* of *vayad* rather than that of *baharad,* and that the reason for establishing the *molad baharad* was for pedagogical reasons. And his statement about the pedagogical purpose in establishing *baharad* is comparable to the view of Rabbenu Isaiah [di Trani] the younger which was cited by the author of *Shilṭe ha-Gibborim.*[111] He writes: "When the supreme law court was abolished, they no longer established the new-moon days by observation. Instead there was a computation known to all the people of the Diaspora which the former sages had established for them such that everybody had a uniform fixed computation." A similar statement is made by the author of the *Aqedah*[112] He writes: "The experts in the calendar established the *molad* of *baharad*—from their statements, it is clear that it corresponds to the *molad* of Tohu." Furthermore, in this chapter I cited the Semag and Abudarham who held that the tradition was based on the *molad* of Nisan; but since we need to know the *molad* of Tishri of Tohu, we deduct 2d 4h 438p and arrive at *baharad.* Then I also cited Ramban of blessed memory who wrote in his *Animadversions* that none of the sages' works on this subject refer to tradition or Mosaic *halakhah.* At any rate, then, there is no prophetic tradition with regard to *baharad* or the two associated formulae. Rather, as we said, it was a convention agreed upon by the formulators of the calendar. On the basis of this, together with the other evidence which shall be brought to your notice in the rest of the chapter, you will realize that the tradition about *baharad* cited by Rabbenu Baḥya in his commentary[113] lacks the basis which is distinctive to the kabbalists. Study the passage. It can also serve as a premise by means of which one can understand his other statements. Now the commentator on the Laws of the Sanctification of the New Moon,[114] cites a proof to justify the position of those who begin from the *molad* of Adam on Friday at the end of the second hour. He refers to the statement of the rabbis of blessed memory that at the third

110. Cf. Lev. 27:33.
111. Joshua Boaz, *Shilṭe ha-Gibborim* to Alfasi R.H. 4v.
112. Isaac Arama, *Aqedat Yiṣḥaq,* gate 3, 5 (30a).
113. Baḥya ben Asher to Gen. 1:2 (20). De' Rossi's point is that Baḥya, whose commentary is replete with kabbalistic notions, singles out *baharad* as an astronomical computation that is totally fictitious.
114. *Perush* to Qiddush ha-Ḥodesh VI:8.

hour He created him; thus the *molad* of the moon and the creation of Adam took place one second after the beginning of the third hour. However, with all due respect to him, you should know that this is an erroneous and unfounded comment. He did not give us initially a correct representation of what the rabbis of blessed memory said. The saying about Adam's creation at the third hour is nowhere to be found in any text. Rather, the following statement is found in six passages with some variation between some of the texts, although they are all the same in that not one of them speaks of the third hour as he does. In the eleventh chapter of Pirqe d'Rabbi Eliezer and in Sanhedrin[115] which is also cited by Rabbenu Baḥya, it states: "In the first hour He collected the dust for Adam, in the second He formed it into a mass, in the third He gave it its shape, in the fourth hour, He cast a soul into it." In Vayiqra Rabbah,[116] Tanḥuma,[117] and Midrash Tehillim[118] and the Pesiqta,[119] on the verse, *Your word, O Lord stands forever* (Ps. 119:89) which is cited by Ran of blessed memory,[120] there is the statement: "In the first hour the idea of creating man came into His mind; in the second hour, He took counsel with the angels; in the third hour He collected Adam's dust; in the fourth hour, He formed it into a mass; in the fifth hour, He gave it shape; in the sixth hour, He made it into a lifeless body; and in the seventh, He cast a soul into him." Thus, by attributing the words "in the third hour He created him" to our rabbis of blessed memory, the commentator was presenting false testimony against his teachers.[121] As for the creation, the essence of which is the endowing of his actual form, namely, the casting of the soul, it took place, according to all their statements, only after the third hour; therefore the creation of man could not have coincided with the *molad* of the moon. And you might be able to say that the gathering of his dust is tantamount to creation; but even this gathering, according to the Gemara in Sanhedrin and Pirqe d'Rabbi Eliezer, took place in the first hour. Thus there would be no consensus with regard to the hour of his creation; rather it would be a matter of dispute. How then could we set it as a fixed point on which the record of all the days of the earth depends? But the true reason which led people to begin the count from the *molad* of *vayad* (or one might say *yov* as we said before) is because by adding 4d 8h 876p to the imaginary *baharad,* the *molad* of the third year would fall on Tuesday at 10h 876p. Thus by subtraction, those *moladot* would occur one before the other in a backward progression. Accordingly, it makes no difference as to which of these three starting points you take with regard to the conventional anno mundi computation; it is just a question of adding one or two years as was said above. Furthermore you should understand that there is not even one scholar who would not evaluate this and all comparable sayings of theirs as expressing the inner meaning of apposite subjects divorced from any literal significance; they would consider anyone who interprets it at face value as beyond the pale. You certainly know that although the scriptural verses explicitly describe the works of creation as produced

115. B. Sanh. 38b. (Also ARN, ch. 1, rec A (4), rec. B (8).
116. V.R. 29:1 (669).
117. Tanḥuma, Shemini, 8 (Buber, 13).
118. Mid. Teh. to Ps. 92:1.
119. Pes. Rabbati 47:2 (187b); Pes. d'R. Kah. 23:1 (334).
120. Rabbenu Nissim to Alfasi R.H. 3a to B. R.H. 16a.
121. 'A false . . . teachers,' cf. Deut. 19:18.

separately over six days, many world scholars, both Jewish and gentile, consider that the entire creation actually took place simultaneously without any separation as we mentioned in chapter 6. How then could you imagine that the blessed Lord measured out and conceived the creation of mere man, who is like a breath, over twelve hours from morning to evening, or for the manifestly greater part of that time? This gains greater credibility given that the divine scriptural text pronounces that the beasts, cattle, and creeping creatures preceded Adam's creation on the sixth day itself. And in Bereshit Rabbah,[122] they say that six things were created on the sixth day: Adam and Eve, the creeping creatures, the cattle, beasts, and demons. Surely a specific hour was required for the four latter things which preceded his creation in order to ensure that the impure did not contaminate the pure. And if they really believed that this was what actually happened, who was the first to declare it that we may take note; after all, this information was not conveyed or transmitted to us by any one of the prophets. But there must be something in the rabbis' statement, and if you look, you will discover the point. You might say that the implication of their statement is that man is beloved to the Highest God, and his creation is so essential that He as it were devotes an entire day to it. In a similar fashion, the rabbis of blessed memory say:[123] "The entire world was created by ten sayings. And what is the meaning of Scripture? To requite the ungodly and to give a fine reward to the righteous [who sustain the world that was created by ten sayings]." In the same way, Rabbi Aḥa's statement in Sanhedrin[124] conveyed the idea that the creation of man was in His image, and out of love He expended time in creating him. Having appreciated this observation, you will undoubtedly not take the literal sense of the saying as evidence of a historical happening. You should also adopt this method for all sayings of a similar nature; then you will reach an incisive understanding as to how the true basis for comprehending such material is, as we indicated in chapter 15, to be acquainted with the words of the sages, their enigmas, parables, and rhetoric. The ancient gentile sages also employed this method. For in treating philosophical matters, they would use allegory by inventing stories about incidents that happened to gods or human beings or the animal species. Their purpose was either to conceal these matters from the masses or to amuse the audience with an imaginary tale which would render them memorable, or for other reasons as the wise Rabbi Judah, author of the famous dialogue about Philone e Sophia writes in the second part of his work.[125] It is true that under the impact of Pythagoras, there was a progression from inventiveness of this kind to the symbolic use of arithmetical numbers such as one or two. He was followed by Plato who also moved away from this type of imagery to definitions by means of forms called geometrical in Greek, such as the circle and the square and their components. This becomes clear from his exposition on the elements, the soul, and other subjects. However, the common feature in all three modes is that the language employed is metaphorical and allegorical, which they call symbolic. Thus by

122. B.R. 11:9 (96).

123. M. Avot. 5:1.

124. This is a reference to B. Sanh. 38b about Adam's creation over twelve hours. In the standard text, the passage is ascribed to R. Johanan.

125. Judah Abravanel (Leone Ebreo), *Dialoghi* II (99–100).

using these or similar methods and particularly that of linking the interpretation to Scripture, our rabbis have often succeeded in composing delightful sayings.

The third piece of evidence is taken from the wise Israeli who wrote:[126] "The third fundamental principle is *baharad.* Our predecessors of blessed memory discovered its significance through their research or by means of prophecy. Thus they knew that the moment of the *molad* of the very first Nisan, according to the view that the world was created in Nisan, occurred at 9h 642p. Similarly they knew that the moment of the first *molad* of Tishri, according to the view that the world was created in Tishri, occurred at the end of the fourteenth hour of Friday." Examine the passage. Thus he, may his memory be blessed, correctly stated that our predecessors discovered the formula through their research. And as has already been demonstrated, human research proceeds a posteriori, as we indicated at the end of chapter 35. For the purpose of aggrandizing and enhancing the discipline, however, he added the words "or by means of prophecy." These words of his are simply a product of sheer imagination.[127] After all, he is, in fact, acknowledging that we have no knowledge as to whether this is prophecy or not, particularly when the prophet in question is not known and the prophecy itself is open to doubt. You must surely be surprised at his statement in which he gives two different views. Have you ever heard of prophecies that ride on two steeds?[128] There is no doubt that if it were prophetic inspiration that illuminated us with regard to the question of the very first *molad,* by means of this same illumination it would have also been revealed to us as to which was the first month, Nisan or Tishri, and it would not have become a subject of controversy.

The fourth seal of perfection[129] which strengthens our argument shall be explained to you when you pay attention to what I have to say. You certainly are aware of the great wisdom and stature of the great teacher, Rambam of blessed memory, which is demonstrated in all his statements in general, and in the Laws of the Sanctification of the New Moon in particular. Thus we should not regard the blessed teacher as arrogant, but as he thought, justified, when at the end of the Laws, he goes so far as to apply the verse, *search and read it in the scroll of the Lord* (Is. 34:16) to his own words.[130] And yet in his *Yesod Olam,* the great sage Israeli writes:[131]

> Our teacher Moses [Maimonides] made out a case as to why New Year's day cannot fall on a Sunday, Wednesday, or Friday [Adu] on the basis of the mean and true motion of the two luminaries. This is what he wrote at the end of chapter 7 of the Laws of the Sanctification of the New Moon: "Why does this method of calendrical calculation eliminate Sunday, Wednesday, and Friday from being declared as new-moon days? Because it reckons with the conjunction of the moon and sun based not upon their true position but only on their mean motion. . . . Therefore [the days of declaration are made to alternate with the days of postponement] in order to hit upon the day of their conjunction."

126. *Yesod Olam* IV, ch. 3 (66v).
127. This is a play on the word *nevu'ah* (prophecy) and the expression "sheer imagination" (*divre nevi'ut*) in B. Eruv. 60b.
128. This expression is taken from B. Ket. 55b.
129. Cf. Ezk. 28:12.
130. Qiddush ha-Ḥodesh XIX:16 (Yale Judaica series translation XIX:13).
131. *Yesod Olam* IV, ch. 9 (74v).

In this context Israeli mentions Rabad's criticism and reinforces it. He also produces many proofs based on astronomical methods to demonstrate that the view of Rabbi Moses of blessed memory has no validity whatsoever.[132] In similar fashion he writes in his work *Shaʿar ha-Shamayim* as follows:

> When ordination was abolished at the end of the period of the sages of the Gemara, the elders and sages of that generation produced the tradition which they had received from the prophets (you have already heard what we have to say about these products of the imagination) and transmitted to us this fixed computation for establishing the dates of the new moon and festival days such that it is entirely constructed and based according to the course of the mean motion of the two luminaries. Nowadays, therefore, we do not have to concern ourselves with their true motion as some sages reckoned, who even went as far as saying that the basic reason for the postponement of New Year's day is linked with the true conjunction. But as I demonstrated in the *Yesod Olam,* this is not true.

In general he ratifies the view of Rabad of blessed memory that the reason for the postponement is to ensure that the day of the willow [Hoshanah Rabbah] does not fall on the Sabbath and that the Day of Atonement does not fall on the Sabbath eve [Friday] or at the conclusion of the Sabbath [Sunday]. Ran [Rabbenu Nissim] also writes in this way[133] although the Semag does accept Rambam's reasoning. This difference of view is of great significance, for according to Rabbi Moses, the postponement derives from astronomical principles, whereas the view of his opponents is that it is a convention agreed on authority of a valid law court following the scriptural statement, *These are the set times of the Lord, the sacred occasions which you shall celebrate each at its appointed time* (Lev. 23:4). Even the wise commentator of the Laws of the Sanctification of the New Moon, for whom[134] it would have been appropriate to defend the master, raised his own objection to his [Maimonides'] principle at the end of chapter 7 and then said that there could be no response to make in his favor until the righteous teacher comes.[135] Similarly, in his *Yesod Olam,* he [Israeli] discusses the question regarding the [geographical] location on which the calculation of the time of the seasons and *moladot* is based, an issue of great controversy among two groups of sages of our people. He wrote: "Rabbi Hasan the judge and Rabbi Isaac ben Rakufel demonstrated that the location under investigation is in the eastern part of the *oiḳoumene.* Rabbi Abraham bar Ḥiyya the prince agreed with them. Now I, the author, used to be of the same opinion until I discovered that Rabbi Isaac son of Rabbi Baruch had annulled their statements and arguments and gave his verdict that the location on which the reckoning of the *moladot* and seasons is based is not in the east as they thought." He then continues: "And the author of the *Kuzari* as well as the author of the *Maʾor,* as I have shown you (that is at the end of section 2, chapter 17, and section 4, chapter 3), said that the reckoning of the

132. The issue of the postponements was a subject discussed by Münster and Scaliger (see Grafton, *Joseph Scaliger II,* 328–29). De' Rossi who is sympathetic to Maimonides' view refers to the subject again in his *Maṣref la-Kesef* (2, ch. 14, 110) where he refers to Münster's discussion: "Indeed, I noticed that a Christian sage who translated our calendrical system for the benefit of his own people [i.e., the *Kalendarium Hebraicum,* Basel, 1527] became quite contemptuous . . . which one cannot be when speaking about Maimonides' explanation."

133. Rabbenu Nissim to Alfasi Meg. 10a to B. Meg. 30a.

134. Cassel wrongly reads *lo* (not) instead of *lo* (for him).

135. *Perush* to Qiddush ha-Ḥodesh VII:7.

moladot is based on the midpoint of the Land of Israel. But these people also strayed from the path of reason. . . . Accordingly it appears that there is no reason to rely on either of the two views regarding this matter." Examine the passage. Then in chapter 3, after having disproved, according to his thinking, the view given in the *Kuzari* and the *Ma'or,* he writes: "I have used scientific methods to investigate the times of the eclipses of the moon and discovered that the reckoning of the times of the seasons and *moladot* is based on the navel of the earth." Accordingly, there are three views regarding this question. One is the view of the judge and ben Rakufel and Rabbi Abraham that it is based on the eastern side of the *oikoumene.* The second view is that of the *Kuzari* and the author of the *Ma'or* that it is based on the midpoint of the Land of Israel. The author of the *Ma'or* also simply calls it "the navel of the earth," as though the Land of Israel is truly in the center of the world. Rambam, too, in the eleventh chapter of his Laws of the Sanctification of the New Moon[136] and in his commentary on the first chapter of Rosh ha-Shanah, which is cited by the commentator[137] on the subject of the six hours in which the new moon is not visible,[138] adopts this method, but he explicitly states that Jerusalem is not at the center of the world. Examine the passage. The third view, that of Israeli, is that it is based on the center of the world, namely, the true center of the world and not the center of the *oikoumene* which is in the north. This is why he writes:[139] "The point at which the line of longitude, which is the meridian, and the line of latitude, which is the equator, intersect each other into two halves is called the navel of the world. You should give the utmost consideration to this location in the *oikoumene* and be familiar with it since we shall be dealing with it extensively in this book." But for my part, I have already alerted you to his controversial position regarding this center in chapter 11 of part 1.

Now intelligent reader with all this information at your disposal, you are asked now to make an a fortiori reasoning. The end point of the reckoning which stems from *baharad* was established and formulated quite recently in the time of Rabbi Hillel and his law court—for it was like yesterday that our ancestors were with them around the time of the closing of the Gemara when these controversies broke out, and not only among them, but also among the great authorities mentioned above. While we do know the computation, we do not know on what it is based. Thus ibn Ezra demonstrated profound wisdom when he raised the questions for which he is renowned in his introduction to this commentary on the Torah where he describes the second method of exegesis,[140] as well as in his commentary on Exodus 12 and Leviticus 23.[141] Examine the

136. Ibid. XI:17.

137. Ibid. VII:1.

138. In B. R.H. 20b, it is stated that the moon is invisible for twenty-four hours, and that in the land of Israel, six of these hours belong to the new moon and eighteen to the old (and vice versa in Babylon). In the commentary to R.H. ascribed to Maimonides, it is explained that in the land of Israel, the new moon appears six complete hours after its birth.

139. *Yesod Olam* II, ch. 3 (21v).

140. In this section of his introduction, ibn Ezra is attacking Karaites and other anti-traditionalists who do not accept the traditions of the Oral Torah as transmitted by the rabbis which are needed in order to fulfill the written Torah. Among the issues he raises are those related to the calendar which, as he argues, cannot be fully understood by simply relying on Scripture.

141. In his commentary to Ex. 12:1 and Lev. 23:3, ibn Ezra demonstrates how the Jewish calendrical system is derived and developed from biblical laws.

passages. How then can you allow yourself to believe that we are in possession of a priori knowledge regarding the origin of the universe before the creation of our first ancestor when it is not mentioned at all in prophetical utterances and in the Gemara? As I showed you, Ramban, too, in his *Animadversions* states that there is no record of such a tradition. How then can this amazing matter be known when the Lord has not spoken of it? Did not the blessed Lord say to Job and likewise to every human being, *Where were you when I laid the earth's foundations?* (Job 38:4) *Do you know the laws of heaven?* (ibid. v.33). And the sage of the *Kuzari* showed great wisdom when, as is demonstrated in part 1,[142] he based all his inspired words in that book on the divine statement at the beginning of the ten commandments, *I am the Lord the God who brought you out of the land of Egypt* (Ex. 20:2): for all this you have seen through personal experience. It does not say, *I am the Lord who created heaven and earth* for you would then say we cannot know that which our ancestors and their ancestors never saw.

But the truth regarding the *baharad* formula is as we have said. Rabbi Hillel was one of those who sanctified the new moon on the basis of observation according to the true *molad.* And as we know from Rambam of blessed memory, in order to know the true conjunction, one must first calculate from the mean conjunction according the mean motion.[143] This confirms that he [Hillel] must have also known the mean conjunction in his time. He then calculated all the mean *moladot* from his time retrospectively until the end point of the calculation at creation which he collated on the basis of the years which are counted in the Torah, Prophets, and from the statements of our rabbis just in the way he found that they had been authorized—for there was indeed no reason to cast doubt on them by way of clarification, as we have described in our previous comments. Indeed, for the end point of this accepted calculation, he obtained the *baharad* formula based on 1d 12h 793p which is the mean measure for all mean *moladot,* future and past, and he transmitted it to us as a fundamental principle. It is in itself logical that if at that time he had decided to count fewer or more years from creation, so too without doubt would his calculation have concluded, together with its assigned mnemonic symbol, according to that calculation. In any case, all the fixed dates of the calendar and appointed days and embolismic years would have fallen in exactly the same times as they are also today.[144] For example, if he chose to add a 19-year cycle to his calculation, he would have subtracted 2d 16h 595p once from *baharad* such that he would reach 6d 12h 689p as the end limit, and that figure would now be used as the basic stem instead of *baharad.* For when you want to know the *molad* of the beginning of the next cycle, you add 2d 16h 595p to the *molad* that you have. Similarly, when you wish to find the *molad* at the beginning of the past cycle, you subtract it from the beginning of your present cycle; thereby with the addition of one cycle you obtain 6d 12h 689p. If there would be an addition of two cycles, you obtain 3d 20h 94p; in the case of three cycles, 1d 3h 579p and so on. And if there is also an addition to the years of an incomplete cycle you must deduct 4d 8h 876p for every ordinary year and 5d 21h 589p for every

142. *Kuzari* I, par. 25.
143. Qiddush ha-Ḥodesh, VI:1; XV:1.
144. All the calculations given in the following section are clearly explained in ch. 6 of Maimonides' Qiddush ha-Ḥodesh.

embolismic year. Their order should be according to Rabbi Hillel's method from the end of the cycle to its beginning, i.e., he begins from the nineteenth year which is embolismic and proceeds to the eighteenth which is ordinary and then to the seventeenth which is also an embolismic year as is known. And the mnemonic symbols for the embolismic years together with the addition of an incomplete cycle would change from the third, sixth, eighth, eleventh, fourteenth, seventeenth, and nineteenth years which are linked to *baharad.* Nevertheless this would indeed not result in any real alteration. For all the embolismic years[145] and all the festivals and the like[146] would still occur exactly as they are nowadays, linked to *baharad* according to the system described by the commentator of the Laws of the Sanctification of the New Moon regarding those who set the *molad* at either 6d 14h (*vayad*) or 3d 10h 876p as the fundamental principle rather than *baharad.*[147] Examine the passage. To what should this be compared? To one who says: "I shall go from one end of a district to the other," imagining that the journey ends in a certain location. For although subsequently he may go a long way on his journey from that location to the other, in his daily travels, throughout the entire journey, he never actually changes the place of his overnight stays, one of which would undoubtedly be the place that he imagines to be the final destination. However, he will just continue to depart from there until he comes to the end of the road. Similarly, if you add the years and the *moladot* back to *baharad,* however many they are, you are always calculating and going from a prescribed *molad* of your times to the previous *molad,* and likewise from one fixed time to the other invariably, until you reach *baharad* which will never be dislodged nor disappear from Israel. But you should not regard it then as the real starting point,[148] for you can go even further back and calculate until you reach the mnemonic symbol which, according to the amount of years, one obtains at the final count as the basic stem. And you might wish to know any *molad* of your time on its basis according to the way which Rabbi Moses of blessed memory taught us in chapter 7 of his Laws of the Sanctification of the New Moon. Instead of counting complete cycles by taking 2d 16h 595p [for each cycle] for the 280 cycles which have elapsed until this time, you might think, for example, that there are an extra 100 years which are equivalent to 5 complete cycles and 5 years. Then, you should count 285 cycles and for the 5 years which since one proceeds retrospectively, they are the last years of the imaginary cycle, one should begin with the nineteenth year and also the seventeenth, the embolismic years, which is not the case with the 3 other years, the eighteenth, the sixteenth, and the fifteenth. One should then take 5d 21h 589p twice and 4d 8h 876p three times according to the known method of calculation. In this way, your calculation will reach the actual position which you also obtain today by calculating from *baharad.* There will be no alteration either in days, hours, or even one minute in any *molad,* festival, or *ibbur* whether you wish to proceed from your own time to the past by subtracting, or whether you wish to proceed from that principle to the future by

145. In B. de' Rossi crossed out the word *ha-qeviot* and changed it to *ibburim.*

146. Here too, in B de' Rossi has crossed out the words *be-yamim uve-regaim* and inserted *ve-ḵol ḥaggim ve-ḵahem.*

147. *Perush* to Qiddush ha-Ḥodesh VI:8.

148. 'Real starting-point,' lit. as a head and prince. Cf. 1Chr. 11:6.

way of addition. A mnemonic for this is that those engaged on a religious errand will not suffer either on their outward or return journey.[149] And if the figure of 5 years used in the given example is not acceptable because the embolismic year is prevented from occurring in one of those years, then add to that figure until you find the year which you consider to be appropriate. {After all, the calculation is questionable anyway and there is no need to use it to diverge from the methods of Rabbi Hillel and his conventional computation.} Thus there is no need for the intelligent person to become contemptuous and say: "By heaven, you have acknowledged that *baharad* itself is the imaginary *molad.* How then can one think to impose yet another line of chaos (Tohu) and stones of emptiness (Bohu)[150] by adding imaginary years beyond that." The reason as to why *baharad* serves nowadays as our end limit for the years such that there is no more room to maneuver[151] is the convention authorized by Rabbi Hillel which was to ensure that we only count, 4,000 years from his times backwards. However, if he had decided to say that there were 130 more imaginary years, then *baharad* would have occurred exactly at the time of Seth's birth, when Adam was aged 130 years, which would mean that the *molad* of that time would have actually occurred and was not imaginary. Moreover, 130 years would remain which one would have to pass until one reaches the end limit, and this would necessarily generate another basic stem. And likewise the same thing would have happened if Rabbi Hillel had thought to deduct from the figure that he had chosen. For he fixed his symbol from *baharad* onwards, and by deducting one cycle for example, he would have obtained at the end limit 4d 21h 799p which results when you add 2d 16h 595p to *baharad* according to the normal procedure. But it remains our basic stem and no *molad* and no fixed time can ever be changed as we have written. Then there is the statement of Rabbi Isaac bar Aaron[152] in his *Sefer ha-Ibbur.** Speaking about the imaginary *molad* in the year 5028 [1268], he said that the *molad vayad* would fall in the *molad* of Iyyar in the third year of the 772 cycle, and the rest of the *moladot* would fall in turn according to the same measurement of time. In this way a person can acquire knowledge as to when every specific *molad* occurred and will occur. Moreover, by adding and subtracting, one would likewise obtain the *anno mundi* figure according to the basic stem. Everything is always understood in relation to the mean *molad* in that before Rabbi Hillel's time, they were only concerned with the true *molad* and the observation contingent on it. And so, before the number of cycles reaches the number 772, may it please God to return our exile; then the calendar will not be fixed according to the mean *molad,* but rather we shall sanctify the days on the basis of observation as in the past.

(*I saw his work among the collection of Yehosef, may his redeemer preserve him, son of Rabbi Solomon Ḥazaq of blessed memory.)

149. This expression which occurs in B. Pes. 8b; B. Qidd. 39b, B. Ḥull. 142a, is used by de' Rossi to demonstrate that all these computations are equally acceptable.

150. This is a play on Is. 34:11: *He shall measure it with a line of chaos (Tohu), and with weights of emptiness (Bohu).*

151. 'Such . . . room,' a play on Is. 5:8.

152. De' Rossi read this work in manuscript. It is probably to be identified with the manuscript listed by M. Steinschneider in his *Catalog,* par. 187, 70–71.

Now dear reader, on the basis of these considerations, it appears that you can sum up between the two opposite sides and see both sides of the argument, and say that the *baharad* mnemonic symbol and our anno mundi computation are both correct and incorrect. They are correct in regard to the number of years that was agreed by Rabbi Hillel and his law court and which constituted knowledge, choice, and necessity. "Knowledge" pertains to the years of the calculation of the Greek Empire and era of documents from the day of its initiation 380 years before the destruction of the second Temple until these days. For there is no doubt regarding it and nobody challenges the figure as we said in chapter 23. "Choice" pertains to the figure of 410 years for the duration of the first Temple, even if it is confirmed that it lasted 20 years longer as the commentators hold, or else that the first 8 years of Hoshea's reign should be included in the count. For Rabbi Hillel followed the figure of 410 years given by the sages who followed Scripture as was said in chapter 35. "Necessity," however, pertains to the numbers of the first generations, for without moving one hairsbreadth away from the ways of the perfect Torah as we wrote just before, it is likely that they are open to doubt—it may be that there are fewer or more months to be taken into consideration which may amount to years, but we do not know how many. Also open to doubt is the number of years of the exile in Egypt, as we said in chapter 35, and of the first years of the second Temple. The fact is that the true number of years has not been divulged to us since the lifetime of each one of the first seven [high] priests and the duration of the Persian kingdom during that period is not known, as we said—and we shall discuss it further. However the description "incorrect" is right as far as the true computation itself is concerned, which is only known to the one who knows all secrets, He who is the owner of heaven and earth. For there are doubts concerning it which no sage has any way or method of clarifying with incontrovertible evidence. In any case, from now onwards, be you blessed of the Lord and understand my view in its entirety with regard to everything that pertains to this question and keep it in hand. For I am not casting doubt nor proposing change of any one of the fixed times in any way at all. And likewise I am not attributing any error or foolishness, God forbid, to our early rabbis, nor to Rabbi Hillel and his court. For they all certainly realized and knew everything that we have discussed. It was with wisdom and for the greater good that they came to a consensus concerning the matters which they transmitted to us and which we are obliged to observe until, as ibn Ezra, Ramban and Israeli said, the redeemer and righteous teacher comes to Zion; for then through the volition of our God we shall revert to the sanctification of the new moon by observation according to the true conjunction, if the world still functions in its usual way. From these observations you must surely obtain most precious peace of mind since *baharad* will not pose problems for you, for no prophet or seer divulged information as to how we derived that precise computation from the Tishri before any person was yet on earth, or as to why it was in the following Adar that the sun and moon stood still on high[153] with the result* that the *molad* did not occur in its right time.[154] Using a mystical

153. 'Sun . . . high,' cf. Hab. 3:11. This is the view of those who say that the world was created in Nisan.
154. He is referring to the idea discussed earlier that the *molad* of Nisan only occurred 7d 9h 642p after the moon had been created.

method, we account for this by saying that on account of its reprimand, the moon was covered in darkness for seven days. And the same pertains to other such obscure matters. The fact is that there are a few who do not belong to the category of dreamers who lie down and love to drowse,[155] but on the contrary are intent only on the truth. Such people abstain from absorbing everything that is put into their mouths; they are not satisfied by taking implausible matters on trust, and they delight in discovering how their secrets were sought out and revealed to us.

(*[See p. 507] Examine *Sefer ha-Ibbur* of Rabbi Isaac bar Aaron mentioned above where he makes a distinction between his view and that of the Semag.)

However, you should know that one of the great Italian teachers[156] has already opposed our view in writing. He invoked the tradition that in the fortieth year [of the wandering in the desert], Moses died on Friday on the seventh of Adar, and that on the twenty-eighth of Nisan, they conquered Jericho and so on, and that likewise, on various days according to this calculation, several things happened as is demonstrated in chapters 10 and 11 of Seder Olam. Accordingly, if we add to or subtract from *baharad,* those calculations are brought into disarray. But because I did not grasp how the conclusion could truly be drawn from his premise, I did not take any notice of the criticism. This was for various reasons. First, one cannot make deductions about the time when they sanctified the months by observations from the time when they fixed the calendar according to the *ibbur* which is based on the mean motion, since the beginnings of their months are different as I wrote in chapter 35 in connection with the opinion of Latif of blessed memory, and in this chapter with regard to the statement of Rabbenu Hananel. Furthermore, there are divergent Midrashim concerning the death of Moses our teacher, may he rest in peace, on Friday, and the dating of the other events are contingent on this computation. This implies that it is not a prophetic tradition, but simply a general conjectural statement as Rav Sherira Gaon put it, which we noted in chapter 15. For in Sota, they expound the verse, *I am one hundred and twenty years old this day* (Deut. 31:2):[157] "*This day* are my days and years completed," and they state: "It was the Sabbath when there were two leaders." As Rashi explains: "At the beginning of the day, Moses was in power and at its end Joshua was in power;" in other words, Moses died on the Sabbath. Similarly, the reason for saying [the prayer] "Your righteousness [is an everlasting righteousness]" at the Sabbath afternoon service is explained by the Geonim, and corroborated by Rabbenu Tam of blessed memory[158]—it was at that time that Moses our teacher, peace be upon him, died. This was the moment when divine judgment was passed upon him; therefore one does not fix this hour as a time for study or a meal as is indicated in the Ṭur[159] and the Mordechai.[160] So these Midrashim are mutually contradictory and each one has its own drift, as long as it can be jus-

155. 'Dreamers . . . drowse,' cf. Is. 56:10.

156. This is a reference to the critique of Moses Provenzali (Cassel, 494) which was appended to a revised print of the *Me'or Enayim* by order of the Venetian rabbis and to which de' Rossi wrote a response.

157. B. Sota 13b.

158. Cf. Tos. to B. Men. 30a s.v. *mi-ḳan* where this tradition is cited in the name of Sar Shalom Gaon.

159. *Ṭur,* Oraḥ Ḥayyim, par. 292:2 (and not 282 as in the printed text).

160. Mordechai ben Hillel to Pes. ch. 4, 37 col. a. Mordechai states that this tradition is found in the Geonic *Responsa.*

tified. However, when you can see the truth of the explanation because the issues are clear or the reasoning convincing, one need not be concerned that the arguments are forced. {This is what Rabbi Moses wrote at the end of his letter to the sages of Marseilles[161] concerning the reason for the divergent views that he mentions. Finally, he states there that a person should never abandon his reason.[162]} This is comparable to what the esteemed authority Alfasi wrote with regard to a stove whose ashes are not cleared away,[163] and to what is written in the *Kuzari;* namely, when the general principles are consistent, we should not allow ourselves to become confused by the details.[164]

Now I undertook to divulge to you the meaning of the wise Israeli's statement that they [the sages of old] were in possession of a prophetic tradition about the *ibbur.* From his words, it would appear that he was referring to the seven embolismic years in every cycle which are to ensure that the courses of the sun and moon ultimately equalize—this emerges from the last chapter of part 2 of his *Yesod Olam.*[165] Moreover, in part 4,[166] he speaks about an Arabian gentile, a great astronomer called ibn Said[167] who wrote the following in one of his works: "I discovered that the Jews are in possession of a fixed principle and true epoch which is set for the conjunctions of the moon and the equinoxes and solstices of the sun. It is constructed and arranged according to a nineteen-year cycle which they call *ibbur.* I do not know how and from where it came to their hands, but they claim that it was transmitted to them by the true prophets." A similar idea is conveyed in the seventh chapter of Pirqe d'Rabbi Eliezer when he says: "10d 21h 204p are the excess of the days of the solar year over the days of the lunar year and the *ibbur* is introduced in order to equalize them." And in the eighth chapter, he speaks about several of the ancients each of whom were initiated into the secret of the *ibbur* and who intercalated the year.[168] Examine the passage. And you should take note of what he wrote in chapter 8. He said that [knowledge of] the seasons, cycles, and intercalations was transmitted prophetically until Joseph, and was forgotten during the bondage in Egypt. Then the Holy One blessed be He taught them again to Moses, and so too they [i.e., knowledge of the intercalations] would in the future gradually diminish at the end of the fourth kingdom, until the advent of the Messiah.

Thus it appears that we have already lost the benefit that we enjoyed in those days, particularly if, as those who calculate the end of time would have it, our salvation is imminent.[169] And Rabban Gamaliel did not describe the 1d 12h 793p which is the most fundamental principle of the fixed calendar as a Sinaitic tradition but said that he had it

161. This is the Letter on Astrology which Maimonides wrote to the sages of Montpellier. De' Rossi is following the ed pr. of Maimonides' *Teshuvot* which reads Marseilles and not Montpellier.

162. *Iggrot ha-Rambam* (ed. J. Shailat, vol. 2, 488).

163. Alfasi to Shabb. 16b to B. Shabb. 36b.

164. *Kuzari* III, par. 43.

165. *Yesod Olam* II, ch. 17.

166. Ibid. IV, ch. 7 (70r).

167. This is a reference to the writer Sa'id al-Andalusi (1029–70), best known for his work on the classification of the sciences and of the nations, but who also wrote a work in which he suggested corrections of earlier astronomical tables.

168. The ancients described are Adam, Enoch, Noah, Shem Abraham, Isaac, Jacob, Joseph, and his brethren.

169. He is referring to the messianic predictions about the year 1575, which he attacks in ch. 43.

"on authority of the house of my father's father."[170] This formulation refers to a tradition which basically derived from the scholarship of scholars. He did not say as did Nahum the scrivener in Pe'ah regarding the two kinds of wheat:[171] "I have received a tradition from Rabbi Measha who received it from his father who received it from the pairs who received it from the prophets as a *halakhah* given to Moses at Sinai." Nor did he speak in the manner of Rabbi Dosa in tractate Yevamot[172] who regarding the applicability of the purity laws to Ammon and Moab on account of Sihon[173] said: "I call heaven and earth to witness that upon this mortar sat the prophet Haggai." Indeed, Rabban Gamaliel's turn of phrase may be compared to their statement in Berakhot:[174] "I have this tradition on authority of the house of my grandfather that even if a sharp sword [rests on a man's neck he should not desist from prayer]." And in Bava Batra [the priest of] Micah (Jud. 18:3) states:[175] "I have the tradition on the authority of the house of my grandfather that a person should always hire himself out to idolatry rather than find himself dependent on human beings." Comparable, too, is their statement in Megillah:[176] "We are in possession of a tradition from our ancestors that Amos and Amaziah were brothers"; "we are in possession of a tradition from our ancestors that wherever we find the term "and it was" [*va-yehi*] it indicates that there was trouble [*vai-hi*]."[177] These examples are patently not Mosaic traditions from Sinai. {Nor were they prophetic statements in any form. In fact, the chief passage of all must surely be that in tractate Berakhot:[178] "[Once the son of Rabban Gamaliel fell ill. He sent two scholars to ask Rabbi Ḥanina ben Dosa to pray for him. . . . The fever left him. They said to him: 'Are you a prophet?' He replied]: 'I am neither a prophet nor son of a prophet, but I had the tradition on authority of the house of my grandfather that if prayer is fluent on my lips, I know that it is accepted.' " Purity of heart corroborates this,[179] in other words, it yields the belief that the dictum of Rabban Gamaliel's ancestors was a tradition of outstanding wisdom which was not prophetically transmitted. For indeed at the end of these notes, you will see that the wise Ralbag [Gersonides] diminished the length of the 793 parts by one fifty-eighth of a part. While it is a tiny amount, he would have rightly taken care to protect his life had he believed that these words of Rabban Gamaliel were an emanation drawn from on high. Surely everybody knows that not an atom of what the Lord says remains unfulfilled? In any case, we will not take notice of his opinion, as if he was exceedingly wise [in this matter]; for the only figure that will remain intact for our monthly computation is 1d 12h 793p. Indeed, he [i.e., Ralbag] should say: "Bring me an atonement for I diminished the moon."[180]}

170. B. R.H. 25a.
171. M. Pe'ah 2:6.
172. B. Yev. 16a.
173. The Israelites were permitted to take possession of Ammon and Moab which previously had been forbidden to them, when they defeated Sihon who had occupied those lands (cf. B. Ḥull. 60b).
174. B. Ber. 10a.
175. B. B.B. 110a.
176. B. Meg. 10b.
177. Ibid.
178. B. Ber. 34b.
179. In other words, fluency in prayer is a sign of purity of heart. Cf. Pr. 22:11 and Job 17:9.
180. This is a rhetorical play on the aggadah (to which de' Rossi has been referring) in B. Ḥull. 60b in which God says: "Bring an atonement for Me for making the moon smaller."

Now you can read a passage in Rabbi Abraham the prince's *Sefer ha-Ibbur*[181] in which he sets out to demonstrate the wisdom of our sages with regard to the 1d 12h 793p. He states that he saw a reference in Ptolemy's works to a certain gentile sage called Hipparchus who lived 80 years after the death of Alexander of Macedon.[182] He [Hipparchus] examined all the computations of the ancients over 400 years with regard to the eclipses of the moon and the *moladot.* Finally, the result of his scholarship was that he was able to delimit the hours, minutes, parts, and seconds such that his general calculation coincided exactly with that of Rabban Gamaliel regarding the 1d 12h 793p. In that context Rabbi Abraham the prince discusses Rabban Gamaliel's statement, "This is what I received on authority of the house of my grandfather," and comments as follows: "It is known that his grandfather lived at the beginning of the second Temple period. And so this Hipparchus who lived 126 years after the building of the second Temple was younger than Rabban Gamaliel's grandfather and must have learned about it from him." However, I do not know how it could be that Rabban Gamaliel's grandfather could have lived before the building of the second Temple. After all, Rabban Gamaliel was a contemporary of Rabbi Joshua and Rabbi Aqiva at the time of the destruction of the Temple. At any rate, the turn of phrase used by Rabban Gamaliel himself indicates that he was recipient of this teaching through the scholarship of his ancestors as we mentioned. Now we find that the sixth [seventh] chapter of Pirqe d'Rabbi Eliezer and the *Baraita* attributed to Samuel[183] according to its citation by the prince and by ibn Ezra,[184] refer to two-thirds of an hour which is equivalent to 720p and not 793p. It is possible that it was not only because the heavens were covered by clouds on the twenty-ninth of the month, as is explained in the *baraita* in chapter 2 of Rosh ha-Shanah cited in the Gemara,[185] but also on account of this that Rabban Gamaliel used the expression "*not less* [than 29 and a half days and two-thirds of an hour and 73p]." We could, however, utter the view of the prince who stated:[186] "You will discover that all the computations in that *Baraita* [of Samuel] are only counted according to the figure of 29d 12h and two-thirds of an hour. And we cannot say that this was the opinion of Rabbi Eliezer and Samuel for they did not dispute with the sages in regard to this controversy. But the purpose of this *Baraita* was to demonstrate the view of the Persian sages who used this computation." However, in my opinion, this statement of his is not correct. And I did not claim that the expression "not less" means, as the commentator of the Laws of the Sanctification of the New Moon held,[187] that Ptolemy only posited 792 parts. For I saw that in the same context the prince states that according to Ptolemy, the

181. *Sefer ha-Ibbur* II, gate 2 (37–38).

182. Hipparchus was born in the first quarter of the second century B.C.E. and died after 127 B.C.E. Knowledge of Hipparchus's theories is mostly derived from Ptolemy's works.

183. The *Baraita* of Samuel which deals with the secret of intercalation dates from the ninth century, but was attributed to the third-century Amora Samuel.

184. Ibn Ezra to Ex. 12:2.

185. B. R.H. 25a: "Our rabbis taught: Once the heavens were covered with clouds and the likeness of the moon was seen on the twenty-ninth of the month The public wanted to declare the new moon . . . , but Rabban Gamaliel said to them: I have it on authority." In other words, according to Rabban Gamaliel, it was not possible that the public had seen the new moon.

186. *Sefer ha-Ibbur* II, gate 2 (36).

187. *Perush* to Qiddush ha-Ḥodesh VI:3.

Egyptian sages originally held that there were 792p, and then subsequently Hipparchus convinced them that there were 793p.[188] Examine the passage. In the light of these matters, the statement of the sage of the *Kuzari*[189] that the principle of the revolution of the moon and its renewal was handed down from the House of David is not an inevitable conclusion from the dictum of Rabban Gamaliel and we do not know anything else about it apart from what he said. You have also heard that this fact was disseminated among the gentiles more than 300 years before the destruction of the Temple.

I thought that I could not withhold from the reader the astonishing fact that I discovered on studying the work on the reform of the calendar written by the Christian Samotheus.[190] This short work was published at the end of his works. I discovered that he presented the calendar from the beginning of the world and established that the calculation of Samuel's season [*tequfah*] which we follow[191] and which is constructed on the basis that the solar year is 365 and a quarter days (and it also set down thus in the sixth chapter of the Pirqe d'Rabbi Eliezer) was already instituted by Julius Caesar 45 years before the birth [of Jesus].[192] In his honor, they changed the name of the fifth (*quintilis*) month to Julius as Macrobius notes in his *Saturnalia.*[193] For after his conquest of Alexandria in Egypt, he derived knowledge of the computation of that *tequfah* from the scholars of Alexandria which was also based on the view of an ancient sage called Callippus.[194] The same holds for the entire computation of Rav Adda's *tequfah.*[195] (The intelligent person realizes that his wisdom consists of the fact that Rav Adda apportions the 1h and 485p, which are in excess in Samuel's cycle, among the 76 seasons of every cycle such that he reaches 20p 45 secondary parts—each of which equals one seventy-sixth of a part*—the result of which is that by the end of the cycle all those excesses are eradicated.) This computation [of Rav Adda] had already been articulated and instituted after the time of that Caesar by Ptolemy who lived in the year 132 of the Christian era in the time of Hadrian. His calculation of the *tequfah* is published by him in the third part of his *Almagest.* Similarly, in his book *Ḥeshbon ha-Mahalakhot,* Rabbi Abraham the prince writes:[196] "We depend on the view of Ptolemy, the greatest astronomer, for the number of days of the solar year since for the most part his view accords with that of our rabbis, and he bases his calculation of the solar year on the words of Rav Adda bar Ahavah on which the secret of the *ibbur* (i.e., the intercalation of seven years

188. *Sefer ha-Ibbur,* II, gate 2 (36–38).

189. *Kuzari* II, par. 64.

190. This is a reference to the *Epitoma emendationis calendarii Romani pro Pascha rite celebrando* (194v) printed at the end of Johannes Lucidus Samotheus' *Opusculum,* 194r–198v.

191. In B. Eruv. 56a, Samuel states that the average interval between an equinox and a solstice amounts to 91d 7½h which multiplied by 4 corresponds to a Julian year.

192. Lucidus, *Opusculum* 195r: "Iulius quippe Caesar ante Christum annis 45 . . . instituit annum solarem constare ex diebus 365 et quarta diei."

193. Macrobius, *Saturnalia* I, 12, 34.

194. Calippus established this computation in the fourth century B.C.E.

195. The length of the solar year according to the view ascribed to Rav Adda is 365d 5h 997p and 48 secondary p, the secondary p being 1/76 of a primary p (see Qiddush ha-Ḥodesh X:1 in which Maimonides gives the computation without mentioning Rav Adda's name). For more information, see n. 1 to the Yale Judaica series translation of the text (97).

196. Abraham bar Ḥiyya, *Sefer Ḥeshbon,* gate 8 (46).

in every cycle) is constructed. Similarly, his view on the course of the moon follows that of Rav Adda which concurs with that of our rabbis." Now, intelligent reader, it is clear to you now that this Ptolemy lived in the time of Hadrian the emperor as he himself professed and about which the wise Israeli also testified in the introduction to his work the *Yesod Olam.*[197] You would therefore rightly think that although the Tosafists wrote that there were two people of the name Rav Adda bar Ahavah, one living before the other,[198] Ptolemy lived prior to them both. You should make your own appraisal as to which of them ought to be considered the follower and which the disciple. Similarly, you should judge as to the source of the commentator's statement on the tenth chapter of the Laws of the Sanctification of the New Moon which I also saw in the prince's *Sefer ha-Ibbur.*[199] For they say that there are two *tequfot,* the secret one of Rav Adda bar Ahavah and the public one of Samuel. The significance and reason for keeping it secret [i.e., Rav Adda's *tequfah*] was to prevent witches from using this knowledge in order to render their witchcraft efficacious. You will most certainly consider this to be children's and old wives' talk since knowledge of it was clearly disseminated.

(*[See p. 512] If this had not been the case Rav Adda would not have divided up the part into the alien figure of 76 secondary parts.)

{Incidentally you should also consider the statement of the prince of blessed memory who wrote:[200]

> Whenever you hear people say that if the *tequfah* coincides with a certain star, such and such a thing will occur in the universe, you should not take notice of it. For this does not relate to this *tequfah* which accords with the view of the experts in astronomy (that is, Samuel's *tequfah* as explained above). And likewise, the custom of these countries (i.e., his birthplace, France) to desist from drinking water is nonsensical for nobody can know the time of the *tequfah* in his location unless he knows its latitudinal position from the east and this cannot be established by anybody. And we cannot find any record of the ancients on this subject in which a reason was devised in order to account for it.[201]}[2]

Now subsequent to Caesar and Ptolemy, the scholars discovered that both these computations were not completely correct. And as to the question about the amount of the original difference between Samuel and Rav Adda, the correct response to your question should be your answer and do not go any further, that is to say, 20 parts and 45 secondary parts indicated by the letters *ḳmh.* It is certainly the case that because of the many years that have elapsed since then, the parts and secondary parts are daily increasing, amounting to hours, days, and two weeks. Thus the commentator on the Laws of the Sanctification of the New Moon wrote:[202] "If you find it problematic that after many years the *tequfah* [of Nisan] will occur in the month of Iyyar, we would say

197. *Yesod Olam,* bk. 1, ch. 1 (5v): "The scholar Ptolemy lived about 70 years after the destruction of the Temple."

198. Tos to B. Ta'anit 20b, s.v. *amar.* They were Babylonian Amoraim of the third and fourth centuries respectively and thus certainly lived later than Ptolemy.

199. *Sefer ha-Ibbur* III, gate 5 (93–94).

200. Ibid. III, gate 3 (86).

201. The custom of not drinking water at the time of the change of the season is given e.g. in the gloss of Moses Isserles (the Rema) on *Shulḳhan Aruḳh,* Yoreh Deah 116:5.

202. *Perush* to Qiddush ha-Ḥodesh IX:3.

that this is how it has to be until the righteous teacher will come and inform us as to the correct way to deal with it." In the year 1251 of the Christian era, King Alfonso innovated and instituted another computation in his well-known tables. However, there was also an Arabic sage al-Battani,[203] who lived 743 years after Ptolemy, who had already invented another computation which was more correct than Alfonso's, but which Alfonso did not know for he had not seen his works.[204] According to these later computations, the correct calculation is the true *tequfah* of our calendar about which Rabbi Moses of blessed memory writes:[205] "The fact, however, is that both values of the *tequfah* (i.e., that of Samuel and Rav Adda) which have been explained are only approximate, based on the mean motion of the sun and not on its true position. For the *tequfah* of Nisan according to the true position of the sun in our times occurs about two days before the *tequfot* which results from the calculation that we mentioned." These words of his are similar to those of ibn Ezra on the two *tequfot* in his commentary.[206] Study the passages. Now we have heard from these two reliable witnesses that our present calculation of the *tequfah* is not based on the course of the sun in its true position, but according to its mean motion. Now as I have already informed you, these people as well as Israeli made a similar statement regarding the conjunctions of the moon. It does now indeed emerge that with ease and pleasure you may now have the option to relate our statements in these chapters to the anno mundi computation which is also not according to its true course; rather, using appropriate rhetorical language it may be designated as the mean figure. It is as though the authority of the calendar in its entirety is only valid as long as our storm-swept community is in exile and disdained in her affliction and sorrow.[207] You will therefore acknowledge the superior wisdom of our rabbis whose souls are at rest and the extent to which they have helped us in these oppressive times. For when they realized that we are unable to have what we desire, they taught us to desire that which we can attain. We should bless our God who took the precaution to ratify and establish that which they should do in his Torah until such time, as those three sages said, that His spirit emanates over us, and He raises the horn of our salvation. At that time, He will trim away and lop off all the twigs and branches of this ravaged vine[208] which have multiplied on account of the hard times and the oppression of the exile and He will give rest from the exhausting weariness. He will be a light for us and as Isaiah His prophet said, *Your ears will heed . . . saying: This is the road; follow it whether you deviate to the right or to the left* (Is. 30:21).

But let us now resume the subject we were treating. The intercalation of seven years in the nineteen-year cycle is held by us to be a great secret. According to the prince Rabbi Abraham, they acquired their knowledge and training in this computation from Hipparchus the gentile sage who lived in year 80 of the era of documents. Then subsequently, it was ratified by Julius Caesar, and the Christians also use it in their

203. Al-Battani (Albategnius) was an outstanding and influential astronomer of the ninth century living in northwest Mesopotamia.

204. This opinion which de' Rossi probably derived from Lucidus whose work he cites more than once in this chapter, is incorrect; a Spanish translation of Al-Battani's work was made by order of Alfonso.

205. Qiddush ha-Ḥodesh X:7.

206. Ibn Ezra to Ex. 12:2; Lev. 23:3.

207. Imagery from Is. 49:21 and Lam. 1:7.

208. Imagery from Hos. 10:1 and Is. 18:5.

calendar and they call it the *numero aureo,* that is the golden number.[209] The only difference between the Christians and ourselves is the starting point of the cycle; for they begin the cycle from the birth [of Jesus], namely, three years before us, which results that in every fifth and sixteenth year of the cycle, their Easter falls many days after our Passover. They have written specific works on the reform of the calendar which is required in order to ensure that the dates correspond to the true *tequfah.*[210] And as Rambam said in the fore-mentioned passage, this would also be necessary for us. This subject has been discussed at length by many of their scholars, and in particular by Samotheus in the work that we cited.[211] Moreover, in their works on the *ibbur,* some of our sages note, as does Isaac bar Aaron at the end of his book mentioned above, as follows: "The intelligent person realizes that like us, the Christian scholars use the lunar cycle of nineteen years and intercalate the third, sixth, eighth, eleventh, fourteenth, seventeenth, and nineteenth year in order to make the lunar and solar years compatible. But they begin their cycle three years earlier, as indicated in the verse, *Let my lord go on ahead of his servant* (Gen. 33:14)."[212] It is a true fact that the Israelites were a numerous and powerful nation in Alexandria at the time of Caesar, having seventy gilt chairs for the members of their Sanhedrin as we wrote in chapter 12 of the first section of the book. It is therefore quite plausible that he [i.e., Julius Caesar] was taught by them. But it is also true that the sage Hipparchus lived two hundred years or slightly more before Julius Caesar. Since Julius Caesar instituted the computation of the year according to the mode of Samuel who lived after him,[213] it would appear to me to be proof that Samuel's *tequfah* was given to the supreme law court at that time, and not that of Rav Adda which, as Rambam of blessed memory wrote, was more accurate, although ultimately, it too requires the two adjustments described by ibn Ezra.[214] Had their *tequfot* been a prophetic tradition, they would have been precise to the very last second since, as is known, nothing is too difficult for the Lord. It happens that Samuel's *tequfah* is beneficial for the common people for it is easy to divide and arrange despite ibn Ezra's criticisms of it in his commentary.[215] Examine the passage. He says: "Nothing was hidden from Samuel, but he employed the method which approximated that used by the people of the time." The prince writes in a similar vein:[216] "Our rabbis transmitted to us the computation of the *tequfot* based on the mean motion to make it easier for us. They gave us two traditions about the *tequfot:* the one followed the experts in astronomy who say that the solar year is 365 and a quarter days—this corresponds to Samuel's *tequfah*; the second follows one of the two views of those who are precise in the computation—this corresponds to Rav Adda's *tequfah.*" At the end of gate 3, he

209. The "golden number" (which term is of medieval origin) is the number of any year in the Metonic lunar cycle of 19 years which was used in the ecclesiastical calendar to determine the location of the new moon in the Julian year.

210. For a discussion of the Gregorian reform of the calendar of 1582 and the debates which led up to the reform, see J. North, "The Western Calendar," 75–113.

211. Lucidus (*Opusculum,* 195v) states that the equinox had moved fifteen days by his own day.

212. In this verse, Jacob symbolizing Israel is addressing Esau who symbolizes Christianity.

213. In B, de' Rossi crosses out the word Samuel which is erroneously repeated after the word 'after.'

214. Ibn Ezra to Ex. 34:22.

215. Ibn Ezra to Ex. 12:2.

216. *Sefer ha-Ibbur* III, gate 3, 81.

writes:[217] "What remains to say is simply that this *tequfah* is constructed on the view of the experts in that discipline according to which the majority of peoples compute their years. And we find that the ancients who spoke about the secret of the *ibbur* transmitted the computation of the *tequfah* in this way.}[2] And from the prince's citation of Rabbenu Hai, it would appear that he inclines to this view. He writes:[218] "Although our predecessors used to intercalate the year on account of three indications,[219] they commanded us to adopt the computation of the *tequfah* which results in [an excess] of 1h 485p for every cycle." This only refers to Samuel's *tequfah*. But I am unable to uphold this view since nowadays we see that Samuel's *tequfah* for Nisan for the years between the intercalated years occurs after Passover, and thus Passover falls in the *tequfah* of Tevet and not in the spring month as we have been commanded. You should also know that according to Plutarch,[220] and from my reading of the first book of Macrobius's *Saturnalia,*[221] the ancient pagans also used to declare their new-moon days and feast days according to the lunar calendar. They called the first day of the month Kalends which means "to call out" in Greek. This was because on every first day of the month, their priest used to stand on the Capitol and proclaim the days of the feasts and everything that was needed for the regulation of their community during that month. And as I have already informed you in this chapter, all the Arabs also keep to Rabbi Hillel's enactment or something like it for the fixing of their calendar.

But let us return to the subject of *baharad*. It could be that some intelligent person would take the opportunity to claim that I have overstepped the limit in my explanation of a simple matter, citing an unnecessary number of witnesses. But he should remember that for the purpose of satisfying passionate interest, one takes the trouble to find a scriptural verse to prove the point, even when it can be inferred by *a minori* reasoning. This is illustrated in chapter 1 of Qiddushin.[222] At any rate, this action may be adopted for dealing with the alleged sin of casting doubt on the duration of the second Temple and when you reject this defense which is based on the computation of Rabbi Hillel and his law court, as was said. And it may be that with the feet of the innocent, you will trample and tread on all the statements of the writers mentioned above. And you may refute the proofs which have been put forward on the basis of the literal meaning of Nehemiah's words regarding the number of high priests and Persian kings, adopting the view of the antagonist which we mentioned. Now {the five Jewish sages did add to the duration of the bondage in Egypt and}[2] the four did add twenty or so years to the duration of the first Temple. And when you add to these years, in view of the statements of the Seder Olam and the four commentators who use its method, we have all the more reason to necessitate the addition of the first eight years of Hoshea's reign, as was explained in chapter 35. There is then indeed no option but to uphold this

217. Ibid., gate 3, 85.

218. Ibid., gate 7, 97.

219. This is a reference to the passage in B. Sanh 11b: "A year may be intercalated on three grounds: on account of the premature state of the corn crops, or that of the fruit trees or on account of the lateness of the *Tequfah*."

220. *Moralia* (Quaestiones Romanae) 269c: "Is it that on the Kalends the officials used to call the people and announce the Nones for the following fifth day, regarding the Ides as a holy day?"

221. *Saturnalia* I, 15, 9–12.

222. Cf. B. Qidd. 4b where a scriptural verse is used to prove that betrothal may be effected by money.

defense or to search for one of a similar nature which would be reasonably acceptable as vindication of our rabbis. For whether the additional years are more or less, the fixed point has already been dislodged. In general, we say that even if it is conceded that the number of years counted from creation in relation to the duration of the two Temples are too few, they [the rabbis] certainly should not be regarded as guilty of error. On the contrary, it was a sign of their outstanding wisdom—you shall hear more from me on this matter in chapter 42. The most important point is that as far as the commandments of the Torah and its laws are concerned, subtraction from or addition to the total [number of years] is not of the slightest consequence.

CHAPTER FORTY-ONE

That we do not have real confidence in any computation given by any scribe for the duration of the second Temple. That it is possible to take notice of the numerical intimation in the angel's words to Daniel about the seventy weeks (Dan. 9:24).[1]

Now in the light of any one of the preceding investigations, it would appear that the figure of 34 years is too small—even though we would prefer to take it on trust—and that therefore the length of the second Temple period was longer. Nevertheless, it is true that we are in no position to settle for any other figure which one of those other chroniclers suggested. For we see that Josephus counts 639 and a half years for the entire duration of the Temple period;[2] at the end of his commentary on chapter 7 of Daniel, Ralbag [Gersonides] writes that its duration was 437 and a half years; according to Samotheus, some Christian sages count 587 years.[3] Moreover, on examining the comments of other Christian sages, you will notice that in many cases, each person selects his own method and chooses his own figure, be it greater or smaller. And since it is clear, as we indicated in chapter 24, that the era of documents of the Greek empire is by all peoples unanimously declared to be correct, the uncertainty, then, must pertain to the duration of the Persian Empire which immediately preceded it at the beginning of Temple times. And thus it is that different writers, using their own individual methods provide testimony against each other, which proves that we ought to regard their statements as questionable. This is particularly the case when we are confronted with the fact that in the computation of the Persian kings and their reigns which is one of the basic elements in selecting the figure, they are not in proximity to each other, but rather each individual removes and installs kings[4] as they see fit. And even Yedidyah [Philo], who is regarded as an accurate writer, and on whose statements all who glory in the truth construct the edifice of their calculation, made unreasonable claims in his account of the length of the lifetime of Mordechai the righteous, as is seen in his work *On the Times* which we translated.[5] It is not simply that his accounts are unique and that he

1. De' Rossi's use of Daniel's prophecy for his chronological argument may also be seen as an implicit refutation of some Christian interpretations of the prophecy according to which the 70 weeks correspond to the period ending in the crucifixion of Jesus. See, e.g., Johannes Lucidus, *Opusculum,* bk. VII, ch. 3 (which de' Rossi often cites), "De impletione hebdomadum Danielis."

2. *Bellum* VI:270.

3. Johannes Lucidus, *Opusculum,* bk. II, 29v.

4. 'Remove . . . kings,' cf. Dan. 2:21.

5. In contemporary discussions of the interpretation of Daniel's prophecy of the 70 weeks, the length of Mordechai's lifetime is often raised as part of the crucial evidence. (Lucidus who is quoted by de' Rossi

was not accepted by our sages, but that we do not know whether somebody holding a particular bias on this subject tampered with that work and a long time ago put his own view into his [i.e., Philo's] mouth. And the wise Don Isaac, as we know, diverged from his ways. Examine the passage in question.[6] The fact is that as long as we feel that we should take note of the doubts that arise in connection with this subject, familiarizing ourselves with every aspect, the truth must be as follows. Should a person ask his colleague as to whether he could provide us with a correct assessment of the length of the duration of the Temple and on that basis, the anno mundi computation, also taking into account the length of the bondage in Egypt, he would honestly have to answer in the negative. In the light of all that has been said, and following the view of the one who considers that the matter is open to doubt as I said, I saw fit and considered that it was only right and proper—having defended my view and having refuted all other opinions—not to forgo an examination of holy Writ. For we rely on it—even though we cannot be certain to have understood it properly—in preference to all the notions of any human being. And thus when we study the angel's words to Daniel regarding the 70 weeks, it is possible for us to procure a middle path which agrees neither with those who would decrease the figure or those who would add to it. For even if we come to add to the figure of 420 years because the period of 34 years is too limited for encompassing those six generations of priests and the reigns of the Persian kings—these two issues were the kernel of the problem—we should not then inflate it, obtaining such figures as 640 or 587 years which others demarcate. Rather, we should be satisfied by adding 70 years to the period of the second Temple. Thus, even if one would consider adding a certain number of years to the duration of the bondage in Egypt and the 20 or 9 years to the duration of the first Temple as we said, the total figure for the anno mundi computation would not be increased by more than about 100 years, give and take a few more or less.

Now in his work on the end of days, Ramban of blessed memory[7] cites our rabbis' view in Nazir[8] (according to the two explanations of the author of the *Arukh* under the entry for *sbʿ*[9]) that the 70 weeks include the 70 years of the exile and the 420 years of the duration of the Temple. He notes that many people found this amalgamation of years strange, questioning the connection between the two periods. Moreover, at the end of chapter 29 [28], the author of Seder Olam raised another problem,[10] namely, as to why

---

also uses the Annian forgery of Philo on this point. See bk. VII, ch. 3, 56r.) Ps. Philo states that Mordechai lived 18 years longer than Isaac, namely, 198 years. It should be noted, however, that in his revised notes to ch. 32, he states that this figure agrees with B. Men. 64b that implies that Mordechai lived to a very great old age.

6. De' Rossi is referring to *Mayyane ha-Yeshuʿah,* 10, tamar 8 (376, col. a): "Furthermore, according to their opinion [i.e., Christian writers], in regard to the the Persian kings and the length of their reigns, . . . Mordechai who lived from the time of Jehoiachin's exile until the time of Ahasuerus must have lived 280 years which is impossible."

7. Nahmanides, *Sefer ha-Geʾulah* in *Kitve Ramban* (281).

8. B. Nazir 32b. In this passage it is implied that Daniel's prophecy of the 70 weeks indicated that the 70 weeks of years referred to the period from the beginning of the 70-year Babylonian exile to the end of the second Temple period of 420 years, a total of 490 years.

9. Nathan ben Yehiel, *Aruhk,* s.v. *sbʿ*. In the first interpretation, Nathan ben Yehiel explains the passage in Nazir and then gives an alternative interpretation of the 70 weeks.

10. Seder Olam, ch. 28 (130–31).

he [i.e., Daniel] mentions the 70 years which had already occurred—after all what is past is past—together with the 420 years that were to come.

And so, after showing due deference to every other more legitimate opinion and interpretation, I decided, without dogmatically claiming that I was in possession of the truth, that it would not be regarded as far-fetched, but rather in the realm of possibility and appropriate to relate the entire 490-year period to the duration of the Temple. In this way, it would be completely divorced from the time of the exile. Thus the period would begin on the day when they began to build the Temple in the second year of Darius's reign, as is written at the end of chapter 4 of Ezra, and would be completed at the time when we were exiled from our land by Titus. Accordingly, the length of Persian rule in Temple times would come to 104 years—we shall explain this in greater detail in the course of this chapter. For this angel came to give him a general intimation as to how the blessed Lord does not willfully bring affliction[11] but desires the wicked to repent in order to attain prosperity and well-being. Now they did deserve a heavier punishment than that exile. Thus, by extricating them from the burdens of Babylon,[12] He chose to show forebearance and granted them considerable time[13] in which to resort to one of two days. Either *until the measure of transgression is filled and that of sin complete* (Dan. 9:24), that is to say, when their sins would reach the culminating point, when the measure would be full. As a result, they would deserve much greater affliction and protracted exile. Alternatively, when they would purify their ways and return to cling to Him, another generation would atone for their iniquities, and their sins would become as white as snow. Accordingly, the righteousness which He began to show them in this visitation, by putting them to the test, would become everlasting and perpetual righteousness, and He would fulfill His promise conveyed by every seer and anoint the Holy of Holies.[14] This could be an allusion to the aggrandizement of *the glory of this latter House*[15] and its enhanced holiness when the five objects which it lacked, as the rabbis of blessed memory state in Yoma,[16] and even more than these, would be restored. Then the situation would become as described by the Gaon of blessed memory, given that the expression *This shall be the anointment* (Lev. 7:35) is rendered "greatness" in the Targum.[17] Alternatively, it could allude to the coming of the Messiah who will remove the yoke of all the nations from their neck, once and for all selah. In any case, there is no doubt that those words, *until the measure of transgression is filled and that of sin complete* signify the completion of the iniquity until its very end. The same idea is expressed in the statement, *for the iniquity of the Amorites is not complete* (Gen. 15:16). Ibn Ezra of

11. 'How affliction,' cf. Lam. 3:33.

12. 'Burdens of Babylon,' an expression used in connection with Egypt. Cf. Ex. 6:6.

13. 'Enough time,' lit. for a time and a season. Cf. Dan. 7:12.

14. This is a reference to the second part of the verse under discussion, *and eternal righteousness ushered in; and prophetic vision ratified and the Holy of Holies anointed.*

15. A reference to Hag. 2:9: *The glory of this latter House shall be greater than the former one* which is the subject of ch. 51.

16. B. Yoma 21b. According to one view in this passage, the ark cover, Cherubim, fire (these form one unit), the Divine Presence, and the Urim and Tumim were missing from the second Temple.

17. De' Rossi is referring to Saadiah Gaon's commentary on Daniel (9:24) and, in particular, to his interpretation of the phrase *and the Holy of Holies anointed* which he interprets in the light of the meaning of the similar phrase in Lev. 7:35 as a reference to its aggrandizement. Both Targum Onkelos and ps. Jonathan render the word *anointment* as "greatness."

blessed memory gives the same interpretation.[18] And there is reliable proof for this—for Daniel himself was consistent in his own thinking when he said in the previous chapter, *And when their kingdoms are at an end, when the measure of transgressors has been fulfilled* (8:23) which in the context must undoubtedly mean that the sins would reach their end without forgiveness. Our rabbis of blessed memory explicitly state in Sota,[19] Giṭṭin,[20] and Arakhin:[21] "The Holy One blessed be He does not punish a nation until his measure is full as it says, *In the fullness of his sufficiency he shall be in straits* (Job 20:22). In the passage in Arakhin the same idea is applied to the individual: "The Holy One blessed be He does not punish man until his measure is full, as it is said, *In the fullness of his sufficiency he shall be in straits.*" And as we know, one of the benevolent methods of the blessed Lord is to grant the sinner reprieve, as is said of the generation of the flood, *let the days allowed him be one hundred and twenty years* (Gen. 6:3). And the preacher says likewise, *the fact that a sinner may do evil a hundred times and it* [i.e., the punishment] *will still be delayed* (Eccl. 8:12). For God desires to be gracious in the hope that the wicked person might abandon his mode of behavior and obtain a reprieve. The letter *vav* [and] which is in the word *u-le-khapper* [*and to expiate*] in the verse, *until the measure of transgression is filled and that of sin complete and to expiate iniquity* (Dan. 9:24) functions as the word "or." {The *vav* is used in this way in the expression [*He who kidnaps a man—whether he has sold him and [vav] is still holding to him—shall be put to death*] (Ex. 21:16). In his *Sefer ha-Riqmah,* in the section on the functions of the *vav,* Jonah ibn Janaḥ[22] states that the meaning of the expression is *whether he has sold him or is still holding to him.*}[2] All commentators agree that in the verse, *he who strikes his father and [vav] mother shall be put to death* (Ex. 21:15), the *vav* must be interpreted to mean *he who strikes his father or mother,* since he would be guilty of a capital sin whichever of his parents he struck.

Now it is clear that the starting point of these weeks is the second year of the reign of Darius king of Persia, when he issued the edict for the return and the rebuilding of the Temple. For when the 70 years of the desolation of Jerusalem had been nearly completed, that is to say, in the second year of Darius's reign, Daniel as his designation *a man of desireableness* (Dan. 10:11) indicates, desired and yearned that the Lord should fulfill His promise. One year previously he had anticipated this through his prayer addressed to the attribute of mercy. He wrote about it at the beginning of chapter 9, *In the first year of Darius son of Ahasuerus . . . [in the first year of his reign I, Daniel consulted the books concerning the number of years . . . the term of Jerusalem's desolation—seventy years]* (Dan. 9:1–2). Then the angel came to tell him that he did not need to prolong his prayer and supplications; for as he embarked on his entreaties, not only had the decree already been inscribed for the salvation of our people, but the word had issued from the mouth of the King the Lord. He then continued with his intimation saying, *You must*

18. Ibn Ezra to Dan. 9:24.
19. B. Sota 9a.
20. There is no such passage in tractate Giṭṭin.
21. B. Arak. 15a.
22. *Sefer ha-Riqmah* gate 6 (vol. 1, 66). The author of the work was the eleventh-century grammarian Abu al-Walid Marwan, Jonah ibn Janaḥ. His work was translated into Hebrew by Judah ibn Tibbon. De' Rossi read the work in manuscript.

know and understand (9:25). For since this trial to which the Lord intended to submit Israel would be gradual, he should not expect that all the good fortune would be granted instantaneously. Indeed, from the building of the Temple which would be completed by Zerubbabel in the second year of Darius's reign until the coming of the anointed leader who would contribute to the good fortune by building the walls of Jerusalem, would be a period of 7 weeks which is equivalent to 49 years. And 62 years of weeks would further elapse in which the city would acquire a square and its walls would be surrounded by a moat. It would be destroyed for a time and again rebuilt as a result of the vicissitudes it would experience during the wars with several Greek monarchs as well as Romans. For as is well known, even before the battle with Titus, there were hostilities in the time of Pompey their general. Finally, in the last week, the city and Sanctuary which was built by the anointed one would be extirpated in the decreed destruction.

Now who was the *anointed* alluded to in the phrase *until the anointed leader* (9:25)? One could suggest that it refers to Nehemiah who, writing in an autobiographical manner, stated (2 Ezra 5),[23] *Furthermore from the day I was commissioned to be governor* (i.e., leader) *in the land of Judah.* It was he who built the walls in the twenty-first year of Artaxerxes' reign as is evident from the second chapter of 2 Ezra. He was surely a leader and also anointed—such is the connotation of the word in the verse *Do not touch My anointed ones* (Ps. 105:15). Alternatively it might be a reference to Artaxerxes himself, and not to the beginning of his reign, but rather an allusion to his twenty-first year in which he gave his permission and assistance for the building of the walls as is explained in the context. And the words, *From the issuance of the word [to restore and rebuild Jerusalem until the anointed leader is seventy weeks]* (9:25), ought, according to this interpretation, proceed in the same vein, as though to say *until the work of the anointed leader is issued.* In other words, it was he who would pass the decree about the building of the walls. And it designates him as leader in the same way that Titus is described as leader in the phrase, *the leader who is to come [will destroy the city and Sanctuary] but its end will come through a flood* (9:26). And it is not far-fetched to suggest that the anointed leader alludes either to Nehemiah or to Artaxerxes as was said; after all, Don Isaac states[24] that there are many views as to his identity: Josephus writes that he is Jeshua ben Jehozadak;[25] Rashi writes that he is Cyrus; Ibn Ezra and Ramban interpret it as a reference to Zerubbabel, and so on.[26] And at the end of his commentary on Daniel, our teacher Saadiah describes one interpretation which identifies the person in question as Ezra and, in the same context, corroborates our view that the 70 years of the exile are not included in the computation of the 70 weeks. In his commentary on the 70 weeks, ibn Ezra, too, writes about the 70 weeks as follows:[27] "And now I shall explain the 70 weeks which begin from the promulgation of the word at the beginning of Daniel's supplications." Examine the passage. On all problematic matters, many people propose

23. I.e., Neh. 5:14.
24. *Mayyene ha-Yeshuʿah,* 10, tamar 6 (373, col. b–374, col. a).
25. This is also Jerome's interpretation.
26. In fact Abravanel ends the section with a reference to Ps. 105:15, which is also cited by de' Rossi, and interprets it in the same manner as does de' Rossi.
27. This is a reference to the last sentence of ibn Ezra's commentary to Dan. 9:24.

many views. However, from the drift of the verses and their content, a final decision as to their meaning may be concluded. The next statement [i.e., in Dan. 9:27] about Titus, *During one week he will make a firm covenant,* may also be read in terms of God's kindness whereby He grants sinners time [to repent]. As is stated by our rabbis of blessed memory in tractate Moʿed Qatan in the Palestinian Talmud with regard to the verse, *For in seven days' time I will make it rain upon the earth* (Gen. 7:4),[28] the Holy One blessed be He preserved His world for another 7 days. It could be that when the waters reach the soul,[29] they would return to seek God, thus averting the wrath which He was about to discharge against them. Was this not also the case with the destruction of the first Temple? The process began in the time of Jehoiakim, transferred to Jehoiachin, but was not fulfilled until the time of Zedekiah.

Now from these chapters it has already been confirmed that 386 years elapsed from the time of the transference of the Persian Empire to Alexander until the destruction of the second Temple. The angel promised that the Temple would stand for 490 years; it thus transpires that the Persian kingdom lasted 104 years during Temple times as we said. In other words, 49 of these years elapsed from the second year of Darius who built the Temple until Nehemiah's arrival in Jerusalem, or until the twenty-first year of Artaxerxes, for they both were involved in the rebuilding of the ruins.[30] From this time, 55 years elapsed until Alexander brought about the downfall of Darius the last. We cannot ascertain the length of Artaxerxes' reign which lasted for more than 32 years. Similarly, all writers testify to the fact that Darius who was captured had already reigned for 6 years. It is also possible that others reigned between the reigns of these two monarchs which would extend the total number of years. In any event, given all these uncertainties, it is appropriate to rely on the message intimated by God's angel. We are provided with valuable support by Eusebius the Caesarean whom we cited in chapter 32. For he said that Artaxerxes Memnon who is thought to be the Artaxerxes under discussion, reigned 40 years; he was succeeded by Ochus for 26 years, who was succeeded by Arses for 4 years, and finally succeeded by Darius who was captured and reigned for 6 years. Furthermore, you should set yourself the task of calculating from the twenty-first year of this Artaxerxes' reign until the sixth year of the last Darius, and you will reach the exact total of 55 years as we mentioned. Moreover, Metasthenes the Persian, who was cited in chapter 31, gave the same list and chronological data for these last four kings. The only difference was that he wrote that Memnon reigned for 55 and not 40 years—it may be that an error crept into this part of his book. In any case, we may accept more than half which is the greater part, for it is patently of great importance for our purpose. Similarly, you will see that the 49 years that we mentioned may have elapsed from the time of Darius who built the Temple until Nehemiah and the twenty-first year of Artaxerxes' reign. For even if you deny that the Darius in question reigned 25 years, there were, according to the writers mentioned, many kings of Persia. Thus it could be suggested that some of them reigned between the reigns of Darius and Artaxerxes. At any rate, we should be receptive to that part of their statements which is

28. P. M.Q. 3 (5) 82c.
29. Cf. Ps. 69:2.
30. 'Rebuilding . . . ,' cf. Job 3:14.

relevant to holy Writ, and for the rest we should not be concerned. The truth of the matter is that in many of the accounts in which they stake their positions, they demolish each other's views. You should realize that by means of the methods we have employed, Nehemiah's descriptions of those six generations now fall into place. For he lived in the time of the third [priest] Eliashib who built the sheep gate as is shown in the third chapter of Nehemiah. Regarding Jeshua and Joiakim who lived before him, he gave a faithful account of what he had been told. With regard to Joiada, Jonathan, and Jaddua, he presented a completely honest[31] description of that which he saw and knew. One can conjecture that he died at the beginning of the days of Jaddua and consequently made no reference to his [Jaddua's] involvement with Alexander and the downfall of Darius. Indeed there is no need at all to pick holes and to raise questions as to the meaning of the number of 70 weeks and to divide them into the three stages that he mentions, for this was what the Lord in His wisdom had decreed. You know what the author of the *Guide* states about the number of the sacrifices. He writes:[32] "Know that wisdom rendered it necessary—or if you like to say, necessarily occasioned it—that there would be parts for which no cause can be found. Why should seven be prescribed and not eight? For they could ask as to why more or less had been chosen." Examine the passage for it is lengthy. This is comparable to Rabbi's response to Antonius in Sanhedrin[33] who asked as to why the sun rises in the east and sets in the west. He said to him: "Were it the reverse, you would ask the same question." And in Bemidbar Rabbah[34] and Shir Rabbah[35] a gentile asked Rabbi Joshua as to why the Holy One blessed be He spoke from the bush. To which he answered: "If he had spoken to him from a carob tree or sycamore, you would have asked me the same question." Furthermore, in his *City [of God],*[36] the greatest Christian doctor counters those who uphold the notion of the eternity of the world and question as to why man was only created five thousand years ago thereabouts. His response was that even if he had been created countless ages ago, the same question would be raised. (However, if the truth be known, the question is actually invalid since time which includes past and future was one of the parts of creation. This is held by many of those who assert the truth, and in particular, by the Christian sage Dante in the beautiful section of his *Paradiso,* canto 29.[37]) And so, we ought not to pose the question as to why the number of those weeks was not smaller or greater. But if nevertheless, you should desire a reason, examine the words of Don Isaac[38] who wrote in a persuasive manner on this matter and merits the greatest approbation.[39] Furthermore, as far as my own view is concerned, I shall not desist from demonstrating it whatever it is. It concerns the fact that we already mentioned in chapter 35 on authority of the wise Don Isaac that from the day on which Saul

31. 'Completely honest,' lit. honest weight. Cf. Lev. 19:35.
32. *Guide* III, ch. 26.
33. B. Sanh. 91b.
34. Bem. R. 12:4.
35. S.S.R. to S.S. 3:10.
36. Augustine, *De civ. Dei,* 12, ch. 13 (*P.L.* XLI, col. 360).
37. *La commedia, Paradiso,* canto 29, 19–36. In this passage Dante states that there is no point in asking questions about the time before creation since time is only relevant after creation.
38. *Mayyene ha-Yeshuʿah,* 10, tamar 6.
39. 'Greatest approbation,' lit. 'and the lips would kiss.' Cf. Pr. 24:26.

was anointed as king until the destruction of the Temple was a period of 493 years. It is therefore possible that God in His supernal wisdom thought it right to allow them another period of time of the same duration in keeping with the sentiment, *Truly, God does all these things two [or three times] to a man* (Job 33:29). His intention would be to put them to the test in order to ascertain whether they would return to Him, directing themselves heavenwards.[40] Is it not the case that the blessed Lord employs cycles of recurring sevens as indicated in the passage in the Zohar which we cited in chapter 11.[41] And it would appear that there is no reason to be concerned about the truncation of the 3 years. For it is established that the Torah did not take individual figures into account with regard to the number of the hosts of the children of Israel, which according to reason, should have amounted to several more hundreds and fifties.[42] It is also possible that the text can be taken literally. Moreover, in his commentary on the verse, *Saul was one year old when he became king* (1 Sam. 13:1), the wise Don Isaac writes in a way which implies that those 493 years were actually 490 years.[43] And furthermore, the statement in Daniel, *For half a week he will put a stop to the sacrifice* (Dan. 9:27) ought perhaps to be taken separately from the 490 years. Examine the passage. This is the extent to which I wish to speak about that great vision which is appropriate to investigate in the light of all the data that I have supplied.

40. 'Return . . . heavenwards,' cf. Hos. 7:16.

41. Zohar III, 9b to Lev. 3:1: "At the time of creating the world the Holy One blessed be He created seven upper firmaments, seven lower earths, seven rivers, seven days, seven weeks, seven years seven times multiplied, seven thousand years for the duration of the world, and the Holy One blessed be He exists in the seventh of them all."

42. This is a reference to his discussion in ch. 35 of Num. 11:21 in which the exact figure of the Israelite hosts is not given.

43. In this context Abravanel states that Saul reigned 17 years until his death, while in his introduction to Kings he states that he ruled 20 years.

CHAPTER FORTY-TWO

Discussions between the author and his friend regarding the person who casts doubt on our anno mundi computation.[1]

Now for the further instruction of the intelligent person, I shall not refrain from giving an account of the discussions on these topics which I recently had with one of the upstanding sages of our times. He initiated the discussion in the following manner:

I shall not examine the separate proofs that you gave with regard to the anno mundi computation and make an appropriate and truly balanced evaluation of each piece of evidence. But the case I wish to present is of a general nature and regards the question of casting doubt [on the anno mundi computation]. In Shemot Rabbah, it is stated:[2] "Akylas said to Hadrian: 'I wish to convert.' He said to him: 'What do you see in them?' He said to him: 'The lowliest of them knows how the Holy One blessed be He created the world and what was created on the first and second day and how long it is since the world was created. Moreover their Torah is true.' "

Furthermore, in Midrash Tanḥuma, this statement of Akylas or Onqelos is repeated,[3] with the explicit assertion that the lowliest of us knows how long it is since the world was created. Now Onqelos or Akylas was held in the highest esteem and particularly because, as is stated in tractate Megillah,[4] he translated the Torah under the guidance of Rabbi Eliezer and Rabbi Joshua.

I responded in the following way. Brother, your final comment leads me to begin by making a differentiation between these two saintly converts [i.e., Onqelos and Akylas] so as not to ascribe the statement of the one to the other. However, to prevent us

1. Given de' Rossi's arguments in this chapter regarding the fictitious nature of the literary dialogue, it could be argued that de' Rossi's dialogue, too, never actually took place. However, it should also be considered that his friend Judah Moscato, whom he mentions elsewhere, wrote a commentary (*Qol Jehudah*) on Judah Halevi's *Kuzari* which is partly the focus of the argument in the first part of the chapter. It could be suggested that the some of the contents of this chapter may have been stimulated by de' Rossi's discussions with Moscato. It is perhaps significant that in his *Qol Jehudah,* Moscato often implicitly disagrees with de' Rossi's views. (See, e.g., his observation on *Kuzari* III, par. 65).

2. S.R. 30:12.

3. Tanḥuma, Mishpaṭim 5 (Buber, 3). As Buber comments, de' Rossi is referring to the Tanḥuma printed in Mantua in 1563 in which the words "Onqelos the proselyte" are added. Although the Tanḥuma text contains the discussion between Hadrian and Akylas, it omits the passage about creation.

4. B. Meg. 3a.

becoming confused about the main subject by introducing other issues into the discussion, it is preferable to treat this commendable topic on another occasion.[5] As for the reader, you will find that there is a separate chapter following these chapters of the "Days of the World" in which I deal with this subject in the manner that I intimated to him.[6] Now we shall return to solve our problem.

I said to him: Dear brother, regardless of whether it was Akylas or Onqelos, rightly described by you as a great person, who made the comment that Israelites know how long it is since the world was created, you should please take note that his words do not contradict what was said above. His true aim was to refer to the years that are explicitly given in the Torah and Prophets until the time of Moses and until the time of the first Temple and so on. It was indeed correct when he spoke about how the Holy One blessed be He created the world, what He created, and how that their Torah is true. However, for the subsequent period we lack the Holy Spirit which could illumine this and other subjects; the verification of the number of years is simply a matter that we must determine as best we can.

He continued to raise objections and said: Your heart articulates wisdom such that you rightly adopt the anno mundi computation like any one of us. But by your insistence on finding some way of justifying those doubts, you surely turn out to be breaking faith with the wise author of the *Kuzari* with whose crowns on so many occasions you adorn your head. For he told the king that those discussions of his would be dated by us to the year 4500 [740 C.E.], which date no two Jews would dispute.[7] This surely proves that the anno mundi computation was used by our ancestors even before the time of Rav Sherira Gaon. It is likewise clear that this sage used that computation because it was true and correct; and one cannot claim that an error has arisen since then. And I did not remind you that in several places in his *Yad Ḥazaqah,* the magnificent glory, the Rambam of blessed memory, gave the anno mundi computation according to our reckoning. For you would have responded with the statement you made about him [Rambam] and Rashi in chapter 14 and at the end of chapter 37, namely, that since their writing postdated that of the Gemara, it was appropriate for them not to deviate from the ways of our rabbis. And yet in his *Kuzari,* Rabbi Judah shows himself to be independent of such an attitude—so why did you argue with him?

I replied: My brother and leader, I will answer you by taking your first point first, and you will be able to regard me as faithful to the covenant and goodness.[8] You should know that although at the beginning of his book Rabbi Judah ascribes his entire text to the rabbi he mentions,[9] there is no doubt that it was a complete invention and product of his own profound wisdom. But he followed in the footsteps of such outstanding persons as Plato and Cicero who used the dialogue, putting some of their own ideas in the mouth of Socrates or Cato and other qualified and renowned contemporaries of theirs. Thus he, too, ascribed those sacred dialogues of his to an ancient sage whom he

5. 'Commendable . . . occasion.' A play on the talmudic expression (e.g., B. Qidd. 33a).
6. I.e., ch. 45.
7. *Kuzari* 1, par. 47.
8. 'Faithful . . . kindness,' cf. Neh. 9:32.
9. *Kuzari* I: "As I found that many of the rabbi's arguments appealed to me and were in harmony with my own opinion, I resolved to write them down exactly as they had been spoken."

took as an exemplary figure; according to the author of the *Sefer ha-Emunot,* he was called Isaac Sangari.[10] Thus at the beginning of his book Rabbi Judah says: "I resolved to write down the discussion exactly as it occurred and the wise will understand." In other words, they should infer from this statement of mine that the entire enterprise is my own production. In the same way, to my mind, the book of Job was the composition of one person; namely, according to rabbinic view, Moses our teacher, may he rest in peace. For he ascribed it to one who was known in his days as a fitting subject of that story on account of his stature and experience. This conclusion is most certainly to be deduced from the view according to which it is claimed that Job never existed.[11] Thus both views are equally correct. The proof is that all the interlocutors of the dialogue speak in the same style. You would know if they had been different persons, since it is the pen that distinguishes the individual. Even two prophets do not prophesy in an identical style;[12] moreover, when one person is reproducing the words of many people, even then he ought to adopt each individual's method. Now Rabbi Judah was a contemporary of ibn Ezra,[13] and according to report, he was his father-in-law.[14] In his [ibn Ezra's] commentary he refers to a question "put to me by Rabbi Judah, may he rest in paradise."[15] And at the end of his commentary on Exodus, ibn Ezra wrote that he completed it in the year 913 [1153], that is, 418 years ago.[16] Accordingly you will realize that the figure 4500 [given by Judah Halevi] was simply made up for the purposes of the moment in order to give the impression that the book was written in the past. Now we have seen that in his *Epistle,* the Gaon Rav Sherira dates the generations of the year 4500 according to the Greek era which was in use in those times. Even if we concede as you said that this method of dating was used thousands of years ago, and we did not deny this possibility, none of this detracts in the slightest from the importance of those statements cited above. However, inasmuch as you are resolved in your claim that the sage [i.e., Halevi] set that figure as a fixed linchpin, I can in fact show you that it contains an inherent contradiction which emerges in relation to his statement about the Men of the Great Synagogue in section 3.[17] But these words of yours will aid me in that I judged that the book contained an error through the fault of the translator as was demonstrated in chapter 36 in which I also mentioned many esteemed authorities who likewise challenge our customary computation. It is thus apparent that the consensus about which you spoke does not exist. When you delve into the meaning of those

10. He is referring to the *Sefer ha-Emunot,* written by Shemtov ibn Shemtov (1390–1440). The passage to which he refers is not in the introduction, but in gate 2, ch. 4, 15v. He refers to Rabbi Isaac ha-Sangari who was a friend of the king of the Kazars who converted to Judaism and states that the records of the discussions of the rabbi with the king were used by Judah Halevi in his *Kuzari.*

11. See B. B.B. 15a: "Job never existed and never lived but is simply a parable."

12. Cf. B. Sanh. 89a.

13. Judah Halevi was born in 1075 and ibn Ezra in 1090.

14. For a discussion of the legend that Halevi was ibn Ezra's father-in-law, see N. Ben Menahem, *Inyyane ibn Ezra,* 224–40.

15. Ibn Ezra to Ex. 20:2.

16. The statement is printed at the end of ibn Ezra's commentary on Exodus in the ed. pr. Naples, 1488, but it is not clear whether it was written by ibn Ezra himself or by the copyist.

17. In ch. 36, de' Rossi quotes *Kuzari* III, par. 65 in which Halevi states that Simeon the righteous was in the generation after the Men of the Great Synagogue and thus, by implication, rejects the rabbinic computation of the second Temple period.

statements of his, it become clear that his only purpose was to demonstrate the truth of creatio ex nihilo with regard to the years that are universally counted from creation, regardless of whether they were actually more or less. His statement in the first section of the book clarifies this point, for he states:[18] "If an upholder of the Torah is compelled to admit to eternal matter and the existence of many worlds prior to this one, it would not be regarded as a defect in his belief; for it is sufficient that he believes that this world was created at a specific time and that Adam and Eve were the first of us human beings." He therefore discounts the view of the Indians which he quotes in a later passage (par. 37) whose calculations go back countless years.[19] A similar statement is made by the greatest Christian doctor in book 18 of his *City [of God]* where he ridicules the Egyptians who boast that their astronomical science is more than one hundred thousand years old.[20] He also pours scorn on them in book 12[21] where he demonstrates their deception with regard to the years from creation which are manifestly proven from Scripture—there is, however, a slight discrepancy between his and our computation. In particular, he exposes the lie of the writer who mentions the letter written by Alexander to his mother Olympia in which he claimed that thousands of years ten times over had elapsed since the world began. And thus, if you were to add a few years to the figure given by the sage of the *Kuzari,* he would not criticize you since you would not be deviating in the slightest from his main point about the truth of creatio ex nihilo.

The scholar continued to confront me with the following statement. And yet the gentiles report, and in one of your chapters you present their view, namely, that Alexander ruled 430 years after the foundation of Rome. Now it was not until the sixth year of his reign that he subjugated Darius, which means that the Persian Empire came to an end 436 years after the foundation of Rome. Our rabbis of blessed memory state[22] that when Solomon married Pharaoh's daughter, Gabriel (and some say Michael, the arch prince) descended and planted a reed in the sea and it accumulated a bank around it, and when Jeroboam made the two calves, the city of Rome was built on its ground. Thus 374 years elapsed from the foundation of Rome until the end of those 34 years. Four hundred and ten years from Jeroboam until the end of the period of the first Temple, in addition to the 70 years of the exile and the 34 years of Persia come to a total of 478 which is 42 years more than the 436 years that were mentioned. Although this excess is problematic according to all opinions, the fact is that the problem becomes magnified as more years are added to the duration of the Persian Empire.

I answered him: My brother, the way you begun this part of the argument was not well advised since you set alight your own arrows. For you will discover that those who count 430 years from the foundation of Rome until Alexander do not date its foundation from the calves of Jeroboam, as you claimed on authority of our rabbis. Rather, as I

18. *Kuzari* I, par. 67.

19. Ibid., par. 60: "The Indians have antiquities and buildings which they consider to be millions of years old."

20. *De civ. Dei,* 18, ch. 40. "De Aegyptiorum mendacissima vanitate quae antiquitati scientiae suae centum millia annorum ascribit."

21. Ibid., 12, ch. 10 "De falsitate eius historiae quae multa millia annorum praeteritis temporibus ascribit."

22. De' Rossi refers to B. Shabb. 56b; B. Sanh. 21b; S.S.R. to S.S. 1:6. He also refers to Berakhot, but his citation is not exact.

shall divulge to you, they connected it by means of other calculations. At the beginning of the section on the record of the history of Rome in his *Sefer ha-Qabbalah,* Rabad states that its foundation and rule began at the time of the exile of the ten tribes in the ninth year of the reign of Hoshea ben Ela who was the sixth king to reign after Hezekiah. This was appropriate, insofar as the working of the attribute of justice is concerned; the rod of the taskmaster for the remnant of Israel was being set in readiness at that time, should they rebel as had the first lot.[23] But let us put aside Rabad and his line of thinking. We should give our attention to Eusebius the Caesarean and Samotheus. They counted the same 430 years, and in their chronological tables they wrote that the foundation and sovereignty of Rome begins from the time of Romulus in the fourteenth year of the reign of Jotham son of Uzziah. This information was also given by the reliable historian Curtius who devoted his work to the history of Alexander. It is true that at the beginning of his second book,[24] he dates the beginning of Alexander's reign to the four hundred and twenty-sixth year after the foundation of Rome, but this is only due to a certain discrepancy in the way historians count Olympiads. In any case, a difference of a mere 4 years is not something we have reason to be concerned about at the moment. In other words, the starting point of the calculation as set by those writers does not accord with your view. And if you resolve to take it back to the time of Jeroboam's calves, you will also augment your calculation, as far as their view is concerned, to more than 426 or 430 years as we mentioned. And thus the problem lies only with our rabbis' computation. Moreover, if one were to proceed on this path, the problem will be compounded from another perspective. My point is that according to the writers mentioned above, the translation of our Torah by the seventy elders was accomplished in the five hundredth year after the foundation of Rome. In their view, the truth of this assertion may also be made clear by reference to the the fact that another 500 years elapsed from the time of the translation until Philip the twenty-seventh emperor—according to the work on the *Lives of the Caesars,*[25] he reigned 176 years after the destruction of the Temple—which brings us to a total of 1,000 years. It was then the second year of Philip's reign,[26] and he arranged festivities and theatrical entertainment on a large scale because the birthday of Rome, that is to say, the thousandth anniversary of its foundation, was to fall in his days. Similarly, you will discover that the seven hundred years of Rome's history which was the subject of the works of the great historian Titius Livius came to completion in the time of the wars of Julius Caesar and Pompey, the captain of the Roman army. This was an apposite moment in time, set approximately midway between the 500- and 1,000-year period. Thus in this way you reach the total of years which elapsed from the foundation of Rome before the building of the second Temple until the time of the translation [of the Septuagint] which was accomplished long after the Temple had been built. Now using the data

23. I.e., according to Rabad, the foundation of Rome at the time of the exile of the ten tribes prefigured the later persecution of the Jews by Rome.

24. The second book of Curtius Rufus is not extant, but in sixteenth-century editions, this book (and the other missing parts of the work) were reconstructed and put as Supplementa to the text. "Anno ab urbe condita 426, . . . Alexander . . . assequutus est imperium" (*De rebus gestis,* 17).

25. This is a reference to Pedro Mexía's *Le vite di tutti gl'imperadori* (294–95). Mexía counts Philip as the twenty-ninth (not twenty-seventh) emperor, but usually he is listed as the thirty-sixth emperor.

26. I.e., the year 247.

given by those writers, or that of Rabad who gives 133 years for the regnal years of the kings of Judah from the beginning of Rome until the destruction of the first Temple and the 70 years in which Jerusalem lay in ruins and the 34 years of Rabbi Jose which came to an end in the sixth year of Alexander—that was when he defeated Darius—the sum total is a mere 261 years. And if you proceed further and add the last 6 years of Alexander and the 36 years of Ptolemy son of Lago who succeeded him as sovereign of Egypt and the 31 years of Ptolemy Philadelphus to arrive at the time of the translation, there is a total of 334 years. Accordingly, Rabbi Jose's 34 years is the only questionable figure and therefore requires augmentation, but we do not know the precise amount. I admit, my dear, that there are other writers who date the origin of Rome to a time before Romulus—this information is readily available in the entry for Rome in the Latin dictionary.[27] But there is a modification that I should make to this declaration. For you will notice that in the tables of the chronologers, they begin their computation from Romulus, and if one were to predate its origin, the figure of 430 or 426 that we mentioned would become augmented. Furthermore, having lead you on this alien path, there is another examination of a similar nature that you should take into account for the topic under discussion. Consider the dates of any important person who lived either a short or long time before the second Temple and, likewise, what is known in relation to him once the Temple was built. All this information is taken from writers who are regarded as objective narrators of past events in world history. You count the years, as you did, from the foundation of Rome in conjunction with the years which had elapsed by the beginning of the Temple era. You could take Plato as an example. Examine the work entitled *History of the World* by the Christian writer Dolce.[28] On authority of the four ancient writers, Laertius, Dionysius, Plutarch, and Apuleius, he wrote that Plato was born 500 years before the destruction of the second Temple.[29] And in his *City [of God]*[30] the greatest Christian doctor wrote that Plato lived 81 years and died 60 years before the translation of our Torah. Now given that he lived 81 years—and all others who write about Plato give the same indication—his death, according to rabbinic calculation, must have occurred in the year in which the Temple was built. And on the basis of the confirmation given above that the Septuagint translation was produced 79 years after the beginning of the Alexandrian Empire and 60 years after the death of Plato, we must necessarily conclude that Plato lived 7 years after the 12 years of the Alexandrian Empire had ended. Now if Plato's lifetime came to an end in the year of the construction of the Temple, how could it be feasible that Alexander, who died 7

27. He is referring to Calepino's *Dictionarium* in which three views for the origins of Rome are given: from the time of Evander (whose name is said to mean strong man which would correspond to the Greek meaning of the word Rome, i.e., strength); the name of a captive girl from Troy; or from Romulus. For a discussion of the legends about the origins of Rome, see A. Momigliano, "The Origin," 384–88, and in the context of sixteenth-century chronological debates, A. Grafton, *Joseph Scaliger II,* 134–35, 656–57.

28. This is a reference to the *Giornale delle historie del mondo* of the translator and verse and prose writer Lodovico Dolce (1508–68).

29. *Giornale* (133): "L'anno inanti Christi 427. Nacque Platone philosopho nel terzo anno della guerra del Peloponneso. Laertio e Dionisio Halicarnaseo, Plutarcho Appuleio nella vita di Platone." De' Rossi has made his own calculation based on Dolce's data, namely, that Plato was born in the third year of the Pelopennesian war, in 427 B.C.E.

30. *De civ. Dei,* 8, ch. 11 (*P.L.* XLI, col. 235).

years earlier, could, in his sixth year, have been brought by the high priest into the Sanctuary a number of years after it had been built, when stone had not yet been put on stone? We must perforce conclude that 500 years before the destruction of the Temple, they approximately began to build the temple, either a little before or after—we do not know exactly. And although there is a certain discrepancy between those writers, through their lattice some light on these calculations is shed.[31] So as long as they have some semblance of reliability, I have spoken well for it was better for us not to give them our consideration lest we become like diggers of a pit who fall into it.[32] And there is all the more reason. For apart from the question which arose on account of the regnal years counted by Metasthenes the Persian in his book *On the Order of Times* which we translated in chapter 31 and also raised at the end of chapter 39, there is the statement of the Arab al-Farghani at the end of the first gate of his *Astronomy.*[33] It is not in the Latin translation which omits the words in question but is contained in the Hebrew translation of Rabbi Jacob bar Anatoli. I saw a copy of it which belonged to the heir of the wise Cases of blessed memory[34] and the heirs of Rabbi Nethanel da Norzi of blessed memory and Rabbi Ezra da Fano,[35] may his rock protect him. It states that more than 350 years elapsed between the reign of Nebuchadnezzar and the beginning of the empire of Alexander of Macedon. This statement prompted the translator to append the section with the following observation: "The author al-Farghani ended this gate with a statement about the years of all eras and it contains an error with regard to the creation of the world both from the standpoint of our people and tradition as well as the tradition of the Romans, but we left it."

{In the *Almagest,* Ptolemy also mentions the positions of various stars which appear two or three times in specific years. In the third section of the work regarding the rotations of the sun (that is, in the Latin version which was translated from the Greek text itself), he writes as follows:[36]

> From the reign of Nabonassar to the death of Alexander is a period of 424 years; from the death of Alexander until the reign of Augustus is a period of 294 years; and from the first year of Augustus's reign, on the first day of the Egyptian month called Thoth (that is our Tishri) and half a day—since we wish to begin the epoch from midday—until the seventeenth year of Hadrian's reign on the seventh day of the month Athyr (which is Kislev), 2 equatorial hours after midday is a period of 161 years and 66 days, and 2 equatorial hours. Thus from the first year of Nabonassar, midday of the month Thoth, until the time of the autumn equinox which we indicated (in the seventeenth year of Hadrian) is a period of 879 years, 66 days, and 2 equatorial hours.

In chapter 8 of the fourth section he writes in a similar vein on the subject of the position of the moon in its mean motion. And in chapter 4 of the tenth section he writes

31. Play on Pr. 7:6.
32. 'Diggers . . . it,' cf. Eccl. 10:8.
33. As indicated in ch. 23, de' Rossi read the Hebrew translation in manuscript.
34. This is probably a reference to Samuel ben Moses Cases who was rabbi in Mantua and Bologna.
35. Ezra da Fano was a rabbi of Mantua.
36. *Almagest* III, ch. 7 (in George of Trepizond's translation which De' Rossi used, the passage is in ch. 8).

about the movements of Mars[37] and states as follows: "There were 884 years from the reign of Nabonassar until Antonius." Furthermore in his fifth section, chapter 14, he writes in regard to a certain subject[38] as follows: "We know that this is true in respect to two eclipses, one of which occurred in the fifth year of Nabopolassar, 127 years after Nabonassar; and the second took place in the seventh year of Cambyses, 225 years after Nabonassar." The truth of the matter is that we have reason to express some scruples regarding the names. There is a Christian scholar, Gerhardus Mercator, who wrote a chronology of world history both on the basis of holy Writ and the best gentile writers and on the basis of the eclipses and the stars whose rotations according to Ptolemy are regular. He printed the book in Cologne in the year 1569 according to their era.[39] On folios 1^{v}[40] 55, and 70 he demonstrates that Ptolemy's Nabonassar is called Salmanassar in holy Writ (2Kings 17) who lived about 120 years before Nebuchadnezzar the Great who destroyed the Temple. And he shows that all the figures mentioned, namely, 424 years from the death of Alexander, and 225 years from the seventh year of Cambyses, and 879 from the seventeenth year of Hadrian, and 884 from Augustus retrospectively arrive at exactly the beginning of the reign of Salmanassar.[41] And he also shows that the positions of the stars relevant to this question coincide exactly. One ought to add that Nabopolassar whose name is not found in holy Writ nor mentioned by any other gentile writer must be Nebuchadnezzar who is otherwise not mentioned in the *Almagest.* Thus it follows that from Nebuchadnezzar until the seventh year of Cambyses, the son of Cyrus, is a period of about 100 years, and from Cambyses until the death of Alexander about 200 years. Disregarding Nebuchadnezzar's years with which we are not concerned, there is also the further confirmation that from Salmanassar who exiled Hoshea son of Ela in the sixth year of Hezekiah, 133 years elapsed before the destruction of the first Temple, as we said in chapter 35, and 203 years when they left Babylon after 70 years of exile and up until the death of Alexander comes to a total of 424 years according to his view. Thus from the end of the 70-year period which is the beginning of the Persian Empire until the death of Alexander, 6 years after he had extirpated Darius, is necessarily a period of 221 years; and this is the duration of the Persian Empire in Temple times which is the main subject of our inquiry. There is no doubt in my mind that the Arab al-Farghani followed the computation of the *Almagest* in chapter 1 of his *Astronomy;* indeed, his [i.e., Ptolemy's] words served as his guide. However, the Jew who translated the *Almagest* from the Arabic text and not from the Greek original—and it was he who translated al-Farghani's *Astronomy*—thought that the name Nabatnassar, which is given in the Arabic in both texts instead of Nabonassar,

37. The chapter deals with the movements of Venus not Mars.

38. I.e., on the magnitude of the apparent diameter of the sun, moon, and stars during the syzygies.

39. Gerhardus Mercator (1512–90) was a cartographer, printer, and chronologer. De' Rossi's description of the book is a free transcription of the title of the book *Chronologia. Hoc est Temporum demonstratio exactissima ab initio mundi usque ad annum Domini MDLXVIII ex eclipsibus et observationibus astronomicis omnium temporum, sacris quoque Bibliis et optimis quibusque Scriptoribus summa fide concinnata.*

40. *Chronologia,* cap. 1: "A condito mundo tempora certis dimensionibus continuavimus usque ad Nabugodonosorem. . . . A Nabugodonosoris anno 5 ex Ptolemei demonstrationibus retrocessimus ad initium Nabunassari qui in libris Regum et Paralipomenon est Salmanassar."

41. For a discussion of this subject, see Grafton, *Joseph Scaliger II,* 124.

referred to Nebuchadnezzar and in that way the discrepancy becomes magnified to about 120 years.[42] No writer of any distinguished nation came to realize this, and that is why he chose to omit it, as we mentioned.[43] In any case, it is most probable that one can confirm that either due to the information at their disposal regarding the succession of kings, or from the conclusion drawn from their astronomical reckoning of the paths of the stars, both Ptolemy and al-Farghani alike advanced the same reckoning, interposing about 300 years between Nebuchadnezzar and Alexander. The same dating was also given by Metasthenes the Persian whose text we gave in chapter 31. This figure is therefore 170 years more than Rabbi Jose's 34 years for the computation of the length of the Persian Empire during Temple times. And we have already indicated in chapter 36 that two sages belonging to our people, Yedidyah the Alexandrian in his work *On the Times* and Josephus in his *War* gave approximately the same figure as the Persian, Greek, and Arab writers that we mentioned. The duration of the second Temple was thus, according to their view, 600 years and more. And since we have had occasion to mention Josephus, it would seem appropriate to note that in his glosses on the *Sefer Yuḥasin* which he printed in Constantinople, Rabbi Samuel Shullam sometimes gives the designation "the great Josephus" and sometimes, "the long Josephus." This designation, as is evident from his statement in his introduction, is identical with our "Roman Josephus"—from his sporadic references to him it is clear that he is the same person.[44] Therefore, one could suppose that it was translated into Hebrew in the past, and the text was found in the environs of Turkey. Likewise, his books of *Against Apion* were translated into Hebrew and reproduced at the end of *Sefer Yuḥasin.*[45] As regards our previous statement that Thoth corresponds to the month of Tishri and Athyr to the month of Kislev, it is clear from the statement of the Christian translator [Jerome] in his commentary on the book of Ezekiel that Tebe is the fifth Egyptian month.[46] Thus following the order of their months as given in Mercator's introduction, it would appear that Thoth/ Tishri, is the first of the Egyptian months and this explains why the blessed Lord pronounced Nisan as the first of the months, *This month shall mark for you the beginning of the months* (Ex. 12:2); *for you,* that is, for you my people who are coming out of Egypt.[47]}[2]

My friend then answered me and said. In their own way, these investigations do appear to have some basis. However, when we agree to uphold the notion expressed in the statement, *Do not learn to go the way of the nations* (Jer. 10:2), as you yourself indicated at the end of chapter 39, everything goes wrong and these calculations be-

42. Joseph Scaliger came to the same conclusion. See Grafton, *Joseph Scaliger II,* 303.

43. De' Rossi refers to ch. 40, 137. He is actually referring to ch. 42, 137 in the first edition and to the translator's gloss in which he discusses the differences between the Latin and Hebrew al-Farghani.

44. Shullam does give occasional references to Josephus in his glosses on the text.

45. The translation of *Contra Apionem* is at the end of the work, 166r–174v. Shullam explains that he included the text whose purpose was to sanctify the Holy one of Jacob and His holy Torah and to aggrandize the glory of Moses who received it at Sinai.

46. Jerome, *Commentaria* to Ezk. 29:1–2 (*P.L.* XXV, col. 277): "Porro iuxta LXX decimus mensis qui Hebraice appellatur tebeth et apud Aegyptios Tothi apud Romanos Januarius dicitur."

47. In other words, Nisan as opposed to Tishri became the first of the months of the Jewish calendar to indicate separation from Egypt and the Egyptian bondage and the start of a new era.

come altogether abhorrent.[48] Your statements regarding our wise rabbis and specifically Rabbi Hillel and his law court are certainly correct. In other words, they were not unaware of the doubts regarding both the length of the bondage in Egypt and the duration of the two Temples; they therefore wisely and voluntarily agreed to uphold the figures that were widely used by our people. The same is true of your demonstrations in chapters 38 and 40 that any feasible addition to the anno mundi computation would not affect belief in creatio ex nihilo or the fixed festivals. These arguments would be considered correct by the understanding person and silence anybody who would try to speak arrogantly against these chapters of yours. However, three aspects of this question disquiet me. Please give me your response and I will grant you a covenant of friendship. The first matter regards what happened to our ancestors. For from 380 years before the destruction of the Temple until this day, the figure for the era of documents has been known and not been questioned or disputed, while those few years between the beginning of the Temple period until the death of Alexander have generated the questions that you discussed. The second point is that if the rabbis of blessed memory, as you wrote, voluntarily and wisely closed their eyes to those generations of high priests, how will you absolve yourself when in the future you will have to account for having divulged that which they concealed? There is the comparable case in tractate Shabbat where Rabbi Eliezer responds to Rabbi Aqiva who thought it right to divulge the name of the "gatherer of wood,"[49] and who, in the Palestinian Talmud, revealed the identity of Elihu son of Berakhel.[50] Thirdly, I am agitated about the entire investigation. For although you are, in actual truth, free of any sin as I showed, when the ignorant masses get word that our customary anno mundi computation is in disarray, one has reason to fear that they will take the argument one stage further and learn to invalidate other things and the sin will lie at your door.

I answered the first point and said. You should realize, my dear, that the era of documents was not only in use among our people but also among many others, as is clear from the first and second book of Maccabees[51] and from Josephus.[52] In this way, it was prevented from falling into oblivion and disarray for there was constant recourse to it. However, the length of the first part of the second Temple period which was not explicitly documented in Scripture nor regarded by other peoples was adopted by us through tradition. Such is the impact of the troubles and reprimands that have struck us with stupor, that as with other matters of importance, these things have become confused. There are the statements of our sages of blessed memory about the letters *mnspk*[53] and about the Aramaic translation of the Torah which were forgotten and later

48. Cf. Ps. 14:3.

49. B. Shabb. 96b. Rabbi Aqiva identified the "gatherer of wood" (Num. 15:32) as Zelophehad. Rabbi Judah b. Batyra said to Rabbi Aqiva: "You will have to give account. If you are right, the Torah shielded him while you reveal him; and if not, you cast a stigma on a righteous man."

50. P. Sota 5 (6) 20d. R. Aqiva identifies Elihu as Balaam and Rabbi Eleazar ben Azariah chides him for having divulged that which God had concealed.

51. 1Macc. 1:10; 2Macc. 1:7, 9 (and not ch. 9 as de' Rossi states).

52. *Ant.* XII:321.

53. These are the letters which have a double form according to whether they are placed at the end of the word or not. In B. Shabb. 104a, B. Meg. 2b–3a, and P. Meg. 1 (9) 71d, it is suggested that the use of the medial and final forms of the letters had been forgotten and later reinstituted.

reinstituted.[54] And also with regard to the blowing of the Shofar [ram's horn] you should know the content of Rabbenu Hai's responsum which is cited by Asheri [Asher ben Yehiel]:[55] "Do not think that the doubt regarding this matter occurred in Rabbi Abbahu's days." Indeed, in his Laws,[56] the great teacher Rambam of blessed memory concludes that the doubts we have regarding the mode of blowing the Shofar is due to the passing of time and the long duration of the exile. So when our ancestors returned from the Babylonian exile which only lasted 70 years, as Ezra and Nehemiah describe, *they were unable to tell whether their father's house and descent were Israelite,*[57] and the priests *searched for their genealogical records but they could not be found.*[58] Now if this is what happened in the three cases which befell the entire nation in all places and times, and what happened to those families who were justifiably mindful of the rolls containing their genealogical records, it is surely easy for us to realize, from whatever perspective we come, that as a result of the many dispersions and troubles, we became confused about the calculations of those years of remote antiquity. Moreover we should not blame Rabbi Jose, the author of the statement about the 34 years, although some astonishment is not out of place; after all his testimony was not that of an eyewitness. Rather, it was based on tradition which was not Sinaitic—for it would be impossible to make such a claim—but instead derived from other sages of the world whether his compatriots or foreigners, and this is how it came to be transferred to us.

Now with regard to calculations of dates, you should pay particular attention to the following point, wise man, and evaluate it. In tractate Taʿanit of the Palestinian Talmud it is stated:[59]

> It is written: *On the ninth day of the fourth month [the walls of] the city were breached* (Jer. 39:2). But you say it was on the seventeenth of the month. Rabbi Tanḥum said: "The dates here are in disarray. It is written, *In the eleventh year on the first of the month the word of the Lord came to me. O mortal, because Tyre gloated over Jerusalem* (Ezk. 26:1–2). You cannot say that it was the first of Av, for the Temple had not yet been burnt; and you cannot say it was the first of Ellul. For could the *baldar* (this means captain of the army)[60] go from Jerusalem to Tyre in one day and night? Rather it is obvious that the dates here are in disarray.

Rashba [Solomon ben Adret] comments on this passage as follows:[61] "The dates were in disarray, that is to say, [the breaching of the walls] did indeed take place on the seventeenth of the month both in the case of the first and second Temples. However, due to the great calamity, they erred in the calculation and the dates fell in disarray. They thought that it occurred on the ninth of the month and the scriptural statement is given according to the popular reckoning." The Tosafists also wrote about the passage from the Palestinian Talmud. They said: "This is at variance with our Mishnah. It means that because of their troubles the people erred in their calculation and thought

54. B. Meg. 3a.
55. Asher b. Yehiel to R.H. 4:8. He states that already in Mishnaic times there was a question about the notes blown on the Shofar.
56. *Mishneh Torah,* Shofar III:2.
57. Ezra 2:59; Neh. 7:61.
58. Ezra 2:62; Neh. 7:64.
59. P. Taʿanit 4 (5) 68c.
60. *Baldar* is the Hebrew calque of *veredarius* which means courier.
61. This comment of the Rashba is given in Jacob ibn Ḥabib's *En Yaʿaqov* to B. R.H. 18b.

that it was then the ninth of Tammuz, but the prophet did not want to deviate from what they thought." The final part of the statements of both sages is comparable to the statement in the *Kuzari*[62] regarding the verse, *They found written in the Torah* (Neh. 8:14; 13:1), where it is explained (at the end of section 3) that it was the people who did the finding [but not the intellectual elite]. As in the case of the day on which the first Temple was destroyed, Josephus's reckoning of the day on which the second Temple was destroyed is also confused. For in the seventh book of his *Wars* he writes that the Temple was burnt on the tenth day of the month of Augustus.[63] However, we can take part of his statements into account, for, like the sages of blessed memory, he does express the view that they put a torch to the Temple towards evening.[64] Now this was explicitly told by a prophet regarding a day of communal calamity which, as is the way of the world, becomes engraved on the heart. Therefore arrangements for fasting and crying on the very days that these things happened to the Jews were established. Nevertheless the rabbis did not refrain from declaring that with regard to these events the calculations were in disarray. In a time of emergency, then, it is surely appropriate to make the same claim about Rabbi Jose's declaration which he heard secondhand, and not make him culpable for his error as we said. Although an end should be put to words, I cannot refrain from interposing here with the passage from tractate Niddah[65] in which Rabbi Jose said that the giving of the heave-offering in the present time is only a rabbinic enactment. They questioned his view on the basis of the teaching in Seder Olam (ch. 30) for the verse, *Which your fathers possessed and you shall possess it* (Deut. 30:5) indicates that it is a pentateuchal obligation.[66] Rabbi Johanan then stated: "Who is the author of Seder Olam? Is it not Rabbi Jose?" They replied: "He may have been its compiler, but he himself did not hold this view. This may also be supported by a process of reasoning" This is also cited by Rabbenu Isaiah the elder in his first gloss on chapter three of Makkot.[67]

{There is also the passage in Baba Meṣia[68] regarding a marriage contract which is found in the street. On this matter, Rabbi Jose is said to have given his view in accordance with that of the rabbis. Then in tractate Nedarim concerning vows of self-denial,[69] it is suggested that Rabbi Jose may have been questioning them according to their own view.}[2] Accordingly, also with regard to the subject under discussion, it is not far-fetched to consider that he conveyed the view that he was given, although he himself may have entertained another idea about it.

As regards your second criticism, you will rightly consider that I should be completely exonerated. For before our own times this was a matter which was contested by gentile chroniclers and Christian doctors as well as by the sages of our own people of

62. *Kuzari* III par. 54 ff.
63. In Gelenius's edition, the passage is in *Bellum* VII:9 but in Niese's ed. VI:250.
64. B. Taʿanit 29a: "towards dusk of the ninth day, they set fire to it."
65. B. Nidd. 46b.
66. I.e., since the biblical text repeated the word "possess," it was inferred that it referred to a repossession of the land which remained in perpetuity. Since the land remained sacred, the obligation to give the heave-offering also remained in force.
67. This is a reference to Isaiah ben Mali di Trani (b. 1200) whose work de' Rossi read in manuscript.
68. B. B.M. 7b.
69. B. Ned. 81a.

more recent times. Thus it would appear to be a kindness and no crime to publicize the defense and to demonstrate that the defect cannot be made good,[70] as is the case of every impossible thing which is sustained by its own nature.[71]

{Moreover I am able to cite reliable witnesses—Tannaim, Amoraim, and Geonim—to prove that it was only in the case of public expositions that our sages were concerned about divulging matters which they had kept hidden. In these situations, one might be anxious about [its impact on] the audience of common people, but this would not apply to written works which were for the consumption of the learned. The discussion among the Tannaim in the first mishnah of tractate Berakhot illustrates my point. Having mentioned the teaching of the sages which had been transmitted orally that the time of the reciting of the [evening] *Shema* extends until midnight, Rabbi then continues to write down the true *halakhah* as revealed by Rabban Gamaliel: "Moreover, wherever the sages prescribe 'until midnight,' the duty (also from his [i.e., Rabbi's] own point of view) lasts all night." The reason for stating "until midnight" was not halakhically determined but "to keep a person far from transgression." Similarly, I can use your own argument which you employed in raising the question about the passage from tractate Shabbat. For you can see that the author of the *baraita* did not refrain from publishing Rabbi Aqiva's statement identifying the "gatherer of wood" with Zelophehad. And yet he himself concludes the passage with Rabbi Judah ben Bathyra's angry reaction to this statement and his rebuke of Rabbi Aqiva. The same argument applies to the passage from the Palestinian Talmud that you cited. It is obvious that Rabbi Eliezer took Rabbi Aqiva to task for his identification of Elihu with Balaam because it was made in public, as is clearly indicated there by the expression, "And Rabbi Aqiva expounded." All this is proof that their only concern was that the information would reach the ears of the masses, but not that it would be put in writing. Moreover you should consider the nature of the man Rabbi Aqiva. For he was not deterred by the tepid attack[72] on him about the gatherer of wood but went on to give his teaching about Elihu in the desire to reveal what he regarded was the truth. However, in the final analysis, one should describe these statements as mere conjecture—this is Rabbenu Sherira Gaon's term which we have cited on many occasions. For he was of the belief that the truth should not be hidden from anybody, and that he who wishes to err will only rage against his foolishness but not against the sages who will publicize it. A similar case involving Amoraim and Geonim arises from the passage in Nedarim in which they say:[73] "He who desires that his vows should be rendered invalid should stand at the beginning of the year and declare." They derived this view from a precise reading of the Mishnah of Rabbi Eliezer ben Jacob. For it is taught in that context: "Rav Huna wished to lecture [on this subject] at the public session." (The commentator[74] notes here: "He intended to lecture on the lesson, 'He who wishes that his vows are rendered invalid.' ") Rav then said to him: "The Tanna has deliberately obscured the issue so that vows should not be taken lightly, while you want to teach it in the public

70. Cf. Eccl. 1:15.
71. De' Rossi is using the concept of the impossible as described by Maimonides in the *Guide* III, ch. 15.
72. 'Deterred . . . attack,' lit. he was not scalded by the tepid water. Cf. B. Ber. 16b.
73. B. Ned. 23b.
74. De' Rossi is referring to the commentary on Nedarim which was wrongly ascribed to Rashi.

session." Thus notwithstanding this reprimand, the Gemara in this selfsame passage and others, all the Geonim and codifiers without exception, did not refrain from recording it overtly in writing. This may be seen in the relevant texts of the Rambam,[75] the Semag,[76] and the Ṭur[77] and all other codifiers who did not employ subterfuge in their discussion of the issue. Then there are also other passages in Nedarim regarding a person who vows by the Torah[78] or by a fishing net.[79] When such vows are made by the ignorant, they are suspected. Then they also say:[80] "The soft part of linseed is good with preserve, but this may not be told to the ignorant." Then in tractate Menaḥot it is stated:[81] "[Even though a man reads the *Shema* morning and evening he has fulfilled the precept], *This book of the law shall not depart from your mouth* (Josh. 1:8:). It is forbidden to say this in the presence of an ignorant person. Abbaye cursed the one who says this in the presence of an ignorant person." There are other such passages and yet the editors of the Gemara did not refrain from recording all these details in writing for the edification of the knowledgeable. Such then should be your appraisal of other cases of a similar nature which they indicated should be kept private. Then there is the statement at the beginning of the *Guide* in which the teacher writes: "Now if somebody explained all those matters in a book, he will in effect be expounding them to thousands of people." You who are living can only understand it through expositions on the Chariot [Ezk. 1:4ff)] or the creation about which he [Maimonides] speaks in that context in agreement with the precautions laid down by our rabbis in Ḥagigah.[82] The reasons for these precautions were the extreme difficulty of the subject matter or else the self-destructiveness of people who are so powerfully motivated to acquire even the slightest bit of knowledge of profound topics, or for some other reason.}[2]

Now as regards your third criticism which you raised after having included a defense of my position in the course of your argument, I shall be content with the following response. What wise man is there who with regard to our discourse would take the slightest notice of any common person and those who sit at street corners who have no knowledge or understanding? Surely it would be appropriate for him to divert them with appropriate words and to say that everything is enacted in accordance with the view of our ancestors as we explained. For in the end, the masses are merely the trumpets of the learned and the sound they produce is determined by how much they blow into them.

Now by means of this study, we have achieved the three advantages that we delineated in chapter 29.[83] You should therefore now consider the statement of our rabbis of

75. *Mishneh Torah,* Nedarim II:4.
76. Moses of Coucy, *Sefer Miṣvot ha-Gadol* (*Semag*), negative commandment 242.
77. Jacob ben Asher, *Tur,* Oraḥ Ḥayyim, par. 619; Yoreh Deʿah, par. 211.
78. B. Ned. 14b.
79. B. Ned. 20a.
80. B. Ned. 49a.
81. B. Men. 99b. But it should be noted that the statement in Abbaye's name is not in the Talmud but in the passage as cited in the Yalqut II, par. 6 to Josh. 1:8.
82. M. Ḥag. 2:1: "The forbidden unions may not be expounded before three people nor the story of Creation before two nor the Chariot before one alone unless he is a sage that understands his own knowledge."
83. I.e. to acquire the truth, to explain Scripture and to understand the futility of computations regarding the messianic era.

blessed memory in Bava Batra[84] which regards the mishnah in chapter 17 of Kelim.[85] Discussing the subject of fraudulent representation, Rabbi Johanan ben Zakkai said, "Woe to me if I should speak. [Woe to me if I should not speak]." Finally he did speak, basing his decision on the verse, *for the paths of the Lord are straight; [the righteous can walk on them while sinners stumble on them]* (Hos. 14:10). Then in Bereshit Rabbah[86] Moses is described as having reservations about writing the verse, *And God said: let us make man* (Gen. 1:26): "The Holy One blessed be He said to him: "Write, *But those who in the crookedness act corruptly [let the Lord make them go the way of evildoers]* (Ps. 125:5)." And in tractate Avodah Zarah the elders respond to the Romans:[87] "Should the Holy One blessed be He destroy the world because of fools?" For the intelligent person will not refrain from his actions or statements by which he hopes to benefit thoughtful people in the fear that fools will embark on wrongdoing and make gashes on their flesh.[88] Rather, they should keep company with the wise and become wise.

Now, good friend, it would appear that I have disposed quite properly of all the criticisms that you raised against me. And yet I shall bless you all my life and regard it to your credit that you did not spontaneously concede and agree with the view of the antagonists which we mentioned. At any rate, it was indeed my intention to repair the customary reckoning without casting aspersions, in the same spirit with which they sent the message from there [i.e., the Land of Israel to the Diaspora] telling that they should be careful not to forsake our mother's Torah.[89] In particular you should know how, for the purpose of the moment, I had given a discourse on this subject in the presence of my close friend, a great Italian teacher. When, for brevity's sake, he was told the chapter headings, he said that one ought to abolish the view of anybody who raises doubts about the statements of the rabbis of blessed memory with regard to this subject. In his opinion, one should pay no attention to the authorities who lengthen the period of the bondage in Egypt nor to those who lengthen the duration of the first Temple to 430 years. Likewise one should not take notice of anybody who, on the basis of the literal account of Scripture, contradicts their view about the length of the second Temple period, and still less consideration should be given to the rumblings of any chronicler who produces new records. The reason he gave was that it was always our duty to accept all their statements at face value and to be completely confident that they were aware of everything that we saw; nevertheless, their point of view was grounded in the knowledge that it was right and correct. We, on the other hand, could not grasp how they worked, since they possessed a broader knowledge than us. This was the main thrust of his views which we should indeed corroborate and asseverate, as the

84. B. B.B. 89b.

85. M. Kel. 17:16.

86. B.R. 8:8 (61). In all the texts of B.R. as noted by Theodor and Albeck, the Psalm verse is not given, but rather the statement "Write, whoever wishes to err may err."

87. B. A.Z. 54b. The elders are asked as to why God does not destroy the objects of idolatry to which the elders respond that since people worship the sun and moon among other things, God would therefore have to destroy the entire world.

88. 'Make gashes on their flesh,' cf. Lev. 21:5.

89. B. Beṣ. 4b. In this passage, they are discussing the need for the observance of two new-moon days in the Diaspora. A message was sent from Palestine to the Diaspora urging them not to depart from ancestral custom.

words of a holy and blessed man. For we know the truth of their statement in Yoma.[90] "The fingernails of the ancients were superior to the belly of the moderns." We discussed all this in chapter 14. Accordingly we could certainly say that when the sages mentioned by us augment the length of the bondage in Egypt and the duration of the first Temple, the restraint appears to be removed such that we can also augment the length of the second Temple period—for it is inconsequential whether the addition to the total is small or large. This has all the more justification given that the essence of any law or belief, as we demonstrated, is not affected. Thus anybody whose thoughts and conduct are irreproachable may have taken on board the responses we have tendered concerning the first 9 years of Hoshea's reign which should be counted with the 410 years, the length of the first Temple and the problematic years of the second Temple. Nevertheless, he may choose to discard into the bottom of the sea all the statements of the authorities and writers that we have cited, and without hypocrisy or flattery declare that we should only take heed of the sages' words who gave life to our spirit and who constantly directed us on the paths of righteousness. May he be blessed by our God and live by his faith in eternal pleasantness. In fact, Rambam of blessed memory has already indicated to us that this is the best path to take. For in the tenth chapter of the Laws of the Sabbatical Year,[91] he states that the sabbatical year occurs in a specific year according to the correct figure at our disposal. But he then says, "All the Geonim, however, have said that they have a tradition," and he agrees with their view. Moreover in one of his responsa[92] he states that the only sabbatical year is the one which he gives in their name. After all, as he said,[93] "tradition and practice are the great pillars in the legal decision process and it is right to rely on them." By the same token, we should not remove the fixed nail of the anno mundi computation which is also an arbitrary figure, and not even in our thoughts should we deviate from ancestral custom. The fact is that anyone who embarks on a critique of their statements and tries to refine them like silver would be best advised not to abandon them halfway through the research and get an erroneous impression of them. Rather he should persevere to grasp and fathom their ideas until he is in a position to justify them which is what we endeavored to do previously in chapters 35 and 40. Now with all other religious or philosophical subjects which the sages of every generation have treated correctly or wrongly, they have produced enlightening arguments about the pure and impure, sometimes decisively, sometimes not. As for me, with integrity and within the bounds of my limited intelligence, in the thrust and parry of the argument, and in the honest debates about which view to accept even in the case of majority opinion, I have submitted several responses before my teachers in all humility[94] in the course of all these chapters of mine. In Ḥullin[95] and tractate Demai of the Palestinian Talmud[96] our rabbis of blessed memory

90. B. Yoma 9b.
91. *Mishneh Torah,* Shemiṭṭah X:5.
92. *Teshuvot,* 389 (vol. 2, 667–68).
93. Shemiṭṭah X:6.
94. 'In all humility,' lit. on the ground. Cf. B. Sanh. 17b where the same expression occurs in reference to Simeon the Temanite to show that he was allowed to take part in the discussion although he was not of the same status as the rabbis.
95. B. Ḥull. 6b.
96. P. Demai 2 (1) 22c.

have told us the story about the tithing of fruits in Bethshean in which Rabbi's brother and other members of his family joined forces to complain against the holy Rabbi and said to him: "Will you regard the place which was regarded as subject to tithes as not liable to tithes? He then submitted to them an exegesis of the following verse, *And he* [Hezekiah] *broke in pieces the brazen serpent that Moses had made, for until those days the children of Israel did offer to it* (2K. 18:4). He posed the question as to how it came to be that from Moses until Hezekiah, no righteous person had come to destroy it. And he concluded: "Surely it must be that his [i.e., Hezekiah's] ancestors left something undone whereby he [Hezekiah] could distinguish himself." Likewise, if generally in this work and specifically in these chapters, the intelligent will find something of benefit which gives reason for rejoicing, we should praise the Lord for good is He who is eternally blessed selah. Then we should express our acknowledgement of the ancients who left us a way by which to distinguish ourselves. In particular we should give that credit to the wise Don Isaac who had intended, as we mentioned previously,[97] to undertake a study of the anno mundi computation; for he thereby opened up this gate through which we could proceed with our heads erect as may be done with any law which they disregarded and permitted.[98] And if our statement on this subject appears either totally or partially void and valueless from the perspective of the sages, may it appear like the letter *vav* written on a trunk as they say in Zevaḥim,[99] and may it be accorded the value given to Rabbi Aqiva's statement in tractate Niddah,[100] the purpose of which was to sharpen the wits of the students so that with good and knowledgeable arguments they would present their witnesses and be vindicated. And even Rabbah, as it states in tractate Berakhot[101] and many other places, used to test the wits of Abbaye. But my pact is with those[102] who posit that everything which has been pronounced in repudiation of the customary anno mundi computation should be taken as right and true until the content of the following useful chapter has been perused.

97. I.e., in ch. 35.
98. Cf. P. Shabb. I (4) 3c.
99. B. Zev. 19b. Since the letter *vav* has a rough-lined surface, it is not visible on a tree-trunk. The expression is therefore used to denote futile discussion.
100. B. Nidd. 45a.
101. B. Ber. 33b.
102. Cf. Is. 59:21.

CHAPTER FORTY-THREE

That one should not expect the advent of the Messiah in the year 5335 [1575] in preference to any other year. Rather, now as always, all times are equally dependent on our God's will.[1]

IN view of the doubts we have raised regarding the aera mundi computation—that the duration of the latter part of the bondage in Egypt, the middle years of the first Temple, and the first years of the second Temple period should be increased—there is good reason to claim that the year 335 of the sixth millennium [i.e., 1575] has passed not simply by a few years, but by decades. I observe the band of sons of prophets[2] who expect the year 5335 to be a day of the Lord in which He shall effect a joyous salvation for his people that will last forever. These men are stirred to array themselves against me with the warrior's sharpened arrows. With one voice they address me thus:

> Jew, this is what we think is right, so why do you produce these visions of yours whereby you disturb the people depriving them of their source of comfort? And why do you dislodge the hope which they hold? For a "goodly man" [i.e., Daniel][3] enunciated that this year 5335 that is nearly upon us would be the end when he said, *Happy is the one who waits and reaches*—once the four thousand years of nothingness and Torah have elapsed—*one thousand three hundred and thirty-five days* (12:12) of the two thousand years of the messianic era.[4] This is further confirmed by those who give a symbolic exegesis of Scripture by counting the numerical value of those two last verses in Daniel (12:12, 13) which come to a total of 5335. Moreover the words "at the end of days"[5] (*le-qeṣ yamin*) amount exactly to 335. Thus one might suppose that Daniel was referring to the figure 1335 as implied by the numerical value of those two verses. And the statement of our patriarch the elder [Jacob], *until he comes to Shiloh* (Gen. 49:10), also somehow supports such a view.[6] The same figure is reached by interpreting the phrase, *And I will keep my countenance hidden* (Deut. 31:18)

1. For a discussion of this subject and the historical background to de' Rossi's treatment, see D. Tamar, "Expectation," 61–88.
2. 'Band . . . prophets,' cf. 1Sam. 19:20.
3. Dan. 10:11.
4. This is a reference to the statement of the Tanna d've Eliyahu (B. A.Z. 9a): "The world is to exist six thousand years: the first two thousand years are void; the next two thousand years are the period of the Torah, and the following two thousand years are the period of the Messiah."
5. I.e., the words which occur in the verse, *But you go on to the end; you shall rest, and arise to your destiny at the end of days* (12:13).
6. The numerical value of Shiloh (but discounting the letter *yod* in the word) is a total of 335. This phrase which occurs in Jacob's blessing of Judah is traditionally interpreted as a reference to the coming of the Messiah.

according to its numerical value.[7] Again the expression *a time, times [and a half]* (Dan. 12:7) is meant to refer to two disparate periods of time, namely, the 480 years that span the period from the exodus from Egypt to the building of the first Temple, and the 410 years during which the Temple stood. This gives a period of 890 years to which is added half of that figure amounting to 1335. And there are many other such examples by means of which our ancestors, the guardians of the faith, gave us indication concerning our time, a time of love,[8] in order to ratify prophetic vision[9] and usher in our righteous Messiah. Particularly relevant is the fact that the kabbalist and expert in Torah, who is the glory of his time, Rabbi Mordechai Dato, recently wrote a work devoted to this subject. He entitled it *Migdal David* after the name of his brother.[10] In the work, he corroborates and confirms the view that there is considerable reason for Israel to expect the beginning of the redemption and the rebuilding of the Temple in the year [5]335. He bases his view on the statement in chapter 28 of Pirqe d'Rabbi Eliezer that the duration of the four kingdoms Persia, Greece, Edom [i.e., Rome], and Ishmael [i.e., the Mohammedan Empire] will last one day according to the time scale of the Holy One blessed be He, less two-thirds of an hour.[11] And he also uses chapter 48 of the same work[12] to demonstrate that 1,000 years are 12 hours for God. Consequently, one complete day of 24 hours is equivalent to 2,000 years for the blessed Lord. Subtract two-thirds of an hour which is equivalent to 55 years, 6 months, and 20 days, and 1544 years, 5 months, and 10 days are counted from the beginning of the Persian Empire, namely, 52 years after the destruction of the first Temple, as is stated in the Seder Olam[13] which is 18 years before the building of the [second] Temple. This implies that the era of the domination of the four kingdoms will come to an end on the tenth of Adar 335. He also provides additional support for his view from Midrash ha-Neʿelam which is included in the Zohar where it is stated that redemption will take place in the sixth millennium.[14] And it is taught in that context: "The building of the Temple will precede the ingathering of the exiles and the ingathering of the exiles will precede the resurrection of the dead as is written, *The Lord rebuilds Jerusalem,* and after that, *He gathers in the exiles of Israel,* and after that, *He heals their broken hearts* (Ps. 147:2, 3)."[15] And it is further taught: "The ingathering of the exiles will precede the resurrection of the dead by 40 years."[16] This is all described at length in this passage. Thus the aforementioned sage [i.e., Dato] was right in his judgment that the Temple would be rebuilt in the year 335, that in the year 368 the ingathering of the exiles would take place, and that in the year 408 our

7. The verses read: *Then my anger will flare up against them and I will abandon them. . . . Yet I will keep my countenance hidden on that day because of the evil they have done in turning to other gods* (Deut. 31:17, 18). The implication of the numerical value of the expression *Yet I will keep my countenance hidden* which amounts to 1,336 is that when that period of time has elapsed, the period of punishment will be completed and the new era begun.

8. 'Our time, a time of love.' The expression is based on Ezk. 16:8. De' Rossi is clearly taking into account the Targum which renders the expression, "a time of redemption."

9. Cf. Dan: 9:24.

10. Mordechai Dato (1529–91?) was a noted Italian kabbalist. Most of his works are still in manuscript and the *Migdal David* is in the Bodleian Library (Ms. Opp. Add. 153). On Dato, see R. Bonfil, "A Sermon."

11. *PRE,* ch. 28. One day of God is equivalent to one thousand years—this calculation is based on Ps. 90:4, *For in Your sight a thousand years are like yesterday.*

12. Ibid., ch. 48: "The Egyptians only enslaved the Israelites for one hour of the day of the Holy One blessed be He, i.e., eighty-three and a third years." If God's day equals one thousand years and there are twelve hours to the day, the hour of God's day equals eighty-three and a third years.

13. Seder Olam, ch. 27 (123).

14. Zohar, Midrash ha-Neʿelam I, 139, col. d.

15. Ibid. I, 139, col. b.

16. Ibid.

dead would be resurrected. And he proves his view from several other statements and hints of our sages. Support is offered us by Rabbenu Hananel whose opinions are based on tradition and whose view is mentioned by Rabbenu Baḥya in his commentary.[17] So you[18] who we know to be waiting for salvation just like us, by virtue of upholding a contradictory view, are undermining our position and are removing the anchor of hope which has been held fast securely for us.[19] What prompts you to behave in this fashion? What has happened to your common sense and where is your compassion?

Truly, you who are wise and who in your integrity can take consideration of everything which is found to be impaired, please pay attention to my replies to these good men. First, it is appropriate to mention the case of Rabbi Hillel. Even he had the audacity to claim that there is no Messiah for Israel.[20] This is an unparalleled wicked statement. When he put forward the reason for his view, namely, that they had already enjoyed the messianic era in the time of Hezekiah, the sages of his time did not devour him,[21] nor did they charge him with wickedness. On the contrary, they prayed for his welfare and said, "May the Lord forgive him," thus implying that he belonged to the category of the righteous mortal who deserves absolution for his sins. In adducing proof of the falseness of his words, they articulated and laid down[22] an irrefutable response, namely: "Hezekiah lived in the time of the first Temple. Yet Zechariah, prophesying in the time of the second Temple proclaimed, *Rejoice greatly, O daughter of Zion, O daughter of Jerusalem, behold your king comes to you* (9:9)." Thus anyone who offers a reason for his views such that they appear to be well founded and not heretical will receive the approbation of the sages, and his mistake will not be regarded as a sin. After all, not everybody can be an expert in all cases,[23] and once the error has finally been exposed either of itself or when the teachers's opinion is heard, the truth of the matter from which we will not deviate shall be clarified.

My next point is as follows. It is surely probable that the wise who consider all matters to their logical conclusion might regard our statement about the additional years, which signifies that the date 5335 has already passed, as not only posing no danger but may, with divine help, prove advantageous, yielding fruit which in its due season will taste sweet to every palate. There will be the essential benefit that is gained from resolving the doubts which were raised with regard to holy Writ and from elucidating Scripture, as we said. But not only this—for there will be the means of saving many souls and preventing the mindless from stumbling into the disaster which lies in wait for them, God forbid. May they be far removed from wickedness.

This is indeed my opinion. For all informed people are aware that in the past, many

17. Baḥya ben Asher to Ex. 12:40 argues that three figures are found for the duration of the Egyptian exile: 210, 400, 430. The duration of the exile will therefore also have three terms which are enumerated in Dan. 12:11, 12, namely, 1150, 1290, 1335. The exile could not extend beyond the last date.

18. This is allegedly addressed to de' Rossi.

19. 'Anchor . . . fast,' cf. Is. 22:25.

20. B. Sanh. 99a.

21. De' Rossi is playing on the word *akhlu* (which literally means ate), thus echoing the statement of Rabbi Hillel: "They already *akhlu* the Messiah in the time of Hezekiah."

22. 'Laid down.' The expression used by de' Rossi is "*im ha-sefer*" which is a quotation from Esther 9:25, an obscure expression which appears to mean "by letter."

23. Lit. not everybody can learn the laws of all matters.

Jews of complete integrity calculated the end of time and set a final end to our exile. You are familiar with the statement of our sages of blessed memory that our rabbis used to expound the verse, *until a time and times and the dividing of time* (Dan. 7:25) [for the purpose of determining the date of the advent of the Messiah], whereas Rabbi Aqiva quoted the verse, *In just a little while longer, I shall shake the heavens and earth* (Hag. 2:6) [for the same purpose].[24] Of a similar nature is the statement:[25] "Rabbi Ḥanina said: 'If four hundred years have elapsed since the destruction of the Temple and somebody tells you [to buy a field which is worth one thousand dinars for one dinar, do not buy it.']" This is explained by Rashi in a similar vein.[26] However, it is possible to interpret all or some of these opinions in accordance with Elijah's statement to Rav Judah:[27] " 'The world shall not exist less than eighty-five Jubilees and in the final Jubilee [the son of David shall come.' He asked him: 'At the beginning or the end?' He replied: 'I do not know.' He asked: 'Shall it be completed?' He said: 'I do not know.'] Then Rav Ashi addressed him: 'Before that do not expect him; afterwards you may wait for him.' " I discovered that in his *Sefer ha-Mahadurot,* Rabbi Isaiah [di Trani] the elder makes the following point with specific reference to Rabbi Ḥanina's statement: "The teacher (i.e., Rashi) explained this statement in connection with the final redemption. But according to Geonic responsa which I read, it was prompted by the fact that it was a period of great oppression and bloodshed for Jews. This seems to me to be the essential meaning of the passage." I would agree with him since in the *Epistle* of Rav Sherira[28] and Rabad's *Sefer ha-Qabbalah,*[29] it is recorded that in the year 781 of the Seleucid era, Amemar was put to the gallows[30] and that many troubles and disasters befell our people.

And yet it was not only these Tannaim and Amoraim and others of their ranks who chose to impose on us a fixed point for redemption.[31] There were also such comparatively modern and recent authorities as Rabbenu Saadiah,[32] Rashi, Ralbag [Gersonides] in his commentary on Daniel,[33] Rabbi Abraham [bar Ḥiyya] the prince in his work *Megillat ha-Megalleh,*[34] Ramban [Nahmanides] in his *Sefer ha-Qeṣ,*[35] Rabbi Abraham Zacuto in his discourse on astronomy[36] and his brother-in-law Rabbi Abraham

24. B. Sanh. 97b. Various verses are used in this passage to determine the date of the advent of the Messiah, but R. Nathan claims that all the calculations are false and that the three verses quoted here (Hab. 2:3, Dan. 7:25, Hag. 2:6) refer to the Hasmonean, Herodian, and Bar Kokhba periods.

25. B. A.Z. 9b.

26. In other words, the one dinar would be wasted because this would be the time for the final redemption.

27. B. Sanh. 97b.

28. *Iggeret,* 96.

29. Abraham ibn Daud, *Sefer ha-Qabbalah* (41–42).

30. Sherira and ibn Daud both refer to Amemar's murder, but they do not state that his death was by hanging.

31. De' Rossi uses imagery from Ezk. 9:4, *and put a mark on the foreheads of the men who moan and groan because of all the abominations.*

32. Saadiah Gaon (882–942) treats the subject in the eighth chapter of his *Emunot ve-Deot,* in his commentary on Daniel and in his *Sefer ha-Galui.*

33. Gersonides maintains that there is a clear reference to the final redemption in Dan. 12.

34. Abraham bar Ḥiyya (d. 1136). De' Rossi read his *Megillat ha-Megalleh* in manuscript.

35. De' Rossi read the work which is also called *Sefer ha-Ge'ulah* (written about 1263) in manuscript.

36. Abraham ben Samuel Zacuto. According to M. Beit-Arié and M. Idel, "Ma'amar al ha-Qeṣ" (174–75), this is a reference to the work which de' Rossi himself transcribed (his copybook is in the National

Halevi in his work *Meshare Qitrin,*[37] and they were succeeded by the great community leader Don Isaac [Abravanel] in his work *Mayyane ha-Yeshuʿah.*[38] Each of these writers set a final end to the darkness of exile, in truth following the precedent set by the Tannaim who deserved to experience this great event. It is all accessible in their works which have been disseminated among our people. And yet, as we ourselves have witnessed, due to the numerous transgressions, God did not act with us according to their predictions. Many years have passed and every pronouncement regarding the "valley of vision"[39] has failed and nullified is their hope and prospect[40] that they conceived in our regard. As to whether even one of these predictions of theirs was valid and opportune, or rather served as a wicked stumbling block and fraudulent exploitation of some of those embittered persons who wait for that day, historians will give their verdict either orally or in writing; for I would not venture to speak on this matter.

Now, in recent times, these pious men, following in the wake of those who were the first to take this course, have also set the time for the year 335 as we said. Amen, may God act out of kindness to us according to their views. May that "Citadel of David"[41] be a strong and sturdy citadel and not an ephemeral one. However, with all due respect to those distinguished authorities who initiated such speculations, it would appear that their desire got the better of them, and that, beguiled by their human fallible wisdom, some of them were led to erect a monument which had no validity in the holy place.[42] If they did read, they did not read it in sufficient depth nor did they heed that which is taught in Sanhedrin:[43] "Rabbi Nathan said: 'This verse pierces and descends to the abyss, *For the vision is yet for an appointed time, but at the end it shall speak and not lie; though he tarry, wait for him because it will surely come, it will not tarry* (Hab. 2:3).' " As Rashi of blessed memory commented: "Just as the abyss is infinite, so too, there is no person who can fathom the depths of this verse." Of a similarly maledictory nature is the statement of Rabbi Jonathan: "Blasted be the bones of those who calculate the end and thereby delay the time of redemption."[44] In other words, God alone knows about that day, and we should be content in the knowledge that the blessed Lord is waiting to enlighten us and to show us compassion. We shall speak about this further. The true sage Rambam of blessed memory gave a similar treatment of the main points of this subject at the end of his *Yad Ḥazaqah* and in his commentary on Mishnah Sanhedrin and at length in his *Letter to Yemen.* How much more serious is the error of certain sages such as Rabbi Abraham bar Ḥiyya (in his *Megillat ha-Megalleh*) and Don Isaac (in his gate of heaven)[45]

Library Jerusalem Ms. 3935) which contains Zacuto's eschatological calculations for the years 1504–31 derived from the book of Daniel and a description of eclipses and their astrological significance and a horoscope which Zacuto composed in Tunis for the years 1504–17.

37. Abraham ben Eliezer Halevi (1460–1528?). The *Meshare Qitrin* is a commentary on Daniel.
38. *Mayyane ha-Yeshuʿah* which Abravanel wrote in 1496 is a commentary on Daniel.
39. Cf. Is. 22:1.
40. Cf. B. Eruv. 21b.
41. A playful reference to the title of Dato's work.
42. I.e., they used their human wisdom to make calculations which belong to God's domain.
43. B. Sanh. 97b.
44. Ibid.
45. This is a reference to the subdivision into gates which Abravanel inserted into his Mayyene ha-Yeshuʿah from the twelfth mayyan onwards (402, col. b).

at the end of his commentary on Daniel, who imagined that they could bring this arcane matter to light by means of the laws that govern the stars and the great conjunctions of the heavenly hosts. Although they did preface their statements with a partial defense, going so far as to make clear that their opinion was certainly not dependent on this [i.e., astrology], yet the entire subject was surely of itself forbidden;[46] it would have been more appropriate that their writing never saw the light of day. Who would pay attention to them when Scripture is replete with verses which demonstrate that God apportioned the heavenly constellations to the gentiles, but not to us His chosen people—it is the nations that are dismayed by them, not Israel,[47] for ever since He formed this people for Himself, whatever happened to them whether for good or bad was determined[48] by the mouth of God. The verse, *Those nations that you are about to dispossess do indeed resort to soothsayers and augurs; to you, however, the Lord your God has not assigned the like* (Deut. 18:14), prompted our sages of blessed memory to state that Israel is immune from both universal and individual influence of the planets.[49] How then can they attribute this central event of redemption totally or partially to the aspect of amity or to the favorable position of the light-bearing stars; it is the Lord alone who determines whether it should come to pass. This is all the more the case nowadays when the experts in this discipline put forward views and hypotheses on this subject that are contradictory and mutually exclusive. The two fore-mentioned sages claim that our ancestors were redeemed from Egypt when the great conjunction[50] was under the influence of the planet Pisces and that this conjunction always signifies the rise and prosperity of Israel. But the great astrologer ibn Ezra wrote as follows: "The phrase *who is bringing you out [from the labors of the Egyptians]* (Ex. 6:7) signifies that it was due to the conjunction of the great configuration of the uppermost [i.e., Saturn and Jupiter] planets[51] that they were still in exile." Similarly he wrote:[52] "It was due to the configuration of the conjunction that their exile in Egypt was prolonged. But because they cried out to the Lord, He saved them. This is what happens to the individual and therefore happy is the one who keeps the Torah."[53] In his previous comment on the incident of the golden calf which of course happened in the year of their exodus from Egypt, he wrote: "Astrologers say that the great conjunction of the uppermost planets was then

46. Lit. a piece of prohibition. De' Rossi is using the talmudic phrase in B. Ket. 22a which is used to refer to a woman who declares herself married and then retracts. In the same way, the writers used astrological data to determine the time of redemption and then retracted by declaring their view as nonauthoritative.

47. Cf. Jer. 10:2.

48. 'Determined,' lit. encamped and journeyed. Cf. Num. 9:20, *they remained encamped at a command of the Lord, and broke camp at a command of the Lord.*

49. B. Shabb. 156a; Tanḥuma, shofeṭim, 10.

50. I.e., the conjunction of Saturn and Juppiter.

51. Lit. servants. According to Y. Tzvi Langerman, "Astrological themes," 52 and n. 61, the use of the word "servants" to denote the planets indicates ibn Ezra's view of the slavish, inflexible nature of the celestial bodies.

52. Ibn Ezra to Ex. 33:21.

53. See Langermann's discussion ("Astrologial themes," 54–56) of ibn Ezra's treatment of this theme. Ibn Ezra is concerned with explaining the method of avoiding astral decrees by calling for reliance on God who may direct the people as to how to avoid astral decrees.

under Taurus. This is false—it could only have been under Aquarius, for according to the science of astrology this is Israel's star. Many people over the centuries have experienced this to be the case and I, too, have observed this phenomenon."[54]

So, reader, you should take stock and realize that the basic opinions of these three sages batter each other with the flank and shoulder,[55] and that the specific content of their views are similarly contradictory. We will therefore stand by our view[56] and assert that Israel's well-being is not dependent on the heavens. When the Lord desires to effect salvation for those that fear Him, He has no desire that the stars and planets should from that moment suddenly give indication of His action.[57]

An even more extreme illustration of this point may certainly be observed in the statement of the holy sage, the author of the *Kuzari.* In section 4, on the basis of the *Sefer Yeṣirah* attributed to our patriarch Abraham[58] he demonstrates that the blessed Lord used the sibillant letters [i.e., *he, vav, yod*] for the creation of His world and that according to certain philosophers, there was a chain of emanation of an angel from an angel and spheres from angels—this is Avicenna's view which is cited and refuted by the Christian doctor Aquinas.[59] Then the king raised the question:[60] "Why are the letters *alef, vav, yod,* or an angel or a sphere required when we believe in the simple will of God. As we say, *Through His bounty He constantly renews every day the work of creation.*[61] The holy sage then replied: 'You are quite right, king of the Kazars. This is the truth, the real faith, and everything extraneous to it should be abandoned. Perhaps this was Abraham's point of view before . . ."[62] The subject is elucidated at length. A similar view is expressed by Bar Sheshet in his responsum (157).[63] Study the passage. The wise author of *Aqedat Yiṣḥaq*[64] already completely decried the astronomical views connected with the time of our redemption as expressed by the author of the *Megillat ha-Megalleh* and those who follow in his wake. Previously, ibn Ezra in his commentary to Daniel and the great sage Rambam in his *Epistle to Yemen* (as will be shown presently) had completely undermined their view;[65] in their estimation, the star-gazing people who

54. Ibn Ezra to Ex. 31:18.

55. Cf. Ezk. 34:21.

56. Lit. stand by our burnt offerings, cf. Num. 23:6.

57. 'Suddenly give indication of His action,' lit. suddenly shoot him. Cf. Ps. 64:5.

58. Judah Halevi (*Kuzari* IV, par. 25). De' Rossi, unlike Halevi, is clearly doubting the ascription of the work to Abraham by using the words "attributed to." The work is a mystical cosmogony using the letters of the Hebrew alphabet, variously dated between the third and ninth centuries.

59. Thomas Aquinas, *Summa theologica* I, quaestio 47, articulus 1: "Utrum rerum multitudo et distinctio sit a Deo."

60. *Kuzari* IV, par. 26.

61. The question is taken from the liturgy for the daily morning service.

62. *Kuzari* IV, par. 27. Halevi goes on to say that prior to God's revelation to Abraham, he used astrology, but after revelation, he understood that his only endeavor should be to strive for understanding of God without the aid of astrology and the like.

63. Isaac bar Sheshet Perfet, *She'elot* (67, col. b). In this responsum addressed to his friend Amran b. Mervan Efrati of Oran, Bar Sheshet discusses the question of the kabbalists' use of *Sefirot* in their prayers. They "direct one prayer to one *Sefirah,* another to another *Sefirah.*" He then states: "Who introduced this [form of prayer] to us? Is it not simply better to pray to the blessed Lord who knows how to refer each petition to the proper agency."

64. Isaac Arama, *Aqedat Yiṣḥaq,* pequde, gate 56 (207a ff.).

65. Lit. swung the axe against him. This is a talmudic phrase (B. Pes. 32b et al.).

vaunt their expertise in giving timely predictions[66] of future events are fools. In the *Epistle* mentioned above, Rambam of blessed memory also derides all those who would propound a similar view, namely, that the lack of knowledge and inadequate cultivation of learning in his time was to be attributed to the fact that the Jews were under the influence of the earthly trigon.[67] (I.e., they were under the influence of the three earthly signs of the Zodiac—Taurus, Gemini, Capricorn[68]—as is demonstrated in the work on judicial astronomy written by the Arabic writer Alcabitius[69] as well as in the *Ephemerides* of Moletius.[70]) Thus they were not under the influence of the fiery trigon (i.e., Aries, Leo, Sagittarius). For the fact is, as the Rav [i.e., Maimonides] proves, in his days of the patriarchs "who are the chariot,"[71] which means that they carry the Throne of Glory in their hearts and have a true apprehension of God, and likewise in the days of David and Solomon and other such notables, they were under the influence of the earthly trigon; and yet, as is well known, they were wise and discerning.

The main point is that Israel's actions or expectation for their redemption cannot be dependent on the constellations; rather, it is the Lord alone who effects our salvation and it is He who knows the time of its occurrence. It might even occur today, if, as that old man[72] said, you will listen to His voice.[73] He has no dealings with the stars whatsoever. By the Lord, while we do not claim that He will use them as the agents of His will in these lower regions, this does not mean that before that moment they can indicate that which the Lord might ordain them to do in the future at a moment's notice. For this is not an event that will take place and come to pass in like manner to the other happenings which affect human beings. What then remains to be said regarding the sages of our generation to whom we shall now return, who, as we wrote, were determined to set the year 5335 as the date of redemption? It is surely evident that they should have desisted from that endeavor and dismissed it from their thoughts by taking into consideration the experiences and examples of the sages themselves on whose authority they relied. It is indeed true that anyone who has not set eyes on Ramban's *Sefer ha-Ge'ulah* in which he assembles proofs and reasons for the year 118 [1358] on the

66. 'Timely predictions.' De' Rossi uses the obscure phrase in Is. 50:4 which commentators such as Kimḥi explain as signifying "to speak timely words."

67. *Iggeret Teman,* 160. The Zodiac was divided into four quarters which were called trigons, and three of the twelve signs of the Zodiac were located in each trigon.

68. The earthly trigon consists of Taurus, Virgo (not Gemini), and Sagittarius.

69. Alcabitius is the Latin name for al-Qabisi abd al-Aziz ibn Uthman (fl. 950 Aleppo). His introduction to the art of astrology was translated in Latin by John of Spain in 1144 and entitled *Alcabitii ad Magisterium Iudiciorum Astrorum Isagoge.* It was widely disseminated and printed many times in the fifteenth and sixteenth centuries. De' Rossi refers to Differentia Prima, section 4 of the work in which Alcabitius describes the trigons (*triplicitates*).

70. This is a reference to Josephus Moletius (Moleto: b. 1531) who was an important mathematician and was involved in the formulation of the Gregorian calendar. De' Rossi refers to the first book of his *Ephemerides* which deals with the trigons, "De Triangulis sive triplicatibus signorum."

71. Maimonides is using the statement in B.R. 82:6 (983): "The patriarchs are God's chariot for it says, *and God went up from him* (Gen. 17:22)."

72. I.e., Elijah.

73. This is a reference to the discussion in B. Sanh. 98a about the time of the Messiah's arrival. Joshua ben Levi is told that the Messiah will come "today." He goes to Elijah and expresses his disappointment that this had not happened. Elijah then explains that the promise is conditional as is demonstrated by the verse, *today, if you will listen to His voice* (Ps. 95:7).

basis of Scripture and kabbalistic works, has never seen the date for redemption established and fixed on such a firm basis.[74] And this is quite apart from the fact that he was a great authority. Now had I, who read the book three times over (I have really absorbed it thoroughly), been present [i.e., in Ramban's time], I would have humbly reiterated Rav Joseph's words of prayer: "May he come and may I be worthy of sitting in the shade of the dung of his ass."[75] This is all the more reasonable given that several distinguished authorities agreed with him. As the wise Don Isaac mentioned:[76] "The Gaon Rav Saadiah, the prince Rabbi Abraham bar Ḥiyya, Rashi, Ramban, and Ralbag calculated that the Messiah would come in the year 118 [1358]." Similarly, in his commentary, Rabbenu Baḥya puts forward what he regards as substantial evidence for that final date culled from holy Writ and rabbinic statements.[77] Reading those passages, you would become convinced of their coherence; this, then is how they came to their dictum that the Messiah would come in the year 118. And Zacut and the author of *Meshare Qitrin* set the date for 5250 [1490]. They all had sweet dreams, but their expectations for salvation were deluded. The wise Don Isaac who followed in their wake also imagined that he could pinpoint the end, but his vision was likewise deluded. And although it was according to instructive indications that they all established their opinions on a firm intellectual basis and with a variety of proofs, ultimately it was realized that they were on a flimsy foundation since not one of us knows those secret matters. Their views were presumptuous and unacceptable to the Lord. Thus it would have been right and proper for these later authorities to have become regarded as true sages by refraining from uttering such views and disassociating themselves from the four generations mentioned in Shir ha-Shirim Rabbah on the verse, *I adjure you, O daughters of Jerusalem* (S.S. 2:7) who tried to hasten the end and came to grief.[78] Our argument has all the more validity given that they are asserting that it is about to happen in our generation within a few days—with God's help it is imminent. They are not saying that we shall confront it in the distant future which would have engaged the defense of Rabbi Moses [Maimonides] of blessed memory. We shall discuss this presently with regard to Rabbenu Saadiah and other like-minded people. With regard to the hope that they gained from the final words of Daniel, you who are wise should please consider that the angel in the book of Zechariah expressed his wonder about the brief period of 70 years [of the Babylonian exile] in the following words, *How long will You withhold pardon from Jerusalem and the towns of Judah which You placed under a curse seventy years ago?* (1:12). And in the book of Daniel the holy being says, *How long will the vision last [the regular offering be forsaken because of transgression, the Sanctuary be surrendered and the host be trampled?]* (8:13). This referred to the three years and few days when Antiochus Epiphanes abolished the continual offering and set up his appalling abomination [in the Temple]. (In his

74. This is a rhetorical flourish based on such expressions in B. Sukk. 51b as "He who has not seen the double colonnade of Alexandria has never seen the glory of Israel."

75. B. Sanh. 98b.

76. Abravanel, *Mayyane ha-Yeshuʿah,* 11, tamar 10 (398 col. b).

77. Baḥya ben Asher to Gen. 2:3 (53–58) quoting Nahmanides argues that the Messiah son of Joseph will come in 1358.

78. S.S.R. to S.S. 2:7. The oath mentioned here is also repeated in S.S. 3:5, 5:8, and 8:4 and is homiletically interpreted to correspond to the four attempts at hastening the end: in the time of Amram, [Eliezer bar] Dinaeus, Bar Kokhba, and Shutelach son of Ephraim.

commentary on Daniel, the Christian translator states that he placed a statue of Jupiter there.[79]) And as to the prophecy that was to take about 250 years to come to pass,[80] the angel says to Daniel, *I am going to inform you of what will happen when wrath is at an end for it refers to the time appointed for the end* (8:19). He then says, *Now you keep the vision a secret for it pertains to far-off days* (8:26). The angel sets a limit to his words, namely, 70 weeks [of years] (9:24). You will notice that in the first chapter of the first book of Maccabees, which is entirely devoted to the events related to Antiochus, they specifically refer to the appalling abomination which he placed in the Sanctuary.[81] Josephus, too, like many of our commentators, interprets those verses in relation to Antiochus.[82] Ibn Ezra interprets the verse, *For twenty-three hundred evenings and morning—then the Sanctuary shall be cleansed* (8:14) in the following way:[83] "In my view, the correct meaning is that Israel suffered great tribulation for six years and [some] months in the time of Antiochus—this is what is written in the Greek book. The figure given here refers to actual days. *Twenty-three hundred mornings* signifies six solar years, three months, and [some] days or three and a half lunar years. . . . This is what the angel said, *And the vision about evenings and mornings is true* (8:26)." He corroborates this interpretation in his commentary on the Pentateuch.[84] Now we already mentioned that chapter 1 of the first book of Maccabees—in my opinion this is the Greek book to which ibn Ezra refers—describes Antiochus's oppression of Israel from the year 143 of the Seleucid era to the year 148. In the year 149, as is described in books one and two of Maccabees,[85] he was broken by supernatural means for he was gripped by pains, his flesh was covered by worms, and he wasted away. It was in the year 145 that calamity on calamity befell us—it was then that the continual offering was abolished and the appalling abomination placed in the Sanctuary. According to Josephus's *War,* this happened over a period of three and a half years.[86] Rabad also writes in his *Sefer ha-Qabbalah* that the verse, *From the time the regular offering is abolished and an appalling abomination is set up* (Dan. 12:11) refers to Antiochus's time.[87] Furthermore, in his commentary on Daniel, the Christian translator [Jerome] cites the view of a Greek [Porphyry] who explained all those verses including the last two as a reference to this Antiochus.[88] In the same way, he also explains the expression, *a time, times, and half a time* (Dan. 7:25) which is equivalent to *a time, times, and half a time* (ibid. 12:7) in connection with the *seven times* that correspond to the number of these days.[89] And in

79. Jerome, *Commentaria* to Dan. 8:13 (*P.L.* XXV, col. 537): "Unus angelus interrogat alterum angelum . . . usque ad quod tempus Dei iudicio sub Antiocho rege Syriae templum futurum sit desolatum, et simulacrum Iovis staturum in templo Dei."

80. I.e., the 250 years from Daniel to Antiochus.

81. 1Macc. 1:54.

82. *Ant.* X:276.

83. Ibn Ezra to Dan. 8:25.

84. Ibn Ezra to Gen. 4:4 (the comment refers to the expression in Gen. 4:3 *And it was at the end of days*).

85. 1Macc. 6:8; 2Macc. 9:8,9.

86. *Bellum* I:32.

87. Ibn Daud does not refer explicitly to this verse in any part of the *Sefer ha-Qabbalah.*

88. Jerome, *Commentaria* to Dan. 12:11 (*P.L.* XXV, col. 579). De' Rossi does not point out that Jerome does not agree with Porphyry's view.

89. Ibid., (cols. 577–78). Jerome alludes to the *seven times* of Dan. 4:13, 20, 29 as seven years, i.e., three and a half and three and a half.

his *Recognitio,*[90] the bishop Eugubinus cites Theodoretus, an early Christian from Greece[91] who interpreted the phrase, *Ships come from the quarter of Kittim; they subject Asshur, subject Eber. They, too, shall perish forever* (Num. 24:24) as a reference to Alexander. For at the beginning of the first book of Maccabees, it is explicitly stated that he came from the land of Kittim[92] which is (according to Josephus[93]) the island of Cyprus—for in his time there was an ancient city in that location called Kittim. And he states that Balaam prophesied that the Greek Empire would subjugate Asshur, namely, that with the downfall of Darius, all Syria and Assyria would come under his power. He also states that Greek kings would subjugate the Jews who are called the sons of Eber during the episode with Antiochus and that he, too, would finally perish forever[94] as is known to have happened. One must accept, however, that these explanations are not conclusive for all mysteries are not divulged to us.[95] However, it may be that they do contain some slight truth. The statement, *From the time the regular offering is abolished . . . it will be a thousand two hundred and ninety days. Happy the one that waits and reaches one thousand three hundred and thirty-five days* (Dan. 12:11, 12) alludes to the forty-five following days which is the difference between the two figures [i.e., 1290 and 1335]. For perhaps the battles of Judah the Maccabee were prolonged this amount of days before the Jews had rest from their enemies and he had cleansed the land of his people by the purification of the Sanctuary—for surely, there is nobody who can wait and reach such a number of years.[96] Now inquiring scholar, please apply your mind and consider what implication this might have for us. Praised be the Lord—for even if these final words of Daniel do not relate to this exiled force,[97] there are in fact the earlier prophecies about the stone that was not hewn out by hands (2:34) and the human being who came with the clouds of heaven (7:13) and several other prophecies of other prophets which are collated in an intelligent and thoughtful manner by the wise Don Isaac in his work *Mashmia Yeshuʿah.* These prophecies fortify the faltering and encourage the fainthearted to be strong and courageous.[98]

The letter *nun* that occurs in the expression *leqeṣ yamin* [at the end of days] (Dan. 12:12) is likewise found in *lamḥot melakhin* (to destroy kings; Pr. 31:3) and in *lo yaʾamin ba-ḥayyin* (may he live with no assurance of life; Job 24:22). {And as Ibn Janaḥ points out in his *Sefer ha-Riqmah,*[99] there are many other usages of this final *nun* (in 1K. 11:33; Ezk. 4:9; 26:18; Lam. 1:4; Job 36:10).} In Midrash Tehillim, our rabbis of blessed

90. Augustinus Steuchus, *Recognitio,* 171v.
91. Theodoretus of Cyrus (b. 393) was Bishop of Lyons.
92. 1Mac. 1:1: *After Alexander son of Phillip the Macedonian who came from the land of Kittim.*
93. *Ant.* I:128.
94. 'Perish . . . forever,' cf. Num. 24:20.
95. Cf. Dan. 4:6.
96. In other words, nobody can live to see a thousand and more years; consequently the verse refers to days rather than to years. Thus, de' Rossi disagrees with the views of many of the commentators, such as Rashi and Nahmanides, who interpret the days as years and use the figure to calculate the date of the advent of the Messiah.
97. 'This exiled force,' cf. Ob. 1:20. I.e., these verses in Daniel do not relate to our final redemption.
98. In other words, the many prophecies about the final redemption give reason for hope, and one should not be affected should the one prophecy in Daniel, as understood by Dato and others, prove to have failed to come to pass.
99. Jonah (Abulwalid Merwan) ibn Janaḥ, *Sefer ha-Riqmah,* gate 7 (vol. 1, 111).

memory did not interpret the final *nun* [in Dan. 12:13] in a numerological sense but as an allusion to the verse, *Deliver with Your right hand [yeminkha] and answer me* (Ps. 60:7).[100] Study the passage for yourself. But as regards the phrase "until he come to Shilo," disregarding the fact that everybody imposes great significance to the incidence of the letter *yod*[101] in the word "Shilo," it is actually enough to inform them of its rendering in the Targum [ps.] Jonathan ben Uzziel which reads, "until the King Messiah comes, the youngest of the sons." This is certainly an allusion to David who was the youngest son. He derived this rendering from the expression *The afterbirth (u-ve shilyatah) [that issues from between her legs]* (Deut. 28:57). He then concludes his rendering of the verse [i.e., *and the homage of peoples be his* (Gen. 49:10)] "and because of him the peoples will melt away." For he understands the words "the homage" (*yiqhat*) in the sense of the word *tiqehenah* in the phrase, *his teeth shall be blunted* (Jer. 31:28). Now if one prefers Kallir's interpretation,[102] that he [the Messiah] is David himself—which accords with the view that the verse, *and my body will rest secure* (Ps. 16:9) is a reference to David—there was no need for a second birth and the renewal of the soul of the Messiah. All this is cited by the Rav Recanati on pericope *va-yeshev* with regard to the sons of Judah.[103] What then can one suggest? In view of this,[104] the prediction that the staff shall not depart from Judah perhaps then refers to the preeminence of Judah over the tribes and princes, *Let [the tribe of] Judah go up first* (Jud. 1:2) and *Though Judah became more powerful than his brothers and a leader came from him* (1Chr. 5:2). Moreover, you will notice that in his Laws of the Kings,[105] Rambam mentions the rabbinic interpretation of Balaam's prophecy in which they describe David as the Messiah who was designated as savior of our people. And as regards the passage in Midrash ha-Neʿelam, you have heard my observations about the work in chapter 19.[106] However, you should know that in chapter 1 of Eduyot in the Tosefta it is taught:[107] "Of the number of the generations that have gone before him he is the end. Even though the days and hours are like a hairsbreath in the eyes of the Omnipresent, He only counts generations as it says, *He who announced the generations from the start* (Is. 41:4). And while it states, *And they shall be enslaved and oppressed four hundred years* (Gen. 15:13), it also states, *And the fourth generation shall return here* (ibid. v. 16)." This clarifies the statement in the second chapter of Mishnah Eduyot which reads:[108] "The father endows the son with the merit of the number of generations that have gone before him [and of them he is the end.]" This is brought out in Rambam's interpretation of the

100. Mid. Teh. 137:7. In the course of this homily there is a play on the expression *at the end of days,* in which the word for days can also be read as right hand.

101. Lit. see the *yod* as a town. Cf. B. Qidd. 16b.

102. This is a reference to the poem for the service of Hoshanah Rabbah (the seventh day of the festival of Tabernacles) written by the liturgical poet Eliezer Kallir. The poem which begins "Your true salvation has come" contains the line: "A man has sprung forth and the branch is his name—it is David himself."

103. Recanati, *Perush* (34, col. a).

104. I.e., since Jacob's blessing of Judah does not refer to the messianic era.

105. *Mishneh Torah,* Melakhim XI:1.

106. In ch. 19, de' Rossi argues that there were later interpolations in the texts of the Zohar and Midrash ha-Neʿelam. He is thus implying that the interpretation of Jacob's blessing as a reference to the messianic era need not be taken as an authentic view of the Tannaim.

107. T. Ed. 1:14.

108. M. Ed. 2:9.

passage and with even greater clarity in the explanation of Rabad [Abraham ben David] of blessed memory who writes as follows:[109] "All the termini which the Holy One blessed be He assigns for the number of generations He assigns, even though He fixes an end to the years." And in the Mekhilta[110] and the Tanḥuma[111] they compare *And they shall be enslaved and oppressed four hundred years* (Gen. 15:13) with *And the fourth generation shall return here* (ibid. v.16) and state: "How [can both these verses be upheld]? If they repent, I will redeem them after the generations, but if not, I will redeem them after the number of years." Now according to these people who calculate the end, the prophets set a limit to the years, but nothing is said about the generations. In other words, they had decided at that time that he would come when the generation would be totally wicked. If that is the case, our rabbis were engaged in futile controversy about the generation that is totally righteous[112] and to no purpose was their exegesis of the verse, *I the Lord will hasten it in its time* (Is. 60:22):[113] "If they are worthy I will hasten it, if not he will come at the due time." The problem then arises as to why this, the exile of the longest duration, should be deprived of being circumscribed by the number of generations which is the definitive end. It was their axiom that all the termini concerned both years and generations. Thus we learn that it is certainly better to say in unison with our rabbis,[114] "Let my heart not reveal it to my mouth." There is all the more reason to think this way. For according to the Zohar[115] and chapter 30 of Pirqe d'Rabbi Eliezer, various omens will be seen close to the time of the redemption; and yet despite their claim that we have reached that watershed, we have not seen one such omen.

However, apart from everything that has been said, I have a question to put to those sages which they should kindly answer. If, in accordance with Rav Shila's statement, [116] the time of Shilo will really come and mislead us such that it will leave us just as it came to us, and we, God forbid, will not have been saved, how will the messengers of a nation respond?[117] How will the people of impoverished intellect, the downhearted and stubborn restore their faith? What will have come of our dignity? I regard my position on this matter to be correct and consider that our God will regard my action as an acceptable and charitable deed. For I have taken preemptive action and spread my opinion abroad. In other words, according to the computation which was established by the formulators of our calendar as has been discussed above, the year 335 has not yet arrived. However, if those imbued with the Holy Spirit really did prophesy about this time, they were certainly referring to the correct year 335; and there is no doubt that

109. Rabad to M. Ed. 2:9.

110. Mekhilta d'Rabbi Ishmael, bo, pisḥa, 14 (I, 111).

111. Tanḥuma, bo, 9.

112. An allusion to the discussion B. Sanh. 98a: "The son of David will only come in a generation that is either altogether righteous or altogether wicked."

113. B. Sanh. 98a.

114. In B. Sanh. 99a, it is stated "I have revealed it to my heart but not to my limbs." But the version given by de' Rossi is found in Mid. Teh. 9:2.

115. Zohar, shemot, II, 16b–17a.

116. B. Sanh. 98b: "The school of R. Shila said: His [the Messiah's] name is Shiloh for it is written *until Shilo come.*"

117. Cf. Is. 14:32.

this date has already passed by an unascertainable number of years. This then is the sign for us that there was no vision about it for the fact is that God's word never fails to come to pass instantaneously. And all those who look forward to that year should not weary themselves with such thoughts, and those who wait for it should not be deluded. In any case, whether it has already come or is still to come they should not wait for it and in particular should not pin their hopes on it. But from now and always they should, as in the past continually lift their eyes towards the Holy One of Israel. He, the blessed Lord, knows when He will bring the end to these secret matters. And they should take note that Daniel himself was told explicitly that all such things remain hidden and sealed until such time as it pleases the blessed Lord to implement the word of his servants, the true and just prophets. Then, in an instant, there shall be light for all the children of Israel. Such is our God's power which was evinced in all works of the creation which were created instantaneously, fully developed and appropriately shaped.[118] And so that righteous person will repose and sleep with the consolation that he can know nothing about the end of these terrible trials.[119]

Now we see that Rav, whose greatness was such that he was regarded as both Tanna and Amora,[120] pronounced even by his own time that all the predestined dates had passed and that the matter only depended on repentance.[121] And Rabbi Jonathan[122] who was even greater than he, said, and we quoted the passage previously,[123] "The verse pierces and descends to the very abyss, *For the vision is yet for an appointed time, but at the end it shall speak and not lie.*" And Rabbi Nathan[124] said: "Blasted be the bones of those who calculate the end and thereby delay the time of redemption." And in the same context,[125] and in Midrash Tehillim,[126] Rabbi Samuel teaches in the name of Rabbi Judah: "If a man should tell you when the day of redemption will come, do not believe him for it says, *For a day of vengeance is in my heart* (Is. 63:4). If the heart does not disclose its secrets to the mouth, to whom can the mouth disclose it?" When Rav Zeʿera would find the rabbis engaged in messianic calculation, he would say: "I beg of you, do not postpone it for it has been taught: Three things come unawares—Messiah, a lost object, and a scorpion."[127] And in tractate Ketubot,[128] such a notion is derived from the verse, *I adjure you, daughters of Jerusalem by the gazelles and by the hinds of the field that you do not awaken nor stir up love until it please* (S.S. 2:7). And in Tanḥuma,[129] it is stated that they should not reveal the end nor force the end. And there is a *baraita* which is edited and

118. Cf. B. Ḥull. 60a.
119. 'Terrible trials,' cf. Dan. 12:6.
120. Rav (Abba Arikha) was a first generation Amora (d. 247 C.E.). The statement, "He is a Tanna and may dispute (the view in the Mishnah)" is often said of him. See B. Eruv. 50b; B.B. 42a; B. Sanh. 83b.
121. B. Sanh. 97b.
122. The Talmud reads "R. Nathan."
123. B. Sanh. 97b.
124. The Talmud reads "Rabbi Jonathan."
125. B. Sanh. 99a.
126. Mid. Teh. 9:2.
127. B. Sanh. 97a.
128. B. Ket. 111a. The adjuration is interpreted with regard to those who calculate, force, or preempt the time of redemption.
129. Tanḥuma, Devarim 4 (Buber, 3).

preserved in the Mekhilta,[130] Pesaḥim,[131] and Midrash Qohelet[132] with regard to the verse, *Just as you do not know how the lifebreath passes into the limbs within the womb of the pregnant woman so you cannot foresee the actions of God who causes all to happen* (Eccl. 11:5). It states: "Seven things are hidden from human beings: the day of death, . . . when the Davidic dynasty will be restored and when the wicked kingdom (i.e., the evil inclination which is called an old and foolish king[133]) will come to an end." Accordingly, how can anybody who comes after these outstanding people be more correct than they? Is it not the case that on their authority, the reeds and rushes of those who fabricate lies on this subject have withered[134] and their scrolls been completely erased, for there is no longer any prophet. So profound are the thoughts of our God that the seed that serves Him cannot trace them and seek to know that which He has not told us. As for he that is incapable of inquiring about the details or is disinterested in endeavoring to comprehend them, he will appreciate the truth of the principle enunciated by the wise ibn Ezra in his comment on the passage close to the end of the book of Daniel. He writes:

> Ben ha-Yoṣer wrote a book about the time of the end and I completely shattered his words like a vessel which is shattered by the craftsman before it is brought to completion.[135] For his hope was fixed on a time which has already passed. I would pronounce that his statements on the end are all vanity and a striving after the wind. Such is also my judgment on the view of Solomon ibn Gabirol who wanted to connect the end to the great conjunction of the two uppermost stars, and the view of Abraham the prince which he presented in his work on the ends, and the view of ha-Yoṣer and Rabbi Isaac ben Lev and all those who make numerical computations by means of words and letters and *gematria.* For Daniel did not know when the end would be and still less so his successors. The angel alluded to it but was not explicit as to the time of its occurrence.

Such are the words of a gracious sage which are completely lucid and absolutely true. And in his commentary on Mishnah Sanhedrin,[136] Rambam sums up everything in two words: "The twelfth principle is the messianic era. One should not assign a date to it nor should one work out the time of the advent of the Messiah by reasoning based on scriptural verses." However you should know that in his *Epistle to Yemen,* with regard to the restoration of prophecy to our people, even Rambam of blessed memory does not refrain from recording his ancestral tradition according to which we should attain this favor from our God in the year 4972 a.m. [1212].[137] The basis of this calculation is Rabbi Ḥanina's statement in the Palestinian Talmud, tractate Shabbat:[138] "It appears that half the days of the universe had elapsed by the time that Balaam the wicked announced,

130. Mekhilta d'Rabbi Ishmael, vayassa, 6 (II, 125).
131. B. Pes. 54b.
132. Qoh. R. to Eccl. 11:5. The reference to the restoration of the Davidic kingdom is not listed here.
133. This identification is given in Qoh. R. to 4:13. However, the expression "wicked kingdom" usually refers to Rome.
134. 'Reeds . . . withered,' cf. Is. 16:4.
135. This is all an elaborate play on the Ben ha-Yoṣer (son of the craftsman).
136. He is referring to Maimonides' long introduction to ch. 10 of Sanhedrin in which he lists the thirteen principles.
137. *Iggeret Teman,* 172.
138. P. Shabb. 6 (9) 8d.

Jacob is told as the present time, yea Israel what God has planned (Num. 23:23). A further period, "as the present time,"[139] is told to Jacob." Balaam was prophesying in the thirty-eighth year after the exodus from Egypt which corresponds to the year 2486 anno mundi. This is all to be found in the *Collectanea* of ibn Ḥabib in which he cites the passage from the Palestinian Talmud tractate Shabbat (p. 173).[140] Now Rabbi Ḥanina used discretion by speaking in tentative and not absolute terms. For not everything that "appears" is necessarily of substance. And I would defend the Rav of blessed memory, assuming that the reason for his overstepping the limit was because he came across a valley in the land of Yemen whose circumstances were such that he had to safeguard it.[141] However, if one word is worth one *sela,* silence is certainly worth two *selas.*[142] For there is every indication that that specific tradition was false, being a mere conjecture, and had not been transmitted to us as something which was sure and precise. So wherever you turn, one thing becomes clear with regard to every promise and goodness that we hope to receive through the kindness of our God. Anybody who marks out an end limit on the basis of whatsoever proof and indication from Scripture or from the [numerical value of the] letters of the years is in error, misleads others, and incurs guilt. For he transgresses the words of the sages who in olden times looked to the future when they said, "Blasted be the breath of those who calculate the end." Thus the correction to the computation of years that we have suggested in order to show that it is in truth open to doubt is most certainly not a deleterious correction. Rather, the computation was established as a convention for the greater good and therefore should not be synchronized with words of prophecy, as has been said. On the contrary, not only is it unlikely to cause any damage or harm, but on account of such an explanation and by abstaining,[143] we shall receive a reward for protecting those embittered people from falling into the debris. Who knows whether at a time like this, it has been opportune for us to write on this subject and our loins will be encircled with a girdle of justice.[144] Will not every intelligent person be pleased and content that thank God we have not fallen into the pit into which the Christian doctor Lactantius Firmianus fell? For in his seventh book,[145] he cleverly managed to ratify and confirm the decree, analogous to the

139. Balaam is said to be prophecying in the year 2486. This figure is doubled on the basis of the word *as* in the expression *as the present time.*

140. From this precise indication, it is clear that de' Rossi was consulting the Venice, 1566, edition (173, col. b) of Jacob ibn Ḥabib's compilation of Aggadot of the Talmuds with commentaries, entitled in this edition *Bet Yisrael.*

141. In 1167, Maimonides received a letter from Jacob ben Nathanel al-Fayyumi on behalf of the Jews of Yemen whose existence had been threatened by a fanatical Muslim movement. A person claiming to be the Messiah had come forward as their savior. Among other things Maimonides was asked to comment on this claim and to give his opinion as to whether the advent of the Messiah could be predicted by astrology. Maimonides' response is noted for its humanity and the care with which he encouraged the Yemenite community not to succumb to messianic delusions. De' Rossi is therefore right in seeing Maimonides' offer of a date for the redemption, which was clearly contradictory to his own ideas about the Messiah, as a means of giving some consolation and hope to a desperate community.

142. Cf. B. Meg. 18a.

143. This phrase, based on B. Pes. 22b, means that by explaining the calculations in this way and abstaining from such views, he deserved a reward for thereby protecting others.

144. 'Loins . . . justice,' cf. Is. 11:5.

145. Lactantius, *Divinarum Institutionum lib.,* bk. VII, ch. 14, "De mundi temporibus primis ac postremis" and ch. 15, "De mundi vastatione et mutatione imperiorum."

statement of the Tanna d've Eliyahu, that the world will exist for six thousand years and will lie desolate for one thousand years.[146] He stated that the six days of creation and the seventh day on which God rested from His work are indicative of the significant amelioration and rest from all tribulation that will occur in the seventh millennium.[147] By the same token, the Tanna most certainly implied that the desolation of one thousand years was to facilitate the repair. It is comparable to the one statement in Sanhedrin:[148] "Just as the sabbatical year brings release, so too, one thousand years out of seven brings release as it says, *A Psalm and song for the Sabbath day* (Ps. 92:1)." The explanation of Rashi of blessed memory is of a similar nature. He writes: "The world is decreed to exist for six thousand years corresponding to the [six] days of the week, and the rest of the seventh day corresponds to the seventh millennium in which the world will have rest." In reference to the verse, *Bela son of Beor reigned in Edom* (Gen. 36:32), the wise Recanati also wrote as follows:[149] "One can deduce from this[150] that the statement of our rabbis of blessed memory in Bereshit Rabbah, about God constructing worlds and destroying them, does not signify real destruction. Rather, it is as though He sets them to one side until He has restored the countenance of Supernal Man."[151] Study the passage. Likewise Lactantius's lengthy passage on the disasters that are to come in the latter days[152] corresponds to the statements of the rabbis of blessed memory at the end of tractate Sota,[153] Sanhedrin,[154] and Shir Rabbah.[155] From one perspective, however, he was confused and blundered. He follows the Septuagint for his computation of the years of the world from Adam to the deluge, and according to that version, we would have already commenced the seventh millennium by more than a hundred years. In his own day, that time was remote in the future. But since, according to his own thinking, we would have today been well into that time, the later Christians were justified in exposing him as a deluded prophet. Eugubinus, in particular, in his comment on the verse, *let me inform you what this people will do to your people in the latter days* (Num. 24:14), said that although Lactantius's statement about the future of the world in the seventh millennium could be reconsidered in a favorable light and regarded as true and correct by God since it had also been predicted by two of ten Sibyls and the old Hystaspes [Hydaspes] king of Media[156] and before him, Hermes Trismegistus (about whom we spoke in chapter 4), God would not hasten to act as Lactantius

146. B. R.H. 31a; B. A.Z. 9a; B. Sanh. 97a. This statement is given in the name of Rav Qattina, while a similar idea is also expressed by the Tanna deve Eliyahu.

147. This passage from Lactantius, together with the statement of the Tanna deve Eliyahu is often cited in sixteenth-century world chronicles, and in Ferentilli's *Discorso,* which de' Rossi cites in ch. 16. They are even mentioned on the title page.

148. B. Sanh. 97a.

149. Recanati, *Perush* to Gen. 36:32 (32c).

150. Recanati is referring to his citation from the Zohar.

151. 'The countenance of Supernal Man.' This refers to the kabbalistic conception of the divine world of the Sefirot.

152. *Divinarum Institutionum lib.,* bk. VII, ch. 16, "De mundi vastatione eiusque prodigiis."

153. M. Sota 9:15.

154. B. Sanh. 97a.

155. S.S.R. to S.S. 2:13.

156. 'Hystaspes Medorum rex antiquissimus' is mentioned by Lactantius as one of the ancient prophetic theologians. The name Hydaspes which Steuchus uses is a tributary of the Indus and occurs as the name of a king in Vergil, *Georgica* 4, v.211.

had thought. The reason was that the time that he had calculated had already passed while the world remained as it always been, and the expected change had not been witnessed. Thus we would not have made this kind of pronouncement nor would we have set down a figure of great proportion that would result in the removal of our hope, God forbid. On the contrary, with the ninety or one hundred years at the most which we thought could possibly be added to the total we are closer to the latter days in which His deed will be seen by the servants of God.[157] {Of particular note is the statement in the Zohar on the verse, *The Lord took note of Sarah as He had promised* (Gen. 21:1) on page 117:[158] "In the six hundredth year of the sixth millennium, the gates of wisdom will be opened."} Moreover, for the support of the frail and fearful, we should note that apart from their statement, "If they are worthy I will hasten it, if not he will come at the due time," there is also their statement in Shir Rabbah on the verse, *hark my beloved there he comes leaping over mountains* (S.S. 2:8). The passage impresses us, for while it might be thought that the time of redemption which we await is fixed, the Lord is a great God and abounds in mercy such that He may hasten its advent without regard to any calculation or limit nor even to the good behavior that is to our credit. Thus they say:

> When Moses said to Israel: "In this month you are to be redeemed," they said to him: "How can this be so? Only 210 years have elapsed." He said to them: "Since the Holy One blessed be He, desires your redemption, He takes no heed of your reckonings (and later in the same passage it states, "and He does not consider your deeds"); rather, *he leaps over the mountains.* The "mountains" and "hills" mentioned here refer to the termini and intercalations. He skips over the calculations and termini and you are to be redeemed, as it says, *This month shall mark for you the beginning of the months* (Ex. 12:2).

At any rate, may the Lord deal with His flock as He so desires, whether to castigate or to be merciful. Every sage and understanding person should grasp the truth of these ancient and true words which regard the termini which any sage may assign for the date of our redemption. I discovered a passage at the end of gate 2 of the *Sefer ha-Geʾulah* by Ramban of blessed memory. His words are more precious than gold and sweeter than honey. Despite their length, I desired to transcribe them here particularly because few people have access to the book.[159] Now Ramban of blessed memory is reputed as a worthy and respected authority such that everything he has to say is heeded and taken into consideration by all wise people of these times. He said as follows:

> Know that God will come to your help. We might admit to ourselves that our transgression and the sin of our ancestors has deprived us of all consolation and that God will prolong the exile interminably. Likewise, we might say that God wanted to afflict us in this world by subjecting us to the kingdoms either for His own pleasure or for beneficial ends. All this, however, will not impair the principle of the Torah in any way. The ultimate goal of our reward in the messianic era does not consist of indulging in the fruits of the earth and bathing in the hot springs of Tiberias and other such pleasures. Neither are the sacrifices and the Temple service His ultimate goal for us. Rather our recompense and

157. 'His . . . God,' cf. Ps. 90:16.
158. This is a reference to the first edition of the Zohar published in Mantua, 1558–60.
159. De' Rossi quotes the work from manuscript which differs slightly from the text published by Chavel.

> expectation should be for the eternal life and spiritual delight, which is called the Garden of Eden, and to be spared punishment in Gehinnom. Notwithstanding all this, we persist in our hope for the redemption because it is a well-known truth for those who uphold the Torah and prophecy, and by means of it, we shall arouse those who are mesmerized by the disasters and shut the mouths of the heretics. Happy in its proofs and delighting in its words we await it in the hope that it will bring us near to God as we come into His Temple with its priests and prophets, and that we shall partake of the purity and sanctity in the chosen Land and that His presence will rest on us. This will exceed anything we could achieve nowadays since we are filled with wrath over the calamities and events that oppress us. At that time in the messianic era the evil inclination shall be abolished such that we will be able to apprehend the truth as it really is or for some other deep mystical reason which I mentioned. This is our fundamental goal and longing with regard to the messianic era. In addition, our desire and longing for those days is augmented by the fact that the Torah explicitly told us that as long as we sin, we will remain in exile in order to receive correction, but when we serve correctly, God will again deal bounteously with us as He did to our ancestors, and to an even greater degree. However the craving of our soul for those days is also aroused for the sake of proving to those who would argue against it that we are in possession of the truth. This desire of ours enshrines an important precept. That is, we desire to demonstrate the sanctification of God's name to all the peoples of the earth. Now the sages of blessed memory considered the one who denies the recompense of the messianic era as a heretic who is deprived of the world to come, since it is only his denial of reward as laid down in our Torah that is the cause of his heresy. Such a person is mad, contradicting the express statements of Scripture and denying the words of our rabbis.

This is what he says and he writes in a similar vein in the gate of recompense which is the last gate of his book *Torat ha-Adam.* But I was surprised that he did not include another most important reason for our longing for the redemption which accords with his own thinking. I am referring to the fact that at that time we shall be in a position to observe the precepts that must be performed in the Land [of Israel]. He, blessed be his memory, writes about these precepts in his commentary on the verses, *and let the land not spew you out* (Lev. 18:28), and *These are the laws and rules that you must carefully observe in the land* (Deut. 12:1). In his *Responsa,* the Rashba [Solomon ben Adret] also writes:[160] "The Land is the pivot of all the precepts to the extent that some of them can only be fulfilled there." We cited this towards the end of chapter 11. Be that as it may, one can summarize the passage by Ramban of blessed memory as follows. Our only goal in the messianic era is the observance of the Torah and the reward that we hope to gain from God by whatever means and at whatever time. Accordingly, whether our redemption comes soon or is delayed so long that it is deleted from our thoughts, we shall not deviate from all the words of the Torah. As the psalmist said, *I shall have an answer for those who taunt me, for I have put my trust in Your word. Do not utterly take the truth away from my mouth. . . . I will always obey Your Torah* (Ps. 119:42–44). Through it, we shall prolong our days and from it springs all salvation and desire.

160. Solomon ben Adret, *Teshuvot,* responsum 134 (vol. 1, 54, col. b).

CHAPTER FORTY-FOUR

On the statement that the world will exist for six thousand years and lie desolate for one thousand years.

Now we ought not remain silent on the subject of the six thousand years that we mentioned. For indeed, whatever its consequences and however it appears to us, the statement that the world will be destroyed at the end of six thousand years is upheld by the one who regards that Tanna d've Eliyahu as having been enkindled by the spirit of prophecy to speak the truth.[1] However, according to the author of the *Guide,*[2] Yedidyah the Alexandrian in his work *On the Eternity of the World* and other philosophers both of our people and from the ranks of the Christians, this is a strange statement which they cannot uphold. They argue that the Creator of the world is eternal and, according to His will, may bring about its destruction, or let it remain in existence for a length of days, for eternity. On rational grounds, one is rather inclined to the verdict that the blessed Lord desires its existence. Indeed, certain verses demonstrate such a view, for example, *He established the earth on its foundations [that it shall never totter]* (Ps. 104:5); *But you O Lord, are enthroned forever, Your throne endures through the ages* (Lam. 5:19). I myself can produce additional proof to corroborate such a view, for there are hosts of verses in the Torah that cry out[3] to *those who keep His commandments to the thousandth generation* (Deut. 7:9). Moreover, there is the verse in the Decalogue, *but showing kindness to thousands* (Ex. 20:6) which signifies two thousand generations. This is the way it is understood in tractate Sota in the Palestinian and Babylonian Talmuds.[4] They say that he who acts out of fear will reap the consequences for a thousand generations; but he who acts out of love, for two thousand generations. And likewise there is the explicit scriptural statement in the Hagiographa, *the promise He gave for a thousand generations* (Ps. 105:8).

Now we need not pay attention to [ps.] Xenophon the Greek who in his work *On*

1. Throughout this discussion, de' Rossi quotes interchangeably from the statement of R. Qattina: "Six thousand years shall the world exist and lie desolate for one thousand years" and that of the Tanna d've Eliyahu: "The world is to exist six thousand years: two thousand of desolation; two thousand years of Torah; and two thousand years of the messianic era."

2. *Guide* II, chs. 27, 28, 29. De' Rossi also refers to *Mishneh Torah,* Teshuvah VIII:8.

3. This is a play on Is. 33:7.

4. B. Sota 31a. In P. Sota 5 (5) 20c, there is a discussion about serving God out of love and fear, but there is no reference to the Decalogue.

Synonyms[5] explains that according to the Egyptians, the duration of a generation is thirty years, and twenty-five years according to the Greeks. From the twelfth book of the *Metamorphoses* by the Roman poet Ovid, it would appear that the Romans held that the duration of a generation is one hundred years.[6] But for a definition of a generation, see[7] ibn Ezra's discussion of the verse, *And they shall return here in the fourth generation* (Gen. 15:16): He states that the idiom of the our holy tongue implies that a generation (*dor*) is the length of time in which a person lives (*yador*) in the world. Kimḥi also gives the same explanation of the word under the entry for the root letters *dvr.*[8] And even if the lives of a father and his son are terminated simultaneously, one need only count the number of years of the father which had transpired before the birth of the son. This view may be gleaned from the statement of Rambam [Maimonides] of blessed memory in his commentary on the mishnah in tractate Eduyot:[9] "A father endows his son . . . with the number of generations that have gone before him [and of them he is the end]." He [Rambam] states: "After a number of generations, one procreating the next, the predicted event will come to pass." In any case, the years in which the revolution of Saturn is completed[10] will be exceeded countless times in a thousand generations and still more in two thousand generations. I know that the kabbalists considered that a generation lasts fifty years. They explained the verse, *to a thousandth generation,* as a reference to the year of the final Jubilee which in their view will occur at the end of fifty thousand years.[11] Rabbi Todros ha-Levi gives this view in his discussion of the statement that the world will exist for six thousand years in his work entitled *Oṣar ha-Kavod.*[12] But according to the view expressed by our rabbis of blessed memory in the Palestinian and Babylonian Talmuds, tractate Sota, with regard to the verse, *but showing kindness to thousands*—which is equivalent to two thousand generations—that Jubilee year [of the kabbalists] would be surpassed unless the revolutions of the universe go on forever, a view that we shall discuss. It would also appear feasible to endorse this opinion on the basis of the proof given in chapter 2 of Daniel concerning the kingdom which is predicted to arise after the overthrow of the four kingdoms. It states: *And in the time of those kings, the God of heaven will establish a kingdom that shall never be destroyed* (2:44). And with regard to that kingdom, he says in chapter 7,[13] *All peoples and nations of every language must serve Him. . . . His dominion is an everlasting dominion that shall not*

5. This is a reference to ps. Xenophon's *De Aequivocis* (17) forged by Annius of Viterbo.

6. *Metamorphoses* XII, lines 187–88: "vixi / annos bis centum nunc tertia vivitur aetas." In this context, the speech of Nestor, the word "*aetas*" means "generation."

7. This is a play on Jer. 2:31.

8. David Kimḥi, *Sefer Shorashim,* s.v. *dvr.*

9. M. Ed. 2:9.

10. Cf. B.R. 10:4 (76): "There is a planet which completes its circuit in thirty years; it is Saturn."

11. The notion of the cosmic cycles or *shemiṭṭot* (sabbatical years) was a widely held kabbalistic doctrine which was articulated in the thirteenth-century work *Sefer ha-Temunah.* Each sabbatical is governed by one of God's attributes and in the Great Jubilee, that is, after seven sabbaticals, God's creative powers are manifested. Each of these cycles lasts for seven thousand years and in the fiftieth millennium, all creation returns to nothingness. See G. Scholem, *On the Kabblah,* 77–83. For a discussion of the various kabbalistic notions on this topic, see E. Gottlieb, *Studies,* 332–39.

12. Todros Halevi Abulafia (thirteenth-century Spanish kabbalist) *Oṣar ha-Kavod,* to B. R.H. 31a (34, col. a).

13. De' Rossi refers to ch. 8 instead of ch. 7.

pass away (7:14). Such words cannot be applied in any way to the world of the souls where there are no series of generations and different monarchies which are a necessary feature of this world alone. The wise Recanati alluded to this when citing some of the kabbalists of more recent times.[14] He said: "They were troubled by the fact that Israel's messianic era should be of such a short duration, being less than a thousand years, when according to its due, the days of peace should last a thousand times longer than the days of adversity which we have endured for the sake of the sanctification of the name of God." Examine the passage.

And even with all this diversity of opinion, there are in fact yet other views. For the divinely inspired among the Christian doctors did not divide up the years of the world which is a macro-man into six equal periods of a thousand years as did our sages, but into six ages which they called *aeta[te]s.*[15] Each age was of a determined length but one was long, the other short, just as the lifespan of man, who is a microcosm, is of variable length. This undoubtedly accounts for the diversity that we mentioned. Starting their reckoning from birth, the sixth age is compared to old age, the length of which cannot be known—rather there are some of the elderly who enjoy an old age which is of equal duration to most of their preceding years. After the sixth age, the time will come which is compared to the Sabbath in its relation to the other days of the week. Thus in their view, this sixth age, which is the world's old age, could exceed six thousand years by a considerable amount more than we imagined. Their doctors Augustine (at the end of the last chapter of his *City of God*)[16] and Aquinas (in the fourth part of his commentary on the *Liber Sententiarum*)[17] demonstrate all this; and Contractus treated the subject at greater length at the beginning of his chronicle which was printed after Eusebius's chronological tables.[18] The divine philosopher Plato held another view, namely, he believed in the cyclical notion. In the *Statesman,* he wrote as follows:[19] "During a certain period of time, the blessed Lord keeps a hold on the world and at a certain moment, releases it when He sees that a requisite number of the cycles of time have revolved." He expresses a similar view in disparate passages throughout the *Timaeus* which were collated by Eusebius the Caesarean in the eleventh book of his *Praeparatio.*[20] He states: "Time was created when the heavens were made so that they would also dissolve at the same time." Then in the next passage, he puts an imaginary speech in the mouth of the

14. Recanati, *Perush,* behar (68d).

15. The subject of the ages of the world was very popular. De' Rossi would have also read the chapter (bk. 1, ch. 3) entitled "De temporibus et aetatum saeculi distinctione" in Johannes Lucidus Samotheus's *Opusculum.* For a general discussion of the subject, see G. W. Trompf, *The Idea of Historical Recurrence.*

16. *De civ. Dei,* 22, ch. 30 (*P.L.* XLI, col. 804).

17. De' Rossi is referring to the commentary (Aquinas's authorship is doubtful) on the *Libri Sententiarum* of Petrus Lombardus. He refers to lib. IV, distinctio 43, articulus 1, and distinctio 47, quaestio 1, articulus 1, in which the author speaks of the time of judgment at the end of the world's existence for which humans must prepare themselves since they do not know when it will occur.

18. De' Rossi is referring to the chronicles published by Sichardus. Hermannus Contractus's *Chronicon* is not printed directly after Eusebius's tables, but after the work of Cassiodorus. Contractus gives a detailed description of each of the ages.

19. *Politicus* 269c.

20. De' Rossi read this work in George of Trepizond's Latin translation where the passage indicated is in bk. XI, ch. 17 (*P.G.* XXI, bk. XI, ch. 32, cols. 929/30–934). Eusebius also refers to the passage from the *Politicus.*

highest God addressing the heavenly hosts in which he says: "You are my handiwork, but it is your own nature that will in the future bring about your disintegration." We shall mention this again presently.

In any case, I would first like to give you information lest you are under the widespread misapprehension that the Elijah who taught us these things was the Tishbite who went up to heaven. For he is actually to be identified with the Tanna indicated by Rambam of blessed memory in connection with Ḥoni the circle-drawer at the end of chapter 7 in his introduction to the order of Zeraʿim.[21] Then there is the statement in tractate Pesaḥim:[22] "Tanna d've Eliyahu: Rabbi Nathan said: The whole of the *oikoumene* is under one star." I would then like to say that the author of the *Guide* should forgive us if we do not heed him in this matter. For, as we noted previously, the expression "lie desolate" does not imply absolute destruction, but rather mutation to a higher level in accordance with God's will. But apart from this, we can see that the kabbalists uphold the opinion of the Tanna d've Eliyahu, which is not an individual's opinion formulated according to a particular way of thinking as he [i.e., Maimonides] describes it in chapter 29.[23] Among other passages, there is the statement at the end of tractate Tamid:[24] "On the Sabbath, they sang *A Psalm: a song for the sabbath day* (Ps. 92). A Psalm, a song for the time that is to come, for the day that shall be all Sabbath and rest for eternity." And they say that the Tanna here is expressing the view indicated in the saying, "six thousand years the world will exist."[25] Similarly, commenting on the verse, *When the woman saw that the tree was good for eating* (Gen. 3:6), it is written in he Zohar:[26] "Come and see. This is the sabbatical year . . . because it is from the left side it has no firm basis until the time of the seventh millennium." There is likewise another statement from the Zohar on Genesis (I could not find the passage in our printed edition), which is cited by Don Isaac:[27] "Rabbi Eliezer and Rabbi Aqiva were going on a journey . . . [and in the sixth and seventh millennium there will be a sabbatical for the desolate world and in the eighth, the world will be restored as of old . . .], until *those who remain in Zion and are left in Jerusalem* (Is. 4:3)." Furthermore, the true kabbalist Ramban [Nahmanides] wrote in a similar vein in his commentary on the verse, *on it God ceased from the work of creation He had done* (Gen. 2:3). And ibn Ezra writes that the verse, *so long as the earth endures . . . day and night shall not cease* (Gen. 8:22), "indicates that there is a fixed end to the existence of the earth." And he explained the phrase "a sabbath of the Lord" (Lev. 25:2) when he wrote: "It is like the Sabbath day, and the mystery of the days of the world is alluded to in this context." Similarly there is Rabad's

21. Maimonides, *Perush* (Introduction, ch. 7).

22. B. Pes. 94a.

23. *Guide* II, ch. 29. Maimonides argues that the prophetic and rabbinic texts do not demonstrate that there will be a permanent change in the nature of the world. The expression, "and one thousand years lies desolate" indicates that time remains. He then dismisses the statement as an individual's opinion "according to a certain manner of thinking."

24. M. Tamid 7:4.

25. Cf. B. Sanh. 97a (and B. R.H. 31a). Using Ps. 90:4, they understand the word "day" as referring to one thousand years and thus the "day that is all sabbath" refers to the period of complete desolation.

26. Zohar I, 50b.

27. Abravanel, *Mayyene ha-Yeshuʿah,* 11, tamar 10 (399, col. a). S. Leiman pointed out to me that the passage quoted by Abravanel is taken from Zohar Ḥadash, Midrash ha-Neʿelam, bereshit, 16c–d.

[Abraham ben David's] critique of the teacher of blessed memory [Maimonides] at the end of chapter 8 of the Laws of Repentance,[28] although the sages of Lunel did come to his defense as is indicated there.[29] The Rashba [Solomon ben Adret] also upholds this view in his *Responsa* because it was the tradition of our sages.[30] The most stringent attack on Rambam of blessed memory was launched by the wise Recanati.[31] He proved the validity of the statement by adducing many statements of the rabbis of blessed memory on this subject which were based on holy Scripture. Study the passage. Now in his *City [of God],* the greatest Christian sage [Augustine] ridicules Plato for saying that existence reverts to its own levels at the end of a certain number of cycles. Likewise he ridicules his belief in the transmigration of souls. His statements are explained by the commentator Vives. And yet in the third part of his Dialogue of Philone e Sophia, the wise Messer Leone cites Plato's view that the heavens will also be subject to decay in the future;[32] and he expatiates at length on the cyclical theory, explaining that it is an ancient tradition which had been transmitted from Enoch and Noah.[33] And he demonstrates that the precepts of the Torah recur in sevens: there are seven days [of creation], seven weeks of the sheaf-offering, seven months of the year,[34] the sabbatical years, the sabbatical years of the Jubilee—all these are indication and reliable testimony to the cycles of six thousand years until forty-nine thousand which correspond to the cycles of the sabbatical years and the Jubilee.[35] As we have already indicated, the wise ibn Ezra referred to the secret of the days of the world about which you should read the book entitled *Meqor Ḥayyim.*[36] How much more significant then is the statement of Rabbi Meir in tractate Shabbat in the Palestinian Talmud:[37] "Once every seven years, the Holy One blessed be He changes His world." In the course of his various laudations of the number seven in his work *On the Creation of the World,*[38] Yedidyah the Alexandrian writes that according to Solon the lawgiver of the Greeks and Hippocrates the greatest of the physicians, the seventy years of a man's life are divided up into ten qualitative phases. These are described by him in commendable rhyming verse. It is thus all the more likely that the world in its entirety will not fail to pass through the remarkable

28. *Mishneh Torah,* Teshuvah VIII:8. In this passage Maimonides states that the expression "world to come" does not imply the destruction of this world and the advent of that world, but rather refers to the immortality of the soul. This is glossed by Abraham ben David who accuses Maimonides of refuting the idea of the renewal of the world after a period of destruction as indicated in the statement about the universe lying desolate for one thousand years.

29. De' Rossi is referring to the comment on the passage by Shemtov ibn Gaon in the *Migdal Oz* in which he refers to the sages of Lunel who defended Maimonides on the grounds that the statement under discussion was not an explicit and unanimously held tradition.

30. Solomon ben Adret, *She'elot,* responsum 9 (5 col. a ff.).

31. Recanati, *Perush* (68, col. a–69, col. d).

32. Leone Ebreo (Judah Abravanel), *Dialoghi,* 3 (245).

33. Ibid. (248).

34. Leone makes no reference to months.

35. Leone, *Dialoghi,* 3

36. Samuel ibn Ṣarṣa (fourteenth-century Spanish philosopher). This is a reference to his super-commentary on ibn Ezra's Bible commentary, *Meqor Ḥayyim,* to Lev. 25:2. Ibn Ṣarṣa (83 col. c–84 col. d) interprets ibn Ezra's words as a reference to the notion of the seven millennia.

37. P. Shabb. 1 (3) 3b.

38. *Op.* 104–5.

change assigned to it by our sages. And they state in the Zohar:[39] "Come and see—At the time of creating the world, the Holy One blessed be He created seven upper firmaments, seven lower earths, seven rivers, seven days, seven weeks, seven years seven times multiplied, seven thousand years for the duration of the world, and the Holy One blessed be He exists in the seventh of them all." The fact is that both regarding this final end and the end of our exile, which we discussed in the previous chapter, and all such esoteric and profound matters, we are bound to make the following declaration. It is beyond all doubt that there is no advantage in studying and investigating this subject in any depth or to any extent. Rather we should assign this task to the will of our Father in heaven—we know that He is wise, desirous of doing good and omnipotent. Now the wise Socrates used to say (this is ascribed to him by the Xenophon the Greek in the fourth part of work entitled *On the Deeds and Sayings of Socrates*)[40] that in all fields of learning and knowledge, there is a certain limit and goal that a person ought to attain but not surpass.[41] He likewise said:[42] "One should dissuade all people from endeavoring to know the nature of the heavenly hosts, their constellations and the laws that govern them. One should particularly deprecate the desire to discover what it is that God desires to do in His universe at one point in time rather than at another. This is a difficult concept for man to grasp and one which is alien to his nature. Moreover man's audacity to disclose that which He determined in His wisdom to hide and conceal from us is regarded as a great evil by the deity." This old man practiced what he preached as is shown by his behavior when he was first imbued by the spirit of wisdom and discovered that the ancients were engrossed in the investigation of physics and metaphysics. He departed from their way and said that the study of that which is higher than us is an unsuitable activity for us and him. He then directed himself to inquiry into human ethics and the necessary perfection of world society. The wisest man of all time said, *just as you do not know how the lifebreath passes into the limbs . . . so you cannot foresee the actions of God* (Eccl. 11:5). Indeed, there are two different stories told in the Babylonian[43] and Palestinian[44] Talmuds regarding those who know something but not everything. One of the great sages addressed somebody of comparable stature and said: "In the future you will have to justify yourself for having disclosed that which the Torah concealed." We quoted the passage in chapters 15 and 42. As for those who expound on delightful subjects, or essential matters (*ḥamurot*) according to Rashi's reading,[45] it is stated:[46] "What does the expression *and for stately clothing* (*li-mekhasseh atiq*) (Is. 23:18)

39. Zohar III, 9b–10a.

40. Xenophon, *Memorabilia.* In the Latin translation which de' Rossi used the title is *De factis et dictis Socratis memoratu dignis.*

41. *Memorabilia* IV, 7, 1.

42. Ibid. IV, 7, 5–6.

43. B. Shabb. 96b.

44. P. Sota 5 (6) 20d.

45. De' Rossi is referring here to an expression used to denote a school of exegetes or allegorists in B. Pes. 54a; B. Ber. 24a; B. Ḥull. 134b. Strangely, he does not use the term *dorshe reshumot* but only refers to Rashi's statement to B. Ber. 24a in which he states: "We read *dorshe ḥamurot* instead of *dorshe reshumot,* but both are the same." On the identity of these exegetes, see J. Lauterbach, "The Ancient Jewish Allegorists."

46. B. Pes. 119a.

mean? It refers to him who conceals [*mekhasseh*] the things which the Ancient [*atiq*] of days concealed." If one who declares the truth is held in this light, what then would be the judgment on a prophet whose dreams bring false predictions? Let us then act in obedience to the fine dictum attributed to Ben Sira in Ḥagiga. They said:[47] "Do not investigate that which is too difficult for you." This notion is developed in the third chapter of his work which the Christians call Ecclesiasticus. May the Lord God who is true bring it to completion for us and through us, may His purpose prosper.[48]

[END OF SECTION THREE]

47. B. Ḥag. 13a.
48. 'And through . . . prosper,' cf. Is. 53:10.

SECTION FOUR

CHAPTER FORTY-FIVE

On the difference between Onqelos and Akylas. How that Akylas only translated into Greek, and that he is to be identified with Aquila, who was renowned as a translator among the gentiles. That there were two people called Onqelos and two called Aquila.

In one of the chapters of the section entitled "Days of the World,"[1] I intimated that I had delightful material on the subject of Onqelos and Akylas and promised to devote a chapter to the topic. I am presenting it to you here, sagacious reader; may you consider it in a favorable light.

I have heard it said that these two names belong to one and the same person for in the simpler Jerusalemite idiom mentioned at the beginning of Bava Qama,[2] Onqelos is sometimes called Akylas. In the same way, Eleazar is called Lazar in the Jerusalemite idiom, Judah is called Juda and there are other such examples. Particularly relevant is the passage in tractate Demai of the Tosefta:[3] "If a proselyte and gentile inherit the estate of their idolatrous father, . . . Onqelos took his share to the Dead Sea." The identical story is related in the Palestinian Talmud, but in the name of Akylas.[4] Similarly, in our [i.e., Babylonian] Gemara,[5] it is stated: "Onqelos the proselyte translated the Torah under the jurisdiction of Rabbi Eliezer and Rabbi Joshua." However, in the Palestinian Talmud, the name of Akylas is given[6]—this is our point. Moreover, there are different versions of the story about Akylas's conversion in Midrash Tanḥuma, some of which read "Akylas," others "Onqelos,"[7] and not one of them gives precedence to the other. Accordingly, in order to facilitate our understanding of the matter and to avoid being misled by scribal and printing errors such as to suppose that they were one creation, sharing one soul, I thought it right to explain the real truth of the matter, and to differentiate between these two holy persons.

Now Onqelos was a righteous proselyte who received instruction[8] from Hillel and Shammai as is evident from the passage in the Zohar on the verse, *My rules alone you shall observe, and faithfully follow My laws* (Lev. 18:4) regarding the prohibition of

1. I.e., ch. 42.
2. B. B.Q. 6b: "This Tanna was a Jerusalemite who employed an easier form."
3. T. Dem. 6:12–13.
4. P. Dem. 6 (7) 25d.
5. B. Meg. 3a.
6. P. Meg. 1 (5) 71c.
7. Tanḥuma, Mishpaṭim 5 (Buber, 3). See ch. 42, n. 2.
8. 'Received instruction,' lit. one who knows how to read. Cf. Is. 29:11.

teaching gentiles. It reads:[9] "Peace be on the fathers of the world, Hillel and Shammai, for thus they said to Onqelos, and they did not teach him a word of Torah until he was circumcised." I take this as indication that Onqelos must have set eyes on Jonathan ben Uzziel. For in Bava Batra,[10] Jonathan is described as having quarreled with Shammai the elder about a person who gave his estate to him because of the misconduct of his sons. There is also a story in tractate Shabbat in the Tosefta[11] and Avodah Zarah[12] which would date Onqelos to the time of Rabban Gamaliel the elder. It reads: "It is told that when Rabban Gamaliel died, Onqelos the proselyte burnt [garments] worth seventy Tyrian *minae.*" These examples shed light on the identity of the Rabban Gamaliel mentioned in the Tosefta, tractate Miqvaʾor,[13] who took a ritual bath together with Onqelos, and again in the final section of tractate Kelim of the Tosefta[14] in which Onqelos's cook brought his board [on which he kneaded bread] to Rabban Gamaliel. In both cases the reference must have been to Rabban Gamaliel the elder. From the first chapter of Shabbat[15] we also know that Hillel, Simeon [his son], the Gamaliel under discussion, and Simeon all officiated as patriarchs over a period of one hundred years during Temple times. Gamaliel, as Rambam [Maimonides] also notes in his introduction to the Mishnah,[16] did not live to see the destruction of the Temple. Akylas, on the other hand, according to Shemot Rabbah,[17] said to Emperor Hadrian, "I wish to become a proselyte." There is also the passage in the Tanḥuma cited above and in Bereshit Rabbah[18] that is also cited in Midrash Qohelet[19] which indicate that he did not convert until the time of Hadrian, his sister's husband,[20] who destroyed Betar 52 years after the destruction of the Temple, and only began to study Torah in the time of Rabbi Eliezer and Rabbi Joshua. Thus it reads:[21] "Akylas said to Hadrian: 'I wish to convert. . . .' He went off to the Land of Israel and began to put questions to Rabbi Eliezer and Rabbi Joshua." To one of his questions, Rabbi Eliezer responded in a patronizing manner (in Avot d'Rabbi Nathan[22] and tractate Shabbat,[23] Shammai is said to have behaved in the same manner towards another potential convert), whereas Rabbi Joshua (like Hillel in the corresponding story) was kind and patient. It is as clear as sunlight to me that this Akylas is to be identified with the person whom the gentiles call Aquila. For the reason I gave in chapter 8, he made another Greek translation of the Torah, his being the first of the three translations which were composed after the Septuagint. Now I have noted that several writers and in particular, the bishop of

9. Zohar III, 73a.
10. B. B.B. 133b.
11. T. Shabb. 7:18.
12. B. A.Z. 11a.
13. T. Miq. 6:3.
14. T. Kel., Bava Batra, 2:4.
15. B. Shabb. 15a.
16. Maimonides, *Perush* (Introduction, ch. 4).
17. S.R. 30:12.
18. B.R. 70:5 (802).
19. Q.R. to Eccl. 7:8.
20. The text should read "the son of Hadrian's sister."
21. Tanḥuma, Mishpaṭim 5 (Buber, 3).
22. ARN, ch. 15 (rec. A, 60–61).
23. B. Shabb. 31a.

Mondognedo,[24] in the second part of his volumes of *Letters,* claim that this Aquila was a pagan priest from the island of Pontus which is located in Magna Grecia. He became a righteous proselyte in the fourth year of the reign of the emperor Hadrian [*sic*],[25] in the year 104 of the Christian era, 31 years after the destruction of the Temple. It is however true that Mondognedo remarks pointedly that Aquila's action was motivated by his love for a fair maiden of our people. And truly did he indeed speak, if he would allow us to interpret the maiden as a synonym for Torah whose breasts gave him satisfaction.[26] He further remarks that Jews held his translation of little account since it was written by a foreigner, and that it was completely disregarded by the gentiles. In his prefaces to holy Writ, and specifically, the prefaces to the book of Ezra[27] and Job,[28] the Christian translator [Jerome] wrote that Aquila's translation indicated a Jewish bias for he suppressed some of the mysteries which, in their view, it contains. And in his introduction to the translation of the chronological tables of Eusebius the Caesarean,[29] he writes disparagingly of Aquila's literal rendering since, according to initiates in the esoteric, such a method of translation is considered to be inappropriate since it can only distort the meaning of the text. In my opinion, this was also one of the reasons which prompted our rabbis of blessed memory to state in Qiddushin[30] and tractate Megillah of the Tosefta:[31] "Whosoever translates a verse exactly according to its structure is a liar." Under the entry for Pontus, the compiler of the Latin dictionary writes:[32] "Aquila, the ancient translator came from the island of Pontus." Our rabbis also said that Akylas came from the island of Pontus. In Torat Kohanim,[33] it is stated: "*And your cattle and the beasts in your land you may eat all its yield* (Lev. 25:7). You may eat that which is "in your land," but not that which Akylas took out to his servants in Pontus." Although this is said to discredit him somewhat for having transgressed the prohibition against taking produce out of the Land of Israel, one might say in his defense that after they had warned him, he desisted. Moreover, I am convinced that this Akylas did not translate any part of holy Writ into Aramaic. He only translated into Greek, speaking, as it were, his native tongue. Indeed, it is a fact that among our numerous tomes, there is no Aramaic translation bearing his name. There is sure proof of this; for in the passages in which an Aramaic Targum is given, the words are in Aramaic, but when Akylas's translation is given, the rendering is invariably in Greek.[34] Thus in Bava Qama, it states:[35] "*How are*

24. Antonio de Guevara, *Libro secondo delle lettere,* 402: "Aquila, naturale dell'Isola di Ponto, la cui conversione al giudaismo non fu gia nel vero per salvar l'anima sua, ma per potersi maritar con una bella Ebrea."

25. The text should read "Trajan."

26. 'Breasts . . . satisfaction.' This phrase based on Pr. 5:19 is used in B. Eruv. 54b as an allegory for Torah study.

27. Jerome, Praefatio in Ezram, (*P.L.* XXVIII, col. 1404).

28. Idem, Praefatio in librum Job, (*P.L.* XXVIII, col. 1082).

29. Eusebius, *Chronicon,* Praefatio Hieronymi, (*P.L.* XXVII, col. 35).

30. B. Qidd. 49a.

31. T. Meg. 4:41.

32. Ambrosius Calepinus, *Dictionarium,* s.v. Pontus: "Ex Ponto fuit Aquila veteris testamenti translator et interpretes."

33. Sifra, Behar, 1:9 (106, col. c).

34. In all the following examples, therefore, the renderings of Rav Joseph are all in Aramaic.

35. B. B.Q. 3b.

his hidden places sought out (Ob. 1:6). Rav Joseph translated, How were his hidden treasures exposed." And in Qiddushin it is stated:[36] "*And a bastard shall settle in Ashdod* (Zech. 9:6): Rav Joseph translated, The House of Israel shall dwell in safety." And in Moʿed Qatan, it is stated: "*My father, my father, chariot of Israel* (2K. 2:12). Rav Joseph translated, My master, my master, who was better to Israel." And in Sanhedrin,[37] it is stated: "*Because this people refuse the waters of Shiloah* (Is. 8:6). Rav Joseph said: 'If it were not for the Targum of this verse [I would not know its meaning]. Because this people have cut down the Davidic dynasty.' " And at the end of Menaḥot,[38] it is stated: "What is meant by *the town of Heres* (Is. 19:18)? Rav Joseph rendered it, The city of Bet Shemesh which is destined to destruction." And in Megillah it is stated:[39] *In that day, the wailing in Jerusalem shall be as great as . . .* (Zech. 12:11). Rav Joseph said: "Were it not for the Targum [we would not know its meaning]. In that time . . ." And in Sota,[40] Rav Sheshet translated the phrase as "bees do" (Deut. 1:44), "As bees spring forth and fly into the heights of the world." And in Nedarim,[41] it is stated: "*for I am a herdsman* (Amos 7:14). Rav Joseph translated, 'For I am an owner of flocks.' " {There is also the passage near the beginning of Midrash Ruth ha-Neʿelam in which it states:[42] "*If your father had spat in her face, would she not bear her shame for seven days* (Num. 12:14). Jonathan translates the verse, 'He shall surely put her to shame.' "}[2]

These then are seven key passages in which the Aramiac words employed are also used in the Targum of Jonathan ben Uzziel. As the Tosafists[43] and Ritba [Yomtov ben Abraham] state,[44] they are attributed to Rav Joseph because he possessed great proficiency in Targum since he was blind and it is forbidden to recite the written text [of Torah] from memory. The same reason could also be given for the occasional attribution of Targum to Rav Sheshet for, according to the statement in Megillah[45] and Bava Batra [*sic*], he too was blind.

As regards Akylas, there is the passage about circumcision in Bereshit Rabbah[46] where the expression *El Shaddai* (Gen. 17:1) is translated by Akylas as *aḳios inqos [aḳsios hiḳanos]* sufficient and enough), which are Greek words that indicate the eternal and indestructible. This idea is conveyed by the rabbis of blessed memory who interpret the verse: "The word and its fullness is insufficient for receiving My Godhead." In other words, all existence in its entirety is incapable of withstanding the likes of Me. In the translation of the Pentateuch which was printed in Constantinople for the Greek Jews,[47]

36. B. Qidd. 72b.
37. B. Sanh. 94b.
38. B. Men. 110a.
39. B. Meg. 3a.
40. B. Sota 48b.
41. B. Ned. 38a.
42. Midrash Ruth ha-Neʿelam col. 75d. De' Rossi discusses this passage more extensively in ch. 9.
43. Tos. to B. B.Q. 3b, s.v. *ḳi-demetargem.*
44. Ritba to B. Meg. 3a (cols. 25–26).
45. B. Meg. The expression "afflicted" that Rav Sheshet uses of himself is understood by Rashi to mean that he was blind. Rav Sheshet is also reputed (see B. Shev. 41b; Eruv. 67a) to have known a vast amount of traditional teaching by heart.
46. B.R. 46:3 (461).
47. The Pentateuch printed in Constantinople in 1547 contained Onqelos, Rashi, Ladino, and Greek translations in Hebrew characters. (On this edition, see E. D. Goldschmidt, "Judaeo-Greek," 131–34).

the words *El Shaddai* are rendered *ego theos yiqanos [hikanos]* which is equivalent to the rendering in our Italian version,[48] "God who is capable of doing whatsoever He wishes." In the Palestinian Talmud,[49] Akylas translates the word *hadar* in the expression *fruit of a goodly (hadar) tree* (Lev. 23:40) as *hydor* which means water in Greek, thus referring to a tree which grows by water, namely, the Etrog. Study the entry for *hadar* in the *Arukh*. In Vayiqra Rabbah,[50] with reference to the verse, *You shall not wrong one another* (Lev. 25:14), Akylas translates the phrase *Death and life [are in the power of the tongue]* (Pr. 18:21) as *mistera mekerin [mustron makhairis]* which are Greek words denoting spoon and knife. Then towards the end of the same passage, the expression *To her that was worn out with adultery* (Ezk. 23:43) is rendered by Akylas as *paliah [palaia porne]* (old harlot).[51] The Midrash concludes with the explanation that it signifies a worn-out harlot (*mebalya giraya*), meaning that she wears out fornications, that is, the tool of fornication. Study the fourth entry for *gr* in the *Arukh* where the Targum for the expression *he who commits adultery* (Pr. 6:32) is *gayyer itteta*. It may be that it is of the same derivation as the expression *gir* [scum] of the lees used in the Mishnah[52] to denote the spurt of the lees. Study the second entry for *gr* and the entries *pl'h* and *prn* in the *Arukh*.

In the Palestinian Talmud[53] and in Vayiqra Rabbah,[54] Akylas renders the expression *He will lead us evermore (almut)* (Ps. 48:15) as *at[h]anasia* which signifies a world without death. Similarly, in Shir ha-Shirim Rabbah,[55] Akylas translates the word *alamot* in the phrase, *maidens (alamot) playing timbrels* (Ps. 68:26) as *at[h]anasia* and surprisingly fails to distinguish between *alamot* and *almut*.[56] Again in the Palestinian Talmud, tractate Qiddushin,[57] you find that he does not distinguish the letters *he* and *ḥet*. It reads as follows: "Akylas the proselyte translated in the presence of Rabbi Aqiva and rendered the word *neḥerefet* in the phrase, *and she is a woman designated (neḥerefet) for a man* (Lev. 19:20), as pounded before a man as though it read, *And she scattered groats (harifot) on it* (2Sam. 17:19). It is as though his version read *neherefet* with the letter *he*. Nevertheless, this does not really present a problem since in the Palestinian Talmud[58] there is the statement of the rabbis of blessed memory: "The rabbis were not loathe to substitute *he* for *ḥet* in their exegesis so that the expression *holiness hillulim* (praises) [*of the Lord*] (Lev. 19:24) became *ḥillulim* (profanations). Similarly, in tractates Maʿaser Sheni and Shabbat of the Palestinian Talmud,[59] it is stated: "*These (eleh) are the precepts* (Ex. 35:1) alludes to the thirty-nine categories of work" as though the word *eleh*

48. The Italian version of the Bible published by Niccolò de Malermi in Venice in 1471 was translated by the humanist Bartolomeo della Fonte (Fonzio). The rendering of the phrase is "Io signor Omnipotente."
49. P. Sukk. 3 (5) 53d.
50. V.R. 33:1 (756).
51. Ibid. 33:6 (767).
52. M. Men. 8:7.
53. P. M.Q. 3 (7) 83b; P. Meg. 2 (4) 73b.
54. V.R. 11:9 (241–42).
55. S.S.R. to S.S. 1:3.
56. De' Rossi appears to have misread the Midrash. Aquilas's interpretation is given in reference to the phrase *almut*, not *alamot*.
57. P. Qidd. 1 (1) 59a.
58. P. Pe'ah 7 (6) 20b.
59. P. Maʿaser Sheni, 5 (2) 56a; P. Shabb. 7 (5) 9b.

was written with a *ḥet.*[60] This example is also cited in the *Arukh* under the entry for *av.* And in Megillah, they say:[61] "Hataḥ is Daniel because they demoted him [*hateḥuhu*] from his position, or else, because all matters of state were decided (*neḥtakhim*) by him." At the beginning of Aḥare Mot Rabbah,[62] the phrase, *I said to wanton men (la-holelim)* (Ps. 75:5) is interpreted as *la-ḥolelim,* "those whose heart is full of wicked intrigues [*ḥolḥaliot*]" which according to the *Arukh* means "thoughts." And in the Pesiqta,[63] the expression "with your wealth" (*me-honekha*) in *Honor the Lord with your wealth* (Pr. 3:9) is interpreted, "with what he has endowed you (*mi-ma she-ḥananekha*)." The same case arises in the passage from Qiddushin quoted above; for after citing Akylas, the passage concludes: "Rabbi Eleazer son of Rabbi Simeon explained Akylas's words to the sages: *A maidservant designated for a man* means that she is pounded before a man in the sense conveyed by the expression, *with a pestle among the groats* (Pr. 27:22)." The device used in enigmatic sayings of substituting *ḥet* for *he* is found in the passage in Eruvin:[64] "Prepare me a bull in judgment on a poor mountain (*ṭur misken*)." Bull corresponds to *tor,* judgment to *din,* from which the word *tardin* is formed which means beet. Mountain corresponds to *har,* poor to *dal* which forms the word *ḥardal,* mustard,[65] although "*ṭur misken*" can actually only mean "poor mountain."[66] Then there is a number of cases in which, according to the compiler of the *Arukh,* the word *memaheh* (threadbare) is written with the letter *he* but understood as though spelled with a *ḥet,* meaning "erased." The Targum on the verse, *Those whom God's hands have produced* (Job 12:6) may assist you. It reads: "God will bring a plague (maḥata) in his hand." And in Taʿanit,[67] they read the expression *distilling (hashrat) of waters* (2S. 22:12) with the letter *ḥet* instead of *he* such that they say with regard to the waters of the ocean that are sweetened by the clouds, "Take away the letter *kaf* in *hashkat,* add it to the word written with the letter *resh,* and read *hakhsharat (drinkable).*"

All this is not due to error or variant readings. Kimḥi of blessed memory justifiably expressed his surprise at Ḥayyuj in the entry for the root *rhb.*[68] Rather, it is that there are people who speak in their local unintelligible language and pronounce *he* as *ḥet* and vice versa. In like manner the natives of Haifa and Bet Shean and the Tibbonim are mentioned in tractate Megillah[69] as pronouncing *alef* as *ayin* and vice versa. Thus in that context, that sage [R. Ḥiyya] reproved his colleague with regard to the pronunciation of the verse, *And I will wait for the Lord* (Is. 8:17).[70] I had already come to know

60. The numerical value of *eleh* spelled with a *ḥet* rather than a *he* amounts to 39.

61. B. Meg. 15a.

62. V.R. 20:2 (445).

63. Pesiqta Rabbati 25:2.

64. B. Eruv. 53b.

65. The word *ḥardal* is spelled with a *ḥet,* whereas the word *har* is with a *he.*

66. The first expression "poor mountain" is in Aramaic and is then transferred into the two Hebrew words *har* and *dal* on which the play with the interchanging of the *he* and the *ḥet* is based.

67. B. Taʿanit 10a.

68. David Kimḥi, *Sefer ha-Shorashim,* s.v. *rhb.* Kimḥi disagrees with the Hebrew grammarian Judah Hayyuj who read the word *raḥav* which occurs in Is. 60:5 as though it was written with a *he* rather than a *ḥet.*

69. B. Meg. 24b.

70. He was unable to pronounce the *ḥet* in the word *ve-ḥiketi* and would therefore say blasphemously *ve-hiketi* (I shall smite).

about this through an old man from Apulia* who when asked the reason for this phenomenon, ascribed it to local custom.

(*On this question I cannot refrain from telling those who are fatigued from study[71] about an incident that happened to him which illustrates my point. One day he was reciting the section *All these blessings shall come upon you and take effect* (Deut. 28:2) in the presence of the fluent-speaking Rabbi Eliezer of Pisa. As was his custom, he pronounced the *kaf* which is like the *ḥet* as a *he.* Rabbi Eliezer appeared to keep his peace. On another occasion, he heard him read the response to Job, *She leaves her eggs on the ground* (Job 39:14). Then he gnashed his teeth, smiting him with a grievous curse. He [the old man] said: "You black pot,[72] if you will not bless me, you should also not curse me.")

And so, some sages of the Land of Israel who spoke in these ways would use some of the words for exegetical purposes or support in accordance with the consonantal text or the traditional pronunciation of Scripture. Thus, as Rashi of blessed memory comments, Jonathan ben Uzziel provides a twofold translation for *the town of Heres* (Is. 19:18). For he renders it "the city of Bet Shemesh" [*ḥeres* means glow] and "that which is bound for destruction" [i.e., from the root *hrs*]. Similarly, at the end of Menaḥot[73] (and it is cited by the compiler of the *Arukh* under the entry for *ḥeres*), it is stated: "How do we know the meaning of this word *ḥeres?* It signifies sun as in the verse, *Who commands the sun* (heres) (Job 9:7). Similarly in Keritot, they say:[74] "And where do we find that the term "designated" [*neḥerefet*] implies that a change has taken place? (Rashi explains that the woman's natural condition has been changed by sexual intercourse, namely, by the pounding.) Because it is written, *Even if you pound the fool in a mortar with a pestle among the groats* (Pr. 27:22)—a change is effected by means of the pounding. Indeed, the interchanging of letters was a very common practice and the entire phenomenon is undoubtedly to be considered from the perspective that we gave. Accordingly, the statement of the wise ibn Ezra on the verse, *Who commands the sun* is rendered invalid; for he expresses surprise at the substitution of *he* for *ḥet.* He must be alluding to the Targum of Jonathan ben Uzziel and the anonymous statement in Menaḥot. Moreover, I put great store by it, and in my opinion, it will be appreciated by Christian intellectuals and the learned of our own people. For from this root, a sprout will come forth for their wise translator [Jerome] with his rendering "until he who is sent[75] will come."[76] However, the Septuagint which in many instances he uses as his model renders, "until he to whom it belongs does come," namely, whose scepter it is.

But let us now resume the subject of Akylas. You will notice that in Shir ha-Shirim Rabbah,[77] the word *riqmah* (embroidered garments) in the verse, *I clothed you with*

71. 'Fatigued . . . study,' cf. B. Eruv. 28b.
72. An expression taken from B. A.Z. 16b.
73. B. Men. 110a.
74. B. Ker. 11a.
75. Jerome thus renders Shiloh in the verse *until he comes to Shiloh* (Gen. 46:10) as though Shilo is spelled with a *ḥet* and not a *he.*
76. Jerome translates Gen. 46:10 "donec veniat qui mittendus est." In this sentence redolent with mesianic vocabulary ("sprout"), de' Rossi appears to be saying (using terminology from Is. 11:1) that Jerome's rendering would suggest that the Messiah is yet to come.
77. S.S.R. to S.S. 4:12.

embroidered garments (Ezk. 16:10) is rendered as *iplekta [empoikilta]* by Akylas. According to the reading given in the *Arukh,* he rendered it *pukreton, poilikton.* And in Midrash Esther,[78] he renders the words "white" [*ḥur*] and "fine cotton" [*karpas*] (Est. 1:6) as *eirinon karpasinon* (woollen and flaxen). And in the Palestinian Talmud, tractate Shabbat,[79] Akylas renders the expression *bate ha-nefesh* (perfume boxes, lit. receptacles of the soul; Is. 3:20) as *stomakheia* which, according to the explanation in the *Arukh,* means "something which is placed on the location of the soul." And in tractate Yoma[80] of the Palestinian Talmud, Akylas renders the expression *in front of the candlestick* (Dan. 5:5) as *lampados.*

These then are the thirteen key Greek expressions employed by Akylas. No doubt there are other such examples in the Gemarot and Midrashim. It is therefore obvious that Akylas did not translate into Aramaic, but only into Greek, his native tongue. Furthermore, in the conversation between Hadrian and Akylas, recorded at the end of the passage from the Tanḥuma cited above, he says to him: "You give the *isteratilates annona*" which means "you give a gift[81] to the commander." Thus in the Palestinian Talmud, in Megillah,[82] with regard to the teaching of Rabban Simeon ben Gamaliel that it is only permitted for scrolls of Torah to be written in Greek, Rabbi Ḥiyya said: "Akylas the proselyte translated the Torah before Rabbi Eliezer and Rabbi Joshua and they praised him and said, *You are fairer than all men* (Ps. 45:3)." The compliment was apposite since the rabbis of blessed memory connect the term "fair" (*yofi*) with Greek when they say in Megillah:[83] "Let the beauty of Yafet [i.e., Greece] dwell in the in the tents of Shem [Israel]."[84] And it is indeed beautiful as we demonstrated at the end of chapter 8. Particularly noteworthy is the statement of Rabbi Abbahu in the name of Rabbi Johanan in tractates Pe'ah[85] and Shabbat[86] of the Palestinian Talmud: "It is permitted for a man to teach his daughter Greek for it will be an ornament for her." The passage does, however, continue with the statement of Rabbi Simeon bar Ba who says: "Because Rabbi Abbahu wants to teach his daughter Greek, he transfers the responsibility for it on Rabbi Johanan." Finally, Rabbi Abbahu responds: "May [evil] befall me if it is true that I did not receive this tradition from Rabbi Johanan."

You may take this as additional proof that Onqelos and Akylas were two individuals, composing different translations; the one composed an Aramaic translation, the other a Greek one. As Avicenna[87] and the author of the *Kuzari*[88] wrote: "Distinctive actions point to potencies that are also distinctive." I consider it most worthwhile that I began this useful section with this observation. For should you come across the entire transla-

78. Est. R. 2:7 to Est. 1:6.
79. P. Shabb. 6 (4) 8b.
80. P. Yoma 3 (8) 41a.
81. The Latin word *annona* means rations or pensions. *Isteratilates* is a loanword from the Greek *stratelates.*
82. P. Meg. 1 (9) 71c.
83. B. Meg. 9b.
84. This is a play on Gen. 9:27.
85. P. Pe'ah 1 (1) 15c.
86. P. Shabb. 6 (1) 7d.
87. De' Rossi is referring here to the Hebrew translation of Avicenna's *Canon* which was first printed in Naples in 1491. The passage to which he refers is bk. 1, Ofan 1 (= fen 1), Limmud (= doctrina) 6 (ch. 1).
88. *Kuzari* V, par. 4.

tion of Aquila which is only to be found in royal collections, you will find relevant new material and be pleased with yourself for having appropriated it.[89] What is more, the lips of Akylas, as the rabbinic saying goes, will murmur in the grave[90] and blessings sent by him from heaven will fall on me. For after 1,466 years have elapsed since his circumcision, I will have rejuvenated him like an eagle [Aquila = eagle];[91] with our sages, he will be remembered for good, and I will have reclaimed him from the nations. In a short while, you will be able to consider passages from the *Hebraicae Quaestiones* of the Christian translator [Jerome][92] which are in part 3 of his *Opera* and from the *Recognitio* of Bishop Eugubinus, both of whom cite many examples from Aquila's translation which they treat in its own right, separately from other translations. According to the translator's statement in the first preface to Chronicles, the Christian doctor Origen who lived in the generation before Jerome, collated the four Greek translations which were known at that time—the Septuagint, Aquila, Symmachus, Theodotion—and arranged them in four columns in one book. You are sure to remember what I wrote about them in chapter 8. In his work cited above, the bishop of Mondognedo[93] writes that the ancients also possessed a work which contained six columns [Hexapla], for two other translations were included. There is the translation which is well known nowadays, whose author remains unidentified (although I did hear that some Christians are of a different opinion). He claims that in past times, one of their patriarchs called Joannes Budaeus discovered it hidden underground in the city of Jericho—that is why some call it "Hierichontina," namely, of Jericho.[94] The other translation was Origen's collation of all four translations that we mentioned. Now from that time, the Christian bishops gave preference to the Jericho translation, thus causing the disappearance of all the other translations from the public eye. Nevertheless, the translator [Jerome], who was a great doctor and leader from the highest ranks of the Christians, actually saw the translation of Aquila and studied it in depth. And so where appropriate, in his *Hebraicae Quaestiones,* he cites some of its renderings and also those of all the other translations. Now in these times, during the reign of Pope Clement the seventh,[95] the bishop, author of the *Recognitio* served as custodian of the great collection of books stored in Rome, nowadays known as the holy Palace.[96] He actually saw the translation there, and thus was in a position to cite passages from it which were not mentioned by the translator. He also gives some citations from Greek commentators on the Bible which had not yet been sullied by the eye. If God deems me worthy, I shall

89. 'Pleased . . . it,' cf. Pr. 4:8.

90. Sanh. 90b: "The lips of he whose *halakhah* is mentioned in this world will murmur in the grave."

91. A pun based on Ps. 103:5.

92. The *Hebraicae Quaestiones* appear in the third volume of both the Basel 1516 and Rome 1565 editions of Jerome's *Opera Omnia.*

93. Antonio de Guevara, *Libro secondo delle lettere,* 403.

94. On this, see ch. 7, n. 56.

95. De' Rossi is incorrect. Steuchus was appointed librarian of the Vatican by Paul III (1534–49) in 1543. Moreover, Steuchus himself states in the preface of his *Recognitio* which he dedicated to Cardinal Domenico Grimani that he had discovered these rare texts in the library of the cardinal, which had been transferred to Venice while he was custodian of the Sant'Antonio library. Although part of Grimani's library was brought to Rome, it is obvious that Steuchus was utilizing Grimani's library while he was in Venice.

96. I.e., Bibliotheca Palatii Apostolici.

undertake a study of the works of both these sages and will translate all the passages in which they cite Aquila and put them together with the citations of Akylas mentioned by our ancestors.

And so now, I cannot refrain from providing you with some indications and proof by plucking buds and shoots from either author. In the *Recognitio,* the bishop writes that Aquila translated the expression *tohu va-vohu* as *ḳenoma ḳai out[h]en* which means emptiness and nothing, a rendering which appears to follow the meaning as expressed in Onqelos's Targum. This is all the more likely, given that their lifetimes overlapped—the former being an older colleague and the latter, a younger student of Rabbi Eliezer and Rabbi Joshua. And there is no doubt that in his Greek translation, Aquila followed in the footsteps of Onqelos's Aramaic Targum and sometimes that of Jonathan ben Uzziel who also translated the Torah as we wrote in part 1, chapter 9. Now I noticed that the Targum of Jonathan ben Uzziel as well as the Palestinian Targum which is at the end of the Rabbinic Bibles,[97] did not contain the Targum quoted above about the bees flying into the height of the world. Also missing is the Targum used in the controversy between Rav and Levi in Zevaḥim[98] as to whether the altar was built on Benjamin's territory or not. In that context, Rav quotes the Targum:[99] "In his heritage shall the altar be built." Levi quotes the Targum: "In his heritage shall the Sanctuary be built." (In my opinion, this was not their own interpretation, but a version of a Targum that was known in their day.) This Targum is not found in the Targum of Jonathan ben Uzziel nor in the Palestinian Targum. I therefore concluded that there must have been another version extant among our people in those times. Therefore the Targum about the bees is attributed to Rav Sheshet and not to Rav Joseph who is quoted as Targumist in all the other passages—for the two Targumim are dissimilar. At any rate, the fact is that this pair of pious sages, Onqelos and Akylas, with the approval of Rabbi Eliezer and Rabbi Joshua, both translated the expression *tohu va-vohu* as emptiness and nothingness. I also noticed that Jonathan ben Uzziel rendered it: "The land was empty and void, devoid of human beings and void of any creature." And even Symmachus and Theodotion, as the bishop states in the same context, agree with Akylas's translation but use different words. These then come to a total of eight noble men.[100] So go and inform those who interpret the words as matter and form, manipulating the words of the living God with Greek inventions, using the concept of *hyle* and its various forms, that with all due respect for their teaching, this is not the way to come to understand the actions of our God.[101] Now with the information given you in chapter 25, you now know that according to its literal meaning, the word *bereshit* signifies "in bygone times." You can therefore claim that the verse is conveying the idea that the part of

97. He is referring to the Venice 1517 edition of the *Rabbinic Bible* in which the Targum Yerushalmi is printed at the end of the second volume.

98. B. Zev. 54a.

99. I.e., they discuss the meaning of the verse about Benjamin, *And he rests between his shoulders* (Deut. 33:12).

100. 'Noble men,' cf. Micah 5:4.

101. Interestingly, this attack on the use of Greek notions is made by Steuchus himself against certain Jews and is counterattacked by de' Rossi himself in ch. 5 in his critique of Philo. Here, de' Rossi, concerned to provide proof of the identity of Aqylas (i.e., he does not need to attack or defend Philo), feels free to use Steuchus's argument for his own purposes.

existence which is now our earth was once empty and devoid of all matter and being. Similarly, the abyss which is regarded as the lowest part of existence was covered with darkness and void. Nothing existed save the spirit of God and His throne of glory which, according to Rashi's explanation based on statements of our rabbis, was hovering in the imaginary upper air on the face of existence—once created, this was called waters which encompass and surround the whole earth. At this point, the blessed Lord made His first utterance, *Let there be light*—before this, nothing whatsoever had been created. In the same context, the bishop makes the fine observation that the darkness and abyss mentioned in this passage can only mean nothing and nonexistence.[102]

In his *Quaestiones,*[103] the noble translator explains the expression "coat of many colors" (Gen. 37:3) and writes that Aquila rendered it with the word *astragleion* which means a long garment that reaches the tips, namely, the fingers and ankles. This is certainly an apposite interpretation, for Scripture describes Joseph from the perspective of Jacob, as a son of his old age, because he had the wisdom[104] and composure of an old and melancholic man. According to the philosopher [Aristotle] in his work, the *Magna Moralia for Eudemus,*[105] the special character of such a person is that he has dreams that come true. This is why his father gave him a long coat such as is worn by devotees of learning and the self-composed. It is the mode of dress of the noblemen of the renowned city of Venice who perspire in their robes.[106] Thus Joseph also wore it when he traveled. I was delighted to discover that the term is interpreted in the same way in Bereshit Rabbah. It reads:[107] "*Passim* indicates that it reached as far as his wrist (*pas yado*)." Moreover, the third of the three translators called Symmachus as is indicated in the *Quaestiones* rendered it as *manicuta,* which signifies a garment with sleeves which reach the wrist. Such an interpretation demonstrates that the upright commentator Redaq [Kimḥi] was confused in his explanation of the statement about Tamar. *On her was a ḳetonet passim for so maiden princesses were customarily dressed in such meʿilim* (2S. 13:18). For he said that when the term *meʿil* is used without qualification, it is identical with the long cloak of the high priest that reaches the feet, but here the expression "for so" indicates that it also refers to the *ḳetonet.* Furthermore a novel idea is conveyed in the verse, *His mother would make him a little robe* (*meʿil*) (1Sam. 2:19). By clothing him [Samuel] in this outfit, she was preparing him for the composure and peace of mind which is required for the holy ministry. Likewise he was girded with a linen efod (ibid. v.18) which is a garment used for the same purpose. The efod of the high priest contained the colors blue and purple, the characteristic of nobility and true holiness.

102. *Recognitio,* 101: "Chaos itaque et thou et bou et nihil idem sunt."

103. *Heb. Quaest.* (*P.L.* XXIII, cols. 994–95): "Pro varia tunica, Aquila interpretatus est . . . id est tunicam talarem." The expression does not, as de' Rossi claims, indicate a long-sleeved garment.

104. This interpretation is given in Targum Onqelos ad loc. and is cited by Rashi.

105. De' Rossi's confused reference to two difference works, namely, the *Eudemian Ethics* and the *Magna Moralia* was probably due to the conflation of these works in a work circulating under the title *De bona fortuna* which was first published in Venice in 1482. In this short compilation, bk. 8 ch. 2 of the *Eudemian Ethics* is conflated with bk. 2 ch. 8 of the *Magna Moralia.* The passage to which he refers is *Eudemian Ethics* 8, 1248a–b: "That is why the melancholic even have dreams that are true, for it seems that when the reason is disengaged, the principle has more strength" (Loeb, trans. Rackham).

106. 'Perspire . . . robes,' cf. Ezk. 44:18.

107. B.R. 84:8 (1010).

Likewise, those who garb themselves in His image and likeness, in mere linen, which is not holy, as it were, approach and surrender themselves to holiness in this way. In my opinion, this was the reason why the priests of Nob were clad with the linen efod (1Sam. 22:18) and David, too, wore the linen efod (2Sam. 6:14). Rambam of blessed memory puts forward a similar explanation[108] and the passage in tractate Yoma in the Tosefta is apparently even more accommodating to such a view.[109] Similarly in the episode with the necromancer, Samuel is described as *an old man coming up wrapped in a robe (meʿil)* (1Sam. 28:14). The word *meʿil* refers to a long robe, and since it is worn over other clothes, it may be derived from the root *al* as in the expression *over (meʿal) his garment* (1Sam. 17:39). The Romans call it *pallium* which according to the compiler of their Dictionary derived from the word *palam* which means open or disclosed in their language.[110] The same explanation could be applied to the *ketonet* since it is described in this way in the expressions, *the coat (ketonet) of many colors which was on him,* and *on her was the ketonet.*

Now intelligent reader, you should accept three more examples of Akylas's renderings which I saw in the work of the bishop and reap the benefit. The expression *sevenfold* in the verse *If Cain is avenged sevenfold* (Gen. 4:24) is rendered *[h]eptaplos,* namely, in seven parts.[111] In other words, Cain who killed his blameless brother will receive his punishment in only seven installments. I, Lamech, who killed a lad for wounding me and bruising me (as the Septuagint renders it), should I therefore not have my punishment allocated in seventy-seven installments such that I will not feel any pain? This is certainly a fine interpretation which provides for leniency similar to Onqelos who rendered it "over seven generations." The real meaning of *shivatayim* (sevenfold) is *beshivatayim* (in seven times), just as the expression *Six days God made the heavens and earth* (Ex. 31:17) actually means *in six days.*

The expression *Then there was a beginning* (Gen. 4:26) is rendered *tote erkhetai [erkheto]*[112] which means "then it was begun" which corresponds to ibn Ezra's explanation that they began to pray [to God]. And then the expression *ḥamushim* [armed][113] in the verse, *Now the Israelites went up armed out of the land of Egypt* (Ex. 13:18) is *enoplismenoi* which, like Onqelos's rendering, means "armed." The Septuagint, however, renders "in the fifth[114] generation," although Scripture is explicit that *the fourth generation shall return* (Gen. 15:16). When Morenu ha-Rav Phineas Elijah, may his rock and redeemer guard him, son of Morenu ha-Rav Zemaḥ da Melli[115] of blessed memory heard the explanation of the word "sevenfold," he was pleased and said that a similar

108. *Mishneh Torah,* Kele ha-Miqdash X:13: "and thus you find that the priests who wore the linen efod were not high priests. For the high priest's efod was not made of linen. And even the Levites wore it for Samuel the prophet was a Levite. . . . Rather this efod was worn by the sons of prophets and by whosoever was inspired by the Holy Spirit."

109. He is probably referring to T. Yom ha-Kipp. 4:20 which describes how spittle on the high priest's vestments disqualified him from ministering on the Day of Atonement.

110. Ambrogio Calepino, *Dictionarium,* s.v. Pallium: "Pallium dictum est quod palam hoc est foris gestaretur."

111. Steuchus, *Recognitio,* 38r.

112. Ibid., 39r.

113. Ibid., 116r.

114. I.e., the word is connected with *ḥamesh* (five).

115. Phineas Elijah da Melli was a scribe of the community of Mantua.

view is expressed by the author of the *Iqqarim*[116] with regard to the verse, *visiting the guilt of the parents of the children upon the third and upon the fourth generations of those who hate Me but showing kindness to the thousandth generation of those who love Me* (Ex. 20:5, 6). He gave the following interpretation. In the case of those who hate God, the visitation of the iniquity is only allocated over four generations at the most; but to those who love Him, He allocates His kindness over thousands of generations in the manner described by our rabbis of blessed memory.[117] "It is like a man who lends a thousand *zuz*; from his enemy, he collects the debt in one sum, but from his friend, he will collect payment in installments." As is known, the word "Targum" means interpretation into any language that is understood. As is stated in Shabbat:[118] "Rav Ḥisda interpreted it [*tirgemah*]." The verse, *For there was a meliṣ (an interpreter) between them* (Gen. 42:23) is translated by Onqelos: "There was an interpreter (*meturgeman*) between them."

Now on the basis of the above information we have obtained the following conclusions. Onqelos and Akylas are different individuals. Akylas is to be identified with Aquila and, as we said, only translated into Greek and not into Aramaic. Accordingly, the scholar may emend scribal errors as is required and as far as it is possible. If, nevertheless, somebody asserts aggressively that the two names are interchangeable and that Onqelos is called Aqylas in the Jerusalemite idiom and that in the Babylonian idiom Akylas is called Onqelos, we may respond without hesitation that these two translators were two different individuals with two different life histories. Now once the truth of this is made clear to you, you will find that on occasions, the expression "Akylas translated" is followed by a Hebrew word. For example, in Bereshit Rabbah it states: [119] "*And one holy being said to whomever (la-palmoni)* (Dan. 8:13). Akylas translated: "He spoke to him who was within (*li-penimi*) which refers to Adam [whose partition was within that of the ministering angels]." Consequently, you would rightly conclude that the author of the statement omitted the Greek word and gave the rendering in his own native tongue. Likewise in Bereshit Rabbah, it is stated:[120] "*Like golden apples in silver settings* (Pr. 25:11). Akylas the proselyte translated the verse: "Like apples of gold on a silver plate (*diskarion*)." Rashi explained the word *diskus* as meaning table. If this reading is correct, the example belongs to the category mentioned before. That is, the author of the statement thought it sufficient to inform us that the word *diskarin* is the Greek for table—the Italian equivalent is *desco*—while the rest of the statement is in Aramaic, the language of the sages. Now under the entry *dsqr,* the author of the *Arukh* cites the passage in the name of Onqelos, but we can dismiss this as an error, knowing full well that he translated only the Pentateuch.[121] Nor could it be attributed to Jonathan ben Uzziel, for he did not translate the Hagiographa as is indicated in tractate Megillah.[122] The Tosafists therefore decided that the extant Targum of the Hagiographa was written by somebody we are unable to identify. In fact,

116. Joseph Albo, *Sefer ha-Iqqarim,* bk. 4, ch. 38 (377).
117. B. A.Z. 4a.
118. B. Shabb. 115b.
119. B.R. 21:1 (198).
120. B.R. 93:3 (1152).
121. I.e., the translation under discussion is of a verse from Proverbs.
122. B. Meg. 3a.

this verse [i.e., Pr. 25:11] is rendered, "Golden apples in vessels of beaten metal" and does not correspond to the rendering given in Bereshit Rabbah. A problem does arise with regard to the comment on the verse, *If the clouds are filled* (Eccl. 11:3) in Midrash Qohelet. It reads: "*And I will command the clouds* (Is. 5:6). Akylas translated: "I will command the prophets that they shall prophesy to them no more prophesies." Do not be mistaken—this is a textual error,[123] and the translation should have been attributed to Jonathan in whose Targum this rendering is to be found. In any case, mere doubt cannot detract from absolute certainty which is as clear as the light of the sun.

Now you should not mistake this Aquila with his namesake mentioned in their Acts of the Apostles[124] and in their Letter to the Romans.[125] But, dear reader, I should make you wise to the fact that although the names are the same, and both came from the island of Pontus, the one is the opposite of the other. The former was a Jew who, according to those two passages, became an apostate; whereas the latter was a gentile who converted to Judaism. The former lived during the reigns of the emperors Claudius and Nero before the destruction of the Temple; the latter during the time of Hadrian after the destruction. In any case, the Aramaic translation of the Pentateuch was composed by Onqelos and not by Akylas as is stated in Megillah: "Onqelos the proselyte translated the Torah under the jurisdiction [lit. from the mouth of] of Rabbi Eliezer and Rabbi Joshua." The expression "from the mouth of" cannot be interpreted as similar in meaning to the statement of Baruch son of Neriah *from his mouth he recited to me all these words and I would write them down* (Jer. 36:18). For otherwise, the authorship of the Targum would be ascribed to them, just as Jeremiah [and not Baruch] is ascribed with the authorship of those prophecies. Rather, the expression is indicative of their approbation, namely, they saw and praised it. Likewise they said to Onqelos, "You are the fairest of men." Now it is made clear in the Pesiqta that Hillel lived 120 years, 80 years of which he was engaged in study.[126] Thus it is not problematic for us that Onqelos lived at the end of his lifetime, during the days of Rabban Gamaliel, before the destruction of the Temple, and also later, in the time of Rabbi Eliezer and Rabbi Joshua. Furthermore, we have undeniable proof that Onqelos and Rabbi Eliezer were both present at the time of the death of Rabban Gamaliel the elder. The tradition is given in Moʿed Qatan:[127] "There is a story about the death of Rabban Gamaliel. As soon as they went out of the door of his house, Rabbi Eliezer said to them, 'Overturn your beds.' After the rolling slab had closed up the entrance, [Rabbi Joshua said to them, 'Overturn your beds.' They said to him, 'We have already overturned them as instructed by the Elder [Rabbi Eliezer].' " As for the Onqelos who, according to tractate Giṭṭin, raised up his uncle Titus by necromancy, he is certainly not the Onqelos we know. For that Onqelos only converted after the death of Titus who destroyed the Temple. The passage reads:[128] "He wanted to convert. He raised Titus from the dead by

123. I.e., it is in Aramaic and therefore, according to de' Rossi's argument, cannot be ascribed to Akylas.

124. Acts 18:2: *There he [Paul] fell in with a Jew named Aquila, a native from Pontus.*

125. Rom. 16:3: *Give my greetings to Prisca and Aquila* (also 1Cor. 16:19; 2Ti. 4:19).

126. *Pesiqta Zuṭarta (Leqaḥ Ṭov),* Zot ha-Berakhah, to Deut. 34:7 (135).

127. B. M.Q. 27a. De' Rossi is implying that Onqelos was one of the mourners at Rabban Gamaliel's funeral, possibly on the basis of the passage in the Tosefta (Shabb. 7:18) quoted at the beginning of the chapter.

128. B. Giṭṭ. 56b.

necromancy. He said to him, 'What then, should I join them?'" The additional name Bar Kalonikos that he is given is even more indicative. Moreover, since he was the son of the sister of Titus, he is descended from a Roman mother and according to all probability, his father was also Roman. In any case, we can now assert that Akylas is identical with Aquila. Should we hear Christian doctors refer to him, we shall strain ourselves to listen and become a most receptive audience.[129]

129. 'Receptive audience,' lit. make our ear like a hopper. Cf. B. Ḥull. 89a.

CHAPTER FORTY-SIX

Controversies among our commentators regarding the design of the priestly vestments.

THE purpose of this chapter is to collate the opinions of our sages, the commentators and codifiers, blessed be their memory, on the subject of the priestly vestments. We shall consider their descriptions of the vestments and the specific points which became a bone of contention among them. The subsequent chapters will treat any other opinions on the subject which may contain decisive information for the resolution of some of the controversial issues.

Now the robe (*meʿil*), in Rashi's opinion,[1] was a garment, like the tunic (*ketonet*), but the *ketonet* was a body-clinging garment, while the *meʿil* was worn on top. Ramban (Nahmanides) criticized his view and asserted that it enfolded the body,[2] an opinion which appears to have been held by Rambam (Maimonides).[3] This was also the view expressed by Don Isaac (Abravanel) in his commentary on Exodus.[4] But Rabad (Abraham ben David), author of the *Animadversions*[5] appears to agree with Rashi's interpretation as does the wise Rabbi Elijah Mizraḥi in his *Novellae.*[6] Ralbag (Gersonides) wrote as follows:[7] "The design of the *meʿil* is known to have been completely sleeveless; there was an opening through which the head was inserted, one half hanging over the back, the other half over the front." Regarding the verse, *The opening for the head shall be in the middle of it . . . it shall be like the opening of a coat of mail—so that it does not tear* (Ex. 28:32), Rabbi Obadiah Sforno wrote:[8] "The neck opening in the material was not cut lengthwise, but was circular; for the expression *tear* would be used in connection with something which opened lengthwise as in the verse, *and cut out windows* (Jer. 22:14)."

Furthermore, with regard to the bells which were on its hems, Rashi wrote:[9] "Each

1. Rashi to Ex. 28:4.
2. Ramban to Ex. 28:31.
3. *Mishneh Torah,* Kele ha-Miqdash IX:3.
4. Abravanel to Ex. 28 (277, col. b).
5. In his gloss on Rambam, Kele ha-Miqdash IX:3, he simply says that he does not know the source of Rambam's view.
6. Elijah Mizraḥi (1450–1526), *Perush Rashi* 28:4 (456).
7. Gersonides to Ex. 28:32 (381).
8. Sforno to Ex. 28:32 (195).
9. Rashi to Ex. 28:33.

bell was placed in between two pomegranates." Rambam of blessed memory,[10] the Semag,[11] Ralbag,[12] and Mizraḥi[13] all concurred in this opinion. But Ramban[14] writes that the expression "in between them" in the verse, *On its hem make pomegranates of blue, purple, and crimson yarns, all around the hem with bells of gold in between them all around* (Ex. 28:33) implies that the bell was placed within the pomegranate. Both the author of the *Aqedah* (Isaac Arama)[15] and Don Isaac agreed with his opinion.

The design of the turban (*miṣnefet*) and headtire (*migbaʿot*), according to Rashi's view, was like a helmet.[16] Ramban, however, objected that it was described as being sixteen cubits long which could hardly fit such a description. In his opinion, it resembled the turban which was wound round the head in many coils. Rambam wrote[17] that Aaron's *miṣnefet* was identical to the *migbaʿot* worn by his sons. The only difference was that the high priest wound it around the head as though bandaging a fracture, whereas his sons wrapped it round like a helmet, and it was therefore called *migbaʿot.* Ralbag gave a similar description. Rabad criticized this view and asserted that the two items were not made in the same way: the *miṣnefet* was long and bound many times around the head in Arabic fashion whereas the *migbaʿot* was designed like the hats we wear which are pointed at the top and low. The wise Don Isaac put forward a similar view.[18] He wrote that since the *migbaʿot* was a head covering like the *miṣnefet,* the term *miṣnefet* was also applied to it. Regarding the verse *and you shall wind migbaʿot on them* (Ex. 29:9), he wrote:[19] "The *migbaʿot* they wore on their head was instead of the *misnefet* of Aaron; as is familiar, they were high and were called *migbaʿot* because they were like two hills with a dip between them and were tied with a sash under the chin. The *miṣnefet,* on the other hand, was wound around the head, with the crown on which the oil was poured left bare." He may have been referring to the headgear worn by cardinals when he spoke of the familiar sight of the high *migbaʿot.* The Tosafists cited the view of Rabbi Eliezer ben Jacob[20] as does the Semag that the only difference between the two head coverings was their size: that of the lay priest which came down to the point on the forehead on which the phylacteries are put was called *migbaʿot;* that of the high priest which allowed for hardly any space for the phylacteries between it and the gold plate was called *miṣnefet.* Rabbi Isaac explained that there was no difference between the two head coverings. Rather, Scripture sometimes used the term *miṣnefet* to denote the idea of encompassing the head like a turban, and sometimes *migbaʿot* to signify a head covering which resembled a helmet. This view is cited in his name by Mizraḥi in his *Novellae.* The interpretation of Rabbi Eliezer ben Jacob is also given in the Pisqe Tosafot on tractate Zevaḥim.[21]

10. Kele ha-Miqdash IX:4.
11. Moses of Coucy, *Sefer Miṣvot ha-Gadol* (Semag), positive commandment, par. 173.
12. Gersonides to Ex. 28:33 (382).
13. Mizraḥi to Ex. 28:33 (467).
14. Ramban to Ex. 28:31.
15. Isaac Arama, *Aqedat Yiṣḥaq* (164b).
16. Rashi to Ex. 28:4.
17. Kele ha-Miqdash VIII:2.
18. Abravanel to Ex. 28 (278, col. b).
19. Ibid. (284, col. b).
20. Tos. to B. Giṭṭ. 7a, s.v. *bi-zeman.*
21. Pisqe Tosafot to Zev. 2, n. 10.

Likewise with regard to the cord (*patil*) mentioned in connection with the plate,[22] Rashi, the Semag, and Rabad spoke uniformly—it was inserted at either end of the plate and through the middle and the three ends were fastened at the back of the neck. Ramban[23] and Don Isaac[24] in their commentaries and Rambam[25] in his code all agreed that the plate was pierced at either end and a blue cord inserted underneath from one hole to the other so that it could be tied with the cord against the back of the neck. They made no reference to the middle cord which passed over the top of the head. Indeed, on examination, the view of Rashi and the Semag cited above appear to be their own original idea, an attempt on their part to resolve the contradiction in Scripture.[26] What I found most surprising was the failure of all codifiers and commentators of blessed memory to give consideration to the statement of the sages of blessed memory in Ḥullin:[27] "A woollen hat (*kippah*) was placed on the head of the high priest, and the plate was put on it in order to fulfill what is said, *You shall put it on a cord of blue* (Ex. 28:37). Now I was frightened that it was I who was mistaken and that in my naivety, I had put them in the wrong. Thus it was of great importance to me to see that in his wise comments on Rambam's statement in the Laws of the Temple Furniture, the distinguished Caro wrote:[28] "'And his hair was visible between the plate and the *miṣnefet*.' This is in chapter 2 of Zevaḥim.[29] Know that in Ḥullin it is taught: 'A woollen hat.' I do not know why our teacher [Rambam] omitted this reference." These are the words of a wise man. But one should not explain his statement as implying that in addition to the plate and the cord, the teacher omitted to add the reference to the other cord which our rabbis of blessed memory called *kippah* (hat). In that case, the high priest would have been wearing too many garments [nine instead of eight], and one would have to ask oneself how our rabbis came to such a view. Rather, the point of the wise Caro's statement is that the teacher had omitted the interpretation of the rabbis of blessed memory and their way of describing the cord (*patil*) connected with the plate which was nothing more than a hat. Thus we learn that Ramban of blessed memory, a chief spokesman, blocked the view of our rabbis by following the lines of his distinguished predecessors such as Rashi, and none of his successors gave access to their view. It is true that Rashi's main idea is that it was designed in the shape of a helmet, but I do not know how three cords, such as they were, could be designed in the shape of a helmet. In the language of the sages, a hat [*kippah*] suggests an exact semicircular shape. In fact, Rashi himself, commenting on that passage states explicitly: "A *kippah* is a small hat which is called *feltrin* in the French vernacular." One could also question his explanation of their statement that the plate was placed on it since according to his understanding he should have said that they tied the plate by means of it. Now I

22. *And you shall put it on a blue cord that it may be on the miṣnefet; it shall remain on the front of the miṣnefet* (Ex. 28:37).

23. Ramban to Ex. 21:37.

24. Abravanel to Ex. 28:6 (271, col. a).

25. Kele ha-Miqdash IX:2.

26. He is referring to the contradictions mentioned by Rashi between Ex. 28:37 and Ex. 39:31 in which it is stated that the *patil* should be placed on the plate.

27. B. Ḥull. 138a.

28. *Kesef Mishnah* to Kele ha-Miqdash X:3.

29. B. Zev. 19a.

perused the wise Mizraḥi's *Novellae* on Rashi's commentary to discover whether he had any observations about this cord. I noticed the following comment:[30] "On the expression "to fasten it on the *miṣnefet,*" Rashi states, "He put it on the *miṣnefet* by means of the cords. I explained this in the pericope *teṣave.* Examine the passage." But there was no mention of this matter in the designated passage. I therefore took it as an indication that he had already raised various matters with regard to Rashi's interpretation of the cord. Then subsequently, being the scholar he was, when he realized that Rashi's statements on the scriptural passage were not consistent with what he said with regard to the talmudic passage, and having tried unsuccessfully to accommodate the different views, he let the incident pass in silence. However, one might also suggest that he actually made an error. For Rashi writes that the *miṣnefet* was a kind of domed helmet which is called *coiffe.* To this comment Mizraḥi observes: "He explains that it was a kind of hat which is a helmet in accordance with the statement about the woollen hat. Rashi explains that this was a helmet." One must object to this statement, however, since he is hanging that which has been distinctly taught on that which has not been distinctly taught: the *miṣnefet* which was made of linen and not of wool was worn by the high priest and lay priests alike. But the hat mentioned in the talmudic passage was blue and was the special garb of the high priest and is put forward by the sages of blessed memory as an explanation of the word *patil* (cord). Furthermore, it would appear that an objection could be raised against the interpretation of those who claim that the third cord passed from the middle of the brow to the neck. For this would surely imply that it would have protruded on the point between the eyes on which the phylacteries are placed. We could then refute this by the statement in Avodah Zarah[31] with regard to the crown of Milcom[32] which was on David's head. There it is said that it was necessary for him to put on the phylacteries; you may conclude therefore that a partition renders it impossible for him to do so. The great luminary Alfasi of blessed memory discusses the strand of the woollen hat which is mentioned in relation to garb which may be worn by women on the Sabbath. He writes:[33] "The woollen hat was made of woollen strands which were woven together, i.e., embroidered work, in the form of a network of cords. Like the plate, it measured two fingers in width, as is stated: 'A woollen hat . . . was placed on the plate.' " Under the second entry for *kph,* the compiler of the *Arukh* gave a similar explanation, stating that the woman's woollen hat was made of woollen strands which were woven together in a plaited form and like the plate was two fingers wide as is stated in Ḥullin. On the basis of these two explanations, it may be deduced that the hat of the high priest was not semicircular in shape such that it even covered the crown of the head. Rather, it was two fingers wide like the plate and even encompassed the side of the forehead on which the golden plate was attached. However, according to the first entry for *kph* in the *Arukh,* it refers to a simple hat, namely, a semicircular hat that covers the head. One might therefore surmise that the high priest's woollen hat was

30. Mizraḥi to Ex. 39:31 (586).

31. B. A.Z. 44a: "He used to wear the crown in the place of the phylacteries and it fitted. Rabbi Samuel b. Isaac said: 'There is sufficient room for two sets of phylacteries.' "

32. *The crown of Malcam* [Milcom] . . . *was placed on David's head* (2Sam. 12:30). De' Rossi reads Milcom (and not Malkham as Cassel). Cf. 1K 11:5.

33. Alfasi to B. Shabb. 57b (26b).

similar in shape, and this would also conform to Rashi's description in Ḥullin. As is known, the wool which our rabbis of blessed memory identify as the blue [cord], is explained in various passages as wool dipped in the blood of the conchiferous fish which produces a pale green dye as Rashi comments in his commentary on the Torah. Furthermore, with regard to that passage in Ḥullin,[34] he writes that it was blue wool.

The term "plate" (*ṣiṣ*) could be related to the word *ṣiṣit* in the expression *by the hair (be-ṣiṣit) of my head* (Ezk. 8:3). However, the wise Don Isaac[35] as well as Rabbi Abraham ibn Ezra[36] wrote that it is related to *meṣiṣ* as used in the expression *He looks (meṣiṣ) through the lattice* (S.S. 2:9), on the grounds that it is placed on the part of the brain in which is located the imaginative faculty. But it is more reasonable to relate it to the expression *ṣiṣ ha-sadeh* (flower of the field; Is. 40:6) and *piṭṭure ṣiṣim* (budding flowers; 1K. 6:18,29,32,35).

The diadem (*nezer*) undoubtedly refers to the wreath or crown which encircles the entire head. Accordingly, since the frontplate was a golden plate which was only semicircular in shape, the question arises as to the meaning of the two scriptural expressions, *the gold plate, the holy diadem* (Lev. 8:9). The fact is that our rabbis' description of its shape is cited by the codifiers and commentators of blessed memory and of particular note is Rambam's comment:[37] "How was the frontplate made? A gold plate two fingersbreadth wide and reaching from ear to ear was made, and on it was inscribed in two lines: *Holy to the Lord* (Ex. 28:36)—*Holy to* on the bottom line and *the Lord* above."[38] The distinguished authority Caro glosses this comment by noting its source in tractates Shabbat[39] and Sukkah.[40]

The efod is discussed by Rashi of blessed memory in the following manner:[41] "I have neither heard nor discovered a description of its design in a *baraita*. My own feeling is that it was tied at the back in the fashion of the apron worn by women on horseback. He fastened it behind him opposite the heart and it had the width of a man's back. It hung down as far as the heels." The Semag cites these words of Rashi of blessed memory in the name of Rashi himself. Rambam also concurred with this view. Likewise the author of the *Aqedah* of blessed memory wrote:[42] "The efod was hung over the back of the high priest from the belt and down to the lowest part of a man's body." Ralbag wrote:[43] "The efod was as wide as a man's back; and at his back it stretched from under the armpits as far as the feet, and two hands, as it were, emerged from it and served as a sash—this was already explained in the seventh chapter of Yoma.[44] Now Rashi wrote that he was unable to find a description of its design. At any rate, I cannot be convinced as to whether this conjecture of the commentators cited here is valid and

34. Rashi to B. Ḥull. 138a.
35. Abravanel to Ex. 28 (278, col. a).
36. Ibn Ezra to Ex. 28:37.
37. Kele ha-Miqdash IX:1.
38. De' Rossi has slightly misread Rambam who reads "*Holy* on the bottom line; *to the Lord* above."
39. B. Shabb. 63b.
40. B. Sukk. 5a.
41. Rashi to Ex. 28:6.
42. Isaac Arama, *Aqedat Yiṣḥaq* (164a).
43. Gersonides to Ex. 28:33, to'elet ha-sheni, shoresh 1 (390).
44. B. Yoma 71b.

correct. Moreover, their explanations of the expression "meʿil ha-efod" (Ex. 28:31) is inadequate. In his explanation of its design, the wise Don Isaac does not indicate that it hung down from the sash as far as the feet; simply that it was worn over the back with raised shoulders. Kimḥi of blessed memory appears to have been of the same opinion. Under the root *ʾfd*[45] which he elucidates in relation to the verse, *and he put the efod on him . . . girded him* (Lev. 8:7), he then concludes, "It was called *efod* because it was tied." Ibn Ezra of blessed memory is eclectic in the opinions he follows regarding the design of the vestments. He writes that the *meʿil* was a cloak, and this was the view of Ramban; in contrast he states that every bell was placed between two pomegranates and vice versa—this was not Ramban's opinion. He wrote:[46]

> The *migbaʿot* and *miṣnefet* were not identical; the *migbaʿot* resembled the headgear worn by males in these countries which cover the head and are high, as the word suggests. But the *miṣnefet* was a thin and long garment which was only wrapped around the head. One could hardly imagine that it was like the *miṣnefet* worn by women in these parts; for in Africa, Egypt, Babylon, and Bagdad the *miṣnefet* is worn by the male nobility and not by women, while the aristocrats wear a golden headplate on the *miṣnefet* on the brow such that no other cord is required in order to keep it in place on the brow. Aaron alone wore the *miṣnefet* and the *migbaʿot* were worn by his sons.

Examine the passage. He has nothing to say about the shape of the efod apart from the comment that it was bigger than the breastplate.

Rabbi Sforno wrote: "The efod was a garment that was drawn downwards over the man's limbs; the upper hem was made in the design of a girdle whereby the one who donned it would attach the efod to the *meʿil.*" Examine the passage.

Furthermore we should not conceal the fact that neither the Tannaim nor the Amoraim have anything to say about the nature of the Urim and Tummim. There is simply the passage in tractate Yoma in which an explanation of their name is put forward:[47] "Because they ratified[48] and fulfilled their message." They also taught us about their method of questioning, the type of question, and the method of response. One rabbi said: "The letters in the breastplate stood out in relief." The other said: "The letters were joined." According to Ritba,[49] these statements are not contradictory. Again in Yoma[50] as well as tractate Sota,[51] they speak about the time during which the Urim and Tummim were used. For during the second Temple period, they were missing, together with the five other objects which are connected with *I will be glorified* (Hag. 1:8) which is spelled without the letter *he.*[52] But all this information does not satisfy my voracious curiosity to know about the nature of these objects and what it was

45. David Kimḥi, *Sefer ha-Shorashim,* s.v. *ʾfd.*
46. Ibn Ezra to Ex. 28:36.
47. B. Yoma 73b.
48. In the talmudic text, it states "made their message clear," thus linking the word Urim to the word *or* (light).
49. *Ḥiddushe ha-Ritba* (cols. 399–400).
50. B. Yoma 21b.
51. B. Sota 48b.
52. The numerical value of the letter *he* is 5, and the verse speaks about God's glorification in the Temple. Since the word *I will be glorified* is spelled without the customary *he,* it is taken to refer to the objects that had been used in the first Temple but were supposed to be missing from the second Temple.

that deprived the people of the second Temple from hope of acquiring them. Turning my attention to the commentators and codifiers blessed be their memory, I found Rashi's assertion that they were inscribed with the Ineffable Name, but he did not disclose the source of his statement. However, I did find the Targum of [ps.] Jonathan ben Uzziel on the verse, *And you shall put in the breastplate* (Ex. 28:30) which he rendered:

> And you shall put in this breastplate the Urim which illuminate their words and reveal the secrets of the House of Israel, and the Tummim which complete their deeds for the high priest who, by means of them, seeks instruction from the Lord. For on them is engraved and articulated the great and holy Name by which the 310 worlds were created and which was engraved and articulated on the foundation stone by which the Lord of the world sealed up the mouth of the great deep in the beginning. Whoever invokes that holy Name at a time of necessity shall be delivered and initiated into the mysteries, and they shall be set on the heart of Aaron.

The great commentators, such as Ramban, author of the *Aqedah,* the noble Don Isaac, Mizraḥi, and others, follow the opinion of Rashi of blessed memory. The wise Recanati also writes:[53] "I discovered a statement in the name of Rabbi Eliezer that the letters of the Urim and Tummim have the same numerical value as the Name of seventy-two letters." However, ibn Ezra discarded such interpretations and, using astrological terms, described the Urim and Tummim as an astrolabe. Ralbag tended towards a definition in terms of natural philosophy. He wrote:[54] "The Urim are the material principles, the Tummim are the formal principles. . . . Alternatively the Urim would be types of natural heat which every existing being possesses . . . and the Tummim are the forms. . . . Alternatively, the Urim would be the stars and the Tummim the forms of the heavenly bodies." All these views are put forward by these two authorities. However, in my opinion it is a waste of time to examine them since their entire treatment of this subject is completely worthless and nonsensical. As Ramban states in connection with ibn Ezra's view, on the grounds of balanced reason, this view should be repelled from the holy countenance.

{However, beloved reader, I cannot refrain from informing you of the statement of the wise d'Estella, author of the *Migdal David* which I mentioned in chapter 14.[55] He spoke disparagingly about their interpretations (in paragraph 32) and then wrote:

> In relation to their view that the efod represents the Zodiac [lit. belt of the planets] and the breastplate the observatory instrument, one could draw a comparison with the purpose of our precepts regarding the sacrifices which was aimed at weaning us away from idolatry to the worship of God. (He was following the view of the teacher of the *Guide* in part 3, chapter 3). Similarly, one might say that in order to eradicate the notions of the star-gazers such that we do not put our trust in their governance, He commanded us to examine these kind of predictive observations when He said, *Those nations that you are about to dispossess do indeed resort to soothsayers and augurs; to you, however, the Lord your God has not assigned the like* (Deut. 18:14).}[2]

53. Recanati to Ex. 28:30 (51, col. a).

54. Gersonides (379).

55. De' Rossi refers to him in ch. 6 (not 14). David b. Samuel d'Estella (Kokhavi) was probably from Navarra. The manuscript of *Migdal David* is in the Biblioteca Palatina of Parma (Parmense 3540–42), (ed. Hershler, p. 115).

Now ibn Ezra wrote:[56] "Rabbenu Solomon [Rashi] explained that they were inscribed with the Ineffable Name. But had he seen the responsum of Rabbenu Hai, he would not have made such a statement." Regarding this comment, Ramban wrote:[57] "With regard to Rabbi Abraham's statement about Rabbenu Hai's responsum, we have already seen that responsum and considered it. We know that it is Rabbi Abraham's view that does not conform to it." These words and those of ibn Ezra indicate that Rabbenu Hai is not in agreement with either of them, but that there must be a third opinion of which we are ignorant. Now Rambam wrote:[58] "The Urim and Tummim were made in the second Temple in order to complete the eight vestments even though they were no longer consulted . . . because of the absence of the Holy Spirit." He makes the same point in the Laws of the Temple.[59] The wise Don Isaac corroborates this view in his commentary on Haggai.[60] But here they were at variance with Ritba who wrote in his commentary on Yoma:[61]

> There was no mention of making with regard to the Urim and Tummim; it was simply said, *you shall put them on the breastplate,* for they were not of human workmanship but the work of God, and inscribed. They were transferred to Moses with the command that they were to be placed within the folds of the breastplate. Consequently they were missing from the second Temple, but this did not constitute an obstacle. For the vestments of the high priest were there, but not the Urim and Tummim. Therefore the Urim and Tummim are not mentioned in the Mishnah in connection with the high priest's donning of the garments and only after the reference to the priestly vestments, is it taught:[62] "And in them were the Urim and Tummim consulted," for the inquirer had first to be clad in the eight garments.

The Semag wrote: "According to Rashi's interpretation, it was an inscription of the Ineffable Name which was put in the folds of the breastplate by means of which it illumined and completed its pronouncements. The breastplate must have been used in the second Sanctuary for it was impossible for the high priest to minister without being garbed in the requisite number of garments. But that Name was not on it, and yet, the breastplate of judgment owed its name to the inscription of the Name, for it served as the instrument by which Israel was judged and shown whether to act or not." In any case, a problem does arise if, as Rashi and his party claim, the Ineffable Name was inscribed on them. It is surely true that they also knew it in second Temple times. As is stated in Yoma[63] and in tractate Megillah of the Palestinian Talmud:[64] "What is meant by great in, *And Ezra blessed the Lord, the great God* (Neh. 8:6)? He magnified Him by pronouncing the Ineffable Name." And in Midrash Tehillim, with reference to the verse, *Continue Your kindness to those that know You* (Ps. 36:11), Rav Abba said:[65] "Two

56. Ibn Ezra to Ex. 28:5.
57. Ramban to Ex. 28:30.
58. Kele ha-Miqdash X:10.
59. Bet ha-Beḥirah IV:1.
60. Abravanel to Hag. 1:8 (186, col. b).
61. Ritba to B. Yoma 73b (col. 401).
62. M. Yoma 7:5.
63. B. Yoma 69b.
64. P. Meg. 3 (7) 74c.
65. Mid. Teh. to Ps. 36:11.

generations used the Ineffable Name: the Men of the Great Synagogue and the generation of the persecution. . . . Some say it was also used by the generation of Hezekiah, for it is said, *I am going to turn around the weapons in your hands* (Jer. 21:4). [What weapon could He have meant except His Ineffable Name.]" In Yoma[66] we learn that after the death of Simeon the righteous, his brothers, the priests, refrained from pronouncing the Name in their blessing. Rashi explains that they did not pronounce the Name because the people were not worthy. And even after the destruction of the Temple, certain special individuals had knowledge of it. This is evident from Midrash Qohelet[67] where it is said that Rabbi Ḥanina and a physician of Sepphoris possessed knowledge of the Ineffable Name. Then there is a unit of Talmud in tractate Qiddushin demonstrating their knowledge of the Name of four, twelve, and forty-two letters.[68] Rava thought of lecturing about it at the public session. A certain old man said to him: "*[This is My name forever]* (Ex. 3:15)." The word "forever" [*le*ʿ*olam*] is written *le*ʿ*allem* [to keep secret].[69] Then there is the description of Ben Qamṣar in Yoma[70] whose skill with the pen [was such that he could join up the letters with one stroke]. The efficacy of this skill is explained by Ḥayyat in *Ma*ʿ*arekhet ha-Elohut.*[71] Examine the passage.[72] Apart from this, it is generally acknowledged that the power of prophecy was retained in Israel for forty years after the rebuilding of the Temple, as we have noted many times throughout these chapters. Accordingly, why did they not do what was most appropriate and write it down and place it between the folds of the breastplate? After all, there may have been some future occasion in which the Holy Spirit would alight on a certain high priest. If Rambam also held that they wrote down the Ineffable Name, they must have done this.

Now I heard the following view which was given in the name of Rabbi Obadiah Sforno: "There were two names on the breastplate; when the high priest would gaze on the one which was called Urim, the letters through which the answer would be composed would light up. Since it was possible to join the letters in different ways, he would then look at the one called Tummim which would complete the letters and enable the high priest to understand properly the order of the letters through which the answer was composed. The nature and function of the Urim were similar to that of the auguries of the pagan priests which were called oracles in antiquity—but this is all said with due distinction between holy and profane, impure and pure." Following the several introductions to his commentary on the Torah entitled *Ir David,* the erudite scholar Rabbi David Provenzali wrote:[73] "The exalted God gave the Torah which was written in His presence with black fire on white fire secretly to Moses, the faithful one of His house. By divine command, Moses put the so-called Urim and Tummim into the breastplate just as he put the tablets into the Ark. Since no human eye save that of

66. B. Yoma 39b.
67. Qoh. R. to Eccl. 3:11.
68. B. Qidd. 71a.
69. I.e., the word *le*ʿ*olam* is written defectively, without the letter *vav,* and thus can be read as though it read *le*ʿ*allem.*
70. B. Yoma 38b.
71. Judah Ḥayyat, *Ma*ʿ*arekhet ha-Elohut,* 2, 5b–6a.
72. I.e., he was able to take four pens and write the four-letter Name with one stroke.
73. Once again, de' Rossi is referring to a work of his friend David Provenzali which does not appear to be extant.

Moses has seen them, it is not clear whether they were his handiwork or whether He gave them to him; nor do we have explicit information about the nature of the material of which they were made and their form and inscription." So much for his words which are even more enlightening[74] in their context.

The subject of the inscription of the names of the tribes on the shoulder-stones in order of age was also controversial. Rashi wrote that the first six were inscribed on one shoulder and the six others on the other shoulder.[75] Mizraḥi gives the same interpretation in his *Novellae.*[76] Rambam[77] wrote that Reuben was engraved on one shoulder, Simeon on the other shoulder, and so on. The Semag cites both views without passing judgment.

Now I have not been able to reach any definitive conclusion with regard to the majority of the problems that have been raised and particularly as regards the nature of the Urim and Tummim. Nevertheless, I considered it worthwhile to discuss them alongside our other sacred vestments. In the end, every intelligent person who sees the divergence of opinion among the sages that we cited would take stock of the situation. Then he would lament for the children who have been exiled from the House of their heavenly Father, were he to ask himself if the Temple were to be built speedily, and it would devolve on us to reinstate the high priest with the Urim without the help of another righteous teacher, which writer of all those experts in Torah we should adopt and according to his instruction robe him in the priestly finery. Now an objection could be pronounced against the person who could nowadays entertain such high ambitions. One could express surprise, as Rav Joseph [Rava] did in Zevaḥim,[78] with regard to the case of *piggul*[79] in respect of a rite which is performed outside [i.e., in the Temple court] and in Sanhedrin[80] with regard to a priest's daughter who transgressed the sexual laws, and describe it as messianic *halakhah.* Likewise in Yoma,[81] regarding the question as to the order in which Moses clothed Aaron in his vestments, they objected that what is past is past and that in the future, when Aaron and his sons will come, they will be accompanied by Moses. It is all well and good when the outcome of the discussion is a prohibition as in the passage in Qiddushin[82] in which the *halakhah* is concluded in favor of Rabbi Jose's view that unidentified *mamzerim*[83] will become pure in the future, and the practical implication is that one should not estrange those families whose descent is not known as the Tosafists wrote.[84] In such cases it is right to make a decision about messianic *halakah.* But as regards the subject of our inquiry, nothing by way of permit or prohibition may be concluded from it. Yet both in the passage in Sanhedrin and that

74. De' Rossi is punning here, alluding to the Urim.
75. Rashi to Ex. 28:10.
76. Mizraḥi, *Perush Rashi* (460).
77. Kele ha-Miqdash IX:7.
78. B. Zev. 45a.
79. *Piggul* is the term used to describe a sacrifice which is unfit because of an improper intention on the part of the officiating priest.
80. B. Sanh. 51b.
81. B. Yoma 5b.
82. B. Qidd. 72b.
83. The offspring of an incestuous or adulterous union.
84. Tos. to B. Zev. 45a; B. Sanh. 51b s.v. *hilkheta.*

of Yoma mentioned above, a response to our question is juxtaposed. The response is that one should investigate such matters for the sake of elucidating Scripture. In other words, one should resolve the verses in order to achieve consistency, if not for another reason, that is, to expound and receive reward. Otherwise, all the material about slaughter of sacrifices (as Abbaye states there)[85] would not be studied. But the reverse is the case. Go and read, for the sages of blessed memory encourage us to study it. As they wrote in Menaḥot:[86] "Why is it written, *[I will dedicate it to Him for making incense offering . . .] as Israel's eternal duty* (2Chr. 2:3)? These are the sages who study the laws of the Temple service and the laws of the sin offering and guilt offering and it is imputed to them as though the Temple were built in their days." Now in tractate Niddah,[87] the Alexandrians ask Rabbi Joshua whether the dead would require sprinkling on the third and seventh day in the hereafter. He responded: "When they will be resurrected we shall go into the matter." Others say: "When our master Moses will come with them." But the question itself had already been described as foolish[88] and lacks proof-texts to which we should pay attention.

Now our blessed God has granted the people of our times to become acquainted with the writers of antiquity who wrote in their own context and with authors whose works have lain hidden and buried away from the sight of our people.[89] It was as though they had been completely obliterated since they were written in the Greek script and language which was not understood in the assemblies of our later sages of blessed memory. In the Laws of the Phylacteries, Rambam of blessed memory goes so far as to say:[90] "The Greek language was lost from the world; it became corrupted and then disappeared." Indeed, there is some semblance of proof that the Babylonian sages, and specifically those who lived far from Greek-speaking countries, did not know the language. For we see that they took apart the word *diatheqe* which is mentioned in the Mishnah[91] and interpreted it as *da tehe le-meqam,*[92] and *hupotheqe* as *afo tehe qa'e.*[93] We could, however, explain these definitions as rhetorical devices, as shall be mentioned in chapter 57. Now the writers to whom we alluded were speaking impartially about the design of some of the vestments that we mentioned. There is, for example, the book of Aristeas that we translated previously, the works of Yedidyah the Alexandrian (Philo) and the statements of the Pharisee Josephus. All these writers lived in Temple times; their statements were not guesswork or hearsay, but rather what they and not others actually witnessed.[94] To my limited understanding it seemed that it could only be beneficial and something in which the Omnipresent and intelligent beings would find pleasure, if we were able by means of their accounts to arbitrate with regard to all or

85. B. Sanh. 51b.
86. B. Men. 110a. In this citation, de' Rossi has conflated various statements in the same passage.
87. B. Nidd. 70b.
88. Ibid., 69b "Twelve questions did the Alexandrians address to Rabbi Joshua ben Hananiah: three were mere nonsense."
89. This is an explicit reference to the recovery of the works of classical antiquity in the Renaissance.
90. *Mishneh Torah,* Tefillin I:19.
91. M. B.M. 1:7.
92. B. B.M. 19a.
93. This play on the Greek word is given by Rashi to B. B.Q. 11b.
94. Cf. Job 19:27.

some of the problems that have been raised. For any form of comfort is permissible, and this would be for the purpose of eludicating Scripture, an endeavor for which one should receive a fine recompense from our God. It is true that this Aristeas was a gentile; but as we learnt in chapter 2, he and others like him are deserving of being used as some support in a time of emergency. Moreover, it is certainly appropriate to decide the matter in some way according to the dictates of reason on the basis of the evidence of the two Jewish witnesses, especially since Josephus was a priest with expert knowledge of the Temple furniture. When he describes how Herod opened up the grave of King David, on him be peace, and extracted large sums of [silver] from it—I shall mention this again with the help of the Creator in the chapter on the splendor of the Temple[95]—he says of himself:[96] "Indeed I am a priest to the highest God and of royal extraction (for at the beginning of his *Autobiography,* he wrote that was of Hasmonean descent on his mother's side). Why then should I attach rubbish and disgrace to my worthy name and write in jest and that which would turn out to be false." Now you, reader, who are adept in the truth through which you will attain the good,[97] come bless the Lord and in the forthcoming chapters we shall examine and look together at the discourses of those ancient writers which have recently come to light.

95. I.e., ch. 51.
96. *Ant.* XVI:187.
97. 'Adept . . . good,' cf. Pr. 16:20.

CHAPTER FORTY-SEVEN

An abstract of Aristeas's statements about the design of some of the priestly vestments.

Now the following is a synopsis of Aristeas's statements about Eleazar the high priest. He wrote:[1]

> Was he not an amazing spectacle, distinguished by the magnificent impression created by the grandeur of the coat (*meʿil*) which he wore and the precious stones with which it was studded. Behold, from this long garment, which stretched to the feet, hung golden bells which produced a harmonious sound, and between each bell was placed a pomegranate adorned with flowers of various hues. He was girt with a girdle . . . and on his breast he wore. . . . Now his head was covered by the so-called *sudar* [*cidaris*] and above it was the mitre which was wrought with inimitable artistry, a most splendid regal ornament and on it, brought out in relief, was a golden plate which was inscribed with the name of God.

The text is in "Splendor of the Elders," which we presented above. You who are intelligent should consider his words for what they are. If you query as to why he fails to mention the tunic, girdle, or breeches, we for our part have a response. He was only describing what was visible and was thus in no position to see and describe the undergarments. Indeed, he mentions the beautiful girdle which corresponds to the band of the efod, and he also refers to the breastplate which was patently visible. However, he thought that the cloak and the efod were one garment, since to the eye, the two seemed to be one garment which hung from around the neck down to the feet. This points to the fact that the efod did not hang down from the belt, as Rashi and his band of colleagues claimed. Rather, as Don Isaac said, whose opinion we cited, it hung from the shoulders as far as the girdle at the back, and doubled at the front to allow for attachment to the breastplate, as is well known. From his description it also becomes clear that the bells were not placed within the hollow of the pomegranates, as Ramban and Don Isaac said; rather, as all the other commentators claimed, one bell was placed between every two pomegranates and between every two bells, a pomegranate. From his description it is also clear that the *miṣnefet* that was put on the high priest's head was called *sudar.* This word occurs in Curtius's description of the ornaments of Darius who was captured by Alexander.[2] The

1. Aristeas 96–97.

2. Quintus Curtius, *De rebus gestis* III, 3, 19: "Cidarim Persae vocabant regium capitis insigne; hoc caerulea fascia albo distincta circumibat."

Persians called it *cidaris* which is equivalent to *sudar* in the language of our rabbis, who also regarded it as an ornament of distinction as is evident from tractate Shabbat:[3] "*Sudra: sod adonai li-re'av.* (The secret of the Lord is revealed to those that fear Him.)" In particular, it would appear from tractate Qiddushin[4] that a married person should not be seen without a *sudar* covering his head. Since the verb employed here is "to cover," it would seem that there is no reason to say that it was wrapped around the head, but that it only covered it. The same word is used in Megillah to denote a curtain.[5] The two interpretations are given by the compiler of the *Arukh* under the entry for *prs.* And the Palestinian Targum renders the word "veil" in the verse, *and he put a veil over his face* (Ex. 34:33) as *sudra.* The word *migba'ot* is therefore a fitting description of the high priest's *sudar*—we shall comment on this again in the next chapter. Aristeas's description also makes clear that above the *sudar* on the brow was the mitre on which the gold plate was set. You should know that according to Latin lexicographers, the mitre often refers to a pointed and slightly curved helmet which was the customary head covering of men and women in Egypt.[6] Sometimes it simply refers to the encircling like a crown which does not cover the top of the head. These two definitions correspond to the hat (*kippah*) to which our rabbis refer when they speak of the woollen hat donned by the high priest. For under the entry for *kph,* the compiler of the *Arukh* presents his first interpretation as simply a hat similar to a helmet which even covers the top of the head. In the second interpretation, he follows Alfasi. Having demonstrated that the blue cord mentioned in connection with the plate could not have been wider than the plate itself which was two fingers in breadth, he said that the hat mentioned by our rabbis and which was also discussed in relation to women's ornaments, must have been a cord of braided work, of two fingersbreadth as we mentioned above. But you should take into account, intelligent reader, that the juxtaposition of the word "cord" in this context misled many commentators. For they believed that it referred to only one cord and so they endeavored to interpret the cord of the plate according to that meaning without relating it to the hat as did our rabbis. It is true that it does sometimes simply denote "cord" as in the expression, *and cut cords [to be worked in the designs . . .]* (Ex. 39:3). Usually, however, it denotes an ornament or cord or anything big or small which is fashioned from many cords braided together, or else something wound around an object, the head, for example, just as one strand is called cord because it is itself twisted. In fact under the root *ptl,* Kimḥi writes as follows:

> *A lid that is fastened (patil)* (Num. 19:15) means a small piece of cloth and in the Mishnah[7] there is the comparable expression "a cord (*petilat*) of a garment." Similar in meaning, as I think, is the expression *your signet and your cord* (Gen. 38:18) which refers to his cloak or to the turban on his head. The translator of the Targum had the same notion when he rendered the word as *shoshifakh* [your coarse cloak]. The same word is used to render the

3. B. Shabb. 77b.
4. B. Qidd. 29b: "Said he to him . . . 'Why have you no *sudar?*' 'Because I am not married.' "
5. B. Meg. 26b: "I used to think that the curtain is an accessory."
6. See Calepino, *Dictionarium,* s.v. *mitra:* "Dictio barbara qua significatur quoddam capitis ornamenti genus. Hoc est pileus incurvus quo primum Maeronii deinde Aegyptii, Syri, Phryges et Lydi usi sunt. Aliquando tamen et pro mulieri corona ad ornatum capitis adulescentularum accipitur."
7. M. Shabb. 2:3.

word "cloak" in *he wrapped his cloak around his face* (1K. 19:13), and for the word "mantles" in Isaiah (3:22) and the word "cloth" in *and they shall spread out the cloth* (Deut. 22:17).

Rashi also renders *your cord* (Gen. 38:18) as "the garment in which you are robed." The term derives from the fact that the garment itself was woven from cords in braided work, or else fashioned by cords wrought together and not because it signifies the prayer shawl with fringes—if this were true, Ramban and Mizraḥi of blessed memory would have reproached him [Judah].[8] Ramban himself wrote: "Perhaps the word 'your cord' " refers to the small *sudar* which is wrapped twice round the head and owes its name to the fact that it is as short as a cord. In his commentary on the precept of wearing the fringes (Num. 15:38), ibn Ezra chews peppers as is his wont and devises a polemical stand.[9] Examine the passage. The author of the *Mikhlal Yofi,*[10] who produced a compilation of citations from the best commentators, wrote about the term "your cord" which was said in connection with Judah as follows: "It would appear that the garment or turban were made by means of two or more [cords] for which reason the plural form of the word is used in *whose seals and cords . . . are these?* (Gen. 38:25). But we would account for it in our own manner and say that it was fashioned from the many cords of the material, distinguishable as a braided and quilted design or made with twisted cords as we said. Thus on the basis of Aristeas's account, we can understand that the cord of the plate was not simply a cord, but rather, a hat, as our sages said, may their memory be for a blessing, according to either one of the two explanations. With the help of the Creator, we shall discuss this further in chapter 49 which is dedicated to Josephus. In fact, the design of the crown and the plate is not elucidated at all in his [Aristeas's] description. With regard to that wonderful artifact, he does not indicate whether it contained those patterns and budding flowers and we are therefore unable to judge whether such descriptions are apposite. However, we shall present a comparative study, if God so helps us, in chapter 49. But first of all, we shall see what the text of Yedidyah the Alexandrian [contributes and adds to the discussion].

8. Ramban and Mizraḥi to Gen. 38:18 express their horror at the thought that Judah would have had intercourse with Tamar while dressed in the prayer shawl.

9. Ibn Ezra to Num. 15:39. In his interpretation of the word *patil* in the verse, *Let them attach a patil of blue to the fringe at each corner,* ibn Ezra does not refer to the definitions given by the other commentators with reference to Gen. 38:18. He is only polemical with regard to the observance of the precept.

10. Solomon ibn Melekh, *Mikhlal Yofi.* The work contained explanations of all difficult words and grammatical forms in the Hebrew Bible.

CHAPTER FORTY-EIGHT

An abstract of the statements of Yedidyah the Alexandrian on the design of some of the priestly vestments.

In the third chapter [book] of his *Life of Moses,* Yedidyah the Alexandrian wrote:[1]

After this, the craftsman Bezalel,[2] whom we mentioned, prepared for the high priest a supremely beautiful holy vestment which was wonderfully woven from various textures. It did in fact consist of the robe and the efod as it is called in the Torah.[3] The robe was made of only one texture; it was entirely blue except for the hems which were studded with flowers,* pomegranates, and golden bells. But the efod was a most beautiful artifact, made with amazing artistry from the above-mentioned textures: blue, scarlet, purple, and white linen. It was interwoven throughout with gold: for they beat out gold plates and cut out fine threads which were inserted with all kinds of yarn. On his shoulder tops were affixed two most precious onyx stones on which were engraved the names of the twelve tribes, six on either shoulder. Similarly, on his heart, other precious stones were to be seen, shimmering with different colors like seals on hidden objects,[4] three stones on each of four rows. These were placed on the ornament known as the breastplate of judgment. This was square and doubled so as to bear the two virtues, that is, the revelation of the secret and truth,[5] and was attached by two golden chainlets from the shoulder straps of the efod and fastened to it to ensure that it did not come loose. He also made for him a golden plate which bore great resemblance to a crown, and it was engraved with the four letters of the Name which may only be heard and pronounced by those who in wisdom have purified their ears and tongue and who stand in the holy precincts. Theologians say that it is the tetragrammaton, possibly because it symbolizes the first four numerals, one, two, three, and four. For the square comprises everything—point, line, surface, solid—and is the measure of all things. This is particularly evident in the case of concordant harmonies in music; for example, the epitrite is in the ratio of four to three, the fifth in the ratio of three to two, the octave in the ratio of four to two, and the double octave in the ratio of four to one. The number four has many other properties, many of which we discussed in our discourse on numbers. Now this Name was attached to a mitre so that it did not touch the

1. *Mos.* II, 109–16 (In the Latin translation, bk. III, 568).
2. De' Rossi adds the name of Bezalel.
3. De' Rossi uses the traditional term "Torah" where the Latin translation reads "Scriptura."
4. The Latin text reads "similes signaculis" (like seals).
5. Philo gives here the LXX rendering of the Urim and Tummim.

head. His head was covered by a *sudar* [*cidaris*] which is worn by eastern monarchs in preference to the diadem.

(*[See p. 601] He is undoubtedly referring to the flowers on the pomegranates which, as the rabbis of blessed memory explain, had not yet opened up.[6])

According to the Latin lexicon, the diadem is a turban resembling a band which is wrapped around the head leaving the crown bare.[7]

Then further on in the same passage he writes:[8] "This *sudar* rather than the diadem was on his head so that in conducting his office and performing his rites, he becomes preeminent not only above ordinary men, but also above all earthly monarchs. Over his countenance was the golden plate which was engraved with the four letters which according to theologians denotes the Name of being; for nothing can come to be without the invocation of the name of God by whose loving-kindness all that is above and below exist." Yedidyah expatiates on how the priestly vestments symbolize the universe both in its entirety and in its parts. Thus when he [the high priest] approaches God, it is as though he is accompanied by and arrayed with the myriads of His creatures who assist him in the quest for grace and loving-kindness. On behalf of them all, as it were, does he ascribe praise to their Creator and prays for their everlasting existence.

In his work entitled *De monarchia,*[9] that is, *On Government,* he writes as follows:

The priests wear the tunic and breeches. The tunic is to cover his nakedness which if exposed at the altar, would be a source of shame. The other garment is designed so as to enable him to perform his duty expeditiously,* for once the priest is robed in the cloak, he would feel that he has greater freedom of movement to perform all the actions required for the divine service. The high priest is also commanded to wear such a vestment when approaching the altar to offer the incense because unlike wool, the linen from which the garments are made is not a material derived from creatures subject to death. Then, there is yet another garment which is multicolored whose design appears to commemorate all parts of the universe in one. Indeed, the uppermost garment which he wraps around him is blue, and hangs down to the feet and thus represents the air which is naturally darkish in color. Similarly, the efod is like a garment which stretches from the environs of the moon down to the recesses of the earth. On the cloak he wears the woven breastplate which covers the chest and symbolizes the heavens. For on his shoulders are two onyx stones, circular in shape, one on each shoulder, which represent the two parts of the sphere, one of which is above, the other below, the earth. On his heart, he wears twelve precious stones of different colors, arranged in four rows of three which is comparable to the Zodiac which is divided into four seasons of the year with three signs for each season. Indeed, this part of the dress as a whole on which the stones are attached is called the breastplate of judgment, a most apposite name; for each part of the heavens was made in wisdom and its splendor and luster is the result of the rational principles and agents which work in conjunction with each other. Indeed nothing is made to no purpose. This breastplate with its twofold construction has two different designations, one of which is clarity, the other truth. By this [truth], we are shown that no falsehood is allowed to ascend to heaven; rather

6. B. Zev. 88b.

7. Calepino, *Dictionarium,* s.v. *diadema:* "gestamen capitis . . . erat enim fascia quaedam qua caput circumligabatur."

8. *Mos.* II, 131 (570).

9. *Spec.* I:83–98 (690).

it has all been banished to the nethermost parts of the earth where it wanders to and fro in[10] the souls of the impious. Clarity indicates that our actions will be clear because they are endowed with the clarity of the firmament without which they would be engulfed with darkness. Is it not known that if the sun does not rise, we would have no means of perceiving the qualities of the many physical things, the various types of colors and forms and of distinguishing between days and nights, months and years? In sum, the only marker of the times are the sun, moon, and stars. The magnitude of the wisdom which determines their cyclical movements cannot be fathomed by man. How could we come to comprehend the nature of different numbers without the knowledge of those divisions of time that we mentioned. Those who go down in ships on the great wide sea can only plot the course by means of the laws which govern the celestial lights. And so there are several phenomena whose secrets have been penetrated by thoughtful men who have also recorded their information in writing: whether stormy winds or gentle breezes would prevail; whether there would be famine or plenty, hot or cold; whether the hot days of summer and the cold days of winter would be moderate or intolerable; whether the earth's produce and the offspring of flocks would be fertile or unprolific; and so on. For all earthly things are betokened by the heavens.

(*[See p. 602] This contradicts the statement of the author of the *Aqedah* who wrote:[11] "The tunic reached to the heel; the steps of the one who wore the garment were made smaller in order to retard his steps.")

Now on the hems of the cloak are appended golden bells, pomegranates, and flowers which symbolize water and earth. The flowers symbolize the earth from which they grow; water is represented by the pomegranates, the nature of which is indicated by the word "flowing" as they are designated in Greek. The bells with their harmonious sound represent the concordant bond and harmonious relation between the orders of existence. All these images are arranged with wondrous artistry on the uppermost ornament, that is, the breastplate, representing the heavens that are also located on high. Under the breastplate hangs the cloak which is blue throughout just as the air which also is darkish in color is the next chain in order of existence below the lowest parts of the heavens. The flowers and pomegranates, however, are put on its hems just as the water and earth are located in the lowest part of the entire universe.

These are the woven vestments of the high priest whose splendor denotes the world in its entirety when we regard them either with the eye or with the mind. Indeed, just as from the point of view of appearance, size, and variety, this woven work transcended anything else we possess, so, too, the representations of all its parts were the embodiment of wisdom and understanding which is amazing in our sight. Thereby the high priest is taught that by his comprehension of the design of the entire universe in whose splendor he is robed, he should endeavor to ask for its continued existence by means of his sacrifices as nature would wish. Likewise, he would bear in mind that the entire universe would be among his helpers in the quest for grace and loving-kindness from God. It is indeed fitting that in presenting his supplications and confessions before the heavenly father, he should join his son who is the universe in its entirety and be unified with him.

Furthermore there is a third mystery to these vestments which should not be overlooked. The priests of other nations only seek the welfare of their beloved ones and fellow countrymen in their ministry. But the high priest of the Jews does not pray only for the

10. Isaac Arama, *Aqedat Yiṣḥaq,* gate 51 (164v).
11. Cassel erroneously reads "like" instead of "in."

> welfare of the human species, but also for the divisions in nature: fire, air, and earth are included in his prayer and are praised by him. For he reckons (as is indeed true) that this world is his birthplace and that he should therefore implore the Creator of all to preserve it intact.

Simply, consider my findings[12] from Yedidyah; in my opinion it confirms many of Aristeas's views on the priestly vestments which were given in the previous chapter. There is no need to go from the one to the other.[13] After all, knowledge comes easy to the one with understanding.[14] And now we shall address ourselves to Josephus as we promised.

12. 'Simply . . . findings,' cf. Eccl. 7:29.
13. He bases his statement here on the expression from B. Ket. 110a, "Why change bags of equal weight from one side of the animal to the other?"
14. Cf. Pr. 14:6.

CHAPTER FORTY-NINE

An abstract of Josephus's statements on the design of some of the priestly vestments.

In book three (chapter 8) of his *Antiquities,*[1] Josephus writes as follows:[2]

Now that we have described the Tabernacle, it is appropriate that we should discuss the vestments both of the general body of priests whom we call *kahane,*[3] and those of the principal priest who is called *kahana rabbah.* However, our first task is to speak about the vestments of the ordinary priests. The priest who proceeds to perform the sacrifices is purified and cleansed according to the precepts of the Torah. First of all, he dons the vestment of spun linen, called *makhnesin,* which covers and goes round the pudenda. His feet are fitted into it and it is drawn over his limbs and then fastened. Over this, he wears a linen garment of double texture which is called *ketuna,* a word which derives from the root *kitan* which means linen in our language. This is a long garment reaching the feet; it envelops the body and has two sleeves which are not very baggy. Around his chest, below his armpits, it is tied with a sash, four fingers in breadth, gauzy in texture, which is fashioned like a serpent's skin and decorated with colored flowers—scarlet, purple, blue, and spun linen—while its warp is made entirely of fine linen. This sash is bound twice under his armpits as was said and then, provided that the ritual is not in process, it sweeps down to his feet in such a way as to contribute to the splendor of the decoration. But when he proceeds to perform the service, he throws it over his left shoulder so that it does not impede him in his various actions. Moses called this sash *avneṭ*; we have learnt from the Babylonians to call it *hemyan* for so it is designated by them. The tunic mentioned above is not pleated. It has an opening at the neck and the ends are fastened on each of the shoulders both at the front and at the back by means of clasps. It is also called *mashabṣa.** He wears a hat on his head that is not peaked, and it covers only slightly more than half of his head—it is called *maṣnefta.* It is fashioned such that it appears like a thick band of linen folded around many times and stitched. On it, another linen vestment, which is very flimsy, comes down to the forehead so as to cover the entire surface of the head and thus conceals the unsightly stitching. It is firmly attached so that it does not slip off during the sacred ministry. Here we have described the vestments of the ordinary priests.

1. *Ant.* III:151–87.

2. As in other cases where de' Rossi translates from Josephus (particularly in his section on the *Letter of Aristeas*), he follows Gelenius's Latin translation in the main but also refers to Ruffinus's translation.

3. De' Rossi has not followed the Latin transcription of the Aramaic words but used the correct Aramaic forms.

(*[See p. 605] You should not be surprised that *mishbeṣot* is rendered in Onqelos's Targum as *meramṣa*. For the Jerusalemites used the word *meshabṣa,* as you may gather from the entry *shbṣ* in the *Arukh.*)

Now all these vestments are donned by the high priest, and above them he wears another blue vestment that reaches the feet and which we call *meʿila.* It is fastened with a sash made from the same colors that we mentioned, but is also interwoven with gold. The hems are embroidered with a border on which pomegranate designs are distributed and from which golden bells hang down such that every pomegranate is placed between two bells and every bell between two pomegranates. This garment is not made of two pieces which would necessitate stitching at the back[4] or at the sides. It is one long whole garment in one piece and the slit is not made crosswise, but lengthwise at the top down the back, and at the front as far as the middle of the chest. There is a border of stitching around this slit and similar slits through which the arms are passed. Above this vestment, he puts on yet a third garment, called efod, which resembles the cloak which the Greeks call *epomidi* [*epomis*] which refers to a shoulder ornament. Its design is as follows. It is multicolored with an inset of gold which is one cubit long. In the front, a gap is left in the weaving on the middle of the chest, and it has sleeves like the tunic. This gap is filled with a piece of cloth measuring a span in length and width in the colors mentioned above, and with a golden inlay as with the efod. It is called *ḥushena* or *logion* in Greek which means ornament of judgement.[5] It fits exactly into the place in the fabric of the efod which, as indicated, was left vacant. It is fastened to the efod by golden rings which are placed on its corners and on those of the gap and bound together by a blue* band (meshiḥah). There are two onyx stones each of which protrudes at the edge of the shoulder with golden pegs which are used for suspending the chain and on them are enscribed the names of the children of Israel in the letters** which are specifically used for our own native language. Six names are engraved on each stone, that is, the names of the six older sons on the right shoulder and the six younger on the other. Similarly,† the breastplate itself is distinguished by twelve stones of extraordinary size and beauty; it is an ornament which by reason of its exceeding worth cannot be replicated in anything else we possess. In each of four rows, three stones are set which are enclasped in gold to hold them in position. The first row contains sardonyx,‡ topaz, and emerald. The second row comprises carbuncle, jasper, and sapphire. The third row contains amber, amethyst, and agate. The fourth row contains chrysolite, onyx, and beryl. The stones are engraved with the names, in order of age, of the children of Israel, that is, our tribal chiefs. Since the two rings which are on the edge of the breastplate as we said, are not strong enough to bear the weight of the stones, two more rings protrude at the ends of the breastplate near the neck. On these are placed golden chains of wrought work which are inserted into the tops of the shoulders by means of golden twine. The ends of these chains are passed back on the shoulders and hang down from the back and are joined to the border at the back of the efod, and this secures the breastplate. But the edges of the breastplate are stitched with a band of the same colors with a golden inlay. It is tied round the body twice and fastened in front on that seam and both its ends hang down to the ground. All the pegs that we mentioned are fastened on the two sides with golden twine, a most beautiful sight.

(*Note that he interprets the cord (*patil*) as a band.)

4. 'At the back.' The Latin (and Greek) texts read "in humeris" (on the shoulders).

5. De' Rossi is using the Ruffinus rendering here: "quod Graeca lingua Logion, Latina rationale significat."

(**[See p. 606] He is referring to the script of the holy tongue.)

(†[See p. 606] Ruffinus's translation, however, reads:[6] "In the breastplate, twelve stones." You will understand this translation when you reach the end of chapter 3 [i.e., of Josephus].)

(‡[See p. 606] The rendering of these stones in the Septuagint is exactly the same as that given in the Italian translation.[7])

Now he wears a hat like the other priests, but over this is placed another one which is embroidered in blue. A three-tiered golden crown bedecks this hat and on it appears golden calyxes similar to those we see in the grass which we call *dachharus* and the Greeks *[h]yoscyamus.* I consider it in order for me to provide a description of this plant for the benefit of those who have seen it without taking note of it fully, or for those who have heard of it but have never seen it. It* is a plant which grows to a height of about three spans from the ground. Its root is like that of the turnip, and its foliage like that of parsley. Out of its branches, it puts forth a small calyx which remains attached to them and is enveloped in the husk and then detaches itself when the fruit ripens. This calyx is as big as the joint of the little finger and is circular like a bowl. For further elucidation for the ignorant, I would like to say that the lower part at the stem is like the emerging part of a sphere[8] which curves upwards until it reaches the rim where it broadens out again at its rim which is indented like the tip of a pomegranate, and it is covered with a lid so well rounded that it appears to be of human workmanship.[9] Its spikes are high and jagged like the tip of the pomegranate to which I referred and culminate in a point like the end of a sword. Beneath their lid is the fruit which fills that small calyx, resembling the seed of the herb *sideritis,* while its flower may be compared to the poppy. The crown was fashioned in a similar manner, extending from the neck to the two temples without covering the forehead; instead there was a wide plate of gold which was engraved** with the sacred letters of the divine name. These are the holy vestments of the high priest. In view of all this, I am amazed at the nations of the world who hate us Jews on account of fictitious lies with which they charge us. It is as though we are guilty of the foolish crime of deriding the divine service that they venerate. Surely anyone who comprehends the construction of the Tabernacle, the priestly vestments, and the vessels which are used for the holy ministry will becomes convinced that our lawgiver was a true man of God and that the charges of impiety leveled against us are false. For on proper examination, it will emerge that it is a representation of all parts of nature. There is the Tabernacle which is thirty cubits long and is divided into three parts; two of these, which may be used as a thoroughfare for the priests, are, as it were, not regarded as holy ground and thus symbolize the sea and land which may be traversed by humans. The third section, however, is reserved for God alone like the heavens to which none of those who dwell on earth can ascend. Again, the twelve loaves that are laid on the table represent the year which is divided into twelve months. The candelabrum composed of seventy parts symbolizes the twelve planets through which the luminaries pass in turn.[10] The seven lamps represent the seven planets. The curtains that are fashioned with four designs represent the four sublunar elements: the flax symbolizes the earth from which it grows; the purple is the sea which is dyed with the blood of the fish; the blue is air; while the scarlet is fire. Similarly, the priest's tunic which is made of flax

6. Ruffinus: "Inserti sunt autem in Essin, id est in rationali, duodecim lapides."
7. He is referring to the *Biblia vulgare* (translated by Niccolò de Malermi).
8. Both the Greek and Latin texts describe the lower half of a divided sphere.
9. The Latin text reads "quasi de industria" (as though on purpose).
10. This passage is problematic in all versions.

represents the element earth for us; the blue cloak is the firmament; the pomegranates, lightening; and the bells, thunder. The efod also represents nature in all its entirety, for it is composed of four designs. In my opinion, the gold with which they are overlaid is meant to represent the all-pervading light. The breastplate is placed in the middle just as the earth is the center of the heavens.[11] The girdle which he ties around his body is comparable to the ocean which encompasses the whole earth. The two onyx stones on the shoulders of the efod signify the sun and the moon, while the twelve stones on the breastplate may possibly symbolize the twelve months or twelve parts of the planetary circle known as the Zodiac. The hat represents the heavens, specifically because it is blue in color; otherwise, the name of God would not have been engraved upon it, and it irradiates light on the golden plate just as in truth light dwells with the exalted God,[12] selah. This discourse of ours is only one of several topics that we shall treat in our demonstration of the wisdom of our lawgiver.

(*[See p. 607] Examine the fine description of [the calyx] in the fourth book of Dioscorides.[13] However, the plant is found in our country, but not in the Land of Israel.)

(**[See p. 607] From Ruffinus's translation, you gain the clearest impression that these flowers which he describes as calyx-like in shape were many and scattered over the part of the crown which extends from the back of the neck.[14])

Thus far Josephus. Now in book 12[15] he discusses Alexander of Macedon's meeting with Jaddua the high priest and states: "He saw the tiara on his head, that is, the royal crown, and on its front was the golden plate on which was engraved the name of God." And in the sixth book of the *Wars*,[16] he refers to the vestments of the high priest: "His head was covered by a linen hat embroidered in blue and it was encircled by another crown of gold imprinted with the sacred letters, that is, the four vowels to facilitate our pronunciation."[17]

All this constitutes Josephus's treatment of the priestly vestments. You shall hear our comments on it, if God so wills. And if you have benefited from our discussion so far, do not refrain from continuing with the following chapter.

11. 'Heavens.' The Latin reads: "terra medium locum mundi obtinet."

12. 'Light . . . dwells,' cf. Dan. 2:22. The Latin reads: "propter splendorem quo maxime Deus delectatur."

13. Pedacius Dioscorides (physician of the first century C.E.), *De materia medica,* bk. 4, ch. LXIX. There is reference to the Tuscan designation of the plant. There were many editions of the work.

14. Ruffinus reads: "Habet autem flores similes plantigini per circuitum tota corona his floribus est caelata ab occipitio usque ad utrumque tempus."

15. *Ant.* XI:331.

16. *Bellum* V:235.

17. 'Vowels . . . pronunciation.' This is de' Rossi's circumlocutory rendering of the Latin phrase "elementa vocalia" for which he also uses an expression echoing B. Yoma 19b used in relation to the high priest. It is not clear why Josephus describes the tetragrammaton as the four vowels.

CHAPTER FIFTY

An abstract of the statements of the Christian doctors on the design of some of the priestly vestments. On the relevant citations from our rabbis which relate to Scripture, and also on the evidence of the writers that we have cited.[1]

In tractates Sukkah[2] and Shabbat,[3] it is taught: "The *ṣiṣ* was like a plate of gold, two fingers in breadth which went round from ear to ear. On it was an inscription of two lines, with the words "Holy to" on the lower line and "the Lord" on the upper line." In tractate Yoma in the Palestinian Talmud,[4] there is an additional statement: "It was like a king who sits on his throne. Rabbi Eleazer bar Yose said: 'I saw it in Rome and the words "Holy to the Lord" were written in one line.' " There is also the statement about the curtain in the Tosefta, tractate Yoma[5] and in the Talmud:[6] "Rabbi Eleazar said: I saw it in Rome and it was bespattered with drops of blood." And at the end of Avot d'Rabbi Nathan[7] it is stated: "The mortar of the house of Abtinas,[8] the table, the candelabrum, and the curtain are still kept in Rome." So much for the statements of the rabbis of blessed memory from which it emerges that our precious and valuable objects, the holy vessels, were kept in Rome. We are given the specific information that they remained there until the time of Rabbi Eleazar who lived many years after the destruction of the Temple, as is made clear in Rambam's introduction to Zerʿaim. The circumstances in which he was able to see the vessels is mentioned by Rashi of blessed memory in the passage about Ben Temalion in tractate Meʿilah.* {The above-mentioned statements are corroborated by a passage in the work entitled *De deis gentium* by the Christian writer Giraldo (section 1, p. 31).[9] He writes: "There is a well-disseminated

1. Once again de' Rossi is treating a subject of contemporary interest, both to Christian and Jewish scholars. Arias Montanus wrote a treatise on the vestments in book 8 of the Plantin Polyglot, asserting that knowledge of the actual appearance of the vestments must precede any investigation into their symbolism. In his *Shilṭe ha-Gibborim,* Abraham Portaleone discussed the stones of the ephod and the breastplate and their colors.
2. B. Sukk. 5a.
3. B. Shabb. 63b.
4. P. Yoma 4 (1) 41c.
5. T. Yom ha-Kipp. 3:8.
6. B. Yoma 57a.
7. ARN, ch. 41 (rec. A, 133).
8. They were experts in compounding incense.
9. This is a reference to the *De deis gentium* written by Lilio Gregorio Giraldo which was first published in Basel in 1542. De' Rossi may be referring to the edition of Lyons, 1565, where the passage in question is in Syntagma 1, 33: "In hoc templo [pacis] sunt qui tradunt D. Hieronymum secuti vasa et donaria templi Hierosolymitani a Tito et Vespasiano reposita fuisse."

report that Vespasian and Titus placed the vessels plundered from the Temple in the Temple of Peace in Rome.}

(*[See p. 609] In tractate Meʿilah,[10] Rashi writes: "A miracle was performed by Rabbi Eleazar. He healed the Roman emperor's daughter into whose body a demon by name of Ben Temalion had entered. They brought him to the treasure house of the emperor to take whatever he desired. There he saw the Temple vessels.")

It occurred to me that some Christian doctors may have seen them either at that time or at some later date, and for some reason or other may have left a written record with information relating to their design which is the subject of our present inquiry. I thought that they might yield some elucidation (if not valid proof). I therefore delved into their works and gave particular consideration to the work entitled *Catena aurea* by Lippomano[11] who produced a compilation from all fields of Christian exegesis. Now I did not find anything which was sufficiently noteworthy or significant to warrant a full-length translation as was the case with these three pleasant persons[12] whose works were presented above. But their investigation did not lack novel information, and so I have presented a synopsis which I submit for your consideration.

Their greatest exegetes were all of the opinion that the *patil* which is mentioned in reference to the plate was not a twisted thread but rather a hat or band and that on it was placed the golden plate which reached from ear to ear on the brow.[13] You have read my discussion of the word *patil* in chapter 46. And in chapter 49 you were shown that Josephus interprets the *patil* in *the breastplate shall be held in place by a patil* (Ex. 28:28)[14] as a band.

They describe the efod as a coat of mail which covered the body from back to front, from the shoulders to the navel or thereabouts and it was tied with a girdle, namely, the *ḥeshev.*[15]

However, they refer to the opinions of our commentators on the subject of the Urim and Tummim, and the view of some Jewish sages that the actual stones of the breastplate were called Urim because of the light they irradiated, whereas the Tummim or settings were so called because they filled the breadth of the breastplate. In the final analysis there were at a loss as to what they were.

In their translator's [Jerome's] epistle addressed to Fabiola which is in part 3 in the collection of his epistles published in his works,[16] he writes about the *miṣnefet* as follows:[17] "The fourth garment which all the priests wore was a rounded hat which was

10. B. Meʿilah 17b.

11. Aloysio Lippomano, *Catena.* See ch. 35, n. 35.

12. This is a play on Gen. 9:19, *These three were the sons of Noah.* De' Rossi has spelled Noaḥ in a plene form, thus rendering the word for pleasantness. He appears to be identifying Aristeas, whom he thought to be a gentile, with Ham; Philo, as a product of Greece, with Japhet; and Josephus with Shem, the ancestor of the Jews.

13. Lippomano, *Catena,* 292r: "Nec mireris quod dictionem pethil, fascia vitta vel filum reddatur omnia enim haec significat."

14. "It is fastened to the efod by golden rings which are placed on its corners and on those of the gap and bound together by a blue band."

15. Lippomano, *Catena,* 282r.

16. The *Epistolae* of Jerome were arranged in three sections by Teodore de' Lelli Piceno (1427–66) and this division was retained in the sixteenth-century editions of Jerome's *Opera Omnia.* (Erasmus's division of the books in his edition of 1524–26 was revised by Claude Chevallon in the edition of 1533–34. Chevallon published only genuine works of Jerome in the first three volumes.)

17. *Epistolae* (*P.L.* XXII, ep. LXIV, col. 614).

shaped like that which Ulysses is depicted as having worn. That is to say, it was practically hemispherical like a bronze helmet[18] and the Hebrews call it *miṣnefet.* It was not pointed at the top nor did it cover the entire head, but was left bare at the brow, and they tied it at the back of the neck with a band* to prevent it slipping from the head.

(*[See p. 610] It is perhaps with reference to this band that Josephus wrote: "And they attach it.")

Another work which won great acclaim among them called *Rationale divinorum officiorum*[19] treats our priestly vestments in the last chapter of the third section of the book.[20] He described the *ṣiṣ* as a peaked hat called *petalus* (they undoubtedly derived it from the word *patil*). Around its edges was a golden diadem decorated with pomegranate blossoms. On his front was a golden plate shaped like the crescent of the moon which was engraved with the four-letter Name.[21] As for the breastplate, he said that it was called the breastplate of judgment on account of the brightness of the stones which indicated whether God was favorably disposed to them or not.

So much for all the statements of these sages, whether non-Jewish or Jewish, but which were not recorded by our rabbis, and in particular, the first three writers who were eyewitnesses. Intelligent reader, I wish to inform you that in relation to all these passages in which the sages of blessed memory treat the subject of these priestly vestments, whether based on visual testimony or tradition, are lucid. There is no doubt that all other accounts are worthless and a striving after the wind. In my opinion, the views of our later commentators, which were based on a judicious and reasoned examination of Scripture or study of rabbinic dicta, should also be taken into consideration as long as their claims can be supported by the scriptural verses and the statements in the Gemara. This is a particularly valid approach when the beautiful soul[22] assesses the profit that a generation gains in relation to their reconstruction [i.e., of Scripture and Gemara] as imagined by some of our commentators. According to the verdict of both Rashi and the Semag, the efod is conceived as hanging down to the feet from the back, and the *ṣiṣ* tied with three strands. Now I am constrained to say that in the eyes of any socially aware person, this could hardly have been its appearance nor was it an appropriate adornment for a servant of God and leader of our people. It is certainly accepted that if the precious precept explicitly entailed that the high priest should put a studded shoe on his head and worn and shabby garments over his clothes, these would constitute his beauty, glory, majesty, and splendor. There is also no question that once we are able to explain the object of the Omnipresent's pleasure such that it also becomes human beings' pleasure, it is right to act accordingly and follow the dictates of the intellect with which He in His kindness has instilled us.

Now I was surprised that Ramban of blessed memory could conjecture and hold that the *patil* mentioned in connection with the *ṣiṣ* was simply a thread. He said: "The main

18. 'Bronze helmet.' This detail taken from 1Sam. 17:5 is not in Jerome.

19. This very popular work by the liturgist Guglielmus Durandus (1237–96) was first published in Mainz, 1459.

20. *Rationale,* bk. III, ch. 19, "De indumentis legalibus seu veteris testamenti."

21. *Rationale,* 82v: "aurea lamina quam petalum dicunt ad modum lunae dimidiae in qua scriptum est nomen Domini."

22. De' Rossi uses the expression 'beautiful soul' on various occasions throughout his work to denote the . . . scholarly lover of the truth.

point is that the meaning of Scripture is only to demonstrate that the cord is drawn through the holes of the *ṣiṣ*." But in his explanation of the *patil* of Judah,[23] he was content to apply the statements of our sages of blessed memory about the woollen hat and to depict its splendid design in the usual manner. He writes:[24] "The word "your patil" refers to a small *sudar* which enfolds the head." Then he goes on to speak of the Targum rendering "coarse cloak" and states: "The nobility would stretch it over their headdress and tiaras, and to this day it is still the customary dress in eastern lands." I would therefore propose that as regards the *ṣiṣ* and the *patil* which is mentioned in connection with it, that we should ground our position on the statement of our rabbis: "A woollen hat was placed on the head of the high priest on which was set the *ṣiṣ* in order to fulfill the command, *and you shall place it on a blue patil* (Ex. 28:37)." We should therefore be convinced that the *patil* mentioned in the Torah is to be identified with this hat as we wrote previously. And you may opt for the interpretation of Rav Alfasi which is equivalent to the second listed entry for *kph* in the *Arukh:* "The hat was completely rounded and two fingers broad and the upper part left uncovered." Accordingly, this ornament may rightly be described as the holy diadem and also crown as in the verse, *Remove the turban, and lift off the crown* (Ezk. 21:31). This is how Don Isaac interpreted it. By skilled workmanship, a golden headplate was attached to it on the brow. Now the compiler of the *Arukh* and Alfasi both agree that this hat was somehow made by being interlaced with threads. In this case we cannot refute Josephus's statement that the warp of this ornament consisted of three cords or one might say meshes, one on either side and one in the middle, which were decorated with those flowers. Therefore it was also appropriately designated *ṣiṣ* as used in the expression *budding flowers* (*piṭṭure ṣiṣim*). According to this interpretation, its design would be as illustrated here.

צד המצח

צד העורף

Alternatively, one might be inclined to adopt the interpretation of the compiler of the *Arukh* according to which the *kippah* was a hollowed out semicircular hat. This was also the way Rashi of blessed memory interpreted the passage in the Talmud which I discussed in chapter 46. However, in his commentary on the Torah, he was simply

23. See ch. 47 for his discussion of the story of Judah and Tamar.
24. Ramban to Gen. 38:18.

content to explain the word *patil* as a type of helmet. We could therefore propose that such an interpretation approximates that of Josephus when he writes that this diadem, namely, the circumference which measured two fingers, ornamented with flowers, was totally wrought in gold even at the back of the neck. {Such an interpretation gains credibility on noting that the expression *Give a ṣiṣ to Moab* (Jer. 48:9) is rendered in the Targum as "Remove the crown from Moab."}[2]

It is true that there were the two parts, one which extended from the back of the neck to the ears, the other, which is the plate, emerged from the brow and was attached to the other as the making required. This is why he [Josephus] said: "The crown was fashioned in a similar manner." Examine the passage. The entire diadem was placed on the edges of the *kippah* which was semicircular and blue as we mentioned. Josephus's terminology implies that he imagined this *kippah* as the tiara of the lay priests when he said, "but over this was placed another." It might be deemed therefore that it was modeled by means of protruding plaited and braided strands and thus the designation *patil* was particularly apposite. But our sages were only interested in describing the golden part which bore the holy inscription. At any rate, the statement of the blessed Lord about the vestments in general, *Note well and follow the patterns for them that are being shown you on the mountain* (Ex. 25:40) indicates that not all the requirements were given in writing. Now I have already cited ibn Ezra's view who wrote: "The aristocrats wear a golden head-plate on the *miṣnefet* on the brow such that no other thread is required in order to keep it in place on the brow." Accordingly, this would have been its design.

Now it occurred to me that once you had appreciated the truth of the exposition in our way, you would find that the verses, *You shall put it on a patil* (Ex. 28:37) and *and he put on the miṣnefet the golden ṣiṣ, the holy diadem* (Lev. 8:9) would fall into place. For all these examples refer to mere positioning and do not involve binding with cords and fastening with loops. And it would also fit with the statements of the rabbis of blessed memory: "The *kippah* was set [on the head of the high priest] and on it was placed the *ṣiṣ*." This implies that the precept was fulfilled by simply "placing" and not by binding. In fact, according to the commentators we have cited, the question would be raised as to how Scripture or Talmud would not have omitted any reference to any kind of binding as was the case with the breastplate about which it states, *The breastplate shall be held in place by a cord* (Ex. 28:28) and *They attached to it a cord of blue* (Ex. 39:31). Such an objection then is easily resolved particularly in relation to the second explanation which offers the idea that the *patil,* namely, the *kippah,* was higher than the ṣiṣ which is placed on its hems. The *patil* is intended to be placed on the *miṣnefet* from above. The statement, *Let a pure diadem be placed on his head* (Zech. 3:5), is certainly not a reference to the common priest's *miṣnefet,* but to the special headgear of the high priest, namely a blue *kippah* with the *ṣiṣ*." This is entirely consistent and indicates that the *patil* is the diadem which was put on his head only after they had dressed him in the vestments which comprise all the priestly vestments.

Now you might object to the second explanation that the gold also went round the back of the neck extending from ear to ear on the grounds that it is contrary to rabbinic opinion. But one could propose that the braided work of the *kippah* was visible on its edges and even at the back of the neck and that the plate (only the front part) was attached to it by the requisite artisanship. Moreover, according to those commentators it would also be necessary to surmise that the ends of the plate had to be pierced by holes through which the *patil* was passed, although such an idea is not explicitly found in Scripture. Indeed, there would then be no reason for its description as a *ṣiṣ,* diadem, or crown. Now there is no doubt that the statement of the rabbis of blessed memory, "His hair was visible between the *ṣiṣ* and the *miṣnefet* on which he laid the phylacteries" would be completely consistent with the first explanation but leave the second one open to question. It is not impossible that the implication of their statement is that although the nature of the helmet is such that it also covers the bend of the head towards the brow, they folded the *kippah* slightly in the middle so that his hair would be visible and he would be able to fulfill the precept of the donning of the phylacteries. The phrase, *You shall put it on a patil* (Ex. 28:37) is rendered in the Targum of [ps.] Jonathan ben Uzziel as "And it shall be on the *miṣnefet* above the phylacteries on the head." Now you might think that the two doubled threads which according to Rashi and the Semag were inserted at the two ends of the plate with the cord which passed over the crown of the head were not meant as simple cords, but were woven together by braided work. This was described by Rashi as a type of helmet. If such is your opinion, I am in agreement with you and congratulate you. Otherwise, the function of the third thread mentioned by Rashi and the Semag which passed over the crown of the head is inexplicable.

Now the pomegranate designs which, according to Josephus, decorated the diadem were either blue as in the first interpretation of the *kippah,* or golden if the second interpretation is followed. You already know that representations of whole pomegranates were put on the hems of the tunic and its warp was divided into three leashes, one above the other, as we said. We have no compelling reason to refute this interpretation. Who knows whether they do not symbolize the three crowns that we are familiar with from tractate Yoma which represent Torah, priesthood, and kingship.[25] Alternatively, they symbolize the Pentateuch, Prophets, and Hagiographa, or, with agreement of the kabbalists, they could be attributed to the three uppermost *sefirot*—I do not know. Although the statement I am about to make does not offer conclusive proof, it does contain allusive evidence. For the mitre worn by the Christian high priest which is in three tiers filled with flowers, made of precious stones between each tier, bears some resemblance to the *ṣiṣ* of the holy diadem. In fact, the author of *Rationale divinorum officiorum* wrote that there was some similarity between the vestments used by them and those of our high priest.[26] Perhaps they decided that they should not be completely identical for the reason expressed by some of their doctors regarding the dating of Easter. In the chapter on Victor, the fifteenth pope, the writer Platina[27] states that although many of their esteemed authorities thought that it was right to celebrate it on the fourteenth of Nisan like us, as a result of a great debate on the question,[28] it was decided to postdate Easter by one day to avoid all identification with us. Thus with all the more reason did they change the structure of headplate and therefore decided to bring the three crowns to a sharp point and this became known as their particular head emblem. You will indeed notice that their high priest, like ours, was given a title which contained the word "holy" in view of the verse, *And you must treat him as holy . . . he shall be holy to you for I the Lord who sanctify you am holy* (Lev. 21:8). He therefore commanded that his brow should bear the words *Holy to the Lord,* a designation which did not only apply to the *ṣiṣ,* for all garments were referred to as *sacral vestments* (Lev. 16:4), but to the priest himself who embodied the will of God. This ornament was not only a golden plate, but also, as shown by the first interpretation, a woven fabric, and could therefore appropriately be described in the terms used by our rabbis of blessed memory in connection with the son of Jose ben Joezer who married the daughter of King Jannai's wreath-plaiter.[29] Rashi explains the term as a binder of crowns. The crown is also mentioned in connection with women's jewelry in tractate Shabbat,[30] and there are the braided crowns of brides in tractate Sota.[31] This clearly indicates that it was their custom to wear braided crowns. Enough now has been said about our conception of the *ṣiṣ* and the *patil.*

However, as regards the efod, study of the secular writings that we have cited reveals that they did not believe that it hung down from the girdle which appears to be the view of some of our commentators, but not that of Rashi and his colleagues. There is nothing in the Torah or Gemara to contradict their view and it is also consistent with

25. In B. Yoma 72b, the reference is to three crowns: that of the altar, the ark, and the table which are interpreted to represent priesthood, kingship, and Torah respectively.

26. *Rationale,* 82v.

27. Bartolomeo de' Sacchi (Platina), *De vitis,* 21–22.

28. I.e., at the Council of Nicaea.

29. B. B.B. 133b.

30. B. Shabb. 59b.

31. B. Sota 49b.

reasoned opinion.[32] On examination of the statements of all those writers, and in particular those of Josephus who was a priest, arbitration in the controversies of our commentators of blessed memory over the design of the *miṣnefet* is achieved. For their verdicts on the subject concur and are correct. In other words, it was braided all around but stitched such that it was unnecessary to thread it each time. But you should imagine the *ḳippah* and *migbaʿot* as an erect helmet as Rashi of blessed memory states. Similarly they provide conclusive evidence regarding the order in which the names of the tribes were engraved on the shoulder bands of the efod, which concurs with Rashi's view, but not with Ramban's. Again Rashi's and not Ramban's view is confirmed by their view on the positioning of the bells between the pomegranates. Study and discover the facts for yourself. There are also other matters related to the design of these priestly vestments which become somewhat elucidated once we give them our consideration.

Now I shall speak about the Urim and Tummim, but only on the condition that nothing will pass my lips which might be contrary to the refined word of God whether of the written or oral variety. Having submitted to the most plausible opinion, I would say that I cannot settle for Rashi's opinion that they bore an inscription of the Ineffable Name because of the problem that I raised in chapter 46. I find it most satisfactory to hold that they are the actual onyx stones which are put between its folds. I came to this opinion because the designation *stones for setting* (Ex. 25:7) implies that they filled the breastplate. For if, according to Rashi, they filled those encasings, so too, the onyx stones could have the same function. Furthermore, the commandment about the making of the onyx stones only speaks about the fact that they should be put *on* the shoulder pieces which indicates that they are put on the exterior. In contrast, when the stones of the breastplate are mentioned, the copula *be* (in) or the word *el* (to) is always connected to it. Examine the following examples: *You shall set in it* (Ex. 28:17); *They set in it* (Ex. 39:10); *you shall place inside the breastplate* (Ex. 28:30); *he shall put into the breastplate* (Lev. 8:8). This last example corresponds to the phrase *and into the arḳ* (Ex. 25:21); *and Aaron shall carry the names . . . in the breastplate in his heart* (Ex. 28:29). And the expression *in his heart* indicates their concealment just as the phylacteries of the hand are said to be in the heart.[33] And in pericope *va-yaqhel,* in which there is an elaborate explanation of various details of less importance than these, it states, *they set in it four rows of stones* (Ex. 39:10), and this is not followed by reference to the Urim and Tummim. Conversely, in pericope *ṣav* in which they are mentioned, *he put the breastplate on him and put into the breastplate the Urim and Tummim* (Lev. 8:8), there is silence on the subject of the stones. Then there is the repetition in pericope *teṣaveh.* At first it is stated, *And you shall set in it mounted stones in four rows of stones* (Ex. 28:17), and then at the end it again states, *In the breastplate of judgment you shall place the Urim and Tummim so that they are over Aaron's heart* (Ex. 28:30). The last clause, namely, the additional words *over Aaron's heart,* was necessary. You must surely know about the repetition of the description of the rings for the ark in pericope *terumah* and Rashi's comments on it.[34] Another possible reason for

32. The Cassel edition has a faulty reading here, *en* (not) instead of *hem* (they).

33. De' Rossi is referring here to the commandment about the phylacteries as expressed in the first two paragraphs of the *Shema* (in particular Deut. 6:5–8; 11:18).

34. I.e., to Ex. 25:12 where Rashi explains that the repetition serves to explain where the rings were fixed.

the repetition is that it explains that the precept *And you shall set in it mounted stones in four rows of stones* (Ex. 28:17) could only be fulfilled after the ornament had been completed and placed on the priest. This is evident from the passage in pericope *ṣav* in which it states, *He put the breastplate on him* and only afterwards, *and put into the breastplate the Urim and Tummim* (Lev. 8:8). The doubled breastplate must have looked like a bulging bag and so rhetorically we could apply to it the verse, *Honest scales and balances are the Lord's; all the weights in the bag are His work* (Pr. 16:11). There is additional support for the view that the Urim and Tummim are the stones themselves. For the words of Rambam of blessed memory which, on many occasions, are spoken with a "still small voice" but have the force of the "cry of a multitude" appear to be really compatible to such a view. For in chapter 9 of the Laws of the Temple Vessels, which contains instruction about the making of all the vestments, he writes as follows:[35] "In it were set the four rows of precious stones." But he makes no reference to the Urim and Tummim. Then in chapter 10 which was not the context for the design of the vestments since he had already treated it in chapter 9, he remarks that the Urim and Tummim were made in the second Temple.[36] The reference to the making of the Urim and Tummim certainly did not provide new information from that given in the previous chapter; rather, its purpose was to explain that they were made in order to complete the required number of vestments even though they were no longer used for seeking counsel. Now we know that the answer issued from the stones and their letters. One might propose that these precious stones were called Urim because of the strong natural light which emanated when they were all connected; it may also have been called thus because of the splendor of the divine light that irradiated from them on propitious occasions—we shall discuss this presently. The word "Tummim" may derive from the word for twins as in the phrase *there were twins* (*tomim*) (Gen. 25:24) because they were of equal size and value just as the tribes whose names were imprinted on them were of equal standing before God. And there is the particularly apt explanation of the rabbis of blessed memory:[37] "Urim because they made their words enlightening and Tummim because they fulfill them." In any case, the basic name for them was simply "Urim" as in the verse, *who shall on his behalf seek the decision of the Urim before the Lord* (Num. 27:21). I do not know what objection could be raised against this view. Although we said that the stones were concealed within the folds of the breastplate, at the moment when the response was given, they were able to stand out in relief, irradiate, and combine without being impeded by the iron partition. In particular there is the *baraita* in the Palestinian Talmud about the method of questioning where one Tanna taught:[38] "A voice was heard as is written *[When Moses went into the Tent of Meeting to speak with him,] he heard the Voice addressing him* (Num. 7:89)." Who knows whether there was a gap in between the meshes in the breastplate's embroidery from which the light could emanate. In any case one could also suggest that the stones were not placed within the folds of the breastplate, but upon it—a plain reading of the discussions of the three writers would agree with such an interpretation. Now in

35. Kele ha-Miqdash IX:6.
36. Ibid. X:10.
37. B. Yoma 73b.
38. P. Yoma 7 (3) 44c.

tractate Qiddushin in the Palestinian Talmud they comment on the verse, *until a priest with Urim and Tummim should appear* (Ezra 2:63):[39] "Were there Urim and Tummim in the second Temple? No, it is as though somebody refers to the resurrection of the dead or to the advent of the Messiah." This in no way contradicts the view of Rambam of blessed memory or our own words, for since the response was withheld, it was indeed as though they had disappeared. Similarly the Tosafists write:[40] "They did have the Urim and Tummim in the second Temple for otherwise, the high priest would not have had the required number of vestments; but they did not give any responses." Now you should know that since the question raised in the Palestinian Talmud is not taken up in the Babylonian Talmud, we must conclude that its view was not upheld—we shall want to discuss this at the beginning of chapter 51 with the authority of Alfasi and the Rosh [Asher ben Yehiel]. On the contrary, on the basis of the verse which was quoted, it is clear that for a certain time at the beginning of the second Temple period, the Urim and Tummim answered their requests as in bygone days and that fire also descended from heaven and this continued for some time until on account of their sins, the sacred words gradually decreased. I shall develop this discussion towards the end of chapter 51.

In conclusion, I must tell the readers that I have never forced them to accept my opinion; rather each and every truly intelligent person will decide for himself. I am particularly in agreement with the author of the *Kuzari*[41] who said that if at this present time we were issued with the command to offer the sacrifices, we would not know about the vestments and their makeup and so on. Under the entry for the word *or,* Kimḥi writes:[42] "We do not know what the Urim and Tummim were. Rashi of blessed memory said that they were inscribed with the Ineffable Name, but the truth of the matter is not clear." Now with regard to the construction of the Tabernacle, the blessed Lord said, *[Note well and follow the patterns for them] that are being shown you* (Ex. 25:40). As I said, this indicates that the written word alone cannot provide adequate explication as to what they were, but that they also had to be seen with the eye. It is therefore our duty to study, investigate, and explain Scripture with all the powers of the intellect. I am fully aware that I have not satisfied the reader for I have not given an exhaustive and adequate treatment of all the vestments. However, he should be content with the little if anything he has gained. There was more than a little work involved in presenting him with all those passages from the works of the Jewish and gentile sages. Now whoever is interested has the simple task—he can refer back to those passages, sift their contents, and be all the wiser for it.

Now I noticed that in the *Antiquities,* Josephus speaks about the stones of the efod and the breastplate. If his information is true, it serves as a novel and fitting contribution to our study. I though it write to translate the passage at this juncture and it shall constitute the conclusion to our treatment of these holy vestments. In chapter 9 of book 3[43] he writes:

39. P. Qidd. 4 (1) 65b.
40. Tos to B. Yoma 21b, s.v. *ve-Urim.*
41. *Kuzari* III, par. 57.
42. David Kimḥi, *Sefer ha-Shorashim,* s.v. *or.*
43. *Ant.* III:214–18.

> I shall now describe the design of the priestly vestements that was not relevant to our previous discussion. Dressed in this garb, priests were deterred from lying and defrauding others under a sham and fraudulent guise. Indeed, he himself displayed to all who saw him, to strangers or natives, sure sign as to whether God was with the priest who was thus clad, or not. Of the two onyx stones that were on the shoulders, the nature of which is familiar and known, the one on the right shoulder irradiated such an extraordinary blaze of light that it was visible even from afar. So amazing was this spectacle that all intellectuals who despised the divine service retracted from their false suppositions. But there was an even more wondrous phenomenon. By means of the twelve stones that were affixed to the heart of the high priest on the breastplate, God used to disclose to the children of Israel on the eve of battle that they were to be victorious. For before the armed forces went into motion, a dazzling light emanated from them which was an obvious indication to all the people that God was with them and would be near at hand to all those who called on Him in truth. Hence Greek sages who do not ridicule the way we worship God, call that ornament *logion* which means oracle, namely, a response of God.[44] Now these blazened-out letters, both of the stones of the breastplate and those of the efod, completely disappeared about two hundred years before I composed this work, for God was angry that the laws which He had given us had been transgressed.

Such is Josephus's description. From his account and that of the author of *Rationale divinorum officiorum,* it would appear that they were of the opinion that the high priest who inquired of the Urim could know whether the response was favorable or not according to the strength of the light that emanated from the stones. However, two of the greatest Christian doctors, Augustine[45] and Aquinas[46] his disciple, derided those who believe in this. Suidas, on the other hand, one of their great interpreters of antiquity,[47] confirmed and ratified the entire account of Josephus, as can easily be seen from the *Catena aurea* on Exodus 28.[48] Josephus also gives a lengthy description of the structure of the Tabernacle and all its furniture. The scholar can read it for himself. But there is a passage he wrote which I should like to mention. At the end of chapter 6, he describes the Cherubim in the following manner:[49] "The Cherubim were in the form of winged creatures, a new species the likes of which has never been seen. But Moses saw their form on the throne of God. In the Ark he deposited two tablets which contained the ten commandments, five on each of them, and two and a half on either side."

Now for the final scenario and as our closing words, I would not entertain the idea that on seeing the crowd of foreigners, any one of the perfect and faithful of Israel, indeed those holy people who do not look at the effigy of a coin,[50] would hesitate to

44. The words 'a response of God' are de' Rossi's addition.

45. *Quaestionum . . . libri,* bk. 2, CXVII (*P.L.* XXXIV, col. 637). "Fabulantur tamen quidam lapidem fuisse cuius color, sive ad adversa, sive ad prospera mutaretur quando sacerdos intrabat in sancta."

46. *Summa theologicae prima secundae,* quaestio 102, articulus 5: "Iudaei tamen fabulantur quid in rationali erat lapis qui secundum diversos colores mutabatur secundum diversa quae debebant accidere filiis Israel."

47. Suidas or Suda is the name of a lexicon or literary encyclopaedia of Greek learning and civilization which was compiled at the end of the tenth century.

48. Lippomano, *Catena,* 287v. quotes Josephus and the Suda.

49. *Ant.* III:137–38.

50. 'The holy . . . coin.' This expression is from B. Pes. 104a and refers to those who refrain from looking at the effigy on a coin in case it contains an idolatrous image.

extend a listening ear to any innovation regarding Torah studies. For such has been the vision which has been given through these chapters and indeed in all the contents of this book. For the fact is that there is but one measurement for all the curtains[51] and each person would therefore make the blessing pronounced by those who have derived benefit. He would pronounce the blessing which Ben Zoma, whose memory is blessed, made on the Temple Mount[52] "Blessed be He who created all these to serve me." And yet, I shall now reiterate the statement that I made previously. While we value and will listen to the opinions of others, we shall not relinquish the tradition of our rabbis in any respect. May God be kindly disposed towards His people and speedily restore the service in love to the oracle of His Temple. At such a time, all these matters and many others besides will become clarified and elucidated and the fire-offerings of Israel and their prayer will be perpetually acceptable before His splendid glory.

51. 'One . . . curtains,' cf. Ex. 26:2. I.e., de' Rossi has used non-Jewish material for all his investigations.

52. B. Ber. 58a. Ben Zoma sees 'a crowd' on the Temple Mount, and de' Rossi turns this crowd into the crowd of foreigners whose works he cites throughout the book.

CHAPTER FIFTY-ONE

Concerning the pronouncement of Haggai the prophet: *The glory of this latter House shall be greater than that of the former.*[1]

As we know from the "Splendor of the Elders," King Ptolemy contributed great splendor to the Temple of our God. He dispatched gifts consisting of the table, flagons, wonderfully constructed bowls, one hundred talents as payment for the cost of the sacrifices, the repair of the Temple, and the valued offering for the officiating priest. In addition, he donated gifts for the elders who translated the Torah and he released one hundred twenty thousand oppressed Jews, all of whom he compensated with money from the royal treasuries. This story stimulated me to reflect on the Sanctuary's enrichment and embellishment by many other kings on many occasions and in a variety of ways. There is no written evidence that the first Temple received such treatment from any earthly king. I therefore reached the verdict that it was with reference to this fact or also because of it that in his fulfillment of the Lord's mission, Haggai the prophet pronounced that happy prediction, *In just a little while longer . . . the glory of this latter House shall be greater than that of the former one* (Hag. 2:6, 9). I shall explain this presently.

Now it is known that the sages of the Babylonian Gemara considered that this verse referred to the second Temple. In tractate Bava Batra,[2] Rav and Samuel disagreed about the interpretation of the word "greater." One said that it referred to the size of the Temple, the other, to its duration. Moreover, in Shir ha-Shirim Rabbah, with regard to the verse, *The blossoms have appeared in the land, the time of pruning has come; and the song of the turtledove is heard in our land* (S.S. 2:12) it is stated: "*The blossoms have appeared in the land*—these are Mordechai and his associates; Ezra and his associates. *The time of pruning has come*—this refers to the time which has come for the destruction of the Babylonians and the rebuilding of the Temple as is written, *the glory of this latter House shall be greater. And the song of the turtledove is heard in our land*—this is the voice of the good guide, namely, Cyrus. Furthermore, with regard to the verse, *We have a little sister and she has no breasts* (S.S. 8:8), they state:[3] "This refers to the five things by

1. It should be noted that while de' Rossi explicitly criticizes some Jewish interpretations of the prophecy, he is also indirectly undermining a dominant Christian approach to the verse as given by Augustine (to whom he refers) and anti-Jewish polemicists such as Pietro Galatino and Sebastian Münster who, like de' Rossi, interpreted the verse in reference to the second Temple, but on the grounds of its glorification on account of Jesus' presence.

2. B. B.B. 3a–b.

3. S.S.R. to S.S. 2:12.

which the latter House fell short of the first." The fact is that both the wise author of the *Aqedah* (gate 50)[4] and Don Isaac [Abravanel] in his commentary on Haggai (fourth question)[5] and in his explanation of the literal meaning of the verses, both dissented from rabbinic opinion and asserted that the verse referred to the third Temple—may it be rebuilt soon. Don Isaac, in particular, gives the reason for his dissent when he states that there is no glory but the Divine Presence which brings riches and glory. Furthermore, he said that the explicit expression "latter House" must refer to the third Temple. We can adduce statements of the kabbalists as support for their view. In *Sefer ha-Tiqqunim*[6] and the *Zohar,*[7] there is the passage about the three questions raised by that clever but ignorant man. (In my opinion, the author of the *Kuzari* used their response for the formulation of that wonderful saying of his,[8] "Israel is among the nations like the heart among the limbs.") They gave a similar interpretation. Referring to the verse, *Unless the Lord build the House, its builders labor in vain on it* (Ps. 127:1), they asserted that the two first Temples were destroyed because they were of human workmanship, whereas the third and last one is described as *The sanctuary, O Lord, which Your hands established* (Ex. 15:17); *the dwelling place of the eternal God* (Deut. 33:27); *The Lord rebuilds Jerusalem* (Ps. 147:2)—for He shall sustain it as a wall of fire and therefore it is stated, *The glory of the latter House shall be greater than that of the former.*

However, as was said, the sages of the Gemara and the Midrash who saw and understood the words of Rabbi Simeon bar Yoḥai disagreed with his opinion. One might say that this was not a question involving a practical decision such as the case of eating meat products after milk, which appeared to be forbidden according to the Zohar[9] on the basis of the verse, *You shall not boil a kid in its mother's milk* (Ex. 23:19). For once a permit had been issued as given in tractate Ḥullin,[10] general practice followed the view prescribed in our Gemara. In a similar manner, Alfasi[11] and Rosh [Asher ben Yeḥiel][12] of blessed memory discuss the treatment of the law regarding knocking on doors on the Sabbath in the Palestinian [lit. the Westerners'] Gemara: "Although they prohibited it, our [i.e., the Babylonian] Gemara permitted it and we therefore do not take notice of their prohibition since their expertise in the Palestinian Gemara was greater than ours. If they had not regarded their opinion on this matter as one that should not be supported, they would not have issued their permit." With regard to our subject, then, we have all the more justification in our position given that the best exegetes interpret the verse according to its literal sense as referring to the second Temple. This evaluation of the text also appears to be correct in the light of the

4. Isaac Arama, *Aqedat Yiṣḥaq,* gate 50, terumah (153b).
5. Abravanel, to Haggai (183, col. b–184a).
6. *Sefer ha-Tiqqunim* 8, 24a; 12, 27a.
7. *Zohar,* Pinḥas, II, 220b–221a. "One day a certain clever non-Jew came and said: 'Old man, old man, I want to ask three questions of you. One is how can you maintain that another Temple will be built for you, whereas only two were destined to be built. A third and a fourth you will not find mentioned in Scripture, but it is written *Greater shall be the glory of the latter house.*' "
8. *Kuzari* II, par. 36.
9. Zohar II, 125a.
10. B. Ḥull. 108a.
11. Alfasi to B. Eruv. 104a (35b).
12. Asher ben Yeḥiel to Eruv, ch. 10, par. 20.

Midrash of the rabbis of blessed memory on the verse, *I am that which I am* (Ex. 3:14):[13] "The Holy One blessed be He said to Moses: 'I am with them in this adversity as I will be with them during the enslavement of the exiles.' He said to Him: 'Sovereign of the universe, sufficient is the evil in the time thereof.' Then He said to him: 'You have spoken well.'" In this case, then, Haggai's intention was to comfort them about the second Temple; how then could one imagine that he would have wanted to distress them by referring to the third Temple which would imply that the present Temple was to be destroyed? This would be most surprising. Moreover, according to Josephus and others who like him believe that the second Temple stood for more than 420 years, as we have discussed in the previous chapters, the word "great" in this context could not refer to the number of years as the one sage would have it. Such an interpretation would be unacceptable on logical grounds for those who classify different sayings into categories of the how and the when. I therefore felt that my method of proceeding was justified and I decided to present a synopsis of the written evidence that I had discovered with regard to the great glory which had been bestowed on the second Temple in a multiplicity of ways by several monarchs of the three great kingdoms of Persia, Greece, and Rome before sin had taken its effect. Previously the first Temple, as far as is known from Scripture, had not received such treatment from the kingdom of Assyria and Babylon. On the contrary, for the length of its duration until the decisive war came to an end, no good, but only evil, befell it. And so we are led to the belief that in all probability Haggai the prophet was alluding to the glory with which foreigners aggrandized that Temple.

The term "latter" is not problematic. The plain meaning of the word can be satisfactorily explained in two ways.[14] First, it is true that with the Almighty's help, the third Temple is to be built after the second. As they state in Nazir[15] with regard to the verse, *The Temple of the Lord, the Temple of the Lord, the Temple of the Lord* (Jer. 7:4), the Temple of the Lord is repeated three times to refer to the first, second, and third Temples; two were destroyed and the third will stand forever. Nevertheless it must be that the second Temple is called last in comparison to the first Temple which preceded it. Likewise it is written in Jeremiah, *Israel are scattered sheep, harried by lions. First the kings of Assyria devoured them,*—this refers to the exile of the ten tribes—*and this last one Nebuchadnezzar king of Babylon [crunched their bones]* (Jer. 50:17). Now it is known that the Babylonian exile was not the last, for it was followed by that of Titus, but it is called last in relation to the former one. Likewise, the expression "last" used in reference to the second Temple is only relative to the first one and does not carry the sense of final. Moreover, on consultation of the work *Me'ir Nativ,*[16] you will discover that the word is used in this comparative sense throughout Scripture with the exception of the word issuing from the holy mouth, *I am the first and I am the last* (Is. 44:6). Examine the

13. B. Ber. 9b.

14. The word *aḥaron* under discussion may be used in either a comparative or superlative sense; hence, de' Rossi's discussion.

15. B. Nazir 32b.

16. This is the first Hebrew concordance of the Bible compiled between 1437 and 1448 by Isaac b. Kalonymus (or Mordechai Nathan). The books of the Hebrew Bible are listed according to the order of the Vulgate in order to facilitate its use by those involved in polemics with Christians.

statements: *[putting the maids and their children first] Leah and her children last* which then ends *and Rachel and Joseph last* (Gen. 33:2); *And the later generation among them* (Deut. 29:21); *and their children of the last generation* (Ps. 78:4); *You have acted well with your last act of kindness* (Ruth 3:10); *that you shall tell the last generation* (Ps. 48:14); *that the last generation of children may know* (Ps. 78:6). In each of these examples the word "last" is not used in an absolute sense.

The other explanation is as follows. In the previous passage, Haggai states, *Who is left among you who saw this House in its former splendor?* (Hag. 2:3). The word "former" refers to the splendor. It is therefore also appropriate by way of a literal interpretation to understand the terms "former" and "latter" in this verse as a reference to the splendor itself and not to the Temple. If this is the case, its purpose may be to demonstrate how the luster of the Temple became more and more resplendent as was indeed the case until the perpetration of sins put an end to it. Thus all the latter splendor exceeded that of the first, as it increased steadily. According to the dictates of the intellect, I am brought to the view that with all our conviction that Herod's construction was a wondrous spectacle—thus it is described by Josephus[17] and our sages of blessed memory in tractates Bava Batra[18] and Sukkah[19]—its magnificence was only relative to Zerubbabel's construction which was very modest according to Josephus.[20] Perhaps it was for this reason that they made the one-cubit partition with the two curtains as is explained in chapter 4 of Middot.[21] However, in comparison to Solomon's construction, it was unquestionably on a lesser scale, just as the riches of Herod were inferior to those of Solomon. For according to the scriptural evidence, his riches and wisdom exceeded that of any other king of the world. This fact is further corroborated insofar as we know that David left him great wealth which was to be spent on the construction of the Temple; and then there is Solomon's message to the king of Tyre, *The House that I intend to build will be singularly great inasmuch as our God is greater than all gods* (2Chr. 2).[22] And there is even greater confirmation from Josephus's statement in book 7,[23] if true, that Solomon buried his father David with great pomp and inserted a large quantity of gold and silver into the ornate grave. He said that eight hundred[24] years later, King Hyrcanus the Hasmonean was in need of large sums of money in order to ward off Antiochus's forces and opened one of the chambers of the tomb and extracted three thousand talents. Again, after many years had elapsed, King Herod opened another chamber and also extracted a large amount of money. Neither of them, however, tampered with the grave itself. He repeats the story of Hyrcanus in the first book of the *Wars*.[25] In book 16 (chapter 11) of the *Antiquities*[26] he gives a lengthier version of the story about Herod who entered the cave secretly at night, only accompanied by his

17. *Ant.* XV:391ff.
18. B. B.B. 4a: "He who has not seen the Temple of Herod, has never seen a beautiful building."
19. B. Sukk. 51b.
20. *Ant.* XI:81.
21. M. Midd. 4:7. The two curtains were divided by this one-cubit partition.
22. De' Rossi combines vv. 4 and 8.
23. *Ant.* VII:392.
24. The text reads 1300 not 800.
25. *Bellum* I:61.
26. *Ant.* XVI:179–87.

two lads. Fire issued from the grave and burnt his lads, while Herod who had been waiting outside made a quick escape for his life. Frightened about the sin he had perpetrated, he rebuilt the grave and constructed an amazing edifice out of yellow, black, and white marble.[27] Nevertheless, ever since the time of that crime, all his deeds went from bad to worse. This is surely indicative of the fact that his wealth lacked a solid foundation. For he was prepared to risk his life and to break into the caves of the dead for the sake of the living. Such a person can certainly not be compared to the one for whom money is of no consequence. But I have no need to continue with this conjectural kind of evidence. Our sages have made an explicit pronouncement about it in Bemidbar Rabbah[28] and Shir ha-Shirim Rabbah.[29] They state: "Rabbi Isaac said: It is taught (in chapter 4 of Middot) that the whole of the Temple was overlaid with gold except the backs of the doors in the second Temple. But in the first Temple, even the backs of the doors were overlaid with gold. It is taught: Seven kinds of gold were used: good gold . . . gold of Parvaim. This was red like the blood of a bullock (*par*) while others say that it yielded fruit (*perot*)." The last statement is also in Bemidbar Rabbah. Now Rashi, Kimḥi, and the Septuagint understand Parvaim as a place name.[30] In my opinion, it must be reference to the country of Peru which was discovered in our days by the Spaniards—I discussed this in chapter 11. Come what may, there is no doubt that at the time of its construction, the riches of the first Temple exceeded those of the second Temple as we said. Moreover, according to the statement of our sages of blessed memory in Yoma,[31] the Divine Presence and the five precious objects were in the first, but not in the second, Temple and undoubtedly endowed and invested it with incomparable grandeur. But in our view, the glory which is designated here by Haggai does not refer to the Temple's own glory but to its enrichment from the sacrifices and gifts brought time and time again by foreign kings and nations. He therefore states in that same context, *Silver is Mine and gold is Mine—says the Lord of Hosts* (2:8), the implication being that what is "Mine" is God's to increase and expand however small its beginning, as is known. The same message is conveyed by Malachi's address to Israel, *Now if I am a father, where is the honor due Me?* (1:6) and then further on, *For from where the sun rises to where it sets, My name is honored among the nations, and everywhere incense and pure oblation are offered to My name* (v.11). In other words, they are coming or sending from all places to offer incense and oblation in Jerusalem for great is My name among the nations.

Now the gentiles were still idol-worshippers in the time of the second Temple. Nevertheless, several gentile writers wrote that Numa Pompilius, the second king of Rome—according to the chronological tables of Eusebius and Samotheus [Johannes Lucidus], it is clear that he was a contemporary of the provocative Manasseh—found that his subjects were completely dissipated and lacked religious piety of any kind nor did they worship the gods that had been conceived by the ancients. They were even less

27. The Latin text reads "e candido marmore." De' Rossi is using the expression in B. Sukk. 51b about Herod's Temple.
28. Bem. R. 12:4.
29. S.S.R. to S.S. 3:10.
30. LXX. 2Chr. 3:6.
31. B. Yoma 21b.

inclined to offer sacrifices in our God's Temple. Now we should look carefully at Zephaniah's pronouncement, *And I will wipe out . . . those who have forsaken the Lord and those who have not sought the Lord and have not turned to Him* (Zeph. 1:4,6). He is speaking of two classes of people: the idolators and those who have completely severed themselves from any yoke. Now with regard to the providence which our God extends to the nations of the world it is stated, *Behold the Lord God has His eye upon the sinful kingdom* (Amos. 9:8). It is thus not an implausible deduction that He pays more attention to those who have no object of veneration than to those who worship idols or the heavenly hosts which He assigned for all nations. For to any form of religious piety there is some advantage[32]—for they are more likely to refrain from destroying the world which He created for habitation, not to lie waste.[33] As ibn Ezra wrote with regard to the first commandment:[34] "He who does not believe in the Lord commits a greater sin than an idolator." Now, in those days, whether because of the tale he invented according to which he was familiar with the nymph Egeria who spoke to him with divine words, or because of his prowess with the mighty sword, Numa began to persuade his subject nations to revert to the worship of certain heavenly powers as had been the practice in remote antiquity. He instituted a hierarchy of high priests and lay priests and specification for the sacrifices and festive days together with statutes and laws which were undoubtedly meaningless and worthless. And yet he did wean them away from absolute anarchy to control and restraint. While pasturing the asses, he discovered the objects and rites that inspired them with fear and trepidation.[35] All this is described at length by Livy in the first book of his *Decades*[36] and by Lactantius Firmianus in the last chapters of his work entitled *De falsa religione*[37] and by many other exemplary people. Thus, as the generations went by, those peoples became increasingly entrenched in their worship of the gods and the powers. And so, in second Temple times, they would have also had the opportunity, as we have said, to have come to hear about the name of our blessed God. So it was that many kings and peoples sent their gift and sacrifices together with a regular assignation of food or offering as is documented by chroniclers. This was not the situation in the first Temple, but rather the reverse. It is to this phenomenon that the prophet rightly alluded when he spoke of "the glory of this latter House." So reader, please first pay attention to the words of Ezra the scribe and his true account of the Median and Persian kings. In the sixth chapter he wrote how that on the authority of the written edict of his predecessor Cyrus, who had expressed the same wishes, Darius had issued the command, *the expenses are to be paid to these men with dispatch out of the resources of the king. . . . Let them be given daily, without fail, whatever they need so that they may offer pleasing sacrifices to the God of heaven and pray for the life of the kings and his sons* (Ezra 6:8,9,10). And then later in chapter 7, he told that Artaxerxes had issued the order *to bring the silver and gold which the king and*

32. A play on Pr. 14:23.

33. 'Create . . . waste,' cf. Is. 45:18.

34. Ibn Ezra to Ex. 20:2.

35. This is a play on Gen. 36:24, *Anah who discovered the mules in the wilderness while pasturing the asses of his father.* In B. Ḥull. 7b, the word *mules* (*yemim*) is connected with the word *emah* (fear).

36. *Decades* (1, 21).

37. Lactantius, *Divinum Institutionum lib., De falsa religione,* lib. 1, chs. XIX–XXII (*P.L.* VI), and particularly, ch. XXII.

his advisors gave as a freewill offering to the God of Israel (7:15), and the entire chapter goes on in the same vein. Then in the light of all this, Ezra states, *Blessed is the Lord God of our fathers who put it into the mind of the King to glorify the House of the Lord in Jerusalem* (7:27). Now after the time of Ezra, the faithful scribe, there were no longer prophets among us nor were there those who spoke under divine inspiration. As is stated by the author of the *Kuzari,* prophecy came to an end forty years after the Temple had been erected—we discussed this previously. As result, a state of doubt was engendered by the lack of receptiveness to the divine. And so, in the absence of other people, we shall endeavor to see the relevant information that is provided by those who write without superhuman powers, only from the perspective of our own understanding and the common wisdom they display. For ultimately, those who compose iniquitous documents[38] will be battered on their heads by other writers. For it is simply that they are jealous of our God's glory.[39]

Now having considered the glory that was bestowed on that Temple by the kings of Persia and Media, we should turn our attention to a matter of common knowledge. I am referring to the great deeds of Alexander of Macedon in his encounter with the high priest who came from Jerusalem to meet him. For contrary to the expectation of his servants, Alexander prostrated himself before him, and while he waged tempestuous wars with all nations of the world, he behaved with great kindness and love towards us. With great veneration he approached the Sanctuary with the priest and donated a meal offering and pleasing sacrifices[40] and he requested the Lord regarding the final outcome of his wars with Darius. Thus, in my opinion, the primary purpose of Haggai in his prophecy, *In just a little while longer* (2:6) and in his second prophecy, *I am going to shake the heavens and the earth* (2:21) was to allude to the exploits of Alexander. For after the second Temple had been standing for some time, his wars shook all nations and he overthrew the imperial throne.[41] He came to Jerusalem together with the highest nobility and the kings that were in his train, who were indeed *the gem of all the nations* (Hag. 2:7) for that generation, and their best representatives. He wanted to offer the priest gold and many precious jewels for the purpose of erecting a commemorative statue of him in the Sanctuary. But he was told that this was not acceptable to God who is the source of silver and gold. While the entire world was steeped in the pain of wars, he brought peace and quiet to that place. Likewise all his successors to the throne who also deserved the designation "gem of all the nations" continued to bestow honor on this Temple—this shall be elucidated further. One should also not neglect to examine the words *And I will shake [all the nations]* (Hag. 2:7) and *I am going to shake [the heavens and the earth]* (ibid. v.21) which do not imply that they shook of their own accord. Rather, they alert one to the understanding that although the main reason for that war was, to all appearances, to free the king of Macedon from paying the customary tribute to Darius, the real and principal cause was effected by the Creator by whom actions are weighed. A similar appraisal should be made in all comparable issues. Now from the work the *Splendor of the Elders,* we have already been apprised as to the grandeur,

38. Cf. Is. 10:1.
39. This statement may be a veiled allusion to Christian interpretations of the verse in question.
40. 'Meal offering . . . sacrifices,' cf. Dan. 2:46.
41. 'Overthrew . . . throne,' cf. Hag. 2:22.

honor, and distinction that was contributed to this Temple after the time of Alexander by Ptolemy Philadelphus, the son of one of the four kings who came to the throne after "the horn was broken."[42] There is no reason to elaborate on this for the contents of this work are well known. Additionally, however, go and read book 12 of Josephus (chapter 3).[43] There he gives a lengthy account of how Antiochus the great, king of Greece, the grandfather of Antiochus Epiphanes the wicked, published a royal edict with regard to the respect to be shown the Temple. He wrote: "All non-Jews should take great care not to approach the Sanctuary contrary to the law of the Jews. Nor shall any person have the audacity to bring the flesh of any of the creatures which they regard as unclean into Jerusalem, nor to breed them in the city, nor should their hides be brought there, and the only animals that may be killed within the city are the animals and birds which are permitted for Jews to offer to the great God who is there." Again in book 13 (chapter 5) he refers to the honor bestowed on this temple by Demetrius, a Greek king of the days of Jonathan the Hasmonean high priest. He issued a royal edict concerning the Jews which was endearing and precious. It included the following statement:[44] "And in addition, I dedicate a yearly sum of fifteen thousand silver sheqels from my own revenue for the acquisition of sacrifices. And I abrogate my right to the ten thousand sheqels that my predecessors on the throne used to receive from the Temple and give them over to the priests. Any person who takes refuge in the Temple and Sanctuary to which it is connected may not be apprehended by the officers even when they have debts to the king. If any repairs must be done to the Temple, I desire that the necessary costs should be defrayed by us." He also mentions the Samaritans, who set up the altar on Mount Gerizim in the time of Alexander of Macedon, and the representatives of the community of Alexandria in Egypt who defended the Jerusalem Sanctuary. The case of both parties was brought to Ptolemy Philometor who had to adjudicate as to which temple should be given precedence. In addition to the proofs based on Torah in favor of the preeminence of the Temple, the Jews also used the following arguments. They said:[45] "Our Lord, consider that this Temple is the supreme one; for all the kings of Asia have honored it with dedicatory gifts time and time again." The outcome of the debate was that the defenders of the altar were left like dumb dogs and were punished by death according to royal edict. {Who knows if this were not one of the arguments referred to by our rabbis of blessed memory in Sanhedrin.[46] However there, due to their disinclination to transmit an accurate version of the story they were told, they impute that the debate took place with Alexander.}[2]

Then in the second book of *Against Apion,*[47] he writes that after his conquest of the entire domain of Syria, Ptolemy III, surnamed Euergetes, did not offer sacrifices of thanksgiving to the Egyptian gods, but came to Jerusalem and there offered numerous sacrifices through the ministry of the priests in accordance with the statutes of our

42. 'Horn . . . broken,' cf. Dan. 8:8.

43. *Ant.* XII:145–46.

44. *Ant.* XIII:55.

45. Ibid. 78.

46. B. Sanh. 91a. He is referring to the passage in which various peoples are said to have brought lawsuits against the Jews before Alexander of Macedon.

47. *Contra Apionem* II, 48.

Torah. In the *Wars,*[48] he describes how Alexander, the father of the emperor Tiberius,[49] invested a large amount of money on the adornment of the gates of the Sanctuary and, in particular, on the gate of the special compartment of the women who would come to worship opposite the Sanctuary. The edifice of the door had a height of forty cubits which, taken with the decorations of gold and silver with which it was overlaid, reached a height of fifty cubits. The whole construction was of consummate beauty. Then in the first book of the *Wars*[50] and in the Hebrew Josephus,[51] he relates the story of the capture of Jerusalem by the great general Pompey during the quarrel between the brothers Aristobulus and Hyrcanus, the sons of Alexander Jannaeus. The fact is that he entered the inner Sanctum with the captains of his legions. But there is also a praiseworthy aspect to this shameful behavior of Pompey. For when he saw all the holy furniture and took account of their magnificent worth, out of veneration for the place[52] he departed without touching anything. In fact, the following day, he reinstated Hyrcanus as high priest and ordered him and the Levites to cleanse the Temple forthwith and to resume their customary offices. Now it is true that in his oration *Pro Flacco,*[53] Cicero denies that Pompey's forebearance in this matter was due to his veneration for that place, but rather that he did not wish to get the reputation as a profiteer. However, he [Cicero] falsely alleged that he hated the Jews and vaunted the fact that their worship of God was not superior to his worship of the gods and that each state has its own religious worship which should be adhered to by all its citizens. All this emerges from his oration. But you should address this orator with a question about the rule of war. What shame would have Pompey incurred had he plundered and taken possession of that which fell within his grasp? After all, it is a military rule that each person can keep his booty for himself.[54] But had he regarded it as a violation and rapine to set hands on any Jewish possessions, why did he not deter both himself and his soldiers from taking the rest of the booty and loot? Thus his intention is recognizable from his actions. It could only have been veneration for the place and the fear of God that impelled him to refrain from profaning the splendid Sanctuary by relinquishing the spoil. Such a view gains greater credibility in the light of his enthusiasm in restoring the ministry of the priests and the choir of the Levites. In relation to that moment, one can rightly claim that Pompey bestowed glory on that Temple and honored it. Now you will hear that in his *City [of God],*[55] the doctor Augustine inclines to Cicero's view.[56] But be assured that he did not say this because he regarded that holy ground as profaned. It is simply that he read Cicero's oration and adopted his line of thinking. Another

48. *Bellum* V:205.

49. The text refers to Alexander, father of Tiberius, namely, the Alabarch of Alexandria and brother of Philo. His son Tiberius is not the emperor of that name, but a staff officer in the Roman army.

50. *Bellum* I:131–54.

51. *Josippon,* bk. 5, ch. 39 (136–38).

52. The expression "out of veneration for the place" is de' Rossi's addition.

53. *Pro Flacco,* 28:66–69.

54. 'Booty . . . himself,' cf. Num. 31:53.

55. *De civ. Dei,* 18, ch. 45 (*P.L.* XLI, col. 607): "Pompeius . . . templum reserat, non devotione supplicis, sed iure victoris, et ad sancta sanctorum quo nisi summum sacerdotem non licebat intrare, non ut venerator, sed ut profanator accedit."

56. Interestingly, de' Rossi does not point out that in this chapter Augustine interprets Haggai's prophecy in reference to Jesus.

response is to be culled from the last section of the work of Yedidyah the Alexandrian which is entitled *On the Embassy to Gaius.* In the course of his discourse, he relates how King Agrippa the first endeavored to plead the cause of his people before Emperor Gaius and to dissuade him from placing a statue of himself in the holy precincts. Although he was in Rome at the time, he became ill from his extreme distress about the calamity, took to his sickbed, and was unable to speak face-to-face with him as would have been appropriate in such a crucial situation. From his sickbed he wrote a fine and most appealing supplicatory letter. In one of his persuasive pleas,[57] he mentioned that the emperor Augustus had paid honor to that place while being aware that it was devoid of any effigy and ordered that at his cost, priests should offer daily offerings of one bullock and two lambs as a burnt offering in his name. His wife Julia Augusta had followed his example and contributed golden vials, libation bowls, and other magnificent vessels of consummate beauty to that holy Temple.

Furthermore in book 16 of the *Antiquities,*[58] Josephus expatiates at length on the various privileges granted by this same Emperor Augustus and by some of his officers to the large Jewish population of the lands remote from Jerusalem.[59] He allowed them to send their bundles of donations annually to the house of God, contrary to the wishes of the peoples who endeavored to prevent them from taking state money out of the countries. He also permitted them to have regular public meetings and to erect meeting places although the other peoples were warned against such activities.[60] The reason for this edict was that all Jewish activities were not done with the intention of rebelling against the Roman Empire, but rather in order to adhere to their ancestral observances by glorifying the great God who is in Jerusalem.

You should also know and understand that all world monarchs, and specifically Cleopatra, queen of Egypt, contributed to the glory of this House by their magnificent presents and donations. In book 14 of the *Antiquities*[61] and in the Hebrew Josephus,[62] he describes how on his march against the Parthians, Crassus, the captain of the Roman army, passed through Jerusalem, and, unlike Pompey, carried off the treasures of the Lord's Sanctuary. He took 2,000 talents of silver, 8,000 golden talents, and gold bars weighing 300 minae—the mina (he refers there to the mina of the Jews) is worth 150 ounces.[63] Finally he writes:[64] "One need not wonder at the great wealth contained in the Sanctuary for many kings of the world and their dignitaries sent presents of golden and silver vessels to God's Temple every year to glorify it and to seek assistance. Many peoples also paid tribute regularly to the holy Sanctuary. . . . In those days Mithridates, king of Armenia, sent to the city of Cos which is on the extremity of Asia and sequestered the gold which Queen Cleopatra had deposited there and dedicated to the

57. *Leg.* 317–19.
58. *Ant.* XVI:160–73.
59. I.e., to the Jews of Cyrene, Ephesus, and Sardis.
60. This detail is not in Josephus but appears to be derived from Philo's *Leg.* 158 where a similar account of Augustus's decrees is given, although in relation to the Jews of Rome.
61. *Ant.* XIV:105–6.
62. *Josippon,* bk. 5, ch. 42 (142–43).
63. I.e., according to Josippon, the *mina* is two and a half pounds, and one pound is sixty ounces.
64. The passage he gives here is virtually a transcription of the text of the Josippon which is somewhat different from the parallel text in Josephus (110–12).

Lord our God." You can also have confirmation that the emperor Tiberius also paid honor to the holy Sanctuary. Agrippa's letter to Gaius which we cited contains the following statement:[65]

> Did your grandfather Tiberius not evince his good disposition towards our Temple. During the twenty-three years of his reign he was prepared to maintain the service of the Temple without dislocating any part of it.[66] Tiberius did treat me very badly, but because of my love of the truth,[67] I cannot refrain from recounting his praises in relation to this matter. A case in point is when Pilate was procurator of the beautiful land [Judaea] and wanted to place golden shields in our holy Sanctuary.[68] No forbidden form was depicted on them but only the names of the donors and those in whose honor they were donated. But when this came to the notice of the people, four sons of the king and chiefs congregated against Pilate to appeal to him to remove those disgraceful shields which had been placed in the Temple in infringement of our law. The enemy and adversary refused to hear their plea and so they addressed their supplication to Tiberius in writing.

On reading the missive, his fury was aroused and he sent Pilate a letter full of reproaches and rebukes and ordered him to remove all the shields from the Sanctuary at once and to transfer them to the royal palace which was located there.[69] And he wrote as follows:[70] "Now in that Holy of Holies, a high priest prays once a year on behalf of the entire world. And any Jew or even priest directly below the high priest and even the high priest himself who would enter it on more than that one occasion, would be punishable by death from the God of heaven. On account of the extreme sanctity of that place, the lawgiver decreed that it should be preserved from becoming a mere thoroughfare. And so with all the more reason ought the person who would dare to place a statue there, slaughter his wife and children, and then instantly immolate himself upon their corpses." At the end of this same section in which Yedidyah recounts the great honor which the emperor Augustus and all his ministers honored the holy Sanctuary through their sacrifices, he concludes as follows:[71] "All these procedures were even maintained in the time of the emperor Tiberius although his governor Sejanus was intent on inciting him against us. But after the death of that troublemaker, Tiberius came to realize that all the charges imputed against us were false slanders which were concocted with the purpose of obliterating us from the city of Rome. He therefore charged all his people not to harm the Jews and to leave them to observe the laws of their God and His laws, the sole purpose of which was to promote lasting peace and quiet among the people." Again, among the foreign kings that honored the second Temple and came from distant lands to worship and sacrifice to the Lord of Hosts was Monobaz the king and Queen Helena, as Josephus writes in book 20. Our sages refer to them in the statement:[72] "King Monobaz saw to it that all the handles of all the vessels

65. *Leg.* 298–306.
66. 'Without . . . it,' cf. 1Sam. 25:7.
67. This is not an accurate rendering of the Latin which refers also to Gaius's love of the truth: "Sed amica est et tibi quoque grata veritas."
68. The Latin text reads: "in Herodis regia."
69. The Latin text reads: "in Caesaream maritimam."
70. Philo, *Leg.* 306–8.
71. Ibid., 159–61.
72. M. Yoma 3:10.

used on the Day of Atonement were made of gold. His mother Helena had a golden candlestick made over the door of the holy Temple. She also had a golden tablet made on which the portion about the suspected adultress was inscribed." This same Monobaz is mentioned in the Palestinian Talmud, tractate Pe'ah,[73] the Tosefta,[74] and in Bava Batra[75] where they state: "Our rabbis taught: There is a story about King Monobaz who gave away all his own stores and those of his fathers [in years of scarcity]." There is a similar passage in Menaḥot which we shall discuss presently. It is true that the great luminary Rashi of blessed memory comments on the passage in Bava Batra and states: "King Monobaz, the son of Queen Helena, was of Hasmonean extraction." But it is not so, my father.[76] For this woman and her son were gentiles who became righteous proselytes and were neither from priestly nor Israelite stock. Go and consult the chroniclers regarding the succession of kings and priests of the second Temple period. You will not discover any reference to Helena and Monobaz, apart from Monobaz son of Agrippa the last who was of Herodian stock and who together with his father the king was killed at the time of the destruction of the Temple. And it is known that not one of the Hasmoneans regained power in Jerusalem after the Herodian period. There is incontrovertible proof that they were not kings of the Hasmonean dynasty. For Helena lived in the days when the disciples of Hillel rose to leadership in the holy Land, in order to instruct the Jews as sages of the land; and they certainly would not have dared to do this while their teacher Hillel was still seeking justice and zealous for equity.[77] There is an explicit Mishnah in Nazir which you should read:[78] "It once happened that the son of Queen Helena went to war. She said: 'If my son returns safely I shall be a Nazirite for seven years.' Her son returned and she became a Nazirite. . . . She went up to the Land [of Israel] and the House of Hillel taught her that she had to be a Nazirite for another seven years." And in Shabbat[79] we are told that Hillel served as patriarch for 100 years during Temple times; in other words, during the reign of the House of Herod which according to tractate Avodah Zarah[80] and Seder Olam[81] lasted 103 years. Similarly, at the beginning of book 15[82] and towards the end of chapter 13,[83] Josephus writes that Herod honored Hillel and his disciple Shammai, the heads of the Pharisees, because on realizing the immense danger that would result from the revolt, they helped him to make his rule acceptable without resort to force. Now the Hasmonean dynasty preceded that of Herod as is stated in Avodah Zarah and in Seder Olam. Accordingly, the disciples of Hillel and this woman could hardly have lived in Hasmonean times, but rather later in the time of Herod. And there is the explicit statement of our rabbis of

73. P. Pe'ah 1 (1) 15b.
74. T. Pe'ah 4:18.
75. B. B.B. 11a.
76. 'But . . . father,' cf. Gen. 48:18. De' Rossi calls Rashi 'father' in order to mitigate his criticism.
77. 'Seeking . . . equity,' cf. Is. 16:5.
78. M. Nazir 3:6.
79. B. Shabb. 15a.
80. B. A.Z. 9a.
81. Seder Olam, ch. 30 (142).
82. *Ant.* XV:3.
83. Ibid. XV:370, but the closer parallel is in XIV:176.

blessed memory in Bava Batra[84] that no man or woman of Hasmonean extraction remained alive during the reign of Herod. However, you should know that the Tosafists discuss the passage in which the House of Hillel legislated regarding her, and in a devious manner endeavored to correct the idea that she was a Hasmonean when they said:[85] "Even though she was a Hasmonean, she was the mother of King Monobaz as is stated in Yoma, and the Herodian dynasty lasted 103 years during Temple times. Hillel's patriarchate extended to 3 years after the Herodian dynasty. As is stated in the first chapter of Shabbat, Hillel, Simeon, Gamaliel, and Simeon wielded their patriarchate for 100 years during Temple times. In any case, Hillel had already acquired disciples at that time and they made the decision regarding her case." But all this does not help them.[86] I see the argument, but do not see the solution. For while the rabbis of blessed memory do say in Yoma that Helena was the mother of Monobaz, they do not say that Monobaz was a Hasmonean king. How could it be feasible when, according to the *On the Times* of Yedidyah, the Roman and Hebrew Josephus, and all the writers to the last man,[87] and in particular Rabad [Abraham ben David] in his *Record of the Second Temple*, it is known for certain that the last incumbent of the Hasmonean house was Hyrcanus son of King Jannai and Queen Alexandra and that having ruled for thirty-four years, he was put to death by his father-in-law Herod. There is no doubt in my mind that had the Tosafists read the chronicles (which they did not read in order to ensure that they did not distract themselves for one second from the laws of Torah) they would have become apprised of the fact that Helena and her son were of gentile extraction and had become righteous proselytes. With God's help, the next chapter will make clear the turn of events which brought them to take refuge under the wings of our God in the time of the emperor Claudius about twenty-five years before the destruction of the Temple. At that time, Agrippa was king and Ishmael son of Fiabi, who gets favorable mention in tractate Pesaḥim[88] and in the Tosefta, tractate Yoma,[89] was high priest. Josephus also refers to him in book 20. Of particular note is the passage in book 3 of the *Antiquities*[90] in which Josephus writes that in the time of Claudius and Ishmael son of Fiabi the high priest, there was a devastating famine which was so severe that a tenth part of flour was sold for four drachmas which according to what he writes in chapter 9 is equivalent to a holy sheqel.[91] And in book 20, he explicitly states that it was during this time of famine that Queen Helena and Monobaz provided for our people.

84. B. B.B. 3b. This is a reference to the story of the woman [presumably a distorted reference to Mariamme] who threw herself off the roof when she saw that Herod wanted to marry her, exclaiming: "Whoever comes and says I am from the Hasmonean house is a slave since I alone am left of it and I am throwing myself down from this roof."

85. Tos. to B. Ket. 7b, s.v. *horuhah.* Their gloss refers to the statement in Ket. 7a: "The school of Hillel gave a decision regarding her that she should be a Nazirite yet another seven years."

86. 'All . . . them,' cf. Est. 5:13.

87. 'To the last man,' cf. Gen. 19:4.

88. B. Pes. 57a.

89. T. Yom ha-Kipp. 1:21.

90. *Ant.* III:320.

91. *Ant.* III:195.

In addition to everything, reader, in the next chapter, you shall see for yourself a passage from Bereshit Rabbah in which the rabbis of blessed memory speak about circumcision with regard to King Monobaz. It serves as decisive evidence that Helena, as was noted by Josephus, who also was a Jewish sage, was queen of the peoples of Adiabene who live in the land of Ararat where Noah's ark came to rest. Monobaz ruled in succession to his father and one of his brothers. She went to Jerusalem with her other son called Izates who was younger than Monobaz and his predecessor on the throne. And he was the true Monobaz as you shall see, and they made extravagant acts of charity and offered precious gifts to the holy Sanctuary. I considered it right to bring such a meritorious and notable incident to the notice of ourselves and our children and chose to translate it in the separately designated chapter. And so, for the moment, I shall forgo speaking on that topic.

Now in book 2, chapter 17[92] and in book 6 of the Hebrew Josephus,[93] Josephus writes that the impious emperor Nero also used to send the priests burnt offerings and sacrifices to be offered on his behalf to ensure his prosperity. One day it happened that a daring leader of the brigands of the partisans of Ananias, the high priest called Eleazar, entered the Temple and saw that they were sacrificing burnt offerings for Nero, and in rage he threw them out. He reproached and chastized them, claiming that only the sacrifices of our people should be offered in that place. Although his father and the elders of the city rebuked him and earnestly explained to him that he should be mindful of his words lest disaster befall him and he become responsible for causing harm to all the people, he remained obdurate. According to Josephus, this incident was the main reason for our downfall; for the Romans then became anxious to fight to the end and bring about their complete exile, as is known. I think it likely that it is to this incident that the rabbis of blessed memory alluded in Midrash Ekhah[94] and in Giṭṭin[95] when they said that on account of Qamṣa and Bar Qamṣa Jerusalem was destroyed: "He went and said to the emperor: 'The Jews are rebelling against you.' He said to him: 'How can I know?' He said to him: 'Send them an offering.' . . . He sent Vespasian against them." In other words, Nero the emperor sent Vespasian his general against them and the outcome was what it was. It has already become clear that in stories of this kind one should not be concerned about divergencies in detail as long there is consensus about the general issues.

Intelligent reader, in presenting these main points, I have given you the benefit of what I know about this subject. You might judge that there are some aspects that were not described by the writers or of which I was ignorant. But it is enough that you realize, as Haggai said, that the second Temple was honored by foreigners on a much larger scale than was the first Temple. And so we are not far off the mark when we say that purpose of the divine statement communicated by Malachi, *For from where the sun rises to where it sets, My name is honored among the nations* (1:11) corresponds to that of the rabbinic statement in Menaḥot,[96] "They call Him God of Gods." Now the scriptural

92. *Bellum* II:409. There is no reference to Nero.
93. *Josippon,* bk. 6, ch. 66 (241–42).
94. E.R. to Lam. 4:1.
95. B. Giṭṭ. 55b–56a.
96. B. Men. 110a. This statement is in the context of a discussion about the nations' acceptance of

passage concludes, *and everywhere incense and pure oblation are offered to My name.* According to rabbinic exegesis,[97] this refers to the scholars who devote themselves to study of the Torah wherever they are. But in addition, the point expressed here is that from all over the world, the nations of that time were donating and sending presents and offerings to His holy Sanctuary, offering Him incense to savor and whole-offering on His altar.[98]

It may be that when you sit down to contend with a dominating and self-composed sage[99] using conciliatory words, and you explain these words in accordance with these observations, he will regard you as a peacemaker, particularly when you make clear that you are not insisting that your opinion must be accepted and that you are not damaging the statements of others.

And for the sake of making my analysis of the verse in question most admissible, I would disclose to you that having reached this juncture in the chapter, Rabbi Judah Moscato scanned it and at the time commended it to Rabbi David Provenzali. That dear friend of mine then told him: "I also adopted the same line in my interpretation of Song of Songs on the verse, *Whither has your beloved go turned? Let us seek him with you* (6:1).[100] This is the nations' address to Israel while the second Temple was standing." And this is indeed the case; for two great men have come and given their stamp of approval.

However, we would also say that Haggai's prediction of the aggrandizement of the glory of this House is also confirmed by the oracular voice which was heard on many occasions. In tractare Sota in both the Palestinian and Babylonian Talmuds,[101] it is stated: "When the latter prophets Haggai, Zechariah, and Malachi died, the Holy Spirit departed from Israel; nevertheless they used the oracular voice." Now in the same tractate[102] and in chapter 11 of Megillat Taʿanit[103] and in Midrash Shir ha-Shirim[104] they recount:[105] "Johanan the high priest heard an oracular voice issue from within the Holy of Holies announcing: 'The young men who went to wage war in Antioch have been victorious.' It also happened that Simeon the righteous heard a voice issue forth from the Holy of Holies announcing, 'Annulled is the decree which the enemy intended to introduce in the Temple. Caskalgus [Caius Caligula] is killed and his decrees annulled.'" Then again on one occasion elders entered the upper chamber of Gurya's house in Jericho. An oracular voice issued and pronounced: "There is in your midst [one man who is deserving . . .] They looked at Samuel the little."

"Israel and their Father in heaven." R. Shimi quotes Mal. 1:11 to which Rav responds with the statement cited by de' Rossi.

97. Ibid.

98. 'Offering . . . altar,' cf. Deut. 33:10.

99. 'Sit . . . sage.' This is a play on Pr. 23:1: *When you sit down to dine with a ruler.*

100. David ben Abraham Provenzali's commentary to Shir ha-Shirim is still in manuscript; the manuscript held in the Cambridge University Library is identified by Schiller-Szinessy, as Provenzali's commentary. (See Reif, 74.)

101. P. Sota 9 (13) 24b; B. Sota 48b.

102. B. Sota 33a.

103. Meg. T., 344.

104. S.S.R. to S.S. 8:9. "The intention of the enemy is frustrated and Caius Caligula is slain and his decrees are annulled."

105. De' Rossi presents a combination of these sources. The last example about Samuel the Little is also in B. Sota 48b.

This is the only thread of love that remains for us during this exile of ours as a sign and testimony to the fact that the Lord will not forsake His people. As they state in Eruvin:[106] "An oracular voice issued and pronounced: 'Both statements are the words of the living God, but the *halakhah* follows the school of Hillel.'" In fact, in tractate Berakhot,[107] when an objection was raised to the sage who said that the *halakhah* follows the school of Hillel, it was said: "This is self-evident [for the oracular voice issued and proclaimed that it was so]." Then there is the passage in Ḥullin[108] in which the oracular voice said: "The cup of wine over which the benediction has been said is worth forty gold coins." In Ketubot,[109] the oracular voice announced: "That fuller is also destined for life in the world to come." Then with regard to the case of the oven of Akhnai in Bava Meṣia,[110] the oracular voice pronounced: "Why do you dispute with Rabbi Eliezer when the *halakhah* agrees with him." There is the statement of Rabbi Johanan in Megillah:[111] "How do we know that we may avail ourselves of an oracular voice. Because it says: *Your ears will heed the command behind you* (Is. 30:21)." This must refer to Hezekiah's time, 103 years before the destruction of the first Temple.[112] It is therefore obvious that it is another kind of divinatory voice, while the scriptural verse is used as a mere support. This is how Rashi explained it: "If one is intending to embark on something and hear a voice that tells you yes, yes or no, no, follow its advice—it is not a case of witchcraft." Likewise the Tosafists who cite the Palestinian Talmud[113] state: "*You shall not practice divination* (Lev. 19:26). Although it does not fall into the category of divination, there is an omen. And only when there are three omens. . . ." That is, the passage in Megillah concludes: "This only applies if one hears the words of a voice of a man in a town and the voice of a woman in a field and only if it says yes, yes or no, no." But as for the ten miracles which according to the fifth chapter of Avot[114] happened in the Temple, they obviously also occurred in the first Temple. For in Yoma when they ask whether there were any more [miracles], it is stated:[115] "The crop [of birds], the feathers and the ashes removed from the inner altar and fragments of earthenware were swallowed up in the place in which they were. The shew-bread was in the same state when it was removed as when it was put on." And there were other miracles. Among them are listed: "The place on which the ark stands is not included in the measurement;[116] it is by sheer miracle that the cherubs were standing." These were definitely in the first Temple.

Likewise there was the adornment and glorification in the time of the Hasmoneans on account of the miracle of the eight lights of the days of Hanukkah, the memory of

106. B. Eruv. 13b.
107. B. Ber. 51b.
108. B. Ḥull. 87a.
109. B. Ket. 103b.
110. B. B.M. 59b.
111. B. Meg. 32a.
112. I.e., Isaiah was prophesying in the time of Hezekiah.
113. P. Shabb. 6 (9) 8c.
114. M. Avot 5:5.
115. B. Yoma 21a.
116. The room was twenty cubits, and the cherubs were placed to the right and the left of the ark. Since the spread of the wings of the cherubs was twenty cubits, the placement of the ark and the cherubs would appear to have been by miraculous means.

which shall never be obliterated from our seed. In chapter 9 of Megillat Taʿanit and in tractate Shabbat,[117] the sages of blessed memory recount the tradition about the miracle of the cruise of oil that lay under seal, which bears affinity to the well-known story of the Shunamite woman's jug of oil (2K. 4). Now I was surprised that the books of the Maccabees, the whole thrust of which is to recount the story of Antiochus, make no allusion to this miracle of the oil. I am thinking specifically of chapter 4 of the first book and chapter 10 of the second which is nothing but an account of God's great act of salvation by which He delivered them from the enemy. In the concluding passages it states that on the twenty-fifth of Kislev, in the year 148 of the Greek era, the priests purified the Temple and made new vessels and dedicated it on the very day that the Greeks had profaned it. And they fixed the celebration of the dedication of the altar for eight days because not long before they had been unable to celebrate the festival of Tabernacles since they were forced to flee to the mountains and deserts on account of their numerous oppressors. Josephus, who apparently derived his account of the miracle from this source, mentions in book 12[118] that the day of the purification of the Sanctuary in the year 148 of the Greek era in Olympiad 155 was the selfsame day on which three years previously, Antiochus the wicked with his army had desecrated it. And in conclusion, he suggests that it was called the festival of lights to commemorate the light which after the days of darkness and gloomy despair, God in His kindness shone over them to bring them peace and salvation. Now the episode of Judith and the captain Holofernes is not mentioned in conjunction with this miracle by any of the chroniclers, nor is it related to any of the other events in which the Hasmoneans were involved. It is possible that the incident occurred in the days of one of the Persian kings,[119] as is noted in the actual scroll of Judith which is part of the Christian canon—Samotheus the Christian writes as much.[120] The king sent Holofernes, the captain of his army, to conquer the nations of the world for him. Ravished by her beauty, he fell into the hand of Judith who cut off his head. Later, in the time of Ahasuerus the first, the enemies of Judah who drafted the indictment against the Temple wrote to him, as is apparent from the first book of Ezra: *so that you may search in the records of your fathers and find in the records and know that this city is a rebellious city and harmful to kings* (Ezra 4:15). This is an allusion to the murder of Holofernes and undoubtedly would have been recorded at the time in the royal archives. There is no doubt that our ancient sages did well not to accept that scroll which was not written under divine inspiration. In any case, it is necessary to give it some consideration—we have demonstrated this in our earlier discussion about such works.[121] In fact, you will note that the book of Wisdom [of Solomon] which is not part of our canon was given primary significance by Ramban of blessed memory in the introduction to his commentary on the Torah, where he translates two long sections from chapter 9 of the book in support of his arguments.

117. B. Shabb. 21b.

118. *Ant.* XII:321.

119. According to the book of Judith, the incident is supposed to have occurred in the time of Nebuchadnezzar.

120. Johannes Lucidus Samotheus, *Opusculum,* bk. II, ch. 12, 27r. De' Rossi also refers to bk. IV, ch. 1, but I could not find any reference to Judith there.

121. I.e., in ch. 2.

Now in the book of Judith, the name of Nebuchadnezzar is mentioned in conjunction with the title "king of Assyria." However, the Christian mentioned above [Samotheus] solves the problem by explaining that the name is an honorary title of the kings of Babylon and Assyria just as Pharaoh is the title of the kings of Egypt[122] for the reason given by Josephus in book 8 (chapter 2).[123] While it may not have been a specific title of the kings of Assyria, it is certainly possible that after his conquest of the kingdom of Babylon which was at the time greater than Assyria, he rose to distinction and his name became an honorific title. Now it is also known that Babylon and Assyria were one kingdom for hundreds of years as we noted in chapter 21 and that in holy Writ the same person is called king of Babylon, king of Assyria, as well as king of Assyria as we proved in chapter 38 of section 3. According to the book of Judith, the incident occurred while Joiakim was serving as high priest.[124] In his book *De temporibus* which we translated [*On the Times*] Yedidyah states that this Joiakim succeeded his father Jeshua who had gone to press for permission to rebuild the Temple. Jeshua wrote this scroll which, like the book of Tobit, according to the Christian translator [Jerome], was written in Aramaic since Aramaic was their vernacular at that time—as we shall see in the course of some of these chapters. Now Ran (Rabbenu Nissim) wrote about the passage in Shabbat[125] which stated that [the precept of the Hanukkah lamp is obligatory on women] for they too experienced the miracle. He wrote:[126] "According to a midrash, the daughter of Johanan gave the leader of the enemy cheese to eat in order to make him drunk. And she cut off his head and they all fled. This is why they are accustomed to eat a cooked cheese dish on Hanukkah." He does not mention the source of the midrash. I detect that he has mixed up different passages. In chapter 6 of Megillat Taʿanit which deals with the miracles that occurred in the month of Ellul it is stated: "Mattathias son of Johanan the high priest had a daughter. When she came of marriageable age, a soldier came to defile her, but he was deterred by Mattathias and his sons, and they observed that day as a festival. And in chapter 9 for the month of Kislev, it mentions the miracle of the lights, but nothing more. Clearly the episode occurred in Ellul and this story of Judith is not connected with Hanukkah as certain commentators wrote. You will observe that Rashi of blessed memory crosses this river on foot[127] without referring to Judith. At the end of Pesaḥim, Mordechai [ben Hillel] of blessed memory cites the statement in the Palestinian Talmud[128] that the women were in the same difficulty, and explains it with reference to that miracle. In other words, he states that they experienced the same danger as the men. Indeed, the only prayer of thanks-

122. *Opusculum,* 27v: "Et non te perturbet quod iste Assuerus vocetur Nabuchodonosor in libro Judith quia ut ubi dicitur et Philo scribit Artaxat invaserat monarchiam tenebatque Assyrios, Medos et Persas et hic Assuerus solam Babyloniam ubi rex communi appellatione dignitatis vocatur Nabuchodonosor, sicut in Aegypto Pharao."

123. *Ant.* VIII:155: "Pharaoh in Egyptian signifies king."

124. Judith 15:8.

125. B. Shabb. 23a.

126. Rabbenu Nissim to Alfasi, Shabb. 10a (to B. Shabb. 23b).

127. 'Crosses . . . foot,' cf. Ps. 66:6, i.e., Rashi makes light of it.

128. P. Meg. 2 (5) 73b. The statement regards women's obligation to hear the recitation of the scroll of Esther.

giving[129] which they instituted was that [which includes the words] "and You vindicated their cause" and subsequently states, "Afterwards, Your children came [into Your Sanctuary and cleansed the Temple]." In any case, it is possible that after the abolition of the Scroll of Fasts, the authorities of the times decided to include reference to various other miracles in the context of the celebration of Hanukkah. These included the episode with Judith whenever it took place, or that of the daughter of the Hasmonean which occurred in Ellul, or the miracle of the oil, and above all, our deliverance from the hands of Antiochus.

We can also claim that this House was glorified by the miracle that took place in the time of Onias the high priest. Seleucus the king of Greece was incited by a Jewish informer of the tribe of Benjamin called Simeon and despatched Appollonius to remove all the money found in the Temple. Angels of God then smote him and inflicted blows on him in the holy precincts and the only means by which he could be healed was through the agency of Onias's prayer. All this contributed to the glorification and aggrandizement of the Temple as is described in book 2 (ch. 3) of Maccabees and in Josephus's specific work entitled *De Machabaeis*[130] and in the Hebrew Josephus.[131] It would appear that this Onias was favored by God and an expert in miracles. For in the second book of *Against Apion,*[132] there is reference to a miracle he performed when Ptolemy Physcon who was at war with Cleopatra, and infuriated that Onias had come to her aid by despatching his army, arrested the Jews who were in Alexandria at the time and bound them naked before ravaging elephants which he let loose on them. But by divine will, the reverse occurred. The elephants desisted from destroying the Jews and turned and rushed on Physcon's troops[133] who had bound them before the elephants. Physcon then repented of his sin and throughout all the years of their residence in Alexandria, the Jews commemorated that day as a festival.

Among the miracles that occurred in second Temple times that remain to be mentioned is the one recounted to us by our ancestors in chapter 3 of tractate Taʿanit[134] and in the Mekhilta [*sic*] on the verse, *And I will grant your rains* (Lev. 26:4).[135] They state: "It happened in the days of Herod when they were occupied with the rebuilding of the Temple that rain would fall at night while the next day the wind would blow and disperse the clouds and the sun shone and everybody rose early to go about their work." This demonstrated that they were engaged on a sacred enterprise.

As regards the tradition about the five objects that were missing from the second Temple, transmitted in Yoma[136] and in Qiddushin and Taʿanit in the Palestinian Talmud,[137] we are in a position to say that according to the statements of the rabbis of

129. This is the prayer which gives a summary of the event which begins "In the time of Mattathias" and is recited in the Amidah prayer and the grace after meals throughout the days of Hanukkah.
130. I.e., 4Macc. 4.
131. *Josippon,* bk. 3, ch. 16 (66–67).
132. *Contra Apionem* II, 51–56.
133. The Latin (and Greek) texts read "amicos."
134. B. Taʿanit 23a.
135. The reference is to Sifra, baḥuqotai 11:1 (110, col. d).
136. B. Yoma 21b.
137. P. Taʿanit 2 (1) 65a.

blessed memory, they were there for some of the time. For at the end of the first chapter of Yoma in our Gemara [i.e., the Babylonian Talmud][138] they say that fire from heaven lay like a lion in the first Temple, but like a dog in the second Temple. And when the exegesis of the verse which proved that the five objects were missing was questioned, the response is given that they were there, but were not as helpful. The quality of the fire of the second Temple was certainly less than that of the first Temple. And yet, these objects were present for some of the time—we also mentioned this fact towards the end of chapter 50.

Now if we are to believe the authors of the books of the Maccabees (2Macc. 1:19ff.) and the Hebrew Josephus,[139] it happened that Ezra and Nehemiah prayed for fire to come from heaven. An old man showed them a cave in which Jeremiah had hidden at the time of the destruction of the Temple, and it was like water or thick oil[140] and they took it. But they were unable to find the Ark, for Jeremiah had also hidden it on Mount Nebo[141] but had sworn that the place would remain hidden until the ingathering of the exiles—this is explained in chapter 2.[142] But in tractate Yoma in both the Babylonian[143] and Palestinian[144] Talmuds, you will see that the [location of the Ark] is a matter of controversy. In his commentary on Haggai (1:8), Don Isaac also describes the story of the fire which he appears to have derived from the [Hebrew] Josephus.[145] Now in the previous chapter, we quoted Josephus's description of the answer of the Urim and Tummim and the letters which were seen on the two shoulder-stones. He claimed that they were still in existence until two hundred years before his own time. It was then that the sins of our nation caused the rupture. The heresy of the Sadducean sects sprung forth at that time. In the same way, as the sages of blessed memory explain in Yoma,[146] the miracles which occurred in the second Temple ceased when Simeon the righteous died. We may therefore be in a position to claim that the sages of blessed memory meant that the objects were only absent intermittently and occasionally. If it were not for the passage from the Palestinian Talmud, tractate Qiddushin that I cited towards the end of the previous chapter with regard to the verse in Ezra, *until a priest with Urim and Tummim should appear* (2:63):[147] "Were there Urim and Tummim in the second Temple?" I would have said that they were there at the beginning of the period when the spirit of the Lord still alighted on our people. The evidence is provided by the prophets Haggai, Zechariah, and Malachi and their entire holy assembly who undoubtedly made the Urim and Tummim according to their prescriptions and which, on being consulted, would have given responses as in the past. For this is what is meant by the phrase, *until*

138. B. Yoma 21b.

139. *Josippon,* bk. 1, ch. 3 (22).

140. In 2Macc. 1:20 it states: "And when they reported to us that they had not found fire, but thick liquid."

141. The detail about the mountain is only in the *Josippon.*

142. 2Macc. 2:7.

143. B. Yoma 53b.

144. The passage is in P. Sheq. 6 (1) 49b–c.

145. Abravanel to Hagg. 1:8 (186 col. b). He refers to the *Josippon* and claims that the story does not contradict rabbinic opinion on the matter.

146. B. Yoma 39a.

147. P. Qidd. 4 (1) 65b.

a priest with Urim and Tummim should appear. And when the rabbis of blessed memory transmitted the tradition that they were missing from the Temple (with the allusion to this by the missing *he* in the word "and I shall be honored," they were only referring to the latter period. For it is possible that during the many wars with the Greeks, all the holy vessels and holy vestments were plundered by the enemy and when they made them anew according to prescription, prophecy had already come to an end, and by then we also lacked the Urim and Tummim, namely, the faculty of being in receipt of the divine response. It is also certainly possible that the spikes[148] that were put on the parapet of the Sanctuary as is stated in Middot,[149] the purpose of which is explained by the compiler of the *Arukh* under the entry *kl,*[150] was not done in the time of Haggai and his colleagues, but only after a certain period of time had elapsed, once they realized that its holiness has been withdrawn on account of our sins.

Now we should not remain silent about the obvious, namely, that all the predictions of any prophet are to be understood in conjunction with the condition enunciated by Zechariah, *Men from afar shall come and take part in the building of the Temple of the Lord . . . if only you will obey the Lord your God* (6:15). Otherwise, as Jeremiah makes clear, *At one moment I may decree that a nation [shall be uprooted . . . but if that nation turns back from its wickedness,] I shall change My mind* (18:7–8). The rabbis of blessed memory cast the same idea in rhetorical language which is cited by the author of the work *Sha'are Orah* (f.32)[151] and by the author of *Sha'are Ṣedeq* (f.25).[152] "The Holy One blessed be He passes a decree and [it is abrogated by] the sefirah *binah,* that is repentance which is called *who can abrogate it* as it says *For the Lord of Hosts has planned, who then can abrogate?* (Is. 14:27). Likewise the opposite is also true. That is, each one of us has the power to reverse the attribute of anger or love by corrupt or upright action. As Ezekiel said, *So too if a righteous person turns away from his righteousness . . . [shall he live?]* (Ezk. 18:27) and *and if a wicked person turns back [from his wickedness . . .] such a person shall save his life* (ibid.). A similar notion is found in the Tanna d've Eliyahu[153] and in Mo'ed Qatan:[154] "I rule man; who rules me? It is the righteous for I pass a decree and he annuls it." Accordingly, it is feasible that in saying, *the glory of this House would be greater,* Haggai the prophet also had in mind to demonstrate that it would remain standing and really be the last and that they would receive from God that which there was in the first Temple and more. But this could only come about on the understanding that the Israelites, too, would not deviate from doing that which for their part was appropriate,

148. 'Spikes,' lit. 'a form consuming the raven.'

149. M. Midd. 4:6.

150. Nathan ben Yehiel, *Arukh,* s.v. *kl:* He explains that this was not needed in the time of the first Temple because its holiness prevented birds from flying over it which was not the case with the second Temple, when they erected the spikes to keep the birds away.

151. The author of *Sha'are Orah* is Joseph ibn Gikatilla (1248–1325), a Spanish kabbalist whose works were very influential. De' Rossi is referring to the printing of Mantua, 1561.

152. De' Rossi is referring to the printing of Riva di Trento, 1561, in which the authorship of *Sha'are Sedeq* is ascribed to Joseph ben Karnitol, although the work was probably written by Joseph ibn Gikatilla.

153. De' Rossi is referring to Tanna deve Elijahu (ch. 2, Braude translation, 54) which like B. M.Q. 16b quotes 2Sam. 23:3, *He who rules men justly he who rules with the awesomeness of God* and then states: "The righteous man whose self-rule overcomes the evil impulse within him achieves a share of God's power and rules alongside the awesomeness of God."

154. B. M.Q. 16b.

and would connect themselves to that good such that they should be worthy of it. Speaking in a similar vein, the sage of the *Kuzari* gives a fine response in section 2[155] to the question as to why the divine objects[156] were missing from the second Temple. He states that it was due their limited desire to attain them. The fact is that the divine was ready for His part, as is expressed in the momentous promise of Zechariah, *Sing and rejoice* (2:14). He then concludes by stating: "Divine providence only rests on the person according to his receptiveness; if it be small, he obtains little, and much, if it be great." It is certainly true that while we may claim that Haggai did not prophesy about the last Temple that is yet to be built, there is no lack of true prophets who did, particularly Ezekiel, who in his concluding words spoke at length about the structure of the Temple and all the laws that apply to it. It is one of the prophecies which the prince Don Isaac of blessed memory wisely and intelligently collated in his work *Mashmia Yeshu'ah.* There is no doubt that they have not yet come to pass. Moreover the Eternal of Israel does not deceive and will not change His mind[157] about them; rather He shall keep the written promise for His own sake, if not for ours. This is what I saw fit to write as explanation of the verse—the discerning person will choose the good and gain wisdom.

155. *Kuzari* II, par. 24.

156. Halevi does not actually refer to the objects, but rather to the state of impurity in the country during the second Temple period.

157. 'The eternal . . . mind,' cf. ISam. 15:29.

CHAPTER FIFTY-TWO

How Helena queen of Adiabene and her sons converted to Judaism as described by Josephus in book 20 (chapter 2)[1] of the *Antiquities*. The concluding part of the chapter regards the false prophet called Theudas.

In those days, Helena queen of Adiabene and her son Izates adopted the religion of the Jews in the following circumstances:

Monobaz king of Adiabene surnamed Bazaeus conceived a passionate desire for his sister. He married her and she became pregnant. It happened that on one occasion, as he lay sleeping beside her and his hand was covering her belly, he thought that he heard a voice addressing him and commanding him to remove his hand from her belly so as not to crush the fetus whose start in life was not without divine volition and whose end was also destined to be most propitious. Monobaz was disquieted by this voice. As soon as he awoke, he told his wife what had happened. He called the child that was born to him Izates. Now another child had previously been born to this same Monobaz by his wife and he was also called Monobaz. He also had other children by his other wives. Nevertheless, it was obvious to all his acquaintances that all his sympathy lay with Izates. Consequently, his brothers began to be jealous of him and their hatred for him increased daily, for each one them was troubled that Izates took precedence in his father's affections. Although Monobaz the king was aware of all this, he judged the behavior of those sons of his in a positive light, claiming that it was not motivated by arrogance, but by their great desire to be loved by him to the same degree. Yet the brother's hatred made him fear for Izates' safety. He therefore sent him, laden with numerous gifts, to Abemerigus [Abennerigus], who was then the ruler of the fort of Spasinus, as the locals called it, with the request that he should look after the boy. He gave him a welcome reception, and was so well disposed towards him that he gave him his daughter called Samacho in marriage. As a dowry, he conferred on them a fertile estate that would yield a satisfactory income.

The day came when Monobaz the king felt the pressure of old age and he desired to see his son before he went the way of the world. So he summoned him and received him most affectionately, presenting him with a plot of land called Caeron where the amomum trees grow profusely. On this land are preserved the remains of the ark in which, according to report, Noah saved himself from the waters of the deluge. In fact, they are still there today on show for all to see. Izates lived in that land until the death of

1. *Ant.* XX:17–99.

his father the king. On the day of his death, his widow Helena summoned the satraps and commanders of the army and addressed them thus: "You must surely be aware that it was the wish of the king my husband that Izates should be heir to the kingdom, for he deemed him worthy of this honor. However, I also wanted to know your wishes for I am of the opinion that he is blessed who is crowned not through the wishes of one person alone, but of the many who willingly give him their support. Her motive in putting such a request to them was to become apprised as to the direction in which the decision of the gathering was going. On hearing her words, the satraps first did obeisance to her, as is fitting before royalty, and then replied that they would ratify all her decrees and would gladly accept Izates as their king in the knowledge that he had been chosen in preference to his brothers by his father and by the unanimous vote of the entire nation on account of his virtuous behavior. They also volunteered, should that be her wish, to begin by killing his brothers and kinsmen to ensure that the new king would be seated on the throne on a secure basis. In this way, he would have no reason to fear the hatred and jealousy they might bear him in this regard. In response to these words, Helena expressed her pleasure and gratitude to all of them for such a demonstration of benevolence. Nevertheless, she was unwilling to make any final decision about putting the brothers to death, saying, "My son should come and decide their fate." The satraps then advised her that in any case the best course in the meantime would be to imprison them to ensure the security of her son's throne. They also counseled her that until his arrival, she should appoint a regent of her choice who would administer the realm. Helena approved of their advice and chose her eldest son Monobaz to be the regent as they had agreed. The royal diadem was put on his head and he was given the ring and staff[2] of his father the king, and she bade him take charge until the arrival of his brother Izates. The latter, on hearing of the death of his father, did not delay his departure and with Monobaz's consent, became their king.

Now while he had been living in the fort of Spasinus, a Jewish merchant called Ananias used to visit the women of the court and teach them to worship God in accordance with the Torah[3] of the Jews. It was through these noble women that Izates gained his friendship and also became inspired by this doctrine. When he was recalled to the land of Adiabene, he [Ananias] acceded to his persuasive plea to accompany him. It so happened that Helena, too, who had been instructed by another Jew, had become attached to the Torah of God and its precepts. On his return to his native country of Adiabene, he was enraged to discover that his brothers and their kinsmen had been imprisoned. He regarded it as unjust to kill them or to keep them in permanent imprisonment; and yet, there was a danger that they would unjustifiably take revenge on him should he let them free. So he sent some of them together with their own children[4] to the emperor Claudius in Rome, and some of them to Artabanus* the king

2. 'Staff.' The Greek and Latin text read "sampsera," a golden shield which was a symbol of sovereignty.

3. De' Rossi uses the word "Torah" throughout his translation where Josephus uses expressions such as "according to Jewish tradition" or "laws" or "rites."

4. 'With their own children' (cum propriis filiis)—there is a slight error in de' Rossi's text which reads "with their own sons of his."

of the Parthians; in both cases, as hostages from the people of Adiabene. Subsequently, when he realized how much pleasure his mother derived from the Jewish religion, he decided to follow her example and to convert. Furthermore, he took stock of the fact that he could not be a true Jew unless he was circumcised, and so he resolved to remove his impurity. However, when his mother came to know of his plan, she made every attempt to dissuade him, telling him that it would only increase the precariousness of his situation and that his people would plot to take his life. She said that they would use the fact of his devotion to an alien god as a strong reason for removing their allegiance from him. They would not tolerate the rule of a Jew on any account. For several days, then, his mother prevailed on him, and she urged him to relinquish his desire in this matter. His friend Ananias whose advice he sought also espoused Helena's view and threatened to leave him if he did not renounce his desire. For he [Ananias] was afraid that all the guilt would be laid at his door should these secrets become generally known. It would be said: "You are responsible for having taught the law and practices of your people to the king." He also told him that it was possible to worship God without being circumcised as long as he embraced the Torah of the Jews with complete integrity and total devotion—for the divine worship to which he aspired depended more on spiritual perfection than on the correct state of the base body. God would forgive him for having been compelled to forsake this, His covenant, in order to prevent the insubordination of the people which would unsettle and disrupt the entire country. So in this manner, over several days, he dissuaded him from executing his desire in this regard. Later, however, his craving still unquenched, another Jew from Galilee, Eliezer by name, who was renowned as an upholder of the Torah, persuaded him to complete the fulfillment of the precept on which he had embarked. On one occasion, he was given an audience with him and found him reading from the scroll of the Mosaic Torah. He said to him: "My lord king, do you not realize the extent of your fraudulent behavior towards the Torah and thereby, towards God? It is not enough to know about its ways; one has to observe its precepts. How long will you tolerate the reproach of your uncircumcised flesh? If you have not yet read about the precept of circumcision, come and read it now, for then you will appreciate the extent of the damage incurred by setting it aside." As soon as he heard these words, he no longer put off the fulfillment of his duty. He withdrew into a room and summoned a reliable physician and was circumcised forthwith. Then he summoned his mother and teacher Ananias and told them what he had done. They were overwhelmed by fear and consternation, for they were frightened that the people might come to hear about it and that certain individuals might dislodge Izates from the throne. They argued that gentiles would not suppress their indignation about having a man who worshipped an alien god as king. They also feared for their own lives since with but one voice they would be charged: "You agreed to this act and were even accomplices in the deed." The fact is that God ensured that these fears did not materialize. For He saved Izates and his children and all that he had from several perils and many troubles. When they thought the situation was beyond repair, He showed them pity and brought them respite. And so they came to the realization that all who trust in Him and dedicate themselves to Him alone will have their trust rewarded. But let us put aside this subject for the meantime; we shall discuss it in a short while.

(*[See p. 644] In tractate Pe'ah in the Palestinian Talmud,[5] Artaban is the name of the friend of Rabbi, but he is certainly not the same person.)

Now Helena, the king's mother, saw that the affairs of state were secure and stable and that thanks to divine assistance, her son was loved and blessed in the eyes of all his acquaintances, by foreigners and natives alike. She longed to see Jerusalem and the Temple whose fame had reached all lands, and to worship God there and to pay her freewill offerings. She encountered no difficulty in obtaining permission for this journey from the king her son. After making lavish preparations and providing herself with many supplies, she went to Jerusalem. Her son accompanied her for a few days to put her on her way. Her arrival turned out to be most opportune for the natives; for the country was in the grip of a severe famine and many were dying from starvation. Queen Helena acted swiftly and sent some of her servants to Alexandria to procure corn and bread, while others were sent to Cyprus to get dried figs. They all returned in haste and she distributed the provisions which they had brought among the poor of the land. For this kindness she gained an everlasting reputation among our people and will never be forgotten. Her son Izates, who saw that people in the grip of the disastrous famine, likewise sent a large sum of golden dinars to the leaders of Jerusalem. We shall have reason to speak further about the many good deeds which this royal pair performed with great kindness for our compatriots.

It was about this time that Artabanus king of Parthia became aware that his [supposedly] loyal[6] satraps were preparing to rebel against him. Unable to live safely in his own land, he decided to entrust himself to the charge of Izates and to ask him to come to his rescue and, if possible, to restore to him a stable and secure throne. Accompanied by about a thousand friends and reliable dependents, he went and met him [Izates] on the way. He actually recognized him, but Izates, however, did not for he had never set eyes on him. As he approached him, before uttering a word, he prostrated himself in accordance with native custom and then proceeded to pour out his plea which went as follows:

> My King, do not despise your servant, who is entreating your Honor. Do not scorn the affliction of the needy who has no means of repaying your help.[7] The fact is that cast from the heights of sovereignty to low estate, I have fled to take refuge in your help. Therefore, you should consider how the wheel of the human condition can suddenly turn. You should also give thought to your own affairs, in the knowledge that we are all subject to reversals of fortune. If you leave me now and do not take revenge on my enemies, insubordination of slaves against their rulers will surely become widespread. Who will be able to guarantee for himself that he will live in security.[8]

With tears on his cheeks and with bowed head, he addressed him thus. When he had been told his name, and saw the great King Artabanus standing as a suppliant for his life, Izates got down from his chariot[9] and said to him: "My lord, the king, be strong

5. P. Pe'ah 1 (1) 15d.
6. 'Supposedly loyal,' cf. Job 33:23.
7. 'Who . . . help' is de' Rossi's addition.
8. 'Who . . . security' is de' Rossi's addition.
9. De' Rossi has used the word "chariot" where Josephus writes "horse."

and of good courage. Do not despair on account of this calamity that has befallen you and behave as though there is no remedy. For your sorrow will suddenly disappear and you will find a better friend and colleague than you hitherto expected. I will not rest until I have restored the Parthian crown to you; otherwise, I shall certainly abandon my own realm, and divest myself of crown and tiara." So saying, he brought Artabanus into his chariot and he set out to accompany him on foot. For he thought that he was a greater king than himself and ought therefore be shown such respect. But Artabanus found the situation greatly to his distaste. He swore by the salvation that he hoped for and by the royal crown that he would descend immediately and go on foot unless the other would get into the chariot and precede him. Then respecting his wishes, Izates got into the chariot and they gradually[10] made their way to his royal palace and quarters. Artabanus was regaled with royal dainties and given the chief seat at banquets. For he [Izates] did not have regard for his present situation, but rather his former position. He reflected that a happening of this kind might suddenly befall any person who prided his dignity.[11] So he fulfilled his promise and wrote to the Parthian satraps and appealed to them not to delay in reinstating their king who, for his part, would disregard everything they had done to him, and even bind himself by an oath so as to dispel all their fears. The satraps were not opposed to reinstating the king, but they extended their apologies for not being in a position to do so since they had already crowned another by the name of Cinnamus as king. They feared that if the former sovereign were to be reinstated there would be an outbreak of civil war. Now when Cinnamus, who had been brought up by Artabanus and possessed an upright and virtuous character, became aware of the wishes of the princes, he wrote to Artabanus that he should put his trust in him and return, and the diadem on his head would sparkle as in days of old. Reassured, he returned. Cinnamus came to meet him, prostrated himself and addressing him as king, removed the crown from his own head and placed it on that of Artabanus.

And so aided by Izates, he regained the realm from which he had been banished by peaceful means. Nor was he forgetful of the kindness he had received, and he lavished the highest of honors on Izates as was the custom in those countries. He was pleased that like himself, he should wear the lofty tiara and sleep on a golden bed, privileges which were the special mark of distinction of the Parthian kings. He also gave him a fertile and extensive plot of land called Nisibis which he had sequestered from the king of Armenia. On that land, in former times, the people of Macedon had founded the city of Antioch which was called Mygdonia. This was all given to Izates by Artabanus in repayment for all the kindness he had showed him.

A few years later, the life of Artabanus came to an end. He left his kingdom to his son Vardanes. Now Vardanes was contemplating war with the Romans and went to ask Izates to form an alliance with him. But he failed to realize his scheme because Izates was aware of the power and might of the Roman Empire and considered such an enterprise as useless and a striving after the wind. He was also unwilling because he had already sent away five of his sons to acquire knowledge of our language and the laws of

10. 'Gradually' is de' Rossi's addition.
11. 'Prided their dignity,' lit. the sons of the proud (cf. Job 28:8). The Latin reads "mortales."

our people and besides, his mother was absent, having gone to worship and offer sacrifices in Jerusalem. He was therefore disinclined to go to war at that particular moment. He endeavored to dissuade Vardanes from his plan. He recounted the exploits of the Romans and the extent of their power in an effort to frighten him from proceeding with hostilities. But Vardanes who was set in his purpose reacted to Izates' words as to a prickly briar. In a sudden outbreak of anger, he furiously vented his wrath on Izates and challenged him aggressively: "Fill up your ranks and come out."[12] But his wicked intentions were frustrated, for it was divinely willed that all that he had set up was soon to be destroyed. When the Parthian nobles got to hear of Vardanes' intention to take the field against the Roman troops, they put him to death and transferred the government to his brother Cotardes. Not long afterwards, he, too, was murdered as a result of a conspiracy and Vologeses ruled in his stead. He divided his kingdom between his two real brothers who were the offspring of the same womb. He gave Media to Pacorus the elder and Armenia to the younger, Tiridates.

It was in those days that the king's brother Monobaz and his other relatives saw that because of his dedication to the worship of God, Izates succeeded in all his enterprises and had won a great reputation among all men. They therefore reflected that it would also be to the benefit of them all if they abandoned the religion in which they had been nurtured and adopt the Torah of the Jews. When rumor of this reached the satraps, they were extremely angry but refrained from disclosing their secret thoughts, nursing them vigilantly until an occasion would arise to break out against him with a treacherous revolt. Consequently, they wrote to Abdias king of Arabia, promising him a large sum of money if he were to come and fight against Izates. They offered to desert their king at the first engagement of troops—for their only purpose was to take revenge on him for having forsaken the ancestral covenant. After they had bound themselves to allegiance to him, they encouraged and urged him to make haste and expedite the matter. Abias consented to their request and came with a strong force to take the field against Izates. When his army were in sight of the city, the people did not wait for the engagement of troops, but immediately deserted their king. They gave the impression of having been seized by a sudden panic and that overwhelmed by the presence of the enemy had all taken to flight in haste. Izates, however, was not discouraged when he realized that the satraps had deserted him in battle. He made a thorough investigation as to who was responsible for the treason and who were the ringleaders. He arrested many of those who surrendered to the enemy's standard. He passed judgment on them and they were all together impaled in public.[13] The next day, he braced himself for battle and fought his enemies. Many were slain by him while the rest, overwhelmed by the fear of God, fled. He pursued the king himself and barred the roads so that he was forced to flee into the fort of Arsamus. He made an assault on the wall, and then captured the place and took much plunder and booty. He returned with song and the timbrel in glory to Adiabene. He was unable to capture Abdias alive—he chose the bitterness of death in preference to be taken captive by the enemy.

12. 'Fill . . . out,' cf. Jud. 9:29.

13. 'Impaled . . . public,' lit. impaled in face of the sun. Cf. Num. 25:4 where this punishment is meted out for the people who worshipped Baal Peor.

Now although God had foiled them on this occasion and their leaders had been delivered into the hands of Izates, the satraps were not deterred from devising a new outrage against him, and a trap was prepared for him once more. They wrote to Vologeses the king of Parthia, urging him to use all his power to eradicate Izates and to appoint any other person[14] of Parthian origin as their king. They told him that they could not possibly tolerate Izates as their king because he had substituted the object of their veneration for another god. Hearing these words, he delightedly agreed to their request and devised a plan of attack. Looking for a pretext [for belligerency], he demanded that Izates return the lands which in bygone times, Artabanus his father had given him in perpetuity[15] as repayment for the great kindness Izates had showed him. He said that if he were to refuse, he should realize that he was preparing a day of darkness for him. Izates was most shaken by this message. To his mind, it would be contemptible and infuriating to yield to fear and to surrender the gift he had attained in honor. Besides, he knew that even if he acceded to his wishes, the enemy would not replace the sword in its sheath. So he decided to commit his fate to the hands of God, for even on this occasion, he would put everything he had in the balance. Confident in this support, he put his children and wives in a fortress and stored all the produce inside the towers. He then burnt all the other grain and produce of the land in the areas on the periphery of the cities and waited for the arrival of the aggressor. The king of Parthia arrived with a large and powerful force sooner than expected. He pitched his royal camp by the river which separates Media from Adiabene. Izates also entrenched his forces which consisted of six thousand sword-bearing cavalrymen not far off. When the camps had been pitched in the places mentioned, the king of Parthia sent a messenger to inform Izates of his army's size and strength and to let him know that he had recruited all sword-bearing youth from the entire span of the cities of his realm which extended from the city of Bactria to the river Euphrates. Then he threatened him that he would pay the penalty for his ingratitude towards his masters, and that even the god on whom he relied would be unable to save him this time. The emissary did not omit any part of his king's orders and transmitted this entire message. Izates answered that he was perfectly aware that the king of Parthia's force was too strong and powerful for him to engage in hostilities, but that he was also confident that God is greater and more powerful than any man on earth. With this message, the emissary was dispatched on his return journey. And he [Izates] proclaimed a fast and time of mourning for himself, his children, and members of his household and then flung himself on the ground, covering his head with burnt ashes. He entreated God with these words: "God, my God, if it has not been in vain that I have endeavored to entrust myself to Your attribute of goodness—it is You, alone, the Most High (as is indeed fitting) that I have proclaimed the Lord of the whole world—hasten to deliver me, not in order to defend me from my enemies, but rather for the sake of the glorification of Your great name. You will crush the arrogance of their uncircumcised hearts, they who with impious words, have dared to assail Your mighty power with pernicious words." Then God saw his affliction and listened to his plea. On that very night, Vologeses received letters informing him that

14. Lit. a son of Tabeel. Cf. Is. 7:6 where this term is used to refer to a "good for nothing."
15. 'In perpetuity' is de' Rossi's addition.

while the king was not there to block the way, the Dariae [Dahae] and Sacae had invaded and overrun Parthian territory. At a moment's notice, he left the encampment without perpetrating his plan and returned to the cities of his realm with all his troops. The entire population was confronted with the fact that the sudden deliverance of Izates was due to divine providence.

Not long afterwards, Izates' life was drawing to an end, and at the age of fifty-five and in the twenty-fourth year of his reign, he was gathered to God. Although he was survived by five sons, he had ordered that his elder brother Monobaz should succeed him as a reward for all his kindness in keeping the throne for him when Izates was previously in foreign parts, at the time of the death of their father Monobaz. We wrote about this. When Helena his mother heard the news in Jerusalem of the death of her son, the delight of her eyes, she was racked with grief. But she was rightly consoled by the news that her eldest son had succeeded him on the throne. A few days later she came to see him, but not long after her return to the land of Adiabene, she too was gathered to her people, just a few years after the death of Izates. Monobaz sent her bones and those of his brother to Jerusalem with the instruction that they should be buried in the mausoleum of three towers[16] which she had had erected about three furlongs from the city. We shall give an account of the remaining part of Monobaz's reign in a more appropriate context.

During the period when Cuspidus Fadus, the captain of the Roman army was procurator of the land of the Jews, a certain sorcerer called Theudas incited the masses to take all the most valuable of their possessions and to follow him to the banks of the river Jordan. He boasted that he was a prophet and said that he could split the river and enable them to cross it easily on foot. Many were beguiled by these lies of his. But Fadus the procurator of the land did not allow this folly of theirs go unpunished. Unexpectedly, he dispatched an armed squadron of cavalry against them; they killed many of them, and took many alive and brought them to Fadus. Theudas the magician was also one of those slain by the sword; his head was brought to Jerusalem. These are the events that befell the Jews during the time of this ruler Cuspidus Fadus.

Such is Josephus's account in that chapter. While I translated the greater part in order to speak in praise of the righteous, I did not refrain from including this small passage which refers to the disgrace of the wicked. In fact, even I will get honor through the slaughter of Theudas,[17] for thereby I will be able to discern that the wicked will not prevail ultimately,[18] whereas the righteous will flourish like foliage.[19] I reached the verdict that it was to this man that the person Gamaliel was alluding in the fifth chapter of the Christian Acts.[20] He describes how that Theudas had a following of about four hundred men who in a moment were all slain and annihilated. There is also another story of a similar nature in book 20 of Josephus's *Antiquities*[21] about an Egyp-

16. The Greek and Latin texts refer to three pyramids.
17. This is a pun of the phrase, *He who sacrifices a thanks offering* (*zevaḥ todah*) *honors me* (Ps. 50:23).
18. 'Wicked . . . ultimately,' cf. Pr. 24:20.
19. 'Righteous . . . foliage,' cf. Pr. 11:28.
20. Acts 5:36.
21. *Ant.* XX:169–72.

tian Jew who vaunted his prophetical powers. He ensnared several Jews whom he lead out to the Mount of Olives which is situated about five-sevenths of a mile from Jerusalem. If you read that chapter and the subsequent ones, you will be sure to acknowledge our God's justice and pronounce Him perfect in His action over the destruction of the Temple which was due to the sin of those Jews.[22]

Now I noticed that the passage about the precept of circumcision in Bereshit Rabbah, presents an account which definitely tallies with that told by Josephus. I felt it important to transcribe it and set the two accounts side by side in order to lend them more credence. Should there be discrepancies between the accounts, any person of discretion will attribute the fault to one of the two narrators. For the person who brings the sheaves of his tradition, consisting both of straw and cut grain, to the threshing floor, is himself responsible for the damage. At any rate, we shall regard the two accounts as one. The rabbis of blessed memory state:[23]

> There is a story about Monobaz the king and Zotus (he is certainly to be identified with Izates), the sons of King Ptolemy. While sitting and reading the book of Genesis, they came across the verse, *You shall circumcise the flesh of your foreskin* (Gen. 17:11). One of them turned his face to the wall and began to weep, and the other turned his face to the wall and wept. They both went and were circumcised. Some days later, they were sitting and reading the book of Genesis when they came across this same verse, *You shall circumcise.* One said to the other, "Woe to you, my brother." The other said to him, "The woe is yours my brother, but not mine." They then disclosed to each other what they had done. When their mother came to know what had happened, she went and said to their father, "Your sons had a sore (*nomi**) on their bodies and the physician decided that they should be circumcised." He said: "Let them be circumcised." How did the Holy One blessed be He repay him? Rabbi Phineas said: "When he went out to battle, and a band prepared a ditch (*piston***) for him, an angel came down and saved him.

(*According to the interpretation given in the *Arukh,* the word means "wart.")
(**According to the interpretation given in the *Arukh,* the word means "trap.")

Now in awe the sage will conclude that the drift of both these versions of the story is the same. As the rabbis of blessed memory say:[24] "The truth will out."

Now, as we wrote in the previous chapter, Rashi and the Tosafists of blessed memory wrote that Monobaz and his mother Helena were priests of the Hasmonean dynasty. However, they can all be justified on the grounds that they received one report, but did not see the other. In this context, the mention of Ptolemy seems surprising to me, and perhaps is comparable to the case of the Ptolemy who is mentioned at the end of chapter 10 of Bereshit Rabbah[25] which I discussed in chapter 7 of this book.

22. The subsequent chapters contain descriptions of disputes between high priests, ordinary priests, and popular leaders and the stoning of James ordered by the high priest Ananaus a Sadducee. The main target of de' Rossi's statement is therefore difficult to ascertain. He is attacking messianic pretenders and Jewish sectarians who brought dissension among the Jews and these disputes may also include the rifts caused by the rise of Christianity as exemplified in the stoning of James.

23. B.R. 46:10 (467–68).

24. B. Sota 9b.

25. B.R. 10:9 (85). De' Rossi demonstrates that the name of Ptolemy is a scribal error.

Know that the mausolea[26] of Helena and her sons are mentioned again by Josephus in the sixth book of the *Wars*[27] in his topography of Jerusalem and its precincts. He also speaks about the beautiful palace which belonged to Helena's heirs in Jerusalem.[28] During the capture of the city by Titus and his troops, they were setting fire to many of its palaces indiscriminately. The sons and brothers of King Izates, together with a group of nobles, pleaded with Titus to leave it intact. Although he was incensed at the many defectors, he gave them preferential treatment on learning of their noble descent, and granted them a pledge to protect that house. This is surely the legacy of the servants of God who is eternally blessed, selah.

Now, reader, connecting the content of the previous chapter with the beginning of this one, which refers to Monobaz, the ancestor of them all, by the name of Bazeus, you may deduce that Monobaz was a royal title, just as Pharaoh and Abimelech are the titles given to Egyptian and Philistine kings respectively. Accordingly, the "Monobaz of the storehouses" mentioned by our sages may be identical to Izates who, as king, was also called Monobaz. This would be compatible with the account of the donations he sent to the people of Jerusalem during the famine after Helena his mother had sent her contributions. Then there was his brother Monobaz who was his successor to the throne. The descendants of Monobaz who settled in Jerusalem after converting to Judaism are given favorable mention by our sages in tractate Niddah:[29] "The house of King Monobaz did three things for which they are given honorable mention: They examined their beds during the day (according to the opinion that marital intercourse [during the day] is forbidden),[30] they examined their beds with wool of Parhava,† and they observed the laws of impurity and purity in the case of snow." Then in Menaḥot, with regard to the precept of the *mezuzah* which cannot be fulfilled by hanging it on a stick, they state:[31] "The household of King Monobaz used to do this when staying in inns to remind themselves of the precept of the *mezuzah*." Study the *Nimmuqe Yosef*[32] on the *Halakhot Qetanot* of Alfasi. From experience we know that whatever precept proselytes fulfill, they are more meticulous than born Jews. This is one of the reasons which prompted the statement of the sages,[33] "Proselytes are as distressful to Israelites as a running sore." Even though it may be wishful thinking, it is possible that it was one of the children of these proselytes who was given the ancestral name of Monobaz that argued in the presence of Rabbi Aqiva in Torat Kohanim[34] and in tractate Shabbat[35] with regard to the sacrifice of unwitting transgressors. Examine the passage.

26. 'Mausolea,' lit. graves of craving. Cf. Num. 11:34.
27. *Bellum* V:147.
28. *Bellum* VI:355.
29. B. Nidd. 17a.
30. According to a second opinion, marital intercourse during the day is permissible, and the practice is ascribed to the house of King Monobaz.
31. B. Men. 32b.
32. Joseph Ḥabiba was a fifteenth-century Spanish talmudist whose commentary on Alfasi's *Halakhot* was first printed in Constantinople in 1506. De' Rossi is referring to his comment on the cited passage which is given in Hilkhot Mezuzah in which he states that it is not necessary to put up a *mezuzah* while staying at an inn since it is a temporary residence.
33. B. Qidd. 70b.
34. Sifra, meṣorah, 1 (70 col. a).
35. B. Shabb. 68b.

(†[See p. 652] This is pure wool according to the explanation given in the *Arukh.*)

This is what I saw fit to relate about the Monobaz men and the clever woman, their parent. My pleasure in this endeavor was comparable to that which I derived from demonstrating the merits of the two proselytes Onqelos and Akylas. May they all, together with ourselves, be assured a blessed and lasting name.

CHAPTER FIFTY-THREE

Josephus's enumeration of all high priests who officiated from Aaron the priest until the destruction of the Temple, may it be rebuilt soon in our days.

In previous chapters, I mentioned Josephus's opinion regarding some of the high priests. I thought it was appropriate at this juncture to translate his entire enumeration as presented at the end of chapter 8 of book 20 of the *Antiquities.*[1] But first, you should be aware that this account of his is actually not free of errors—some of the obvious passages shall be indicated by marginal glosses on the page. The rest of the book is in a similar condition; for there is no doubt that for whatever reason, a significant part was tampered with.[2] As I wrote in chapter 19, this is also what happened to his extant Hebrew text *[Josippon].* So I cannot resist applying the words of Rabbi Moses [Maimonides] of blessed memory to our case. For at the beginning of chapter 25 of his work on medicine entitled *Chapters of Moses,*[3] he collected various errors which in his opinion are to be found in the works of Galen. Conscious that he was handling versions of Galen's works that had been translated from Greek into Arabic, he wrote as follows:[4] "Perhaps it was not Galen who was in error, but rather the translator, or I the reader." And in this context we might add, "or the scribes or the printers." In any case, this chapter is not without worth, and for this reason I have set it before you:

> Now it was fitting that we should give information about the high priests in these histories: who was the first, to whom was this office given, and how many there were up to the end of the war that we have described.
>
> Now the first who served as priest to God was Aaron, the brother of Moses. After his death, his sons officiated, for a covenant of everlasting priesthood was granted to his descendants. The office of God's priesthood was only transmitted to the seed of Aaron and could not even be held by kings of another lineage. Thus eighty-three priests officiated from Aaron until Phineas whom some of the people[5] appointed as high priest during the war that we have described. Of these, thirteen officiated from the time that Moses, by

1. *Ant.* XX:224–51.
2. De' Rossi may be implying that there are Christian interpolations in the text. It may also be an oblique reference to the famous Testimonium Flavianum.
3. De' Rossi read the work in the Hebrew translation of Nathan Hameati (1283) in manuscript. He may have also had access to the Latin translation which was first published in Florence in 1488.
4. *Pirqe Mosheh* (325).
5. 'Some of the people.' The Greek and Latin texts refer to the revolutionaries (seditiosi). De' Rossi may have regarded Josephus's designation as too extreme.

divine command, erected the Tabernacle in the desert. At first, the new high priest was only selected after the death of his predecessor. But in the course of time, the institution fell into disarray such that the predecessor was still alive when his successor served in the holy place. The thirteen who were direct descendants of the two sons of Aaron retained their original office in succession. In those days, the people were governed by the judges. Then came the rule of the national kings, i.e., such monarchs as Saul and David.[6] Later, they were ruled by kings ruling over specific regions.[7] Six hundred twelve* years elapsed from the time of the exodus of the children of Israel under the leadership of Moses until they embarked on the construction of Solomon's Temple. After these thirteen high-priests, eighteen others held office from the time they embarked on the construction of Solomon's Temple until the destruction of the first Temple at the hands of Nebuchadnezzar. Jehozadak who was high priest at the time was exiled with the rest of the people. These held the office of high priesthood for 466 years,** 6 months, and 10 days. During this time the people were governed by kings. After 70 years of captivity, Cyrus was willing to liberate the Israelites and to send them back to their land. He also gave them permission to rebuild the Temple. Since his father had died,[8] Jeshua son of Jehozadak officiated as high priest. Jehsua and his descendants, fifteen successive generations in all, held the high priesthood and administered† the people until the reign of Antiochus Eupator, for a period of 413 years. Then Antiochus and his general Lysias seized Onias the high priest, who was also called Menelaus, and deprived him of his life and priesthood in a place near of the city of Berytus. They even excluded his son Onias from holding onto that office, and in his place they appointed Jacimus who was in Aaron's line, but not of the same family. Consequently, Onias son of the murdered Onias, the high priest, and who bore the same name as his father, fled to Egypt. After winning the favor of Ptolemy and his wife Cleopatra, he succeeded in erecting an altar in Alexandria which was modeled on the Jerusalem Temple as we have discussed elsewhere. Jacimus died after officiating for three years. He had no successor and for seven years, the city and Sanctuary were without a high priest.

(*This figure is patently wrong since it is stated, *In the four hundred and eightieth year [after the Israelites left the land of Egypt . . . Solomon began to build the House of the Lord]* (1K. 6:1).)

(**We spoke about this figure in chapter 14.)

(†I.e., together with the princes, Zerubbabel, and his descendants.)

During the reign of the Hasmoneans who revolted against the Greeks and drove them out, a group from the Jewish community elected Jonathan as high priest. After he had held office for seven years, Tryphon devised a plot against him and killed him, and Simeon his brother became high priest in his stead. When he, too, died, from the poison with which his son-in-law had contaminated his food, he was succeeded by his brother Hyrcanus who officiated for thirty-one years. Having become advanced in years, he bequeathed the priesthood to Judah the Hasmonean who was also called Aristobulus. He officiated both as high priest and king for one year, and then his brother Alexander succeeded him to the high priesthood and throne. He was high priest and king for twenty-seven years. Before his death, he entrusted his wife with the appointment of a high priest of her choice. She gave the position to her son Hyrcanus, while she herself retained the throne for nine years after which she was gathered to her people. But Hyrcanus was not able to retain the office

6. The Latin text simply reads "monarchas."
7. I.e., the kings of Israel and the kings of Judah. The Latin text simply reads "reges."
8. 'Since . . . died,' is de' Rossi's addition.

of high priest. After the death of their mother, his brother Aristobulus managed to demote him to the position of ordinary priest, while he himself took both the high priesthood and the throne. After he had held these offices for three years and three months, Pompey captured Jerusalem and sent him with his children in chains to Rome. He reinstated Hyrcanus to the high priesthood and gave him sovereign powers, but only on the condition that he did not wear the crown. Thus, in addition to the nine years that we mentioned, he ministered for a further twenty-three years. Subsequently, [Bar] Zapharses and Pacorus, the rulers of Parthia, crossed the river Euphrates, made war on Hyrcanus, captured him alive, and brought him to their territories and appointed Antigonus, the son of Aristobulus as king. After three years and three months, Herod assisted by the general Mark Anthony killed Antigonus at Antioch. With Roman assistance Herod had enforced his rule over the Jews. Unwilling to appoint those of Hasmonean lineage to the high priesthood, he gave the office to ordinary priests. It is true, however, that he temporarily appointed Aristobulus, the grandson of the Hyrcanus who had been captured by the Parthians, and sister of his wife Mariamme; in this way, the people sought to retain the memory of his grandfather Hyrcanus. But later, he became frightened that the people would turn their allegiance to Hyrcanus. So he devised a plot to kill him while he was swimming near Jericho, as we recounted above. From that time onwards, he refused to entrust the office of high priest to any of Hasmonean extraction. After his death, Herod Archelaus his successor followed his father's policy, as did the Roman officers who agreed that none of Hasmonean lineage would be able to serve as high priest in the Sanctuary.

CHAPTER FIFTY-FOUR

On the phenomenon of omens that sometimes foreshadow great blessings or calamities.

MEN of virtue have said that the lover does not forget. And so, my beloved reader, though I have tarried in fulfilling the promise I gave you at the beginning of the book, I always kept it in mind—that must surely be of some importance—and now it is to be accomplished once and for all. I am referring to Herod's address to his troops in which he stated that great disasters ought to be preceded by indicative omens.[1] I promised that I would demonstrate that this is true and correct in one of these chapters. We preferred not to do so at the time, because it was not appropriate for us to introduce material which, if kept brief, could not have been complete and, if developed, would have taken the reader on a digression beyond the scope of the chapter.

You should know that in the Zohar, our sages also express this idea when they comment on the verse, *A new king arose* (Ex. 1:8), and not only in regard to disasters, but also in regard to future blessings which, they say, are heralded by a heavenly portent. They states as follows:[2] "Rabbi Ḥiyya said: 'Thirty days before power comes to a nation on earth, or before destruction comes to a nation on earth, it is announced in the world. Sometimes the news is communicated by children, sometimes by those devoid of knowledge, and sometimes by the birds. And they pronounce it to the world and nobody heeds it. When the people are righteous, it is heralded by the righteous leaders of the world in order to inform them that they should return to their Lord. But when they are not righteous . . .'" Examine this lengthy and fine passage. The same idea is expressed in the Zohar on the verses, *When an ox or a sheep or a goat is born* (Lev. 22:27) and *When Jacob saw that there was food rations* (Gen. 42:1). In Yoma[3] and Sheqalim in the Palestinian Talmud,[4] the rabbis of blessed memory write explicitly that a long time before the destruction of the first Temple, Josiah found the scroll of the book of the Torah which Hilkiah discovered open at the verse, *The Lord will drive you and the king you have set over you [to a nation unknown to you . . . where you shall serve other gods]* (Deut. 28:36). He quickly went and hid the Ark, the bottle of manna, the

1. He discusses this subject in the "Voice of God."
2. Zohar II, 6b.
3. B. Yoma 52b.
4. P. Sheq. 6 (1) 49c.

anointing oil, and the other objects. With regard to the second Temple, it is stated in Yoma[5] and in Sheqalim in the Palestinian Talmud[6] that when the priests would shut the doors of the Temple in the evening, which were so heavy that every time three hundred priests (this is hyperbole) had to make a concerted effort to move them, they would sometimes be found open in the morning as is said, *Open your doors, O Lebanon* (Zech. 11:1). The passage continues with the speech by Johanan ben Zakkai. In the seventh book of the *Wars,* Josephus testifies to this phenomenon along with other portents which he describes. He states:[7] "The doors of the eastern gate of the inner court were made of brass and were so massive that it was with difficulty that twenty priests would close them in the evening. They were fastened with iron bars and many bolts were fixed into the large stone which was on a block under the gate. At the sixth hour of the night it was observed that these opened of their own accord." I had thought of presenting a translation of the other disconcerting presages of doom which at that time, according to Josephus, appeared in the heavens and on earth, but they were too numerous; moreover, it was enough to have instructed you to read them. But here is one exception which is enlightening.[8] After the great citadel of Jerusalem had been captured, the troops[9] continued to make the Temple building into a fortress until it became a four-angled edifice. Subsequently, they reflected about the tradition in holy Writ that the city would fall to the enemy when the Sanctuary would be built with square parapets. Now the statement of the rabbis in Sheqalim in the Palestinian Talmud,[10] in Yoma[11] and Menaḥot[12] is already known: "Forty years before the Temple was destroyed, the lot [for the Lord] would not come up in the right hand, the crimson-colored strap did not go white and the western light did not shine and the doors of the Temple opened of their own accord. Then Rabban Johanan ben Zakkai rebuked them, 'Temple, Temple, [why is it you who are setting the alarm?']." And it was not only supernatural events of the kind that were regarded as portents of the future. Even natural phenomena such as eclipses which are caused by the moon's interposition between the sun and the earth, or the earth's interposition between the sun and the moon, would be designated in this way. A patent example is the passage in Sukkah[13] and in the Mekhilta[14] where the rabbis of blessed memory state that the eclipse of the sun is a bad omen for the gentiles, and the eclipse of the moon, a bad omen for Israel.[15] If the face of the sun is red like blood, it is a portent of the sword; if it is like sackcloth, it is a portent of famine. This will come about unless they act in accordance with the Omnipresent's wishes; for then,

5. B. Yoma 39b.
6. The passage is not in Sheq., but in P. Yoma 6 (3) 43c.
7. *Bellum* VI:293–96.
8. *Bellum* VI:310–11.
9. I.e., the Jews.
10. See n. 6.
11. B. Yoma 39b.
12. De' Rossi refers to B. Men. 109b, but whereas it does contain some of the same material from B. Yoma 39b, it does not contain the cited text.
13. B. Sukk. 29a.
14. Mekhilta d' Rabbi Ishmael, bo, 2 (I, 19).
15. The text reads "enemies of Israel" euphemistically for Israel.

as is made clear in that context, and also in tractate Shabbat,[16] "the idolators will be dismayed, but not Israel." Likewise, with regard to the rainbow, Ramban (Nahmanides)[17] writes: "We must believe the Greeks who say that a rainbow results from effect of the sun's rays in the moist air, just as a container of water standing in the sun gives the impression of the rainbow." Nevertheless, go and see the greatness of God who testified to this phenomenon when He said, *and it shall serve as a sign of the covenant* (Gen. 9:13). Equally, we find that this was ordered by the blessed Lord as part of the constellations of heaven when He said, *they shall serve as signs* (Gen. 1:14). Now the gentile nations, who practiced divination, recount many stories of supernatural happenings and omens which they call auguries, portents, and prodigies[18] which presaged blessings or disasters for kings and princes or great cities. You will notice that in his *Lives of the Kings,* Plutarch describes many such cases which would take too long to narrate. But you can easily find all the references by consulting the table of contents. Similarly, the ancient Roman writer Valerius Maximus refers to many stories from each of the three categories of portents of good and calamitous happenings. It seemed right to me to present to you one example about Plato at the end of chapter 4.[19] He says that when the baby Plato was lying in his crib, bees came and made their honey in his mouth as though he had temporarily become a beehive. The magicians of the time said that this was an indication of great wisdom and that he would be gifted with mellifluous eloquence and thought. This story bears great affinity to the statement of our sages in the Palestinian Talmud, tractate Taʿanit,[20] Ekhah Rabbati,[21] and the Pesiqta:[22] "[Forty years before the exile, palm trees were planted in Babylon to indicate] that sweet varieties of fruit accustom the tongue to Torah."

Now at the beginning of the book, I discussed the philosophers' treatment of the natural and unnatural prognostications of the earthquake and made particular mention of the book written by the physician Buoni (par. 305).[23] Then there is also the Christian scholar Marsilio Ficino, a Platonic philosopher and distinguished physician. At the end of his short erudite book on the plague and its remedies, he states[24] that the great plague occurred in his lifetime in the year 1477 according to their era. And he said that a month earlier, he had predicted its occurrence to his people when he saw the unnatural and unprecedented phenomena of those days.[25]

Now we the community of the children of Israel should be happy and rejoice. For we have sinned greatly like all the nations, and it may be that the heavenly portents and

16. B. Shabb. 156a.
17. Ramban to Gen. 9:12.
18. De' Rossi uses the Italian words: *auspicii, nuntii, prodigii.*
19. Valerius Maximus, *De i detti e fatti (Memorabilia* 1, 6, 3). De' Rossi refers to ch. 4 (rather than ch. 6) of bk. 1 which would seem to indicate that he read the work in an early Italian translation (e.g., Rome, 1539) in which the said passage is in ch. 4 entitled "De li prodigii cioe miracoli." On the unknown translator, see M. T. Casella, "Il Valerio massimo."
20. P. Taʿanit 4 (8) 69b.
21. E. R. Proem 34.
22. Pes. d'R Kah. 13:10.
23. Antonio Buoni, *Del terremoto,* 3 par. 305.
24. *Il consiglio,* ch. 23, 37r. (The ed pr. was printed in Florence, 1481.)
25. Ibid., 37v.

other omens are intended for us all equally. But the fact is that when we perform the will of our Father in heaven who has given us preferential treatment as His treasured people, no augury or divination as Balaam the gentile said[26] can govern or affect us. And as the Jewish prophet of skilled tongue[27] said, *Do not be dismayed by the portents in the sky* (Jer. 10:2).

26. Num. 23:23.
27. 'Skilled tongue,' cf. Is. 50:4.

CHAPTER FIFTY-FIVE

How the Jews follow the prophets' injunction and ancestral custom to pray constantly for the welfare of those who govern them. And in our present exile they pray that God should grant peace and tranquility to all nations.

All peoples should know that as long as we are strangers and sojourners in a land that is not ours, we, the surviving remnant, are obliged by injunction of the true prophets and ancestral custom, which is Torah, to pray for the welfare of the governing powers to whom we are subject. They should also know that particularly at a time like this, when we have been scattered to the four winds of heaven on account of our iniquities, we should request God that the world should be at peace and that nation should not lift sword against nation. Accordingly, I thought it worthwhile to collate the testimonies and illustrative examples which I discovered and came across in divergent sources. May the judicious person gain knowledge.

In fulfilling his divine mission regarding Babylon, the first kingdom to bring about our downfall, Jeremiah commanded the Jews and said, *And seek the welfare of the city to which I have exiled you and pray to the Lord in its behalf; for in its prosperity, you shall prosper* (29:7). And in the first book of his disciple Baruch which was accepted by the Christians, but not by us, it is made clear that those Jews who had been the first to be exiled with Jeconiah collected contributions from everybody which they sent to the rest of the people who had stayed in Jerusalem with the high priest. The gifts were dispatched with the following message: "We send you money with which you should pay for burnt offerings and incense . . . and pray for the life of Nebuchadnezzar king of Babylon and for the life of Belshazzar his son that their days on earth should be like the days of heaven. . . . And that we shall serve them many days and be in receipt of their kindness (1:10–12)."[1] Now in the book of Ezra, we are told that Darius the king ratified Cyrus's written decree, *and at the expense of the king . . . let them give daily without fail . . . sacrifices to the God of heaven and pray for the welfare of the king and his sons* (6:8–10). There is no doubt that this decree was enforced, as is attested by Josephus in book 11 (chapter 4).[2] And in Yoma[3] and chapter 9 of Megillat Taʿanit,[4] they refer to the twenty-first[5] of Kislev

1. De' Rossi does not give a complete citation of these verses.
2. *Ant.* XI:16–18.
3. B. Yoma 69a.
4. Meg. T. 339.
5. In Yoma, the date given is 25 Tevet, but in B. Tamid 27b and Meg. T. the incident is listed for 21 Kislev.

as the Day of Mount Gerizim. On that day, the Cutheans had asked Alexander of Macedon to destroy our God's Temple and thereby give precedence to the sanctuary which they had erected for themselves on Mount Gerizim. Simeon the righteous then came and addressed him thus: "Is it possible that those Cutheans can mislead you into destroying the place where we pray for you and for the preservation of your kingdom?" Then in the first book of Maccabees,[6] there is the description of how Demetrius king of Greece sent his general Nikanor against the Jews at the instigation of the wicked Alcimus who had tried without success to get appointed as high priest. He [Demetrius] was met on Mount Zion by some of the priests and members of the Sanhedrin who in the course of their appeals drew his attention to the sacrifices and burnt offerings that were offered for the welfare of the king. And in the second book of the Maccabees (ch. 3), in Josephus's work dedicated to the Maccabees,[7] and in the Hebrew Josephus,[8] there is an account of the incident which occurred after Simeon a Benjamite had incited Seleucus king of Greece to divest the Sanctuary of its splendid riches. On his arrival, Heliodorus, Seleucus's general, received the following appeal from Onias the high priest: "My lord and prince, it is surely against your best interest to damage this place in which we pray daily on behalf of the king, his children, and friends that God should continue to grant them peace and quiet." And the Hebrew Josephus also recounts how the Asian Jews sent books and presents to Hyrcanus the priest and the princes of Judah saying:[9] "Accept our donation for the glory of our God, and pray for the life of our lord Augustus, emperor of Rome, and for the life of his friend Mark Anthony." In his last work entitled *On the Embassy to Gaius,* Yedidyah the Alexandrian [Philo] records the letter sent by Agrippa king of the Jews to the emperor Gaius [Caligula] asking him to desist from putting a statue of himself in the holy place. He wrote:[10] "Our lord king, do not the Jews make votive offerings for the welfare of your kingdom and offer meal offerings with the sacrifice of the burnt offerings not only at the noted feast days but also with the daily sacrifices that we offer to our God?" In book 2 of the *Wars,*[11] Josephus wrote that when Petronius, the captain of Gaius's army, wanted to put a statue of the Caesar in the Sanctuary, the Jews implored him saying: "Do we not offer burnt offering and sacrifices to God for the sake of the peace of the Caesar and all the people of Rome?" And in the second book of *Against Apion,*[12] he makes the general statement that we Jews are accustomed to pay honor and homage to all the emperors and the Roman people and to offer burnt offerings and sacrifices on their behalf, not only with those which are for the community at large or for particular individuals,[13] but also, on many occasions, as exclusive dedications for the glory of the emperors, a privilege which is not extended to any other person on earth. And as is stated by the founding fathers:[14] "Pray

6. 1Macc. 7:33.
7. 4Macc. 4.
8. *Josippon,* bk. 3, ch. 16 (67).
9. Ibid., bk. 6, ch. 47 (158–59).
10. *Leg.* 280.
11. *Bellum* II:197.
12. *Contra Apionem* II, 76–78.
13. The Latin reads "filiis."
14. M. Avot 3:2.

for the welfare of the state; for were it not for fear of it, a man would have swallowed up his fellow alive."

There is an even greater dimension to this: for our ancestors did not only make supplications on behalf of our rulers; but also, when we ourselves were in power, they were not loathe to pray for those kingdoms that were among the ranks of those who were kindly disposed towards us. For example, in the first book of Maccabees, it is described how Jonathan the high priest formed an alliance with the Spartans who claimed that they were of Abrahamic descent and kinsmen of the Jews. In his letter to them he wrote:[15] "We remember you on the feast days during the offering of the sacrifices, since it is right that we should remember our brothers."

Furthermore, we pray to God to extend His loving-kindness not only towards sovereigns and friends, but to all citizens of the world. Such a view is expressed by Agrippa in his letter to the emperor Gaius[16] when he wrote that on the Day of Atonement, the high priest is accustomed to pray that all mankind should be granted a year of blessing and assured tranquillity. And in his book *On Government,* Yedidyah also states:[17] "The priests of other nations pray only for their own people, but the high priest of the Jews seeks blessing and bounty not only for all humankind, but also for all parts of nature and its elements." Likewise in his work *On Sacrifices,* he writes:[18] "Some of the sacrifices are offered for our nation[19] and some for the entire human species. For the two daily offerings alongside the meal offerings and libations constitute a declaration of gratitude on behalf of all human beings for the benefactions of the Creator which He bestows on them day and night." In *Against Apion,*[20] Josephus also writes: "The request for the good and prosperity of the entire world takes precedence over our own particular needs in our sacrifices and outpouring of prayer. For we know that prayer for the general good which comes before that of the individual is particularly acceptable to our God." A similar statement in made by Eusebius the Caesarean in book 8 of his *Praeparatio.*[21] You should give these words due consideration for they are fine sentiments.

Henceforth, sagacious reader, you should extol our ancestors for their institution of the prayers which are said at the beginning of the year with regard to the entire coming year: "Reign over the entire universe. . . . Shine forth in splendor . . . and every creature will understand . . . to establish the world under the reign of the Almighty, for to You every knee must bend . . . and everybody shall take the yoke of Your kingdom upon themselves." All these and other such proclamations serve as our substitutes for the sacrifices which were offered in righteousness. Speaking on the subject of resurrection

15. 1Macc. 12:11.
16. Philo, *Leg.* 306.
17. *Spec.* I:97.
18. Ibid., 168–69.
19. The Latin text reads, "pro universa gente," namely, for all people, but de' Rossi has taken it in a more particularistic sense.
20. *Contra Apionem* II, 196.
21. De' Rossi, using George of Trepizond's translation of the *De ev. praep.* refers to bk. 8, ch. 2: "in quibus pro communi prius salute oramus deinde pro nostra. Gratissimus enim deo est qui communem salutem suae anteponit" (*P.G.* XXI, col. 618).

in his work *Naḥalat Avot* with regard to the mishnaic statement[22] "All is His," Don Isaac refers to these prayers with great joy.[23] Since this is so,[24] it is fitting and acceptable that He should endeavor to bring all human beings back to Him as it says, *The Lord is good to all and His mercy is upon all His works* (Ps. 145:9). Then in the prayer that is recited without fail three times a day, we say,[25] "And saturate the world with Your blessings." For it is only right that with pure heart Israel should walk on the paths of our God, who does not desire that anyone should die,[26] but rather that he who has gone away from Him should relinquish his ideas and return to the Lord who will show him mercy. As reinforcement of this idea, there is the custom practiced in certain communities to recite a blessing for their rulers and all those connected with government. This was actually the custom of the pious of old, the purpose of which was to obtain the favor and understanding of God and man.

Certain prayers also express the desire to eliminate the power of arrogance and to uproot and exterminate its sway such that the spirit of impurity is eradicated. We ought to praise such sentiments and understand what is being conveyed, namely, that the recovery of the sick person is achieved by the removal of the sickness. For there is no doubt that arrogance and the sin of pride is identical with the evil inclination and the angel of death which constantly lurks at the gate of our mind in readiness to ensnare us. But when we subjugate it, it is stamped out and brought under God's sway. Consider the statement, *Should a man act presumptuously . . . [that man shall die]* (Deut. 17:12) *[If the prophet speaks in the name of the Lord and the oracle does not come true, . . .] the prophet has uttered it presumptiously* (ibid. 18:22). If it [i.e., arrogance] is kept away from us, like a gazelle, we can set our sights on the streams of good works on which our spiritual life depends.[27] As the divine poet said, *Let sins*[28] *disappear from the earth* (Ps. 104:35), which sentiment is praised by the rabbis of blessed memory on the understanding that the verse refers to sins and not to sinners.[29] A similar idea is expressed in one of the wise proverbs of the gentile sage Seneca:[30] "It is most praiseworthy to eradicate sin and transgression rather than sinners."

It is characteristic of holy Writ to ascribe a role and power to the embodiment of sin and arrogance. There is the explicit statement by Ezekiel, *The rod has blossomed: arrogance has budded* (7:10) and by Jeremiah, *Insolence will stumble and fall* (50:32). According to our rabbis,[31] the expression *There is a little city* (Eccl. 9:14) refers to the body, while the expression *and to it came a great king* (ibid.) refers to the evil inclination. The verse *if the wrath of a lord flares up against you* (Eccl. 10:4) is rendered in the

22. M. Avot 4:22: "They that have been born are destined to die and they that are dead are destined to come to life. . . . He is the Creator . . . for all is His."

23. Abravanel interprets the Mishnah as referring to the time of resurrection when the words of the New Year's day liturgy will be fulfilled.

24. I.e., "all is His."

25. De' Rossi is referring to the prayer as recited according to the Italian rite.

26. 'Desire . . . die,' cf. Ezk. 18:32.

27. This passage makes rhetorical use of Ps. 42:2 and Is. 38:16.

28. The word can be read as "sinners" or "sins."

29. B. Ber. 10a.

30. "Res optima est, non sceleratos extirpare, sed scelera."

31. B. Ned. 32b.

Targum: "If the spirit of the evil inclination has power over you." It is also possible that the Christian lawgiver [Paul] who was himself a Jew was influenced by this approach when he wrote in his Letter to the Romans, *Let not sin reign in your mortal body* (6:12). Indeed when there is still a remnant of the nations left in the land, our hope for the remnant of our people will come about as predicted by Daniel, *Dominion, glory, and kingship were given to him; all peoples and nations of every language must serve him* (7:14).[32]

Now since everything we have said is absolute truth, and it is known that all of us, the surviving remnant, are scattered and dispersed from one end of the world to the other, our attitude should not be to hope for the prosperity of one power at the expense of another. For should one fall, only wretchedness will ensue and after all, the blood of us all is equally red[33] and precious to our God. Therefore it is a duty to obey the words of the wise and the counsel given in antiquity by the true and faithful prophets. That is, we should proclaim in exultation and prayer that for the sake of the governing powers, the Lord should remove all dissension and envy from their heart and grant peace on earth. For when they are at peace, He will appoint peace for us as well. Everybody will see and give thanks that through His kindness He will exalt our horn and the sprout of David his servant will soon flourish. Towards the end of chapter 5 we raised the subject of the interpretation of the verse, *You shall not curse God* (Ex. 22:27) according to the rendering of the Septuagint, Yedidyah, and Josephus. In that regard we pointed out that in everything that relates to faithfulness and the divine, it is honorable for a person to desist from dissension. A similar idea is expressed in the verse, *You shall be very careful not to provoke them* (Deut. 2:4,5). By such behavior we shall ensure the security of our tents[34] until such time as God desires to deliver us.

32. In the context of the vision of the four beasts, Daniel sees the human being to whom *dominion, glory . . . were given.* De' Rossi sees this as the final stage that must take place before Israel's salvation will occur as predicted in Dan. 7:27: *The kingship and dominion belonging to all the kingdoms under heaven will be given to the people of the holy one of the Most High.* Therefore, to this end, they should pray for the welfare of the nations.

33. 'Blood . . . red,' a saying from B. Pes. 25b.

34. 'Security of our tents.' De' Rossi has used and reversed the idea in Job 12:6: *Robbers live untroubled in their tents, and those who provoke God are secure.*

CHAPTER FIFTY-SIX

Concerning the characters of the *ever ha-nahar* script and the holy sheqel.[1]

Now that we have grown old we are like children.[2] For as we approach the end of this book, we shall introduce some real novelty which will also have bearing on certain issues raised in these chapters; so we shall begin to learn about the form of the [Hebrew] characters. We shall not deal with our script, but rather with the Hebrew (*ivri*) script as the rabbis of blessed memory call it in Megillah[3] and Sanhedrin[4]—that is, the script of those who are "on the other side of the river" (*ever ha-nahar*). The Libunaʾah script is another name for it, which according to Rashi, refers to large letters which are like those used for amulets and *mezuzot.* In his commentary on Mishnah Yadayim,[5] Rambam [Maimonides] of blessed memory wrote that this script was used by the people who are called al-Samira, that is, Samaria. Now I looked at the document which a trustworthy person from the beautiful land [i.e., the Land of Israel] had transcribed for the Rav, Rabbi Petachiah Yada of Spoleto at the time when he was also teaching him the Arabic language. It was his son Moses the physician who showed it to me here in Ferrara. Subsequently, when I was in the city of Mantua, the scholar Rabbi Samuel of Arles showed me the actual autograph of the itinerary to the holy Land written by Rabbi Moses Basola of blessed memory which contains a description of the novel things that he saw on that journey.[6] Then while I was in Mantua, the scholar Rabbi Reuben of Perugia also showed me a text from an ancient work which they hold to be reliable and which he had been given by a Christian scholar in the city of Bologna. It is the Samaritan alphabet, the form of which is given below. This is what Rabbi Moses Basola states:[7] "These are the Cuthean [Samaritan] characters which are

1. This chapter was of interest to seventeenth-century Christian scholars, who often referred to it in their work on the Samaritans and on Jewish coins. In addition, M. Gaster translated a portion of the chapter into English ("Jewish knowledge").

2. A saying from B. B.Q. 92b.

3. B. Meg. 8b.

4. B. Sanh. 21b.

5. M. Yad. 4:5.

6. Moses b. Mordechai Basola (1480–1560) was rabbi of Ancona and went to the land of Israel on two occasions. His work *Massaʿot* was first published anonymously in Livorno in 1785 and then in his name by I. Ben Zvi, Jerusalem, 1938.

7. *Massaʿot,* 91.

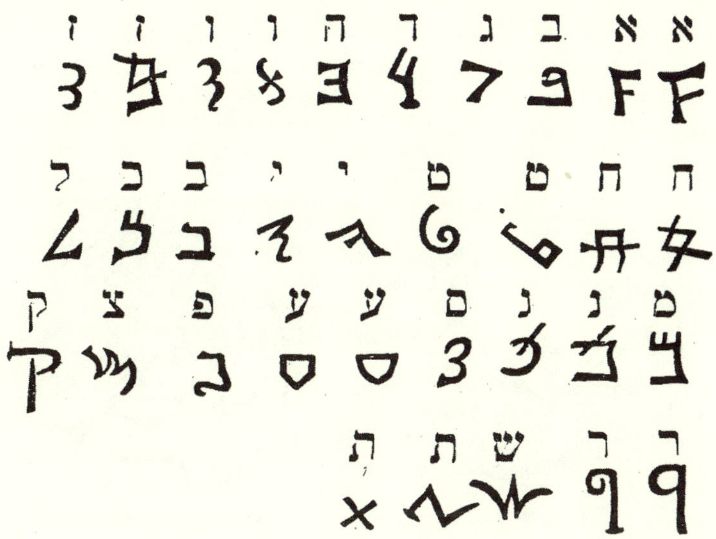

enscribed on the coins."[8] Now at the end of his commentary on the Torah, Ramban of blessed memory writes as follows:[9]

> With the Lord's blessing I reached Acre and I discovered that some of the elderly locals had a silver coin which was engraved. On one side, it had a figure of a branch of an almond tree, and on the other side, that of a flask and around both sides there was a very clear inscription. They showed the writing to the Samaritans who could read it at once because it was the Hebrew script which had been preserved by the Samaritans as is mentioned in Sanhedrin. On the one side, it read "Sheqel of Sheqels," and on the other side, "Jerusalem the holy." And they claim that the one emblem denotes the blossoming almond rod of Aaron, and that the second is the flask of manna. We weighed it on the banker's scales and it came to ten pieces of silver which is equivalent to half an ounce as Rashi indicates.[10] I have also seen a coin with the same emblems and inscription which was half the weight with which they would weigh out the half sheqel that was used for the sacrifices.

However, I the writer, thanks be to God, have seen one such sheqel which was in the possession of the widow of the pious merchant Isaac Haggio the Sefardi of blessed memory who lived in Ferrara. With the crown of a good name,[11] he went to Jerusalem and there he died and was buried in the valley of Jehoshaphat, about a mile outside the Zion gate. This woman who had to care for her dependent children, went to stay with her eldest son Rabbi Yomtov of blessed memory, who managed the estate of his father here in Ferrara. On the contours of the coin I saw the inscription "Sheqel of Israel" written in the same characters, and in the center, a chalice with the letters *shin dalet*

8. It is interesting to note that Basola was a friend of Guillaume Postel who also reproduced the Samaritan alphabet and the sheqel discussed below in his *Linguarum . . . alphabetum,* 38. On de' Rossi's discussion of the coin and the alphabet and contemporary interest in Samaritan, see my article, "Azariah de' Rossi and Septuagint Traditions," 25–28.

9. This passage is printed at the end of his commentary (vol. 2, 507).

10. Ramban refers to this statement of Rashi in his commentary to Ex. 30:13.

11. Cf. M. Avot 4:13.

which in my opinion stand for the words "Sheqel of David."[12] On the obverse, the words *yerushelayim ha-qedoshah* (Jerusalem the holy) or *yerushelaimah qedoshah,* and in the center, a rod with three blossoms as seen in the illustrations of either side of the coin given here.

I believe that Rav Naḥmani [i.e., Nahmanides] of blessed memory mistakenly wrote "Sheqel of Sheqels" instead of 'Sheqel of Israel."

Now both the readings *yerushelayim ha-qedoshah* and *yerushelaimah qedoshah* may be upheld. For it is stated in Megilla in the Palestinian Talmud:[13] "Rabbi Simon and Rabbi Samuel bar Naḥmani both say: 'The Jerusalemites used to write *yerushelayim* as *yerushelaimah* [lit. to Jerusalem] and were not concerned about doing so, and likewise they wrote *ṣafonah* (northwards) for *ṣafon* (North) and *temanah* (southwards) for *teman* (South).' " In the light of this you can understand the statement in Yevamot in the Palestinian Talmud[14] on the mishnah,[15] "The school of Shammai permit [levirate marriage] between the co-wives and the brothers."

> Rabbi Simon said that the school of Shammai based their position on the verse, *[When brothers dwell together and one of them dies and leaves no son] the wife of the deceased shall not be married outside (ha-ḥuṣah) to a stranger* (Deut. 25:5). The outsider (*ha-ḥiṣonah*) shall not be a wife to a stranger. Thus the school of Shammai is in agreement with the Cutheans who apply the levirate marriage to the betrothed women and exempt the married women, for they expound the word *ḥuṣah* (outside) as *ha-ḥiṣonah* (a woman outsider). How then do the school of Shammai uphold the expression *and he leaves no son?* Rabbi Jacob the southerner said in the presence of Rabbi Yose: "He has no son from the woman to whom he was married. The one who is an outsider should not marry a stranger." Rabbi Jose said to him: "They may put you to shame for being a Cuthean for you uphold their interpretations of Scripture." Rabbi Simeon ben Eleazar taught: "I remarked to the Cuthean scribes: 'How come that you erred for you do not interpret Scripture according to Rabbi Nehemiah's teaching. For he taught that any word which requires a *lamed* (to) as a prefix and it has not been supplied, a letter *he* is put at the end of it. For example, there is the word *la-ḥuṣ* and *ḥuṣah* (to outside) and *le-seir* and *seirah* (to Seir), *le-sukkot* and *sukkotah* (to

12. The identification of the letters is correct, but they stand for "*shanah dalet,*" i.e., year four, and refer to the fourth year of the first revolt against the Romans, i.e., 70 C.E.

13. P. Meg. 1 (9) 71d.

14. P. Yev. 1 (6) 3a.

15. M. Yev. 1:4.

> Sukkot).'" They responded to Rabbi Nehemiah: "It is written, *The wicked will return to Sheol (li-she olah)* (Ps. 9:18), that is, to the nethermost part of Sheol."

The last part of this passage is also found in Midrash Tehillim.[16] The main point here is that the Cutheans do not agree that the letter *he* at the end of a word is a substitute for a *lamed* at the beginning. They therefore explain the word *ḥuṣah* as outsider, and the school of Shammai appear to give a similar exegesis of the verse. The implication of Rabbi Jose's comment to Rabbi Jacob is "Let the Cutheans not curse you." For I discovered in the log book of the beautiful land[17] to which I referred that their expression "may shame be upon him" is another way of saying "may a curse be upon him." Perhaps the expression *Lest he who hears it reproach you* (Pr. 25:10)[18] is of the same type. There is also Ramban's statement on this subject.[19]

There is another fundamental passage about the form of these characters in tractate Megillah in the Palestinian Talmud:[20] "Rabbi Levi said: According to the view that the Torah was given in *raʿaṣ* characters, the letter *ayin* was a miraculous phenomenon. But according to the view that the Torah was given in Assyrian characters, the *samekh* was a miraculous phenomenon." In tractates Sanhedrin[21] and Megillah of the Tosefta and in our Gemara[22] and in Megillah in the Palestinian Talmud,[23] there is a controversy among the Tannaim as to the characters in which the Torah was given on Sinai. We shall discuss this again in chapter 58. Rabbi Jose and Rabbi Nathan said that they were in the *ever ha-nahar* script, whereas Rabbi Simeon ben Eleazar, Rabbi Eleazar ben Parṭa, and Rabbi Eliezer of Modin and Rabbi, who expressed the general view, said that it was given in the Assyrian script. Therefore Rabbi Levi said that according to the view that the Torah was given in the Assyrian script, the *samekh* was a miraculous phenomenon. The allusion here is to Rav Ḥisda's statement in our Gemara[24] that it was miraculous that the *mem* and the *samekh* remained in place in the tablets. For according to the rabbis of blessed memory, the statement *they were inscribed on one side and the other* (Ex. 32:15) implies that the letters went right through from side to side.[25] Such a view fits their explanation in the Babylonian Talmud that the script is called Assyrian (*ashuri*) "because its letters are excellent (*meʾushar*)"; alternatively, as they say in the Tosefta and the Palestinian Talmud, "because its script is excellent." In other words, it is excellent and distinguished, as Rambam of blessed memory explains on Mishnah Yadayim.[26] And according to the view [that it was given] in the *raʿaṣ* characters (which must

16. Mid. Teh. to Ps. 9:18.
17. I.e., Moses Basola's account.
18. The verb *ḥsd* here means "to reproach."
19. Ramban to Lev. 20:17. Ramban is commenting on the word *ḥesed* (disgrace) which is used in connection with the forbidden unions.
20. P. Meg. 1 (9) 71c.
21. T. Sanh. 4:8.
22. B. Sanh. 21b–22a.
23. P. Meg. 1 (9) 71c.
24. B. Meg. 2b–3a.
25. Cf. B. Shabb. 104a. The miracle that occurred was that the closed letters, namely the *mem* and the *samekh,* did not fall out, although the engraving of the tablets went right through from one side to the other.
26. Maimonides, *Perush* M. Yad 4:5. Maimonides explains the unparalleled distinctiveness of the letters and the script.

correspond to the *ever ha-nahar* script), the *ayin* was a miraculous phenomenon—for as you see, it is perfectly circular in shape like the *samekh* we use. The other explanation, namely, that it was called Assyrian because they brought it with them from Assyria, would also apply to this view. In the same vein they say in the Palestinian Talmud in Rosh ha-Shanah[27] that they imported the names of the angels and the months from Babylon. Moreover it is stated in the Palestinian Talmud:[28] "Assyrian has a script but no language; Hebrew has a language but no script. So they chose the Assyrian script and the Hebrew language." There is no doubt that the meaning of the statement that there was no language or no script is that it had no remarkable characteristics. The Tosafists gloss the statement[29] "they do not possess a language or script" and write: "In Megillah they state, *I will wipe out from Babylon name and remnant* (Is. 14:22). Name refers to the language. What is meant by this, for they still speak and use the Aramaic language. Rather the reference must be to the imperial language." And the compiler of the *Arukh* explains the word *raʿaṣ* as though it is read from back to front, to mean *ṣaʿar* (distress); alternatively we could read it as *daʿaṣ* which means to squeeze or push which is the idea conveyed by distress. In any case, it is evident that *raʿaṣ* refers to the *ever ha-nahar* script. And when they say in Sanhedrin that it was changed into the *roʿaṣ* script which according to Rashi is connected with the word tiraṣ, as in, *you shatter the foe* (Ex. 15:6), it implies that it is the antithesis of the Assyrian script which brings blessing to those who hold onto it.[30] Alternatively the word *raʿaṣ* derives from a Samaritan word which must denote the form of that script in one way or another. Now in his *Iqqarim,*[31] Rabbi Joseph Albo tends to take the view that the Torah was given in the *ever ha-nahar* script. But there is no doubt that his view is completely unfounded, whereas the opinion of the sages whom we shall mention in chapter 58 that it was given in the Assyrian script will always meet with approval.

With regard to this question, I cannot desist from informing you of a comment made by Rabbi Moses al-Ashqar in his *Responsa.* He writes:[32] "Know that various different types of coins, the sheqel and the half-sheqel, came into my possession. Some of them bore the inscription "year so and so for the comfort of Zion," "year so and so of king so and so." And on one of them I saw the symbol of a bound lulav with an etrog by it.[33] A certain Jew who was a competent reader of that script told me that on one side there was an inscription in Greek with Greek arms engraved on it, and the other side had an inscription in the Hebrew script. Evidently, this coin must date from the time of their subjugation to the Greeks." Examine the passage. Now the characters, which the author of *Miqneh Abraham*[34] reproduces at the beginning of the book, are certainly not

27. P. R.H. 1 (2) 56d.
28. P. Meg. 1 (9) 71b.
29. B. A.Z. 10a. This is said about the Latin language and script.
30. This is a play on the phrase in Pr. 3:18 in which the root *ashr* (to be happy) is used.
31. *Sefer ha-Iqqarim,* III, ch. 16 (143–46).
32. Moses b. Isaac al-Ashqar, *She'elot,* Responsum 74, 138a–b.
33. I.e., the palm branch, myrtle, and willow tied together and the citrus all of which are used for the ritual on Tabernacles.
34. Abraham ben Meir de Balmes (1440–1523) was a physician, philosopher, translator, and grammarian. His grammar *Sefer ha-Diqduq, Miqneh Abraham* was translated into Latin with the title *Peculium Abramae.*

the same characters which were on the sheqel described above.[35] Furthermore, I would also like to mention Rashi's comment on the expression *thirty pieces of silver* (Ex. 21:32). He writes: "A sheqel weighs four gold coins which is equivalent to half an ounce." However in his commentary to the beginning of pericope *ḳi tissa* (Ex. 30:13), he refers to *zuzim* rather than gold coins (*zehuvim*). Then in his first book of *On the Special Laws,* Yedidyah the Alexandrian (Philo) discusses the scales of valuation and states that the sheqel is equivalent to four pieces of silver.[36] In his *Antiquities,*[37] Josephus writes that the sheqel used by Jews is equivalent to four Athenian drachmas. In my opinion the sixty thousand drachmas mentioned in chapter 2 of Ezra (v.69) and the thousand darics mentioned in chapter 8 (v.27) are all the same currency. Whosoever has a desire to obtain exact information about all the weights mentioned in the Torah and by our rabbis as well as all the different kinds of measurements, both the dry and liquid quantities, should consult chapter 15 of *Kaftor va-Feraḥ*[38] which provides an elaborate and precise explanation of this topic with reference to all opinions on the subject.

35. De Balmes reproduces an alphabet from an ancient work written in a script which he describes as the *ever ha-nahar* script.
36. *Spec.* II:33.
37. *Ant.* III:195.
38. On Estori (Isaac ben Moses) ha-Farḥi and his *Kaftor Va-Feraḥ,* see ch. 23.

CHAPTER FIFTY-SEVEN

On the antiquity of the holy tongue and the use of the Aramaic language among our people.[1]

IN some of the previous chapters I offered to treat some relevant issues regarding our holy tongue, and its letters, vowels, and accents. I shall now fulfill my promise. May the good God give me a response[2] and show me kindness. I shall devote separate chapters to each topic in order to give respite to the reader between each topic. This shall be my discussion of language.

I would say that although there were certain members of the community of our ancient sages who held that all 70 languages preexisted the generation of the dispersion (this shall be clarified presently), the prevailing opinion, and that to which all the upright subscribe, is that it was only in the time of Peleg that these languages were introduced by divine instigation. Before that time, the holy tongue was the only language in the world. Examine the statement of the rabbis of blessed memory in Bereshit Rabbah concerning the verse *[She shall be called woman (ishah) for from man (ish) she was taken* (Gen. 2:23):[3] "This proves that the world was created with the holy tongue. Have you ever heard *gyne, gynea, antrope antropea, gavra gevarata?*[4] No, but there are the words *ish* and *ishah* because the one word is connected with the other." Now it is true that the wise author of the *Aqedah* challenged this statement. He wrote:[5] "This proof does not make sense, for who told us that it was not transcribed from another language." But he then adapts their statement to the point of view that he held to be correct.[6] Examine the passage. Nonetheless, we have another way of considering the matter which is most plausible and

1. For a discussion of de' Rossi's views on language, see my article, "Azariah de' Rossi and the Forgeries of Annius of Viterbo," 264–67. For a recent study of general Renaissance views on the subject, see M. Tavoni, "La linguistica rinascimentale," 216–42.

2. 'Give . . . response,' lit. answer me with a voice. Cf. Ex. 19:19.

3. B.R. 18:4 (164–65); 31:8 (281).

4. This is a play on the Greek and Aramaic words for man and woman, where the one word cannot be modified to express the corresponding male or feminine form.

5. Isaac Arama, *Aqedat Yiṣḥaq,* gate 8 (66a–b).

6. Arama explains that the rabbinic explanation could be challenged on the grounds that the example given is comparable to the word *par* (bull) and *parah* (heifer) and also that the words could simply have been transcribed from another language. However, he argues that the relationship between *ish* and *ishah* is different because the letter *yod* in *ish* is omitted in *ishah* and merely indicated by a *dagesh.* The word *ishah* thus demonstrates the nature of woman as an inextricable conjunct to man. This idea is reflected in the midrashic statement, "because the one word is connected with the other."

acceptable. For over time and in the course of the narrative, the names are always derived in the following manner: *He formed Adam from the earth (adamah)* (Gen. 2:7); *Eve (Ḥavva), because she was the mother of all living (ḥai)* (Gen. 3:20); *Cain . . . I have gained (qaniti) a man from the Lord* (Gen. 4:1); *Seth, God has established (shat) another seed for me* (Gen. 4:25); *Peleg for in his days the earth was divided (niflagah)* (Gen. 10:25). We notice that when those narratives were translated into foreign languages, the actual names were not changed; rather all peoples retained the proper Hebrew form of such names as Adam, Cain, and Noah. Thus clearly all nations provide us with convincing proof and reliable testimony that the first language in which these names were formulated was the holy tongue. Furthermore, intelligent reader, you should be receptive to the proof that Rabbi Judah Moscato demonstrated to me. He argued that the perfect should be the recipient of the perfect, particularly when the donor, that is the Creator, is Himself perfect.[7] Experts in natural science give a similar reason to account for the rotundity of the heavens. As is explained in book 2 of *De caelo,*[8] they assert that it is appropriate that the most perfect matter should be endowed with the most perfect form. Similarly, we are justified in our claim that the blessed Creator who ensured that His world lacked nothing it needed, did not refrain from endowing the first man who was perfect of his species (as is explained in section 1 of the *Kuzari*),[9] with this language which owing to its various attributes is of the greatest perfection. In particular, it excels in expressing the innate meaning and qualities of what is named. For example, the word for eagle (*nesher*) denotes its keen eyesight as expressed in the word *ashureno* in *I shall see him (ashureno) but not nigh* (Num. 24:17); it also signifies the shedding of its wings which, as is known, occurs in the process of its rejuvenation.[10] And as demonstrated in the introduction to the *Sefer ha-Tiqqunim*[11] and in Tiqqun 69,[12] the word for hand (*yad*) corresponds to the number of its parts and related meanings and the other attributes with which it is endowed. As for the name of the blessed Lord, it is well known that the kabbalists have endowed it with a multitude of distinctive attributes, a phenomenon which is not paralleled in any other language. Similarly, its letters excel in representing the true nature of every being, inferior or great. This has all been explained by Ramban (Nahmanides) with regard to the verse, *and whatever the man called each living creature that would be its name* (Gen. 2:19),[13] and applies equally to the language and the letters which were undoubtedly created with him. I shall explain this matter further in the next chapter.

7. Judah Moscato, de' Rossi's mentor and friend, expresses a similar view in his commentary *Qol Yehudah* on the *Kuzari* (I, par. 95): "Indeed Adam is described as endowed with perfect matter and form and bound together by a perfect agent. Indeed, all that is perfect is created through a perfect executor." Cf. his long commentary to *Kuzari* II, par. 68. Moscato's discussion bears greater resemblance to de' Rossi's own arguments.

8. Aristotle, *De caelo* II, ch. 8 (290b).

9. *Kuzari* I, par. 95.

10. This is a reference to Ps. 103:5 *And my youth is also renewed like the eagle.* Rashi ad loc. explains that the eagle's wings are refurbished every year. He refers to a myth (perhaps a version of the phoenix myth) about a certain species of eagle which becomes rejuvenated as soon as it reaches old age.

11. *Tiqqune ha-Zohar* (9a). The symbolism of the hand is described in relation to the donning of the phylacteries.

12. Ibid., 101b. The various attributes of the right and left hands are discussed here.

13. Ramban to Gen. 2:20: "The Holy One blessed be He brought all the animals of the field and fowl of heaven to Adam and he discerned their nature and gave them appropriate names."

Similarly, the modes by which the meaning of words is expressed, namely, metaphor, as the Greeks and Romans call it, is exemplified in the incredibly shrewd expression used by Jacob in anticipation of his death, *And I shall lie with my fathers* (Gen. 47:30). Inherent in these words are two important basic tenets. Several scholars and scribes have struggled to write books on the truth which they embody but still have been unable to do justice to the subject. The use of the term "lying" as a description of death does indeed imply that there will be a resurrection of the dead, an awakening and rising, just as in the normal course of things, a person who lies down will probably get up again unless he is blighted by the curse, *And now that he lies, he shall rise no more* (Ps. 41:9). And if I could have been present during the discussion of the sages reported in tractate Sanhedrin,[14] I could have also offered my own contribution and given this verse as yet another indication that the notion of resurrection of the dead can be derived from the Torah.[15] The expression "with my fathers" which is equivalent to "gathered to one's people" certainly signifies the immortality of the soul. For otherwise, where could one locate his fathers and people? In chapter 10,[16] I showed you how the first Indian sage (that is, according to the version of the story reported by Plutarch and Clement) was asked by Alexander: "Who do you think are more numerous, the dead or the living?" He answered, "The living, for the dead no longer count." Furthermore, the phrase *since his life is bound up with his life* (Gen. 44:30) does indeed contain all the ideas developed by scholars in their books about true love between two people. Such subjects as these which are regarded as a particularly relevant concern of scholars can actually be learned from the simple expressions of the holy tongue. Accordingly, Rashi of blessed memory did well in explaining the verse, *And the earth was one language* (Gen. 11:1) as a reference to the holy tongue. You will notice that the sum of the letters [of the words "one language"] is equivalent to that of [holy tongue] although the latter has one extra letter.[17] The sage in the *Kuzari* has an excellent discussion of this subject in part 2 (par. 34)[18] and 4 (par. 33)[19] of the work.

Of the Christians who also treated this topic was the great doctor Augustine. In his *City [of God],*[20] he wrote that from Adam until the dispersion, there was one language in the world. But when presumptious people of the generation sinned with their boastful assertion *Come [let us build a city . . . to make a name for ourselves* (Gen. 11:4),[21]

14. B. Sanh. 90b.

15. De' Rossi appears to discount the fact that in B. Sanh. 90b, a similar verse *Behold you shall sleep with your fathers and rise up* (Deut. 31:16) is also quoted in the course of the discussion as proof of resurrection. However, ibn Ezra to Deut. 31:17 does indicate that the syntactical structure of the verse does not allow for such an interpretation.

16. In this chapter, he discusses the description of Alexander the Great's meeting with the Gymnosophists as recounted by Plutarch and Clement of Alexandria and a parallel story in the Talmud.

17. The phrase *one language* has the numerical value of 794, and *Holy Tongue,* 795. In this type of *gematria* or numerical symbolism, the extra digit is disregarded. Cf. Jacob ben Asher ad loc. and Profayt Duran in ch. 3 of *Ma'aseh Efod* who mention this *gematria.*

18. The reference must be to *Kuzari* II, par. 68.

19. According to Cassel, the reference is to III, par. 67; but more appropriate to the argument is IV, par. 25 in which he speaks about the perfection of Hebrew and its characteristics.

20. *De civ. Dei,* 16, ch. 4 (*P.L.* XLI, col. 482); ch. 11 (cols. 490–92).

21. De' Rossi alludes to God's speech, *Let us then go down and confound their speech there* (Gen. 11:7), but must have meant to refer to Gen. 11:4.

the punishment they received was likewise through language. However, Eber and his family who had not associated themselves with the mockers were able to retain their first language. In fact, it was not the legacy of the entire family of Eber but was passed only through the Abrahamic line, and then not to all Abraham's family but only to his chosen seed, Isaac, and then not to all Isaac's family but only through the line of Jacob. For God was to ensure that the holy tongue should remain with the holy seed.[22] These words of Augustine bear affinity to the statement in the *Kuzari* that the chosen people came from special stock.[23] The author of the *Aqedah* also touches on this subject in many of the gates of his work, as does Yedidyah [Philo], at the end of the tenth part of his works[24] in his comment on the verse, *And Noah awoke* (Gen. 9:24). Please consult the passages I have indicated and be grateful.

Now it is true that both Augustine[25] and Annius in his commentary on the second book of Berosus the Chaldean[26] say that there were 72 languages. For it was their contention that this figure comprised the number of the children of Shem, Ham, and Japhet about whom it is written, *each with its language* (Gen. 10:5). Annius derides one of their commentators[27] for his adherence to our sages' opinion regarding the figure of 70 which is derived from the verse, *[When the Most High gave nations their homes and set the divisions of man,] He fixed the boundaries of peoples* (Deut. 32:8). Furthermore, one of their [i.e., Christian] great exegetes, Tostatus, commented on the pericope on the dispersion and wrote:[28] "Scripture is not explicit as to the number of language divisions, nor is it known whether any language was lost over the course of time as a result of the native speakers' annihilation in battle, or whether another language was invented by human agreement. But insofar as the children of Noah about whom it is written, *each with its language* were 72 in number, it is universally agreed that there must have been 72 languages." In my opinion, the discrepancy between their figure and ours arose because they included Assyria and Philistia in the count, while we do not. I noted this in the Pesiqta d'Rav Kahana which was together with the Midrashim of Avkir and Abba Gorion[29] in an old volume which I read in the academy of Messer Isaac da Fano, a native of Ferrara.[30] In the section entitled "On the Festival of Tabernacles," the individual

22. De' Rossi omits Augustine's reference in ch. 11 to Jesus' descent from the same line.

23. *Kuzari* I, par. 95.

24. I.e., *Sob.* 65. (As always, de' Rossi refers to the order of the books in Gelenius's Latin translation.)

25. In *De civ. Dei,* 16, ch. 3 (col. 481), Augustine distinguishes between nations and individuals and counts 72 nations.

26. Annius of Viterbo's forgeries are used quite extensively by de' Rossi in this chapter. The reference here to Annius's commentary to bk. 2 of ps. Berosus (97) is not quite accurate since Annius counts 74 which includes Noah, Shem, Ham and Japhet.

27. Nicholas de Lyra is 'one of their commentators.' Annius who disliked de Lyra's use of Jewish interpretations, accuses de Lyra of misunderstanding Gen. 46:27, *all the souls of the house of Jacob who came into Egypt were three score and ten.*

28. Tostado's commentary to Genesis is in vol. 1 of his *Opera.* De' Rossi refers to quaestio 12 entitled "Quot linguae datae fuerant" (56, col. b). Tostado also says that Hebrew was the common language before the deluge and, like Augustine, traces the transmission of Hebrew from Eber through the direct line of descent to Jesus: "et non mansit in omnibus discendentibus ab Heber, sed in solis illis qui erant in recta linea per quam venit Christus."

29. Only fragments of Midrash Avkir are known; Midrash Abba Gorion, a Midrash on Esther was printed by Jellinek in his *Bet ha-Midrash.*

30. This passage is not in the printed editions of the Pesiqta d' Rab Kahana. In his edition (Lyck 1868,

figures are given—14 to Japhet, 30 to Ham, 26 to Shem—which amount to 70.[31] As we indicated, Assyria and Philistia are omitted from the list of Ham's sons. This appears to be correct because these two were included with others which had already been counted. In any case, we cannot dissent from the agreed opinion of our sages that there were 70 languages, nations, and their princes. [Ps.] Jonathan ben Uzziel's rendering of the verse, *Thus the Lord scattered them from there* (Gen. 11:8) makes this point particularly clearly: "And the word of the Lord was revealed concerning the city and its people: seventy angels for 70 nations and each one with its language and character of its script in hand and they were scattered from there." A similar idea is expressed in chapter 24 of the Pirqe d'Rabbi Eliezer: "Seventy angels for 70 peoples, and to each nation its own script and language." And in Bemidbar Rabbah it is stated that the weight of the basin was 70 sheqels to correspond to the 70 nations who live from one end of the world to the other.[32]

Now the above-mentioned Berosus could not attribute the confusion of languages to God's agency because he was not acquainted with the name of God. But at the beginning of book 4,[33] he wrote that when Noah saw that humans had begun to proliferate, he divided Asia, Africa, and Europe among his progeny and dispatched each man and his family to his own designated country. He said that 131 years after the deluge, Nimrod founded the city of Babel and the wondrous tower but was unable to complete their construction. Towards the end of book 3,[34] he wrote that Noah was also called Janus, a name derived from the word for "wine" (*yayin*). His wife who was called Tithea was also given the name Aretia, a derivative of the word for "earth" (*ereṣ*) because she was the mother of all inhabitants of the earth. After her death she was called Esta, a name connected with fire (*esh*) because of her ascension to heaven, the highest of all the elements. There are other examples of this kind which indicate that the holy tongue was used in those generations.

According to Cato whose work is printed in the second volume of Berosus's works, the name Aretia was also given to a city of great antiquity called Aretia di Toscana.[35] Similarly, in his work entitled *On the Origin of the Tuscan Language,*[36] the Italian author first proves the antiquity of that region [i.e., Tuscany] and that the human race began with Noah, and then he gives about a hundred examples of words in that language [Tuscan] which derive from the holy tongue: e.g., *besora, ambasceria; mesura, misura,*

XXIII, n. 20), Buber conjectured that the reference was to a reading of the Pesiqta Rabbati to which de' Rossi had access.

31. These figures also found in Bem. R. 9:14. Cf. B. Sukk. 55b where the 70 nations are said to be represented by the 70 bullocks which are sacrificed over the 7 days of Tabernacles.

32. Bem. R. 14:12. "Seventy symbolizes the 70 nations who descended from him [i.e., Noah]."

33. Annius, *Berosus,* bk. 4, (129, 132).

34. Ibid., bk. 3, 122. This was a typical euhemeristic treatment of biblical personalities which provided a link between classical mythology and biblical history. On Annius's euhemerism, see H. J. Erasmus, *The Origins,* 41. See also, R. Fubini, "L'ebraismo."

35. This is another forgery of Annius of Viterbo entitled *M. Catonis Fragmenta de originibus.* De' Rossi is referring to vol. 2, 107.

36. The unnamed author is Pierfrancesco Giambullari (1495–1555). The work to which de' Rossi refers, *Il Gello,* asserts the linguistic autonomy of Italian from Latin by ascribing Etruscan and ultimately Hebrew or Aramaic as the ancestral language of Italian. Giambullari uses the forgeries of Annius to support his thesis.

ḥarbone qayiṣ, carbone, etc.[37] There is a fine Aramaic grammar written by one of their scholars who shall remain anonymous[38]—from the introduction to Baḥur's [Elijah Levita's] *Meturgeman,* it is evident that he [Münster] pilfered the idea [to write the grammar] from him.[39] In his introduction,[40] he writes that at the time of the dispersion several Hebrew words remained interspersed throughout many of the new languages in a corrupt form. He said that the languages spoken in the vicinity of the scene of the dispersion, such as Aramaic, Arabic, and those of the nations of the adjacent eastern areas, bore greater affinity to the holy tongue. But the languages of the more remote countries, such as Germany and the other western regions, were correspondingly more dissimilar, the further the distance, the greater the dissimilarity. A similar view is expressed by the sage Efodi at the end of chapter 3. He writes:[41] "There is no doubt that when the nations came to an agreement about the 70 languages, they used some of the words and verbs of the language which had been used since antiquity."

Furthermore, among the scholarly works written by Rabbi David Provenzali, a standard- bearer of Torah in the city of Mantua,[42] is his *Dor ha-Pelagah* in which he recorded more than two thousand Hebrew words some of which were integrated into Latin, others into Greek, Italian, and other languages.[43] Among the Latin examples are the words *uxor* (wife) derived from *ezer ḳe-negdo* (a helpmeet); *axillae*[44] from *aṣile yadai* (my arm joints). From the word *pilegesh* (concubine) is the Greek and Latin word *pellex; ospedale* (hospital) from *osef dalim* (a gathering of the sick). The name of the muse of music, Calliope, the first of the nine guardian muses, is, according to the compiler of the Latin dictionary,[45] derived from the expression *qol yafeh* (a beautiful voice). Similarly, he says that the word *ḳalendae* derives from the word *qol* as we wrote at the end of chapter 40 in section 3 of the book.[46] The word *accademia* is derived from a combination of the words which make up the expression *bet eqed roʿim*[47] which is rendered as "a meeting place of shepherds" in the Targum of Jonathan, and thus of men—in other words, an assembly of people is meant. I proffered this information with regard to the

37. The etymologies given here are in Giambullari (55): "Diciamo noi adunque, ambasciata, imbasciadore ed ambasceria da bascer che a loro significa nuntiare . . . carbone da carbon ch e la estrema et ultima siccita arsiccia." The mesura-misura etymology is not given by Giambullari but is found in Augustinus Steuchus, *Recognitio,* 9r ("Mensura enim nomen est Hebraicum").

38. This is a reference to the *Chaldaica grammatica* written by the Protestant hebraist Sebastian Münster, a disciple of Elijah Levita. In the seventh rule of the Tridentine Index of 1564, it was conceded that heretics' books could be cited, but only anonymously.

39. This is a reference to Elijah Levita's *Meturgeman.* In the introduction, Levita states that he had begun to write an Aramaic grammar, but that the sack of Rome brought a halt to his work and he lost all his manuscripts. Thus Münster became the writer of the first Aramaic grammar.

40. *Chaldaica Grammatica,* "De affinitate et differentia Chald. et Heb." (9).

41. Profayt Duran (Efodi), *Maʿaseh Efod,* ch. 3 (31). De' Rossi read the work in manuscript.

42. De' Rossi plays on the Italian form of the name, Mantova, dividing it into *min* (of) *ṭovah* (goodness), yet another indication of his appreciation of his Italian environment.

43. De' Rossi mentions his friend David Provenzali on several occasions throughout the work, particularly in reference to his work on Philo. The Dor ha-Pelagah does not appear to be extant.

44. De' Rossi gives here the Italian form *ascelle.*

45. Ambrogio Calepino, *Dictionarium,* s.v. Calliope. Calepino states that Calliope is "a pulchra voce" and does not refer to Hebrew.

46. Calepino states that the word derives from the Greek *ḳaleo* (to call), and in ch. 40, de' Rossi only refers to its Greek derivation.

47. The expression is in 2K. 10:12 and means "shearing house of shepherds."

academy which had recently been founded here in Ferrara.[48] The first lecturer had described the institution as an academy. Somebody then objected that he found it anomalous that a Jewish society should bear a Greek name. When I told him that the word might have derived from Hebrew, he was appeased and satisfied.

Thus in addition to the proofs that we put forward earlier, these data supply us with substantial evidence that the holy tongue is the antecedent and father of all other languages since its imprint is particularly recognizable and has left its mark on each of those languages. And so one can justifiably assess the benefit that accrues to those who are masters of Hebrew; by means of it and as a result of it, they can also be familiar with many words of other languages and therefore be in a position to say truthfully, *The language that I did not know, I can understand* (Ps. 81:6). But their great poet Dante put false words into the mouth of Adam in chapter 26 of *Paradiso* when he said:[49] "The language which I used to speak was utterly eliminated before the completion of the tower." It has indeed survived, and, thanks be to God, it is in our possession. In fact, according to the enunciation of the holy Rabbi Simeon bar Yoḥai, the opposite would appear to be the case, and all those languages are destined to disappear while this one will remain. For he states that the confusion of tongues brought contention to the world—ibn Ezra speaks in a similar vein when he relates the story of the dispersion to the verse, *and speak the language of his own people* (Est. 1:22)[50]—and then he [Simeon bar Yoḥai] concludes:[51] "But what is written with regard to the time to come? *For then I will make the peoples of pure speech so that they all invoke the Lord by name* (Zeph. 3:9). This alludes to the fact that the sum of the letters of the expression "pure speech" equal that of the words "holy tongue," bar one which has no significance for the total count as you know.[52] I also was told that in one of his works, the great Christian doctor Aquinas said that the holy tongue would be the only language to survive once God had accomplished the restoration of His world in accordance with His age-old desire.

Now in tractate Megillah in the Palestinian Talmud,[53] it is written: *And the whole earth was one tongue and single things* (Gen. 11:1): "Rabbi Eleazar and Rabbi Johanan had a discussion. One said that they were speaking the 70 languages, and the other said that they were speaking the language of the unique one, that is to say, the holy tongue." Likewise it is stated in Bereshit Rabbah:[54] "Single things"—things held in common.

48. The accademia was a widespread phenomenon in Italy from the fifteenth century onwards. The humanists accademia was essentially formed by a group of friends who met to discuss classical texts, languages, or philosophy. The yeshivah in Italy was comparable to the accademia. (See Elijah Levita's *Tishbi,* s.v. *yeshivah* where he calls the head of the yeshivah "presides academiae." See R. Bonfil, *Rabbis,* 18.)

49. Dante, *La commedia, Paradiso* 26, ll. 124–27: "La lingua ch'io parlai fu tutta spenta / inanzi che al'ovra inconsummabile / fosse la gente di Nembròt. attenta." But cf. *De vulgari eloquentia,* 1, vi, 5ff. where Dante expresses his idea of the development of the Hebrew language, i.e., Adam's language was spoken by all his descendants until the tower of Babel after which time it was only spoken by Jews. Cf. H. Reinholder, "Dante."

50. Ibn Ezra to Gen. 11:6: "For when laws are changed, jealousy, and hatred are resuscitated and this is what happens when language is changed. It was for this reason that the king of Medes and Persians pronounced that his edict should be promulgated *according to the language of each people.*"

51. Zohar I, 76b.

52. The numerical value of *pure tongue* is 798, *Holy Tongue,* 797. See n. 17.

53. P. Meg. 1 (9) 71b.

54. B.R. 38:6 (354).

What one possessed was at the other's disposal and vice versa. Some rabbis say that it means "one language." For with unsullied divine speech, namely, this verse, *And the whole earth was one tongue and single things,* a situation arises as described by the author of the *Guide*[55] with regard to the word *avh* which means to desire in Hebrew, but to refuse in Arabic. But additionally, it is also true, as he wrote at the beginning of his treatise on resurrection,[56] that two speakers of the same language will each understand the same verse according to their own light and arrive at diametrically opposed interpretations. Similarly in the case of this story of the dispersion, one of the two pairs of our sages may possibly have noticed that even before the construction of the tower, Scripture refers to the progeny of each of Noah's sons with the words *each with his language, their clans and their nations* (Gen. 10:6). It may be that he then found it difficult to reconcile the fact of their sudden dispersion with their acquisition of language which was so swift that they had an adequate vocabulary with which to speak. Accordingly, he felt justified in eliciting an entirely consistent interpretation of Scripture and therefore asserted that the expression "one language" meant that they all spoke uniformly—however many the parts of speech, they were all common knowledge. Thus despite the slight amount of dissension cast among them by the working of the attribute of justice, causing separation between individuals and families, they nevertheless clung to their own particular language for life. Nevertheless, as I said, the former opinion prevailed and was confirmed by our ancients. I am alluding to the view of "the other" who said that they were all speaking the holy tongue. Likewise, the verse, *And the earth was one language* was rendered in the Targum of [ps.] Jonathan ben Uzziel and the Palestinian Targum as follows: "And all the earth was one language and one speech and one order of the holy language by which the world was created from the beginning."

Now I do not know of any gentile sage who took it upon himself to distort the correct literal meaning of the story of the dispersion. The only exception is Yedidyah the Alexandrian who, as I suggested in chapter 6, has an anomalous status [lit. like an antelope][57] among the speakers and is a creature is his own right in respect to our sages. For in his book on the confusion of languages, his own statements are confused.[58] He virtually claims that the story is merely a representation of the confusion of false opinions which are generated by material thoughts that are antagonistic to the Lord of all the earth—I discussed this in chapter 5. Nevertheless, he does acquit himself somewhat at the end of that section[59] when he says that there is also no harm in believing in the literal meaning of the story as long as this belief is accompanied by the realization that divine words are like bodies which conceal treasures the value of which correspond to that of the souls they enclose.

55. Maimonides, *Guide* II, ch. 29.

56. At the beginning of his *Ma'amar Teḥ. ha-Met.,* Maimonides refers to the contradictory interpretations of Deut. 6:4, *The Lord is our God, the Lord is one,* by Jews and Christians, as a preamble to his discussion of the different Jewish interpretations of the anthropormorphic designations of God in the Bible.

57. In B. Ḥull. 80a, it is discussed whether the antelope belongs to the genus of cattle or to that of beasts of chase. Similarly in his critique of Philo, de' Rossi remains neutral in his attitude towards Philo, refusing to call him "Rav or sage, heretic or sceptic."

58. *Conf.* 14ff.

59. Ibid. 190.

Now in the passages indicated above, the divine author of the *Kuzari* wrote wisely and perceptively. For he said that the particular meaning of the words in the vocabulary of the holy tongue was not determined by convention; rather, it was formed and became current speech ever since there was breath, "a speaking breath," as Onqelos puts it.[60] Indeed, at the very moment of his creation, Adam was like a twenty-year-old, as the rabbis of blessed memory state in Bereshit Rabbah,[61] Bemidbar Rabbah,[62] and Shir Rabbah on the verse, *Go forth and gaze* (S.S. 3:11). But even though he was the only one, he had to be able to hear the voice of God speaking to him about the tree of life and knowledge. Such a voice (as is stated in the *Kuzari* about the sounds which were heard at Sinai)[63] cannot be defined in terms of philosophers' notions about prophecy, namely, the end of the process of distillation of the thoughts of the soul which then becomes attached to the active intellect. Rather, it is heard when by divine volition the air which touches the prophet's ear is fashioned with the forms of the letters which will convey the matters He wishes to communicate. The wise Recanati also wrote in a similar vein with regard to the verse, *And all the people witnessed the thunder* [lit. sounds] *and lightning.* (Ex. 20:18).[64] Yedidyah the Alexandrian also pressed home this idea in his work entitled *On the Ten Commandments*[65] and supports their statement in Shir Rabbah[66] that the actual speech was engraved by itself and its sound was heard [from one end of the world to the other]. This was why Adam needed to understand the language, as we said.

The question as to whether the other languages preexisted the generation of the dispersion was a bone of contention among the Amoraim mentioned above. One could suggest that they were the product of human selection and convention and could also describe them as divinely ordered if they were bestowed and produced for their families in their due time. They were not a new creation, but the result of inspired teaching which, as it were, propelled individuals among them to bring about the mission according to what was known. This was the drift of the citations from Jonathan ben Uzziel and the Pirqe d'Rabbi Eliezer. In other words, the angels, the providential messengers, taught each nation its language. I was also pleased to see that one of the early Christians, Origen, wrote the following in his eleventh homily[67] on Numbers:[68] "Various angels dealt with the language and speech of different nations. One could virtually say that one angel assigned the Babylonian language to one man, while another assigned the Egyptian language to another and so on with all the languages. Consequently, the language which originally had been given to Adam remained with the seed whose designated portion was neither an angel nor prince, but the divine."

60. This is Targum Onqelos's rendering of Gen. 2:7: *and man became a living soul.*
61. B.R. 14:7 (130).
62. Bem. R. 12:8.
63. *Kuzari* I, par. 89; II, par. 6.
64. Recanati, *Perush,* Gen. 22:3 (26, col. a): "The word moved in the air and the people saw the speech and the form of the letters as it is said *and all the people saw.* Indeed when somebody speaks on a cold day, the letters seem to issue from his mouth and engrave the air."
65. Philo, Dec. 32–35.
66. S.S.R. to S.S. 1:2.
67. The text reads "olympia" (i.e., Olympiad), but this must be a typographical error for "omilia."
68. Origen, *Super Numeros Homiliae* XI (*P.G.* XII, cols. 648–49).

Now having established that this chosen language was the legacy of Jacob's community alone, one should also know, as is stated in the *Kuzari,*[69] that from the time of our father Abraham, two languages were in the possession of both Abraham and his children: there was Hebrew, the language exclusively used by his descendants as a holy tongue, and Aramaic, their secular language. This situation pertained particularly to the time when they were strangers and sojourners in those countries. Although they embraced an extensive area and one region spoke a purer form of the language than the other—one might say that the Aramaic vernacular of the Chaldeans had the same status as the vernacular of children of Meshech [Tuscans] in Italy[70]—the entire or majority of the area was Aramaic speaking. In his introduction to the Aramaic grammar cited above, the author who shall remain nameless wrote as follows:[71] "The Aramaic language was used not only in the countries of Babylonia, but also in Mesopotamia (i.e., Aram Naharaim), Assyria, the cities of Arabia, and other places." And if you consult the entry for Syria in the Latin lexicon, you will have no difficulty in realizing that the name Aram embraces an incalculable number of countries.[72] Our ancestors who named the cities and places Adonai Yireh, Rehovot, Gilead, Mispeh, the tribes, the children of Joseph, and the children of Moses used etymologies for this purpose which were based on their own exclusive language. Likewise, the names of the patriarchs themselves, and particularly the names Abraham and Sarah, were actually constructed from the natural form of the language which was used by the Holy Spirit. Disregarding ibn Ezra's pronouncements about the name of Moses,[73] we should take account of the statement of Yedidyah the Alexandrian who undoubtedly knew Egyptian, and who wrote at the beginning of his *Life of Moses*[74] that the Egyptian word for water is *mos.* Such information is consistent with the given explanation for the name *[She named him Moses explaining] I drew him (meshitihu) out of the water* (Ex. 2:10), whether the Egyptian word for "water" or the Hebrew word for "drawing out" is taken into account.

Now the Israelites entered the Land [of Israel] in the time of Joshua after those who had been born in the wilderness had been cleansed of the impurities with which they became contaminated in Egypt and of their barbarous speech which resulted from their long stay in the country. For so, in my opinion, was it decreed according to His wise providence. In addition, there is the statement of the rabbis of blessed memory in chapter 48 of Pirqe d'Rabbi Eliezer,[75] Mekhilta d'Rabbi Ishmael,[76] the Tanḥuma,[77] and

69. *Kuzari* II, par. 68.

70. Ibn Ezra to Ps. 120:5 cites the *Josippon* as identifying the children of Meshech with the Tuscans (as does David Kimḥi, *Sefer ha-Shorashim,* s.v. Meshech). But according to all editions of the *Josippon,* Tubal is named as the ancestor of the Saxons.

71. Münster, *Chaldaia grammatica,* 2.

72. Calepino, *Dictionarium,* s.v. Syria: "Regio Asiae quae ab oriente fluvio Euphrate ab occidente nostro mari et Aegypto terminatur a septentrione habet Ciliciam et partem Cappadociae."

73. Ibn Ezra to Ex. 2:10: "The name Moses was translated from Egyptian into Hebrew; in Egyptian his name was Monios, as is written in the work on agriculture which was translated from Egyptian into Arabic."

74. *Mos.* I, 17.

75. PRE ch. 48: "By merit of three things did the children of Israel come out of Egypt: they did not change their language."

76. Mekhilta d' Rabbi Ishmael, bo, 5 (I, 34).

77. Tanḥuma, Balaq 16 (Buber, 25).

Shir ha-Shirim Rabbah[78] that even while they were in Egypt they did not change their language. It is therefore credible that everybody, including the common people, continued without fail to speak the holy tongue. Various reliable testimonies can be brought forward: *Then say shibbolet; but he would say sibbolet* (Jud. 12:6); then there is the expression *leḥi ḥamor* (jawbone of an ass) which is connected with *ḥamor ḥamoratayim* (heap upon heaps)[79] and there are many names of peoples and places such as Gilgal, Jerubaal, Ramat Lehi, Samuel, and Yedidyah. Similarly, as Josephus writes in book 5 (chapter 11),[80] the name Obed [lit. he who serves] which according to the women neighbors signified that he would serve Naomi in her old age was consequent on their statement *A son is born to Naom* (Ruth 4:17). There are many other such examples. While the narratives were translated into other languages, the actual names were not altered from their original form. Hezekiah's men said to Rabshakeh, *Please speak to your servants in Aramaic,* for although he is a foreigner in our land, *we understand it; do not speak to us in Judean* (which is the holy tongue) *in the hearing of all the people* (2K. 18:26). Some time ago I saw the ancient coins which belonged to the Mantuan David Finzi. The collection contained a silver coin. On one side there was a representation of a man's head, and its contours were inscribed in square Hebrew characters with the words "King Solomon," and on the obverse was a Temple and on its contours the inscription "the Temple of Solomon."[81]

Now if there is some authenticity to the book of Eldad the Danite who came from the ten tribes[82]—despite everything ibn Ezra wrote about it[83]—I could most certainly claim that the ten tribes as well as the children of Moses spoke the holy tongue.[84] Thus even on foreign soil they preserved the language which they had originally used in their own land. The same description is found in chapter 13 of 4 Ezra which is part of the Christian and Greek canon.[85] For after they had been removed into exile, they became determined to return to God and no longer intermingle with any of the gentile nations who had corrupted them. To this end, they maintained their self-imposed decision to go far away from the place to which they had been exiled.[86] A similar description is given in the work on Hebrew poetry, *Darkhe No'am,*[87] where he discusses the inscrip-

78. S.S.R. to S.S. 4:12.

79. This is a reference to Samson's statement *with the jawbone of an ass, heaps upon heaps, with the jawbone of an ass I have slain a thousand men* (Jud. 15:16) where there is a pun on the word *ḥamor* from which root words meaning both "ass" and "heaps" may be derived.

80. *Ant.* V:336.

81. The coin was probably a counterfeit.

82. Eldad the Danite, professed to belong to the tribe of Dan, living in Havilah, near Ethiopia. In *Sefer Eldad* which was first printed in Mantua, 1474–77(?) and reprinted with other legendary accounts in Venice, 1544, he describes the ten tribes, their whereabouts, and their way of life.

83. Ibn Ezra to Ex. 2:22 classifies the book of Eldad the Danite with other legendary accounts such as the book of Zerubbabel as fictional stories. Rashi and other authorities regarded it as a genuine account of the ten lost tribes.

84. Eldad describes the "sons of Moses" who were cut off from the world by the impassable river Sambatyon and spoke only Hebrew (39r).

85. 2 Esdras (or 4 Ezra) was included in the Apochrypha in the majority of Bibles but was excluded from the canon of the Greek Church. The earliest edition in the West was Jerome's Latin translation of a Greek version of the text. On 4 Ezra, see A. Hamilton, "The Book."

86. See 4 Ezra 13:40–42.

87. Moses ibn Ḥabib, *Darkhe No'am* was first printed in Constantinople in 1510 (and reprinted in

tion on the tomb of the commander of Amaziah's army. We shall write about it in the chapter on poetry, and as you shall see, it provides substantial confirmation of our argument and is most instructive. Jeremiah's words, *Thus you shall say to them* (10:11), unusually for him, were in Aramaic because he wished to make himself understood by the gentiles themselves, the inhabitants of Babylon. It is as though he were saying: "Convey these words of mine to them in a language which they understand."

There is also another point. At the beginning of the Babylonian exile, Nebuchadnezzar ordered the children to be taught the literature and language of the Chaldeans, namely, Aramaic, which implies that they did not know it previously. Daniel's sole motive in recounting the Chaldeans' discussion with the king in their own language was to demonstrate that among the various benefactions he received from the Lord was the ability to gain mastery of the language, a fact which was of even greater significance since its purity was exemplary as is easily seen by comparing Daniel's Aramaic with that which is used in Ezra or any other text we have.[88]

However, there is no question that during the seventy years of exile, all the masses of Jews who were entrenched in various foreign countries adopted a different language. In particular, they learned the Aramaic of Babylon and its environs. Such was the state of affairs until the distress about the exile caused the next generation to eschew the iniquities of their fathers who, while the first Temple was standing, had abolished and forgotten the Torah and its commandments. And so, Jehoshaphats's princes went to teach in the cities of Judah as is written in book two of Chronicles, *They offered instruction throughout Judah, having with them the Book of the Torah of the Lord* (17:9). In the time of Josiah, the priest Hilkiah as one who had news to tell pronounced, *I have found a scroll of the Torah in the House of God* (2K. 22:8). And Scripture is explicit: *Because you have forgotten the Torah of your God* (Hos. 4:6). While they were in exile, the only books and methods by which they could study the Torah were in the Aramaic tongue. They were familiar with a translated and interpreted version, a product dependent on the abilities and knowledge of certain scholars. This version contained many variant readings in vocabulary and, to a certain extent, in subject matter, for such is the fate of everything of a popular nature which gets passed from one recipient to the other. When they were again the object of God's compassion, Ezra the scribe was stirred to reinstate the Torah in an unadulterated and pure form in the Assyrian script and the holy tongue. According to the *Kuzari,*[89] it had been memorized by the priests and the Sanhedrin since there was the need to teach the true laws. But the common people, and particularly those who lived in the border towns, knew and understood only the Aramaic texts to which they had become accustomed, and this state of affairs resembled former times. In fact, from the concluding words of Nehemiah, it is evident that as a

---

Rödelheim in 1806 together with de' Rossi's ch. 60 on poetry). Ibn Ḥabib records that he saw an ancient gravestone of an army commander of Amaziah king of Judah in Valencia. The legible part of the inscription was composed in Hebrew verse. De' Rossi uses ibn Ḥabib's evidence here to corroborate the use of Hebrew in antiquity.

88. The same point is made by Levita in his introduction to the *Meturgeman* in which he declares that the Aramaic of the books of Daniel and Ezra is purer than Babylonian Aramaic which is interspersed with foreign words.

89. *Kuzari* III, par. 31.

result of the majority's minimal observance of Jewish regulations, some used to tread the wine presses and load their asses on the Sabbath[90] and half their children spoke the language of Ashdod and did not know how to speak Judean, but only the language of each and every people.[91] The Aramaic idiom was also retained by the Jerusalemites for the entire duration of the Temple period. Indeed, a hundred years before the destruction of the Temple, Hillel the elder used the vernacular for his sayings, "A name made great is a name destroyed";[92] "because you drowned [others, they drowned you]."[93] Likewise, in his description of the priests and their vestments, Josephus states:[94] "In our language (namely, in Aramaic, their language at that time), they are called *ḳahane, ḳahana rabbah, maḳhnesin, ḳetuna.*" I referred to this passage in section 1, chapter 9 and cited the actual text in chapter 49 in this fourth section. In Sanhedrin[95] and Soṭa,[96] Samuel the little, about to die, said [in Aramaic]: "Simeon and Ishmael will meet their death by the sword and his sons[97] will be executed . . . and many troubles [will come upon the world.]" And even when the oracular voice pronounced on secular matters with regard to certain saints, the words employed were Aramaic as is mentioned in Sota in the Palestinian Talmud[98] and in our Gemara[99] and in chapter 11 of Megillat Taʿanit:[100] "Johanan the high priest heard an oracular voice issue from within the Holy of Holies announcing: 'The young men who went to wage war in Antioch have been victorious.' It also happened that Simeon the righteous heard a voice issue forth from the Holy of Holies announcing, 'Annulled is the decree which the enemy. . . .' " Now I have already treated the material relevant to this topic in chapter 5 in my treatment of Yedidyah the Alexandrian, and in chapter 9 regarding the translation of the Torah. A significant point is the reference to the Aramaic expressions used by the Christian apostles. Rather than transfer the material from there to here, the reader ought to consult the passages in context for they provide essential data for the argument.

Now the widespread use of Aramaic at that time is demonstrated by the Christian translator [i.e., Jerome] in his introduction to the books of Judith and Tobit which are part of their canon, but not ours. He wrote that he had translated those books from the original Aramaic. Indeed, these persons and their story belong to the period following the Babylonian exile. This is not the case with the book of Baruch, who was a disciple of Jeremiah in Temple times.

There is the book *Ḥoḳhmeta rabbata di-Shelomoh* which is called the book of Wisdom[101] to which Ramban refers in his introduction to his commentary on the Torah, with the words "I saw an Aramaic translation of the work." He quotes from chapter 7

90. Neh. 13:15.
91. Neh. 13:24.
92. M. Avot 1:13.
93. Ibid., 2:6.
94. *Ant.* III:151–53.
95. B. Sanh. 11a.
96. B. Sota 48b.
97. The standard reading is "his colleagues" and refers probably to other martyrs at the time of the Hadrianic persecutions.
98. P. Sota 9 (13) 24b.
99. B. Sota 33a.
100. Meg. T., 345.
101. I.e., the Wisdom of Solomon in the Apocrypha.

of the work.[102] I think that it is likely that it was not translated; rather, King Solomon wrote it in Aramaic with the intention of sending it to an eastern monarch. However, Ezra handled only works which were written by the prophets under divine inspiration and in the holy tongue, and our sages wisely and judiciously adopted only the books ratified and authorized by him.

It would also appear that this practice was continued by the remnant left in Jerusalem and its environs after the destruction of the Temple. An example is the language of the books of the Zohar written by Rabbi Simeon bar Yoḥai and his colleagues; then Rabbi Johanan compiled the Palestinian Talmud in a simple Aramaic. As the rabbis of blessed memory said in Bava Qama and Megillah:[103] "Rabbi Johanan said [in Aramaic]: I remember that when I was young . . ." It was also the language used in the Mishnah and Baraita for civil documents regarding issues relating to "male and female offspring"[104] and acquisition "from the depths of the earth"[105] as is mentioned by the author of *Sefer Keritut.*[106] In this context, there is no reason to refer to the Aramaic of our Gemara and of some of our prayers. After all, that was the language of the Babylonian sages and the orders of the prayers formulated by them in Babylon. As the Tosafists said in the name of Rabbi Isaac,[107] the Qaddish[108] was [in Aramaic] because the common people in Babylon only understood Aramaic which was their language.

Indeed, at the time of the destruction of the second Temple, the Lord acted kindly; His mercy was not spent.[109] And so, to ensure that His holy Torah, with its script and language, was not erased from the memory of His seed, He inspired all the sagacious Tannaim, in particular our holy Rabbi,[110] and among other traditions, they transmitted the holy tongue and holy script to us in its correct state. This was the case for the text of the Pentateuch, Prophets, and Hagiographa (these, at any rate according to the response of Hillel the elder to the proselyte, we received from them[111]) as well as for the Mishnayot, Baraitot, and Toseftot among which there was total consistency—the tongue of the righteous is choice silver.[112] Moreover, on many occasions, the study of *halakhah* becomes directed through the realization that the anonymous talmudic

102. I.e., 7:4–6, 17–21. Ramban was the first Jewish commentator to refer to the Wisdom of Solomon. In his edition of Wisdom (8), Reider conjectures that Ramban's references are to a Syriac version transliterated into Hebrew characters.

103. B. Meg. 5b. There is no such passage in B. B.Q.

104. This is an allusion to M. Ket. 4:10–11 in which the legacy arrangements for male and female offspring in the marriage contract are discussed in Aramaic.

105. This is a reference to B. B.B. 63b which is about the selling of an apartment. The expression, "Acquire for yourself possession from the depths of the earth to the height of heaven," must be inserted into the contract.

106. Samson of Chinon, *Sefer Keritut,* leshon limmudim, 2, par. 36 (252–53).

107. Tos. to B. Ber. 3a, s.v. *ve-onim.*

108. The Qaddish is an Aramaic prayer recited by mourners during the daily and festival services. It is also recited between major units of the public liturgy and after particular study sessions.

109. 'His . . . spent,' cf. Lam. 3:22.

110. I.e., Judah the patriarch, the compiler of the Mishnah.

111. In B. Shabb. 31a, Hillel proves the need to accept the authority of the tradition of the oral Torah to a prospective proselyte. One day he taught him the order of the Hebrew alphabet, and the next day reversed the order. When the prospective proselyte objected, he replied: "Must you then not rely on me? Then rely on me with respect to the Oral Torah as well."

112. 'Tongue . . . silver,' cf. Pr. 10:20.

authority inserts some Aramaic words into the statements of the Tannaim that we mentioned. Perhaps it was with a view of reinforcing this point that they also aroused the people's sentiments with regard to public prayer. For although it belonged to the category of things which may be said in any language, they laid down (particularly since it corresponded to the continual sacrifice[113]) that it could only be said in the distinguished language instituted by the Men of the Great Synagogue,[114] and not in the Aramaic language. As they said in Berakhot [*sic*][115] and Sota:[116] "A person should never make a request in the Aramaic language because the ministering angels will not pay attention to him." They also said that the angels do not understand Aramaic, which, as the Toasafists say,[117] is a rhetorical way of demonstrating that in their opinion, the language was too inferior to be used as a vehicle for conveying our prayers into the holy Sanctuary. The entire objective was to ensure that any public invocation in the name of the Lord, whether through the reading of the Torah or prayer, should no longer be effected by means of a corrupt Aramaic version which they had used in the past. Rather, as far as was possible, the Torah would be reinstated in its inn which had been furnished precisely.[118] Perhaps the story recounted in the Palestinian Talmud tractate Shabbat[119] and in chapter 15 of tractate Soferim,[120] is to be assigned a reason of this kind: "It happened that Rabban Gamaliel was standing on the precincts of the Temple Mount when they brought him the Aramaic version of the book of Job. He said to the builder: 'Bury it under the rubble.'" It stands to reason that it must have been one of the popular versions which did not provide an exact rendering of the text of holy Scripture. However, in an effort to ensure that the common people did not cease to understand the Torah according to their own ability, it became the practice in certain places to provide a *meturgeman* (a translator). And so in Berakhot,[121] they instituted that the reading of the pericopes should be completed by a recitation of Targum Onqelos which was purged of any errors seven times over. You are aware of the statement of the Semag and his colleagues[122] that some people hold that [Rashi's] commentary is more relevant for us than Targum.

But let us resume our discussion of the holy tongue. It is fitting that we should mention in this connection the statement in Megillah in the Palestinian Talmud[123] and in Midrash Esther:[124] "Four languages are appropriate for general use: the vernacular

113. Cf. B. Ber. 26b: "The daily prayers were instituted to correspond to the daily sacrifices."

114. In B. Ber. 33a, it is said that the Men of the Great Synagogue established the prayers for Israel.

115. B. Shabb. 12b.

116. B. Sota 33a.

117. Tos. to B. Shabb. 12b, s.v. *she-en*. This is only implied by the Tosafists who claim that the angels must surely know all human thoughts.

118. This is a play on an expression in B. B.M. 85a: "Torah seeks its inn."

119. P. Shabb. 16 (1) 15c.

120. Sof. 15:2.

121. B. Ber. 8a. The Targum Onqelos is not specified here, but since it was later custom to read Targum Onqelos, de' Rossi inferred that it was to this Targum they were referring.

122. Moses of Coucy, *Sefer Miṣvot ha-Gadol,* positive commandment, 19. Semag states that he considered that [Rashi's] commentary was more useful than the Targum, although this was not the opinion of Rabbi Isaac and Rav Amram on the authority of Rav Natronai who said that the Targum was worthy of being given at Sinai.

123. P. Meg. 1 (9) 71b.

124. Est. R. 4:12 to Est. 1:22.

for song; Roman (Latin) for war (*qerav*); Sorsi (Syriac) for lament (*ileya*); Hebrew for speech." The term "vernacular" signifies the Greek vernacular. However you should know that there is a specific literary Greek as well as the spoken language.[125] Our rabbis of blessed memory referred to it in Megillah[126] when they said that the Greek vernacular is valid for all [Jewish] people.[127] I discovered that our sages used both forms of the language on different occasions. For example, there is the word *asemon* which means bullion;[128] *moros,* a fool, used in the Pesiqta[129] for the expression "hear you fools" which is the vernacular. From this word, in my view, is derived the expression "books of Miros" used at the end of Yadayim[130] and in Ḥullin[131] meaning "books of nonsense." Then there is also the word *diateqe* which means a covenant, in other words a contract. Therefore in Bava Meṣia[132] they say *da tehe lemeqam* (this shall be established and executed)—this etymology is only used because the Aramaic is clearer than the Greek. A similar play on words occurs with the word *apoteqe* which they refer to as *apo tehe qa'e*[133] and *qapendriah* (a shortcut):[134] "Instead of going round the block, I will go through here,"[135] and there are other examples. These are certainly Greek words, but they nevertheless made mnemonic forms of the words in Aramaic. But the word *hydor* which we mentioned in the chapter about Aqylas which means "water": and the word *ariston* which means "dinner" are examples of the literary language.

There is no doubt that "Roman" means Latin. And the meaning of the word *qerav* is public oration as they say in Sukkah[136] and in Shir Rabbah with regard to the verse, *Who is this that comes up . . . with the powders of the merchant* (S.S. 3:6): "What is meant by "powders of the merchant"? One who is learned in Scripture and Mishnah, a leader in prayer (*qarov*) and poet."

It is clear from the Mekhilta[137] and chapter 3 of Pesaḥim[138] that Sorsi means Aramaic: "Rabbi Josiah said: *[In proportion to the number of persons] you shall contribute (taḵhossu) for the lamb* (Ex. 12:4). This is a Syrian expression, and is to be illustrated by a man who says to his friend, 'Slaughter (*ḵos*) this lamb for me.' "[139] And in Bava Qama it is stated: "The Syrian language has its share of glory in the Pentateuch with the

125. It is highly unlikely that the rabbis were making a distinction between written and spoken Greek. Perhaps de' Rossi became aware of these kind of distinctions from the humanists' discussion of whether there was a difference between the spoken and written language of the ancient Romans. (On this, see M. Tavoni, *Latino.*) He may have also had in mind the difference between *ḵoine* and classical Greek.

126. B. Meg. 18a.

127. I.e., regardless of whether they are Greek speakers or not.

128. B. B.M. 44a.

129. Pes. d' R. Kah. 14 (246–47).

130. M. Yad. 4:6: "We complain about you Pharisees for according to you the holy Scriptures defile the hands, whereas the writing of Miram do not." The word Miram or Hamiram has no connection with *moros.* In ch. 2, de' Rossi also connects the word *moros* with the name of Homer.

131. B. Ḥull. 60b: "There are many verses which to all appearances ought to be burnt like the books of Miram." The expression "books of Miram" is missing from some texts as a result of censorship.

132. B. B.M. 19a.

133. See Rashi to B. B.Q. 11b.

134. The word *compendiaria* is actually Latin.

135. This etymology based on Aramaic is given in B. Meg. 29a.

136. As Cassel notes, de' Rossi is referring to Pes. d'R. Kah. 27 (for Tabernacles) 27:1 (404).

137. Mekhilta d'Rabbi Ishmael, pisḥa, 3 (I, 28).

138. B. Pes. 61a.

139. I.e., *taḵhossu* means "you shall slaughter."

expression *yegar sahaduta* (Gen. 31:47), and in the Prophets [with the Aramaic expression], *Thus you shall say to them* (Jer. 10:11). In his commentary to the end of tractate Sota, Rashi wrote:[140] "The Syrian language is akin to Aramaic, and I would say that it is the language of the Palestinian Talmud and the Arabs call it Syriac." And Rabbenu Tam may have been right when he said that the purest and best variety of Aramaic is that spoken in the vicinity of Syria.[141] {The word *ileya* is a Greek word for the sound of moaning and dirges. Thus in Arakhin there is the statement: "It was *ileya* that came to his mouth." According to Rashi, the word *ileya* means dirge just as the word *qinah* in the verse, *Take up a lament (qinah) on the heights* (Jer. 7:29) is rendered in the Targum by the word *ileya.*}

And what is last is best,[142] the Hebrew language—that is, the holy tongue—which is beautiful for speech. What greater quality and beauty can there be than the language which was actually part of the nature of the first man when he came out of the womb of his mother earth, and which was also the language of his offspring, the fruit of his womb, until the sin was perpetuated in the time of Peleg? How can its excellence be surpassed when we find that it was used by the living God to pronounce all the words of Torah and prophecy and is unique to the holy people and the holy Land. Thus the statement of Ramban of blessed memory at the beginning of pericope *tissa* is correct,[143] and so too, Efodi at the end of his work,[144] in the company of the most authoritative grammarians, who said that it was for this reason that our rabbis called it the holy tongue. Furthermore, the teacher of the *Guide* (part 3, chapter 8) is not wrong when he said that it was designated in this way because it did not contain the primary nouns and verbs relating the pudenda. And in my eyes, there is reason to be surprised at ibn Ezra's comment on the verse in Isaiah, *In that day there shall be five towns in the land of Egypt speaking the language of Canaan* (19:18). He states that it implies that the Canaanites were speaking the holy tongue.[145] Regarding the verse [said by Joseph to his brothers], *You can see for yourselves . . . that it is indeed I who who am speaking to you* (Gen. 45:12), Ramban also states that the language in question is the language of Canaan.[146] But Isaiah's prophecy refers to Onias's altar which was erected in the city of Alexandria in Egypt with the sanction of Ptolemy of which our rabbis of blessed memory speak at the end of Menaḥot[147] and which we have discussed in some of these chapters.[148] He therefore implies that due to the large immigration of Israelites to those cities, they would learn the language of Israel, the inhabitants of Canaan, namely, the Aramaic language which was used by the Jews at that time during the second Temple period. A

140. Rashi to B. Sota 49b, but most editions read "nations of the world" (rather than "Arabs").

141. Tos. to B. B.Q. 83a.

142. This is a common saying, cf., e.g., B.R. 78:8 (925).

143. Ramban to Ex. 30:13.

144. Profayt Duran, *Maʿaseh,* ch. 33 (177–78).

145. Ibn Ezra to Is. 19:18 and a similar statement is made by Elijah Levita in his *Meturgeman.* In the preface, he states that when Abraham and his children came to Canaan they spoke the native language which was Hebrew.

146. Ramban, unlike Rashi, Ibn Ezra, and Kimḥi believed that Joseph spoke to his brothers in Hebrew, i.e., in the Canaanite language.

147. B. Men. 109b.

148. Chs. 21 and 22.

similar interpretation is given by Rashi when he says:[149] "The language of Canaan is the language spoken by Jews in the land of Canaan." He does not categorically state that it was the Israelites' language, but simply the language of the Jews during their stay in the land of Canaan. And Ramban's use of the verse, *it is indeed I who who am speaking to you* to prove his position is refuted by our sages of blessed memory in Tanḥuma, in Vayiqra Rabbah and Shir Rabbah when they state that despite their dispersion from one place to another, our ancestors did not change their language. Accordingly, as Rashi states regarding the verse under discussion, the reference is to the holy tongue.

Now I have a valuable and original idea to contribute to the explanation of those sages to account for the application of the term "holy" to our language. It is as follows. From the very beginning it was a divine creation for Adam, as we noted, and was not formulated by human convention as were the other languages, for although they were lent divine assistance they are, as with everything human, all subject to destruction. As we have already written in this chapter on the basis of the passage quoted from the Zohar, it alone will remain together with the other parts of creation about which it was said, *And God saw all that which He had made and it was very good* (Gen. 1:31). The appellation "holy" is therefore most apt because it signifies duration and eternity. The verse, *[And those who remain in Zion and are left in Jerusalem—all who are inscribed for life in Jerusalem] shall be called holy* (Is. 4:3) is glossed by our sages of blessed memory in Sanhedrin:[150] "Just as the Holy One endures forever, so too the righteous will live forever."

You should know that every person regards his own method as flawless and that natives appreciate their own place of residence.[151] In the first five chapters of the second book of *De pulsuum differentiis,*[152] Galen the Greek physician had the audacity to write that the beauty of the Greek language surpasses all other languages, not only in its scope and richness of resources, but also in its spoken idiom, in comparison to which they all sound like the roaring of the animal species or the chirping of birds and insects.[153] However, the teacher Maimon [Maimonides] of blessed memory who wherever possible stands up for us, takes him to task for this at the end of his book on medicine, the *Chapters of Moses.* In the same passage[154] he gives him deserved castigation for his attack on the servant of the Lord, Moses, about the function of eyebrows in chapter 14 of the eleventh book of his *De usu partium.*[155] Through his censure of Galen, we come to appreciate the virtue and humility of the teacher of blessed memory [i.e., Maimonides]. For despite his fury at these faults of his, he never refrains from describing him as a person who has total mastery of his profession, namely, medicine, which is the subject

149. Rashi to Is. 19:18.

150. B. Sanh. 92a.

151. This expression is used in B. Sota 47a in response to the problem raised as to how the men of Jericho (2K. 2:19) could say that *the situation of the city was pleasant when the water was nothing and the ground barren.*

152. *De pulsuum differentiis* II, 5 (vol. VIII, 586).

153. This passage is also quoted by Johanan Alemanno (fifteenth-century mystical philosopher) in his discussion about the Hebrew language. See M. Idel, *Language,* 137–38.

154. *Pirqe Mosheh,* ch. 25 (372ff.).

155. *De usu partium* XI, 14 (vol. III, 904). Galen suggests that according to Moses, God ordered that the hair of the eyebrows should not grow long. On Maimonides' response, see R. Walzer, *Galen,* 33–35.

of that book. He merely says that he was afflicted with the common disease of imagining that because he is a master of one discipline, he is also a master and expert critic in other subjects.[156] At any rate, we do have a future and great hope regarding our holy tongue contained in the positive prediction which was uttered by the Lord about the time in which we are to come from darkness to a great light: *For then I will make the peoples pure of speech so that they all invoke the Lord by name and serve him with one accord* (Zeph. 3:9). Amen, may He fulfill this promise soon in our own days.

156. *Pirqe Mosheh* (363).

CHAPTER FIFTY-EIGHT

On the antiquity of the characters of the holy tongue.

Now the fact is that an explicit mishnah in the fifth chapter of Avot[1] and two *baraitot* of a similar nature in Pesaḥim[2] indicate that the characters must date back to the time in which Adam set foot on earth. It reads: "Ten things were created on the eve of the Sabbath: the writing and the script." Although the entire section is replete with matters worthy of investigation as is evident from the wise Don Isaac's commentary to Avot entitled *Naḥalat Avot,* there is no doubt that Rashi's interpretation of the mishnah conveys their meaning. He said that the "writing" refers to the letters and the "script" to the words. And in his gloss on the Pesaḥim passage, he makes the additional statement that the "letters" are those which were inscribed on the tablets. Examine the passage. Rambam [Maimonides] of blessed memory interpreted the mishnah in a similar way when he said: "The writing is the Torah about which it is stated *[and I will give you the stone tablets with the teachings and commandments] which I have written* (Ex. 24:12). The script refers to the writing on the tablets about which it is said, *and the writing was God's writing* (ibid. 32:16)." The argument that we put forward previously certainly pertains here. Just as Adam needed to be able to understand the language which he heard and spoke, so too he needed to know the letters of the script to ensure that something precious would remain imprinted for himself or for his descendants, whether close or distant, both in life and death. Therefore it was essential that the first letters to be formed were applied to our unique language which was the holy tongue as we said. The sage of the *Kuzari*[3] spoke about them when he wrote that just as the language embodied the specific nature of what was named, so the shapes of its letters are not accidental and without purpose, but are completely congruent with every letter for which reason it was called God's writing. He also writes in the same context: "The grouping of the letters accords with the order of the macrocosm and microcosm." All these statements of his are undoubtedly said on authority of the *Sefer Yeṣirah* which was followed by all the true and righteous kabbalists. Go and examine the wise Ḥayyat's commentary on the *Maʿarekhet ha-Elohut* where in the section on names[4] he cites many

1. M. Avot 5:6.
2. B. Pes. 54a.
3. *Kuzari* IV, par. 25.
4. Judah ben Jacob Ḥayyat, *Minḥat Jehudah,* Commentary to *Maʿarekhet ha-Elohut,* ch. 3.

important passages from the *Sefer Yeṣirah,* the *Bahir,* and the *Zohar* and other holy writings where they take their signs as indication[5] that the letters were in existence ever since the day that the Lord God made the earth and heavens. As ibn Ezra wrotes in his famous riddle about the four brothers[6]—they are the letters *alef, heh, vav, yod*—on the day when Adam was created, these were created. In chapter 57 I already mentioned the Targum of [ps.] Jonathan ben Uzziel on the verse, *thus the Lord scattered them* (Gen. 11:8) and Rabbi Eliezer's statements in his Chapters where they speak about the seventy angels who were appointed over the seventy nations at the time of the dispersion: "and each one with its language and character of its script in hand." It would appear that in their view, each nation's language and script were both invented under divine inspiration. In that case, there can be no doubt that Adam was endowed with the holy tongue and script from remote antiquity.

This subject is even treated by Pliny, a great pagan writer. In the seventh book of his *Natural History* he wrote:[7] "I believe that the Assyrian letters always existed." He cited proofs of the great antiquity of the Egyptian letters, which implied that the Assyrian letters must have preexisted them by seven hundred years. However, it is not known who initiated their use. He therefore came to the conclusion that they always had existed.

Similarly, in his *Questions on Exodus*[8] and in the fifteenth book of his *City of God,* Augustine ratified the opinion expressed above. And in book 18[9] he pours scorn on those who hold that the language of the Jews came into use from the time of Eber and the letters from the time of Moses on the grounds that the transmission of both the letters and the language was simultaneous.

Furthermore, at the beginning of book 1, the ancient writer Berosus the Chaldean wrote that sages predicted the deluge and inscribed their prophecies on marble.[10] Josephus writes in a similar vein in chapter 3 of book 1[11] when he says that the sons of Seth, who was the son of Adam, constructed two pillars, one of marble and one of stone, on which they inscribed their inventions. He reported that he had seen the marble pillar in the land of Seiris.

Likewise, in his letter of rules,[12] one of the Christian apostles mentions these two pillars and alleges that Enoch engraved the one of stone, the other of bronze, with predic-

5. 'Take . . . indication.' This is a play on the word for letter and sign (*ot*) based on Ps. 74:4.

6. This is the grammatical riddle which was published at the beginning of the Bomberg Rabbinic Bible (1524–25) among others, at the end of ibn Ezra's preface to his Commentary on the Bible.

7. *Nat. hist.* 7, 56: "Litteras semper arbitror Assyrias fuisse."

8. *Quaestiones ad Exodum,* 69 (*P.L.* XXXIV, col. 620).

9. *De civ. Dei,* bk. 18, ch. 39 (*P.L.* XLI, col. 598).

10. Annius, *Berosus* (vol. I, 74). The text reads "stone" not "marble": "Tum multi praedicabant et vaticabantur et lapidibus excidebant."

11. *Ant.* I:70–71.

12. In Jude 14:3 there is a vague allusion to this prophecy: *And Enoch, . . . saying, Behold the Lord comes with ten thousand of his saints,* and v.15 *to execute judgment upon all.*" But de' Rossi's source is predictably Annius, commentary to *Berosus,* bk. I (vol. 1, 69): "Nam, ut patet Genesis, sanctus propheta Enoch natus est ante inundationem terrarum anno 34 supra mille qui teste Iuda Apostolo cognomine Thadeo in sua canonica prophetavit de iudicio futuro tam aquarum diluvii quam ultimae conflagrationis et ea teste Josephi in primo de antiquitate Iudaica inscribit duabus columnas, altera aerea, altera lateritia."

tions of two major catastrophes, a flood and a conflagration. Furthermore, at the beginning of book 3,[13] Berosus wrote: "So now we should speak about how the world, which was left desolate and empty, had been replete with inhabitants and tillers of the soil. Indeed, as was right, Noah and his family descended from Mount Gordio to the plain below which was full of corpses. Thus until this day, it is called Mryi Adam. (I.e., of the children of Adam whose entrails issued forth. Since they were speaking the holy tongue at that time it may be that the word derives from the word *murato* (Lev. 1:16) which is translated in the Targum as 'its [the bird's] crop.')[14] And he commemorated the event by inscribing it on stone, and the local inhabitants call that place 'the issue of Noah.' "

Indeed, the antiquity of the practice of engraving in stone as memorials in perpetuity is also attested by [ps.] Xenophon the Greek in his work *On Synonyms*[15] in his discussion of the word "generation" [*aetas*]. He writes that the famous Queen Semiramis, who was the fourth ruler from Nimrod, erected a pillar as a monument to herself and engraved it with the names of all her forbears from Noah onwards. Annius supplies the same information derived from Archilochus in his introduction to the work of Berosus.[16] Furthermore, under the entry for Adam on whom he lavishes praise, their ancient commentator Suidas[17] writes that Adam undoubtedly invented the letters and that subsequently, after their dispersion over the earth, it was from him that each one learned [the letters] in his own language.

Thus there is no lack of witnesses in all the languages of the nations, the good, the pure, and impure alike,[18] as to the fact that all the letters are of ancient origin. In particular, we learn that the characters that pertain to the holy tongue were not only in existence from the time of the giving of our Torah, but even from the six days of creation; in fact, even earlier, if one would accept that it is possible, taking our sages' saying literally, which was cited by Rashi in his comment on the passage in Pesaḥim quoted above, that the Torah preexisted the world, written with black fire on white fire. But in any case there is no doubt that it is appropriate to believe that the saying contains an arcane allusion. For according to all those who know how to interpret,[19] time, which is a prerequisite for a conception of before and after, was included together with all the hosts of heaven and earth as part of the creation.

However, the question of whether these were the letters in which our Torah was given from Sinai in the holy tongue, on the Tablets or in the book which our master Moses wrote as is known, was a bone of contention among the ancients, first among the Tannaim and subsequently among the Amoraim. And if the author of *Iqqarim*[20] is worthy of being given a central place in this study, we could also say that the later

13. Ibid., 117.

14. The passage in brackets is de' Rossi's gloss.

15. Annius, [ps.] Xenophon, *De aequivocis* (vol. 1, 17).

16. Ibid., 58.

17. De' Rossi also refers to the *Suidas* as though it was the name of a person. He would have consulted a Latin translation of the work. See Hieronymus Wolfius's translation, Basel 1564, s.v. Adam, col. 17–21.

18. 'The good . . . alike,' cf. Eccl. 9:2.

19. 'Those who know . . . interpet' is an allusion to 1Chr. 12:32 where the expression is used of those who know how to interpret the times.

20. I.e., Joseph Albo.

authorities were also divided on this issue. The basic Tannaitic passage is in the Tosefta, in tractate Sanhedrin,[21] and it is cited in Gemara Sanhedrin which reads as follows:[22]

> Rabbi Jose said: "The Torah would have been given through Ezra because of his merit, had Moses not preceded him. And even though the Torah was not given through him, the script was changed by him as it says, *And the writing of the letter was written in Aramaic* (Ezra 4:7). And it is written: *And they could not read the writing* (Dan. 5:8)—this means that he gave it on that very day.[23] And it is also written, *And he shall write the copy (mishneh) of the Torah* (Deut. 17:18), that is, in a script which is destined to be changed (*le-hishtanot*). And why was it called Assyrian? Because it was imported by them from Assyria."

The Tosefta reads: "The script and language were also given through him, as it says, *And the writing of the letter was written in Aramaic and translated into Aramaic.*" Likewise in tractate Megillah of the Palestinian Talmud, they cite Rabbi Jose's words and then add: "Rabbi Nathan said that the Torah was given in the *raʿaṣ* script which view accords with that of Rabbi Jose." We have already discussed the meaning of the word *raʿaṣ* in chapter 56. Furthermore, in chapter 2 of Sanhedrin in the Babylonian Gemara, it states:[24]

> The Torah was given in the Assyrian script, but when they sinned it was substituted by the *roʿaṣ* script (and in the Tosefta it states, "and when they sinned, their language was changed"). When they repented in the days of Ezra, it was changed back into the Assyrian script as it says, *And he shall write for himself a copy of the Torah,* that is, a script which is destined to be changed. Rabbi Simeon ben Eliezer said on authority of Rabbi Eleazer ben Parṭa in the name of Rabbi Eleazar of Modin: "This writing was never changed at all as it says, *The vavs* (hooks) *of the pillars* (Ex. 27:10). Just as the pillars were not changed, so too the *vavs*[25] were not changed." And it is also stated: *And to the Jews according to their writing and language* (Est. 8:9). Just as their language did not change, so too their script was not changed. Then how can I understand the expression "a copy of the Torah"? This refers to the two copies of the Torah which one writes. (But then they raise objections). According to the one who says that the script was never changed at all, what can be the meaning of the phrase *they could not read the writing.* (A solution is given.) It was written in *gematria.*

And in the Palestinian Talmud as well as in the Tosefta the reading is as follows: "Rabbi said: 'The Torah was given in the Assyrian script' " and it then concludes: "Rabbi Simeon ben Eleazar said: 'The Torah was given in the Assyrian script.' What is the meaning of the expression *the hooks of the pillars?* The *vavs* of the Torah are like the pillars."

Thus the controversy between Rabbi Jose, Rabbi and Rabbi Simeon are presented in the same passage of the Tosefta. Rabbi Jose and likewise Rabbi Nathan whose view is cited in the Palestinian Talmud cited above agree that Ezra found that they were using the *raʿaṣ* script, that is, the *ever ha-nahar* script in which the Torah was given, which is also described as the Libonaʾah script, whether its interpretation is according to Rashi

21. T. Sanh. 4:7.
22. B. Sanh. 21b.
23. I.e., only Daniel could read the script which means that the letters were not promulgated until Ezra's time.
24. B. Sanh. 22a.
25. This is a play on *vav* meaning "pillar" and the letter *vav.*

of blessed memory that they were large characters similar to those used for amulets or according to the Tosafists, that it was the name of a place. Similarly, he found that they were using the Aramaic language which they had learned during their exile in Babylon. He [Ezra] transposed the script and language and gave them the Assyrian script and the Hebrew language, that is the holy tongue. But our holy Rabbi and Rabbi Simeon on authority of Rabbi Eleazar and Rabbi Eliezer agreed that the Torah was given in the Assyrian script. We need not be concerned about the disagreement between Rabbi and Rabbi Simeon as to whether it was changed in the period between Sinai and the time of Ezra. It is enough that they agree that it was given in the Assyrian script at Sinai. In chapter 56 we noted that the holy sheqel was inscribed in the *ever ha-nahar* script and the holy tongue. Perhaps that coin was minted during the first Temple period. If so, it would fit with Rabbi's view that the script was changed between the time of Moses and Ezra. In view of this controversy it states in the Palestinian Talmud in Megillah: "Rabbi Levi said: According to the view that the Torah was given in *raʿaṣ* characters, the letter *ayin* was a miraculous phenomenon. But he who says that the Torah was given in Assyrian characters, the *samekh* was a miraculous phenomenon." We discussed this in chapter 56. It is true that in his commentary on Sanhedrin, Rashi of blessed memory endeavored to manipulate Rabbi Jose's view and argued that he too held the view that the Torah was given in the Assyrian script. I would also love to be able to hold such a view. But it is problematic since the opinions of Rabbi Jose, Rabbi, and Rabbi Simeon are presented in the Tosefta in the form of a controversy between all three. According to his [i.e., Rashi's] view, Rabbi's opinion that the Torah was given in the Assyrian script but was changed for the *raʿaṣ* script when they sinned is identical with Rabbi Jose's view. And if you say, as emerges from his commentary that there were those who forgot it, there is the explicit pronouncement in the Palestinian Talmud about Rabbi Nathan's view that it was given in the *roʿaṣ* script which accords with that of Rabbi Jose's. And then there is Rabbi Levi who said: "He who claims that the Torah was given in *roʿaṣ* characters, the letter *ayin* was a miraculous phenomenon" this refers then to the *ever ha-nahar* script. Then there is the view of Mar Zuṭra[26] that the Torah was given in the Hebrew script. Now you might grant that Rabbi Jose's view is being expressed by Mar Zuṭra. But if you claim that Rabbi Jose's view is the same as Rabbi's, whose view can one rely on since all the Tannaim contradict his opinion? Accordingly, Rabbi Jose and Rabbi Nathan or at least Rabbi Nathan alone is of the opinion that the Torah was given in the *ever ha-nahar* script.

Likewise there is a controversy among the Amoraim. We read in Sanhedrin:[27] "Mar Zuṭra said or some say Mar Uqba: Originally the Torah was given to Israel in the Hebrew script and in the holy tongue. The Torah was restored to them again in the time of Ezra in the Assyrian script and the Aramaic language. They selected the Assyrian script and the holy tongue for Israel, and the Hebrew script and the Aramaic language were left for the *hedyotot*. Who were the *hedyotot?* Mar Ḥisda said: the Cutheans." In the same context as well as in tractates Shabbat[28] and Megillah,[29] Rav

26. I.e., in B. Sanh. 21b.
27. B. Sanh. 21b.
28. B. Shabb. 104a.
29. B. Meg. 2b–3a.

Ḥisda states that the *mem* and the *samekh* which were in the tablets stood by a miracle. In other words, it was in the Assyrian script. Likewise in tractate Megillah in the Palestinian Talmud[30] Rabbi Levi said: "In the Torah of the ancients, neither the *he* nor the *mem* was closed, which means that the *samekh* was closed." I saw an explanation for this phenomenon, as I think (if there is no error in the reading), in a work which is actually in my possession. It is about the characters of thirteen languages and was written by brother Theseo of Pavia and printed in 1539 according to their era.[31] It contains two kinds of alphabets which are used by the inhabitants of Syria[32] (i.e., Suria or Sorsi as was said previously[33]), who are known to have come from the land of Israel. The most common form of the *he* is closed thus ܗand likewise the *mem* ܡ. Rabbi Levi therefore meant that the script of the ancient [lit. first] Jews did not contain these two closed letters—in other words they did not use this script which subsequently, in the time of Rabbi Levi himself, was used in Syria. Rather, the *samekh* was closed, which meant that they were using the Assyrian script as Rav Ḥisda said. When he speaks of the closed *mem,* he is referring to the earliest form of the *mem,* for in the Assyrian script one is open and the other closed, whereas in the Syrian script there is only one form which is closed. Indeed, it is known that no other script apart from the holy script contains the letters which have both a medial and final form. Therefore he said that the ancients did not always have a closed *mem.* Thus, Mar Zuṭra's view accords with that of Rabbi Jose and Rabbi Nathan, whereas Rav Ḥisda and Rabbi Levi agree with that of Rabbi Simeon and Rabbi.

Among the latter authorities, Rabbi Joseph Albo tends to espouse the view of Rabbi Jose. Ritba [Yomtov ben Abraham] expresses the view of the Tosafists[34] who basing themselves on various kabbalistic notions, ascribe the highest esoteric meanings to the forms of the letters and other evidence which they assemble.[35] They therefore adamantly refuse to entertain the idea that the Sinaitic Torah was given in any other than the Assyrian script. You, reader, do not find it burdensome to draw water from their sources in joy for they are sweeter than honey and sacred. Similarly, the responsum (74) of Rabbi Moses al-Ashqar[36] contains citations of the Geonim, Rav Sherira, and Rav Hai who go to lengths to prove that the Torah was written in the Assyrian script. And in the responsum, Rambam of blessed memory is cited:[37] "It is forbidden to write in the Assyrian script in which the Torah was indeed given. The only exceptions are the holy Writings. Jews have always taken great precautions to maintain this rule. In fact, their letters, secular books, and inscriptions on coins and holy sheqels are all in the Hebrew script. That is why the Sephardim are accustomed to use other characters with the result that a totally different script was reconstructed which is permitted for use." And

30. P. Meg. 1 (9) 71c.
31. Theseo Ambrogio (Albonesius), *Introductio.* (This was the book that de' Rossi used to learn Syriac.)
32. *Introductio,* 9. "Chaldaeorum literae qui Syriam incolunt quae etiam Syriacae dicuntur."
33. See ch. 57 and his discussion of P. Meg. 1 (9) 71b.
34. De' Rossi writes in error: "The Ritba in the name of the Tosafists."
35. *Ḥiddushe ha-Ritba* to B. Meg. 2b (col. 23). De' Rossi also refers to his comment in Sanhedrin.
36. Moses b. Isaac al-Ashqar, *She'elot,* responsum 74 (137r–138v).
37. Ibid., 138r–v. He cites the letter as quoted in the *Orḥot Ḥayyim* by the fifteenth-century Provençal scholar Aaron of Lunel.

al-Ashqar himself concludes thus:[38] "However, the scrolls and all the books of the Samaritans are written in the Hebrew script and even nowadays, they insist that the Torah was given in that script, and that they have in Shechem a scroll of Torah which goes back to the time of Phineas ben Elazar. They make many other claims of a similar nature." And in his introduction, the wise Efodi of blessed memory writes about the ninth of the fifteen methods of improving the memory for the study of Torah[39] "which is to facilitate study of Scripture and Gemara by means of the biblical text written in the Assyrian script which has the most excellent of characters and in which the divine Torah was given according to the view of the holy Rabbi, and it is true." This statement is comparable to their saying[40] that the declaration of a rule implies that the subject was a matter of controversy. Indeed, I was amazed that any controversy should arise with regard to this matter since in the passage which we quoted from the Palestinian Talmud it is stated: "The letters *mnṣpḵ* derive from Sinai. What are these letters? That which the watchers instituted for you. Who were those watchers? It happened on a stormy day when the scholars did not come to the school, the children . . ." This story is also related in the Gemara in Shabbat[41] and there they raise the question. "Surely, since it is written *These are the commandments* (Lev. 27:34) no prophet is henceforth permitted to make any innovation." They then reach the solution: "Rather they had forgotten them and then they came and reinstituted them." Indeed, these double letters are not found in any Hebrew, Arabic, or Aramaic script apart from the Assyrian script as we noted. If it is the case that they forgot them after they had been given at Sinai and then they were reinstituted, how come that they became a matter of controversy? If you consult the passage in chapter one of the Laws of the Phylacteries of Rambam of blessed memory in which he states that phylacteries and *mezuzot* may only be written in the Assyrian script,[42] you will notice that the glosses[43] contain references to many statements of our rabbis in Shabbat and Menaḥot[44] and in Ḥagigah in the Palestinian Talmud[45] and Bereshit Rabbah[46] where they are concerned about the forms of the characters. There they discuss and expound the reason as to why the letter *he* has a crownlet and the roof of the *ḥet,* a vertical stroke, and why the *bet* has two pointed strokes, and so on. Thus in addition to the other relevant aspects of this topic that we have raised or not, we are brought to the point where we can truly conclude that the tablets and the Torah were given in none other than the Assyrian script. And I was surprised at Rabbi Jose, who on various occasions says that he has deep reasons for whatever he says,[47] could have been the initiator of this debate. And I was also surprised

38. Ibid., 138v.
39. Profayt Duran, *Ma'aseh Efod,* Introduction, 21.
40. Cf. B. Ber. 33b.
41. B. Shabb. 104a.
42. *Mishneh Torah,* Tefillin I:19.
43. I.e., the *Haggahot Maimuniyyot* from the school of Meir b. Baruch of Rothenburg which was first printed with the *Mishneh Torah,* Constantinople, 1509.
44. B. Men. 29b.
45. P. Ḥag. 2 (1) 77c.
46. B.R. 1:10 (9).
47. E.g., B. Giṭṭ. 67a; B. Bek. 37a.

at Rabbi Nathan about whom it is said in Bava Meṣia,[48] "he is a judge and has penetrated the depths of civil law" and who is also described as *av bet din* in Horayot.[49] Furthermore, how could Mar Zuṭra or Mar Uqba who were the chief exponents of the Amoraim have entered into this quarrel. Surely they were of the opinion that all those pedantic and esoteric points were unfounded? And even if it were supposed that they would interpret Rabbi Jose's statement in accordance with Rashi's view, Rabbi Nathan and Mar Zuṭra were certainly not illiterate[50]—so how did they come to express such a view.

By a stroke of good luck, I discovered the kernel of the pomegranate[51] in the epistle which the Christian translator [Jerome] wrote to Marcella [*sic*][52] about the ten holy Names—they are also discussed in chapter 33 of Avot d'Rabbi Nathan.[53] Speaking about the tetragrammaton, he declared that its letters *YHV* were engraved on the headplate (*ṣiṣ*) and he reproduces the letters in the excellent Assyrian script. Perhaps he saw the *ṣiṣ* while he was in Rome as did Rabbi Eleazar bar Jose. It stands to reason that they should have made it anew in the second Temple. While the common people would also have used the characters of the *ever ha-nahar* script, they must have retained the form of the original headplate which was certainly known to their prophets in its inscription in Assyrian characters. This fact also reflects the situation regarding all the other holy writings. Indeed, in his commentary to the Torah, the sage ibn Shuaib[54] first mentions the question raised by the Tosafists on the statement that the Torah was given in the Hebrew Libunaʾah script in relation to the *mem* and the *samekh* in the tablets, and then writes:[55] "With all due deference to them, it must be said that Rabbi Moses [Maimonides] of blessed memory had already resolved this problem. He said that the intention was to refer to the book of the Torah which Moses wrote and gave to Israel; they then wrote their own text in the Hebrew script, thus avoiding use of the holy script and the holy tongue." The Rav, ibn Ḥabib also expressed a similar idea in the name of the Ritba on the first chapter of Megillah.[56] But if you, the reader, consider that the plaster which has been daubed [over the problem] served to repair the breach, peace be on you and peace be on your helpers. For my part, all this does not satisfy me. Let this bewilderment remain until Elijah comes or when the dust will be removed from the eyes of those sages at the time of the resurrection of our dead.

48. B. B.M. 117b.

49. B. Hor. 13b. According to tradition, the *av bet din* was the vice president of the Academy.

50. 'Illiterate,' lit. cut reeds in a meadow. Cf. B. Shabb. 95a; B. Sanh. 33a.

51. Cf. B. Ḥag. 15b, where concerning R. Meir's instruction from the "heretical" Elishah ben Abuyah it is said: "He found a pomegranate: he ate the fruit within it and threw away the peel."

52. The Epistle to Marcella on the ten names of God does not contain the passage to which de' Rossi is referring, but it is in his *Epistolae,* Epistula ad Fabiolam (*P.L.* XXII, col. 617): "Octava est lamina aurea, id est SIS ZAAB in qua scriptum est nomen Dei hebraicis quatuor literis Jod He Vav He."

53. ARN, rec. A ch. 34, 99.

54. Joshua ibn Shuaib was a Spanish scholar of the first half of the fourteenth century whose sermons were frequently cited.

55. *Derashot,* shelaḥ lekha, 43, col. a.

56. Jacob ibn Ḥabib, *En Yaʿakov,* to B. Meg. 2b.

CHAPTER FIFTY-NINE

On the antiquity of the vowel points and the accents of the holy tongue.[1]

Now the subject of the vowels and accents is treated by the great grammarian of our times Rabbi Elias ha-Baḥur [Elijah Levita][2] in his work *Massoret ha-Massoret.*[3] In the third introduction he investigates the question of when they were put into the holy Writings, and he cites various different views. He says that according to majority opinion, they were put in place in the time of Ezra, a view which is based on the passage in Nedarim:[4] "*And they read from the scroll of the Torah of God* (Neh. 8:8)—this is Scripture; *distinctly*—this refers to the Targum; *making it intelligible*—these are the divisions of the sentences; *so that they could understand Scripture*—this refers to the dividing accents, or according to others, these are the traditional spellings and pronunciations of the text (*ha-masorot*)." But he rejects their evidence by claiming that the passage simply means that when Ezra and his colleagues read out the Torah to the Israelites, they translated it orally into Aramaic which was their language at the time, and that they made divisions between one verse and another in accordance with the tradition which they had received from Moses. But there is no reference to the accents which we use nowadays. He refers to Kimḥi who, at the end of the section on the *hitpael* conjugation in his *Mikhlol,* wrote that the vowels should not be changed from the form in which they were given to Moses at Sinai.[5] But he points out that in his treatment of the *niphal* conjugation, Kimḥi states: "The people who instituted the vocalization,

1. The subject of the antiquity of the Hebrew vowels became a hotly debated issue among all denominations of Christians in the seventeenth century. Levita's arguments (see below) and de' Rossi's counterarguments were extensively cited and used for the basis of discussion. For a recent treatment of the subject, see Burnett, *From Christian Hebraism,* ch. 7.

2. Elijah Levita (often called by the name Baḥur, which was the title of the Hebrew grammar he wrote in 1518) was a pioneer in massoretic studies and lexicology and a fine exponent of Hebrew grammar. He was born in 1469 in Neustadt in Germany, spent most of his life in Italy, and died in Venice in 1549. He taught Hebrew to Christians and his work was adopted and disseminated by the great Christian hebraists of his time such as Sebastian Münster and Paulus Fagius. See G. E. Weil, *Elie Levita.*

3. The work was first published in Bomberg in Venice, 1538, and presents a pioneering discussion of the technical terms and signs of the Masorah. A vocalized text with Latin translation of the three prefaces was produced by Münster in Basel, 1539. C. D. Ginsburg edited and translated the work into English, and it was reprinted with his edition and translation of Jacob ibn Adonijah's *Introduction.* All references will be to the 1968 edition.

4. B. Ned. 37b.

5. *Massoret,* 122.

made a distinction." He [i.e., Levita] thus concludes that one ought to realize that Kimḥi's reference to the vocalization signifies the sounds and not the vowel points themselves. He refers to the author of the *Sefer ha-Semadar,* the author of *Horayot ha-Qoreh,* and Rabbi Moses the punctuator who said that they were given with the Torah at Sinai, but were forgotten and then reinstituted by Ezra. He rejects their idea by claiming that the book of the Torah which Moses wrote did not contain the vowels and accents. And he refers to the sage ibn Ezra who in his *Sefer Ṣaḥot* casts some doubt as to whether the accents were put in place in the time of Ezra, and both in this work and in his *Sefer Moznayim* appears to incline more to the view that it was the work of people living after Ezra's time. Similarly, the statements of the authors of *Ṣaḥ Sefatayim* and the *Kuzari,* that the correct pronunciation and reading were transmitted from Sinai, lend the impression that the vowel points and the accents, which were simply used as a mnemonic, were only put in place at a later date by one or by more individuals—since it is not clear whether they believed that Ezra or one of his successors set them down. In the wake of all these opinions, Baḥur wrote his own view that they were not put in place until after the closing of the Gemara. His strongest proof is that in all the statements of the rabbis of blessed memory in the Gemara, Aggadot, and Midrashim there is no reference or allusion to any vowel point or accent. And he explains that their statements,[6] "There is the authority for the traditional rendition and there is the authority for the scriptural text"[7] and "Any verse that Moses our teacher on him be peace did not divide, we may not divide" refer to their oral study of the text according to its traditional reading. Furthermore, if the accents and vowels had been in existence in that time, the teacher of Joab would not have been killed as is stated in Bava Batra[8] on account of the difference between the word *zekher* and *zakhar.* Moreover, the fact that all the names [of the vowels and accents] such as *ṣere, segol, melofum, mapiq* are in Aramaic indicates that they were not given on Sinai, for Aramaic would have been of no relevance at Mount Sinai. In general then, he is of the conviction that over the generations they learned the correct reading of the text by regular study without vowels and accents.[9] He says that this was also the method by which the Chaldeans learn how to read their books—he derived this information from Chaldeans who came during his lifetime to Pope Leo from the country of Prester John.[10] Thus, in his view, this state of affairs continued after the close of the Talmud until the time of the Massoretes, that is to say, the Tiberians, who were highly versed in Scripture and had a greater purity of language than all other Jews as Rabbi Jonah the grammarian attests. It was they who instituted and formalized the vowel-point system. Nevertheless the names of the vow-

6. B. Sukk. 6b, i.e., the traditional reading of the unvocalized text or the reading of the text irrespective of its spelling.

7. B. Meg. 22a.

8. B. B.B. 21a–b. Joab is said to have killed all the males in Edom (1K. 11:16) because he had been taught by his teacher to read *zekhar* (male) in *You shall blot out the males of Amalek* (Deut. 25:19) rather than *zekher* (remembrance). According to one report, Joab then went and killed his teacher for having allowed him to read the text incorrectly.

9. Levita, *Massoret,* 129.

10. Ibid., 130. Levita states that while he was in Rome, at request of Pope Leo X, three Chaldeans came from the land of Prester John to show their Syriac version of the Bible and were able to read the Psalter without vowels.

els and the accents were changed subsequently by the sages of the generations, some calling the *ḥireq, shever* and the *ḥolem, melofum,* and there are other such examples.

This is the basic drift of his discussion. However, in my view, the meaning of the statement of the rabbis of blessed memory, "*distinctly*—this refers to the Targum" is that the Targum of those texts which had become widely disseminated was reduced to writing. As we proved in previous chapters, they had a text of the Torah which was written in the language of Targum [i.e., Aramaic]. The rest of the statement [in Nedarim] is in the same vein and means that they punctuated the text with the accents and divisions. There is also a version of the passage given in Nedarim in the Palestinian Talmud which reads as follows:[11] "*making it intelligible*—these are the accents; *so that they could understand Scripture*—this refers to the traditional spellings and pronunciation, and some say these are the syntactical constructions, while other say that these are the beginnings of the verses." And in Bereshit Rabbah at the end of pericope *bereshit,*[12] they say: "*Making it intelligible*—these are the accents; *so that they could understand Scripture*—this refers to the beginnings of the verses. Rav Huna[13] said: 'These are the [disputed] syntactical constructions and the arguments for and against.' And the rabbis of Caesarea said: 'Here we have an allusion to the traditional text.' " There is no doubt that the expressions "these are the accents," "these are the grammatical constructions and the arguments for and against" lend greater support to the contention that the rabbis of blessed memory were referring to the actual form of the accents and not simply to the pronunciation. This view gains greater credibility in the light of Ibn Adonijah's Introduction to the Rabbinic Bible,[14] where on the basis of various masterly demonstrations, he proves that the Gemara and Masorah are at variance in many places with regard to the defective and *plene* spelling of words. He cites 1Sam. 2:24, Gen. 25:6, and Deut. 6:9 among other examples.[15] He finally raises the question as to whose authority we should follow for the writing of our Torah.[16] At first glance it would appear that we should opt to follow the Gemara which is our received authority. But he also mentions passages in which the two great guides Rashi and the Tosafists rely on the Massoretic text as against the Gemara. On this basis, then, one should believe that the Massoretic text was received from the Men of the Great Synagogue as implied in the expression "these are the traditional readings (*masorot*)." Accordingly, just as their reference to that traditional massoretic rendition implied a written and not an oral text, so too the accents and the syntactical constructions of the text and the other things they mentioned certainly had reference to a written text.

However, notwithstanding these criticisms, it should be noted that from the outset, Rabbi Elias himself put forward the statement, "I shall succumb to the will of any

11. P. Meg. 4 (1) 74d.

12. B.R. 36:8 (342–43).

13. This is the reading in the first edition, but other texts read Rabbi Ḥiyya bar Lulianus.

14. Jacob bem Ḥayyim ibn Adonijah was originally from Spain and eventually came to Italy and to Venice in 1517 where he worked in the printing press of Daniel Bomberg. His Rabbinic Bible of 1524–25 was based on manuscript readings and massoretic notes and was acknowledged as the most accurate massoretic text in print.

15. In all these cases, he refers to the citations of the verses in rabbinic texts where the spelling is different.

16. Ibn Adonijah, *Introduction,* 66.

person who can disprove my argument against our rabbis." So we would say to him: "Who will uncover the dust from your eyes, Baḥur, you who are chosen from the people."[17] Since the kabbalistic works to which we shall refer were not yet in print in his lifetime, how he would have defended his position is obvious.[18] But today, blessed be God, the eye can see and the ear hear the entire texts of the *Bahir,* the *Zohar,* the *Tiqqunim,* and the *Maʿarekhet ha-Elohut* (whose content is based upon the activities of Rabbi Neḥuniah ben ha-Qanah, and Rabbi Simeon bar Yoḥai before the Mishnah was composed). These texts, as is known, supply a variety of unsullied sayings regarding the forms and names of the vowel points and the accents. Consider the citation of the *Bahir* by Rabbenu Baḥya[19] and Ḥayyat:[20] "The vowel points in the letters of the Torah of Moses are comparable to the soul which exists in the human body."[21] {I saw the following passage in the Bahir:[22]

> It is impossible to have one square within another square. But a circle within a square can move. And if a square is within a circle it cannot move. What are the things that are circular? The vowel points in the Mosaic Torah for these are all round. Their relation to the letters is like the soul in the human body. For it is impossible for him to have any life whatsoever unless the soul exists within him, and it is impossible for him to produce a word, small or great, without the soul. The same is true of the vowel point, for the letters are given life by the vowel point, and it is impossible to say a word, great or small, without the vowel point. Every vowel point is round and every letter is square and the letters come to be through the vowel points and have life through them. This vowel point comes by way of the channels to the letters by means of the scent of the sacrifice and it immediately descends as it is written, *a sweet scent to the Lord,* for the Lord descends towards the Lord[23] and therefore it is written, *The Lord our God, the Lord is one* (Deut. 6:4).

The meaning of the concluding part of this passage is elucidated by Ramban in his commentary to the verse, *and offering by fire of pleasing scent to the Lord* (Lev. 1:9), particularly if you also consult the interpretation of the esoteric parts of his commentary by the author of *Me'irat Enayim*[24] who cites the passage from the *Bahir.* At the same time, this text shows you the antiquity of the vowel points of the letters and the preeminence of the square Assyrian script. It also demonstrates that the Torah was not given in the *ever ha-nahar* script, a view that we cited in chapter 56.}[2] And in the Zohar on Song of Songs it states:[25] "It is not permitted for all the letters to move to this or the other side without the vowels. All the letters are like the body without a soul. When the vowels come, the body is upright in its stature." And in the introduction to the *Sefer*

17. De' Rossi is playing on Levita's penname Baḥur by means of Ps. 89:20 and using the expression "who will uncover" from M. Sota 5:2.

18. In other words, Levita would have argued for an early date for the vowel points had he been able to read the kabbalistic works which were replete with references to the points and were attributed to sages of the second century.

19. Baḥya to Gen. 18:3; Deut. 7:2. De' Rossi refers to the wrong passage.

20. Judah ben Jacob Ḥayyat, *Minḥat Jehudah,* Commentary to *Maʿarekhet ha-Elohut,* 20a. On this subject, see G. Scholem, *On the Origins,* 63–65.

21. *Bahir* (par. 115, 51–52).

22. Ibid., (pars. 114–15).

23. This refers to the two incidences of the tetragrammaton in Ex. 34:6.

24. Isaac b. Samuel of Acre, *Me'irat Enayim,* (186, col. b).

25. *Zohar Ḥadash,* Shir ha-Shirim 73 col. c.

ha-Tiqqunim:[26] "The accents are the breath, the vowels are the spirit and the letters are the soul,[27] the one propelled towards the other, . . . thus *one higher than the other* (Eccl. 5:7)." Now if you were to claim that the vowels and accents about which they are speaking are simply the pronunciations and pauses which we learn orally, go and examine *Sefer ha-Tiqqunim,* Tiqqun five, and Tiqqun eighteen, and also the Zohar on the verse, *And God called the light* (Gen. 1:5)[28] and *And God said Let us make man* (Gen. 1:26),[29] and in the Cremona edition[30] on the verse, *And Adam knew* (Gen. 4:1). For in every text the names of the vowels and the accents in the forms that are known to us are written down not once nor twice. The specific passages from *Sefer ha-Idra*[31] and *Ṣeniuta d'Sifra*[32] are quoted also by Ḥayyat,[33] and he says that the letters come from the *sefirah* of *binah* and the vowels from *ḥokhmah* and the accents from *keter*—he writes about this in the same context.

Thus Baḥur's view is patently undermined since we have intimations to prove that the different kinds of vowels and accents were in existence not only before the close of the Gemara, but even before the composition of the Mishnah. And if he were with us today, he would certainly submit to our view. Even the opinion of those who claim that the vowels of the letters of our holy tongue, namely, the Hebrew script, were invented at Sinai or in the days of Ezra but did not exist prior to that time, according to my limited understanding, appears to be nonsensical. This view is corroborated by a comparative study. For when we examine all other known languages, we find that the letters have notations of sound and pronunciation. These are either indicated by actual letters as is the case with Italian, Latin, and Greek used in our countries, and also in Armenian and Persian as I saw in the *Introduction to Languages* written by brother Theseo whom I mentioned before.[34] Alternatively, there are points, lines, and markers which are put above, below, and in the middle, as in Hebrew, which was the first language to have this system. It was then adopted by Arabic and Aramaic which are later corruptions of Hebrew. In the case of this second group [of languages], educated people frequently omitted the points and the markers without confronting any difficulty. But this does not imply that the languages intrinsically lacked the vowel points. In fact, reading the book entitled *Introduction,* I noticed, and whosoever is interested can see for himself, that Arabic and Aramaic have the points and markers which are used by the speakers of those languages. Since these languages bear affinity to Hebrew

26. *Sefer ha-Tiqqunim,* 8a.

27. The passage refers to the kabbalistic notion of the tripartite soul: the *nefesh* (soul) is the lowest part, close to the body and nourishing it; the *ruaḥ* (spirit) is an intermediate power which illuminates the nefesh; the *neshamah* (breath) is a spiritual force that "draws man near to God and preserves the bonds between them" (I. Tishby, *The Wisdom,* vol. 2, 685).

28. Zohar I, 16b.

29. Ibid. 24b.

30. I.e., the edition of the Zohar, Cremona 1559–60, cols. 152–54. This edition was printed about the same time as the Mantuan edition (1558–60). For the most part, subsequent printings were based on the Mantuan edition. See Tishby, *The Wisdom,* vol. 1, 97–99.

31. Part of the Zohar in which the hints and allusions of the preceding chapter are developed and explained.

32. A six-page section in the Zohar, containing a commentary on the first six chapters of Genesis.

33. *Ma'arekhet,* 22b–23a.

34. Theseo Ambrogio (Albonesius), *Introductio.*

and derive from it, we may logically deduce that they too have vowel points from antiquity. Yet we should not make conclusions about that which is structured from that which does not belong in that category and about that which is essential from that which is accidental. For how could it be rationally tenable that the first man who invented the letters in order to produce the appropriate words in the holy tongue would not have invented modes and indicators whereby the reader could distinguish and recognize the difference between *shelemah, shalmah, shelomo, shalamah,* etc. Likewise the letters of all languages were also originally constructed with the indicators of their pronunciation either by vowel letters or by points, lines, and markers as was said. Now through habitual reading and comprehension of the context, it is easy to read unvocalized texts in those languages whose vowels are indicated by points and lines. Thus after a time, the vowels came to be omitted except in those cases where they are required. This is the method we have sometimes adopted here. When the vocalization of the words might be uncertain, we insert the vowel points to ensure that the words are read correctly. Now Moses our teacher did not write the Torah with the pronunciation indicators despite the fact that the reading of certain words might become open to question. He had an important reason for doing so. He wanted to ensure that people's understanding of its precepts would only be in conjunction with the Oral Tradition as the wise author of the *Kuzari* wrote. Therefore Moses also began with the simple text with which we were to begin. In addition, it is known that there are seventy faces to the Torah. This idea is given greater corroboration by Ramban [Nahmanides] who wrote in the introduction to his commentary to the Torah: "We are in possesion of a mystical tradition that the whole of the Torah consists of the names of the Holy One blessed be He for the letters separate themselves into [divine] names when divided in a different manner." The special characteristics of the tetragrammaton, in particular, as all the kabbalists indicate, is that it may be read in many different ways. And so if one mode of reading was imposed on the words of Torah, it would supersede all other possible readings. Thus it is apposite to consider this in rhetorical fashion in the light of their statement in Menaḥot:[35] "Sometimes the cessation from Torah is its very foundation, [for it is written, *the tablets that you smashed* (Deut. 10:2)]. The Holy One blessed be He said to Moses: 'You did well to smash them.' "

And yet, we cannot suppress the fact that from that time, the different kinds of vowel points were written into some of the texts according to requirement, and particularly, on the stones, as the author of *Semadar*[36] states with regard to the verse, *And on those stones you shall inscribe every word of this Torah most distinctly* (Deut. 27:8). Had they not been vocalized, the reader would have been unable to understand them and who could have explained them to him as he stood there at the river's side?[37] Now the Jews, including the common people, continued to speak their holy tongue until the destruction of the first Temple as we noted in the previous chapter. As a result of their abandonment of the Torah and its recitation, it is all the more plausible that its vowels

35. B. Men. 99b.

36. This is the passage quoted by Levita, *Massoret,* 122–23.

37. In Deut. 27, they are told to inscribe the stones with the words of Torah once they had crossed over the Jordan.

were forgotten until Ezra's time. While restoring to them the Torah written in the Hebrew language which during the Babylonian exile together with the Torah had been forgotten by the populace, he also restored its vowels. Nevertheless throughout the second Temple period they continued to speak the Aramaic language, even for matters of Torah as we demonstrated. Consequently, the vowels gradually disappeared and became unfamiliar to all but a few, conspicuous among whom are the kabbalists as we noted. Thus it is no wonder that the reading of some words became doubtful for some as is exemplified in the statement:[38] "Ishmael, my brother, how do you read *For your love is better than wine* (S.S. 1:2)?"[39] There is also the case of Rabbi Eleazar ben Arakh whose learning had vanished because the phenomenon of the vowels was not widespread[40] and who read, *Their heart was silent* [instead of *This month shall be to you* (Ex. 12:2)].[41] This may also have happened to Joab in first Temple times and they therefore became unsure about the reading of the verse, *You shall blot out the memory of Amalek* (Deut. 25:19).[42] This state of affairs continued until after the close of the Gemara (as Baḥur wrote) when the Tiberian sages or others, whom they knew, decided that it was right to produce some form of safeguards for the correct modes of reading the text. Such precautions had been taken by the Babylonian academy when they closed the Gemara and by Rabbi Hillel and his law court in the Land of Israel when they instituted the fixed calendar as we noted in some of these chapters. For in His compassion for us few who remain, God implemented the favor of allowing us a support and stay[43] until the time of love arrives and He sets up the fallen booth of David.

Now Baḥur produced evidence from the people who came from the land of Prester John[44] and who were reading from Aramaic texts without vowels and accents. However, you should know that the author of the Aramaic grammar, who shall remain anonymous,[45] set out in his introduction to disprove categorically that the language of Prester John was Aramaic.[46] He wrote:[47] "Know that there is one India in the east in the furthermost part of Asia which is not encompassed by the hemisphere in which we live. And there is another India in the south, located in Africa, with the Red Sea, east of it, near Arabia Felix, but separated by the Arabian gulf. It lies adjacent to Egypt in the north and to Ethiopia in the west. This very extensive region belongs to Prester John." Who knows whether the rabbis of blessed memory who make different comments about these two countries with regard to the verse, *from India (Hodu) to Ethiopia (Kush)*

38. M. A.Z. 2:5.

39. The word *your love* may be masculine or feminine according to its vocalization.

40. This is a play on 1Sam. 3:1.

41. B. Shabb. 147b. Because Rabbi Eleazar had neglected his learning, he had forgotten how to read the words with the proper vocalization, and had also confused some of the letters.

42. B. B.B. 21a–b.

43. I.e., the massoretic text.

44. Prester John was the legendary Christian ruler of the Far East. The people to whom Levita refers were probably Nestorians or Maronites.

45. I.e., Sebastian Münster.

46. Münster used the works of the Ethiopic scholar Johannes Potken and the traveler Bernard Breidenbach for this subject.

47. *Chaldaica grammatica,* 14–15.

(Est. 1:1) were actually agreeing[48] and did not hold different views.[49] And in that passage[50] the scholar reproduces the letters of their alphabet and demonstrates how the vowel system is like ours.

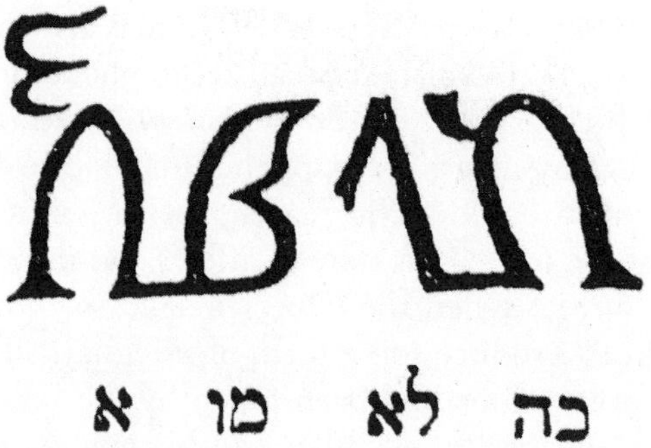

In other words, when they put a dot to the right of a letter in the middle, it is to be read as a *shureq;* and if the dot is at the side of a letter below, it is a *ḥireq;* and above, it is a *ḥolem.* This is how their vowel system is constructed. Thus their script is read backwards and not frontwards as in Italian. Furthermore, you will notice that certain letters have shapes which are not vocalized in any other way but have an in-built vocalization such that one can know whether it should be read as a *ḳameṣ* or a *ḥolem* and so on. This is why they have more than a hundred letters. Their books are written with these characters such that they can be read without vocalization except that the letter that has been elided is substituted by a dot. He gives examples of some words with the Hebrew and Aramaic equivalents. I thought it best to show you one of these words, *amolaḳah.* While in Hebrew the word would read *elo'ah* and in Aramaic *elaha,* Prester John would say *amoloḳah.* In my opinion, this is equivalent to *Molech, the abomination of the Ammonites* (1K. 11:7). My idea is ratified by the passage in Yevamot and Berakhot where it speaks of Judah the Indian, the Ammonite proselyte.[51] Indeed, in his description of the language, some of their words do bear affinity to Hebrew and Aramaic, but

48. 'Agreeing' (hodu). De' Rossi is deliberately using a verb that resembles the place-name Hodu (India).

49. B. Meg. 11a: "One said that Hodu is at one end of the world and Kush at the other, and the other said that Hodu and Kush adjoin each other."

50. Münster, *Chaldaica grammatia,* 14.

51. As Cassel notes, neither in B. Yev. 76b nor in B. Ber. 28a does this combination of names occur. In B. Yev. 76b there is a reference to an Ammonite proselyte, and in B. Ber. 28a to a Judah, an Ammonite proselyte. Judah the Indian appears in B. Qidd. 22b, but he is not called the Ammonite proselyte.

they are few. In fact, he reproduces the verse, *Have mercy on me, O Lord for I call to You all day long. Bring joy to your servant's life* (Ps. 86:3) in their language and script.[52] Of these ten words, only two bear any affinity to Hebrew, namely, the word *ḳol* (all) which is *chulo* and *nefesh* (life) which is *nafscha.* But for the rest there is no point of comparison at all. In sum, his statements prove conclusively that Baḥur deceived us when he said that these people's language and script was Aramaic. Indirectly we also come to understand why sometimes they read without any vowels and accents. For in fact, they do have vowel points which function like those we use.

Now all this refers to the vowels which are necessary for learning to read correctly, and particularly for those who are beginners in the language. However, I would not categorically pronounce that the accents, which are only the auxiliaries for understanding the subject matter and serve as *baladhur*[53] against forgetfulness, are of the same antiquity. Rather, it is possible that they were invented in some previous century. You should consider the statement of the Tosafists at the end of Megillah[54] where they say that the ancients used chant even in their study of Mishnah so as to aid the memory. Now in the past, when I was a censor,[55] I came across two Mishnah texts which were five hundred years old that contained the vowels and dividing accents. Moreover, while I was in the alma mater[56] of Bologna, I was present while a Christian taught geometry to a large number of students. In unison with them he would chant aloud the multiplication tables[57] which they were required to memorize. Time after time, he would strike a block with a hammer, which as I myself experienced, was the final test that those lessons had actually been committed to memory. Indeed, given that the kabbalists also ascribed esoteric significance to them [i.e., the vowel points], it is possible that they were received at Sinai, but that subsequently they were also invented by one of us. The Lord knows whether human designs are futile. In the light of this method of mine, all the sages' statements that we put forward at the beginning of the chapter are all equally justifiable: the vowel points were given at Sinai, in the time of Ezra and after the close of the Gemara. In other words, when the vowels were rediscovered at those moments in time, after a period in which they had been forgotten or had fallen into disarray in the hands of the people, it was as though they had been given on that very day. Also correct would be our impression that they were instituted with the letters of the script from the time of creation. There was a continual process of neglect and restoration. As the wise and experienced sage stated, *Sometimes there is a phenomenon of which they say: Look this one is new—it occurred long since, in ages that went before us* (Eccl. 1:10). Now naming that is not divinely inspired is arbitrary, and as the wise Galen states in many passages of his works, one should not be concerned about names but only about the

52. Münster, *Chaldaica grammatia,* 16.

53. *Baladhur* was one of the most popular drugs for the treatment of forgetfulness in the Middle Ages and was often prescribed by Arabic and Jewish physicians. On *baladhur,* see G. Bos, "*Baladhur,*" 229–36.

54. Tos. to B. Meg. 32a, s.v. *ve-ha-shoneh.*

55. As a safeguard against Catholic censorship of Hebrew books, Jews implemented their own censorship, omitting any material that might be regarded as offensive or dangerous.

56. 'Alma Mater' was the motto of Bologna University.

57. The expression de' Rossi uses for multiplication tables, *ha-misparim ha-mukhim zeh al zeh,* is derived from the Arabic, first used by Judah ibn Tibbon, See Sarfatti, *Mathematical Terminology,* 174 (par. 226). On the teaching of mathematics and number theory, see Grendler, *Schooling,* 311.

matters which they denote.[58] I do not find it problematic, therefore, that according to the region or teacher, a vowel may be designated a *ḥireq* by one sage and *shever* by another, and *melofum, ḥolem,* and so on. Do we not see that scholars of Spain and France differ in their grammatical methodology and even in matters regarding biliteral roots, and yet the final outcome is the decisive factor,[59] and their statements balance equally in the scales of rhetoric and poetry.

In fact I saw a statement by the Christian translator [Jerome] which is relevant for this topic. I shall not refrain from communicating it to you, relying on the fact that you are prepared to hear the truth from whichever quarter it comes. In his introduction to the book of Samuel he writes:[60]

> The Hebrews have a twenty-two-letter alphabet, as is also attested by the language of the Syrians and Chaldeans to which it bears great affinity. For their alphabet also has twenty-two characters which are homophonous with those of the Hebrews but different in form. Similarly, the Samaritans, namely, the Cutheans,[61] write the Mosaic Pentateuch with the same number of characters, although they differ in their shapes and vowel points. It is well known that after the rebuilding of the Temple in the time of Zerubbabel, Ezra the scribe discovered another script which is still used by the Jews. Before his day, however, the Jews and the Samaritans used an identical script. Some Greek tomes that are still extant reproduce the tetragrammaton in the original script to which we referred.

In his Epistle to Marcella,[62] he wrote that there is some resemblance between the *yod* and the *he* in the Samaritan script and the Greek *pe* and *yod.* Consequently, on seeing the name [i.e., the tetragrammaton] reproduced in Samaritan letters in Greek tomes, some people used to read it as PIPI. For the Greeks have one type of writing where the letter *pi* is *X* and resembles the Hebrew *yod* that we reproduced in chapter 56. And if you examine Bishop Eugubinus's discussion of the burning bush in his *Recognitio,*[63] you will come to understand his view that of the three holy letters of the Name, only the *yod* and *he,* written twice over, were represented.

Now in his letter to his friend Evagrius,[64] the translator discusses the word "Shalem" in the verse, *And Jacob arrived safe [shalem]* (Gen. 33:18) which some of them read as *shalim* and writes: "It does not matter whether it is read as Salem or Salim since the Jews use the vowel letters very seldom. The different pronunciations stem from the fact that each region has its own usages."[65] At any rate, then, these passages reveal that contrary to Baḥur's opinion, the vowels were in existence even before his time although

58. Galen's distaste for terminological disputes is manifested throughout his works. See, e.g., *Methodus medendi* I, 5, 9.

59. De' Rossi is probably referring to the fact that Rashi adhered to the notion of biliteral roots in Hebrew, whereas in Spain it was no longer fashionable to do so.

60. Jerome, Praefatio in Samuelem (*P.L.* XXVIII, cols. 547–50).

61. 'The Cutheans' is de' Rossi's gloss.

62. *Epistolae,* 25 (*P.L.* XXII, col. 429).

63. Steuchus, *Recognitio,* 107v–108a. Steuchus argues on the basis of the expression *I will be that which I will be* (Ex. 3:14) that the tetragrammaton was originally spelled as though it read literally "he will be" (*yhyh*), and that later the *yod* became elongated into a *vav.*

64. *Epistolae,* 73 (*P.L.* XXII, cols. 680–81).

65. Jerome is referring to the letters *alef, yod, vav,* the *matres lectionis* and not to the vowel points in general. Theseo Ambrogio, *Introductio* (10) states that according to some opinions, the *matres lectionis* are vowels, and according to others, consonants.

they were used rarely. Similarly, you will note that both the Hebrew and Samaritan script have a built-in vowel system by means of dots, or lines or markers although their forms are different from those illustrated in the *Introduction to the Languages* that we mentioned. Even so, as demonstrated in a previous chapter, the words "Jerusalem the holy," "Sheqel of Israel," were engraved on the holy sheqel, but the coin was not imprinted with vocalization of any kind. For often they relied on knowledge which had been acquired through usage, while on occasions they also wrote the letters together with their vowels. A similar phenomenon occurred with the holy Writings although from that time onwards, the Assyrian script that we use did have vocal points and lines. Before dismissing the subject, intelligent reader, I thought it right to inform you about the passage from the *Kuzari* which is cited by Baḥur. It reads:[66] "Seven main vowels and accents were placed as signs for those vowels which they had received through Mosaic tradition." In an ancient version of the text, I noticed that there was an alternative reading: "which men had transcribed from Moses." Such a reading lends support to the contention that it was his [i.e., Halevi's] view that those vowels and accents, and not simply the dispositions for them, were transmitted from Moses. May the wise person gain greater wisdom.

66. *Kuzari* III, par. 31.

CHAPTER SIXTY

On the poems composed in the holy tongue.[1]

WHILE treating the subject of our holy tongue and its letters and vowels, I also consider it worthwhile to channel the discussion into a study of the nature of the poems, both modern and ancient, which have been composed in that language. Now, towards the end of section 2,[2] the author of the *Kuzari* uses tradition and logical reasoning to demonstrate the preeminence of our language over all other languages. He then concludes that in more recent times, some of our sages endeavored to embellish their poems by means of melodic compositions in different kinds of meter, in long and short vowels, which are not congruent with the Hebrew language but derive from Arabic. In fact, they are alien to Hebrew whose innate structure is achieved by means of the accents which indicate the sense. He states that those sages who regarded poetic compositions in terms of meter, as was said, only generated discord,[3] and he elaborates on this subject in that context.

Such a view is also espoused by the wise Don Isaac [Abravanel]. In his comment on *Let me sing for my beloved* (Is. 5:1), he presents a threefold classification of poems written in our holy tongue.[4] The first class comprises the metered poems with feet and rhymes which are customary usage nowadays—these are not modeled on the verses in holy Writ but are borrowed from Arabic poetry and are even more commendable. The second class comprises the songs which differ from the rest of Scripture, not by reason of the words themselves or any other characteristic, but because they have a melody and are actually sung as exemplified by the song of the Sea (Ex. 15), *ha'azinu* (Deut. 32), the song of Deborah (Jud. 5) and the song of David (2Sam. 22). The distinguishing mark of the third class of poems is not determined by the words or the voice of the singer, but only insofar as they are not meant to be taken literally. In fact, its best part is its

1. This chapter which was an important contribution to the understanding of the parallelism of biblical poetry has received much attention: Johannes Buxtorf II translated it into Latin at the end of his edition of the *Kuzari* (415–24), Robert Lowth refers to it in his *De sacra poesi,* vol. 1, prael. XIX, 258–60, and translates and discusses it in his Preliminary Dissertation to his translation of Isaiah, XXVIII–XXXVI. See also, J. Kugel, *The Idea,* 200–3; A. Berlin, *Biblical Poetry,* 42–44, with an English trans. of this chapter, 144–53; id. "Azariah de' Rossi and Biblical Poetry."

2. *Kuzari* II, pars. 66–68.

3. Ibid., par. 73.

4. Abravanel to Is. 5:1 (39–40).

subterfuge,[5] as is exemplified in the Song of Songs and the song of Isaiah (5). The designation "poetry" essentially and primarily belongs to this category which is treated by the "philosopher" [Aristotle] in his famous work, the *Poetics*.[6] Indeed, these sages, namely, the author of the *Kuzari* and Don Isaac, appear to be correct since we cannot detect even one example of those types of poems in the holy Writings.

A converse view, however, is expressed by Yedidyah the Alexandrian [Philo] whom we dated to the period prior to the destruction of the second Temple, in his work entitled *On the Contemplative Life*. He describes the sects of men and women who segregated themselves from worldly desires and committed themselves to the service of God and the quest for wisdom in like manner to the Christian orders of brothers and sisters that exist in our time. He said as follows:[7] "In addition to their dedication to contemplation, they compose songs in all kinds of meters which are appropriate for singing during the divine service." Then several pages later in the same book, he writes:[8] "When the president sees that the studies have been completed and the voices of the discutants have abated, he then rises and sings a psalm in praise of God, either a new composition of his own, or else one taken from those written by a prophet[9] in the past. For the ancients had many kinds of hymns in trimeters and songs of praise with their melodies which were sung during the ritual at the altar."

Likewise, Josephus[10] writes in book 2 that the song of the Sea is written in hexameters, namely, verses written with six feet [to a line]. And in book 4,[11] he also writes that the poem in pericope *ha'azinu* is written in hexameter verse in the holy tongue. Furthermore, in his *Praeparatio*,[12] the Caesarean [i.e., Eusebius], who lived about two hundred years after the destruction of the Temple, wrote: "Plato said that poems recited in honor of God should be in meter and harmonious. This advice which we learn from him in theory is demonstrated to us in practice by the Jews. For the only form of metrical hymns and odes which they deem acceptable for the divine service are the compositions of the divinely inspired prophets."

Similarly, in his Epistle to Paula,[13] the Christian translator [Jerome] wrote that some of the Psalms are in trimeters and some in tetrameters. Likewise the song in *ha'azinu* as well as those in Proverbs and Lamentations are in meter, but of different types. For in chapters 1 and 2,[14] one verse contains three versicles. The third chapter is written in trimeter, with triplets of verses [each beginning with the same letter] and the fourth is

5. This saying was often repeated by theoreticians of poetry such as Moses ibn Ezra and derives from Arabic tradition which partly also derives from Plato's definition of poetry in bk. 10 of the *Republic*. See Kugel, *The Idea*, 187–89.

6. *Poetics*, 1451a–b where Aristotle states that the poet's function is not to report things that have happened, but rather that which might happen. Poetry deals with universals.

7. *Cont.* 29.

8. Ibid., 79–80.

9. Although the Greek text reads "poet," Gelenius's Latin translation reads "prophet" (754): "aut desumptum ab aliquo vatum veterum."

10. *Ant.* II:346.

11. *Ant.* IV:303.

12. De' Rossi refers to bk. 12, ch. 16 of the *De ev. praep.* which corresponds to the divisions in George of Trepizond's free Latin translation of the work. (*P.G.* XXI, bk. 12, ch. 22, col. 989.)

13. *Epistolae*, 30 (*P.L.* XXII, cols. 442–43).

14. De' Rossi mistakenly refers to ch. 4 instead of ch. 2.

like the first two. And in his preface to the book of Job,[15] he writes that the beginning and ends of the book are written in prose[16] but that the dialogues are written in different forms of hexameter verses which he compares to many of the poems written by Roman masters. And he says that if anyone regards his view that holy Scripture contains metered verse as implausible, he should take into account the testimony of Yedidyah, Josephus, Origen, and Eusebius. Similarly, in his preface to the Caesarean's *Chronicon,*[17] he speaks about the preeminence of our holy tongue and the difficulty of translating it on account of its mellifluous character as compared to all other languages, and then states: "Which book is as melodious as the Psalter that is comparable to the poems of the Latin Horace and the poems of the Greek Pindar. Sometimes, indeed, it flows in iambics and sometimes it has the feel of the Alcaic meter, and sometimes it swells like Sapphic verse, and sometimes moves in half feet. Which song is as beautiful as the song of Moses in Deuteronomy and the song of Isaiah 5. Which poems have the grandeur of the poems of King Solomon and are as finished as those of Job? All these poems are written in hexameters or pentameters as Josephus and Origen wrote." There is a booklet printed together with grammatical treatises entitled *Darkhe Noʿam* which was written by ibn Ḥabib.[18] It contains the following statement:[19]

> When I was in the kingdom of Valencia, in the community of Murviedro, all the people in the gate and the elders informed me that there was a tombstone of the commander of Amaziah the king of Judah. I then hastened to look at it. It is a stone monument on the peak of the mountain. After great effort I was able to read the writing which was a poetic epitaph. It read: "Raise a lament with embittered voice for the great prince whom the Lord has taken." I was unable to read any more, but the poem ended "to Amaziah." Then I was convinced that this mode of metrical poetry was used since the days our forefathers lived in their own land.

Thus, according to these sages, poems with measure and meter are not extraneous to our holy tongue, which has been used for this genre since early times, not only by reason of the melody in which they are sung as Don Isaac said, but also in respect of the actual words. Some examples are to be found in holy Scripture.

Nevertheless, I questioned many of the scholars of our time as to whether they could detect any measure and meter in the texts and they were unable to provide me with a response. However, everybody admitted that they were conscious of a poetic melodiousness while reciting them and that their cantillation differed from that of the rest of the Pentateuch, Prophets, and Hagiographa. But nobody knew how to appraise them. I grew more preoccupied[20] in my desire to resolve these views and to discover something of what I was looking for. My heart told me that the songs of holy Scripture do undoubtedly have measures and structures, but that they do not depend on the number

15. Praefatio ad Job (*P.L.* XXVIII, cols. 1081–82).
16. 'Prose,' lit. simple style. The Latin reads "prosa oratio est."
17. Eusebius, *Chronicon,* Praefatio Hieronymi (*P.L.* XXVII, col. 36).
18. Moses ibn Ḥabib (b. Lisbon) wrote his *Darkhe Noʿam,* a treatise on poetry, in 1486 in Bitonto. It was first printed in Constantinople (1520?) and reprinted with vocalization in Venice (1546) together with his Hebrew grammar *Marpe Lashon.* On ibn Ḥabib, see J. Kugel, "The Influence," 308–25.
19. *Darkhe Noʿam,* sig. iiii, 2, 4.
20. Cf. Ps. 94:19.

of long or short vowels, as is the norm with poems of our own times. As the author of the *Kuzari* wrote, these are imitations of the poems written in Arabic which is a corrupt form of our own language. Rather, their structure and measures consist in the number of ideas and their parts, subject and predicate, and its adjunct in every sentence and clause. In some cases, the clause will have two measures which together with the second to which it is attached amounts to four; other have three feet and with the second part amount to six complete feet. For example,[21] *Your right hand, O Lord* (Ex. 15:6) which is a clause in its own right and has two units, or one might say, two feet; *wondrous in might* is the same and attached to it, which comes to four. Similarly, the second *Your right hand, O Lord* has two other feet. *You shatter the foe* is two more which come to four. In like manner, *The foe said, I will pursue, I will overtake, I will divide the spoils, my desire shall have its fill of them. I will bare my sword, My hand shall subdue them. You make Your wind blow,* and so on. But the song of *ha'azinu* (Deut. 32) is in two sets of three which come to six, namely: *Give ear of heavens, let me speak, let the earth hear the words I utter; may my discourse come down as rain, my speech distill as the dew,* and so on. Sometimes, a single verse, and even more so, one song, will contain these two kinds of measures, namely, two-two and three-three, according to the inspiration of the prophet and also because the variation may fit the meaning. One such example is (Ex. 15:8): *At the blast of your nostrils, the waters piled* which are two-two; *The floods stood straight like a wall, The deeps froze in the heart of the sea* which are three-three. Similarly, there is the song at the well (Num. 21:17–18) which begins three-three and continues two-two. Likewise, the prayer of Habakkuk which is in the mode of Shigionot (Hab. 3) like the Shiggayon of David (Ps. 7:1), and which he gave to the leader to play with the appropriate melodies when he says, *for the leader with my melodies* (Hab. 3:19) is composed in the three-three mode:[22] *God is coming from Teman, The Holy One from Mount Paran selah, His majesty covers the skies, His splendor fills the earth* (Hab. 3:3).

Now the intelligent person must realize that for some reason or other, certain words in some of the utterances do not fall into the category of those measures. This is exemplified by the song of *ha'azinu, And He said, I will hide My countenance from them* (Deut. 32:20). *And He said* is a separate entity, and therefore *I will hide My countenance from them* are three feet and *And see how they fare in the end,* another three, and so on. And the two incidences of the tetragrammaton in the prayer of Habakkuk in the verse, *O Lord I have heard of Your renown, I am awed, O Lord by Your deeds* (Hab. 3:2) in each case stand alone, and therefore the adjoining clauses are three-three. And the verse, *Though the fig tree does not bud* (3:17) goes according to another mode, that of subject and predicate. For "the figtree" is the subject and "does not bud" is the predicate. Likewise every verse which contains twelve utterances can be reduced to six distinct sentences. You should not count the feet nor the words, but only the ideas, and thus it often happens that a small word converges with the adjoining word. Similarly, the verses of the Psalms keep to the order that we have described: *Have mercy upon me O God as befits Your faithfulness* are three, [and likewise] *in keeping with Your abundant compassion blot out my transgression* (Ps. 51:3); *In God whose word I praise, in the Lord*

21. The example is from the Song of the Sea, Ex. 15:6ff.
22. In the Hebrew, each phrase contains three words.

whose word I praise (Ps. 56:11). And again in the Proverbs of Solomon, *Wisdom cries aloud in the streets, raises her voice in the squares* (Pr. 1:20).

It does not surprise me that there are many verses which I am unable to fit into the systems described above—perhaps the exceptions outnumber those that are applicable. However, following the lines of this discourse of mine, the intelligent people will gain enlightenment and go on to discover that which escaped me. At any rate, we do indeed have reason to believe that all the songs of holy Scripture—the song of the Sea, the song of the Well and the Song in *ha'azinu* and the song of Deborah and the song of David and books of truth [i.e., Job, Psalms, and Proverbs][23]—undoubtedly adhere to an arrangement and structure, one with one mode and the other with another, or one in its own right containing different measures. On reciting them, we sense that they have a wonderful special quality even though we cannot fully apprehend their structures. In like manner, we speak, get up, and sit down without knowing which nerves and natural faculties enable us to perform those actions, for their function in us is due to divine wisdom. There is no doubt that the Davidic songs, particularly those recited at the Lord's altar, as the author of the *Kuzari* said,[24] used to be set to music and there [at the altar] indeed, it [i.e., the music] reached its culmination, and there, for such is its distinctive quality, it would arouse the soul. You should not be surprised at our statement that the same song consists of different measures. Once acquainted with the nature of the poetry written by pagan sages such as Horace and Terence, it will become clear to you that they also composed in this way. Everything is determined by that which suits the purpose of the subject and the variations which occur in the course of the song are due to the movements of the body and soul.[25]

Know, intelligent reader, that I was eager to hear how a notable and erudite authority of the time, particularly an expert in poetics, would speak about this topic. I therefore discussed this study of mine with the sagacious and third of the Provenzali brothers who are the luminaries of Mantua, my land. I am referring to Rabbi Judah who wrote the book *Nefuṣot Yehudah*.[26] In the name of the Lord, I read out to him the text that I had written from the beginning of the chapter until this juncture. As he said (and he is not the man to lie), that in his estimation, my method is correct and useful. He also made his own contribution to the topic. He said that rather than claiming that our later authorities borrowed the relevant poetical techniques from the nations of antiquity, we could rather enhance the honor of our own language and people and put forward a contrary argument, namely, that the nations of antiquity had already borrowed the material from the ancients of our people. You can provide support for such an idea from the statements of the teacher of the *Guide*[27] and from the author of *Dere*ḵ*h*

23. De' Rossi is using a popular acronym based on the first letters of the names of these books.

24. *Kuzari* II, par. 64.

25. See Lowth, *Isaiah* (XXXV–XXXVI): "I agree therefore with Azarias in his general principle of a rhythmus of things: but instead of considering terms or phrases or senses in single lines, as measures; I consider only that relation and proportion of one verse to another, which arises from the correspondence of terms, and from the form of construction; from whence results a rhythmus of propositions, and a harmony of sentences."

26. Judah was brother of David and Abraham Provenzali. His work appears not to be extant.

27. Maimonides, *Guide* I, ch. 71.

Emunah[28] that the Jews originally had many disciplines but that when we were subjugated by the nations, these came into their possession. Thus when we learn something from them, we gain the impression that this knowledge was theirs in the first place, but in fact the reverse is true.

Be that as it may, we have so far established that the words of the *Kuzari* and Don Isaac which we cited at the beginning of the chapter who deny that the holy songs are built on quantitative meter which is used nowadays, are the words of true sages who have attained knowledge. Notwithstanding all this, we cannot refrain from admitting that they do, without question, have other measures that are dependent on the ideas in the manner that we described. The result are verses which are superior and more notable than those that depend on syllabic feet. Moreover, once you have grasped the truth of the view put forward in the *Kuzari,* you will notice that it has some bearing on what we have written. You will notice that there is an added advantage to the different kinds of prophetic poems. It is actually possible to translate some of them into another language and to preserve their meter, at least approximately, which is impossible to achieve with poems where the rhythm is dependent on the number of syllables, as is obvious to all those who are knowledgeable. And so, if the story about Amaziah's commander is true,[29] we cannot deny that from that time, even the contemporary modes of writing poems (which according to the *Kuzari* and Don Isaac are borrowed from the Arabic) would have been used by some of the people for compositions of a popular nature, but not by the poets who composed under divine inspiration.

Now among the things that should be taken into consideration with regard to this subject—although I am not aware that contemporary poets are mindful of it—is the following point. You will discover that the peoples who are settled in their habits[30] and organize their disciplines in appropriately systematic modes, compose poems with the meter which suits the subject matter. There is a difference between the meter used for joyful poems, lyric poetry as they call it, the so-called elegiac meter for poems of mourning and the heroic meter in which they compose poems to extoll and glorify heroes or mighty kings, comparing them to divine beings. Such is their method of employing the different meters. Likewise, when we compose poems with meter we should ensure that their structures fit their purpose—not every meter will be suitable for any subject that comes to our mind. For example, the rhythm which the best poets of today and their predecessors used for poems of joy or praise or prayer ought not to be applied to dirges or epitaphs and the like. For the words of the poem must suit the voice, just as the voice must suit the purpose to which it is put. You should certainly consider the correct observation that we made above with reference to the verses of the book of Lamentations. For every verse in chapters 1 and 2 of Lamentations comprises three distinct clauses, and each clause comprises subject, predicate, and all that goes with it. Chapter 3 similarly preserves the same mode since it is attached to them, but it is divided into three main sections. But chapter 4 does not include its ideas in every

28. Abraham ben Shemtob Bibago, *Derekh Emunah,* gate 3.

29. De' Rossi's skepticism is naturally well founded. On the inscription, see F. Cantera and J. M. Millas, *Las inscripciones,* 394–403.

30. 'Settled in their habits,' lit. settled on their lees. Cf. Zeph. 1:12.

verse but is divided into two lots of two which come to four. Look and you will discover this for yourself, and come to realize that this was their method of composing dirges. Similarly, Josephus wrote[31] that Jeremiah composed his dirge for Josiah in a rhythm[32] that gave expression to mourning and sorrow. But chapter 4 of Lamentations which is a prayer is obviously constructed in another style, namely, one-one, like the verse of the books of Job, Proverbs, and Psalms, as we noted. Likewise, the song of *ha'azinu* and Deborah's song preserves one measure of three-three, amounting to six, comparable to the heroic meter which they regard as the best and most majestic of meters. Now I have not been constrained by the fact that these words of mine are but a tiny part of vast subject, a mere drop from a bucket. Yet the sage will pay attention to them and contribute to the subject with discretion and knowledge.

Similarly, one of the various relevant considerations that should be observed in the writing of verse epitaphs, which we mention since the subject has arisen, is that they ought to be composed with a view to the true purpose and benefit to which they are put. You are familiar with the statement of our rabbis of blessed memory in Sheqalim in the Palestinian Talmud[33] and in Bereshit Rabbah[34] with regard to the verse, *Over her grave Jacob set up a pillar* (Gen. 35:20): "It is taught: Rabbi Simeon ben Gamaliel said: 'Monuments are not erected for the righteous for their words are their memorial.'" From this it would appear that the custom of erecting tombstones for the dead is practiced by the ignorant and has no basis. Such a view gains credibility when considered from the perspective of the deceased's honor. The fact is that the dead are completely oblivious to it, and what was, was. Thus all the eulogies applied to them, telling that they are descended from a line of sages or from kings of antiquity are regarded as futile and of no account. In contrast, however, in the same context,[35] it is said that the surplus [of funds] may be used to erect a monument over his grave. And in Eruvin,[36] they mention these tombstones with regard to the Sabbath laws about extended city boundaries. Scripture is explicit: *Over her grave Jacob set up a pillar.* And in 2 Kings, a grave of a man of God is noted: *What is the marker that I see there?* (2K. 23:17). These are indications that the custom was already widespread in antiquity. Therefore we would say that Rabbi Simeon ben Gamaliel's purpose was not to censure outright the act of erecting monuments for the righteous; rather, the relevance of his statement lay in the reason which he gave. In other words, his statement referred to the intention of giving him a memorial by means of that monument with the implication that otherwise, no blessing or remembrance of him would remain. A memorial of this nature would thus be comparable to Absalom's monument in Samuel (2Sam. 18:18),[37] *For he said, I have no son to keep my name alive.* But neither Rabbi Simeon ben Gamaliel nor any later sage was troubled about the kind of monuments that we are about to discuss, which serve a beneficial purpose in some way.

31. *Ant.* X:78.
32. Cassel's edition erroneously reads *miqṣat* (some) instead of *miqṣav* (rhythm) as in the first edition.
33. P. Sheq. 2 (5) 47a.
34. B.R. 82:10. This passage is not in any of the manuscripts.
35. See nn.33 and 34.
36. B. Eruv. 53a.
37. *Now Absalom in his lifetime, had taken the pillar . . . and set it up for himself, for he said, For I have no son to keep my name alive.*

Now in the *Antiquities,*[38] Josephus refers to the death of one of the kings of the second Temple and his burial. He relates that during the burial procession, the people walking behind the coffin sprinkled it with various different kinds of spices, time after time. This was Jewish custom of the day, which indicated and reminded us that our dead will live again. It may also account for the story recounted about King Asa in 2 Chronicles (16:14), who, while alive, had filled the grave which he had prepared for himself with spices and perfumes of sweet scent. Thereby he implied that a time was still to come when he and his acquaintances would approach one by one to speak to each other as in former times without being deterred by a mouldy and offensive smell since it would be obliterated by the sweet scent given off by the choice spices.

This subject is treated in a similar vein by Christians. In his commentary on the fourth book of the *Sententiae* (distinctio 15 and 45),[39] Aquinas writes that gravestones are constructed in order to betoken the future resurrection, and to prompt those who set eyes on them to pray for the salvation of the soul. In the first of his *Tusculans,*[40] the orator Cicero also expresses similar views when speaking about ancient pagan custom with regard to tombstones. But let us put aside these authors and concentrate on the statement of the rabbis of blessed memory in Taʿanit:[41] "Why do they go to the cemeteries? One said, 'because we are as dead before You.' The other said, 'That they should ask for mercy on our behalf.' " And in the Zohar they say:[42]

> At the time when the world needs mercy, the living go and tell the souls of the righteous, and they weep by their graves and they are fitting to be informed in this way. Why? Because they [i.e., the souls of the righteous] dedicate their will to join one soul to another.[43] Then the souls of the righteous are aroused and they gather together and they go and wander off to those who sleep in Hebron[44] and inform them of the distress of the world, and they all go up to the gateway of the Garden of Eden and inform the spirit, and those are the spirits that are crowned in the Garden of Eden and the celestial angels are among them and all inform the Soul and the Soul informs the Holy One blessed be He and they all ask for mercy for the living and the Holy One blessed be He has mercy on all the world for their sake and concerning this Solomon said, *Then I accounted those who died long since more fortunate than those who are still living* (Eccl. 4:2).

An illustration of this is given in Sota where it speaks about Caleb who prostrated himself over the graves of our ancestors.[45] Accordingly it is to our advantage to distinguish between one who serves God and one who does not, according to the criterion that we learn from their saying,[46] "Everyone with whom human beings [are pleased,

38. *Ant.* XVII:199, describes Herod's funeral and simply mentions that there were "500 servants carrying spices." However, the detail given by de' Rossi is in the *Josippon,* bk. 6, ch. 61 (220).

39. *Super quatuour libros Sententiarum* (of Petrus Lombardus) lib. 4, distinctio 45. I cannot find a substantial reference to this subject in distinctio 15.

40. *Tusc. Disp.* 1, XLIV, and particularly, "Let the living, however, attend to funeral observances to the extent to which they must make a compromise with custom and public opinion, but with the understanding that they realize that no way does it concern the dead" (Loeb, trans. J. E. King).

41. B. Taʿanit 16a.

42. Zohar, aḥare mot, III, 70b–71a.

43. On the nature of the soul, see above ch. 59, n. 27.

44. I.e., the patriarchs.

45. B. Sota 34b.

46. M. Avot 3:13.

God is pleased with him]." How, then, shall the location of the burial ground of those who are regarded as men of piety be known? By seeking out the place marked by the monuments and gravestones which are erected over them, one will find that the ground on which he stands is holy.

In the light of these matters, my heart is astir. The verses written on tombstones should not be composed with a view of lavishing exaggerated and vain praises on noble lineage and the distinction of honor, riches, and the like. The only purpose should be to remind the one who comes to stand there that the soul does not die with the body and that his righteous actions will be kept in mind by the God of recompense; or alternatively, that at the time of resurrection he will move about among those who stand[47] and that every person must in the future give account of himself before the King, the Lord. These and other such doctrines of Torah the living should take to heart. In these cases, the tombstone is not spurned by a rational person, but rather will have good associations.[48] For the fact is that the words and the aims that we mentioned are right and correct. It is to the honor of the dead and the living to instill exemplary notions into the minds of the people, for example, that the spirit returns to God, that every action will be judged and that at the end of days, the righteous will attain his portion of everlasting salvation.

Now in this context, I cannot desist, dear reader, from making mention here of a poem which, being still among the living, I was inspired to compose for my own tombstone. For as Job said (19:24), *Incised on a rock forever with iron stylus and lead:* first *with iron stylus,* and then filled *with lead.* But the motivation [to write such an epitaph] was not, God forbid, like that which inspired the monument of Absalom. On the other hand, I did not write it because I consider myself a righteous man or in order to ascribe praise and repute to my family name de' Rossi which according to family tradition is one of the four noble families that were exiled to Rome by Titus.[49] For ultimately, to use apposite rhetorical language, one would say, *Though he goes along weeping, carrying the seed bag, he shall come back with songs of joy, carrying his sheaves* (Ps. 126:6). As Rav Perida said in Menaḥot:[50] "If he is a learned man, it is fine." And Yedidyah the Alexandrian speaks in the same vein in the section *On Nobility.*[51] But it occurred to me that I should indicate that, like all other humans, I shall in the future be held to account for my actions by the Lord of all creatures, and together with this I trusted in His mercies which are everlasting, and this as we said, is one of the purposes [of tombstones]. Read it out aloud. It is as follows:[52]

47. Cf. Zech. 3:7.

48. 'Will have good association,' lit. will be remembered for good. The expression is used when mentioning the dead.

49. Other families which according to this medieval tradition, claimed this lineage were the de Pomis, de' Vecchii, and de' Mansi.

50. B. Men. 53a. The implication of this statements is that lineage is not important, but only the qualities of each individual.

51. *Virt.,* particularly 189–91.

52. With regard to his epitaph, de' Rossi states in B that he had modeled his text on the inscription that Cardinal Contarini had prepared for his own grave: "Venimus ad portum, spes et fortuna valete / nil mihi vobiscum, illudite nunc alios." (We have reached port; farewell hope and fortune / I have nothing more to do with you; now make play with others.) On the inscription, see my introduction.

From the storm-tossed sea yea to the shore
I have come and no hurricane need fear
I laugh at the vicissitudes of false time
My God will no more be strange to me
It may be asked if my merchandise find favor
With the Prince who calls all by name
But He it is who created me, I shall not want
For He His grace does lavish on every creature

And on the tombstone of the dear son of my daughter I wrote:

The lot of a precious child of noble lineage
buried until at days' end he like saplings will blossom forth.
Among those whose ways are pure, deserving of rest
The God, creator of spirits, called him Benjamin

Now let us put aside these matters and return to the main purpose of the chapter. The principle that we have reached is as follows. The poems based on rhythm with feet and quantities, numbered according to rules, are not truly congruent with the nature of our language. The sage of the *Kuzari* was right to say that they are antithetical to its supreme character. For generally they move when there should be a pause, and pause where there should be movement; they separate that which should be connected and connect that which is separate. These and other such discreditable things come about if one is not sufficiently heedful. But the poems that suit it are those which preserve their harmonies by means of the content as is shown by the words of the prophets that we mentioned. God in His goodness will open our eyes and we shall see[53] in his Torah wonders enough on account of His great mercy which endures forever, selah.

Now I would like to end with a blessing, thus mirroring the opening of the book about the earthquakes which erupted here in Ferrara. Now we have already demonstrated how they begun on the night of Thursday, leading to Friday 17 November [5]331 [i.e., 1570], between the ninth and tenth hour. Indeed, they continued intermittently, on new moon and Sabbath, at times of assemblies,[54] once or twice until the end of the year. Now at the very same time, as the year drew to its close, that is on the holy Sabbath, the following day being 17 November [5]332 [1571], in the first half of the night between the fourth and fifth hours, there were likewise six minor quakes, with hardly an interval between them, the last of which was the strongest. It brought the entire populace into a state of terror lest it would continue and persist in its raging, God forbid, as in the previous year. But, thanks be to the Lord, it then abated and the earth was at rest. Accordingly, the reign of these earthquakes to date was twelve months, namely, one whole year, the years of a hired laborer,[55] from midnight of the second day to midnight of the first as we related. Now the year having come to its close, and its curses ceased, may it please my God to usher in a good year with its blessings. However, should it henceforth erupt again may it not come to pass like those quakes mentioned

53. Cassel reads *nabia* instead of *nabbit* (we shall see) as in the first edition.
54. 'New . . . assemblies,' cf. Is. 1:13.
55. 'Like . . . laborer,' cf. Is. 21:16.

by the sage ibn Rushd (Averroes) towards the end of book 2 of the *Meteorologica* which continued for three years in the city of Cordova[56] or if, as we hope, God will respond with mercy to the plea for the earth[57] and the raging will not recur, chroniclers shall record the events for the generation who will inform us of what occurs.[58] We shall bless God who until now has protected us. So may He lovingly take us under His wing, continually watching over all the seed of those who serve Him and shield us from all troubles and distress. For He, the blessed Lord, is indeed our rock and salvation who answers us in time of adversity and delivers.

I, Azariah de' Rossi, a Mantuan, in the name of the eternal God, conceived this book on the eve of Passover in the year [5]331 [1571]. With His blessed aid, I brought it to fruition at the end of eighteen months in the month of Ethanim[59] in the year 5333 [1572]. In other words, I wrote it within one year and labored six months to revise it. May God who granted me the strength to write it, bestow His glorious kindness upon me that I shall be happy with my lot, and so too all those who call on Him with loving kindness.

As a conclusion to the book, I have composed the following poem of twenty lines:

I shall bless You, blessed Lord, living God, high above all holy beings
who have brought me in peace to the end of my work, to gladden spirits.
Sure I am that all the learned will delight in it and seek it out,
Knowing well that all my utterances here are for the sake of truth, each necessary to its purpose.
The wise, indeed every man, whoever he is, will find in it what pertains to him.
But to the fools or hypocrites and those clothed in falsehood,
let me make a pact with them that they touch it not, for they will surely bite it like serpents.
With mighty justice will it break their fangs and enchant them with its words.
Let them curse but the Almighty God will bless; I shall rejoice and they are garbed in shame.
Honor enough there is, if an error is mine, let it be struck down midst a hundred warriors of truth.[60]
For it will draw its sword alone against a fifty-square span
I began it in the spring, the first of the months, the year of the tamarisk,[61] made famous by the earthquakes
and finished it in the month of God's appointed times, at the end of twice nine months.
I considered it my firstborn, for a double length of time I've carried it within me long the brimming days of gestation.
It irradiates light to me in this world and merits my soul to join celestial beings.
Elders basked in its splendor and wise old men in its "Words of Understanding"[62]

56. *Aristotelis Opera,* 444v, col. a.
57. 'God . . . earth,' cf. 2Sam. 24:25.
58. 'For the generation . . . occurs' combines Ps. 22:31 and Is. 41:22.
59. 'Ethanim,' i.e., the month of Tishri, six months after Passover.
60. I.e., his error is negligible in comparison with the numerous correct data that he provides.
61. The numerical value of the letters of the word for "tamarisk" is 331, i.e., 5331 (1571).
62. This is play on the titles of the sections of the book "Splendor of the Elders" and "Words of Understanding."

Its chapters form a perfect number* of tens, let any error that there is be annulled midst the sixty.[63]

(*Some hold that six is a perfect number[65] and sixty is a perfect factor of ten.)

And if my Rock will decree me for life, productive will I be and will not forsake my studies.
With a second, yea third revision, I shall build it up again and again[64]
As my name Azariah, I hope God is my help, and again new songs shall I sing to Him.

THE END

Blessed is the Lord forever Amen Amen

63. The book contains sixty chapters. De' Rossi plays here with the halakhic concept according to which something becomes neutralized when the quantity in which it is mixed is sixty times as large.
64. The imagery is from the description of the construction of Noah's ark.
65. See Philo, *L.A.* I, 3.

CHRONOLOGICAL TABLES

Biblical chronology from the flood to the destruction of the second Temple in Seder Olam Rabbah reckoned from the creation of the world

1656	Flood
2048	Birth of Isaac (400 years until)
2448	Exodus from Egypt (480 years until)
2928	Building of the first Temple (410 years until)
3338	Destruction of the first Temple
3408	Consecration of the second Temple (420 years until)
3828	Destruction of the second Temple

Kings of Judah		Kings of Israel	
Rehoboam	928–911 B.C.E.	Jeroboam I	928–907 B.C.E.
Abijah	911–908	Nadab	907–906
Asa	908–867	Baasha	906–883
		Elah	883–882
		Zimri	882
		Omri	882–871
Jehoshaphat	867–846	Ahab	871–852
		Ahaziah	852–851
Jehoram	846–843	Jehoram	851–842
Ahaziah	843–842	Jehu	842–814
Athaliah	842–836		
Jehoash	836–798	Jehoahaz	814–800
Amaziah	798–769	Jehoash	800–784
Uzziah	769–733	Jeroboam II	784–748
Jotham	758–743	Zechariah	748–747
		Shallum	748–747
Ahaz	758–743	Menahem	747–737
		Pekahiah	737–735
		Pekah	735–733
Ahaz	733–727	Hoshea	733–724
Hezekiah	727–698	Samaria captured by Shalmaneser V	(722)
Manasseh	698–642		
Amon	641–640		

Kings of Judah		Kings of Israel
Josiah	639–609	
Jehoahaz	609	
Jehoiakim	608–598	
Jehoiachin	597	
Zedekiah	595–586	

Persian Kings during the Second Temple Period	
Cyrus	559–530 B.C.E.
Cambyses	530–522
Darius I	522–486
Xerxes I	486–465
Artaxerxes I	465–424
Xerxes II	424–423
Darius II	423–404
Artaxerxes II	404–359
Artaxerxes III	359–338
Arses	338–336
Darius III	336–330

GLOSSARY

Aggadah (pl. aggadot): The nonlegal material in the classical rabbinic corpus.

Amora (pl. Amoraim): Post-Mishnaic rabbinic authority of the third to sixth centuries C.E. active in Palestine and Babylon.

Baraita (pl. baraitot): Any ruling or tradition attributed to Tannaim which is not included in the official Mishnah.

Gaon (pl. Geonim): Title of the leaders and teachers in the rabbinic academies of Babylonia in the post-talmudic period from the seventh to the eleventh centuries. The title was also used as a purely honorific designation.

Gemara: A substitute term for the talmudic commentary on the Mishnah.

Halakhah (pl. halakhot): the legal material in the classical rabbinic corpus.

Ibbur: (1) the intercalation of a month or year; (2) the science of the fixed calendar; (3) the regulation of the calendar.

Kabbalah: (1) Religious tradition; (2) the mystical and esoteric tradition.

Masorah: The traditional text of the Hebrew Bible which was systemized, established, and transmitted by a school of scholars known as the Massoretes in the early Middle Ages.

Megillat Taʿanit: Scroll of fasts which lists thirty-six days on which fasting is not permitted, referring to events of the Maccabean and Roman periods. The name is also given to a list of fast days, probably dating from the Geonic period.

Men of the Great Synagogue: The body of sages who according to rabbinic tradition were authoritative during the prerabbinic period in the first years of the second Temple.

Mezuzah: Piece of parchment containing passages from Scripture affixed to the doorposts of the house (Deut. 6:9).

Midrash (pl. Midrashim): Rabbinic exposition of Scripture. The term is applied both to the method of exegesis and to the actual product(s), incorporated in the Talmuds and in the various collections of Midrashim, such as the Mekhilta d'Rabbi Ishmael, Sifra, Sifre, Midrash Rabbah (on the Pentateuch and the five Scrolls), Midrash Tehillim (on Psalms), Tanḥuma, and Yalqut Shimoni.

Mishnah: The authoritative corpus of Jewish law compiled about 200 C.E. attributed to Rabbi Judah the patriarch.

Miṣvah (pl. miṣvot): Precept of the Torah.

Seder Olam Rabbah: A midrashic chronology attributed to Rabbi Jose ben Ḥalafta which imposes dates on biblical events.

Talmud: Corpus of Jewish learning presented as a commentary on the Mishnah of which there are two compilations: the Palestinian Talmud (redacted in the first half of the fifth century) and the later and more authoritative Babylonian Talmud (redacted in the sixth century).

Tanna (pl. tannaim): Name given to the rabbinic authorities of the first two centuries C.E. in Palestine whose views are recorded in the Mishnah, Baraitot, and Tosefta.

Tosafists: The French and German glossators on the Talmud between the twelfth and fourteenth centuries.

Yeshivah (pl. yeshivot): School or academy in which Talmud is studied.

BIBLIOGRAPHY

AUTOGRAPH MANUSCRIPTS OF AZARIAH DE' ROSSI

Bodleian Mich. 308: Azariah de' Rossi, *Maṣref la-Kesef; Elegie per la morte della madama Margarita duchessa di Savoia;* Italian translation of ch. 35 of the *Me'or Enayim.*

National Library, Jerusalem Ms. 3935: Copybook belonging to Azariah de' Rossi containing transcriptions of various works and fragments.

Angelica Library, Rome, Narducci Ms. 1948: Azariah de' Rossi, *Osservazioni di Buonaiuto de' Rossi ebreo sopra diversi luoghi degli Evangelisti nuovamente esposti secondo la vera lezione siriaca* (1577).

PRINTED EDITIONS OF THE *ME'OR ENAYIM*

Mantua, 1573–75 (ed. pr.).

Berlin, 1794 (ed. I. Satanov).

Vienna, 1829–30 (ed. A. Schmid).

Vilna, 1863–65 (ed. I. Benjacob).

Vilna, 1864–66 (ed. D. Cassel; rpt. Jerusalem, 1970).

Warsaw, 1899 (ed. D. Cassel, with additional notes by Z. H. Jaffe).

DE' ROSSI'S SOURCES IN THE *ME'OR ENAYIM*

The listing of the Hebrew sources is according to the entries in the *Encyclopaedia Judaica.*

The listing of the non-Hebrew sources is mainly according to the entries in the British Library catalogue. All references to patristic works are according to Migne's *Patrologia Graeca* and *Patrologia Latina* series.

* = edition(s) consulted by de' Rossi.

[Ed.] = modern or standard edition(s) indicated in the notes in conjunction with fifteenth- or sixteenth-century edition(s).

Where it was impossible to establish which sixteenth-century edition of a work de' Rossi cited, a late sixteenth-century edition has generally been consulted in line with the dating of the other editions which have been identified.

Hebrew Sources

Aaron ben Elijah, *Keter Torah* (read in ms.). Goslaw, 1866–67.

Aaron ben Joseph, *Sefer ha-Mivḥar* (read in ms.). Goslaw, 1835.

Aaron ben Joseph Halevi (attrib.), *Sefer ha- Ḥinnukh.* Venice, 1523. [Ed. H. D. Chavel, 7th ed. Jerusalem, 1966.]

Aboab, Isaac, *Menorat ha-Maʾor.* Constantinople, 1514. [Ed. *Menorat ha-Maʾor,* 4th ed., ed. J. Prijs-Ḥorev. Jerusalem, 1961.]

Abraham ben David of Posquières (Rabad), *Hassagot al Mishneh Torah.* See Maimonides, *Mishneh Torah.*

——, *Perush Eduyyot.* See *Talmud Bavli.*

*Abraham ben Eliezer Halevi, *Meshare Qitrin.* Constantinople, 1510.

Abraham bar Ḥiyya, *Megillat ha-Megalleh* (read in ms.), ed. A. Poznanski. Berlin, 1924.

——, *Sefer Ḥeshbon ha-Mahalekhot ha-Kokhavim* (read in ms.), ed. J. M. Millás-Vallicrosa. Barcelona, 1959.

——, *Sefer ha-Ibbur* (read in ms.), ed. H. Filipowski. London, 1851.

*Abravanel, Isaac ben Judah, *Mashmia Yeshuʿah.* Salonika, 1526. [Ed. *Mashmia Yeshuʿah.* Tel Aviv, 1960.]

——, *Mayyane ha-Yeshuʿah.* Ferrara, 1551. [Ed. *Mayyane ha-Yeshuʿah.* Tel Aviv, 1960.]

——, *Naḥalat Avot.* Venice, 1545. (Rpt. Jerusalem, 1970.)

——, *Perush al ha-Torah* [on Pentateuch] (read in ms.), *Perush al ha-Torah.* Jerusalem, 1964.

——, *Perush al Neviʾim Rishonim* [on former Prophets]. Pesaro, 1511–12. [Ed. *Perush al Neviʾim Rishonim.* Jerusalem, 1955.]

——, *Perush al ha-Neviʾim Aḥaronim* [on latter Prophets]. Pesaro, 1520. [Ed. *Perush al Neviʾim Aḥaronim.* Tel Aviv, 1960(?). Ed. *Perush al Neviʾim u-ketuvim.* Includes commentary on minor prophets. Tel Aviv, 1960.]

Abudarham, David ben Joseph, *Sefer Abudarham.* Venice, 1566. [Ed. *Perush ha-Berakhot veha-Tefillot Sefer Abudarham ha-shalem,* ed. S. Wertheimer. Jerusalem, 1963.]

Abulafia, Meir ben Todros, *Yad Ramah. Pesaqim al Bava Batra* (read in ms.). Salonika, 1790.

Abulafia, Todros ben Joseph Halevi, *Oṣar ha-Kavod* (read in ms.). Warsaw, 1879. (Rpt. Bene Berak, 1987.)

Adret, Solomon ben Abraham (Rashba), *Ḥiddushe ha-Rashba,* ed. Leon A. Feldman. Jerusalem, 1991.

——, *Sheʾelot u-Teshuvot.* Venice, 1545.

Ahmad ibn Muhammad ibn Kathir (al-Farghani), on astronomy (no title) (read in ms.).

*Al-Ashqar, Moses ben Isaac, *Sheʾelot u- Teshuvot.* Sabbioneta, 1553.

Albo, Joseph, *Sefer ha-Iqqarim.* Venice, 1544. [Ed. *Sefer ha-Ikkarim, Book of Principles,* ed. and trans. Isaac Husik. 5 vols. Philadelphia, 1946.]

*Alfasi, Isaac, *Halakhot,* with Jonah Gerondi, Nissim Gerondi, Asher ben Jehiel, Joseph Ḥabiba, Mordechai ben Hillel, Zerachiah Halevi, Joshua Boaz, Isaiah di Trani. Constantinople, 1509. [Ed. *Sefer ha-Halakhot.* Vilna, 1880–86.]

Amram ben Sheshna, *Seder Rav Amram* (read in ms.), ed. Daniel Goldschmidt. Jerusalem, 1971.

Anav, Zedekiah ben Abraham, *Shibbole ha-Leqeṭ* (read in ms.), ed. S. Buber. Vilna, 1886. (Rpt. New York, 1958.)

Arama, Isaac, *Aqedat Yiṣḥaq.* Venice, 1546. [Ed. *Aqedat Yiṣḥaq.* Pressburg, 1849. (Rpt. Jerusalem, 1961.)]
——, *Ḥazut Qashah.* Sabbioneta, 1551.
Asher ben Yehiel (Rosh/Asheri), *Pisqe ha-Rosh.* See *Talmud Bavli.*
Avot d' Rabbi Nathan. See *Talmud Bavli.* [Ed. *Avot d'Rabbi Nathan,* ed. S. Schechter. Vienna, 1887.]
Bahir, Sefer ha-, 2d ed. (read in ms.), ed. R. Margaliot. Jerusalem, 1978.
Baḥya ben Asher, *Beʾur al ha-Torah.* Venice, 1566. [Ed. *Beʾur al ha-Torah,* ed. H. D. Chavel. Jerusalem, 1966–68.]
Baruch ben Isaac, *Sefer ha-Terumah.* Venice, 1523.
Basola, Moses, *Massaʿot Ereṣ Yisrael* (read in ms.), ed. I. Ben Zvi. Jerusalem, 1938.
Benjamin bar Jehudah (Anav), *Perush al Divre ha-Yamim* (read in ms.).
Bertinoro, Obadiah di, *Perush ha-Mishnayot.* See *Mishnah.*
Biba, Samuel, *Perush ibn Ezra* (read in ms.).
*Bibago, Abraham b. Shemtov, *Derekh Emunah.* Constantinople, 1521.
**Bible, Pentateuch* in Hebrew and Greek and Spanish translation in Hebrew characters. Constantinople, 1547.
**Bible, Pentateuch* in Hebrew with Targum Onqelos, Rashi, Arabic, Persian translations in Hebrew characters. Constantinople, 1546.
**Bible, Rabbinic,* with Targum Yerushalmi on Pentateuch and Targum on Prophets, Abraham Farissol on Job, etc. Venice, 1517.
**Bible, Rabbinic,* with introduction by Jacob ben Ḥayyim ibn Adonijah, Ḥidah of ibn Ezra, and commentaries of ibn Ezra and (ps.) Saadia on Daniel, etc. Venice, 1524–25.
Caro, Isaac ben Joseph, *Toledot Yiṣḥaq.* Mantua, 1558.
Caro, Joseph, *Bet Yosef.* Jacob ben Asher.
——, *Kesef Mishneh* (read in ms.). Venice, 1574–76.
Dato, Mordechai, *Migdal David* (autograph ms. in Bodleian Opp. Add. 153).
*De Balmes, Abraham ben Meir, *Miqneh Avram,* with Latin translation *Peculium Abrae.* Venice, 1522.
D'Estella, David ben Samuel (Kokhavi), *Migdal David* (read in ms.), ed. Hershler, Jerusalem, 1982.
Duran, Profayt, Isaac ben Moses, *Ḥeshev ha-Efod* (read in ms.).
——, *Maʿaseh ha-Efod* (read in ms.), ed. J. Friedländer and J. Kohn. Vienna, 1865.
Eldad ha-Dani, *Sefer Eldad ha-Dani.* Venice, 1544.
*Estori ha-Parḥi ben Moses, *Sefer Kaftor va-Feraḥ.* Venice, 1546–50. [Ed. *Sefer Kaftor va-Feraḥ,* ed. J. Blumenfeld, New York, 1958–60.]
Farissol, Abraham, *Magen Avraham* (read in ms.).
——, *Perush al Iov.* See *Bible, Rabbinic* (1517).
*Gershon ben Solomon, *Sefer Shaʿar ha-Shamayim.* Venice, 1547.
Gersonides, Levi ben Gershon, *Milḥamot ha-Shem.* Riva di Trento, 1560–61.
——, *Perush ha-Torah.* Mantua, 1474–77. [Ed. *Perushe ha-Torah le-Rabbenu Levi ben Gershom (Ralbag).* Jerusalem, 1992–94.]
——, *Perush al Daniel.* Rome, 1469–72.
——, *Toʿaliyyot.* Riva di Trento, 1560.
*Gikatilla, Joseph ben Abraham, *Shaʿare Orah.* Mantua, 1561.

——, *Shaʿare Ṣedeq*. Riva di Trento, 1561.

Ḥabiba, Joseph, *Nimmuqe Yosef*. See Alfasi.

Ḥayyat, Judah ben Joseph, *Minḥat Yehudah*. See Perez.

*Husain ibn Abd Ablah (ibn Sina-Avicenna), *Qanon ha-Gadol,* trans. Joseph ben Joshua Lorqi and Nathan ben Eliezer Hameati. Naples, 1491.

*Ibn Bibago, Abraham, *Derekh Emunah*. Constantinople, 1521.

*Ibn Daud, Abraham, *Sefer ha-Qabbalah*. Mantua, 1513. [Ed. *The Book of Tradition Sefer ha-Kabbalah,* ed. and trans. Gershon D. Cohen. London, 1967.]

Ibn Ezra, Abraham, *Ḥidah*. See *Bible, Rabbinic* (1524–25).

——, *Perush Daniel*. See *Bible, Rabbinic* (1524–25).

——, *Perush ha-Torah*. Naples, 1488. [Ed. *Perush ha-Torah,* ed. A. Weiser. Jerusalem, 1976.]

*Ibn Ḥabib, Jacob, *En Yisrael u-Vet Yisrael (En Yaʿaqov)*. Venice, 1566.

*Ibn Ḥabib, Levi. *Sheʾelot u-Teshuvot*. Venice, 1565.

Ibn Ḥabib, Moses ben Shemtov, *Darkhe Noʿam*. Venice, 1546.

Ibn Janaḥ, Jonah, *Sefer ha-Riqmah* (read in ms.), ed. M. Wilensky and D. Tene. Jerusalem, 1964.

*Ibn Moṭoṭ, Samuel ben Saadiah, *Megillat Setarim, Perush al Perush R. Avraham ibn Ezra*. Venice, 1553.

Ibn Shemtov, Joseph, *Perush Sefer ha-Middot I-Aristo* (read in ms.).

Ibn Shuaib, Joshua, *Derashot al ha-Torah,* Constantinople, 1523.

Ibn Tibbon, Samuel ben Judah, *Maʾamar Yiqqavu ha-Mayim* (read in ms.), ed. M. L. Bislichis. Pressburg, 1837.

Isaac bar Aaron, *Sefer ha-Ibbur* (read in ms.).

Isaac ben Samuel (of Acre), *Meʾirat Enayim* (read in ms.), ed. H. Erlanger. Jerusalem, 1975.

Isaac ben Sheshet-Perfet (Ribash), *Sheʾelot u Teshuvot*. Riva di Trento, 1559.

Isaac Nathan ben Kalonymus (also called Mordechai Nathan), *Meʾir Nativ*. Venice, 1523.

Isaiah ben Mali di Trani (the elder—Rid), *Sefer ha-Mahadurot* (i.e., *Hịddushim al ha-Talmud*) (read in ms.), ed. *Piske ha-Rid, Piske ha-Riaz*. Jerusalem, 1964–.

Isaiah ben Elijah di Trani (the younger—Riaz), *Pesaqim* (read in ms.), ed. *Piske ha-Rid, Piske ha-Riaz*. Jerusalem, 1964–.

——, *Perush al Ezra* (read in ms.). [Ed. *Der Commentar zu Ezra und Nehemia von Jesaja di Trani,* ed. E. Schächter. Königsberg in Pr., 1892.]

Israeli, Isaac ben Joseph, *Shaʿar ha-Shamayim* (read in ms.).

——, *Yesod Olam* (read in ms.), ed. J. Shklover. Berlin, 1777. (Rpt. Jerusalem, 1970.)

*Isserles, Moses ben Israel, *Sefer Torat ha-Olah*. Prague, 1569.

Jacob ben Asher, *Arbaʿah Ṭurim* with *Bet Yosef* of Joseph Caro. Venice, 1566–64–67.

Jacob ben Ḥayyim ibn Adonijah. See *Bible, Rabbinic* (1524–25).

Jeshua ben Joseph Halevi, *Halikhot Olam*. Venice, 1544. [Ed. *Halikhot Olam*. Warsaw, 1883.]

Jose ben Ḥalafta. See *Seder Olam Rabbah*.

Joshua Boaz ben Simon Baruch, *Shilṭe ha-Gibborim*. See Alfasi.

**Josippon*. Mantua, before 1480; Constantinople, 1510; Venice, 1544; Basel, 1541 (ed. with Latin trans. by Sebastian Münster).

*Judah ben Yehiel (Messer Leon), *Nofet Ṣufim*. Mantua, before 1480. [Ed. *The Book of the Honeycomb's Flow,* ed. and trans. I. Rabinowitz. Ithaca and London, 1983.]

Judah Halevi, *Sefer ha-Kuzari.* Venice, 1547. (Also read in ms. Hebrew translation of Judah ibn Cardinal.)

Kaspi, Nathaniel ben Nehemiah, *Perush ha-Kuzari* (read in ms.).

Kayyara, Simeon (attrib.), *Halakhot Gedolot.* Venice, 1548. [Ed. *Halakhot Gedolot,* ed. E. Hildesheimer. 3 vols. Jerusalem, 1988.]

Kimḥi, David (Redak), Commentaries on Bible. See *Bible, Rabbinic* (1517). (Also read in ms.)

——, *Sefer ha-Shorashim.* Venice, 1546.

Latif, Moses, *Derashot* (read in ms.).

Levi ben Gershom. See Gersonides.

*Levita, Elijah ben Asher (Baḥur), *Massoret ha-Massoret.* Venice, 1538.

*——, *Meturgeman.* Isny, 1541.

Maimon of Montpellier, *Qiṣur al-Farghani* (read in ms.).

Maimonides (Moses ben Maimon, Rambam), *Mishneh Torah,* with *Hassagot* of Abraham ben David; anonymous *Haggahot; Migdal Oz* of Shem Tov b. Abraham; *Maggid Mishneh* of Vidal of Tolosa; Obadiah b. David on *Kiddush ha-Ḥodesh.* Constantinople, 1509.

——, *Moreh Nevukhim (Guide of the Perplexed),* with commentaries of Shemtov ben Joseph, Profayt Duran. Venice, 1551. [Ed. *Guide of the Perplexed,* trans. S. Pines. Chicago, 1963.]

——, *Perush al ha-Mishnah.* See *Mishnah.*

——, *Pirqe Mosheh* (read in ms.), ed. Süssmann Muntner. Jerusalem, 1959.

——, *Shemonah Peraqim.* See *Mishnah.*

——, *Teshuvot She'elot ve-Iggrot.* Venice, 1545. *Iggeret Teman. Iggeret le-Ḥakhme Marsilia. Ma'amar Teḥiyyat ha-Metim.* [Ed. *Teshuvot ha-Rambam,* ed. J. Blau. Jerusalem, 1957–86. Ed. *Iggrot ha-Rambam,* ed. M. D. Rabinowitz. Jerusalem, 1974. Ed. *Iggrot ha-Rambam,* ed. J. Shailat. Jerusalem, 1988.]

Maimonides (Moses ben Maimon, Rambam) (attrib.), *Perusho shel ha-Rambam le-massekhet Rosh ha-Shanah* (read in ms.), ed. J. L. Maimon. Jerusalem, 1969.

**Megillat Ta'anit* (together with *Seder Olam* and *Sefer ha-Qabbalah* of Abraham ibn Daud). Mantua, 1513. [Ed. *Megillat Ta'anit,* ed. Hans Lichtenstein. *HUCA* 8–9 (1931–32): 318–51.]

Mekhilta de'Rabbi Ishmael. Venice 1545. [Ed. *Mekhilta de'Rabbi Ishmael,* ed. J. Z. Lauterbach. Philadelphia, 1933.]

Meshullam ben Moses, *Sefer ha-Hashlamah,* (read in ms.) vol. 3, ed. J. Lubetzky. Pietrokov, 1910.

Midrash Abba Gorion (read in ms.).

Midrash Avkir (read in ms.).

Midrash ha-Ne'elam al Megillat Ruth. See *Zohar.*

Midrash Rabbah (on Torah and Megillot). Venice, 1566.

Midrash Bereshit Rabbah, with (ps.) Rashi and Abraham ben Asher. Venice, 1567. [Ed. *Midrash Bereshit Rabbah,* ed. J. Theodor and C. H. Albeck. Berlin, 1912–36. (Rpt. Jerusalem, 1965.) *Midrash Vayiqra Rabbah* Ed. *Midrash Vayikra Rabbah,* ed. M. Margulies. Jerusalem, 1953–60. *Midrash Devarim Rabbah* Ed. *Midrash Devarim Rabbah,* ed. S. Lieberman. Jerusalem, 1974.]

Midrash Mishle. See *Midrash Tehillim.*

Midrash Tanḥuma Yelammedenu. Constantinople, 1520–22; Venice, 1545; Mantua, 1563.

Midrash Tanḥuma Yelammedenu, ed. S. Buber. Vilna, 1885. (Rpt. Jerusalem, 1964.)

**Midrash Tehillim,* with *Midrash Shemuel* and *Midrash Mishle.* Venice, 1546. [Ed. *Midrash Tehillim,* ed. S. Buber. Vilna, 1891. (Rpt. Jerusalem, 1966.) Ed. *Midrash Mishle,* ed. B. L. Visotzky. New York, 1990.]

*Minz, Judah ben Eliezer Levi, *He lakhem zera li-Ṣedaqah Pesaqim u-She'elot.* Venice, 1553.

Mishnah, with commentary introduction, including *Shemonah Peraqim,* of Maimonides and commentary of Obadiah di Bertinoro. Riva di Trento, 1559.

Mizraḥi, Elijah ben Abraham, *Perush Rashi.* Venice, 1545.

Mordechai ben Hillel Hakohen. See Alfasi.

Moses ben Jacob (of Coucy), *Sefer Miṣvot ha-Gadol.* Venice, 1547. [Ed. *Sefer Miṣvot ha-Gadol,* ed. H. D. Chavel. Jerusalem, 1983.]

Moses ben Maimon. See Maimonides.

Moses ben Nahman. See Nahmanides.

Nahmanides (Moses ben Naḥman, Ramban), *Be'ur ha-Torah.* Venice, 1545. [Ed. *Perush ha-Ramban,* 17th ed., ed. H. D. Chavel. Jerusalem, 1989.]

——, *Hassagot al Sefer ha-Miṣvot.* Venice, 1550–51. [Ed. *Sefer ha-Miṣvot le-ha-Rambam im Hassagot ha-Ramban,* ed. H. D. Chavel. Jerusalem, 1981.]

Nahmanides (Moses ben Naḥman, Ramban), *Derashah le-Rosh ha-Shanah* (read in ms.), ed. *Derashah le-Rosh ha-Shanah,* in *Kitve Rabbenu Moshe ben Naḥman,* vol. 1, ed. H. D. Chavel. Jerusalem, 1963.

——, *Sefer ha-Ge'ulah* (read in ms.), ed. *Sefer ha-Ge'ulah,* in *Kitve Rabbenu Moshe ben Naḥman,* vol. 1, ed. H. D. Chavel. Jerusalem, 1963.

——, *Sefer ha-Vikuaḥ* (read in ms.), ed. *Sefer ha-Vikuaḥ,* in *Kitve Rabbenu Moshe ben Naḥman,* vol. 1, ed. H. D. Chavel. Jerusalem, 1963.

——, *Sha'ar ha-Gemul* (from *Torat Adam*). Naples, 1490, ed. *Sha'ar ha-Gamul,* in *Kitve Rabbenu Moshe ben Naḥman,* vol. 2, ed. H. D. Chavel. Jerusalem, 1964.

Nahmanides (Moses ben Naḥman, Ramban) (attrib.), *She'elot u-Teshuvot.* Venice, 1518–23.

Nathan, Mordechai (Nathan, Isaac). See Isaac Nathan ben Kalonymus.

Nathan ben Yehiel, *Arukh.* Venice, 1531.

Nissim ben Reuben Gerondi (Ran), on Alfasi. See Alfasi.

Nissim ben Reuben Gerondi (Ran), *Ḥiddushin al Nedarim.* See *Talmud Bavli.*

Obadiah ben David ben Obadiah. See Maimonides, *Mishneh Torah.*

Perez ben Yiṣhaq (attrib.), *Ma'arekhet ha-Elohut,* with commentary of Judah Ḥayyat. Mantua, 1558.

Pesiqta de'Rav Kahana (read in ms.), ed. *Pesikta de'Rav Kahana,* ed. B. Mandelbaum. New York, 1962.

Pirqe de'Rabbi Eliezer. Sabbioneta, 1567. [Ed. *Pirke de Rabbi Eliezer,* ed. G. Friedlander. London, 1916.]

Provenzali, David ben Abraham, *Dor ha-Pelagah* (read in ms.).

——, *Ir David* (read in ms.).

——, *Perush al Shir ha-Shirim* (read in ms.).

Provenzali, Judah, *Sefer Nefuṣot Yehudah* (read in ms.).

Rambam. See Maimonides.

Ramban. See Nahmanides.

Rashi. See Solomon ben Isaac.
Recanati, Menahem ben Benjamin, *Perush al ha-Torah.* Venice, 1545. [Ed. *Perush al ha-Torah* in *Levushe Or Yeqarot.* Jerusalem, 1961.]
Reuben ben Ḥayyim, *Perush Aggadot* (read in ms.).
Saadya ben Joseph Fayumi (ps.). See *Bible, Rabbinic* (1524–25).
Samson ben Isaac (of Chinon), *Sefer Keritut.* Cremona, 1558. [Ed. *Sefer Keritut,* ed. J. M. Sofer. Jerusalem, 1983.]
Samuel ben Isaac ha-Sardi, *Sefer ha-Terumot* (read in ms.). Salonika, 1596.
Samuel ben Meir (Rashbam), *Perush al-Pesaḥim.* See *Talmud Bavli.*
*Ṣarṣa, Samuel ibn Seneh, *Meqor Ḥayyim.* Mantua, 1559.
**Seder Olam Rabbah* (attrib. to Jose ben Ḥalafta). Mantua, 1513. [Ed. *Seder Olam Rabbah,* ed. B. Ratner. Vilna, 1897. (Rpt. New York, 1966.)]
Seder Tannaim ve-Amoraim (read in ms.), ed. K. Kahan. Frankfurt am Main, 1935.
Sefer Torah, in *Talmud Bavli.* [Ed. *Massekhtot Qeṭanot,* ed. M. Higger. New York, 1930.]
Sforno, Obadiah ben Jacob, *Beʾur al ha-Torah.* Venice, 1567. [Ed. *Beʾur al ha-Torah,* 4th ed., ed. Z. Gottlieb. Jerusalem, 1990.]
*Shemtov ibn Shemtov, *Sefer ha-Emunot.* Ferrara, 1556.
*Sherira Gaon, *Iggeret Rav Sherira,* in Abraham Zacuto, *Sefer Yuḥasin.* Constantinople, 1566. [Ed. *Iggeret Rav Sherira,* ed. B. M. Lewin. Frankfurt, 1920. (Rpt. Jerusalem, 1972.)]
Sifra. Venice, 1545. [Ed. *Sifra,* ed. I. Weiss. Vienna, 1862.]
Sifre Bemidbar. Venice, 1545. [Ed. *Siphre d'Be Rab* with *Siphre zutta,* ed. H. S. Horovitz. Leipzig, 1917. (Rpt. Jerusalem, 1966.)]
Sifre Devarim, with *Sifre Bemidbar.* Venice, 1545. [Ed. *Siphre al Sefer Devarim,* ed. L. Finkelstein. Berlin, 1939. (Rpt. New York, 1969.)]
Siphre zutta, ed. S. Lieberman. New York, 1968. [Ed. See *Sifre Bemidbar.*]
Soferim, in *Talmud Bavli.* [Ed. M. Higger. New York, 1937.]
Solomon b. Abraham Parḥon, *Maḥberet he-Arukh* (read in ms.), ed. S. G. Stern. Pressburg, 1844.
Solomon ben Isaac (Rashi), *Perush al ha-Talmud.* See *Talmud Bavli*
——, *Perush al ha-Torah* (read in various mss. and editions). See *Bible, Rabbinic* (1517). [Ed. *Rashi al ha-Torah,* 2d ed., ed. A. Berliner. Frankfurt am Main, 1905. (Rpt. New York, 1969.)]
Solomon ben Isaac (ps.), *Or ha-Sekhel* (Commentary on Midrash Bereshit Rabbah). Venice, 1567.
*Solomon ibn Melekh, *Mikhlal Yofi.* Constantinople, 1549.
Talmud Bavli, with Rashi, Tosafot, Maimonides on Mishnah, Nissim Gerondi, and Samuel ben Meir. Venice, 1520–23. [Ed. *Talmud Bavli.* Vilna, 1880–86.]
Talmud Yerushalmi. Venice, 1523–24. [Ed. *Talmud Yerushalmi,* ed. Krotoschin, 1866. (Rpt. Jerusalem, 1969.)]
**Tiqqune ha-Zohar.* Mantua, 1557. [Ed. *Tiqqune ha-Zohar,* ed. R. Margaliot. Jerusalem, 1978.]
*Tobiah ben Eliezer, *Pesiqta Zuṭarta o Rabbata.* Venice, 1546. [Ed. *Leqaḥ Ṭov,* ed. S. Buber. Vilna, 1880.]
Tosefta. See Alfasi. [Ed. *Tosefta,* ed. M. S. Zuckermandel. Pasewalk, 1880. (Rpt. with *Tashlum Tosefta.* Jerusalem, 1970.) Ed. *Tosefta,* ed. S. Lieberman. New York, 1955–73.)]

*Treves, Johanan ben Joseph, *Kimḥa d' Avishuna* on *Maḥzor Romi.* Bologna, 1540.

**Yalqut Shimoni.* Salonika, 1521; Venice 1566.

Yomtov ben Abraham of Sevile (Ritba), *Ḥiddushe ha-Ritba al ha-Shas* (Yoma, Megillah, and Beṣah), ed. E. Lichtenstein. Jerusalem, 1976.

*Zacuto (Zacut), Abraham, *Sefer Yuḥasin.* Constantinople 1566. [Ed. *Sefer Yuḥasin ha-Shalem,* ed. H. Filipowski, introduction and indices Abraham H. Freimann. Frankfurt am Main, 1924.]

Zerechiah ben Isaac Halevi. See Alfasi.

**Zohar, Sefer ha-*. 3 vols. Mantua, 1558–60.

**Zohar, Sefer ha-*. Cremona, 1558. [Ed. *Sefer ha-Zohar,* ed. R. Margaliot. 3 vols. Jerusalem, 1964.]

Zohar, Midrash ha-Ne^celam (on Ruth). Venice, 1566.

Non-Hebrew Sources

Abd Al-Aziz ibn Uthman al-Kabasi (Alkabitius), *Ad magisterium iudiciorum astrorum isagoge.* Paris, 1521.

Abravanel, Judah (Leone Ebreo), *Dialoghi d'amore.* Rome, 1535.

*——, *De amore dialogi tres,* nuper a loanne Carolo Saraceno latinitate donati. Venice, 1564. [Ed. *Dialoghi d'amore,* a cura di Santino Caramella. Bari, 1929.]

Aesop, *Corpus fabularum Aesopicarum,* vol. 1, ed. Augustus Hausrath. Teubner. Leipzig, 1957.

Ahmad ibn Muhammad ibn Kathir, Al-Farghani, *Compendium, id omne quod ad astronomica rudimenta spectat complectens,* Ioanne Hispalensi interprete. Paris, 1546.

*Albonesius (Theseo Ambrogio), *Introductio in Chaldaicam linguam, Syriacam, atque Arenicam et decem alias linguas. Characterum differentium alphabeta . . . Mystica et cabalistica quamplurima scitu digna etc.* Pavia, 1539.

Al-Farghani. See Ahmad ibn Muhammad.

*Annius, Joannes (Nanni) Viterbensis, *Berosi Chaldaei sacerdotis reliquorumque consimilis argumenti autorum, de antiquitate Italiae ac totius orbis, cum F. Ioann. Annii Viterbensis theologi commentatione tomus prior (alter).* Lyons, 1554.

*Aristeas, *Aristeas Ptolemei Egyptiorum regis auricularius, . . . disserens ad Philocratem fratrem.* Paris, 1514. [Ed. *Aristeas to Philocrates,* ed. H. St. J. Thackerary and trans. Moses Hadas. Jewish apocryphal literature. New York, 1951.]

*——, *De legis divinae ex Hebraica lingua in Graecam translatione per Septuaginta interpretes historia, nunc primum Graece edita . . . ,* cum conversione Latina autore Matthia Garbitio. Basel, 1561.

*——, *De settanta due interpreti,* tradotto per M. Lodovico Domenichi. Florence, 1550.

Aristotle, *De animalibus historia,* ed. L. Dittmeyer. Teubner. Leipzig, 1907.

——, *De coelo libri IV. On the Heavens,* trans. W. K. C. Guthrie. Loeb Classical Library. London and Cambridge, Mass., 1939.

——, *De physico auditu libri VIII. Physics,* trans. Philips H. Wicksteed and Francis M. Cornford. Loeb Classical Library. London and New York, 1929.

——, *Ethicorum Nicomacheorum libri X. The Nicomachean Ethics,* trans. H. Rackham. Loeb Classical Library. London and Cambridge, Mass., 1934.

——, *The Eudemian Ethics,* trans. H. Rackham. Loeb Classical Library. London and Cambridge, Mass., 1935.

——, *Meteorologicorum libri IV. Meteorologica,* trans. Henry P. P. Lee. Loeb Classical Library. London and Cambridge, Mass., 1962.

——, *Poetica. Poetics,* trans. W. Hamilton Fyfe. Loeb Classical Library. London and Cambridge, Mass., 1927.

——. *Politicorum libri VIII. Politics,* trans. H. Rackham. Loeb Classical Library. London and Cambridge, Mass., 1959.

Arrianus, Flavius, *De rebus gestis Alexandri Magni libri VIII,* Bartholomaeo Facio interprete. Lyons, 1552. [Ed. *Anabasis Alexandri,* ed. Carolus Abicht. Teubner. Leipzig 1889.]

*Augustine, *Omnium operum D. Aurelii Augustini primus [-decimus] tomus.* Basel, 1543: *De civitate Dei* (with commentaries of Vives); *Homiliae; Enarrationes in Psalmos; De Genesi ad litteram; Contra Epistolam Manichaei quam vocant fundamenti; Quaestionum in vetus instrumentum libri XII.*

Averroes. See Muhammad ibn Ahmad.

Avicenna. See Husain ibn Abd Allah.

Berosus. See Annius.

Biblia Regia. Paris, 1532.

Biblia vulgare, nuovamente stampata et corretta, per N. de Malermi. Venice, 1546.

*Borro, Girolamo (Alseforo Talascopio), *Dialogo del flusso e reflusso del mare.* Lucca, 1561.

*Buoni, Jacomo Antonio, *Del terremoto dialogo.* Modena, 1571.

Caesar, Julius, *Commentariorum C. Caesaris elenchus, De bello Gallico libri VIII, De bello civili Pompeiano libri III, De bello Alexandrino Liber I, De bello Africano liber I, De bello Hispaniensi liber I.* Paris, 1533.

Calepino (Ambrogio da Calepio, Ambrosius Calepinus), *Dictionarium nunc demum . . . repurgatum atque . . . adauctum et locupletatum.* Venice, 1557.

Cassiodorus, *Chronicon.* See Sichardus, Joannes.

Champier, Symphorien, *De triplici disciplina cuius partes sunt philosophia naturalis medicina theologia moralis philosophia.* Lyons, 1508.

Cicero, *Epistulae ad familiares. The Letters to His Friends,* trans. W. Glynn Williams. 3 vols. Loeb Classical Library. London and Cambridge, Mass., 1927–29.

——, *Paradoxa Stoicorum,* trans. A. G. Lee. Loeb Classical Library. London, 1953.

——, *Philippicae. The Philippics,* trans. Walter C. A. Ker. Loeb Classical Library. London and New York, 1926.

——, *Pro L. Valerio Flacco,* ed. T. B. Webster. Oxford, 1909.

——, *Pro Sexto Roscio Amerino,* ed. St. George Stock. Oxford, 1931.

——, *Tusculanae Disputationes. The Tusculan Disputations,* trans. J. E. King. Loeb Classical Library. London and New York, 1927.

Cicero (attrib.), *Rhetorica ad Herennium, de ratione dicendi,* trans. Henry Caplan. Loeb Classical Library. London and Cambridge, Mass., 1954.

*Clement of Alexandria, *Liber adhortatorius adversus gentes. Stromatum libri octo. In Omnia quae quidem extant opera, a paucis iam annis inventa. . . .* Gentiano Herveto Aureliano interprete. Basel, 1556.

Contarini, Gasparo, *De elementis et eorum mixtionibus libri V.* Paris, 1548.

Contractus, Hermannus. See Sichardus, Joannes.

Corpus iuris canonici, vol. 2, ed. A. Friedberg. Leipzig, 1881.

Corpus iuris civilis. Digesta, ed. P. Krueger and T. Momsen. Berlin, 1954.

*Cratander, Andreas, *Sacra Biblia ad LXX interpretum fidem* diligentissime tralata, per Andream Cratandrem. Basel, 1526.

Curtius, Quintus Rufus, *De rebus gestis Alexandri magni opus . . . Accesserunt enim antehac nunquam visa, duorum in principio librorum, qui desiderantur, supplementum compendiosum, finis in quinto libro atque fragmentorum in decimo restitutio,* per Christophorum Brunonem. Basel, 1545. [Ed. *Historia Alexandri Magni,* trans. John C. Rolfe. 2 vols. Loeb Classical Library. London and Cambridge, Mass., 1946.]

Dante Alighieri, *La divina commedia cum commento Christophori Landini.* Florence, 1481. [Ed. *La commedia secondo l'antica vulgata,* a cura di Giorgio Petrocchi. Milan, 1966–67.]

Dio Cassius, *Romanae historiae libri tot enim hodie extant,* Gulielmo Xylandro interprete. Lyons, 1559. [Ed. *Roman History,* trans. Earnest Cary. 9 vols. Loeb Classical Library. London and New York, 1914–27.

Diodorus Siculus, *Bibliothecae historicae libri XV.* Basel, 1559.

[Ed. *Bibliothecae historiae libri XVII. The Library of History,* trans. C. H. Oldfather. Loeb Classical Library. London and Cambridge, Mass., 1968.]

Diogenes Laertius, *De vita et moribus philosophorum libri X.* Lyons, 1566. [Ed. *Lives of the Eminent Philosophers,* trans. R. D. Hicks. 2 vols. Loeb Classical Library. London and Cambridge, Mass., 1964.]

Dioscorides, Pedacius, *De medica materia libri sex,* J. Ruellio interprete, nunc primum ab ipso Ruellio recogniti. Paris, 1537. [Ed. *De materia medica, libri quinque,* ed. Max Wellmann. 3 vols. Berlin, 1907–14.]

*Dolce, Lodovico, *Giornale delle historie del mondo.* Venice, 1572.

Durandus, Gulielmus, *Rationale divinorum officiorum.* Lyons, 1565.

Epiphanius, *Opera . . . Contra octoaginta haereses opus . . . De mensuris ac ponderibus,* Iano Cornario . . . interprete. Basel, 1560.

Eusebius, Pamphilus Caesariensis, *Chronicon.* See Sichardus, Joannes.

——, *De evangelica praeparatione,* a Georgio Trapezuntio traductus opus. Venice, 1501.

——, *Historia ecclesiastica Latine,* interprete Rufino a Gaufrido Boussardo emendata et correcta. Paris, 1497.

Eutropius, Flavius, *De gestis Romanorum libri decem.* Paris, 1539. [Ed. *Breviarium ab urbe condita libri X,* ed. F. Rühl. Teubner. Leipzig 1887.]

*Ferentilli, Agostino, *Discorso universale . . . per le sei età e le quattro monarchie . . . dal principio del mondo sino all'anno MDLXIX nel fine del quale si mostra con diligente calcolo de'tempi quanto habbia da durare il presente secolo, seguitando in ciò l'opinione di Elia rabino e di Lattantio Firmiano.* Venice, 1570.

Fernelius, Joannes Ambianus (Fernel), *Medicina.* Paris, 1554.

Ficino, Marsiglio, *Il consiglio di M. M. Ficino contra la pestilentia con altre cose aggiunte appropriate alla medesima malattia.* Siena, 1522.

*Foresti, Jacobus Philippus, *Supplementum. Supplementi de le chroniche,* per Francesco Fiorentino vulgarizato e historiato. Venice, 1520.

Galen, Claudius, *Opera . . . omnia quae extant.* Basel, 1562. [Ed. *Opera Omnia,* ed. C. G. Kühn. Leipzig, 1833. (Rpt. Hildesheim, 1965): *De naturalibus facultatibus; De pulsuum differentiis; De usu partium corporis humani; In Hippocratis librum de acutorum victu commentarius; Methodus medendi.*]

Galen (ps.), *Definitiones medicae.*

Gellius, Aulus, *Noctes Atticae.* Lyons, 1566. [Ed. *Noctium Atticarum libri XX,* ed. C. Hosius. Teubner. Stuttgart, 1967.]

Giambullari, Pierfrancesco, *Il Gello: Ragionamenti de la prima et antica origine della toscana et particolarmente della lingua fiorentina.* Florence, 1546.

Giraldi, Lilio Gregorio, *De deis gentium libri sive Syntagmata XVII.* Lyons, 1565.

Guevara, Antonio de, *Libro di Marco Aurelio con l'horologio de principi distinto in quattro volumi.* Venice, 1562.

——, *Libro primo [-libro secondo] delle littere del A del G,* tradotte dal A. di Catzelu. Venice, 1556–57.

Guicciardini, Lodovico, *Descrittione . . . di tutti i paesi bassi, altrimenti detti Germania Inferiore.* Antwerp, 1567.

Hermes Trismegistus (ps.), *Pimander de potestate et sapientia Dei. Eiusdem Asclepius de voluntate Dei,* Marsilio Ficino interprete. Basel, 1532.

Herodotus, *Histories,* trans. A. D. Godley. 4 vols. Loeb Classical Library. London and Cambridge, Mass., 1971.

Honorius Augustodunensis, *Libri septem . . . quorum De aetatibus mundi chronicon.* Basel, 1544.

Husain ibn Abd Allah (ibn Sina-Avicenna), *Liber canonis,* translatus a Magistro Gerhardo Cremonensi ab Arabico in Latino. Strasburg, 1475.

Isidore, *Liber ethymologiarum.* Basel 1489.

Jerome, *Opera Omnia.* Paris 1533–34: *Commentaria (in Sacram Scripturam); Epistulae; Praefationes (in Sacram Scripturam); Quaestiones Hebraicae in Genesim.*

Josephus, *Antiquitatum Iudaicarum libri XX interprete Ruffino. Eiusdem De bello Iudaico libri VII. Contra Apionem libri II. De Machabaeis liber unus ab Erasmo recognitus.* Cologne, 1534. [Ed. *The Life,* trans. H. St. J. Thackeray. Loeb Classical Library. London and Cambridge, Mass., 1966. Ed. *Against Apion,* trans. H. St. J. Thackeray. Loeb Classical Library. London and Cambridge, Mass., 1966. Ed. *The Jewish War,* trans. H. St. J. Thackeray. Loeb Classical Library. London and New York, 1927. Ed. *Jewish Antiquities,* trans. H. St. J. Thackeray et al. 6 vols. Loeb Classical Library. London, 1930–63.]

*——, *Los veynte libros de F. Josepho de las antiguedades Judaycas; y su vida por el mismo escripta . . . todo nuevamente traduzido de Latin en Romance Castellano.* Antwerp, 1554.

*——, *Opera, in sermonem latinum, iam olim conversa, nunc vero ad exemplaria graeca denuo summa fide diligentiaque collata ac plurimis in locis emendata,* cura S. Gelenii. Basel, 1567.

Justinus, *Ex Trogi Pompei historiis externis libri XLIIII.* Basel, 1543. [Ed. *Epitoma Historiarum Philippicarum Pompei Trogi,* ed. Otto Seel. Teubner. Leipzig, 1935.]

Justin Martyr, *Operum quae extant omnium* per Ioannem Langum . . . e greco in latinum sermonem versorum. *Oratio ad Graecos sive Gentiles, Ad senatum Romanum Christianorum defensio . . . Pro Christianis apologia.* Basel, 1565.

Lactantius, Lucius Coelius Firmianus, *Divinarum institutionum lib. VIII . . . , omnia ex castigatione H. Fasitelii . . . pristinae integritati restituta.* Lyons, 1548.

Leone Ebreo. See Abravanel, Judah.

*Lippomano, Luigi, *Catena in Exodum ex auctoribus ecclesiasticis.* Paris, 1550.

Livius, Titus, *Decades tres cum dimidia, seu libri XXXV.* Paris, 1552. [Ed. *Ab urbe condita,* ed. Robertus Maxwell Ogilvie. Oxford, 1974.]

Lucidus, Johannes Samotheus, *Opusculum de emendationibus temporum ab orbe condito ad usque hanc aetatem . . .* Venice, 1537.

Macrobius, Ambrosius Theodosius, *In somnim Scipionis lib. II; Saturnaliorum lib. VII* Venice, 1565.

——, *Saturnalia [et] Commentarii in somnium Scipionis libri,* ed. Jaobus Willis. 2 vols. Teubner. Leipzig, 1963.

*Mauro Fiorentino, *Annotationi sopra la lettione della spera del Sacro-bosco, con una nuova traduttione di detta Spera . . .* Florence, 1550.

*Mercator, Gerardus, *Chronologia: Hoc est temporum demonstratio exactissima ab initio mundi usque ad annum Domini MDLXVIII ex eclipsibus et observationibus astronomicis omnium temporum, sacris quoque Bibliis et optimis quibusque scriptoribus summa fide concinnata.* Cologne, 1569.

Metasthenes. See Annius.

Mexía, Pedro, *Historia imperial y Cesarea en la qual en suma se contiene las vidas y hechos d'todos los Cesares Emperadores de Roma. . . .* Seville, 1547.

——, *La selva di varia lettione,* tradotto di Spagnolo per Mambrino da Fabriano. Venice, 1547.

——, *Le vite di tutti gl'imperadori e da Lodovico Dolce tradotte aggiuntavi la vita dell'Invitissimo Carlo Quinto Imperatore, descritta dal medesimo L. Dolce.* Venice, 1561.

Modestinus. See *Corpus Iuris Civilis.*

Moleto, Giuseppe, *Ephemerides J. Moletii annis viginti inservientes, incipientesque ab anno 1564 . . . ad annum 1584, ad meridianum inclytae Venetiarum urbis exacte supputatae.* Venice, 1564.

Muhammad ibn Ahmad (ibn Rushd-Averroes), *Aristotelis Opera cum Averrois commentariis.* Venice, 1562.

*Münster, Sebastian, *Chaldaica grammatica antehac a nemine attentata sed iam primum per S.M. conscripta et aedita non tam ad Chaldaicos interpretes quam Hebraeorum commentarios intelligendos Hebraicae linguae studiosis utilissima.* Basel, 1527.

——. See Ptolemy, Claudius, *La geografia.*

Origen, *Super Job libri tres . . .* [suppositious]. *Eiusdem Homiliae,* Hieronymo et Hilario interpretibus. Venice, 1513.

Orosius, *Adversos paganos . . . historiarum libri VII.* Cologne, 1536. [Ed. *Historiarum adversum Paganos libri VII,* ed. C. Zangemeister. Vienna, 1868.]

*Ortelius, Abraham, *Theatrum orbis terrarum.* Antwerp, 1570.

Otto (Bishop of Friesing), *Rerum ab origine mundi ad ipsius usque tempora gestarum libri octo.* Strasburg, 1515.

Ovid, *Metamorphoses,* trans. Frank J. Miller. 2 vols. Loeb Classical Library. London and Cambridge, Mass., 1968.

Pagninus, Xantes, *Thesaurus linguae sanctae.* Lyons, 1529.

Perez de Valencia (Pharez), *Expositiones in centum et quinquaginta psalmos Davidicos ad illustrationem fidei nostrae.* Paris, 1518.

Petrarch, Francesco (ps.), *Chronica delle vite de pontefici et imperatori romani* . . . Venice, 1507.

Petrus d'Abano, *Conciliator differentiarum philosophorum.* Venice, 1565.

*Philo, *Lucubrationes omnes* . . . nunc primum Latinae ex Graecis factate per S. Gelenium. Lyons, 1555.

Philo (ps.), *Breviarium de temporibus.* See Annius.

——, *Libri antiquitatum, Quaestionum et solutionum in Genesin, De Essaeis, De nominbus Hebraicis* (divo Hieronymo interprete), *De mundo* (G. Budaeo interprete). Basel, 1527. [Ed. *The Biblical Antiquities of Philo,* trans. M. R. James (1917), prolegomenon by Louis H. Feldman. New York, 1971.]

Philostratus, *De vita Apollonii Tyanaei* [trans. A. Rinuccinus]. Lyons, 1504. [Ed. *The Life of Apollonius of Tyana,* trans. F. C. Conybeare. 2 vols. Loeb Classical Library. London and New York, 1912.]

Phrygio, Paulus Constantinus, *Chronicon regum regnorumque omnium catalogum, et perpetuum ab exordio mundi temporum seculorumque series complectens ex optimis quibusque Hebraeis, Graecis et Latinis autoribus congestum.* Basel, 1534.

Pico della Mirandola, Giovanni, *Commentationes J. Pici Mirandulae in hoc volumine contentae: Heptaplus . . . Apologia . . . Tractatus de ente et uno . . . Epistolae . . . Deprecatoria ad Deum . . . Disputationes adversus astrologos.* 2 pts. Bologna, 1496, 1495.

——, *De studio divinae et humanae philosophiae* (with *De morte Christi*). Bologna, 1497.

[Ed. *Disputationes adversus astrologiam divinatricem,* a cura di Eugenio Garin. 2 vols. Florence, 1946, 1952.]

Platina. See Sacchi, Bartholomaeo de'.

Plato, *Omnia . . . Opera,* tralatione M. Ficini. Basel, 1551. [Ed. *Critias,* trans. R. G. Bury. Loeb Classical Library. London and New York, 1929. [Ed. *Laws,* trans. R. G. Bury. 2 vols. Loeb Classical Library. London and New York, 1926.] Ed. *Phaedo,* trans. H. N. Fowler. Loeb Classical Library. London and New York, 1921. Ed. *Politicus.* ed. Lewis Campbell. 2 pts. Oxford, 1867. [Ed. *Republica.* trans. Paul Shorey. 2 vols. Loeb Classical Library. London and New York, 1930. [Ed. *Symposium,* trans. W. R. M. Lamb. Loeb Classical Library. London and New York, 1925. [Ed. *Timaeus,* ed. R. D. Archer-Hind. London, 1888.]

Plinius secundus, Caius, *Naturalis historiae libri XXXVII,* a Paulo Manutio multis in locis emendati. Venice, 1558–59. [Ed. *Natural History,* trans. H. Rackham. 10 vols. Loeb Classical Library. London and Cambridge, Mass., 1979.]

*Plutarch, *Alcuni opusculetti de le cose morali . . . in questa lingua nuovamente tradotti* (per M. Giovanni Tarcagnotta). Venice, 1559.

——, *Graecorum, Romanorumque illustrium vitae.* Paris, 1558.

——, *Opuscula (quae quidem extant) undequaque collecta et diligentissime iam pridem recognita.* Basel, 1530.

Plutarch (ps.), *De placitis decretisque philosophorum naturalibus libri V.* In *Opuscula.* Basel, 1530.

Ptolemy, Claudius, *Almagestum seu magnae constructionis mathematicae opus plane divinum . . . ,* Latina donatum lingua ab Georgio Trapezuntio. Venice, 1528.

*——, *La geografia . . . con alcuni comenti ed aggiunte da Sebastiano Munstero . . . altre nuove*

aggiuntevi di Gastaldo . . . ridotta in volgare Italiano da M. Pietro Andrea Mattiolo Senese. Venice, 1548. [Ed. *Geographia universalis vetus et nova . . . succedunt Tabulae Ptolemaicae, opera S. Munsteri novo paratae modo. His adiectae sunt plurimae novae tabulae.* Basel: H. Petrus, 1540. (Rpt. with introduction by R. A. Skelton. Amsterdam, 1966.)]

*——, *La geografia di Claudio Tolomeo Alessandrino,* nuovamente tradotta di Greco in Italiano da Girolamo Ruscello. Venice, 1561.

Quintilianus, Marcus Fabius, *Oratoriarum institutionum libri XII.* Basel, 1568. [Ed. *Institutio oratoria,* trans. H. E. Butler. 4 vols. Loeb Classical Library. London and New York, 1920–22.]

Reisch, Georg, *Margarita philosophica nova totius philosophiae rationalis, naturalis et moralis principia dialogice duodecim libris complectens.* Basel, 1508.

*Richerius, Ludovicus Coelius Rhodiginus (Ricchieri), *Lectionum antiquitatum libri XXX.* Basel, 1542.

Ruscello, Girolamo. See Ptolemy, Claudius.

Sacchi, Bartholomaeo de' (Platina), *Historia de vitis Pontificum Romanorum . . . usque ad Paulum Papam II.* Venice, 1562. [Ed. *De vita Christi ac omnium Pontificum,* a cura di G. Gaida. Storici italiani III. Città di Castello, 1913.]

Sacrobosco, Joannes de, *The "Sphere" of Sacrobosco and Its Commentators,* ed. Lynn Thorndike with English translation. Chicago, 1949. (Also see Mauro.)

Sansovino, Francesco, *Gl'annali overo le vite de' principi et signori della casa Othomana.* Venice, 1571.

Seneca, Lucius Annaeus, *Ad Lucilium Epistulae Morales,* trans. Richard M. Gummere. 3 vols. Loeb Classical Library. London and New York, 1917–25.

——, *Naturalium quaestionum ad Lucilium libri septem.* Paris, 1540. [Ed. *Naturales Quaestiones,* trans. Thomas Corcoran. 10 vols. Loeb Classical Library. London and Cambridge, Mass., 1971.]

*Sichardus, Joannes, ed., *En Damus Chronicon divinum plane opus . . . Eusebii Pamphili Hieronymo interprete, Hieronymi Presbyteri, Prosperi Aquitanici, M. Aurelii Cassiodori, Hermanni Contracti, Matthaei Palmerii Fiorentini, Matthaei Palmerii Pisani.* Basel, 1529.

*Solinus, Caius Julius, *Delle cose maravigliose del mondo,* tradotto dall' S. Gio. Vincenzo Belprato. Venice, 1557. [Ed. Solinus, *Collectanea rerum memorabilium,* ed. T. Momsen. Berlin, 1895.]

Steuchus, Augustinus (Steuco), *Recognitio Veteris Testamenti, ad Hebraicam veritatem, collata etiam editione Septuaginta interprete, cum ipsa veritate Hebraica, nostraque translatione . . .* Venice, 1529.

Strabo, *De situ orbis libri XVII,* a Guarino Veronensi et Gregorio Trifernate latinitate donati. Lyons, 1557. [Ed. *The Geography of Strabo,* trans. Horace L. Jones. 8 vols. Loeb Classical Library. London and New York, 1917–32.]

Suetonius Tranquillus, Caius, *XII Caesares.* Lyons, 1548. [Ed. *The Lives of the Caesars,* trans. John C. Rolfe. 2 vols. Loeb Classical Library. London and New York, 1914.]

Suidas (Suda), *Historica caeteraque omnia quae ulla ex parte ad cognitionem rerum spectant,* nunc primum opera . . . ac studio H. Wolfii in Latinum sermonem conversa. Basel, 1564.

Tartagni, Alexander de Imola, *Consiliorum libri primus [=septimus].* Venice, 1570.

Theseo Ambrogio. See Albonesius.

Thomas Aquinas, *In Aristotelis libros: De caelo et mundo, De generatione et corruptione, Meteorologicorum expositio,* ed. Raymundus M. Spiazzi. Turin and Rome, 1952.

——, *Summa theologica,* ed. Pietro Caramello. 3 vols. Turin, 1963.

——, *Super epistolas S. Pauli lectura,* 8th rev. ed., ed. P. Raffaele Cai. Turin and Rome, 1953.

——, *Super quarto libro Sententiarum* (of Petrus Lombardus). Venice, 1481.

Tostado Ribeira, Alonso, *Opera omnia quotquot in Scripturae sacrae expositionem . . . inventa sunt.* Venice, 1596.

*Ulloa, Alfonso de, *La vita dell'invitissimo imperator Carlo Quinto.* Venice, 1560.

Valerius Maximus, *De I detti e fatti memorabili,* tradotto di latino in toscano da Giorgio Dati Fiorentino. Rome, 1539. [Ed. *Factorum et dictorum memorabilium libri IX,* ed. C. Kempf. Teubner. Leipzig 1888.]

Virgil, *Georgica. Georgics.* trans. H. Rushton Fairclough. Loeb Classical Library. Cambridge, Mass. and London, 1978.

Vives, Joannes Lodovicus, *De civitate Dei cum commentariis Ludovici Vivis.* In *Omnium Operum divi Aurelii Augustini . . . ,* tomus V. See Augustine.

Xenophon, *Opera . . . omnia in Latinam linguam conversa.* 2 vols. Basel, 1553: *De paedia Cyri Persarum regis lib. VIII.* [Ed. *Cyropaedia,* trans. W. Millar. 2 vols. Loeb Classical Library. London and New York, 1914.] *De Cyri minoris expeditione lib. VIII.* [Ed. *Anabasis,* trans. E. C. Marchant. Loeb Classical Library. London and Cambridge, Mass., 1953.] *De factis et dictis Socratis memoratu dignis.* [Ed. *Memorabilia,* ed. L. Dindorf. Teubner. Leipzig, 1886.]

Xenophon (ps.). *De aequivocis.* See Annius.

BIBLIOGRAPHY OF WORKS CITED IN NOTES

Abravanel, Isaac, *Mirkevet ha-Mishneh.* Sabbioneta: Tob. Foa, 1551.

Aescoly, Aaron Z., *Sippur David ha-Reuveni.* Jerusalem: Bialik, 1940.

Alon, Gedaliah, *The Jews in Their Land in the Talmudic Age* (trans. from the Hebrew). 2 vols. Jerusalem: Magnes Press, 1980–84.

Altmann, Alexander, "Ars Rhetorica as Reflected in Some Jewish Figures of the Italian Renaissance." In *Jewish Thought in the Sixteenth Century,* ed. Bernard Dov Cooperman. Cambridge: Harvard University Press, 1983, 1–22.

Amatus Lusitanus (Rodrigues João de Castelo Branco), *Curationum medicinalium centuriae quatuor, quarum duae priorae ab auctore sunt recognitae, duae posteriores nunc primum editae.* Basel: H. Froben, 1556.

Apfelbaum, Abe, *Toledot R. Yehudah Moscato Rav be-Mantova lifne 300 shanah.* Drohobycz: A. H. Zupnik, 1900.

Arias Montanus, *Phaleg, sive de gentium sedibus primis, orbisque terrae situ liber.* Vol. 8 of the Antwerp Polyglot. Antwerp: Plantin, 1572.

Armellini, Mariano, *Bibliotheca Benedictino-Casinensis, sive scriptorum Casinensis congregationis . . . ad haec usque tempora floruerunt, operum ac gestorum notitiae.* 2 pts. Assisi, 1731–32.

Ashtor (Strauss), Eli, *Toledot ha-Yehudim be-Miṣraim ve-Suryah taḥat Shilṭon ha-Mamelukim,* vol. 1. Jerusalem: Mossad Harav Kook, 1944.

Assaf, Simḥah, *Meqorot le-Toledot ha-Ḥinnukh,* vol. 2. Tel Aviv: Devir, 1930.

Azulai, Hayyim D., *Maḥaziq Berakhah.* Livorno: Abraham Isaac Castello, Eliezer Sadon, 1785.

Bacchini, Benedetto, *Dell'istoria del monastero di S Benedetto di Polirone nello stato di Mantova libri cinque.* Modena: Il Capponi e gli EE del Pontiroli, 1696.

Baer, Fritz, "Don Isaac Abrabanel ve-Yaḥaso el Baʿayot ha-Historiyah ve-ha-Medinah." *Tarbiz* 8 (1937): 241–59.

Baer, Seligman, ed., *Avodat Yisrael,* 2d ed. Berlin: Schocken, 1937.

Balletti, Andrea, *Gli ebrei e gli Estensi,* 2d ed. Reggio Emilia: Anonima poligrafica emiliana, 1930.

Bamberger, Bernard J., "A Messianic Document of the Seventh Century." *HUCA* 15 (1940): 425–31.

——, *Proselytism in the Talmudic Period.* Cincinnati: Hebrew Union College Press, 1939.

Barnes, Robin B., *Prophecy and Gnosis. Apocalypticism in the Wake of the Lutheran Reformation.* Stanford: Stanford University Press, 1988.

Baron, Salo W., "Azariah de' Rossi: A Biographical Sketch." In *History and Jewish Historians: Essays and Addresses.* Philadelphia: Jewish Publication Society of America, 1964, 167–73.

——, "Azariah de' Rossi's Attitude to Life." *History and Jewish Historians: Essays and Addresses.* Philadelphia: Jewish Publication Society of America, 1964, 174–204.

——, "Azariah de' Rossi's Historical Method." In *History and Jewish Historians: Essays and Addresses.* Philadelphia: Jewish Publication Society of America, 205–39.

Bataillon, Marcel, *Érasme et l'Espagne: Recherches sur l'histoire spirituelle du XVIe siècle.* Paris: Librairie E. Droz, 1937.

Beit-Arié, Malachi, "Iggeret me-Inyan Shevaṭim me-Et R. Avraham ben Eliezer Halevi ha-Mequbbal mi-Shenat rpḥ." *Qoveṣ al Yad,* n.s. 6 (1966): 371–78.

Beit-Arié, Malachi, and Idel, Mosheh, "Ma'amar ha ha-Keṣ." *KS* 54, 1 (1979): 174–94.

Benayahu, Meir, *Copyright, Authorization and Imprimatur for Hebrew Books Printed in Venice* (Hebrew). Ramat Gan: Makhon Ben Zvi and Mossad Harav Kook, 1971.

——, "The Polemic Regarding the *Me'or Enayim* of Azariah de' Rossi" (Hebrew) *Asufot* 5. Jerusalem, 1991, 213–65.

Benedini, Benedetto, *I manoscritti polironiani (anteriori all'anno 1200) della Biblioteca comunale di Mantova.* Atti e Memorie n.s., vol. 30. Mantua: Academia Virgiliana di Mantova, 1958.

Benjacob, Abraham "Shirim me-R. Azariah min ha-Adumim" (Hebrew). *Halevanon* 7 (1870): 47–48, 63–64.

Ben Menahem, Naftali, *Inyane ibn Ezra.* Jerusalem: Mossad Harav Kook, 1978.

Bergmann, Judah, "Gedichte Asarje de' Rossi's." *Zeitschrift für Hebräische Bibliographie* 3 (1898): 53–58.

Berlin, Adele, "Azariah de' Rossi and Biblical Poetry." *Prooftexts* 12 (1992): 175–83.

——, *Biblical Poetry through Medieval Eyes.* Bloomington: Indiana University Press, 1991.

Bickermann, Elias, *Chronology of the Ancient World,* London: Thames and Hudson, 1980.

——, "The Septuagint as a Translation (1959)." In *Studies in Jewish and Christian History,* pt. 1. Leiden: Brill, 1976, 167–200.

Blatt, Franz, ed., *The Latin Josephus:* I *Introduction and Text.* Copenhagen: Universitetsforlaget I Aarhus ajnar Munksgaard, 1958.

Bonfil, Robert, "Expression of the Unity of the People of Israel in Italy during the Renaissance" (Hebrew). *Sinai* 76 (1975): 36–46.

——, "How Golden was the Age of the Renaissance in Jewish Historiography?" In *Essays in Jewish Historiography,* ed. Ada Rapoport-Albert. *History and Theory* Beiheft 27. Middletown, Conn.: Wesleyan University, 1988, 78–102.

——, "New Information about the Life of Rabbi Menahem Azariah da Fano" (Hebrew). In *Studies in the History of Jewish Society in the Middle Ages and in the Modern Period Presented to Professor Jacob Katz,* ed. E. Etkes and Y. Salmon. Jerusalem: Magnes Press, 1980, 98–135.

——, *Rabbis and Jewish Communities in Renaissance Italy* (trans. from the Hebrew). Oxford: Oxford University Press, 1990.

——, "A Sermon in the Vernacular by Rabbi Mordechai Dato." *Italia* 1, 1 (1976): 1–XXXII.

——, "Some Reflections on the Place of Azariah de' Rossi's Meor Enayim in the Cultural Milieu of Italian Renaissance Jewry." In *Jewish Thought in the Sixteenth Century,* ed. Bernard Dov Cooperman. Cambridge: Harvard University Press, 1983, 23–48.

——, ed., *Kitve Azariah min ha-Adumim. Mivḥar Peraqim mi-tokh Sefer Me'or Enayim ve-Sefer Maṣref la-Kesef.* Jerusalem: Mossad Bialik, 1991.

Bos, Gerrit, "Baladhur (Marking-Nut): A Popular Medieval Drug for Strengthening Memory." *Bulletin of the School of Oriental and African Studies,* 59, 2 (1996): 229–36.

Burke, Peter, "A Survey of the Popularity of Ancient Historians, 1450–1700." *History and Theory* 5 (1966): 135–52.

Burnett, Stephen G., *From Christian Hebraism to Jewish Studies, Johannes Buxtorf (1566–1629) and Hebrew Learning in the Seventeenth Century.* Leiden: Brill, 1996.

Busi, Giulio, "Il terremoto di Ferrara nel Meor Enayim di Azaryah de' Rossi." In *We-zo't le-Angelo, raccolta di studi giudaici in memoria di Angelo Vivian,* a cura di Giulio Busi. Bologna: AISG, 1993, 53–92.

Buxtorf, Johannes II, *Kuzari.* Basel: Georg Decker, 1660.

Campani, Romeo, *Alfragano, Il "libro dell' Aggregazione delle stelle," secondo il codice Mediceo-Laurenziano, Pl29, cod. 9, contemporaneo a Dante.* Città di Castello: S. Lapi, 1910.

Cano, Franciscus Melchor, *De locis theologicis, libri duodecim.* Louvain: S. Sassenus, 1564.

Cantera Burgos, Francisco, and Millás Vallicrosa, José María, *Las inscripciones hebraicas de España.* Madrid: C. Bermejo, 1956.

Carpi, Daniel. "The Expulsion of the Jews from the Papal States in the Time of Pope Pius V and the Inquisition Trials against the Jews of Bologna 1560–1569" (Hebrew). In *Scritti in memoria di Enzo Sereni,* a cura di Daniel Carpi et al. Jerusalem: Editirice Fondazione Sally Mayer, 1970, 145–65.

Carucci Viterbi, Benedetto, "La polemica tra Azariah de' Rossi e il Maharal di Praga sul significato delle Aggadot." In *Scritti sull'ebraismo, in memoria di Emanuele Menachem Artom,* ed. J. Sierra and Elena L. Artom. Jerusalem: Sinai Publishing, 1996, 89–123.

Casella, M. T. "Il Valerio massimo in volgare dal Lancia al Boccaccio." *Italia medioevale e umanistica,* 6 (1963): 49–136.

Cassuto, Umberto, *Gli ebrei a Firenze nell'età del Rinascimento.* Florence: Tipografia Galletti e Cocci, 1918. (Rpt. Leo S. Olschki, 1965).

Charlesworth, James H., ed., *The Old Testament Pseudepigrapha.* 2 vols. London: Dartman, Longman & Todd, 1983, 1985.

Chayes, Zvi H., *The Student's Guide through the Talmud* (trans. from the Hebrew). London: East and West Library, 1952.

Copenhaver, Brian P., *Corpus Hermeticum. Hermetica, the Greek Corpus Hermeticum and the Latin Asclepius in a New English Translation with Notes and Introduction.* Cambridge: Cambridge University Press, 1992.

Coüasnon, Charles, *The Church of the Holy Sepulchre in Jerusalem* (trans. from French). London: Oxford University Press, 1974.

David, Abraham, "Le-Toledot ha-Pulmus saviv ha-Sefer Me'or Enayim." *KS* 59, 2–3 (1984): 641–42.

De Benedetti Stow, Sandra, "Due poesie bilingui inedite contro le donne di Semuel de Castiglione (1553)." *Italia* 2, 1–2 (1980): 7–64.

De Pomis, David, *L'Ecclesiaste di Salomone nuovamente tradotto . . . dall'eccellente physico.* Venice, 1571.

De' Sommi Portaleone, Judah, *Quattro dialoghi in materia di rappresentazioni sceniche,* a cura di F. Marotti. Milan: Edizioni Il Polifilo, 1968.

Del Medigo, Joseph Solomon, *Mikhtav Aḥuz.* In *Melo Ḥofnayim,* ed. A. Geiger. Berlin: Witzig, 1840.

Dienstag, Israel J., "Perush le-Rosh ha-Shanah ha-meyuḥas le-Rambam." In *Reverence, Righteousness and Rahmanut: Essays in Memory of Rabbi Dr. Leo Jung,* ed. Jacob J. Schachter. Northvale, N.J.: J. Aronson, 1992, 353–65.

Dionisotti, Carlo, "Appunti su Leone Ebreo." *Italia medioevale e umanistica* 2 (1959): 409–28.

Discours sur l'espouventable, horrible et merveilleux tremblement de terre. Paris, 1571.

Duran, Simeon ben Zemaḥ, *Sefer Tashbeṣ.* Amsterdam: Naftali H. Levi, 1738–39.

Emden, Jacob, *Mor U-Qeṣiah.* Altona, 1761–68.

Erasmus, Desiderius, *Opus epistolarum Des. Erasmi Roterodami denuo recognitum et auctum* per P. S. Allen. Oxford: Clarendon Press, 1906–47.

Erasmus, Hendrik J., *The Origins of Rome in Historiography from Petrarch to Perizonius.* Assen: Van Gorcum, 1962.

Farissol, Abraham, *Iggeret Orḥot Olam.* Venice, 1586.

Feldman, Louis H., "Prolegomenon." In *The Biblical Antiquities of Philo,* New York: Ktav, 1971.

Finkel, Joshua, "Maimonides' Treatise on Resurrection: The Original Arabic and Samuel ibn Tibbon's Hebrew Translation and Glossary." *PAAJR* 9 (1939): 63–101.

Finkelstein, Louis, *Jewish Self-Government in the Middle Ages,* 2d ed. New York: Philip Feldheim, 1964.

——, *The Pharisees; The Sociological Background of Their Faith,* 2d ed. New York: Jewish Publication Society, 1950.

Finus (Finus) Hadrianus, *In Iudaeos flagellum ex sacris scripturis excerptum.* Ferrara, 1537.

Fishman, Talya, *Shaking the Pillars of Exile: "Voice of a Fool," an Early Modern Jewish Critique of Rabbinic Culture.* Stanford: Stanford University Press, 1997.

Flusser, David, *Sefer Josippon.* vols. 1 and 2. Jerusalem: Mossad Bialik, 1978, 1980.

Freudenberger, Theobald, *Augustinus Steuchus, Augustinerchorherr und päpstlicher Bibliothekar, 1497–1548, und sein literarisches Lebenswerk.* Münster in Westfalen: Aschendorffsche Verlagsbuchhandlung, 1935.

Friedberg, Bernhard, *History of Hebrew Typography in Italy, Spain-Portugal, and the Turkey. From Its Beginning and Formation about the Year 1470. Biographies of the First Printers, and Their Assistants and Successors,* 2d ed. (Hebrew). Tel Aviv: M. A. Bar-Juda, 1956.

Friedenwald, Harry, "Two Jewish Physicians of the Sixteenth Century, The Doctor Amatus Lusitanus, the Patient Azariah dei Rossi." In *The Jews and Medicine, Essays.* 2 vols. Baltimore: Johns Hopkins Press, 1944, vol. 2, 391–403.

Fubini, Riccardo, "L'ebraismo nei riflessi della cultura umanistica: Leonardo Bruni, Giannozzo Manetti, Annio da Viterbo." *Medioevo e Rinascimento,* Annuario II 1988 (1989) 283–324.

Galatinus (Columna), Petrus, *Opus toti christianae reipublicae maxime utile de arcanis catholicae veritatis contra obstinatissimam ludaeorum nostrae tempestatis perfidiam, ex Talmud aliisque hebraicis libris nuper excerptum et quadruplici linguarum genere congestum.* Ortone: Hieronymus Suncinus, 1518.

Gans, David. *Sefer Ṣemaḥ David,* ed. M. Breuer. Jerusalem: Magnes Press, 1983.

Gaster, Moses, "Jewish Knowledge of the Samaritan Alphabet in the Middle Ages." In *Studies and Texts in Folklore, Magic, Medieval Romance, Hebrew Apocrypha and Samaritan Archaeology,* vol. 1, collected and reprinted by M. Gaster. London: Maggs, 1925–28, 600–613.

Ginsburg, Christian D., *Jacob ibn Adonijah's Introduction to the Rabbinic Bible, Hebrew and English with Explanatory Notes and the Massoret ha-Massoret of Elias Levita,* prolegomenon by N. Snaith. New York: Ktav, 1968.

Ginzberg, Louis, *Legends of the Jews.* 7 vols. Philadelphia: Jewish Publication Society of America, 1909.

——, *On Jewish Law and Lore.* Philadelphia: Jewish Publication Society of America, 1955.

Giorgio, Francesco, *In Scripturam sacram problemata.* Venice: Bernardinus Vitalis, 1536.

Goldfeld, Lea N., *Moses Maimonides' Treatise on Resurrection: An Inquiry into Its Authenticity.* New York: Ktav, 1986.

Goldschmidt, Daniel, "Judaeo-Greek Bible Translations of the Sixteenth Century." *KS* 33, 1 (1957): 131–34.

——, ed., *Seder Rav Amram Gaon.* Jerusalem: Mossad Harav Kook, 1971.

Goldstein, Bernard R., *The Astronomy of Levi ben Gerson (1288–1344).* New York: Springer Verlag, 1985.

Goldstein, Jonathan A., "Alexander and the Jews." *PAAJR* 59 (1993): 59–101.

Gottlieb, Ephraim, *Studies in Kabbalistic Literature* (Hebrew), ed. Joseph Hacker. Tel Aviv: Daf-Chen Press, 1976.

Grabbe, Lester, *Etymology in Early Jewish Interpretation: The Hebrew Names in Philo.* Atlanta, Ga.: Scholars Press, 1988.

Grabois, A., "The Legendary Figure of Charlemagne in Jewish Sources of the Middle Ages" (Hebrew). *Tarbiz* 36 (1967): 22–58.

Graetz, Heinrich, "Alexander and His Gold-Lettered Scroll." *JQR,* o.s. 2 (1890), 102–4.

Grafton, Anthony, *Defenders of the Text, the Traditions of Scholarship in an Age of Science, 1450–1800.* Cambridge: Harvard University Press, 1991.

——, *Forgers and Critics: Creativity and Duplicity in Western Scholarship.* Princeton: Princeton University Press, 1990.

——, *Joseph Scaliger. A Study in the History of Scholarship II: Historical Chronology.* Oxford: Oxford University Press, 1993.

Grendler, Paul F., *Schooling in Renaissance Italy: Literacy and Learning 1300–1600.* Baltimore: Johns Hopkins University Press, 1989.

Gruterus, Janus. *Lampas sive Fax artium liberalium, hoc est thesaurus criticus in quo infinitis locis, theologicis iurisconsultorum, et scriptae supplentur, corriguntur.* 7 vols. Frankfurt am Main, 1603–34.

Guidoboni, Emanuela, "Riti di calamità. Terremoti a Ferrara nel 1570–4." *Quaderni storici,* n.s. 55 (1984), 107–35.

Gutwirth, Eleazar, "The Expulsion from Spain and Jewish Historiography." In *Jewish History: Essays in Honour of Chimen Abramsky,* ed. A. Rapoport-Albert and S. J. Zipperstein. London: Peter Halban, 1988, 141–61.

Habermann, Abraham M., *Studies in the History of Hebrew Printers and Books.* (Hebrew). Jerusalem: Rubin Mass, 1978.

Halberstam, Solomon J., "Sheloshah Ketavim al Devar Sefer Me'or Enayim u-Mikhtav eḥad el R. Azariah mi ha-Adumim." In *Festschrift zum achtzigsten Geburtstage Moritz Steinschneiders.* Leipzig: Otto Harrassowitz, 1896, 1–8.

Hamilton, Alastair, "The Book of 'Vaine Fables': The Reception of 2 Esdras from the Fifteenth to the Eighteenth Century." In *Essays on Church History Presented to Prof. Dr. J. van den Berg,* ed. C. Augustijn, et al. Kampen: J. H. Kok. 1987, 45–62.

Hammond, Nicholas G. L., *Sources for Alexander the Great: An Analysis of Plutarch's* Life *and Arrian's* Anabasis Alexandrou. Cambridge: Cambridge University Press, 1993.

Harrington, Daniel J., *Ps. Philon, Les Antiquités bibliques.* Paris: Éditions du Cerf, 1976.

Hefele, Carl J. von, and H. Leclercq, *Histoire des Conciles: Les Décrets du Concile de Trente,* vol. 10. Paris: Librairie Letouzey et Ané, 1938.

Hoffmann, Karl, *Ursprung und Anfangstätigkeit des ersten Päpstlichen Missionsinstituts im sechzehnten Jahrhundert . . . ,* Münster in Westfalen: Aschendorffsche Verlagsbuchhandlung, 1923.

Idel, Moshe, "Enoch is Metatron" (Hebrew). In *Early Jewish Mysticism,* ed. Joseph Dan. *Jerusalem Studies in Jewish Thought,* vol. 6, 1–2. Jerusalem, 1987, 151–70.

——, *Language, Torah and Hermeneutics in Abraham Abulafia* (trans. from the Hebrew). Albany: State University of New York Press, 1989.

——, "The Magical and Neoplatonic Interpretation of the Kabbalah in the Renaissance." In *Jewish Thought in the Sixteenth Century,* ed. Bernard Dov Cooperman. Cambridge: Harvard University Press, 1983, 186–242.

Ioly Zorattini, Pier C., *Processi del s. uffizio di Venezia contro ebrei e giudaizzanti (1571–1580).* Florence: Olschki, 1985.

Jacobs, Louis, *Theology in the Responsa.* London: Routledge and Kegan Paul, 1975.

Jeauneau, Edouard, *Nani sulle spalle di giganti.* Naples: Guida, 1969.

Jellicoe, Sidney, *The Septuagint and Modern Study.* Oxford: Clarendon Press, 1968.

Jones, Christopher P., *Plutarch and Rome.* Oxford: Clarendon Press, 1971.

Kajanto, Iiro, *Classical and Christian Studies in the Latin Epitaphs of Medieval and Renaissance Rome.* Helsinki: Suomalainen tiedeakatemia, 1980.

Katz, Peter, *Philo's Bible: The Aberrant Text of Bible Quotations in Some Philonic Writings and Its Place in the Textual History of the Greek Bible.* Cambridge: Cambridge University Press, 1950.

Kaufmann, David, "Contributions a l'histoire des luttes d'Azaria de' Rossi." *REJ* 33 (1896): 77–87.

——, "La défence de lire le Meor Enayim d'Azaria de' Rossi." *REJ* 38 (1899): 280–81.

——, "Eliezer et Hanna de Volterra dans le poème d'Avigdor de Fano." *REJ* 34 (1897): 309–11.

——, "La Famille de Yehiel de Pise." *REJ* 31 (1895): 62–73.

Kisch, Guido, ed., *Pseudo-Philo's Liber antiquitatum biblicarum.* Latin ed. and introduction. Notre-Dame: Notre Dame Press, 1949.

Klibansky, Raymond, "Answer to Query: Standing on the Shoulders of Giants." *Isis* 26 (1936): 147–49.

Kraye, J., "Heinsius and the Author of *De mundo.*" In *The Uses of Greek and Latin:*

Historical Essays, ed. A. C. Dionisotti, A. Grafton, and J. Kraye. London: Warburg Institute, University of London, 1988, 171–97.

Krochmal, Nachman, *Moreh Nevukhe ha-Zeman,* ed. Leopold Zunz. Berlin: Louis Lamm, 1923.

Kugel, James L., *The Idea of Biblical Poetry. Parallelism and Its History.* New Haven: Yale University Press, 1981.

——, "The Influence of Moses ibn Ḥabib's *Darkhei No'am.*" In *Jewish Thought in the Sixteenth Century,* ed. Bernard Dov Cooperman. Cambridge: Harvard University Press, 1983, 308–25.

Lamarche, Pierre, "La Septante." In *Le Monde grec ancien et la Bible,* ed. C. Mondésert. Paris: Beauchesne, 1984, 19–35.

Langerman, Y. Tzvi, "Some Astrological Themes in the Thought of ibn Ezra." In *Rabbi Abraham ibn Ezra: Studies in the Writings of a Twelfth-Century Jewish Polymath,* ed. Isidore Twersky and Jay Harris. Cambridge: Harvard University Press, 1993, 28–85.

Lauterbach, Jacob, "The Ancient Jewish Allegorists in Talmud and Midrash." *JQR,* n.s. 1 (1910–11), 291–333, 503–31.

Le Déaut, Roger, *Targum du Pentateuch, Traduction des deux recensions palestiennes complètes avec introduction, parallèles, notes et index,* avec la collaboration de Jacques Robert, vol. 1. Paris: Éditions du Cerf, 1978.

Le Moyne, Jean, *Les Sadducéens.* Paris: Librairie Lecoffre, 1972.

Leibowitz, Joshua O., "A Probable Case of Peptic Ulcer as Described by Amatus Lusitanus (1556)." *Bulletin of the History of Medicine* 27, 3 (1953): 212–16.

Leiman, Sid Z., *The Canonization of the Hebrew Scriptures: The Talmudic and Midrashic Evidence.* Hamden, Conn.: Archon Books, 1976.

——, "From the Pages of Tradition: Dwarfs on the Shoulders of Giants." *Tradition* 27 (1993): 90–94.

Levi della Vida, Giorgio, *Documenti intorno alle relazioni delle chiese orientali con la s. sede durante il pontificato di Gregorio XIII.* Studi e Testi 143. Vatican City, 1948.

Lewin, Benjamin M., *Oṣar ha-Geonim.* Haifa, 1928–62.

Lichtenstein, Hans, "Die Fastenrolle: Eine Untersuchung zur jüdisch-hellenistischen Geschichte." *HUCA* 8–9 (1931–32): 257–351.

Lieberman, Saul, *Greek in Jewish Palestine: Studies in the Life and Manners of Jewish Palestine in the II–IV centuries* C.E., 2d ed. New York: Philip Feldheim, 1965.

——, *Hellenism in Jewish Palestine: Studies in the Literary Transmission, Beliefs and Manners of Palestine in the I Century* B.C.E.*–IV Century* C.E., 2d ed. New York: Jewish Theological Seminary, 1962.

——, *Shkiin,* 2d ed. Jerusalem: Wahrman Books, 1970.

Lieberman Saul, ed., *Tosefta Ki-feshuta: A Comprehensive Commentary on the Tosefta* (Hebrew). 8 Vols. New York: Jewish Theological Seminary, 1955–73.

Loew ben Bezalel, Judah (Maharal of Prague), *Be'er ha-Golah.* Jerusalem: Jahadut, 1971.

——, *Neṣaḥ Yisrael.* London: L. Honig, 1960.

Löwinger, Samuel, "Recherches sur l'oeuvre apologétique d'Abraham Farissol." *REJ* 105, 2 (1940): 23–52.

Lowth, Robert, *De sacra poesi Hebraeorum Praelectiones academicae* (1753). Oxford: Clarendon Press, 1810.

——, *Isaiah: A New Translation with a Preliminary Dissertation* (1778). London: William Tegg, 1848.

Luria, Ben'Zion, ed., *Megillat Taʿanit with Introduction and Notes.* Jerusalem: Bialik, 1964.

Luzzatto, Samuele Davide, "De scriptura Samaritana." In R. Kirchheim, *Karme Shomron.* Frankfurt am Main: J. Kaufmann, 1851, 109–16.

——, *Hebräische Briefe,* ed. Eisig Gräber. Przemysl: Zupnik and Knoller, 1882.

——, *Philoxenus, sive de Onkelosi chaldaica Pentateuchi versione.* Vienna: Anthon Schmid, 1830.

Maccoby, Hyam, *Judaism on Trial; Christian Disputations in the Middle Ages.* Rutherford: Fairleigh Dickinson University Press, 1982.

Mahler, Eduard, *Handbuch der jüdischen Chronologie.* Leipzig: Max Schmerson, 1916.

Manasseh ben Israel, *Dissertatio de fragilitate humana.* Amsterdam, 1642.

Marcus, Ralph, "A Sixteenth-Century Critique of Philo." *HUCA* 21 (1948): 29–71.

Margolioth, Mordechai, "Moʿadim, ve-Ṣomot be-Ereṣ Yisrael u-ve-Bavel bi-Tequfat ha-Geonim." *Areshet* 1 (1944): 204–16.

Marzi, Demetrio, *La questione della riforma del calendario, nel quinto concilio lateranense, 1512–1517, con la vita di Paolo di Middelburg scritto da Bernardino Baldi.* Florence: Università di Firenze, 1896.

Medini, Hayyim, *Sede Ḥemed.* New York: Kehot, 1959–60. (Rpt. of Warsaw 1891–1912.)

Mehlman, Yisrael, "Saviv Sefer Meʾor Enayim le-Rabbi Azariah min-ha-Adumim be-Italiah." In *Genuzot Sefarim: Maʾamarim Bibliografiyim.* Jerusalem: Jewish National and University Library Press, 1976, 21–39.

Merton, Robert K., *On the Shoulders of Giants: A Shandean Postscript, etc.* New York: New York Free Press, 1965.

Meyer, Johannes, *Seder Olam Rabba Seder Olam Zuta, sive Chronicon Hebraeorum maius et minus.* Amsterdam: Joannes Wolters, 1699.

Modena, Leon. *The Autobiography of a Seventeenth-Century Venetian Rabbi: Leon Modena's Life of Judah,* trans. and ed. Mark R. Cohen. Princeton: Princeton University Press, 1988.

Modona, L., "Une lettre d'Azaria de Rossi." *REJ* 30 (1895): 313–16.

Momigliano, Arnaldo D., "Greek Culture and the Jews." In *The Legacy of Greece; A New Appraisal,* ed. M. I. Finley. Oxford: Clarendon Press, 1981, 325–46.

——, "The Origins of Rome." In *Settimo contributo alla storia degli studi classici e del mondo antico.* Rome: Edizioni di storia e letteratura, 1984, 384–436.

——, "The Place of Ancient Historiography in Modern Historiography." In *Settimo contributo alla storia degli studi classici e del mondo antico.* Rome: Edizioni di storia e letteratura, 1984, 13–36.

Monfasani, John, *George of Trepizond: A Biography and a Study of His Rhetoric and Logic.* Leiden: Brill, 1976.

Moore, George Foot, "The Vulgate Chapters and Numbered Verses in the Hebrew Bible," *Journal of Biblical Literature* 12 (1893). In *The Canon and Masorah of the Hebrew Bible: An Introductory Reader,* ed. Sid Z. Leiman. New York: Ktav, 1974, 815–20.

Moscato, Judah, *Nefuṣot Yehudah.* Venice: Zuan Bragadini, 1589.

——, *Qol Yehudah.* Venice, 1594.

Neher, André, *Le puits de l'Exil.* Paris: Albin Michel, 1966.

Neubauer, Adolf, "Where Are the Ten Tribes?" *JQR,* o.s. 1 (1889), 14–28, 95–114, 185–201, 408–23.

Nikiprowetzky, Valentin, *Le Commentaire de l'écriture chez Philon d'Alexandre: Son caractère et sa portée, observations philologiques.* Leiden: Brill, 1977.

North, John, "The Western Calendar, 'Intolerabilis, horribilis et derisibilis': Four Centuries of Discontent." In *The Gregorian Reform of the Calendar,* ed. George V. Coyne et al. Vatican City, 1983, 75–113.

Olitzki, M. "Die Zahlensymbolik des Abraham ibn Ezra," *Jubelschrift zum siebzigsten Geburtstag des Dr. Israel Hildersheimer,* Berlin: H. Engel, 1890, 99–120.

Orlinsky, Harry, "Studies in Talmudic Philology." *HUCA* 23, 1 (1950): 499–514.

Parente, Fausto, "Il liber *antiquitatum biblicarum* e i falsi di Annio da Viterbo," *Paideia Christiana. Studi in onore di Mario Naldini,* Rome: Gruppo Editoriale internazionale, 1994, 153–72.

Pedersen, Olaf, *A Survey of the Almagest.* Odense: Odense University Press, 1974.

Pelletier, André, *Flavius Josèphe, adapteur de la Lettre d'Aristée, une réaction atticisante contre la Koiné.* Paris: Librairie C. Klincksieck, 1962.

Perani, Mauro, "Due biblioteche di ebrei a Bologna nel Quattrocento." In *Banchi ebraici a Bologna nel XV secolo,* ed. Maria G. Muzzarelli. Bologna: Il Mulino, 1994, 255–68.

Pesaro, Abramo, *Memorie storiche sulla communità israelitica ferrarese.* Ferrara, 1878.

Petrarch, Francesco, *De sui ipsius et multorum ignorantia,* ed. Luigi M. Capelli. Bibliothèque littéraire de la Renaissance 6. Paris, 1906.

Portaleone, A. *Shilṭe ha-Gibborim.* Mantua, 1612.

Postel, Guillaume, *Linguarum duodecim characteribus differentium alphabetum introductio ac legendi modus.* Paris: D. Lescuier, 1538.

Purvis, James D., *The Samaritan Pentateuch and the Origin of the Samaritan sect.* Cambridge: Harvard University Press, 1968.

Rabbinowicz, Raphael N., *Diqduqe Soferim,* pts. 1–15. Munich, 1867–84.

Rahmer, Moritz, *Die biblische Erdbeben-Theorie, Eine exegetische Studie.* Magdeburg: Robert Friese in Leipzig, 1881.

Reider, Joseph, ed. and trans., *Wisdom of Solomon.* New York, Harper and Brothers, 1957.

Reif, Stefan C., *Hebrew Manuscripts at Cambridge University Library.* Cambridge: Cambridge University Press, 1997.

Reinholder, Hans, "Dante und die Hebräische Sprache." In *Judentum im Mittelalter. Beiträge zum christlisch jüdischen Gespräch,* ed. Paul W. Wilpert et al. Miscellanea mediaevalia Bd. 4. Berlin: De Gruyter, 1966, 442–57.

Reusch, Franz H., *Die Indices librorum prohibitorum des sechzehnten Jahrhunderts.* Tübingen, 1887.

Rice, Eugene F., *St. Jerome in the Renaissance.* Baltimore: Johns Hopkins Press, 1985.

Rizzo, Silvia, *Il lessico filologico degli umanisti.* Rome: Edizioni di storia e letteratura, 1973.

Rossi, Giovanni B. de, *Mss Codices Hebraici.* 3 Vols. Parma: ex publico typographo, 1803–4.

Rowley, Harold H., *Darius the Mede and the Four World Empires in the Book of Daniel: A Historical Study of Contemporary Theories.* Cardiff: University of Wales Press Board, 1935.

Ruderman, David B., "An Exemplary Sermon by a Jewish Teacher in Renaissance Italy." *Italia* 1, 2 (1978): 7–38.

——, *Jewish Thought and Scientific Discovery in Early Modern Europe.* New Haven: Yale University Press, 1995.

——. *The World of a Renaissance Jew: The Life and Thought of Abraham ben Mordechai Farissol.* Cincinnati: Hebrew Union College Press, 1981.

Sarfatti, Gad B., *Mathematical Terminology in Hebrew Scientific Literature of the Middle Ages* (Hebrew). Jerusalem: Magnes Press, 1968.

Schiller-Szinessy, Solomon M., *Catalogue of the Hebrew Manuscripts Preserved in the University Library Cambridge,* vol. 1. Cambridge, 1876.

Schirmann, Jefim, ed., *Mivḥar ha-Shirah ha-Ivrit be-Italia.* Berlin: Schocken, 1934.

Schmidman, Michael A., "The Abot Commentary of R. Shem Tob ben Joseph ibn Shem Tob." In *Reverence, Righteousness and Rahmanut: Essays in Memory of Rabbi Dr. Leo Jung,* ed. Jacob J. Schachter. Northvale, N.J.: J. Aronson, 1992, 277–91.

Scholem, Gershom, "The Author of the Forged Zohar Fragment in the Time of Rabbi Abraham Halevi (Hebrew)." *KS* 8, 1 (1931–32): 262–65.

——, "The Cabbalist Rabbi Abraham ben Eliezer Halevi" (Hebrew). *KS* 2, 4 (1925): 101–41.

——, "Gematria." In *Kabbalah.* Jerusalem: Keter, 1974, 337–43.

——, "Gilgul: The Transmigration of Souls." In *On the Mystical Shape of the Godhead: Basic Concepts of the Kabbalah,* ed. and trans. J. Chipman. New York: Schocken, 1991, 197–250.

——, *On the Kabblah and Its Symbolism* (trans. from the German). London: Routledge and Kegan Paul, 1965.

——, *On the Origins of the Kabbalah* (trans. from the German). Princeton: Princeton University Press, 1987.

Schreckenberg, Heinz, *Bibliographie zu Flavius Josephus.* Leiden: Brill, 1968.

Schürer, Emil, *The History of the Jewish People in the Age of Jesus Christ,* rev. ed., ed. Geza Vermes and Fergus Millar, vol. 1. Edinburgh: T. and T. Clark, 1973.

Schwab, Simon, "Comparative Jewish Chronology." In *Jubilee Volume Presented in Honour of the Eightieth Birthday of Rabbi Dr. Joseph Breuer,* ed. Marc Breuer and Joseph Breuer. New York: Philip Feldheim, 1962, 177–97.

Secret, François, *Les Kabbalistes chrétiens de la Renaissance.* Paris: Dunod, 1964.

Segal, Lester A., *Historical Consciousness and Religious Tradition in Azariah de' Rossi's Me'or ʿEinayim.* Philadelphia: Jewish Publication Society of America, 1989.

Segal, Mose H., ed., *Sefer Ben Sira ha-Shalem,* 2d ed. Jerusalem: Mossad Bialik, 1958.

Segre, Renata, *The Jews in Piedmont,* vol. 1: 1297–1582. Jerusalem: Israel Academy and Diaspora Research Institute, 1986.

Septimus, Bernard, *Hispano-Jewish Culture in Transition; The Career and Controversies of Ramah.* Cambridge: Harvard University Press, 1982.

Shalem, Nathan, "Una fonte ebraica poco nota sul terremoto di Ferrara del 1570." *Rivista geografica italiana* 45 (1938): 66–76.

Sherrington, Charles S., *The Endeavour of Jean Fernel.* Cambridge: Cambridge University Press, 1946.

Simon, Richard, *Histoire critique du texte du Nouveau Testament, où l'on établit la vérité des actes sur lesquels la Religion Chrétienne est fondée.* Rotterdam: Reinier Leers, 1689.

——, *Histoire critique du vieux testament* (1678). Amsterdam: D. Elzevir, 1680.

Simonsohn, Shlomo, *History of the Jews in the Duchy of Mantua* (trans. from Hebrew). Jerusalem: Kiryath Sefer, 1972.

Solerti, A., "Il terremoto di Ferrara." *Rassegna Emiliana* 2, 2 (1889): 517–28.

Sonne, Isaiah, *From Paul V to Pius V* (Hebrew). Jerusalem: Mossad Bialik, 1954.

——, "Excursions into History and Bibliography" (Hebrew). In *Alexander Marx Jubilee Volume on the Occasion of his Seventieth Birthday,* ed. Saul Lieberman. New York: Jewish Theological Seminary, 1950, 209–35.

——, *Expurgation of Hebrew Books—the Work of Jewish Scholars: A Contribution to the History of the Censorship of Hebrew Books in the Sixteenth Century.* New York: New York Public Library, 1943.

Steinschneider, Moritz, *Die arabische Literatur der Juden.* Frankfurt am Main: J. Kauffmann, 1902.

——, *Catalog der hebräischen Handschriften in der Stadtbibliothek zu Hamburg und der sich anschliessenden in anderen Sprachen.* Hamburg: Otto Meisner, 1878.

——, *Catalogus Librorum Hebraeorum in bibliotheca Bodleiana.* Berlin: Ad. Friedländer, 1852–60.

——, *Die heb. Übersetzungen des Mittelalters und die Juden als Dolmetscher* (1893). Graz: Akademische Druck-U. Verlagsanstalt, 1956.

Stern, Menachem, "Sicarii and Zealots." In *The World History of the Jewish People, Society and Religion in the Second Temple Period,* ed. Michael Avi-Yonah and Zvi Baras. London: W. H. Allen, 1977, 263–301.

Stow, Kenneth, "The Burning of the Talmud in the Light of Sixteenth-Century Catholic Attitudes toward the Talmud." *Bibliothèque d'humanisme et Renaissance* 34 (1972): 435–59.

Tamar, David, "Expectation for Redemption in the Year [5]335 in Italy" (Hebrew). *Sefunot* 2 (1958): 61–88.

——, "Peraqim le-Toledot Ḥakhme Ereṣ Yisrael v'Italia u-le-Toledot Sifrutam." *KS* 33, 3 (1958): 378–79.

Tavoni, Mirko, *Latino, grammatica, volgare: Storia di una questione umanistica.* Padua: Editrice Antenore, 1984.

——, "Renaissance Linguistics." In *History of Linguistics,* vol. 3 (trans. from the Italian), ed. G. Lepschy. London: Longman, 1990, 1–108.

Teicher, Jacob, "Il principio Veritas filia temporis presso Azariah de' Rossi." *Rendiconti della reale accademia nazionale dei Lincei,* Rome ser. 6, 9 (1931), 268–75.

Tishby, Isaiah, *The Wisdon of the Zohar* (trans. from the Hebrew). 3 vols. Oxford: Oxford University Press, 1989.

Trompf, Gary W., *The Idea of Historical Recurrence in Western Thought from Antiquity to the Reformation.* Berkeley: University of California Press, 1979.

Twersky, Isadore, *Rabad of Posquières; A Twelfth-Century Talmudist.* Cambridge: Harvard University Press, 1962.

Urbach, Ephraim E., *The Tosafists, Their History, Writings and Methods,* 4th ed. (Hebrew). Jerusalem: Bialik Institute, 1980.

Vaccari, Alberto, "La fortuna della lettera d'Aristea in Italia." In *Scritti di erudizione e di filologia,* vol. 1. Rome: Edizioni di storia e letteratura, 1952, 1–23.

Veltri, Giuseppe, "The Humanist Sense of History and the Jewish Idea of Tradition:

Azaria de' Rossi's Critique of Philo Alexandrinus." *Jewish Studies Quarterly* 2, 4 (1995): 372–93.

Vermes, Geza, *Scripture and Tradition in Judaism,* 2d ed. Leiden: Brill, 1973.

Vidal-Naquet, Pierre, *Du bon usage de trahison (La guerre des juifs).* Paris: Éditions de Minuit, 1977.

Villalpandus, Joannes Baptista, *Apparatus urbis ac templi hierosolymitani,* vol. 3 of H. Pradus and J. Villalpandus, *In Ezechielem Explanationes.* Rome: Carolus Vulliettus, 1602.

Vorstius, Guglielmus H., *Chronologia sacra-profana a mundi conditu ad annum M.5352 vel Christi 1592, dicta Zemah Dawid Germen Davidis auctore David Gans.* Leiden: Joannes Maire, 1644.

Walker, Daniel P., *The Ancient Theology: Studies in Christian Platonism from the Fifteenth to the Eighteenth Century.* London: Duckworth, 1972.

Wallach, Leopold, "Alexander the Great and the Indian Gymnosophists in Hebrew Tradition." *PAAJR* 11 (1941): 47–83.

Walter, Nikolaus, *Der Thoraausleger Aristobulos, Untersuchungen zu seinen Fragmenten und zu pseudepigraphischen Resten der jüdisch-hellenistischen Literatur.* Berlin: Akademie-Verlag, 1964.

Walzer, Richard R., *Galen on Jews and Christians.* London: Oxford University Press, 1949.

Weil, Gérard E., *Élie Lévita, humaniste et massorète (1469–1549).* Leiden: Brill, 1963.

Weinberg, Joanna, "An Apocryphal Source in the Me'or'Enayim of Azariah de' Rossi." *Journal of the Warburg and Courtauld Institutes* 56 (1993): 280–84.

——, "Azariah de' Rossi and LXX Traditions." *Italia* 5, 1–2 (1985): 7–35.

——, "Azariah de' Rossi and the Forgeries of Annius of Viterbo." In *Essential Papers in Jewish Culture in Renaissance and Baroque Italy,* ed. D. Ruderman. New York: New York University Press, 1992, 252–79.

——, "Azariah dei Rossi: Towards a Reappraisal of the Last Years of His Life." *Annali della Scuola Normale Superiore di Pisa,* ser. 3, vol. 8, 2 (1978): 493–511.

——, "The Quest for the Historical Philo in Sixteenth-Century Jewish Historiography." In *Jewish History: Essays in Honour of Chimen Abramsky,* ed. A. Rapoport-Albert and S. Zipperstein. London: Peter Halban, 1988, 163–87.

——, "The Voice of God: Jewish and Christian Responses to the Ferrara Earthquake of November 1570." *Italian Studies* 46 (1990–91): 69–81.

Weiss Halivni, David, *Peshat and Derash: Plain and Applied Meaning in Rabbinic Exegesis.* Oxford: Oxford University Press, 1991.

Wilson, Charles W., *Golgotha and the Holy Sepulchre.* London: Palestine Exploration Fund, 1906.

Wirszubski, Chaim, ed., *Flavius Mithridates, Sermo de Passione Domini.* Jerusalem: Israel Academy of Science and Humanities, 1963.

Wolfson, Harry A., *Philo: Foundations of Religious Philosophy in Judaism, Christianity, and Islam,* 4th ed. Cambridge: Harvard University Press, 1968.

Yaari, Abraham, *Studies in Hebrew Booklore* (Hebrew). Jerusalem: Mossad Harav Kook, 1958.

Yassif, Eli, *The Tales of Ben Sira in the Middle-Ages: A Critical Text and Literary Studies* (Hebrew). Jerusalem: Magnes Press, 1984.

Yates, Frances A., *Giordano Bruno and the Hermetic Tradition.* London: Routledge and Kegan Paul, 1964.

Yerushalmi, Yosef Hayim, "Clio and the Jews: Reflections on Jewish Historiography in the Sixteenth Century." *PAAJR* 46–47 (1979–80): 607–38.

——, *Zachor: Jewish History and Jewish Memory.* Seattle: University of Washington Press, 1982.

Zinguer, Ilana, "Historiographes juifs de la Renaissance italienne lecteurs d'Antonio de Guevara." *REJ* 146, 3–4 (1987): 281–97.

Zollicofferus, Johannes, *Quaestiones quaedam de terraemotu, ex Hebraeorum atque Arabum scriptis eruta.* Zurich, 1651.

Zucchetti, Giuseppe, ed. *Il Chronicon di Benedetto (989–1000), monaco di S. Andrea del Soratte e il libellus de imperatoria potestate in urbe Roma.* Rome: Fonti per la storia italiana, 1920.

Zunz, Leopold, "Toledot Rabbi Azariah min ha-Adumim." *Kerem Ḥemed* 5 (1841): 131–58 (with additional notes by S. Rapoport); 7 (1843) 119–24. Rpt. in the editions of *Me'or Enayim* by I. Benjacob, and Z. H. Jaffe.

GENERAL INDEX

Abraham ben Eliezer Halevi xiv, 546–47
Abravanel, Isaac
    Days of the World 432–34, 451–52
Abravanel, Judah 13–14
Adam, creation of 498–500
Aesop in Aggadah 301
Ages of man 564
Aggadah xxvi–xxvii 279–95
    authority of 289–90
    di Trani on 279–80, 293
    evaluation of 285–88, 291–95
    Maimonides on 281, 291, 302–3
    purpose of 288–89
    as rhetoric 284, 299–300
    and scientific truth 297–98
    Sherira on 288
Aggadot
    discrepancies 296–97, 508–9
    and Josephus 342–45
Agrippa, see Caligula
Akylas and Onqelos 526–27, 571–85
Alexander of Macedon 3
    and the elders of the South 197–98
    and the high priest 4, 352–54, 361–62
    and the Indian sages (Gymnosophists) 198–200
    massacre of the Alexandrian Jews 240–41
Alexander Romance 199
Alexandria
    and Abravanel 243–45
    altar 342–44
    foundation of 241–43, 247–48
    Jews of 239–40, 252–54
    massacre of the Jews 239–41, 243, 245–47, 250–51
    No Amon 244, 248
    and Tosafists 242–48
Alfonso, king 514
Alḥarizi, Judah xv
Almagest and Maimonides 234–35
Amatus Lusitanus xv–xvi
Annius of Viterbo xxvii, xxxix–xl, 2, 343, 346–47, 412
Aquila 193–94, 573, 579, 581, 584–85
Aramaic 129, 182, 185–87, 681
    in New Testament 190–92
    as vernacular 683–86
Aristeas, *Letter of* xvii, 1, 31, 33–77
    translations of 4–6, 33, 42
Aristobulus 188–89
Aristotle the Jew 354–55
Artaxerxes 466–68, 470
    identification of xxvii, 314–15, 319–22
Arukh 47, 90, 206, 257, 302, 328, 367, 372, 408, 519, 576, 577, 583, 589, 599, 606, 612, 641, 653
Ashkenazi, Eliezer xvi, 152
Astrology 548–50
Astronomy
    and Gersonides 235
    and Maimonides 235–36
    Ptolemean 234–35
    stars, movement of 203–5
    sun, movement of 204–5, 207, 209, 218
Authority, rabbinic
    and human disciplines 268–70, 278, 391
    and medieval exegesis 270–75
    and Sinaitic tradition 267–69, 392–94, 398–401

Babel 678–79
Baharad 448–50, 488, 497–98, 516
Baron, S. xiii, xix, xxii, xxiii, 209
Baruch of Peschiera 370
Benjamin, see Judah and Benjamin
Ben Sira 87–89, 357, 568
  Alphabet of xiv
Bereshit, translation of 369–70
Bergman, J. xiii
Bethar, destruction of 240–41, 248–49, 254
Bible (Greek),
  Versions of 166, 172–74, 193–94, 574, 579–80
  See also Septuagint
Bible (Hebrew), variant readings 163
Bible (Italian) 575
Boethusians 102–6, 109–10, 144–45
Bologna xvi, 30
Boncompagni, Giacomo xviii
Bonfil, R. xiii, xv–xvi, xxii, xxvi, xxix, xxx, xxxi, xlii, xliv, 98, 406, 544
Buoni, Antonio xxx, 14, 22, 301–2, 659

Calendar 484–517
  and Abraham bar Ḥiyya 511
  fixed calendar 484–85, 492–93, 502, 504–6
  and intercalation 485, 514–15
  Julian 512, 515
  and the land of Israel, 502–3
  Maimonides on, 501
  non-Sinaitic, 501, 503–4
  observation 487
  and postponements 501–2
  and Rabban Gamaliel, 486, 509–12
  reform 512
  and Sabbatical year 487–88
Calepino, Ambrogio xlii, 47, 199, 242, 531, 582, 599, 602, 677, 681
Caligula and Agrippa 255
Caro, Joseph 89, 363
Carthage 212–14
Cases, Samuel 532
Cassel, D ix, xiii, xvii, xxi, 7, 9, 14, 36, 38, 49, 82, 84, 103, 105, 106, 113, 126, 131, 137, 138, 146, 147, 158, 214, 220, 282, 283, 287, 295, 324, 339, 349, 363, 387, 400, 425, 442, 444, 454, 458, 490, 494, 502, 508, 603, 616, 674, 687, 706, 716, 719
Cattaneo, Stefano xvii–xviii
Chronology xxvii–xxviii, xxxi
  and *baharad* 448–50, 495–96, 507–8
  errors in 536–37
  and foundation of Rome 529–31
  interregna 441–42
  rabbinic 440, 442–46, 450, 536
  in Septuagint 127, 188
  synchronic 529–32
Contarini, Gasparo xxv, 718
Cosmography 201–238
  antipodes 233
  cosmos, size of 398–99
  earth, shape of 201–11, 400–1
  Gehinnom 207–8, 233
  heavens, shape of 206–9
  in Pirqe d'Rabbi Eliezer 205–6, 208–9
  spheres 216–18
  spheres, upright and oblique 230
  in Zohar 209–10, 230
Creation 529
  month of 488–91, 501
  Platonic views on 134–37
Cutheans 344–45, 668–69
Cycles, cosmic 563–65
Cyrus 468–469
  identification of xxvii, 314, 319–21

Dama b. Netina 97, 181
Daniel, seventy weeks 519–25, 551–53
Darius 4
  identification of xxvii, 314–15, 319–21
Dato, Mordechai 544–45
De' Rossi, Azariah
  under attack xvii–xviii, 303–4, 322,
  copybook of xiv–xv
  elegies xvii
  epitaph xix, 718–19
  Hebrew style xlv
  Letter of Aristeas xvii, 1, 31–32
  life xiii–xix, 30
  Maṣref la-Kesef xliv
  poetry xviii
  Ṣedeq Olamim xliv
  Syriac Gospels xviii, xxxi
  333, 341, 395
  wife of 27–28
De' Sommi, Judah xvii, 322
Derashot, see Aggadah
Dialogue
  in Job 276–77
  in *Kuzari* 527–28

Earthquake
  Ferrara xvi–xvii, 7–11, 26–32, 719–20
  Greek philosophers on 14–15
  Josephus on 21, 24–26
  Pythagoras on 22

rabbinic views on 16–24
in Scripture11–14
Easter, date of 615
Ecclesiastes 277–78
Egyptian bondage, duration of 426–31
End of days, calculation 547, 556–60
Maimonides on 557
Epitaphs 716–19
Era, Creation xxviii, 369–77, 405–6, 408–9, 452–53, 527
Seleucid 4, 359–65, 366–68, 452–53
starting-points of 369–71
Era of documents, see Seleucid era
Essenes 102–3, 106–10
Euphrates 225–27, 228–29
Ezra 328, 341, 396–97
and Chronicles 475
Torah Scroll of 195–96

Fano, Avigdor da xiv
Fano, Ezra da 376, 532
Ferentili, Agostino xxviii
Ferrara, earthquake of xvi–xvii, 7–11, 26–32, 719–20
Eliseo Capys, inquisitor of xviii
yeshivah of xvi 331
Friedenwald, H. xv

Galatinus, Petrus. xv, 326
Garden of Eden 138–39, 152, 208, 226
Gelenius, Sigismund 1, 3, 111, 117, 422
Genazzano, Elijah da xiv
Gentiles, reward for 465, 468–69
Geography, Ptolemean 212–15, 222–23
George of Trepizond 19, 38
Government, forms of 124–25
prayer for 661–65
Grafton, A. xxvii–xxviii, xxxi, 412
Greek 578, 596
literary and spoken 687
rabbinic attitude to 179–80

Hadrian and Jerusalem 249–50
massacre of the Alexandrian Jews 240–41, 249
Haggai and Temple 621–42
Hai Gaon 91
Halakhah, messianic 406
Hanukkah 636–39
Hebrew 672–90
first language 672–75, 680
and other languages 676–79
primacy of 673, 688–90
pronunciation 576–77
as vernacular 681–83
Hebrew vowels and accents
antiquity of xxix, 699–709
in Jerome 708
in Kabbalistic texts 702–3
Helena, queen 631–34, 643–53
Hermes Trismegistus 115–17
High priests
in Josephus 420–22, 654–56
number of 339–41
in second Temple 352, 420–22
succession of 457–65, 481–82
Hilkhot Sheḥiṭot u-ṭerefot xiv
Hillel II 375–76, 485, 496, 506–7
History, rabbinic approach 384–88
Hoshea, reign of 437–39, 442, 447, 516
Hyperbole xxvii, 333–39

Ibbur (calendrical) 486–87, 509
Ibbur (kabbalistic), see Impregnation, secret of
Ibn Ezra, criticism of 478
Ibn Ḥabib, Moses and tombstone 682–83, 712
Ibn Zabarra, Joseph b. Meir xiv
Impregnation, secret of 318–19
Isaac Nathan ben Kalonymus, see *Me'ir Nativ*
Issereles, Moses, criticism of 236–38

Jaddua 3, 353–54, 463–64
Jaffe, Z.H. ix, 295, 333, 368
Jannaeus, see Jannai
Jannai 347–50
Jeconiah, descendants of 474–79
Jerusalem 220–23, 226
Job and knowledge of God 276–77
Jose [ben Ḥalafta] 380–83, 445, 536, 537
Josephus, Flavius 3
translations of 422, 654
Josippon 3, 331–32
Judah and Benjamin, numbers of 253–57, 262–64
Judah b.Yehiel, Messer Leon 98
Judah the Gaulonite 102–3
Judith 637–39

Kallir 315, 554
Kalonymus b. Kalonymus xv
Karaites xliv, 110, 142
Ketiv-Qeri 397–98
Kimḥi, *Sefer ha-Shorashim* 563, 576, 591, 618
Kings of Judah and Israel 436–43
Kuzari, dialogue in 527–28
translations of 453–54

Land of Israel 222–25, 227, 229, 231–33
Language, confusion of 674–80
Latif, Moses 427–29
Leiman, S. 88, 89, 125, 204, 238, 565
Leone Ebreo, see Abravanel, Judah
Levita, Elijah xxix,
 critique of 699–709
Lex Hieronymiana 146–47
Liber antiquitatum biblicarum, see pseudo-Philo
Light of the Eyes xvii
 Christian texts in xxxviii–xli
 classical texts in xli–xlii
 content xxiii–xxv
 controversy over xlii–xliv
 fortuna xx–xxii
 Hellenistic texts in xxxvi–xxxvii
 literary style xxii–xxiii, 81–85
 post-Talmudic texts in xxxiv–xxxvi
 purpose xxv–xxxi
 rabbinic texts in xxxiii–xxxiv
 sources in xxxii–xlii
Literature, profane 86–94
Livy 384
Luzzatto, Samuel David xix

Maccabee, etymology of 343–44
Maccabees, fourth book of 58
Maharal of Prague xxii, xxv
Maimonides, dates of 377
Margaret of Savoy xvii
Marini, Marco xviii
Masora 25–26, 177–78, 195–96
Massaran Hayyim 292
Me'ir Nativ 623
Melli, Phineas Elijah da 580
Men of the Great Synagogue 351–53, 455–56
Mercator, Gerardus 533
Messianism 406, 543–61
 medieval and later views on 546–47, 550–51
 rabbinic views on 545, 547, 556–57
Metasthenes, on the *Order of the Times* 412–14
Midrash, see Aggadah
Miracles 28
Mishle Sindebar xiv
Modena, Avtalion 478
Modena, Leon xix, 24
Molcho, Solomon 261
Momigliano, A. xxxi, xxxvi–xxxvii, 35
Monarchy 124–25
Monobaz 631–34, 643–53
Moscato, Judah xvi, xliv
Mount Gerizim, altar of 344–45, 347
Münster, Sebastian xl, 677

Nathan b. Yehiel, see *Arukh*
Nebuchadnezzar, identification of 533–34
Nehemiah 470, 475, 524
New World 209, 211–15
Norzi, Nethanel da 532
Numa 625–26
Number-symbolism 137–38

Omens 657–60
Onias 3
Onqelos, see Akylas
Oral Torah 392–96

Pagninus, Xantes 149
Perez de Valencia xxix
Persian Empire, duration of 352, 371, 533–34
Persian kings 466–73, 480–81
 Abravanel on 472–73
 in the Bible 411
 and Daniel 472–73
 Eusebius on 423–24
 Josephus on 420–2
 rabbinic view of 480–84
 and the *Seder Olam* xxvii, 466–67, 473
 Xenophon on 410–11
Peru, biblical references to 211–12
Peshaṭ, see Scripture, plain meaning of
Pharisees 102–3, 108–10
Philo 101–2, 110, 111–59
 allegorization 137–40
 defence of 146–59
 and Essenes 154, 158
 ignorance of Hebrew and Aramaic 129–30, 133
 on angels and souls 154–58
 on creation 134–35, 151
 follower of Plato 111, 135
 on God 114–15
 on immortality of the soul 112–14
 and Karaites 143–44
 on names of God 114
 and Oral Torah 141–44
 on Torah 117–20
 use of lxx 128, 130–32, 172
Pico della Mirandola, Giovanni xxviii, 24
Pisa, Yeḥiel Nissim da 105
Poetry, biblical 710–16, 719
 and Abravanel 710–12
 and Jerome 711–12
 in *Kuzari* 710–11, 715

Polirone, Abbazia di xvi, 189
Pompey 378–80
Prester John 260, 700, 705–6
Priestly vestments 586–620
  Aristeas on 598–600
  and Christian equivalent 615
  Christian writers on 609–11
  efod 581–82, 590–91
  Jewish commentators on 586–97
  Josephus on 605–8, 618–19
  me'il 581–82, 586
  migba'ot 587, 591
  miṣnefet 587, 589, 591, 613–14
  nezer 590
  patil 588–589
  Philo on 601–4
  ṣiṣ 590, 609, 611–13
  Urim and Tummim 591–96, 616–18, 640–41
Procreation, classical authors on 309–10
  Fernel on 310
Procreation of primevals
  Augustine on 308–9
  di Trani on 312–13
  Maimonides on 308
  rabbinic views on 305–13
Prophecy 390
  Bat Qol 356, 388–89, 635, 684
  cessation of 389–90, 453
Provenzali (brothers), on Philo 189
Provenzali, David xliv, 677
Provenzali, Judah 714
Provenzali, Moses xliii
Pseudo-Philo
  LAB xxx, 120–23, 125–27
  The Book of the Times 415–19
Ptolemy 511, 513
Ptolemy Philadelphus 3, 160–62, 181, 189
Purim games 461

Rabbinic tradition and scientific truth 218–20, 398–401
Redemption
  Nahmanides on 560–61
Resurrection
  Maimonides on 105–6
Reuveni, David 261–62
Rieti, Moses da xiv
Ruffinus 3, 41

Sadducees 102–6, 108–10, 144
Salmanassar 533
Samaritans, see Cutheans
Sarteano, Abraham da xiv
Santoro, Giulio xviii
Scaliger, Joseph xxvii–xxviii, xxxi
Script
  antiquity of 691–98
  Assyrian and Hebrew 128–29, 185–87, 666–71, 693–98
  and Jerome 698
  Samaritan 666–67
Scripture, plain meaning of 279, 283–84, 294–95, 394
  allegorization 140
Sects, Josephus on 102–4, 107–8, 180
Seder Olam xxvii, 323–24, 537
  Abravanel on 271, 273
  author of 445
Segal, L. xxii, 269
Semiramis 346–47, 471, 693
Septuagint
  Christian writers on 174–75
  inspiration of 166–67, 169
  Josephus on 33, 41
  translated from Aramaic 189–93
  as translation of Pentateuch 167–69
  transmission of 176–79
  variant readings 171, 178
Septuagint-origins
  Christian writers on 165–67
  Philo on 165
  rabbis on 160–63
Sheqel 667–68, 670–71
Sherira, Epistle of 367
Shilo 543, 554
Simeon the righteous 3–4, 351–53, 356–58, 455–56, 458, 460–61, 463–64, 640
Simon, R. xx
Simonsohn, S. xiii
Sinaitic tradition 95, 97, 267
Steuchus, Augustinus xl–xli, 579
Study 81–84
  of Torah 385–88

Tanna d've Eliyahu xxviii, 558–59, 562–68
  and Lactantius 558–59
Targum 182–85
  Jonathan ben Uzziel 183–85, 192
  Onqelos 183, 185
  Yerushalmi 183–85, 192
Tarquin, massacre of the Alexandrian Jews 240–241, 245
Temple, first
  duration of 431–48
Temple, second
  duration of 451–56, 518–25

Ten tribes 252
  in 4 Ezra 259–60
  and Ortelius 260
  return of 257–64
Tribes 252–64, see also Judah and Benjamin,
Tequfah
  and Rav Adda 512–16
  and Samuel 512–16
Tetragrammaton 114, 133, 148–50, 698
Textual corruption 323–32
Tiqqun Soferim 326–28
Titus in Aggadah 296–304
  Roman historians on 298–99
Tohu va-vohu 150–51, 580
  Steuchus on 136
Trajan, Massacre of the Alexandrian Jews 239, 241, 245–47
Tribes, see Judah and Benjamin and Ten tribes

Wisdom
  Greek 90–92
  of Solomon 637, 684–85
  sources of 94–96, 98

Yedidyah, see Philo
Yerushalmi, Y.H. xix, xxii

Zacuto, Abraham, astrology xiv, 546
  Sefer Yuḥasin 2, 534
Zohar, authorship of 329–30
Zunz, L. xiii, xxi

INDEX OF SOURCES

HEBREW BIBLE

(references are exclusively to biblical passages discussed by de' Rossi)

Genesis

1:1 369
2:8 225
6:2 414
9:7 257
10:6 679
33:2 624
35:26 494
44:30 674
47:30 674

Exodus

10:19 227
12:40 426ff
15:6 713
15:8 713
20:6 562
25:40 613, 618
23:31 214, 226
33:13 280, 440

Leviticus

4:3 391
4:22 391
18:28 561
26:23–24 22

Numbers

11:21 443
21:17–18 713

Deuteronomy

2:4,5 665
2:8 213
7:9 562
10:16 293
10:22 494
11:22 226, 229
11:24 226
12:1 561
17:12 664
18:22 664
22:23 397
25:5 308
28:27 397
28:30 397
32 713
32:26–27 262

Joshua

1:8 386

2 Samuel

18:18 716
24 256

1 Kings

6 444
6:1 494
6:38 444
10:22 211
16:23 438
17 28
22:49 213

2 Kings
4 28, 637
4:27 389
5 28
7:1 437
15:29 438
17:6 252
18:26 682
22:8 683
23:17 716
23:25 468
23:29 468

Isaiah
1:1 457, 481
8:23 437
9:11 226
13:13 20
19:19 344
23:4, 14 214
24:18–20 13
30:21 514
38:5 346
38:21 28
41:25 223
44:6 623
45:1 468
54 255, 262
56:7 346
66:19 213

Jeremiah
2:2 534
10:2 660
10:10 20
10:11 683
16:15 224
18:7–8 641
18:13 298
25:38 346
29:7 661
46:16 346
49:36 361
49:38 361, 382
50:3 224
50:9 223, 224
50:16 346
50:32 664
51:27 224
51:63 225

Ezekiel
1:18 13
7:10 664
27:12 212
27:23 226
36:37 262
37 258

Hosea
4:6 128, 683

Amos
2:1 16
2:13–16 11–13
3:2 23
3:12 13
3:15 11–13
6:11 11–13
9:8 626

Jonah
1:3 212

Habakkuk
3 713

Zephaniah
1:4,6 626
3:1 347
3:9 690

Haggai
2:6,9 621–642

Zechariah
1:12 466, 551
2:14 262
2:15 263
3:7 461, 464
4:10 13
6:15 253, 641
7:1 389
8:4 461
14:5 25

Malachi
1:6 625
1:11 625, 634

Psalms
12:1–2 419
6:2 419
41:9 674
48:8 212, 213
48:14 624

51:3 713
56:11 714
78:4 624
78:6 624
81:6 678
104:5 562
104:32 13
104:35 664
105:8 562
105:15 522
116:11 218
116:69 393
119:42–44 561
126:6 718

Proverbs
1:20 714
10:27 460

Job
19:24 718
33:29 525
38:2 277
40:9 277
42:7 277
42:8 237–38

Song of Songs
7:3 302–03
7:5 302

Lamentations
5:19 562

Ecclesiastes
1:7 227
1:10 707
7:20 218
11:5 567

Esther
3:7 470
10:2 472

Daniel
2:34 553
2:44 563
7:5 471–72
7:13 553
7:14 563–64, 665
7:27 665
8:13 551
8:19 552
8:22 381
8:26 552
9:1–2 521
9:24 518–525, 552
9:25 522
9:26 522
9:27 525
10:11 521
11:2 361, 381, 411, 471, 480
11:4 381
12:11–12 553

Ezra
2:1 397
2:59 536
2:62 536
2:64 252
4:5–6 321
4:6 411
4:7 411
4:15 419, 637
4:24 466
5:2 466
6:8,9,10 626, 661
6:14 320
6:15 466
6:22 471
7:1 321, 466, 470
7:15 627
7:27 627
8 252
8:1 471

Nehemiah
3:29 478
5:14 522
7:5 397
7:61 536
7:64 536
7:66 252
12 397, 457
12:10 481
12:10–11 352
12:26 481
13 466–67
13:6 456, 461, 470–71, 482

1 Chronicles
3:17–24 474
3:21 477–78, 480
5:26 252, 258
7:15 397
8:29 397

1 Chronicles (*cont.*)
9:1 263
9:3 263
21:5 256

2 Chronicles
2 624
3:1 250
9:22 211
15:9 263
17:9 683
20:36, 37 213
22:10 419
30:18 263
33:11 471
34: 263
36:23 381

APOCRYPHA AND PSEUDEPIGRAPHA

4Ezra
13:39–46 259–60, 262

Judith
15:8 638

Wisdom of Solomon
7:4–6 685
7:17–21 685

Sirach
3:2 87
6:6 87
11:1 87
11:29 87
13:15 88
24:26 49
26:3 87
42:9 87
50:25 345

Baruch
1:10–12 661

1 Maccabees
1:6–8 360
1:7 4, 360
1:10 535, 360
1:54 552
4:52 452
6:8 552
7:33 662
12:11 663
14:27 358

2 Maccabees
1:7 535
1:9 535
1:19ff 640
1:20 640
2:7 640
9:5–10 299
9:8–9 552
14:3ff 343

4 Maccabees
4 639, 662

NEW TESTAMENT

Matthew
23–33 106

Mark
12:18–27 106

Luke
19:44 302
20:27–36 106

John
19:13 190
19:18 190

Acts
1:19 191
2:1–13 191
5:37 102
18:2 173
23:8 106

2 Thessalonians
2:15 267

Romans
6:12 665

BIBLE VERSIONS

Septuagint

Gen. 5:2 191
Ex. 1:5 191
Ex. 13:18 582
Ex. 21:22 141

Ex. 22:27 142, 664
2K 21:19 435
Jonah 3:4 17
Zech. 14:5 25
2Chr. 3:6 625
2Chr. 33:21 435

Aramaic versions

Targum Onqelos
Gen. 1:1 369
Gen. 2:7 672
Gen. 2:8 225
Gen. 42:23 582
Ex. 13:18 582
Ex. 20:5 122
Lev. 1:16 693
Lev. 7:35 520

Targum [pseudo–] Jonathan
Gen. 1:1 369
Gen. 1:2 580
Gen. 1:7 208
Gen. 2:24 192
Gen. 4:8 192
Gen. 11:1 679
Gen. 11:8 692
Gen. 13:3 369
Ex. 4:25 184
Ex. 28:37 614
Ex. 34:10 261
Lev. 7:35 520
Num. 12:14 184

Targum Yerushalmi
Gen. 2:24 192
Gen. 4:8 192
Gen. 11:9 679
Ex. 4:25 184
Lev. 27:10 185

Targum Jonathan
1K. 8:2 123, 489
2K. 10:12 677
Is. 1:26 369
Jer. 7:29 688
Jer. 46:25 244
Jer. 48:9 613
Ezk. 16:55 369
Ezk. 30:14 244
Nahum 3:8 244
Zech. 3:7 461
Zech. 14:5 25

Targum Ecclesiastes
10:4 665

Targum Psalms
102:26 369

RABBINIC SOURCES

Mishnah
Berakhot
1:5 85
5:3 273
9:2 9

Pe 'ah
2:6 510

Terumot
3:9 468

Shabbat
2:3 599

Eruvin
1:5 95
5:4 396

Pesaḥim
5:5 143
9:6 396

Sheqalim
8:5 338

Yoma
3:10 187, 631
7:5 593

Rosh ha-Shanah
1:1 371
1:2 491
1:7 270
2:6 486
2:8 486, 489

Ta'anit
3 29
3:8 20

Megillah
2:1 129, 182
4:9 326

Ḥagigah
2:1 197, 539
2:2 108

Yevamot
1:4 668
6:6 306
8:3 258, 394
10:9 308

Nedarim
9:10 330

Nazir
3:6 632

Sota
5:2 702
9:14 249
9:15 102, 559

Bava Qama
8:1 28

Bava Meṣia
1:7 596

Sanhedrin
1:6 374
4:2 480
6:4 142
10 105
10:1 86, 87, 105, 149, 168, 387
10:3 258

Eduyyot
1:3 390
1:4 267
1:6 342
2:2 381
2:9 554, 563

Avodah Zarah
2:5 705
3:1 210

Avot
1:3 104
1:6 82, 348
1:8 348
1:13 684
1:16 82
2:6 684
2:8 302
3:2 662
3:11 334
3:13 717
4:1 82
4:13 390, 667
4:22 664
5:1 138, 231, 500
5:5 636
5:6 146, 691
5:8 231
5:21 311, 476
5:22 292, 385
6:3 5
6:8 291

Zevaḥim
3:1 143
5:2 104
12:4 381

Menaḥot
8:7 575

Keritot
3:9 258, 394

Tamid
2:2 339
7:4 565

Middot
4:6 641
4:7 624

Kelim
17:16 540

Parah
1:1 396
3:5 2

Yadayim
4:5 666
4:6 90, 687

Tosefta
Pe'ah
4:18 632

Demai
6:12–13 571

Shabbat
7:18 572

Yom ha-Kippurim
1:21 633
3:8 609

Sukkah
3:1 109
4:5 302
4:6 241

Megillah
4:41 573

Sota
13:2–6 388
13:6 356
15:8 91

Sanhedrin
4:7 694
4:8 669
7:7 284
13:2 469
13:5 105

Eduyyot
1:4 342
1:14 554

Miqva'ot
6:3 572

Mekhilta d'Rabbi Ishmael
pisḥa 2 489, 658
pisḥa 3 687
pisḥa 5 681
pisḥa 14 160, 426, 555
beshalaḥ 1 122
beshalaḥ 3 122, 240
beshalaḥ 9 289
shirata 6 326
shirata 7 122
vayassa 2 357
vayassa 6 287, 557
amalek 3 463
baḥodesh 1 370
baḥodesh 4 293
neziqin 8 141
neziqin 9 141
neziqin 17 152
kaspa 1 142

Sifra (ed. Weiss)
6a 143
19a 391
76c 440
79a 459
80a 294
83a 458
95a 143
106c 573
110c 250
110d 639
112b 258
112c 258

Sifre Bemidbar (ed. Horovitz)
64 371
131 339, 460

Sifre Zuṭa (ed. Horovitz)
10 340

Sifre Devarim (ed. Finkelstein)
32 293
37 221
49 288
156 123
292 141
317 287

Seder Olam Rabbah (ed. Ratner)
1(4–6) 426
1(7) 272
2(12) 272
2(13) 311
3(14) 121
3(56) 271
4(18–19) 488
4(21) 495
5(22) 428
13(58) 270
20(88) 389
22(96) 438
22(98–99) 437
23(99–100) 437
27(123) 544
28(130) 271
28(130–131) 519
29(131) 252
30 52
30(136–137) 314, 456
30(140) 360
30(141–143) 4, 273, 452
30(141–46) 323

Seder Olam Rabbah (ed. Ratner) (*cont.*)
30(142) 63
30(144) 356

Megillat Ta'anit
4 104
5 104
7 372
9 344, 460, 661
10 103
11 348, 356, 635, 684

Palestinian Talmud
Berakhot
2(1)4b 85, 463
2(3)4d 113
5(1)8d 1
7(2)11b 87
9(2)13c 17

Pe'ah
1(1)15b 277, 632
1(1)15c 90, 97, 179, 387, 578
1(1)15d 5, 646
1(1)16b 335
2(4)17a 290
7(6)20b 575
8(7)21a 85

Demai
1(3)21d 268
2(1)22c 541
6(7)25d 571

Shevi'it
1(7)33b 277
4(3)35b 23

Ma'aser Sheni
5(2)56a 575

Bikkurim
2(1)64c 270

Shabbat
1(3)3b 566
1(4)3c 542
6(1)7d 578
6(4)8b 578
6(9)8c 636
6(9)8d 557
7(5)9b 575
16(1)15c 287, 686

Sheqalim
2(5)47a 85, 716
4(2)48a 351
5(1)48c–d 268
5(2)48d 85, 419
6(1)49b–c 640
6(1)49c 657

Yoma
1(1)38c 337, 339, 459
1(1)38d 458
2(5)40a 440
3(8)41a 578
4(1)41c 609
6(3)43c 658
6(3)43c–d 342
7(3)44c 617

Sukkah
3(5)53d 575
3(12)54a 463
4(1)54b 277
5(1)55a–b 239

Rosh ha-Shanah
1(1)56a–b 370
1(1)56b 444, 495
1(2)56d 490
1(3)57b 484
2(3)58a 216

Ta'anit
2(1)65a 639
2(14)66 447
4(2)68a 163
4(5)68b–69a 240
4(5)68c 122, 147, 536
4(5)68d 248
4(5)69a–b 334
4(8)69b 659

Megillah
1(5)71c 571
1(9)71b 670, 678, 686, 696
1(9)71c 173, 179, 578, 669, 696
1(9)71d 161, 535, 668
1(10)72a 458
1(13)72b 165
2(4)73b 575
2(5)73b 638
3(2)74a 165
3(7)74c 593
4(1)74d 701

Mo'ed Qatan
3(5)82c 523
3(7)83b 575

Ḥagigah
1(8)76d 290
2(1)77c 697
2(2)78a 396

Yevamot
1(6)3a 399, 668
7(1)8a 270
12(1)13a 82

Nazir
5(5)54b 87

Sota
3(4)19a 113
5(5)20c 562
5(6)20d 317, 535, 567
5(7)20c 121
5(7)20d 288
7(2)56b 280
9(13)24b 356, 358, 388, 635, 684

Qiddushin
1(1)59a 575
4(1)65b 618, 640

Sanhedrin
10(1)28a 88

Avodah Zarah
3(1)42c 210
3(3)42d 122
5(4)44d 345

Horayot
3(2)47d 458
3(5)48c 290

Babylonian Talmud
Berakhot
3a 157
5a 23
6b 286
8a 686
9b 623
10a 286, 510, 664
16a 295
16b 538
17a 268
18a 113, 407
20a 93
24a 567
26b 686
28a 395
29a 347, 348
33a 456, 686
33b 143, 153, 542, 697
34b 510
44a 348
48a 87, 347
51b 636
54b 254, 299
55a 8
57b 334
58a 96, 304, 620
59a 16, 23, 26, 92
63a 373
63b 82, 83
64a 178

Shabbat
8a 95
10a 387
12b 686
13b 31, 338
15a 380, 477, 572, 632
21b 637
22a 284
23a 638
26a 331
30a 475
30b 280
31a 256, 267, 318, 572, 685
39b 354
49b 615
50b 194
55a 194, 406
55b 19
56b 529
61a 331
63a 83, 140, 295
63b 590, 609
65b 225
68b 652
77b 599
85a 94
87b 428
88a 443
92a 389
96b 288, 535, 567
104a 535, 669, 695, 697
105b 335

Shabbat (*cont.*)
108a 109
112b 268
113b 230
115b 583
118b 334
119a 339
119b 334, 387, 390
139a 23
147b 705
156a 548, 659

Eruvin
2b 334
4a 282
13b 636
14b 95
19a 208, 222
21b 547
50b 556
53a 82, 268, 716
53b 91, 576
54b 83, 573
56a 207, 512
60b 501
65a 88
67a 574

Pesaḥim
7b 97
8b 506
22b 558
25b 665
32b 549
44b 477
54a 567, 691
54b 557
57a 338, 633
61a 687
62b 283, 334, 338
64b 253
87b 98, 122
94a 202, 207, 269, 334, 398, 565
94b 203, 207
103b 194
104a 619
110a 157
118a 468
119a 271, 567

Yoma
5b 241, 406, 595
9a 4, 271, 336, 337, 351, 380, 431, 459
9b 268, 541
18a 348, 349, 460
19b 104, 387
21a 636
21b 520, 591, 625, 639, 640
35b 333
38b 594
39a 351, 640
39b 94, 658
47a 458
52b 657
53a 104, 460
53b 640
54a 94, 231
54b 221
57a 609
66b 113
69a 243, 344, 351, 661
69b 406, 456, 593
71b 590
72b 615
73b 591, 617
77a 335
82a 307
83a 381
86a 89

Sukkah
5a 590, 609
6b 700
8a 95
28a 209, 387, 391
29a 658
49b 334
51b 240, 254, 333, 551, 624, 625
53a 302
55b 676

Beṣah
4b 540
24a 306

Rosh ha-Shanah
2a 371
2b–3a 315
3b 314, 456, 469
10b 123
10b–11a 494
12a 489, 490
16a 123

17b 335
18b 180, 536
20a 429
20b 95, 503
21a 375, 484
25a 484, 486, 510, 511
27a 489
31a 321, 559, 563, 565

Ta'anit
5b 270, 279, 293, 475
7a 82
7b 23
9a 123, 385
10a 202, 207, 576
16a 717
18a 104
18b 302
22a 20
23a 639
29a 537

Megillah
2b 669, 696, 698
2b–3a 535, 669, 695
3a 97, 183, 188, 390, 526, 536, 571, 574, 583
5b 685
6b 337
8b 666
9a 180
9a–b 160
9b 179, 578
10b 361, 510
11a 358, 706
11b 319, 420
12a 391, 452
14b 257, 258, 259
15a 231, 274, 317, 318, 336, 419, 576
15b 441
16a 96
16b 320
18a 330, 558, 687
22a 326, 700
24b 576
25a 326
26b 599
29a 687
32a 636

Mo'ed Qatan
16a 491
16b 641
17a 89, 292
26a 250
27a 584
28a 270

Ḥagigah
4b 19
7a 441
10b 97
12a 201, 216
12b 157, 387
13a 87, 568
14a 287, 288, 291
15a 335
15b 90, 91, 338, 698
16a 387
16b 108

Yevamot
12b 307, 309
16a 338, 399, 510
17a 257
24a 140, 295
47b 180
52b 282
61a 348
63a 23
63b 87
64b 245, 306
65b 301
77b 143
82b 445
96b 85
97a 304
103a–b 93
105a 82
121b 96

Ketubot
3a 387
5a–b 281
8b 311
19b 323
22a 548
23a 381
55b 353, 501
68a 336
85b 98
103b 636
106a 388
110a 15
110b 87

Ketubot (*cont.*)
111a 294, 556
111b 294

Nedarim
14b 539
20a 539
23b 538
32b 664
37b 129, 182, 699
38a 574
39b 334
40a 225, 335
49a 539
81a 537

Nazir
23b 93
32b 519, 623

Sota
5b 26
9a 521
9b 651
11b 257
12a 122
13b 123, 493, 508
22b 349
31a 562
33a 173, 356, 388, 635, 684, 686
34b 717
41a 349
41b 236
45a 388
47a 347, 689
48b 574, 591, 635, 684
49b 91, 249, 615

Giṭṭin
7a 346
10b 97
19b 97
24b 356
28b 96
55b–56a 634
56a 348
56b 296, 584
57a 254, 295
57b 240, 254, 333
58a 254, 302
60a 287
67a 697
79b–80a 372

Qiddushin
4b 516
12b 432
16b 395, 554
22b 706
25a 443
29b 599
29b–30a 311
31a 97, 181, 286, 468
31a–b 124
32b 91
33a 527
39b 506
40b 23
49a 573
49a–b 284
51a 82
66a 110, 348
69a 221
69b 252
70b 180, 652
71a 594
72a 472
72b 245, 357, 574, 595

Bava Qama
3b 574
6b 571
11b 596
51a 269
54b–55a 481
55a 286
82b 91
83a 179
83b 141
92a 164
92b 88, 334, 666

Bava Meṣia
7b 537
16a 136
18b 356
19a 596, 687
33a 47
44a 687
49a 308
59b 97, 636
61b 101
84b 334

85a 84, 686
85b 95, 335
85b–86a 159
114a 388
117b 698

Bava Batra
3a–b 621
3b 633
4a 390, 624
9b 286, 334, 336
10b 441, 469
11a 632
11b 386
12a 140, 324, 365, 389
12a–b 390
14b 81
14b–15a 2
15a 258, 277, 475, 477, 528
15b 121
16b 26
19a 320
21a–b 292, 700, 705
25a 229
25a–b 400
25b 205, 206, 223
42a 556
58b 279
63b 685
65a 399
73a–b 299
73b 279
74a 208
78b 281
89b 540
91a 121
98b 87, 89
110a 510
111b 320
115b 103, 104
133b 347, 572, 615
145b 288
146a 87
156a 306
158b 232

Sanhedrin
7a 335
11a 374, 388, 684
12a 91
14a 338
17a 92
17b 541
20b 123
21b 129, 185, 194, 529, 666, 694, 695
21b–22a 669
22a 178, 694
24a 84
27b 122
34a 279
37b 475
38b 201, 338, 489, 499, 500
39b 180
43b 152
46a 396
51b 406, 595, 596
64a 406
64b 461
68a 93, 337
69b 305, 311, 312, 476
83b 556
87a 392
89a 167, 528
90a 105
90b 85, 106, 579, 674
91a 628
91b 524
91b–92a 167
92a 85, 689
93a 136
93b 475
94b 574
95b 368
95b–96a 300
96a 468
97a 102, 556, 559, 565
97b 546, 547, 556
98a 550, 555
98b 551, 555
99a 326, 545, 555, 556
100b 86, 87, 88, 282, 357
101a 293
102a 300, 391
105a 469
106a 123
106b 338
107b 347
109b 123

Makkot
7b 141
10a 82
12a 391

Shevuʿot
4a 443
16a 399
36a 99
41b 574
46b 287

Avodah Zarah
2a 122
3b 387
4a 481, 583
8a 489, 490
8b 338, 379, 380
9a 273, 324, 352, 369, 371, 425, 431, 448, 451, 543, 559, 632
9b 546
10a 4, 359, 371, 372, 381, 670
11a 572
18b 387
19a 83
33b 375
37b 409
44a 589
54b 540

Horayot
11b 458
13b 698

Zevaḥim
19a 588
19b 542
44b–45a 406
45a 595
54a 580
88b 602
107b 399
113a 121
116b 206
118b 431, 435, 445

Menaḥot
29b 375, 468, 697
32b 652
53a 718
64b 91, 519
65a 92, 104, 318
65b 419
85a 116
99b 90, 147, 387, 539, 704
109b 342, 351, 658, 688
109b–110a 342
110a 214, 574, 577, 596, 634

Ḥullin
6a 344
6b 541
7b 626
16a 320
18b 82
24a 441
24b 463
43a 477
45b 298
58a 297
58b 334
60a 309, 489, 490, 556
60b 291, 491, 510, 687
80a 679
87a 636
89a 288, 585
90b 254, 279, 333
91b 121
95b 333
97a 95
98b 477
105b 157
108a 622
115b 142
129b 395
134a 95
134b 567
137b 441
138a 588
142a 506

Bekhorot
31b 85
37a 697
57b 254, 338

Arakhin
12a 271, 445
12b 431, 435
13a 467
15a 521
15b 334, 335
32b 362

Temurah
16a 97, 338

Keritot
11a 577

Tamid
27b 661
29a 339
31b–32a 197
32a 214, 381

Niddah
13a 334
13b 180
15a 442
17a 652
23a 97
30b 380
31a 231
45a 307, 308, 477, 542
46b 271, 324, 445, 537
47b 306
61a 261, 316
69b 302, 596
70b 596

Avot d' Rabbi Nathan, rec.A (ed. Schechter)
1,4 499
5,26 103
9,41–42 25
11,46 82
15,60–61 572
25 337
29,7 285
34,99 698
34,101 328
41 609

Soferim
1:2 109
1:7 161
1:9 187
6:4 163
15:2 686
16:2 285, 287

Sefer Torah
1:10 187

Bereshit (Genesis) Rabbah
1:1 115
1:1 244
1:6 207
1:10 697
2:4 352
3:7 150
3:8 157
4:2 400
4:5 49, 209
4:7 216
6:6 217
6:8 207
8:2 87
8:8 540
8:11 161
10:4 563
10:7 296
10:9 132, 162, 651
11:5 262
11:9 500
12:4 153
14:2 178
14:7 490, 680
14:8 221
15:3 225
16:3 49
17:4 112
17:8 231
18:1 206
18:4 672
18:5 283
19:5 309
20:7 283
21:1 583
30:8 317
31:8 672
32:6 495
34:10 233, 353
35:2 351, 456, 460
36:8 701
37:1 86
37:4 26
37:7 409
38:6 678
38:13 121, 136
38:28 121
44:12 121
44:15 456
46:3 574
46:10 162, 651
49:7 327
56:6 291
57:4 121
60:8 268
61:4 282
63:9 283
64:10 301
65:21 240
70:5 572
71:10 143
74:17 443

Bereshit (Genesis) Rabbah (cont.)
78:1 291
78:8 422, 688
81:2 82
81:2 82
81:3 345
82:6 550
84:8 581
82:10 716
85:4 316
91:3 347
91:9 152
93:3 583

Shemot (Exodus) Rabbah)
5:9 83
9:4 116
14:1 122
18:11 426
24:4 358
29:9 16
30:12 526, 572
31:9 468
40:3 318
40:4 24, 318

Vayiqra (Leviticus) Rabbah
1:3 282
11:9 575
13:5 161, 243, 319, 351
17:6 32
19:6 475
20:2 576
20:19 458
21:9 339, 444
22:3 296
27:1 214
29:1 499
33:1 575
33:6 575

Bemidbar Rabbah (Numbers Rabbah)
3:13 328
9:14 676
9:48 113
11:2 229
12:4 207, 524, 625
12:8 216, 490, 680
13:20 122
13:14 210
13:15 118
14:12 676
14:4 89
19:20 315
19:30 123

Devarim Rabbah (Deuteronomy Rabbah)
3:13 249
8:6 387
9:9 330

Shir ha-Shirim (Song of Songs) Rabbah
1:2 680
1:3 575
1:6 529
1:15 289
1:15 121
2:7 551
2:12 621
2:13 102, 559
2:17 241
3:10 524, 625
3:11 216, 490
4:12 577, 682
7:1 443
8:9 356, 388, 635

Ekhah Rabbah (Lamentations Rabbah)
Proem 5 438
Proem 34 659
1:5 249
1:16 240, 348
2:2 240, 247; 248; 254, 333, 338
3:5 240
3:10 240
3:22 291
4:1 634
4:18 206

Qohelet (Ecclesiastes) Rabbah
1:1 277
1:5 245, 357
2:5 221
2:8 282
3:11 594
6:2 290
7:8 267 572
7:12 347
10:20 124
11:5 557
12:7 244
12:12 88

Esther Rabbah
Proem 3 240

Proem 4 241
1:6 578
4:12 686
6:3 317

Pesiqta d' R. Kahana (ed. Mandelbaum)
2:5 180
13:10 659
14:5 687
23:1 499
27:1 687
(Suppl.) 2 217

Tanḥuma (ed. Buber)
bereshit 12 17
bo 9 426
mishpaṭim 3 526, 571, 572
vayaqhel 10 338
pequde 3 249
shemini 13 499
qedoshim 10 95, 221
emor 9 214
balaq 25 681
devarim 3 556
devarim 7 249
zot ha-berakhah 208

Tanḥuma
shemot 13 317
mishpaṭim 5 526, 571, 572
terumah 9 272
tissa 13 24
vayaqhel 7 338
pequde 4 249
shemini 8 499
qedoshim 8 95, 221
emor 6 214
ḥuqqat 1 296
balaq 16 681
devarim 4 556
shofeṭim 10 548

Pesiqta Rabbati (ed. Friedmann)
6:3 274, 317
25:2 576
47:2 499

Tanna d've Eliyahu
2 641

Midrash Tehillim (Psalms)
9;2 556
9:7 251, 463
9:18 469, 669
18:7 351
22:4 285
28:5 286
36:11 351, 456, 460, 593
104:7 157
104:32 17
137:7 554

Midrash Mishle (Proverbs)
Pr.1:1 294
Pr. 26:24 328

Pirqe d'Rabbi Eliezer
3 225, 228
5 206
6 400, 491
7 491
8 373, 491
20 226
28 544, 186
47 443
48 122, 681
52 294

Yalqut Shimoni
II, par. 6 539
II, par. 236 445
II, par. 300 469
II, par. 738 426
II, par. 906 323
II, par. 1064 324
II, par. 1067 419
II, par. 1068 274

GREEK AND LATIN SOURCES

Aesop (ed. Hausrath)
I,161 301

Aristeas
30 189
96–7 598
187–294 197
302 164

Aristotle
De Caelo
II,289b32–34 204
II,297a2ff 205

De physico auditu
449

Ethica Eudemia
8,1248a–b 581

Ethica Nicomachea
1,1098b7 247
7,1153b25–30 407

Historia animalium
V,544b25 309

Meteorologica
7365a14–369a9 14
365a15ff 203

Poetica
1451a–b 711

Politica
VII,1335a25 309

Aristotle, pseudo-
De mundo
4,396a 14

Arrian
De rebus gestis
II,2 469
III,1 242
III,21 360

Caesar, pseudo-
De bello Alexandrino
7 177

Cicero
Epistulae ad familiares
V,12 84
VI 8
VII 8
XII 84

Tusculanae disputationes
I 112
I,44 717
II,27 31

Paradoxa
III,1 453

Pro L. Valerio Flacco
28,66–69 629

Pro Sexto Roscio Amerino
XVI,47 300

Topica
X,45 336

Cicero (attrib.)
Rhetorica ad Herennium
III,12 84
IV,33 336

Corpus iuris civilis
I, vii 310
I, xxii 441

Curtius, Quintus Rufus
De rebus gestis
I,5 362
II 530
III,3 598
IV 124
IV,7 332
IV,8 242
V 360
X,5 470

Dio Cassius
Romanae historiae libri
37,15–17 378
86, 26 298

Diodorus Siculus
Bibliothecae historicae libri
II,4–20 346

Diogenes Laertius
De vita et moribus philosophorum
V,23 354

Dioscorides
De materia medica
4,LXIX 608

Eutropius
Breviarium
7 298
8 245

Galen
De naturalibus facultatibus
2,9 99

De pulsuum differentiis
II,5 689

De usu partium
XI,14 689

In Hippocratis librum de acutorum victu commentarius
1,19 83

Gellius, Aulus
Noctes Atticae
7 177
17 366

Hermes, pseudo- (ed.Ficino)
Pimander
45 8

Herodotus
Historiae
1,213–24 483

Homer
Iliad
II,204–5 124

Josephus
Contra Apionem
I,131ff 414
I,26 175, 407
I,177–81 355
II,31–32 176
II,48 628
II,51–56 639
II,76–78 662
II,82 419
II,134 379
II,196 663
II,199 283
II,237 142
II,263 135

Antiquitates
I,12 168
I,70–71 692
I,82 172
I,128 553
II,346 711
III,137–38 619
III,151–53 684
III,151–87 605
III,153 190
III,195 633, 671
III,214–18 618
III,320 633
IV,181 118
IV,207 142
IV,223–24 124
IV,303 711
V,336 682
VI,60–61 124
VII,392 624
VIII,155 638
IX,223–27 24
IX,290 186
X,78 716
X,147 431
X,220–21 414
X,248 420
X,276 552
XI,16–18 661
XI,31 420
XI,49 356
XI,81 624
XI,120 3, 421
XI,120ff 470
XI,133 259
XI,183 421, 475
XI,184ff 421
XI,297 421, 456
XI,301 420
XI,309–11 345
XI,313 421
XI,321 421
XI,322–24 458
X1,329 243
XI,331 608
XI,333–5 362
XI,337 361
XI,340 347
XI,347 422
XII,1 56
XII,11–118 3
XII,14 190
XII,22 36
XII,24 36
XII,28 35
XII,32 37
XII,43 357, 422, 464
XII,57 40
XII,64 42
XII,72 42
XII,86–119 167

Antiquitates (*cont.*)
XII,94 57
XII,97 58
XII,119 360
XII,145–46 628
XII,156–58 343
XII,157 422
XII,157ff 3
XII,224 357
XII,237–41 343
XII,321 452, 535, 637
XII,385–87 343
XII,413 343
XII,413ff 379
XIII,55 628
XIII,62–72 344
XIII,74–79 345
XIII,78 628
XIII,171–73 102
XIII,256 458
XIII,288–92 348
XIII,297–98 102
XIII,320 348, 349
XIII,372–98 110
XIV,40ff 379
XIV,105–6 630
XIV,114–18 255
XV,3 103, 632
XV,121–46 21
XV,370 103, 632
XV,373–79 108
XV,391ff 624
XVI,160–73 630
XVI,179–87 624
XVI,187 597
XVII,175–79 349
XVII,199 717
XVIII,4 102
XVIII,11–25 102
XVIII,16 106
XVIII,18–23 107
XVIII,23–25 102
XVIII,259 158
XX,17–99 643
XX,102 103
XX,169–72 650
XX,180–81 460
XX,213 349
XX,220 339
XX,224–51 654
XX,231 431
XX,235–41 459
XX,261 414

Vita
9–12 172
9–13 103
10–12 103
337 97

De bello Judaico
I,32 552
I,33 344
I,61 624
I,78–80 108
I,131–54 629
I,138ff 379
I,370–79 21
II,113 108
II,119–61 107
II,119–66 102
II,154–57 108
II,197 662
II,409 634
II,487–98 246
II,488 243
V,136ff 45
V,147 652
V,205 629
V,235 608
VI,250 537
VI,270 454, 518
VI,293–96 658
VI,310–11 658
VI,355 652
VI,420 253
VI,422–26 253
VII,426–32 344
VII,9 537

Justinus
Epitoma
II,1 224
XI,11 332

Livius, Titius
Decades
praefatio 10 384
I,21 626
VIII,24 242

Macrobius, Ambrosius Theodosius
In somnium Scipionis
5,6 138

Saturnalia
I,12 512

I,15 516
II 138

Ovidius, Publius Naso
Metamorphoses
1,48–51 215
2 209
12,187–88 563

Philo
De Abrahamo (Abr.)
71 192
119ff 114
133ff 119
167ff 119
258 12

De aeternitate mundi (Aet.)
4 111, 231
5 135
56 287

De agricultura (Agr.)
51 115

De Cherubim (Cher.)
1 130
27–28 114

De confusione linguarum (Conf.)
14ff 679
50 132
62 133
168–70 114
170 124
174 114
174–75 155
190 679
190–91 139

De congressu eruditionis gratia
120 117
137 141

De vita contemplativa (Cont.)
28–9 144
29 711
78 118
79–80 711
245–49 115

De decalogo (Decal.)
32–5 680

121–22 126
154 117
159 143
175 117

Quod deterius potiori insidiari soleat (Det.)
1 130, 192
125 287
160 131

Quod Deus sit immutabilis (Deus)
20 130
23–24 112
31–32 115
47–48 119
86ff 131
108 134
145 132

De fuga et inventione (Fug.)
54–57 113
68–70 114
149 131
178 ff 128

De gigantibus (Gig.)
6–7 139
6–11 114
6–15 154
8 114
55 127
65 130, 192

Quis rerum divinarum heres sit (Her.)
2 131
173 126
198 132
224 217
237 131

De legatione ad Gaium (Leg.)
3 119
4 130
76 255
159–61 631
170 176
280 662
281–83 255
298–308 631
306 663
317–19 630

Legum allegoriae (L.A.)
I,2 130
I,2–4 137
I,3 721
I,8–15 138
I,16 132
I,28 128
I,43 138
I,80 131
III,10 151
III,169 131

De migratione Abrahami (Mig.)
14 132
89–93 118
199 131, 146
215 131

De vita Mosis (Mos.)
I,17 681
I,75 150
I,130 131
II,12ff 118
II,14–16 118
II,25–29 129
II,26 189
II,31–44 165
II,99–100 114
II,109–16 601
II,115 133
II,131 602
II,132 1, 133
II,135 115
II,203–4 132
II,224 143
II,267 151
II,290–92 478

De opificio mundi (Op.)
13 137
16–18 115
21–3 134
26 115
89 ff 138
104–5 566
129 130
154 138
171 362

De plantatione (Plant.)
14 155
25–26 157
36–37 138
78 133
134 131

De praemiis et poenis (Praem)
8 287
14 130
162ff 119

Quod omnis probus liber (Prob)
68 132
69 118
175–91 107

De sacrificiis Abelis et Caini (Sac)
5 113
6 131

De sobrietate (Sob.)
65 675

De somniis (Som.)
I,21–24 111
I,30–32 112
I,31 112
I,133ff 119
I,138–146 156
I,139 113
I,159 132
I,180 113
I,230 150
I,254 113

De specialibus legibus (Spec.)
I,41 132
I,53 142
I,83–98 602
I,97 663
I,110 143
I,162ff 119
I,163 55
I,168–69 663
I,255 143
II,33 671
III,8 126
III,32–3 142
III,64 144
III,120 141
III,151 142

De virtutibus (Virt.)
65 287
134–51 143

142–44 143
189–91 718

Philo, pseudo-
Liber antiquitatum biblicarum (Book of Biblical Antiquities)
III,9–10 125
VI,16–18 121
VII,4 121
VIII,8 121
XVIII,5 121
VIII,14 121
IX,8 128
IX,12 127
IX,13 122
X,I 122
XI,2 122
XI,6 122
XII,5 122
XII,7 122
XIII,6 122
XIII,7 123
XVI,3 123, 126
XVIII,2 123
XVIII,6 121
XVIII,13 123
XIX,16 123
XX,8 123
XXV–XXIX 123
XXXI,1 123
XL,5–8 123
LIX,2 123
LX1V,5–7 126
LXI,9 123

Philostratus
De vita Apollonii Tyanaei
6,32 299

Plato
Leges
712b 1

Phaedo
114b–c 114

Politicus
269c 564
302e 125

Plinius, Secundus Caius
Naturalis historiae libri
II,81–86 14
VII,2 309
VII,56 692

Plutarch
Vitae
Alexander
36 242
64 198
Pericles
33 164
Theseus
3 100

Moralia
269c 516
814d 243

Plutarch. pseudo-
De placitis philosophorum
2, ch. 11, 13 216
3, ch. 10 203
3, ch. 15 15

Ptolemy
Almagest
1, ch. 4 205
3, ch. 7 532
13, ch. 2 234

Geographia
1, ch. 5 215
15a 212
63b 212
72a 223
93a 213
102b 212
103a 222
105a 214
107a 224
108 214

Quintilian
Institutio oratoria
I,12 84
VIII,6 336
IX,4 84

Seneca, Lucius Annaeus
Naturales Quaestiones
6 14

Epistulae ad Lucilium
II,4–5 83

Solinus, Caius Julius
Collectanea
49 49, 226, 261
65 309
471

Strabo
De situ orbis
XI,14 226

Suetonius Tranquillus, Caius
Caesares XII
Titus
X 298

Tibullus
Elegiae
I,7 347

Valerius Maximus
Facta ac dicta memorabilia
1,IV,7 242
1,VI,3 659

Virgilius, Publius, Maro
Georgica
1,233–34 215
I,242–43 224

Xenophon
Cyropaedia
I:II,1 410
VIII:VIII,1 410,411

Anabasis
I,1 411

Memorabilia
IV,VII 567
IV,VII 216

EARLY CHRISTIAN SOURCES

Augustine
De civitate Dei
2, ch. 17 153
8, ch. 11 531
12, ch.10 529
12, ch. 13 524
15, ch.9 338
15, ch. 11 174
15, ch. 12 490, 309
15, ch. 13 127, 174
15, ch. 15 308
16, ch. 3 675
16, ch.4 674
16, ch. 9 233
16, ch.11 309
18, ch. 39 692
18, ch. 40 529
18, ch. 42 166, 190
18, ch. 43 173
18, ch. 44 174
18, ch.45 629
22, ch. 30 564

Homiliae De tempore
CCV (col. 1044) 254

Enarrationes in Psalmos
Ps. 40 (col. 463) 174

De Genesi ad litteram
5:3 (col. 322–3) 153.
8:1 (col. 371) 152

Contra Epistolam Manichaei
Col. 176 268

Quaestionum in vetus instrumentum libri XII.
2 (col.620) 692
2 (col. 637) 619

Cassiodorus
Chronicon (ed. Sichardus)
160v 298

Clement of Alexandria
Stromata
I; ch. 22 (col. 148) 167
VI ch. 4 (cols. 255–58) 198

Contractus, Hermannus
Chronicon (ed. Sichardus)
177r 298

Epiphanius
Contra octoaginta haereses opus
1:14 104

De mensuris ac ponderibus
3 (cols. 241–44) 167

Eusebius, Pamphilus Caesariensis
Chronicon
I. cols. 177–78 360

I, col. 208 108, 181
II, cols. 399–400 362
II, cols. 471–74 366
II, cols. 475–76 186
II, col. 499 357
II, col. 501 357

De evangelica praeparatione (De ev. praep.)
7, ch. 8. 151
8, ch.1 38, 167
8, ch. 2 663
8, ch. 3. 189
8, ch. 5 19
8, ch. 12 107
8 ch. 60 55
9, ch. 5–6 355
11 ch.17 564
12, ch.16 711

Historia ecclesiastica
5:8 166
11:42 111

Irenaeus
Contra haereses
III col. 947–49 166

Isidore
Ethymologiae
6:4 col. 236 166

Jerome
Hebraicae Quaestiones
Gen. 4:8 col. 945 192
Gen. 32:27–8 130
Gen. 37:3 581
Gen. 46:26 146

Commentaria
Gen. 46:10 577
Is. 38:10 191
Is. 38:19 191
Ezk. 5:5 222
Ezk. 29:1–2 534
Dan. 1:1 129
Dan. 8:13 552
Dan. 9:24 382
Dan. 11:2 424
Dan. 12:11 552

Praefationes
In Pentateucho Moysi
167
In libros Samuelem et Malachim
186, 373, 708
In Ezram
573
In librum Job
573
In Evangelio
190
In librum chronicorum Eusebii
172, 573, 712

Epistolae
XXV 149, 708
XXX 711
LXIV 610, 698
LXXII 440
LXXIII 708

Justin Martyr
Cohortatio ad Graecos
VI, col. 271–74 135
VI, col. 273 124

Justin Martyr, pseudo-
Oratio paraenetica
VI col.265–8 165

Lactantius
Divinarum institutionum lib.
1:6 135
1:22 626
7:8 113
7:14 558
7:16 559

Origen
Super Numeros homiliae
XI 680

Origen, pseudo-
Super Job
col. 374 120

Orosius
Adversus paganos
6:15 177
7:12 246
7:13 248

MEDIEVAL JEWISH SOURCES

Aaron ben Elijah
Keter Torah
2,59a–60d 144

Aaron ben Joseph
Sefer ha-Mivḥar
III,38a 144

Aboab, Isaac
Menorat ha-Ma'or
Introduction 288

Abraham ben David of Posquières (Rabad)
Perush Eduyyot
2:9 555

Abraham bar Ḥiyya
Sefer ha-Ibbur
II, gate2 (36) 511
II, gate 2 (36–38) 512
II, gate 2 (37–38) 360, 511
III, gate 3 (81) 515
III, gate 3 (85) 516
III, gate 3(86) 513
III, gate 5(93–94) 513
III, gate 7(96–97) 497
III, gate 7(97) 363, 374, 450, 485, 516

Ḥeshbon ha-Mahalekhot ha-Kokhavim
8 364, 512

Megillat ha-Megalleh
546, 549

Abudarham, David ben Joseph
Sefer Abudarham (ed. Wertheimer)
378 490

Abulafia, Meir ben Todros
Yad Ramah
61 292

Abulafia, Todros ben Joseph Halevi
Oṣar ha-Kavod
31a 563
60a 285

Adret, Solomon ben Abraham (Rashba)
She'elot u-Teshuvot.
134 233, 561

Ḥiddushe ha-Rashba
B. Rosh ha-Shanah 18b 536
B. Bava Batra 78b 281

Al-Ashqar, Moses
She'elot
74 670, 696
96 269, 401
117 106

Albo, Joseph
Sefer ha-Iqqarim
3, ch. 16 185, 670
3, ch. 22 327
4, ch. 38 583

Alfasi, Isaac
Halakhot
Bava Meṣia 13b 184
Shevu'ot 1a–b 291
Shabbat16b 509
Shabbat 26b 589
Eruvin 35b 622

Amram ben Sheshna
Seder Rav Amram
Ta'aniyot
91, par. 49 161

Anav, Zedekiah ben Abraham
Shibbole ha-Leqeṭ
18a 268

Arama, Isaac
Aqedat Yiṣḥaq
3,20bff 138, 498
7 119, 139, 140
37 203, 388
50 622
51 587, 590, 603
56 549
98 256

Ḥazut Qashah
7 139, 140
8 139, 672
10 140
11 140

Asher ben Yehiel (Rosh/Asheri)
Pisqe ha-Rosh
Rosh ha-Shanah
4:8 536
Eruvin
10 622

Sefer Torah
1,13 173, 325

Baḥya ben Asher
Be'ur al ha-Torah
Gen. 1:2 445, 498
Gen. 2:3 551
Gen. 18:3 702
Ex. 12:2 487
Ex. 12:40 426, 545
Ex. 25:8 444
Num. 41:30 316
Deut. 7:2 702

Bahir, Sefer ha-
114 702
115 702

Baruch ben Isaac,
Sefer ha-Terumah
Avodah Zarah 135 445

Benjamin bar Jehudah (Anav)
Perush al Divre ha-Yamim
1Chr. 3:21 478

Biba, Samuel
Perush ibn Ezra
Num. 23:1 137

Boaz, Joshua
Shilṭe ha-Gibborim
Rosh ha-Shanah 4a 498
Avodah Zarah 15b 279

D'Estella, David ben Samuel
Migdal David
32 592
181 153

Eldad ha-Dani
Sefer Eldad ha-Dani
262

Estori ha-Parḥi ben Moses
Sefer Kaftor va-Feraḥ
6 364
51 363, 364

Gershon ben Solomon
Sha'ar ha-Shamayim
1,7 14
2,2 297
8 310

Gersonides, Levi ben Gershom
Perush ha-Torah
Gen. 15:13 429
Ex. 12:40 429
Ex. 28:32 586
Ex. 28:33 587, 590
Dan. 7 271
Dan. 7:24 431
Dan. 7:25 453
Dan. 8:14 431

To'aliyyot
8 431

Milḥamot ha-Shem
5 235

Gikatilla, Joseph ben Abraham
Sha'are Orah
32 641

Sha'are ṣedeq
25 641

Halakhot Gedolot (ed. Hildesheimer)
38a 161

Halevi, Judah
Kuzari
1 527
1, par. 25 504
1, par. 47 527
I, par. 60 529
I, par.67 150, 433, 529
I, par. 89 680
I, par.95 673, 675
I, par. 111 468
II, par.6 680
II, par. 18 232, 484
II, par. 20 52, 223, 650
II, par. 23 179
II, par. 24 642
II, par. 36 622
II, par. 57 454
II, par. 64 512, 714
II, par. 66–68 710
II, par. 68 674, 681
II, par. 73 710
III, par. 31 683, 709

Halevi, Judah (*cont.*)
III, par. 41 267
III, par. 43 509
III, par. 54 276, 537
III, par. 57 276, 618
III, par. 59 276
III, par. 61 276
III, par. 65 110, 389, 453
III, par. 67 245
III, par. 68 276
III, par. 73 391
III, par. 69 278
III, par. 73 290, 300
IV, par. 25 549, 691
IV, par. 26 549
IV, par. 27 549
IV, par. 29 278
V par.4 578

Ḥinnukh, Sefer ha-
negative commandments
36 96

Ibn Daud, Abraham,
Sefer ha-Qabbalah (ed. Cohen)
3 491
6 271, 433, 444
7 431
8 477
13 389
16 353, 455
16–17 361
17 345
19 349
41 194
41–42 546
43 375
58 367
60 272
87 293

Zikhron Divre Romi
246, 298

Ve'eleh Divre Malkhe Yisrael
345

Ibn Ezra, Abraham
Commentary on the Torah
Introduction 140, 503
Gen. 1:1 11
Gen. 1:6 220
Gen. 1:11 147
Gen. 1:14 111
Gen. 1:28 282
Gen. 3:24 140
Gen. 4:4 552
Gen. 6:3 317
Gen. 11:6 678
Gen. 22:4 272
Gen. 33:10 484
Gen. 38:1 224; 272; 307
Gen. 46:23 494
Ex. 2:10 681
Ex. 2:22 682
Ex. 12:1 503
Ex. 12:2 484, 487, 511, 514, 515
Ex. 20:2 528; 626
Ex. 25:5 273
Ex. 28:5 593
Ex. 28:36 591
Ex. 28:37 590
Ex.31:2 272
Ex .31:18 549
Ex. 33:21 548
Ex. 34:22 515
Lev. 11:44 149
Lev. 23:2 486
Lev. 23:3 503, 514
Lev. 25:9 489
Num. 13:17 223
Num. 15:39 600
Num. 23:1 137
Deut. 1:2 478
Is. 19:18 688
Amos 1:1 11
Nahum 3:8 244
Zech. 14:5 25
Dan. 1:1 497
Dan. 9:24 521, 522
Dan. 11:2 320
Ps. 24:2 219
Ps. 120:5 681

Ḥidah
699

Yesod Mora
7 144

Ibn Ḥabib, Jacob
En Yisrael u-Vet Yisrael (En Ya'akov)
P. Shabbat 558
B. Berakhot 59a 18
B. Megillah 2b 698

Ibn Janaḥ, Jonah
Sefer ha-Riqmah
6 521
7 553

Ibn Moṭoṭ, Samuel ben Saadiah
Megillat Setarim
Gen. 38:1 224

Ibn Shemtov, Shemtov
Sefer ha-Emunot
2, 14 528

Ibn Shuaib, Joshua,
Derashot al ha-Torah
43a 698

Ibn Tibbon, Samuel ben Judah
Ma'amar Yiqqavu ha-Mayim
19 111

Isaac ben Samuel (of Acre)
Me'irat Enayim
77 355

Isaac ben Sheshet-Perfet (Ribash)
She'elot u Teshuvot
9 566
45 90
157 549
171 335
284 26, 163, 163

Isaiah ben Mali di Trani (the elder-Rid)
Sefer ha-Mahadurot
Sanhedrin 69b 312

Nimmuqe Ḥumash
495

Isaiah ben Elijah di Trani (the younger-Riaz)
Perush al Ezra
315
Pesaqim
Sanhedrin 279

Quntres Re'iyyot
115–23 91

Israeli, Isaac ben Joseph
Yesod Olam
1, ch. 1 211, 513
2, ch. 2 219, 360, 511, 512
2, ch. 3 215, 220, 503
2, ch. 9 235
2, ch. 17 223, 509
3, ch. 3 513, 515, 516
3, ch. 5 513
3, ch. 7 363, 374, 450, 485, 497, 516
4, ch. 3 223, 501
4, ch. 5 374
4, ch. 9 374, 485, 501
4, ch. 18 163, 353, 364, 477

Sha'ar ha-Shamayim
II, 2 297

Jacob ben Asher
Arba'ah ṭurim
Oraḥ ḥayyim
par. 292 508
par. 580 161
par. 619 539
Yoreh De'ah
par. 211 539
Ḥoshen Mishpaṭ
par. 43 359
Even ha-Ezer
par. 127 372

Jeshua ben Joseph Halevi
Halikhot Olam
2 327
5 354, 365

Jonah Gerondi
Perush Alfasi
Ber.42 21

Josippon
1, ch. 3 640
1, ch. 4 470
1, ch. 5 243, 353, 362
2, ch. 5 353
2, ch. 11 200
3,ch. 15 87
3, ch. 16 639, 662
3, ch. 17 43, 168, 332
4,ch. 19 58
4, chs. 25–30 325
5, ch. 39 379, 629
5, ch. 42 630
6, ch. 47 662
6, ch. 55 108
6, ch. 63 158
6, ch. 66 634
6, ch. 77 332

Kaspi, Nathaniel ben Nehemiah
Perush ha-Kuzari
II, par. 57 454

Kimḥi, David
Commentary to Torah
1Sam. 28:25 126
1K. 8:2 489
2K. 14:22 432
Jer. 1:13 272
Ezk. 5:5 222
Amos 1:1 12
Nahum 3:8 244
Hag. 1:1 474
Zech.14:5 25
Ps. 24:1 219

Maʿarekhet ha-Elohut
22b–23a 703
129a 335

Maimonides
Perush al ha-Mishnah
Introduction 105, 399, 565, 572
Terumot
3:9 468
Yoma
8:2 307
Sanhedrin
7:4 334
Intro. to ch. 10 139
10:1 87
Avot
1:3 109, 110, 144
Ḥull.1:2 109
Bekhorot
7:3 256
Ṭoharot
Introduction 311
Yadayim
4:5 669

Mishneh Torah
Haqdamah 2
Yesode ha-Torah
III:1 217
X:3 24
Deʿot
III:3 94
Talmud Torah
IV:8 284
Teshuvah
III:14 335
III:5 469
III:6 105
IV 336
V 59
VIII:3,4 298
VIII:8 562, 566
Tefillah
IX:7 273
Tefillin
I:19 596, 697
Sefer Torah
VIII:4 195
Shofar
III:2 536
Qiddush ha-Ḥodesh
I:3 429
V:1 375
V:2 429, 492
V:3 373 484
V:10 347
VI:1 236, 429, 504
VI:2 492
VI:3 486
IX:2 490
X:1 512
X:7 514
XI:15 486
XI:16 4, 368
XI:17 503
XV:1 504, 429
XVII:25 99
XVIII:14 229
XIX:16 501
Ḥannukah
III:12 286
Ishut
II 306
Gerushin
I:27 363, 372, 376
Issure Biah
XIV:7 469
XIX:13 143
Shevuʿot
V:22 399
Terumot
I:9 227
Shemiṭṭah
X:3 435, 448, 467
X:4 368
X:5 541
X:6 487, 541
X:8 259

Bet ha-Beḥirah
IV:1 593
Kele ha-Miqdash
V:1 463
V:15 463
VIII:2 587
IX:2 588
IX:3 586
IX:4 587
IX:6 617
IX:7 595
X:1 590
X:3 588
X:10 593; 617
X:13 582
Meʿilah
VIII:8 393
Temurah
IV:13 393
Roṣeaḥ
IV:1 141
IV:4 141
Sanhedrin
VII:4 334
XII:3 250
XIV:12 374
Edut
IX:1 330
XI:10 469
Mamrim
I:2 392
1:3 393, 491
Melakhim
I:2 124
VIII:11 469, 465
XI:1 554
XII:3 263

Teshuvot She'elot ve-Iggrot (ed. Shailat)
2,673 465
2,488 509
2,667–78 541

Iggeret Teman
127 352
160 550
172 557

Ma'amar Teḥiyyat ha-Metim (ed. Rabbinowitz)
341 679
350 105
358–59 376

Ma'amar Teḥiyyat ha-Metim (ed. Finkel)
63–4 106

Shemonah Peraqim
Introduction 99
5 94
8 20

Guide of the Perplexed
Introduction 330, 386, 337, 147, 299, 303
I, ch. 4 142
I, ch. 10 230
I, ch. 31 164
I, ch. 63 131
I, ch. 71 96, 714
I, ch. 73 98, 219; 400
II, ch. 5 491
II, ch. 6 299
II, ch. 8 203, 400
II, ch. 10 228
II, ch. 13 135, 136
II, ch. 16 481
II, ch. 24 234; 236
II, ch. 25 150
II, ch. 29 562, 321, 328, 565, 679
II, ch. 30 150, 153, 273, 370
II, ch. 46 192, 227
II, ch. 47 308
II, ch. 48 465
III, ch. 1 319
III, ch. 4 273
III, ch. 14 203
III, ch. 14 393
III, ch. 14 391
III, ch. 15 538
III, ch. 17 153
III, ch. 26 524
III, ch. 29 93, 136
III, ch. 36 21
III, ch. 41 147
III, ch. 43 281
III, ch. 48 153, 273
III, ch. 50 386

Pirqe Mosheh (ed. Muntner)
325 654
363 690
372 689

Maimon of Montpellier
Qiṣur al-Farghani
Introduction 490

Meshullam ben Moses
Sefer ha-Hashlamah
28a 99

Mordechai ben Hillel Hakohen
Pesaḥim 37a 330, 508

Moses ben Jacob (of Coucy)
Sefer Miṣvot ha-Gadol
Introduction 392
Positive Commandments
par. 19 686
par. 133 227
par. 173 587
Negative Comamndments
par. 242 539

Nahmanides
Commentary on the Torah
Introduction 8, 685
Gen. 1:2 136
Gen. 2:8 225
Gen. 2:20 673
Gen. 5:4 306, 308
Gen. 8:4 274
Gen. 8:5 489
Gen. 9:12 659
Gen. 38:18 600, 612
Gen. 46:15 462
Gen. 47:28 378
Ex. 12:2 489
Ex. 12:42 427
Ex. 21:37 588
Ex. 28:30 593
Ex. 28:31 586, 587
Ex. 30:13 667, 688
Lev. 18:25 233
Lev. 20:17 669
Deut. 22:6 153
Deut. 2:23 226
Deut. 4:3 233
Deut. 11:24 226
Deut. 28:42 378
appendix 250

Hassagot al Sefer ha-Miṣvot (ed. Chavel)
221 492
222 374
226 485

Sefer ha-Ge'ulah (ed. Chavel)
3, 281 519
2, 279–80 560

Sha'ar ha-Gemul (ed. Chavel)
2, 298 139
2, 309–11 298

Sefer ha-Vikuaḥ(ed. Chavel)
1, 308 289

Torat Adonai (ed. Chavel)
1, 162 443

Derashah le-Rosh ha-Shanah (ed. Chavel)
1, 21 489

Nahmanides (Moses ben Naḥman, Ramban) (attrib.)
She'elot u-Teshuvot
232 163, 289

Nissim ben Reuben Gerondi
Perush Alfasi
Shabbat10a 638
Shabbat 15a 206,400
Shabbat 29b 225
Rosh ha-Shanah 3a 491, 499
Megillah 10a 502
Giṭṭin 20a 376
Giṭṭin 42a 372
Shevu'ot 1a-b 291

Ḥiddushin al Nedarim
B. Nedarim 40a 225

Obadiah ben David ben Obadiah
Perush to Mishneh Torah
VI:3 511
VI:8 497, 505
VII:1 229
VII:7 502
IX:2 490
IX:3 513
XI:17 503

Pisqe Tosafot
Zevaḥim. 2 587

Pecanati, Menahem ben Benjamin
Perush al ha-Torah (Jerusalem, 1961)
15a 92
15a–b 140
25d 172
26a 680
32c 559
34a 554

39b 317
49a 221
51a 592
63b 117
68a–69d 566
68d 564
74c 281
77a 91
79d 318

Samson ben Isaac (of Chinon)
Sefer Keritut
5:2 685
3 284
4:2 367
4:3 365
5:3 399

Samuel ben Isaac ha-Sardi
Sefer ha-Terumot
374

Seder Tannaim ve-Amoraim
1 352

Sherira Gaon
Iggeret Sherira Gaon (ed. B. Lewin)
61 375
78 245, 367
84 367
94 194
96 194; 546
109 389

Solomon b. Abraham Parḥon
Maḥberet he-Arukh
42a 397

Solomon ben Isaac (Rashi)
Commentary on Torah
Gen. 1:1 282
Gen. 18:22 327
Gen. 47:2 161; 164; 290
Ex. 6:9 274
Ex. 6:11 465
Ex. 28:4 586, 587
Ex. 28:6 590
Ex. 28:10 595
Ex. 28:33 586
Lev. 10:19 340
Num. 11:20 290
Is. 19:18 689
Nahum 3:8 244
Ezra 6:14 314
Neh. 12:10 2

Commentary on Babylonian Talmud
Shabbat 65b 225
Shabbat 119a 339
Pesaḥim 94a 400
Rosh ha-Shanah 3b 314
Yoma 21b 389
Megillah 9a 162
Sota 41a 350
Sota 49b 688
Bava Qama 11b 596; 687
Bava Batra 25b 206
Bava Batra 115b 103
Sanhedrin 72b 398
Sanhedrin 90a 105
Sanhedrin 97a 102
Sanhedrin 100b 87
Sanhedrin 110b 258
Avodah Zarah 9a 495, 371
Avodah Zarah.10a 359
ḥullin 138a 590
Arakhin 12b 435

Solomon ben Isaac, pseudo-
Or ha-Sekhel
85:4, 167b 316

Solomon ibn Melekh
Mikhlal Yofi
600

Tiqqune ha-Zohar
Introduction, 9a 673
5,8a 703
8,24a 622
12,27a 622
69,101b 673

Tobiah ben Eliezer
Pesiqta Zuṭarta o Rabbata (Leqaḥ Ṭov)
Lev. 21:14 143
Lev. 22:33 324
Num. 15:18 324
Deut. 34:7 584

Tosafot to Babylonian Talmud
Berakhot
3a 685
Shabbat
12b 686

Tosafot to Babylonian Talmud (cont.)
Yoma
21b 618
Rosh ha-Shanah
3b 319, 469
Taʿanit
20b 286, 513
Megillah
9a 162–163
32a 707
Ḥagigah
12a 201
Yevamot
16b 164, 290
16b 164
77b 491
104a 286
Ketubot
7b 633
Giṭṭin
7a 587
56b 297
80a 373
Bava Qama.
3b 574
83a 688
Bava Batra
113a 481
Sanhedrin
51b 595
Avodah Zarah
9b 453
24b 306
Zevaḥim
45a 595
101b 340
Menaḥot
30a 508
64b 318, 419
Ḥullin
6a 345
60a 164
Bekhorot
19b 306
44b 228
55b 228

Yomtov ben Abraham of Sevile (Ritba)
Ḥiddushe ha-Ritba
Yoma 9a 339
Yoma 18a 348
Yoma 38a 247
Yoma 69a 345
Yoma 73b 591, 593
Megillah 2b 185, 696
Megillah 3a 574
Bava Batra 98b 89
Avodah Zarah 8a 290

Ṣarṣa, Samuel ibn Seneh
Meqor ḥayyim
Lev. 25:2 566

Zerechiah ben Isaac Halevi
Sefer ha-Meʾorot
Rosh ha-Shanah 3a 321
Rosh ha-Shanah 5a 484
Avodah Zarah 2a 497

Zohar
I,16b 703
I,24b 703
I,50b 565
I,62a 338
I,72b 92
I,76b 678
I,145b 338, 385
I,191a 115
II,6b 657
II,16b–17a 555
II,17b 1
II,73a 572
II,87b 140
II,125a 622
II,157a 221
II,220b–221a 622
III,9b 525
III,9b–10a 221,567
III,10a 209
III,50a 1, 30
III,70b–c 717
III,152a 140, 385
III,161b 232
III,244b 329

Zohar ḥadash, Midrash ha-Neʿelam
I,16c–d 565
I,139d 544
Shir ha-Shirim
73a 702
73c 702
Ruth
75d 184, 574
81b 114

MEDIEVAL CHRISTIAN SOURCES

Cassiodorus
Chronicon
160v 298

Contractus, Hermannus
Chronicon
173r 243
177r 298

Corpus iuris canonici
2, col. 1123 441

Dante Alighieri
Inferno
XXXIV,110–13 222

Purgatorio
II,1–3 222

Paradiso
26,124–7 678
29,19–36 524

De' Sacchi, Bartolomeo (Platina)
De vitis
16 298
19–20 246
21 248, 615
22 251, 615

Durandus, Guglielmus
Rationale
III, ch.19 611, 615

Honorius Augustodunensis
De aetatibus mundi
V 456

Otto of Friesing
Rerum ab origine mundi libri
ch.42 382

Petrarch, pseudo-
Chronica
298

Sacrobosco, Joannes de
De Sphaera
2 215

Suidas (Suda)
619, 693

Thomas, Aquinas
Summa theologica
I 47,1 362, 549
I 74,2 153
I,2 102,5 619

Super epistulas S. Pauli lectura
Ad Romanos 2, ch.9 175
Ad Titum 2, ch. 3 440

In Aristotelis libros: De caelo
II, XVII, par.254 204

Super quarto libro Sententiarum (of Petrus Lombardus)
IV,43, 1 564

MEDIEVAL ARABIC SOURCES

Ahmad ibn Muhammad ibn Kathir (al-Farghani)
Compendium (Latin version)
1 485, 487
3 210
Hebrew version
364, 532

Husain ibn Abd Ablah (Avicenna)
Canon
I, fen 1 578
I, fen 3 83
III, fen 20 310
III, fen 2 27

Abd Al-Aziz ibn Uthman al-Kabasi (Alkabitius)
Ad magisterium iudiciorum astrorum isagoge
4 550

Muhammad ibn Ahmad (Averroes)
Meteorologica
444v 720

FIFTEENTH AND SIXTEENTH-CENTURY JEWISH SOURCES

Abraham b. Eliezer Halevi
Meshare Qitrin
325, 547

Abravanel, Isaac ben Judah
Perush al ha-Torah
Gen. 15 426

Abravanel, Isaac ben Judah (*cont.*)
Ex. 28 586, 587, 590
Ex. 28:6 588

Perush al Nevi'im Rishonim.
1Sam. 8:1 271
1Sam. 13 271
Introduction to Melakhim 163, 244, 253, 433
2K. 17:1 439

Perush al ha-Nevi'im Aḥaronim
Is.5:1 710
Is.22 273
Amos 1:1 12
Haggai 1 352
Haggai 1:8 593, 640
Haggai 2:6 622
Haggai 2:9 622
Zech. 11:10 163
Zech. 12:6 250
Introduction to Jeremiah 398

Mayyane ha-Yeshuʿah
2, 3 273, 451, 471, 472
2, 2 319
8, 3 472
10, 1 452
10, 6 522, 524
10, 7 452
10, 8 519
11, 10 551, 565

Naḥalat Avot
1:2 353,354,361
1:6 110
1:51 361
4:22 664

Zevaḥ Pesaḥ
426

Abravanel, Judah (ed. Caramella)
Dialoghi d'amore
2 (99–100) 500
2 (109) 135
2 (111) 216
3 (186) 13
3 (245) 566
3 (248) 566

Albo, Joseph
Sefer ha-Iqqarim
3, ch.16 670
3, ch.22 328
4, ch.38 583

Basola, Moses
Massaʿot Ereṣ Yisrael
91 666

Bertinoro, Obadiah di
Perush ha-Mishnayot
Avot 1:1 455

Bibago, Abraham b. Shemtov
Dereḵh Emunah
2, 3 96
3 715

Caro, Isaac ben Joseph
Toledot Yiṣḥaq
Ex. 12:40 429

Caro, Joseph
Bet Yosef
Yoreh Deʿah
par. 334 89
Even ha-Ezer
par. 127 372

Kesef Mishneh
Kele ha-Miqdash
X:3 588
Shulḵhan Aruḵh
Yoreh Deʿah
par. 334:42 89

Dato, Mordechai
Migdal David
544

De Balmes, Abraham ben Meir
Miqneh Avram
670–71

Duran, Profayt
Maʿaseh Efod
Introduction 697
3 674, 677
7 398
33 688

Ḥeshev ha-Efod
497

Farissol, Abraham
Job
26:7 220

Magen Avraham
23 354

Ḥayyaṭ, Judah ben Joseph
Minḥat Yehudah
3 691
2 5b–6a 594
3, 20a 702

Ḥabiba, Joseph
Nimmuqe Yosef
Hilkhot mezuzah 652

Ibn Ḥabib, Levi
She'elot
143 368, 436, 445, 4878–8

Ibn Ḥabib, Moses ben Shemtov
Darkhe No'am
683, 712

Jacob ben Ḥayyim ibn Adonijah
Introduction
66 701

Judah ben Yehiel (Messer Leon)
Nofet Ṣufim
1, 13 98
4, 43 336

Ibn Melekh, Solomon
Mikhlal Yofi
600

Ibn Shemtov, Joseph
Perush Sefer ha-Middot l-Aristo
354

Isserles, Moses ben Israel
Sefer Torat ha-Olah
III, ch.27 237

Latif, Moses
Derashot
427

Levita, Elijah ben Asher
Baḥur
177

Massoret ha-Massoret
122 699
112–23 704
129 700

Meturgeman
677

Minz, Judah ben Eliezer Levi,
Pesaqim u-She 'elot.
8 196

Mizraḥi, Elijah ben Abraham
Perush Rashi
Gen. 11:15 327
Gen. 18:22 327
Gen. 28:4 586
Gen. 28:11 164, 290
Gen. 38:18 600
Ex. 28:10 595
Ex. 28:33 287
Ex. 35:30 308
Ex. 39:31 589
Deut. 4:32 202
Deut. 4:32 202

Provenzali, David ben Abraham
Ir David
594
Dor ha-Pelagah
677

Perush al Shir ha-Shirim
635

Provenzali, Judah
Sefer Nefuṣot Yehudah
714

Sforno, Obadiah ben Jacob
Be 'ur al ha-Torah
Gen. 1:1 370
Ex. 28:2 586

Treves, Johanan ben Joseph
Kimḥa d' Avishuna on *Maḥzor Romi*
163

Zacuto (Zacut), Abraham
Sefer Yuḥasin
11a 2
141b-142a 329

FIFTEENTH AND SIXTEENTH NON-JEWISH SOURCES

Annius, Joannes Viterbensis (Berosus)
De antiquitatibus
74 692
117 257, 476, 693
122 676
129 676
132 676

Commentary to Berosus
69 692
97 675
117 436
186 346, 347
221–22 314

Annius (Cato)
De originibus
107 676

Annius (Philo)
Breviarium de temporibus
379 136
392 130
398–404 349
414 343
406 353
407 349, 357
415 348

Annius (Xenophon)
De Aequivocis
31 248
17 563, 693

Commentary to Pseudo Xenophon
17 563
36–7 346

Borro, Girolamo (Alseforo Talascopio)
Dialogo del flusso e reflusso del mare
42 228

Buoni, Antonio
Del terremoto dialogo
I, par. 29 14
2, par. 239 302
3, par. 305 659
4, par. 339 22

Champier, Symphorien
De triplici disciplina
117

Contarini, Gasparo
De elementis
2, 33r-v 228

Dolce, Lodovico
Giornale delle historie del mondo
133 531

Ferentilli, Agostino
Discorso universale
110–111 299

Fernelius, Joannes Ambianus (Fernel)
Medicina
3, ch.9 297
6, ch.17 310

Ficino, Marsilio
Il consiglio di M. M. Ficino contra la pestilentia
23 659

Hermes
115, 116, 132

Platonis Opera
Timaeus
134, 151
Respublica
138

Symposium
337

Foresti, Jacobus Filippus
Supplementum. Supplementi de le chroniche
114v 188

Giambullari, Pierfrancesco
Il Gello
55 677

Giraldi, Lilio Gregorio
De deis gentium libri
1:8 36
1:33 609

Guevara, Antonio de
Libro di Marco Aurelio
III, ch.10 379

Libro primo [–libro secondo] delle littere
2, 402 193, 573
2 (403) 166, 579

Guicciardini, Lodovico
Descrittione...di tutti i paesi bassi
17–23 228

Lippomano, Luigi
Catena in Exodum
94r 430
282r 610
287v 619
292r 610

Lucidus, Johannes Samotheus
De emendationibus temporis (Venice, 1537)
9v–11v 175
12r–12v 175
24v 435
25v 343
27r 637
27v 638
29v 455, 518
35r–v 346
39r 382
48v 439
55r–58r 518
107r 360
107v 360, 366
107v–112r 181
108r–109r 357
194v–198v 512
195r 512
195v 515

Mauro Fiorentino
Annotationi sopra la lettione della spera del Sacro-bosco
44–49 401

Mercator, Gerardus
Chronologia
533, 550

Mexía, Pedro (Messia)
La selva di varia lettione
III, 19 401

Le vite di tutti gl'imperadori
Vespasiano 302
Tito 298
Traiano, 190 24, 254
Filippo primo 530

Moleto, Giuseppe
Ephemerides
1 550

Münster, Sebastian
Chaldaica grammatica
9 677
14 706
14–15 705
16 707

Perez de Valencia (Pharez)
Expositiones
Ps. 73:12 222

Pico della Mirandola, Giovanni
Apologia
7 121, 177

De studio divinae et humanae philosophiae
2, 2 27, 355

Disputationes
24

Reisch, Georg
Margarita philosophica
7, ch.44 401
9 ch.24 297

Richerius, Ludovicus Coelius Rhodiginus (Ricchieri)
Lectionum antiquitatum libri
2, 2 354

Sansovino, Francesco
Gl'annali 462

Steuchus, Augustinus (Steuco)
Recognitio Veteris Testamenti
5r 121
9r 677
10r 136, 581
21v 128
28v–29r 226
38r 582
39r 582

Steuchus, Augustinus (Steuco) (*cont.*)
73v–74r 188
96v 131
104r 127
106v–108r 150
107v–108a 708
116r 582
144r 169, 171
170v 175
171v 553

Tartagni, Alexander de Imola
Consiliorum libri
233 175

Theseo Ambrogio (Albonesius)
Introductio
9 696
109 148
10 708

Tostado Ribeira, Alonso
Commentaria in Genesim
56b 675

Commentaria in Leviticum
X, 149–50 441
254v 430

Commentaria in lib.III Regum
XVII, 2 438
XVIII, 3 312

Ulloa, Alfonso de
La vita dell'invitissimo imperator Carlo Quinto
182 211

Vives, Joannes Lodovicus
De civitate Dei cum commentariis Ludovici Vivis
8, ch. 11 188
18, ch.42 3
18, ch. 45 378